# LE 1

OTABLES •

**ACROSS**

1. "____ the Knife"
5. Slight breeze
9. Elvis's "In the ____"
15. Star: Fr.
17. Sci-fi film of 1979
19. Bacon unit
20. Best actor 1954, 1972
22. Panels
23. Japanese admiral
24. Elflike beings
25. Sell
27. Infant's word
28. Sumptuous
30. Oscar-winner Begley et al.
31. Temperate
32. German city
33. Puny
35. Oscar-winner Albertson
36. Cushions
37. Base cops: abbr.
38. Oliver's request
39. Norse king
40. Part of a film's credits
43. Stadium yells
44. Rival
47. Yearned
48. Rural structure
49. Radiation unit
50. "____ and Sympathy"
51. Whitman or Wordsworth
52. Best actress, 1948
55. Carpet style
56. Ms. Hogg
57. ____ up (irate)
58. "____ That a Shame" (Fats Domino)
59. Reside
60. Muffle
62. Office error
63. Song part
64. Ventilates
65. Jaw or wish
66. Evergreen
67. Cadiz wives: abbr.
68. Window section
69. Best picture, 1968
72. Shucks!
73. New Jersey city
74. Ibsen character
75. Adam's grandson
77. One of an O'Neill title's trees
78. Meadow mouse
79. South Carolina river
82. Owing
83. Weight watcher
85. Best actor, 1970
88. Existing from birth
89. Paster
90. Accustoms
91. Best picture,
92. Murder
93. ____ precedent

**DOWN**

1. Glum
2. Suffer
3. Wooden shoe
4. Canine hotels
5. Heats
6. Wings: Latin
7. Fishy features
8. Entertainer Mack
9. Drudgery
10. Round of applause
11. Double curve
12. Best picture, 1972
13. Wyoming mountains
14. Actor Welles
15. Oscar winner Jannings, 1927-8
16. Oscar winner O'Neal
18. Beginner
21. Prop for "Arsenic and Old Lace"
26. Large ruminant
29. Best picture, 1948
31. Injures
32. Canaanite god
34. Raced
35. Best actor, 1969
36. Choice role
38. Colt's mom
39. Peck film, with "The"
40. Long-snouted animal
41. "____ to bury Caesar . . ."
42. Best picture, 1960
43. Sprinted
44. Part of QED
45. River ducks
46. Sharp-sighted one
48. Props for "Dracula"
52. Boxer Willard
53. Surprised sound
54. L-P connection
55. Veer
57. Towel word
59. 507, Caesar-style
61. Inlets
62. Author Morrison
65. Rotten guy
66. Rooks
67. Kansas town
68. Walesa's homeland: abbr.
69. Bone: prefix
70. Agnes Moorehead TV role
71. "____ 66"
72. Dunk again
73. Oscar winner Sophia
74. "The Last ____ Man"
76. Movie locales
78. Turn thumbs down
79. "Body and ____"
80. Zone
81. Slave of old
84. Make edging
86. Rwys. up high
87. Director's order

# PUZZLE 2

**• ALL OF A SUDDEN •**

## ACROSS

1. River to the Volga
5. Region: abbr.
9. Pinochle combination
13. Dagger handle
17. "___ at long last love?"
18. Goatsucker
19. Ohio Indians
21. Melville work
22. Unexpectedly
26. Of domestic affairs
27. Soupy Sales dance
28. Remains stationary
29. Novel endings?
30. Alien craft: abbr.
31. Hay and Holme
32. Moment
41. African language group
42. Jujubes
43. Fanon
44. Crafty
45. "There remaineth ___ . . ." (Browning)
46. Morose
47. ___ vivum ex ovo
48. Nasal: prefix
49. ___ Tin Tin
50. French department
51. Riversides
54. Leading
55. Moving sideways
58. Poetry Muse
59. Actress Jackson
60. Immediately
64. Traveling bag
67. "___-porridge hot"
68. Diversion
72. Patti LuPone role
73. Jumping mammals
74. Pose
75. Old river to the Tiber
76. Frosted
77. Natural force
79. Existed
80. Mild cigar
82. "___ Hear a Waltz?"
83. Trap
84. Remote
86. Safaris
87. Instantly
92. Heroic poetry
93. Fr. teacher of the deaf
94. Record
95. Irish county
98. The ___ in the fire
100. Art lover
104. Suddenly
107. Space chimp
108. Faint
109. Metal mixture
110. Eskers
111. Prying
112. Hawaiian goose
113. Philippine skirt
114. Alien: prefix

## DOWN

1. Chinese gooseberry
2. A ___ Abel
3. Diamond wear
4. Nonbelievers
5. Take ___ (scold)
6. List shortener: abbr.
7. Fracas
8. "Make ___ Daddy"
9. Mortal Gorgon
10. ___ and Psyche
11. Biography
12. Condensation
13. Trustworthy
14. Writer Kingsley
15. Assortment of type
16. Fast food order
18. ___ Gorda, FL
20. Marketable
23. Put up ___ up!
24. Mansard and gambrel
25. Hair tint
30. Not new
31. "___ Old Cowhand"
32. Ski lifts
33. World ___
34. Upright
35. Israeli statesman
36. Take care of
37. In the ___ Morpheus
38. Pale
39. Story of the siege of Troy
40. Actress Carter
46. Sound of relief
48. Scarlett's love
50. Contribute a share
51. Indian area
52. Rebelled
53. Scruffs
54. Word of sorrow
56. Congregation
57. "___ Wonderful Life"
59. Indian mountain pass
61. Spartan magistrates
62. Anesthetize
63. Sacred bull
64. Opera composer
65. Airplane: Fr.
66. Restrict
69. Fatuous
70. Borgnine role
71. Unevenly notched
74. U.S. marionette maker
77. Buries
78. Regulations
79. Diminish
80. Pure
81. Meal carrier
83. Brown pigment
84. Tutt'___ (at most): Ital.
85. Celebrations
88. False doctrine
89. Organic compound
90. "___ Nightingale"
91. Suspicious
95. Danish length
96. Boy: Sp.
97. Ring decisions: abbr.
98. Ice sheet
99. Like ___ of bricks
100. ___ in the ointment
101. Otherwise
102. Malay master
103. Architect Saarinen
105. Admit
106. Palm leaf

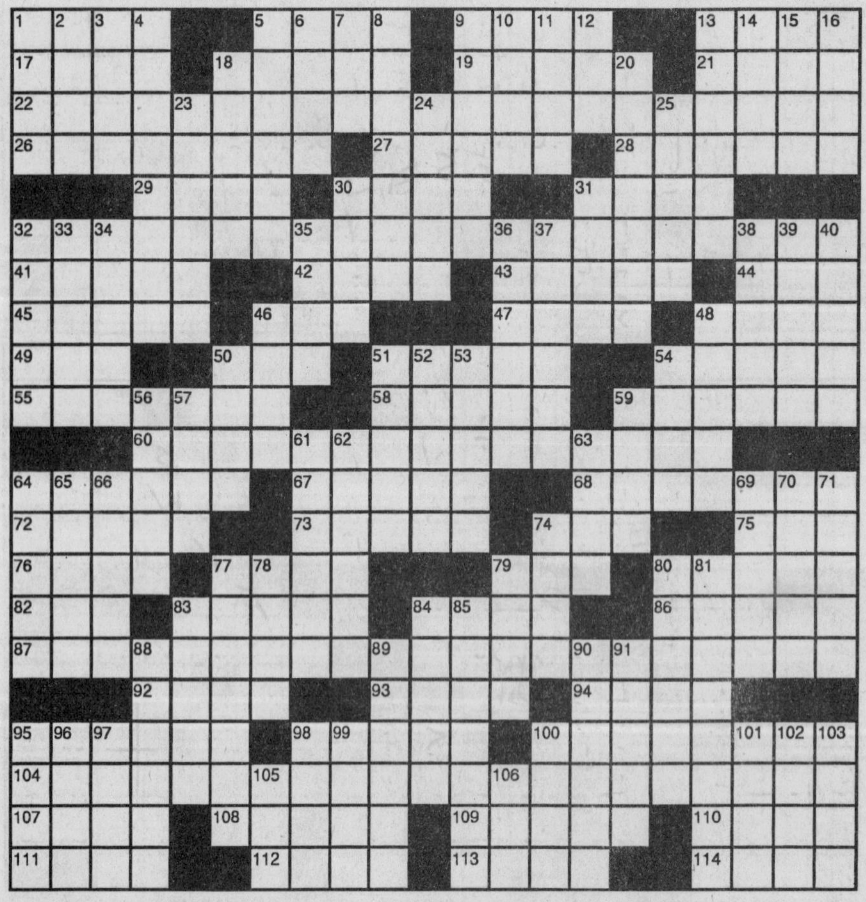

# PUZZLE 3

**• DOWN ON THE FARM •**

**ACROSS**

1. Like a chimp
6. Body joint
9. Humble abode
12. Faith, Hope and Charity's mom
13. Writer Joyce Carol
15. Single unit
16. Don't be impatient!: 3 wds.
21. Take the prize
22. Printers' measures
23. Metal erosion
24. Power group: abbr.
25. Negative
26. Fury
27. Damage
30. Thomas Alva ____
33. Auction offer
35. Dawn announcer
38. At this time
39. American Indian
40. Models
41. Snatches
43. Sun beams
45. Wager
47. Overhead trains
50. Make ready, for short
52. Actress Merkel
53. Everybody
54. Exclamation of discovery
56. Mining product
57. Tear
58. Sheep cry
59. Stitch together
60. Very damp
61. French friend
62. External: prefix
63. Observe
64. Wind direction: abbr.
65. Falls behind
67. Beer barrel
69. Droop, as ears
70. High cards
71. Prevaricated
73. Certain tides
77. Self
78. No, in Scottish
79. In the open air
81. Novel
82. Land owner
84. Third letter
85. Comedian Paulsen
87. "Great Expectations" character
88. Atlas entry
90. Actress Whelchel
91. Ajar, poetically
94. Workers' organization: abbr.
95. Hot-rodder's pastime: 2 wds.
100. Largest deer
101. Dance exhibition
102. Scottish nobleman
103. Kind of bread
104. Put
105. Parts of plants

**DOWN**

1. Feel sore
2. Laborer, of yore
3. Ailments
4. Comedian Caesar
5. Country fun
6. Exclamation of triumph
7. Japanese emperor
8. Miles ____ hour
9. Popular rhyming question: 4 wds.
10. Association
11. Canvas shelter
13. Table scrap
14. Fast plane: abbr.
17. Belonging to us
18. Utilizer
19. Always
20. Depressed
27. Barn sound
28. Donkey
29. Map abbreviation
31. Hostel
32. Cleanser
33. Purchase sight unseen: 6 wds.
34. "____ a Wonderful Life"
36. Choose
37. Language suffix
42. Calm
43. Pastoral
44. Beast
45. Ebon
46. Make happy
48. Calf rope
49. With 45 Down, social outcast
51. Folk-singer Seeger et al.
53. Honest ____
55. Great admiration
66. Burn
68. Large antelope
69. English money: abbr.
70. Years old
72. Kennedy's party: abbr.
74. And so forth: abbr.
75. Peer Gynt's mother
76. Dessert option
77. Encompasses
79. College exam
80. Heroic
82. Baby horse
83. Royal ruler: abbr.
86. Cigar residue
87. Ship's landing
89. ____ for the course
90. Size type: abbr.
91. Migrant worker
92. Hair curling, for short
93. Finishes
96. Affirmative
97. "____ been workin' on the railroad . . ."
98. Squirrel morsel
99. Feline

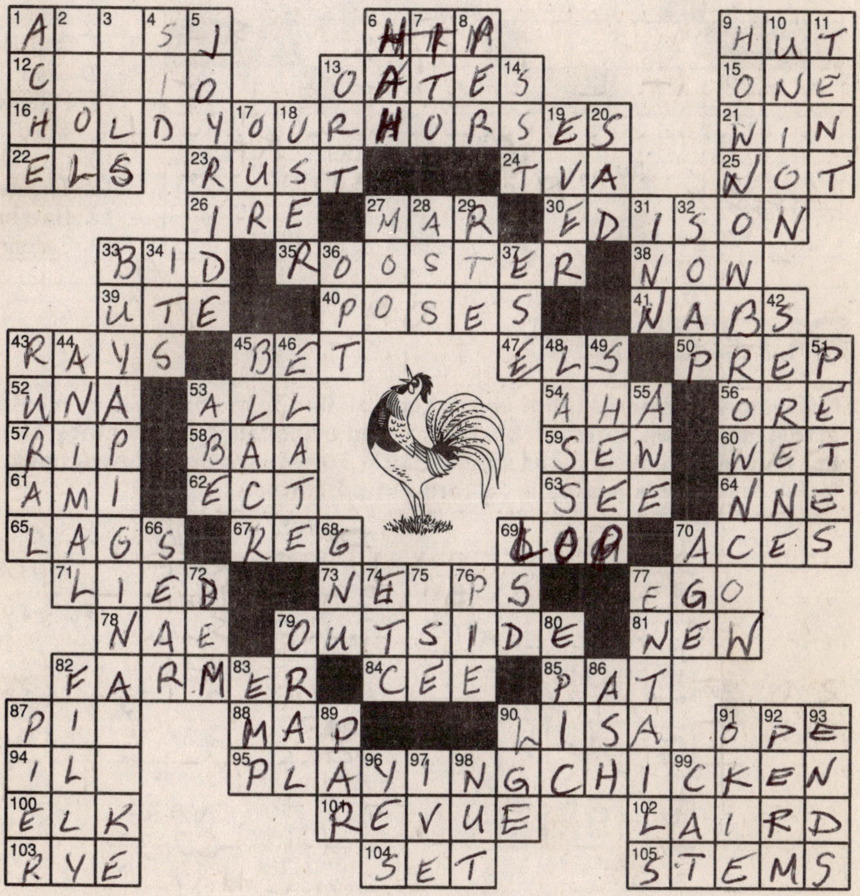

# PUZZLE 4

**ACROSS**

1. Impress
6. Mop
10. Bill of fare
14. Metric volume
15. Buckeye State
16. Graph element
17. In solitude
18. VIP's car
20. Precious stone
21. Thin
23. Famous
24. Peruse
25. Climb, in a way
27. Bounce
30. Informal talk
31. Coach Parseghian
34. Build
35. Portion
36. Victory
37. Scholarly book
38. Range
39. Piquance
40. Sash for Yum-Yum
41. Prop
42. Horse-race prize
43. Seine
44. Native of Warsaw
45. Muse
46. Knotted
47. ___ to the bait
48. Reject with disdain
51. Canvas shelter
52. Actress Ruby
55. Listen secretly
58. Say "I do"
60. Downwind
61. Govern
62. Maltreat
63. Pb
64. Shout
65. Identifies

**DOWN**

1. Metal dross
2. Mah-jongg piece
3. Energy source
4. Stag guests
5. Gift
6. 100%
7. Caprice
8. Goal
9. Halloween word
10. ___-Dixon line
11. Theater sign
12. Baseball team
13. Secondhand
19. Join
22. Dawdle
24. Texas university
25. Form
26. Rapid rodent
27. Put to attack: 2 wds.
28. Investigate
29. Send money in payment
30. Task
31. Grant
32. Wash lightly
33. Dander
35. Berate
38. Sabot or clog
39. Melody
41. Short rides
42. "The ___ Always Rings Twice"
45. Wrestling coup
46. Trapped aloft
47. Drive off
48. ___ of approval
49. Ashen
50. Eye part
51. Ring
52. "The Tin ___"
53. Irish
54. Watches
56. Arid
57. Parisian street
59. Arab cloak

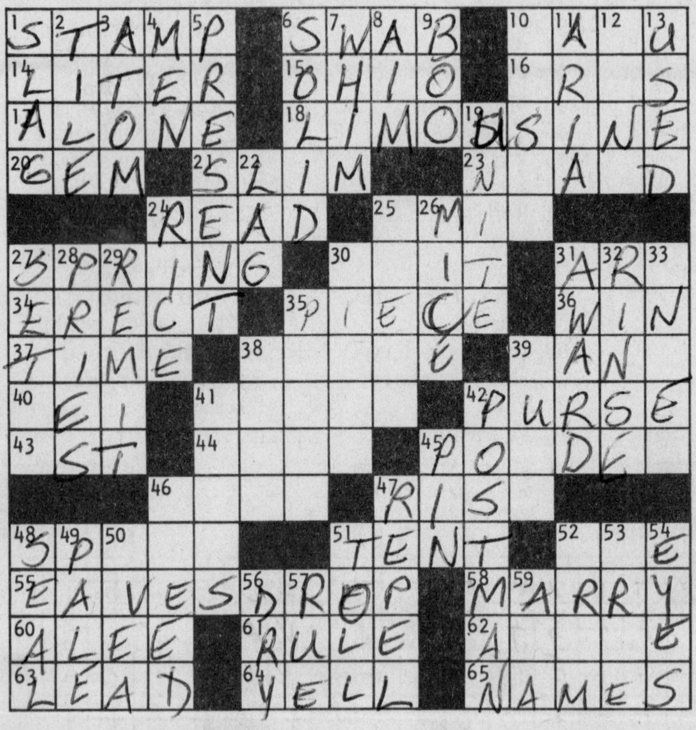

# PUZZLE 5

# ALL FOURS

**How many common 4-letter words can you find in the diagram by moving from letter to adjacent letter across, up, down, forward, backward, and diagonally? A letter may be used more than once in a word, but only after leaving it and coming back. Foreign words, abbreviations, words beginning with a capital letter, and words ending in "s" are not permitted.**

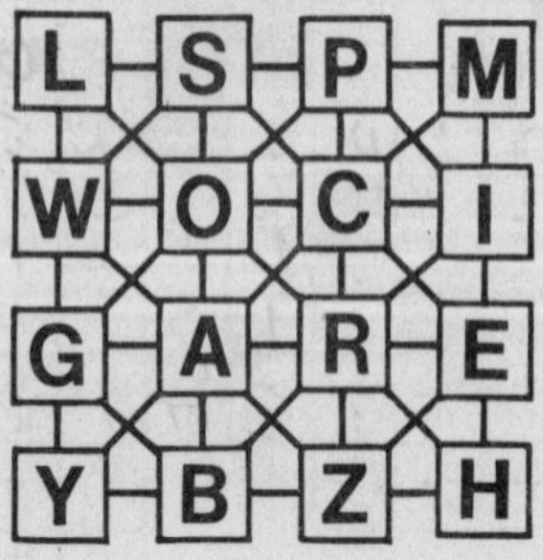


**YOUR WORD LIST**

LOWS WORE GORE PORE CARE HEIR BARE SOAR MIRE MICE PIER CORE LORE SORE SLOW WARB BRAY BRIE RICE ICER SCAR RACE ROWS GARB CARB WARE COPS SLOP LIMPS PIES SLOG COWS SWAG SWAB SWAY AROS CRAB CROP BARE BROS BROW BRIG SPEC MIRE GAZE BARB CAGY

# PUZZLE 6

## NUTTY

**Here is a puzzle with more than the expected crossword challenge—and rewards. Each clue involves a pun or some form of nuttiness. Look out for traps! With a little practice, you will soon catch on to these tricky clues and enjoy the extra challenge.**

**ACROSS**

1. Go back over text slowly
5. Sticky subject
10. Get your thin coin back
14. Sign of things that were reversed?
15. Wire home
16. Singer makes eager comeback
17. "My Beautiful Laundrette," e.g.
19. Unfitting boutonniere for moonstruck lover
21. Door to the left aboard?
23. Vital publication
24. Reverse curve
25. Father goes back to Paris
27. Where residents are canvassed
29. General description
33. Fought poverty
37. Fasted?
38. Not as great as Superior
40. It's shouted about
41. Long trek back
43. From the warden's stylus?
45. It's a plot!
46. Lyon heads
48. Real gone birds
50. Setback
51. Like tennis shoes?
53. Why I hate dis code medicine
55. Tart kinsmen
57. Yes, Virginia, there is a dance
58. Live in a backward way
61. Pied Piper's oath when he wasn't paid
63. Did uplifting work
67. When the brook stopped babbling?
70. Right by your plate
71. Father of invention
72. The raven said more
74. Lamb of a Charles
75. Questions, questions, questions
76. Lose all cents
77. Where you go from here

**DOWN**

1. Raise a glass
2. One who must pay up
3. Famous pup houser?
4. It might suggest where Bill could board
5. Letter reopener
6. Spring up
7. That's the spirit
8. Bracer chaser
9. It pops up in the toaster
10. Old Tokyo brings up a poem
11. Head up the river
12. Burly singer
13. Virginia's last venture
18. The very sort of thing that grates on your nerves
20. Melon has a sour taste
22. What to do before things get you down
26. Uncovered a peach of a pear
28. Means of support
29. Worry worry worry
30. The old bucket wood, like
31. Resident of the U.N.?
32. He gives up
34. Dresses of male
35. Send up
36. In the thick of things
39. Low point in a space career
42. Make a pile
44. He doesn't sport a winning smile
47. A ballerina's is just tutu
49. The most common beef
52. Goes a long
54. Baba and Beatty in a row
56. Like the cost of making tea?
58. Time's up!
59. Get carried away
60. By George, summer drinks!
62. Lay a nest egg
64. My fodder's house
65. She strolls up the bridal path
66. BMOC
68. Weekend test?
69. Fellow Americans, e.g.
73. Down the road a piece

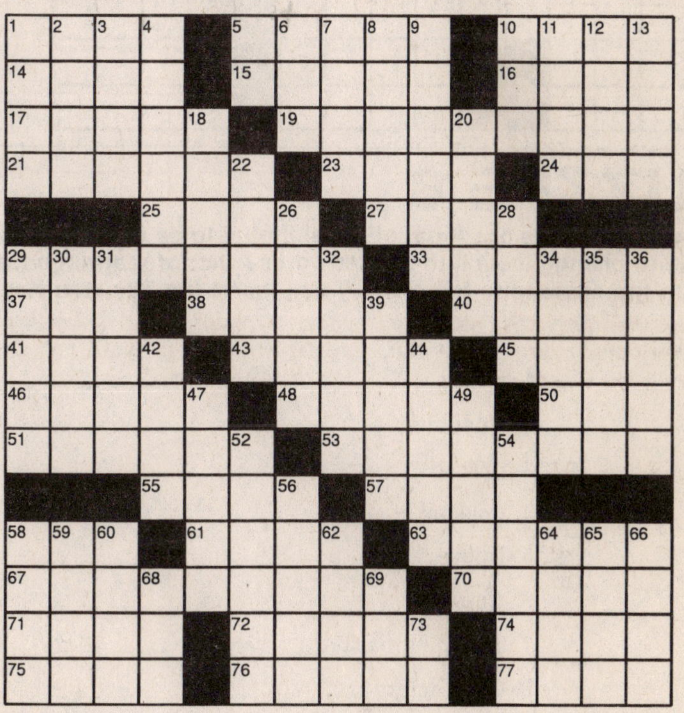

# PUZZLE 7

**• BLOW ME DOWN! •**

**ACROSS**

1. Sail support
5. "___ Shrugged"
10. Scorch
14. Ms. Sheedy
15. Molts
16. Foray
17. Gather a crop
18. Tropical easterlies
20. Restrained, as an animal
22. Aleutian island
23. Bears: Sp.
24. Moslem judge
26. Parka stuffing
29. Tropical cyclone
34. Straightened
36. Scottish cap
37. Gypsy man
38. Fabulous bird
39. Clocked again
42. Wane
43. Year: Sp.
44. Jeanne d'___
45. Mexican dish
47. Westerly
51. Skinflint
52. Cher film
53. Actor John ___
55. Barbecue rod
57. Amazon
61. Shakespeare comedy
64. Ready to pluck
65. Solemn vow
66. Danish islands
67. Opera highlight
68. Curds and ___
69. Small valleys
70. Camera eye

**DOWN**

1. Shopping center
2. Toward shelter
3. Bed board
4. Tropical cyclone
5. Dog on "The Jetsons"
6. Separate wheat from chaff
7. Conduct
8. Append
9. Vane dir.
10. Rex Reed, e.g.
11. Skein
12. Verdi opera
13. Highways: abbr.
19. Dry stream in Africa
21. Glacial ridge
24. Pack full
25. Knight's helmet
26. Iranian town
27. Solitary
28. Loop on lace
30. City on the Mohawk
31. Neighborhoods
32. Exalted
33. Glowing coal
35. Loved ones
40. Hard journey
41. ___ and Pythias
46. Northerly
48. Forge
49. London art gallery
50. House: Fr.
54. Spouses
55. Persian ruler
56. Singer Seeger
57. Actor Richard
58. Irish republic
59. Make thread
60. Sail the seven
61. Pull behind
62. Producing: abbr.
63. Crony

# PUZZLE 8 — Skeleton Key

**Can you guess the one letter of the alphabet to be put into the same place in each of the 4-letter answer words to change them into 5-letter words? Do not rearrange the order of the letters. First, fill in column A with the answers to the clues. Then, insert the Skeleton Key letter to complete column B.**

| | A. | B. |
|---|---|---|
| 1. Finest | _ _ _ _ | _ _ _ _ _ |
| 2. Unadulterated | _ _ _ _ | _ _ _ _ _ |
| 3. Cease | _ _ _ _ | _ _ _ _ _ |
| 4. Footfall | _ _ _ _ | _ _ _ _ _ |
| 5. Injure | _ _ _ _ | _ _ _ _ _ |
| 6. Actuality | _ _ _ _ | _ _ _ _ _ |
| 7. Shopping basket | _ _ _ _ | _ _ _ _ _ |
| 8. Confederate | _ _ _ _ | _ _ _ _ _ |
| 9. Male singer | _ _ _ _ | _ _ _ _ _ |
| 10. Assists | _ _ _ _ | _ _ _ _ _ |

# PUZZLE 9

**ACROSS**
1. Mesh
5. Cove
8. Before: pref.
12. Speck
13. Street: Fr.
14. Take a ____ on
15. Dance move
16. Night-out place
17. Excite
18. Storm
20. Roly-poly
21. Antlered animal
22. Mongrel
23. Bracelet accessory
26. Earthly
30. Hurt
31. Jabber
32. Time of light
33. Tardy
36. Thicket
38. Grimalkin
39. Hairdo
40. Antitoxin
43. Reasonable
47. Carriage
48. Slack
49. Paste
50. Formerly
51. Hail
52. Spouse
53. Adolescent
54. Taproom
55. Berserk

**DOWN**
1. Essence
2. Mechanical procedure
3. Article
4. Natty
5. Zippy
6. Em or Eller
7. Desire
8. Ridiculous
9. Exigency
10. Zip
11. Duane or Nelson
19. Freddy's street
20. Lowest form of humor?
22. Coffee holder
23. Hired car
24. Run like the wind
25. Whole
26. Infatuated
27. Tot up
28. Henpeck
29. Hurricane center
31. Still
34. Shrewdness
35. Beret's kin
36. Embrace
37. Conundrum
39. Pugilist
40. Sally, Dick, and Jane's dog
41. Sea bird
42. Hare and tortoise event
43. Molten rock
44. Mollusk
45. Word before pilot or mobile
46. Onion's relative
48. Type of dog, for short

# PUZZLE 10

**ACROSS**
1. At a ____
5. Pump purchase
8. Ella's singing style
12. White House office
13. TV actress Meyers
14. Roof overhang
15. Andes nation
16. Vereen or Gazzara
17. Shoe or clothes
18. Tooth coating
20. Sherlock's find
22. Apiarists
26. White-sale item
29. Significant time
30. Doze
31. Actor Sharif
32. Holiday lead-in
33. Medal-of-Honor recipient
34. Small colonist
35. Clay, today
36. West Point student
37. Webster book
40. Beatles film
41. Paths
45. Dissolve
47. Greek vowel
49. Rocker Billy ____
50. Pride member
51. Balderdash
52. Knave
53. Assns.
54. Observe
55. Ogled

**DOWN**
1. Canter
2. Microwave
3. Poetess Teasdale
4. Sleep
5. Butler's portrayer
6. "Where the Boys ____"
7. Straightforward
8. Sting
9. Heeled
10. Boulevard: abbr.
11. Football stand
19. Conger
21. Actress Thompson
23. Actor Costner
24. Opposite of well-done
25. Lady Macbeth's problem
26. Adult tadpole
27. All: pref.
28. Nader, for one
32. Some newlyweds
33. Brooke Hayward book
35. Feel poorly
36. "____, the Beloved Country"
38. Adolescents
39. Diminish
42. An apple ____ . . .
43. Harness
44. Coaster
45. "Alice" spinoff
46. Broadcast
48. Low digit

# PUZZLE 11

**• RHYME AND REASON •**

## ACROSS

1. Letter after iota
6. President Johnson in-law
10. June celebrants
14. Handles
18. Cake finishers
19. Asian sea
20. Touch on
21. Webber hit
23. Potentate's desert cooler?
25. Blitherin' bird?
27. Trumpet call
28. Permission
30. Turkish regiment
31. Yale alum
32. Arduous journey
34. Map abbr.
35. Basic
37. Graf ____
40. Estuary
42. Med. tests
44. Sow
45. Part of today's gooseberry crop?
49. Northern constellation
52. "Exodus" hero
53. Star flower
54. Intestinal section
56. Religious symbols: var.
58. Fix the lawn
60. Shensi Province capital
62. Incline
64. Govt. money gp.
65. Thailand, formerly
68. Primitive plant
70. 56, in 56 A.D.
71. Wood sorrels
72. Correspond correctly?
76. Delicious digs?
79. Roll-call word
80. Modern: prefix
81. Counterpart of Eros
83. Exams for H.S. srs.
84. Oriental sash
85. Of the kidney
87. Actress Gray
89. Bits
93. Too, in Toulouse
95. Harden
97. Young mayfly
100. ____ Tse-tung
101. Humiliate
103. Arrowlike narrows?
106. Membrane
108. Volunteer St.
109. Convene
110. Odds' partners
111. Humorous verses
115. Young ladies' org.
117. French lucky number, perhaps
119. Actress Balin
120. Despise
121. Stable sound
123. Stirred up
127. Weather word to a lad?
130. Ordinary surface?
132. King of Troy
133. Actor O'Neal
134. Scottish isle
135. British coins
136. Facility
137. Like some stuffings
138. Lading measures: abbr.
139. Appended

## DOWN

1. Buss
2. Twinge
3. Hammer part
4. Gutenberg, e.g.
5. Inviting one
6. Stadium sound
7. Kind of surgeon
8. Howard of the Senate
9. Ewe, at times
10. Challenge
11. Mideast garment
12. "Tender Mercies" star
13. Sets of fence steps
14. Canal on a foggy night?
15. Polynesian pepper
16. Item for Rosie
17. Inscribed pillar
22. Indigo plant
24. Isaac and Otto
26. Appointed
29. Mid-swerve
33. Singer Eartha
35. Slaves of Mercia
36. Flickertail St.
37. Wound remnant
38. Untainted
39. Goddess of discord
41. Serves untouchably
43. "____ Young Un"
46. "____ Was a Lady"
47. Dickens's Heep
48. Net fabric
50. Bacteria
51. ____ a time
55. Relocates
57. Envelope encl.
59. Bone: prefix
61. Utah ski resort
63. Mideast bread
66. British composer
67. Attitudes
69. Hebrew zither
71. Evict
72. Stallion stopper
73. Kind of puzzle
74. Gaelic
75. Sports fall-guys
77. Twist
78. German town
82. Olio
85. Yield of Frost on frost?
86. Riga natives
88. Indecorous nixes
90. Neighbor of Saudi Arabia
91. Charwoman
92. Topers
94. Cloy
96. Before, to Byron
98. "How sweet ____!"
99. Aft
102. Inventor Howe
104. Flavorless
105. Did over the floor
107. Thespians
111. Speech defect
112. Accustom
113. Craze
114. Nairobi's land
116. Shining
118. "Where's ____?"
121. Big Apple inits.
122. Dwell in as a ghost: var.
124. Touch down
125. Action: suffix
126. Accomplishment
128. Milit. base
129. Henpeck
131. Aviator's concern: abbr.

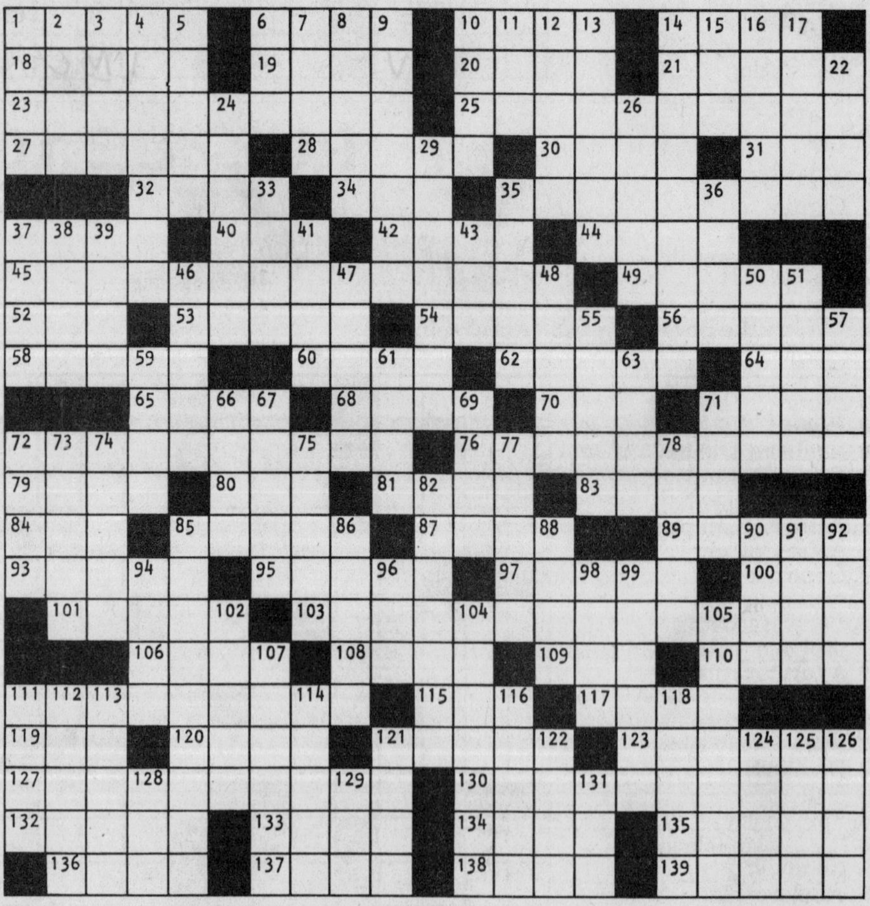

# PUZZLE 12

**ACROSS**

1. Hairless
5. Sky sight, for short
8. Scribble
11. Shampoo ingredient
12. Develops
14. Donated
15. 41st president
17. Sherman Hemsley vehicle
18. Tennis unit
19. Gusto
20. Hospital employee
22. Make impure
23. Dregs
24. Accolade
26. Laboratory containers
28. Autocrats
29. Give a leg up
31. Confidant
33. Greek peak
34. Kurosawa film
35. Ford's running mate
36. Hooray!
37. Stave off
39. Paddock prancer
40. Disagree
42. Chap
43. Closely related
44. Bear or star
46. Stogies
48. Limonite and mispickel
49. Bar bill
52. New Testament book
53. 34th president
56. Fire residue
57. Great fear
58. Read, to Brigitte
59. Texas Governor Richards
60. Append
61. "... were Paradise ___!"

**DOWN**

1. Catches, as game
2. Out of the wind
3. Booty
4. "___ Rosenkavalier"
5. Municipal
6. Spring of water
7. Expressions of pain
8. 11th president
9. Finished
10. Neighbor of Ky.
12. Icy
13. Confidence man's decoys
14. Entrances
16. Machinery parts
21. Undiluted
22. Ancient home of Irish kings
24. Syrian president Hafez al-___
25. 1st president
26. Baptism receptacle
27. French explorer Robert La ___
28. Craggy peak
29. ___ Rabbit
30. Shell's implement
32. Pewter alloy
35. Name in fashion design
37. Off yonder
38. Experienced
39. Jiffy
41. Smorgasbord
42. Composite
44. Sat for the camera
45. Mountain nymph
46. Pedro's house
47. Religious image
49. Romulus, to Remus
50. Starter for gram or bat
51. Concoction
54. Vermont founder Allen
55. Violinist Bull

# Quotagram

# PUZZLE 13

**Fill in the answers to the clues. Then transfer the letters to the correspondingly numbered squares in the diagram. The completed diagram will contain a quotation.**

1. Displays ___ ___ ___ ___ ___ ___ ___ ___ (14 24 20 31 38 5 33 9)
2. Eccentricity ___ ___ ___ ___ ___ ___ (11 4 40 16 35 41)
3. Immature ___ ___ ___ ___ ___ (7 1 37 25 17)
4. Lifting machines ___ ___ ___ ___ ___ ___ (13 39 8 32 22 29)
5. Contribute ___ ___ ___ ___ ___ ___ (18 34 6 3 10 30)
6. Dairy product ___ ___ ___ ___ ___ (27 26 2 21 15)
7. Byron or Betty ___ ___ ___ ___ ___ (19 36 28 12 23)

# PUZZLE 14

## CRYPTIC CROSSWORD

**British-style or cryptic crosswords are a great challenge for crossword fans. Each clue contains either a definition or direct reference to the answer as well as a play on words. The numbers in parentheses indicate the number of letters in the answer word or words.**

**ACROSS**

1. Royalty tracks aloud (6)
4. Larry's head in bizarre suppression (8)
10. Keep us in soil (7)
11. Waves at peculiar slipper (7)
12. A cereal sounds crooked (4)
13. Watch mechanism apes cement mixer (10)
15. He gives a blender, starting off (6)
16. Goes and remedies (7)
19. Fine ink in front of Sharpton and Cobb (7)
20. Severely criticize her about Tom (6)
23. Works with Gary at top of escalator (10)
24. Initially, teal is not the color (4)
26. Ride in explosive missile (7)
27. Reaching a competitor, we hear (7)
28. Act shaky about farm accumulation (8)
29. Made bristly to conceal trash (6)

**DOWN**

1. Dad's weasel just good enough (8)
2. Council repays in shoddy coverage (9,6)
3. Chinese dog heard Italian greeting (4)
5. Endanger muddy earth with sawbuck (8)
6. Soft food is nonsense (10)
7. Lamenter grasps redolent stray dog (6,9)
8. Surrogate hidden by skiers at zenith (6)
9. Gang still has feeling of dread (5)
14. Corruption of Spanish cellar (10)
17. Tail can't sully vast body of water (8)
18. French island in schoolbooks makes fabric (8)
21. Put an end to whiskey (6)
22. Tied up sticker (5)
25. Bonsai in great reef (4)

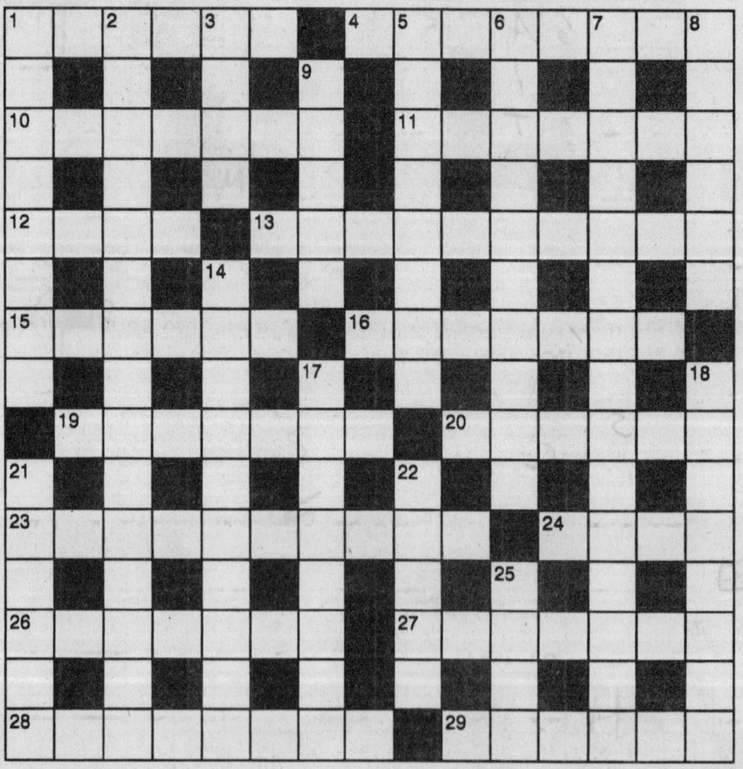

# PUZZLE 15

**ACROSS**

1. Years long past
5. Engage
9. Submit, as a question
12. Prayer conclusion
13. Fifty-fifty
14. Indefinite number
15. Pie filling
17. Waiter's reward
18. Small porch
19. Diminutive
21. Teases
24. Mass of fish eggs
25. Roof overhang
28. City trains
30. Oklahoma town
33. Luxurious resort
34. Obtain
35. Cote call
36. Personality
38. Tar's milieu
39. Posted
40. Ornamental vase
42. Golf hazard
44. Cried, as a donkey
47. Depart
51. Shot at Wimbledon
52. Resumed
55. Annex
56. Reflex site
57. Nuisance
58. Itsy-bitsy
59. Patched
60. Garage event

**DOWN**

1. Sweet potatoes
2. Choose not to include
3. Nevada town
4. Once more
5. Skirt bottom
6. "____ Got a Secret"
7. Harvest
8. Log
9. Steady perseverance
10. Squadron
11. Category
16. Outer: pref.
20. Foot part
22. Entreats
23. Icy rain
25. Snaky shape
26. Gibbon
27. Precious
29. Headliner
31. Charged particle
32. Period
37. Saute
39. Consumes
41. Bottle parts
43. Boxing great
44. Gusted
45. Audition goal
46. Finished
48. Air
49. Young beef
50. Border
53. Modern
54. X

| | | | | | | | | | | | | |
|---|---|---|---|---|---|---|---|---|---|---|---|---|
| 1 Y | 2 O | 3 R | 4 E | ■ | 5 H | 6 I | 7 R | 8 E | ■ | 9 A | 10 S | 11 K |
| 12 A | M | E | N | ■ | 13 E | V | E | N | ■ | 14 | | |
| 15 M | I | N | C | 16 E | M | E | A | T | ■ | 17 T | I | P |
| 18 S | T | O | O | P | ■ | ■ | 19 P | E | 20 T | | | |
| ■ | ■ | ■ | 21 R | I | 22 B | 23 S | ■ | 24 R | O | E | ■ | ■ |
| 25 E | 26 A | 27 V | E | ■ | 28 E | L | 29 S | ■ | 30 E | R | 31 I | 32 E |
| 33 S | P | A | ■ | ■ | 34 G | E | T | ■ | ■ | 35 | O | R |
| 36 S | E | L | 37 F | ■ | 38 S | E | A | ■ | 39 S | | N | A |
| ■ | ■ | 40 U | R | 41 N | ■ | 42 T | R | 43 A | P | ■ | ■ | ■ |
| 44 B | 45 R | A | Y | E | 46 D | ■ | ■ | 47 L | E | 48 A | 49 V | 50 E |
| 51 L | O | B | ■ | 52 C | O | 53 N | 54 T | I | N | U | E | D |
| 55 E | L | L | ■ | 56 K | N | E | E | ■ | 57 D | R | A | G |
| 58 W | E | E | ■ | 59 S | E | W | N | ■ | 60 S | A | L | E |

# PUZZLE 16

**ACROSS**

1. Owl's question
4. Dull pain
8. Touch
12. Slippery fish
13. Satellite
14. Volcano output
15. Quivered
17. Applications
18. Long in the tooth
19. New
20. Cost
23. Inheritor
25. Appear
26. Hairdresser's item
30. Dine
31. Chunks
32. Poem
33. Beginners
35. Skin spot
36. Unwanted plant
37. Drilled
38. Expressions
41. Protrude
42. Pride member
43. Renovate
48. Revise copy
49. Mental faculties
50. Remove moisture from
51. Refuse
52. Bird's home
53. Half of a pair

**DOWN**

1. Damp
2. That woman
3. Bullfighter's cheer
4. Stroll
5. Frosty
6. Garden tool
7. Conclude
8. Brief snow shower
9. Soothe
10. Plumb and Arden
11. Eyelid hair
16. Deride
19. White lies
20. Request
21. Wander
22. Smidgeon
23. Squirrel away
24. Flows back
26. Azure
27. Destitute
28. Lazy
29. Require
31. Visualizes
34. "____ Questions"
35. Wool-eater
37. Pop
38. Scurried
39. General's help
40. Nickel, e.g.
41. New York team
43. Have
44. Compete
45. Bustle
46. Vase
47. Caustic substance

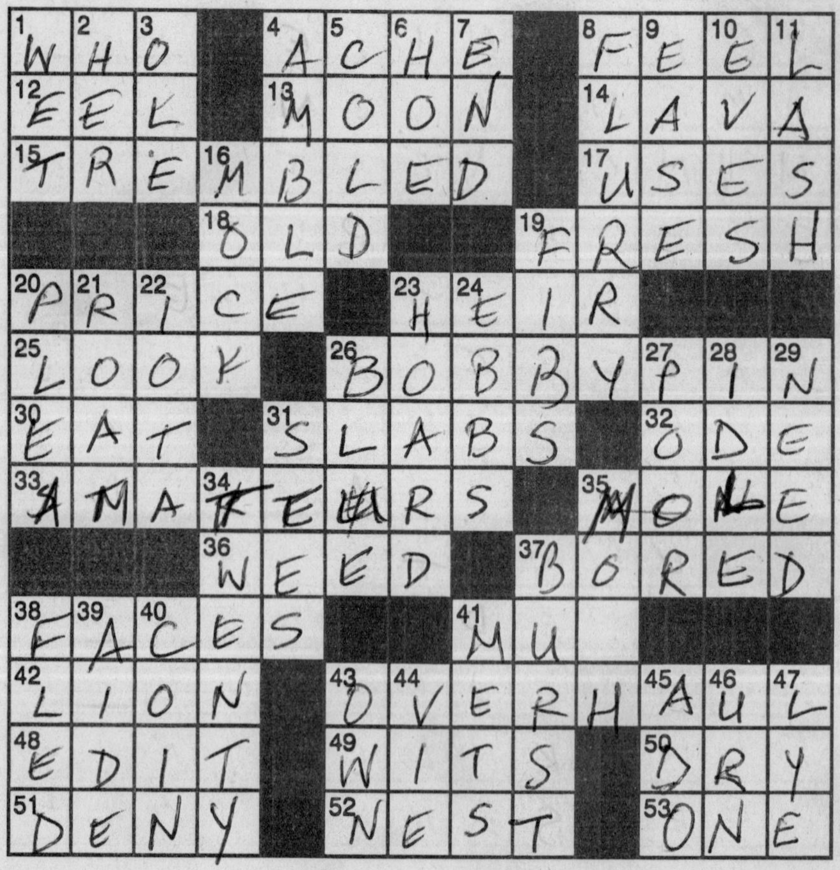

# PUZZLE 17

**ACROSS**

1. Hemingway's nickname
5. Fast plane
8. Those people
12. Amazed
13. "Long, Long ____"
14. Roof edge
15. Mollusk
16. Represents as similar
18. Alaskan natives
20. Unseals
21. Actor Hunter
22. To and ____
23. Stanza
26. Make believe
30. Prior to, to Byron
31. ____ sauce
32. Body of water
33. Young frog
36. Stale
38. ____ an egg
39. Newsman Rather
40. Portly
43. Detachable strongbox fastener
47. Piece of parlor furniture
49. Press
50. Look for
51. Gypsy Rose ____
52. Actress Capshaw
53. Barnyard animals
54. Donkey
55. What ____ is new?

**DOWN**

1. Speed
2. Leather worker's tools
3. Colorado's Pikes ____
4. Owns up
5. Son of Isaac
6. Selves
7. Twain's Sawyer
8. Brewing vessel
9. Rabbit's relative
10. Tied
11. Clutter
17. Skin opening
19. Actress West
22. Cook in fat
23. Animal doc
24. Baseball stat
25. Primary color
26. Writer Edgar Allan ____
27. Curvy letter
28. Butterfly catcher
29. 24 hours
31. Sneaky
34. Pulls off
35. Promise
36. Incensed
37. Dissimilar
39. Challenges
40. Cloth belt
41. Oak or maple
42. Augury
43. Fruit desserts
44. Spoken
45. Campers' beds
46. Jerky joint
48. ____ carte

| | | | | | | | | | | | | |
|---|---|---|---|---|---|---|---|---|---|---|---|---|
| 1 R | 2 A | 3 P | 4 A | ■ | 5 J | 6 E | 7 T | ■ | 8 T | 9 H | 10 E | 11 M |
| 12 A | W | E | D | ■ | 13 A | G | O | ■ | 14 E | A | V | E |
| 15 C | L | A | M | ■ | 16 C | O | M | 17 P | A | R | E | S |
| 18 E | S | K | I | 19 M | O | S | ■ | 20 O | P | E | N | S |
| ■ | ■ | ■ | 21 T | A | B | ■ | 22 F | R | O | ■ | ■ | ■ |
| 23 V | 24 E | 25 R | S | E | ■ | 26 P | R | E | T | 27 E | 28 N | 29 D |
| 30 E | R | E | ■ | ■ | 31 S | O | Y | ■ | ■ | 32 S | E | A |
| 33 T | A | D | 34 P | 35 O | L | E | ■ | 36 M | 37 U | S | T | Y |
| ■ | ■ | ■ | 38 L | A | Y | ■ | 39 D | A | N | ■ | ■ | ■ |
| 40 S | 41 T | 42 O | U | T | ■ | 43 P | A | D | L | 44 O | 45 C | 46 K |
| 47 A | R | M | C | H | 48 A | I | R | ■ | 49 I | R | O | N |
| 50 S | E | E | K | ■ | 51 L | E | E | ■ | 52 K | A | T | E |
| 53 H | E | N | S | ■ | 54 A | S | S | ■ | 55 E | L | S | E |

# PUZZLE 18

**ACROSS**

1. Conforms
5. Picture hanger
9. Neck or cut
13. Proper's mate
17. Touch upon
18. Hautboy
19. "Our Love Is ___ to Stay"
20. Primrose or Penny
21. Waiter's offering
22. Notorious husband
24. Israeli port
25. Indication
27. Dressed
28. Court list
30. Bonnet intruder
31. Use an adz
32. Camper's trek
33. R-rating viewer
36. Versifier
37. Ascetic
41. Tortoise's foe
42. Head honcho
43. Piquant
44. Coach Parseghian
45. Burro
46. Bender
47. Stock in trade
48. Sir Christopher ___
49. Egyptian irrigation device
51. Cash and ___
52. Slip back
53. Coin
54. Sprite
55. Festive affair
56. Remembered ship
58. Tearful
59. Misfortune
62. Polly, to Tom
63. Links locales
64. "Bringing Up ___"
65. Reason Pinocchio's nose grows
66. Debate side
67. "___ of Manhattan"
68. Touch gently
69. Iota
70. Fish in a can
72. Instant
73. Section of plywood
74. Vegas quotes
75. Dandy's mate
76. Coupe, e.g.
77. Metal admixtures
80. Kind of cherry
81. Boasters
85. Cross
86. Uniform hue
89. Celebrity
90. Wear for Cato
91. Palmer's cry
92. Greek liqueur
93. ___ St. Vincent Millay
94. Tore
95. Trends
96. Pith
97. Discharge

**DOWN**

1. TV series
2. Mountain goat
3. Salad fish
4. Trip
5. Aristocratic
6. Up to the task
7. Chit
8. Parasites
9. Inexpensive
10. Peruse
11. Be human
12. June mergers
13. Runs second
14. Ski holder
15. Anent
16. Run into
23. Ink stain
26. Favorite
29. Give permission for
31. Price
32. Sweetheart
33. Cries of discovery
34. Sprint
35. North Star's constellation
36. Disappearing-act sound
37. Join
38. Field covering
39. Danders
40. Staff
42. Riding shoe
43. Linger
46. Tenor
47. Delays' yield
48. Off the ___
50. Power
51. Units for Sherlock

# PUZZLE 18

52. Luck's title
54. Does an office job
55. Chinwags
56. Sketches
57. Nimbus
58. Lawn underminers
59. Sunbathe
60. Quote
61. Sloop steadier
63. Kind of policy
64. Twining plant stem
67. Spruce
68. Realm
69. Agates, e.g.
71. Contraption
72. Grape yield
73. Dance step
75. Fins
76. Henry ____ Lodge
77. Liberal ____
78. Belt holder
79. Carnegie Hall area
80. Basketball's Larry ____
81. ____ Strip
82. General's sidekick
83. Forgotten
84. Piece of cake
87. Mauna ____
88. Parisian street

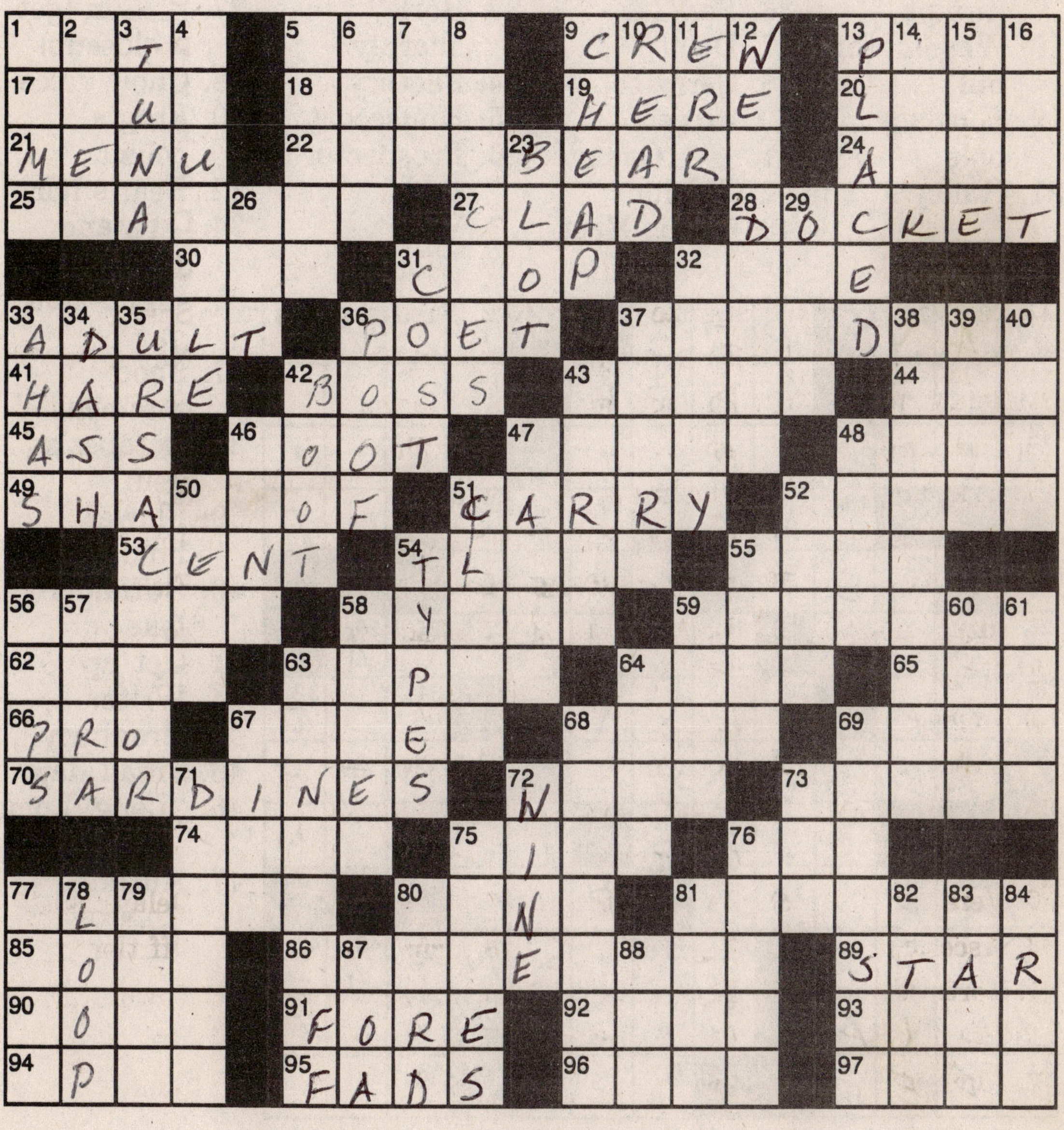

# PUZZLE 19

**ACROSS**

1. Large cove
4. In favor of
7. Close
11. Muhammad ____
12. Body of knowledge
14. Be concerned
15. Set of letters
17. Equips
18. Washington bill
19. Shoelace hole
21. Halley's ____
24. At liberty
25. Hubbubs
26. Gold strike, e.g.
29. Burst open
30. Houston's state
31. Antique
33. Modernize a home
35. Musical symbol
36. Paddles
37. Devil
38. Carry to excess
41. ____ Grande
42. Portion
43. Of the East
48. India's continent
49. Sail support
50. Ripen
51. Ogle
52. Absolutely!
53. Cry of disapproval

**DOWN**

1. Lamb's comment
2. "____ the king's men . . ."
3. Bark sharply
4. Factory
5. Housecoat
6. Prospector's find
7. Veil
8. Greet
9. Prod
10. Large quiz
13. Lasting forever
16. Cultivates
20. Affirmative votes
21. Beret, e.g.
22. Fragrance
23. Sulk
24. Crafty creatures
26. Sleeping chamber
27. ____ in (get a closeup)
28. Choir voice
30. Frog's cousin
32. Bear's lair
34. ____ and pestle
35. Light-tube gas
37. Food regimens
38. October's gem
39. Flower holder
40. Buffalo's lake
41. Get up
44. Writer Bradbury
45. Small flap
46. "Long, Long ____"
47. Author Tolstoy

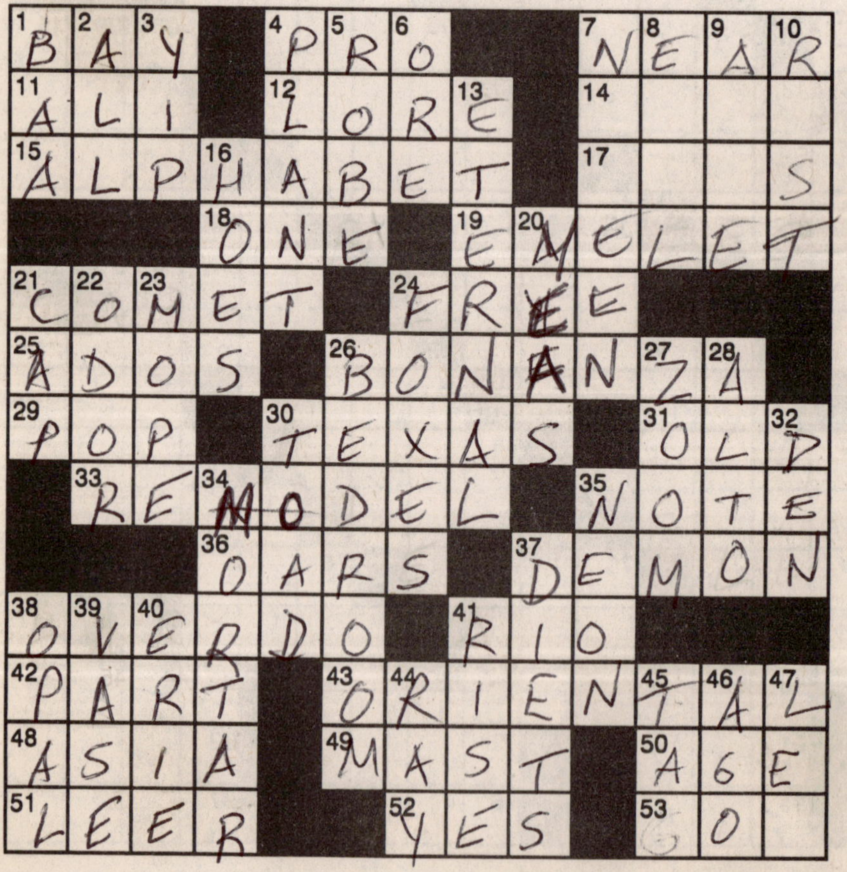

**ACROSS**

1. Plays a role
5. Vale
9. Health resort
12. Ice-cream holder
13. Zone
14. Back talk
15. Amusement
18. Sandra and Ruby
19. Yields
20. Outbuildings
22. Longing
23. Listens to
24. Outcomes
28. One ____ million
29. "____ Miserables"
30. Cereal grain
31. Zebra's features
34. Curves
36. Critic Reed
37. Is deeply fond of
38. Viper
41. Rational
42. Diploma time
47. Make leather
48. Ship's mast
49. Ocean cycle
50. Sault ____ Marie
51. Long time periods
52. Espy

**DOWN**

1. ____ in the hole
2. Pro's counterpart
3. Explosive initials
4. Planted
5. Social engagements
6. Historic times
7. Hawaiian necklace
8. Spears
9. Winter slider
10. Soft wood
11. Rental props.
16. Cincinnati nine
17. Bill of fare
20. Dispatched
21. Get word
22. Absolutely!
23. That man's
24. In medias ____
25. Sole
26. Youngsters
27. Wall and Canal: abbr.
29. Superman's foe Luthor
32. Angered
33. Read
34. Sonny ____ of song
35. Happenings
37. Hideouts
38. Middlemen: abbr.
39. Mild oath
40. Copenhagen native
41. Comedian Laurel
43. Soldier's address: abbr.
44. Short swim
45. Stir
46. So far

# PUZZLE 20

# PUZZLE 21

**ACROSS**
1. Cauldron
4. Brainstorm
8. Snow slider
12. Poet's before
13. Close
14. Optimism
15. Pod vegetable
16. Assigned job
17. Unseal
18. Brief
20. Leg joints
21. Adhesive strip
23. Type of net
25. End a mission
27. European deer
28. Terrier, e.g.
31. Clothes cabinet
33. Indigenous one
35. Decade number
36. Atmosphere
38. Sofa
39. Colorado resort
41. Part played
42. Big
45. Leap about
47. Healing plant
48. Brief note
49. Bottle top
52. College official
53. Lyric poems
54. Cenozoic, e.g.
55. Dispatched
56. "Go ____, young man"
57. Morning moisture

**DOWN**
1. Kind of rally
2. Mineral-bearing rock
3. Chef's measure
4. Involved with
5. Loved ones
6. Spring holiday
7. Clumsy vessel
8. Gleamed
9. Run easily
10. Dueling sword
11. Lairs
19. Towel marking
20. Work, like dough
21. Diplomacy
22. Up to the job
24. Charged particle
26. Ridicule
28. Completely separated
29. Racetrack shape
30. Unit of heredity
32. Gratuity
34. Radial, e.g.
37. Ebb
39. Representative
40. Titles
42. Young fellows
43. Opposite of aweather
44. Horse color
46. Mail
48. Cut the grass
50. "Where the Boys ____"
51. Cat's foot

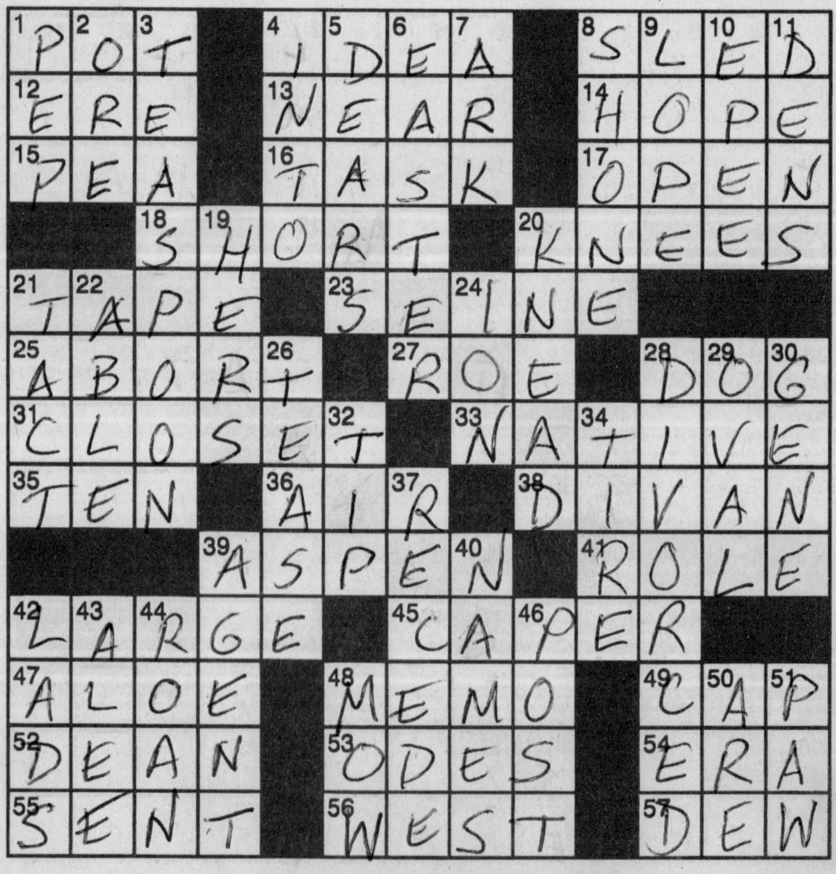

# PUZZLE 22

**ACROSS**

1. Pats gently
5. Buddy
8. Ten-speed, e.g.
12. Iraq's neighbor
13. Top pilot
14. Prayer ending
15. Missile housing
16. ____ Island dressing
18. Unit of heat
20. Tent spike
21. Menagerie
22. Modeling
25. Pasted
28. Moral wrong
29. And not
30. Greases
31. Edgar Allan ____
32. Actor Arnaz
33. Stable morsel
34. Legal decree
35. West Point student
36. Crusoe's companion
38. Daughter's brother
39. Insane
40. Nebraska city
44. Studied closely
47. New York canal
48. Carry
49. Snakelike fish
50. Babble
51. Rams' mates
52. Before, to poets
53. Snow coaster

**DOWN**

1. Record
2. Diva's solo
3. Orb
4. Naps
5. Terrace
6. Dull pain
7. Zodiac lion
8. Military compounds
9. Dreamed up
10. Actor Berry
11. Finale
17. "____ the Roof"
19. Slender pole
22. Baked dessert
23. Snout
24. Course sand
25. Blunder
26. Untruthful one
27. Last
28. Female pig
31. Remit funds
32. Ballerinas, e.g.
34. Refined woman
35. Swindle
37. Wide valleys
38. Move sideways
40. Sly look
41. Spoken
42. Reside
43. Want
44. Had brunch
45. Immediately
46. Zuider ____

# PUZZLE 23

**ACROSS**

1. Melt
5. Cain's brother
9. Head of a suit
12. Crude metals
13. Traveled
14. Samovar
15. Grows older
16. Pennsylvania city
17. Divest
18. Showed the way
19. Profit
20. Checks
21. Concept
24. Australian bird
26. Smudges
28. Cut a rug
32. Macaroni
33. Jeweled headpiece
34. Painter
36. Paid a landlord
37. "Brave ____ World"
38. Periphery
39. Electric lamp feature
42. Lessen
44. Sailor
47. Kind of doll
48. Escape
49. Tramp
50. Petroleum
51. Egg-shaped
52. Do a household chore
53. Snoop
54. Precious stones
55. Colored

**DOWN**

1. Young horse
2. Encourage
3. Most run-down
4. Sibilant letter
5. Stadiums
6. Tedious person
7. Corrected copy
8. Brenda or Bruce
9. Atmosphere
10. Baby bed
11. Remnants
20. Adjusting in pitch
22. Going steady
23. Rub out
25. Paired
26. Place to rejuvenate
27. Scratch
29. Ilk
30. Sooner than, in verse
31. June honoree
35. Number of Apostles
36. Dissenters
39. Actor's tool
40. Lion's home
41. Unattractive
43. Smile broadly
45. Reed instrument
46. 007
48. Mist
49. Covered up

# PUZZLE 24

**ACROSS**

1. Fibs
5. Singer Domino
9. To and ____
12. Israeli port
13. Soothing plant
14. Moo
15. Enter
17. Overwhelm
18. Make over
19. Leave out
21. Saga
24. Gluts
27. Food fish
30. Roadster
32. Roman emperor
33. Elf
34. Mined matter
35. ____ Tin Tin
36. Significant times
38. Bird's bill
39. Hues
40. Valuable
42. Palm fruit
44. Poorboy
46. Kitty builder
49. "The Greatest"
51. Attempt
55. Ballpoint
56. Cicatrix
57. Ginger drinks
58. Quiche ingredient
59. Sawbucks
60. Not as much

**DOWN**

1. ____ dog
2. Froster
3. Marine bird
4. Planted
5. Distant
6. Menu phrase
7. Movie dog
8. "____ Like Old Times"
9. Blarney
10. Squabble
11. Be in the red
16. "____ Gun"
20. Writer Fleming
22. Religious image
23. Had feelings
25. Huron's neighbor
26. "____ and Lovers"
27. ____ butter
28. ____ d'oeuvre
29. Shaming
31. Singer McEntire
37. Understand
39. Of teeth
41. Faith
43. Roofing liquid
45. Previously
47. Fantasy
48. Supplements
49. Copy
50. Table support
52. Newsman Rather
53. Bitter vetch
54. Road turn

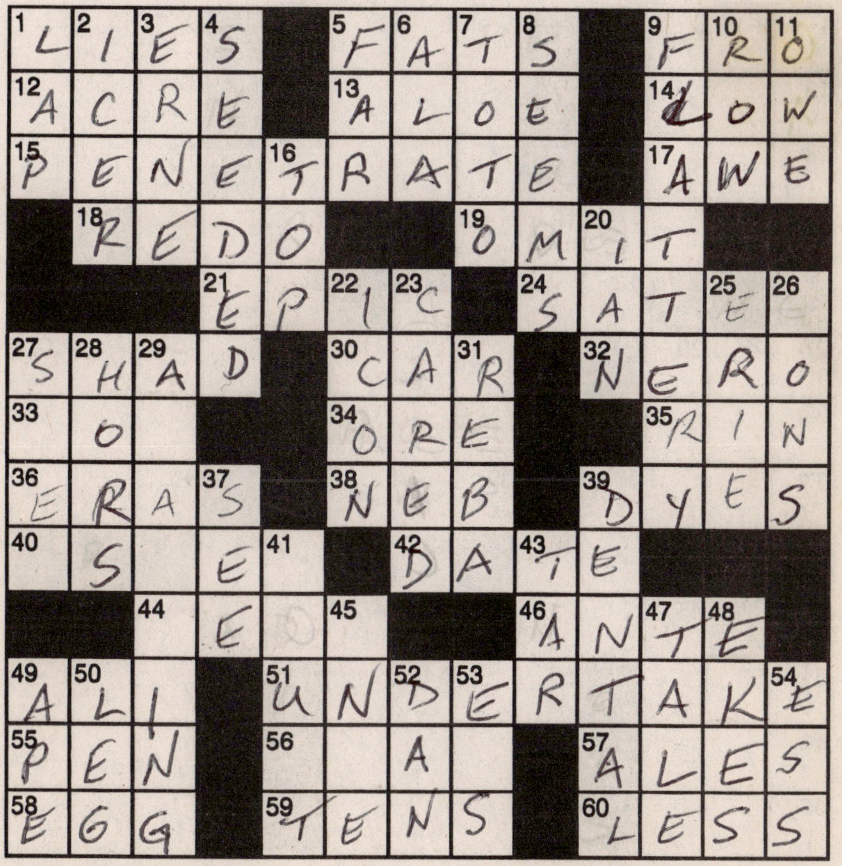

# PUZZLE 25

**ACROSS**

1. Type of package
5. Muscle strain
9. Casey's club
12. Province
13. Mountain animal
14. Hard water
15. Spear or pepper
16. Prickly feeling
17. Comedian Skelton
18. Copyright
20. Gentle
22. Bona fide
24. Expenses
27. Divest
30. Potent particle
32. You ____ what you sow
33. Writer Levin
34. Royal
36. Supplement
37. Use a stop watch on
39. Location
40. Dawn moisture
41. Ski resort
43. Copper coin
45. Verve
47. Bakes
51. Moral wrong
53. Adolescent
55. Folk knowledge
56. "Where the Boys ____"
57. Author Bombeck
58. Warning
59. Attach firmly
60. Inner being
61. Extreme poverty

**DOWN**

1. Group of tents
2. Diva's song
3. Apartment fee
4. Nosher
5. Shakes briskly
6. Canvas bed
7. Taxicab
8. Body of moral values
9. Avian chow
10. One, in dice
11. Edward's nickname
19. Not far
21. Scand.
23. Reason
25. Seize
26. Gush
27. Actress Moreno
28. Blue flag
29. Moistened
31. Motherly
35. Carson's replacement
38. Moray or electric
42. Archibald and Thurmond
44. Eagle's claw
46. Roman fiddler
48. Several
49. Forest plant
50. Transmit
51. Carpenter's tool
52. Fury
54. Ostrichlike bird

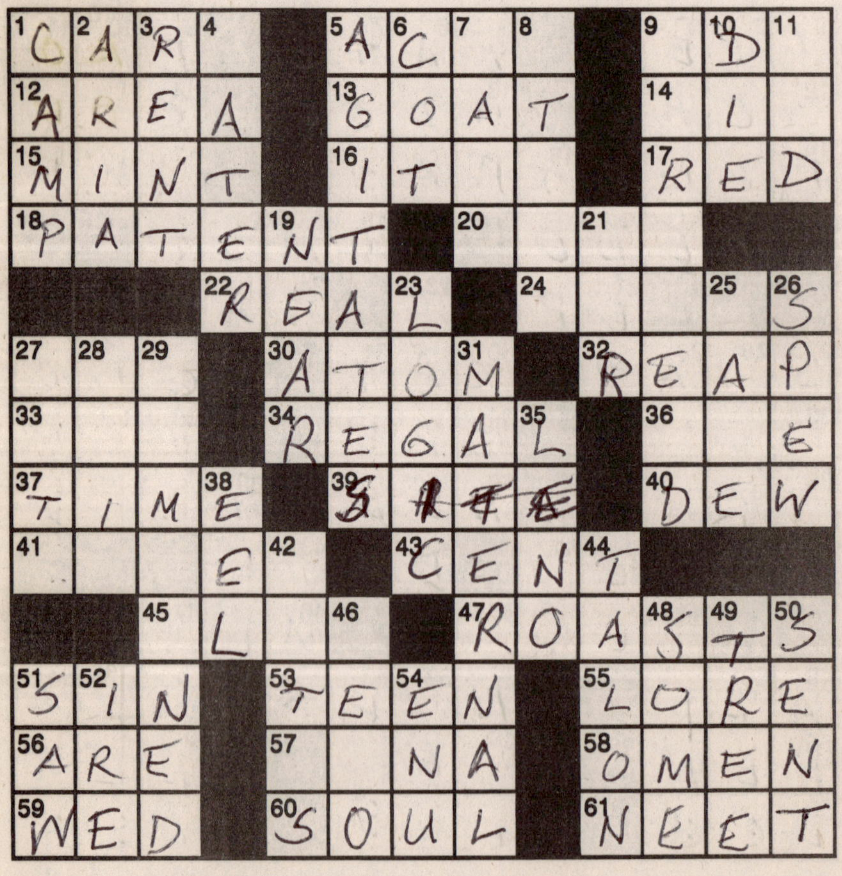

# PUZZLE 26

**ACROSS**

1. Wane
4. Bigwig
8. Skinny branch
12. Whiskey
13. Actor Alan ___
14. Expansive
15. Martin Luther King, Jr., was one
17. Component
18. Tears
19. Wichita's locale
21. Buckets
23. "___ Colors"
24. Minerals
25. Shortly
26. Feminine pronoun
29. Family room
30. "___ the Moon"
31. Santa's delivery
32. Blue
33. Sedate
34. Strong wind
35. Bad actors
36. Sentence components
37. Soak up
40. Botch
41. Close-by
42. Schooling
46. Sunbathes
47. Wicked
48. Caribbean or Caspian
49. "Jagged ___"
50. Transmit
51. Greeting

**DOWN**

1. Slip up
2. Farewell
3. Act as a pal to
4. Angelic instruments
5. "Desire Under the ___"
6. Summer beverage
7. Photographer's milieu
8. Rope
9. Punsters
10. Inspiration
11. Some stones
16. Canola and corn
20. Bee or Clara
21. Whale herds
22. Domain
23. Implements
25. State of disorder
26. Five-armed beach dweller
27. Retain
28. Watches carefully
30. Wound mark
34. Mobster's man
35. Steed
36. "Wayne's ___"
37. Poker move
38. Droplet
39. Warbled
40. Advance
43. Night before
44. Formerly named
45. Merry

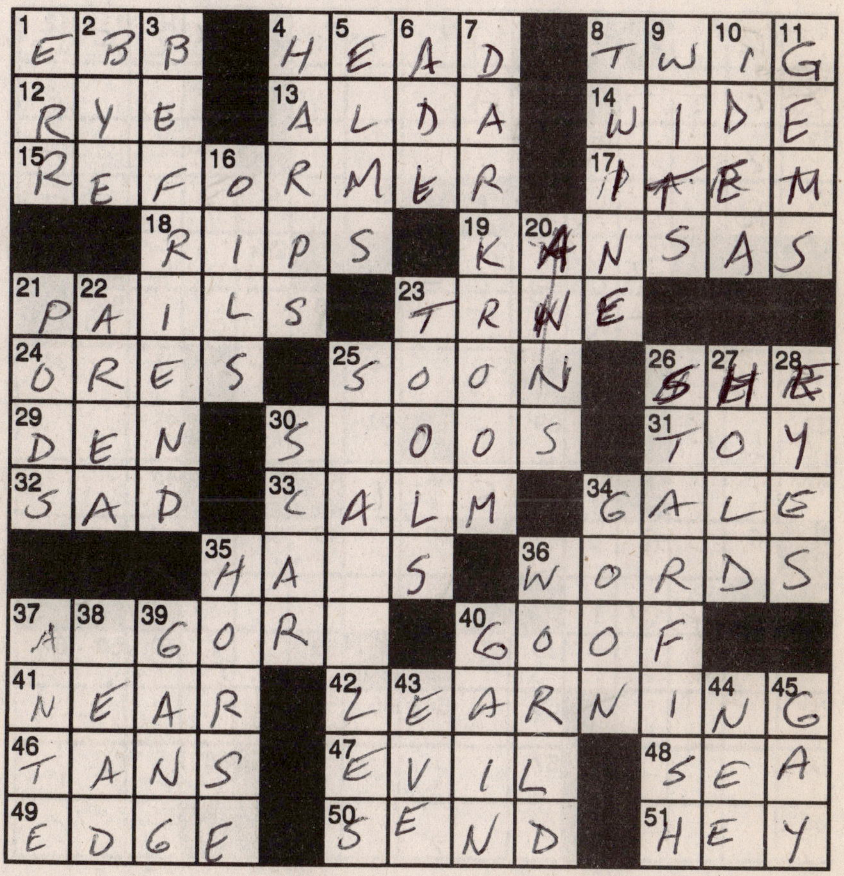

# PUZZLE 27

**ACROSS**

1. Society page word
4. Sends forth
9. Top pilots
13. Rows
15. Indian princess
16. Poi ingredient
17. Greer Garson film
19. Despot
20. Whole
21. Arbitrate
23. Sample
26. Sphere
27. Insane
30. Fights
32. Bridge expert Culbertson
33. Muzzles
35. Exclamation of triumph
37. North Pole worker
38. Deputy: abbr.
40. Thanksgiving dessert
41. Zilch
42. Red or Black
43. Painting surface
45. Auditor: abbr.
46. Agave fiber
48. Batter's place
52. Decay
53. Evade
54. Merchant vessel
58. Car shelter
62. Turkish regiment
63. Bing Crosby film
66. Comedian Foxx
67. Uncanny
68. Wash
69. Ottoman governors
70. Large antelope
71. Affirmative answer

**DOWN**

1. Alaska city
2. Deserve
3. Formerly, of old
4. Author Hemingway
5. ___ tai
6. Bill: abbr.
7. Swarm
8. Dry
9. Apparel
10. Humphrey Bogart film
11. Quod ___ demonstrandum
12. Tender
14. Strike hard
18. Persia, today
22. Drench
24. Camping shelters
25. Old Tokyo
27. Frances and Ruby
28. Model Macpherson et al.
29. Audrey Hepburn film
30. "Agnus ___"
31. Transports
34. Thread holder
36. Winglike expansions
38. Playing marble
39. Thicken
44. Haggard novel
47. Cubes, e.g.
49. Grimaced
50. Mild cheese
51. Green mineral
54. Dress
55. Sheltered
56. Double curve
57. Carol
59. Out
60. Donated
61. Peepers
64. Tax shelter: abbr.
65. Diarist Anais ___

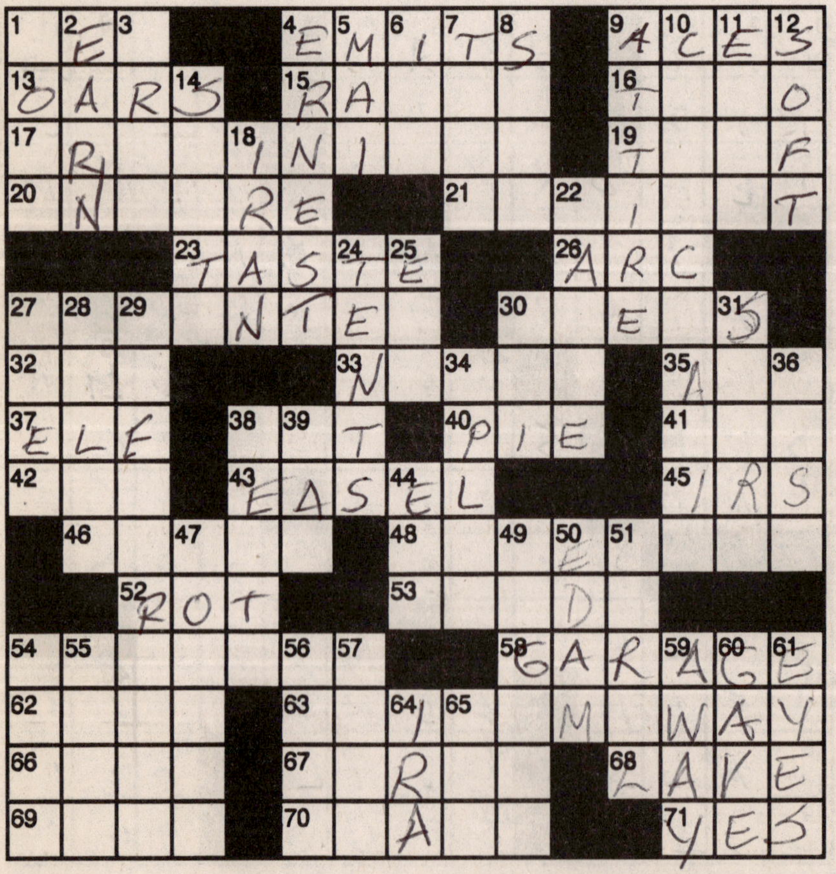

# PUZZLE 28

**ACROSS**

1. "Married to the ____"
4. Forest measure
8. Prayer ending
12. Reverence
13. Twofold
14. Mountain hollow
15. Dawn moisture
16. Encourage
17. Works by Keats
18. Lazy
20. Mother or father
22. Apportion
24. Lower face part
25. Ocean movement
26. Close loudly
27. Lemon drink
30. Singletons
31. Sunbather's goal
32. Surrounded by
33. ____ capita
34. Sand
35. Highway division
36. Baseball feature
37. Consumed
38. Occur
41. Foundation
42. Emerald ____
43. Equipment
45. ____ and downs
48. Tilt
49. Corrupt
50. Knock smartly
51. Country
52. Depend
53. Cunning

**DOWN**

1. Furious
2. Be in debt
3. Perplex
4. Mature
5. Heal
6. Dustcloth
7. Dumbo, e.g.
8. Squirrel's treat
9. Created
10. Equal
11. Birdhouse structure
19. Accomplishes
21. Intention
22. On the apex
23. Draw the ____
24. Assertion
26. Outsider
27. Novices
28. Enjoy a banquet
29. Genesis garden
32. Woeful word
34. ____ whiz!
36. Pay out
37. Ahead of time
38. Road incline
39. Confused
40. Strategy
41. Suspect's release money
44. Christmas ____
46. Buddy
47. Secret agent

| | | | | | | | | | | | | |
|---|---|---|---|---|---|---|---|---|---|---|---|---|
| 1 M | 2 O | 3 B | ■ | 4 A | 5 C | 6 R | 7 E | ■ | 8 A | 9 M | 10 E | 11 N |
| 12 A | W | E | ■ | 13 D | U | A | L | ■ | 14 C | A | V | E |
| 15 D | E | W | ■ | 16 U | R | G | E | ■ | 17 O | D | E | S |
| ■ | ■ | 18 I | 19 D | L | E | ■ | 20 P | 21 A | R | E | N | T |
| 22 A | 23 L | L | O | T | ■ | 24 C | H | I | N | ■ | ■ | ■ |
| 25 T | I | D | E | ■ | 26 S | L | A | M | ■ | 27 A | 28 D | 29 G |
| 30 O | N | E | S | ■ | 31 T | A | N | ■ | 32 A | M | I | D |
| 33 P | E | R | ■ | 34 G | R | I | T | ■ | 35 L | A | N | E |
| ■ | ■ | ■ | 36 S | E | A | M | ■ | 37 E | A | T | E | N |
| 38 H | 39 A | 40 P | P | E | N | ■ | 41 B | A | S | E | ■ | ■ |
| 42 I | S | L | E | ■ | 43 G | 44 E | A | R | ■ | 45 U | 46 P | 47 S |
| 48 L | E | A | N | ■ | 49 E | V | I | L | ■ | 50 R | A | P |
| 51 L | A | N | D | ■ | 52 R | E | L | Y | ■ | 53 S | L | Y |

# PUZZLE 29

**ACROSS**

1. Wine valley
5. Meeting plan
11. Camel's-hair coat
14. Actor Bates
15. Chestnut
16. ____ Yutang
17. Limited thinking
20. Of South American mountains
21. Quenches
22. Memorize
23. Sharp point
26. With an ____
27. Western plant
30. Hoopla
33. Ryan and Dunne
34. "____ on Down the Road"
38. Stubborn
40. Gleam
42. Oppositionist
43. Twitted
45. Country hotel
46. Leased
49. Military cap
52. Unhappy
53. Got up
57. Downy ducks
59. Smoothed
60. Obsesses
64. ____ Aviv
65. Poetess Wylie
66. Official deeds
67. Opposite of NNW
68. Voiced
69. Bodies of water

**DOWN**

1. Twangy
2. Straighten
3. Bearlike animal
4. Maddens
5. Hymn finish
6. Hood's weapon
7. Be wrong
8. Blue Eagle inits.
9. Medics
10. Tarsi
11. Similar
12. IQ name
13. "____ to bed"
18. Hawaiian porches
19. Commotion
23. Wavers
24. ____ Saud
25. Compelled
28. Actress Garbo
29. Theater seater
30. Eureka!
31. ____ Cupid
32. Table scrap
35. Friend: Fr.
36. Japanese coin
37. Sea eagle
39. Shirt front
41. High hopes
44. ____ loss
47. Steeds
48. Plays
49. Irish clans
50. Employs
51. Ms. Astaire
54. In abeyance
55. Actress Berger
56. Norse myths
58. Alone
59. Saucy
61. Writer Anais ____
62. Stop ____ dime
63. ____ compos mentis

# PUZZLE 30

**ACROSS**

1. Easy task
5. Blue or news
10. Obstruct
14. Pueblo Indian
15. Seed anew
16. Italian river
17. Auditory
18. 10th-century emperor
19. Durocher and Gorcey
20. Afternoon break in Kent
22. Rascality
24. Baseball official
25. Falsehood
26. Saw-toothed
30. Patio
34. Revoke
35. Martin and Jones
37. Milit. rank
38. Ascots
39. Hoes
40. Hotness
41. Under the weather
42. Bandleader Shaw
43. Parsonage
44. Snuggles
46. Miser
48. Arab garment
49. Awesome, dude
50. Male felines
54. Kitchen item
58. Rumlike drink: var.
59. Marble man
61. Actor Lincoln
62. Racetrack fence
63. Rajah's wife
64. Author Uris
65. French pronoun
66. Dazzles
67. Kind of devil

**DOWN**

1. Kaput
2. Memo
3. Samoan port
4. Paintings
5. Punctual
6. Network
7. Devotee: suff.
8. Cranny's partner
9. Kind of camera
10. Serving tray
11. Banyan, e.g.
12. ____ about
13. Carnation
21. Muslim priest
23. Affectations
26. Rich cloth
27. Roman magistrate
28. Lively dances
29. Makes revisions
30. Rumors
31. Representative
32. Discontinue
33. Enroll
36. Clockmaker Terry
39. Tab payers
40. Camera type
42. Duchess of ____
43. Farrow et al.
45. Gridiron ploy
47. Groups of three
50. Weed
51. Of the mouth
52. Post
53. Wood strip
54. Ich ____, motto of Prince of Wales
55. ____-bargain
56. Cupid
57. Not any
60. Wildebeest

# PUZZLE 31

**ACROSS**
1. Lab fluid
5. Make small talk
9. Scottish hillsides
14. Colt's mama
15. Routine
16. Weird
17. Prayer ending
18. Black, to a poet
19. Russian kings
20. Dispatched
21. ____ a plea
22. Fence crossings
23. Horse-drawn winter vehicles
25. Walk through mire
26. Actress Lyon
27. Justice
31. Bed boards
34. Country
35. Red on a traffic light
36. Lend an ____
37. Stored up
40. Paddle
41. Bargain-event term
43. Competes
44. Pocket linen
46. Breaks, as a mirror
48. Snoopy or Sandy
49. Scores, in baseball
50. Laments
54. Essences
57. Feel poorly
58. "Pumping ____"
59. Wading bird
60. Poker stake
61. California wine region
62. Traffic sign
63. Resist temptation
64. Gait
65. German steel city
66. Otherwise
67. Hardy heroine

**DOWN**
1. Accumulate
2. Dromedary
3. Goodnight girl
4. Plaque-fighting man
5. Nativity scene
6. Tramps
7. Spin like ____
8. Little Indians count
9. Gambler
10. Gives up a job
11. Asian lake
12. Republic of Ireland
13. Meeting: abbr.
22. Playground chute
24. Pour forth
25. Singer Tommy ____
27. Bus fees
28. British school
29. Drench
30. Agile
31. The seven ____
32. Flog
33. Leontyne's song
34. Lions' resting places
38. Oasts
39. Arabian boat
42. Flaky
45. Opposing
47. Soup dish
48. Remove from print
50. Tastes
51. Angry
52. Slow gallops
53. Breaks
54. Highest point
55. Very, to Pierre
56. Sea dogs
57. Blue dye
60. Cooling drink

# PUZZLE 32

**ACROSS**
1. Defeat
5. Courtier in "Hamlet"
10. Jones or Martin
14. Cupid
15. Office worker
16. Motionless
17. Current
18. Barbarian of film
19. Author unknown: abbr.
20. Criterion
22. Staid
24. Essence
25. Tender
26. Airy
29. Harm
34. Stop
36. Minstrel's instrument
37. By birth
38. Drones
39. German poet
41. Principal
42. Single
43. Shipshape
44. Prevents
46. Remedied
49. Not as good
50. Aspiration
51. Writer Waugh
53. Riviera wear
56. Playfully
60. Norse god
61. Actress Ekberg
63. Neighborhood
64. Gambling city
65. Forty-____
66. Unpleasantly moist
67. Complains
68. Coasters
69. Discontinues

**DOWN**
1. Louisville sluggers
2. Issue
3. Cracker or fountain
4. Ditches
5. Acting award
6. Laid away
7. Tear apart
8. Actress Claire
9. Associated
10. Crown
11. Writer Ferber
12. Thanks ____
13. Bird of Hawaii
21. Morse elements
23. New York canal
25. Overwhelm
26. Work
27. Goddess of peace
28. Avarice
30. Choice group
31. Enroll
32. Approaches
33. Succinct
35. Troupers
40. Lessen
41. Military prison
43. Sign gas
45. Maas that baa
47. African mammals
48. Sped
52. Truth changers
53. "____ Free"
54. Thought
55. Kong of the jungle
56. Penalty
57. OPEC member
58. Furnish
59. Wild oxen
62. Nothing

# PUZZLE 33

**ACROSS**

1. Moiety
5. Sharpen, as a razor
10. Oodles
14. Russian mountain
15. Bouquet
16. Great Lake
17. Very small
18. Infant at a pool
19. Domesticated
20. Morose
21. Flower plot
22. Snuggled
24. Black suit
27. Take legal action
28. Confronted
30. Beet color
32. Printing machine
36. Juice fruit
38. Immediately
40. Use scissors
41. Policeman
42. Maddened
45. Turn right, Dobbin!
46. Employed
48. Polka ____
49. Pattern
51. Family car
53. Snyder or Brown
55. Languished
56. Acquired
58. ____ control
60. Playbill
64. Ignited
65. Double curve
68. Affection
69. Turning point
71. Tuneful threesome
72. Declare positively
73. Omit in pronunciation
74. Man of valor
75. Cravings
76. Makes laugh
77. Paradise

**DOWN**

1. Shanties
2. Opera solo
3. Improved a lawn
4. Go on a jet
5. Cut wood
6. Stockbroker
7. Actor Steiger
8. Foretoken
9. Peels
10. Alphabet symbols
11. Verbal
12. "As ____ Goes By"
13. Kernel
21. Insignia
23. Have an evening meal
25. Writing tool
26. Ted Kennedy, for one
28. Adjust a camera
29. Came forth
31. Terrier, for one
33. Contrived artfully
34. Prolonged attack
35. Lay out money
37. Finish
39. Marry
43. Decay
44. Railway station
47. Sharp weapons
50. Perch
52. And not
54. Tune
57. Records
59. Small insects
60. "____ It Again, Sam"
61. Wander
62. Baking chamber
63. Grinding machine
66. Father
67. Directly
70. By way of
71. Article

# PUZZLE 34

**ACROSS**

1. Bear's hideout
5. Gaucho's rope
10. Spill the beans
14. Summit
15. Bitter-____ (diehard)
16. Russian river
17. Assay
18. Sour
19. Shake-speare's river
20. Flightless bird
22. Truant
24. Syn.'s opposite
25. Youngster
26. Masked mammal
30. Cause ____
34. Touch
35. Strictness
37. Small amount
38. Wager
39. ____ out (renege)
40. "Where the Boys ____"
41. Helm position
43. Pumps
45. Legal claim
46. Wood-eating insect
48. ____ highway
50. Put to work
51. Prattle
52. Church dignitary
56. Came in
60. Distinctive air
61. La ____ (opera house)
63. Acclaim
64. Debt voucher
65. Window type
66. Very: Fr.
67. Willow or walnut
68. Artists' subjects
69. Tug

**DOWN**

1. Roman patriot
2. Copies
3. Waistcoat
4. Pull out
5. Atomic device
6. Move slowly
7. Summer quaff
8. Semester
9. Judge
10. Dynamited
11. Son of Jacob
12. Soon
13. Big ____ theory
21. Sea goddess
23. Mr. Hurok
26. Moroccan city
27. White poplar
28. Prettier
29. Recess
30. Managed
31. Interweave
32. Street show
33. Correct, as texts
36. Sticky stuff
42. Imitate
43. Texan's hat
44. Traffic lights, e.g.
45. Freedom
47. "Rose ____ rose . . ."
49. Large tub
52. Treaty
53. German district
54. Eastern canal
55. Beige color
56. General Robert ____
57. ____ avis
58. Tied
59. Rolltop
62. Live or first

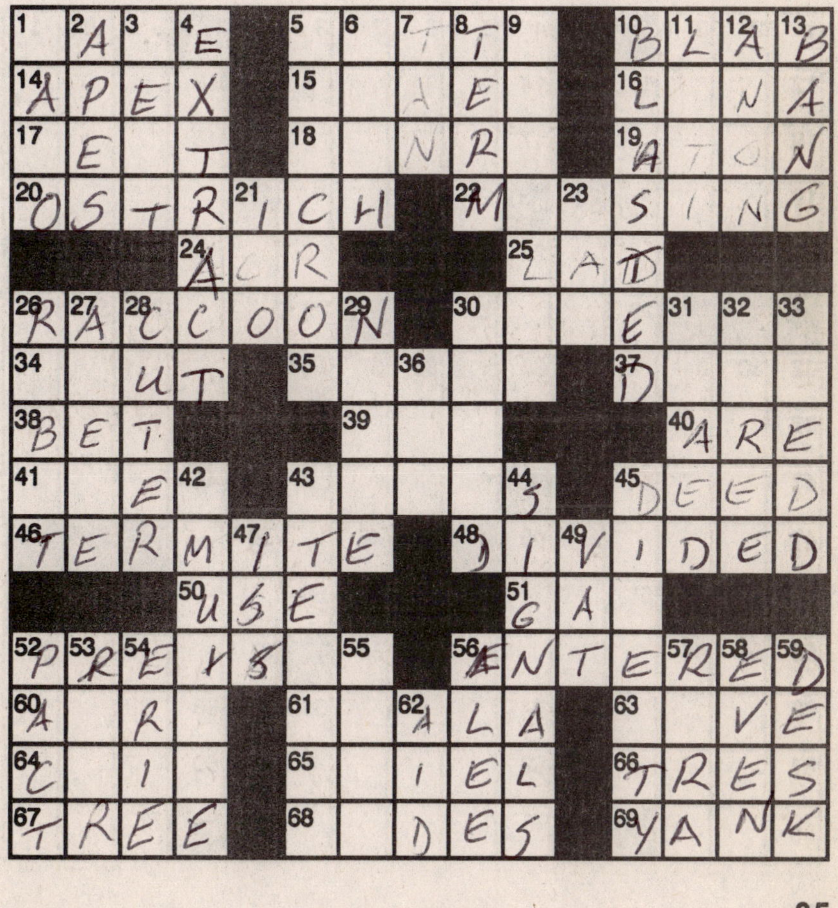

# PUZZLE 35

**ACROSS**

1. To and ____
4. Shock
9. Grand Coulee, e.g.
12. My mistake!
14. Possessor
15. Auction
16. Lost
17. "____ Barbara"
18. Robert ____
19. Deserve
21. Christmas figure
23. Witch town
25. Resound
26. Poems
28. Chore
32. Eternally
35. Page
38. Like a beaver
39. Male sheep
40. List
42. Sooner than, poetically
43. Korean, for one
45. Distance measure
46. Boast
47. Make a home
49. ____ duck
51. Camper's need
53. Highway divisions
56. Splashes
61. Office copies
63. Newsman Sevareid
64. Departs
66. Bad
67. Peril
68. Proportions
69. Descartes
70. Ruler: abbr.
71. Breaks suddenly
72. Normal: abbr.

**DOWN**

1. Froth
2. "The Subject Was ____"
3. Verdi work
4. Distress call
5. "____ the night before . . ."
6. Singer Moffo
7. Bind again
8. Medium's state
9. Surrealist artist
10. Actor Guinness
11. Unassuming
13. Tar
15. Married woman: Sp.
20. Actor Bessell
22. Crowd number
24. Dissolve
27. Appear
29. Curing chemical
30. Roman despot
31. Sketched
32. Epochs
33. Urn
34. Give out
36. Friend, to Francois
37. Complete
40. Estuary
41. Ardor
44. Charge
46. Core
48. Puts in a ledger
50. Pas' partners
52. Man from Austin
54. Roof parts
55. Limit unduly
56. Withered
57. Prudish
58. Speech impediment
59. Actress Hayworth
60. Pace
62. Toboggan
65. Induction initials

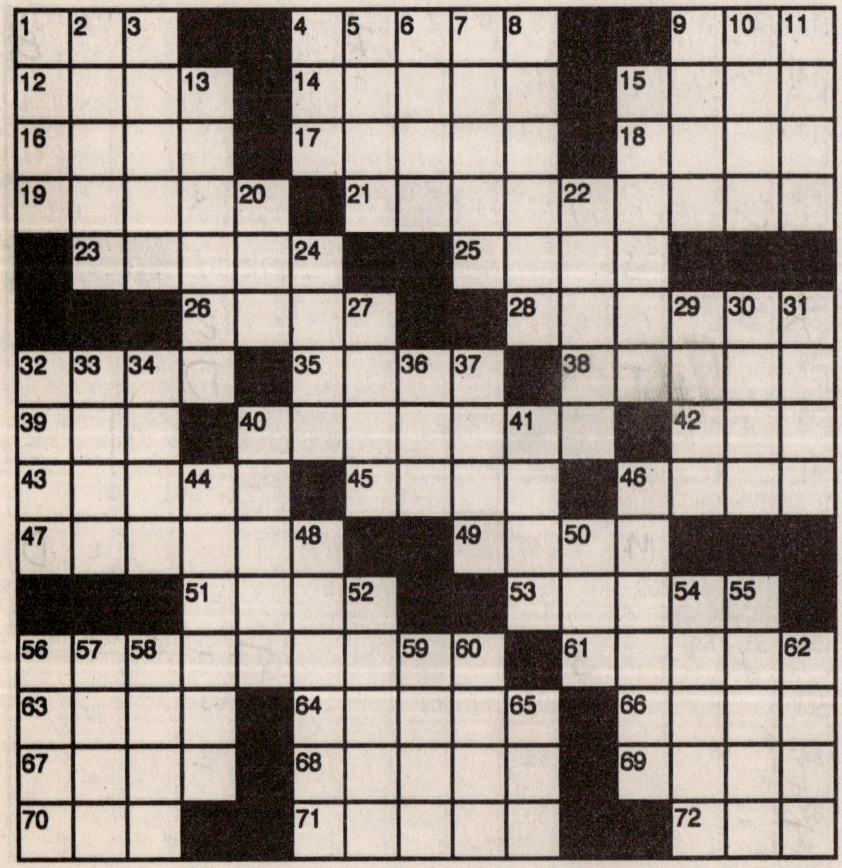

# PUZZLE 36

**ACROSS**

1. Mineral springs
5. Literary collection
8. Neighbor of Cambodia
12. Agreement
13. Singer Falana
15. South American mountains
17. Tolstoy's ____ Karenina
18. "____ Old Cowhand"
19. Tour of duty
20. ____-do-well
21. Grandmas, to some
23. Winds up
24. Now and ____
26. Jewels
28. Mixes
30. Opera song
31. Poisonous snake
34. Goatees' locales
35. Tarkenton et al.
36. Education gp.
37. Put up, as a picture
38. Thin mud
39. Horse gait
40. Assoc.
41. Actress Martha et al.
42. Musical groups
43. Tiny
44. Waiters' rewards
45. Bombard
46. Actor Lugosi
47. Originate
48. Western alliance: abbr.
51. Maliciousness
53. Tattle
57. Actress ____ Dunne
59. Eternally
60. Solitary
61. Grows wan
62. Speak wildly
63. Long periods
64. ____ Trueheart
65. Modern: pref.
66. Locale

**DOWN**

1. Bridge
2. Window glass
3. Complexion woe
4. Commencing
5. Straightens
6. "____ is an island"
7. Actor Alda
8. ____ Vegas
9. Pot fillers
10. Norse god
11. Transport
14. Word scrambles
16. Rds.
22. French river
25. Time units: abbr.
27. Pas' spouses
28. Portion
29. Faint coloration
30. Zodiac ram
31. "____ in Paris"
32. Barroom perch
33. Butter portions
34. Food, informally
35. Adhesive trap
38. Goes to sea
39. Shakes
41. Map line: abbr.
42. Definite article
45. Sound equipment
46. Make no ____ about it
47. Comic Martin
48. Small bite
49. I smell ____!
50. Prefix with vision or phone
52. Tennis's Lendl
54. Circle
55. ____ Domini
56. Top
58. Curvy letter

# PUZZLE 37

**ACROSS**

1. Hullabaloo
5. Quick
9. Speechify
10. Queues
12. Foolishness
13. Stadiums
15. Writing tablet
16. Apportion
18. Moves stealthily
20. Pub drinks
22. Camper's shelter
23. Kingly
24. Skin openings
26. Profound
28. Sandwich shop
29. Respond
31. Uppish one
33. Aug. clock setting
34. Lose one's footing
36. Ooze
38. "My Mother the ____"
41. Golf cry
43. Taunted
47. Filled with wonder
49. Sports group
51. Inane
52. Fray, as threads
54. Loyal
56. Ore-deposit vein
57. Hemingway's forte
58. Come in
60. Marry
61. XI
63. More hackneyed
65. Fashion
66. Downy duck
67. Ball holders
68. Actress Donna ____

**DOWN**

1. Part of TGIF: abbr.
2. Mt. Etna's yield
3. Inclined
4. Rang
5. Knocks down
6. Atmosphere
7. Derisive look
8. Took care of
9. Commands
11. Drooped
12. Claw
14. Closes tightly
15. Mama's mate
17. Change for a five
19. Skirt feature
21. Bastes
25. Ego
27. Bard
30. Mob scene
32. Busy insects
35. Feigns
37. Bucket
38. Find fault
39. Cognizant
40. Uprising
42. Merit
44. More snaillike
45. Senior
46. Colored
48. Gobi, for one
50. Grumble
53. Embankment
55. Uncanny
59. Go on horseback
62. Chemical suffix
64. Rocker Nugent

# PUZZLE 38

**ACROSS**
1. Rope fiber
5. Tear
10. Begone!
14. Mideast bigwig
15. String along
16. ____ and hearty
17. Run for Coe
18. Enthusiastic
19. "Pumping ____"
20. Corks
22. Washed lightly
24. Lends a hand
25. Diamond source
26. Rejects
29. Rear entrance
33. Melodies
34. Rawboned
35. Fib
36. Like the Sahara
37. Spares
38. Scrabble piece
39. Go on pension: abbr.
40. Salad utensils
41. Did a half gainer
42. Memento
44. Furnishes food
45. Scottish girl
46. Harbor
47. Go
50. Railroad employee
54. "Once ____ a time . . ."
55. Boo-boo
57. Gown
58. Simple
59. Turnpikes
60. Singer Fitzgerald
61. Pollinators
62. Feel intuitively
63. "The ____ Hunter"

**DOWN**
1. Corny actors
2. Radiate
3. Venus de ____
4. Boned up
5. Spirited horses
6. Listens
7. From ____ to riches
8. Opposite of WNW
9. Oil-well towers
10. Polished
11. Hatchbacks, e.g.
12. Medicinal plant
13. Baby-sit
21. Bowlers' targets
23. Black
25. Hefty tresses
26. ____ raving mad
27. Processor's output
28. Join
29. River boat
30. Kalamata, for one
31. Tank ship
32. Orchestra section
34. Golf course
37. Pop-up appliances
38. Snickered
40. Autocratic ruler
41. "Wait Until ____"
43. Carpenters' tools
44. Unrefined
46. Urges
47. Stupid
48. Fencing sword
49. Skin opening
50. Wheat husk
51. Tunneler
52. Competent
53. Close
56. Caviar

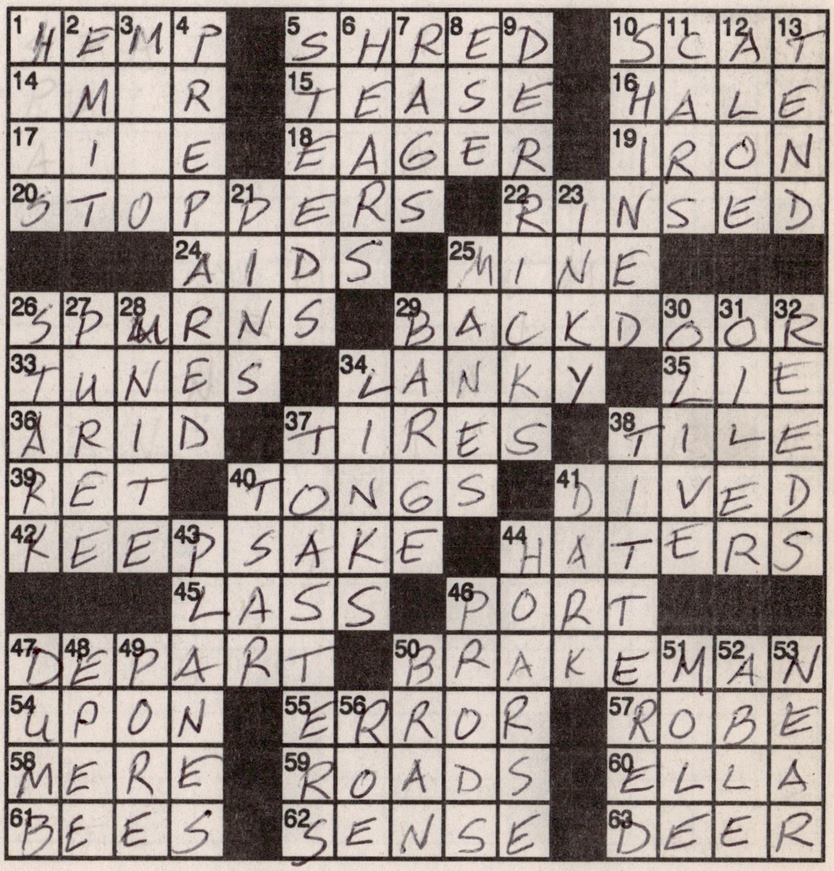

# PUZZLE 39

**ACROSS**

1. Tart
5. Place to rejuvenate
8. Mold
12. Poker stake
13. Towel word
14. Hautboy
15. Green vegetables
16. Enemy
18. Change
20. Total
21. Sahara, e.g.
24. Frost
27. Velocity
30. Negative replies
31. Serving of corn
32. Female birds
33. Supped
34. "____ Karenina"
35. Snaky swimmer
36. Epic poem
37. Ceremonies
38. Muhammad ____
39. Great fear
41. Snow runner
43. More skilled
46. Mentally sound
50. Comic-strip light bulb
52. Ripened
53. Pipe joint
54. Requirement
55. Seed containers
56. Route
57. Goals

**DOWN**

1. Weaken
2. Washington bills
3. Mormon state
4. Dwells
5. Photographs
6. Dice spot
7. Serpent
8. Enamored
9. Mindful
10. Baseball's Darling
11. Ran into
17. Horse fodder
19. Nourished
22. Log
23. Fish beginnings
25. Walking stick
26. Historic ages
27. Mets' stadium, once
28. Rind
29. Signed up
33. Fuss
34. Commercial flying corporation
36. ____ Express ('60s band)
37. Filch
40. Comeback
42. Youngsters
44. Heaven on earth
45. Bamboo shoot
46. Knock sharply
47. In the past
48. Novel
49. ____ carte
51. Paid notices

# PUZZLE 40

**ACROSS**

1. Fruit container
5. Server
9. Risk
13. Burn soother
14. In this place
15. Patriot Deane
16. Sign gas
17. Stagger
18. Contaminate
19. Top prize
21. Greek letter
22. Sight organs
23. Yoko ____
24. Deserve
26. Perfumed
30. Actress Jillian
31. Minute
35. Dreadful
36. "Holiday ____"
37. Batter's coup
39. Female deer
40. Repents
42. "The Way ____"
43. Insert
44. Sweet ____
46. Capri, e.g.
48. Total
49. Wise man
51. Scold
54. Football score
59. Sound judgment
60. Help in a robbery
61. Pierre's friend
62. Approximately
63. Knot
64. Color
65. Bait
66. Plant
67. French summers

**DOWN**

1. Explosive noise
2. Bread spread
3. Yarn type
4. Borrower's friend
5. Blind mice count
6. Robert and Donna
7. Space
8. Cheer
9. Baseball field
10. "I cannot tell ____"
11. Pealed
12. This, in Spanish
15. Rock
20. Chatty bird
23. Happen
24. Boredom
25. Attach
26. Father
27. Wave type
28. Eat away
29. House document
30. Ventilates
32. Wiping cloth
33. Sign
34. Kitten noise
38. Horse sound
41. Wrigley Field, e.g.
45. Choose
47. Calm
49. "Blue ____ Shoes"
50. Behaved
51. Scratch
52. Drifter
53. Frankenstein's assistant
54. Beige and ecru
55. English horn
56. Leave out
57. Grape drink
58. Court dividers

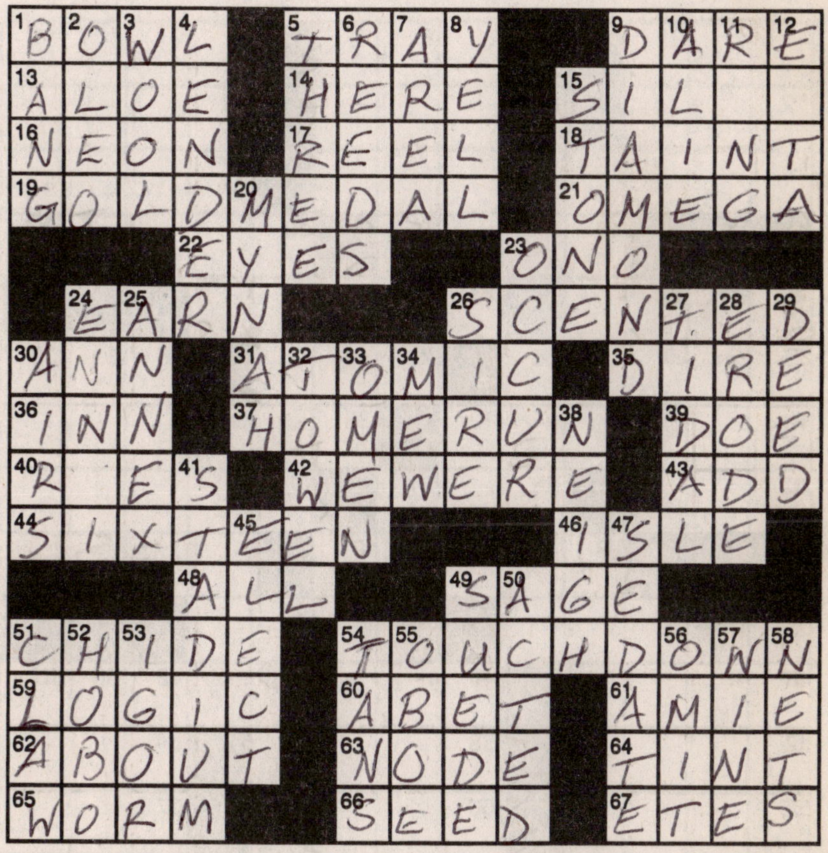

# PUZZLE 41

**ACROSS**

1. Hamilton bill
4. Paris eatery
8. Snow boards
12. Rage
13. Son of Eve
14. Diarist Frank
15. Motherly
17. Chinese staple
18. Suggestive stare
19. Promises
20. Chimney duct
23. Stretch
25. Pound part
27. Cloth coloring
28. "____ on a Grecian Urn"
31. Author
33. Acquired through merit
35. Lease
36. Untrained
38. Dis-tinguished
39. Havana export
41. Shop or language
42. Love
45. Ready for picking
47. Change position
48. Spatters
52. Thought
53. Orange skin
54. Mr. Gershwin
55. Quad building
56. Tags on
57. Fellows

**DOWN**

1. Allen of "Home Improve-ment"
2. Generation
3. Mosquito ____
4. Worry
5. "Li'l ____"
6. Dreaded
7. House wing
8. Abraham's wife
9. Mend, as bones
10. Foot component
11. Looks at
16. Pick
19. Bounding main
20. Chicken
21. Attract
22. Rental
24. Yes
26. Spooky
28. Aware of
29. Act
30. Mac-Donald's partner
32. Fabric scrap
34. Lounging garments
37. Distorted
39. ____ of the crop
40. Vexed
42. Among
43. Extinct bird
44. Above
46. Buddies
48. Healthy place
49. Not her
50. Bard's before
51. ____ Francisco

# PUZZLE 42

**ACROSS**

1. Mound
5. Health spot
8. Traipsed
12. Pungent
13. Dally
14. "The Last American ____"
15. Prescription
17. Actual
18. Spigot
19. Tease
21. Aflame
24. Land measure
25. Clod
26. Move slightly
27. Favorite
30. Scientist's milieu
31. Sandals
32. Fruit beverage
33. City trains
34. Processes leather
35. Valley
36. Obedient
37. Craze
38. Urge
41. "____ of Love"
42. Ajar
43. Vaguest
48. Temporary shelter
49. Samovar
50. Jug
51. Groups
52. Support
53. Moist

**DOWN**

1. Tennis' Shriver
2. Vanilla ____
3. Hat
4. Magazine bigwig
5. Wharf
6. Frying utensil
7. Organizations
8. Trio
9. Hollow grass
10. Word-of-mouth
11. Disburse
16. Crow's call
20. Bungles
21. Qualified
22. Target
23. Flings
24. Make amends
26. Disgraceful
27. Wan
28. Utopia
29. Take care of
31. Luminary
35. Shredded
36. Colors
37. "____ Little Indians"
38. Speckles
39. Sword
40. Forwarded
41. Warble
44. "Where the Boys ____"
45. Ram's mate
46. Embroider
47. Attempt

# PUZZLE 43

**ACROSS**

1. Rock to and fro
5. Clay brick
10. Pleads
14. Huron or Superior
15. Grieve
16. Seldom seen
17. Member of the nobility
19. China's continent
20. Writing tool
21. Diving birds
22. Pre-Christmas period
24. Evergreens
25. Blaze
26. Disentangles
29. Merriment
33. False name
34. Update
35. Mediterranean, e.g.
36. Covered in gold leaf
37. Rationed
38. Tribe
39. Lamprey
40. Sewing joints
41. Spot
42. Certain turtles
44. Some restaurant seats
45. Race segments
46. Cheeky
47. Congressional body
50. River mud
51. Chimpanzee
54. ___ hand (strict control)
55. Anonymously
58. Ceremony
59. Bring out
60. Fencing sword
61. Kernel
62. Engagements
63. Russian emperor

**DOWN**

1. Smack
2. Item of merchandise
3. Similar
4. Of course!
5. Lovers
6. Piers
7. Belonging to us
8. Bikini top
9. Necessitated
10. More courageous
11. Comfort
12. Smile
13. Chair
18. Coin-toss call
23. Stalemate
24. Accomplishment
25. Monetary penalties
26. Fits of temper
27. UFO pilot
28. Country estate
29. Tillers
30. Small land mass
31. Instruct
32. Pulls suddenly
34. Crowd noises
37. Intensified
38. Cluster
40. Squabble
41. Strong point
43. Smoothed, as wood
44. Beauties
46. Fragment
47. Knights' titles
48. New York canal
49. Message
50. Sooty matter
51. Poisonous snakes
52. Court argument
53. Ogler
56. Nabokov novel
57. Hardened

# PUZZLE 44

**ACROSS**

1. Poet
5. Pack away
9. Mineral spring
12. Opposite of aweather
13. Flightless New Zealand bird
14. Heavy weight
15. Star of the show
17. Likely
18. Hint
19. Letter opener
21. Give up, as land
24. Locales
27. Jog
30. Upper limb
32. Give temporarily
33. Tear
34. Wrath
35. "Born in the ____"
36. Frozen fruit desserts
38. Collection
39. Dance move
40. Waiter's handouts
42. Showroom model
44. Kingsley and Vereen
46. Friendly nation
49. "Much ____ About Nothing"
51. Barbara Walters's specialty
55. Pair
56. Wharf
57. First name in scat
58. Cartoon scream
59. Doe's mate
60. Small drinks

**DOWN**

1. "____, humbug!"
2. Actor Guinness
3. Actual
4. Subtract
5. Hit the slopes
6. Can metal
7. Had creditors
8. Telegrams
9. Begin
10. Mom-and-____ store
11. Picnic pest
16. Kathie ____ Gifford
20. Be ill
22. Speaker's platform
23. Misjudged
25. Luxury
26. Clothing fastener
27. Neat
28. Pilaf ingredient
29. Easily-read person
31. Distribute
37. Mystery author Grafton
39. Answers
41. Cuts short
43. Damage
45. Fit of pique
47. Leslie Caron film
48. Puppy's sound
49. Citrus cooler
50. Payable
52. Boston ____ Party
53. Unit of work
54. Existed

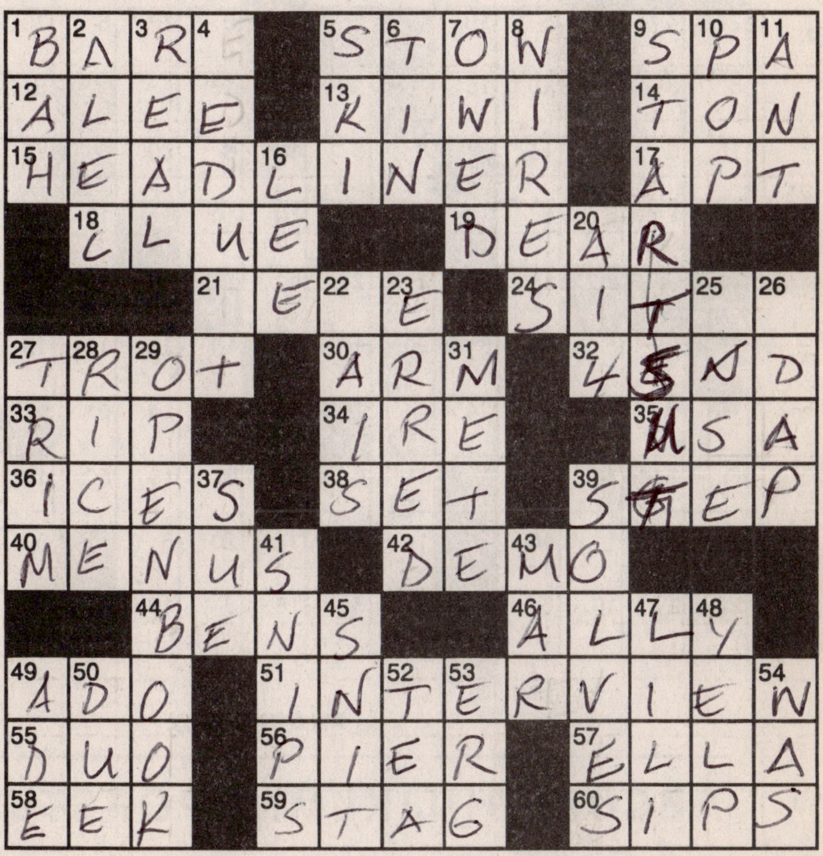

# PUZZLE 45

## CODEWORD

**Codeword is a special crossword puzzle in which conventional clues are omitted. Instead, answer words in the diagram are represented by numbers. Each number represents a different letter of the alphabet, and all the letters of the alphabet are used. When you are sure of a letter, put it in the code key chart and cross it off in the Alphabet Box. A group of letters has been inserted to start you off.**

| | | | | | | | | | | | | |
|---|---|---|---|---|---|---|---|---|---|---|---|---|
| 1 | 2 | 3 | 4 O | 5 | 6 | 7 | 8 | 9 | 10 | 11 | 12 | 13 |
| 14 | 15 | 16 | 17 | 18 G | 19 | 20 L | 21 | 22 | 23 | 24 | 25 | 26 |

| | | | | | | | | | | | | | | |
|---|---|---|---|---|---|---|---|---|---|---|---|---|---|---|
| 5 | 20 | 5 | 10 | ■ | 19 | 6 | 15 | 5 | 13 | ■ | 10 | 20 | 4 | 17 |
| 2 | 5 | 15 | 23 | ■ | 4 | 3 | 1 | 11 | 6 | ■ | 5 | 14 | 19 | 5 |
| 5 | 24 | 16 | 1 | 9 | 14 | 5 | 16 | 6 | 11 | ■ | 22 | 19 | 5 | 8 |
| 19 | 6 | 10 | ■ | 14 | 18 | 20 | 8 | ■ | 6 | 20 | 6 | 15 | 16 | 10 |
| ■ | ■ | ■ | 25 | 6 | 6 | 16 | ■ | 13 | 10 | 8 | 15 | 26 | 6 | ■ |
| 24 | 4 | 12 | 5 | 10 | ■ | ■ | 18 | 5 | 16 | 6 | 19 | ■ | ■ | ■ |
| 6 | 3 | 1 | 10 | 16 | ■ | 22 | 6 | 16 | 5 | ■ | 5 | 19 | 4 | 17 |
| 15 | 6 | 24 | 16 | ■ | 6 | 5 | 10 | 6 | 20 | ■ | 15 | 5 | 18 | 6 |
| 23 | 24 | 6 | 6 | ■ | 13 | 14 | 10 | 10 | ■ | 10 | 23 | 1 | 19 | 16 |
| ■ | ■ | ■ | 19 | 26 | 1 | 24 | 4 | ■ | ■ | 15 | 6 | 11 | 6 | 10 |
| ■ | 20 | 5 | 13 | 6 | 20 L | 10 | ■ | 10 | 13 | 14 | 19 | ■ | ■ | ■ |
| 15 | 5 | 10 | 1 | 24 | 4 O | ■ | 10 | 16 | 14 | 21 | ■ | 16 | 4 | 4 |
| 5 | 24 | 16 | 6 | ■ | 18 G | 6 | 24 | 6 | 19 | 5 | 16 | 1 | 4 | 24 |
| 20 | 5 | 1 | 15 | ■ | 14 | 16 | 1 | 20 | 6 | ■ | 5 | 11 | 7 | 6 |
| 22 | 1 | 19 | 6 | ■ | 6 | 5 | 16 | 6 | 19 | ■ | 21 | 6 | 6 | 19 |

**ALPHABET BOX**

**A B C D E F ~~G~~ H I J K ~~L~~ M N ~~O~~ P Q R S T U V W X Y Z**

# PUZZLE 46

**ACROSS**

1. Men-only party
5. Sound loudly
10. Carbonated drink
14. Hardy cabbage
15. Air again
16. Saudi, e.g.
17. Islands: Fr.
18. Leafy vines
19. Speed
20. Fated
22. Shakespeare's Dane
24. Encourage
25. A Great Lake
26. Bright plaid fabric
29. Wickedness
33. Foreigner
34. Family groups
35. Hole in one
36. Canisters
37. Grass leaf
38. Elderly
39. Actress Arden
40. Savage
41. Stadium
42. Explain
44. Desolate
45. Witches
46. Atmosphere
47. Fleet of ships
50. Sick days
54. Dog's sound
55. Sammy ____, Jr.
57. Donated
58. Lily-family plant
59. Deteriorate
60. Fencing foil
61. Cravings
62. Basted
63. Post

**DOWN**

1. Slide
2. Anecdote
3. Tavern brews
4. Hand movements
5. Carries
6. Dike
7. Desertlike
8. Feel sorrow
9. Consider sacred
10. Singer Miranda
11. Type of exam
12. Tardy
13. Aid in wrongdoing
21. Modern Persia
23. Has bad health
25. Elude
26. Paired
27. Active
28. Eats in style
29. Fill with joy
30. Anxious
31. Play division
32. Family car
34. Nightspots
37. Army units
38. Plans
40. Small nail
41. Swiss river
43. Irritates
44. Moved by motor coach
46. Withstand
47. Not at home
48. Actor's part
49. Full or new
50. Declare openly
51. Superman's garment
52. Level
53. Kernel
56. "You ____ So Beautiful"

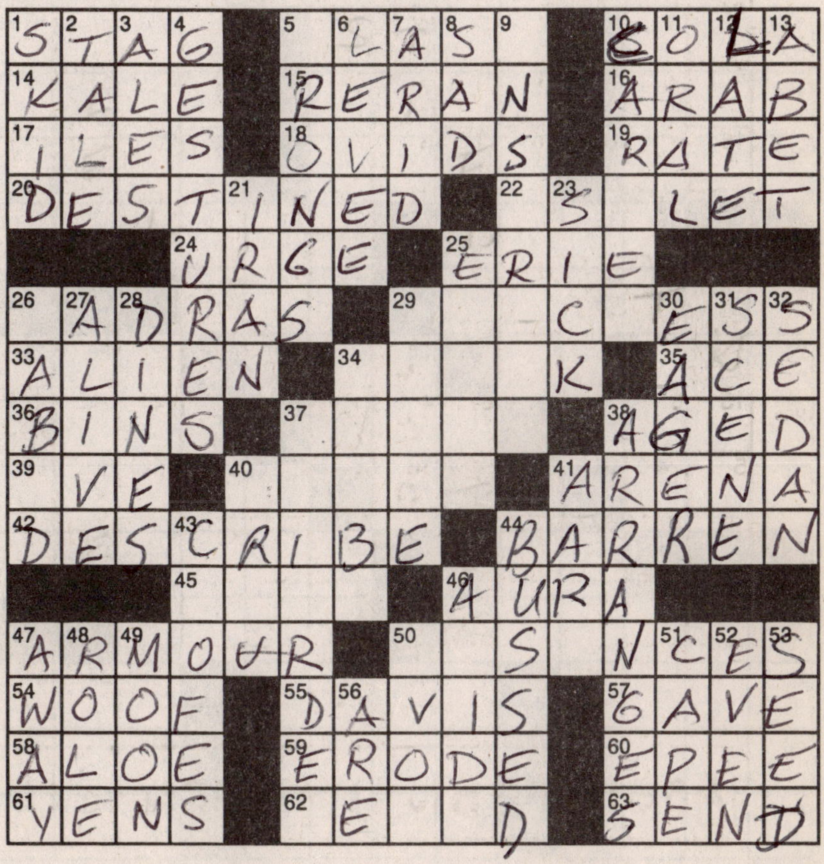

# PUZZLE 47

**ACROSS**

1. Joke
4. Pack away
8. Chowder ingredient
12. Epoch
13. Time and ____
14. Solitary
15. NYC opera house, for short
16. Region
17. Has breakfast
18. Detest
20. Swaps
22. Prepared prunes
24. That girl
25. Healed
26. Flower plot
27. ____ of Tranquility
30. Dollar bills
31. Armed conflict
32. Asterisk
33. Mack or Knight
34. Gear tooth
35. Group of bees
36. Male
37. Oyster treasures
38. LP, e.g.
41. Rave
42. Egg-shaped
43. Like a villain
45. Anger
48. Emcee Parks
49. Go by car
50. ____ and then
51. Concludes
52. Kernel
53. Golly!

**DOWN**

1. Precious stone
2. Exist
3. Formed a congregation
4. Declared
5. Weary
6. Pindar opus
7. Climate
8. "On a ____ Day You Can See Forever"
9. Burden
10. Poker kitty
11. Disorder
19. Overwhelms
21. Danger color
22. Highlander
23. "Name That ____"
26. Satchel
27. Beginning
28. Actor Holliman
29. "A Farewell to ____"
31. Is curious
32. Graceful bird
34. Limousine
35. Made airtight
36. Loses feathers
37. Self-esteem
38. Dressing gown
39. Level
40. One in a deck
44. Compete
46. Fish eggs
47. Female sheep

# PUZZLE 48

**ACROSS**

1. Young bovine
5. ___ Khan
8. Satiate
12. African lily
13. "___ Abner"
14. Opera highlight
15. Maoris, e.g.
18. Double curve
19. Metric measure
20. Perched
21. Greek god of flocks
22. Damage
24. Pitcher Ryan et al.
27. TV's "Remington ___"
31. Commotions
32. Deposited
33. Camper, perhaps
36. Small blackboards
38. Paleozoic or Mesozoic
39. Make ___ while the sun shines
40. Mr. Brokaw
43. Map book
45. ___ of Reason
48. 1965 Herb Alpert song
51. Moreno or Hayworth
52. Spoil
53. Hawaiian goose
54. Made a hole in one
55. Holy people: abbr.
56. Sheep mothers

**DOWN**

1. Walking stick
2. Tavern orders
3. Moos
4. Turkish cap
5. Actor Delon and others
6. Coated with gold leaf
7. Warnings
8. Craze
9. Infuriates
10. Turkish money
11. Endure
16. Verve
17. Tidy
21. Glue
23. Pass on
24. ___ King Cole
25. Keats poem
26. Actor Chaney
28. Dine
29. Falsehood
30. Sullivan and McMahon
34. Part of QED
35. Graders
36. Arrow parts
37. Whip
40. Scarlett's home
41. Of the ear
42. Spouse
44. Booty
45. Afresh
46. Unit of heredity
47. "For Your ___ Only"
49. Unhappy
50. Single

# PUZZLE 49

**ACROSS**

1. Fishing pole
4. Desire
8. Use a towel
12. Be in debt
13. Opera melody
14. Lendl of tennis
15. House wing
16. Those with green thumbs
18. Press
20. Part of a three-piece suit
21. Rich variety of pie
23. Land title
25. First man
26. Not fatty
27. Barracks bed
30. Collection
31. "Beauty and the ——"
32. "Ben ——"
33. Washington bill
34. Give the eye
35. Pedestal part
36. Time gone by
37. Tot's adhesive
38. Meadows
40. Like a lemon
41. Without feelings
44. —— Capades
47. Against
48. Woe!
49. Viewed
50. Church service
51. Telegram
52. Before, in poetry

**DOWN**

1. Fish eggs
2. Pussycat's sailing companion
3. Wash cycle
4. "Paint Your ——"
5. Teheran's land
6. Polite title
7. Owned
8. —— and dined
9. Singer Burl
10. Role
11. Pulver's rank: abbr.
17. Happening
19. Aries
21. El ——, Texas
22. Bible garden spot
23. Gave out, as cards
24. Relaxation
26. Gangster Diamond
27. Berate
28. Evict
29. Oak, for one
31. Brag
35. Saloon
36. Louvre locale
37. Outdated
38. Singer Horne
39. Has a meal
40. Russian ruler, once
41. Deli meat
42. Statute
43. Mr. Wallach
45. Auto
46. She-sheep

# PUZZLE 50

**ACROSS**

1. Pierre's friend
4. Greek vowel
7. Land measure
11. Succotash bean
13. VIP carpet color
14. Male pig
15. Investigated
17. Thrice minus twice
18. Ship's spar
19. Silent
20. Station
23. Role for Faye Dunaway
25. Cupid
26. Actress Moran
27. Mr. Gershwin
30. Itemized
32. Less fat
34. Gave permission
35. Pierre's head
37. Left
38. Piggy-bank filler
40. Walks through water
41. Soft drink
42. Offensive smell
44. Boxing arena
45. Traded
49. On the sheltered side
50. Columnist Landers
51. Alaskan town
52. Seedcases
53. Pleased the cook
54. Hot dog roll

**DOWN**

1. Ginger drink
2. Blend
3. Small demon
4. Makes mistakes
5. Wobble
6. Total
7. Concerning
8. Enclosed
9. Speed contest
10. Bard's before
12. Nearly
16. Morsel for dobbin
19. Pit
20. Valley
21. Clinton's canal
22. Suspended
24. Despicable
26. Adam's address
28. Actor Auberjonois
29. ____ and crafts
31. Sicilian volcano
33. Rouse from sleep
36. Oppressor
39. Perimeters
40. Soaking
41. Farm storage tower
43. Irish lake
44. Knock sharply
45. Sheep's bleat
46. Director Reiner
47. Flightless bird
48. Cozy room

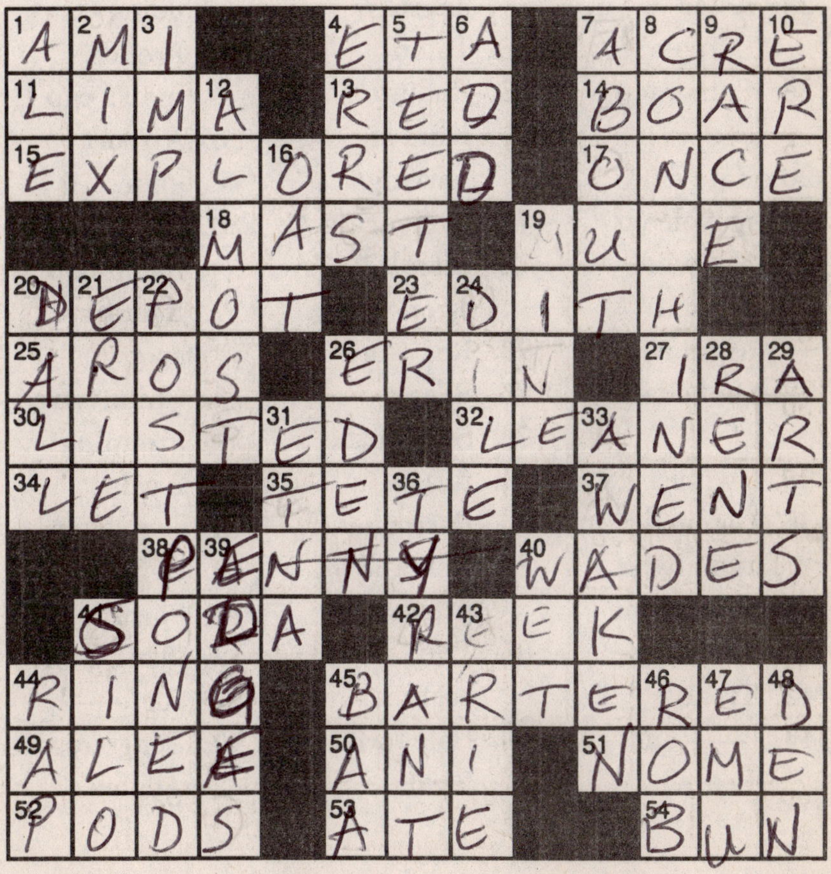

# PUZZLE 51

**ACROSS**

1. Grouchy person
5. Long —— of the law
8. Definite article
11. Lean-to
15. Peignoir
16. Old car
17. Auricle
18. Dissemble
19. Finished
20. Free
22. "The Willow Song," e.g.
23. Actor O'Toole
25. Camera eye
26. Rate of movement
27. Not wild
29. Formal argument
32. On behalf of
35. Twitch
36. Commotion: hyph.
37. Chest bone
40. Territory
42. Tread
45. "—— and Peace"
46. High card
47. Valley
48. Michener epic
50. Combined
52. Intent
54. Feasts
56. Drunkard
57. Cereal coupon: 2 wds.
60. Scrabble pieces
62. Insect
65. Summer beverage
66. Butterfly snare
68. Talon
69. Radiate
70. Kind of herring
71. Unhearing
73. Moral wrong
75. Ref. work
76. Spans
78. Sign of the future
80. Postpone
83. Demand on property
85. Thin cookie
89. Sale term: 2 wds.
90. U-shaped
93. Deep mud
94. —— -mop
95. Possess
96. Mariner's dir.
97. Wickedness
98. Takes to court
99. Diminutive
100. Conceit
101. Refute

**DOWN**

1. Harvest yield
2. Roam
3. Aid in wrongdoing
4. Frenchman's cap
5. Airport abbr.
6. Chose the incumbent
7. Beauty spot
8. Chinaware grouping: 2 wds.
9. —— been
10. Before
11. Form
12. "This Gun for ——"
13. Songstress Adams
14. —— to the world
21. At the —— of one's rope
24. Ship deserter
26. Emporia
28. Fine fog
30. Curtsy
31. Actor West
32. Latest rage
33. Unrefined metal
34. Took a break
37. "Alexander's —— Band"
38. Frozen water
39. Flower plot
41. Dismounted
43. Way out
44. Unreasoning fear
49. Vend
51. Eternal City
53. —— -morning quarterback
55. Spice
57. Chevron
58. "—— on a Grecian Urn"

# PUZZLE 51

59. Hammer head
61. Do the Australian crawl
63. Can metal
64. And so forth: abbr.
67. Childhood game
72. Cat
74. The latest
76. Coarse files
77. Title for Galahad
79. Given a title
80. Fathers
81. Jacob's twin
82. Rickey fruit
84. Fencing sword
86. Quintet
87. —— go bragh
88. Depend
90. "—— to Marry a Millionaire"
91. Reverent fear
92. Modern: prefix

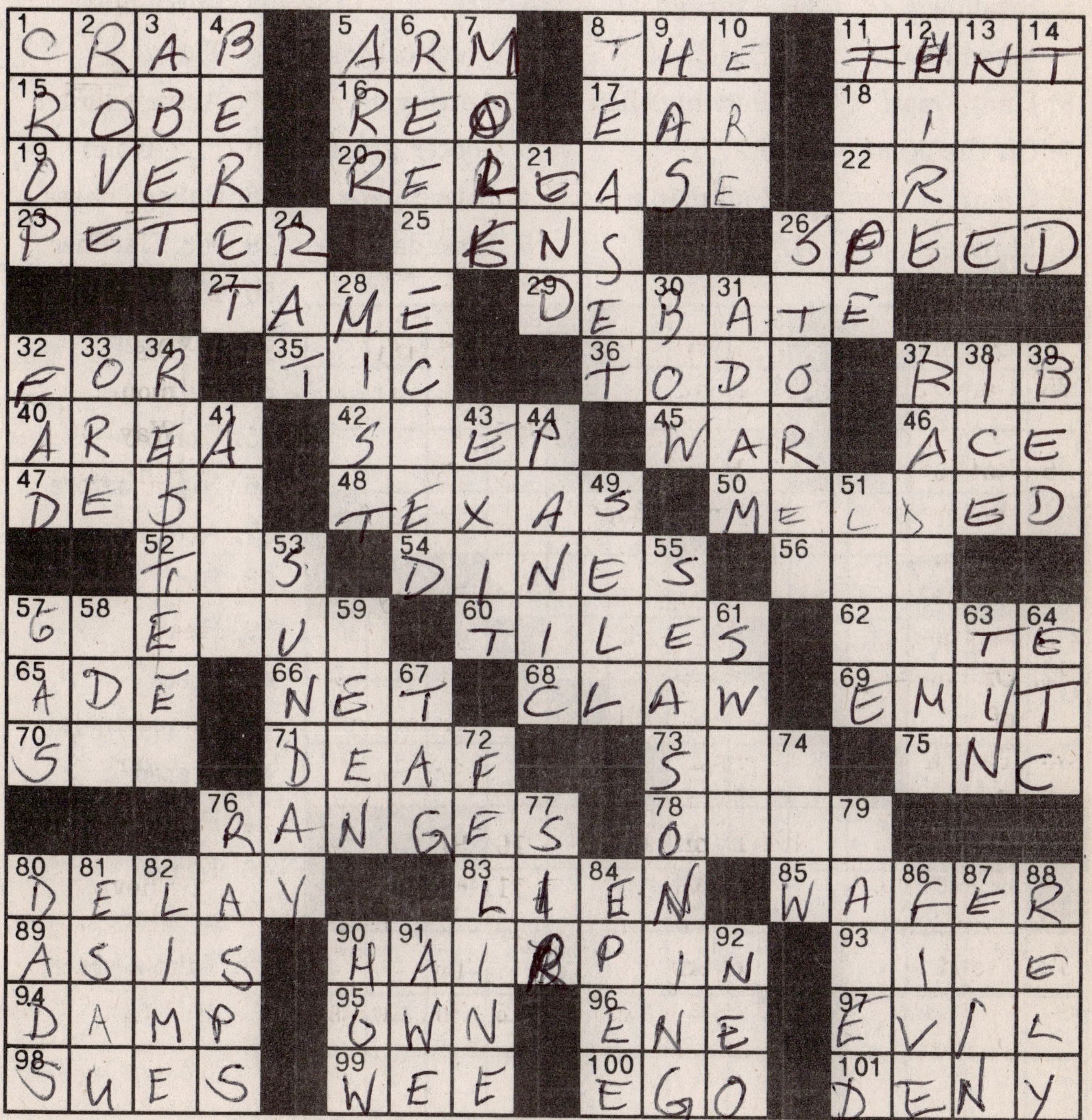

# PUZZLE 52

**ACROSS**

1. Stare
5. Chart
8. Applaud
12. Quiz-master Trebek
13. Make a mistake
14. Wander
15. Swallow greedily
16. Had a meal
17. On the ocean
18. Gourd
20. Minaret
22. Breakfast dish
24. Muffler
27. Squid secretion
28. Laser output
31. Enormous
32. Completion
33. Preserve
34. Affirmative
35. Hatchet
36. Patriot Allen
37. Ratify
39. Fall drink
41. Senses
44. Nimbus
45. Sprite
47. Turf
49. Farm yield
50. Comprehend
51. Niche
52. Camper's shelter
53. Mister
54. Whirlpool

**DOWN**

1. Practical joke
2. Astringent
3. Soccer great
4. Investigate
5. Intended
6. Singer Garfunkel
7. Make believe
8. Go on all fours
9. Misplace
10. Declare
11. Small, round veggie
19. Boor
21. Sturdy tree
23. Forty-niner
24. Timid
25. Actor's hint
26. ____ Khan
28. College cheer
29. Ms. Gardner
30. Hankering
32. Nonstop
33. Spire
35. Gorilla
36. Night before
37. Accustom
38. Bid
39. Heal
40. Press
42. Heavy metal
43. Stated
44. Perform
46. Island necklace
48. Take a crack at

# PUZZLE 53

**ACROSS**

1. Chest bone
4. Stitches
8. Cut wood
12. Wrath
13. Appeal
14. Tresses
15. Crashed
17. Merely
18. Every bit
19. Help
20. Damage
21. Add greater value to
24. Jacket feature
27. Feline
28. Hint
29. Beers' relatives
30. Distant
31. Information
32. Eccentric
33. Metal container
34. Venomous snake
35. Popeye, e.g.
37. Transgression
38. Big hole
39. Home for an American Indian
43. Stable
45. Regular
47. Like some wine
48. Work for money
49. Shovel
50. Performs
51. Zone
52. Watch

**DOWN**

1. Oriental grain
2. Press
3. Pants supporter
4. Coil
5. Church official
6. Very small
7. Unhappy
8. Singing group
9. Disadvantage
10. Lubricate
11. Use a lever
16. Green citrus fruit
19. Picnic pest
21. Lobe locale
22. Adorable
23. Listen
24. Southeast Asian country
25. Hawkeye Pierce portrayer
26. Lineage
27. Is able to
30. Evergreen
31. Ate
33. Highest point
34. Austrian city
36. Touches down
37. Gaze intently
40. Mats
41. Great Lake
42. Rim
43. Evil
44. In the past
45. Caribbean, e.g.
46. Paving liquid

# PUZZLE 54

**ACROSS**

1. Noah's craft
4. Mama's mate
8. Obi
12. Coal receptacle
13. Syria's old name
14. "I cannot tell ___"
15. Agree exactly
17. Disturb
18. Dorm denizen
19. Ribbed
21. Fan
23. Burn
24. Busy time for Brutus
25. Body
29. Mal de ___
30. ___ Mae
31. Footed vase
32. Baby bed
34. "___ My Heart"
35. Waste time
36. Sits for a portrait
37. Ship out
40. Transmitted
41. Doodle
42. Hasten
46. Fence opening
47. Nasty look
48. Night bird
49. Ogled
50. Does simple math
51. ___ de plume

**DOWN**

1. Alphabet starters
2. ___ Grande
3. Bloomers' kin
4. Racing horse
5. Like the Sahara
6. Hippie's abode
7. Violet birthstone
8. Hunting expedition
9. Rueful word
10. Medium or large
11. Obey
16. Negative words
20. Not difficult
21. Branch
22. Thought
23. Foremost
25. Kind of cigar
26. Ask
27. Egg on
28. Son of Seth
30. Designer Christian ___
33. Applied the brakes
34. Small lake
36. One's equals
37. Margin
38. Medical photo
39. Meat paste
40. Did 70
43. Crossed out
44. Pair
45. Shade tree

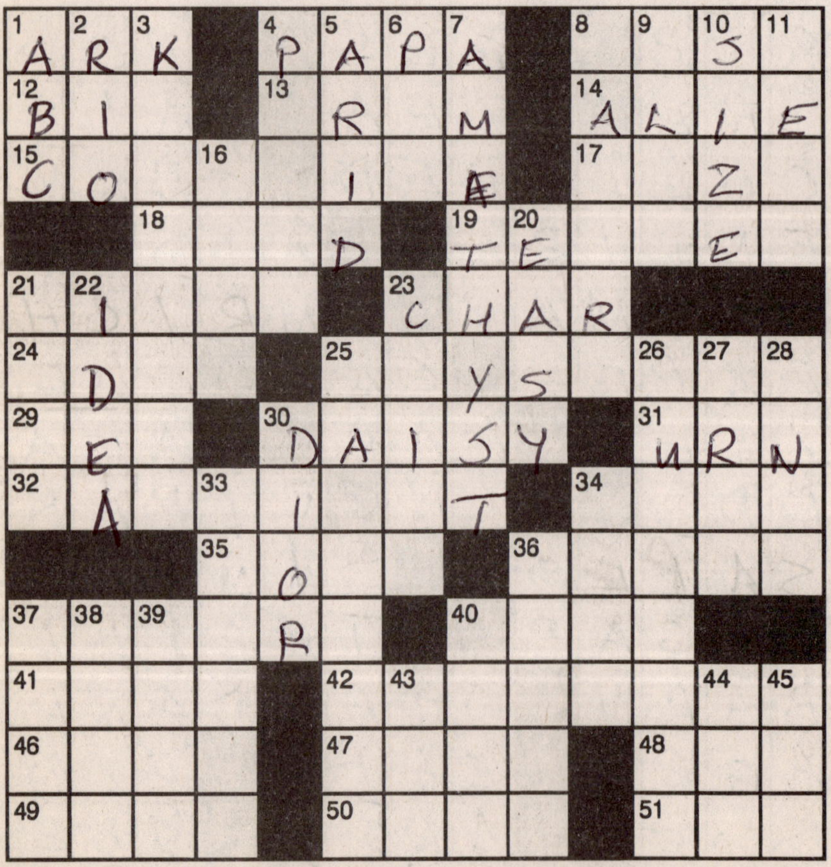

Bank? BANNOCK? What time was she supposed to be here?

# PUZZLE 55

**ACROSS**

1. Information
5. Milk source
8. Tender
12. Zone
13. Be situated
14. Complete
15. Comic Cosby
16. Ancient
17. Hill's opposite
18. Persons
20. Come back from defeat
21. Government office
24. Payload
27. Fury
28. Little dog
31. Toward shelter
32. Climbing plant
33. Spouse
34. ____ and breakfast
35. High card
36. Cart
37. Middle
39. Perspire
43. Not here
47. Car for hire
48. Comic Conway
50. Whisker
51. Eager
52. Alas
53. Bit of land
54. Wagers
55. Belonging to us
56. Glimpse

**DOWN**

1. Steals
2. Iroquoian
3. Healthy
4. Rescue
5. Nearby
6. Lubricate
7. Marry
8. Carbonated beverage
9. Egg-shaped
10. Tripped
11. Low card
19. Dignity
20. Whiskey grain
22. "Casino Royale" star
23. Wail
24. Car for hire
25. Malted brew
26. "Stop" color
28. Sow
29. Flying saucer
30. Write
32. Drink cooler
33. Destroyer or frigate
35. Play part
36. Tangle
38. Circus personality
39. Pierce
40. Ocean ripple
41. Leave
42. Assists
44. Leisure
45. Egyptian river
46. Journey
48. Tango number
49. Chit

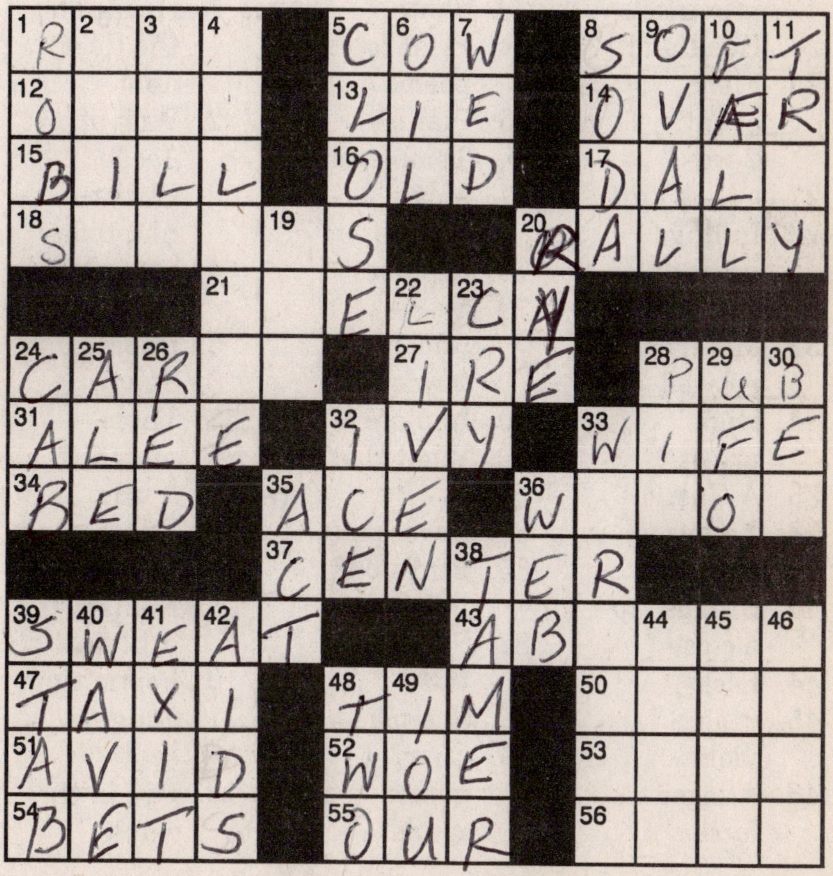

I played BINGO and got skunked! My auntie was here

# PUZZLE 56

## ACROSS

1. —— you care!: 2 wds.
5. Footless one
9. Networks
13. Negotiate
17. Lucie's brother
18. Gambling city
19. Gather a harvest
20. Holly
21. Median strip
22. Unit of weight
23. Italian province
24. Headland
25. Field event: 2 wds.
27. —— a girl!
29. Innings game
31. Temper
32. Maternally related
34. High priest
35. A Castle
38. Young chicken
40. Brought to a close
44. Kick
45. Pine yield
46. Alleged force
48. Spiritual adviser
49. Sign
50. Tender spots
51. Adjust again
53. Clamor
54. Ninepins
56. Game officials
58. Indian mulberry
59. Actress Charlotte
60. Card game
65. Miming game
70. Concealed
71. Motionless
73. Santa
74. Prior to, in poems
75. Pianist Templeton
77. Movie lioness
78. Red deer
79. So —— (amen): 2 wds.
80. Implore
82. What the ——?
84. Beverages
85. Bird's bill
87. Standing tall
88. She-pig
89. Court game: 2 wds.
93. —— Ridge, Tenn.
94. Italian game
98. Curved lines
99. Units of measure
101. Wicked
103. Thought
104. Eat carefully
105. Bucks
106. Calif. fish
107. Like a pin
108. Norse epic
109. Christen
110. Plant start
111. Needlefish

## DOWN

1. Heads of the fleet: abbr.
2. Wife of Jacob
3. Christia- nia, today
4. —— at windmills
5. Debate
6. Saucy
7. Three —— match: 2 wds.
8. Tile game
9. "Greco- Roman" athlete
10. Poetic time
11. Judge's seat
12. Tire in the trunk
13. Doing the samba
14. Biblical well
15. African fox
16. Enumerate
26. Before: Latin
28. Chinese lake
30. —— du Diable
32. Sea raptors
33. Conger catcher
35. Wading bird
36. Grade
37. Sumerian water god
38. Tunnel
39. Tea flower
41. City slicker
42. Pa. port
43. Presses for payment
45. Put in order
47. Swindle
50. Pierces
52. Shreds
55. Bill
57. Cartoonist Gardner
60. Bloke
61. Small brook
62. Notion, in Nantes
63. Coat with gold
64. "—— Dinsmore"
65. Actor Eastwood

# PUZZLE 56

66. Actor Conreid
67. Exploit
68. Assam silkworm
69. Thwarts at bridge
72. Amerind game
73. Jumping game
76. Card game
79. Earl Anthony's game
81. Punta —— Este
83. New Zealand parrot
84. Mr. Hurok
86. The Red ——
88. Waldorf or Caesar
89. Green stone
90. Like a desert
91. Chilled
92. New York college
94. Yearn (for)
95. Greek theaters
96. Approximate
97. Nibbles
100. Certain pol
102. Churchill's letter

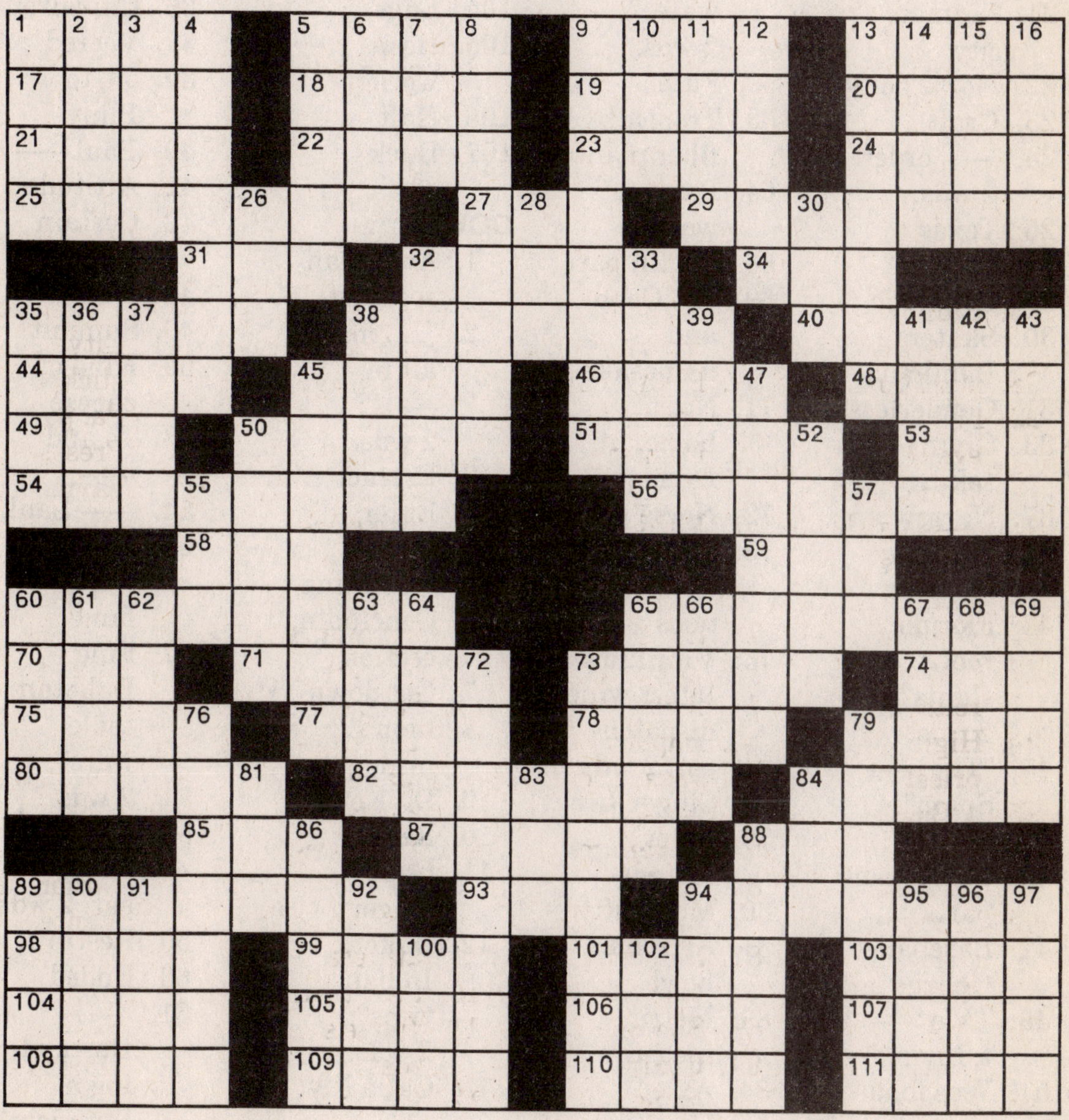

# PUZZLE 57

**ACROSS**

1. Humid
5. Con game
9. Eureka!
12. Full
17. Eastern Indian
18. Piano favorite
19. Mr. Torme
20. Very angry
21. German city
22. Norse deity
23. Craft
24. —— order: 2 wds.
25. Texas cologne?
28. Cenotaph
30. Skater Babilonia
31. Genderless
33. Giving and taking
37. Narrow opening
38. Burning
43. Florida roof sights?: 2 wds.
45. "The —— Spain": 2 wds.
46. Component parts
47. Baseballer Gehrig
48. TV's "—— a Living"
51. Was fond of
52. Remove from print
53. Exhaust ducts
55. Romans and country-men
57. Fine Michigan white water?: 2 wds.
59. Face
63. Tropical fiber plant
64. Pampas weapon
68. Mouth part
69. Mr. Cobb and namesakes
71. Not at home, in Dundee
72. Norse tales
73. Temporary fortifica-tions
75. Virginia's latest wine dispatch-es?: 2 wds.
78. Singer Lee
79. River islands
80. Most nifty
81. Arizona bowl
83. Metric measure
84. Axle breakers
88. Small Arkansas jewel?: 2 wds.
95. Additional
96. Flipped item
98. Hindu garb
99. Mr. Hunter
100. Desolate
101. I, to Claudius
102. Chills
103. Wile
104. Lugs
105. Hosp. workers
106. Halt
107. Duck

**DOWN**

1. American socialist
2. ". . . maids all in ——": 2 wds.
3. Extract
4. Enter
5. Over-whelming
6. Concluding section
7. Got down
8. Lion's pride
9. Dr.'s org.
10. Recluse
11. Choir singers
12. Dakota Indian trips?: 2 wds.
13. Calla lily, e.g.
14. London gallery
15. Harrow foe
16. Skillful
26. Follows
27. Precept
29. Close
32. Unless, legally
33. Move like a cloud
34. Strop
35. Seed coat
36. Chivalrous
37. Veered
39. 53, to Pliny
40. Paul ——
41. Attitude
42. Certain gridders
44. Wealth
49. Summit
50. Kind of cheese
53. To and ——
54. —— Lanka
56. George of "Artie" fame
57. Fine Dakotan table-ware?: 2 wds.
58. . . . purse out of —— ear: 2 wds.
59. Restrain
60. Ended
61. "—— Descend-ing a Staircase"

# PUZZLE 57

62. Custard
64. Riposte sources
65. Kind of arch
66. Statutes
67. Aide: abbr.
70. Fit of pique
72. Eye rudely
74. Genoa, e.g.
76. Kin of etc.
77. Painting style
79. Allocate
82. Certain fisherman
84. Guard's spot
85. Football's Graham
86. Pronoun
87. Roll-call answer
89. Egyptian goddess
90. Savoir-faire
91. Magnolia or willow
92. Egg
93. Job for a lawyer
94. Was aware
97. Uno plus uno

# PUZZLE 58

**ACROSS**

1. Deep hole
4. Noah's niche
7. Routine procedure
12. Fruit drink
13. Reading room
14. Stadium
15. ____ Commandments
16. Rental unit
18. Possesses
19. Film
20. Permit
22. Scarlet
23. Slide
27. Rodent
29. Sovereignty
31. Swift
34. External
35. Speaker
37. In favor of
38. Remove
39. "Born in the ____"
41. High-wire safety device
44. Naples's country
46. Male sheep
48. Skydiver's necessity
52. Pub drink
53. With mouth open
54. Mad Hatter's brew
55. Jr., to Sr.
56. Mimicked a cat
57. Sin
58. Terminate

**DOWN**

1. Lane
2. Perfect
3. Taut
4. First man
5. Give an account of
6. Scoundrel
7. Detest
8. Branch
9. Spelling event
10. Lodge
11. Make lace
17. Carnival contraption
21. Hackneyed
23. Rebuff
24. Ignited
25. Wrath
26. Each
28. "Much ____ About Nothing"
30. Cow's cry
31. Staff
32. "____ You Being Served?"
33. Chum
36. Baseballer Babe ____
37. Hesitate
40. Pan-fry
42. Rub out
43. Claw
44. Chilled
45. Calendar span
47. Darn
48. Actress Dawber
49. Improve, like wine
50. Uncooked
51. Monkey

# PUZZLE 59

Diagramless crosswords are solved by using the clues and their numbers to fill in the answer words and the arrangement of black squares. Insert the number of each clue with the first letter of its answer, across and down. Fill in a black square at the end of each word. Every black square must have a corresponding black square on the opposite side of the diagram to form a symmetrical pattern.

**ACROSS**

1. Strong wind
5. Atop
9. Church officer

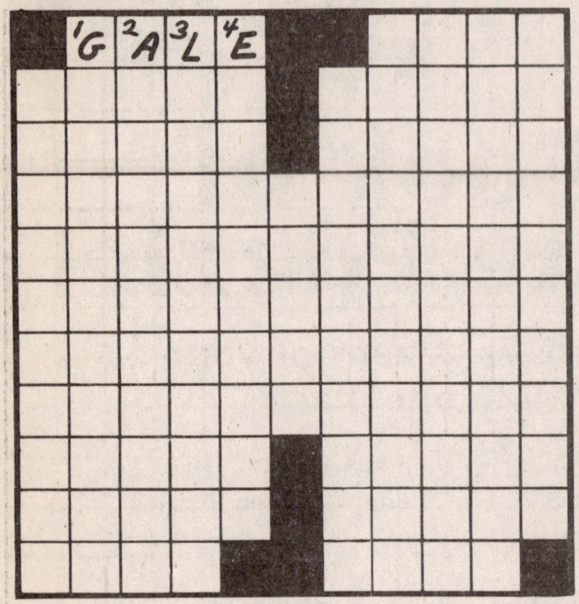


10. Witch's vehicle
11. Fred Allen's medium
12. Tolerate
13. Exist
14. Perched
16. ____ Francisco
17. Feudal drudge
19. Cozy
21. Actress Dunne
23. Seoul's land
25. "Where or ____"
29. ____ a plea
30. Nabokov heroine
32. French boyfriend
33. Anon
35. Poe's bird
37. Assumed name
38. Sphere of activity
39. Treaty
40. Tight spot

**DOWN**

1. Fierce look
2. Venomous snake
3. Hawaiian garland
4. God of love
5. Globe
6. Din element
7. Dave Garroway's time
8. Prophetic sign
9. Historic periods
10. Conductor's wand
15. Out front
18. Douglas or Fraser
20. Gull's cry
22. Brings up
23. Marsupial "bear"
24. Of the eye
26. Refuge
27. Correct
28. Pinta's sister ship
29. Applaud
31. Fine horse
34. Break a fast
36. Mr. Onassis, for short

---

# PUZZLE 60

**ACROSS**

1. Aid and ____
5. Ark builder
6. Droop

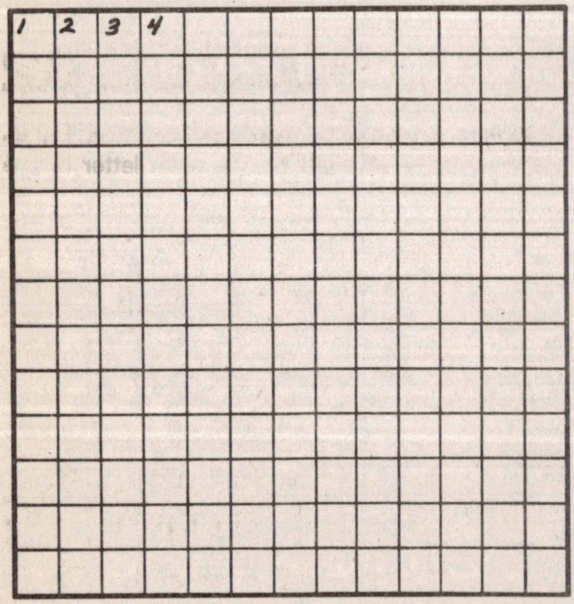


10. Against
11. Concept
12. Instruct
14. Camel's cousin
16. Inspire
19. Ottoman bigwig
21. Heavenly body
22. Banner
23. Quaker pronoun
26. Dickens hero
28. Aviation prefix
29. Desire
30. Instrument
32. London's ____ Vic
33. Glossy finishes
35. An ____ of prevention . . .
37. Uncanny
41. "____ Window"
42. Bye-bye
43. Diminutive ending
44. ____ bien
45. Brewer's oven

**DOWN**

1. Medical-school course: abbr.
2. Wish or jaw
3. . . . I could ____ horse: 2 wds.
4. Stocky
6. Actor Geer
7. Pointless
8. Lamb locale
9. Mexican entree
13. Boffo show
15. Culture medium
17. Siesta
18. Concerted effort
20. Give it ____ (try): 2 wds.
22. Singing voice
23. Duo
24. Sign of an angel
25. Last
27. ____ in the sky
31. Singleton
33. Ella's forte
34. Roll-call word
36. Clear
38. ____ avis
39. Inhabitants: suffix
40. Orient

# PUZZLE 61

**ACROSS**
1. Commercials
4. "____ O' My Heart"
7. Turf
10. Knocks
12. Rescues
14. Swing
15. Snare
16. Dish
17. Tortoise's race opponent
18. Rub out
20. Sandal parts
22. Father
23. Use a straw
24. Ragout
26. Disorder
29. Automobiles
30. Also
32. Tavern drink
33. The whole amount
34. Pod vegetable
35. Slipped
36. Halt!
39. Want
40. Chest bone
42. Dog's foot
43. Blackboards
46. Unwraps
49. Footwear
50. Begin
53. Bellow
55. Otherwise
56. Lone Star State
57. Davenport
58. Little child
59. Assembled
60. Fresh

**DOWN**
1. Mr. Linkletter
2. Venture
3. Box lightly
4. Friend
5. Miss Gabor
6. Receives
7. Exchange
8. Paddles
9. Change color
11. Digging tools
12. Hurried
13. Matched collections
14. Figure
19. Jig or coping
21. Border
24. Auctions
25. Entertain
27. Trite
28. Firm
29. Bottle top
31. Aged
35. Man-made conduits
37. Use a soapbox
38. Deep hole
39. Short sleep
41. Most suitable
42. Cooking vessels
43. Alone
44. "Paradise ____"
45. Watch part
47. High time
48. Secure
49. "You ____ Your Life"
51. Cutting tool
52. Rodent
54. Uncooked

Starting box on page 562

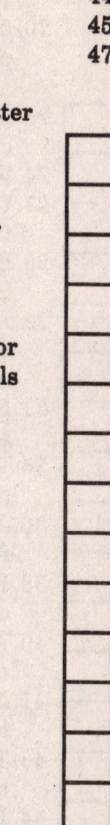

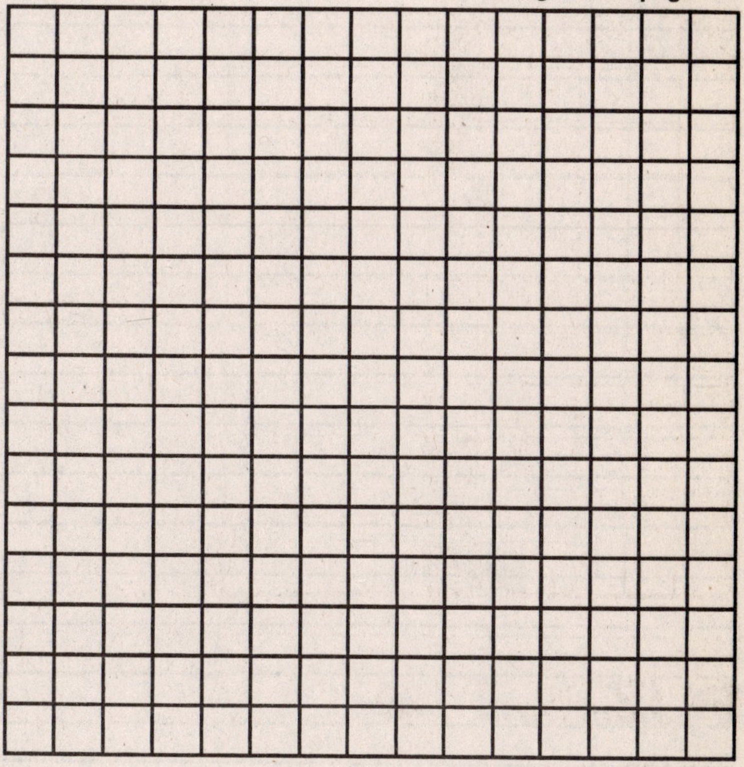

# Top to Bottom

# PUZZLE 62

**Place the letters given below each diagram into the squares to form eight 4-letter words reading from top to bottom from square to connected square. The top letter is the first of all eight words, each letter in the second row is the second letter of four words, and so on.**

**Example:**

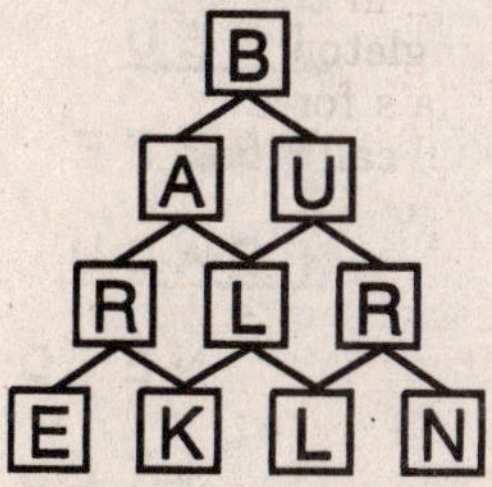

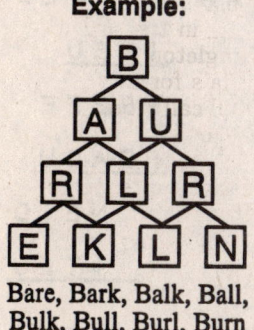

Bare, Bark, Balk, Ball, Bulk, Bull, Burl, Burn

**1.**

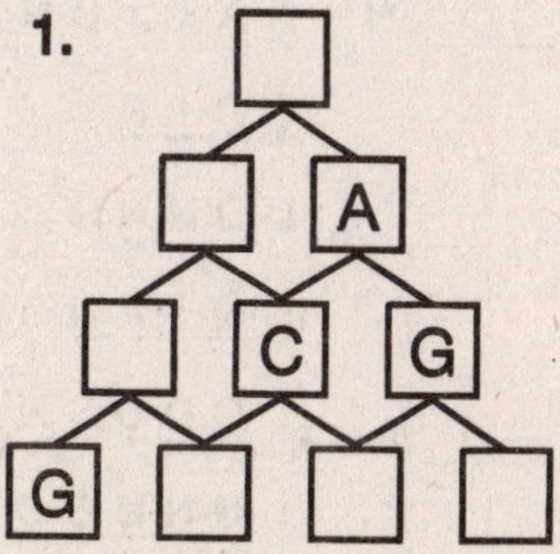


**E I K N R S**

**2.**

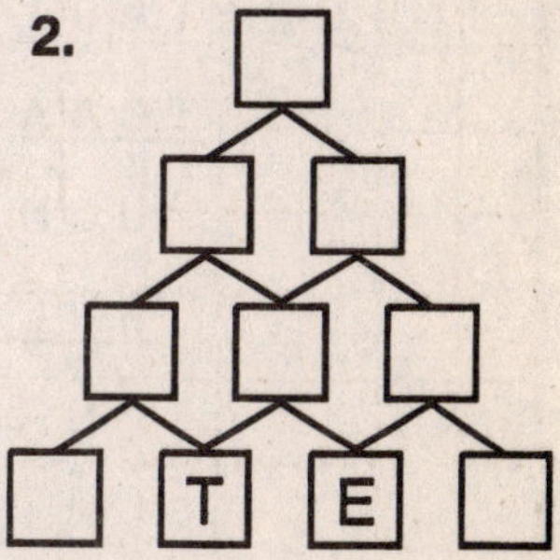


**A C K O P R R U**

# PUZZLE 63

**ACROSS**
1. Use a crowbar
4. Regretted
6. Outskirts
8. What Washington could not tell
9. Midge
12. WWII ally
14. Exhaust
16. English preparatory school
18. Reminder to an executive
20. Chinese philosopher ____-Tzu
22. ____-de-campe
24. Never-ending
27. One of Jacob's twelve sons
28. Saratoga Springs, e.g.
29. American writer of humorous verse
31. Southern sweet potatoes
34. Without dilution
36. Jewelry for a finger
38. Pack aboard ship
40. Actress Salonga of "Miss Saigon"
41. More ostentatious
43. Time before the storm
44. Island off of Florida

**DOWN**
1. Clergyman
2. Flow
3. Itinerant petty thief
5. Parking lot mishap mark
6. Chills and fever ailment
7. Ascent
10. Intention
11. Written works
13. Turn over and over
15. Actor Jannings
17. Hit the ____ on the head
19. Lyrical poems
21. Prophetic sign
23. Catch sight of
25. "One Day in the Life of ____ Denisovich"
26. German river
30. Derby or Stetson
32. Moderately
33. Snick's partner
35. Bridge fee
37. Needlefish
39. Author of "The Caine Mutiny"
42. Rubber plant

Starting box on page 562

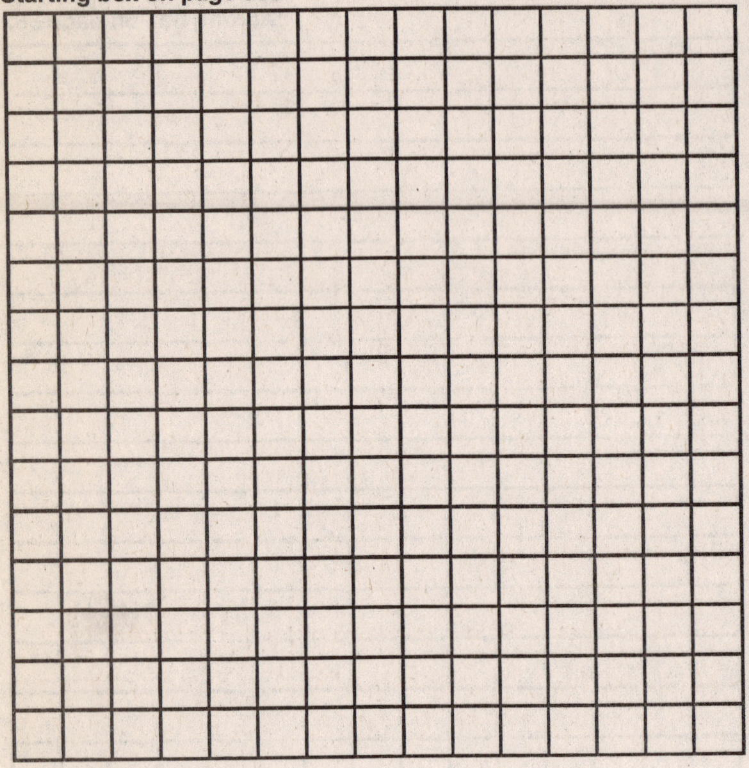

# PUZZLE 64

## Word Math

**In these long-division problems letters are substituted for numbers. Determine the value of each letter. Then arrange the letters in order from 0 to 9, and they will spell a word or phrase.**

**1**

| 0 | 1 | 2 | 3 | 4 | 5 | 6 | 7 | 8 | 9 |
|---|---|---|---|---|---|---|---|---|---|
| | | | | | | | | | |

```
        TUN
NICE | TASTES
       TOAA
        UCNE
        UNLO
         NAAS
         NICE
          ACN
```

**2**

| 0 | 1 | 2 | 3 | 4 | 5 | 6 | 7 | 8 | 9 |
|---|---|---|---|---|---|---|---|---|---|
| | | | | | | | | | |

```
        BIN
COIN | NATION
       COIN
       UDNNO
       DNIAN
        CDOSN
        UNBCC
         CITC
```

**3**

| 0 | 1 | 2 | 3 | 4 | 5 | 6 | 7 | 8 | 9 |
|---|---|---|---|---|---|---|---|---|---|
| | | | | | | | | | |

```
        ANA
FLAN | GIFTED
        ITEU
       FEEFE
       FDADU
         NEID
         ITEU
          LLT
```

# PUZZLE 65

**ACROSS**

1. Spiel
5. Find
7. Doubleday's game
9. Neighbor of G. Brit.
12. Scores 100 on
13. Goal
15. Mr. Sparks
16. ____ Serene Highness
17. Modeled
20. Detest
21. Indigent
22. Painting or sculpture
23. Do kitchen work
24. Trick
27. Flock parent
30. And not
31. Sports locale
33. Gainsay
34. Thankfulness
36. Garden spot
39. Long time
40. Reno cube
41. Whet
42. Hesitant sounds
43. Fees
46. Traps
47. Pung

**DOWN**

1. Also-ran
2. Chills
3. Collar
4. Letter after zeta
5. Dentelle
6. Buoy
7. Pshaw
8. Ignited
9. ____ sanctum
10. High-pitched
11. Singer Nelson
14. Males
17. Parcel's mate
18. On the same wavelength
19. Mr. Buttons
20. Possesses
25. "____ But the Brave"
26. Attempt
27. Diamond miscue
28. Breaks of a habit
29. Tolkien creature
31. Author James
32. Help
33. Musical pairs
35. "____ the season . . ."
36. Filleted
37. Purposes
38. ____ Plaines, Ill.
41. Present
44. Elected ones
45. Mate

Starting box on page 562

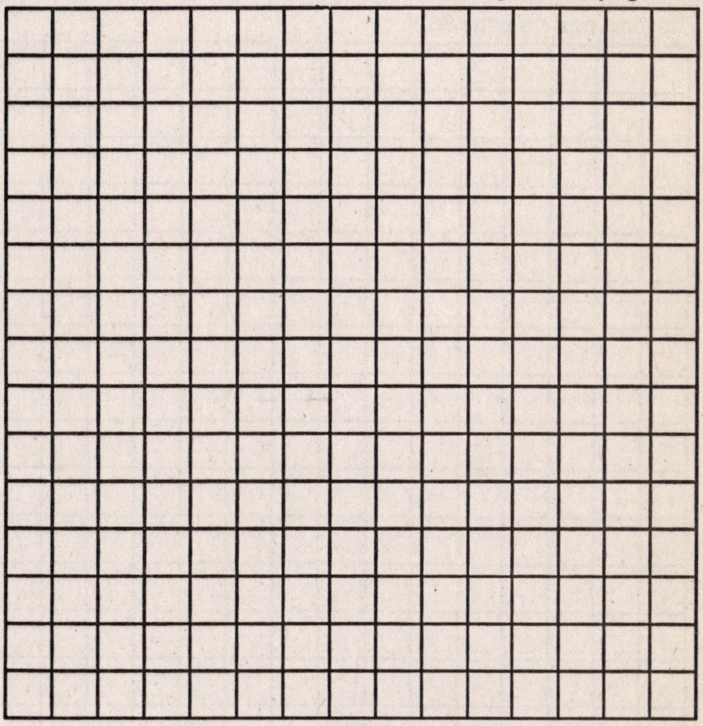

# QUOTAGRAM — PUZZLE 66

**Fill in the answers to the clues below. Then transfer the letters to the correspondingly numbered squares in the diagram. The completed diagram will contain a quotation.**

1. Carried ___ ___ ___ ___ ___ (15 29 1 9 14)
2. Entree ___ ___ ___ ___ (37 31 10 34)
3. Swain ___ ___ ___ ___ ___ ___ (32 24 35 21 16 5)
4. Perfect ___ ___ ___ ___ ___ (28 18 3 12 36)
5. Teach ___ ___ ___ ___ ___ ___ ___ (6 23 19 33 7 27 39)
6. Pertaining to a culture ___ ___ ___ ___ ___ ___ ___ ___ (22 11 2 30 13 25 17 20)
7. Admit ___ ___ ___ ___ ___ (4 38 26 40 8)

| | | | | | | | | | | | | | | | |
|---|---|---|---|---|---|---|---|---|---|---|---|---|---|---|---|
| 1 | 2 | 3 | ■ | 4 | 5 | 6 | 7 | 8 | 9 | 10 | 11 | ■ | 12 | 13 | 14 |
| ■ | 15 | 16 | ■ | 17 | 18 | 19 | 20 | 21 | ■ | 22 | 23 | 24 | 25 | 26 | 27 |
| 28 | 29 | 30 | ■ | 31 | 32 | ■ | 33 | 34 | 35 | 36 | 37 | 38 | 39 | 40 | ■ |

# PUZZLE 67

**ACROSS**

1. Recede, as tides
4. Appearance
6. Ventilate
9. Complains
11. Gangster
13. Give rise to
15. Prize
17. Troll
19. Idolize
21. Pepper's mate
23. "The Raven" poet
24. Tire mishap
27. Wail
28. Chief
29. United
30. Sentence subject, often
31. French resort
32. Go to a restaurant
34. Squid's fluid
35. Small beds
36. "Hazel" actress
39. Hen's perch
42. Rustic
44. Of one's birth
46. Flooring square
47. Aviator
49. Seed container
50. Gambling town
51. Stitch

**Starting box on page 562**

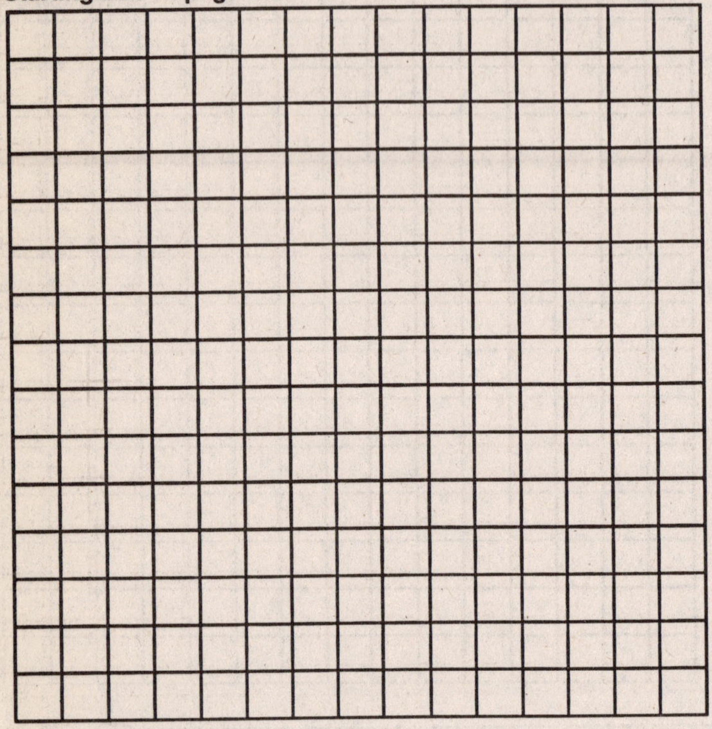

**DOWN**

1. Shade tree
2. Nitwit
3. Plank
5. Realized
6. Cry of triumph
7. Des Moines location
8. Highway
10. Add spice to
12. Leave without graduating
14. Sketch
16. Inundate
18. Deluge
20. Moray
22. Overblouse
24. Withdraw
25. Tell a fib
26. Male singer
27. ___ said a mouthful!
28. Trivial
30. The deal's unacceptable
31. Penpoint
33. Short jacket
37. Vacation jaunt
38. Saint's headdress
40. Recipe word
41. Stories
43. Was winning
45. Sole
48. Pull by rope

# PUZZLE 68

## QUOTAGRAM

**Fill in the answers to the clues below. Then transfer the letters to the correspondingly numbered squares in the diagram. The completed diagram will contain a quotation.**

1. 20-year napper: 3 wds. ___ ___ ___ ___ ___ ___ ___ ___ ___ ___ ___ ___
   2 15 69 27 61 33 51 44 58 22 37 28
2. Thin, like model Hornby ___ ___ ___ ___ ___ ___
   13 19 35 17 25 3
3. Expressing gratitude ___ ___ ___ ___ ___ ___ ___ ___
   1 14 52 30 11 38 24 6
4. Feeling ___ ___ ___ ___ ___ ___ ___ ___ ___
   18 12 60 64 10 47 70 48 45
5. Fugitive-catchers' rewards ___ ___ ___ ___ ___ ___ ___ ___
   53 20 54 16 65 23 32 49
6. Dispossessed ___ ___ ___ ___ ___ ___
   8 63 36 56 40 68
7. Halloween phrase: 3 wds. ___ ___ ___ ___ ___ ___ ___ ___ ___ ___ ___ ___
   7 21 4 62 39 59 42 55 29 50 66 34
8. Alabama's capital ___ ___ ___ ___ ___ ___ ___ ___ ___ ___
   9 57 5 41 46 26 31 71 67 43

| | | | | | | | | | | | | | | | | | | | | | |
|---|---|---|---|---|---|---|---|---|---|---|---|---|---|---|---|---|---|---|---|---|---|
| 1 | 2 | 3 | 4 | 5 | 6 | ■ | 7 | 8 | ■ | 9 | 10 | 11 | 12 | ■ | 13 | 14 | 15 | 16 | 17 | 18 | ■ |
| 19 | 20 | 21 | 22 | ■ | 23 | 24 | ■ | 25 | 26 | 27 | 28 | 29 | 30 | 31 | 32 | 33 | 34 | ■ | 35 | 36 | ■ |
| 37 | 38 | 39 | 40 | ■ | 41 | 42 | 43 | 44 | 45 | 46 | ■ | 47 | 48 | ■ | 49 | 50 | 51 | ■ | 52 | ■ | 53 |
| 54 | 55 | 56 | 57 | 58 | ■ | 59 | 60 | ■ | 61 | ■ | 62 | 63 | 64 | 65 | 66 | 67 | 68 | ■ | 69 | 70 | 71 |

# PUZZLE 69

**ACROSS**
1. Lobe locale
4. Falsehoods
6. Founder of psychoanalysis
8. Electrical unit
12. ____ capita
15. Go in front
17. Blue flag
18. Dry, as the desert
20. Three-sided figure
22. Enter a swimming pool
23. Comes in last
24. Back of the neck
26. Twice fifteen
28. Smoked salmon
29. Jog
30. Male sheep
32. Twine
34. Verbal
36. Weather satellite
37. Metal barrel
39. Stirs up
42. Fodder tower
43. Female knight
44. Sound reverberation
46. Shade tree
47. Drove too fast
48. Domesticates
51. Man of the hour
52. Arrest

**DOWN**
1. Sprite
2. Atmosphere
3. Spool of film
5. Hard fat
7. Loved one
8. Wine plantations
9. Associations: abbr.
10. "____ Abner"
11. Mao ____-tung
12. Cushion
13. ____ go bragh
14. Competitor
16. Designer Christian
19. Banked money
21. Houston baseballer
25. Crowd actor
26. Divide in three parts
27. Barbarian
31. ____ Antoinette
33. Fixed routine
35. Period of calm
36. Clock reading
38. Mother
39. Commercials
40. Space between
41. Persian king
45. Sign of the future
49. Important age
50. Cry noisily

Starting box on page 562

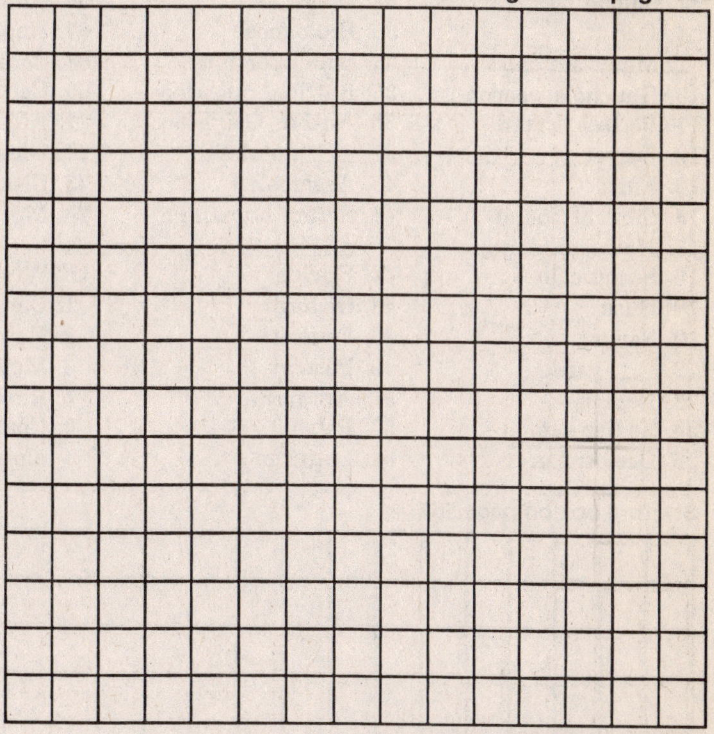

# Word Math

# PUZZLE 70

**In these long-division problems, letters are substituted for numbers. Determine the value of each letter. Then arrange the letters in order from 0 to 9, and they will spell a word or phrase.**

**1**

| 0 | 1 | 2 | 3 | 4 | 5 | 6 | 7 | 8 | 9 |
|---|---|---|---|---|---|---|---|---|---|
| | | | | | | | | | |

```
              D I N
EDGE ) G O A T E E
       T A N T
       D A I M E
       D E M A O
         D T A D E
         D T E R R
             O I G
```

**2**

| 0 | 1 | 2 | 3 | 4 | 5 | 6 | 7 | 8 | 9 |
|---|---|---|---|---|---|---|---|---|---|
| | | | | | | | | | |

```
              E O N
NAIL ) Y E O M A N
       O A R G
       I G N N A
       I O L I N
           L I E N
           A M E N
           I I M M
```

**3**

| 0 | 1 | 2 | 3 | 4 | 5 | 6 | 7 | 8 | 9 |
|---|---|---|---|---|---|---|---|---|---|
| | | | | | | | | | |

```
                  T A N
RASP ) C R A N I U M
       C C U U N
         I T C U
         R A S P
         A P M C M
         A N N T R
           C I C S
```

# PUZZLE 71

## ACROSS

1. Saloon
4. Dab
7. Mountain crest
10. Gaucho's weapon
11. Perfect accord
12. Garret
13. Finis
14. Sibilant sound
15. Hawaiian dance
16. Social calls
18. Buss
19. Sailor
22. ____-garde
23. Regimen
24. Zodiac ram
26. Ocelot, e.g.
29. Italian coffee
32. Opera hero
33. Prologues
34. Small portion
35. Baffling question
36. Author Deighton
37. ____ nutshell
40. Assembled
41. Errare humanum ____
42. Prickle
43. Of birds
46. Favorite
49. Portray
51. Art form
53. Petrol
54. Luggage
56. Revise
57. Handle roughly
59. Rejects a lover
62. Draft initials
63. Twitches
64. Wasteland
65. Daunt
66. Animal pouch
67. Has permission
68. Ceremonial staff
69. Carpet fibers
71. Etching fluid
72. Gloss
73. Clear profit
74. Morse code word

## DOWN

1. Carpentry tool
2. Hero of "Exodus"
3. Moved
4. Swimming places
5. Communications alphabet start
6. Make lace
8. Prepare a salad
9. Metaphysical being
10. Makes empty threats
11. Group of colleges: abbr.
13. Topsy's playmate
15. Hurry
17. "There was not a penny ____"
18. Set of tools
19. Soprano
20. Theater passages
21. Be indignant
23. ____ es Salaam
24. Weapon
25. Distress signal
27. Genetic material: abbr.
28. Corn holder
30. Bishopric
31. ____ excellence
33. Kettle
35. Cage
37. Construction girders
38. Hospital workers
39. Fire crimes
40. Actress West
43. Black cuckoo
44. Martin ____ Buren
45. Catalogued
46. Cribbage marker
47. Chang's twin
48. Transported, formerly
49. Links group: abbr.
50. Ancient
51. "My ____ Sal"
52. Protection
54. Public vehicle
55. Chemical substance
58. One-spot
60. Refrain syllables
61. Pigs' home
63. Unspoken
64. Short race
65. Visage
66. Family member, for short
68. Male
70. Hawaiian wreath

Starting box on page 562

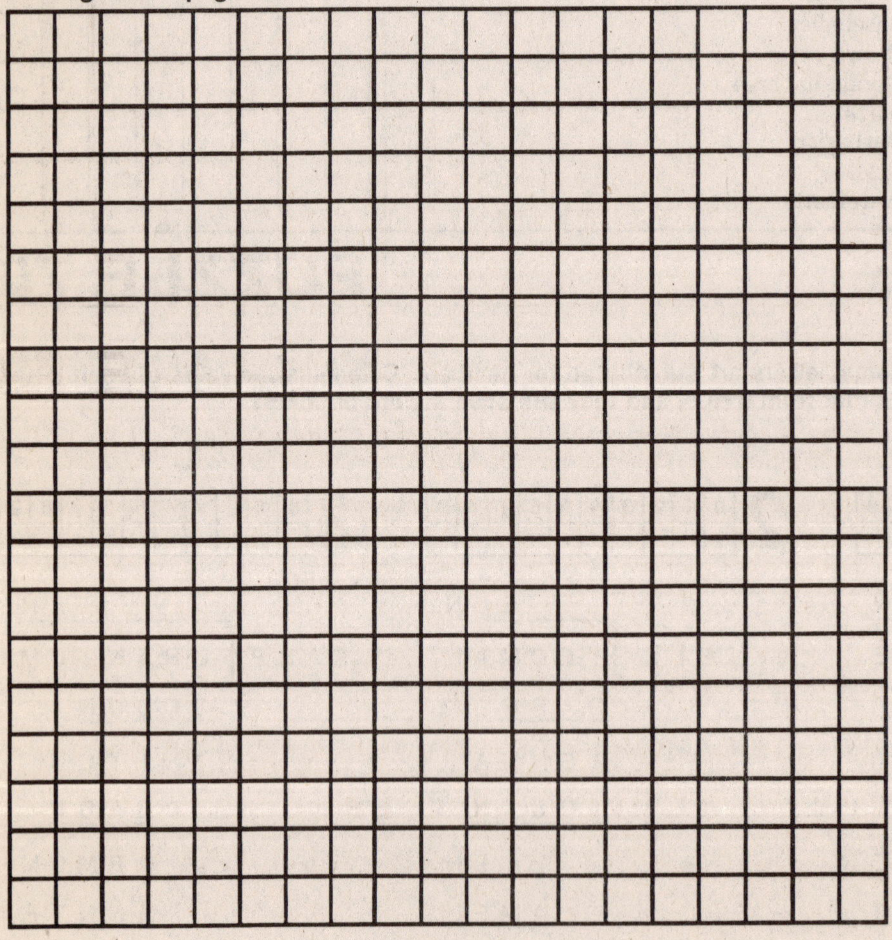

# PUZZLE 72

**ACROSS**
1. Short distance
5. Diva's renditions
10. Portion
11. Schedule
12. Austin citizen
13. School assignment
14. Sandwich shop, for short
15. Law suit
16. "Let's Make a ____"
17. Vapor
18. Cargo weight
21. Vend
22. Stream
23. Dog's foot
25. Actress Gabor
26. Fixed a piano
28. Greek letter
29. Morning moisture
30. "Phantom of the ____"
31. Groove
32. ____ carte
33. Exhausted
34. Have being
35. Likewise not
36. Pitch
37. Night sight
38. Energy
40. Solidify
41. Simpleton
42. Remote
44. Dispense from a pitcher
45. Noah's landing place
48. Intelligent
50. Amateur
51. Third planet from the sun
52. Josh
53. Family lineage chart

**DOWN**
1. Snail's home
2. Hired vehicle
3. Notable time
4. Animal enclosure
5. Grows older
6. Bowling-alley button
7. Those holding office
8. ____ Annie of "Oklahoma"
9. ____ Fernando, Argentina
10. Pilfer
11. Alack's partner
14. Dover's state
15. Food provider
16. Process photography
17. Military rank
19. Telephone-company employee
20. Not artificial
21. Enclosed car
22. Largest planet
24. Irrigate
26. Toddler
27. June honoree
37. Bridge position
39. "____ Blues"
40. Fence door
41. Expertise
43. Confront
44. Peel
45. Pismire
46. Caviar
47. Role on "Evening Shade"
48. Ready, ____, go!
49. Disfigure

Starting box on page 562

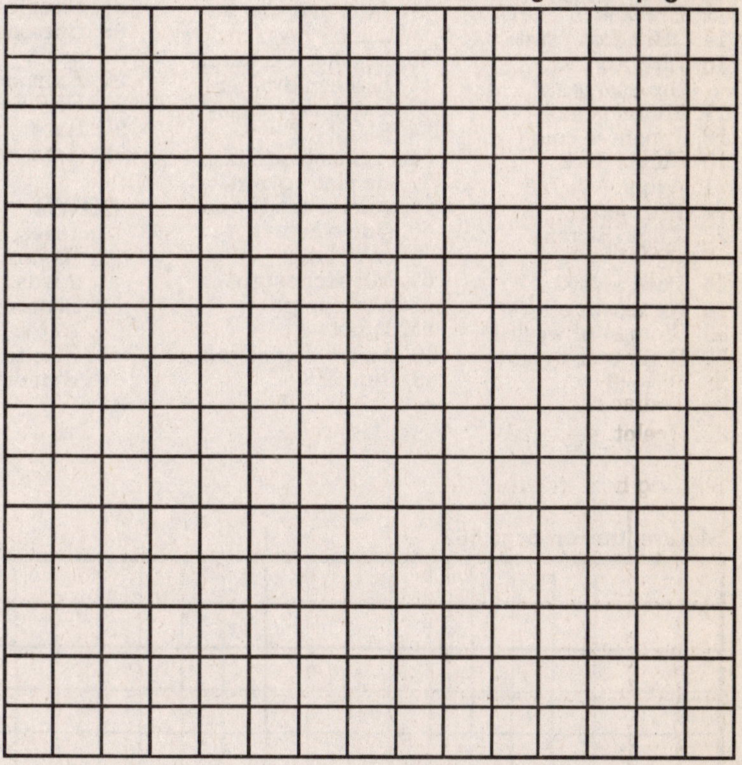

# Crypto-Verse

# PUZZLE 73

**To read this verse, you must first solve this simple substitution code.**

LJ ILJCRMCLER L QZSR TVAQ OVJ
IQRJ L WDZH YVXLCT ILCQ OZCQRM.
L KRZC QLE ZDEXTC RSRMH FZER.
QR JRSRM TRRET CX KXCQRM.
QR DXXUT ZC EXCQRM ZJG NVTC TELDRT.
ZDD CQLT TRRET TCMZJFR CX ER,
OXM IQRJ QR WDZHT ILCQ FMXIJ-VW OXDUT,
QR KRZCT CQRE RZTLDH.

# PUZZLE 74

**ACROSS**
1. Wall angle
6. Chess piece
12. Breathe in
14. "Big Sky" state
15. Literary threesome
17. Melon type
18. Japanese coin
19. Ship's deck
21. Arbor
22. 19th letter
23. Anglo-Saxon slaves
25. Turn away
26. Narcissus's lover
30. Woman of wealth
32. Computer input
36. Pushed
39. Stair post
40. "____ of Grass"
42. Philippine buffalo
44. ". . . and one for ____"
45. Leather workers
46. Kitchen drainer
48. Extremely clean
50. Flank
51. Against: prefix
52. Be clairvoyant
56. Idler's antithesis
60. One who calculates
61. Mr. Burroughs
63. Sea nymph
65. If not
66. Angry dog sound
68. Rancor
69. "A friend in ____ . . ."
70. Disparages
72. Fraternal org.
73. Figure of speech
75. Used up
78. ____ Appia
81. Shield
82. Lose color
83. NCO
86. Sleeplessness
88. Cheese-filled pasta
90. Exhaust
91. Eskimo shoe
92. Rate
93. Grasslike plant

**DOWN**
1. Insect eggs
2. Regarding: 2 wds.
3. Skater Tiffany
4. Actor Holbrook
5. Flee to wed
6. Blunder, slangily
7. Inactive
8. Pigpen
9. Geological angle of fault
10. Singletons
11. What dogs "shake" with
13. Selves
14. Lawn grooming necessity
16. Over there, to Shelley
17. Rude abode
20. Mexican peasant
21. Lox's go-withs
24. Avow
26. Certain N.J. time
27. Cartoonist Young
28. "Ecce ____"
29. Ellipse
31. Sharp tool
32. Jutlander
33. Certain prayers
34. Regions: abbr.
35. Mulelike animal
37. Artists' needs
38. Descendants of the son of Jacob and Bilhah
40. Kind of pie top-crust
41. Perk up
43. Cow's milk bag
45. Scout's rider
47. Snakelike fish
49. Moccasin
52. Precise
53. Leer
54. Regretted
55. Chargers' weapons
56. Eagle's nest
57. Poetic foot
58. Cut short
59. Yugoslavia's late premier
60. Enjoyment
62. "Cheers," e.g.
64. Color the hair
66. Brownish tint
67. Foliage unit
70. Stray calf
71. Vega, e.g.
73. Domesticates
74. Leases
76. Dutch cheese
77. Birthmark
78. Pitcher Blue
79. Noun suffixes
80. Adders
83. Common ailment
84. Promote a product
85. Similar
87. Hurray for Ferdinand!
89. Mamie's hubby

Starting box on page 562

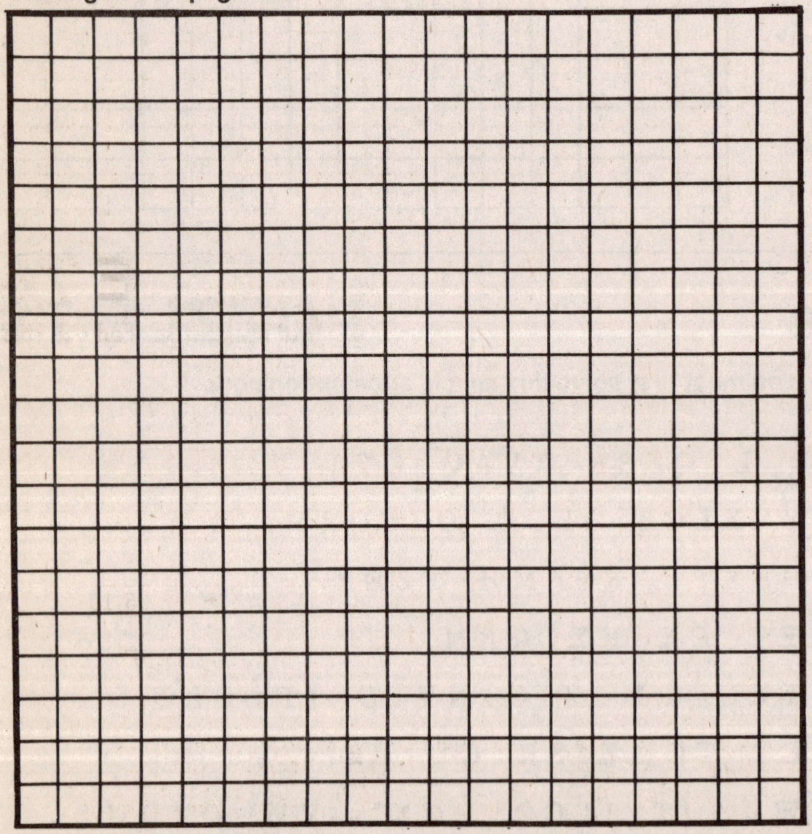

# PUZZLE 75

**ACROSS**
1. Permit
4. Mates for lasses
8. Aft's cohort
9. "God's Little ___"
10. Liquid
11. Wharves
13. Briny
15. Goliath's undoer
17. Accompanying
18. Venus de ___
19. Most swift
22. Religious image
23. Kind of curve
24. Golf club
27. "Untouchable" Eliot
28. Watching wide-eyed
30. Heavenly headwear
33. Tempo
34. Ocean
37. Seed coat
38. Moral
41. Coal source
42. Expunge
43. Appears
45. Blazes briefly
46. ___ Ana, Calif.
48. "The Nutcracker ___"
49. Pleased
50. Factual
51. "Jane ___"
52. Shade tree

**DOWN**
1. Hotel area
2. Cleveland's lake
3. Williams or Mack
4. Splash gently
5. Biting
6. In a reverie
7. Military branch
8. Spark producer
10. "The Mill on the ___"
12. Rural structures
13. Vault
14. Woeful word
16. Knotts and Adams
20. Take a chair
21. Corner
25. Old Danish coin
26. Pleasant
28. With gravity
29. Clear
30. Stage hogs
31. Zodiac ram
32. Ancestry
34. Frighten
35. Facility
36. Pub brews
39. Blimp gas
40. Furious
44. Luminary
45. Roll up
47. Fruit drink
48. Blessed Fr. woman

Starting box on page 562

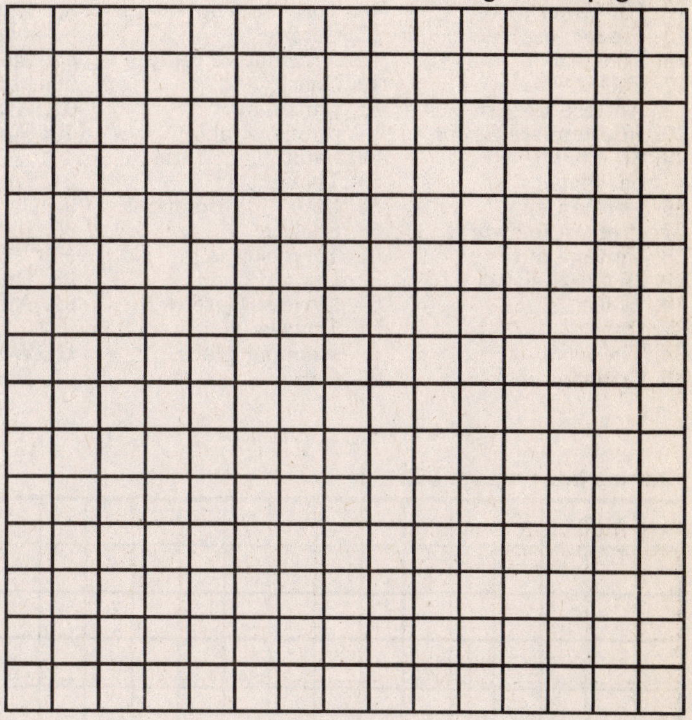

# QUOTAGRAM PUZZLE 76

**Fill in the answers to the clues below. Then transfer the letters to the correspondingly numbered squares in the diagram. The completed diagram will contain a quotation.**

1. Streisand song ___ ___ ___ ___ ___ ___ (21 33 14 18 27 42)
2. Aromas ___ ___ ___ ___ ___ (36 13 29 20 17)
3. Neighbor of Cambodia ___ ___ ___ ___ (26 12 3 39)
4. Wild party: hyph. ___ ___ ___ ___ ___ ___ ___ ___ (8 16 37 15 2 40 30 38)
5. Quite large ___ ___ ___ ___ ___ (9 19 44 11 28)
6. "___ Christmas" ___ ___ ___ ___ ___ (34 32 6 23 22)
7. Dawn goddess ___ ___ ___ ___ ___ ___ (1 24 5 43 35 10)
8. Frogs' kin ___ ___ ___ ___ ___ (31 4 25 41 7)

| | | | | | | | | | | | | | | | | | | |
|---|---|---|---|---|---|---|---|---|---|---|---|---|---|---|---|---|---|---|
| 1 | ■ | 2 | 3 | 4 | 5 | ■ | 6 | 7 | ■ | 8 | 9 | 10 | 11 | ■ | 12 | ■ | 13 | 14 |
| 15 | ■ | 16 | 17 | ■ | 18 | 19 | 20 | 21 | 22 | 23 | 24 | 25 | 26 | 27 | 28 | ■ | 29 | 30 |
| ■ | 31 | 32 | 33 | ■ | 34 | 35 | 36 | 37 | 38 | ■ | 39 | 40 | 41 | 42 | ■ | 43 | 44 | ■ |

# PUZZLE 77

**ACROSS**

1. Science room, for short
4. Aged
7. Tabby
10. Depart
12. Hawaiian food
13. Pindar, e.g.
16. Fool
17. Feel
19. Actress Berger
20. Boutonniere flower
23. St. Louis baseballers
26. German spa
27. Prepare for war
28. Vintage auto
29. Distress signal
30. "Dies ____"
31. Ogle
33. Tin
35. Cribbage jack
37. ____ Angeles
38. Circle segment
41. City oasis
42. Actress Balin
43. Director Burrows
44. Equipment
46. Tortoise's opponent
47. Coterie
48. Affirmative reply
49. Boast
51. Canadian province: abbr.
52. Sault ____ Marie
53. Thought
55. Otto ____ Bismarck
58. Shelter
61. Tennyson, e.g.
62. Dry
64. Lyricist Gershwin
65. Traveler's stopping place
66. Curve
67. Foxy
68. Shade tree
69. British corporation: abbr.
70. ____ a girl!
71. Sea eagle
73. Peruse
75. Toward the rear
78. Actress Merkel
79. Pitcher handle
80. Permit
83. Button-up sweaters
87. Meat eater
90. Musical chord
91. Athletic game
93. Singer Bobby ____
94. Angry
95. "____ Maria"
96. Ruled
97. "____ Miserables"
98. Uncooked
99. Alfonso's queen

**DOWN**

1. Dens
2. Stratford-on-____
3. Phi ____ Kappa
4. Ajar
5. Actor Chaney
6. Phonograph record
7. "____ Fan Tutte"
8. Seaport in Yemen
9. Louise and Turner
10. Vermin
11. Dutch cheese
14. French town
15. Russian news agency
17. "____ to Watch Over Me"
18. Body part sometimes pierced
21. Seaman
22. Natives of Teheran
24. Della and Pee Wee
25. Female deer
30. Printing fluid
32. Cleaning cloth
33. First Family before the Reagans
34. Exist
36. Flying mammal
37. Minstrel's song
39. Confederate soldier
40. Johnny and Kit
41. Chinese mammal
45. Graded
46. ____ polloi
50. Obtain
54. Be sick
55. Capital of Austria
56. Maid of ____
57. Viet ____
58. "____ Abner"
59. Beg
60. Make beloved
61. Favorite
63. Change color
66. Offer
72. Carpet
74. Scottish alder
75. Play beginning
76. Actor Jamie ____
77. Court proceeding
80. "____ Doone"
81. New York canal
82. Baby-sit
84. Fixed appointment
85. ____ of March
86. Box
87. Work gang
88. Not working
89. Conceited
92. Eggs

**Starting box on page 562**

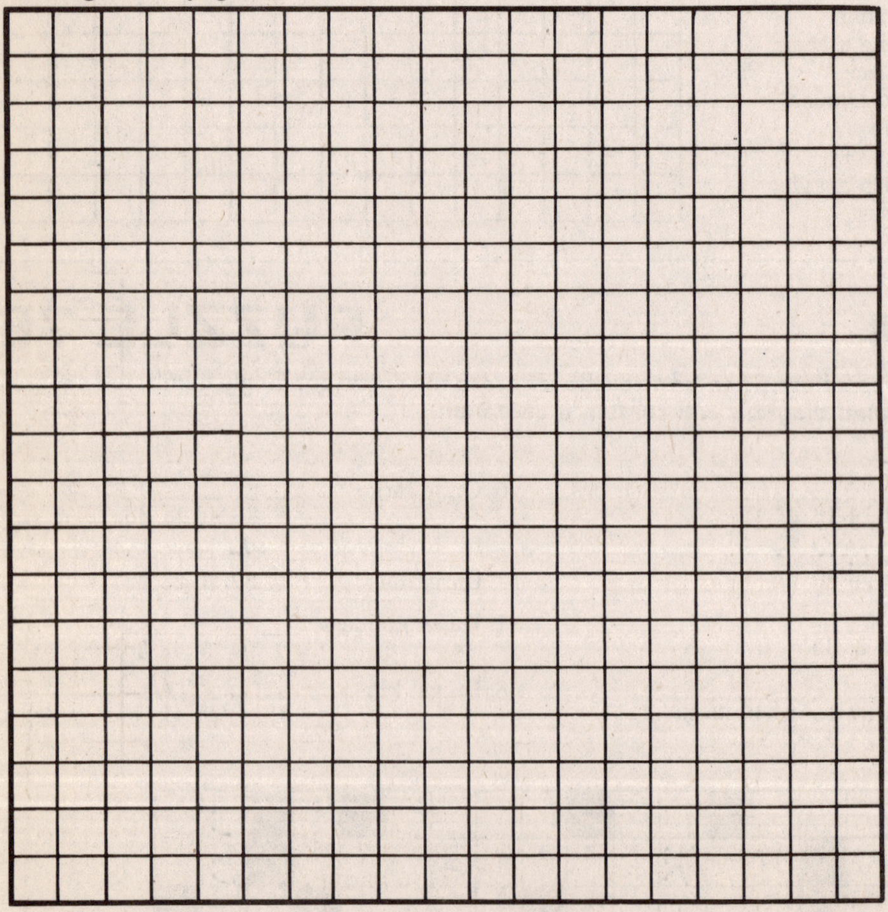

# PUZZLE 78

**ACROSS**

1. Competent
5. Confederates, for short
9. Some soldiers: abbr.
13. "He went ____-a-way"
17. Cut of meat
18. Rock salt
19. Harvest
20. Mythological VIP
21. Slight color
22. Merrill
23. Storyteller's start
24. Angers
25. "Lohengrin" character
26. Conceited
28. File's partner
29. Comes in again
31. Sugar source
32. "____ Shrugged"
33. Lemonwood: var.
34. Female in Liverpool
35. They're scattered
36. Librarian's degree: abbr.
37. Cushions
38. Minute openings
39. Musical exercises
42. Brown bear
43. Dramatizes
45. Brier patch
46. Parade feature
48. Roberts
49. "Paperback ____" (Beatles song)
51. Headless nails
52. Kind of electrode
54. Latin-American dance
55. Moves a camera
57. ____ worth
59. Weird
60. Cowpoke's word
61. Some beers
64. Masts
65. Loyal
66. Ores
68. Tuscany commune
69. Getting ready
71. Suffix for period
72. Few: prefix
73. Evaluate
74. "Picnic" author
75. Russian river
76. Cooked
77. Scent
78. Bambi, e.g.
79. Pluck
80. Breakfast order
81. French waters
82. Misjudges
83. Groom in India

**DOWN**

1. Shorten the sleeves
2. Cooked
3. ____ oil
4. Snarl
5. Coupon word
6. Fr. revolution escapee
7. Sonny et al.
8. Blinds part
9. Tedious talkers
10. Aired
11. Implied
12. Detailed requirement, for short
13. "____ Women" (Dunne film)
14. Messengers
15. Stadiums
16. Chores
27. Footnote abbr.
30. Flavor
32. Eagle's nest
34. Diamond corners
35. Made noise
37. Flower parts
38. On the double
40. Sense of injury
41. El ____
42. Eggheads
44. Compass pt.
47. Trademark
48. Bird life of a region
50. Grazing ground
51. Overwhelming attacks
53. Unpleasant glances
54. Being a pest
55. Penniless ones
56. Neighborhood
58. Ornamental work, as in stone
59. Final commentary
60. Ancient Roman magistrate: var.
61. Dawdle
62. Enrages
63. Serbian
64. Fine porcelain
65. Mark or wind
66. Collier
67. Roofing material
69. Seniors' big event
70. Travel on horseback

**Starting box on page 562**

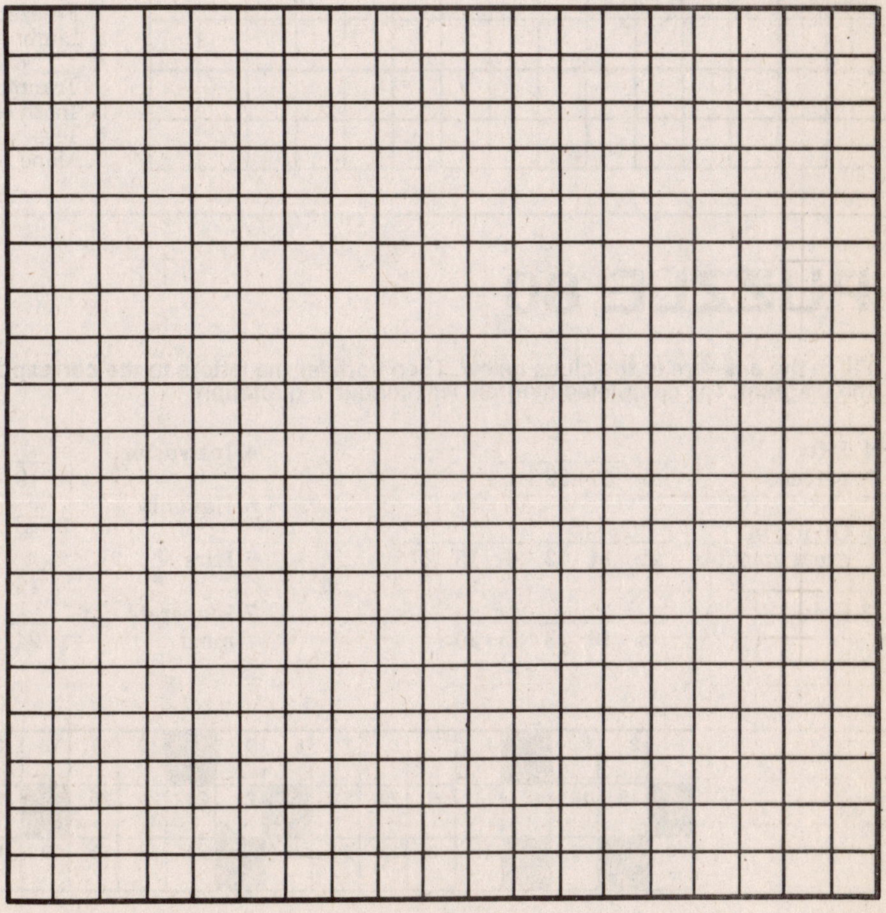

# PUZZLE 79

**ACROSS**
1. Inclination of outlook
5. Other
9. Talon
13. Land measure
14. Midday
15. Heavenly headgear
16. Amazing
19. Skilled
20. Goal
21. Portent
23. Tendon
25. Desires
27. Public transportation
28. Ordinance
30. Restraint
33. Characterized by humor
35. Joke
37. Admire
38. Blunder
39. Bouquet
42. Sass
43. Conflicts
45. Dolt
46. Wand
48. Act
50. Vat
52. Neither's companion
53. Distort
55. Fortunate
57. Abound
59. Payable
60. Pink wine
63. Assemble
69. Icon
70. Toward shelter
71. Concept
72. Disavow
73. Salamander
74. Capricorn

**Starting box on page 562**

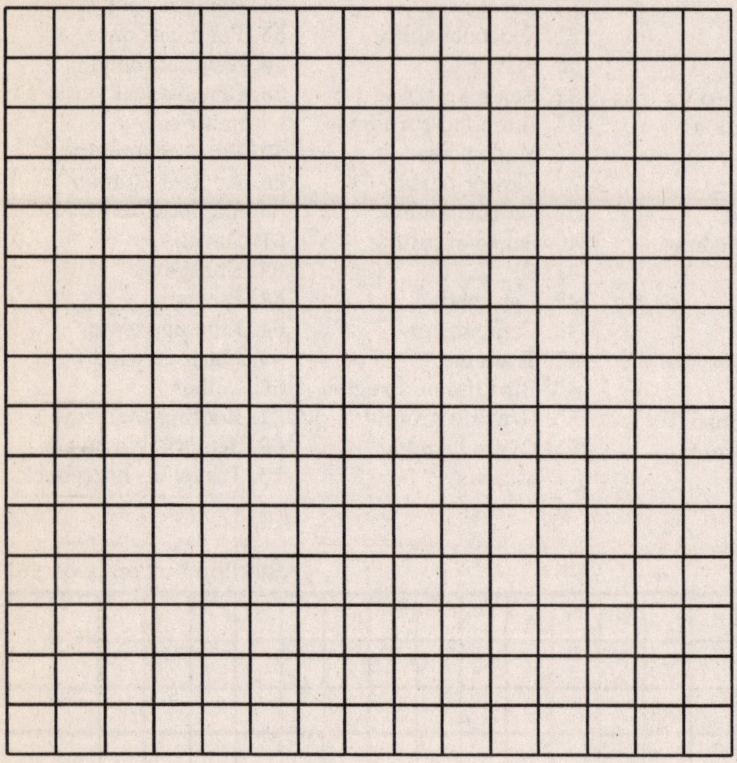

**DOWN**
1. Saloon
2. Freeze
3. Limb
4. ____ of Tranquillity
5. Tooth covering
6. Toss
7. Alone
8. Foe
9. Bed of a stream
10. Research room, for short
11. Every
12. Sorrow
17. Dried grape
18. Family
22. Moray
23. Total
24. Restless
26. Tar
27. Use temporarily
29. Removable hair
31. Epidermis
32. With it
33. Stuff
34. Pigeon murmur
36. Small amount
38. Sheep
40. Perched
41. Northerner
44. Majestic
47. Plaything
49. Before, before
51. Financial plan
54. Nut
56. Mongrel
58. Skin spot
60. Free
61. Poem
62. Progeny
64. Fresh
65. Demerit
66. Commotion
67. Reception
68. Dine

---

# PUZZLE 80

## QUOTAGRAM

**Fill in the answers to the clues below. Then transfer the letters to the correspondingly numbered squares in the diagram. The completed diagram will contain a quotation.**

1. Fifty percent ___ ___ ___ ___ (5 37 32 1)
2. Giving in great amounts ___ ___ ___ ___ ___ ___ (22 14 12 6 15 27)
3. Snivel ___ ___ ___ ___ ___ (3 16 23 35 20)
4. Instructor ___ ___ ___ ___ ___ ___ ___ (19 41 30 31 10 25 38)
5. Haughty ___ ___ ___ ___ ___ ___ ___ ___ (39 18 21 17 36 11 29 4)
6. Hire ___ ___ ___ ___ ___ ___ (13 7 40 34 8 2)
7. Elaborate meal ___ ___ ___ ___ ___ (24 33 28 9 26)

| | | | | | | | | | | | | | | | | |
|---|---|---|---|---|---|---|---|---|---|---|---|---|---|---|---|---|
| 1 | 2 | 3 | | 4 | 5 | 6 | 7 | 8 | 9 | | 10 | 11 | 12 | 13 | | 14 |
| | 15 | 16 | 17 | 18 | 19 | 20 | 21 | | 22 | 23 | 24 | 25 | | 26 | 27 | 28 |
| 29 | | 30 | | 31 | 32 | 33 | 34 | 35 | | 36 | 37 | 38 | 39 | 40 | 41 | |

# PUZZLE 81

**ACROSS**

1. Likely
4. Male cat
7. Lifeless
9. Presage
10. Hair blower
12. Arbor
13. Remove price restraints
15. City drain
16. Tribe symbol
18. Very good
19. Italian city
21. Evaluated
23. Of a satellite path
26. Make a knot
28. At what time
29. Intuit
30. "___ Miserables"
31. Sandy wastelands
34. Capital of Georgia
36. Intercede
38. Wide
41. Single-seeded fruit
43. Circus comedian
44. Gnome
46. Demonstrated
47. Acclaim
49. Legumes
50. Man of the hour
51. Toward the back of a boat
52. Short sleep

**DOWN**

1. Do sums
2. Inca country
3. Contaminate
4. Drying cloth
5. River through Poland
6. Mal de ___
8. Bus station
9. Cereal dish
11. Prepare for different work
12. Hive dweller
14. Dominating principle
15. More mellifluous
17. Small plateau
18. Pigpen
20. ___ volatile
22. Food regimen
23. Hooting bird
24. Mother of Zeus
25. Groom's attendant
27. Overhead trains
29. Special attraction
31. Father
32. Geraint's wife
33. Begin
35. Directed
37. Memorable period
38. Puff up
39. Lines of seats
40. Have title to
42. Actress Burstyn
43. Head cook
45. Zhivago's love
46. Mineral spring
48. Crown

**Starting box on page 562**

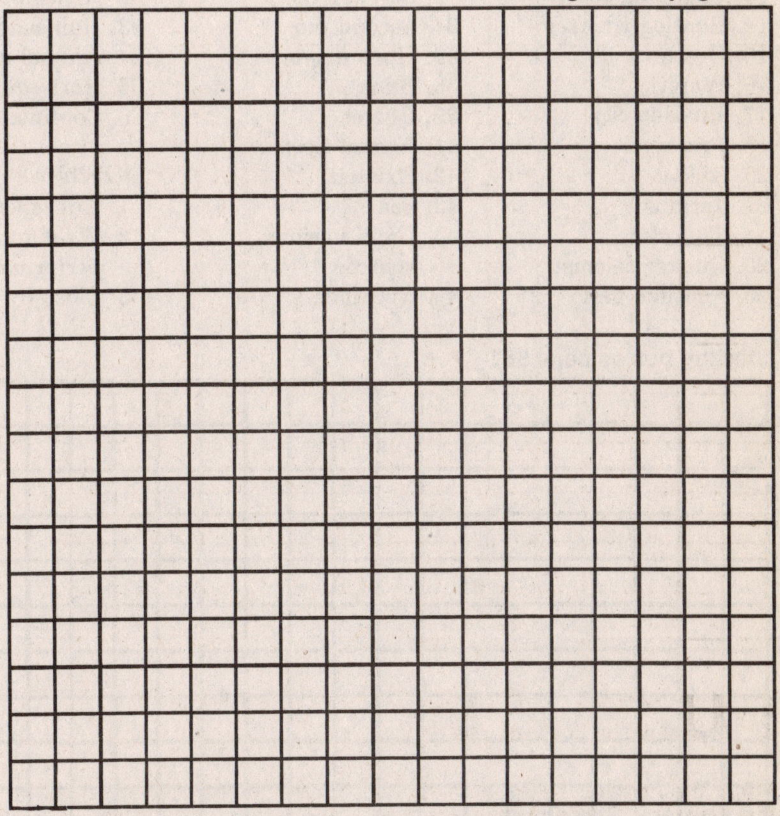

---

# Changaword PUZZLE 82

**Can you change the top word into the bottom word (in each column) in the number of steps indicated in parentheses? Do not change the order of the letters, and change only one letter at a time. Proper names, slang, and obsolete words are not allowed.**

| 1. **LESS** (4 steps) | 2. **GOOD** (5 steps) | 3. **SLOW** (6 steps) | 4. **DUMB** (6 steps) |
|---|---|---|---|
| **MORE** | **BEST** | **FAST** | **WISE** |

# PUZZLE 83

## ACROSS

1. Gasp
5. Appraised
6. Football kick
10. Italian staples
11. Father: Latin
12. Rapid speech
13. Pounding tool
14. Bootleg whiskey
15. Gratuity
16. Wapiti
17. Russian city
18. Profound
20. Assay
21. Jardins ____ Tuileries
22. Quaker colonist
23. Footlike part
24. Half quart
28. Tranquilized state
30. Tom's father
31. Dog's foot
32. Gist
33. "The Second Mrs. Tanqueray" playwright
34. Second mo.
35. Horn player
38. Bunk
39. Bigger
41. Armed fleet
42. Existed
43. Sea
44. From various sources
46. Nuisance
47. Salary
48. Mountain pass
49. Arctic bird
52. Drunkard
53. Swimming place
54. Turkish coins
55. Liner: abbr.
56. Obese
57. "The ____ Cometh"
59. Walk unsteadily
61. Hebrew northern kingdom
62. African antelope
63. Hair ointment
64. Animal skin
65. Norwegian kings
66. Confined

## DOWN

1. Adhesive
2. Went to a performance
3. Close by
4. Football scores: abbr.
5. Honey badger
6. Faux ____
7. Says
8. "____ Bly"
9. Hard journey
10. Hors d'oeuvres spreads
11. Vitality
12. Skin opening
13. Apple seed
14. Seed vessel
15. Drying frame
19. Captivate
20. Sawbuck
22. Church bench
23. Strength
24. Fraternity emblem
25. Emetic
26. ____-crown (crape jasmine)
27. Jogging gait
28. British cavalry swords
29. Writer Fleming
30. Peach seed
31. Serenity
33. Hitchcock film
34. Failure
35. Hundred years: abbr.
36. Hindu cymbals
37. "____ You Under My Skin"
40. Hood's rod
42. Intelligence
44. Nosh
45. Amulet
47. Doorway
49. ____ Semple McPherson
50. River to the Caspian Sea
51. Barbie's friend
52. Fur scarf
53. Face value
54. Guides
55. Tread
56. Nourished
58. Manual skill
60. Explosive: abbr.
61. Hercules's captive
63. Soda water

Starting box on page 562

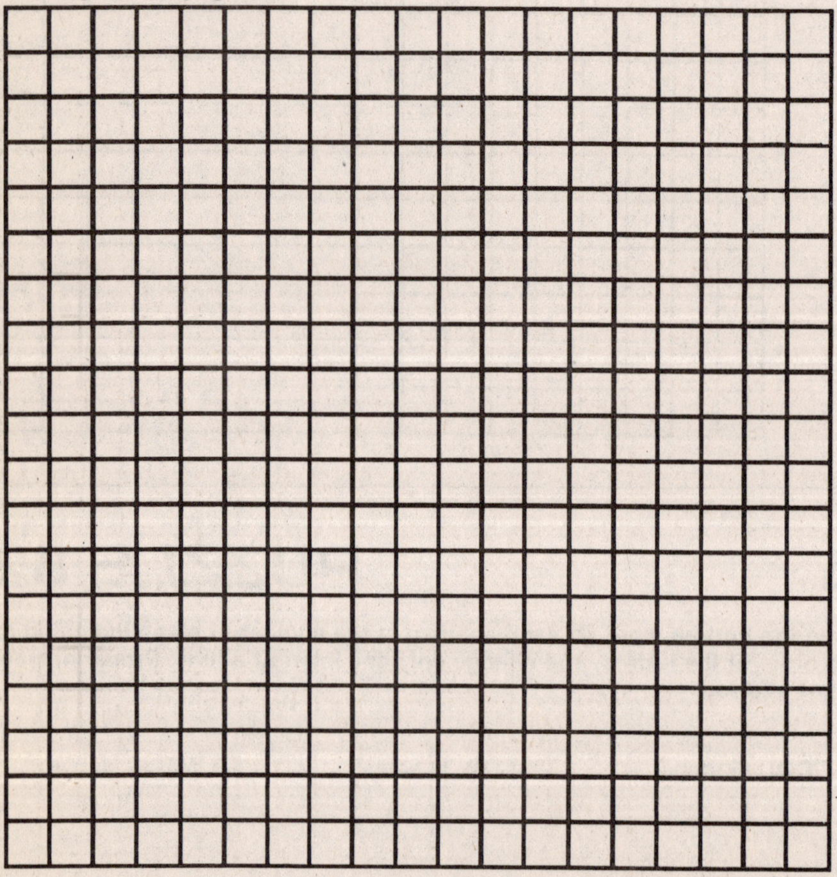

# PUZZLE 84

• AFFAIRS OF STATE •

**ACROSS**

1. Emmets
5. Cager Archibald
9. Mies van der ____
10. Walks in water
15. Elliptical
16. Takes advantage of
17. Actress Tatum ____
18. Altar screen
22. 1851 tune
26. Songstress Sumac et al.
27. Tithe
28. Discharge
29. Beef cattle
31. Ebb and flow
34. Little piggies
35. Cup: Fr.
36. Chest sound
37. GI address: abbr.
38. Relative
39. In the center of
43. Football officials, for short
45. Amphibian
46. Disgrace
47. Works with a shuttle
50. Mental acuity
51. Greek island
52. Neon ____
53. Greenland Eskimo
54. Arab rulers
55. Self-evident truth
56. "It's ____ to Tell a Lie"
57. Less, in music
58. Ex ____ (from one side only)
59. Rainbows
60. Quantities: abbr.
63. "____ Death"
64. Old car
65. Actress Farrow
66. Pubs
68. Mosquito bite
70. Nevada city
74. Wears well
76. Upbeats
77. Seth's father
78. Aegean region
81. Mine yields
82. 1926 tune, with "The"
89. Physics Nobelist
90. Furlough
91. Plaintiff
92. Coup d'____
93. Los Angeles cager
94. Columnist Bombeck
95. Glut
96. Swiss city

**DOWN**

1. In ____ (routinized)
2. Snack
3. 1903 tune
4. Tropical herbs
5. Flickertail
6. State positively
7. Home of ancient Irish kings
8. Height: abbr.
10. Chinese skillets
11. Collection of anecdotes
12. Fender damage
13. Facility
14. Point of view
19. Dexterous
20. Medley
21. Withered
23. Uncommon
24. Mix
25. Legal matter
29. Asterisk
30. Record on a VCR
32. Inventor Howe
33. Transmit
39. "Oh, give me ____..."
40. Yacht basin
41. 1939 film
42. ____ ex machina
44. Burlesque
45. South American monkeys
46. Con game
48. Hurries
49. Identical
50. Badger
52. Bark cloth
56. Sports palace
59. Seed covering
61. Antler point
62. Hangs loosely
67. Pack
68. Marionette maker
69. Locks of hair
70. Sports cheer
71. Dutch cheese
72. Syrian town
73. Persian poet
75. Fishhook line
79. Notion
80. Aleutian island
81. Knockout blow
83. Sherbets
84. Jot
85. Medical subject: abbr.
86. "____ Grown Accustomed to Her Face"
87. Captain of the "Nautilus"
88. Nana

Starting box on page 562

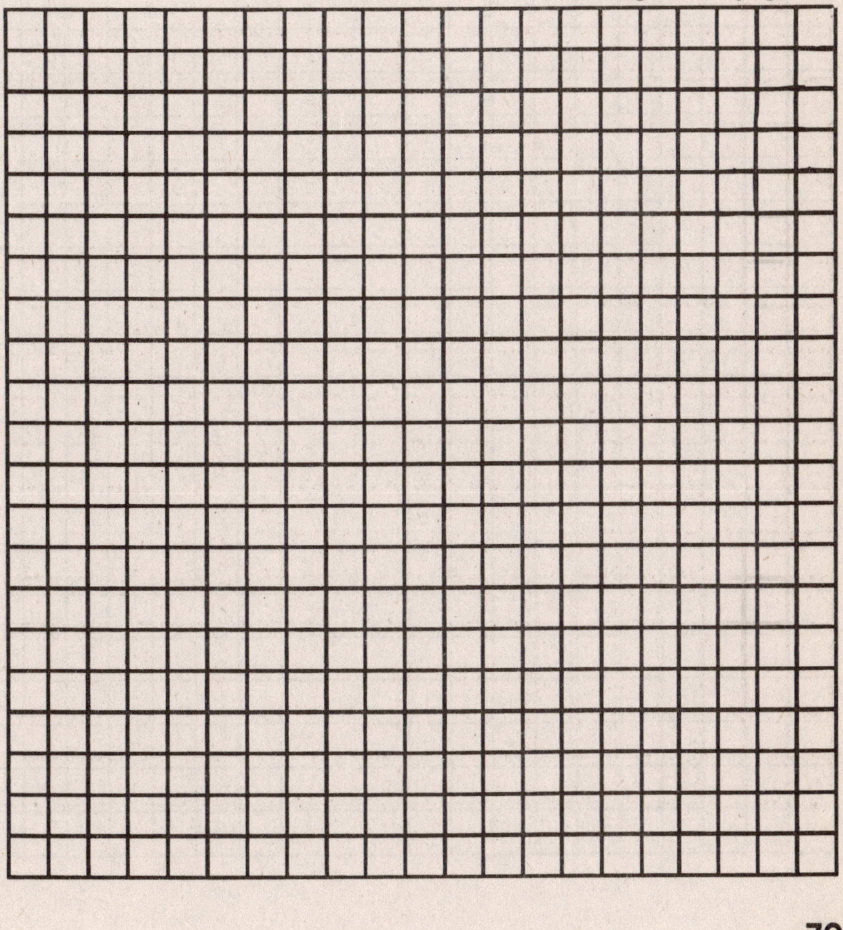

# PUZZLE 85

**ACROSS**

1. Work at (a trade)
4. Morse unit
7. Falsehoods
9. Disjoin
11. Commotion
13. Triple
14. David's instrument
15. Tall story
18. Portrays
19. Palm leaf
20. English prison
22. Military assistant
23. Pipe joint
24. Silk's natural hue
25. Farm measure
26. Leftovers
28. ____ and feather
31. Sloe ____
32. Is obligated
34. Copied
38. Vulgar
41. Art movement
42. Role for Liz
43. Tom Hanks film
45. City on the Oka
46. Blue Jays' home
48. Western state
50. Pious
52. Bring up
53. Italian seaport
54. Flat-topped hill
55. Variety
56. Recipe unit
57. Shed tears
59. Sibilant letter
60. Pennant yielders
65. Gaze narrowly
66. Meat cut
67. "Ay, there's the ____"
70. July 4th noise
71. Cabbage plant
72. Roof finial
73. Cloud type
75. Page
77. L.A. problem
78. "Robin ____"
79. Pick up part of the cost: 2 wds.
81. Untidy
82. Slender
83. Volcano product
84. Conclusion

**DOWN**

1. More than one
2. Speech flaw
3. Thus far
4. Scoff at
5. Gentle
6. Big top, e.g.
8. Crafty
9. Way to the top
10. ____ adjudicata
11. Belle's dance
12. Raring to go
14. Tool for Markham's man
16. Tear
17. Mr. Crosby
18. Agreement
21. Breathing organ
25. Void
27. O'Hare, e.g.
28. Brouhaha: hyph.
29. Emmy or Tony
30. Save
33. Balm
34. Insurance statistician
35. Scheme
36. Eternally, in verse
37. Portals
39. Smears
40. Landed property
43. Vega or Deneb
44. Jack rabbits
47. Modern: prefix
49. Rose fruit
51. Filmdom 29 Down
58. Egg part
60. Extreme poverty
61. Gams
62. Paddock youth
63. Rank's partner
64. Kind of preview
65. Church district
67. Freshen the memory
68. Fairy tale's second word
69. Like some shots
70. Army VIPs
73. Engine part
74. Inspiration
76. Proper
77. Animal hide
80. Senor Guevara

**Starting box on page 562**

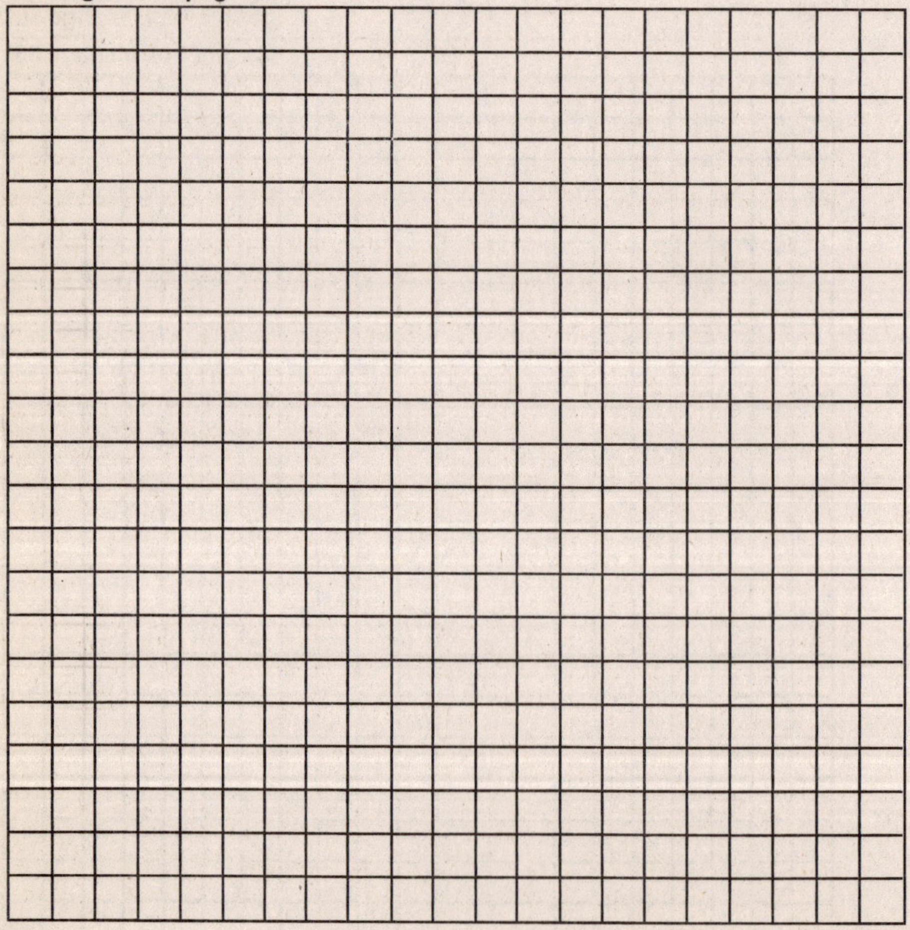

# PUZZLE 86

**ACROSS**

1. I smell ____
5. ____ Strip
6. Medical subj.
7. Sedimentary deposit
8. Necessities
11. Singer's solo
12. Soviet news agency
16. Down with: Fr.
20. Actress Berger
22. "____ a Song Go Out of My Heart"
23. Chest sound
24. Governors of Algiers
25. Parody
27. Inflame
28. Without any delay
31. Ark builder
35. Singer Vaughan
36. Office assistants
37. ____ Major
38. Long areas of churches
40. "Now ____ me down to sleep"
41. Stone figure
43. Heavy cotton fabric
45. Guitarist Lofgren
46. Baseball statistic
49. Hodgepodge
50. Mongolian natives
51. Basil or tarragon
54. Concluded
55. Redact
56. Fulton's power source
58. Actor Calhoun
59. Mil. awards
60. ____ Grosso (Brazilian plateau)
61. Muse of lyric poetry
63. Slangy negative response
65. Greek goddess of strife and discord
66. Desires
67. Rim

**DOWN**

1. High Turkish officials
2. Arrested
3. Blooming shrubs
4. Threadbare
9. Have a repast
10. Woodland deities
12. Yugoslavian leader
13. First Arabic letter
14. Feudal workers
15. Polish seaport
16. Collection of weapons
17. Young baseball attendants
18. Assumed name
19. Spanish muralist
21. Resident of the largest continent
25. Razors
26. Greek goddess of wisdom
29. Road leveler
30. Sun: pref.
31. Crazier
32. Art of public speaking
33. Italian wine region
34. Appeared to as a ghost
39. Sounds of lament
41. Round of gunfire
42. Mild oaths
44. "____ in St. Louis"
46. Lout
47. Suffix for lymph or problem
48. Large tanks
52. Bring up
53. Not ____ (show no surprise)
57. Drove a car
62. Unfolding, poetically
64. To be, in ancient Rome

Starting box on page 562

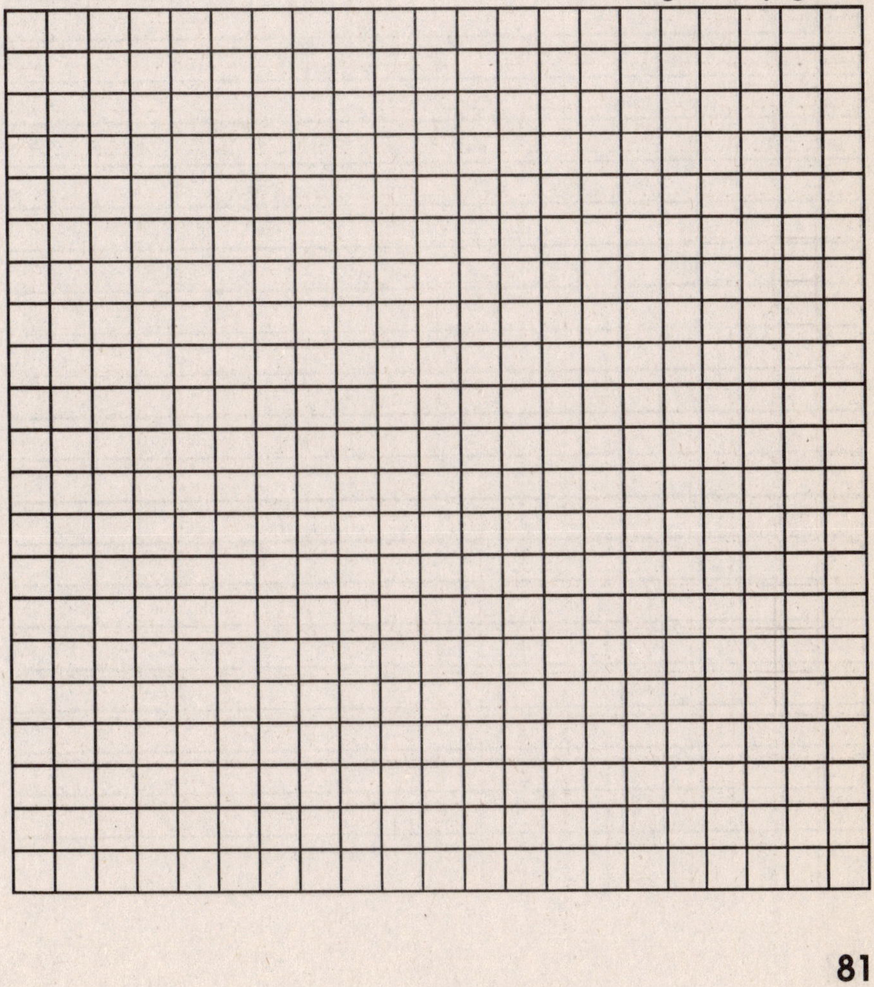

# PUZZLE 87

**• LISTS •**

**ACROSS**

1. Exclamation of triumph
4. Palm leaves
6. Wedding band
10. Drug agent
11. Trojan hero
13. Rare person
14. Recipe list: 2 wds.
16. Playhouse list: 2 wds.
20. 1934 heavyweight champ
22. Street salesman
23. Capital of Norway
24. Oceans
25. Invoices
27. Held session
28. Seamen
30. Historic times
34. Mixed greens
37. Parchment documents
40. Ma Bell list: 2 wds.
43. Court lists
44. ____ und Drang
46. Caresses
47. Italian composer
50. Owned
53. Struck hard
55. Capital of Italia
56. Swiss lake
57. Industrialists
59. Sailors' saint
60. Playbill list: 3 wds.
68. Playhouses
69. River to the Kura
70. Balkan nation
71. Close-by
72. Bulk
73. Mexican Indian
74. Bus station: abbr.

**DOWN**

1. Deans' lists: 2 wds.
2. Pet name for an Irish child
3. Seraglio
5. Fragment
6. Beatty film
7. Data
8. No: Ger.
9. Festive
11. Timetable abbreviation
12. Bishopric
14. Auditors: abbr.
15. ____ Lingus
16. Songstress Reese
17. Mrs. Dick Tracy
18. Thought
19. Bed board
20. Comedian Hope
21. Sale terms: 2 wds.
26. Photocopy
29. Toboggan
30. Aquatic birds
31. Fish eggs
32. White vestments
33. Coin opening
35. Unbalanced
36. Ten: prefix
37. Females
38. Army bunk
39. Tart
41. Parcel: abbr.
42. Malay dagger
45. Club list
48. Works hard
49. Article
50. Israeli dance
51. Roman god of love
52. Actor Andrews
54. Rock group: abbr.
55. Stadium cheers
57. Archaeological date initials
58. Reads quickly
60. Pennies: abbr.
61. Throat-clearing sound
62. Antitoxins
63. Pocket flaps
64. Elevator name
65. Monk's title
66. Essayed
67. Tidal bore

Starting box on page 562

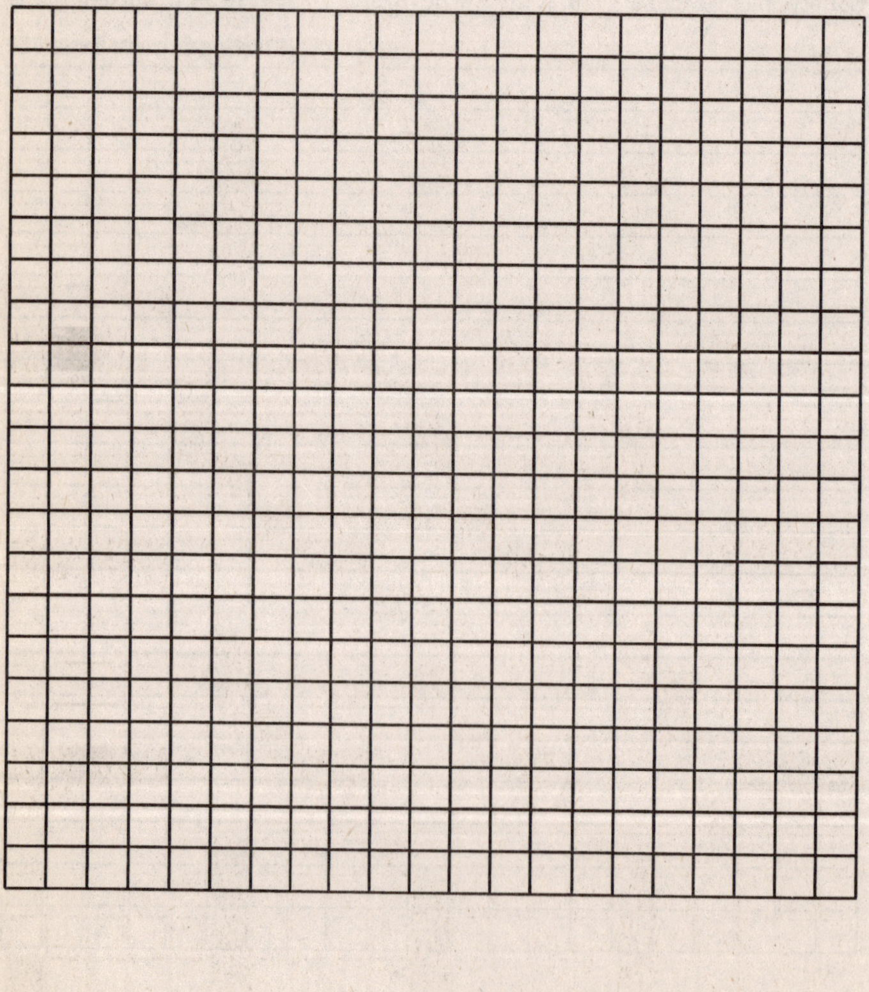

# PUZZLE 88

**• IN ADDITION •**

**ACROSS**

1. Disappear
5. Criticizes
9. Around: pref.
13. Touch
18. New recording
19. Modify
20. Carolina school
21. Mongol
22. Watchful
23. Guy
24. Bright colors
25. Bouquet
26. Eye pencil
27. Collection of sayings
28. Evangelist McPherson
29. Citrus fruits
30. Beyond an executive's duties
34. Vane dir.
35. Durable wood
36. Ultimate
37. Obi
39. Compensation
43. French novelist
45. Tentmaker
47. Toast topping
51. Rectify
52. Stainless
53. Lessen
54. Gridiron unit
55. Valuable violin
56. ___ hit (double, e.g.)
58. "Fur ___"
59. Pickles
61. Chap
62. Puts forth
63. Summer cooler
64. Permission
65. Sept. follower
66. Star flowers
70. Hebrew zither
72. Momentous
78. Scrutinize
79. Arrest
81. Of a region
82. Anklebones
83. Self-evident truth
84. Perfume
85. Record material
86. Egg on
87. Juarez home
88. Fountain find
89. Polish president
90. Hurt
92. ___ Marino
93. Slump
94. Mien
97. Doing more than is required
106. Tart stealer
108. Pitcher Ryan
109. Celtic sea god
110. Nasal passages
111. Composer Reginald De ___
112. Of a time span
113. Volcano feature
114. Compressing device
115. "... ___ of singing birds"
116. Venture
117. Mayberry lad
118. A John
119. Hollows
120. Audacity
121. Marsh matter
122. Detected

**DOWN**

1. Mendelssohn
2. Catkin
3. More horrible
4. Amazing
5. Utterance
6. Italian bell town
7. Rice dish
8. Fr. holy woman
9. Expire
10. Fragrant resin
11. Cowgirl's competition
12. Cruel
13. Postpones
14. Actor Rhodes
15. Element components
16. Christie and Hess
17. Remove
18. Breathing sound
28. Piedmont city
31. Walk
32. Infiltrate
33. Rhine feeder
38. Card game expert
39. 20 quires
40. Madame Bovary
41. Sport
42. Oppositionist
43. Elegance
44. Leftovers
45. Scottish resort
46. Sail holder
48. Secret retreat
49. Formerly, of old
50. Horatian creations
52. "Our Gang" dog
53. Slumbering
57. Spartan square
58. Spendthrift's purchases
60. Madison Ave. products
62. System beginner
64. Standard
65. Ancient Hebrew unit
66. Film pooch
67. Try
68. Large bulrush
69. Writer Wharton
70. Central line
71. Greek portico
72. South of France
73. Short jacket
74. Seed coat
75. Nota ___
76. Songs
77. Educator Young
79. Interrogators
80. Ridd's love
83. Height: pref.
88. Songwriter Sammy ___
89. Combat
91. Representatives
92. Hunts
93. Thoroughfare
94. Babylonian city
95. Hole ___
96. Poe's bird
98. Water wheel
99. Mirror
100. Abscond
101. City in Ohio
102. Bergen's husband
103. Upset
104. Fish garnish
105. Cable TV channel
107. Waistcoat
113. Officer

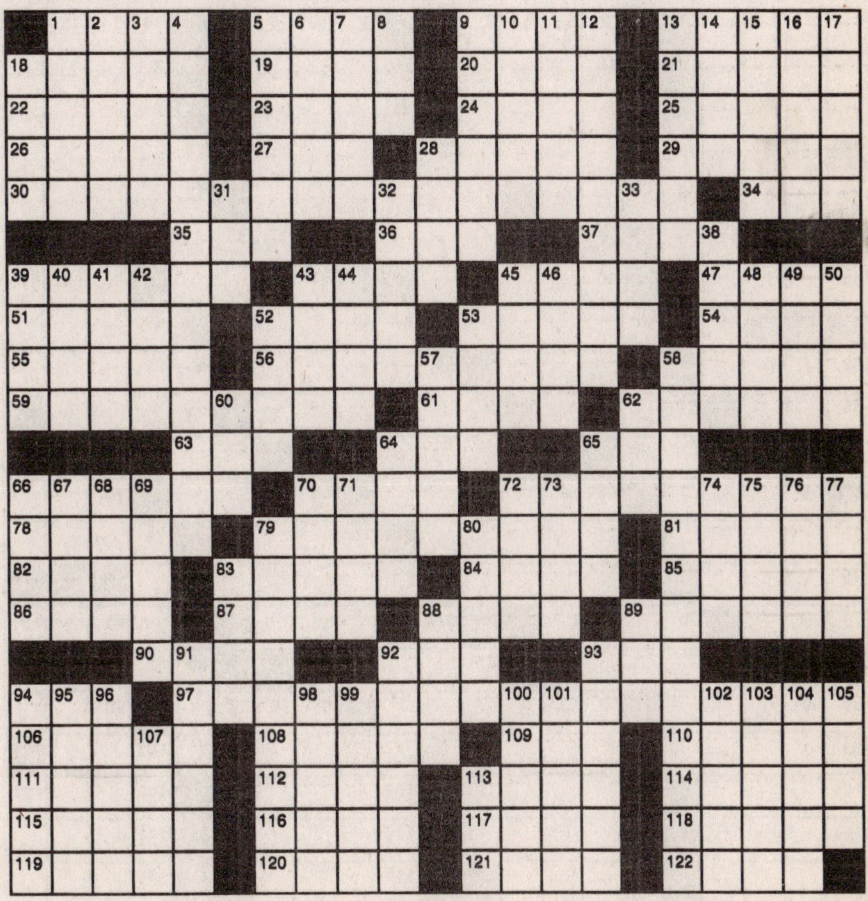

# PUZZLE 89

**• POP CONCERTS •**

## ACROSS

1. Free ticket, for short
5. Indian mountain pass
9. Ohio town et al.
13. Army insects
17. Solo for Sutherland
18. Stratagem
19. "Thine ____"
20. TV knob
21. "____ Eulenspiegels lustige Streiche" by Strauss
22. Actor Navarro
23. Near East coin
24. Field mouse
25. With "The," composition by Rimsky-Korsakov
29. Glory, of old
30. Lion's cry
31. Courteous
32. "... ____ of robins in her hair"
33. Keen
35. Town in Nebraska
37. Declaim violently
39. "____ afraid ..."
40. Biblical song
41. "Three Blind ____"
42. Nativity location: abbr.
45. Of the musical period after the Renaissance
47. Area
49. Wild plum
50. Cockney's steed
53. River to the Java Sea
54. Burial stone
55. Motif
56. Island in Lake Tana
57. Small insect
58. Composer of 86 Down
59. Surgeons' milieu: abbr.
60. Got out of
62. Stirs up
63. "____ Concerto" by Addinsell
65. English school
66. Dozen
68. Photocopy, for short
70. Terminus
71. Mountain ridge
72. Seeps
73. Poem by Tennyson
74. Chances
75. Telegram
76. Greek porticoes
77. Entrance halls
79. "____ Miserables"
80. Cheers
81. Louts
82. Emergencies, slangily
86. Buddy
87. Sudden thrust
88. Composition by Aaron Copland
89. "The Rain in ____" by Rodgers
92. Going out with
95. Copenhagen native
98. Sea bird
99. With "The," composition by Saint-Saens
103. Beige
104. ____ ear ...
105. Like ____
106. U.S. journalist
108. Undiluted
109. Yellow pigment
110. Peruvian Indian
111. Gray's subject: abbr.
112. Genuine
113. Plumbum
114. Female ruffs
115. Hamilton bills

## DOWN

1. "____ Ballou"
2. Opening
3. Water wheel channel
4. Prakrit language
5. Persona non ____
6. Dvorak composition
7. Beginning on
8. Canvas shelter support
9. Excuse
10. Pastry with a hole
11. "____ in Paris" by Gershwin
12. Balkan
13. Arrival
14. Daughter of Tantalus
15. "____ from the Vienna Woods" by Strauss
16. Winter rain
19. Writer St. Johns
22. Town in Italy
26. Actress Garbo
27. Actress Celeste
28. Narrow road
29. Restaurant bill
34. African garment
36. Nothing, in the past
38. Expert
40. Fortified wine
41. French Sudan presently
42. Fortunate
43. "____ Circumstance" by Elgar
44. Sheltered side
46. Foray
47. Neckpiece
48. Livens (up)
49. Restaurateur Toots
50. Horace product
51. Debussy composition
52. "The ____ Waltz" by Waldteufel
54. Switchblades, slangily
55. "____ Old Black Magic"
57. Beginning of the handwriting on the wall
58. Village in Spain
61. Be overly fond
62. ____ Shah Pahlavi
63. African river fed only by rain
64. Dict. entries
66. "Invitation ____" by Weber
67. Courts
68. Composition by Khachaturian
69. Oleo holders
71. Boring tool
73. Synthesizer inventor
74. Christiania presently
76. Met
77. Classical-music lover
78. Violinist Zimbalist
80. Hindu princess
81. Baseball ploy
83. Sweet girl of song
84. "In a ____ Market" by Ketelbey
85. Offspring
86. "____ Waltz" by 58 Across
87. Long-term inmate, slangily
89. Perfume
90. Harness-racing horse
91. Pianist Claudio
93. "____ Oe" by Queen Liliuokalani
94. Mixed paint
96. Celebes oxen
97. Insect egg
100. Old stringed instrument
101. Anglo-Saxon laborer
102. Mongol herdsman
107. City roads: abbr.

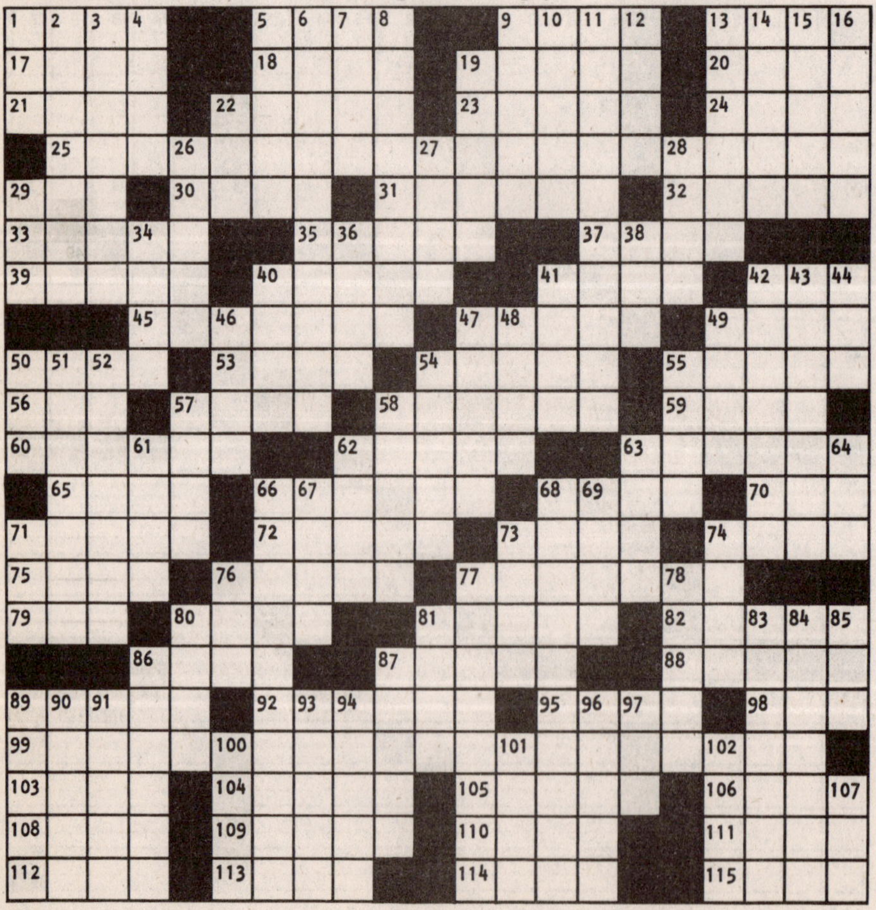

# PUZZLE 90

**• WESTWARD HO! •**

**ACROSS**
1. Crude vessel
6. Nocturnal fliers
10. First spot
14. Actress June ____
19. Suspense
20. Quaker pronoun
21. One-digit number
22. Extant
23. "Fame" role
24. Actress Yothers
25. Did very well
26. Encrypted
27. Tennessee-to-Mississippi path
30. Mongol rulers
31. Gaseous mixture
32. Dilutes
33. Dreams
35. Mottled marking
39. Thai monetary unit
41. Tram passage
42. Month before Nissan
43. Winter mo.
44. Missouri-to-Pacific Northwest path
51. Reasoning power
53. Surface measure
54. Praise
55. Infantry
56. Tabriz native
57. Soak hemp
58. Hoosegows
59. Term exam
60. Deposit with
62. Prickly seeds
63. Biblical dancer
64. Texas-to-Kansas path
68. Reflexive pronoun
72. Blackbirds
73. Many
77. Sheer cotton
78. Vicar's abode
80. Yum-Yum's accessory
81. Singer Gorme
83. Quiche ingredients
84. Finnish bath
85. One-horse carriage
86. Star in Orion
87. New York path
90. Antique car
91. Spoon
92. Actress Hayworth
93. Seek anagram
95. Extent
97. Seat of power
100. Asian mountains
102. Glutton
103. Song of joy
104. Missouri-to-New Mexico path
110. Parroting
111. Facile
113. Hearsay
114. Santa's helpers
116. Riva ____
117. Man Friday
118. Canal of song
119. Twit
120. Adjudicated
121. Baker's shovel
122. Meshes
123. Perception

**DOWN**
1. Eccentric
2. Steel component
3. Byron work
4. Put out
5. Mischief-maker
6. Aquatic mammal
7. Genius
8. Advanced
9. Ransack
10. Make into law
11. Chops
12. Chemical suff.
13. Detective Beaumont
14. Comic Buddy ____
15. Welcome, in Hilo
16. "Burr" author
17. Makes equal
18. Lipstick shades
28. Scurry
29. Prefix for self
33. Revered images
34. Power
35. Famous surrealist
36. Fancy
37. "____ Love Song"
38. Sprigged fabric
39. Flat caps
40. Encourage
41. "I've Got ____ in Kalamazoo"
43. Iran's language
45. Equips again
46. Be
47. Carp
48. Ligurian Sea feeder
49. Muslim priest
50. Football's Alzado
52. Go around
58. ____ Nixon Eisenhower
59. Hesitate
61. "Weird Al" Yankovic flick
62. Miniature tree
63. Nibble's kin
65. Alberta town
66. Gemstones
67. Pedro's pal
68. Thing
69. Fast-food words
70. Expression of sorrow
71. "Lohengrin" heroine
74. Ogling
75. Garden tool
76. Sibling's daughter
78. Not glossy
79. Halo
80. Giant
82. Actress Sommer
84. Flay
88. Maltreated
89. Lanky
94. Word of endearment
95. Morse code dot
96. Herd followers
97. Tropical ungulate
98. Alpine heroine
99. Scope
100. Dramatic comment
101. Classify
102. Snub-nosed dogs, for short
103. Divide
105. Swiss flower
106. Dart
107. Downwind
108. A tsar
109. Minus
111. Lapse
112. Deceive
115. Be a bystander

# PUZZLE 91

• DIRECTIONS •

## ACROSS

1. Marshes
5. Brants, e.g.
10. **Swift horse**
14. Efts
19. Latin I verb
20. "As You Like It" forest
21. Indian queen
22. Spanish month
23. Letdowns
26. Resource
27. Make happy
28. Look fixedly
29. Polanski film
31. Summers: Fr.
32. Moon goddess
34. Violinist Isaac
36. Flee
38. Armada
40. Enthusiastic
42. Harbor vessel
45. High mountain
48. Symbol of Wales
50. Purport
52. Cops
53. Vintage cars
55. Ingenuous
57. Imp
59. Art form
60. Stirs up
62. Check
64. Israeli statesman
66. Spread hay to dry
67. Histories
69. Shrouded
72. Songstress Yma
75. Divans
77. "____ Girls"
78. Warehousing
81. Freshen
82. Populate
85. Chutes
86. ____ volatile
88. Be venturesome
90. Blouse part
92. Adolescent years
93. Away
96. River to the Rio Grande
99. Insipid
101. Greek promenade
102. Cruise ships
104. Tossed greens
106. Attracted
108. Utter
109. Socks
111. Zenith's opposite
113. Pianist Peter
115. Proportions
117. Gripped
119. Buccaneer
123. Applaud
125. Dress-store frame
127. Cook clams
129. Small drum
130. Medieval guild
132. Marquand novel
135. Show financier
136. Fencing sword
137. Annuity: Fr.
138. Italian prince
139. Poor
140. Remove from print
141. Rendezvous
142. Poor grades

## DOWN

1. Loses color
2. Novelist Zola
3. Twangy
4. ____ Island ferry
5. Lacuna
6. Love god
7. Blue-pencils
8. Upper House
9. Beg
10. Metric land measure
11. Carry on
12. Contributed a share
13. Actress Jacqueline
14. ____ Kios, Greece
15. Chamber group
16. USMA students
17. Shoe form
18. Drunkards
24. Punitive
25. United
30. Atlantic food fish
33. Tied
35. Hawaii's state bird
37. Expectant
39. "My Favorite ____"
41. Wandered
43. Israeli port
44. Prepared to drive
45. Rich tapestry
46. Sierra ____
47. Striking distance
49. Capital of the Ukraine
51. "Adam's ____"
54. Roofing material
56. For shame!
58. Scottish girl
61. Luge
63. River to the Mediterranean
65. From soup to ____
68. Beginning
70. Actor Genn
71. See
73. Shed
74. Sky ram
76. Trade
79. Large jib
80. Try
82. Praline ingredient
83. Moo
84. Supplemented
86. Room: Sp.
87. Neat as ____
89. ____ judicata
91. Deserve
94. Regressed
95. Waste allowance
97. King of Norway
98. Cruel person
100. Retain
103. Move
105. Misrepresent
107. Pen
110. Lathered
112. Heavy jacket
114. Spoke
116. Area
118. Marlo's dad
120. Mistreat
121. Rich cake
122. Two Irish lakes
123. Detective Charlie
124. Bowling alley
126. German canal
128. Witty words
131. English cathedral town
133. Born
134. Soak flax

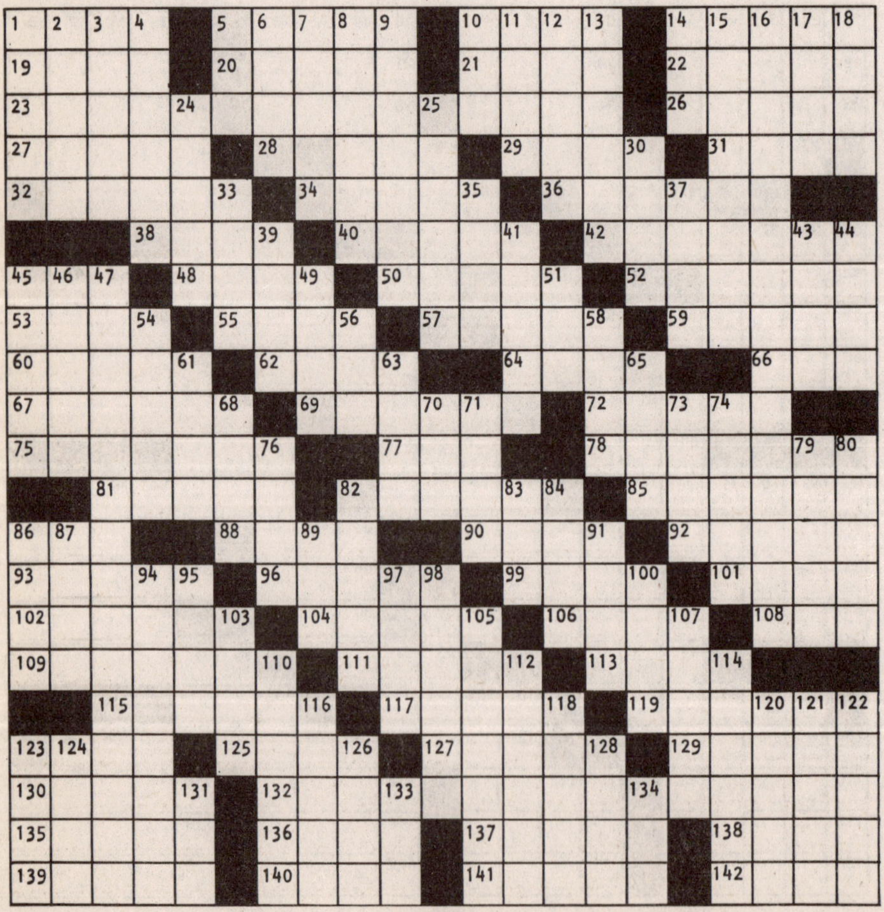

# PUZZLE 92

**• PLAYTIME •**

**ACROSS**

1. Bluenose
6. Go away!
10. Shrewd
14. Cruder
19. Watering place
20. Twist out of shape
21. Saudi Arabia's continent
22. Abridge
23. Manifest
24. Within: pref.
25. Convert to currency
26. Trace
27. Finding game
30. Assembled
31. Type of dance
32. Mexican miss, for short
33. Won
34. Douay and King James
38. Spirit
40. Stake
41. Singer Brickell
42. Circle game
49. Indian chieftain
51. Annex
52. Coastal birds
53. Lamb's nom de plume
54. "____ Were the Days"
55. Lament
56. Pilot
57. Yellow jackets
58. Have more authority than
60. Hawaiian dishes
61. Most invulnerable
62. Marching game
66. Angled fairway
70. Inquires
71. Beginning
75. Spicy stews
76. Fountain treats
78. Canine sound
79. Neutral colors
81. Cut down
82. Urbane
83. Dissemble
84. Oblivious
85. Copying game
89. Actress Talbot
90. Clubs
91. Nicholas, for one
92. Most arid
94. Sires
97. Hawaiian island
99. Edible seed
100. Becomes frayed
101. Tag game
108. Farsi speaker
109. Loam
111. Shackle
112. Fainter
113. Dullards
114. Take on
115. Main church aisle
116. Delight
117. Skulk
118. Vivacity
119. Flock members
120. Had supper

**DOWN**

1. Milne character
2. Musician Shankar
3. Deployed
4. Extreme
5. Legacy
6. Goteborg native
7. Suspend
8. Church calendar
9. New World marsupial
10. Side
11. Japanese city
12. Greek letters
13. Expression of derision
14. Pensioner
15. Strange
16. Recoil
17. Bordered
18. Bulrush
28. Negative answers
29. Perry's creator
30. Trails
33. Join
34. Ernie's friend
35. Spud state
36. Jewel
37. Lowest
38. Egyptian hound
39. Band on a coat of arms
40. Author Rice
42. Frond plants
43. Mementos
44. Galway natives
45. Fall on ____ ears
46. Alternatively
47. Facial feature
48. Final
50. Greek messenger god
56. People
57. Squandered
59. Summer mo.
60. Soft hue
61. Mr., in India
63. Produce offspring
64. More open
65. Surmise
66. Take off
67. Toast spread
68. Four fluid ounces
69. Recline
72. Ancient Briton tribe
73. Corbin's TV role
74. Desires
76. Mongrels
77. Exclamations of delight
78. "Sweet Liberty" star
80. Install in office
82. Hits sharply
86. Monolith
87. Sewing case
88. Senseless
92. Study
93. Spoke hoarsely
94. House of Lords member
95. Circumvent
96. Italian seaport
97. Gourd instrument
98. "Manhattan" star
99. Glass sheets
100. Disencumbers
102. Stalemate
103. Stir
104. Indonesian island
105. ____ Bator
106. Celebration
107. Golfer Couples
109. "____ Drives Me Crazy"
110. Bribe

# PUZZLE 93

**• TUNE IN •**

**ACROSS**

1. Bread unit
5. Splendor
9. Good-bye, in Wales
13. Treaty
17. Bullets
18. Intestine: comb. form
19. Spring bloomer
20. Of a body organ part
21. Oddball
22. Close
23. Photo finish
25. Coeur d'____, Idaho
26. Freed/Brown pop tune
29. Murphy Brown's boss
30. ____-garde
31. Spirit
32. Missing person finders
34. Pertaining to life
37. Sanction
38. Bandage material
39. Gershwin/Gershwin musical
42. Vocalist Frankie ____
43. Guatemalan Indian
46. Graded
47. Tear down, in London
48. Some medications
49. Anecdote
50. Doer: suff.
51. Stop
52. Closes securely
53. Lawful
54. Quench
55. Ajar
56. Actress Bushman from "Just a Gigolo"
57. Opening of "Wonderful Words of Life"
64. Aviator Earhart
65. Shelters
66. Galena and bauxite
67. Beeper
68. Facade
70. Portuguese explorer
71. "The Ghost and Mrs. ____"
75. Mythical monster
76. Saline drops
77. Shred
78. Rich cake
79. Classic auto
80. Fountain drinks
81. "____ Sixpence"
83. Ringers
84. Couple's tune
85. Says
86. Author Alger
89. Fourth down play
90. Bid
92. Rod Stewart's ex
93. "I ____ and judgment" (Psalm 101:1)
99. Infection type
100. Room
101. Fashion magazine
102. African river
103. Smooths
104. Keep the original
105. Israel's Golda ____
106. Privy to
107. Night, in Milan
108. Dobbin's dinner
109. Fusses
110. Cuts off

**DOWN**

1. Thailand's neighbor
2. All: comb. form
3. So be it
4. Assemble
5. Small sailing ship
6. Oily liquid
7. Intended
8. Left, nautically
9. Period between two events
10. Biblical Mount
11. Giant
12. Italian wine center
13. Keep order
14. White poplar
15. Chair worker
16. Lock
20. Childbirth method
24. Necessitates
27. Covered with vines
28. German poet
33. Sprints
34. Violent wind
35. "____ first you don't succeed . . ."
36. Sarge's dog
37. Clenched hand
38. Extreme nerve
40. Angry
41. Witch town
42. Climbing vine
43. Myopic Mr. ____
44. Frighten
45. Fracas
48. Equals
49. Camper's equipment
51. Sunk fence
52. Exhausted
53. Light bender
54. Mix up
55. Potters' needs
56. Is situated
57. Taste
58. Picture
59. Rio ____, Brazil
60. Merriment
61. Smells
62. Leaving
63. Cultivated land
68. Chaps
69. Rodents
70. Depression
71. Paris suburb
72. Egg on
73. "Do ____ Die" by Atlanta Rhythm Section
74. Umps' kin
76. Ankle: comb. form
77. Vittorio ____ (composer)
78. Kind of pole
80. Gold and silver
81. Evening displays
82. Agonizes
83. Type of bicycle seat
84. Pleasant to the ear
86. Rich ones
87. Popeye's Oyl
88. More unique
89. Rio de la ____
90. Leered
91. Manuscript leaf
94. ____ facto
95. Certain worm, for short
96. Splitsville
97. Horse's hoof sound
98. Itches

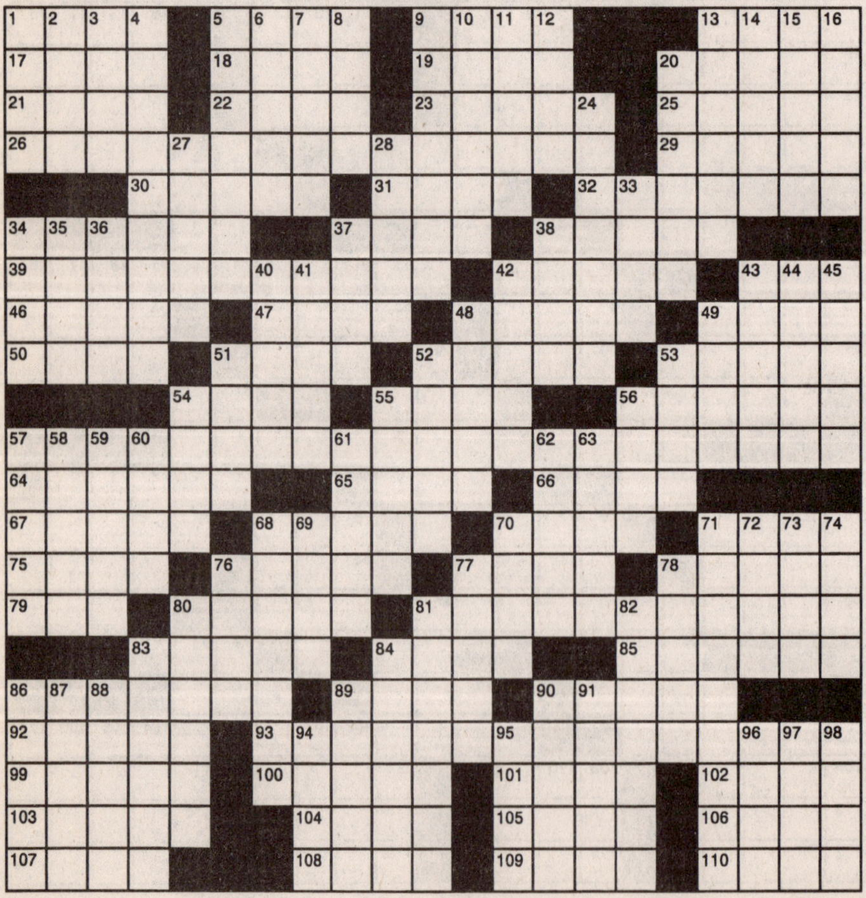

## CIRCULAR CROSSWORD

## PUZZLE 94

**Fill in the answers to the Around clues in a clockwise direction; to the Radial clues, from the outside to the inside.**

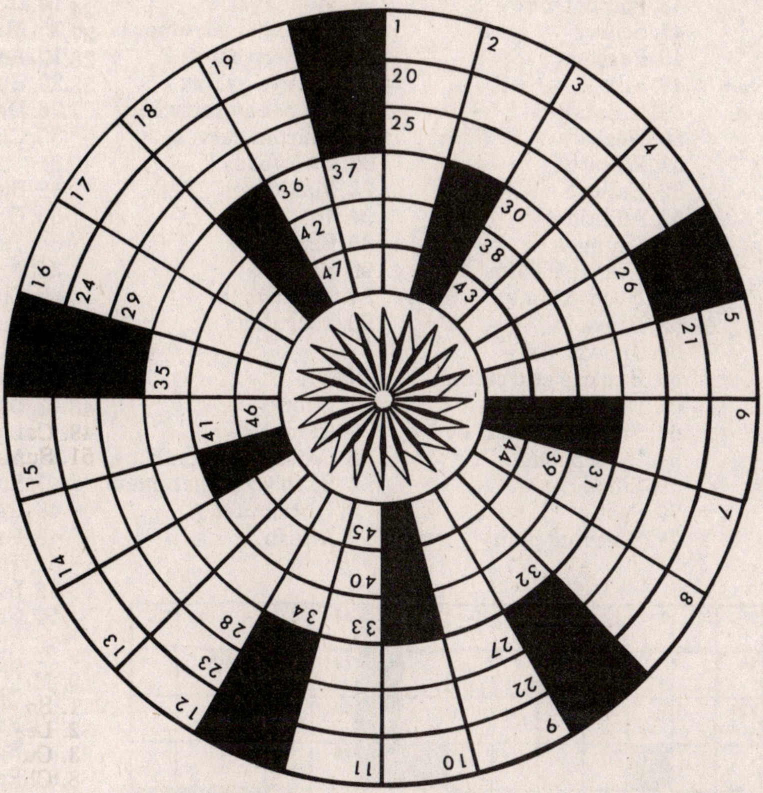

### AROUND (Clockwise)

1. Makes lace
5. Cummerbund, e.g.
9. Squeal
12. Seaweed
16. Atlas entries
20. Matinee or golden
21. Forearm bone
22. Go wrong
23. Notion
24. Leave out
25. Is similar to
27. Afternoon social
28. Force
29. Sup in style
30. The catbird ____
31. To be, in Paris
33. Caring
36. Airport inits.
38. Wicked
39. Old cars
40. Quod ____ demonstrandum
41. Scullers' tools
42. Pop
43. Abnegate
44. Peevish state
45. Knocks
46. Easter's precursor
47. "A Boy Named ____"

### RADIAL (Out to in)

1. Angry speech
2. Humorist George
3. Threw
4. Possible ace locale
5. Unobtrusively
6. Totally
7. Derisive looks
8. Hie
9. Try again
10. Metric measure
11. Kind of bullet
12. Abduct
13. Fiats
14. Unaspirated
15. TV's "Highway ____"
16. Up-to-date
17. Surrounded by
18. Wrestling coup
19. Cavalry mounts
26. Principal
32. King of France
34. Mouths
35. Highland negative
37. Greek letter

*Note to Solvers: This Crossword does not have aids such as "2 wds." and "hyph."*

# PUZZLE 95

**• DRINK UP! •**

**ACROSS**

1. Mandibles
5. Poet Angelou
9. Luau dish
12. Cordial flavoring
17. Table spread
18. At any time
19. Select
20. Roll with a hole
21. Swallow
22. Fragrant blossoms
24. Supply
25. Vacationer's vessel
27. First garden
28. Swear
29. Boor
30. Actress Cheryl ___
31. Norse deity
33. Fierce stare
36. Sculls' instruments
37. Apple
41. Opera
42. Boxers' moves
43. Point of view
45. Scurry
46. Parboils
48. Lift
49. ___ tax
50. Hocks
51. Wreaths
52. Caller
53. Addition
54. Lounges
55. Female lobster
56. Hooded snake
59. Dines
60. Snowbirds
63. Bauxite and cinnabar
64. Hand-warmers
66. Small mound of soil
68. Lyric poem
69. Stops
70. Post
71. Soothing plant
72. Cinema snack
74. Chessman
75. Panel
76. Actress Lanchester
77. Knights
78. Dowel
79. Statesman Stevenson
82. Major league maneuver
83. Twangy instruments
87. Western capital
88. Earth's galaxy
90. It's not a pretty fruit
91. Hairpin curves
92. Everybody
93. Make over
94. Tot
95. Fewest
96. Wield
97. Discovered
98. Yearnings

**DOWN**

1. Chores
2. Came down
3. "Wish You ___ Here"
4. Soup accompaniment
5. Distributed
6. Affirm
7. Affirmative vote
8. Unpaid debt
9. Emulated Naomi Campbell
10. Candid
11. ___ a boy!
12. Escape
13. Temperament
14. Inventor Sikorsky
15. Min. divisions
16. Actress Sommer
23. Bookie's concern
26. Daisy or Fannie
30. Chemists' lairs
31. "___ the night . . ."
32. Suggest
33. Opening
34. Turkish money
35. Arabian gulf
36. Shade trees
38. Pump
39. Anagram for sail
40. Hide
42. Singer Billy ___
43. Loams
44. Mix, as a salad
47. Stew
48. Certain accessories
49. Famous puppet show
51. Takes it easy
52. Inheritance factor
54. Certain punch
55. Shell
56. Pen
57. Church calendar
58. Pager noise
60. Splice
61. Patchouli and linseed
62. Blackthorn
64. Spoils
65. Forearm bone
66. Gullets
67. Lease
69. Most sacred
70. Ones who suffer for a cause
73. Halts
74. In the ___ (healthy)
75. Particle
77. Tarnish
78. Synthetic fabric
79. Cain's brother
80. Portion
81. Singer Stansfield
82. Charge
83. Commanded
84. Fairy-tale heavy
85. Enthusiasm
86. U.S. Admiral William ___
88. Atlas page
89. Small

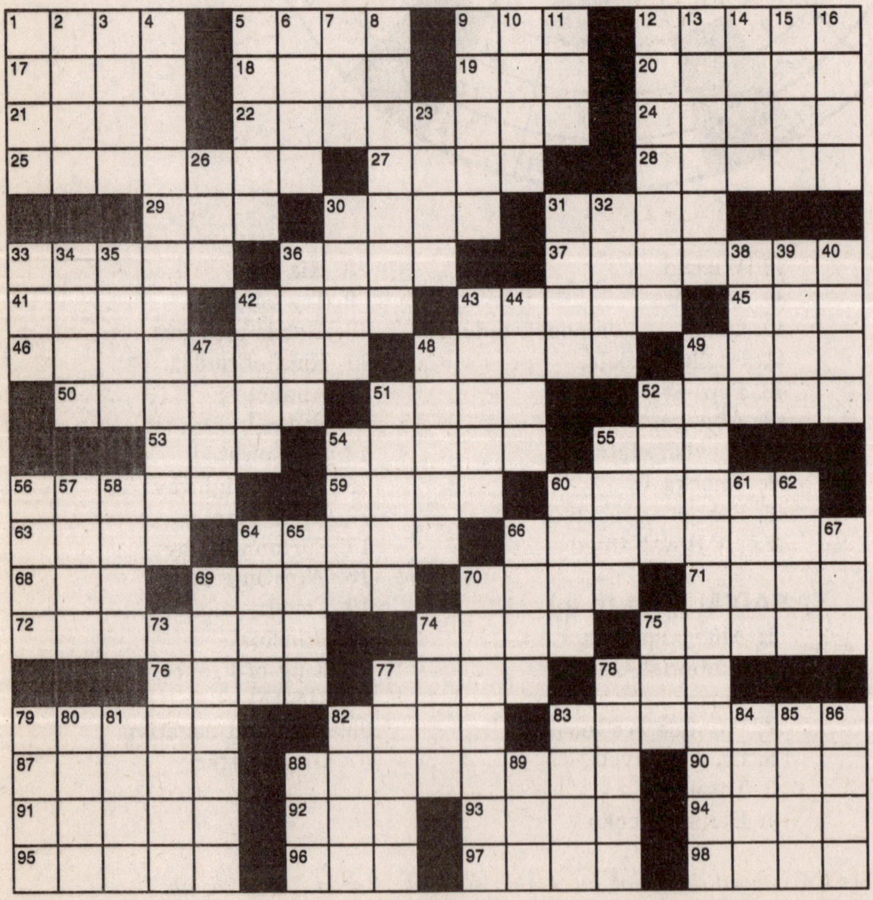

## CODEWORD

# PUZZLE 96

**Codeword is a special crossword puzzle in which conventional clues are omitted. Instead, answer words in the diagram are represented by numbers. Each number represents a different letter of the alphabet, and all of the letters of the alphabet are used. When you are sure of a letter, put it in the code key chart and cross it off in the alphabet box. A group of letters has been inserted to start you off.**

| | |
|---|---|
| 1 | 14 |
| 2 | 15 |
| 3 | 16 |
| 4 | 17 |
| 5 | 18 C |
| 6 | 19 T |
| 7 | 20 |
| 8 | 21 |
| 9 | 22 |
| 10 | 23 |
| 11 | 24 |
| 12 | 25 |
| 13 A | 26 |

| | | | | | | | | | | | | | | |
|---|---|---|---|---|---|---|---|---|---|---|---|---|---|---|
| 26 | 4 | 22 | 2 | 6 | | 15 | 26 | 26 | | 23 | 22 | 10 | 26 | 25 |
| 14 | | 6 | | 13 | | 9 | | 14 | | 9 | | 13 | | 22 |
| 13 A | 15 | 5 | 1 | 17 | 3 | 26 | | 6 | 9 | 1 | 20 | 9 | 13 | 10 |
| 18 C | | 11 | | 10 | | 26 | | 17 | | 24 | | 19 | | 6 |
| 19 T | 9 | 2 | 10 | 5 | | 24 | 1 | 1 | | 26 | 25 | 2 | 19 | 5 |
| | | 12 | | | | 26 | | 25 | | | | 12 | | |
| 13 | 23 | 20 | 7 | 13 | 12 | 5 | | 26 | 20 | 1 | 19 | 2 | 5 | 19 |
| 11 | | | 2 | | 22 | | | | 12 | | 2 | | | 1 |
| 26 | 17 | 1 | 6 | 2 | 12 | 20 | | 4 | 22 | 13 | 17 | 2 | 23 | 8 |
| | | 15 | | | | 9 | | 22 | | | | 12 | | |
| 10 | 13 | 21 | 1 | 9 | | 26 | 3 | 26 | | 26 | 12 | 21 | 1 | 8 |
| 13 | | 26 | | 13 | | 26 | | 9 | | 19 | | 22 | | 26 |
| 5 | 26 | 18 | 19 | 2 | 1 | 12 | | 2 | 12 | 7 | 26 | 9 | 26 | 5 |
| 16 | | 19 | | 12 | | 26 | | 26 | | 2 | | 26 | | 26 |
| 5 | 13 | 5 | 5 | 8 | | 9 | 2 | 25 | | 18 | 1 | 25 | 26 | 5 |

| | |
|---|---|
| ~~A~~ | N |
| B | O |
| ~~C~~ | P |
| D | Q |
| E | R |
| F | S |
| G | ~~T~~ |
| H | U |
| I | V |
| J | W |
| K | X |
| L | Y |
| M | Z |

---

## GUEST STAR

# PUZZLE 97

**Unscramble the letters of each group below to form a 6-letter word and place the word into the correspondingly numbered column reading from top to bottom. Next rearrange the top six letters for the first name and the bottom six letters for the last name of our Guest Star.**

**1.** I B S U M N

**2.** G A S E I N

**3.** G E G L I G

**4.** P R E M O R

**5.** O D O R N I

**6.** B A O E Z G

| 1. | 2. | 3. | 4. | 5. | 6. |
|---|---|---|---|---|---|
| | | | | | |
| | | | | | |
| | | | | | |
| | | | | | |
| | | | | | |
| | | | | | |

**GUEST STAR:** _ _ _ _ _ _   _ _ _ _ _ _

# PUZZLE 98

**• LITTLE GRASS SHACK •**

**ACROSS**

1. Withdrew, with out
6. Carnival
10. Keen
15. Binge
18. Become extremely emotional
19. "___ La Douce"
20. Facial expression
21. Hold sway
22. Stair part
23. Shine
24. Large lily
25. Waxed cheese
26. Join
27. Hoodwinked
29. Eternities
30. Piggery
31. Seine sights
33. ___ and penates
34. Mich.'s neighbor
36. Lots
37. Pugilists' weapons
38. Grouper
42. Fishing vessels
45. Chap
46. Motions
47. Appoints
48. Ditty
49. Small bird
51. Severe
52. Saintly image
53. Adds to a sound track
54. Tight
55. Broad-antlered deer
56. Ginkgo, e.g.
57. Mature
58. ___ ex machina
59. Licoricelike flavoring
63. Bandleader Calloway
64. Pretext
67. Roman dozen
68. Moor flower
70. Poet Ogden ___
71. Baseball's Piniella
72. Cones' partners
73. Was down with
74. Odometer unit
75. Calcium oxide
76. Yemenite port
77. Dairy product
80. Diner sign
81. Hindu deity
82. Sky blue
83. Shelve
85. Swing music
86. Elegant
87. Hightail it
88. Sweetheart
90. Cow chews
91. Cultivate
92. ___ one's style
93. Corn bread
94. Reporter Donaldson
97. Deal with
100. Baseballer Darryl ___
103. Like some letters
105. Culture medium
106. Black wood
107. Comedienne Martha ___
108. Educate
109. Charters
110. Knight's weapon
111. Conceits
112. Singer Ronstadt
113. Retainer
114. More generous
115. Flit
116. Words of consent

**DOWN**

1. Grimm heavies
2. Main idea
3. Delectable
4. Rapier's kin
5. Booms
6. Spoke falsely
7. Zones
8. Muslim priest
9. Perambulating
10. Accompany
11. Stuns
12. Respiratory organs
13. Fashion magazine
14. Prepares
15. Art of self-defense
16. Actor Bates
17. Precious rocks
21. African antelopes
28. Malt dryer
32. ___ Cruces
35. Actress Wood
36. View
37. Bogs
38. Kyoto coin
39. Indonesian islands
40. Scenery
41. Opposite of NNW
42. Pinch
43. Actor Gordon ___
44. Protozoan
45. Comedian George ___
46. Understand
48. Sweetener
49. "Brideshead Revisited" author
50. Bustle
53. Saw socially
54. Strained
55. Follow
58. Telephones
59. Bouquet
60. Mass migration
61. Downy ducks
62. Animator Walt ___
64. Hawn/Beatty film
65. Do a cable stitch
66. Popeye's Oyl
69. British prime minister and family
72. Levels
74. ___ West (life vest)
75. "NBC's Saturday Night ___"
77. Aud., often
78. Morrow or Lowe
79. Hairpin's kin
80. Goal
81. Giggled
82. Passionately
84. Person's being
85. Lintel's companion
86. Press for payment
88. Belgium's neighbor
89. Legal beagle
90. Most coquettish
92. Witch
93. "Stir Crazy" comedian
94. Some trumpeters
95. In reserve
96. Feathered talkers
97. Farm baby
98. Type of molding
99. Top of the head
101. Ski lift
102. Hindu melody
104. Put-in-Bay's lake

# PUZZLE 99

**• ROLE PLAYING •**

**ACROSS**

1. Timber tree
4. Evergreen
7. Baseball's Pee Wee ____
10. Fill with joy
12. Burnett or Channing
13. Drilled
14. Mark Antony portrayer in "Serpent of the Nile"
18. Compete
19. ____ Mahal
22. Climbing rose support
26. Cleaning cloth
29. Hubbub
30. Thug
31. Persia, today
33. Bullfight cheer
34. Humbug!
35. Stardom
36. Review copy
38. Thus far
39. Spike
41. Rain cats and dogs
43. Hit the jackpot
44. For
45. Actor West
47. Circle
48. President Carter's daughter
50. Finn neighbor
53. Heroic poem
55. Newt
58. Football's Marino
59. Bargain
61. Small measure
62. Milne marsupial
63. Tint
64. Actor Peck
66. Use needle and thread
67. Opposite of WSW
68. Calamity Jane portrayer in "The Paleface"
76. Impresario Sol ____
77. Hunter constellation
79. Love
80. Spaghetti, e.g.
81. Groom the greens
82. Viper

**DOWN**

1. Rainbow
2. Char
3. Wife of Zeus
4. Klinger portrayer of "M*A*S*H"
5. Roman way
6. Rose
8. ____ sauce
9. Stately tree
10. Recede
11. Mary ____ Retton
15. Roasting chamber
16. Nothing
17. Supermarket section
19. Flap
20. Oklahoma city
21. Genghis Khan portrayer in "The Conqueror"
22. Male turkey
23. Lobster coral
24. Wrath
25. Heavy-hearted
26. Jesse James portrayer in "Jesse James at Bay"
27. Stout
28. Pick up
30. "Me and My ____"
32. Small bite
35. Certain exam
37. Subject
40. Assist
42. Footed vase
46. Angry
47. Brink
48. Tack on
49. Spring month
51. Dowel
52. Standard
53. Go astray
54. Wages
56. Enemy
57. Type of truck
60. Ogle
61. Moves away
65. African antelope
68. Martial art
69. ". . . pretty maids all in ____"
70. Neither hide ____ hair
71. Scrape by, with out
72. Bribe
73. Important time
74. Actress Bonet
75. Oodles
76. Companion for green eggs
78. Snooze

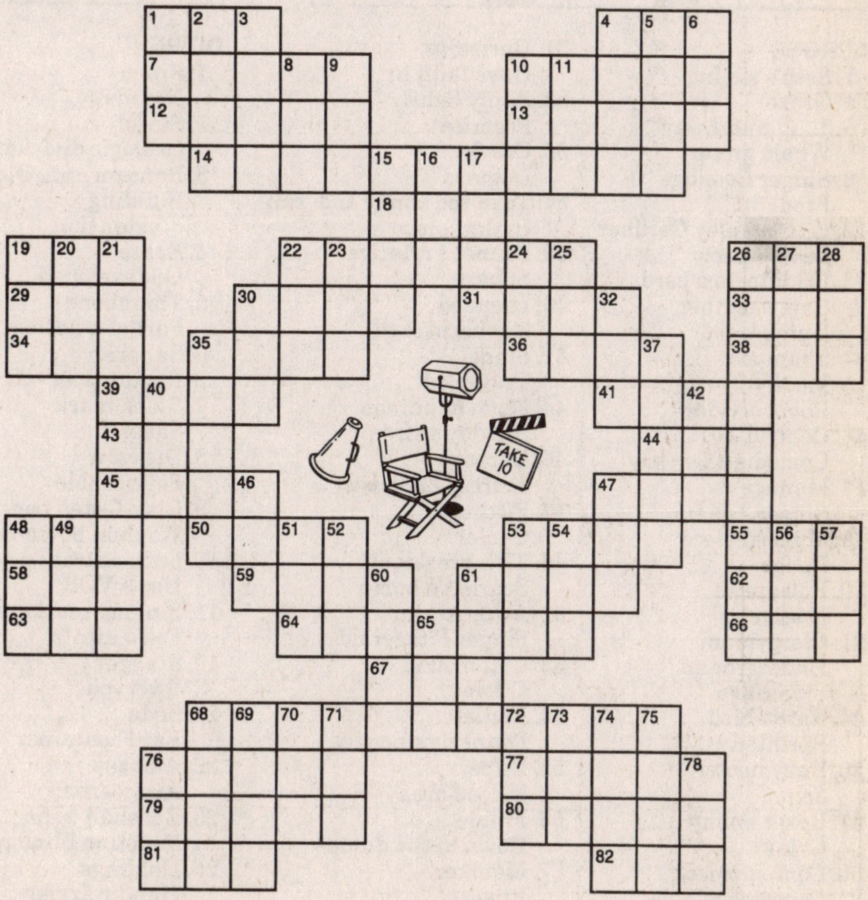

# PUZZLE 100

## TWIN CROSSWORDS

**Two clues for each number and two puzzle diagrams—which answer goes where? That's your dilemma. Answer the clues and then decide in which crossword pattern the answer fits. The first two words have been entered for you.**

A

B

**ACROSS**

1. Seth's sibling
Graze
5. "___ and Away"
Whale group
8. Singer Coolidge
Prod
12. ___ Stanley Gardner
Lavish party
13. Prior to, to a bard
Cain's mother
14. Dutch treat
Shampoo
15. Modify
Room divider
16. Central
Comedian Conway
17. Manage
Singer Adams
18. Musical piece
Dodge
20. Pub brews
Festival
21. Clergyman
Underground passage
24. Ratite bird
Sprinted
26. Baby hooter
Join
27. Boxer Sonny ___
Grins
30. Compartment
Green vegetable
31. Uprisings
Have faith in
33. Apply lightly
Promise
35. Creek
Dogmas
37. Take the honey and run
In that place
39. Sonnet's relative
Sphere
40. Dreaded
Rubbernecked
41. Singe
Trampled
44. Farm buildings
Sunday entree
46. Damage
Actress Lange
47. Fitting
Choler
48. 27th president
Scarlett's home
52. Actor Arkin
Singer Fitzgerald
53. Golf mound
Cravat
54. Radiate
Pennsylvania city
55. Dupe
Raised area
56. Finale
Down in the dumps
57. Moniker
Rive

**DOWN**

1. Ripen
Not many
2. Sinful
Geologic division
3. Ransom ___ Olds
Building extension
4. Erase
Undeveloped
5. Thighbone
Part of a flower
6. Saharan
Roman poet
7. Black mark
Saves
8. Disavow
Serviceable
9. Clay-footed one
Went on horseback
10. Lope or trot
Use a VCR
11. Singing brothers
Foil's kin
19. Stagger
Swerved
21. Soda
Lard container
22. Amazes
Army group
23. Baseball team
Venetian blind part
25. Holdings
Hand warmer
27. ___ Angeles
Whole
28. Eternally
Redolence
29. Back of the neck
Achy
32. Say again
Cottontails
34. Hideaway
Marry
36. Average
Rat or squirrel
38. Scurry
Last one mentioned
40. Liberated
Satisfied
41. Cook
Defrost
42. Circle of light
Actor's goal
43. Singer Guthrie
Iridescent gem
45. Operatic solo
Ajar
49. Doctors' gp.
Metric measure
50. Fish appendage
Curb
51. Corroded
Actor Danson

# PUZZLE 101

**ACROSS**
1. Espy
5. King topper
8. Ticket part
12. Vex
13. Guy's date
14. Facility
15. Lacking knowledge
18. Band that sings the 1983 hit "Rosanna"
19. Jim Morrison's group, with "The"
20. Peak on Crete
22. Knight's title
23. Type of history
26. Rawhide
28. Mom's mate
31. Maine's nickname
34. Kindergartner
35. Assigned part
36. Prayer response
37. Come in first
38. Craggy peak
40. Kate's cohort
43. Zone
46. Antes
51. Meara or Archer
52. Umpire's call
53. Diminutive suffix
54. Crowd noise
55. Princess's annoyance
56. Calendar units

**DOWN**
1. ____ Lanka
2. Liquid measure
3. Margarine
4. Woven fabric
5. Years of life
6. Train unit
7. Hebrew priest
8. Mexican mister
9. Food item for 8 Down
10. Patron
11. Twins, kings, and queens
16. Herd of seals
17. Blue-pencils
21. Cook's wear
22. Winter forecast
23. Choose
24. ____ Grande
25. Pismire
27. Sniggler's quarry
28. Water blockade
29. Dined
30. Room for relaxation
32. Attempts
33. Lingered
37. Broader
39. Tree type
40. At a long way off
41. Carson's replacement
42. Russian river
44. James of jazz
45. Lawyer's abbr.
47. Summit
48. Tint
49. Station letters
50. Of course!

# PUZZLE 102

**ACROSS**
1. Strike
6. Study
9. Precious stone
12. Morning TV show
13. Before, in verse
14. Shad delicacy
15. Worship
16. Gift
18. Coagulate
19. Mineral spring
21. Unknown's name
22. Choice word
24. Globe
26. Put below
29. Tease
32. Flock mama
33. Prohibit
36. Taper
38. Night before
39. Argue
41. Alleviate
43. Batter
44. Bugle call
48. Small amount
50. Twentieth letter
52. Little dog
53. Kind of rally
56. Flash of light
58. Musical sense
59. Hive insect
60. Concise
61. Baboon
62. Light brown
63. Stuffed

**DOWN**
1. Phase
2. Prototype
3. Worshiped objects
4. ____ and feather
5. Potato buds
6. Go away
7. Go astray
8. Requirement
9. Welcomed
10. Eternity
11. Assembled
17. Distress signal
20. Meditate
23. Recede
25. Developed into
27. Hooter
28. Minuscule
30. Relief
31. Mouse's kin
33. Professional charge
34. Egg cells
35. Renovate
37. Brooklyn cager
40. ____ down the hatches
42. Erode
45. Separate
46. Handbag
47. Velocity
49. Obligation
51. Salamanders
53. Green vegetable
54. Knock sharply
55. Body of water
57. Meadow

# PUZZLE 103

**ACROSS**
1. Beef, e.g.
5. ____ bene
9. Enemy
12. Writer Gardner
13. Woe is me!
14. Track cycle
15. Toasted sandwich
18. ____ majesty
19. Delight
20. Lively Cuban dance
23. Syrian river
24. "Long, Long ____"
25. Aquatic animal
28. Turkish generals
32. Gazpacho, for example
35. Once, once
36. Char
37. ____ loss
38. Broadway success
40. Thespian
42. Discolor
45. Italian wine region
47. Poultry dessert?
52. Belonging to us
53. Great Lake
54. Sea eagle
55. Gridiron scores, for short
56. Cowgirl Evans
57. Ascend

**DOWN**
1. Tilly of "The Big Chill"
2. Goof
3. Baba of legend
4. Narrates
5. Turndowns in Edinburgh
6. Ye ____ Shoppe
7. Tic-____-toe
8. Mt. St. Helens emission
9. Dog's pest
10. Hops kiln
11. Fencer's weapon
16. Slightest
17. Inventor Howe
20. Rescue
21. Ripener
22. Cabin rafters
23. ____ breve (musical term)
26. Atlantic coast area
27. Honest ____ Lincoln
29. Nanny or billy
30. Car
31. Shadowbox
33. Moral concept
34. Muse of love poetry
39. Signed
41. Quotes
42. Glasgow native
43. Dull sound
44. Ventilates
45. Indigo plant
46. "Graf ____" (German battleship)
48. Epoch
49. Con's opposite
50. Claire or Balin
51. Always, to poets

# PUZZLE 104

**ACROSS**
1. Comedian Conway
4. "Let's Make a ____"
8. Gallop
12. Past
13. Great review
14. Nevada city
15. Snoopy's nemesis
17. Yemen port
18. Beef or tuna
19. Islamic spiritual leader
21. Give up
23. Make happy
26. Matador's concern
29. Shoshone Indians
31. Spy gp.
32. Corrects
34. Adhesive
36. Berth
37. Engrave
39. Citrus beverages
40. Mother's brother
42. Engine cover
44. Latin dance
46. Threefold
50. Ruckus
52. Operating at a loss
54. Gaelic
55. Novelist James ____
56. Crude metal
57. Go by
58. Scorch
59. Neither's partner

**DOWN**
1. Sailors
2. "____ a Kick Out of You"
3. Style
4. Duck
5. Hearing organ
6. Wading bird
7. Singer Horne
8. Path
9. Blushing
10. "A Chorus Line" song
11. Heavy weight
16. Essayist Francis ____
20. ____ majeste
22. Clean
24. Fork part
25. Diner sign
26. Forbidden
27. Gregory Peck film, with "The"
28. Charitable organization
30. Sound repetition
33. Regard
35. Sierra ____
38. Alter
41. Old string instruments
43. Alternate
45. Partiality
47. Press clothes
48. Fiddling emperor
49. German river
50. Agent, for short
51. Levin or Gershwin
53. "____ and Sympathy"

## DOUBLE TROUBLE

# PUZZLE 105

**Not really double trouble, but double fun! Solve this puzzle as you would a regular crossword, EXCEPT place one, two, or three letters in each box. The number of letters in each answer is shown in parentheses after its clue.**

**ACROSS**

1. Take offense at (6)
4. Stroll (4)
7. Disavow (9)
9. Superstar (9)
11. Symptom (4)
12. Freeway entrance (4)
13. Circle (4)
14. John ___ Passos (3)
15. Campus bigwigs (5)
17. Fatal (6)
19. Put one to sleep (4)
20. Undertakes (7)
22. Struggled (10)
24. Fountain order (4)
26. Hideaway (3)
27. Paint additive (7)
30. Molded dessert (7)
33. Cashbox (4)
34. Quit (6)
36. Apprentice (6)
38. Drying frame (4)
39. Caboose, e.g. (3)
40. Picasso's tripod (5)
42. Yard components (4)
43. Renegades (9)
45. States (8)
47. Watched (6)
48. Spell (6)

**DOWN**

1. Offensive (9)
2. Ship off (4)
3. Regal headgear (5)
4. Kiddie pool activity (6)
5. 100% (3)
6. Related (7)
7. Dwell (6)
8. Synagogue (6)
9. Announced (8)
10. Uneven (5)
16. Give the boot (4)
18. At that time (4)
19. Lout (4)
21. Student's exercise (6)
23. Retaliate (6)
25. "Swan Lake" cast (7)
27. Stout (8)
28. Under the weather (3)
29. Delete (5)
31. High-school subject (5)
32. Obstructing action (12)
33. Swap (5)
35. "___ Poets Society" (4)
37. Brooklyn cagers (4)
39. Furnished food (7)
41. Pick (6)
44. Tear (4)
46. Pasternak heroine (4)

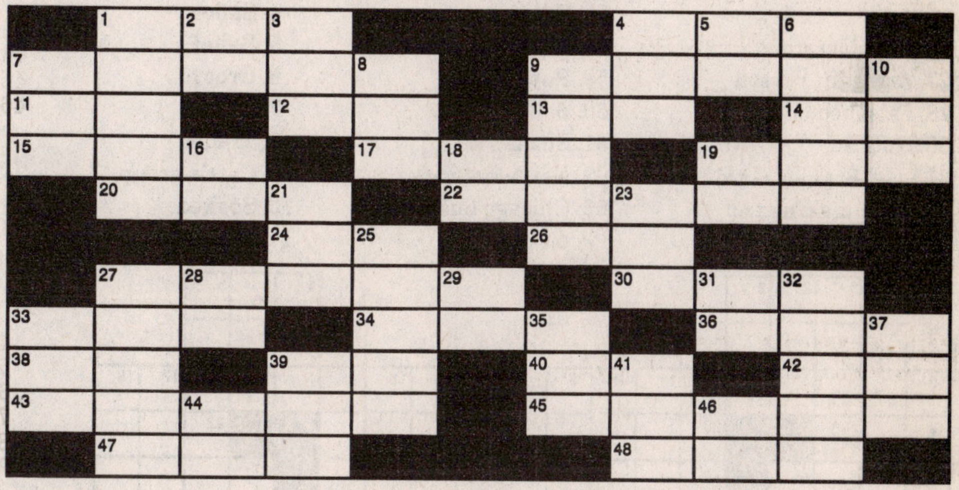

## DEDUCTION PROBLEM

# PUZZLE 106

**• THE BIRTHSTONES •**

Four friends named June, Opal, Pearl, and Ruby were born in four different months of the year. Each girl wore her own birthstone. June was not born in the month of June, and no girl's name was the same as the name of her birthstone. The gems for the months of their births are January, garnet; June, pearl; July, ruby; and October, opal. Ruby was not wearing a pearl, Pearl was not wearing a ruby, and Opal's birthday was later in the year than Ruby's. What gem was each girl wearing?

# PUZZLE 107

**• LIQUID ASSETS •**

**ACROSS**

1. Witty person
4. Twitch
7. Legends
9. Corned beef dish
10. Canals
14. Conduit
19. First lady
20. Away from the wind
21. Actor Sharif
22. FDR program
23. Semester
25. Ago
26. Considerate
27. Arrogant person
28. Falsehoods
30. Noticed
31. ___ Stanley Gardner
32. Hole-making tool
33. Coral reef
34. Kentucky ___
38. Journalist Rather
39. Japanese sash
42. Sweetener
43. Model Carol ___
44. Gardener's need
48. Exclamation of surprise
51. Take it easy
52. Self
53. Reverential fear
54. Send payment
55. Crew members
57. Court
59. Pub drinks
60. Sallow
61. Smell
62. Nerve network
63. Chicago business district
67. Chimed
70. Female sheep
73. Exist
74. Sea eagle
75. Presidential office
76. Head covering
77. Liquor
80. Without moisture
83. Draw wages
84. Bed linen
85. Arid
86. Lubricate

**DOWN**

1. Harbor locale
2. Ripen
3. Needlefish
4. Sailor
5. Belief
6. Groove
7. Rescue
8. Trades
9. Cattle group
10. Soaked
11. ___ mode
12. Affirmative reply
13. Tennis unit
14. Chinese pan
15. "___ Blue"
16. Sunbather's goal
17. Press
18. Catch
24. Factory
27. Stitch
29. Under
30. Utter
31. Etc.'s cousin
33. Ohio Northern University site
34. Written demand for payment
35. Omelet ingredient
36. Speed contest
37. Boast
40. Without clothes
41. Newsy bit
42. Half-dozen
45. Inventor Whitney
46. Rodent
47. Wanderer
48. Steamboat's need
49. Has debts
50. Guitarist Montgomery
54. Caviar
56. Cosmetic ingredient
57. Sprinkled
58. Spanish cheer
60. Persian fairy
61. Stares at
62. British fliers' gp.
63. Slim
64. Table scrap
65. Washington bill
66. For each
67. Use oars
68. Actress Gardner
69. Natalie Cole's father
71. Sunrise direction
72. Rds.
78. Put an ___ to the ground
79. Twisted
81. Greek letter
82. Oahu neckwear

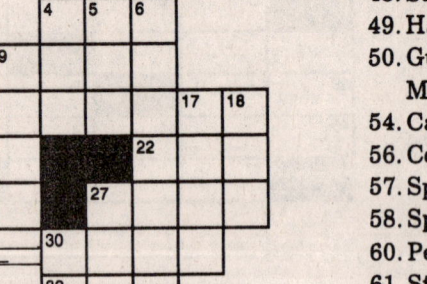

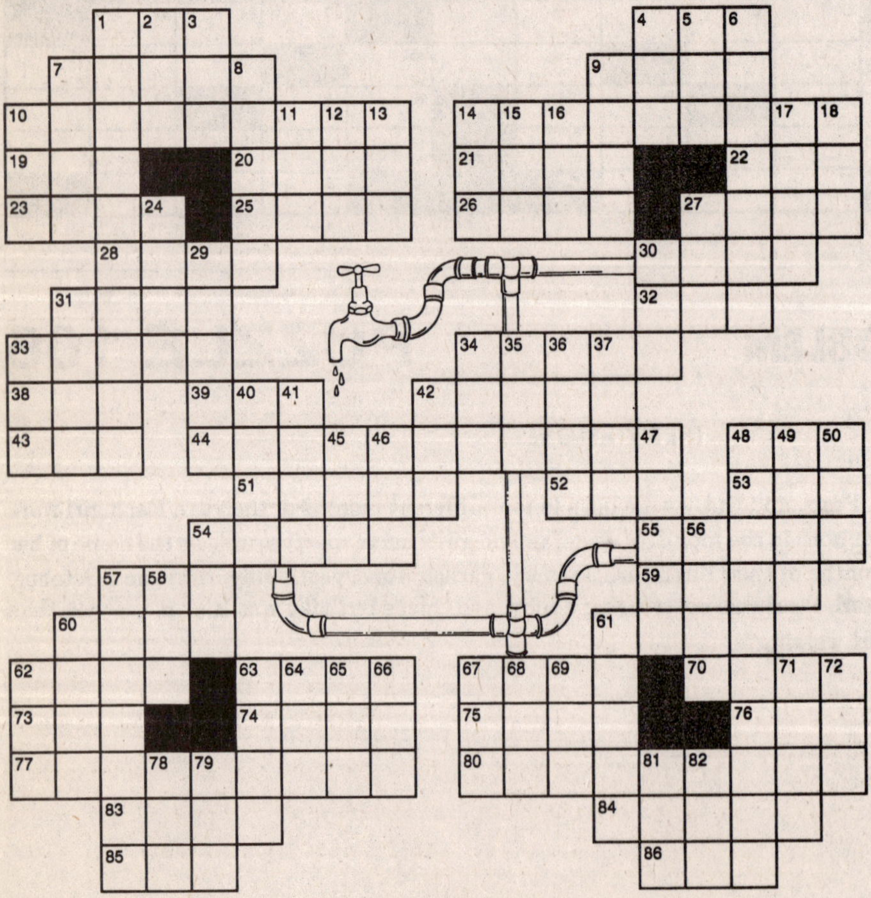

## BRICK BY BRICK

# PUZZLE 108

**Rearrange this stack of bricks to form a crossword puzzle. The clues will help you fit the bricks into their correct places. Row 1 has been filled in for you. Use the bricks to fill in the remaining spaces.**

### ACROSS

1. Mardi ___
   Windy blasts
   Scarlett's home
2. Split
   Poker stakes
   Nefarious
3. Notion
   Infantryman
   Baseball team
4. Violent
   Shelf
5. Sediment
   Intention
6. Disfigure
   Pastures
   Wrinkle
7. Imitated
   Obtrusively
8. Church part
   Tartlike pastries
   Actual
9. Argumentative
   Prophet
10. Military order
    "Younger ___ Springtime"
    Double curve
11. Morning moisture
    Pindaric works
12. Beef animal
    Producing heat
13. Describe
    Zeal
    Temerity
14. Of the ear
    ___ City, Kansas
    March
15. Lacquered metalware
    Influences
    Cabbage salad

### DOWN

1. Coarse sand
   Type of ray
   Reno machine
2. Go by sedan
   Detached
   A Jackson brother
3. Assert
   Musical show
   Actor Jannings
4. Connections
   Deterioration
5. Be unwell
   Computer programmer
6. Flock of geese
   Sped
   Commercials
7. Incapable of being appraised
   Brag
8. Astonish
   Distort
   River in Italy
9. Portable shelter
   Literary collection
10. JFK visitor
    Play parts
    Worships
11. Former money, for Sophia
    King Saul's grandfather
12. Crowded dwellings
    Expressions of relief
13. Eager
    "___ Grows in Brooklyn"
    Flop
14. Peal
    Swings around
    Actress Chase
15. Opposite of aweather
    Those who observe
    Sail corner

### BRICKS

| | | | | |
|---|---|---|---|---|
| S ■ T<br>■ ■ S | F I C<br>A L L | T E R<br>■ ■ ■ | N A V<br>T R U | A N T<br>T ■ ■ |
| S ■ E<br>T ■ N | E ■ F<br>C U L | A S ■<br>B L A | L A N<br>E N T | ■ L E<br>A I M |
| E ■ H<br>S ■ S | N T E<br>R U N | C ■ D<br>E ■ S | ■ T H<br>■ ■ O | V I L<br>I N E |
| M A R<br>A P E | A T E<br>■ ■ ■ | I K E<br>L A W | E R ■<br>N ■ A | S T E<br>L I M |
| E ■ A<br>A ■ G | O D G<br>W A Y | O T I<br>T O L | R U E<br>E E R | C A L<br>R D O |
| A S E<br>D E W | O R I<br>R ■ G | E S S<br>■ ■ ■ | A N ■<br>D E S | ■ L E<br>D ■ ■ |
| D G E<br>■ ■ ■ | M A G<br>S I L | R I V<br>I D E | C R E<br>T A N | A S E<br>T L Y |

### DIAGRAM

| | 1 | 2 | 3 | 4 | 5 | 6 | 7 | 8 | 9 | 10 | 11 | 12 | 13 | 14 | 15 |
|---|---|---|---|---|---|---|---|---|---|---|---|---|---|---|---|
| 1 | G | R | A | S | ■ | G | U | S | T | S | ■ | T | A | R | A |
| 2 | | | | | | | | | | | | | | | |
| 3 | | | | | | | | | | | | | | | |
| 4 | | | | | | | | | | | | | | | |
| 5 | | | | | | | | | | | | | | | |
| 6 | | | | | | | | | | | | | | | |
| 7 | | | | | | | | | | | | | | | |
| 8 | | | | | | | | | | | | | | | |
| 9 | | | | | | | | | | | | | | | |
| 10 | | | | | | | | | | | | | | | |
| 11 | | | | | | | | | | | | | | | |
| 12 | | | | | | | | | | | | | | | |
| 13 | | | | | | | | | | | | | | | |
| 14 | | | | | | | | | | | | | | | |
| 15 | | | | | | | | | | | | | | | |

# PUZZLE 109

**ACROSS**

1. Feel
6. "Mona ____"
10. Tidy
14. Game fish
15. Picnic pests
16. Mayberry kid
17. Caper
18. Read quickly
19. Ocean movement
20. Molar and cuspid
21. Type of cheese
23. Finish
26. School dance
27. Kind of beam
29. Straps
33. Mix
35. Fragrant flowers
39. Hardwood tree
40. Young cow
41. There! in Thierry
42. Asian desert
43. ____ loss for words: 2 wds.
44. ____ salts
45. Musical composition
46. Breakfast food
49. Mails
51. Christmas carol
54. Consume
55. Spaniel type
59. ____ space
64. Margarine
65. Portal
67. ____ a customer: 2 wds.
68. Three-____ salad
69. Stove
70. Baby grand, e.g.
71. Drains
72. Headland
73. Famous violin, for short

**DOWN**

1. Quickly, in a hospital
2. Sea eagle
3. Memo
4. Business wear
5. Engraves
6. ____ Vegas
7. Peruvian Indian
8. Mailing must
9. Actor Ed
10. "____ for Sergeants": 2 wds.
11. Long poem
12. Verdi opera
13. Adolescent
22. Actor Reiner
24. Courage
25. Sag
27. Pale purple
28. Sandy's bark
30. Circles
31. Forbidden: var.
32. Glides on snow
33. Strikebreaker
34. Good-bye, in Britain
36. Family member, for short
37. Run away to wed
38. Pacific island group
42. "I've ____ a Secret"
47. Liver and ____
48. Negative prefix
50. Crouches
52. Urge: 2 wds.
53. "____ It to Beaver"
55. Blubbers
56. Excuse
57. Harvest
58. Roadways: abbr.
60. Military group
61. Rip
62. Sicily's volcano
63. Cross
66. Pulver's rank: abbr.

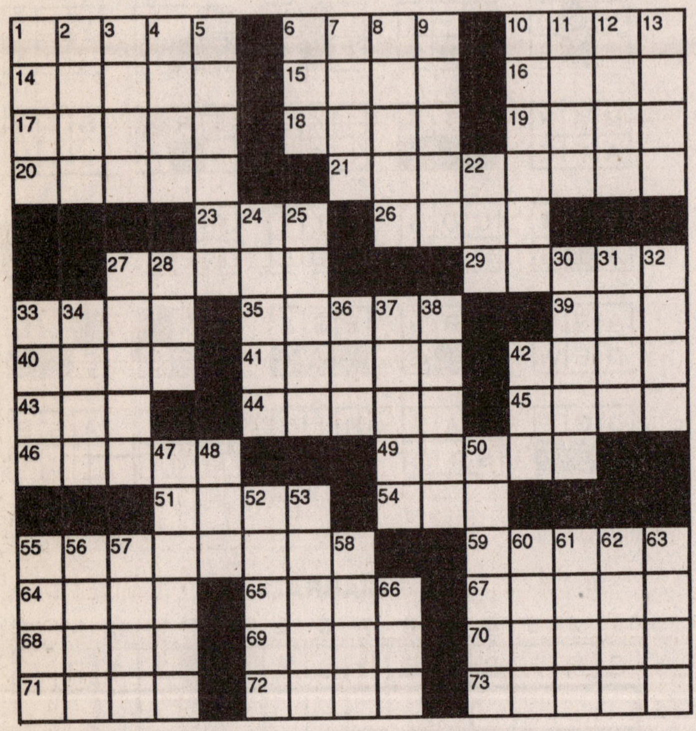

# PUZZLE 110

## SHUFFLE

**In each group of letters below two 6-letter words have been combined, with their letters remaining in correct order. Can you separate them? Helpful hint: the two words in each line combine to form a common 2-word phrase.**

**Example:** BSRHOIWDAELR (BsRhoIwDAeLr) = BRIDAL, SHOWER

1. L L I T E A T G L U E E ________ ________
2. B A D L A N L C E T E R ________ ________
3. S P F L R O W I N E G R ________ ________
4. P U M R A P R T I L N E ________ ________
5. G R M E O N A K E S E Y ________ ________
6. I S N U M D M I E A N R ________ ________

# PUZZLE 111

**ACROSS**

1. Box
5. Hit show
10. Small arrow
14. Comic Johnson
15. Uptight
16. Great Lake
17. Chicago feature
18. Vary
19. 5,280 feet
20. Worker
22. Lives
24. Toward shelter
25. Cruising
26. Set apart
29. Sent back
33. Whimper
34. More tender
35. "Norma ___"
36. Eye part
37. European nation
38. Prima donna
39. Born
40. "___ the Boys Are"
41. Level
42. Border guards
44. Embrace
46. Split apart
47. Evaluate
48. Inquiring
51. Pushed back
55. Flake
56. Rent
58. Hawkeye State
59. Highway fare
60. Go in
61. Gang
62. Only
63. Barrel parts
64. Sea bird

**DOWN**

1. Store sign
2. School dance
3. Upon
4. Supplants
5. Remained
6. Fracas
7. Feed the kitty
8. Wind direction: abbr.
9. Ranch workers
10. Lower
11. Seed case
12. Brook
13. Golf gadgets
21. Bullfight shout
23. Have on
25. High home
26. Rotates
27. Use a blender
28. Stranger
29. Zoo sounds
30. Impel
31. Roof edges
32. College VIPs
34. Go quickly
37. Doctors' signboards
38. Abandoned vessel
40. Small bird
43. 3-bagger
44. Antics
45. Had lunch
47. Bowling button
48. Deeds
49. Scat!
50. Slay
51. Pro ___
52. Old knowledge
53. Pitcher
54. Daybreak
57. Join the army: abbr.

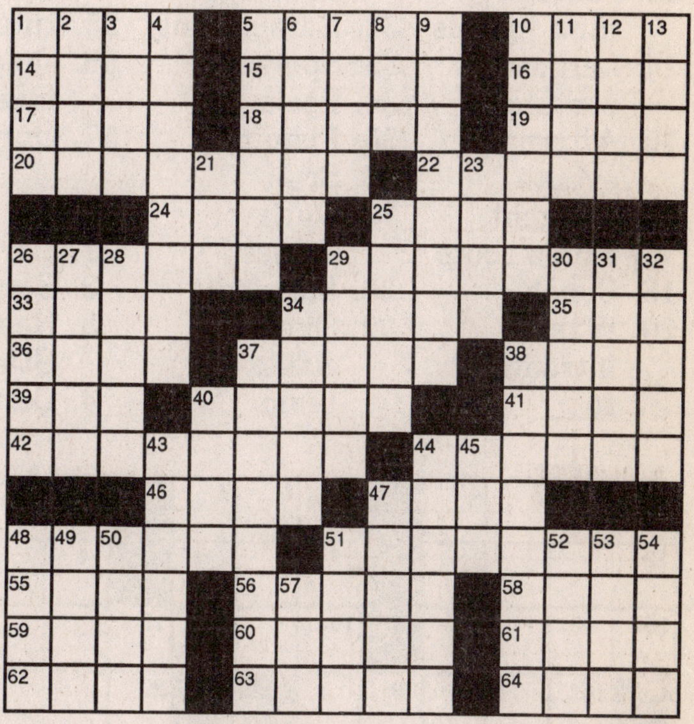


---

## DROP-OUTS

# PUZZLE 112

**The answer to each clue below is the name of a famous person whose initials have been dropped out and replaced with asterisks (*) in that clue. For example: base*all g*eat (base*B*all g*R*eat)—initials B.R.—is Babe Ruth.**

1. Lyric*st for brother *eorge
2. *ild W*st marshall
3. Poi*oned by her *icked stepmother
4. *uch ma*ried star of "Sugar Babies"
5. En*oys *ooking with wine
6. *r. Television *ecame everyone's Uncle
7. Dum*y *econd to Charlie McCarthy
8. *orld War II British *igar-smoker
9. Phil *onahue's fa*her-in-law
10. "National V*lve*" star

# PUZZLE 113

**ACROSS**

1. Rain hard
5. Ruby, for one
8. Lucille ____
12. Involved with
13. Pension fund initials
14. Largest continent
15. Afternoon events
16. Pungent, edible roots
18. Conch
20. Was introduced to
21. Chess piece
24. Lurid newspaper
27. Thunder-head
30. City trains
31. Malt beverage
32. Earsplitting
33. Spoiled
34. Psalm
35. Pismire
36. Scull
37. Outlaw James
38. Married
39. One of Santa's team
41. Cheer for a toreador
43. Particles
46. Slacks
50. Tiny bit
52. Not theirs
53. Baseball stick
54. Side of bacon
55. Interlock
56. Quick farewell
57. Only

**DOWN**

1. Cavity
2. Singletons
3. Beehive State
4. Certain sled
5. Young women
6. Cone's stat
7. Incensed
8. Vile
9. Smokers' receptacles
10. Deceive
11. ____ Cruces
17. Mischief-makers
19. Pot cover
22. Is told
23. Antique
25. Poor box donations
26. Unit of heredity
27. Talon
28. Like a certain ranger
29. Al fresco
33. Bleat
34. Bravery
36. Poetic works
37. Kind of stream
40. Undue speed
42. Luxuriant
44. Burrowing animal
45. Night twinkler
46. Twain's Sawyer
47. Be penitent for
48. Ease off
49. Beam
51. Beame of politics

# PUZZLE 114

**ACROSS**

1. Gasp
5. Hazard
9. Everything
12. Thought
13. Toledo's lake
14. Female deer
15. Caresses
16. Shoeless
18. "____ Wolf" (Michael J. Fox film)
20. Plagues
21. Charm
24. Actor Majors
25. Damp
26. Revere
30. Building shape
31. Like
32. Remarkable time
33. Extra-ordinarily wise man
36. Plugs
38. Stag guests
39. Least found
40. Expect
43. Broad
44. Focused
46. Clique
50. Conclusion
51. Heavy cord
52. English horn
53. Pen
54. Collections
55. Cozy retreat

**DOWN**

1. Apple seed
2. Humorist George ____
3. Rack up
4. Samples
5. "____ Without a Cause"
6. Mideast nation
7. "To ____ With Love"
8. Guardian
9. Fusses
10. Booty
11. Rents
17. Charges
19. Wear away
21. Iowa college town
22. Horseback game
23. Tablet
24. Ship's diary
26. Prevail
27. "____ We Go Again"
28. Annoys
29. Beyond
31. ____ Juan
34. Leave out
35. Gauges
36. Lout
37. Beaver State
39. Carnival attractions
40. Fearless fliers
41. Took off
42. Rooney of "60 Minutes"
43. Sobbed
45. Mass of eggs
47. Actor Vigoda
48. Negative votes
49. Obtain

# PUZZLE 115

**ACROSS**

1. Actress Cheryl ____
5. Louisville sluggers
9. Rate
12. General's helper
13. ____ code
14. Minstrel's song
15. Bestowed
17. Consume
18. ____ 500
19. Medicates
21. Stockpiles
24. Gash
25. Loafs
26. Careened
28. Sun
29. Nautical response
30. Brazilian resort
32. Enigma
35. Fad
37. Manner of running
38. Took on cargo
39. Vise
41. "____ and Lovers"
42. Sizzling
43. Malarkey
48. Stir
49. One of the Great Lakes
50. Sunburn soother
51. ____ capita
52. Sunder
53. Writer Uris

**DOWN**

1. Track circuit
2. Broadcast
3. Ike's monogram
4. Aspiration
5. Prom orchestras
6. Pretentious
7. Pipe joint
8. Burden
9. Befuddled
10. Luxury
11. Organs of sight
16. Remnants
20. Kind of painting
21. Towel word
22. Scent
23. Crocodilian
24. Observe
26. Dark bread
27. Wine and ____
29. Model Carol ____
31. Eccentric
33. Water barrier
34. Big or little constellation
35. Football's Dorsett
36. Scamp
38. Ran easily
39. Fellow
40. Quarry
41. Rotate
44. Cinnabar, e.g.
45. Shout to a toreador
46. Murmur amorously
47. Actor Berry

# PUZZLE 116

**ACROSS**
1. Petrol
4. Feminine pronoun
7. Witch
10. Worry
11. Merchant vessel weight unit
12. Milky gem
14. TV sitcom
15. Canadian province: abbr.
16. Yearn
17. School text
19. Cake toppings
21. New Haven tree
22. Director Howard
23. Bandannas
26. "The Little ____ That Could"
30. Long fish
31. Singer Orbison
32. Bank employee
36. Dairy product
39. Bauxite, for one
40. Trot
41. Pieces
44. Guard
48. Sty sound
49. Sever
51. Satanic
52. Take heed of
53. Employ
54. "Biggest Little City"
55. "To Have and Have ____"
56. Leftover
57. Wind dir.

**DOWN**
1. Pastime
2. Domain
3. "Return to ____"
4. Snow and thunder
5. Dearie, for short
6. Whole
7. Wishing
8. Neat as ____
9. Mob
10. "My Mother the ____"
13. News director in "WKRP in Cincinnati"
18. Sprite
20. Deception
23. Gel
24. Medium grade
25. Entirely
27. Dander
28. Numerals: abbr.
29. Gaze at
33. Pendant
34. Before, in poems
35. Extricate
36. Boxed
37. Hovel
38. Goes in
41. Junior
42. Lahr's Cowardly ____
43. Division preposition
45. Preholiday nights
46. On cloud ____
47. Postal graveyard: abbr.
50. Service branch: abbr.

# PUZZLE 117

## ACROSS

1. File
5. Steal
8. Mutts
12. American Indian
13. "You ____ My Sunshine"
14. Fencing sword
15. Bolted
17. Gasp
18. Ham on ____
19. Men
20. Binge
23. Char
25. Lost one's footing
26. Gab
29. Surpass
30. Brief
31. Tub
33. John Wayne film
35. Only
36. Apple center
37. Healed
38. Belt
41. Future flower
42. '60s musical
43. Tattered
48. Different
49. Podded vegetable
50. Dwell
51. Accomplishment
52. Nevertheless
53. Garden of ____

## DOWN

1. Legal matter
2. Mr. Linkletter
3. ____ Galahad
4. Gazed
5. Garden tool
6. Mine extract
7. Fourposter
8. Leave
9. October gem
10. Siskel or Hackman
11. Collections
16. Nautical response
19. Olympic swimmer Biondi
20. Fast jet
21. "Speed-the-____"
22. Ready to pick
23. Coast
24. Merit
26. "Moonstruck" star
27. Continuously
28. Unusual
30. Traffic sign
32. Senator Kennedy
34. Fearful
35. Confuse
37. Billiard stick
38. Lean-to
39. Saga
40. Ascend
41. Spoiled one
43. 007, e.g.
44. "____ Haw"
45. Acted
46. First woman
47. Bear's home

# PUZZLE 118

**ACROSS**

1. Sprite
4. Switch
8. Unit of land
12. Tiny
13. Poi source
14. Pull the ____ over someone's eyes
15. Bewitch
17. Opposed
18. Guide
19. Roman general Antony
21. Son of Eve
24. Jeopardy
27. A branch of a Scottish clan
30. Eternal City
32. Psyche's mediator
33. Actress West
34. Dispersed
35. Heavy weight
36. Sea eagle
37. Pindar works
38. Breakaway glacier part
39. Provide with a fund
41. Loafer
43. "____ Karenina"
45. Aesthetic sense
49. Transmitted
51. Curb
54. "Thirty days ____ . . ."
55. Binding strip
56. Comedian Sparks
57. Celtic
58. Nova
59. Nineteenth letter

**DOWN**

1. Cote females
2. Fasting season
3. Gala party
4. Gawk
5. Pale
6. Curved line
7. Verse
8. Informed
9. Tangible
10. Rubbish
11. Yale student
16. Remainder
20. Emulated Rich Little
22. Trampled
23. Round openings
25. Dr. Frankenstein's assistant
26. Hanker
27. "Peter Pan" pirate
28. Work for
29. Necklaces
31. Engage, as gears
34. Elevator word
38. Grizzly
40. "Up ____ Roof"
42. Playful mammal
44. Carney and Garfunkel
46. Of sound mind
47. Evens
48. Ceases
49. Andress film
50. Spike of corn
52. Break a fast
53. Health spot

# PUZZLE 119

**ACROSS**

1. Kitchen containers
5. Salary
8. "You ____ There"
11. Place in proper order
13. Stout
14. Young boy
15. Depart
16. Shading
18. Shotgun ball
20. Storm
21. Primate
23. Paddock
24. Urn
25. Fog
27. Garret
29. Lives
31. Staggered
35. Likewise
37. Wither
38. Nourish
40. "____ De-lovely"
42. Sunbathe
43. Pretensions
44. Consequence
46. Ink-absorbing paper
48. Incite
51. Ushered
52. "____ to Joy"
53. Stands up to
54. Before, in verse
55. Pea's place
56. Tidings

**DOWN**

1. Crony
2. Neighbor of Wash.
3. "The Man on the Flying ____"
4. Rescue
5. Title to an invention
6. Descended
7. Hankering
8. Assumed name
9. Expanse
10. Border
12. Sharp, shrill cry
17. Follows the course of
19. Smallest amount
21. Tack on
22. Dog's foot
24. Contest
26. First-born
28. Jogs
30. Jar cover
32. Salad ingredient
33. Time in history
34. Lion's home
36. Having rows
38. Office clerk, at times
39. Deteriorate
41. Ride the waves
43. Adept
44. Decorate again
45. Kind of shark
47. Spinning toy
49. Baste
50. Curvy letter

# PUZZLE 120

**ACROSS**

1. Toward the rear
4. Scientist's workplace
7. Expert
10. Farming implement
12. Be wrong
13. Slammer
14. Use a keyboard of a sort
15. Pierre's pal
16. Thomas ____ Edison
17. Conductor's wand
19. Anagram for lone
20. Generation
23. Astute
25. Neither's sidekick
26. "____ Look Me Over"
27. Kind of ego
31. Seamstress
33. Phonograph envelope
34. Navigate
35. Behave
36. Be under the weather
37. Burn
39. Wily
40. Mineral springs
43. Back of a ship
45. Vagabond
46. Actor Allen of "Home Improvement"
47. Temptation
51. Candid
52. Sooner than, poetically
53. Gas container
54. Moisten
55. In the ____ (losing money)
56. Color

**DOWN**

1. Clever
2. Ride in a plane
3. Spinning toy
4. "____ and Lace" (Stevie Nicks song)
5. Munitions plant
6. Salty liquid
7. Kind of shirt
8. Roam
9. Iridescent gem
11. Spider's trap
13. Wax and wick
18. On land
20. Picnic pests
21. Nanny or billy
22. Border lake
24. Actor Matthau
28. Pekoe and oolong
29. Harmful
30. Depend
32. Pupil's exercise
33. Connived
35. Apparel
38. Organic compound
40. Exposition
41. Vatican leader
42. Be an accomplice
44. Pistachio, e.g.
48. College cheer
49. African antelope
50. Supplement

# PUZZLE 121

**ACROSS**

1. Castle protection
5. Swing back and forth noisily
9. Sprite
12. Not working
13. Fence part
14. Formerly named
15. Shortly
16. Obligated for favors
18. Wined and dined
20. Aura
21. Sign of assent
22. Property
25. Box
28. Mature
29. Fresh
30. Bowlers
31. Large
32. Highest point
33. Behave
34. Hobo
35. Stages
36. Oysters' outputs
38. Used a chair
39. Prompt
40. Branch of mathematics
44. Run through
47. Verb's subject, often
48. Metallic dirt
49. Sudden assault
50. Hill's companion
51. Unite in marriage
52. Health resorts
53. Hearty meat dish

**DOWN**

1. Very fine rain
2. Scent
3. Lotion ingredient
4. Renters
5. Cooked in fat
6. Ground
7. Help
8. Delight
9. Portal
10. Confederate general
11. Nourished
17. Fragment
19. Part of a foot
22. Omelet ingredient
23. Replacement worker, for short
24. Wool producers
25. Fellow
26. Contest
27. Affixed
28. Motive
31. Public transport
32. Is present at
34. Makes dim
35. Droop
37. Actress McClanahan
38. Toboggans
40. Largest continent
41. Watercraft
42. Govern
43. In an updated way
44. Paddle
45. Poet's before
46. Knock

# PUZZLE 122

**ACROSS**

1. Tennis court divider
4. Stare open-mouthed
8. Charmingly attractive
12. Historic age
13. Reed instrument
14. Milky gem
15. Atmosphere
16. Lounge around
17. Crowds
18. Relaxing
20. Closely compacted
21. Soaked
22. Young child
23. Role player
26. More newly made
30. Regret
31. Artfully shy
32. Self-image
33. Betrayer
36. Sword thrust
38. Metal container
39. Numbers: abbr.
40. Male admirer
43. Covered the walls
47. Ocean's rise and fall
48. Somersault
49. Yale grad
50. Finishes
51. Wander
52. In the manner of
53. Nuisance
54. Had debts
55. Chum

**DOWN**

1. Close-by
2. Buffalo's lake
3. Veteran mariners
4. Palmer or Nicklaus
5. Concerning
6. Sampling of opinions
7. Snakelike fish
8. Halley's and Kohoutek's objects
9. "Once ____ a time . . ."
10. Bar bills
11. What ____ is new?
19. Duo
20. Buck's mate
22. Attempt
23. Singer Garfunkel
24. Mongrel
25. Earl Grey, e.g.
26. In favor of
27. Female fowl
28. Omelette ingredient
29. Caviar
31. Swindle
34. Most frozen
35. Light brown
36. Pruned
37. Employ
39. Gullible
40. Stair part
41. Red, white, or rose
42. Tacks on
43. Turn over the soil
44. Harvest
45. Jazz's Fitzgerald
46. Watch face
48. To's companion

# PUZZLE 123

**ACROSS**
1. Possesses
4. Heavy weights
8. Mama's hubby
12. TV personality Linkletter
13. Single entity
14. Actor Guinness
15. Sign of the lion
16. Unwilling
18. Aspect
20. Damage
21. Cabbagelike green
23. Explores
27. Cafe servers
30. Loud sucking noise
31. Hold title to
32. Lend an ____ (listen)
34. Fib
35. Fads
38. Dipped superficially
41. Me, ____, and I
43. Frame of mind
44. ____ Grande
45. General appearance
48. Judged approximately
53. Postal code
54. Astronaut Armstrong
55. Green citrus fruit
56. Yale nickname
57. Refuse
58. Goad
59. Baseball's Darling

**DOWN**
1. 50 percent
2. Length times width
3. Hose
4. Tortoise's cousin
5. First digit
6. None
7. Tree remnant
8. Security tour
9. Chicken ____ king
10. Enclosure
11. Pretend
17. Autos
19. I'll ____ my hat!
22. Bard's before
24. Earthmover
25. New York canal
26. Drove too fast
27. Night crawler, e.g.
28. Not at home
29. Melancholy
33. Ewe's mate
36. Weirdly
37. Slender
39. More daring
40. Call of disapproval
42. Young horses
46. Metric weight measure
47. Twirl around
48. Finish
49. Observe
50. Can metal
51. Hint
52. Flightless bird

# PUZZLE 124

**ACROSS**
1. Palm leaf
4. Rope material
8. Small restaurant
12. Bear cave
13. Evangelist Roberts
14. Amazed
15. Consume food
16. Pleasant
17. Twinge
18. Dueling sword
20. Warns
22. Hold up
24. Fragrance
25. Fusses
26. Arab prince
27. Reporter Donaldson
30. Tombstone initials
31. Play's setting
32. In favor of
33. French summer
34. ____ John Silver
35. Scoop out water
36. Shades of brown
37. Gold measure
38. Open pavilion
41. Country hotels
42. Assert
43. Stallion's mate
45. Mother sheep
48. Bank transaction
49. Graven image, e.g.
50. Male child
51. Hole punchers
52. Copper coin
53. Senator Kennedy

**DOWN**
1. "____ to Joy"
2. Grassland
3. Gazelle, e.g.
4. Bee's product
5. ____ Canal
6. Singer Davis
7. Imploring
8. Prank
9. Lab gel
10. Baptismal basin
11. Omelette ingredients
19. Dance step
21. Traditional legends
22. Venture
23. Revise copy
24. Portents
26. Part of EEC
27. Scantiest
28. Diva's solo
29. Shed feathers
31. Thick slice
35. Outlaw
36. Seabirds
37. Genuflected
38. Festive
39. Declare openly
40. Enthusiasm
41. Wrought ____
44. Fruit beverage
46. Grief
47. Conclude

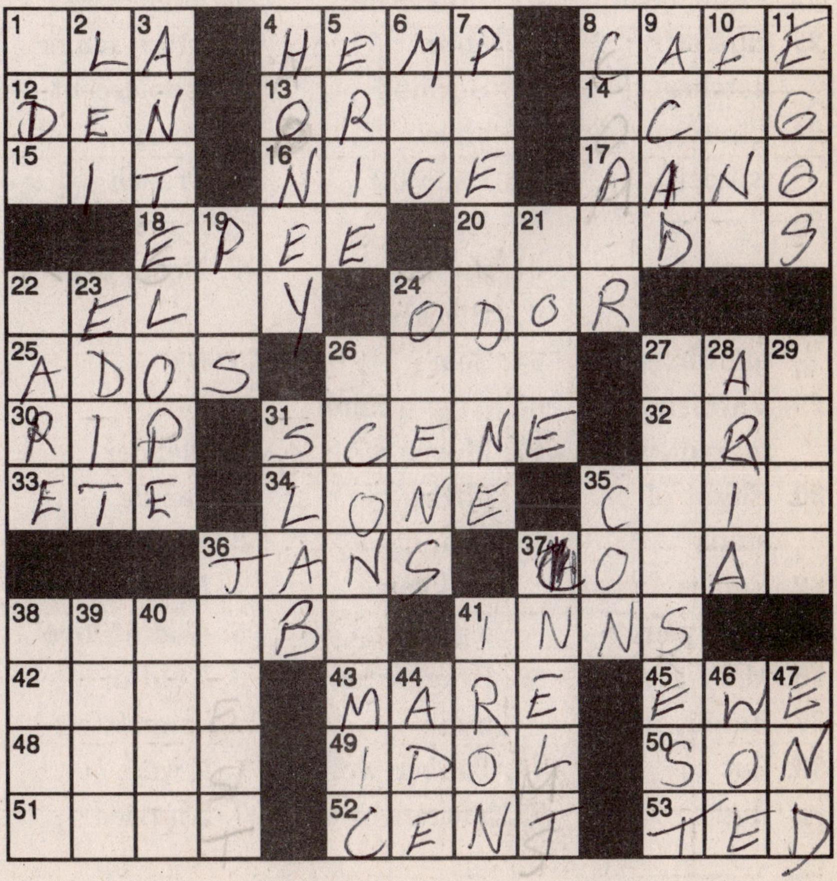

# PUZZLE 125

**ACROSS**

1. Look goggle-eyed
6. Full speed ___!
11. Took effect
16. Particular union
17. Food
19. Mount ___ (highest Adirondack peak)
20. Sign of approval: 5 wds.
22. French soup
23. Butterfly catcher
24. Church council
25. Can be rented
27. Damage allowance
29. Varnish ingredient
30. Flight of steps
32. Espies
33. Epic poetry
35. Most severe
37. Rabbit fur
39. Put to flight
40. Metal fastener
44. ___ of Troy
45. Beam of light
46. Thai or Chinese
47. Make eyes at
48. Neck warmer
49. Algerian city
52. Neighbor of Ore.
53. Summer shirt
54. Mental condition: 3 wds.
56. Before cycle or pod
57. Educating: abbr.
58. Burning glass
59. Palm off
60. Kismet
61. Swelling
63. Blackboard
64. Soars
65. Give a hand
67. Moves with difficulty
68. Hammers and saws, e.g.
69. Braggarts: hyph.
71. Timber wolf
72. Entranceway
75. "The Divine Comedy" author
76. Tourist aid
77. Vale
81. Thurmond and Kennedy. e.g.
83. Trumpeter Armstrong
85. Shad's output
86. Slither
87. Select carefully: 3 wds.
91. Anglo-Saxon laborers
92. Record envelopes
93. More senior
94. Adolescent years
95. French legislature
96. Noble ones

**DOWN**

1. Bias
2. Slender candle
3. Ease off
4. Nonsense!
5. God of love
6. Kind of committee: 2 wds.
7. Scurried
8. ___ tide
9. According to: 2 wds.
10. Make known
11. ___ Alonzo Stagg
12. Melds, in a certain card game
13. Family
14. School, in Rouen
15. Metric units of force
17. Lab burners
18. Flock of geese in flight
21. Hose material
26. War god
28. Indian home
30. Bread: 3 wds.
31. Feel out
34. Wrestling move
35. Piece of the action
36. Rise up
37. Photo captions
38. Asserts without proof
39. Chin wags
41. Kind of duck
42. Ophelia's brother
43. Begrudges

# PUZZLE 125

44. Afternoon refresher: 2 wds.
45. Scrutinize
48. Fr. holy woman: abbr.
49. Deletes
50. ____ and shine!
51. Aardvark's snack
54. Cut, as prices
55. Young horses
60. Surge
62. Misguided
63. Kind of touch?
64. Watch pocket
66. Fuss: hyph.
67. Throat tissues
68. Subject
70. Distorts
71. Praises highly
72. Something of value
73. Jam-packed
74. Foolish
76. "The Water Lilies" painter
78. Deteriorate
79. Also-ran
80. Suggestive looks
82. Hardy girl
83. Volcanic flow
84. Boutique
88. After bee
89. Actor Murray
90. Torero's hurrah

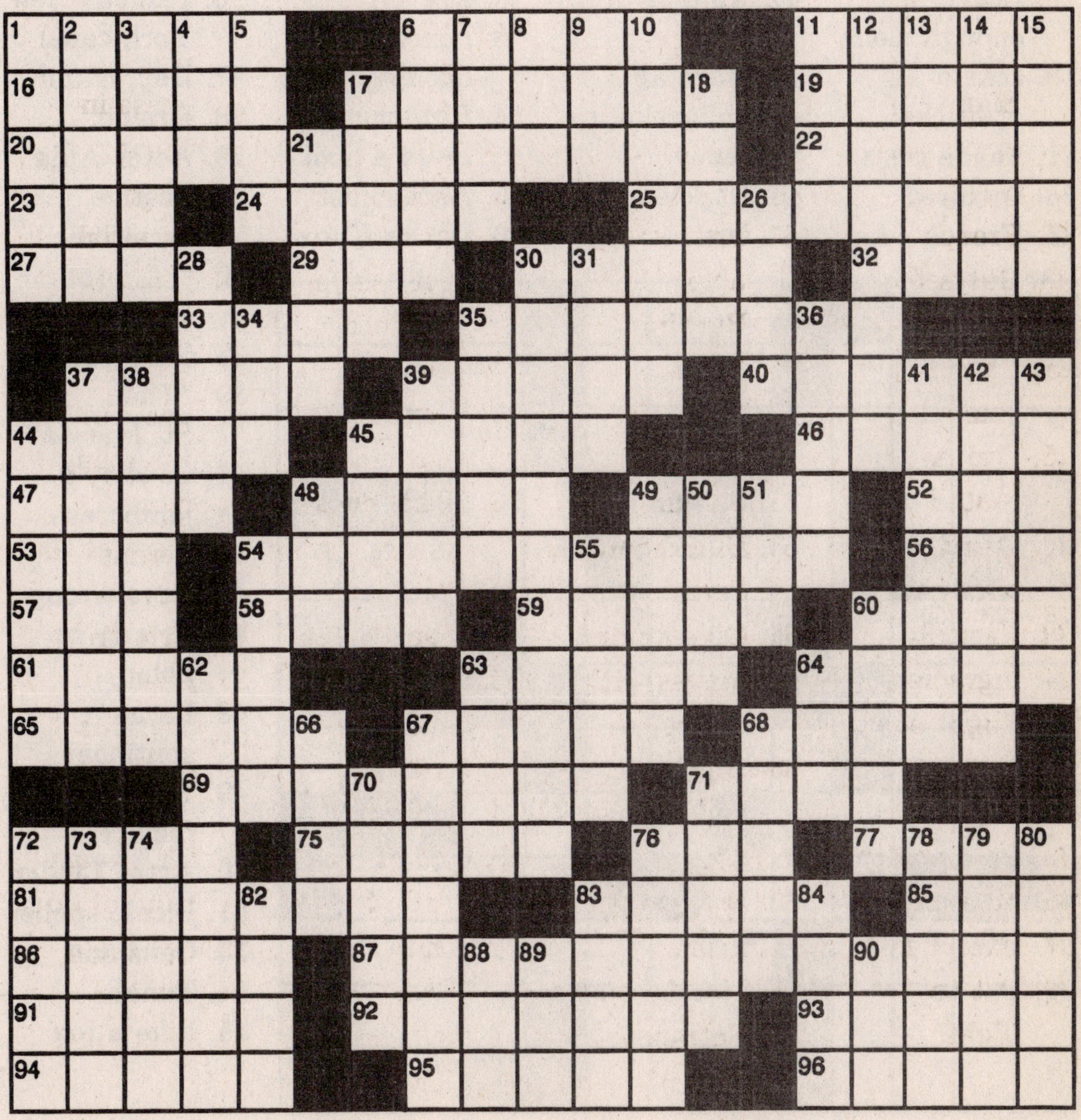

# PUZZLE 126

**ACROSS**

1. Souffle ingredient
4. Light-switch position
7. Time spans
11. Steed breed
13. Court
14. Distasteful
15. Storekeeper
17. Radiate
18. Leave ____ enough alone
19. Like a ____ of bricks
21. Shade trees
24. Inquired
28. Droops
31. Landed
33. Wrath
34. Pie ____ mode
35. Cozy room
36. Can metal
37. Chum
38. Make both ends ____
39. Borsch ingredient
40. Kind of drum
42. Staff
44. Have an obligation to repay
46. Napoleon's isle
49. Roe fish
52. "The Young and the ____"
56. Window unit
57. Good cheer
58. Jib, for one
59. Singing range
60. Porky's pad
61. Beam

**DOWN**

1. Spike of corn
2. Increased in size
3. Fence opening
4. Bird that gives a hoot
5. Antagonist
6. Dix or Knox
7. Ties, as the score
8. Edge
9. Mr. Baba
10. Gel
12. Cotton bundles
16. Under the weather
20. Feed-bag morsel
22. Fabricated
23. Hit the hay
25. Go fly a ____
26. Famous New York canal
27. Depression
28. Drains
29. Actor Alda
30. Festive occasion
32. "____ the Woods"
38. Cat's call
39. "The ____ of St. Mary's"
41. Cowboy's jamboree
43. Permit
45. Goes wrong
47. Grizzly or polar
48. Large continent
49. Health facility
50. Actor Linden
51. Picnic spoiler
53. Consume
54. Timid
55. Like a fox

# PUZZLE 127

**ACROSS**

1. Actress Merrill
5. Agent, for short
8. Pound in
12. Eve's son
13. Grow old
14. Great Lake
15. Authentic
16. Oath
17. "____ Misbehavin' "
18. Unmask
20. Swap
21. Cold season
24. Actor Woody ____
27. Beam of light
28. Health facility
31. Nourish
32. Drill part
33. Bring up
34. Child's game
35. Canary or cat, e.g.
36. Core
37. Teetered
39. Tale
43. Flee
47. Busy place
48. Epoch
50. Alda of "M*A*S*H"
51. Prayer ending
52. Part of L.A.
53. "On Golden ____"
54. Fender bender
55. Brenda or Ruta
56. Observes

**DOWN**

1. Defy
2. Wild mountain goat
3. ____ tide
4. Permitted
5. Black bird
6. Self
7. Sunday seat
8. Salty drop
9. Elaborate solo
10. ____ over matter
11. Guitarist Townshend
19. Transgress
20. Attempt
22. Dull
23. Have a hotdog
24. Toward the back, matey
25. Meadow
26. Support
28. Ocean
29. Average
30. Mr. Carney
32. Spelling contest
33. Porters
35. Snoop
36. "For ____ a jolly good . . ."
38. New ____ on life
39. Food fish
40. Once upon a ____
41. Baking need
42. Landlord's due
44. Bitter herb
45. Window ache?
46. Ceases
48. House addition
49. Fish eggs

# PUZZLE 128

**ACROSS**

1. ____ of the party
5. Recedes
9. "____ to Billy Joe"
12. Scent
13. Song refrain
14. Feather stole
15. Bull, to Juan
16. Boundary
18. Toboggans
20. "The World ____ Me a Living"
21. Criminals
23. Hair style
27. Blunder
29. Painful sounds
30. Swashbuckler Flynn
31. Unfasten
33. Do a cobbler's job
34. Baseball ploys
35. "____ Alibi"
36. Modern: pref.
37. Suffix with kitchen or major
38. Withstand
40. Lamb's pen name
42. Sea duck
45. Displeases
49. Short letter
50. Automobile
51. Curved molding
52. Get one's ____
53. Venture
54. Shredded
55. ____ Stanley Gardner

**DOWN**

1. Oodles
2. False god
3. Position of importance
4. Wear away
5. Fairy
6. British titles
7. ". . . when the wind ____ the cradle . . ."
8. Rational
9. Japanese sash
10. Forest creature
11. Hearing organ
17. Russian rulers
19. Wild plums
22. Of one's ____ free will
24. Entranceway
25. Actor's part
26. Bread spread
27. German river
28. Defeat badly
30. Scary
32. Guide
33. Legal matter
35. Furnace
38. Drummer Starr
39. Char
41. Plunder
43. And others: abbr.
44. Nerve network
45. Perform
46. Distant
47. Saute
48. Japanese coin

# PUZZLE 129

**ACROSS**
1. Highlander
5. Less ornate
10. Composer Franz ____
11. Like a tank
13. Merge
14. Film length
15. Charles Dutton's TV role
16. Sailor's stories
18. ____ Angelo, Texas
19. Ages of note
21. Extra bed
22. Animal hide
23. Wisest
25. Lamprey
27. Single
28. Gain
31. Swab
33. Ballet cheers
35. Spanish painter
38. Wire serv.
40. Like most cagers
41. Pig ____ poke
42. Singer Sinatra
44. Inlet
45. Nuttier
47. Decree
49. Wrecked completely
50. Reduces to tiny bits
51. Appoints
52. Requirement

**DOWN**
1. Spanish women
2. The Windy City
3. Stable morsel
4. Playing card
5. Novelist Charlotte ____
6. Famous cookie man
7. Decay
8. Wipe out
9. Kingly
10. Anglers' needs
11. Hairdo
12. Fender mark
17. Behave
20. City in Alabama
22. Fold
24. ____ Canals
26. Go astray
29. Greed
30. Patrolled
32. Blender products
33. Container
34. Bed boards
35. Main point
36. Tear provoker
37. WWII conference city
39. Cowboy's comrade
42. Manicurist's tool
43. Composer Jerome ____
46. On the ____ (fleeing)
48. Gaming cube

# PUZZLE 130

**ACROSS**

1. Singer Davis
4. Cathedral section
8. Orient
12. Metallic rock
13. Chair
14. Wedding band
15. "____ the ramparts . . ."
16. "The Scarlet Letter" author
18. Armadas
20. Goal
21. Actress Jillian
22. Nevada lake resort
26. Standing
28. Legendary
31. Generation
32. Louvre exhibit
33. "Lifestyles of the Rich and Famous" host
34. Spoil
35. Compete
36. Friendly nation
37. Invoice
38. Abated
40. Clamor
41. Singer Sayer
43. Bachelor's status
46. "Of Mice and Men" author
50. Crumple
51. Harbor
52. Siouan
53. Gardner of "The Night of the Iguana"
54. Yesteryear
55. Breaks bread
56. Thanksgiving vegetable

**DOWN**

1. Once in a blue ____
2. Province
3. "Don Quixote" author
4. Sickly
5. Garden vines
6. Witnessed
7. Jazz songstress James
8. Fragrance
9. Masculine title
10. Hotel kin
11. Season
17. Tether, as a horse
19. Writing fluid
23. "A Farewell to Arms" author
24. Of the mouth
25. British blueblood
26. Praise
27. Song for Sills
28. Lamprey
29. Amigo
30. Frigid
33. Loaded
37. Hamper
39. Select group
40. River embankments
42. Double reed instrument
43. Glasgow native
44. Etna flow
45. Dutch cheese
46. Saboteur
47. Also
48. Misjudge
49. Greek vowel

# PUZZLE 131

**ACROSS**
1. Baste
5. Prone
8. Munch
12. ____ of thumb
13. Beach
15. Turkey's neighbor
16. Quickest
17. Chessmen
19. ____ and bones
20. Pitcher handle
22. Grates
26. Billiards parlor
31. Actor Wallach
32. Ordinance
33. Jerk
35. Fellow
36. Piece (out)
37. Shoving
39. Prospector's test
42. Health facility
43. Soup dish
46. Edge up to
50. Brave
54. Greenish blue
55. ____ hour (last minute)
56. Graceful trees
57. Current
58. Summer shirt
59. Ready for picking

**DOWN**
1. Stumble
2. Air
3. Lobster gripper
4. Doghouse
5. Cigar residue
6. ____ and carrots
7. Chore
8. Porcelain
9. Work in a garden
10. Sounds of hesitation
11. Soaked
14. Move
18. Hindu garment
21. Went by horseback
23. 18-wheeler
24. Blueprint
25. Harmonize
26. Entreaty
27. They begin as acorns
28. Has unpaid bills
29. Frying need
30. Gangs
34. Exceeds
38. Cafe worker
40. Superior
41. Days of ____
44. Custom
45. Stringed instrument
47. Cold cuts shop
48. Torch
49. Otherwise
50. Fido's doc
51. Muhammad ____
52. Took by the hand
53. Haggard novel

# PUZZLE 132

**ACROSS**

1. British beer
4. Mineral spring
7. Let the cat out of the ___
10. Depression
12. Narrow road
14. GI's hangout: abbr.
15. Muttonchops
17. ___ Tin Tin
18. Pester
19. Uptight
21. Fire remains
24. Hardens
25. Sulk
26. Marches
29. Hockey star
30. Snakelike fish
31. Lode load
32. Capitol Hill VIP
35. Dither
36. Golfer's item
37. Strands
39. Washbowl
41. Exist
42. Cigarette residue
43. Kookie of "77 Sunset Strip"
49. Course: abbr.
50. Earth
51. Royal title
52. Smidgen
53. Horse command
54. TV's "L.A. ___"

**DOWN**

1. Paid notices
2. Oahu garland
3. To the bitter ___
4. Punches
5. Golfer's aim
6. Massachusetts cape
7. Puts a match to
8. Sales term
9. Disappeared
11. Doctrine
13. Chemical compound
16. Prohibit
20. Guido's high note
21. Heroic poetry
22. Additional
23. Polished
24. "My ___ Sal"
26. Through
27. City in Pennsylvania
28. Places
30. One billion years
33. Mr. Onassis
34. Sounds
35. Layers
37. ___ of contents
38. Twisted
39. "The Simpsons" son
40. Movie pooch
44. German Shepherd, e.g.
45. Never say ___
46. Nothing
47. Pitcher's concern: abbr.
48. Stitch

# PUZZLE 133

**ACROSS**

1. Olympic medal color
5. Key
9. Highlander's cap
12. Hidden place
13. Ornery
14. Bullfighter's cheer
15. Lab burner
16. Stringed instrument
18. Native Alaskan
20. Rounded roof
21. Apprehends
23. Sale items
26. More reliable
30. Anger
31. Snack
32. Church official
34. Coal weight
35. Stalk
37. Most gung-ho
39. Voice above bass
41. Shade of green
42. Glide
44. Me
48. Correspond
51. Russian emperor
52. Night bird
53. Utopia
54. Soothe
55. Yup
56. Apartment fee
57. Tidy up

**DOWN**

1. Mirth
2. Dobbin's dinner
3. Chain part
4. Empties
5. Not moving
6. Body of water
7. Make shore
8. Donate
9. Permit
10. ___ Baba
11. Blokes
17. Persian poet Khayyam
19. Aussie's buddy
22. Family car
24. Easily bruised items
25. Mailed
26. Evaluate
27. Price
28. Kitchen tools
29. Army
33. Depend
36. Satellite
38. Took it easy
40. Ten-speed bike
43. Tease
45. Isaac's son
46. Young girl
47. Stew
48. Reserved
49. Have money problems
50. Study

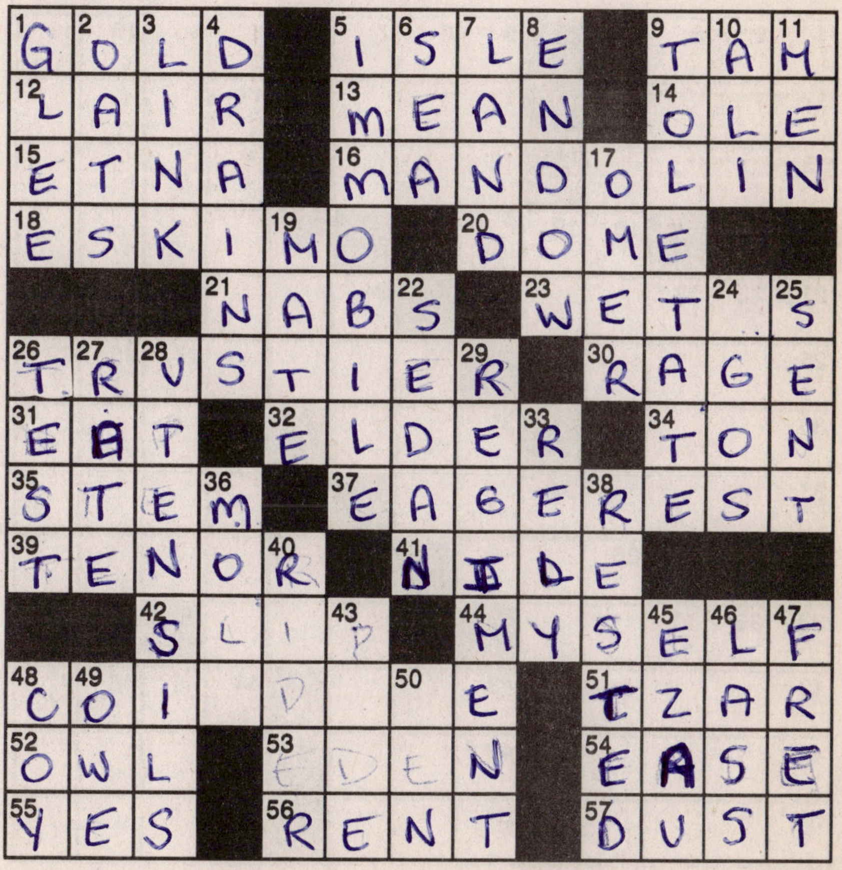

# PUZZLE 134

## ACROSS

1. Winter outerwear
5. ____ Van Winkle
8. Poker word
12. Cry of pain
13. Actress Lupino
14. "____ Homeward, Angel"
15. Elm or maple
16. Mythology
18. Bowling ____
20. Baseball teams
21. Courteous
24. Hog
25. Old saying
26. Escape
30. Hair accessory
31. It's in the ____
32. Floor square
33. Handled
35. Pitcher's powder
36. Pug, e.g.
37. Proofreaders' marks
38. Ragouts
41. Royal splendor
42. Huge
44. James ____ Jones
48. Cain's brother
49. Behave
50. Met song
51. Coral deposit
52. Positive word
53. Mr. Foxx

## DOWN

1. Small bed
2. "____ Town"
3. ____ in the hole
4. "The Three Little Pigs" enemy
5. Firearm
6. Matinee ____
7. School mate
8. Avocado
9. Lunch time for some
10. Ripped
11. ____ out (supplements)
17. Make a sweater
19. Broke bread
21. Agreement
22. Skunk feature
23. Metallic fabric
24. Wooden nail
26. Move about
27. Street smart
28. Touched down
29. Longings
31. Plead
34. Turn's partner
35. Male sheep
37. Young horses
38. Battle reminder
39. "I Want ____ Happy"
40. General Robert ____
41. Walk to and fro
43. Utter
45. "You ____ My Sunshine"
46. Disencumber
47. Young gentleman

# PUZZLE 135

**ACROSS**

1. Clutter
5. Female swine
8. That girl
11. So be it
12. Stalemate
13. Pack away
14. Out of ____
15. Strong beer
16. Leisure
17. Respect
19. Jeopardy
21. Kill
22. Bro's sibling
23. Enraged
27. Pick up
31. Female rabbit
32. Excavate
34. Quilting session
35. Sugary
38. Come before
41. Up-to-date
43. Hole-making tool
44. Haircutter
47. More orderly
51. Lily's relative
52. Inclined
54. Flutter
55. ____ at hand
56. Fixed charge
57. Fencing weapon
58. Jewel
59. Small amount
60. Writing table

**DOWN**

1. Partner
2. Australian birds
3. Forwarded
4. Ahchoo
5. Put an emblem on
6. Lubricant
7. Dandelions
8. Without a date
9. Stocking
10. Pitcher
13. Meaning
18. Hearing organ
20. Be under the weather
23. Newspaper notices
24. At this time
25. Command to a horse
26. Sag
28. Humorist Burrows
29. "The Hunt for ____ October"
30. Society-page word
33. Awarded
36. Smoldering coal
37. Boot tip
39. Ram's mate
40. Scratched
42. Rough sketch
44. Whack
45. Away from the wind
46. Meander
48. Adhesive strip
49. Plumb and Arden
50. Strong smell
53. Black-eyed ____

# PUZZLE 136

**ACROSS**

1. Move the tail
4. Astound
7. Pop
11. Pity!
13. Singer Torme
14. Fragrance
15. Explain
17. Given temporarily
18. Free
19. Large deer
21. Consider
23. "Leave ____ to Heaven"
24. Epic
25. Of currency
30. Molecule part
31. Likely
32. One of the Great Lakes
33. Answering-machine calls
35. Dryer residue
36. Cover
37. Dressed
38. Frenzy
41. "A Boy Named ____"
42. Ahead of the ____
43. Depositor's concern
48. American author
49. Expert aviator
50. Shopper's quest
51. Turn
52. Forget-me-____
53. Bread choice

**DOWN**

1. Roll of money
2. Beer's relative
3. Step on the ____
4. Within
5. Spider's trap
6. Basics
7. Individual effort
8. Some poems
9. Over and ____ with
10. Special skill
12. Shrieks
16. Edge
20. Mine yield
21. Social event
22. I's
23. Wished
24. America's uncle
25. Houdini, for one
26. Bank employees
27. Diva's highlight
28. Skin
29. As of now
34. "The Greatest"
37. Actor's signal
38. Use the beeper
39. So be it!
40. Require
41. Printer's notation
42. Gossip
44. Sgt., e.g.
45. Head feature
46. Shady
47. Short-sleeve shirt

## CAMOUFLAGE

# PUZZLE 137

**The answers to the clues can be found in the diagram, but they have been camouflaged. Their letters are in correct order, but sometimes they are separated by extra letters which have been inserted throughout the diagram. You must black out all the extra camouflage letters. The remaining letters will be used in words reading across and down. Solve Across and Down together to determine the correct letters where there is a choice. The number of answer words in a row or column is indicated by the number of clues.**

| | 1 | 2 | 3 | 4 | 5 | 6 | 7 | 8 | 9 | 10 | 11 | 12 | 13 | 14 | 15 |
|---|---|---|---|---|---|---|---|---|---|---|---|---|---|---|---|
| 1 | G | R | A | T | D | E | B | I | R | D | D | P | N | A | T |
| 2 | S | O | L | I | C | D | E | N | E | W | P | A | R | K | S |
| 3 | P | L | O | P | D | E | L | N | F | O | I | L | R | I | L |
| 4 | E | G | H | E | G | N | U | S | E | O | D | E | I | R | E |
| 5 | A | L | S | T | O | S | E | E | R | R | I | E | S | O | N |
| 6 | C | H | A | R | M | T | S | T | R | E | E | W | E | N | D |
| 7 | P | O | W | E | N | T | I | C | E | S | M | A | N | S | H |
| 8 | I | A | A | L | G | E | N | D | D | A | P | L | A | N | Y |
| 9 | A | P | R | R | O | N | S | L | A | G | E | N | R | I | N |
| 10 | T | E | N | E | R | T | S | A | N | I | D | T | R | I | M |
| 11 | C | R | I | B | L | A | S | T | M | E | E | T | A | R | D |
| 12 | C | H | R | E | D | I | I | T | H | C | O | B | E | R | N |
| 13 | H | O | N | K | E | B | L | E | A | T | R | A | Y | W | E |
| 14 | E | V | P | E | N | L | O | R | R | E | S | P | I | E | S |
| 15 | R | E | G | R | R | E | S | S | T | A | B | B | L | E | T |

**ACROSS**

1. Classify • Winged one • Author Conroy
2. Trustworthy • New Jersey airport
3. Trudge • Sprite • Gusher's output
4. Chick's mom • Manipulated • Wrath
5. Type of saxophone • Weird • Male child
6. Navigation aid • Scatter • Terminate
7. Have debts • French city • Shatter
8. Schedule • Frolic
9. Child's garment • Bar order
10. Dogma • Morose • Comedian Conway
11. Cradle • Final • Encounter
12. Revise • Antler
13. Whet • Flock sound • Unrefined
14. Fifty-fifty • Folk knowledge • Pastry
15. Backslide • Shelve

**DOWN**

1. Vichy, e.g. • Baseball position
2. Tumble • Diamond name • Traipse
3. Island greeting • Alert
4. Ascot • Larch, e.g. • Norm's quaff
5. Actor Ameche • 50th anniversary
6. First home • Camp shelter • Capable
7. Azure • Goes astray • Storage places
8. Map feature • Rackets
9. Allude • Certain cheese • Headgear
10. Eroded • Wise one • Afternoon social
11. Achieved • Hinder • Globe
12. Ashen • Cartoonist Kelly • Spigot
13. Get up • Seed covering
14. Ohio city • Knight's title • Teeny
15. Care for • Religious song

# PUZZLE 138

## FOUR-MOST

**All of the 4-letter entries in this crossword puzzle are listed separately and are in alphabetical order. Use the numbered clues as solving aids to help you determine where each 4-letter entry goes in the diagram.**

**4-LETTER ENTRIES**

ABED
AGES
AINT
AMEN
AMOR
ANTS
AREA
ARIA
ARTS
ASKS
BASE
BRED
CELT
CORN
ENDS
EROS
ESNE
EWES
HALL
HERO
LEAD
LEOS
NESS
PART
PETS
PIER
PITS
RANG
RANT
REAR
ROAN
SATE
SEAN
SODA
SPAT
STAN
STOW
TREY

**ACROSS**

13. Fabulist
17. North Pole resident
18. Supplies place
20. Previous to
27. Flights of steps
30. Riled
33. Heads
34. Pilot
35. Common verb
38. Farmer's output
40. Half a score
41. Daniel or Pat
42. Singer Winwood
43. Repentence
45. Jets
51. Chicken ____ king
54. Actor Cabot
57. Thick books
61. Talk

**DOWN**

4. Period
5. Histories
7. ____ de Janeiro
8. ____ and feather
9. Lifework
12. Beret's kin
14. "The Pickwick ____"
19. Enroll
22. ____ a boy!
25. Sandpiper
28. Meeker
29. Make up for
30. By oneself
31. Consumed
32. Used a car
34. Winter's Jack ____
41. Cooks in water
42. Tilts
44. Asian peninsula
45. Pod vegetable
47. Carols
54. Roads: abbr.
55. La's cohort
56. Actor Hunter
58. Ajar, poetically

# PUZZLE 139

**ACROSS**

1. Macaws
5. Electric power org.
8. Newborn
12. Butterfly's kin
13. Alum
14. Frugal one
15. Rose's love
16. Evaluate
17. Lend ___
18. Aaron's forte
20. Begin
21. Plains abodes
22. Twirl
23. ___ de mer
24. Youth
28. Cast a ballot
31. Great reviews
32. "I love," to Cato
33. Astronaut Shepard
34. Cloaked
35. Slipped
36. Japanese monetary unit
37. Ascetic monk
38. Pillar
39. Grab control of
41. Sequence: abbr.
42. Greek war god
43. Boils over
46. Rooted
48. Off-key sound
50. Lugs
51. Amaze
52. Clinton's veep
53. Like ___ out of the blue
54. Compass direction
55. Pertaining to a time
56. Cleans the floor
57. Before, to a bard
58. Ruby and cerise

**DOWN**

1. Asian nursemaid
2. Android
3. "One Day at ___"
4. Cattle ranchers' competitors
5. Across: pref.
6. Large tubs
7. Summer beverage
8. Top ___ (headliner)
9. State with confidence
10. Defeat
11. Slip up
13. Watery food
14. Glossy fabrics
19. Leaf through
20. Alacrity
22. Cut off
24. Hoglike mammal
25. Football's Sayers
26. Actor Jannings
27. Pestered
28. Huge
29. Olive genus
30. Armored vehicle
31. Garden tools
34. ___ in (surrendered)
35. Odder
37. Wooded region
38. Soothsayer
40. Artists' stands
41. Trick
43. Pickle in brine
44. Van Dyke's costar
45. Fine violin, for short
46. Pitcher Newsom
47. Over
48. Betelgeuse, e.g.
49. Slippery fish
50. Highland cap
51. Bishopric

# Keyword

# PUZZLE 140

**To find the KEYWORD, fill in the blanks in words 1 through 10 with the correct missing letters and transfer those letters to the correspondingly numbered squares in the diagram. Approach with care—this puzzle is not as simple as it first appears.**

| 1 | 2 | 3 | 4 | 5 | 6 | 7 | 8 | 9 | 10 |
|---|---|---|---|---|---|---|---|---|---|
| | | | | | | | | | |

1. B _ I L S
2. F L A I _
3. F A _ L S
4. _ A I L S
5. H E A _ S
6. G R _ V E
7. _ H E E R
8. V O T E _
9. P _ L E S
10. C A R _ S

# PUZZLE 141

**• I'LL FLY AWAY •**

**ACROSS**
1. Billy or nanny
5. On in years
8. School org.
11. Woody's son
12. Debatable
14. Witch
15. Black birds
17. Sooner than, to a bard
18. Make a doily
19. "____ Peace"
21. Shoestrings
24. Studies diligently
25. Spanish gold
26. Threesome
28. Cave dwellers
31. Overcook greatly
33. Conclusion
34. Metal fastener
35. Poet Lazarus
36. "____ Small World"
38. Musical syllable
39. Unlocks
41. Coins, in Chihuahua
43. President Ford
45. Ventilate
46. The Gay Nineties, e.g.
47. Fish-eating duck
52. Soft metal
53. Bench, e.g.
54. Loosen
55. Tennis unit
56. TLC givers
57. Hurried

**DOWN**
1. Car fuel
2. Table scrap
3. Chicken ____ king
4. Rich cake
5. Leave out
6. Actor Chaney
7. Flowering trees
8. Game birds
9. Mountain lake
10. Matured
13. Russian ruler of yore
16. Endure
20. Insurgents, for short
21. Ear part
22. Calla lily, e.g.
23. Diving bird
24. Pub servings
27. Sleigh puller?
29. Tropical root
30. Resorts, of sorts
32. California valley
37. Capital of Western Samoa
40. Stately trees
42. Marine birds
43. Obtains
44. Buffalo's lake
45. G-men, e.g.
48. Bled, as dye
49. Dope
50. Opposite of WNW
51. Scarlet

# PUZZLE 142

**• CAPTAIN COURAGEOUS •**

**ACROSS**
1. Otherwise
5. Automobile
8. Guns a motor
12. Ogle
13. "____ to a Nightingale"
14. Egg-shaped
15. Courageous
17. Actor Arnaz
18. Assist
19. Unwrapped
21. Gleam
24. Butter substitute
25. Peel
26. The jig ____!
27. Wager
30. Noah's vessel
31. Bouts of ill-temper
32. Altar constellation
33. Inlet
34. Suits to ____
35. Journey
36. Whirring sound
37. Fox trot, e.g.
38. Mexican treat
41. Heavy weight
42. Finished
43. Courageously
48. Ripped
49. Charged atom
50. Peter Gunn's girl
51. Is in debt
52. Expected
53. Engrossed

**DOWN**
1. Sprite
2. Confederate general
3. Ocean
4. Mission
5. Dorm dweller
6. Commercials
7. Courageous
8. Cowboy show
9. Level
10. Flower holder
11. Skidded
16. Kindled
20. Fills with energy
21. Snatch
22. Pisa dough, once
23. Black
24. Willow
26. Courageous
27. Farm building
28. Norse explorer
29. Recording
31. Cruise
35. Oiler
36. Exposes
37. "What's up, ____?"
38. Dorothy's dog
39. Assert
40. Only
41. "Name That ____"
44. Comedian Costello
45. Actress Lupino
46. Facial feature
47. Still

## CLAPBOARD

# PUZZLE 143

**In this crossword puzzle, all words in the same row or column overlap by one or two letters.**

**ACROSS**

1. Basilica's kin
8. The Last Frontier
14. Rig
15. Theater machine
16. Good fortune
17. Dnieper River city
18. Wanderer
21. Refrain syllables
22. Waterside plant
24. "Pretty Woman" actor
25. Unearthly
29. Conquistador's quest
30. Texas city
33. Yearly
34. Bowler's target
35. Like some gases
36. Recounted
38. Twist or jerk
39. Color
40. Columnist Bombeck
42. Of a cheek bone
44. Very cold
47. Attack
51. Rim
52. ____ leather
53. Lunchtimes
54. Caravansary
56. Likeness
58. Selfishness
61. Affected
65. Henley and Ho
66. Urbane
67. ____, zwei, drei
68. Supreme Court number
69. White poplar
70. Excuses
71. Take to court
72. Wallows
73. Fodder structures
74. CIA's predecessor
75. Kernel

**DOWN**

1. Wrapper material
2. Zodiac sign
3. Arizona city
4. Increase
5. Skin
6. Lees
7. Meanders
8. Slightly open
9. Myth
10. Estate measure
11. Night twinkler
12. "____-Tiki"
13. Funnyman Johnson
19. Inland sea
20. Vitamin B3
23. German river
26. Laws
27. Litter's littlest
28. Voted in
30. Low numbers
31. Banal
32. Producer Lesser
37. Baby's seat, often
38. Sink outlet
41. Madras queen
43. Italian money, once
45. Lachrymose drop
46. Unworldly girl
48. Saturate
49. "____ or Later"
50. Editions
51. Moon vehicle acronym
52. Window part
55. Fray
57. Originate
58. Dutch cheese
59. Mongolian desert
60. Cay
61. Skirt type
62. Verne captain
63. Little bites
64. Notable act

| | | | | | | | | | | | | |
|---|---|---|---|---|---|---|---|---|---|---|---|---|
| 1 | 2 | 3 | 4 | 5 | 6 | 7 | 8 | 9 | 10 | 11 | 12 | 13 |
| 14 | | | | 15 | | | | | | | | |
| 16 | | | 17 | | | 18 | 19 | | | | 20 | |
| 21 | | 22 | 23 | | 24 | | | 25 | 26 | 27 | | 28 |
| 29 | | 30 | | | 31 | 32 | 33 | | | | | |
| 34 | 35 | | | | 36 | | 37 | 38 | | | | |
| 39 | | 40 | 41 | 42 | | 43 | 44 | | | 45 | 46 | |
| 47 | 48 | 49 | | 50 | 51 | | 52 | | | | | |
| 53 | | | | 54 | | 55 | | 56 | | 57 | | |
| 58 | 59 | | 60 | | 61 | | 62 | 63 | | | | 64 |
| 65 | | | 66 | | | | 67 | | 68 | | | |
| 69 | | | | 70 | | | | | | 71 | | |
| 72 | | | | 73 | | | 74 | | 75 | | | |

# PUZZLE 144

## ACROSS

1. Grinding tooth
6. Pass on
11. Multitude
16. Actress Massey
17. M. Zola
18. Mythological hunter
19. Wise lawgiver
20. Birds sent out from the ark
21. "A Boy ___ Sue" (Johnny Cash song)
22. Disappearing judge
24. Connect notes
25. Electors
26. Led
28. Female zebra
29. Stake at a card game
32. Dispose (of)
33. Tousle
34. ___ result
37. Lugged
39. "___ of the River" (John Garfield fim)
40. Aluminum coin of Italy, once
41. Beside: prefix
42. Penny Singleton role
44. Employee at a posh hotel
45. Turkish title of respect
46. Unusual
47. Not many
48. Take it easy
51. Sparkle
53. Conceit
56. Flabbergasted
57. Golfer's aim
58. Became involved in
60. Thus far
61. Chianti
62. "___ Yeller"
63. Gentle
64. Light
65. Zorba's home
67. Channel
70. ". . . man ___ mouse?"
71. Window in a projecting structure
75. Raise
76. ___-garde
78. Marsh bird
79. Clear the slate
80. Projection
81. "___ of a Wayside Inn"
82. Dealt out sparingly
83. Primp
84. Frozen rain

## DOWN

1. Catchall category: abbr.
2. Swan genus
3. Singer Falana
4. TV's "___ World"
5. Female VIP in India
6. ___ herring
7. Showed feeling
8. Furious
9. On the sheltered side
10. Sycophant's word
11. Reveres
12. Harangue
13. Frost
14. Performer
15. Make ___ meet
23. Seldom
25. Immense
27. Queen of Carthage
28. Clio, for one
29. Expert
30. Downy coating
31. Having three: prefix
33. "___ Night Out" (Joan Fontaine film)
34. Nothing
35. Sooner
36. Use a shuttle
38. Wild goat
39. Mr. Cantor
40. "Burke's ___"
43. ___ prosequi
44. Outlet
45. Naughty
47. Warded (off)
48. Bit of sunshine
49. Fleece source
50. Tennis term
51. Departed
52. Far: prefix
53. Geologic division
54. Prized object
55. Keats output
57. Sword's handle
59. Adjective for Rome
61. Lingered
62. Sherbet flavor
64. Outmoded
65. Student's concern
66. Prices
67. Rural structure
68. Cape chaser
69. Iranian coin
70. Once more
72. 5,280 feet
73. Fencing sword
74. Repose
76. High mountain
77. Decade

## AT 6'S AND 7'S

# PUZZLE 145

**Clues to all the 6- and 7-letter entries in this crossword puzzle are listed first, and they are in scrambled order. Use the numbered clues as solving hints to help you determine where each one belongs in the diagram.**

**6-LETTER ENTRIES**

Hors d'oeuvre
Traps
Cubic meters
Sap
Cut
Put in a common fund
Rascals
Contemporary
Embodiment
Removes
Corrects
Whacked
Value
Loll
Cylindrical
Terence comedy
Last syllable of a word
Beauty shops

**7-LETTER ENTRIES**

Childish
Filters
Having teeth
Mass-transit system
Game bird
Arizona city

**ACROSS**

14. Napoleon's downfall
17. Flows out
18. 1501, to Caesar
21. "____ Got Sixpence"
22. Diagram
24. Hit the trail
25. Amo, ____, amat
26. ____ Wences
28. ____ Moines
29. Watch part
32. In favor of
37. Sass
39. Ooze
41. Chap
42. Photos
44. Weirs
45. Tuns
47. Throw off
48. Tavern quaff
51. ____ de France
52. Reduce in volume
56. Started a paragraph

**DOWN**

2. Without property
3. Gary native
4. Vehicle
5. Finials
6. "____ Be Not Proud"
7. Rise
8. Camera aperture
9. "____ pro nobis"
12. Firemen's needs
15. French female friends
20. Midway attractions
27. Tear again
29. Entrances
31. With it
32. Adversary
34. Indian fan
35. Susa natives
36. Remove hair from
41. Rectory
44. Ancient Roman province
45. Pennies
46. Hawaii, for one
49. Lairs
50. Always
53. English river
55. Southern constellation

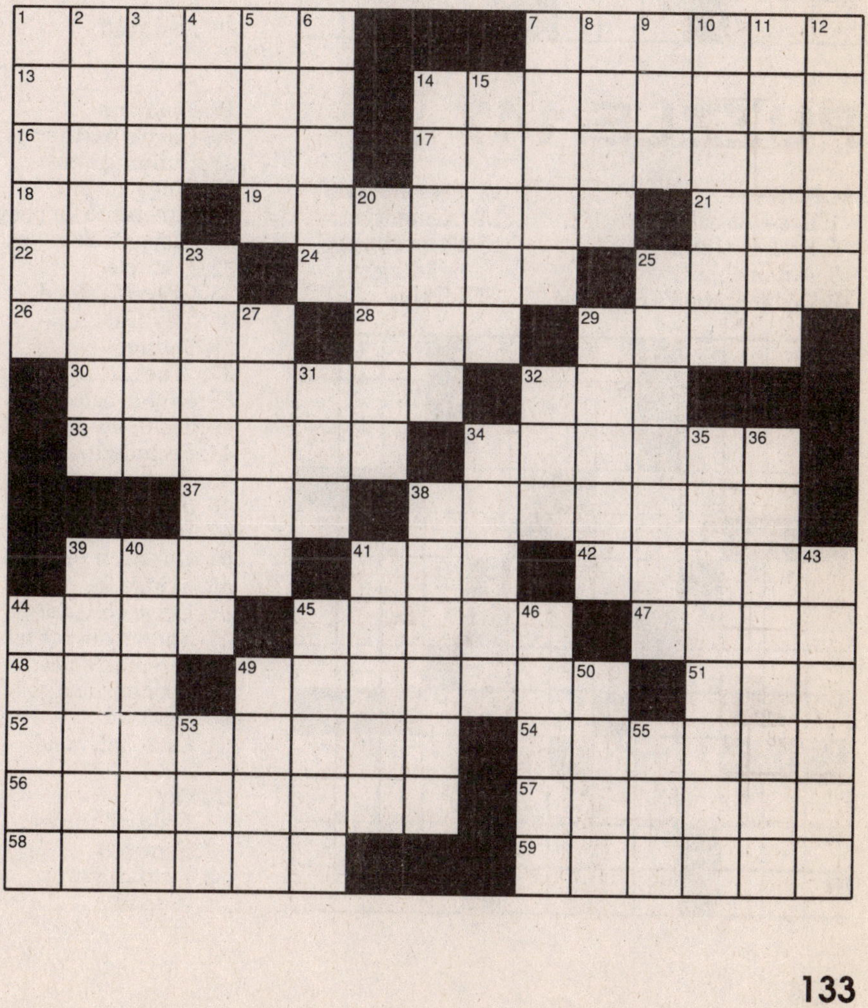

# PUZZLE 146

**ACROSS**
1. Signal
6. Plead
9. Chum
12. Carved stone
13. Raw metal
14. Honest ____
15. Used a keyboard
16. Aborigines
18. Documents of ownership
20. Tennis barriers
21. ____ and bolts
24. Saves
26. Singleton
27. Provided fodder for
28. Rent
32. Phoned
34. Breeding ground
35. Walk like a rooster
36. Kind of window
37. Table support
38. Approaches
40. Give in
41. "Flower Drum ____"
44. Venomous snake
46. Genuflected
48. Opera stars
52. Frozen water
53. Before, in poetry
54. Likeness
55. Senator Kennedy
56. "____ a Mad, Mad, Mad, Mad World"
57. Principle

**DOWN**
1. Perform
2. Secular
3. Current measure, for short
4. Hollow grasses
5. Style
6. Fastened
7. Wipe out
8. Obtain
9. Do road work
10. Egg on
11. Minus
17. Map feature
19. Barely managed, with out
21. Dozes
22. Apartment
23. Rip
25. Clever plan
27. Lavish party
29. Fit
30. Acorn, e.g.
31. Boundary
33. Sudden thrust
34. Hinged fastener
36. Aisle walkers
39. Turn aside
40. Illegal activity
41. Brief play
42. Single time
43. Necessity
45. Prepare for publication
47. Necklace of flowers
49. Moving truck
50. Mature
51. Matched group

# PUZZLE 147

**ACROSS**
1. Brew, as coffee
5. Pack in tightly
9. Automobile
12. Congregation's response
13. Personal castle
14. Commotion
15. Farm storage building
16. Lively
18. Fashions
20. Dash's partner
21. Building sites
23. Sings alone
27. Substance for chewing
30. Cleopatra's river
32. Encircle
33. Graceful steed
35. "My Gal ____"
36. Lounge
37. "The ____ Duckling"
38. Nights before holidays
40. Small number
41. Secluded valleys
43. Bouncing sound
45. Swiss peak
47. Bedevils
51. Question responder
55. Bridge fee
56. Drive obliquely
57. Showroom model
58. Fireman's need
59. Sooner than, to a bard
60. Whirled
61. One-dish meal

**DOWN**
1. Football throw
2. Send out
3. Put faith in
4. Mound
5. Scold
6. Baseball's Darling
7. In the midst of
8. Short notes
9. House pet
10. Citrus drink
11. Staff
17. Coral island
19. Long, long time
22. Hard worker
24. Bread shape
25. Leak out slowly
26. Gush forth
27. Showy ornament
28. Strong impulse
29. Shopping area
31. Part of an atom
34. Organizational edict
39. That girl
42. Snow vehicles
44. Vows
46. Get ready
48. Chimney dirt
49. Additional
50. Many
51. Devoured
52. Neither fish ____ fowl
53. Lay eyes on
54. Flightless bird

# PUZZLE 148

**• RADIO DAYS •**

**ACROSS**
1. Stage article
5. Fountain specialties
10. Islamic laws
14. Make muddy
15. Cross
16. Plate
17. Dexterous
18. Supernatural
19. Singer James
20. Flat-topped hill
21. Radio's member of the RCMP
23. Was located
25. Reservoir
26. Tropical fruit
29. Laconic
32. Large African antelope
33. Swiss river
34. CIA's predecessor
37. Leader of the Secret Squadron
41. New Zealand bird
42. Contend
43. "A poem lovely as ___"
44. Sphere of action
46. Riding horses
47. "A Bell for ___"
50. Newsman Brokaw
51. Radio's master detective
56. Hero
60. In the shape of an egg
61. Bond portrayer
62. End follower
63. Venetian magistrate
64. Actress Potts
65. Unchanging
66. Summers, in Marseille
67. Sully
68. Spanish artist

**DOWN**
1. Baby vehicle
2. Lounging garment
3. Bribes
4. Genial
5. Afternoon nap
6. Portland's state: abbr.
7. Scamper
8. Expecting eagerly
9. Prophet
10. "___ Fideles"
11. Again
12. Merchant John Jacob ___
13. Classic Western
22. Double curve
24. Brazilian tree
26. Gesture
27. Structures like wings
28. California wine center
29. City in Florida
30. Sandusky's lake
31. Cerise or titian
33. Soon
34. Monster in a fairy tale
35. Shack
36. Fr. holy women
38. Clinch
39. Alliance acronym
40. Lists separately
44. Leg joints
45. Bird of myth
46. "Sesame ___"
47. Terminal on a battery
48. Piece of turf
49. "Nor iron bars ___"
52. He loves: Lat.
53. Columnist Barrett
54. Singer Tennille
55. Moran or Gray
57. Peace symbol
58. Humdinger
59. Period after Mardi Gras

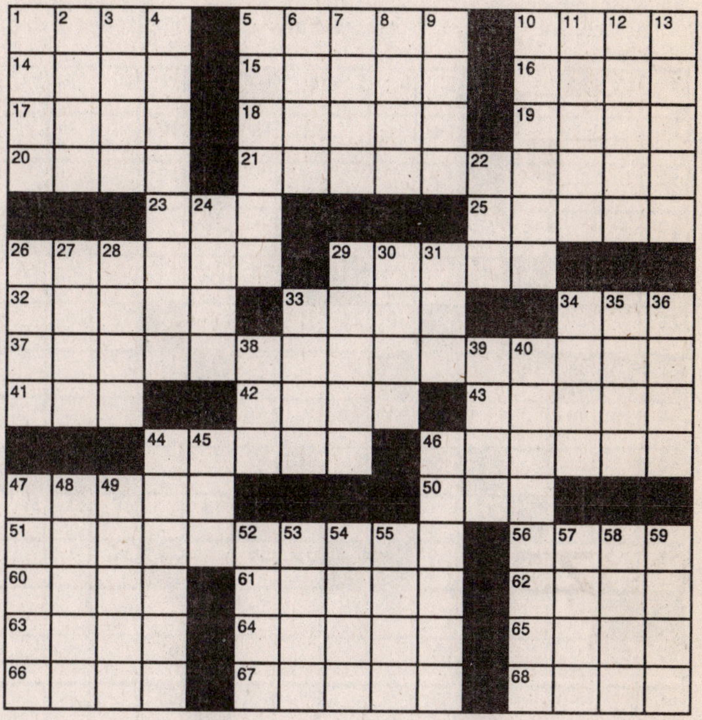


---

# IN THE MIDDLE

# PUZZLE 149

**Fill in the squares to form a word which is the missing link to connect the two given words. For example, if the two given words were CRAB and SAUCE, the missing link would be APPLE (Crab apple, Applesauce).**

1.

2.

3.

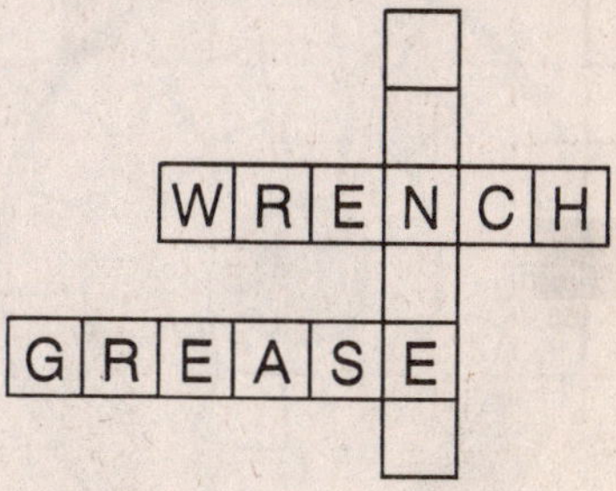

# PUZZLE 150

**• MEN OF LETTERS •**

**ACROSS**

1. "M*A*S*H" actress
5. Troubadour love song
9. Newspaper notice, for short
13. "Falcon Crest" product
14. Carols
16. Entreaty
17. ___ boy!
18. ___ of Langerhans
19. Architect Saarinen
20. Writer Eliot
23. River to the Yangtze
24. Diocese
25. Church services
28. Choose
30. Dripping
33. Exclamation of derision
34. Former nuclear group: abbr.
36. Stooge's name
37. Give medicine to
38. Writer Tolkien
43. French articles
44. Sister
45. Questioning sounds
46. Dry
47. Garret
49. Tank ship
53. Japanese straw mat
55. Swedish village
57. Bullfight cheer
58. Writer Milne
62. Actor Betz
64. Seize illegally
65. Entertainers' union: abbr.
66. Butter substitute
67. Pianist Blake
68. Steal a glance
69. Finest
70. Spool
71. "Rule Britannia" composer

**DOWN**

1. Wrap in bandages
2. Nevertheless, of old
3. Chant
4. Sports group
5. Liqueur flavoring
6. Red-ink items
7. Waistband
8. Away from the weather
9. Lifts the lid
10. Comment after a sneeze
11. Suffix of employment
12. Universal ideal
15. Cattle riot
21. Fall flower
22. Beam
26. Comfort
27. Writer Silverstein
29. Preserves
31. Muscat native
32. Spanish village
35. Go on
37. Bandleader Arnaz
38. Fair
39. Draft classification
40. Metric land measures
41. Kook
42. Valerie Harper role
47. "I ___ Camera"
48. Darling: Fr.
50. Rooming-house tenant
51. Number of football players
52. Clean the yard again
54. Divvy up
56. Oust
59. Supreme Assyrian god
60. Car treatment, for short
61. California valley
62. Corn holder
63. Malt brew

# PUZZLE 151

## Spinwheel

**This game works two ways, inward and outward. Place the answers to the clues below in the diagram beginning at the corresponding number.**

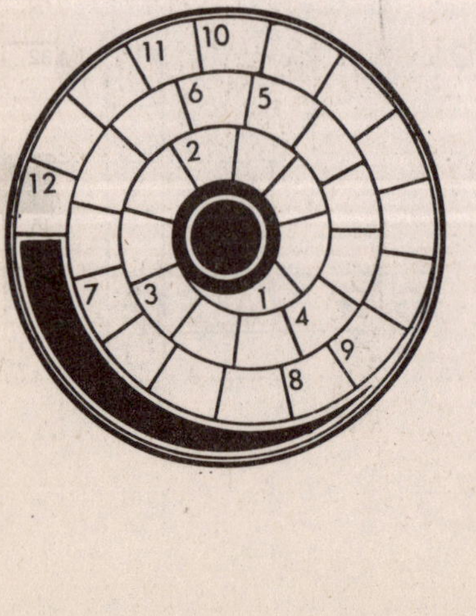

**OUTWARD**

1. Banishes from a country
3. Randomly irregular
5. Drew magnetically
8. Starlet
10. ___ Allan Poe

**INWARD**

12. Dust cloth
11. Sweet course
9. Military student
7. Shopping wagon
6. Unspoken
4. Nab
2. Lassoed

## PUZZLE 152

**ACROSS**
1. Greek or Caesar
6. Cheese
10. Kinds of rust
12. Poles
14. Dakota Indians
15. "I Am a ____"
16. Yen
18. Cerise
19. Computer communication device
23. Gangster's weapon, slangily
25. Gem
26. "Then Came ____"
27. Ogee shape
30. Skulked
33. Emissary
35. NY hours: abbr.
36. See 23 Across
38. Continent
39. African antelope
40. Watchful
41. Ember
44. Amerindians
46. Beetle
49. Hand-on-hip
54. Duke's domicile
55. Peruse again
56. Allot
57. "Inferno" author

**DOWN**
1. Inebriate
2. Woodsman's tool
3. Turned on
4. Fuss
5. Material for jeans
6. Greek letter
7. Beaver's project
8. State
9. Nothing more than
11. Superjet: abbr.
12. Elementary institute
13. Depressed
17. Wail
19. Burrower
20. Musical work
21. Flit
22. Deer
24. Expected now
27. Abate
28. Mix
29. Resting place
31. Caviar unit
32. Waltz subject
34. Young female
37. A pharaoh, for short
40. Queried
41. Snake
42. Sting
43. Healthy
45. Something to lend
47. Rodent
48. Suit's top
50. Author Levin
51. Game pieces
52. Belfry resident
53. Pindar specialty

## PUZZLE 153

**ACROSS**
1. Musical group
5. Male turkey
8. Seasoning
12. Busy as ____: 2 wds.
13. Shoe width
14. Plant of the lily family
15. Pew
16. Circle part
17. Endure
18. Put emphasis on
20. Direction
22. Espy
23. Actor Carney
24. Macaroni
27. Stiffen
31. Fuss
32. Moray
33. Prevent from acting
36. Trick
38. Chart
40. Tiny
41. Take out
44. Fleet of ships
48. Above
49. USNA grad: abbr.
51. Musical collection
52. Vocalize
53. Fido's doc, for short
54. Ripped
55. Otherwise
56. Ram's mate
57. Major follower

**DOWN**
1. Food fish
2. Aid and ____
3. Close
4. Hate
5. Rib
6. 48 Across, to a bard
7. Capital of Hejaz
8. Greet
9. Winglike
10. Defeat
11. French head
19. Caspian
21. Table scrap
24. Writing tablet
25. Summer quaff
26. Drunkard
28. Teacher's group: abbr.
29. Japanese coin
30. Wapiti
34. Come forth
35. Rodent
36. ____ diem
37. Distant
39. Annoyance
40. Squander
41. Amount, as of medicine
42. Wicked
43. Camera part
45. Thanks ____: 2 wds.
46. Filth
47. Excellent: 2 wds.
50. Unused

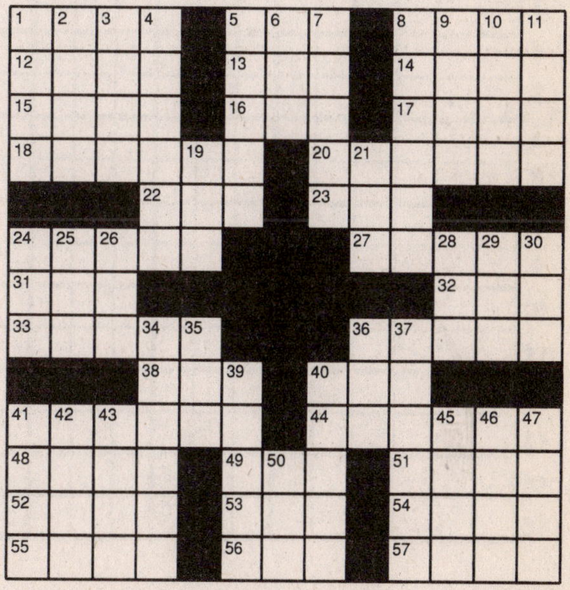

# PUZZLE 154

## BRICK BY BRICK

Rearrange this stack of bricks to form a crossword puzzle. The clues will help you fit the bricks into their correct places. Row 1 has been filled in for you. Use the bricks to fill in the remaining spaces.

### BRICKS

| | | | | |
|---|---|---|---|---|
| AMI<br>NON | NGS<br>UE■ | LOV<br>MEE | ED■<br>TS■ | ■WE<br>■■■ |
| ■GA<br>■AM | LE■<br>MED | ■RA<br>D■R | ■EL<br>EN■ | UNI<br>TEL |
| ESA<br>SER | GRU<br>■ES | D■G<br>■BA | REE<br>NED | ■■■<br>AL■ |
| ITE<br>DAD | TER<br>■■■ | RRE<br>IE■ | D■L<br>E■A | BAR<br>EN■ |
| T■M<br>■VI | OLA<br>NET | YOU<br>■■R | U■T<br>E■■ | ■■■<br>CAT |
| BAR<br>ALI | AD■<br>CAR | CED<br>OVE | IAN<br>SPE | GAB<br>■LI |
| MP■<br>SAY | ON■<br>LS■ | ■EX<br>■DE | AMB<br>R■■ | ILE<br>NSE |

### DIAGRAM

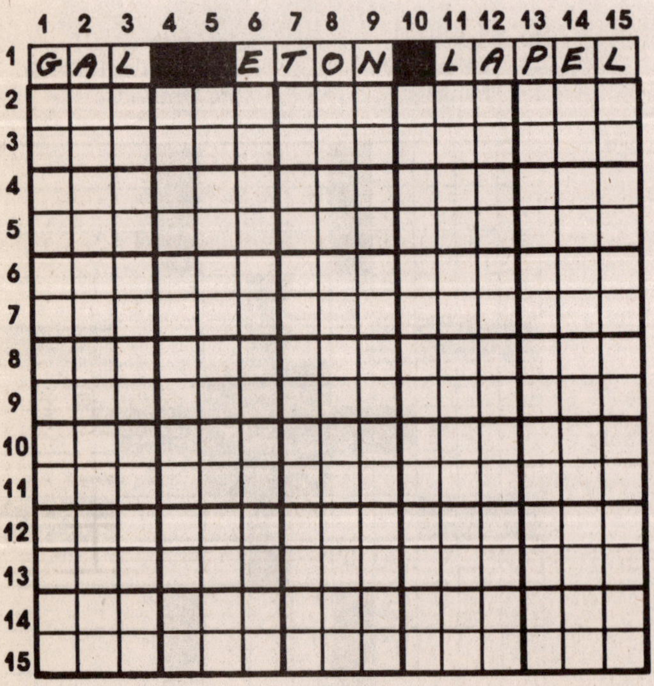


### ACROSS

1. Slangy female
British school
Jacket facing
2. Among
Ms. Falana
Deport
3. Zero
Dill herb
Thick
4. Complain
Whippersnapper
5. Theme
Meadow herb
6. Attic
Sore
7. Garfield, e.g.
Fille's friend
Clergyman
8. Trade ____
Yak
Jet set
9. Recounts
Legal claim
Pop
10. Got hitched
Risk
11. Tavern
Purple Heart, e.g.
12. Savage
Emulated Unser
13. Unfamiliar
Whizzed
Wander
14. Adored
Jacob's sib
Dogwood, e.g.
15. Bumps into
Dry
Newsman Potter

### DOWN

1. Crew
Slice
Ointment
2. Gino's love
Over
Healing plant
3. "Peanuts" kid
Roofing square
Split
4. Certain pols.
Aged
Red root
5. Heathens
Stripes
6. Guido's note
Autumn vegetable
Needlefish
7. Theater award
Outfit
Comes up
8. Pseudo-butter
Kingdom
Chapel recess
9. Mother ____
Baby's wear
Nigh
10. Screwball
Shade source
Expected
11. Shelf
Wood covering
12. Hatchets
Wire measure
Flit
13. Pub order
Tart
Oak source
14. Other
Info
Water barrier
15. Lecher's look
Sunburnt
Exploit

# PUZZLE 155

**• SWEET TOOTH •**

**ACROSS**

1. Appointment
5. Mound
9. Landed
10. Singer Fitzgerald
11. Ice-cream parlor order: 2 wds.
15. Ice-cream parlor order
19. Behave
20. Read quickly
24. Region
25. Ventilated
27. Get away!
28. Frolic
29. Popular desserts: 2 wds.
33. Long time spans
34. "____ for the Seesaw"
35. Bundle
36. Nudge
38. So-so grade
39. Impoverished
41. Texas shrine
43. Tentmaker
44. Temperate
46. Allow
47. Singer Doris
48. Actress Barrymore
50. Glut
51. Coffee or stew
54. Eradicate
56. Possess
58. Ark builder
60. Thunder noise
61. Sedan
64. Falls behind
66. Strawberry ____
70. Notoriety
71. Adhesive
72. Member of nobility
73. Related
74. Out of the wind
75. "My Gal ____"
76. Make over
77. Campfire confection
85. Sinful
86. Assistant
87. ____ Godiva
88. Legal document

**DOWN**

1. Light touch
2. ____ mode: 2 wds.
3. Foil or lizzie
4. Airport abbr.
5. With it
6. Building wing
7. Former ring champ
8. O'Brien or Benatar
12. Brad
13. Land measure
14. Tread
15. Shopping spot
16. Lined up
17. Popular pastry type: 2 wds.
18. Kind of dance
20. Compass pt.
21. Popular dessert: 2 wds.
22. Super: 2 wds.
23. Snout
25. Mimic
26. Scoop of ice cream
29. Help
30. Layer
31. Epoch
32. Scale note
35. ____ diem
37. Water barrier
40. Diner
42. King with the golden touch
43. Ancient
45. Stain
49. Finish first
50. Drain
52. Help!
53. Exclamation
54. BPOE member
55. Actress Charlotte
56. Gymnast Korbut
57. Great ____ of China
59. Fireplace shelf
60. Is able to
62. Surrounded by
63. Splitsville
65. Notice
67. Too hasty
68. Streetcar
69. Soft drink
70. Distant
77. Torme or Blanc
78. Ms. Gardner
79. Disencumber
80. Foxy
81. Boy
82. Fib
83. Poem
84. Married

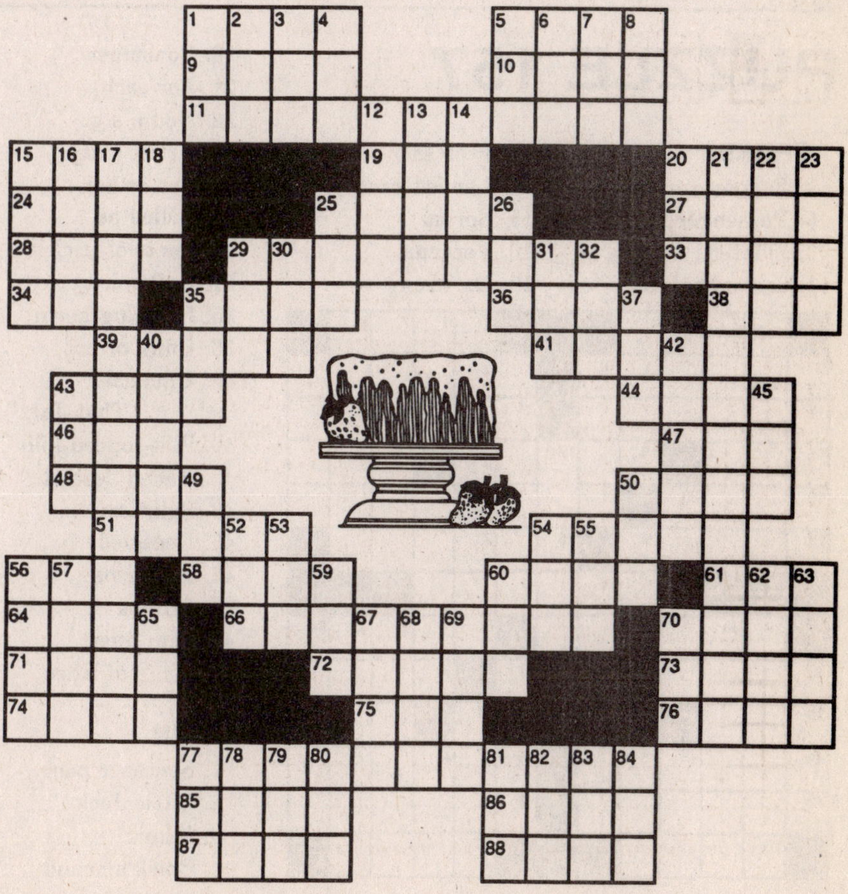

# PUZZLE 156

**ACROSS**

1. Hourglass filler
5. Lager
9. Wharf
10. Kind of race
12. Slice, as a turkey

13. ___ and kicking
14. Pro pilot
15. Pester
17. Hot drink
18. Subtract
20. Camera part
21. Glistened
23. Masculine
26. Stinging plant
30. Drink cooler
31. Doggy doc
32. Above, to a poet
33. "___ Door Canteen"
35. Giant
37. Number of storybook dwarfs
38. Fleecy females
39. Feat
40. Rotunda

**DOWN**

1. The last frontier
2. Ventilated
3. Sagebrush State: abbr.
4. Soak
5. Boast
6. Water wriggler
7. Upper crust
8. Poe's bird
11. Affirmative votes
12. Bounder
16. Make amends
19. Employ
20. Rent
22. Gained
23. ___ Piggy
24. Behaved
25. Depart
27. ___ pole
28. Rent
29. Sea bird
31. Sell
34. Golly!
36. ___ Jima

---

# PUZZLE 157

**ACROSS**

1. Fellow
5. Passenger
9. Slanted
11. "___ Night"
13. Profession
14. Landed property
15. Sprint
16. Veranda
18. Do wrong

19. Consumer
21. For each
22. Noun, e.g.
23. Artist's cap
25. Cat or lion
27. Called on
29. Cents-off ticket
31. Evil spirit
35. Dressing gown
36. Bunk or cot
38. Unusual
39. "___ That Jazz"
40. Flat-topped hills
42. Baked dessert
43. Splinter
45. Deceived
47. Heathens
48. Primps
49. Tear apart
50. "___ of Eden"

**DOWN**

1. Sentence part
2. Little Jack ___
3. Mimic
4. Chick's sound
5. Catch a carp
6. Height: abbr.
7. Cause
8. Whole
9. Scour
10. Let fall
11. "I've Got a ___"
12. Care for
17. Purifies
20. Musical show
22. Broader
24. Gratuity
26. Conducted
28. Becomes serious
29. Shirt part
30. Accommodate
32. Sugar trees
33. The East
34. Requires
35. Grate
37. Moist
40. Darn
41. Father
44. Moving truck
46. Coral or Bering

# PUZZLE 158

**ACROSS**

1. Box
5. Hit show
10. Small arrow
14. Comic Johnson
15. Uptight
16. Great Lake
17. Chicago feature
18. Vary
19. 5,280 feet
20. Worker
22. Lives
24. Toward shelter
25. Cruising
26. Set apart
29. Sent back
33. Whimper
34. More tender
35. "Norma ___"
36. Eye part
37. European nation
38. Prima donna
39. Born
40. "___ the Boys Are"
41. Level
42. Border guards
44. Embrace
46. Split apart
47. Evaluate
48. Inquiring
51. Pushed back
55. Flake
56. Rent
58. Hawkeye State
59. Highway fare
60. Go in
61. Gang
62. Only
63. Barrel parts
64. Sea bird

**DOWN**

1. Store sign
2. School dance
3. Upon
4. Supplants
5. Remained
6. Fracas
7. Feed the kitty
8. Wind direction: abbr.
9. Ranch workers
10. Lower
11. Seed case
12. Brook
13. Golf gadgets
21. Bullfight shout
23. Have on
25. High home
26. Rotates
27. Use a blender
28. Stranger
29. Zoo sounds
30. Impel
31. Roof edges
32. College VIPs
34. Go quickly
37. Doctors' signboards
38. Abandoned vessel
40. Small bird
43. 3-bagger
44. Antics
45. Had lunch
47. Bowling button
48. Deeds
49. Scat!
50. Slay
51. Pro ___
52. Old knowledge
53. Pitcher
54. Daybreak
57. Join the army: abbr.

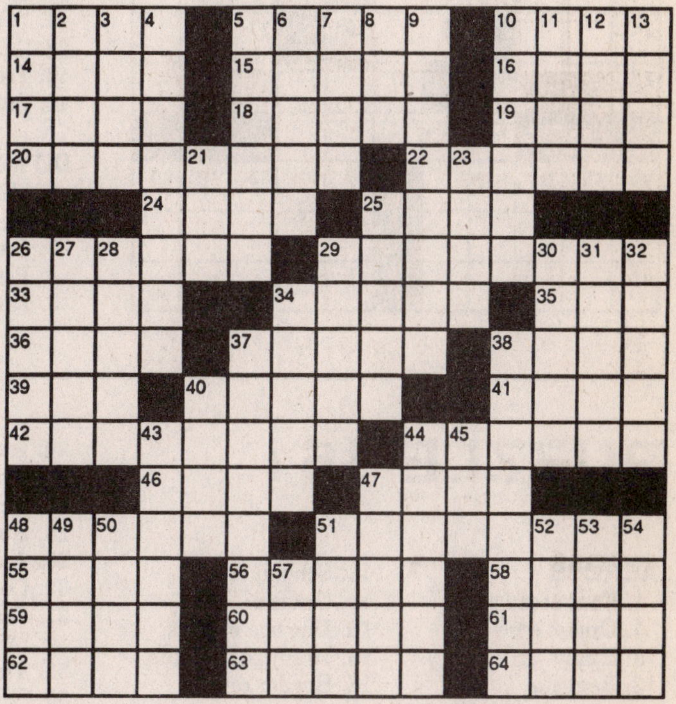

# ESCALATOR

# PUZZLE 159

**Place the answer to clue 1 in the first space, drop a letter, and arrange the remaining letters to answer clue 2. Drop another letter and arrange the remaining letters to answer clue 3. The first dropped letter goes into the box to the left of space 1 and the second dropped letter goes into the box to the right of space 3. Follow this pattern for each row in the diagram. When completed, the letters on the left and right, reading down, will spell related words or a phrase.**

1. Phone user
2. Lucid
3. Contest
4. Spinets
5. Madrid's land
6. Bites
7. Used a razor
8. Coin side
9. Arthur of tennis
10. Omits a vowel
11. Skid
12. Winter vehicle
13. President
14. Auriculate
15. Beloved
16. Method
17. Flower parts
18. Shea team, once

| | | | | |
|---|---|---|---|---|
| | 1 | 2 | 3 | |
| | 4 | 5 | 6 | |
| | 7 | 8 | 9 | |
| | 10 | 11 | 12 | |
| | 13 | 14 | 15 | |
| | 16 | 17 | 18 | |

# PUZZLE 160

**ACROSS**
1. Jeweler's weight
6. Like a zoo animal
11. Green shade

12. Maxim
13. Enlarge
14. Pretend: 2 wds.
15. Resist authority
17. "In the ____" (Presley song)
20. U.S. president
24. Diving bird
25. Tree fluid
27. Bambi's mom
28. Hive dwellers
30. Stirred up
32. West Point student
34. Howled at the moon
37. Kitchen gadget
41. "Goodnight" girl
42. "____ Lucy": 2 wds.
43. Treetop homes
44. Surrendered

**DOWN**
1. Milk producer
2. Actress MacGraw
3. Free (of)
4. Prevent
5. Doctrines
6. Garment for Dracula
7. Grown-up
8. Gangster's gun
9. Self
10. Cozy room
16. Plank
17. Chatter
18. Tint
19. ____ out (supplement)
21. Paid notices
22. Enemy
23. Senator Kennedy
26. Like work by Keats or Yeats
29. Odor
31. Practical
33. Summer drinks
34. Place for coal
35. Exist
36. Affirmative word
38. Up-to-date in the 1960s
39. First woman
40. Cincinnati player

---

# PUZZLE 161

**ACROSS**
1. Fast steed
5. Upper limb
8. Emily ____
12. Regatta
13. Second letter
14. Govern
15. Use the molars
16. In retreat: 3 wds.
18. Border on

20. Item of value
21. Ghost
24. Strike
25. Burdened
26. Army officer
30. Cold cubes
31. Embrace
32. Miss Gabor
33. Thick food: 2 wds.
36. Uncovered
38. Lamb's mother
39. Major crime
40. Little
43. Opera by Verdi
44. Don't touch!: 2 wds.
46. Broad belt
50. Palo ____
51. Plump
52. Leg joint
53. Judge
54. Attempt
55. Seth's parent

**DOWN**
1. Curved line
2. College cheer
3. Top card
4. Watch out!
5. Approximately
6. Monthly payment
7. Assembled
8. Magician's word
9. Yours and mine
10. Twist about
11. Canvas shelter
17. Frozen raindrops
19. Storage box
21. ____ of the tongue
22. Step
23. Notion
24. Pig
26. Saucer's mate
27. Roman emperor
28. Balanced
29. Lord's spouse
31. Color
34. Not often
35. Hooters
36. Cot
37. Baked ____
39. States number
40. Food fish
41. Masculine
42. Poker stake
43. At a distance
45. Frequently, to a poet
47. As well as
48. Caribbean ____
49. Skirt edge

## PUZZLE 162

**ACROSS**
1. Dawber of "Mork & Mindy"
4. Choose
7. Forest tree
10. Zsa Zsa's sister
11. Wing
12. Actress Remick
13. "___ Joey"
14. Military man
16. Mr. Roarke's aide ("Fantasy Island")
18. "Sweet Smell of Success" author
20. Old African kingdom
24. Missing
25. "___ Yesterday"
26. Nightmare
28. Actress Corby
29. "A Man ___ Peter"
31. Comic Don
34. Byrnes of "77 Sunset Strip"
37. Fuss
38. Siamese language
39. Ocean
40. Candle material
41. Common verb
42. North Frederick number

**DOWN**
1. Vim and vigor
2. Gardner of films
3. "The ___ Falcon"
4. Kilns
5. Story line
6. Claw
7. ___ Baba
8. Witness
9. "Leave ___ to Heaven"
15. Twice as much
17. Assault
18. ___ Faithful (geyser)
19. Black beetle
21. Most daring
22. Anger
23. Hollywood's Blyth
27. Island near Sicily
28. ___ the Cow
30. Shakespearean king
31. Uncooked
32. Miss Lupino
33. "Mr. Peepers" portrayer
35. Letter
36. Tough actor Duryea

## PUZZLE 163

**ACROSS**
1. Shoo!
5. Drains energy from
9. Northwestern st.: abbr.
12. Unseen emanation
13. Move by small degrees
14. Decimal unit
15. Let fall
16. Fastened
18. Florida city
20. Frames of mind
21. Fascinate
23. Zing
24. Batter's desire
25. Entreaty
28. Knife wound
32. Eye's colored part
34. Curve
35. Canal or Lake
36. Head-shoulders connection
37. Spouse
39. Dutch commune
40. Little devil
42. Cripples
44. Thin-layered rock
47. Without a script: hyph.
49. Tattler
51. Narrow opening
54. "The bells ___ ringing . . ."
55. Author Hunter
56. Singer Horne
57. Legal matter
58. Tenant's payment
59. First garden

**DOWN**
1. Unhappy
2. Mongrel
3. Sweet-smelling
4. Hoglike animal
5. Thailand
6. Opposed
7. %: abbr.
8. Disgrace
9. Roman emperor
10. Jerry or Donna
11. Finishes
17. Thicket
19. Elec. unit, for short
21. Take it on the ___
22. Employ for pay
23. Treaty
26. Light shedder
27. Period
29. Shook
30. Helper
31. Honey makers
33. Dexterity
38. Building annex
41. Parker's clock
43. Passageway
44. Nightly twinkler
45. In this place
46. Taproom drinks
47. Ladd or Young
48. Small depression
50. Hail to Cicero
52. Individual
53. Sunbather's shade

# PUZZLE 164

## CRISS-CROSSWORD

**The answer words for Criss-Crossword are entered diagonally, reading downwards, from upper left to lower right or from upper right to lower left. We have entered the words MOLD and TOM to show you how.**

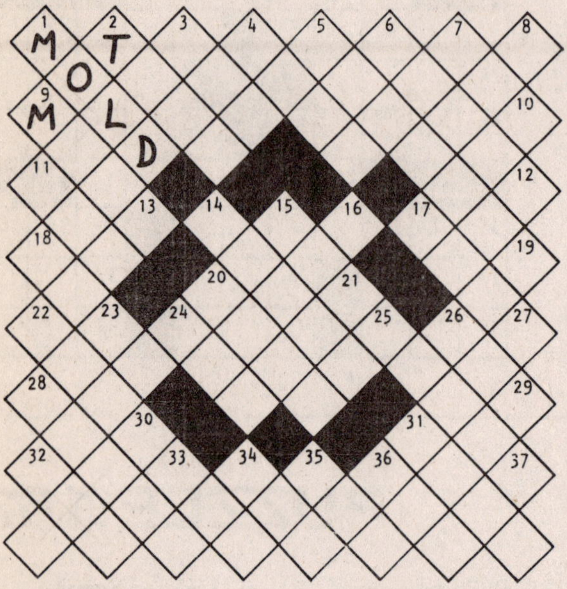

**TO THE RIGHT**

1. Shape
2. Ocean swell
3. "Of Mice and ____"
4. Small thing
5. Weeping trees
6. Writer Oscar ____
7. Modern: prefix
9. Thaw
11. Body of water
14. Pinafore
15. Crackers
17. Actual
18. Apple's "coat"
20. Shopper's aid
22. Respects
24. Performer: suffix
26. Doll material
28. ____ toast
31. Type of duck
32. Kid
34. Fleming
35. Before: prefix
36. Time zone: abbr.

**TO THE LEFT**

2. Male turkey
3. "Five Hundred ____"
4. Interferes
5. Romancer's drink
6. Humor
7. Cleo's river
8. Tattle
10. Scent
12. Female sheep
13. Give and ____
15. Piece of wood
16. Louvre locale
19. Hindu garment
21. Misplaced
23. Doctrine
25. Explosive: abbr.
27. Portable light
29. Silly birds
30. Mr. Kazan
33. Wane
34. "____ Yankee Doodle Dandy"
35. Faux ____
37. Tended baby

# PUZZLE 165

## MATH MAZE

**Find your way through each of these Math Mazes. Start at the top arrow and move through the boxes, across and down, but never diagonally, to the arrow at the bottom so that the sum of the numbers in the boxes will equal the total shown.**

**1.**

| | | | | |
|---|---|---|---|---|
| 2 | 1 | 4 | 6 | 7 |
| 8 | 5 | 2 | 1 | 3 |
| 1 | 1 | 9 | 1 | 2 |
| 6 | 2 | 8 | 1 | 2 |
| 9 | 9 | 3 | 5 | 1 |

**20**

**2.**

| | | | | |
|---|---|---|---|---|
| 7 | 9 | 5 | 1 | 7 |
| 1 | 3 | 2 | 5 | 9 |
| 5 | 8 | 6 | 6 | 3 |
| 6 | 9 | 2 | 4 | 2 |
| 2 | 1 | 5 | 5 | 8 |

**66**

**3.**

| | | | | |
|---|---|---|---|---|
| 1 | 3 | 7 | 6 | 1 |
| 2 | 8 | 9 | 5 | 2 |
| 6 | 7 | 7 | 6 | 8 |
| 8 | 4 | 5 | 2 | 6 |
| 3 | 2 | 1 | 4 | 1 |

**41**

# PUZZLE 166

## STARSPELL

**How many words of 5 or 6 letters can you form by moving from letter to connected letter in the Starspell diagram below? A letter may be repeated in a word, but only after leaving it and coming back. No foreign words, abbreviations, words beginning with a capital letter, or plurals allowed.**

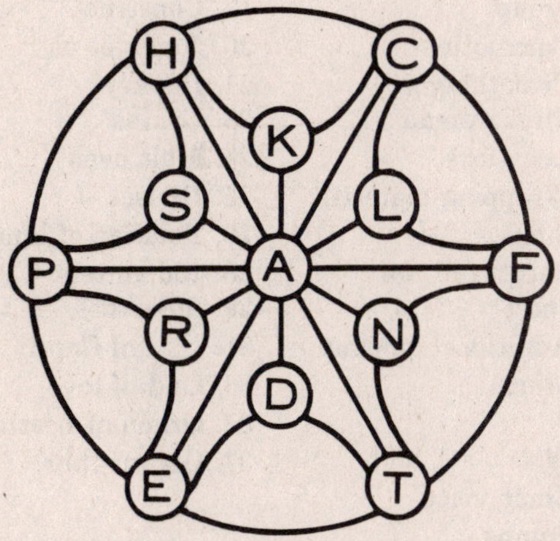


**YOUR WORD LIST**

# PUZZLE 167

## CRISS-CROSSWORD

**The answer words for Criss-Crossword are entered diagonally, reading downwards, from upper left to lower right or from upper right to lower left. We have entered the word TIS and BIS to show you how.**

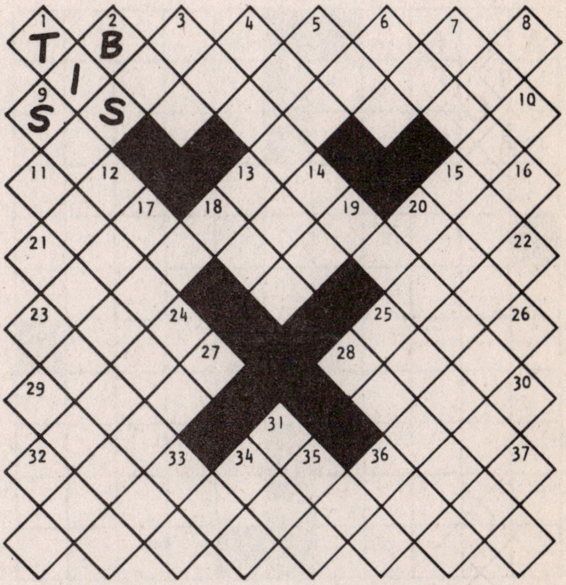


**TO THE RIGHT**

1. "____ the season . . ."
2. However
3. Compromise: hyph.
4. Auction offer
5. Spanish hero
6. Great Lake
7. "What's up, ____?"
9. Endure
11. Nap
13. Mime
15. Take down a ____ (humble)
18. Immediately
20. Almost white
21. Smirks
23. Most profound
25. Grown-up
28. Solace
29. Makes a scarf
31. Story
32. Three, in Rome
34. Unit
36. Letter from Greece

**TO THE LEFT**

2. Encore!
3. Squalls
4. Smidgen
5. Twice LII
6. Child's game: hyph.
7. Dismal failure
8. Pro
10. Held one's own
12. Suffer
14. GI's address
16. Bee's gathering
17. Requisite
19. Untried
22. Rating
24. English river
26. Hawaiian guitar
27. Wish
30. Upper crust
31. Throw
33. Nancy summer
35. Picnic pest
37. "____ for Two"

# PUZZLE 168

Diagramless crosswords are solved by using the clues and their numbers to fill in the answer words and the arrangement of black squares. Insert the number of each clue with the first letter of its answer, across and down. Fill in a black square at the end of each word. Every black square must have a corresponding black square on the opposite side of the diagram to form a symmetrical pattern.

**ACROSS**

1. To shelter
5. Harvest
9. Rent
11. Proprietor
13. Small pies
14. River embankment
15. Choose

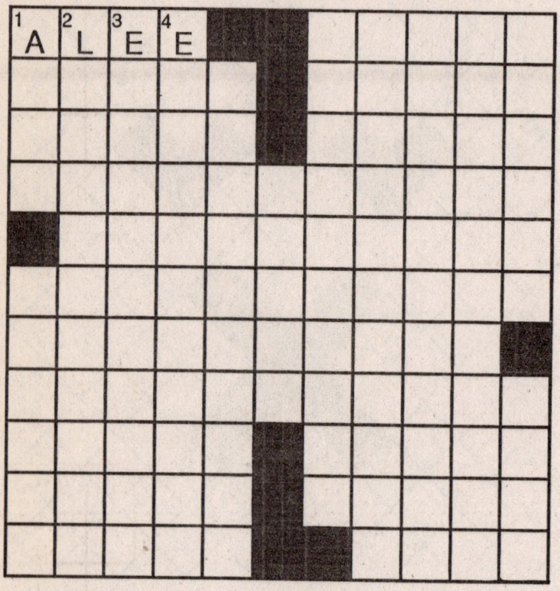


16. Look at
18. Country hotel
19. Clip sheep
21. Too
22. Tinters
24. Lubricates
27. Indian social group
30. Commotion
31. That thing's
32. First woman
34. Locations
36. Wrapping material
38. Sum
39. Shorthand, for short
40. Additional amount
41. Minus

**DOWN**

1. Choir voice
2. Jumps
3. Our planet
4. Superlative suffix
5. Actor's desire
6. Female sheep
7. Blacksmith's block
8. Hammerheads
10. School theme
12. Divorce city
17. Construct
20. Asner et al.
21. Donkey
23. Grates
24. Malt oven
25. Dialect
26. Relative of bingo
28. Indian tent
29. Smoothes
31. ___ of Capri
33. God of love
35. Organ of hearing
37. Ocean: abbr.

# PUZZLE 169

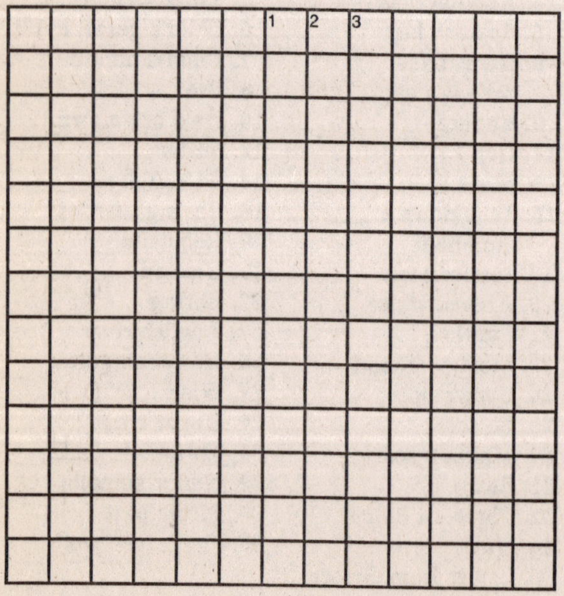


**ACROSS**

1. Domino spot
4. Rescue
5. Water mammal
6. Tumbler
7. Abound
8. Animal doc
11. Turns into
14. Storm
15. Bill
16. Building wing
17. Gymnast Korbut
18. In addition
19. Hilariously funny
21. Strong brew
22. Pastime
23. Copper-zinc alloy
25. Board
26. Belonging to us
27. Fourth letter

**DOWN**

1. Squares of butter
2. Singer Burl
3. For each
4. Stutter
5. Butter substitute
6. Tropical lizard
7. Make fun of
8. Worth
9. Hen products
10. Afternoon drink
11. Telephone inventor
12. Actor Wallach
13. Mottoes
14. Chambers
15. Sheep sound
20. Chore
23. Melancholy
24. Unusual
25. Seed container

# PUZZLE 170

**ACROSS**
1. River craft
5. Footwear
9. Church recess
10. Scorches
11. Sword fight
12. Peels
13. Tossed side dish
16. River's edge
17. Leaning Tower of ____
19. Flightless bird
22. Cupid
23. Ribbon adornment
26. Stronghold
28. Dancer Kelly
29. Cigar
31. Very happy
33. Baking chamber
34. Book sections
38. Sweet potato
39. Floor square
40. Arid
41. Notion
42. Actor Guinness
45. Bend down
49. ____ bear
51. Snatch
53. Cognizant
54. Grade
55. Repair
56. Otherwise

**DOWN**
1. Harmful
2. Musical composition
3. Cruising
4. Relate
5. Actor Connery
6. Listen!
7. Native mineral
8. Double curve
10. Health resort
14. Copycat
15. Dreadful
16. ____ hound
18. Distress signal
19. Mr. Zimbalist, Jr.
20. Night light
21. Footed vase
23. Flag-maker Ross
24. United
25. Marry
27. Ploy
28. Actress Teri ____
29. Bashful
30. Eggs
32. Conducted
35. Secreted
36. Bar orders
37. Type of moss
42. Actor Alda
43. Fat
44. In days gone by, in days gone by
46. Monster
47. Spoken
48. Dabs
49. Actress Dawber
50. Have debts
52. Industrious insect

Starting box on page 562

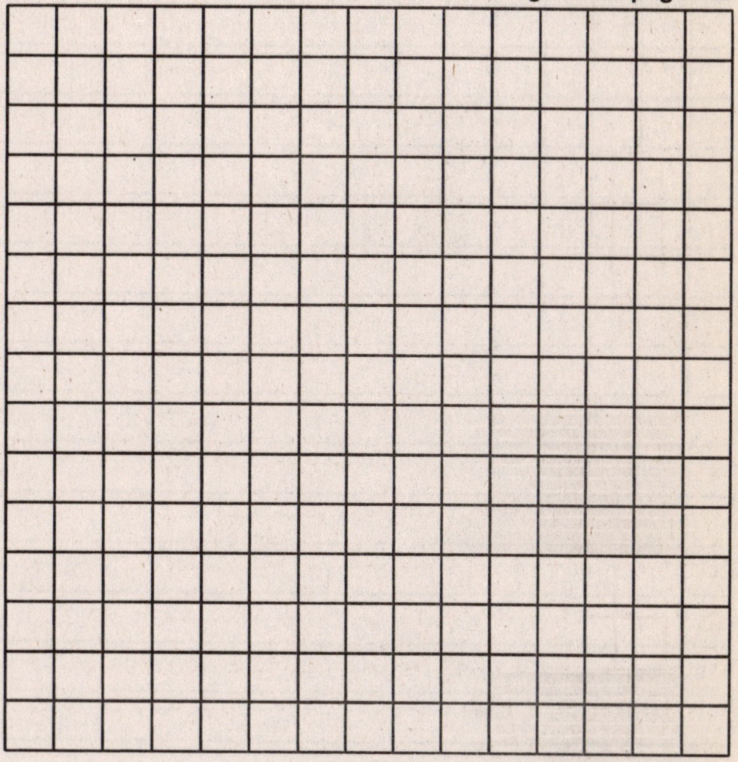

# WORD MATH

# PUZZLE 171

**In these long-division problems, letters are substituted for numbers. Determine the value of each letter. Then arrange the letters in order from 0 to 9, and they will spell a word or phrase.**

## 1

| 0 | 1 | 2 | 3 | 4 | 5 | 6 | 7 | 8 | 9 |
|---|---|---|---|---|---|---|---|---|---|
| | | | | | | | | | |

```
              S U E
S L O E ) L O U V E R
          L U H O
            C E U E
            S L O E
            S S L B R
            S B L C C
              U R O L
```

## 2

| 0 | 1 | 2 | 3 | 4 | 5 | 6 | 7 | 8 | 9 |
|---|---|---|---|---|---|---|---|---|---|
| | | | | | | | | | |

```
                  A N T
D A R T ) L A N T E R N
          T Y Y T R
            A N Y L R
            A A R Y T
              T W A N N
              E A Y N A
                U U W T
```

## 3

| 0 | 1 | 2 | 3 | 4 | 5 | 6 | 7 | 8 | 9 |
|---|---|---|---|---|---|---|---|---|---|
| | | | | | | | | | |

```
                D I D
L I K E ) C L I C H E
          E E C I
            G H D H
            I T K H
              C E F E
              E E C I
                K I T
```

# PUZZLE 172

**ACROSS**

1. Bar or suit
4. Facet
5. Rage
8. Dive
10. Minerals
12. Scope
13. Net
15. Plus
16. Charge
18. Only
19. Blend
22. Simian
23. Vicinity
24. Potato
25. Verify
27. Yearn
29. Submit
31. Set flame to
33. Botch
35. Angler's catch
39. Through
40. Innocent
43. Medicinal plant
44. Tree
45. Faucet
46. Jocund
48. Reason
50. Smooth
51. Give
52. "____ Heat"
53. Superstar
54. Gents

Starting box on page 562

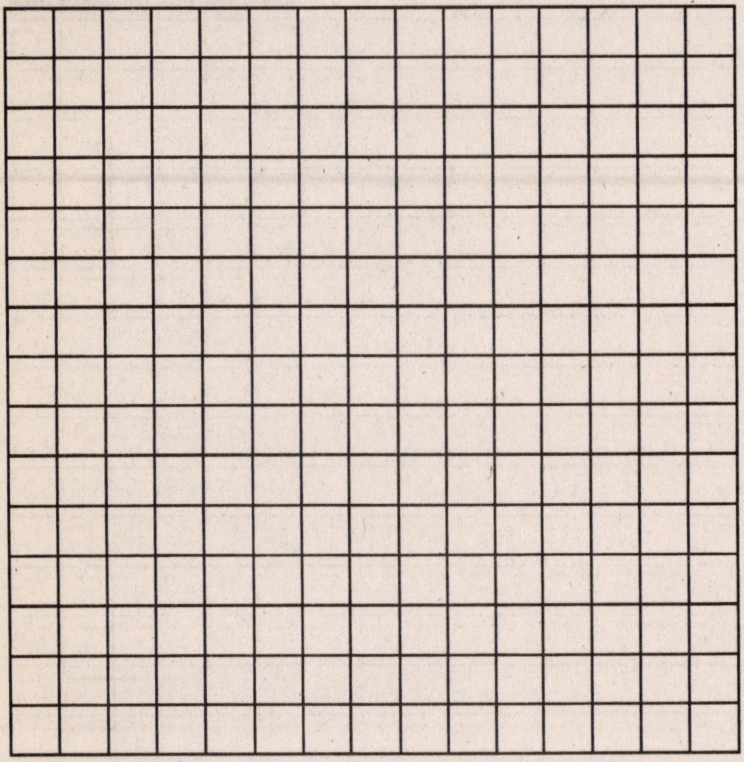

**DOWN**

1. Ell
2. "Jagged ____"
3. Links peg
4. Miscellaneous
5. Pro
6. Smell
7. Postpone
8. Carriage
9. Walkway
11. Father
13. Complaint
14. Pekoe
16. "____ and Away"
17. Time period
20. Space
21. Radiate
25. Risk
26. Heaven on earth
28. New
30. Distinctive time
32. English river
34. Tradition
35. Pouch
36. Pub quaffs
37. Underwater radar
38. English Channel feeder
41. Immense
42. Sword
47. Do sums
48. Zip or Morse
49. Soon
51. ____ sum

# PUZZLE 173 — Quotagram

**Fill in the answers to the clues. Then transfer the letters to the correspondingly numbered squares in the diagram. The completed diagram will contain a quotation.**

1. Egg dish ___ ___ ___ ___ ___ ___ (40 41 11 26 32 19)
2. Gary Cooper film ___ ___ ___ ___ ___ ___ ___ ___ (4 24 16 10 28 30 8 20)
3. "____ Express" ___ ___ ___ ___ ___ ___ ___ ___ (6 14 45 7 42 35 23 1)
4. Excuse ___ ___ ___ ___ ___ ___ ___ (22 5 38 13 33 18 37)
5. Hat ___ ___ ___ ___ ___ ___ (36 2 12 29 39 31)
6. Female ___ ___ ___ ___ ___ (3 21 25 27 34)
7. Wears out ___ ___ ___ ___ ___ (9 17 43 44 15)

| | | | | | | | | | | | | | | | | | | |
|---|---|---|---|---|---|---|---|---|---|---|---|---|---|---|---|---|---|---|
| ■ | 1 | 2 | ■ | 3 | 4 | 5 | 6 | ■ | 7 | 8 | 9 | 10 | 11 | 12 | 13 | ■ | 14 | 15 |
| ■ | 16 | 17 | 18 | 19 | 20 | ■ | 21 | 22 | ■ | 23 | 24 | 25 | ■ | 26 | 27 | 28 | ■ | 29 |
| 30 | 31 | 32 | 33 | 34 | 35 | ■ | 36 | 37 | ■ | 38 | 39 | 40 | 41 | 42 | 43 | 44 | 45 | ■ |

# PUZZLE 174

**ACROSS**

1. Fragrance
5. Wrath
6. Blunders
7. Baseball bag
11. Spirited horses
14. Lamb's pen name
15. Vocalist Turner
17. Guys' counterparts
18. Festivity
20. Hurried
21. Small barrel
22. Decade
23. Speak pompously
25. Existed
26. Choose
27. Wander off
30. Water hole
32. Sixty minutes
33. New plant's start
35. Matured
36. Classified
40. Church service
41. Author Gardner
42. Connery or Penn
43. Dispatched

**DOWN**

1. Mineral deposits
2. Pub game missile
3. Grimm monster
4. Adjusted again
7. Commenced
8. ___ and alack!
9. Fine-grained sand
10. ____ as pie
12. Excavate
13. Vipers
16. Actor Guinness
19. Illuminated
20. Dress edge
22. Duke, earl, etc.
23. Twenty-four hours
24. Simians
25. Hospital areas
27. Trick
28. Ancient Roman garb
29. Regrets
31. Zodiac's lion
34. Attire
37. Oak or elm
38. Dash
39. Fender damage

**Starting box on page 562**

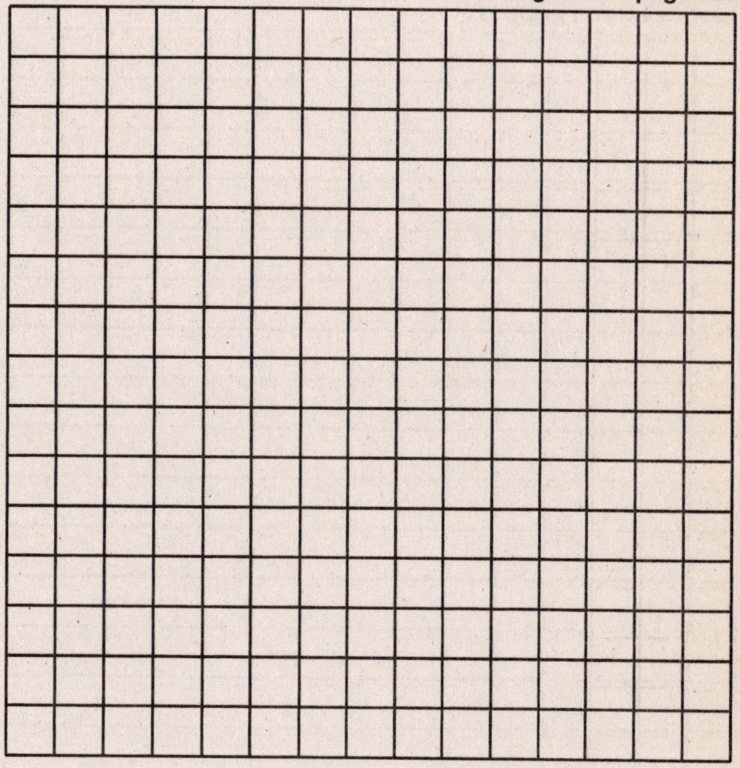

## Progressions

# PUZZLE 175

**Can you follow the mathematical progression to find the fifth number in each series? Read your answers from top to bottom to discover yet another progression.**

| | | | | | | | | | |
|---|---|---|---|---|---|---|---|---|---|
| A. | 15 | 16 | 18 | 21 | ______ | 30 | 36 | 43 | 51 |
| B. | 9 | 3 | 18 | 6 | ______ | 12 | 72 | 24 | 144 |
| C. | 385 | 386 | 193 | 196 | ______ | 54 | 9 | 16 | 2 |
| D. | 8 | 16 | 12 | 72 | ______ | 640 | 628 | 8792 | 8776 |
| E. | 9 | 21 | 30 | 51 | ______ | 132 | 213 | 345 | 558 |
| F. | 200 | 200 | 100 | 200 | ______ | 300 | 200 | 800 | 700 |
| G. | 13 | 2 | 22 | 11 | ______ | 110 | 1210 | 1199 | 13189 |
| H. | 105 | 840 | 120 | 720 | ______ | 576 | 192 | 384 | 384 |

# PUZZLE 176

**ACROSS**

1. Bambi's mother
4. Porcupine spine
6. Crushed
8. Assignment
11. Prompt
12. Incensed
14. Female gametes
15. Malt beverages
16. Heal
17. Competed
18. Beef fat
19. Classifies
20. Traveler's resting place
21. Animal enclosure
22. Turkish hat
23. Outer garment
25. Crafty
26. Ground grain
27. Absorbed
28. Squid squirt
29. Large
32. Overstuff
33. Concerning
36. Otherwise
37. Look intently
38. Barber's call
39. Meadow mouse
40. "Much ___ About Nothing"
41. Small child
42. Supplement
43. For each
44. Not anyplace
48. Irrational
49. Unite

**DOWN**

1. Owed
2. Lubricant
3. Building wing
4. Pursuit
5. Madagascar mammal
6. Female monarch
7. Pub missile
8. Hangout
9. Stove
10. Defective
11. Tip-off
13. Lineage
15. Venomous snake
16. Homey
17. Small container
19. Sailor's instrument
22. Dandy
24. Acorn producer
25. Renown
26. ___ julep
27. Shaving necessity
29. London fellow
30. Wight or Man
31. To the right
32. Ornamental stone
34. Sign gas
35. Applaud
36. All
37. Mountain pass
45. Palindromic super
46. Gardener's tool
47. Finale

Starting box on page 562

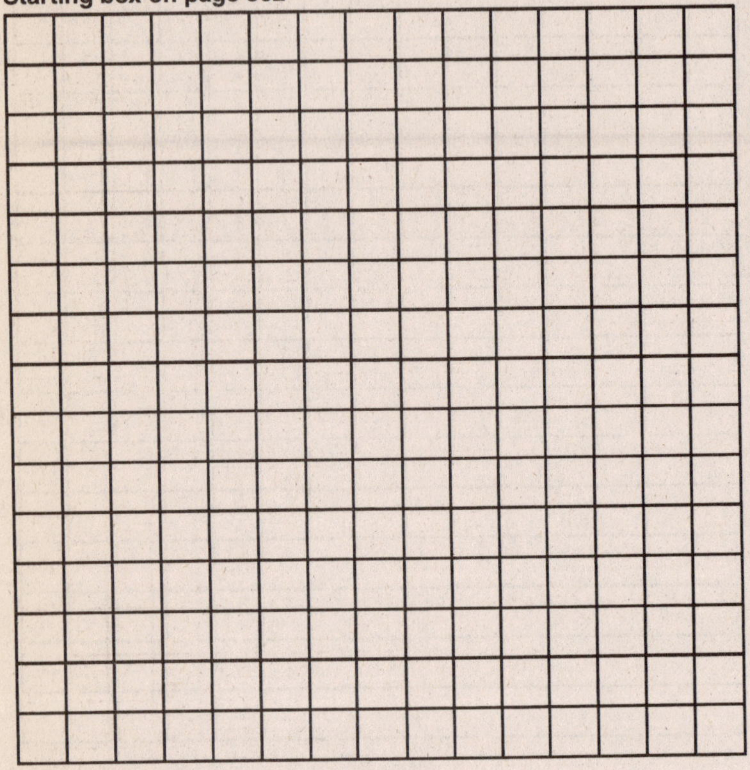

# PUZZLE 177

## Escalator

**Write the answer to clue 1 in the first space. Drop one letter and rearrange the remaining letters to answer clue 2. Put the dropped letter into Column A. Drop another letter and rearrange the remaining letters to answer clue 3. Put the dropped letter into Column B. Follow this pattern for each row in the diagram. When completed, the letters in Column A and Column B, reading down, will spell related words or a phrase.**

| | A | | B | |
|---|---|---|---|---|
| 1 | | 2 | | 3 |
| 4 | | 5 | | 6 |
| 7 | | 8 | | 9 |
| 10 | | 11 | | 12 |
| 13 | | 14 | | 15 |
| 16 | | 17 | | 18 |
| 19 | | 20 | | 21 |

1. Clergyman
2. Indonesian outriggers
3. Shadowbox
4. Choir members
5. Strict
6. Remainder
7. Volcano feature
8. Insertion mark
9. Speed contest
10. Biblical dancer
11. Repasts
12. Shade trees
13. Jog the memory of
14. Bogged down
15. Thin coin
16. Shiny decoration
17. Queues
18. Camera part
19. Oklahoma native
20. Night noise
21. Sea eagles

# PUZZLE 178

**ACROSS**
1. To and ____
4. Walks heavily
6. Large ice mass
8. Amphibian
9. Inert gas
11. Implore
12. Stopper
14. Stews
15. Type of car
17. Intimate
18. Flower part
20. Slice
21. Houseleek
23. Greek god of the forests
24. Finger or toe
26. Requested
29. Adjust again
31. Divide
33. Medieval poem
34. Allude
36. Busy persons
38. Asian country
40. Callas and Sills
41. Fray
43. Wandered
44. Okey-dokey
45. A Karamazov brother
46. Accelerated
48. Utopia
49. Stroll
51. College officials
52. Ocean

**DOWN**
1. Old Glory
2. Fabulous bird
3. Norse god of war
4. Tactics
5. Oozes
6. Shred
7. Functions
8. Not stale
10. Goya subjects
11. Those in favor
13. Stared open-mouthed
14. Football position
16. Lowest point
17. Social rank
19. Olympic sled
20. Mineral spring
22. Deceive
25. ____ for Fears
27. Balanced
28. Put off
30. "My country, ____ of thee"
32. Indemnify
35. Talks wildly
36. Couch
37. Baking chamber
39. Bounds' partner
40. Delaware's capital
42. Type of engine: hyph.
43. Carnival attractions
47. Membership charges
48. Sicilian spouter
50. Laird's no

Starting box on page 562

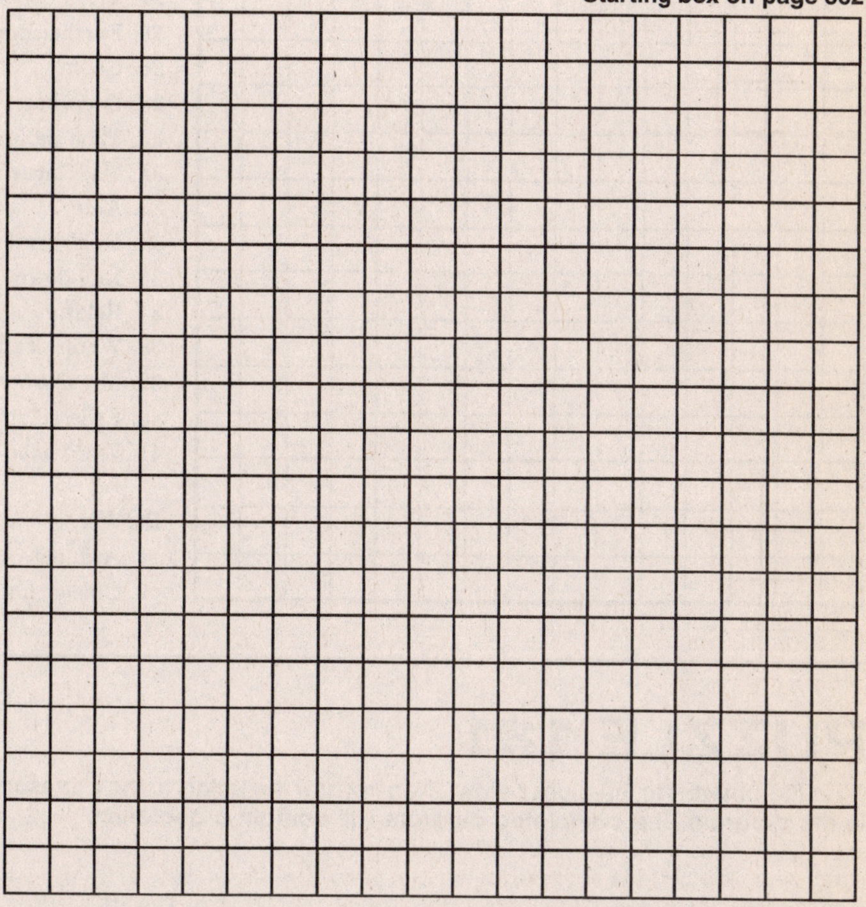

# ROLL OF THE DICE

# PUZZLE 179

**The 6 dice are actually the same die shown from 6 different positions. What 6-letter word is formed by the letters on the 6 bottom faces, reading from left to right?**

# PUZZLE 180

**ACROSS**

1. Chop
4. Wise man
5. "____ Girls"
8. Rid of impurities
9. Decorate again
10. Cattle groups
11. Sloping surface
12. "You ____ My Sunshine"
13. Unfasten
14. Oklahoma city
17. Burrowing animal
18. City in Arizona
20. "Act ____"
21. Verdi opera
25. Furthermore
26. Goofs
28. Deep holes
29. Time periods
32. Ms. Turner
33. Able
34. Hold firmly
35. Run-down
37. Relative
38. Water craft
39. Mr. Durocher
40. Ethereal
41. Everyone

**Starting box on page 562**

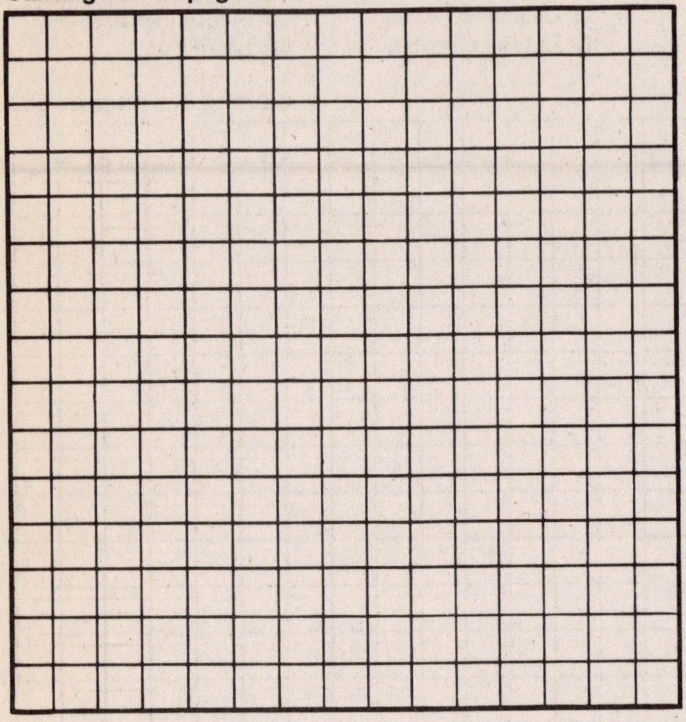

**DOWN**

1. Arduous
2. Omelet musts
3. Very small
4. Of course
5. Embankment
6. Blissful place
7. Impresario Hurok
8. Andean country
9. Well filled
10. Derby, e.g.
11. Daniel ____
15. Big ____
16. French friend
17. Shapes
19. Con
22. Available: 2 wds.
23. Attempt
24. Native metal
27. Security
28. Baby grand
30. Disencumbers
31. Farm pen
32. Accurate
34. "My ____ Sal"
35. Ground
36. Jurist Warren
38. Bleat

# PUZZLE 181

## QUOTAGRAM

**Fill in the answers to the clues below. Then transfer the letters to the correspondingly numbered squares in the diagram. The completed diagram will contain a quotation.**

1. Getting ___ ___ ___ ___ ___ ___ ___ ___ ___ (6 2 30 42 24 35 11 32 33)
2. ____ and fancy free ___ ___ ___ ___ ___ ___ ___ ___ ___ (10 38 28 20 47 4 17 12 44)
3. Since ___ ___ ___ ___ ___ ___ ___ (1 15 25 21 29 39 8)
4. Plug ___ ___ ___ ___ ___ ___ ___ (7 37 45 46 43 48 18)
5. Thwart ___ ___ ___ ___ ___ ___ (19 13 27 41 34 26)
6. Weighty ___ ___ ___ ___ ___ (14 36 31 23 3)
7. "The Man Who ____ Be King" ___ ___ ___ ___ ___ (16 40 5 9 22)

| | | | | | | | | | | | | | | | | | | | |
|---|---|---|---|---|---|---|---|---|---|---|---|---|---|---|---|---|---|---|---|
| 1 | 2 | ■ | 3 | 4 | 5 | 6 | 7 | 8 | 9 | 10 | ■ | 11 | 12 | ■ | 13 | 14 | 15 | ■ | 16 |
| 17 | 18 | 19 | 20 | ■ | 21 | 22 | 23 | 24 | 25 | 26 | ■ | 27 | 28 | 29 | ■ | 30 | 31 | 32 | ■ |
| 33 | 34 | 35 | 36 | ■ | 37 | 38 | ■ | 39 | 40 | 41 | 42 | ■ | 43 | 44 | 45 | 46 | 47 | 48 | ■ |

## PUZZLE 182

**ACROSS**
1. Health resort
4. Finger count
5. Droop
8. Finest
9. Mr. Beame
10. Ranked
12. Not wild
14. Actor Mineo
15. Sick
18. Rude cabin
19. Large tub
21. Edgar Allan ____
22. Metallic rock
23. Lyricist Gershwin
24. Cure leather
26. Conclude
27. Ignited
28. Moist
31. Morning moisture
33. Fencing sword
34. Sixty minutes
38. Noise
40. Landlord's income
41. Or ____!
42. Procure
44. Run into
45. Fish eggs
47. Short sleep
50. Speck
52. Solemn promise
53. Ceased fasting
54. Cowboy Rogers
56. Supplement an income
57. Lid
58. Shoe tip
59. Cooking fuel
61. Precipitation
63. Saber
66. "____ Got a Secret"
67. Woe is me!
68. Comedian Skelton
69. Corded fabric
70. Female deer

**DOWN**
1. Rob
2. Annoying insect
3. Poker kitty
5. Ringed planet
6. Lessened
7. Jewel
8. Bikini top
11. Immerse
13. Wickedness
14. Declared
16. Refugee from Sodom
17. Guide
18. Weeding tool
20. Dry
25. Back of the neck
29. Males
30. Teacher's ____
32. Toupee
34. Skirt edge
35. Bullring shout
36. Secondhand
37. Snappy comeback
39. Jitters
43. Seized
46. Water pitcher
47. Aborigine
48. Made amends
49. Vitality
51. Also
55. Word of permission
59. Potential raisin
60. Classified items
62. Make public
64. Hospital section
65. Butter substitute

Starting box on page 562

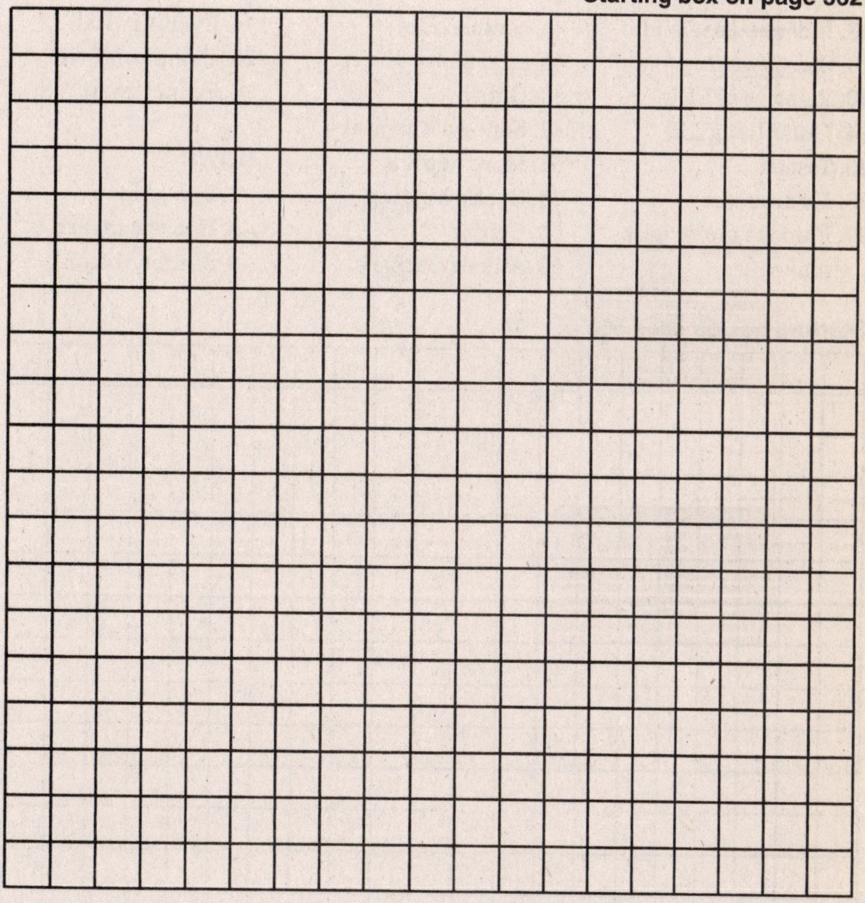

## ONE BY ONE

## PUZZLE 183

**Start with the given word JERK and form a series of common 4-letter words by changing one letter at a time. Do not change the order of the letters. Your goal is to use as many different letters as possible. Cross off each letter of the alphabet as you use it (as we have done for you with the letters of JERK). Once a letter has been replaced, it may not be used again. Our expert used all the letters except X and Q.**

**A B C D ~~E~~ F G H I ~~J~~ ~~K~~ L M N O P Q ~~R~~ S T U V W X Y Z**

# PUZZLE 184

**ACROSS**

1. Spanish surrealist
5. Eden resident
6. Harbors: abbr.
10. Grate
11. Famous Atlanta street
13. Military groups
14. Actor Novarro
18. Indonesian island
19. Secret writing
20. Relative of PDQ
24. "Auld Lang ___"
25. Tossed
26. Madras wear
27. Famous marionette maker
31. War or hope items
32. Arabian sultanate
33. Hebrew measures
35. Imprecations
36. Leg bone
38. Certain waterways
40. Benefit
41. Smooth wholesome complexion
45. ___ bien
46. Gaped
47. Senegal's capital
51. More netlike
54. Book's binding
55. Center
56. Auks' relatives
57. Hied
58. Statesman Abba ___
59. Northern constellation
60. Neighbor of Saskatchewan: abbr.
64. Transmitted
65. Costa ___
66. Sierra ___
68. Dutch cheeses
70. More profound
71. Chives' partner
73. Aware of
74. Evening: Ital.
75. Campus official
76. Tennis great

**DOWN**

1. Pub game
2. Hebrew month
3. Surgery beam
4. Accuses
6. Quarrel
7. Elfin beings
8. Actress Grimes
9. Descendant
12. "From ___ to Eternity"
15. Telegraph developer
16. Playwright Clifford ___
17. Tidings
20. Dating from
21. Alike
22. Composer Khachaturian
23. Locker picture, often
25. Seamstress's need
27. Pele's game
28. Asian nursemaids
29. Mathematician Descartes
30. Lawn material
31. Salad veggie
34. Thin, narrow boards
35. Prepared for spinning
37. Fastens again
39. Clicks, as one's fingers
40. Spectacle
42. Greek god of war
43. Trickle
44. Medieval weapons
48. Honshu port
49. Galway Bay name
50. Landlord's due
51. Sensational
52. Chilean city
53. Fizzy drink
56. Female horse
60. Actor Guinness
61. Ogles
62. Sun helmet
63. Lend ___ (listen)
67. Writer Bombeck
69. Units of sound
70. Male honeybee
72. Neighbor of Arizona

**Starting box on page 562**

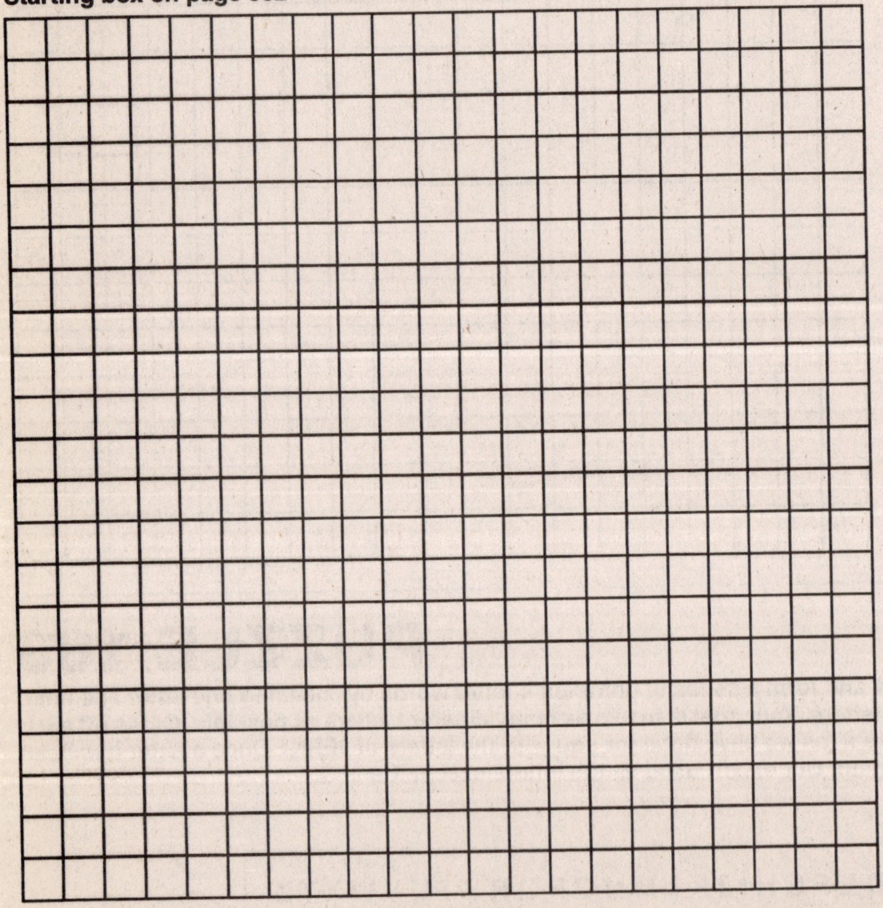

# PUZZLE 185

**ACROSS**

1. Hoover, for one
4. Dismounted
6. Tooth
8. Coach Parseghian
11. ____ of the House
13. Countenance
15. "____ a Yellow Ribbon . . ."
16. Hawaiian bird
17. Inclined
19. Wild hog
20. Turf
21. Famous parter
23. Judge
24. Go beyond
26. Sense of music
29. So be it!
30. "____ of Fury" (Bogart film)
31. Indian weight
32. Treeless plain
34. Rainbow
36. Participating in a Christmas club
40. Orangutan
43. Spring
44. Arab republic
45. Rail
47. Superlative ending
48. ____ avis
49. Continue steadfastly
51. Pithy saying
52. Labors
53. Lawn tool
54. Bert Bobbsey's twin

**DOWN**

1. Regulating device on a stove
2. African lily
3. City in Italy
5. Captures
7. Casino city
8. At a distance
9. Appraise
10. Sour
11. Slender cat
12. Noted Buttons
14. Or ____!
15. Nail or hold
18. Yellow rose's home
19. Cot
22. Peak
23. Playroom
25. Most uncanny
27. "Heidi" setting
28. Give back borrowed money
30. Possessive pronoun
32. Nurse a drink
33. Always
35. Race or trap
37. Muslim title
38. Roman emperor
39. Pesky insect
40. Snake
41. Keats for one
42. Goof
43. Abate
46. Tibetan or Chinese
50. Chase

**Starting box on page 562**

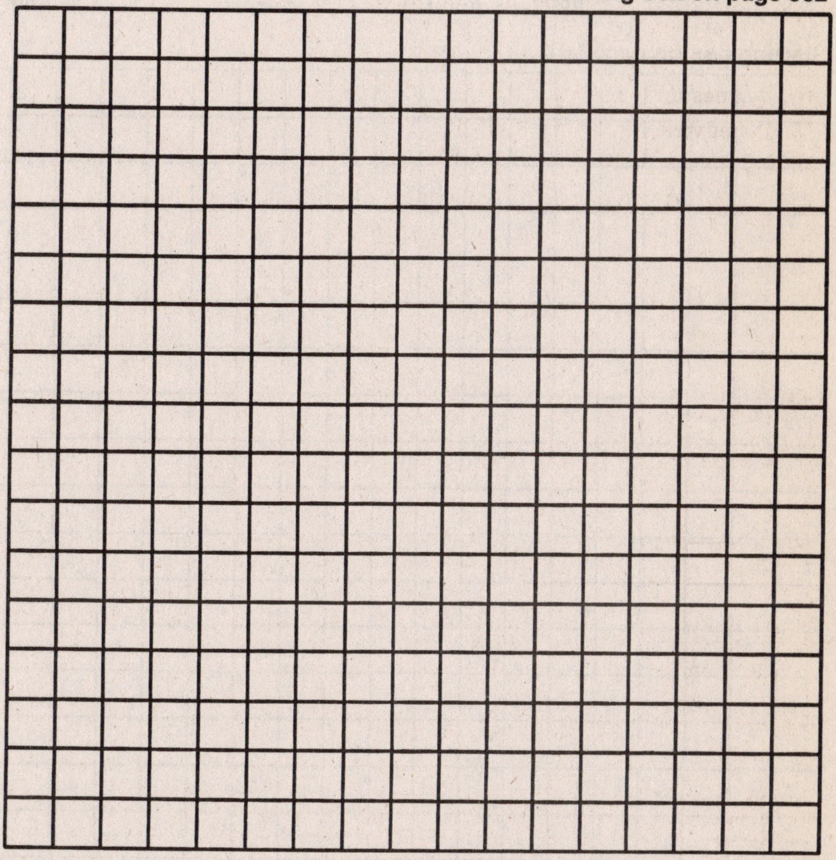

# Changaword

# PUZZLE 186

**Can you change the top word into the bottom word (in each column) in the number of steps indicated in parentheses? Do not change the order of the letters, and change only one letter at a time. Proper names, slang, and obsolete words are not allowed.**

| 1. **HEAT** (4 steps) | 2. **DIET** (5 steps) | 3. **BIRD** (5 steps) | 4. **FLOUR** (6 steps) |
|---|---|---|---|
| | | | |
| **COLD** | **FOOD** | **SONG** | **BREAD** |

# PUZZLE 187

**ACROSS**
1. Splash
8. Ben Hur, e.g.
11. King of the Franks
12. Sheen
13. Football passes
18. Kruger and Preminger
19. Young hare
20. College official
21. Eye part
22. Sty fare
26. Title for Olivier
27. Purify, in a way
30. "Annie Hall" director
33. Preface
35. Loud sound
39. Yarn quantity
40. Dust specks
41. Coast
42. Architectural molding
43. Memory
45. Soft drinks
46. Closest
47. Lawyer: abbr.
48. Fence door
49. Plaits
53. Atlas entries
57. Slices of veal
59. Contradict
60. Playing marbles
62. Writer Katherine Anne ____
63. Question
65. Writing paper
66. Firefighters' aids

**DOWN**
1. California mount
2. Singer Dolly ____
3. French city
4. Row
5. Male turkey
6. And others: abbr.
7. Stately
8. Trough
9. Come in
10. Superman portrayer
11. Lump
14. Soak flax
15. Ascended
16. Russian leader
17. Night sparkler
22. Narrow furrow
23. Pride member
24. Elderly
25. Adorned with feathers
27. Record
28. Dark
29. Stalk
30. Cybele's beloved
31. Property right
32. Suffering defeat
34. Robin Cook novel
35. "____ Eagles Dare"
36. Sharpen
37. Circle segments
38. Convene
41. Beat it!
43. Spin
44. Ocean
45. Swagger
47. Alphabet
50. ____ de France
51. Sandwich shops
52. Be frugal
53. Consolidation
54. Church tables
55. Devoutness
56. Withered
58. Of a bristle
59. Kentucky pioneer
61. "... ____ tabernacle for the sun"
62. Poke
64. Disencumber

Starting box on page 562

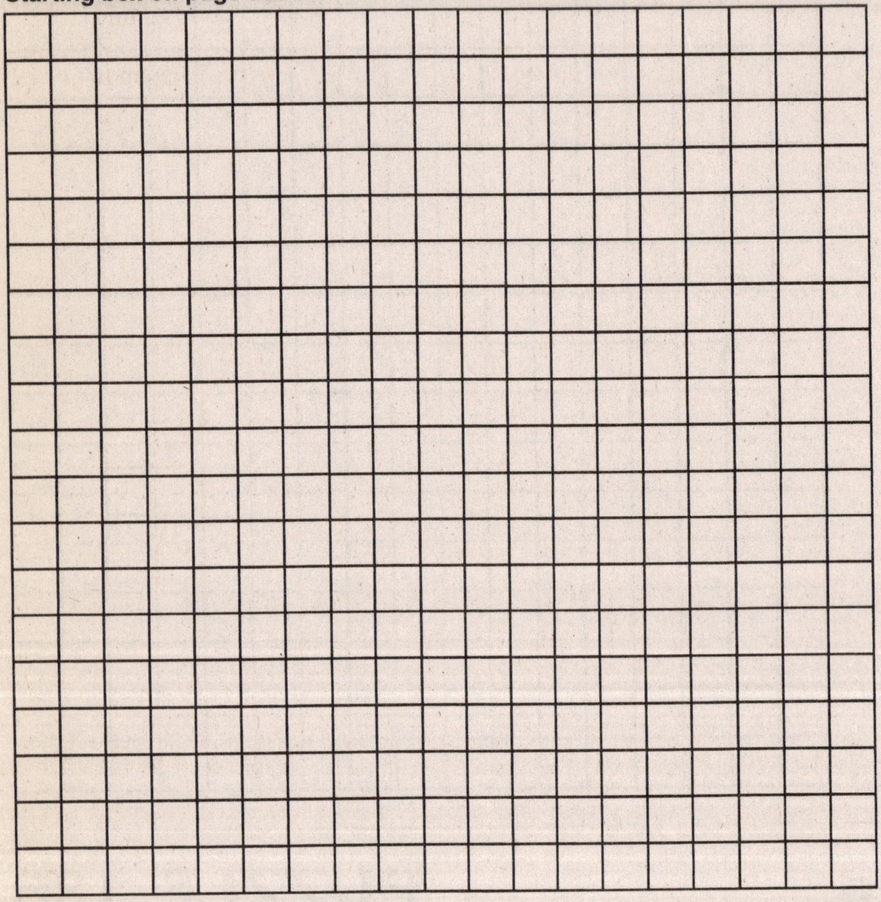

# PUZZLE 188

## One by One

**Start with the given word QUIZ and form a series of common 4-letter words by changing one letter at a time. Do not change the order of the letters. Your goal is to use as many different letters as possible. Cross off each letter of the alphabet as you use it (as we have done for you with the letters of QUIZ). Once a letter has been replaced, it may not be used again. Our expert used all the letters except J.**

A B C D E F G H ~~I~~ J K L M N O P ~~Q~~ R S T ~~U~~ V W X Y ~~Z~~

**QUIZ**

# PUZZLE 189

**ACROSS**

1. Record using a VCR
5. Peaceful
7. Rebuking severely
11. ____ Park (Edison's workplace)
12. Bandleader Shaw
13. Premed subj.
14. Raison d'____
15. Caterpillar hair
16. Throw
17. Distant: pref.
19. Dotted, in heraldry
21. Greek cheese
25. Like
27. Movie house
29. Elementary-school activity
32. Speechifies
33. Meal starter, often
35. Hill dwellers
36. Computer utilizer
38. Dickens character
40. Laughing sounds
44. Mise en ____ (hair set): Fr.
46. Leave out
47. Grain storage structure
48. Hay bundler
50. In front
51. Making a spectacle of
53. Scatters
54. Corn units

**DOWN**

1. Tattlers
2. Woody's son
3. Architect I.M. ____
4. Sicilian town
5. Legislative bodies
6. Wading bird
7. Doctrine
8. Sarge's dog
9. Certain evergreens
10. Cover charges
11. Barker and Bell
18. Flightless birds
20. Resounding sound
21. Monetary penalties
22. Purposes
23. Vietnamese holiday
24. Iowa campus site
26. Israeli dance
27. Suffragist Carrie ____
28. Matty of baseball
30. Pale
31. Profuse
34. Rarees
37. Cures
39. Rice dish
40. Elves
41. Nanking nanny
42. Hawaiian port
43. One-dish meals
45. Turf
49. Ceremony
50. Ripener
52. New Deal initials

Starting box on page 562

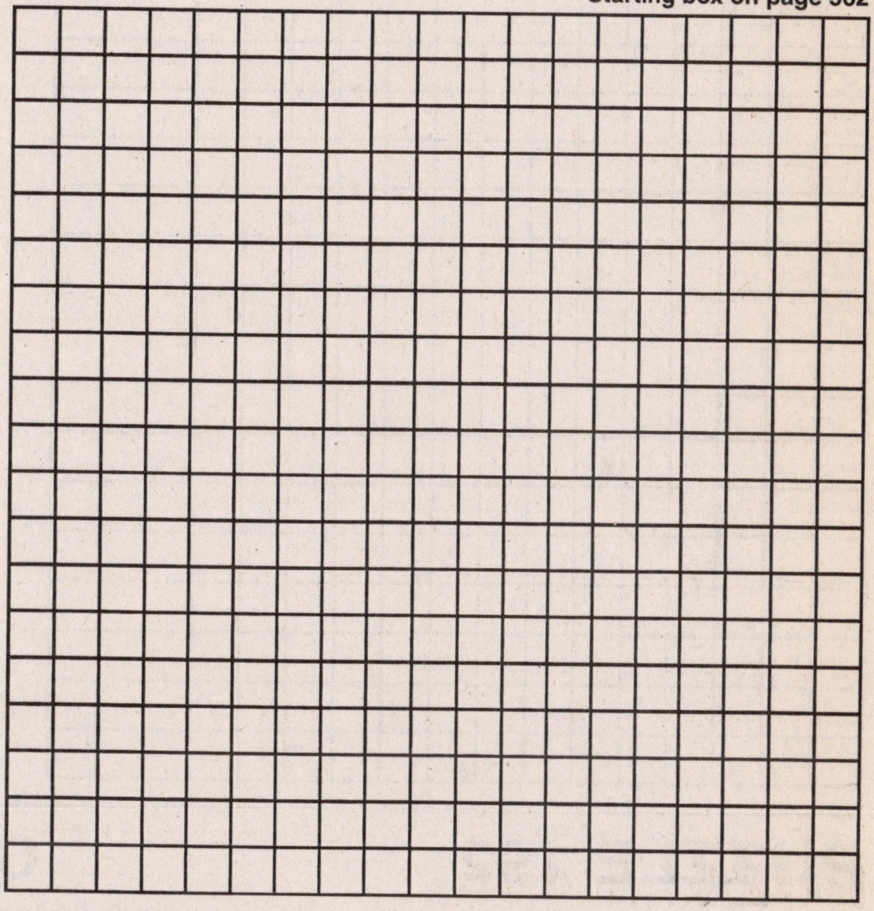

# HOP, SKIP, AND JUMP

# PUZZLE 190

**What is the longest word you can find starting with any letter, moving only from left to right? You may Hop, Skip, and Jump over any number of letters, but once you choose a letter you may not backtrack. A word with 10 or more letters is excellent.**

C F I J N S L G E W F R V K P M R P B I O N T U S

# PUZZLE 191

**ACROSS**
1. Sketch
5. Was obligated
9. Case of puppy love
10. Food
11. Pause
14. Playful
17. Buoy
19. Region
21. Three-sided blade
22. Morose
23. Guru's exercise
25. Emmet
26. Nurse
27. Turf
28. Wag
29. Utah brave
30. Pantywaist
34. Taunting remark
36. Orchard refreshment
37. Gruel grain
38. Of one mind
41. Vintage
42. Indian seasoning
43. Lily root
44. Heaven on earth
45. Crowd
48. Shanty
49. Suitable
52. Garlic section
54. Amigo
55. Error
57. Paid attention to
58. Greasy
60. Fence
62. Young moray
63. Gripping device
66. Drivel
68. Portico
69. Fructose
70. Stepped on it
71. Prophet

**DOWN**
1. Imaginative
2. Out of practice
3. Cleo's snake
4. Clever one
5. Away
6. Brawl
7. Keystone town
8. Hopelessness
9. Sing softly
12. Trinket
13. Seth's son
15. Superman's alias
16. But
17. Motorist's mishap
18. Single
20. Vanity
22. Eland's kin
24. Recess
28. Soggy
30. Blowhard
31. Cretan mount
32. Former boys
33. Cost
35. Cinch
36. Separate
39. Sludge
40. Uranium, e.g.
41. Published
43. Enthusiastic, Wall Street style
45. Method
46. Atop
47. Berth
48. Greet
50. Vegetable container
51. Praise highly
52. Underground chamber
53. Pedal
54. Burst
56. Handful
57. Quibble
59. Abominable Snowman
61. Gaelic gal
64. Fish eggs
65. Dismal
67. Expected

**Starting box on page 562**

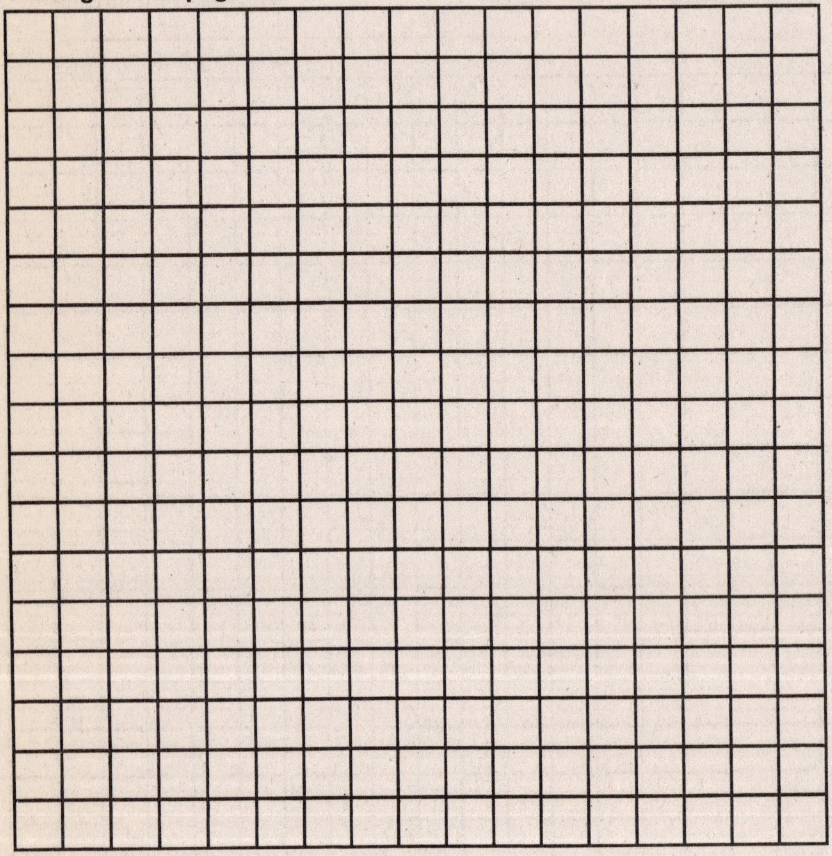

# PUZZLE 192

## Changaword

**Can you change the top word into the bottom word in each column in the number of steps indicated in parentheses? Change only one letter at a time and do not change the order of the letters. Proper names, slang, and obsolete words are not allowed.**

| 1. SNOW (4 steps) | 2. COAT (5 steps) | 3. WOOD (5 steps) | 4. DOWN (7 steps) |
|---|---|---|---|
| SUIT | RACK | PILE | VEST |

# PUZZLE 193

**ACROSS**
1. Once over
6. Possessed
9. Set aside
11. Conceit
12. Gear
14. Wagon
15. Hard covering
16. ____ the sky
18. Metallic rocks
19. French friend
20. Enclose
22. Colorado Shoshonean
23. Photographer Modotti
25. Pool length
28. Come out
30. Party to
31. Greek letter
32. Patriot Allen
33. Barber's cry
34. Lichen
36. Apiece
37. Bargains in court
40. 2000 pounds
41. Not taped
42. "Time" founder
46. Restaurant bar
48. Actress Ullmann
49. October birthstone
50. Commendation
52. Tell fibs
53. Scarlett's home
54. "The ____" (Ross/ Jackson film)
55. Nobleman
57. Sawbuck
58. Region
59. Free
62. Like some seals
64. City on the Rhine
65. Bojangles, for instance
67. And so forth: abbr.
68. Harmful
69. Three-way joint
70. Gibe

**DOWN**
1. Greek crosses
2. Legal document
3. Brat
4. Bivouac
5. "... ____ saw Elba"
6. Encourage
7. See eye to eye
8. Polka ____
9. Spring starter
10. Was certain
12. Stoat
13. Radial
14. Mountain lion
15. "The ____ the Hat"
17. Moniker
21. Personal annoyance
24. Bug
25. Summer quaff
26. Above
27. Go by
29. Zeus's mother
35. Maglie or Bando
37. ____ slaw
38. Capsule
39. MDCCX ÷ XXX
40. Lord Greystoke
42. Destiny
43. Cornered
44. Lifework
45. African antelope
46. Math partner
47. Watch face
51. Jog
54. Scripted
56. Bank offering
58. Assist in wrongdoing
60. The Munsters' dragon
61. Brickell or Sedgwick
62. Son of Seth
63. Wyle E. Coyote's brand
66. Exposure index

Starting box on page 562

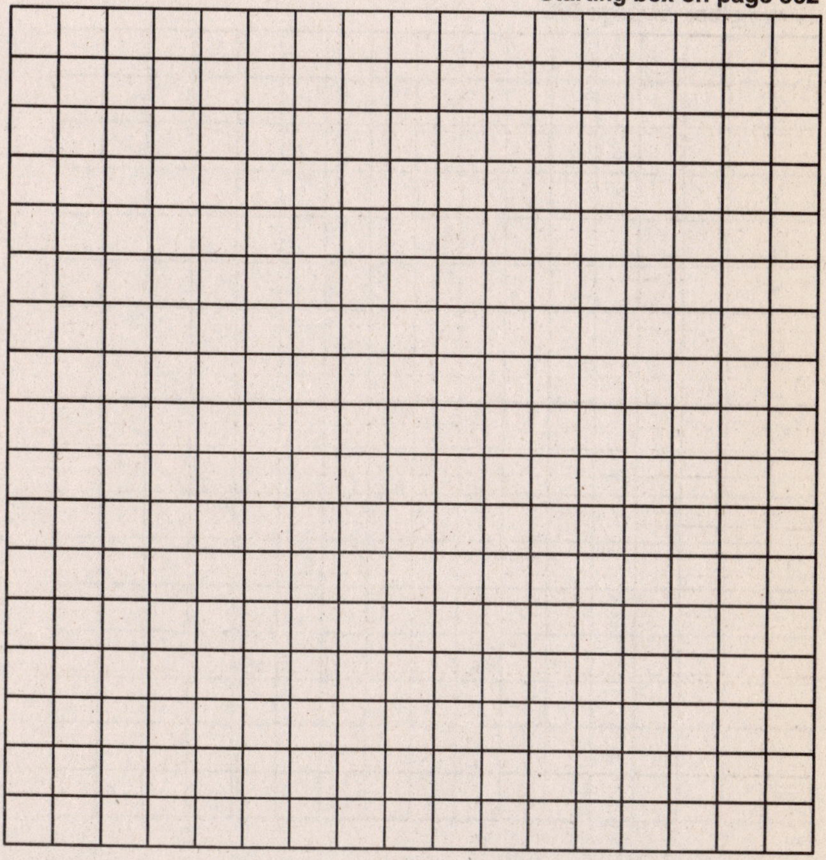

# Changaword

# PUZZLE 194

**Can you change the top word into the bottom word in each column in the number of steps indicated in parentheses? Change only one letter at a time and do not change the order of the letters. Proper names, slang, and obsolete words are not allowed.**

| 1. ROAD (4 steps) | 2. FAST (4 steps) | 3. REST (8 steps) | 4. NEXT (8 steps) |
|---|---|---|---|
| TOUR | LANE | STOP | EXIT |

# PUZZLE 195

**ACROSS**
1. "Of ____ I sing . . ."
5. Priestly vestment
8. Removes rind
9. ____ positive
11. Last scene
12. Masters and doctorates
14. Pursuits
15. Servicemen's group: abbr.
16. Source for help
18. Acquired
19. Fernando or Lorenzo
20. For each
21. Man or Wight
25. Find a sum
28. Fountain treats
30. To the time that
31. Logholder
33. Nightfall, poetically
34. Buckets
35. Consumed
36. Moves briskly
38. Dark bread
39. Graceful waterbird
40. Halloween hoot
41. Movie director Frank
43. Everything
46. Three-wheeler
49. Chinese philosophy
50. Contracted
52. Nutty tree
54. Be agreeable
55. Use the old noodle
56. Unit of weight
57. ____ of these days
58. Younger brother, e.g.

**DOWN**
1. Showing strain
2. Warmth
3. Plumbing joints
4. Compass pt.
5. Thieves' talk
6. Cockney exclamation
7. Dutch South African
8. Bakery treats
9. Mexican money
10. Examine by touch
11. Fuzzy coatings
12. Excavated
13. ____ Flow
14. Football position
17. Breakfast dish
21. Actress Claire
22. Agitate
23. Singer Pons
24. Otherwise
25. Ripens
26. Depict
27. Facts
28. Soldiers
29. "Peanuts" pooch
30. Downs' partner
32. Decade
37. Flaming light
41. Madrid movie
42. Dismounted
43. Do penance
44. Escapade
45. Actress Myrna
46. Stretch of land
47. Trick
48. Ill-fated lover of Narcissus
50. Swing around
51. Female fowl
53. Relatives
54. Soft drink

**Starting box on page 562**

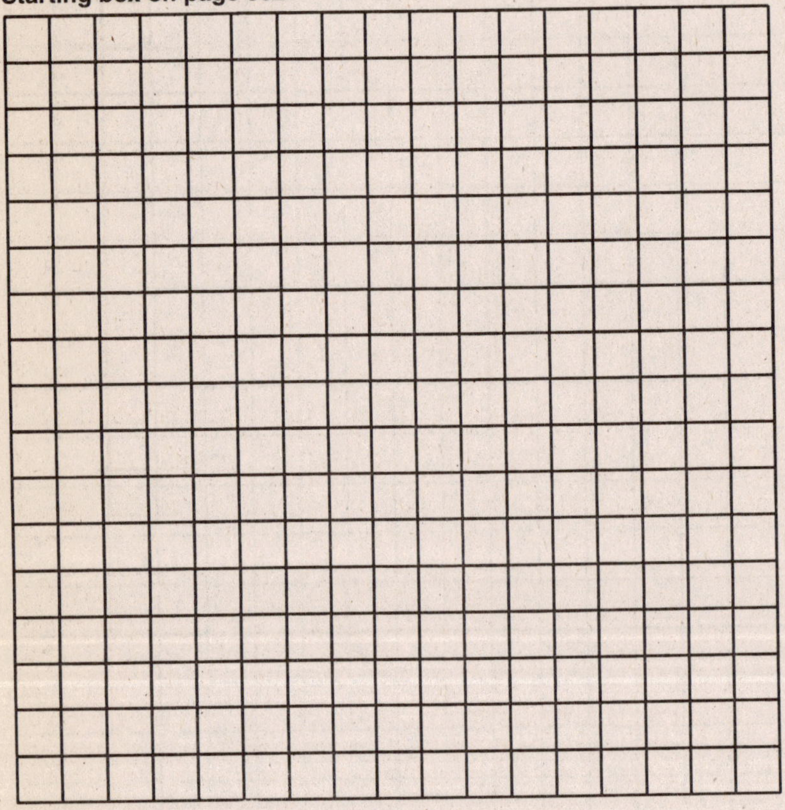

# PUZZLE 196

## KEYWORD

**To find the KEYWORD fill in the blanks in words 1 through 10 with the correct missing letters. Transfer those letters to the correspondingly numbered squares. Fill with care. This puzzle is not as simple as it first appears.**

| 1 | 2 | 3 | 4 | 5 | 6 | 7 | 8 | 9 | 10 |
|---|---|---|---|---|---|---|---|---|---|
| | | | | | | | | | |

1. _ U N C H
2. S _ L L Y
3. T H U M _
4. F L _ S H
5. S T A _ K
6. D _ N C E
7. _ O W E R
8. B R A _ D
9. D R _ V E
10. G R E E _

## PUZZLE 197

**ACROSS**
1. Beanie
4. Small mound
7. Dutch painter
8. Israeli port
10. Details
13. Tropical fruit
14. Old English coin
15. Tease
17. Kind of drum
18. Surfeit
19. Cistern
21. Sacred bull
22. Comrades
23. Snapshot
25. Gumshoe
26. Dissolute man
27. ____ piano
28. Beauty aid: 2 wds.
30. Fine fabric
33. Joust
34. Mr. Hunter
37. Signs
38. Ancient Briton
39. Runny cheese
40. Conjunction
41. Inlet
42. Roman author
43. Kennel sound
45. Indian
46. Child's delight
47. Of the earth
50. Discomfort
51. Expel
52. Witticism
53. Muffin

**DOWN**
1. Freight
2. Choir singer
3. Greek letter
4. Zodiac sign
5. Brilliance
6. Period
7. Suspends
9. Slip
10. Kind of button
11. Cooperative farms
12. London hotel
13. Sulk
16. Portal
17. ____ Masterson
18. Bauble
20. Rocky pinnacle
22. U.S. President
23. Municipal map
24. Self-centered actor
26. Betsy ____
27. Skin
28. Tin
29. Cereal grain
30. TV's Johnson
31. Chinese isle
32. Earn
34. ____ and error
35. "____ Misbehavin' "
36. African ruler
38. Mighty
39. Act sheepish
41. Keepsake
42. Geometric solid
44. Ginger
46. Genuine
48. Merino male
49. Dress, slangily

Starting box on page 562

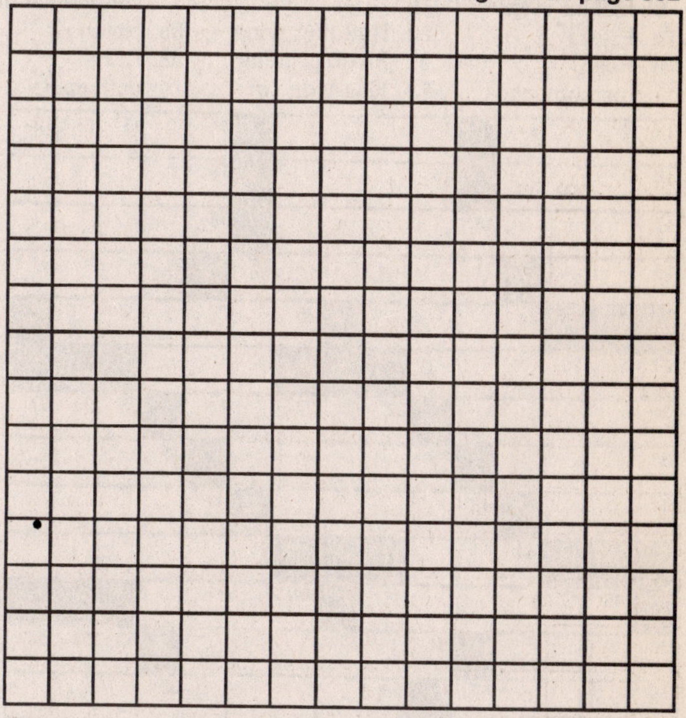

## QUOTAGRAM

## PUZZLE 198

**Fill in the answers to the clues below. Then transfer the letters to the correspondingly numbered squares in the diagram. The completed diagram will contain a quotation.**

1. Upward moves ___ ___ ___ ___ ___ ___ ___ ___ ___ ___
   3 16 50 2 27 39 31 46 32 5
2. Unimportant person ___ ___ ___ ___ ___ ___
   42 49 8 15 36 21
3. Of past events ___ ___ ___ ___ ___ ___ ___ ___ ___ ___
   34 1 52 22 18 44 37 38 13 20
4. Precise ___ ___ ___ ___ ___ ___ ___ ___
   17 25 47 7 29 11 33 35
5. Without hurry ___ ___ ___ ___ ___ ___
   12 51 41 14 9 45
6. Clown ___ ___ ___ ___ ___ ___ ___
   24 28 48 26 4 23 19
7. ____ Thompson ___ ___ ___ ___ ___
   6 43 30 40 10

| | | | | | | | | | | | | | | | | | | | | | |
|---|---|---|---|---|---|---|---|---|---|---|---|---|---|---|---|---|---|---|---|---|---|
| 1 | 2 | 3 | 4 | 5 | 6 | 7 | 8 | 9 | 10 | | 11 | 12 | | 13 | | 14 | 15 | 16 | 17 | | 18 |
| 19 | 20 | 21 | | 22 | 23 | | 24 | 25 | | 26 | 27 | 28 | 29 | 30 | | 31 | 32 | | 33 | 34 | 35 |
| | 36 | 37 | 38 | 39 | 40 | 41 | 42 | 43 | 44 | 45 | | 46 | 47 | | 48 | 49 | 50 | 51 | 52 | | |

# PUZZLE 199

**ACROSS**
1. Couch
5. Injure
9. Italian staple
14. Persia
15. Reed instrument
16. Very pale
17. Shower elements
19. Brief
20. Building wing
21. Most peculiar
23. Has title to
24. Away from the wind
25. Desires strongly
27. Spins
30. Gorilla
31. Half quarts
32. Have confidence in
35. Network
38. Large coffeepots
39. Honking bird
40. Shoe bottom
41. ___ Plaines
42. Drafted a letter
43. Specter
44. Catch sight of
45. Knives
46. "Messiah" composer
49. Row of stitches
50. Be concerned
51. Seesaw
53. Exist
56. Thing of value
58. College teacher
60. Supermarket
61. Roof overhang
62. Shred
63. Uptight
64. Drove too fast
65. Sweet potatoes

**DOWN**
1. King's title
2. Evangelist Roberts
3. Flunk
4. Columnist Landers
5. Throngs
6. Residence
7. Lasso
8. Very untidy
9. Dance step
10. On land
11. Demonstrated
12. Gull-like birds
13. Hill insects
18. "Guys and ___"
22. Make fun of
24. ___ and crafts
26. Likely
27. Potato
28. Metal thread
29. Country hotels
32. Also
33. Decay
34. Utilize
35. Lumber
36. Otherwise
37. Wagers
39. Welcome
40. Counterfeit
42. Marry
43. Blinding light
44. Curls the lip
45. Complained
46. Undue speed
47. Fire crime
48. Runs easily
49. Kitchen range
50. Hurl
52. Snare
53. On the ocean
54. Wander
55. Strays from the truth
57. Ball holder
59. Untidy home

# PUZZLE 200

## Some Sum

**What is the sum of the numbers below? That is for you to guess! Study the numbers for 30 seconds and then try to estimate the sum. There are no 2-digit numbers. You're a winner if your guess is within 30!**

# PUZZLE 201

**ACROSS**

1. More protracted
6. Fish sauce
10. Mr. Martin
14. Lively
15. Roman statesman
16. Italian river
17. Baseball film
19. Arachnid
20. Decided
21. Sun. talk
22. Sharpener food
24. Singer Bandy
26. Figure mug
27. On deck
30. Baseball film
33. Guitar's kin
34. Tall tale
35. "Gimme a Break" gal
37. Besides
38. Loved to excess
39. Cap site
40. Oracle
41. "The African Queen" screenwriter
42. Designer Geoffrey ____
43. "The Pride of ____"
45. Riding horses
46. Units of work
47. Eur. nation
48. Body-hugging dress
51. ____ and away
53. Tango number
56. Dangle
57. Baseball film
61. Matty and Felipe
62. Where the Shannon flows
63. Make up
64. Doctor's amount
65. Split
66. San ____

**DOWN**

1. Scientific rms.
2. Malarial fever
3. Incline
4. Architect's addition
5. Hair color
6. Brazilian state
7. "Cowardly Lion"
8. Delphi vowel
9. Mixture
10. Baseball film
11. Singer Clapton
12. Hero or dote prefix
13. Yuletide tune
18. Like tag-sale items
23. Diminish
24. Baseball film
25. Spanish gold
26. A crowd?
27. Goat's-hair fabrics
28. Hay bundles
29. Start
30. Scolds
31. Actress Adoree
32. Mingle
34. Famous bear et al.
36. Pinky and Peggy
38. Daddy's girl
42. Heat meas.
44. Morsel
45. Gilbert of "Roseanne"
48. Roe producer
49. Salt: pref.
50. Adam's grandson
51. Maidenhair
52. Dill
53. Meadowlands offering
54. Decline
55. Bread spread
58. Hustle
59. Skye cap
60. Large lizard

# PUZZLE 202

**ACROSS**

1. Bessie's home
5. Windstorm
9. Beauty parlor
14. Melville work
15. Caspian Sea feeder
16. Sierra ____
17. Lorre role
18. Go down
19. Synthetic fabric
20. Expanded
23. Liquid meas.
24. "____ Girls"
25. Like some beaches
27. Postponed
31. Farmer, at times
33. Bow's companion
34. Anon
35. "Had I ____ for a century . . ."
38. Problem
39. Easel
40. The Bard's wife
41. Melody
42. Paves
43. French school
44. Summoners
46. Interlocked
47. African desert
49. Grass genus
50. See 41 Across
51. Peace offering
58. Botch
60. Turkish liqueur
61. Matador's foe
62. Tear
63. Seed covering
64. Lulu
65. ____ Ababa
66. Of sound mind
67. Like some lawns

**DOWN**

1. Box-office flop
2. Cupid
3. Sacred Roman ____
4. Lunch time
5. Spewed
6. Sky ram
7. "One if by ____"
8. Nevada county
9. Scheduled
10. Atmosphere: pref.
11. New Jersey resort
12. Ryan or Tatum
13. "____ Bly"
21. Ball of yarn
22. Affect drastically
26. Nautical cries
27. Soviet news agency
28. Pisa's river
29. Highway feeder
30. Open arcade
31. Glides
32. Time periods
34. Lead
36. Type of poison
37. Lack
39. Bargain
43. Limerick man
45. Literary devices
46. Calder creation
47. Israeli
48. Felt sick
49. Illinois city
52. Cleopatra's maid
53. Unit of length: Sp.
54. Speck
55. Taboo
56. Kind of cut
57. Cornucopia
59. Egg: pref.

# PUZZLE 203

**ACROSS**

1. Octagon word
5. Cooking verb
10. Clock face
14. Cavity
15. Whirling
16. Atop
17. Wide-mouthed vessel
18. Layers
19. Colorado Indians
20. Dixie drawl: 2 wds.
23. Conger
24. Above, to poets
25. Hiding places
29. Behave like sheep
32. Forefront
35. Concerning
36. Pretense
37. Sand hill
38. Fiji and Samoa, e.g.: 3 wds.
41. Dancer Miller et al.
42. Small pie
43. Watchful
44. Series
45. Movie dog
46. Stage whispers
47. "____ a Camera": 2 wds.
49. Letter addenda: abbr.
50. 1946 Disney film: 4 wds.
58. Seaweed
59. Path
60. Shelley or Keats
62. Blockage
63. Tapestry
64. Stare
65. Rosebud's rider
66. Hollers
67. Designate

**DOWN**

1. Haggard novel
2. Pulls
3. Bread spread
4. Land of the Incas
5. Washes
6. Spirit in "The Tempest"
7. Clairvoyant
8. Sea bird
9. "Born Free" lioness
10. "Irma La ____"
11. Mediated
12. Solar disk
13. Missing
21. Canines
22. Bashful
25. Houses: Sp.
26. "To a rag and ____": 2 wds.
27. Trusting in: 2 wds.
28. Shanties
29. Scarlett ____
30. Fisherman's need
31. 911 people: abbr.
33. Author Schwarz-Bart
34. Bird sites
36. Subway scarcity
37. Surrealist painter
39. Aves.
40. Lariat
45. I love: Lat.
46. Appraise
48. Marble
49. Flower part
50. Duffel bag
51. Earthen pot
52. Skirmish
53. Raced
54. Fling
55. Above
56. Roman robe
57. Tiller
61. Shirt type

# PUZZLE 204

**ACROSS**

1. Flowery
5. Comedian Wilson
9. European capital
13. Global area
14. Work perk
15. Mixture
16. Gautier novel: 2 wds.
19. Stretch
20. Bay window
21. Odoriferous
23. Handbag
25. Engages
26. Depository
27. Alt. spelling
30. Lucre lover
31. Trade
32. High note: 2 wds.
33. Certain receivers
34. Body section
35. Tidbit
36. Andrea ____ Sarto
37. Sojourn
38. Principle
39. Sooner than
40. Impulse
41. New ____, Ct.
42. French river
44. Cafe chompers
45. "American Bandstand" host
47. Notice
48. Dickens novel: 3 wds.
54. Quarry of the carver's wife
55. Rome's port
56. Zola heroine
57. Court celebrity
58. Polanski film
59. Sprouted

**DOWN**

1. Varnish
2. Dos Passos trilogy
3. Small drink
4. Carolina cape
5. Whim
6. Steal
7. Leb.'s neighbor
8. As thick as ____ soup
9. Tusked animals
10. Holmes novel: 2 wds.
11. ____ and shine
12. December song
14. Moroccan coins
17. Rhone delta city
18. "Murphy Brown" role
21. Brawl bruise
22. George Eliot novel
23. Garden bloom
24. Bring to ruin
26. City in Vermont
28. E.T. and ALF
29. Lost in delight
30. Persian's pal
31. Comic pianist
34. Mountain pool
35. Dividing
37. Finnish port
38. Spud
41. Seaport in 7 Down
43. Napoleon's men
44. ____ Island
45. Cook book
46. Pitcher Tiant
47. Minnesota ____
49. Little one
50. Function
51. Attention
52. From Miami to Hartford
53. Small crow

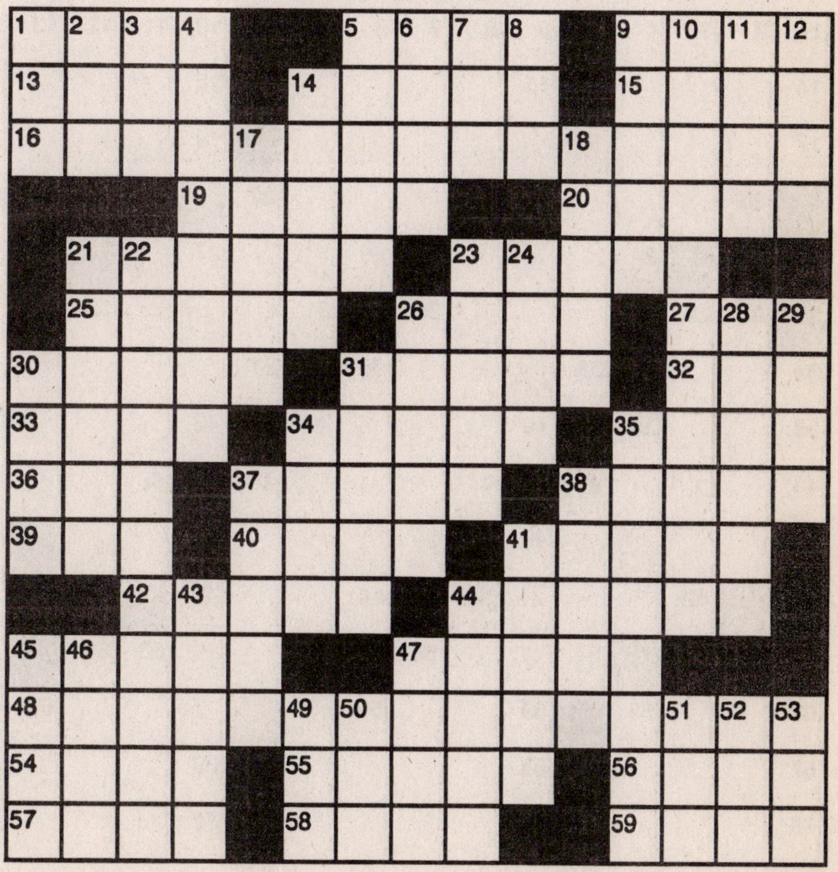

# PUZZLE 205

**ACROSS**

1. Bones
5. NATO and SEATO
10. So be it
14. Soared
15. Permit
16. Golf goal
17. New Year's figure: 2 wds.
19. Normandy town: 2 wds.
20. Water or wine
21. Bog fuel
23. Layer
24. "Metropolis" director
26. Surprised look
28. Encouraged
31. Athens's rival
34. "___ Alibi"
35. Stuffed
37. Upper atmosphere
38. Aphrodite's son
40. ___ eclipse
42. Ilk
43. Ceremonies
45. Diving feats
47. Wallet item
48. Saw
50. Fountain treats
52. Ohio Indians
54. Train-track runner
55. Flub
57. Type unit
59. "Lady and the ___"
62. "GWTW" home
64. Certain reporters: 2 wds.
67. Fiddler on the reef
68. Cape Cod town
69. Isaac's son
70. Detest
71. ___ Hall University
72. Humid

**DOWN**

1. Switch label
2. Reuben ingredient
3. Son of Adam
4. For a bit
5. Type of guidance
6. Jet's elevation: abbr.
7. Football infraction
8. Weighty books
9. Perspires
10. Sounds of surprise
11. Maternity
12. That girl, in Paris
13. Las Vegas light
18. Les ___-Unis
22. Duct ___
25. Outfit
27. Darn it!
28. Penthouse
29. Ronald Reagan film: 2 wds.
30. Jeans' material
32. Gulls
33. Comedian Johnson
34. Spice
36. Senegal's capital
39. Prophet
41. Aunt or uncle
44. Marina offering
46. Rouses
49. Jefferson and religious followers
51. Very happy
53. Put to music
55. Delineate
56. ___ avis
58. Border on
60. Flat-topped hill
61. Hyde Park sight
63. Humorist Burrows
65. Broadway hit sign: abbr.
66. Grab a bite

# PUZZLE 206

**ACROSS**
1. Ear part
5. Athenian
10. Mr. Charles
13. Baal
14. Couple
15. Margarine
17. Space
18. Certain tanker
19. Alpha's follower
20. Refuge
21. Toothpaste holder
22. Panacea
24. New England state
26. TV sitcom
27. Circa
29. Conspiracy
30. Hobby
33. Holy book
34. Lawrence Taylor, for one
35. Mined matter
36. Roman poet
37. Baseball's Dean
38. Connect
39. Singer Shannon
40. Snit
41. Tub occupant
42. French season
43. Ms. Bombeck
44. Belt part
45. Singer Laine
46. Penniless
47. Astrologer's chart
50. Riot
51. Notable time
54. Excited
55. Eagle's weapon
57. October stone
58. Excuse
59. Mountain nymph
60. ____-mell
61. Be human
62. Prepared
63. Playing card

**DOWN**
1. Money in Venice, once
2. Redolence
3. Traveling library
4. Kind of tree
5. Proliferate
6. Clan
7. Story
8. Diamonds
9. Wedding, e.g.
10. Batman's partner
11. Author Haley
12. Sasquatch's cousin
16. Rowboat adjunct
21. Fork part
23. Latvian
25. "____ Lang Syne"
26. "Up ____ River"
27. Home
28. Rosie's fastener
29. Kind of pie
30. Accountant
31. Satellite of Uranus
32. Category
34. One of the "Gremlins"
37. Woody Allen, e.g.
38. Face card
40. Honduran seaport
41. Ocean marker
44. Spirit
45. Proud father's handout
46. Expansive
47. Shoot
48. Gawk
49. Activist
50. Tiny circus performer
52. Chest sound
53. Friend
56. 100 square meters
57. Choose

# PUZZLE 207

**ACROSS**

1. Austen's Woodhouse
5. Rugs
9. British veggies
14. Prone one
15. Atop
16. In disguise: abbr.
17. Catching on: 4 wds.
20. Bird genus
21. El Dorado find
22. Feature of "pfennig": 2 wds.
25. Harems
30. Previous to
31. Sweet treats
33. Clock sound
34. ____ wait (ambush): 2 wds.
35. Scholar's lair
36. Gist: 3 wds.
41. Woodsman's activity
42. Dim
43. Bit
44. Prayer beads
46. Merry: Fr.
49. "The Genius" author
51. Spencer's co-star
53. Madre's sis
54. First name in fictional villains
55. Words of support: 5 wds.
62. Gourmand
63. Russian river
64. Bleaching vat
65. Type of shooting
66. Actress McClurg
67. Riley's life

**DOWN**

1. Go by
2. Above-ground
3. Interfere
4. Take for ____: 2 wds.
5. Coffee holder
6. Fitting
7. Haul
8. Siesta
9. Assign blame to: 2 wds.
10. Rump
11. Be a ham
12. Plant
13. Freud find
18. Yangtze city
19. Son of Zeus and Hera
23. Bound
24. Omega preceders
26. Perfume
27. Proper ____
28. Aussie rock band
29. "Say Anything . . ." actress
32. Ignores
34. Veranda
35. Don't leave!: 2 wds.
36. Uttered
37. Wife: Lat.
38. Bit
39. Listless
40. Parched
44. Bridle part
45. Delphi figure
46. ____ pig
47. Porthos's friend
48. Belong
50. Set in motion
52. In the red
55. Affirmative
56. Sturdy as an ____
57. Shoshonean
58. Carriage spring shape
59. British ref. work
60. Single: pref.
61. Scot's denial

# PUZZLE 208

**ACROSS**

1. Zeno's specialty
8. Cane
13. Limited autonomy: 2 wds.
14. Shot
16. Youngman's specialty: hyph.
17. AL player
18. Fanatical
19. Postulate
21. Stannum
22. ____-and-span
23. Salisbury, for one
24. One trillionth: pref.
25. Lower-case poet's initials
26. Karpov's forte
27. "____ the Family": 2 wds.
28. "Gil ____"
29. Rickles' specialties
31. Lively dance
33. English homework
34. Plaintiff's award
36. Former ruler
37. Foreshadowings
38. Cautious
40. Charade
43. Shred
44. French soldier
45. Peak: pref.
46. Evian, for one
47. Imply: 2 wds.
48. Mohegan chief
49. American Rockies' high point
51. Eastern, for one: 2 wds.
53. Speak indirectly about something: 2 wds.
54. One of the Aleutians
55. Poor
56. Picks

**DOWN**

1. Pacific island
2. Protozoan
3. Dig find
4. Unproductive
5. Demand payment from
6. Certain esters
7. King of Persia
8. Haunter
9. Fixed period
10. MacGraw of movies
11. Naval group
12. Joy
13. Sense or opera
15. Partners of mortises
20. Romanian city
23. Condition
24. Luxurious
26. Dancing shoes
27. Test
28. Wishy-washy
30. Indian leader
31. Strategy: 2 wds.
32. Submissive
34. Part of Wessex
35. Glaswegian
36. Cracker
39. Missing part
40. Confront
41. Model T features
42. " . . . pussycat went ____"
44. Trifling
45. Commonwealth soldier
47. Alum
48. Ubangi feeder
50. Increase
52. ____ de mer

# PUZZLE 209

**ACROSS**

1. Fume
6. Grimalkin
9. Suit fabric
14. Overhangs
15. "____ from the Heart"
16. Lend ____: 2 wds.
17. Ashes
18. Margosa
19. Peruvian ruminant
20. Hair strand, to Medusa
22. Hair ointments
24. Full of vim
26. Ship component
29. Helpful push
30. Nelson or Mary Baker
34. Beverages
35. Places for coins
36. Terrible
37. Wooden nail
38. Great amount
39. Wading bird
41. Ninnies
46. Old wound's leaving
47. Office article
48. Baseballer Hank ____
49. Actor Rip ____
50. Inside info
53. Certain colors
56. Sweet-smelling
60. South American timber tree
61. Boatman's item
63. Disposed
64. Secure
65. "Born in the ____"
66. Rich brown
67. Kills
68. ____ Aviv
69. Automotive lemon

**DOWN**

1. Matched groups
2. Horse
3. Finished
4. Certain zoo employees
5. German industrial city
6. Regulate
7. Tropical bird
8. Storm
9. Game dish
10. Intertwined
11. Interpret
12. Plucky
13. Notable periods
21. Bird beaks
23. Mel's family
25. Stickum
26. Agreeably flavored
27. New cadet
28. Protection
31. "Saturday Night Fever" music
32. Bleak
33. Pine
40. Incomplete
41. British hoosegow
42. Goes to a restaurant: 2 wds.
43. Ahead of
44. Sisterly
45. Geraint's wife
46. Played the lead
51. NYSE memberships
52. Shrubby undergrowth
53. Butter bits
54. Seed covering
55. Legendary account
57. Sorry!
58. Unicorn fish
59. Close tightly
62. "Peer Gynt" character

# PUZZLE 210

**ACROSS**

1. Envelope abbr.
5. Unconstrained
9. Rebuff
13. Hillside, in Dundee
14. Buzz
15. Cato's robe
16. Points
17. Kilns
18. Shortly
19. Anderson/ Weill tune: 2 wds.
22. Dele
23. Den
24. The sun
27. Writer Buntline
30. ____ culpa
31. ____ Beta Kappa
32. Astronaut Shepard
36. Incas' land
38. "Sunshine of Your Love" group
40. Crazy: 5 wds.
43. Unsuitable
44. Poet Khayyam
45. Approval
46. Dunderhead
47. Ocean: abbr.
49. Alkaline substance
51. Pose
52. River nymph
54. Plant of forgetfulness
59. U.S. financier: 2 wds.
63. Recedes
65. Gunwale pin
66. Soft cheese
67. Story
68. Madagascan tree-dweller
69. Miss Kett
70. Spotted
71. Belgian river
72. Film spool

**DOWN**

1. Demean
2. Judge
3. Florida city
4. Aeries
5. Seize
6. Scoundrel
7. Kind of sports
8. Smith of the blues
9. Bandleader Kenton
10. Colorado mountain: 2 wds.
11. Past
12. Kitchen utensil
14. Comic DeLuise
20. Although, poetically
21. Goosefoot
25. Scarlett or John
26. English sailor
28. Antipollution group: abbr.
29. Wrecks
32. Improperly
33. Veranda, in Hilo
34. Equipped to conform
35. Short sleep
37. Aries
39. Greek letter
41. Actor Arnold
42. "____ Freedom"
48. Tensely
50. Pipe joint
53. Mouth: suf.
55. Three-handed card game
56. Rich cake
57. Bring together
58. Filch
60. Secondhand
61. Partially obscure
62. Always, to poets
63. Summer, in Lyon
64. Leaf or window

# PUZZLE 211

**ACROSS**

1. People of Cardiff
6. Buss
10. Tuber
14. Let up
15. Territory
16. Submissive
17. Cattle breed
18. Competed
19. Troubadour's song
20. Therefore
21. Impudent talk
22. Abbey man
23. ___ it (hurry): 2 wds.
25. Marks of behavior
27. Trudge
29. Henry or Lew
32. Sesame plant
35. Leak
37. Transferred legally
38. Father of Seth
40. Type of light
42. Excite
43. Naysaying
45. Brother of Seth
47. Foul place
48. Supplier to equestrians
50. Clipper clink
52. Shone brightly
54. Wind about
58. Revelations of Allah
60. Trough filler
62. "... ___ ready to pardon": 2 wds.
63. Actor Richard
64. Grass bunch
65. Stradivarius's rival
66. Lacerate
67. Porch
68. French impressionist
69. Profits
70. Shuck
71. Overconfident

**DOWN**

1. Night vigils
2. Chicago critic
3. Not petite
4. Sharpens
5. Ahem!
6. South Seas beverage
7. ___ coffee
8. Playground contraption
9. Lugubrious
10. Brings up short
11. Hudson site
12. Shield knob
13. Treasured
21. Reef rover
22. Heap
24. Of the past
26. Tormented
28. Actor Gerard
30. $0.01
31. Vortex
32. Small boys
33. Notion
34. Government donation: 2 wds.
36. ___ Zadora
39. Part of England
41. Decline
44. Actor Bates
46. ___ Yutang
49. Disprove
51. Allure
53. English novelist
55. Town in Guam
56. Pens
57. Archie's dingbat
58. Letterspace
59. Arch type
61. And the other people: 2 wds.
64. Cooking abbr.
65. Diplomat: abbr.

# PUZZLE 212

**ACROSS**

1. Clare Boothe ____
5. Watery color
9. Sad songs
14. ____-and-shut case
15. Revolve
16. Jitterbug
17. Midas's love
18. Chore
19. Include: 2 wds.
20. Prompt: 2 wds.
22. Writer Waugh
24. French season
25. Permit to travel
27. Large deer
29. Purplish red
32. Courage
36. "____ Town"
37. Blunt
40. Andrea ____
41. Pindarics
43. Oven-cook
45. Moisturizes
46. Cambodian money
48. Marked
50. Occur
51. Musical composition
53. Made into law
55. Blemishes
57. Pro ____
58. ____ ideal
61. Racing distance
63. Deep red
67. Adage
69. Against
71. Moslem lord
72. ____ France: 2 wds.
73. Horn sound
74. FDR's dog
75. Choir member
76. Catch sight of
77. Comic Philips et al.

**DOWN**

1. Trademark
2. Onto
3. Irishman
4. Leafy veggie
5. Verifier
6. Sine ____ non
7. ____ Major
8. Leg part
9. Polished
10. Cover
11. Wavy, in heraldry
12. Redact
13. "Auld Lang ____"
21. Penny press
23. Freddy Kreuger's street
26. Hebrew high priest
28. Store
29. Heathlands
30. Sound control
31. Kermit's color
33. Halloween goody
34. Soda measure, abroad
35. Facilitated
38. ____ Paolo
39. Fragrant compound
42. Wallop
44. Perseverance
47. Speech defect
49. Fruit
52. Onassis
54. Wine unit
56. Agenda
58. Send out
59. Wind
60. Yoke pullers
62. Eve's grandson
64. Mosque priest
65. Missile site
66. Time periods
68. Two words in June
70. Acme

# PUZZLE 213

**ACROSS**

1. Obligations
6. Sacred Moslem text
11. Very elegant
15. Eastern greeting
16. Fated
18. Come to light
19. Treatment with drugs
20. "The Hairy ___"
21. Trouble
23. Expiration
24. Abstinence
29. Lacrosse-team number
30. Way to get there
31. Mildewed: var.
33. Church projection
37. Be satisfactory
39. Sticky liquid
40. "King's ___"
41. Watch parts
45. Sweetie, to Andy Capp
47. Corn bread
48. Put an edge on
49. Hawaiian dish
50. Utter
51. Winged
52. Mild oath
53. ___ Hurok
54. Some penguins
56. Low fellow
57. Gel
59. Ireland
60. E major and B flat
62. Anew: Latin, 2 wds.
65. Joplin pieces
67. Greek letter
69. Alter the form of
72. Nutmeg, ginger, etc.
75. Western Indian
76. Trifle (with)
77. Banker's security
80. "The ___ Strikes Back"
83. Contaminant
84. Knocked out
85. Los Angeles athletes
86. Nicks
87. Two-horse teams

**DOWN**

1. Flue-draft controller
2. Charitable
3. Taproom
4. Sticker
5. Blur
6. Kyoto robe
7. United
8. ___ herring
9. Keen
10. Subtlety
11. Greenish crust on old bronze
12. Sashes for 6 Down
13. Kind of gin
14. Egg producer
15. County or driver's
17. Bland
22. Aswan, for one
25. Hesitated
26. Prepare for print
27. Sever
28. Slip by
32. "___ Along with Me"
34. Lengthening
35. Sub detector
36. Pitchers
38. Bugle call
41. Bank item
42. Scoundrel
43. Unfastened
44. "Run ___, Run Deep"
46. Sort
47. Outcast
55. Makes a mistake
58. Craggy hill
61. Overflows
62. Cut calories
63. Safes
64. Canadian prov.
66. Fern parts
68. Begone!
70. Searches for
71. Looked at
72. Popular drink
73. Prune fruit
74. Very dry
77. Train section
78. Hurried
79. Industrious insect
81. Explorer's need
82. Burmese coin

# CRYPTIC PUZZLE 214

**British-style or cryptic crosswords are a great challenge for crossword fans. Each clue contains either a definition or direct reference to the answer, as well as a play on words. The numbers in parentheses indicate the number of letters in the answer word or words.**

**ACROSS**

1. Directions: headless salamanders (4)
3. A contest confronted in reversed direction (5-5)
10. "An animal under cover!" I added (5)
11. Bribe Rose, perhaps, to reveal thefts? (9)
12. Up on deck, Ed, I saw nutty dessert (6-4,4)
14. Proposition is the more confusing (7)
15. Tailless duck in the act figured it out (7)
17. Once more seizes the repeat photographs (7)
19. Be scared and let be Mr. Rocky (7)
20. Being upset, seeing vets, we're getting that good feeling from retribution (7,2,5)
23. Arranges chairs around the first lady for the successful ones (9)
24. Approaches reason, perhaps, with nothing omitted (5)
25. Leader of expert fliers keeps coddler out (10)
26. Employed as second-hand? (4)

**DOWN**

1. Measure flat surfaces for meets (10)
2. Might ten trains be passing through? (9)
4. Ennui of the communist in a time of prosperity (7)
5. Unyielding as the Indian without a weapon? (7)
6. Parisians robing? What sauce! (6,8)
7. Ring in prison? (5)
8. Look, do send a number of pills! (4)
9. Potential friends, the zoo workers have a rule for lost property ownership (7,7)
13. Restive dad upset, as promised (10)
16. Conveyances the taxi somehow clears? (5,4)
18. Propose — it gets Gus confused (7)
19. Possibly reset it in Italy (7)
21. "Hi," etc., is enough to display a principle of good conduct (5)
22. Confine quietly in wetness (4)

# PUZZLE 215

## DOUBLE TROUBLE

**Not really double trouble, but double fun! Solve this puzzle as you would a regular crossword, EXCEPT place one, two, or three letters in each box. The number of letters in each answer is shown in parentheses after its clue.**

**ACROSS**

1. Johnson of "Laugh-In" (4)
3. Supped (5)
6. Celebrated (6)
9. "____ Sera, Sera" (3)
11. Herald (9)
13. Cattle thief (7)
15. Fancy (6)
16. Lying flat (5)
17. Basket fiber (5)
18. Luau garland (3)
19. Ceremonial robe (8)
21. Big ____, California (3)
23. Swimming (6)
25. Journal (8)
28. Spiritualist's session (6)
30. Fool (5)
32. Level, in London (4)
33. ____ four (small cake) (5)
34. Epidermis (4)
35. Law (7)
36. Regular (6)
37. Toe or finger (5)
38. Television part (6)
39. Release (7)
41. Word of dismay (5)
43. Take five (4)
44. Worship (9)
46. God of thunder (4)
48. Equipment (4)
50. Mainstay (6)
51. Wool cutter (7)
54. Informal game (9)
56. Took back words (8)
57. Actor Danson (3)
58. Lean-to (4)
59. Prizes (6)
60. Horse of a certain color (4)

**DOWN**

1. Knight's mail (5)
2. High school student (4)
3. Well-defined (8)
4. Hawaiian bird (4)
5. Lawn tool (5)
6. Facade (5)
7. Fun (9)
8. Give the heave-ho (4)
9. Search (5)
10. Author Gardner (4)
12. Auction (4)
14. Marketing pamphlets (10)
16. Magician (15)
19. Moving vehicle (3)
20. "But ____ for Me" (3)
21. Uncertainty (8)
22. Witty reply (6)
24. Eroded (3)
26. Enthusiast (7)
27. Sharpest (7)
29. Orwell work (10)
31. Charged atom (3)
34. Schuss (3)
35. Prearrange circumstances (13)
37. Unsettle (7)
38. Anatomical pouch (3)
40. Refurbish (4)
42. Pride member (4)
45. Had dull pains (5)
47. Algerian seaport (4)
48. "Beau ____" (5)
49. Bitter (5)
51. ____ butter (4)
52. Of a former style (5)
53. Military fortification (5)
55. Alan Alda show (4)
56. Uncooked (3)

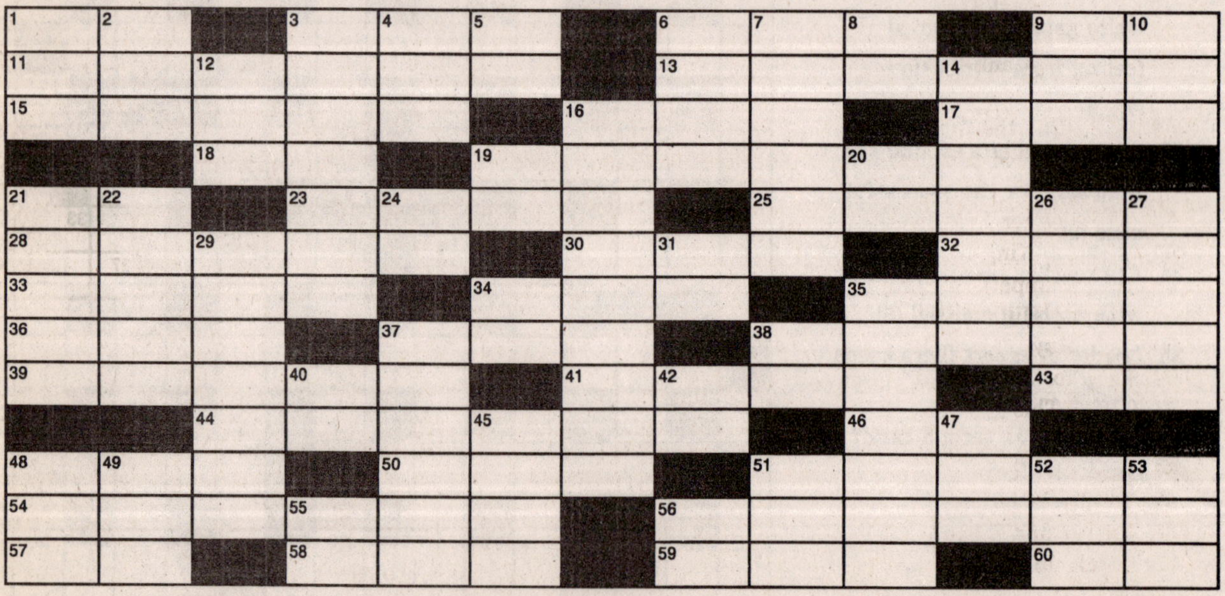

★ ***LOOKING FOR DOUBLE TROUBLE?*** *You've found it! Treat yourself to* ★
*special collections of your favorite puzzles—over 50 in each!*
*To order, see page 63.*

## MOVIES AND TELEVISION

# PUZZLE 216

**ACROSS**

1. "Swiss ___" (1938 film)
5. Dawber and Ewing
9. "___ King" (old TV series)
12. "I cannot tell ___": 2 wds.
13. 1936 Young-Ameche film
15. "White ___ and Tails" (1946 film)
16. Laura or Bruce
17. Actress Susan
18. Sothern or Sheridan
19. Martin and Jones
21. "The ___ Boy" (1961 film)
23. "On Your ___" (1939 film)
25. Actor Gabe ___
26. Mister, to Montalban
29. "High ___"
32. "China ___" (1935 film)
34. Say positively
35. Person in "227"
37. Actress Hagen
39. "My ___ Sal" (1942 film)
40. WWI entertainer ___ Janis
41. "King ___" (1965 film)
42. Reply: abbr.
43. Arthur Godfrey's "___ Scouts"
44. "___ and Gladys" (TV series)
45. "___ Like It Hot" (1959 film)
47. Had supper
48. "___ of Manhattan" (1942 film)
49. "___ But the Lonely Heart" (1944 film)
51. Actor Penn
53. C&W singer Freddy
55. Director King ___
58. ___ Clampett of "The Beverly Hillbillies"
59. ___ May
62. Prop for Julia Child
64. TV's "This ___ House"
65. Stay
66. Director Clair
67. TV Tarzan Ron ___
68. Rather and Dailey
69. Comic Johnson

**DOWN**

1. "___ Max" (1979 film)
2. "___ Three Lives": 2 wds.
3. Father
4. "The ___ Was Indiscreet" (1948 film)
5. "___ Joey" (1957 film)
6. Boyfriend, to Bardot
7. 1970 Elliott Gould film
8. Mortimer ___
9. Half of a famous comedy team: 2 wds.
10. "___ Lady" (1951 film)
11. Longing
13. 1979 Midler film, with "The"
14. "___ Bulldog Drummond" (1939 film)
20. Neither's partner
22. Tavern brew
24. Actress Stevens
26. "The Forsyte ___"
27. Actress Linda of "Dynasty"
28. "New Moon" star: 2 wds.
30. Beginning
31. Actress Ella
33. "___ of the Union" (1948 film)
35. "___ and Sympathy" (1956 film)
36. Court divider
38. Silents actor Roscoe
43. "The ___ Trap" (1955 film)
44. "___ and the Flying Dutchman" (1951 film)
46. "___ Oncle" (1958 film)
48. Skater Babilonia
50. Fished for morays
52. Steady
53. Norman of "Three's Company"
54. "Nine Hours to ___" (1963 film)
56. "___ the Rainbow"
57. Overhead charge
58. ___ Friday of "Dragnet"
60. Author Fleming
61. Town in Serbia
63. Born

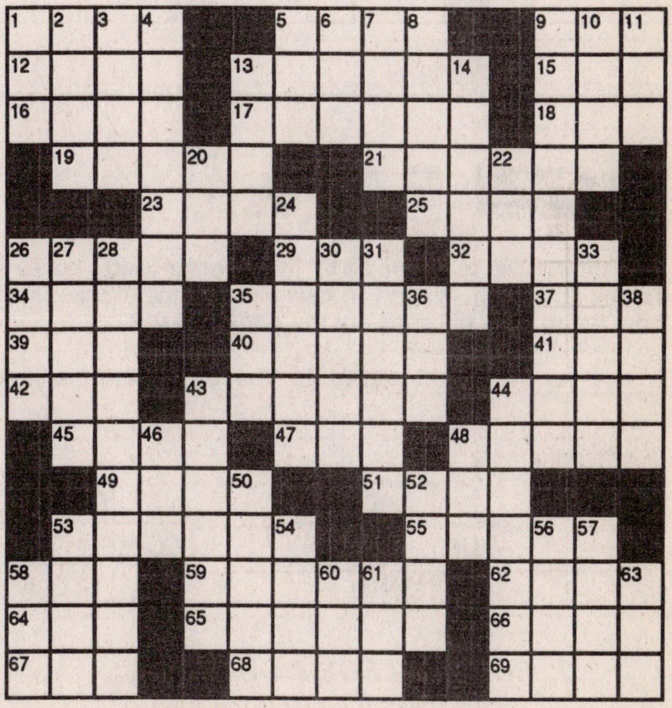

# PUZZLE 217

**ACROSS**

1. Move quickly
5. Up to the time that
10. Paradise resident
14. First-class: 2 wds.
15. Body trunk
16. Sandwich shop, for short
17. Reckless ones
19. Ellipse
20. Abnormal accumulation of fluid
21. Arabian chieftain
23. Vex
24. Greek letter
26. Walk leisurely
28. Makes glum
32. Rebecca or Adam
34. Period
35. Meted
38. Cavalry sword
40. Having curls
42. Titles
44. Calumet
45. Agents
47. Surcoat
49. Brewed drink
50. Fitzgerald
51. Less dense
53. Added garlic to
57. Hit sign
58. Resinous substance
60. Like a cupola
62. Bingolike game
66. Wide jar
68. ____ cake: 2 wds.
70. Ornamental button
71. Wear away
72. Sea bird
73. Cries
74. Church group
75. Colors

**DOWN**

1. Diminish
2. Onus
3. As to: 2 wds.
4. Swarmed
5. Western Indian
6. Exploding star
7. Cuts
8. Small land mass
9. Beaten one
10. Stir
11. Plants with truncated roots: 2 wds.
12. Winged
13. Dairy product
18. Outmoded
22. Uses oars
25. In a short while
27. Vault
28. Toothed tools
29. With mouth wide open
30. Spiny shrub: 2 wds.
31. Blind part
33. Tent
36. Flightless bird
37. Cub packs
39. Behind
41. Dog cry
43. Tastes
46. Stated
48. Reiner et al.
52. Covered over
54. Morse and penal
55. Abrasive
56. English breed of cattle
58. Deprivation
59. Singing voice
61. Prank
63. Whig's opponent
64. Musical sound
65. Keatsian works
67. Newspaper items
69. Conducted

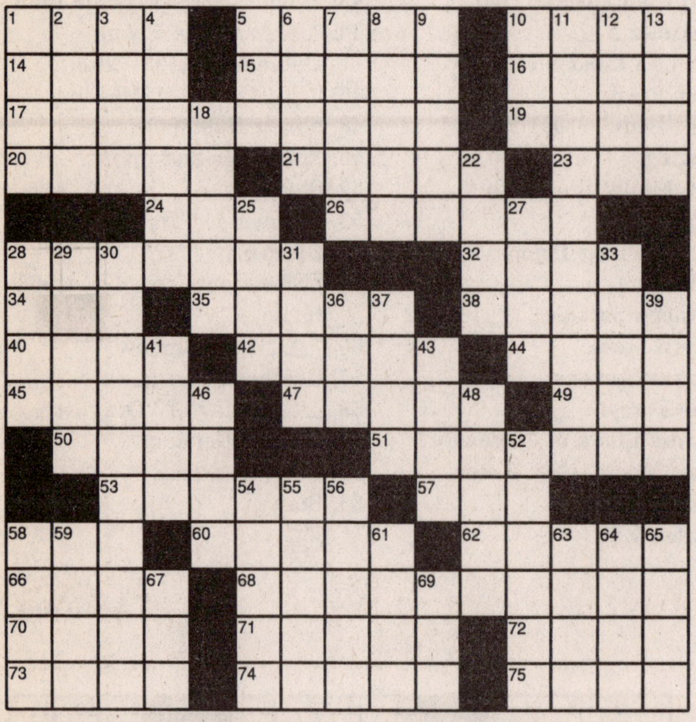

# PUZZLE 218

## CRACKERJACKS

**Find the answer to the riddle by filling in the center boxes with the letters needed to complete the words across and down. When you have filled in the Crackerjacks, the letters reading across the center boxes from left to right will spell out the riddle answer.**

**RIDDLE: What do you call the era of the pony express?**

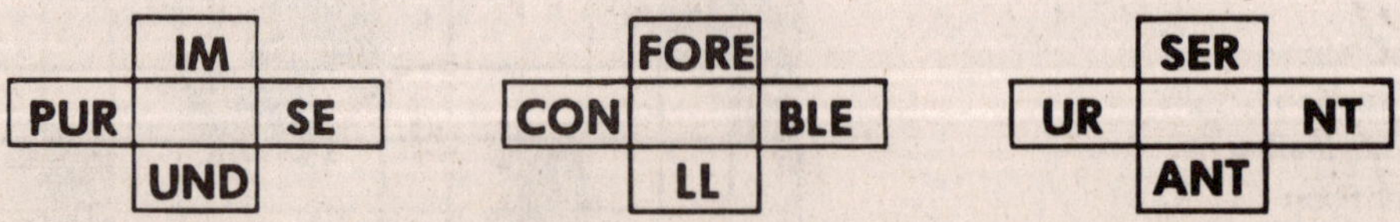


**ANSWER:** ____________

# PUZZLE 219

**• FRATERNALLY •**

**ACROSS**

1. Plumb-bob metal
5. Certain cookies
10. Impulse
14. Highest point
15. Black-gold carrier
16. Crystal gazer
17. "Cocoanuts" quartet: 3 wds.
20. Long time
21. Space
22. Rent again
23. Walked
24. Mittens quantity
26. Kind of squeak
29. Texas flag symbol: 2 wds.
33. The Thing, for one
34. Ship parts
35. Call ___ day: 2 wds.
36. Noah's good-news bringer
37. Underworld
38. "___ Plenty o' Nuthin' ": 2 wds.
39. Opp. of WSW
40. Fulfills
41. Dunne or Pappas
42. Takes back
44. Trapped
45. Actress Sommer
46. Molted
47. Union member
50. Upon
51. Teachers' gp.
54. Joe, Gene, Vic, and Ed: 3 wds.
58. Sweet-singing bird
59. Guide
60. Single entity
61. American Indian
62. Gossip-column entries
63. Actress Rowlands

**DOWN**

1. Tardy
2. Narcissus's spurned lover
3. Prayer ending
4. Rep.'s opponent
5. Woe
6. Turned thumbs down on
7. Canadian prov.
8. ___ diem
9. Theater sign
10. Poe's fallen house members
11. Rod's partner
12. Actor Richard ("Breathless")
13. Long ago, formerly
18. Baseball's Hank
19. Attempts
23. Timber source
24. Models
25. Tiny hill-builders
26. Consumers' friend Ralph
27. Solo
28. Metal bolt
29. Puts on cargo
30. Striped cat
31. Do penance
32. Graded
34. Dull finish
37. Taxi
38. Grandson of Cain
40. "Days of Our Lives" town
41. Bungling
43. Seize again
44. Fires
46. Senator Thurmond
47. French town: 2 wds.
48. Not this
49. Flying prefix
50. Qualified
51. Hawaiian goose
52. Ireland
53. "Thin Man" terrier
55. Before gram or glottis
56. Command to Fido
57. Embrace

# BUBBLES

# PUZZLE 220

**In each of the circles is the name of an animal minus one letter! Find that missing letter to complete the name of the animal. Then arrange the missing letters to spell the bonus name of another animal.**

1. ______________
2. ______________
3. ______________
4. ______________
5. ______________
6. ______________

Bonus: ______________

# PUZZLE 221

## BRICK BY BRICK

**Rearrange this stack of bricks to form a crossword puzzle. The clues will help you fit the bricks into their correct places. Row 1 has been filled in for you. Use the bricks to fill in the remaining spaces.**

### BRICKS

| | | | | |
|---|---|---|---|---|
| E ■ B<br>B ■ R | A N N<br>P E T | E R S<br>R ■ E | A C E<br>E E S | ■ ■ ■<br>A T A |
| ■ G A<br>G A B | S O R<br>T O A | E S ■<br>■ ■ ■ | ■ N E<br>■ ■ S | A W A<br>S H I |
| M A R<br>A N T | L U E<br>A N T | E V E<br>M E L | R I O<br>■ O R | ■ R E<br>■ ■ ■ |
| H O S<br>E N T | S T S<br>T A T | ■ O L<br>I N E | R E S<br>O N ■ | L E ■<br>A T E |
| I E R<br>D A M | S T A<br>T E S | R I V<br>O V E | ■ ■ O<br>M I T | E R I<br>L A M |
| O L D<br>T ■ ■ | T ■ S<br>E A S | ■ ■ ■<br>■ D A | I T S<br>N S ■ | M P ■<br>■ E V |
| T ■ ■<br>S T ■ | E S ■<br>A L ■ | S P S<br>■ ■ P | S ■ R<br>■ ■ T | E O S<br>■ R E |

### DIAGRAM

| | 1 | 2 | 3 | 4 | 5 | 6 | 7 | 8 | 9 | 10 | 11 | 12 | 13 | 14 | 15 |
|---|---|---|---|---|---|---|---|---|---|---|---|---|---|---|---|
| 1 | L | O | A | F | ■ | ■ | B | I | R | D | ■ | ■ | P | A | W |
| 2 | | | | | | | | | | | | | | | |
| 3 | | | | | | | | | | | | | | | |
| 4 | | | | | | | | | | | | | | | |
| 5 | | | | | | | | | | | | | | | |
| 6 | | | | | | | | | | | | | | | |
| 7 | | | | | | | | | | | | | | | |
| 8 | | | | | | | | | | | | | | | |
| 9 | | | | | | | | | | | | | | | |
| 10 | | | | | | | | | | | | | | | |
| 11 | | | | | | | | | | | | | | | |
| 12 | | | | | | | | | | | | | | | |
| 13 | | | | | | | | | | | | | | | |
| 14 | | | | | | | | | | | | | | | |
| 15 | | | | | | | | | | | | | | | |

### ACROSS

1. Bread unit
   Shuttlecock
   Cat's foot
2. Queen ___ lace
   New York waterway
   Dejected
3. Flower part
   Mary's pet
   Speak wildly
4. Vacation spot
   Is in store for
5. Breakfast fare
   Climbs using leg-holds
6. Convulsive breaths
   Margarines
7. Gossip
   Evergreen
   Lariat
8. Highest mountain
   Army man
9. Cantaloupe
   Coast or Indies
   Water barrier
10. Postage mark
    Watering tubes
11. Engagements
    Happening
12. Large streams
    Baltimore ballplayer
13. Above
    Radiate
    Speechify
14. Fourth planet
    Speed contest
    Cozy homes
15. Harvester or red
    Golf gadgets
    Immediately

### DOWN

1. Once around
   Precious stone
   "Arrivederci ___"
2. Unique person
   Donated
   Sofa
3. Poker starter
   Genesis brother
   Ward off
4. Banquets
   Membership lists
5. Boat
   Come in
6. Grates
   State confidently
7. Waist straps
   News bit
   Actress West
8. Writer Levin
   2,000 pounds
   Gibbon
   Cold cubes
9. Basketball-hoop part
   Minus
   Ballots
10. Deflate
    Different
11. Fingerprint circle
    Hamburger garnish
12. Simmered
    Supermarkets
13. Simple
    Helper
    Endure
14. Mother's sisters
    Pekoe and jasmine
    Kett of the comics
15. Soaks
    Furnish weapons to
    Superlative suffix

# PUZZLE 222

**• ILLUMINATION •**

## ACROSS

1. Davis Cup captain
5. " '____' stuck in my throat" ("Macbeth")
9. Spy name
13. Tailed skysight
18. God: Sp.
19. Chess actions
21. Med. course
22. Battery part
23. Genesis phrase
26. Capital whose name means "capital"
27. Like: suffix
28. Son of Seth
29. East wind, personified
30. Golfer's pride
31. Sentimental songs
33. Snarls
34. Coral isle
35. Gaelic
36. Formerly
37. Excellent
40. Acclaim
43. Boats that guide boats
45. 4 qts.
46. Type of joint
47. Express pain
49. River islands
50. "____ be in England"
51. Joplin opus
52. Most pleasant
56. Change
57. Thrown, as a rider
59. Like an egg's center
60. Chic
61. Hair piece
62. Sends telegrams
63. Voice: prefix
64. Like tors
66. Pound part
67. Just bought
70. Kirk and Whelchel
71. Fee for sea service
73. Actress Rehan
74. Author Hunter
75. Wampum
77. Cougar
78. Bambi, grown up
79. U.S. troops sent to Eur. in WWI
80. Type of luminance
84. Disgrace
85. Surgical saw
87. Wild ox
88. Emerald, for one
90. Revolt
91. City vehicles
92. Clown's air-filled bat
96. Lampoon
98. Pacific sound
99. Drip
100. Hail!
101. Workout aftermath, perhaps
102. Cheerful people
105. Top
106. Author Wiesel
107. Fisher
108. "And Then There Were ____"
109. Arranges
110. Forward
111. Geographical seven
112. Penny ____

## DOWN

1. Off-the-cuff
2. Italian province
3. Brolin TV show
4. Id ____
5. Repairs
6. Glum
7. Holiday times
8. Bird beak
9. Coif protector
10. English author ____ Wilson
11. Cheers
12. "Addams Family" cousin
13. Fur hats
14. Even score
15. Beethoven classic
16. Learning: abbr.
17. Before cast or vision
20. Believing, for some
24. Lonely hunter
25. Stagger
30. Paces
32. Jump
33. "____ My Way"
34. Go ____ hammer and tongs
37. Bashfully: var.
38. Archibald et al.
39. Acclaim
40. Raw silk color
41. Kinship unit
42. Airy
43. Placed
44. Oklahoma Indians
47. Not neat
48. Cheers for the matador
50. Actor Warner
52. Remains
53. Hurrying: var.
54. "____ Song Trilogy"
55. Naval power
56. Unaided
58. Type of grinder
60. Bantu language
62. Use a scale
63. Baby buggy
64. Sports-shoe feature
65. Spoon or Moon
66. Come in second
67. Champagne marking
68. Dutch export
69. Salary
72. Hebrew dry measures
75. Composure
76. Sea bird
78. Tool house
80. Hankerings
81. Expressed mirth
82. Map in a map
83. "Faust" author
84. Quench
86. Churchman
88. Michener subject
89. Schedules
91. "Snug as a ____ . . ."
93. Pythias's friend
94. Meet competition
95. Actress Adoree
96. Pouches
97. Height: prefix
98. Carpet feature
99. Put cargo on board
102. "____ Miserables"
103. McMahon et al.
104. Message carrier: abbr.

# PUZZLE 223

• D.C. SHES •

**ACROSS**

1. Driven obliquely, as nails
5. Lawyers' gp.
8. Branches
12. ___ Stanley Gardner
13. Is in debt
14. Space chimp
15. Time periods
16. Cow catcher
18. "Piccolo ___"
19. 34th President's First Lady
22. Position
23. Close
24. Jazz sounds
27. Fast jet
29. Photocopies, for short
33. Two-passenger carriage
35. Bandleader Weems
37. King's title
38. Group: abbr.
39. Road surface
42. Winter month: abbr.
43. Sensory organ
45. ___ Beta Kappa
46. Mute
48. Cubic meter
50. Foul up
52. Music symbols
53. French clergyman
55. Miss Kett
57. 36th President's First Lady
64. Ireland
65. Ambulance horn
66. Lab burner
67. Aroma
68. Giraffe's prominence
69. Incites a dog to attack
70. Takes a snooze
71. Casting mold opening
72. Waste allowance

**DOWN**

1. Pour
2. Odd, in the Highlands
3. Susiana
4. Abstains
5. Expects
6. Harry's wife
7. Concurred
8. Detailed accounts
9. Again
10. Speck
11. Elbe tributary
13. Bread spread
17. Unit
20. Site of an English racetrack
21. Owns
24. Stores
25. Gem weight
26. Geometric corner
28. Part of a flight
30. Helpers
31. English river
32. Religious groups
34. Driver's aid
36. "___ Kapital"
40. Rooting
41. Gaiety
44. Petitions
47. Most thin
49. Fade away
51. Repudiate
54. Encore!
56. Honky-___
57. Author Uris
58. Verdi opera
59. Globule
60. Three: Ger.
61. Mix
62. Formerly
63. Political cartoonist

# PUZZLE 224

## Dial-A-Grams

**These challenging cryptograms are in a number code based on the familiar telephone dial. Each number represents one of the letters shown with it on the dial below. A number is not necessarily the same letter each time.**

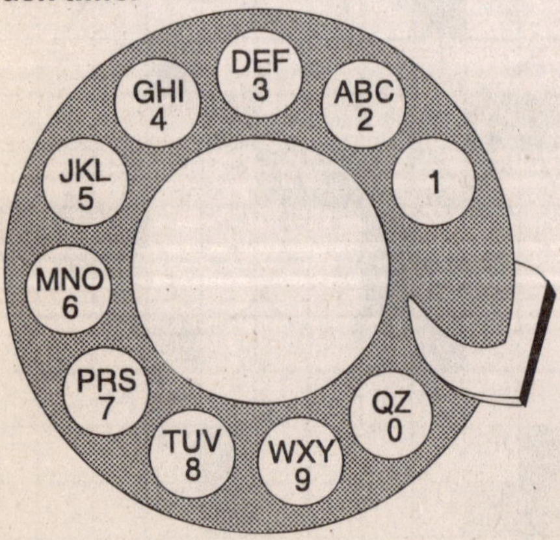


**A.** 43246 47 843 6659 78283 46 843 8.7. 6837 94424 66 3673446 3524 427 3837 35696.

**B.** 663 36556933 29 36789-3483 03767 47 2 082888673324554 66.

# PUZZLE 225

**ACROSS**
1. Large-mouthed fish
5. Preserves
10. Shade trees
14. Volcano site
15. Thrill
16. Control strap
17. Laborious task
18. Up and about
19. Bull or drake
20. Inclination for food
22. Increase by three times
24. Body of water
25. Farm laborer
26. Dark
29. Roamed
33. Urge forward
34. Instant
35. Mexican cheer
36. Self-centered
37. Sty dweller
38. Fail to mention
39. Develop
40. Michigan city
41. Box
42. Young bird
44. Pennant
45. Emulates Big Daddy Kane
46. Muslim prince
47. Scatters
50. Look similar to
55. Vicinity
56. ____ of palm (vegetable)
58. English author
59. Roster
60. Sheeplike
61. Sisters
62. Kindergartners
63. Struck out
64. Head: Fr.

**DOWN**
1. Greek letter
2. Heading
3. Clip
4. Peddlers
5. Done in successive parts
6. Landed
7. Flower vessel
8. Summer, in Nice
9. Independent group of words
10. Costly fur
11. ____ year
12. Factory
13. Dagger
21. Duck
23. Went by horse
25. ____ the town red (celebrate)
26. Couch
27. Picture
28. "____ Like Us"
29. Twist
30. Director Polanski
31. Best of its class
32. Prevent
34. Siamese ____
37. Careless
38. Decoration
40. Imperfection
41. Pen
43. Gives medical aid
44. Stitched loosely
47. Seasoning
48. Singing group
49. Unwind
50. Fence
51. Marine bird
52. "Betty ____"
53. Fluff
54. Comfort
57. Actress Plumb

# CIRCLE SUMS

# PUZZLE 226

**Each circle, lettered A through H, has its own number value from 1 to 9. No two circles have the same value. The numbers shown in the diagram are the sums of the circles which overlap at those points. For example, 12 is the sum of circles G and H. Can you find the value of each circle?**

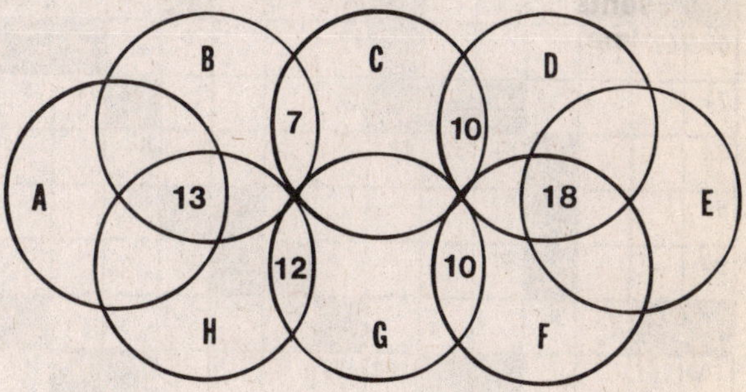

# PUZZLE 227

## • HOME, SWEET HOME •

### ACROSS

1. Ayesha
4. Golfer Tony
8. Hungarian pianist
14. Cause
17. South American republic
20. Dancer Juliet
21. Daydreaming
23. Nodded
24. Winetree
25. Netman Lendl
26. Home-run king
28. Merriment
29. Port
31. Heavy string
33. Art stand
36. Oklahoma native
38. Actor Bert
39. Romance
40. "To ___ with Love"
43. Borneo river
44. Be a match for
45. Hindu garment
46. Single: prefix
47. Urn
48. Pleasure boat
51. Female swan
52. Summer: Fr.
53. Hermit
54. Signal for a taxi
55. Truncates
56. Beau
58. ___ Domingo
59. Charles Augustin ___-Beuve
61. Nabokov book
62. Peevishness
64. Teutonic: abbr.
65. Shack
66. Oxalis
69. Inspirit
71. Choose
74. Story outline
75. Mrs. Copperfield
76. Calced
78. Ax
80. Artificial language
81. 1960 Oscar film
85. Cattle feed
86. Ump's kin
87. National bird
88. English river
89. "___ Kett"
90. Work unit
91. Autographs: abbr.
92. Mousse form
93. Flow
95. Houston baseballer
97. Degrade
99. Cool
100. Piquant
102. Actor David
104. Singer Ives
105. King of Judah
108. Destine
111. Plain cake with fruit sauce
115. Capital of South Dakota
116. Joined
117. Skullcap
118. South Carolina river
119. Susiana
120. Ran into

### DOWN

1. Sail the seven ___
2. Greasy spoons
3. Esse ___ percipi
4. Law: Fr.
5. Annex
6. Place to catch a fly ball
7. Of birds
8. Mineral bath
9. Silver: abbr.
10. Norway, to Norwegians
11. Emphasizes
12. Douay prophet
13. Counsel, of old
14. Record company
15. Oily fruit
16. "___ on Sunday"
17. Roll
18. Concerning
19. "Long, Long ___"
22. Prohibit
27. Gets close
30. Poker kitty
31. South American animal
32. At what time
34. Sheltered
35. Chaldean
36. Economize
37. Harangue
38. Earring locale
39. Motel in "Fiddler on the Roof"
41. Awkward
42. Wash cycle
44. Dialect
45. Ensemble
48. Atoll material
49. Rolled tea
50. Cookstove
53. Ore vein
55. Lo-cal word
57. Dray
58. ___ Zagora, Bulgaria
59. Piece of paper
60. "___ Lang Syne"
62. Rides a bicycle
63. Go to Gretna Green
66. Steeple
67. Earlier in time
68. Lofty patio
70. Sailor
71. Unit of loudness
72. Woman's lapel ornament
73. Seed coat
76. Be cheerful
77. Cattle group
79. Sharp impact sound
81. Quiz
82. Filament
83. Incite
84. New Mexico resort
85. Blackbird
92. Fireplace frame
93. Fruit beverage
94. Diacritical mark
96. Jump
97. English river
98. Ms. Midler
99. Mug
100. Surpasses
101. "___ da Capo"
103. Sherbet
104. River bottom
106. Tizzy
107. Years of life
109. Wrath
110. Born
112. Sky altar
113. Muffin
114. Canine mother

# PUZZLE 228

**ACROSS**

1. Buddy
5. Davenport
9. Heavy weights
13. TV's "____ Shadows"
17. Flexible tube
18. Central Asian lake
19. Step ____!
20. Fifty-fifty
21. Lay bare
22. Large spider
24. Evergreen
25. Relate
27. Sandra and Ruby
28. Pasture
30. Hotel
31. Seth's father
32. Bandy words
33. Turning-point
36. Pother
37. Old joke
41. Golf club
42. Laborer
43. Darken
44. Exist
45. See 1 Across
46. Standard
47. Hillside
48. Arabian gulf
49. Mouse sounds
51. Frighten
52. Refine metal
53. Wheel hub
54. Rock
55. Ooze
56. Burger shape
58. Begin
59. Actor Holloway
62. Regrets
63. Malice
64. Highly organic soil
65. Actress Gardner
66. Metal source
67. Sparkle
68. Modeling material
69. Flower holder
70. In a parade
72. Counterfeit
73. Wharves
74. Brewery ingredient
75. Diving bird
76. Tramp
77. Deprive of weapons
80. Fatigue
81. TV soap opera
85. Religious image
86. Inscriptions
89. Full of energy
90. Green: Fr.
91. Lopez theme
92. Permit to escape
93. Gulf of ____
94. Bohemian
95. Squeal (on)
96. Corn spikes
97. Lease

**DOWN**

1. Cut to bits
2. Expectation
3. Consumer
4. Refer to
5. Glossy cloth
6. Algerian seaport
7. Distant
8. Boy with a magic lamp
9. Indian symbol
10. Burden
11. Nothing
12. Headlong rush
13. Go
14. Greedy
15. Nevada city
16. Recognized
23. Close at hand
26. Hill builder
29. Make less difficult
31. Minute particle
32. Mold
33. Seeds
34. Mideast country
35. Offer one's services
36. Sun. talks
37. Boring task
38. Identification plaque
39. Asian river
40. Canvas home
42. Type of bonnet
43. Viewpoint
46. Dark blue
47. Multitude
48. Augury
50. Breaks bread
51. One of a set of 50
52. Chair part
54. Redford film, with "The"
55. Remain
56. School dance
57. Distinctive air
58. Twirls
59. Rock layer
60. Always
61. Sweet potatoes
63. Freight delivery
64. Course of action
67. Toots ____
68. Hymn
69. Alike
71. Sailor's song
72. Skyrocket
73. Young seal
75. Lawful
76. Takes pleasure (in)
77. Met star
78. Bakery worker
79. Type
80. Mr. Rogers
81. Scorch
82. Current, as of ideas
83. Hot spot
84. Easter season
87. "The Gold Bug" author
88. Shade of green

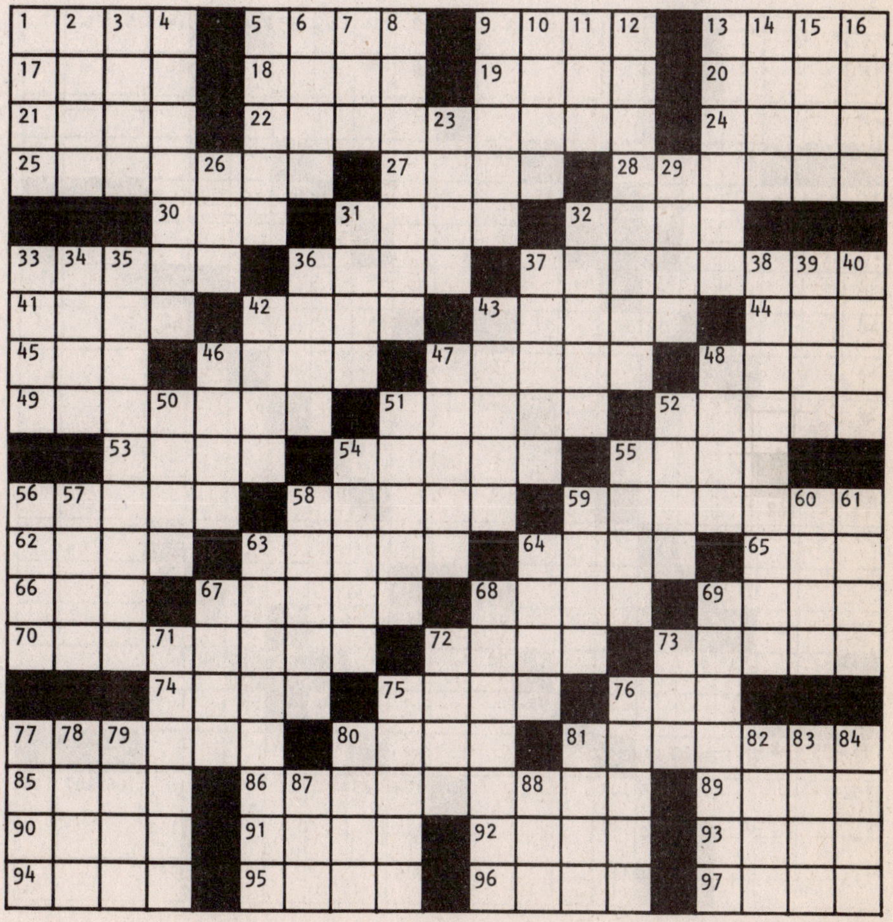

# PUZZLE 229

**• POT LUCK •**

## ACROSS

1. NASA's Sally
5. Understood
10. Tree trunk
14. Gruesome
18. Mine entrance
19. Gladden
20. Bedouins
22. ___ avis
23. Street beggar
25. Interior viewing system
27. Perfect
28. Book designation
30. Actress Dahl
31. Jazz buff
34. Excuses
36. Religious brothers
37. With full force, of old
38. Auricles
39. Rule of conduct
42. Stretching muscle
44. 1957 Verdugo film
46. Metric land measure
48. Ox chariot
49. Just gets by
51. Origination: suffix
52. Snick or ___
53. DDE's command
54. Tumultuous
58. Salt tree
59. Brings into contempt
61. Sins
62. Extorts money from
63. Begin again
64. Balked
65. African carnivore
66. Bar order
68. Behold: Fr.
69. Baby cart
72. Vocal cords, informally
73. Instruments for measuring all angles
75. Topsy's playmate
76. Eight in Bonn
77. Mail
78. Town in Ethiopia
79. "There was not a penny ___"
80. Snow runner
81. Summer headgear
85. Black bucks
87. Shoulder blade
90. Ditto: Latin
91. Town in the Philippines
92. Remove rind
93. Fold
95. Taxi drivers
96. Ocean breeze
99. African antelope
100. Hackneyed
102. Of a digestive gland
104. Slender cigars
109. Pituitary secretion, for short
110. Slaver
111. Senseless
112. Mother of Apollo
113. Korean statesman
114. Handle: Fr.
115. Aeries
116. Hymn coda

## DOWN

1. Seance sound
2. Mount Psiloriti
3. Clamor
4. Student of morals
5. Doctrine
6. Gershwin portrayer
7. Showy lily
8. Native: suffix
9. Jesuit in training
10. Christening
11. Doctoral exams
12. Bowling alley
13. Nigerian tribesman
14. Male salmon
15. Ethnic group
16. Golf club
17. Lion's locks
21. Meagerly
24. "A Bell for ___"
26. Farm vehicle, for short
29. Wadi in Sudan
31. Loathing
32. Riot: Fr.
33. Of mechanical copying
35. Charter
36. Monetary unit of Switzerland
39. Loin muscle
40. Advocacy of Greek political unity
41. Cornered
43. Publishing-house employee
44. Walkers: abbr.
45. Nimble
47. Morays
50. Was cognizant of
52. Sword
54. Sheets of stamps
55. Worth
56. Convex molding
57. Turkish soldier
58. Choir section
60. Bowling button
62. Ballet handrails
64. "9 to 5" actress
65. Roads: abbr.
66. Auditors: abbr.
67. Rubes
68. TV hostess White
69. Photocopy, for short
70. Show clearly
71. Spills the beans about
73. Norman Vincent ___
74. Dutch cheeses
77. Urged on
79. Queen of Castile
82. Supernatural event
83. Yemen seaport
84. Bowler's target
86. Subside
88. Parisian ruffian
89. Brace
93. Advertising awards
94. Lab heaters
95. Quotes
96. Coast Guard woman
97. Apiece
98. Feed the kitty
99. Harrow's rival
101. Torn
103. Sky altar
105. Hydrocarbon suffix
106. Moon buggy
107. Goddess of recklessness
108. Heir

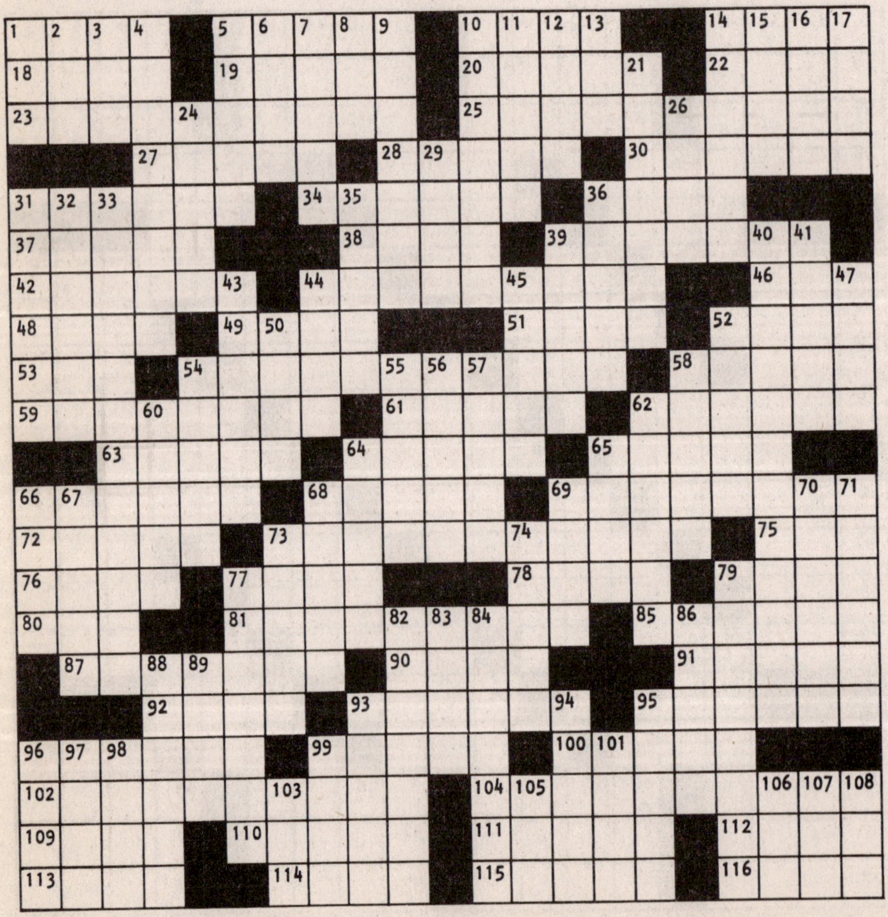

# PUZZLE 230

**ACROSS**

1. Spoken
5. Taj Mahal city
9. Night twinkler
13. Insect stage
17. Corruption
18. Legal claim
19. Fishing rod
20. At a distance
21. Product of heredity
25. Golfer Trevino
26. Not at home
27. Departed
28. Egyptian king
29. Failure
30. Sermon subject
31. Field mouse
32. Broad necktie
35. Battle
36. Bridge player's gaffe
40. German highway
41. Presidential son
45. Old card game
46. Actor Wallach
47. Playwright Coward
48. Arab chieftain
49. ____ as a button
50. Withhold from
52. Gave it a whirl
53. Dewool a sheep
54. Bishop of Rome
55. Fishing basket
56. Stylish
57. Game of skill
59. Highways
60. Attire
63. Seek's partner
64. Boundary
65. Snare
66. Wrath
67. Swiss canton
68. Tasty tidbit
70. Twirl
71. Town in Indiana
73. Curved bone
74. Pondered
75. Outfits
76. Sale terms
78. Storage locker
79. Trembling trees
82. Inquires
83. Is able
84. Cow pasture
87. At a time of crisis
91. Burden
92. S-shaped molding
93. Make comfortable
94. Aid in wrongdoing
95. Hardens
96. Sleep restlessly
97. Blended whiskies
98. Simple

**DOWN**

1. Elliptical
2. Pilaf ingredient
3. Dull pain
4. Aloha State garland
5. Audibly
6. Present
7. Ump's cousin
8. Seaport in Belgium
9. Used money
10. Whistle sound
11. Each and every
12. Children's game
13. Golfer Arnie ____
14. Spaceships, for short
15. Tempo
16. Clumsy boats
22. Sulk
23. Magic spell
24. Farm machine
29. Comedian Rickles
30. Comet's follower
31. Cast a ballot
32. Not yet up
33. Bargain event
34. Contributed one's share
35. Wild cry of delight
37. Good investments
38. Tittle
39. Activist
41. Small, sheltered bay
42. Felt so inclined
43. Girl friends: Fr.
44. Film holder
47. Sharp bites
49. IOU
51. Red flower
52. Characteristic
53. Retail store
55. Stupor
56. Burst of thunder
57. Buddy
58. Employ
59. Ceremonies
60. Nursery bed
61. Toledo's waterfront
62. Transmit
64. Risky venture
65. The one here
68. Sharp tip
69. Refrigerator drawer
70. Earth's star
72. Inclinations
74. Dig ore
76. Fire remains
77. Glide on snow
78. Denudes
79. Piercing tools
80. Oxford or brogan
81. Bog fuel
82. Crack aviators
83. Legal job
84. Ear part
85. Water pitcher
86. Pot money
88. Conceit
89. Speak
90. Beaver's work

# PUZZLE 231

## CODEWORD

Codeword is a special crossword puzzle in which conventional clues are omitted. Instead, answer words in the diagram are represented by numbers. Each number represents a different letter of the alphabet, and all of the letters of the alphabet are used. When you are sure of a letter, put it in the code key chart for easy reference. A group of letters has been inserted to start you off.

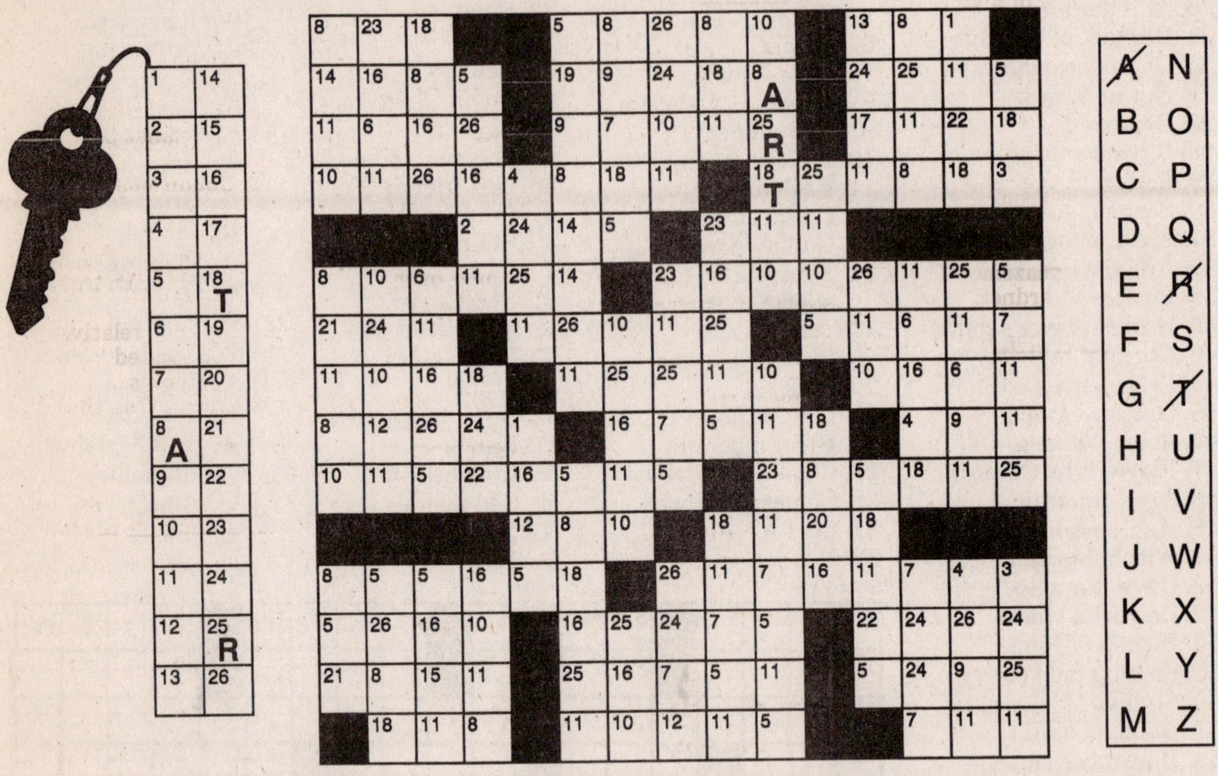

# PUZZLE 232

## Number Cube

Fit the twelve 8-digit numbers into their proper places on the cube in the directions indicated by the arrows.

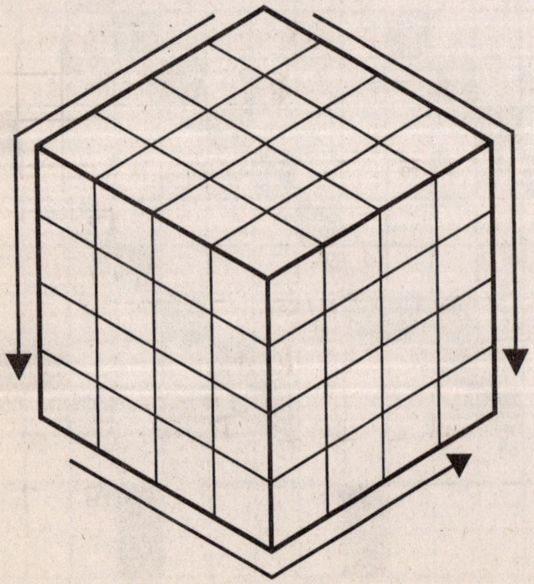

02624107
07341268
16306572
22570391
22815376
30219773

34910652
61273534
70792438
72123630
78359223
91071714

# PUZZLE 233

**• NOISES OFF •**

**ACROSS**

1. Ticket half
5. Taj Mahal site
9. Writer Connelly
13. Large wading bird
17. Without, in Wiesbaden
18. Mint
19. ____ clock
20. Trademark of a kind
21. Raucously
25. Coward
26. Convex moldings
27. Range of colors
28. Downy
31. Part of NFL
33. Not pos.
34. Deliveries from the dais
38. Rich soil
40. Showed amazement
44. Actress Gardner
45. Firm
47. Chancel crucifix
49. French composer
50. God of war
52. ____-arms (soldier)
54. Letter opener
56. Sought office
57. Miss Loos
59. Cupid
61. Rife
63. Utter a taurine roar
67. Bring into conflict
69. Medicinal plant
70. Lively dance
73. Water babies
74. Paw sensors
76. Keep an ____ the ground
79. Fabulous Tibetan creature
80. Baghdad is here
82. Oboist's purchase
84. Service organization members
86. Pilot's record
87. Void
89. Ointment of yore
91. Conic sections
93. Type of grain
95. Shade of blue
97. Unit of force
98. Disney's Lady, e.g.
102. Inter ____
104. Expand
107. Claustrophobe's affliction, perhaps
112. English river
113. Diner's aid
114. Gruff fellow of storyland
115. "____ a song go out . . . "
116. Stain
117. Omit, as a grade
118. Monster
119. Little feller

**DOWN**

1. Miss Piggy is one
2. Skinny
3. Biblical preposition
4. Order
5. Siegfried's sigh
6. Cartoon baby's utterance
7. Wild disorder
8. Composer Dvorak
9. Adversary of the "Merrimack"
10. Connective
11. Garner
12. He wrote "Over There"
13. Bootleg
14. Sudden dash
15. "____ Ideas"
16. Angry
22. Brothers of baseball
23. Asia's ____ Sea
24. Designer Cassini
29. Return address heading
30. Weblike membrane
32. Asian country
34. Mongolian monk
35. Writer Hunter
36. St. Thomas's milieu
37. Tendon
39. Dancer Shearer
41. Analogues
42. Verve
43. Cautionary word
46. Miss Hood of "Our Gang"
48. Prosaic
51. Ending for gang or mob
53. Sheer material
55. Self-satisfied
58. Tipping over
60. Bottoms up!
62. Join in the game
64. Prevaricator
65. Of yore
66. Weird
67. Assam silkworm
68. "September ____"
71. Shoshone Indian
72. Pen pals
75. Pants part
77. Tattled
78. Sole
81. ____ hut
83. Devise
85. Scorch
88. Secular
90. Surrealist painter
92. Allow
94. Conditions
96. Jargon
98. Quick try
99. Comedian Silvers
100. Prefix with tow or plane
101. Onion's relative
103. All excited
105. Unctuous
106. "That Was the ____ That Was"
108. Blackbird
109. Damage
110. Cezanne's summer
111. Sault ____ Marie

# PUZZLE 234

**• MOVING WRITE ALONG •**

## ACROSS

1. Houses: Sp.
6. Fasten with skewers
11. Speaker's platform
15. Printed cotton cloth
16. Small hairpiece
17. Author Bell
19. Author of "Pippa Passes"
21. Incidents
23. Idolize
24. Indian coin
25. "I Remember ___"
27. Portable bed
28. "___ Rhythm"
29. Headed
30. Stove chambers
32. Mauna ___
33. "___ Miserables"
34. Stalks
35. Correct a text
36. Aquatic mammals
38. Fact
40. Author of "Song to David"
41. Louisiana county
42. Author of "Mia Carlotta"
43. "___ and Folk Tales"
44. Bowl or plum
45. Scholarly man
48. Corridors
49. Analogous
52. Adhere
53. Loony
54. ___-Wurttemberg
55. Silkworm
56. Hairdo
57. Author of "Quality Street"
59. "The Ugly Duckling"
60. Delve
61. Chunks of ice
62. Highway
63. Lift
64. Arrests
66. "Ali Baba and the ___ Thieves"
67. Throbbed
68. Pianist Peter's family
69. Aunt: Fr.
70. Augur
71. Plunderer
73. Famous ship
74. Controversial argument
77. Compile
78. Dog's skin problem
79. More painful
80. Assent
82. Common gull
83. Customs
84. Author Terkel
85. Teen-ager's skin problem
86. ___ tempore
87. Actress Anderson
88. Make up for
89. Squash variety
90. Made a goal
92. Author of "The Black Tulip"
96. Cream of society
97. Sermon
98. Pleased as punch
99. Pianist Waller
100. Inscribed slab
101. Coins

## DOWN

1. Freight-train end
2. Watchful
3. Father
4. "___ One"
5. Clearheadedness
6. Pulled
7. Finnish poem
8. Wire service: abbr.
9. Japanese coin
10. Portion
11. Considers
12. Thomas ___ Edison
13. O'Neill work
14. Author of "Ann Vickers"
15. Old coot
16. Drinks excessively
18. Bar seats
19. Banister
20. Card game
22. Hoard
26. Moreover
29. Slanting
30. Sharif et al.
31. Exceedingly
34. Jargon
35. Author of "Wuthering Heights"
36. Author of "Bonjour Tristesse"
37. Epochal
39. "A Bell for ___"
40. Sea dogs
41. Thick soup
43. Goddesses of destiny
44. ___ Hawkins Day
45. Oodles
46. Michael Caine role
47. Author of "Jacob's Room"
48. Horse collar pieces
49. Social gathering
50. Expunge
51. Wrinkled
53. "___ in Toyland"
54. Savage
57. Panel member
58. Main artery
59. Capital of Oregon
61. Antidotes
63. Less polite
65. Last British letters
66. Snake's teeth
67. Stilts
69. Prong
70. Abutted
71. Turnpike exits
72. Punish by a fine
73. Outcasts
74. Author of "Exultations"
75. Revenues
76. Author of "Lord Jim"
78. My: Fr.
79. Unfeeling
81. Lairs
83. Methods
84. Trite
85. Keen
87. Baltic native
88. Botanical angle
89. "___ Bede"
91. Creek
93. Fortune
94. Uncle
95. Biblical judge

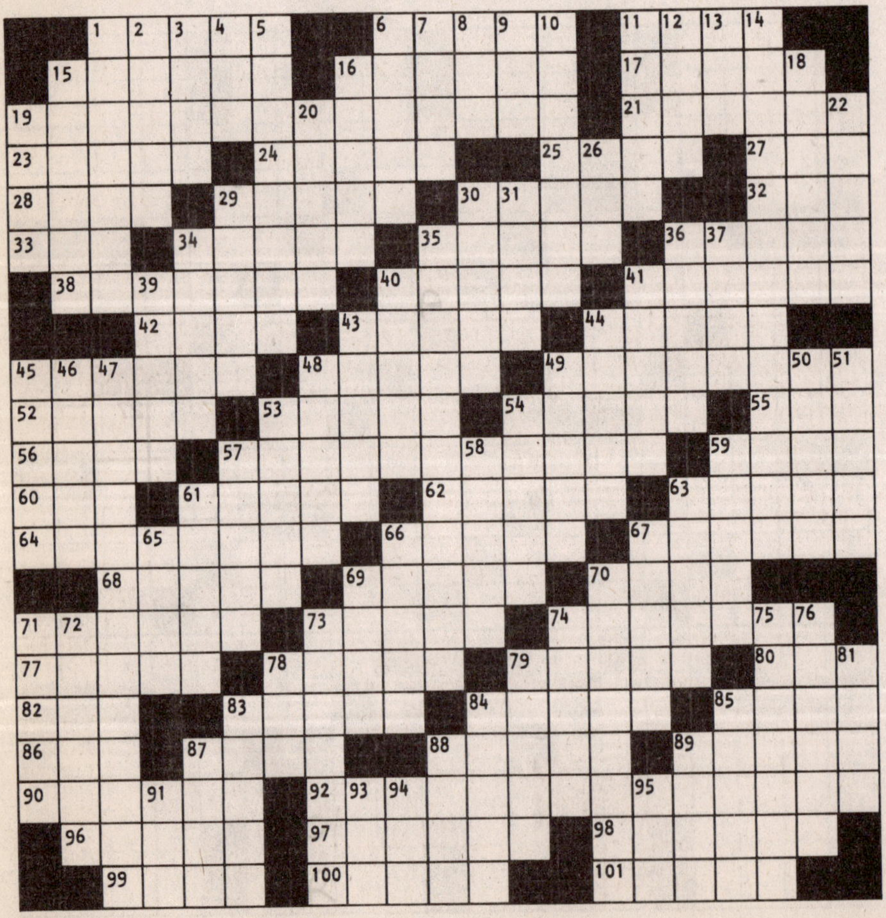

# PUZZLE 235

**ACROSS**

1. Near the ground
4. Casual shirt
7. Fall flower, for short
10. Volcano's dust
11. Vase
12. Half of a pair
13. Crafty
14. Ran, as colors
15. Do the backstroke
16. Throws
18. Lone Ranger's sidekick
19. Toddler's enclosure
22. Custom
25. Historic time
26. Baseball stick
29. Revise text
30. Singer/pianist Charles
31. Nevada city
32. Burglarize
33. Melody
34. Cent
35. Cues
37. Firm
40. Chief male servant
44. Someone who fibs
45. Chest bones
47. Inventor Whitney
48. Large deer
49. "____ to the West Wind"
50. Venomous viper
51. Change the color of
52. 24 hours
53. Payment

**DOWN**

1. Final
2. Capital of Norway
3. The ____ and wherefores
4. Northeastern Oklahoma city
5. Before, to a poet
6. Conclusion
7. Cut, as a lawn
8. Segment
9. Reminding note
14. Pants securer
15. Male child
17. Turning barbecue skewer
18. British beverage
20. Crave
21. Move with leverage
22. That woman
23. Stir
24. Baby's mealtime garment
26. Actor Kingsley
27. Actress ____-Margret
28. Plaything
30. Big truck
31. Relax
33. Assist
34. Addition word
35. Knight's title
36. "____ Road" (Beatles album)
37. Toboggan
38. Greasy
39. Large pond
41. Turn over a new ____
42. Otherwise
43. Mature
45. Curtain or lightning
46. Neighbor of Mont.

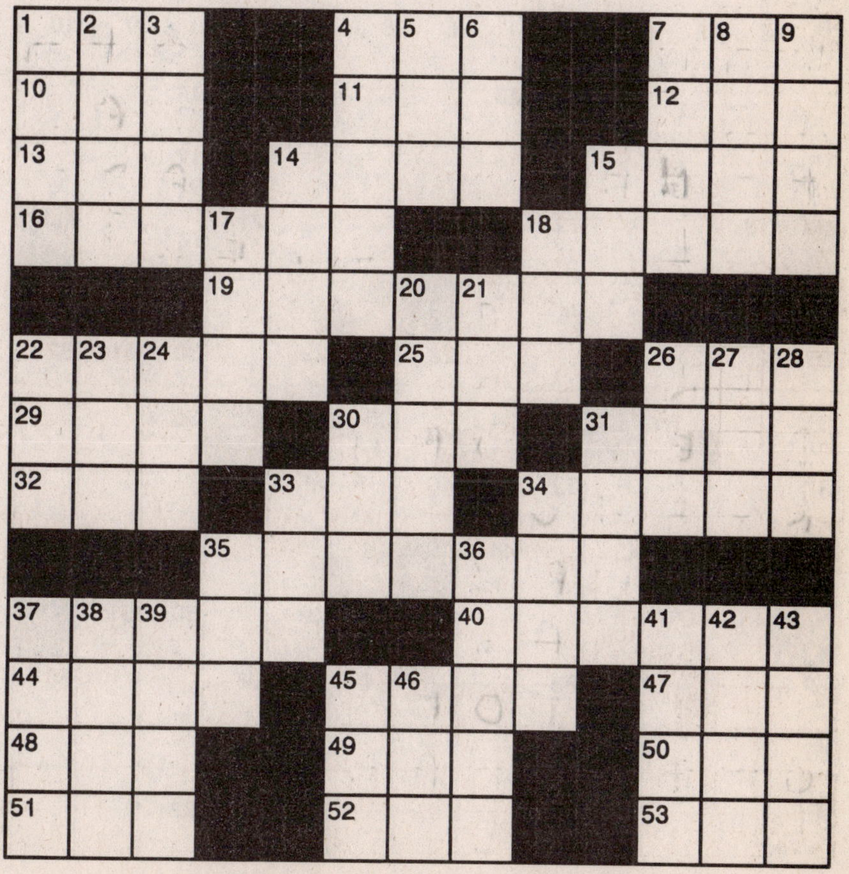

# PUZZLE 236

**ACROSS**

1. Attorney's expertise
4. Towel or sheet
8. Fitness facility
11. Part of the eye
13. Size
14. Faucet
15. Sheet of stamps
16. Control knob
17. Lemon drink
18. Bauble
20. Church tables
22. Swab
24. Stitch
25. Out of control
29. Respond
33. Birthday number
34. Liquid gold
36. Favorable vote
37. Cowboy contest
40. Mexican menu items
43. "Violets ___ blue . . ."
45. Dull
46. Brass and iron
49. Meek one
52. Bounder
53. Foot digits
55. Eagerness
57. "___ to Joy"
58. Milky gem
59. Diminish
60. Stockade
61. Trust
62. Pipe joint

**DOWN**

1. ___ service
2. Swift horse
3. Grape juice
4. Harmful
5. Song for Sills
6. Wild ducks
7. Bridle
8. Asterisk
9. Writing tablets
10. Impersonate
12. Clothing joints
19. Female rabbit
21. Respectful fear
23. Not an amateur
25. Exclude
26. Self-esteem
27. Lipstick color
28. Scout Carson
30. Chum
31. Caustic substance
32. Okay
35. Small boy
38. Consume
39. Speaker
41. Unit of length
42. Surprise
44. Flee, romantically
46. Produced
47. Garden spot
48. Emblem
50. Veal or beef
51. Bottom
52. Police officer
54. Cunning
56. Lawyer F. ___ Bailey

# PUZZLE 237

**ACROSS**

1. Tablet
4. Faucet
7. Health resort
10. Manipulate
11. Melodies
13. Necklace unit
14. Curved chest bone
15. Pat dry
16. ____ upon a time
17. Baby's noisemaker
19. Intense
21. Cherry-colored
22. Flying mammal
23. Refuse
26. Every bit
27. Conducted
30. In the past
31. Carved pole
33. Respectful fear
34. "The ____ Squad"
35. Expert
36. Not shut
37. Ginger drink
38. Fire residue
40. Country house
42. Mortar
46. Animal parks
47. Short letter
49. Cow's sound
50. Low female voice
51. Toboggan
52. Bed-and-breakfast
53. Pod vegetable
54. Begley, Jr. and McMahon
55. Pullover shirt

**DOWN**

1. Contented cat's sound
2. Largest continent
3. Unpaid bill
4. Dining-room item
5. Was sick
6. In favor of
7. Transmitted
8. Tempo
9. Fruit drink
12. Secure
13. Boxing match
18. Attempt
20. Tranquil
23. Beaver's structure
24. Self-image
25. Indicate yes
26. Gobbled up
27. Baby's seat
28. Ram's mate
29. Study
31. High
32. Pacific and Indian
36. Unit of resistance
37. In addition
38. Behaved
39. Kernels
40. Mouselike animal
41. Smidgen
43. Radiate
44. Zip
45. Sound quality
46. Jolt suddenly
48. Bravo!

# PUZZLE 238

**ACROSS**

1. Speck
5. Ernie's friend
9. Pump
13. Stay
17. Arab ruler
18. Turmoils
19. Mama's mate
20. Small guitars
21. Crooned
22. Everest's range
24. Ooze
25. Fire crime
27. Hindu garment
28. Mardi Gras follower
30. "Once ____ a midnight dreary . . ."
32. Swig
35. Fragrant shrubs
39. Embarrassment
43. Rose
45. ____ of the ball
46. Decline
47. Perfumed
49. Hurried
50. Bandleader Shaw
51. Chili ingredient
52. Ewe said it!
54. Witch
55. Troubles
56. Young horses
57. Flow
58. "Butterflies ____ Free"
59. Edited
61. Meerschaum's country kin
63. Overhead trains
65. Sombreros
66. Fold
67. Running mate
70. Cheer
71. Actor Brynner
72. Arboreal mammal
73. Davis or Midler
74. Culture medium
76. Wins over
78. Greek garb
79. Lucky number
81. Circumference
82. Russian soup
83. Puts up
85. Seine
86. Ringing sound
87. Grounded bird
89. Neutral color
91. Sword
96. Honolulu's island
99. Stress
103. Tender
104. Asian range
105. Slide
106. Old Peruvian
107. Potter's oven
108. Pause
109. Bows
110. Nobleman
111. Winter vehicle

**DOWN**

1. Plateau
2. Actor Sharif
3. Cans
4. Therefore
5. Exclamation of contempt
6. Light bulb inventor
7. Numeral type
8. Ruler of yore
9. Healthy spot
10. Hit the ____
11. Role on "All My Children"
12. Artist's stand
13. Victorian fashions
14. Harry's successor
15. Irish Sea feeder
16. Psi power
23. Heeds
26. TLC provider
29. Pen point
31. Lemon meringue, e.g.
33. Charged particles
34. Lobster trap
36. In letter order
37. Prove innocent
38. Marsh plant
39. Gizzard
40. Hoagy
41. Men's cologne
42. Costume
43. Weight-watcher's tool
44. TV personality Norville
47. Judgment and hot
48. Intimidate
51. Moonshine
53. Circle part
56. Con game
57. Browning and Keats

# PUZZLE 238

60. Detective's question
61. Silk or linen
62. Baking chambers
63. Rub off
64. Beer
66. Serving dish
68. Engrave
69. Plague
72. Waterless
73. Villages
75. New member
77. Shark part
78. Large weight
80. Ultimate
82. Rebound
84. Children's author Dr. ___
86. Sea water
88. Singer Paul ___
90. Trim
92. Inquires
93. Simmer
94. Gardner of whodunits
95. Split
96. Boathouse implement
97. London libation
98. Possesses
100. Burrow
101. Ames and Sullivan
102. Corn unit

# PUZZLE 239

**ACROSS**

1. Grouchy one
5. Dill herb
9. Info
13. Come to a halt
17. Western weed
18. Hawaiian goose
19. Ripped
20. Jason's ship
21. Passe: hyph.
23. Portent
24. Cooking fat
25. "Beau ——"
26. Shunned ones
28. Bees
30. Easter meat
32. Paper quantity
33. Inclines
34. Small restaurants
38. Soil
39. Chop off
42. Cereal grain
43. Look-alike
44. Kleptomaniac
46. Record for TV
47. Profess
49. Behind time
51. Adds explanations
53. Lukewarm
55. This evening, in ads
57. East
58. Family member
60. Period
61. Pack away
62. Fastener
65. Alaskan seaport
67. Circus worker
71. Stamp gatherer
73. Hall runners
75. Calif. valley
76. Eye amorously
77. Scout activities
79. Add
81. Stone
82. Court
83. Weathercock
84. Favors
87. Like April
89. Planet
90. Flock mother
91. Dwarfed plant
93. Corsair
95. Israeli seaport
99. In a line
100. Cajole
102. "Bonanza" man: 2 wds.
104. "Peter Pan" pooch
105. Qualified
106. Sicilian resort
107. Be concerned
108. Small valley
109. Told tales
110. Stool
111. Walked

**DOWN**

1. Shoe
2. Debauchee
3. Bible book
4. Bazaar stalls
5. Also
6. Actress Patricia
7. Join: 2 wds.
8. Indian home
9. Tempest
10. Male cats
11. Common verb
12. Boy scout rank
13. Beauty parlor
14. Interpret
15. Monster
16. Peas' homes
22. Banquet
27. Bridge chair
29. Deserter
31. Whimper
33. Legal claim
34. Gravy dish
35. Enthusiastic review
36. On
37. Lariat
38. Eat
40. Unlock
41. Nuisance
45. "Mad" man
46. Formosa
48. Nun's headcloth
50. Withstand
52. Equine gait
54. Miss Evans
56. Charged atom
59. Routine
61. Sweetener
62. Garbage boat

# PUZZLE 239

63. Takeout order: 2 wds.
64. Ultimatum: 3 wds.
65. Gag
66. Canterbury VIP
68. Creche trio
69. Sword
70. Football team
72. Like Tim
74. Buildable lot
78. Battle memento
80. Staircase post
83. By way of
85. Papal vestments
86. Elite
88. Dam town
89. Metaphor or doubles starter
91. Noise
92. Spoken
93. Ashen
94. Lab burner
96. Slightly open
97. Corrida animal
98. Listen carefully
101. Kimono sash
103. Make lace

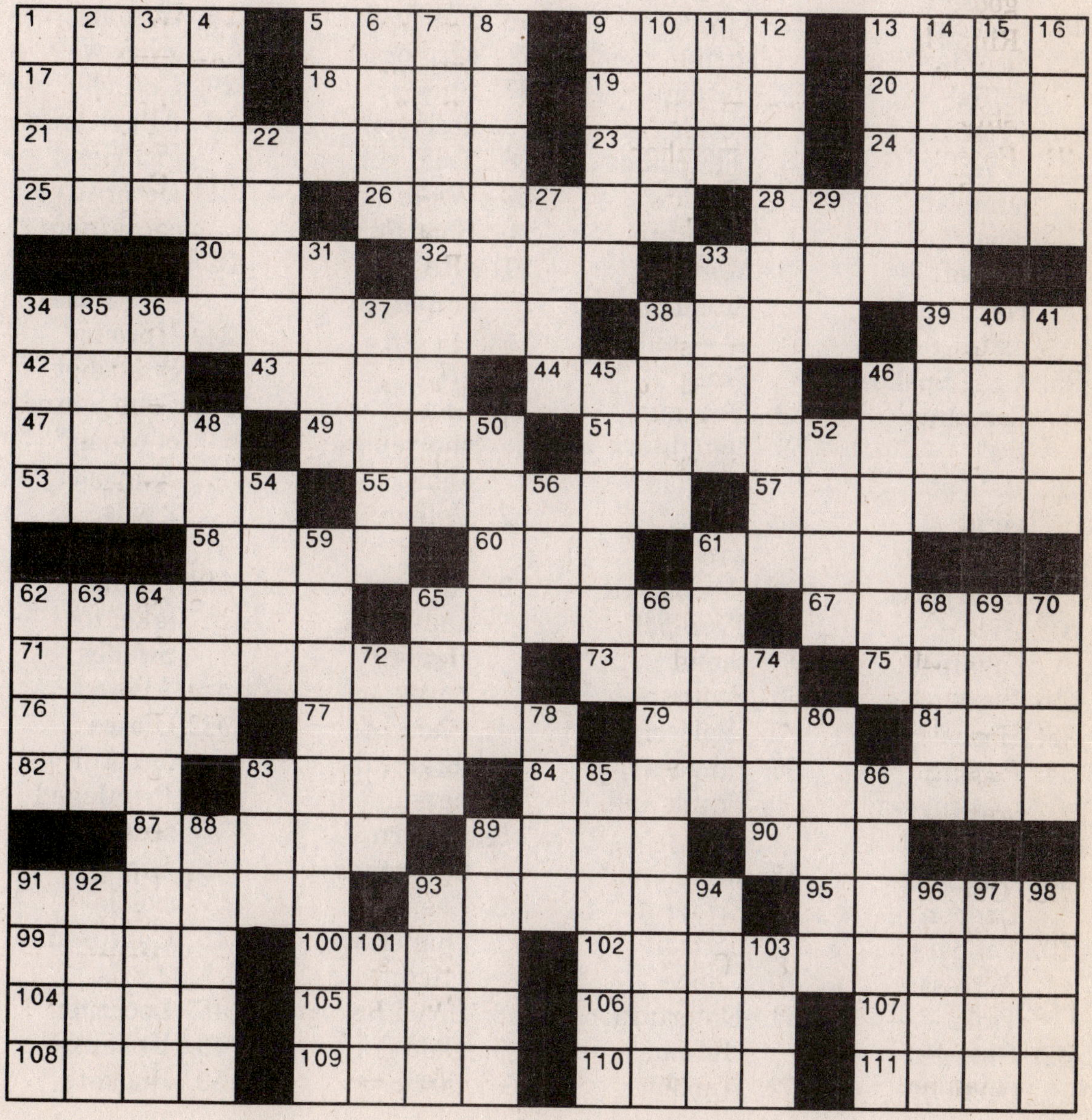

# PUZZLE 240

**ACROSS**

1. Memorable period
4. Lantern
8. Lymph node
13. Small weight
17. —— and feather
18. Polyunsaturated spread
19. Speech disorder: suffix
20. Frost
21. WWII admiral: 3 wds.
24. Site of Napoleon's exile
25. "—— Spake Zarathustra"
26. Eats at eight
27. Fanatic
29. Blue jacks
31. Air openings
32. Woes
33. Highway
34. Paying passengers
35. Can fruit
39. Candidate Landon
40. Ponders
41. Actress Talia ——
42. Charged particle
43. Exchanged in trade
45. Dental thread
46. Official records
47. Limousines
48. Writer Sylvia ——
49. Anesthetic
50. Playwright Harold ——
52. Texas shrine
53. Cardinal Borgia
54. Questioned
55. Window material
56. More confident
57. —— of Pines
58. Not taut
59. Daughters of Atlas
62. Aloha wreath
63. Tea biscuit
64. Trumpet sound
65. Scottish explorer
66. Singers Frank and Nancy
68. Rhymers
69. Sit for a portrait
70. Canoe
71. Entertainer Guinan
72. Knobby
73. Madhouse
76. Candy stripers
77. Tennis star Bjorn ——
78. Pennsylvania city
79. TV interviewer: 2 wds.
84. "Desire Under the ——"
85. Tablecloth material
86. Political cartoonist
87. Ship deserter
88. Trial run
89. Wield
90. Shoe form
91. CIA employee

**DOWN**

1. List shortener: abbr.
2. College cheer
3. Rhythm-and-blues singer: 2 wds.
4. Plant of forgetfulness
5. Tavern beverages
6. Sea: Fr.
7. Dusted with talcum
8. Sparkles
9. Gold fabrics
10. MacGraw, et al.
11. Young insect
12. Beauties
13. Lubrication
14. Small stream
15. Early church desk
16. —— and potatoes
22. Wearing shoes
23. Baseball teams
28. In some other way
29. Grouch
30. Alley Oop's girlfriend
31. Decorative containers
32. "My Wild —— Rose"
34. Uproar
35. Snapshot
36. "The Sound of Music" composer: 2 wds.
37. Elector
38. Finnish lake, to Swedes
40. Alloted
41. Closes forcefully
44. Privileged student
45. Hip bottle
46. Confused: 2 wds.
48. Location
49. Uncanny
50. Buckets

# PUZZLE 240

51. Japanese-American
52. Arkin and Mowbray
53. Prompters
55. Be smug in success
56. Bed boards
58. Mix up
59. Agreeable
60. Life of Riley
61. Germ
63. Portico
64. Pugilist
67. Most talented
68. Hairsplitter
69. Fortified wine
71. River through Rome
72. Actor Nick
73. Sugar vegetable
74. First name in mysteries
75. Loses brightness
76. "Rule Britannia" composer
77. Foundation
80. French city
81. Armed conflict
82. Knock sharply
83. Barnyard area

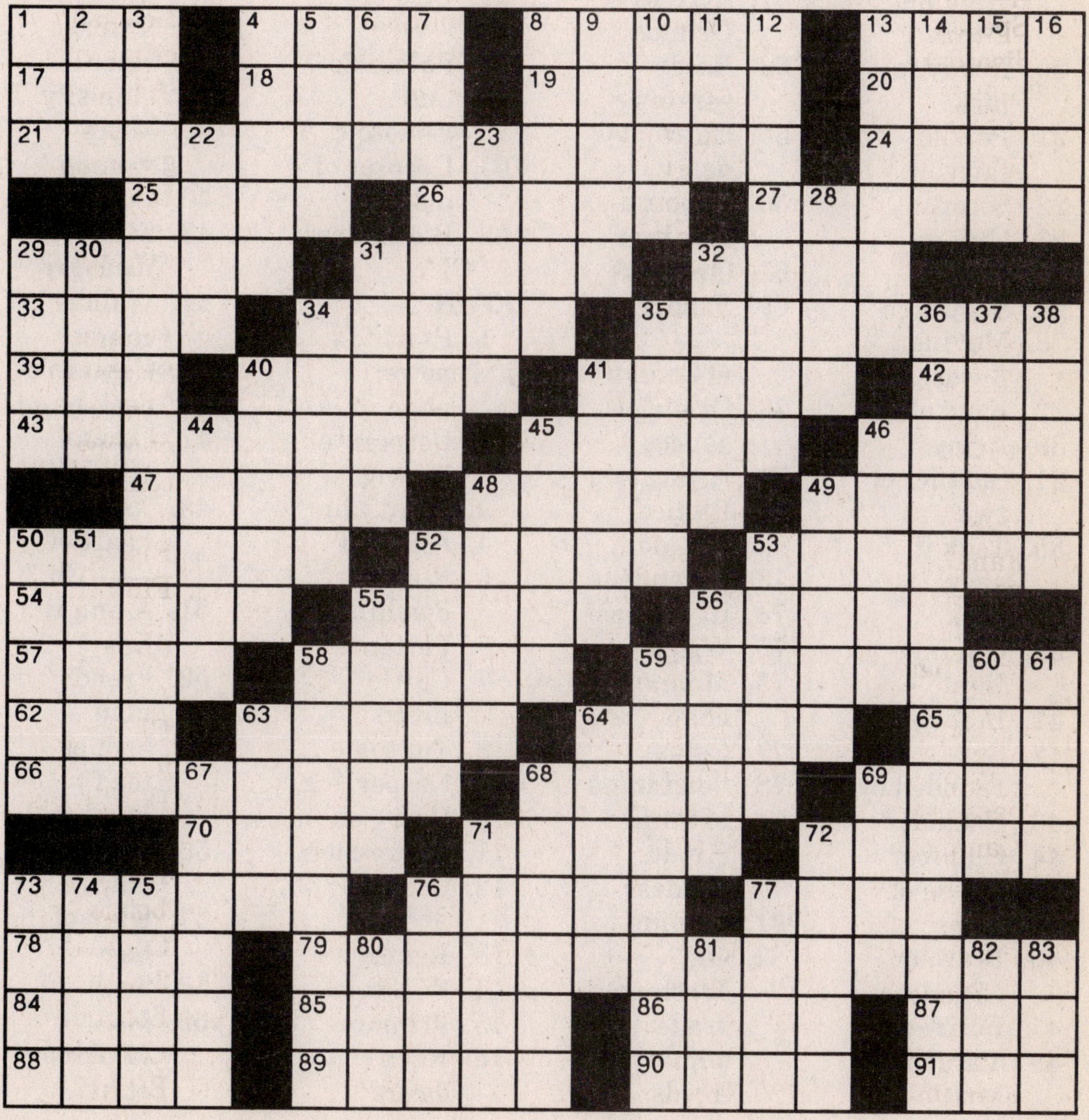

# PUZZLE 241

**ACROSS**

1. Holiday nights
5. Soft drink
9. Hold firmly
13. Strong cart
17. Denomination
18. Roman love god
19. "If I —— Hammer": 2 wds.
20. Ready to pick
21. Persian fairy
22. Stoop
23. Unique chap
24. Shop sign
25. Moving: 3 wds.
29. Kind of ear
30. Army
31. Smaller of two
35. Took it easy
38. Sulk
39. Guiding light
41. In favor
42. Surrounded by
43. Excludes
44. Clamber
45. Theda of films
46. Bravo or Grande
47. Divided
48. Valuable violin
49. —— about: 2 wds.
50. Snoopy's home
52. Personnel worker
53. Dear ones
54. Pioneer transports: 2 wds.
59. Coup d'——
61. Actress Grimes
62. Bacon serving
65. Entrance delay
66. Punctuation mark
67. Overcook
69. Sandra —— O'Connor
70. Oriental sauces
71. Aspiration
72. Biblical kingdom
73. Ascended
74. In the past
75. Wrigglers
76. Mannerly chap
77. Coins
78. Soundness of mind
80. Hindu goddess
81. Decline
82. Old Western trade route: 4 wds.
88. Secular
91. Forbidden thing: hyph.
92. Famous fiddler
93. Crazy bird
95. Roguish
96. Cartoonist of yore
97. Enjoy the joke
98. Sicilian town
99. Bird of ——
100. Paleozoic and Cenozoic
101. Laborer of old
102. Bottomless

**DOWN**

1. Psychic's power: abbr.
2. Corporate bigwig
3. Light tan
4. Affected
5. Rustic dwelling
6. Portent
7. Cattle breed
8. Toilsome
9. Casper, e.g.
10. Carry on
11. Impression
12. Grassy area
13. Refuse
14. —— cord
15. Primate
16. Keen desire
26. Topper
27. Calif. zone
28. Always, in verse
32. Early ranchero: 2 wds.
33. Goof
34. Pride sounds
35. Caper
36. Yvette's chum
37. Utah attraction: 2 wds.
38. Handle clumsily
39. Mean woman
40. Coronet
43. Straw measure
44. Wander off course
45. Captain's deck hands
47. Capitol Hill VIP
48. "Sweetheart of —— Chi"
51. A and B flat
52. French man
55. Foot or toad finisher
56. Packs down
57. Kind of bag
58. Scull
59. Ms. Martinelli et al.

60. N.Y. county
63. Vane direction
64. Some breads
66. Missouri feeder
67. Pine and fir, e.g.
68. Sunbonnet
72. Mixture
73. Delighted
75. Crossed d
76. Heavy's heater
77. Cable ——
79. Eager for action
80. Tie-ups
81. Rock or boulder
83. Go to great heights
84. Vase handle
85. Ireland, to poets
86. Pompeii girl
87. "Carry Me Back to the —— Prairie"
88. Circuit
89. Schedule abbr.
90. Winter hazard
94. Fabric pile

# PUZZLE 241

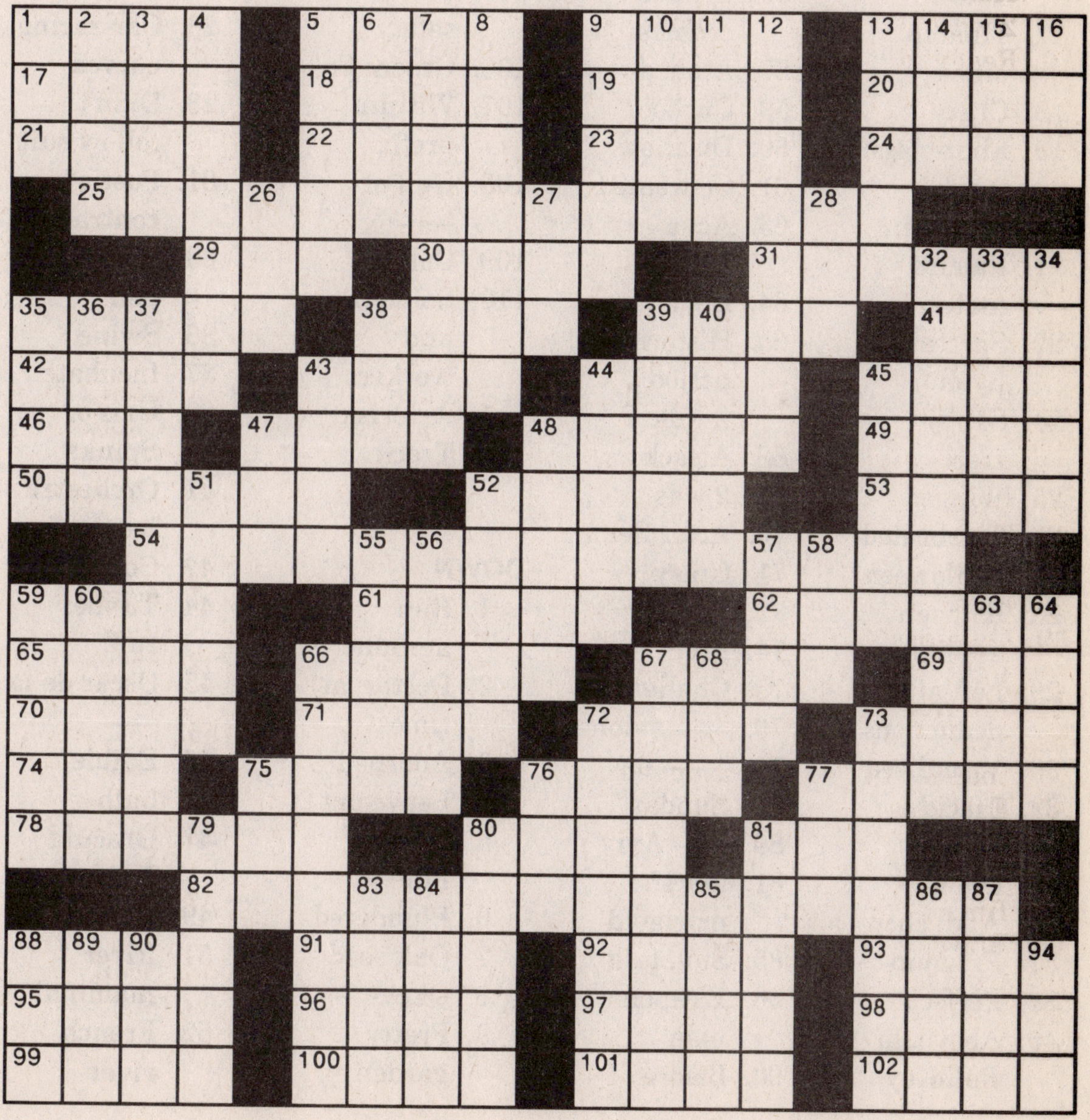

# PUZZLE 242

**ACROSS**

1. Begone!
5. "When I was —— . . .": 2 wds.
9. Stage piece
13. "—— well that ends well"
17. Time in office
18. Crazy
19. First-class: 2 wds.
20. Bumpkin
21. Rajah's mate
22. Spectators: hyph.
24. Sandy tract
25. Winged
27. Celebrated Halloween
28. Kitchen appliance
29. Left after deductions
30. Visualized
32. Placid
34. Harden
35. Did an A.M. chore
37. Pronoun
38. Perfect
40. Above, to F.S. Key
41. Priest
43. Winged insect
44. Ships' fronts
47. Qualified
48. Feast
50. Honker
54. Optical glass
55. Unit of cookies
57. Atoned
59. Cuckoo
60. Disallow
61. Concealed
63. Actor Beatty
64. Bind
65. Historical period: 2 wds.
68. Attack: 2 wds.
70. Actor Sean
71. Crazy
72. Turf
74. Pro
75. Challenges
76. —— avion
78. "—— on Sunday"
80. —— Aviv
81. Marsh marigold
85. Sun. talk
86. Weapons man
90. Before
91. Sullen
93. Exchange premium
94. Compass pt.
95. Lively songs
97. Surplus
99. Tree houses
101. Vein
102. Exhaust
104. Extreme
105. To safety
106. Green: Fr.
107. Within: prefix
108. Gulf of ——
109. Colors
110. Soldiers and workers
111. Asterisk
112. Track event

**DOWN**

1. Run aground
2. Doctor, at times
3. Adorned
4. Leave out
5. "—— of Me"
6. Plundered
7. Oak seed
8. Okey- ——
9. Pretty garden
10. Not a winner
11. Positive poles
12. Urge
13. Actor Robert or Alan
14. Loaf
15. Surges forward
16. Strengthens
23. Comforted
26. Car-racing curves
28. Didn't follow suit
31. Poetic contraction
33. Point of a pen
36. Swine
37. Incubate
39. Uris or Spinks
41. Orchestra location
42. Corn unit
44. Tissue: suff.
45. Oscar de la ——
46. Edible bulb
47. Dracula features
49. Voice
51. River mammal
52. French river

# PUZZLE 242

53. Nice places
55. Bleat
56. Towel word
58. Quill
60. Soothes
62. Put off
66. Bites
67. Many moons
69. High hill
70. —— Alto
73. Meal finales
75. Evil spirit
77. Brazilian resort
79. Swerves
80. Three: prefix
81. Basement
82. Baltimore ——
83. United
84. Established
86. Program
87. Dwell
88. Menu item
89. Take umbrage
92. Apparent
93. FBI man
96. Golf pegs
98. Imitates
100. Yellow cheese
102. Reproductive units
103. "Le Coq ——"

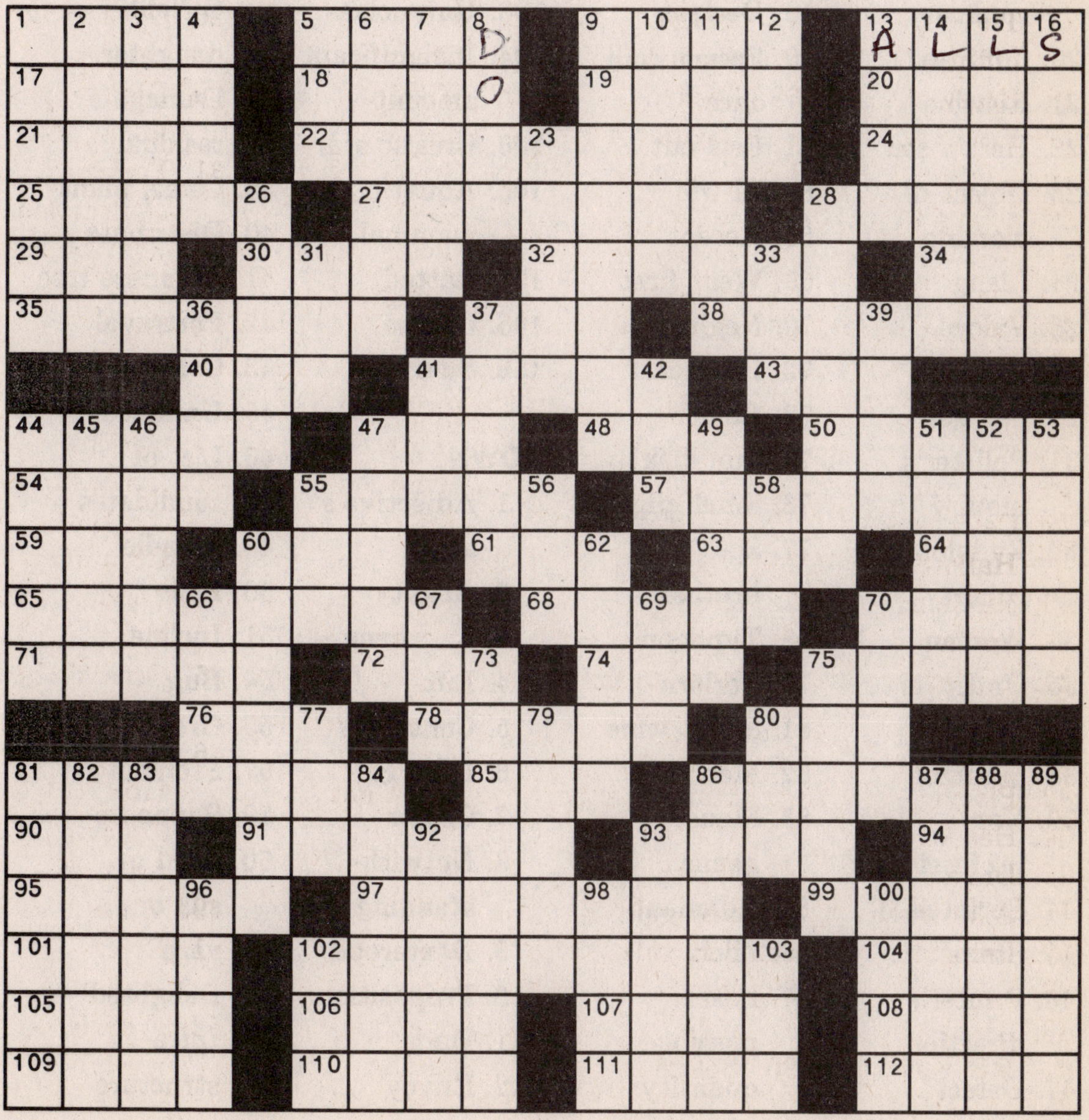

# PUZZLE 243

## ACROSS

1. Weathercock
5. Enthusiastic
9. Retired
13. Assay
17. Environmental sci.
18. Merchant's item
19. Sarcastic comment
20. Confused
21. Routine
22. Hera's son
23. Object of worship
24. Liang
25. Valor
27. Sidekick
29. Sea god
31. Pollster's inquiry
32. Rudolph's cohort
34. Woman
35. Under, in Milan
38. Summon
39. Non-professionals
44. Sprinted
45. Stake
46. Printer's direction
47. Detect
48. Particular
49. Attract
50. Piccolos' cousins
52. Frazier's competitor
53. Model
55. Shine
56. Forfeiter
58. Rd.
59. Declaim
60. French coin, once
61. Feel out
64. Ill will
65. Accept
69. Went first
70. Negligent
72. Downcast
73. Remit
74. Sun disk
76. Small piglet
77. Seth's brother
78. Typhoon
79. Forlorn
81. Sweet wine
82. Men
83. Mouse genus
84. Adamant
86. Zilch
87. Least possible quantity
91. "When I ____ a lad . . ."
92. Casters
96. Directly
97. Moreno of "West Side Story"
99. Electron's home
101. Acknowledge
102. Chinese wax
103. Univ. class
104. Insignificant amount
105. Erratic star
106. Aquatic mammal
107. Ratted
108. Course
109. Swarm

## DOWN

1. Adjective's kin
2. Acidity
3. ____ bene
4. Lift
5. Conscious
6. Diverge
7. Choler
8. Notwithstanding
9. Dexterous
10. Proposition
11. Dark
12. Envoy
13. Squeals
14. Rebekah's son
15. Studied
16. Parable
26. Vanity
28. Split
30. Touch
32. Gross
33. Character
35. Station
36. Eugene O'Neill's daughter
37. Damage residual
38. Cereal plant
40. Distribute
41. Javanese tree
42. Portrayal
43. Commotion
45. Unmixed
46. List of candidates
49. Treadle
50. Pads
51. Incline
54. Bug
55. Ground grain
57. Pronoun
59. Supposes
60. Kind of silk or yarn
61. Delighted
62. Infrastructure

# PUZZLE 243

63. Certain literary works
64. Dirty mark
65. Settled
66. October gem
67. Farewell, to Caesar
68. Glances at
71. Deletions
72. Stall
75. So-called
77. Pirate
78. Chivalrous
80. Scottish chimney
81. Coat type
82. Wire measurement
85. Sharp, nasal tone
86. Drifter
87. Plots
88. Strophanthus product
89. Lopez's theme song
90. Shiny mineral
92. Ecclesiastical court
93. Shout of a Bacchanal
94. Stray
95. Emulated Spitz
98. Great deal
100. Furthermore

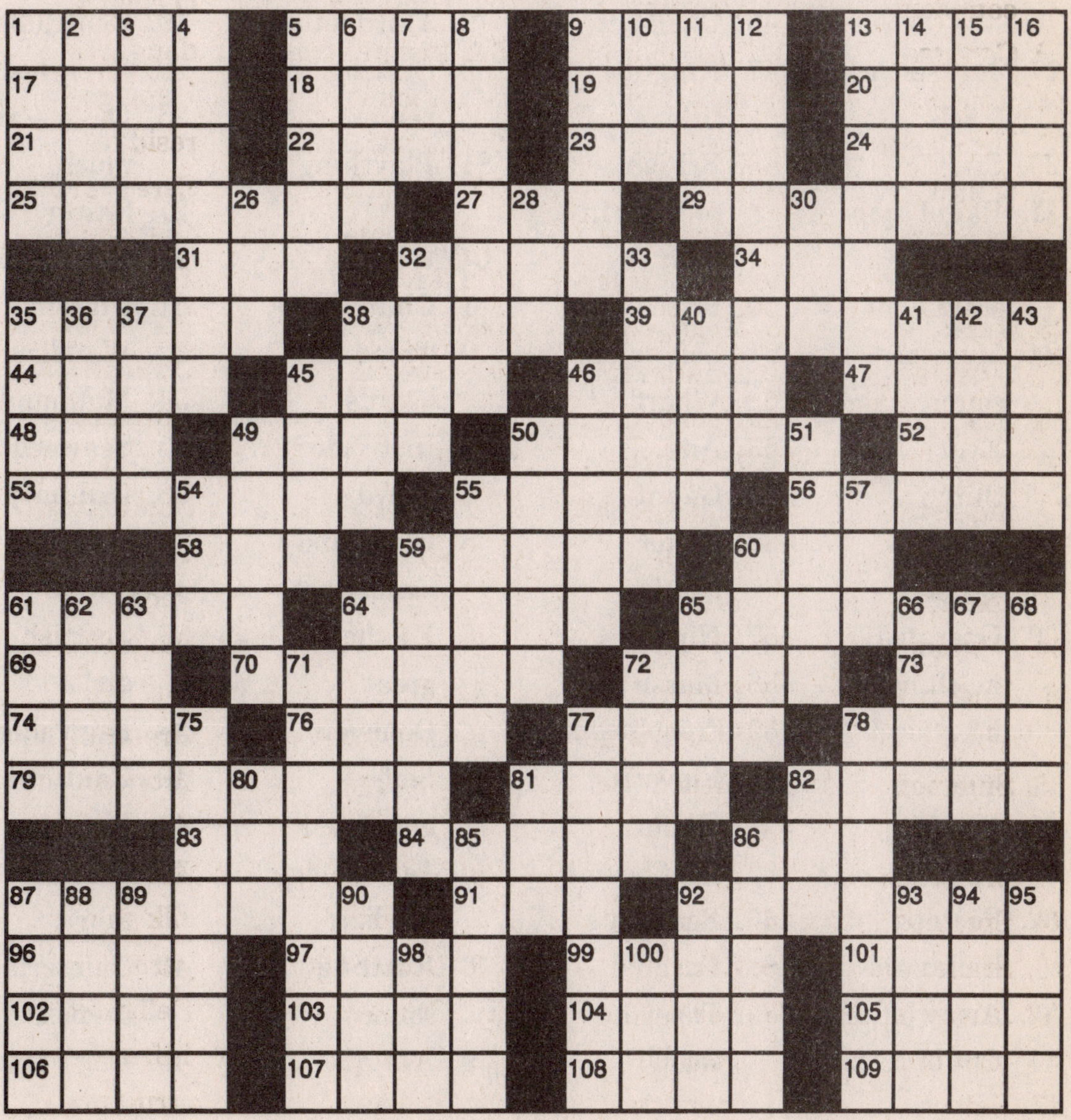

# PUZZLE 244

## ACROSS

1. Spiteful woman
4. Salty drops
9. Out of tune
12. Visage
13. Direction sign
14. Book page
16. —— Fe
17. Jerusalem: 3 wds.
20. Stir
21. Bar of soap
23. Feather scarf
24. Musical sound
25. Every thirty days
27. Quizzes
29. Operated machinery
30. Electrical unit
31. Persian king
32. Poetess Dickinson
34. Army officer
37. Cut of pork
38. Very dry, as champagne
39. Unsymmetrical
40. Caution
41. Noisiest
44. Sound of disgust
45. Endure
46. Chamber
47. Knight's title
48. British soldiers in Bengal
50. Price
51. Soft drink
52. Wharf
53. Any
54. Gaunt
55. Water mains
57. Nip
58. Marsh
59. French coin
60. Flavoring plants
62. Roof beams
66. Penpoints
68. Payable
69. Tapering seam
70. Baseball stick
71. Perry Mason's secretary: 2 wds.
74. Satire
76. Civil disturbance
77. Church path
78. Kitchen basin
79. Third letter
80. Cutting beam
81. Plaything

## DOWN

1. Church law
2. Tread the boards
3. Instructor
4. Dowdy
5. Cleveland's waterfront
6. Football great Donovan
7. Self-appointed Texas judge: 2 wds.
8. Rustling sound
9. Antique
10. Remarkable deed
11. Local candidate: 2 wds.
12. Portuguese dance
15. Crucial exam
16. Yosemite ——
18. Suet
19. Contradict
22. Everybody
26. De —— (too much)
27. Skinny
28. Blood fluid
31. Classify
33. Wet dirt
34. Manhandle
35. Seaweed
36. Ordinary citizen: 3 wds.
37. Scottish girl
38. High shoe
40. Cautious
41. Misplace
42. Chinese fabric
43. Cafeteria utensil
45. Dog's lead

# PUZZLE 244

46. Capital of Italy
49. Billiards stick
50. Folding beds
51. Jargon
53. Place of enforced isolation
54. Radical
55. Remain undecided
56. Less cordial
57. Savage
58. Distant
61. Magazine execs
62. Grader
63. Blackwood
64. Military grade
65. Pig's digs
67. Wild plum
69. Remove from print
72. Took food
73. Nineteenth letter
75. —— de Janeiro

# PUZZLE 245

**ACROSS**

1. Brown paper item
4. Shoo!
8. TV's predecessor
13. Retreats
17. Self
18. Buckeye State
19. Black wood
20. Theater sign
21. Bear up under
23. Goes without food
24. Spanish fruit
25. London apartment
26. "—— of Wax"
28. Broad chisel
30. Train tracks
32. Viking
33. Dishearten
34. Writer Ferber
35. Swell out
36. Basque's hat
37. "—— Day Afternoon"
38. Blouse type
39. Pep up
40. Sacred city
43. Slangy dice
44. Piglike animal
45. Nazimova
46. Table coverings
49. A, E, I, O, or U
50. Heavy blow
51. Does housework
52. All tied up
53. Overcast
54. Peruses
55. County celebrations
56. Swindler
57. With competence
58. Hitchcock villains
59. Confidence
60. Footlike organ
61. Ciphers
62. Crucifix
63. River in Scotland
66. Greek ship launcher
67. Parade sight
68. Cruel
69. Ushers in again
72. Muscular strength
73. Endures use
74. Bay windows
75. Inclined (to)
76. Lemon peel
77. Touched the starting line
78. Encore!
80. Pave the way for: 3 wds.
84. Brink
85. Most unpleasant
86. Thus
87. Atmosphere
88. Pod member
89. Makes wet
90. Sleuth Nancy
91. —— Turner

**DOWN**

1. Wager
2. Time gone by
3. Out on the links
4. Marsh birds
5. Small talk
6. River isle
7. Slight footings: 2 wds.
8. Turn down
9. Make humble
10. Medicinal portion
11. Bank statement abbr.
12. Mollusk fisher
13. Banish
14. Synonym of 13 Down
15. Mets and Yankees
16. Asterisks
22. "—— Cinders"
27. Roman revelry
29. Frank
30. Christmas color
31. "Much —— About Nothing"
32. Undraped statues
33. Lucifer
35. Ties tightly
36. Two-footed animal
38. Complains
39. Front yards
40. Jeer
41. Dodge
42. Woodland deity
43. Like a bad guy's eyes
44. French city
45. On high
46. Quarrel
47. West Point cadet
48. Spanish silver coins
49. Renders null
50. Group
52. Powerful industrialist
53. Bread border
55. Conflagrations
56. Reaction to a pun

# PUZZLE 245

58. Wood-cutting machines: 2 wds.
59. Smoothed plaster
61. Ardent desire
62. Tribe
63. Not showing emotion
64. Spike of corn
65. Half ems
66. Took note
67. Facades
68. Restaurant list
69. Routines
70. Decompose
71. Flock of herons
72. Effervescent
73. Black —— spider
75. India rubber
76. Blow wildly
79. Sticky substance
81. Blunder
82. Aunt, to Pedro
83. Bread morsel

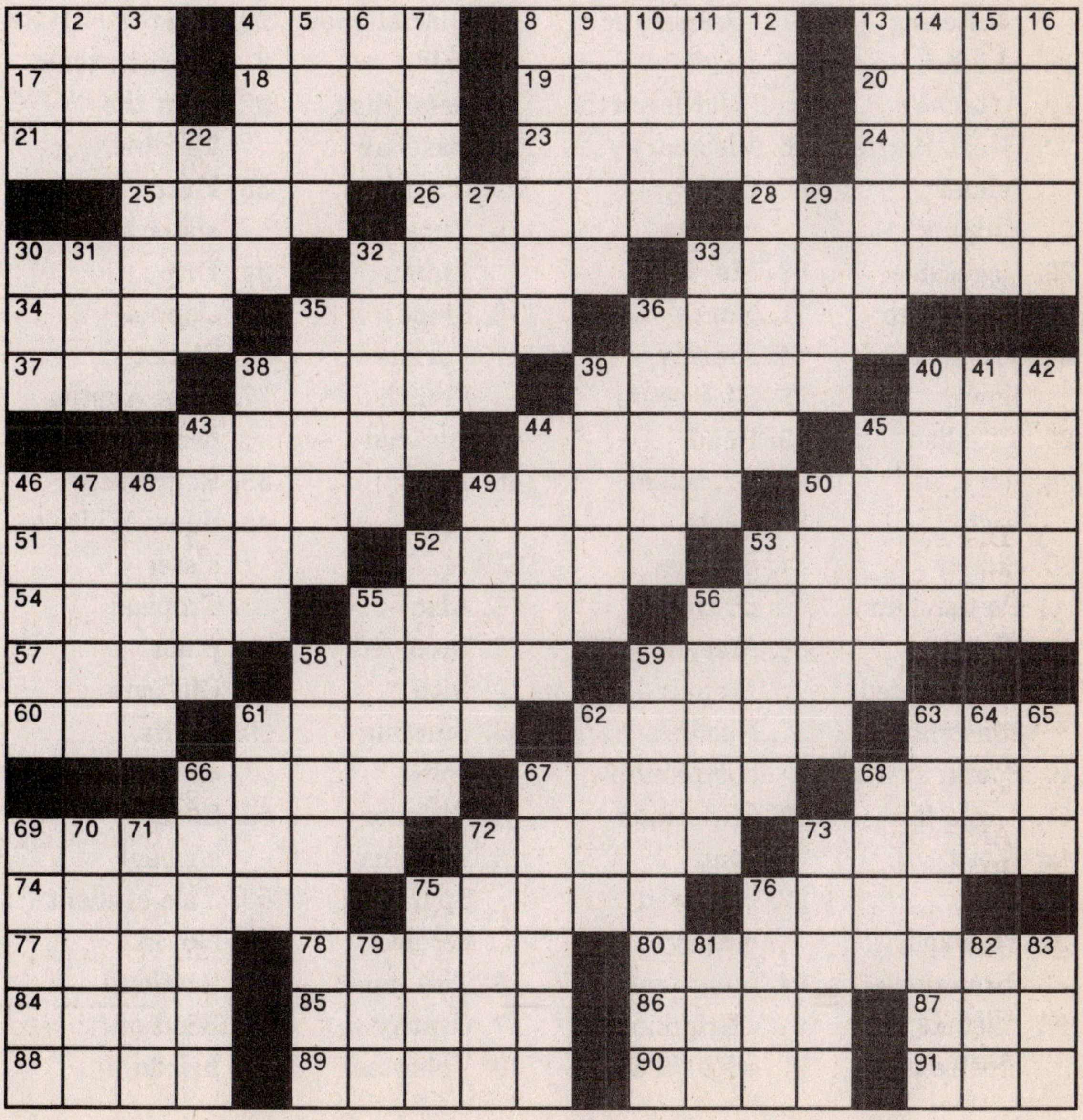

# PUZZLE 246

**ACROSS**

1. A Jackson brother
5. General Arnold
8. Small dogs, for short
12. Lag behind
16. Unique person
17. Do some plastering
18. Shower
19. Attache
20. Great Barrier Island
21. Employ
22. Vegetable
23. Fan's hero
24. Tropical flower
26. TV alien
28. Very, in Vichy
30. Sidney Poitier film
36. Placid
39. Unaspirated consonants
40. Sound system
41. Large bird
42. Weed
44. Seize
46. Thailand, formerly
47. Arabian chieftain
49. New star
51. Tennis star Lacoste
54. ____ out (make do)
55. Memory's route
56. Rug-weaver's knot
59. Palmer's game
61. "A host, of ____" (Wordsworth)
66. Visionary
67. Canary's relative
68. Ms. Kett
71. Youth
74. Freshly
76. Of a poem
78. Bend
79. Drenched
81. Facts
84. Speaker's platform
86. Marvin or Majors
87. Needle's companion
90. Christmas song
92. Followed closely
94. Song from "Brigadoon," with "The"
97. Federal agcy.
98. ____ was saying
99. Ornamental shrub
102. Sunrise
105. Strong drink
107. Heraldic wreath
109. Lodging places
111. Jai ____
112. Glacial snow field
113. Solar disk
114. Baseball team
115. Yucatan Indian
116. Singe
117. Former French marshal
118. Theory

**DOWN**

1. Also
2. Involved with
3. Starting golfer
4. Visionary
5. Johanna Spyri's heroine
6. Tire input
7. Gratify
8. Volunteer
9. Furniture wood
10. Laughter
11. Traps
12. Shastas, e.g.
13. Disencumber
14. Commotion
15. Set
17. Pertaining to Santiago's country
25. Allude
27. Lengthy
29. Newt
31. Football team
32. Ivan the Terrible, e.g.
33. Huron's sister lake
34. Drip
35. Cupola
36. Signet
37. Jane Austen heroine
38. Regretting
43. Snow White's sister
45. Tropical plant
48. Old cars
50. No ifs, ____, or buts
52. Silent consent
53. Yale student
57. No, in Scotland
58. Kind of hairdo

60. Went by jet
62. Grazing ground
63. Hideaway
64. Violin
65. Delay
69. Playhouse locale
70. Emulated Rich Little
71. Wood slat
72. Arthur ___ of tennis
73. Mrs. Copperfield
75. Texas city
77. Countryman
80. Porky Pig's love
82. Scarlet songbird
83. Part of B.A.
85. Casa's room
88. Exclamations
89. Condescends

# PUZZLE 246

91. Buckeye State inhabitant
93. Fighting ___ (Big Ten team)
95. Street show
96. Actor Jack ___
100. Camelot lady
101. "Green Gables" girl
102. Beaver's handiwork
103. Southern st.
104. Method
106. Eggs: Lat.
108. Itinerary: abbr.
110. Red or Yellow

# PUZZLE 247

**• ALL IN THE FAMILY •**

**ACROSS**

1. Gelatin dish
6. Fond du ____
9. Title
12. TV's Reese
17. Wonder Woman's alias
18. London district
19. Elbow
20. Perfect
21. Make law
22. Baldwin of "Beetlejuice"
23. Outstanding
24. Exchanges
25. American painter
28. African animal
29. Slow-moving mammals
30. Appellation
31. Brokers
33. Fascinated
37. Rain
39. Cravats
40. "____ People"
41. Rosalind Russell role
44. Covered
48. Hungarian wine measure
50. Meddle
51. Mosaic parts
52. Vagabond
53. Breathe loudly
54. "____ Pack"
55. Scrap
56. Passengers
57. Prisoners
59. Segment
60. Center
61. Vatican section
65. Soaked
69. Arikaras
70. Marsh
74. Lifts in Vail
75. Mendicant
77. Friend
78. Silas Marner's creator
80. Grain
81. Total
82. Bauxite, e.g.
83. Expanse
84. Paper quantity
85. Important source
88. "Bus Stop" playwright
89. Cadence
90. Exclamations of surprise
91. "Grand ____"
93. Recoiled
96. "____ of Sumatra"
98. Musical sense
99. Talent
100. Treats at carnivals
106. "Blood Wedding" writer
107. Comparable
109. "Boyz N the ____"
110. Meanders
112. Decided
113. Wingless insects
114. Slaughter of baseball
115. "____ Last Night"
116. Web-footed birds
117. Freud's concerns
118. Positioned
119. Irritable

**DOWN**

1. Citrus beverage
2. Harmonize
3. Carson's predecessor
4. Peruvian Indian
5. Sleep
6. Copacabana woman
7. Throat-clearer
8. Tropical fruit
9. Search for water
10. Stringed instrument
11. Foundation
12. Plates
13. Newscaster Newman
14. Bounced
15. Northern Europeans
16. Too
18. Nunn and Donaldson
19. Browning's work
26. Signal for Morse
27. Hindu dress
31. Pointed
32. Thousands
33. Geologic divisions
34. Italian socialist leader
35. Tattle
36. Siren
37. Stickler
38. Black gem
39. Anecdote
41. Cathedral sections
42. Mores
43. Gaiety
44. African republic
45. Jack of "Hawaii Five-O"
46. Genesis brother
47. Amount
49. Contracts
55. Grimace
56. Padding
58. Shallow pan
59. Trepidation
60. Converged
62. Dublin native
63. Citations
64. Lake Erie island
65. Mix up
66. Hautboy
67. Information
68. Small portion
71. Actor Delon
72. Simpleton
73. Lie ____ (out of sight)
75. Gown
76. Routine
77. Winnie the ____
79. Youngster
81. Fed
86. Rub
87. Hooks
89. March
91. Taxi
92. Biblical mountain
93. Inclination
94. Author Bret ____
95. Sieves
96. Narratives
97. Top
98. Purposes
99. Beat
101. Chaplin's daughter
102. Source
103. Roundish projection
104. Thailand's neighbor
105. Dirt
107. "The Greatest"
108. Little goat
111. Dump

# PUZZLE 248

**ACROSS**
1. Collegiate quarters
5. Neck napkins
9. Gp. for F. Lee Bailey
12. On the briny
13. Unruly offspring
14. Prohibit
15. Linen source
16. "Man of ____"
18. Subject
20. Certain sib
21. "Pygmalion" musical
27. "____ Are There"
30. Bob, to Tiny Tim
31. Section
32. Choose
33. See 50 Across
36. Class
37. Lifeless
39. Soupy Sales missile
40. Jolson and Pacino
41. Dickens's "____ Carol"
45. Honest ____
46. "____ Dolly!"
50. With 33 Across, Bernstein's "Romeo and Juliet"
55. Starring role
56. "Diamonds ____ Forever"
57. Seth's son
58. Role for Angela and Lucille
59. Actor Harrison
60. Loch ____ monster
61. Simians

**DOWN**
1. Wacky
2. City in Norway
3. Harvest
4. Axiom
5. Keg: abbr.
6. Private pension fund: abbr.
7. Disney deer
8. Ringo ____
9. TV network
10. Word from Scrooge
11. Santa ____, Calif.
17. Piano novelty
19. Charisse et al.
22. Dieter's dread
23. Take as one's own
24. Operatic solo
25. "The Farmer in the ____"
26. Asian oxen
27. Luke Skywalker's teacher
28. Fuel cartel: abbr.
29. Salt Lake City's state
34. Edge
35. Uh-huh!
38. Darn!
42. "A Doll's House" author
43. Parisian river
44. Alabama city
47. Ballet move
48. Gold cloth
49. Poems of praise
50. Armed conflict
51. Before, long ago
52. Gender
53. John ____ Passos
54. Double curve

# PUZZLE 249

**ACROSS**
1. The law's is long
4. Traffic tie-ups
8. Wave, as a wing
12. "Till There Was ____" (40 Across tune)
13. "The Thrill ____ All"
14. Misplace
15. Bobbsey twin
16. Space shuttle org.
17. Step ____ (rush)
18. 40 Across locale
21. Ideology
22. Mute approval
23. 1982 Disney flick
26. Above, to Keats
27. Time
30. Star of 40 Across
34. Officeholders
35. Apatite, for one
36. "____ and the Tramp"
37. Court
38. ____ rule
40. Meredith Willson hit
45. Rev. Roberts
46. Commanded
47. Marshall's hit
49. Professor Harold ____ (of 40 Across)
50. Legal attachment
51. TV Tarzan
52. Tipplers
53. Otherwise
54. Rep.'s opponent

**DOWN**
1. Novelist Rand
2. Bellow
3. Actor Paul ____
4. 40 Across star Shirley ____
5. "Old MacDonald had ____"
6. Catchall word: abbr.
7. Furniture finisher
8. Boxer Patterson
9. Burt's ex
10. Siberia's location
11. Teacher's ____
19. Clingy plant
20. Ripped
23. Prefix with angle
24. 40 Across child star Howard
25. Out-of-date: abbr.
26. Unclosed, to a poet
27. Greek letter
28. Mr. Serling
29. "____ Which Way But Loose"
31. Space
32. Pool, in 18 Across
33. Bridge coup
37. Water sources
38. Assistants
39. Act part
40. Half a sextet
41. Marching order
42. Take the sloop
43. In the sack
44. Cleo's stream
45. Sounds of surprise
48. Rocky's hangout

# PUZZLE 250

**• ARTIST'S MARKET •**

**ACROSS**

1. Disagreement
5. Ice unit
9. Metric quart
14. Wager
17. "To Sir With Love" singer
18. Confused
19. Desert plant
20. Obligated to
21. Yemen's neighbor
22. Craves
23. Pentateuch
24. Zuider ___
25. Arizona plateau
28. Oak fruit
30. Coastal bird
31. Pass over
32. Belt
34. Indication
38. Doze
40. Ragged
44. For shame!
45. Fuzzy nectarine
48. Lomond, e.g.
50. Stories
51. Babble
53. Plunder
55. Hawaiian dish
56. Recognized
57. Affirmatives
59. Tag
61. Myths
63. Agree
65. Copier need
67. Grange of football
68. Gourmet
72. Underwater radar
74. Oklahoma city
78. "Persistence of Memory" artist
79. Nabokov heroine
81. Kind of pudding
82. "___ Richard's Almanac"
83. Fingertip feature
84. Dog's relative
86. Approaches
89. Parcel of land
90. Plowable
92. Bleat
94. Fine
96. Rest on one's ___
98. Throw
101. Calloway of song
102. Substitute
105. Barbecue
111. Web-footed bird
112. Lowed
114. Musician Shankar
115. Opera song
116. Zadora or Lindstrom
117. Venerate
118. Nirvana
119. Album
120. At all
121. Scruffs
122. Bronte character
123. Witness

**DOWN**

1. Spill
2. Cougar
3. Jai ___
4. Burrow
5. Pepper
6. Applied
7. Curves
8. Artist's stand
9. Of the side
10. Composer Stravinsky
11. Little pies
12. Topsy's playmate
13. Go over
14. Dunce
15. Water pitcher
16. "___ Angel"
26. Stumble
27. Bask
29. Scored
33. More colorless
34. Uncertain
35. Egyptian river
36. Parrots
37. Audacity
39. Soda
41. City on the Rhine
42. Reared
43. Evergreens
46. Jacket
47. Vagrants
49. Mountain pass
52. Student's container
54. Choir voice
58. Old coin
60. Russian revolutionary
62. Acquire
64. Bureau part
66. Marathon
68. Author Ferber
69. TV host Jack ___
70. Remus's mother
71. Tokyo, formerly
73. Glean
75. Hang loosely
76. Carbon deposit
77. Affected
80. Priest's garment
85. Fronts
87. Lie
88. Barrier
91. Amateur
93. Bern's river
95. Scrape off
97. Shovel
99. Loose rock
100. Sycophant
102. Father
103. Destroy
104. Approve
106. Roll call answer
107. Swear
108. Spring bloom
109. Programming acronym
110. Frilly
113. ___ Mae Brown (Goldberg role)

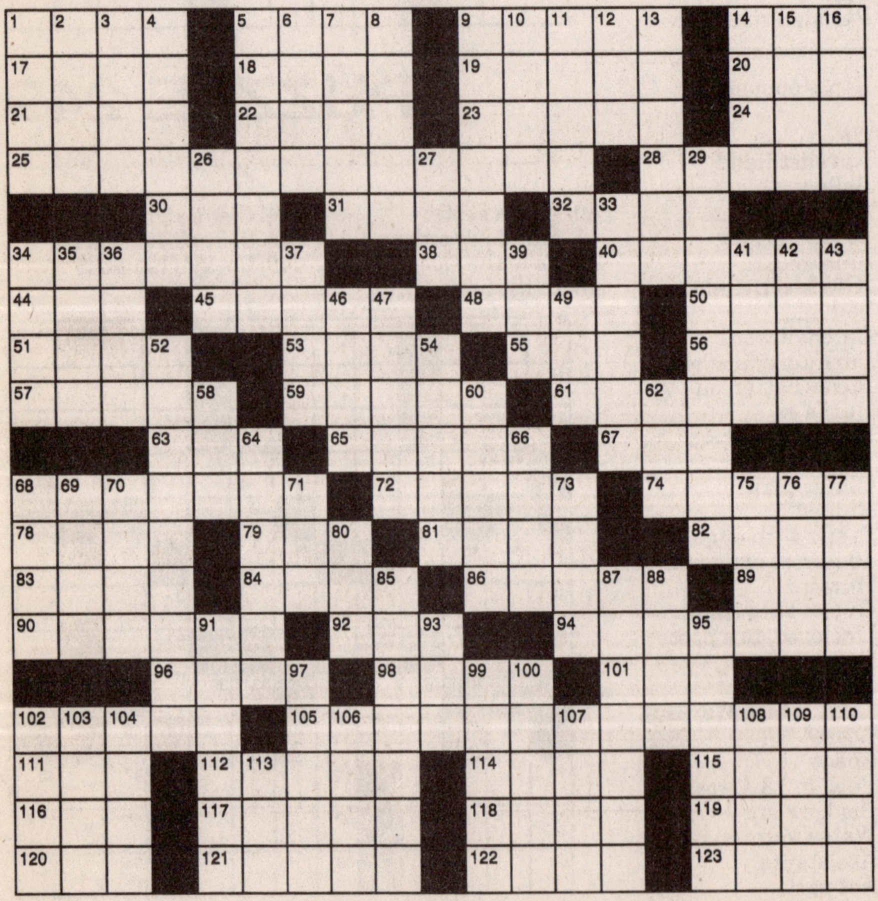

# CRYPTIC CROSSWORD

# PUZZLE 251

**British-style or Cryptic Crosswords are a great challenge for crossword fans. Each clue contains either a definition or direct reference to the answer as well as a play on words. The numbers in parentheses indicate the number of letters in the answer word or words.**

**ACROSS**

1. Chief honcho in shocking pink (7)
5. Chubby, the lady's parents (7)
9. Demolished English school, by the sound of it (5)
10. Country Englander reformed (9)
11. High spot makes the First Lady pause (7)
12. Well-behaved man and fish (7)
13. Warmest state Otis changed (9)
15. In South Dakota, sheep in stitches (5)
17. Walk around end of lake and soak (5)
19. United islands—ones in Asian country (9)
22. Boo, in case it's the last car (7)
24. Check around Monday for chair part (7)
25. Horse cart upset band (9)
26. "Love Bug" brought back to dance (5)
27. Treason destroyed politician (7)
28. General Electric gets in ahead of time, avidly (7)

**DOWN**

1. Sharpest New Hampshire town street (7)
2. Emendator emended college (5,4)
3. Strong-smelling comedian (7)
4. Dark squirming thing (5)
5. Interrupted by octet, Astaire carried cargo (9)
6. Apartment residents—a number of bugs (7)
7. Wipe out "Times" error (5)
8. Burdened tot put into sled (7)
14. Long story to record focal point (9)
16. Occidental person makes the two of us more serious (9)
17. Areas of corsets burst (7)
18. Bug consumes garbage object (7)
20. ID sentry returned (7)
21. Trollope misprinted not any "H" (7)
23. Meat prohibition engulfs company (5)
24. Saw "Advertising Age" (5)

# PUZZLE 252

**ACROSS**
1. Food fish
5. Bathe
9. Nicholson role
14. Enormous
15. Spindle
16. Animated
17. Type of history
18. "____ of the Dragon"
19. Spirit
20. Jelly
22. Bill of fare
24. Moose
25. Actress Remick
26. Possesses
29. Blockhead
31. Color
33. Bit
37. Risky
41. Achievement
42. Messenger of the gods
43. Goof
45. Association
46. Dust
47. Ornamental shoulder piece
49. Pond
52. Rift
53. Regret
54. Desire
55. Sphere
58. Emerald, e.g.
61. Double
64. Match
66. Accumulate
68. Volume
71. Destroy
72. Sprite
73. Always
74. Picture
75. Be frugal
76. Tresses
77. Watch over

**DOWN**
1. Reef
2. Swear
3. Wide open
4. Sandwich shop
5. Course
6. Hatchet
7. Shut
8. "____ Comes the Sun"
9. Large cat
10. Violinist Bull
11. Cattle, once
12. Corrupt
13. Smell
21. Scorch
23. "____ Without My Daughter"
27. Adjutant
28. Night noise
30. Move restlessly
31. Minister
32. Color remover
34. Exploit
35. Pre-Easter season
36. Border
37. Mound
38. Solo for Sills
39. Vitality
40. Sudsy
44. Regulation
48. Boundary
50. Origin
51. ____ Kids on the Block
55. Liquid measure
56. Radioactive gas
57. Like Nick Nolte
58. Holes
59. Utter
60. Skirt type
62. Thing
63. Scientific TV series
65. Resign
67. Transgress
69. Game pieces
70. Before

# PUZZLE 253 Quotagram

**Fill in the answers to the clues. Then transfer the letters to the correspondingly numbered squares in the diagram. The completed diagram will contain a quotation.**

1. Kingston's locale ___ ___ ___ ___ ___ ___ ___ (54 44 12 19 32 22 1)
2. Timepieces ___ ___ ___ ___ ___ ___ ___ (15 24 48 18 43 55 30)
3. Tomahawk ___ ___ ___ ___ ___ ___ ___ (28 3 21 42 16 47 57)
4. Actress Carol ____ ___ ___ ___ ___ ___ ___ ___ ___ (8 49 11 33 14 7 45 26)
5. Obligated ___ ___ ___ ___ ___ (53 17 52 25 37)
6. Floated ___ ___ ___ ___ ___ ___ (38 13 2 6 50 34)
7. Sore ___ ___ ___ ___ ___ ___ (35 56 23 9 40 46)
8. Goolagong's sport ___ ___ ___ ___ ___ ___ (41 27 4 20 29 10)
9. Builder in stone ___ ___ ___ ___ ___ (31 5 51 39 36)

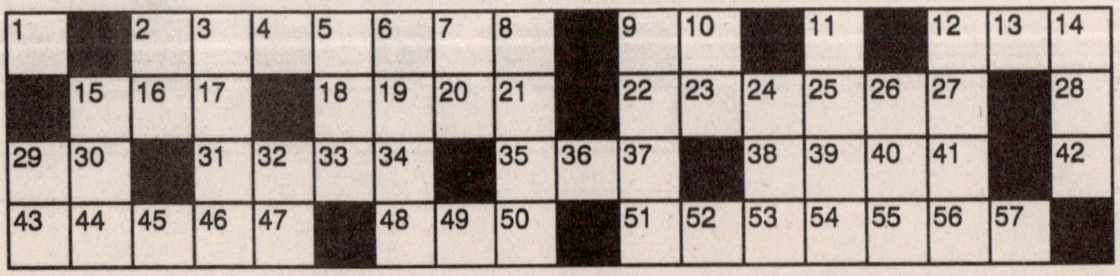

# PUZZLE 254

**• BIRD NAMES •**

**ACROSS**

1. Long fish
5. Complete failure
9. Horse's gait
10. Paddle
13. Kind of bean
14. Birchbark boat
15. Contend
16. Warning
18. "____ Joey"
20. Bird comedian?
23. Recede, as the tide
26. Alack
28. Paddock
29. Statute
30. Pound
31. Unique
32. Each
33. Song gal
35. "The ____ of Night"
36. Radiate
37. Donkey
38. Force open
39. "Damn Yankees" role
40. Happy's comrade
41. Adorable
42. Stop
44. Moist
45. Of an age
47. Singer/actress Carter
49. Beach grains
50. Portico
51. Slice
52. Corrode
53. Turkish garment
55. Science room, for short
57. Wound's leftover
59. Keystone comic
62. Roman emperor
64. Bandleader Kyser
66. Baking vessel
67. Spanish pot
68. Cinders of the comics
69. Cincinnati to New York direction: abbr.
70. Actress Jillian
71. Beatty and namesakes
72. Descended
73. Author Fleming
75. Caesar's seven
76. Iowa town
77. Competed in a road race
78. Bird in "The Graduate"?
83. Metallic rock
84. Welcome
86. "____ of La Mancha"
87. Rose's protection
89. Cigar follower
90. "The ____ of the Needle"
91. Ireland
92. Doe
93. Wander

**DOWN**

1. Station letters
2. Sea birds
3. Booty
4. Most precipitous
5. Utensils
6. Leslie Caron role
7. Middle Eastern nation
8. Average
10. Kiln
11. Strive
12. Genuine
14. Bird in "Silence of the Lambs"?
17. Bird Globetrotter?
18. Cut
19. San Antonio landmark
21. Stanza
22. Scrape
24. Reveille instrument
25. Sheep noise
27. Movie locale
30. Actor Gibson
32. Bird on "Perry Mason"?
34. Bird Steeler?
41. Venice feature
43. Discourage
46. "Norma ____"
48. Mauna ____
53. Close, in poetry
54. Politician Abzug
56. Railing
57. "Lady of ____"
58. Container
60. More aged
61. Out of fashion
63. Cereal grass
65. "It Was a Very Good ____"
67. Three ____ match
74. Alaskan town
75. Climbing plant
78. Distribute
79. Nerve network
80. Inlet
81. Toledo's state
82. Author Ephron
85. Maroon
88. Sleep state: abbr.

# PUZZLE 255

**ACROSS**

1. Orchestra ___
4. Long ___ of the law
7. Created
8. Cruiser
10. Claw
11. Small role
13. Amusing
14. Land parcel
16. Slopes
18. Shortly
20. Pied Piper follower
22. Gerbil or hamster
23. Chanced
25. Fabric strips
28. Fish eggs
30. Golfer's goal
31. Pertains
35. Risk and Monopoly
39. Adam's wife
40. Chatter
42. Ocean motion
43. Attract
46. Guy's date
48. Pose
49. Acting parts
51. Metal fastener
53. Tidy
54. Close by
55. Parched
56. Fast plane

**DOWN**

1. Chum
2. Object of worship
3. Male singer
4. Alphabet trio
5. Lion sound
6. ___ mia!
7. Estate
9. Beat
10. Canned fish
12. Unfold
13. Passing fashion
15. Sailor
17. Rds.
19. Rome's fiddler
21. ___ of the iceberg
24. Actor Johnson
26. Sack
27. Unruly child
29. Hen product
31. Lay odds
32. By any possibility
33. Sour fruit
34. Droop
36. Stingy person
37. Modify
38. Matched pair
41. Farm buildings
44. Begged
45. Eye drop
47. Reclines
50. Place for a pig
52. Cauldron

# PUZZLE 256

**ACROSS**

1. Actor Guinness
5. Used to be
8. Told a fib
12. Prison room
13. Actress Lupino
14. Unemployed
15. Day after today
17. Be defeated
18. ____ sauce (Oriental condiment)
19. Greeted
21. "The ____ Musketeers"
24. Was attired in
25. Film critic Rex ____
26. Petted
30. Saving plan
31. Oklahoma city
32. Month after April
33. Frozen treat on a stick
35. Deep affection
36. Addition word
37. Confined, as in a zoo
38. High regard
41. However
42. Sky's color
43. Cookout
48. Musical group
49. Self-image
50. Couch
51. Remain
52. Utilize oars
53. Horn sound

**DOWN**

1. Play a role
2. Zodiac lion
3. Shady tree
4. Shut
5. Lean and sinewy
6. Fuss
7. Carpenter's steed
8. Easter flowers
9. Worshipped object
10. What ____ is new?
11. Feat
16. Fish eggs
20. Vicinity
21. Voyage
22. Savior
23. Harvest
24. Building partitions
26. Pickle vegetable
27. Polluted air
28. Roof overhang
29. Tinted
31. Flooring material
34. Rapid
35. Most tardy
37. Baby bear
38. Subsides
39. Strip of wood
40. Salad fish
41. Forehead
44. In the past
45. Pigeon's cry
46. Flying saucer
47. Dine

# PUZZLE 257

**ACROSS**

1. Mineral spring
4. Parka
8. Tempo
12. Short sleep
13. Loafing
14. Shoestring
15. ____ for the books
16. School official
17. Locality
18. Hunk of cheese
20. Mix
22. Handicraft
24. Fragrant wood
28. College housing
31. Classify
34. Hatchet
35. Spiny houseplant
36. In the past
37. Building extensions
38. "The ____ Badge of Courage"
39. Fencing sword
40. Root vegetable
41. Meddlesome
43. Small amount
45. Abandoned
48. Small land masses
52. Greeting or credit
55. Corn, peanut, and vegetable
57. Actress Arden
58. Orchestra instrument
59. Film spool
60. Veto
61. Malt beverage
62. Advantage
63. Clever

**DOWN**

1. Skiing surface
2. Glass section
3. Mimicked
4. Apple drink
5. "____ to the West Wind"
6. Oh dear!
7. Temporary shelter
8. Shriek
9. Spike of corn
10. Untouchable serve
11. "____ and Sympathy"
19. Monopoly, e.g.
21. Polar abundance
23. Pitfall
25. Cowgirl Evans
26. Wheel connector
27. Musical pause
28. Mend
29. Muffin topping
30. Serling and Taylor
32. Period in history
33. ____ the line (obeyed)
37. Recedes
39. Gaze
42. More advanced in years
44. Corridor
46. Golf cry
47. Finished together
49. Magnifying glass
50. Sinister
51. Shapely
52. Corn core
53. Honest ____ Lincoln
54. Expensive eggs
56. Lower limb

# PUZZLE 258

**ACROSS**

1. Tent stake
4. Fitness clubs
8. Donkey's sound
12. Historic period
13. Put on the payroll
14. Tempt
15. Be ill
16. Once again
17. Matures
18. Kingdom
20. Horned vipers
22. Fire residue
24. Alternate
28. Tennis-game divisions
31. Corrosive substance
34. Woolly female
35. Fusses
36. Also
37. Given without charge
38. Victory
39. Curved
40. British nobleman
41. Be at the wheel
43. Dined
45. Put on cargo
48. Grownup
52. Ace or jack, e.g.
55. Above
57. Female pig
58. Woodwind instrument
59. Act
60. Personality
61. Tinier
62. Just
63. Distress-signal letters

**DOWN**

1. ". . . partridge in a ____ tree"
2. A Great Lake
3. Festival
4. Frauds
5. Diaper fastener
6. Length x width
7. Stitches
8. Explosion
9. Floor covering
10. "Just the Way You ____"
11. Opposite of no
19. Young girl
21. Pea container
23. Dislike intensely
25. Brave one
26. Vase-shaped jug
27. Film critic Rex ____
28. Woodworkers' tools
29. Make text corrections
30. Musical pitch
32. Partner of pro
33. Tiny amount
37. Escaped
39. Bikini top
42. Older person
44. Late
46. Extinct flightless bird
47. Level
49. Employs
50. Advertising symbol
51. Pairs
52. Dairy animal
53. Honest ____ (Lincoln)
54. Fish eggs
56. Snaky fish

# PUZZLE 259

**ACROSS**

1. Estate
6. Play it by ____
9. Plus
12. Worship
13. Soap-making substance
14. "____ Whom the Bell Tolls"
15. News anchor Jennings
16. Merry
18. Firearm
20. Shops
21. Smelly window-cleaning solution
25. Gasoline and kerosene
26. In the near future
27. Baking and bread-making need
29. Small jump
30. Motionless
31. "The Old Man and the ____"
34. Trifled
35. ____ of Mexico (body of water)
36. Leather band
39. Closest
41. Choruses
43. ____ Grande (Texas river)
44. Put back
46. Mist
50. Function
51. Denial
52. Go away from
53. Sleeping place
54. First number
55. Boundaries

**DOWN**

1. Atlas entry
2. Fruit drink
3. Believe it or ____!
4. Washington's southern neighbor
5. Television-show encore
6. Santa's helper
7. Yes votes
8. Tranquil
9. Burning
10. Work of fiction
11. Put on clothes
17. Guided trip
19. Neat!
21. Dustlike fire-place residue
22. Cow's sound
23. Broom's wet cousin
24. Stranger
28. More ancient
30. High female voice
31. Take to court
32. Overhead railways
33. Fore and ____
34. Dog's wagger
35. Fumbled
36. Rub vigorously
37. The items here
38. Lassoed
40. Wedding walkway
42. Read hastily
45. Organ of sight
47. Tattered cloth
48. Blvd.
49. Of course!

# PUZZLE 260

**ACROSS**

1. "____ Old Man"
5. Beach color
8. Going, going, ____
12. Staff member
13. Utilize
14. Opera tune
15. Alibi
16. Letter before tee
17. Carry on
18. Blackboards
20. Lunchroom furniture
22. Not happy
23. Place for a workout
24. Ink stick
27. Dustcloth
29. Long-plumed bird
33. Neighborhood
35. Up to now
37. Ireland, in Gaelic
38. Proportion
40. Damage
42. Animal's cave
43. Split
45. Exclude
47. Taste
50. Take me to your ____
54. Butter substitute
55. Wonder
57. Make do
58. Raise upright
59. Decay
60. On an ____ keel
61. Campground item
62. Brown or Paul
63. Swamp grass

**DOWN**

1. Dances like Hines
2. Mound
3. Scheme
4. Ticket-holders' claims
5. After Monday
6. Burro
7. Birds' shelters
8. Refuse
9. Word-of-mouth
10. Eight plus one
11. Consumes
19. Cauliflower ____
21. Monkey
24. Standard
25. Division of history
26. Veil fabric
28. Sparkler
30. Do away with
31. Bard's before
32. Finger count
34. JFK or Newark, e.g.
36. Pills
39. Salad dressing
41. "Norma ____"
44. Oyster's jewel
46. Speed contestant
47. Separate
48. Helm position
49. Ornery
51. Bird of peace
52. Blade for Zorro
53. Tatter
56. Sorrow

# PUZZLE 261

## ACROSS

1. Ripens
5. Purple fruit
9. Saloon
12. IOU
13. Go up
14. Expert
15. Decorate with needlework
17. That girl
18. Lincoln's nickname
19. Excessive desire for wealth
21. Scratched
24. Sign before Virgo
25. Crummy
26. Detective story
30. Vase
31. Itty-bitty
32. Fib
33. Separating
36. Spaghetti, e.g.
38. Host Linkletter
39. Indian dwellings
40. Popular game of chance
43. Rowboat necessity
44. Caviar
45. Fast, small warship
51. Be obligated to
52. Toledo's Great Lake
53. Ill-famed Roman emperor
54. Roll of money
55. Beach feature
56. Simmer

## DOWN

1. Lemon drink
2. Precious stone
3. Subside
4. Soda-sippers
5. Opened with leverage
6. Cap
7. Purpose
8. Combines
9. Military station
10. Tooth-ailment symptom
11. Marsh plant
16. Submit to
20. Decay
21. Social organization
22. Knowledge
23. Cousin's mother
24. Soap-making ingredient
26. Grown boys
27. Differently
28. Ritual
29. Yes votes
31. Moisten
34. Shake
35. Wears away
36. "... partridge in a ____ tree"
37. Cooks' garments
39. Carried
40. Forehead
41. Site of Des Moines
42. Require
46. Time period
47. Transgression
48. Still
49. Before, to a poet
50. Line

## CAMOUFLAGE

## PUZZLE 262

**The answers to the clues can be found in the diagram, but they have been camouflaged. Their letters are in correct order, but sometimes they are separated by extra letters which have been inserted throughout the diagram. You must black out all the extra camouflage letters. The remaining letters will be used in words reading across and down. Solve Across and Down together to determine the correct letters where there is a choice. The number of answer words in a row or column is indicated by the number of clues.**

| | 1 | 2 | 3 | 4 | 5 | 6 | 7 | 8 | 9 | 10 | 11 | 12 | 13 |
|---|---|---|---|---|---|---|---|---|---|---|---|---|---|
| 1 | P | A | L | U | F | S | E | K | A | N | O | V | W |
| 2 | I | G | T | N | O | D | R | W | E | X | F | A | R |
| 3 | L | N | O | U | D | Z | E | I | R | A | T | G | E |
| 4 | G | I | N | S | Y | I | S | T | R | I | J | D | H |
| 5 | F | L | E | K | E | A | T | C | A | L | E | B | M |
| 6 | E | K | R | U | J | P | I | T | G | F | H | A | N |
| 7 | A | E | F | L | A | R | M | O | N | I | N | G | S |
| 8 | R | Z | O | A | S | C | T | U | D | X | I | E | T |
| 9 | M | D | U | B | S | I | H | Y | S | A | M | R | I |
| 10 | A | S | S | J | E | K | V | N | T | W | O | A | R |
| 11 | P | A | I | L | S | I | A | T | B | S | E | L | N |
| 12 | J | G | O | T | R | O | W | A | G | C | F | T | D |
| 13 | P | E | U | W | T | T | H | Y | Y | O | N | I | M |

**ACROSS**

1. Hesitate • Be aware
2. Disregard • Distant
3. Noisy • Angry
4. Demand • Disencumber
5. Swift • Beer's kin
6. Burst forth • Devotee
7. Wages
8. Cook in an oven • Count calories
9. Soft • Robe of India
10. Concur • Rower's need
11. False name
12. Get bigger • Perform
13. Trivial • Over there

**DOWN**

1. Steal • Road guide
2. Nimble • Wise
3. Burdensome
4. Out of the ordinary
5. Lyric poem • Declare
6. Small drink • Public melee
7. Once, of old • Defrost
8. Cat's name • Negative vote
9. Mission • Pigpen
10. Carpenter's spike • Major failure
11. Frequently • Charged particle
12. Saying • Ship deserter
13. Small songbird • Mix

# PUZZLE 263

**ACROSS**

1. Poor-box donations
5. Sweetheart
9. That woman
12. Ooze
13. Does sums
14. Cape ____, Massachusetts
15. New Zealand bird
16. Turkey part that's pulled apart
18. Gold leaf
20. Gobbled up
21. Role players
24. Blunder
25. Travel course
26. Bugs
30. Rowdy crowd
31. Weird
32. "Butterflies ____ Free"
33. Pancake flipper
36. Mutiny
38. Plus
39. Ferret or mink, e.g.
40. Gravy
43. Gets hitched
44. Upper-lip hair
46. Subsides
50. Lode load
51. Took to court
52. Plumbing problem
53. Auto fuel
54. Some evergreens
55. Remain

**DOWN**

1. Inquire
2. Hawaiian garland
3. Kitten's cry
4. Faucet
5. Sobs loudly
6. Correct text
7. Magazine fillers
8. Theater employees
9. Glasgow native
10. Sharpen
11. Genesis garden
17. Unclothed
19. Fury
21. Upper limbs
22. Poultry pen
23. Large brass horn
24. Finish
26. Wash.'s neighbor
27. Taxis
28. Poplar or pine, e.g.
29. Vend
31. On in years
34. Diplomacy
35. Worried
36. Strawberry color
37. Artists' stands
39. Unwanted plants
40. City air problem
41. Ambiance
42. Manipulates
43. Expression of relief
45. Stage signal
47. Wager
48. Lamb's bleat
49. Heavens

# PUZZLE 264

**ACROSS**

1. "____ first you don't succeed . . ."
5. Chops
9. Neighbor of Ore.
12. Logical
13. Region
14. Neither here ____ there
15. On cloud ____
16. Prissy
17. "Desk ____" (Tracy film)
18. Clear
21. Be extravagant
22. Lessen
25. Mom's baby carrier?
28. Plus
29. Yearned
30. Passes a bill
32. Like some pretzels
33. Buns
34. Paving goo
35. Blue yonder
36. "____ Cinders"
37. Mallards
39. Sneaky
44. Not skinny
46. Poker term
47. Camp helper
48. Caustic liquid
49. Slant
50. Book leaf
51. Marriage-proposal answer
52. Singing brothers
53. Sleigh

**DOWN**

1. "____ It a Pity"
2. Carnival
3. Actress Magnani
4. Prom attendees
5. Takes place
6. Chore
7. Spooky
8. Alike
9. Moments
10. Buck's mate
11. Actor Carney
19. Disputes
20. Singer Young
23. Look for
24. Guitarist Duane ____
25. Large rabbit
26. Matinee hero
27. Fouls
29. Winter jacket
31. Blueprint
32. Drawer fresheners
34. Before neck or dove
37. Coarse blue cloth
38. Crackles
40. Statistics
41. Radio feature
42. Border
43. Action
44. Outfielder's catch
45. Okay, at sea

# PUZZLE 265

**ACROSS**

1. Head topper
4. Lively party
8. Sub sandwich
12. "You ____ My Sunshine"
13. On the sheltered side
14. Egg-shaped
15. Meadow
16. Approach
17. Split
18. Florida bay city
20. Animal's burrow
22. Hotels
25. Loans
29. Pedicurist's concern
32. Shop
33. Tack on
34. Deep hole
36. 2,000 pounds
37. Scoundrel
40. Idea
43. Fad
44. Fencing sword
45. Poisonous serpent
47. Couches
51. Young sheep
54. Attic
57. Novelist Levin
58. Religious statue
59. Medicinal plant
60. Moral wrong
61. Cupola
62. Must-have
63. Possessed

**DOWN**

1. Stop
2. Locale
3. Crew
4. Yellow tropical fruit
5. Brewed drink
6. Mediter-ranean, e.g.
7. Group of cattle
8. Type of wasp
9. Actress Arden
10. Dashed
11. Elderly
19. Brooch
21. Chicago trains
23. Small bite
24. Piece, as of bread
26. Memo
27. Fall sharply
28. Transmitted
29. Small pie
30. Smell
31. Rim
35. Blouse
38. Not capable
39. McMahon and Sullivan
41. Made a home, as a bird
42. Corporate bigwig: abbr.
46. Scheme
48. Trout or bass, e.g.
49. "Aida" solo, e.g.
50. Beach soil
51. Cover
52. Hubbub
53. ____ and apple pie
55. Spanish cheer
56. Opponent

# PUZZLE 266

**ACROSS**

1. Near the ground
4. Spouse
8. Feathery scarves
12. Actress Marie Saint
13. Heroic tale
14. Small brook
15. Joke
16. Look suggestively at
17. Comrade
18. Slumbered
20. Coffee server
22. Requests
25. Brim
28. Male foal
31. Deserve
33. Paddle
35. Commotion
36. Opposite of a credit
37. "Born in the ____"
38. Animal's cage
39. Woes
40. Piece of news
41. Stitched
43. Snakelike fish
45. Skirt border
47. Fossilized resin
51. Volcano's output
54. Sign
57. Citrus drink
58. Spoken
59. Knowledge
60. "Live With Regis and Kathie ____"
61. Actor Hackman
62. Foot parts
63. Conclude

**DOWN**

1. Table supports
2. Egg-shaped
3. Pay
4. Thaws
5. Mimic
6. Make a knot in
7. Very light beige
8. Mark on cattle
9. Petroleum
10. Every bit
11. Crafty
19. Mrs. Nixon
21. Landlord's income
23. ____ over (fall over)
24. Expensive fur
26. Inflammation of the small joints
27. Relax
28. Baseball hat
29. Certain poems
30. Solitary
32. Ascend
34. Lamb's father
36. Eat
40. Doctrine
42. Large aquatic mammal
44. Bowling-alley features
46. Shed feathers
48. Bundle, as of hay
49. Biblical garden
50. Actress Donna ____
51. Wood for a fireplace
52. "Where the Boys ____"
53. Small bus
55. Cow's call
56. Before, in poetry

# PUZZLE 267

**ACROSS**

1. Maple genus
5. Greek mountain
10. Lab burner
14. Traversed
15. Wedding-party member
17. Keen
18. Like Austria
19. Pledge
20. Nullify
21. Swindle
22. Deterioration
24. More inexperienced
25. Flood
26. Shape, in Britain
27. Porcupine protector
28. Madness
29. ____ de guerre
32. Asian river
33. Mob
34. Lucy's love
35. Slippery fellow
36. Pluto's realm
37. Attics
38. Liliaceous plant
39. Split
40. Foreign traveler's need
43. Different
44. Average
45. Minute
46. Freezer product
47. Devotee
49. Former Dutch coin
50. Acrobatic action
51. Greek drink
52. Beginning
53. Cardinal number
54. Fortune-teller's words?

**DOWN**

1. Ballet pose
2. Shelter
3. Newspaper department
4. Basketball's Auerbach
5. Flowering
6. Retinue
7. Hart's mate
8. Weird
9. Autonomy
10. Hosted a show
11. Occupied
12. Female relative
13. Math student, at times
16. Only
20. Glass container
23. Peddle
24. Olympic medals
26. Edible mushroom
28. Dutch violinist
29. Wicked
30. Shun
31. Holiday hanger
33. "There's no ____ between us"
34. Fool
36. Balloon filler
37. Tax
38. Used cloves
39. Indicate
40. Stockpile
41. "Robinson Crusoe" author
42. Stop on ____
43. Move furtively
45. Bull: pref.
48. Nope
49. "____ Love You?"

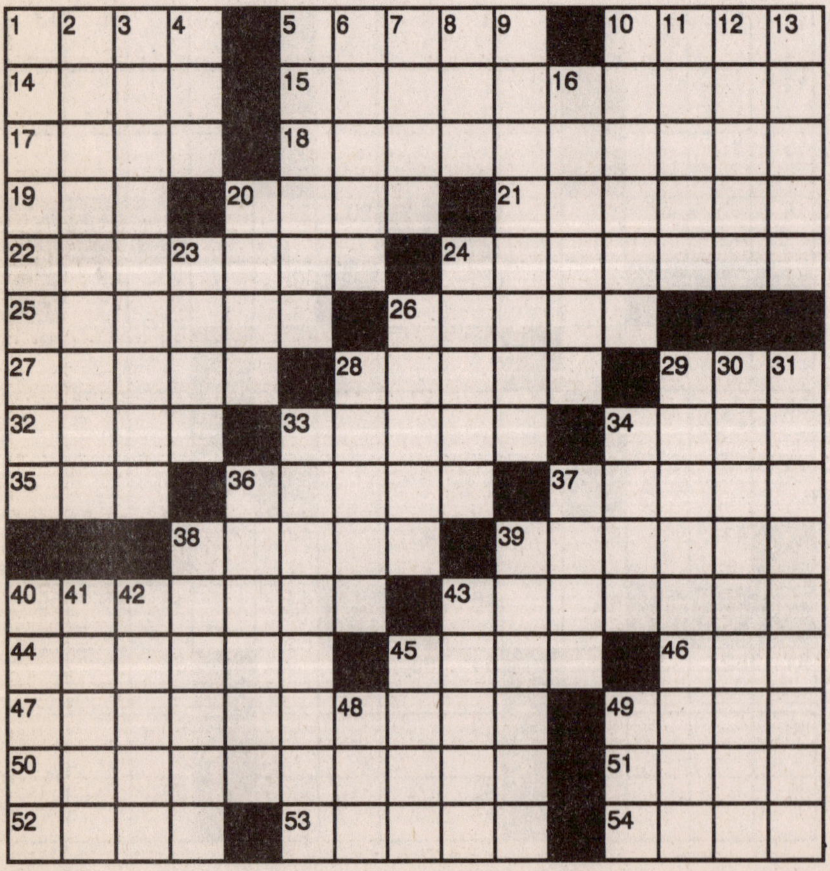

# PUZZLE 268

**ACROSS**

1. Panache
5. Fundamental
10. Racing boat
14. Until: 2 wds.
15. Actress Verdugo
16. Roue
17. 19th-century luggage
19. Spring blossom
20. Inspectors' tools
21. Feminine suffix
23. Favorite
24. Brenda or Bart
25. Christmas meanie
28. Mixture
30. Prima ____
33. Almond cookie
37. Packing box
38. Levin and Gershwin
39. Author Loos
41. Actress Rowlands
42. Kit ____
44. New Jersey town
46. "____ Gantry"
47. Commedia dell'____
48. School for Pablo
51. Slipknot
56. Coolidge's nickname
58. Hill builder
59. Figure shaper
60. Mr. Gemayel
62. Thanksgiving kit: 2 wds.
65. Repetition
66. Bis
67. Assistant
68. Supplemented
69. Pound portions
70. Mysterious loch

**DOWN**

1. Conduits
2. Asunder
3. Groove
4. Aspiring one
5. Wagers
6. Church vestment
7. Black or Red, e.g.
8. Bitterness
9. Roper's rope
10. ____ Lanka
11. Cabinet-maker
12. "____ from Muskogee"
13. Mr. Greeley's direction
18. Faux pas
22. Fountain drink
25. Hebrew nation: var.
26. Like a dunce hat
27. Canyon
29. Bank transaction
31. Not a soul
32. Med. school subj.
33. Mickey and Minnie, e.g.
34. Asian sea
35. White friar
36. Mule sires
37. Two-wheeled wagon
40. "GWTW" plantation
43. Killer whale
45. Mortise's partner
49. Remove the top
50. French floor
52. Church instrument
53. Actor Davis
54. Plants
55. Diminutive endings
56. Give a rap
57. Out of control
59. Movie: Spanish
61. Sparks or Beatty
63. Operated
64. Singer Damone

# PUZZLE 269

**ACROSS**

1. Place
5. Crunchy
10. Ragout
14. Arabian gulf
15. Large artery
16. Put on the payroll
17. Happy medium: 2 wds.
19. Forearm bone
20. Building wing
21. Trouble
22. Busybody
24. Understand
25. Very cold
26. Apple drink
29. Library
30. Corrupt
34. Neighborhood
35. Decompose
36. Esprit de corps
37. Batter
38. Self-service restaurant
40. Scarf
41. Immediately: 2 wds.
43. Pledge
44. Puts on
45. Doctrine
46. Confronted
47. Dalai Lama's land
48. As yet: 2 wds.
50. "Sanford and ——"
51. Unconventional person
54. One-spot
55. Parseghian
58. Fr. river
59. In apple-pie order: 4 wds.
62. Vocalize
63. Small snake
64. Departed
65. Hitch
66. At liberty
67. Border

**DOWN**

1. Wise man
2. Matinee ——
3. Relate
4. Remnant
5. Hiawatha's craft
6. Eternal City
7. Wrath
8. Flower part
9. Jury
10. Quake
11. Cultivate
12. Sea flier
13. Tear's partner
18. Pitcher
23. Piece of turf
24. Caspian, e.g.
25. Recover from: 2 wds.
26. Gem weight
27. Angry
28. Werewolf
29. Speck
31. Powerful person
32. Isolated
33. Smallest amount
35. Regret
36. Animal's throat
38. City near London
39. Witty saying
42. Rainy day fund: 2 wds.
44. Clamor
46. Manage: 2 wds.
47. Little piggies
49. Last
50. Frighten
51. Foreman
52. —— go bragh
53. Ms. Magnani
54. Sweetsop
55. Copied
56. Circle
57. Before: prefix
60. Bustle
61. Solemn wonder

# PUZZLE 270

**ACROSS**

1. Statesman Eban
5. Salvages
10. Swindle
14. Actress Patricia
15. Knowing
16. Poorly
17. Countrywide: abbr.
18. Biblical food
19. Castle ditch
20. Reliable source
23. Highway
24. Peruvian peaks
25. Sausage herb
27. Allan-____
30. ____ me tangere
31. Upper House
33. "The Gold Bug" author
36. Great, to oldsters
39. Ad-____ committee
40. Igneous rock
41. "____ It Romantic?"
42. Speculation
43. Knowing about
44. Moral system
47. Forest member
49. Timid
55. Chain segment
56. Rows
57. "____ corny . . ."
59. Poker kitty
60. Tie holder
61. Quote
62. Exam
63. Start of a toast
64. Worry

**DOWN**

1. Miss Sothern
2. Rhythm
3. English spa
4. Hyper-sensitive
5. Pacific islands
6. Grant
7. Moving trucks
8. Sea bird
9. Vast expanses
10. Actress ____ Signoret
11. On ____ nine
12. Having wings
13. Legends
21. Weeding tool
22. Men
25. London area
26. Actor Guinness
27. Mr. Sadat
28. Arlene of filmdom
29. Keep ____ (persevere)
30. Highest degree
31. Doe's mate
32. To be: Lat.
33. Scourge
34. Yes ____?
35. Superlative suffix
37. Taken ____ (surprised)
38. Science of motive forces
42. Croquet hoop
43. "____ the ramparts . . ."
44. Brilliance
45. "To ____ own self be true"
46. Suggestions
47. Concise
48. Grates harshly
50. Engrave
51. Egyptian river
52. Get wind of
53. Give off
54. Palm fruit
58. Embroider

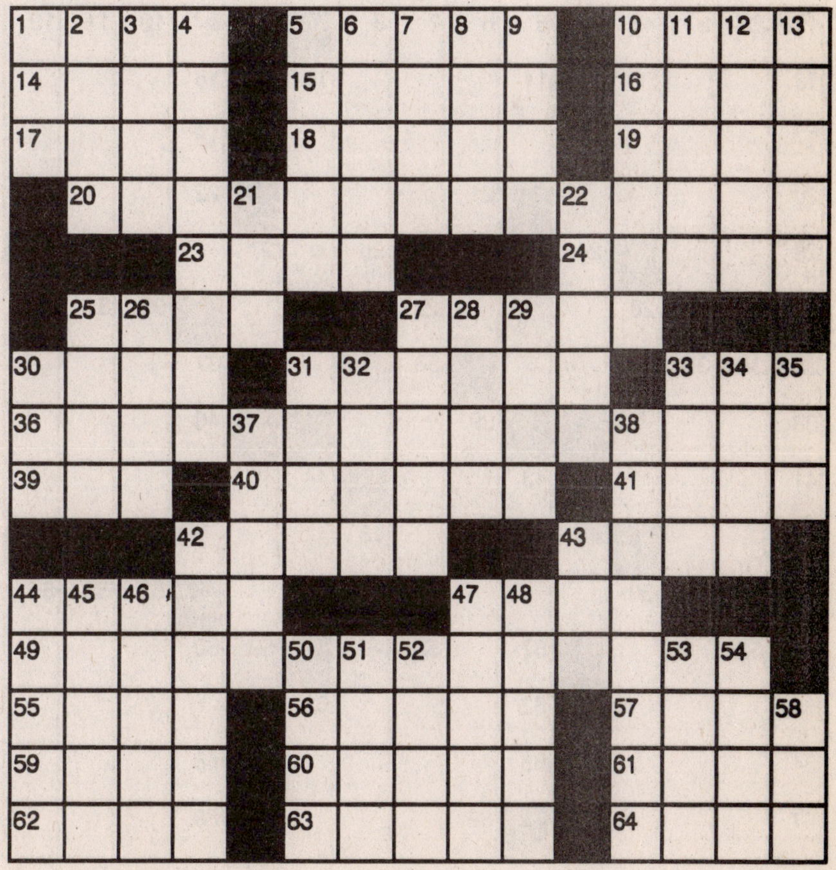

# PUZZLE 271

**ACROSS**

1. Metallic fabric
5. ____ facto
9. Wound covering
13. Organic compound
14. Debonair
16. ____ breve
17. ____ parmigiana
19. Kiss
20. Diner
21. Gumbo ingredient
22. Reed instrument
23. Vetch
24. Sprite
26. Smudges
28. Ragout
30. Reception
33. Repair shoes
36. Lock openers
38. Eight: Sp.
39. ____ leaf
40. Informer
41. Hurdle top
44. Fence posts
46. Big ____
47. Entree
49. Clan chief
51. Writer Rand
52. Sault ____ Marie
55. Songstress Irene ____
57. Israeli statesman
59. Western movie
61. News item, for short
62. Entree
64. Toga
65. Threaded nail
66. Wigwam
67. Disarrange
68. Composer Jerome
69. Russian city

**DOWN**

1. Reception
2. Lend ____
3. Castle ditches
4. French pronoun
5. Ames campus: abbr.
6. Delay
7. Polio-prevention pioneer
8. Wear out a welcome
9. Wooden shoe
10. Aka Delmonico
11. As well
12. Foundation
15. Troop camps
18. Fishing basket
25. Golfer Trevino
27. Sounds of pain
28. Sounds of disapproval
29. Flash
31. Rochester's love
32. Invites
33. Aerial bombs
34. Beige
35. Entree
37. Hilltop
39. Saddleless
42. Health oasis
43. Goofs
44. Timid
45. Like a ____ bricks
48. Mouth sore
50. Detests
52. One of a flight
53. Arizona city
54. Iraqi town
55. Crocus bulb
56. "____ Ben Adhem"
58. Land measure
60. Palo ____
63. Have title to

# PUZZLE 272

**ACROSS**

1. Scads
6. Shopper's paradise
10. Tax gp.
13. Wrath
14. Extent
15. Dill
16. Be of use
19. Leave in print
20. Wanes
21. Other: pref.
22. Mama sheep
23. Depots: abbr.
24. Scorn
25. L.A. team
27. Meadow
28. Roman bronze
29. Zodiac lion
30. Moccasin
31. Norm: abbr.
32. Entertainment
35. Heir
36. ____ League
37. Goddess: Lat.
38. His: Fr.
39. Epoch
40. Recliners
44. Blab
46. Gasp
47. Bolt holder
48. Across the keel
49. ____ the Red
50. Handle
51. Work
54. Fasting time
55. Locale
56. Roman official
57. Double curve
58. Plodded
59. Slackened

**DOWN**

1. Expired
2. Boxing punch
3. Consented
4. Skillful
5. Theater sign: abbr.
6. African snakes
7. Swift horses
8. Not so much
9. New Guinea port
10. Induct
11. Tapered off
12. Cubic meters
15. Affirm
17. Ignite, at stage-separation time
18. Ostrich's kin
23. Astrologer
24. Corruption
26. Valley
27. Take it on the ____
30. Snoop
31. Beat it!
32. Back doors
33. Eggs
34. Bird's home
35. Naval builders
38. Paper holder
39. Sailor's saint
40. Poured
41. Boredoms
42. Steal cattle
43. Lingered
45. 27th president
46. Foremost: pref.
49. Eastern VIP
50. Egyptian skink
52. Q-U fillers
53. Bishopric

# PUZZLE 273

**ACROSS**

1. "L.A. ___"
4. Shoo!
8. Shade of green
11. Constrictor
14. Came down
16. Soap plant
17. Alabama city
19. Unlucky person
20. Actress Powers
21. Aka William Bonney
23. Robt. ___
24. Wallet
26. Skid-row dweller
27. October gem
29. "The Man ___"
30. Coal holder
31. Hindu princess
32. Navy engineer
34. FBI agents
36. Eileen or Walter
39. Sailor's saint
40. Demeanor
41. Certain deer
42. Bushed
44. Occupied
45. Mingo's friend
47. Fearful filly
49. Felix Unger's daughter
50. Flurry
51. "Golden Boy" star
54. D.C. figure: abbr.
55. Store fodder
57. Charged particles
58. Worthy
60. Woody's son
61. Armor
63. Passable
64. Lion constellation
65. Grin
66. Ant attracters
69. High trains
72. Perennial pinks
77. "___ a Living"
79. Stadium sounds
81. Beer mug
82. Score constituents
83. Show approval
84. Uprisings
86. Toward the stern
87. Actor Glass
88. High, in Roma
89. Breakfast offerings
91. Cozy rooms
92. Stocky tropical bird
94. Kodiak, e.g.
95. Jitney
96. Illinois city
97. Collection suffix
98. Rhine feeder
100. Cara or Anson
103. Thwart
105. NFL member
109. Part of QED
110. Actress Sheedy
111. Sting
112. Wadi
113. June 6, 1944
114. Petrol
115. ___ rata
116. Sunken fence
117. Sault ___ Marie

**DOWN**

1. Mary's pet
2. Russian range
3. Fred of "Julia"
4. Funt's admonition
5. Freezing
6. 100%
7. Author Josephine
8. Hammer head
9. Nevada town
10. Bon ___
11. Pool
12. Individual
13. Halberd
15. Chest-on-chest
16. Superior in rank
17. Tibia's locale
18. Love rapturously
19. Barbara Eden's TV role
22. Carbon copy
25. Enemy
28. Gasp
30. Ohio town
32. Biblical country
33. Dodge
34. British pokey
35. Short skirt
36. Seethes
37. Rattan
38. Hawaiian goose
41. River in France
43. Dapper gent
45. Waves
46. Bread spread
47. Pot or hot
48. Betterments
51. Cables
52. Crockett and Tubbs's city
53. Impulse

# PUZZLE 273

56. ____ volatile
59. Mr. Brokaw
61. Kind of point
62. Sheer fabric
63. Cicatrix
65. Complains
67. Road signs
68. Say
69. Stray
70. Non-professional
71. African birds
73. Kin of etc.
74. Old harps
75. Boxer Spinks
76. Fleming and McShane
78. Primer pooch
80. Irregular
83. Lugged
85. Actor Penn
90. Mecca men
91. Fence
92. Galas
93. Suffer
95. Devilish child
96. Eyelashes
98. Remote
99. Hair style
100. Desire
101. Justice deity
102. Eye problem
103. Valise
104. Wing
106. Ref's kin
107. Admiring sound
108. Flock cry

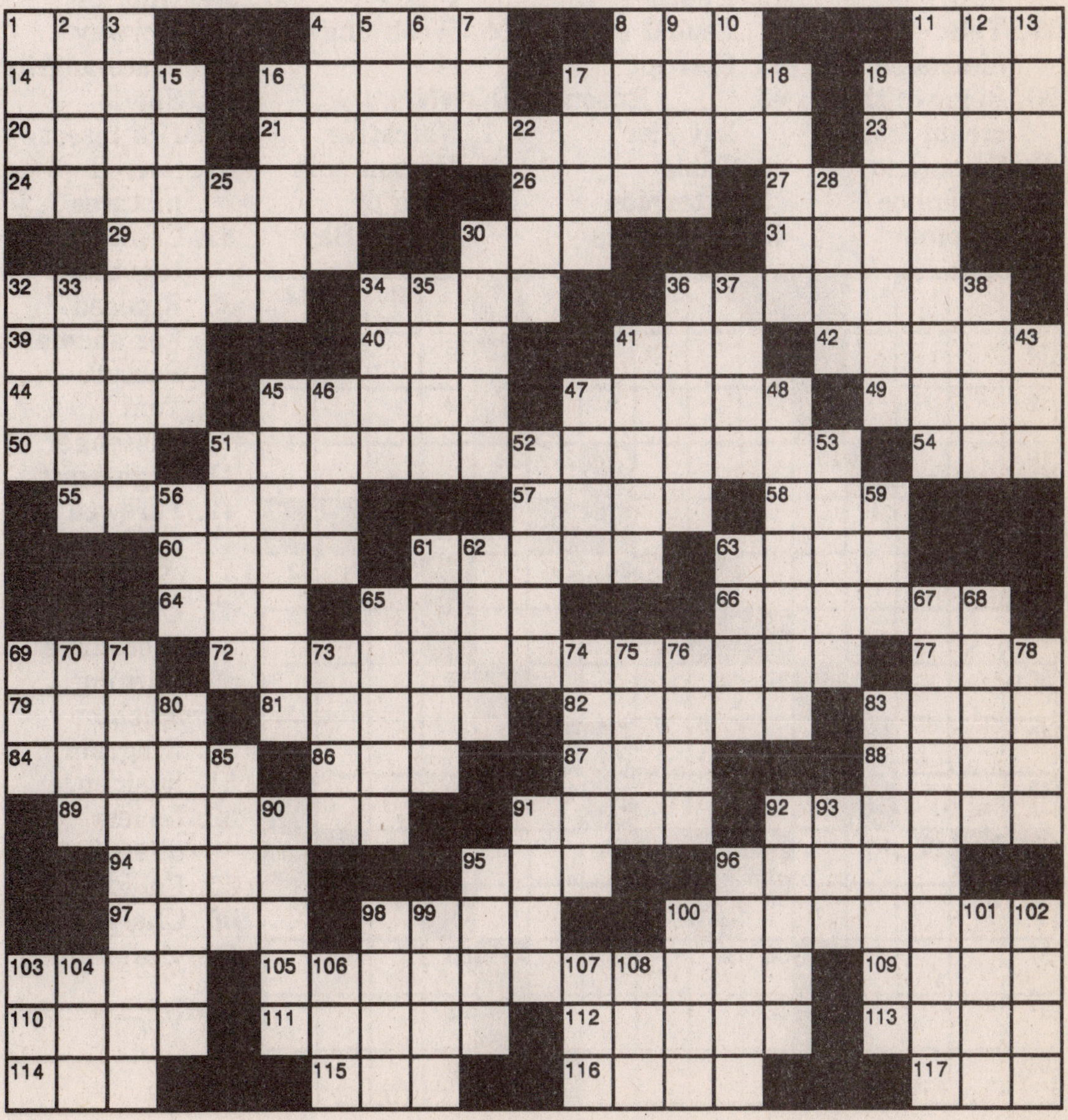

# PUZZLE 274

**ACROSS**

1. Booby ___
5. Stride
9. Slightly open
13. Assistant
14. Western lake
15. Assumed part
16. Nightstand light
17. Expiate
18. Ostrichlike bird
19. Yale nickname
20. Remove the cream from
21. Smoothed
23. "Ivanhoe" heroine
25. Horned viper
26. Festive affairs
27. Counterfeit
30. That chap
33. Actor Arbus
34. Sixth month
35. Skating surface
36. Fishing hook
37. Navy
39. Berg
40. Epoch
41. Feudal estate
42. Corrupt
43. "___ Rosen-kavalier"
44. Table extension
45. Complains
46. Be contrite for
48. Delights
50. Aspects
53. Frog genus
54. Dope
57. Theater box
58. Stickum
60. Blend
61. River to the Okhotsk
62. Hawaiian greeting
63. Court great
64. Court dividers
65. Prong
66. Week units

**DOWN**

1. Narrative
2. Iranian coin
3. Hero of Mobile Bay
4. Spunk
5. Glossy fabric
6. Third president
7. Very long time
8. Chirp
9. Rich tapestry
10. The March King
11. Downwind
12. Interpret
14. Captures
20. "___ Lake"
22. Limping
24. King of Norway
26. Stare angrily
28. Shade
29. Hill insect
31. Sacred pictures
32. Come together
33. Ripened
37. For shame!
38. Pasture
39. Taxi passenger
41. Hightail it
42. Farewell
45. Capital of Crete, once
47. Utility customers
49. Turning machine
50. Diagram
51. Residence
52. Lovers' quarrel
55. Pallid
56. Charges
59. Muhammad ___
60. Vogue

# PUZZLE 275

**ACROSS**

1. Dawdle
4. Walks in water
9. Violence
13. Dollar bill
14. Actor Andy ____
15. Tied
16. "____ Little Indians"
17. Florida fruit
18. Peddle wares
19. Turn aside abruptly
21. Sports officials
23. Road, in Paris
24. Throbs
26. Tadpole's mom or dad
28. Cream-filled pastry
29. Tears apart
33. ____ Angeles
34. Singer Perry
35. Inform positively
36. Kimono sash
37. Wing
38. Batman and Robin, e.g.
39. Water tester
40. Idaho or Irish
42. Scorch
43. Rocker Stewart
44. Format
45. Actress Turner
46. Lulus
47. Instructs
49. Away
50. Bears witness
53. "The ____ Strikes Back"
56. High-priced
57. Capital of Canada
60. Rowing blade
61. Valley
62. Closer
63. Footed vase
64. Hill coaster
65. Go in
66. Understand

**DOWN**

1. Scads
2. Afresh
3. Unselfishness
4. "The Way We ____"
5. Actress Gardner
6. Commotion
7. Overwhelm
8. Appears
9. Makes a new version of
10. Declare positively
11. Kelly or Hackman
12. Remnants
14. Bird of peace
20. Braided or hooked
22. Human being
24. Cougar
25. Mystery craft?
26. Complete failures
27. R2D2, e.g.
28. Horseback game
30. Good for you
31. Slouch
32. Plants
34. Provides food
35. Atmosphere
38. Demands payment from
41. Made different
42. Prohibit
45. Lend an ear
46. ____ tent (two-man tent)
48. Make amends
49. Actor Sharif
50. Says further
51. Small river duck
52. Yarn
53. Vase-shaped jug
54. Uncommon
55. Sea eagle
58. Make lace
59. Land measure

# PUZZLE 276

**ACROSS**

1. D.E.A. agent
5. Canter
9. Applications
13. Actor Sharif
14. Unique person
15. Coral island
16. Canfield, e.g.
18. March king
19. Look over
20. Bridge strategy
22. French cheese
23. Roman three
24. Black suit member
26. Chemin de fer
31. Cheap cigar
32. Went down
33. Speed
34. Nudge
35. Apertures
36. Ibsen woman
37. Scottish uncle
38. Labyrinth
39. Chair worker
40. 4 Down, e.g.: 2 wds.
43. Like Batman
44. Eternally, in verse
45. Board competition
46. Two-deck rummy
50. Adore
54. Verbal exams
55. Bridge holding
57. Engraved stone
58. Canadian Indian
59. Choreographer White
60. Upper: Ger.
61. Mister: Ger.
62. Negatives

**DOWN**

1. Face part
2. Chinese seaport
3. Murmur
4. Competition involving pegs
5. Hockey defender
6. Old-womanish
7. Comparative suffix
8. Elm, e.g.
9. More's opus
10. Type of food
11. Literary lion
12. Murder
15. Brit. sonar
17. Late
21. Notches
24. Leaf pore
25. Five-card stud, e.g.
26. Billiard-table material
27. Pay the kitty
28. French river
29. Ventilated
30. Rend
31. On ____ (on approval): abbr.
32. Bridge coup
35. ____ aleck
36. Pastime involving chips
39. Yule song
41. Distributor
42. Plaster
43. Sponger
45. More choice
46. Tropical palm
47. Semite
48. "____ That Tune"
49. Author Sholem
51. Pay ____ mind: 2 wds.
52. Region
53. Spanish queen et al.
56. Anger

# PUZZLE 277

**ACROSS**

1. Church recess
5. Stage
10. Pliable
14. Asian land
15. Actors' parts
16. Sharif
17. Burden
18. Available: 2 wds.
19. Bill of fare
20. Success
21. Fencing sword
22. Juice fruit
24. Friend of Aeneas
26. Twofold
27. In favor of
28. Cell divisions
32. Sacred book of Islam
35. Singer Shore
36. Immerse
37. Always
38. Jury
39. "Nana" author
40. Pig's home
41. Kind of energy
42. Tree pest
43. —— fish
45. Vegetable drawer
46. H.H. Munro
47. Malicious
51. Burning
54. Withered
55. Hawaiian guitar, for short
56. Letters
57. S. Amer. animal
59. Turkish generals
60. Particle
61. Slur over
62. Spray
63. Decades
64. Prepare spicy eggs
65. Fr. holy women: abbr.

**DOWN**

1. Don Ho's hi
2. Sudden fear
3. Dixie
4. Curve
5. Right
6. Sharpens
7. Der —— (Adenauer)
8. Shore or horse
9. Betrothal
10. African native
11. Portent
12. Long tooth
13. Quiz answer
21. Type of coat
23. Impetuous
25. Distant
26. Eatery
28. Ultimate
29. Aroma
30. "Death on the ——"
31. Mast
32. Retained
33. Finis
34. Nevada city
35. —— Lama
38. Filched
39. Region
41. Thailand, once
42. Nibble
44. Sacred songs
45. Gun part
47. Shirley Temple role
48. Tempus ——
49. Decree
50. Poetic conjunctions
51. Amo, amas, ——
52. Kismet
53. Jungle king
54. Jailbird, in Britain
58. Ginger ——
59. Mornings: abbr.

# PUZZLE 278

**ACROSS**

1. Chinese noodles
5. Clans
11. Brink
14. Director Preminger
15. "Lifeboat" actor
16. Cry of triumph
17. Unit in a brazier
20. Daughter of Loki
21. Fabric trademark
22. Provo's state
23. Up in the air
25. Those complying with RSVPs
28. Sculls
31. Red Sea gulf
32. Melville novel
35. High credit rating
37. Catnappers
41. '40s radio show
44. Jewelry-box item
45. Totally
46. Chef
47. Greek love god
49. "Star Wars" princess
51. Sea gods' scepters
55. Batter's dry spell
59. King of Thailand
60. In a muddle
63. Modern prefix
64. Printed
68. Apple dessert
69. Counted calories
70. Fraternity letters
71. Stop
72. Bandleader Tommy
73. Depend

**DOWN**

1. Coffee-chocolate flavor
2. Singer Merman
3. Novelist Calvino
4. Neither's companion
5. Thunder god
6. Stable hue
7. Lazybones
8. Gideons' texts
9. Sound receiver
10. Snow glider
11. "___ 66"
12. "Do ___ a Waltz"
13. Garment varmints
18. Down: pref.
19. Puzzled
24. Piano feature
26. Cloudburst remnant
27. Trotsky
29. "Don't ___ My Parade"
30. ___ Clemente
32. Fall mo.
33. Printemps month
34. Unlock, poetically
36. Medical org.
38. The self
39. 17th Greek letter
40. Wall St. commodity
42. Leeds's river
43. Under the weather
48. One who bets
50. "___ Mommy Kissing . . ."
51. Inferior stuff
52. Took to jail
53. Fix securely
54. Sports-page figures
56. Combine
57. "Full ___ Jacket"
58. Metrical composition
61. Partner of snick
62. Ocean motion
65. Do sums
66. AFL's partner
67. Ship pronoun

# PUZZLE 279

• FAVORITE PASTIME •

**ACROSS**

1. Equine sound
5. Traynor et al.
9. Expiate
14. Portuguese cape
15. Part
16. Fountain offerings
17. Armadillo
18. ___ instant: 2 wds.
19. Use a lever
20. Spiel: 2 wds.
23. Position
24. Plow inventor
25. Vetch
27. Get comfy
31. Topsoil
33. Orson or Roy
36. Always, in a sonnet
37. Rough-estimate numbers: 2 wds.
41. Fix
42. Active one
43. Les Etats-___
44. Lawrence of ___
47. Hebrew measure
49. One year's record
52. Related nuclide
56. Make progress: 4 wds.
59. Zest
60. Blue-green hue
61. ___ Major
62. Plus
63. "Beanstalk" villain, e.g.
64. Pung
65. Office-pool member
66. Require
67. Soft throw

**DOWN**

1. Coarse
2. Onetime-Yankee Ed
3. Fla. horse-breeding center
4. Part of PG
5. Early reader
6. Hebrides isle
7. African antelope
8. Feel
9. Hope
10. Rich cakes
11. Of a Pindar poem
12. Dramatist Thomas
13. Language suffix
21. Little devil
22. Finnish coin
26. River of Spain
28. Actress Garr
29. Dregs
30. Vocal pauses
31. Wolf's abode
32. Gymnast Korbut
34. Supplement
35. Hairdo
37. Bikini part
38. Hersey's bell town
39. Visitor
40. Frail
45. Secure, asea
46. All told: 2 wds.
48. Deceived
50. Burns's "sweet" river
51. Feudal lord
53. Actress Thomas
54. Certain curves
55. Enjoys a book
56. Puff of wind
57. To be, to Brutus
58. Like diamonds
59. Auto fuel

# SLIDE-O-RAMA

# PUZZLE 280

**Slide each column of letters up or down independently to form as many different words pertaining to articles of clothing as you can. The word will appear in the middle row where SARI is now.**

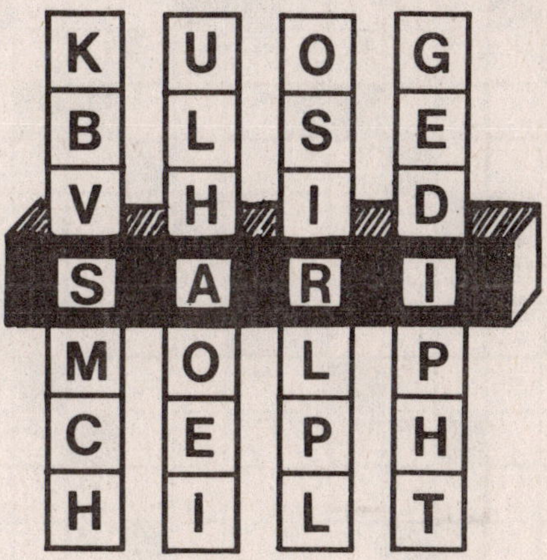

# PUZZLE 281

**• OVERLAPPING •**

**ACROSS**
1. Runyon
6. Salt measure
10. Norm
13. Lackaday
18. "South Pacific" hero
19. Toward
20. Saudi region
21. "The ___ Warrior" (Kingston novel)
22. Jane, Vic, Bob, David, Henry
26. Georges
27. Cuckoopint, e.g.
28. Outsiders
29. Bend
30. Conceit
31. Cheese town
32. French city
33. Children
35. Seth's father
36. Grain pit
37. Actor James ___
38. John, Barry, Amy, Duke
47. Kind of wrench
48. Of late
49. Bargain
50. Iron, for example
51. Russian river
52. Noted
54. Hazy
55. Rani's attire
57. "___ Skylark"
58. Shrill
59. Struggle
60. Revealed
61. Kit, Ryan, John, Bob
66. Actor James ___
69. Personal
70. Stained
71. Digs
74. Paris street
75. Speed
77. Light-show essential
79. Set
80. Old car
81. Shamo
82. Mound
83. Chinese carnivore
84. Al, Lloyd, Michael, Sam, Susan
90. Wheel part
91. Sorts
92. "Desire Under the ___"
93. Londoner's deckhand
96. Protection
98. Station
99. Paragon
102. Busy as ___
103. Delhi princesses
105. Accomplishes
106. Enclosure
107. Henry, George, Walter, Havelock
111. Cuts and splices
112. Descended
113. Animal sci.
114. Lariat
115. Foreboding
116. Female ruff
117. Needlefish
118. Placates

**DOWN**
1. Flanders's creator
2. Inside
3. Actor Sal ___
4. Auto pioneer
5. Federal humanities org.
6. Museum habitat exhibit
7. Per ___
8. Source
9. In what way?
10. Tommy Dorsey hit
11. Author of "The Moffats"
12. "___ Yankees"
13. Grass spike
14. Bonding
15. Acid type
16. Church member
17. Joins together
20. Sanctify
23. Feminine title
24. Actress Jean ___
25. Assault
31. Nirvana
32. Ached
34. Preserve
35. Out to lunch
36. Trig ratio
37. Ground
38. Hinder
39. Oil: pref.
40. Bone
41. North Korean city
42. English king (946-955)
43. Yarn measure
44. Body of water
45. Molding
46. Shortcoming
52. Kind of seed
53. Roman copper
54. Baseball's Hodges
55. Flew
56. Flight: pref.
58. Cut
59. Turkish lake
60. Again
61. Hint
62. ___ a million years
63. Kwa language
64. Ford
65. Brood of pheasant
66. Find fault
67. Olive genus
68. Political coalition
71. All: pref.
72. Opera character
73. Haul
75. Function
76. Arab garment
77. Connects
78. "___, Babylon"
79. Camera movements
81. Rule
82. Like Walesa
83. Splendor
85. Swallows
86. Inverness nix
87. Comprehend
88. Spots
89. Douse
93. Roasts
94. Persevere
95. Distillation remainder
96. Anoint, of old
97. Strange
98. Locating device
99. Affairs
100. Choice
101. Plains
104. Seaweed product
105. Merrill
106. Request
108. Quality: suff.
109. Nod
110. Bard's before

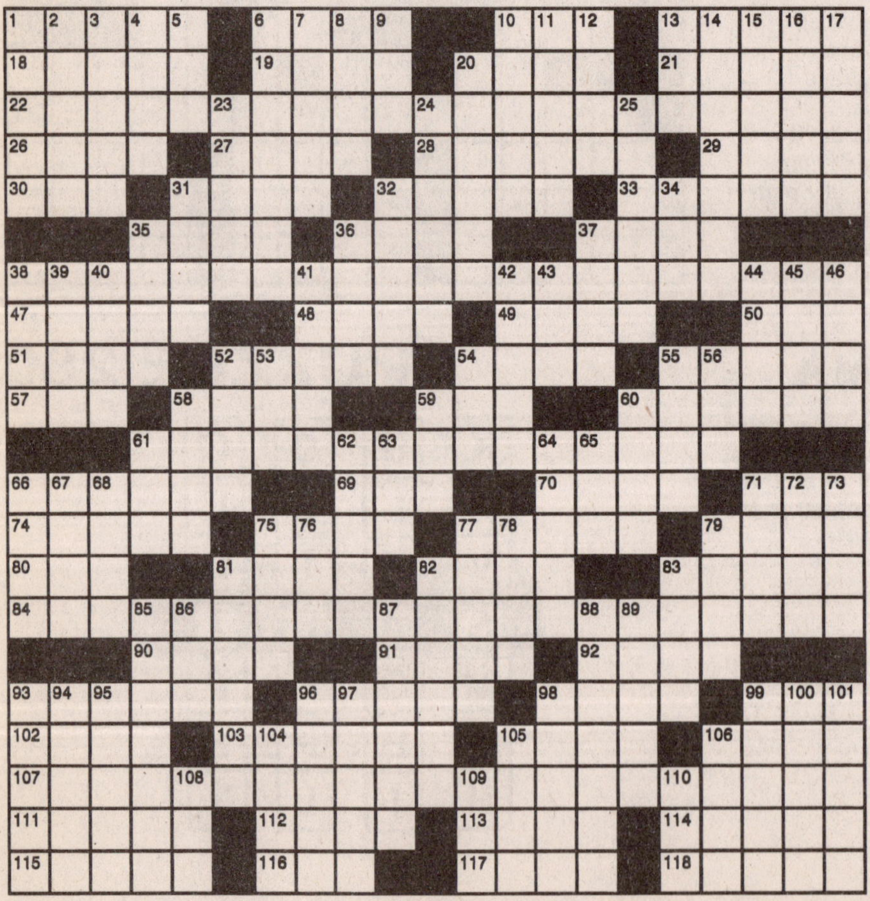

## CAMOUFLAGE

# PUZZLE 282

**The answers to the clues can be found in the diagram, but they have been camouflaged. Their letters are in correct order, but sometimes they are separated by extra letters which have been inserted throughout the diagram. You must black out all the extra "camouflage" letters. The remaining letters will also be used for words in the Down column. Solve Across and Down together to determine the correct letters where there is a choice. The number of answer words in a row or column is indicated by the number of clues.**

| | 1 | 2 | 3 | 4 | 5 | 6 | 7 | 8 | 9 | 10 | 11 | 12 | 13 |
|---|---|---|---|---|---|---|---|---|---|---|---|---|---|
| 1 | P | E | L | E | N | D | G | E | M | O | I | N | E |
| 2 | A | D | Y | R | O | I | N | T | I | R | L | I | S |
| 3 | T | R | A | M | B | E | L | E | S | A | N | G | S |
| 4 | R | I | D | C | F | R | A | N | C | T | U | R | E |
| 5 | A | N | D | G | R | E | S | F | L | I | R | E | S |
| 6 | F | L | E | E | U | D | O | L | G | O | S | V | E |
| 7 | O | K | N | I | S | T | S | O | R | M | E | A | N |
| 8 | F | O | R | D | L | A | M | C | E | R | E | N | D |
| 9 | I | E | L | N | C | G | A | P | A | N | D | A | L |
| 10 | L | S | T | E | A | M | K | A | N | T | S | A | S |
| 11 | O | H | U | N | T | G | E | R | T | O | E | D | N |
| 12 | N | O | N | E | H | E | B | L | O | P | A | D | O |
| 13 | R | E | S | W | E | N | R | E | S | T | E | Y | U |

### ACROSS

1. Promise • Excavate
2. Skilled • Part of the eye
3. Talk aimlessly • Without
4. Free • Break
5. South American mountains • Evergreen trees
6. Vendetta • Affection
7. Osculate • Seaport in Algeria
8. Body structure • Completion
9. Peruvian Indian • Bearlike animal
10. Water vapor • Sunflower State
11. Actress Kim • Having foot digits
12. Zero • Cushion
13. Female sheep • Repose

### DOWN

1. Jar sealer
2. Beverage • Brogan
3. Scaling apparatus • Cask
4. White fur • Novel
5. Bewilder
6. Dreadful • Water barrier
7. Tumbler • Manufacturer
8. Nice summer • Ziegfeld • Trim
9. Villains
10. Fixed portion • Make a choice
11. Accustomed • Vast expanse
12. Great bliss • Append
13. To be: Latin • Transmits

# PUZZLE 283

**ACROSS**
1. Sorrowful exclamation
5. Mocks
9. Eliot's "cruelest month"
14. Uncommon
15. Peaceful
16. Goad
17. Woodwind
18. Fencing sword
19. Back sides of coins
20. Nonflowering plant
21. Harm
23. Seine
24. Regions
26. Eliminate
28. Reddy's "I Am ___"
31. Basic commodity
35. Head cover
38. Fender imperfections
40. Foreteller
41. Refined
43. Picture-taking tools
46. Nothing more than
47. Extra
49. Explosive material: abbr.
50. Legislative body
53. Go in
55. Harshness
57. Succinct
61. Father
64. Courses of travel
67. Greek letter
68. Colosseum center
70. Story
71. Always
72. Bashful
73. Central idea
74. Attract
75. Clay brick
76. Single bills
77. Transmit

**DOWN**
1. Smell
2. Work
3. Got up
4. Playground toy
5. Got a hole in one
6. Father
7. Component part
8. Daub
9. Bear witness
10. Round green veggie
11. Precipitation
12. Atoll
13. For fear that
22. Car fuel
25. Pop
27. Relieve
29. Males
30. Social insects
32. Sassy
33. Thin
34. Soonest, long ago
35. Makes a skirt border
36. Toward shelter
37. Sea swallow
39. Skim
42. Toothed wheel
44. Actor Carney
45. Sports competition
48. Relate
51. Harangue
52. Self-image
54. Defies authority
56. Expense
58. Musical
59. Severe
60. Having hearing organs
61. Computer input
62. Parched
63. Band's first record, for short
65. Other
66. Puts
69. Pen point

# PUZZLE 284

## STAR WORDS

**Place 5 of the 8 words given below into the diagram in the direction of the arrows so that the words share letters as indicated by the diagram.**

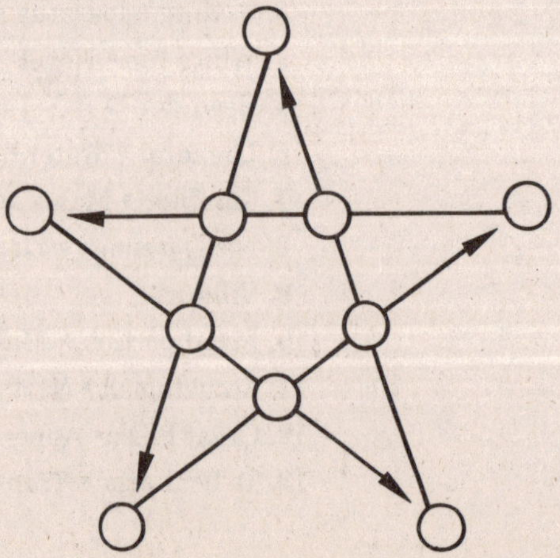

DENT
KNEW
MEEK
MEET
TEEM
TENT
WEED
WENT

# PUZZLE 285

**ACROSS**

1. Apiary
5. Current measure, for short
8. Facts
12. Image
13. Female antelope
14. Parched
15. Clique
16. Arsenal
18. Anticipate
20. Pulse
21. Join
23. Headed
24. Suppresses
25. Nourished
26. Fashion
29. Labyrinth
30. Tarry
31. Wise men
32. "We ___ the World"
33. Baronet's title
34. Noblewomen
35. Baking measurement
36. Consummate
37. Thin
39. Groans
40. Noodle covering
42. Units of resistance
45. Kitty builder
46. Beerlike beverage
47. Jump
48. Sentry's station
49. Sunburned
50. Novelist Ferber

**DOWN**

1. Towel word
2. Sherbet
3. Voice
4. Twist
5. Confess
6. Castle feature
7. Tent stake
8. Startled
9. Diva's song
10. Hue
11. Citrus drink
17. Resting
19. Beast of burden
21. Ms. Bombeck
22. Singer/actress Holly ___
23. Appendage
25. At a distance
26. Malnourished
27. Eternity
28. Platter
30. Facial feature
31. Underground access
33. Warbled
34. Excavate
35. West Pointer
36. Dismissed
37. Funnyman Jay ___
38. Ingests
39. Shopper's bonanza
40. Occurrence
41. Lobe locale
43. "The Music ___"
44. Mineral spring

# PUZZLE 286

**ACROSS**

1. Split
4. Band instrument
8. Landed
12. Journalist Wells
13. Distantly
14. Wholesome
15. Conjunction
16. Fine china
18. Cake toppers
20. Disturb
21. ___ Zeppelin
22. Thing
24. Reduction
26. Self
27. Mr. Ruth
31. Flock member
32. Bullring cry
33. Chemist's lair
34. Additions
36. Biblical land
37. Chunk
38. Bolivian coin
40. Standoff
41. Indian ___
44. Fabricated
47. Promenade
50. Mine extract
51. Skiff's need
52. African lily
53. Make fun of
54. Otherwise
55. Stitched
56. Still

**DOWN**

1. Fight site
2. Golden calf
3. Geometric term
4. Recorded
5. Foreign visitors?
6. Saloon
7. Bow
8. Confidence
9. Hawaiian feast
10. Blue bloom
11. Type of dress
17. Before, to a bard
19. Last letter
22. Inuit dwelling
23. Pigeon-___
24. Comprehend
25. Piercing tool
26. Many moons
28. Fable
29. Bleat
30. Recede
35. Skimpy
37. Respectful title
39. Goal
40. Memento
41. Reed instrument
42. Ember
43. Pitcher parts
44. Gush
45. Huron's neighbor
46. Mortgage
48. No longer is
49. Stout

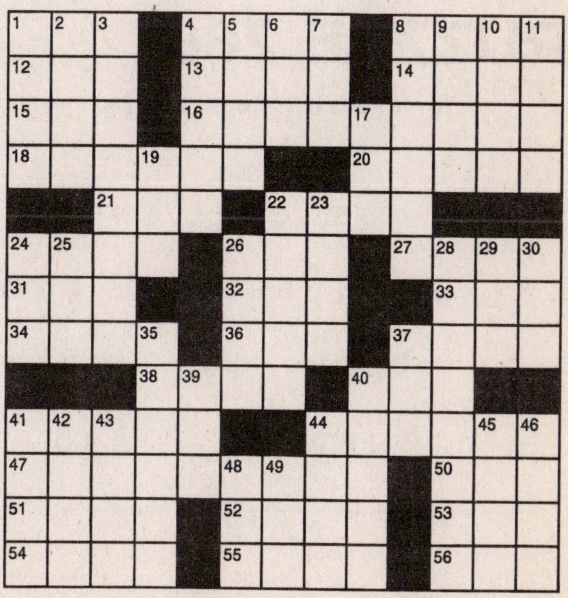

# PUZZLE 287

**ACROSS**

1. "M*A*S*H" star
5. Flat-topped hill
9. Lookout
14. Piquant
15. Indigo
16. Type of pants
17. Presidential office
18. Cay
19. "Love Story" star
20. Peggy Wood role
21. Severe critic
23. Snoop
25. Previous to, to Keats
26. Spy Hari
28. Mast
31. Food fish
35. Deserves
37. Bellicose god
39. Tokyo, once
40. Jakarta's land
43. Opposite of NNW
44. RBI, e.g.
45. Heckle
46. Morays
48. Crude metals
50. "Baked in ___"
51. Buckeye college
53. Muslim judge
55. Separate checks
60. Cabot ___ (Jessica Fletcher's town)
64. Television diner waitress
65. Weapons
66. Natty
67. Took a risk
68. Yawn
69. You are something ___!
70. Lollapaloozas
71. "Lohengrin" heroine
72. Cherished

**DOWN**

1. Molecule part
2. Molten rock
3. Apothecary measure
4. Ocean that Columbus crossed
5. Household employees
6. Follows
7. Sediment
8. Fish sauce
9. Search thoroughly
10. French resort
11. Oil cartel acronym
12. River to the Caspian
13. Mosaic piece
22. Included
24. Vows
26. French river
27. Workers' collective
29. Artificial gem glass
30. Composer Garfunkel
32. Spyri heroine
33. An Astaire
34. Potion
35. Gds.
36. Embark
38. "Slammin' Sammy"
41. Swiss river
42. Described
47. Pele's sport
49. Imps
52. Molts
54. "Dames ___"
55. Wall section
56. German lancer
57. Grow weary
58. Violent anger
59. Of an epoch
61. Heraldic bearing
62. Passport endorsement
63. German river

# PUZZLE 288 Crypto-Limerick

**To read this humorous verse you must first decode it as you would a regular cryptogram.**

S GEQQAJ XSTAL FDYCCAJ TKWSQA
MSF JSRELDI RYQQEXC PX MAECGQ
FSEL QGA KPSKG, SX PDL LYWWAJ,
"IPY'JA CJASQ, OYQ IPY FYWWAJ
WJPT QPP TSXI QJERF QP QGA RDSQA."

## CODEWORD

# PUZZLE 289

The directions for solving are given on page 91.

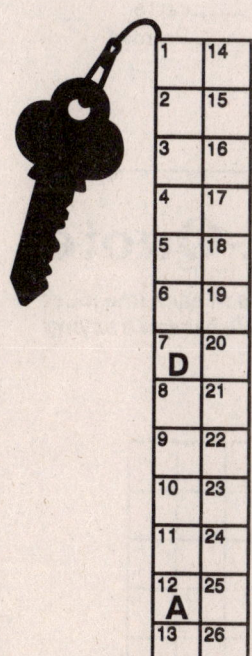

| | |
|---|---|
| 1 L | 14 |
| 2 | 15 |
| 3 | 16 |
| 4 I | 17 |
| 5 | 18 |
| 6 | 19 |
| 7 | 20 |
| 8 | 21 T |
| 9 | 22 |
| 10 | 23 |
| 11 | 24 |
| 12 | 25 |
| 13 | 26 |

| | | | | | | | | | | | | |
|---|---|---|---|---|---|---|---|---|---|---|---|---|
| 20 | 8 | 26 | 24 | 10 | 8 | 5 | 20 | | 13 | 19 | 19 | 2 |
| 19 | | | 7 | | 18 | | 15 | | 8 | | | 19 |
| 1 | | | 22 | 4 | 10 | 10 | 7 | 21 | 23 | | | 3 |
| 11 | 2 | 19 | 19 | | 1 | | 8 | | 23 | 19 | 2 | 12 |
| | | 25 | | 11 | 19 | 19 | 24 | 20 | | 13 | | 2 |
| 7 | 26 | 21 | 4 | 1 L | | 1 | | 14 | 1 | 19 | 8 | 21 |
| 26 | | 2 | | 4 I | 18 | 8 | 5 | 19 | | 14 | | 19 |
| 8 | 6 | 19 | 2 | 21 T | | 21 | | 26 | 12 | 21 | 19 | 24 |
| 9 | | 18 | | 20 | 21 | 19 | 1 | 19 | | 12 | | |
| 8 | 2 | 19 | 8 | | 17 | | 19 | | 24 | 2 | 12 | 3 |
| 2 | | | 20 | 15 | 7 | 19 | 8 | 22 | 16 | | | 12 |
| 19 | | | 17 | | 5 | | 6 | | 19 | | | 26 |
| 20 | 19 | 25 | 16 | | 20 | 3 | 19 | 19 | 24 | 9 | 8 | 16 |

| | |
|---|---|
| A | N |
| B | O |
| C | P |
| D | Q |
| E | R |
| F | S |
| G | ~~T~~ |
| H | U |
| ~~I~~ | V |
| J | W |
| K | X |
| ~~L~~ | Y |
| M | Z |

---

## CODEWORD

# PUZZLE 290

| | |
|---|---|
| 1 | 14 |
| 2 | 15 |
| 3 | 16 |
| 4 | 17 |
| 5 | 18 |
| 6 | 19 |
| 7 D | 20 |
| 8 | 21 |
| 9 | 22 |
| 10 | 23 |
| 11 | 24 |
| 12 A | 25 |
| 13 | 26 |

| | | | | | | | | | | | | |
|---|---|---|---|---|---|---|---|---|---|---|---|---|
| 19 | 2 | 21 | 13 | 14 | 18 | | 15 | 12 | 21 | 1 | 13 | 9 |
| 12 A | | 2 | | | 5 | | | 22 | | | | 25 |
| 7 D | 25 | 16 | 13 | | 12 | 17 | 12 | 22 | 13 | 12 | | 10 |
| 23 | | 2 | | | 6 | | 10 | | | 18 | 26 | 13 |
| 13 | 20 | 21 | 12 | 3 | 14 | | 22 | 25 | 21 | 1 | | 6 |
| | | | 20 | | 13 | | | | 6 | | | |
| 10 | 2 | 21 | 1 | 13 | 6 | | 12 | 16 | 12 | 2 | 22 | 18 |
| | | | 22 | | | | 20 | | 17 | | | |
| 21 | | 11 | 13 | 12 | 6 | | 12 | 18 | 8 | 22 | 26 | 3 |
| 6 | 25 | 13 | | | 26 | | 22 | | | 12 | | 13 |
| 26 | | 20 | 13 | 12 | 9 | 22 | 8 | | 24 | 26 | 2 | 9 |
| 3 | | | | 2 | | | 17 | | | 23 | | 13 |
| 19 | 25 | 4 | 13 | 6 | 18 | | 13 | 2 | 9 | 5 | 13 | 6 |

| | |
|---|---|
| ~~A~~ | N |
| B | O |
| C | P |
| ~~D~~ | Q |
| E | R |
| F | S |
| G | T |
| H | U |
| I | V |
| J | W |
| K | X |
| L | Y |
| M | Z |

# PUZZLE 291

**ACROSS**

1. "The Glass Menagerie," e.g.
5. Disagree
10. Wheat husk
14. Traditional knowledge
15. Dreads
16. Adore
17. Affirmative responses
18. Michigan city
19. Tavern orders
20. Metal container
21. Navigate
22. Put into
24. Springy
26. Release
27. Possessive pronoun
28. Convey
32. Assert
35. Shred
36. Ring great
37. Slope
38. Gibe
39. Look over
40. Point
41. Hue
42. Pay out
43. Pamphlet
45. "____ Send Me"
46. Not theirs
47. Carriers
51. Tiaras
54. Smack
55. Explosive noise
56. Volcanic flow
57. One who ascertains a point in time
59. Rich vein
60. At any time
61. Extraterrestrial
62. Passed with flying colors
63. Resist
64. Units of length
65. Loafer, e.g.

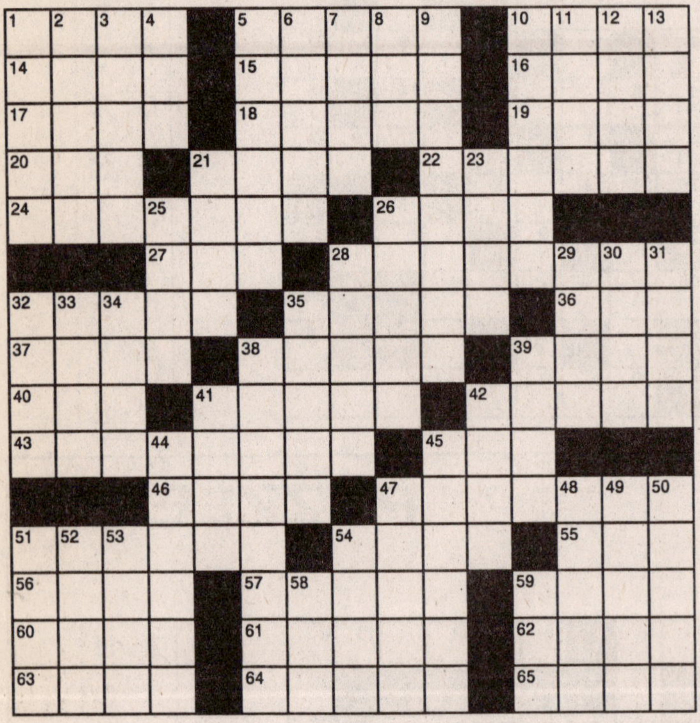

**DOWN**

1. Location
2. Faithful
3. Sports stadium
4. Affirmative answer
5. "An ____ to Remember"
6. Keepsake
7. Author Goodwin
8. Vase
9. Guess
10. Criticizes strongly
11. Actor's part
12. State with confidence
13. Bird abode
21. Stalk
23. Diamond number
25. Ocean vessel
26. Efface
28. Exchange
29. Confront
30. Gusto
31. Fruit skin
32. Complain
33. Burrow
34. Bullets, for short
35. Engine wheels
38. Maundy ____
39. Urge
41. Avoid
42. Cleansing agent
44. Fearful person
45. Longs
47. Become diffused
48. Period of history
49. Cowboy show
50. Stockholm native
51. Musical symbol
52. Speak enthusiastically
53. Kitchen appliance
54. Ado
58. ____ carte
59. ____ Palmas

---

# PUZZLE 292

## Build-A-Quote

**Fill in the diagrams by putting the lines of letters VERTICALLY into their squares. The letters in each line must remain in the same order. The lines are given in jumbled order. When finished, you will be able to read a saying ACROSS the rows in the diagram.**

**1.**

HIHTHR
TNGRTO
ESTHED
EIENW
PMIAS

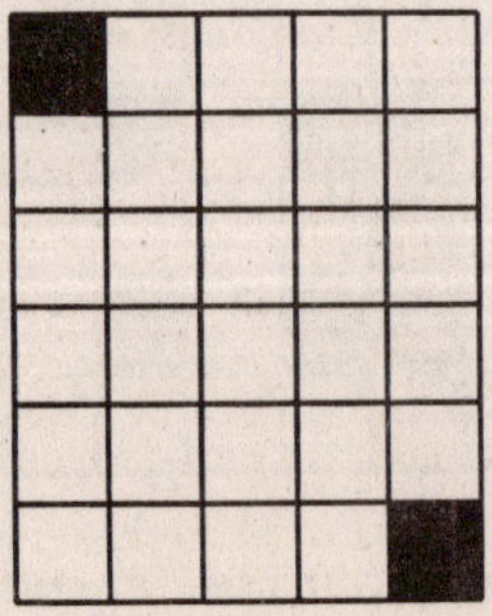

**2.**

SOSAU
WWNKM
NLOTAE
ELEMSR
OADOEM

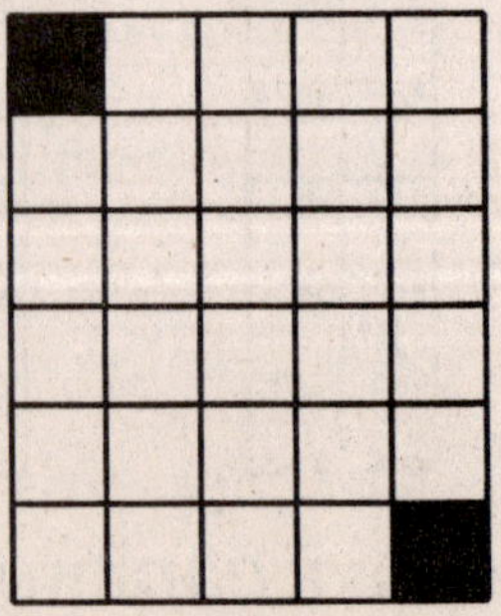

# PUZZLE 293

**ACROSS**

1. Contend (with)
5. Chose
10. Nero's 1,102
14. Swedish coins
15. Gay ____
16. Food for mares and does?
17. Bog
18. '
20. Miss Piggy's pronoun
21. Quahog
22. Dog-faced ape
23. Isolated
25. Parsley unit
27. "The ____ Drum"
30. Roman magistrate
32. Newborn lamb
33. Cause of ruin
34. Prints over the edge
36. Large packages
37. Gift-wrapping items
40. Printing machines
42. Blue dyes
43. "____ Carrie"
45. Cleaver
46. Comfy room
47. Gaze
50. Asian fete
51. Henry, Jane, or Peter
53. Tibetan capital
55. "____ Cheatin' Heart"
57. Being, in Barcelona
59. For what ____ worth
60. &&&&
63. Ginger cookie
64. Misstates
65. Bone cavities
66. Singer Seeger
67. What a model strikes
68. Type of beam
69. Arabian gulf

**DOWN**

1. ,
2. Baltimore ____
3. .
4. Opposite of WNW
5. Fiery stone
6. Daddies
7. Walked heavily
8. Shoe widths
9. Keep waiting
10. Mullins of comics
11. UPPER CASE LETTERS
12. Irish ancestor
13. Function: suff.
19. Joplin opus
21. Instruments for Casals and others
24. Eat like a mouse
26. Files
28. Arrow poison
29. Loch ____
31. Poetic time of day
33. Iraqi port
35. Krupp works locale
36. Scarab
37. Swimmer's platform
38. Concerning
39. Groups with the same genetic traits
41. Directions: abbr.
44. Starts a paragraph
46. On the back
48. Showered
49. Holdings
51. Animal's coat
52. German skater Hoffman
54. Poplar
56. Bacteriologist's wire
58. Russian emperor
60. Lofty mountain
61. "O Sole ____"
62. Literary selections
63. Belgian resort town

# PUZZLE 294

**ACROSS**

1. Picked
6. Desert beast
11. Rood
16. Split
17. Harden
18. Lariat
19. Kilns
20. Harmful
22. Hang
23. Guitarist Paul
24. Needing scratching
25. Allotments
29. Margarine
30. Blurred
33. Mexican cheers
34. Army rank: abbr.
35. Pleasing
39. N. American Indian
40. Last month: abbr.
41. Stooge Howard et al.
42. "The ____ Squad"
43. Want
45. Burn
46. Bank transactions
48. Sparkling
51. Secret agents
53. Summer drinks
54. Quit work
57. Raw material
58. Wheel part
59. Morose
60. Religious sister
61. Gull-like bird
63. Spelling contest
64. Gaming cubes
65. Breakfast item
66. Work: Latin
68. Small tavern
70. To the left, matey
72. Craggy hill
73. Crowd
77. Foreordained
80. Biblical pause
81. Closes
82. Draw out
83. Chalcedony
84. Weeds
85. Cozy homes
86. Showed consideration

**DOWN**

1. Cut short
2. Wasp's nest
3. Kitchen item
4. Dispatches
5. Printer's measures
6. El ——
7. Anoints
8. Softens
9. Strays
10. Hawaiian garland
11. Greek island
12. Italian composer
13. Vow
14. Abide
15. "My Gal ——"
21. Actress Hayley
26. Maids of paradise
27. Comic Steve ——
28. Soak, as flax
29. "Aida," for one
30. Flop
31. Follower: suffix
32. More untidy
34. Embers
36. Dream
37. Pro and ——
38. Asner and Ames
41. Free-for-all
44. Chill
45. Edge up to
46. German songs
47. Canadian prov.
49. Government's share
50. Handbill
51. Barfly

# PUZZLE 294

52. Prior to: prefix
55. Mat
56. Chang's twin
58. Touches
59. Female sib
62. Soup ingredient
64. As the crow flies
67. Iron
68. Extra
69. Last Greek letter
70. Space
71. Fruit
72. Sea movement
74. Having wings
75. Fill
76. Molt
77. Seattle hours: abbr.
78. Decade
79. —— Moines
80. Pouch

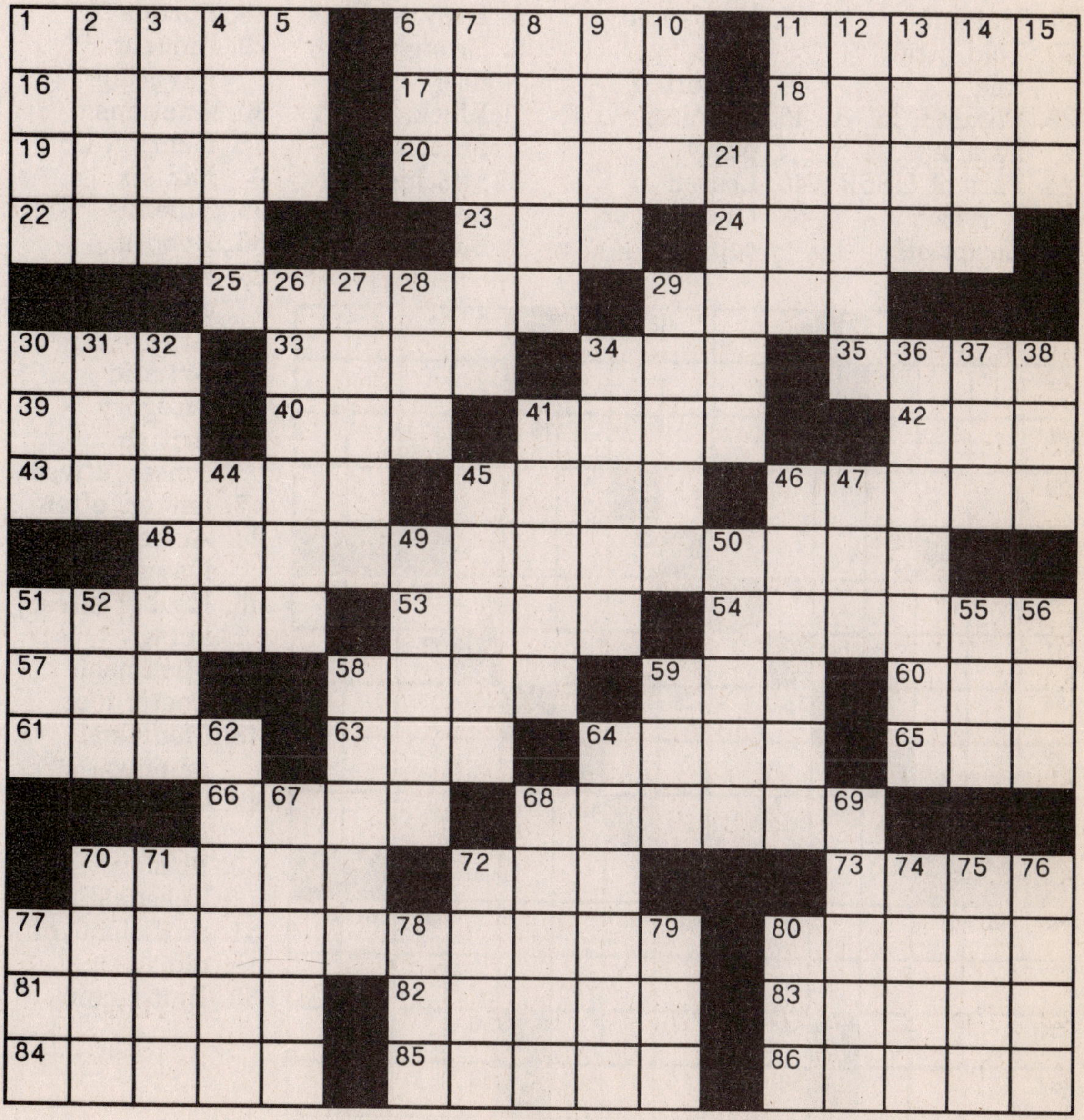

# PUZZLE 295

**ACROSS**

1. Route
5. "____ Magnolias"
10. "The frost ____ the punkin"
14. Inter ____
15. Put aside
16. Make well
17. Police power
20. Ocean hue
21. Hubbub
22. Told a tall tale
23. Figured, in heraldry
24. Part of USSR
27. Porticos
31. Leads off
32. Made on a loom
33. Three ____ match
34. Cherry type
35. Quoted
36. Wind
37. Conclude
38. Footloose one
39. Furze
40. Brought back
42. Eyepieces
43. Yours and mine
44. Distorted
45. Evening party
48. Lessen
52. Undercover cop
54. Put the watch on
55. Sapor
56. Beginner
57. Blubbers
58. Guide
59. Cabbage salad

**DOWN**

1. Buddies
2. Salve plant
3. Actress Louise
4. Sharp bargaining
5. Easy or Fleet
6. Brought to heel
7. Black, to Milton
8. Mischievous one
9. Schooled
10. Deliverers of yore
11. Pacific sea
12. Evangelist Roberts
13. Eft
18. Sign between Pisces and Taurus
19. Mortal
23. Discontinue
24. Serious
25. Say one's piece
26. Markets
27. Cast a ballot
28. Portals
29. Liqueur flavoring
30. Auctions
32. Henry VIII had six
35. Emends
36. Events
38. French cathedral city
39. Artistic category
41. British conservatives
42. Leerer, often
44. Actress Davis
45. Harbor sites: abbr.
46. Mishmash
47. Poetic foot
48. Medicinal amount
49. Chemical group
50. Poet Teasdale
51. Sufficient, of old
53. Baltic coin

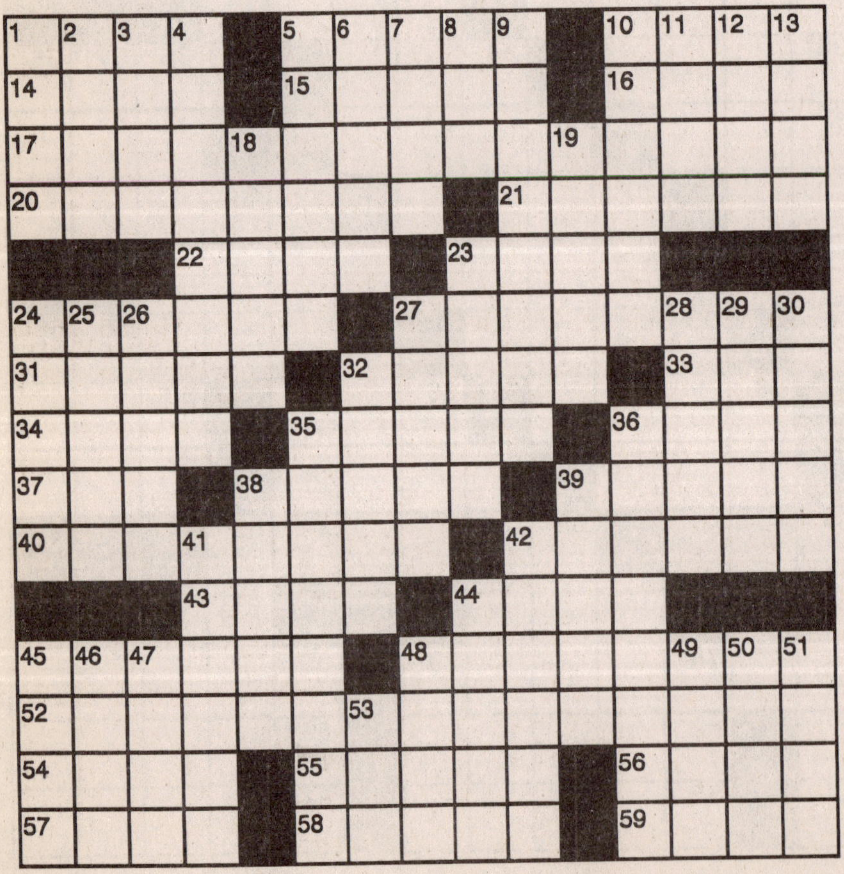

# PUZZLE 296

**ACROSS**

1. Cubic measure
6. "—— and Lovers"
10. Gamble
13. Public esteem
14. Oak or elm
15. Fit to ——: 2 wds.
17. "—— in an hold . . ." (2 Sam. 23:14): 4 wds.
20. Soldiers' meal
21. Pub orders
22. Articles
23. Lulu
24. Succinct
25. Bell sound
28. Accelerated
30. Uproar
31. "The —— Lagoon"
33. Was first
36. "As a piece of —— . . ." (Sol. 6:7): 3 wds.
40. Cub Scout unit
41. Assists
42. Off-white
43. Run in neutral
45. Minus
46. "Gloria ——"
49. Scottish hillside
52. —— -of-roses
53. Winter vehicle
54. Type size
58. "And —— the fifth seal . . ." (Rev. 6:9): 4 wds.
61. Saint Philip ——
62. Carolina rail
63. Propelled a boat
64. Kind of room, for short
65. Actress Anna ——
66. Lock

**DOWN**

1. Fake
2. Dial sound
3. Purposes
4. Fishing gear
5. Victorian or Roman
6. Fence steps
7. Arrangement
8. Information
9. Vast area
10. Took one's swings
11. Anesthetic
12. Rains hard
16. Scot's otherwise
18. Front
19. Location
23. Evil giant
25. Gull
26. Press
27. —— de plume
28. Stars
29. Shade of green
30. Trendy movement
31. Soft cheese
32. "——: A Dog"
33. Asian country
34. Goes wrong
35. Actress Susan
37. "My —— Sal"
38. Floor-covering unit
39. Actress Arden
43. Peaceful
44. Plate
46. Chess piece
47. Jacob's son
48. Voila!
49. Trumpet sound
50. Fortification
51. Fuss
53. Worn out
54. Bosc or Anjou
55. Concerning: 2 wds.
56. So-so grades
57. Appends
59. Kind of curve
60. Kitty

# PUZZLE 297

**ACROSS**

1. Antlers
6. Asian sea
10. Neon is one
13. Knocked for ___: 2 wds.
14. ___ Raton
15. Left
16. Lend-___
17. Oklahoma city
18. Girl of Green Gables
19. 1983 Pia Zadora film: 2 wds.
21. Clairvoyant
22. Ms. Remick
23. Dutch theologian
25. Uncle Miltie et al.
29. Player ___
31. Greek classic
32. 1975 Streisand film: 2 wds.
36. The Swedish Nightingale
37. English coins
38. Simone's friend
39. One-time fiancee of Prince Charles: 2 wds.
41. Minnesota city
42. Covered with fluff
43. Actress Janet
44. Open the port
47. ___ days
48. Mr. Griffin, of TV
49. 1941 Ann Sothern film: 3 wds.
56. French cheese
57. Canyon mouth
58. Swiss river
59. Nights before
60. ___ Bien Phu
61. Russian ruler
62. Thing, in law
63. Conifers
64. Irish poet

**DOWN**

1. Foyer
2. Bread topping
3. Horse hue
4. Sniffer
5. Took the place of
6. White poplar
7. Gossip-columnist Barrett
8. Amino
9. ___ Grey (descendant of Henry VII): 2 wds.
10. Heredity factors
11. Year, in France
12. Violinist Isaac
15. "That ___, that was my wife": 3 wds.
20. Affirmative
24. Some
25. Tab
26. Director Kazan
27. Peel
28. Inamoratas: 2 wds.
29. Like some bad jokes?
30. Peruvian resident
32. Acrobatic accomplishment
33. ___ Gemayel of Lebanon
34. Producer De Laurentiis
35. Leap or fiscal
37. Mild cocktail: 2 wds.
40. Manager: abbr.
41. With enthusiasm
43. Sailor
44. Palette color
45. Courage
46. Sobs
47. Miss Cannon et al.
50. He had an Irish Rose
51. Sketched
52. Buffalo butter
53. Mrs. Chaplin
54. Sleep ___: 2 wds.
55. Family rooms

# PUZZLE 298

**ACROSS**
1. Bashaw
6. Jaguarundi
10. Health club
13. Something else
14. High shoes
16. Otto's domain: abbr.
17. Acts as bouncer: 4 wds.
20. Female hog
21. On and on
22. Latitude
23. Old ascetic
25. English novelist
27. Sheep genus
28. Fiery
29. Redact
32. Go berserk
34. Julia Ward ——
35. Gold: Sp.
36. Russian river
37. Hocks
38. Squadron
39. —— Vegas
40. Rivers: Sp.
41. Tenet
42. Rudiments
44. Pixie
45. Disorder
46. Literary works
48. Slip by
51. Actress Dahl
53. Charter
55. Guided
56. Revealing plans: 3 wds.
59. That lady
60. River boats
61. Peruvian district
62. Word of consent
63. Toward dawn
64. Surfaces

**DOWN**
1. —— comitatus
2. Musketeer
3. Betrays inner feelings: 3 wds.
4. Fell
5. Poison
6. Nigerian native
7. Caesar-Coca program: 4 wds.
8. Go bad
9. Sportsmen
10. Established pecking order: 3 wds.
11. Malay boat
12. Ethereal
15. Prophet
18. Actor Montand
19. English sand hill
24. Machiavellian
26. Villages
30. Rhizome plant
31. Crocus, e.g.
32. Actress Negri
33. Iraqi
34. —— Selassie
37. Attendance
38. Sky bear
41. Keyboard instrument
43. Eject
45. Only
47. Les Etats-——
49. Cassia plant
50. Scandinavian literary works
51. Wan
52. Korean statesman
54. Academy: abbr.
57. Part of India
58. —— Tuv, Israel

# PUZZLE 299

**ACROSS**

1. Hardy heroine
5. Solemn promise
8. Poke
11. Old sayings
15. Body of troops
16. Bon ——
17. Native metal
18. Beehive state
19. Miss Foch
20. Decade
21. Shoshone
22. Horseback game
23. Highly skilled
25. Close
27. Overturn
29. Of little depth
31. Transgression
32. Take to court
33. Vacillated
37. Atlas entry
39. Veracity
43. Slippery surface
44. Quick swim
46. Papal name
48. Adversary
49. Lone Star State
52. Talk idly
54. Military unit
57. Forty winks
59. Pilfer
61. Expire
62. Coal bucket
66. Four-poster
68. Spacious
72. "—— Town"
73. Sweet potato
75. Spinning toy
77. Affirmative
78. Comedian Hill
81. Clumsy boat
83. Stemmed glasses
86. —— de Cologne
88. Bother
90. Legume
91. Scatters
94. Colored
96. Moved sideways
100. Bone-dry
101. Actress Lupino
103. Shred
105. Prima donna
106. Bosun's whistle
107. Sally Field's TV role
108. Impair
109. At all times
110. Raced
111. —— whiz
112. Tricky
113. Lease

**DOWN**

1. Canned fish
2. Writer Bagnold
3. Trig ratio
4. Fastener
5. Large container
6. Augury
7. Claret and Chablis
8. Daily record
9. Actor Carney
10. Borscht base
11. Late meal
12. Upon
13. NYSE street
14. Brake part
24. High mountain
26. Goal
28. On strike
30. Marry
33. Humor
34. The Red Baron, e.g.
35. Irritate
36. Excavate
38. Vivacity
40. Flying saucer
41. Overly
42. Barnyard fowl
45. Golf term
47. Ancient
50. Picnic pest
51. Convened
53. Newhart or Crane
55. Be unwell
56. Pekoe
58. Layer
60. Wager
62. Weep

# PUZZLE 299

63. Pool stick
64. Coffee pot
65. Have dinner
67. Poodle
69. Deli bread
70. Acquire
71. Sibilant sound
74. Unimaginative
76. Explosive sound
79. Required
80. Deviate temporarily
82. Wide inlet
84. Contest
85. Portable steps
87. Exploiting
89. Microbes
91. Devitalizes
92. Journey
93. Ready to pick
95. Watch face
97. Donate
98. Balanced
99. Tapered seam
102. Payable
104. Use a crowbar

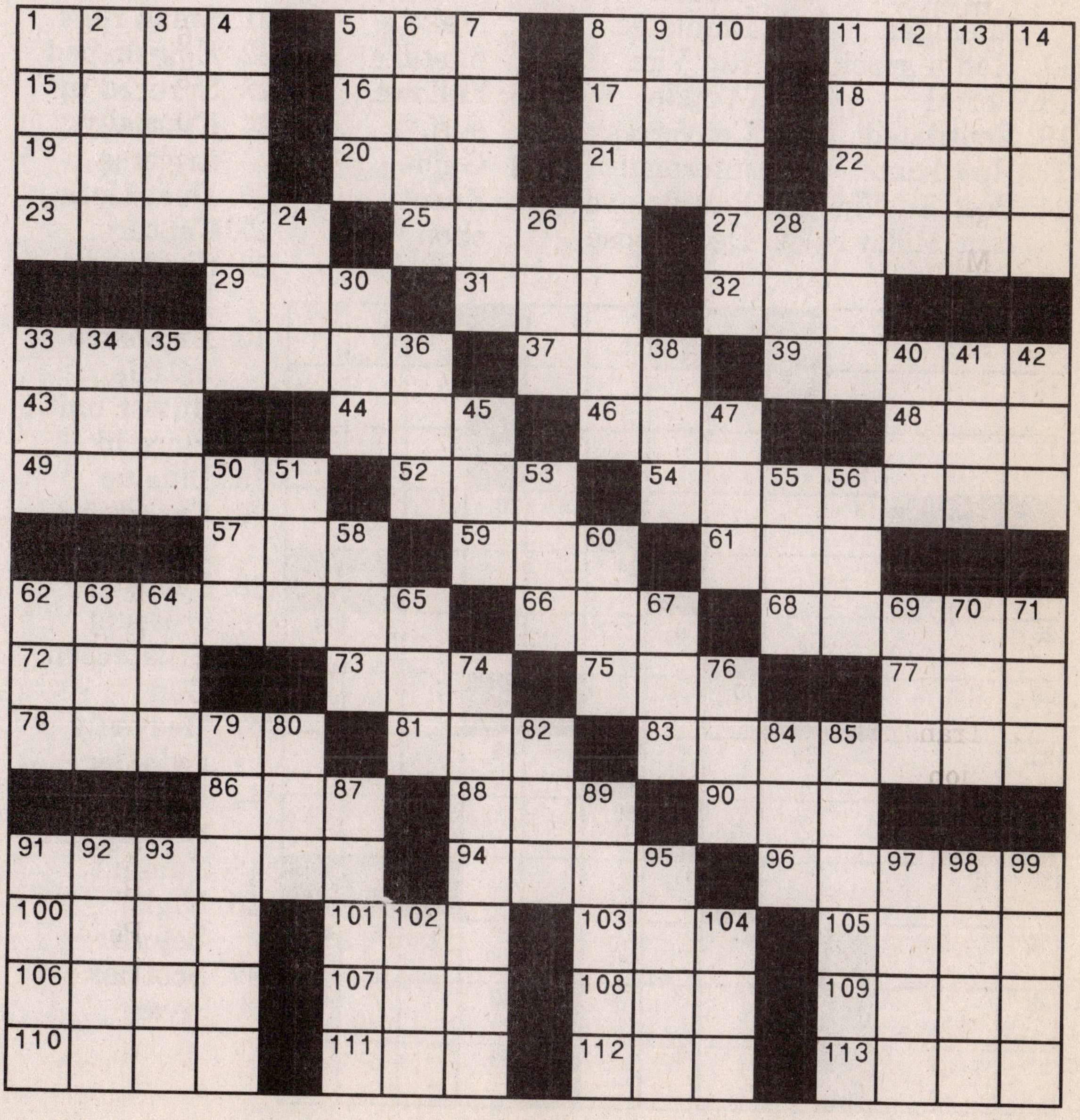

# PUZZLE 300

## ACROSS

1. Astronaut Armstrong
5. Dance move
9. Obtain
12. Commedia dell'____
13. Cain's brother
14. Colorado brave
15. Huron or Michigan
17. Had a snack
18. Portal
19. Ventilated
21. Up-to-date
24. Poet St. Vincent Millay
25. Turn aside
26. Takes offense at
29. Tic-____-toe
30. Roofing substance
31. ____ la la
32. Tilted
35. Dairy product
37. Rave's partner
38. Emulates Rip Van Winkle
39. Converses informally
41. Fawn's dad
42. Decompose
43. Judged approximately
48. Pub drink
49. Genuine
50. "____ Me Tender"
51. Garden plot
52. Biblical weed
53. Fencer's weapon

## DOWN

1. Find fault
2. Make a mistake
3. Follower: suff.
4. Guide
5. Beauty shop
6. Skier's tow: hyph.
7. Comic book scream
8. Begs
9. Promise
10. Diminutive suffix
11. ____ off (started a golf game)
16. Wrongful injury
20. Pertaining to: suff.
21. Small rugs
22. Egg-shaped
23. Spruced up
24. Eternally, in verse
26. Dust cloth
27. Capture
28. Spade and Houston
30. Explosive initials
33. Butter unit
34. Place in
35. Bivalve
36. Entertain lavishly
38. Fence crossing
39. Crustacean
40. Gap
41. Heavenly twinkler
44. Mediterranean ____
45. Summit
46. Night before
47. Scottish river

# PUZZLE 301

**• SUGAR-COATED •**

**ACROSS**

1. Medicated
6. Fairy-tale figure
11. Hatfield, to McCoy
14. Restful day: abbr.
17. Sadat
18. High home
19. Embody
21. Pioneer in plow-making
22. Increase poker stakes
24. Takes care of
26. Yes, indeed!
27. Unique people
28. Pieces of information
29. Mister, in Munich
31. "Guiding Light," e.g.
33. One of four of fifty-two
34. Part of H.R.E.
35. Restaurant for celebrity-watching
37. C.P. or Phoebe
39. Himalayan cedar
41. She-pigs
43. Lowest lake in the world
48. Game pieces
50. Barnum structure
52. Looks threatening
53. Place for a partridge
56. Sound receivers
58. Glossy
59. Quantity: abbr.
60. Annual climbers
63. Second person
64. Unconstrained
67. One-armed bandit feature
68. Filled to the gills
71. Forever, to Shakespeare
73. Hosiery mishap
75. Start afresh
76. Remains
78. Sight in Sitka
80. Undivided
83. Sportsman Bobby and family
85. Prepares to pray
87. Fall behind
88. Petition at a penny pond
92. Algerian port
94. Reader's selection
95. Countertenor
96. ____ of roses
98. Donkeys, in Dijon
100. Melted-cheese dish
102. To the point
105. TV features
107. Foreshadow
108. Cup in Cannes
109. Promotion writers
110. Unkempt place
111. Family mem.
112. Leaves as is
113. Cluttered

**DOWN**

1. June celebrity
2. Former
3. Ocarinas
4. Produces as profit
5. ____ Scott
6. Winery worker
7. Says another way
8. W. U.S. state
9. Doubtful tales
10. "Oh come ____ adore him"
11. ____ dandy
12. Can. province
13. Yodeler's feedback
14. Apt. overseer
15. Regard as saintly
16. Palmer or Ross
20. Spring season
23. Subject of much poetry
25. Participants
28. Retiring place
30. Problem for the police
32. Edgar et al.
35. Type of pork
36. Flattery
38. Some mil. women
40. S. on a vane, e.g.
42. Brittle cookie
44. Amer. money
45. Garden bloomers
46. Nice student
47. Wanted to know
49. Bastes
51. Very, in Versailles
53. Not as colorful
54. Overact
55. Wrigglers
57. Moselle feeder
61. Long times
62. Pennsylvania athlete
65. Asian title of respect
66. Within: prefix
69. Wayfarers' havens
70. Aged, to Pliny: abbr.
72. Continental prefix
74. Mannerly bloke
77. Shopping, banking, etc.
79. "Mommie ____"
81. Babys' playthings
82. Kind of trip
84. Dune dust
86. Causes to be euphoric
88. Stingers
89. "Some Like ____"
90. Bedtime ritual for a tot
91. Politician Gary
93. Chirpers' homes
95. Remain
97. Road-map abbrs.
99. Pursue a fly
101. Dutch cheese
103. Black bird
104. Nationality suffix
106. Ship's curved planking

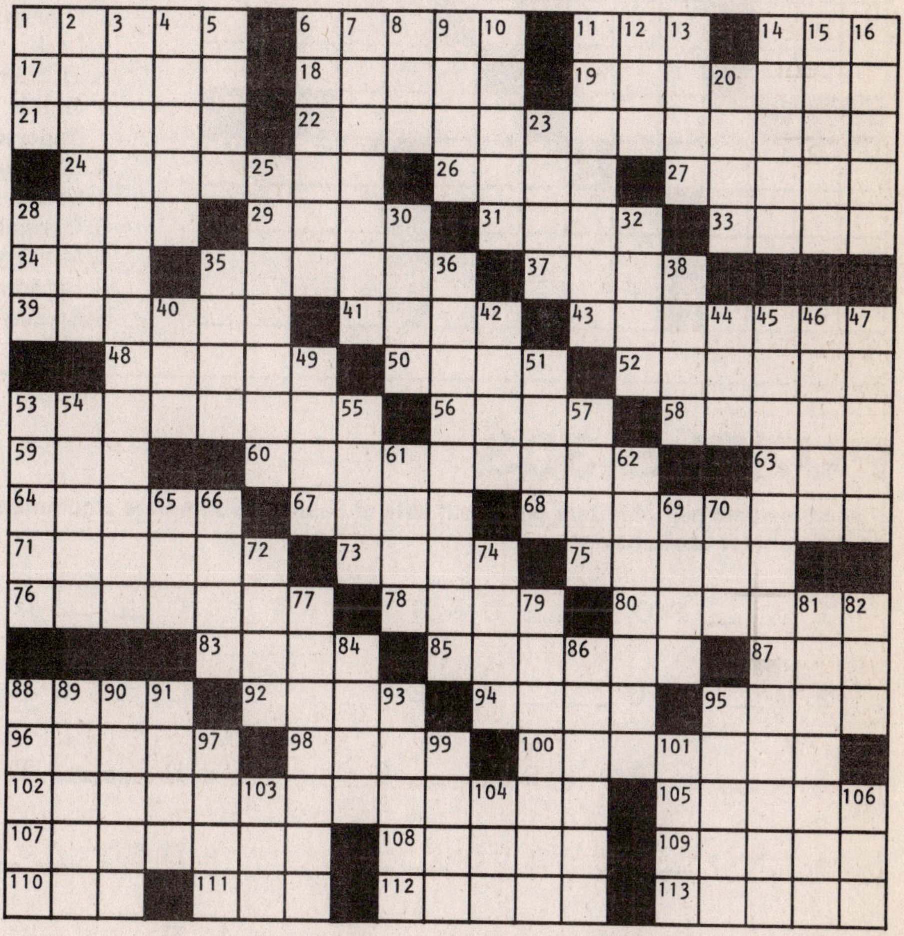

# PUZZLE 302

**ACROSS**
1. Finishes
5. Respond
10. At what time
14. Hurdle
15. Blooper
16. In this place
17. Large van
18. Rhythm
19. Leave out
20. Idyllic place
21. Frosty
22. Throbs
24. Type
26. Stand up
27. Sculptor's product
30. ___ the music
31. Play section
34. Turret
35. Dinner course
36. Cow utterance
37. Stench
38. Refrigerate
39. Garment feature
40. Red or pin follower
41. Glistening
42. Feel
43. Tint
44. Exited
45. Elegant meals
46. Channel
47. Sketched
48. Comment
51. Route
52. Hairstyle
56. Eager
57. Creme de la creme
59. Neckwear
60. Transmit
61. Recommend
62. Wicked
63. Target
64. Plants
65. Gambling town

**DOWN**
1. Otherwise
2. Lack
3. Title for Judith Anderson
4. Old maid
5. Go to bed
6. Upright
7. Military group
8. Beat walker
9. Steamy
10. Entire
11. Borders
12. Great Lake
13. Butterfly catchers
23. Secondhand
25. "___ Town"
26. Bounce back
27. Tolerated
28. Morning show
29. Became active
30. Swoon
31. Prayer words
32. Shoreline
33. Heavy books
35. Adjustment
38. Board game
39. Ocean liquid
41. Slanderous statement
42. Witness
45. Certain chickens
46. Sugar ___
47. Passe
48. Rough file
49. At any time
50. Coal source
51. Spouse
53. ___-and-dime
54. Constraint
55. Norway's capital
58. Golfer Trevino

# PUZZLE 303

## Pairs

**Place the same pair of letters onto both sets of dashes to complete a common word. The pair of letters will be different for each answer.**

1. ___ ___ F O ___ ___ D E D

2. M ___ ___ G ___ ___ E S E

3. H ___ ___ R T B R ___ ___ K

4. I N D ___ ___ T R I O ___ ___

5. M ___ ___ N T ___ ___ N

6. C ___ ___ D I T I ___ ___

7. ___ ___ L ___ ___ T Y

8. D ___ ___ T I N G U ___ ___ H

9. D E P ___ ___ D ___ ___ C E

10. H ___ ___ D W ___ ___ E

# PUZZLE 304

**ACROSS**

1. Film starring Cher
5. Lady of Spain
9. Hep ones
13. As soon as
14. Pitcher
15. Betel palm
17. All-he party
18. Wagon
19. Boca ____
20. Gawain's title
21. Fall sight: 2 wds.
23. Large African antelope
25. Indicates, in a way
26. Greet
28. Some signs
30. Sausage
31. Fly alone
32. Recipe amt.
35. Swedish name for Turku
36. Fall, in Paris
39. Tick-tack-toe win
40. Evergreen tree
41. Impudence
42. Illuminators
44. Habituate
46. Metal-worker's shop
47. Borrowed car
50. Japanese city
51. "When the frost is ____": 3 wds.
54. File
57. Diminished
58. Stir up
59. Gumbo
60. Springe
61. Away from the wind
62. Neb
63. ____ Scott
64. Lad's love
65. "Auld Lang ____"

**DOWN**

1. Shade of green
2. Con
3. Bolger role
4. Beer barrel
5. Pour gently
6. Prize
7. Host Griffin
8. Comedian Johnson
9. Box
10. One Musketeer
11. Dakota Indian
12. Dart
16. Miller and Jillian
21. ____ la vista
22. Table implement
24. ____ Alamitos
26. Not home
27. Lump of ice
28. Slipknot
29. "Desire Under the ____"
31. Bill-topper
32. Nervous male, around Thanksgiving: 2 wds.
33. Frosh's senior
34. Nosegay
37. Take wrongfully
38. Violinist Mischa
43. Broadcast
44. Be an organic part
45. Lacked
46. Subway gates
47. Tennis shots
48. ____ off (intermittently): 2 wds.
49. Rose essence
50. Steinbeck figures
52. Asian river
53. 1916 hit
55. Mediterranean port
56. Pacific island
59. Archaic: abbr.

# CROSS ARITHMETIC

# PUZZLE 305

**Can you figure out what digit, 0 through 9, each letter stands for so that the arithmetic solves correctly across each line and down each column? The number substitution is different for each of the puzzles.**

1.

| | | | | |
|---|---|---|---|---|
| FAKC | + | ACHHF | = | ABGHB |
| + | | + | | + |
| EBAK | + | FGEKK | = | AKKAK |
| = | | = | | = |
| BJAC | + | HEKCHF | = | HEBGGB |

2.

| | | | | |
|---|---|---|---|---|
| DDEHE | ÷ | HE | = | AKC |
| − | | X | | + |
| CKBG | − | FEH | = | FBBF |
| = | | = | | = |
| KCBCJ | − | KEJCE | = | CCEJ |

# PUZZLE 306

**ACROSS**

1. Honey holder
5. Kind of bar
10. Eh?
14. Region
15. ____ con carne
16. Midwest state
17. Church rite
18. Cures
19. Hammer, e.g.
20. Otherwise
21. Paddle
22. "One, two, ____ my shoe"
24. Disposition
26. Be quiet!
27. Charm
30. Be concerned
31. Pub brew
34. Sorehead
35. Ecstasy
36. ____ rummy
37. Littlest of the litter
38. Blackboard
39. Pre-Easter period
40. Conclude
41. City of the Dolphins
42. Big loser
43. Sargasso, for one
44. Totals
45. Larder
46. Gratis
47. Ms. Evans
48. Expose
51. "____ Miniver"
52. Window part
56. ____ estate
57. Blockhead
59. Midwest state
60. ____ and crafts
61. Pigment
62. Additional
63. Misplace
64. Shade of green
65. Facial orbs

**DOWN**

1. Arrived
2. By mouth
3. Confusion
4. Cellar
5. Learning institution
6. In front
7. Fibber
8. Everyone
9. Pay out
10. Crone
11. Fastener
12. Military acronym
13. Story
23. Applications
25. Mighty tree
26. West Indian republic
27. Land measures
28. Trim away
29. Zoo celebrity
30. Mollusks
31. Broker
32. Cruise ship
33. Foyer
35. Sword
38. Chum
39. Sad and solitary
41. Red planet
42. "My ____ Sal"
45. Bakery offering
46. Misleading
47. Slobber
48. Asian river
49. Roman fiddler
50. Wilander of tennis
51. Flour factory
53. Nautical greeting
54. Father
55. Works in the garden
58. Female deer

# PUZZLE 307

## Dash It

**Put the listed words onto the dashes to form eight hyphenated phrases. Some of the words may be appropriate on more than one dash, but, dash it, there's only one combination which uses each of the listed words only once.**

| | | | |
|---|---|---|---|
| AIDE | DO | HEELS | TOUCH |
| CAMP | DOORS | JACK | TRADES |
| CUFF | DOWN | OFF | WILL |
| DIE | GO | OUT | WISP |

1. ________ -O'-THE- ________
2. ________ -DE- ________
3. ________ -OF- ________
4. ________ -AND- ________
5. ________ -OF-ALL- ________
6. ________ -THE- ________
7. ________ -AT-THE- ________
8. ________ -OR- ________

# PUZZLE 308

**• BEFORE AND AFTER •**

**ACROSS**

1. Crowlike bird
4. Clean the deck
8. Pen name of H.H. Munro
12. Uprights for sailing vessels
17. Capek play
18. Mr. Agnew
19. Companion of the "Santa Maria"
21. Summon
22. Uris character
23. Trumpet-playing bandleader/U.S. President
26. Expert skill
28. Hindu woman's garment
29. Entreaty
30. Movie dog
31. For each
32. Ingredient for a molded salad
35. Dreaming stage of sleep
38. Resort
40. Breezy
41. Periods of time
43. "Paradise Lost" author/Mr. Television
49. Large flightless bird
50. Parrot
51. Figurative expression
52. Miss Kett
53. Hags
56. Energy
57. Astrological scales
58. Caustic substance
59. Debases
60. Med. student's course
62. Immobilize by lack of wind
64. Viewed
65. Wind dir.
66. "____ Lucy"
67. ____ vitriol
70. Breakfast item
73. Declare to be true
75. Darker from the sun
77. Dull in color
79. Judicial order
82. Fowl
83. Solemn vows
86. Consumed
87. Entertained
88. Traditional knowledge
89. Dickens's Mr. Heep
90. Author of "Annabel Lee"
91. Floor cleaner
92. The Duke/Trapper John portrayer
95. Slanted
97. Disco dance
98. Obtain
99. Ram's mate
100. Instruct
102. Hustle and bustle
104. Opera highlight
108. Plant base
109. Bergen's Mortimer
111. Looking shortsightedly
114. Lamb Chop's puppeteer/"Through the Looking Glass" author
119. Poem
120. Subway disc
121. Item for a library
122. Chief Justice Warren et al.
123. Can
124. Birthday celebrations
125. Depend
126. What rain does
127. ". . . ____ on a tuffet"

**DOWN**

1. Theater offering
2. Emanations
3. Arm joint
4. Shadowbox
5. Lean and tough
6. Airport info.
7. "The ____ from Brazil"
8. Extra
9. Pointer
10. ". . . with a banjo on my ____"
11. "____ Now or Never"
12. Wife of Jason
13. Steer a plane
14. 3 dots, 3 dashes, 3 dots
15. Bout ender: abbr.
16. Tokyo Exchange unit
18. Haggard novel
20. Unit of electrical current
24. Nippon
25. Confederate
27. Mountain lake
32. ____ monster
33. Actress Dunne
34. Title giver
36. Actor Jannings
37. The south of France
38. Saver
39. Crushed apples
40. Comic Johnson
42. Figure out, to a Brit
43. Main island of Indonesia
44. Suggest
45. Macho one
46. Ad ____
47. Ringer
48. Origin of a word
53. Musical symbol
54. Fish eggs
55. Held the title to
61. Shreds
63. In a backward direction
64. Troop movement to attack
66. Give attention to
68. Sen. Daniel K. ____
69. Memorized
71. Wine fruit
72. Croc's relative
74. Victory sign
76. One more time
78. Buzzers
79. Lady of Spain
80. Give a hammy performance
81. Emissary of love
82. Santa's expression
84. Tortoise's opponent
85. Reveal
88. Theater box
92. Wrote down hurriedly
93. Greek marketplace
94. Tackle
96. Happy cat
97. Prison
101. Dime and penny
102. Famed photographer Adams
103. Belittle
105. Uproars in the streets
106. Gandhi's country
107. Representative
109. Location
110. Miss Barrymore
111. Ship's destination
112. Building extensions
113. Overhead trains
114. Pen
115. Gardening tool
116. Alias designation: abbr.
117. Feud
118. "Norma ____"

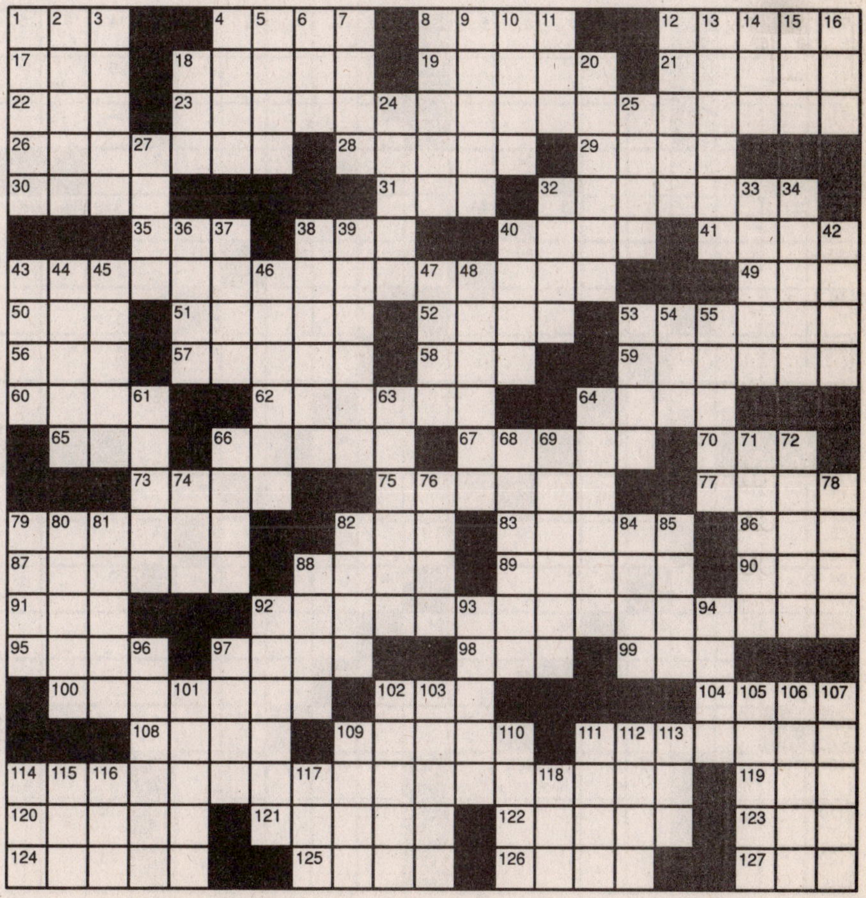

# PUZZLE 309

**ACROSS**
1. Scribble
4. Shore
9. Demon
14. Fuss
17. Hail!
18. Out of practice
19. Marconi's invention
20. Sun god
21. Tavern
22. Flammable liquid
23. Represent in a play
24. Type of shirt
25. Wander
27. Schools of whales
29. Gauge
31. Flier
34. Decorative fabric
36. Insurrection
39. Yellow flower
41. Eastern mental discipline
43. Greasy spoon
44. ____ Baba
45. Change color again
47. Bag
49. Affection
50. Argued in court
52. Bowler
54. Without hearing
56. "Stouthearted ____"
57. Spring and neap
59. Dissident
61. Meandered
63. Long span of time
65. Closes
67. Piece of corn
68. Magic lamp holder
72. Theatrical production
74. Conference site
78. Malicious assertions
79. Sleeveless Arab garments
81. Brainy
83. Grease
84. Roof part
86. Door base
88. Edgar ____ Poe
90. Vogue
91. Floats
93. Take it easy
95. Tart drink
97. Climb
99. Arab prince
101. Siberian dog
102. Oriental
104. Legumes
106. Puff up
107. Airliner
109. More generous
111. Author Sontag
113. Typewriter key
116. Tavern order
117. Furnace
118. Serenity
119. Prosecute
120. Clear
121. Cigar
122. Supply with fuel
123. Scratch

**DOWN**
1. Punch
2. Reproductive cells
3. Afraid
4. Inventor
5. Obsolete
6. Coal residue
7. Pace
8. Austrian Alps
9. Sistine Chapel sights
10. Singer Janis ____
11. Cheese from Holland
12. More congenial
13. Sprinkled with
14. Star study
15. Female goat
16. Bullfight shout
26. Klutz
28. "A Foggy ____"
30. Wicked
31. Modify
32. Four Seasons singer
33. Passenger
35. Yikes!
37. River bank
38. Tendency
40. Greek stringed instruments
42. High cards
46. Diminished
48. Actress Nelligan
51. Title
53. "Two ____ Before the Mast"
55. Brawl
58. Fizzy beverage
60. South American animal
62. Sea east of the Caspian
64. Penpoints
66. Picayune
68. One-celled animal
69. Hawaiian feasts
70. Recommended
71. Spike
73. City on the Rhone
75. French general
76. Occupation
77. Totaled
80. ____ gin
82. Larch
85. "Lyin' ____"
87. Eel
89. Candidate
92. Smells
94. Exclamation of disapproval
96. Negative responses
98. Fortuneteller's aid
100. Grates
103. Roman emperor
105. Animal fat
107. Disturb
108. Yale student
110. Omelet ingredient
112. ____ Paulo
114. Clumsy boat
115. Ciao

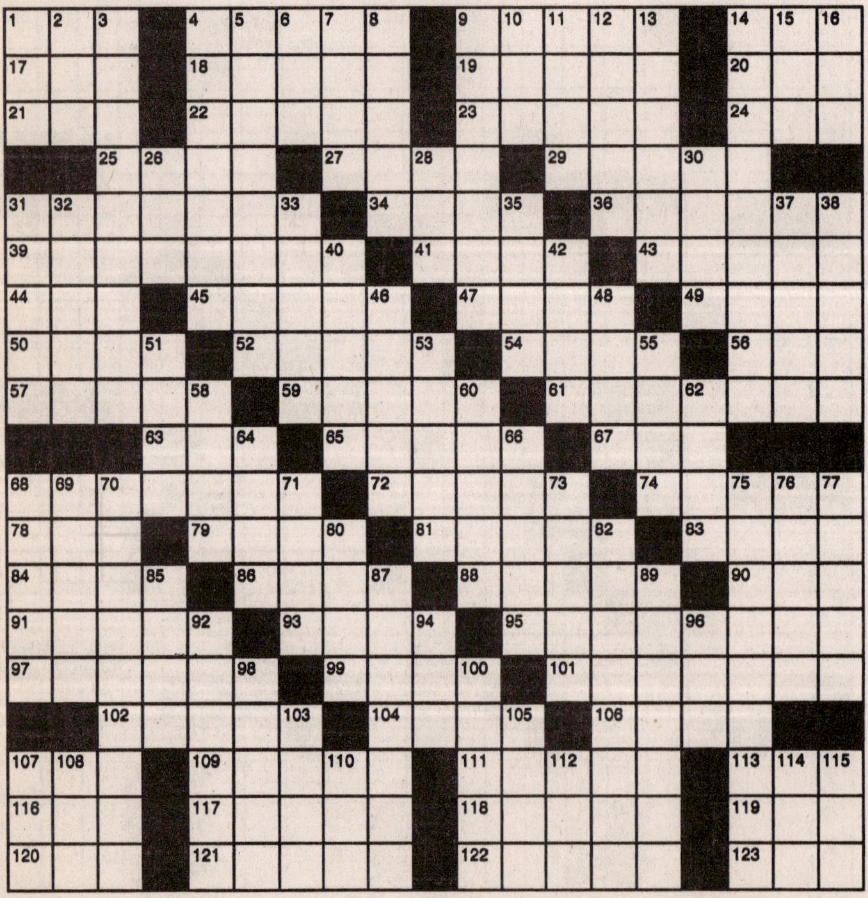

# PUZZLE 310

**• PLEASANT MELODIES •**

**ACROSS**

1. Rainbow
4. Sheep call
7. "Norma ____"
10. Peeled
13. Finish
14. Unmoving
16. Julie Andrews film
19. Adolescent
20. "Penny ____" (Beatles song)
21. Sault ____ Marie
23. Form
27. Curvy letter
30. Persian ruler
32. Weird
33. Audition tape
35. Skin opening
36. Groups of six singers
38. Ebb ____
40. First man
41. Thither
42. Collection
44. Winter toy
45. Canadian-American lake
47. Movie lobby sights
49. Soft drink
50. Poi root
51. Presidential advisory group
54. Dutch cheeses
56. Oil cartel: abbr.
57. ____ Vegas
59. "____ So Easy" (Ronstadt song)
60. Provo's state
63. Semester
64. Cellos, e.g.
68. Stuffing herb
69. ____ dunk
71. Summer TV fare
72. Golf club
73. Compass pt.
74. Violin maker
75. King topper
76. Jai ____
79. Adjective for Wilt Chamberlain
82. Good news
89. Cove
90. Exist
91. Residences
92. "____ and Night"
93. Golf gadget
94. Keats work

**DOWN**

1. Clever
2. Stadium cheer
3. Mediterranean island
4. Big ____
5. Also
6. Fuss
7. Sow again
8. Onassis, to pals
9. Catchall abbr.
11. Natives: suff.
12. John or Jane
14. Miss Hogg
15. Religious woman
17. Hidden
18. Armadas
21. Conductor Caldwell
22. Robert Preston film
24. Bewitch
25. Columnist Buchwald
26. ____ in the sky
28. Orchestrates
29. "Candid Camera" word
30. Health resort
31. Brick carrier
34. Baltic feeder
36. Instrumental compositions
37. Groups of seven singers
39. Newspaper people: abbr.
41. Sing, Swiss-style
43. Amphibians
46. Actor Ely
48. Spanish Mrs.
51. Rollaway bed
52. Primates
53. Uncle Miltie
55. Look hard
58. Narrow waterway
59. Light
61. Past
62. Layer
65. Sleep phenomenon: abbr.
66. Author Levin
67. Pecan, for one
70. Skimpy
75. Texas shrine
77. Fib
78. Behave
80. Bat wood
81. Durocher
82. In the center of
83. Actress Merkel
84. Cereal grain
85. Raw mineral
86. Born
87. ____ herring
88. Wind dir.

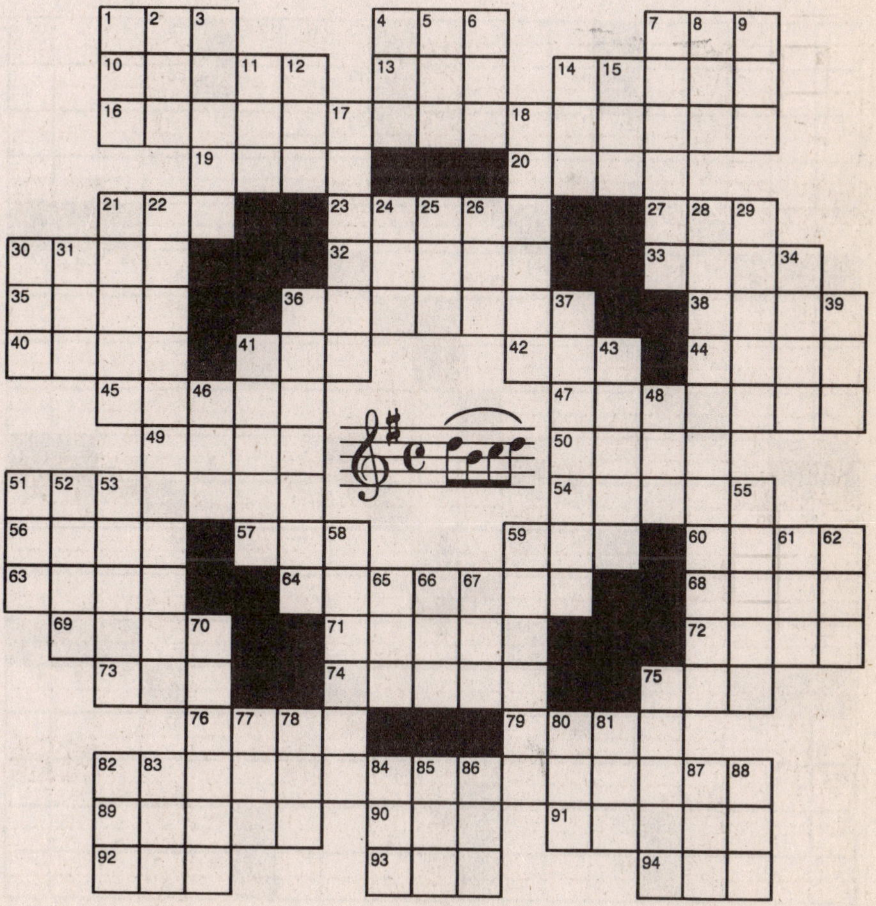

# PUZZLE 311

**ACROSS**

1. "The ____ John B"
6. Baths
10. Toward the stern
13. Town, in Holland
17. Delhi dialect
18. Record
19. Household god
20. "Ruy Blas" author
21. Perform precipitately: 3 wds.
23. Handel masterpiece
25. Sea songs
26. Supported: 3 wds.
28. Laotian money
29. "____ gratia artis"
30. McNamara of the comics
31. Guido's note
32. White lie
33. Eft
34. Perforates
38. Mark of the comics
41. British Olympic runner
42. Place for potatoes
43. Oven
44. Dam
45. Chinese house idol
46. "Have ____ Will Travel"
47. Bright and cheerful
48. Paddle
49. Angular
50. Rattlesnake
52. Black suit
54. Dawn goddess
55. Sycophant
56. Risers' places: 2 wds.
59. Seniors' dance
60. "____ Stop"
63. Wore: 2 wds.
64. Actress MacGraw
65. Coaster
66. Orient
67. Church corner
68. Sign
69. Cultivator
70. Panoply
71. Hits the right cards: 2 wds.
73. Tiff
75. Stein
76. ____ Browne belt
77. Movie
78. Underworld god
79. Grand ____, Nova Scotia
82. Musical comedy: 2 wds.
86. Hard metal: 2 wds.
88. Asian shrub
89. Declared a loser: 2 wds.
91. Bring up
92. LBJ dog
93. Seine tributary
94. Lariat
95. Wheel shaft
96. George Smiley, for one
97. Short or spare items
98. Artist's stand

**DOWN**

1. Lean-to
2. Chinese fruit
3. Ready to go: 2 wds.
4. Norse god
5. Type of duck
6. Remains
7. Bridge call
8. Likely
9. Teeter
10. Take ____ (glance): 2 wds.
11. Gambling game
12. Used car: hyph.
13. Hunt for bargains: 2 wds.
14. Sod
15. Exchange premium
16. Portal
22. Sage, e.g.
24. California bulrush
27. Explosive
30. River of England
32. Evergreen
33. Snooping
34. Evergreen: 2 wds.
35. Check-out counter buy: 2 wds.
36. Serf
37. River in the Ukraine
38. "____ Gentlemen of Verona"
39. Turmeric
40. Pilot in training: 2 wds.
41. Unchanging
42. Laughable Abbott
45. Careers
46. Soldiers: abbr.
47. Thailand, once
49. Scald
50. Help!
51. Copse
53. Biggest portion: 2 wds.
54. Steeple topping
56. Rug type
57. Domesticated
58. Wapiti
59. Scheme
61. "Born in the ____"
62. Messy place
65. Fake
66. Unit of work
68. Showy, yellow insects: 2 wds.
70. Spartan
72. Skimmers
73. Polite address
74. Kind of mine
75. Light fog
77. Transport to Staten Island
78. Jutland natives
79. Malay boats
80. Circuit
81. Inner
82. Tree snake
83. Holm oak
84. Terrestrial
85. Coop sound
86. Sidewalk edge
87. Notion
90. Yes, madame!

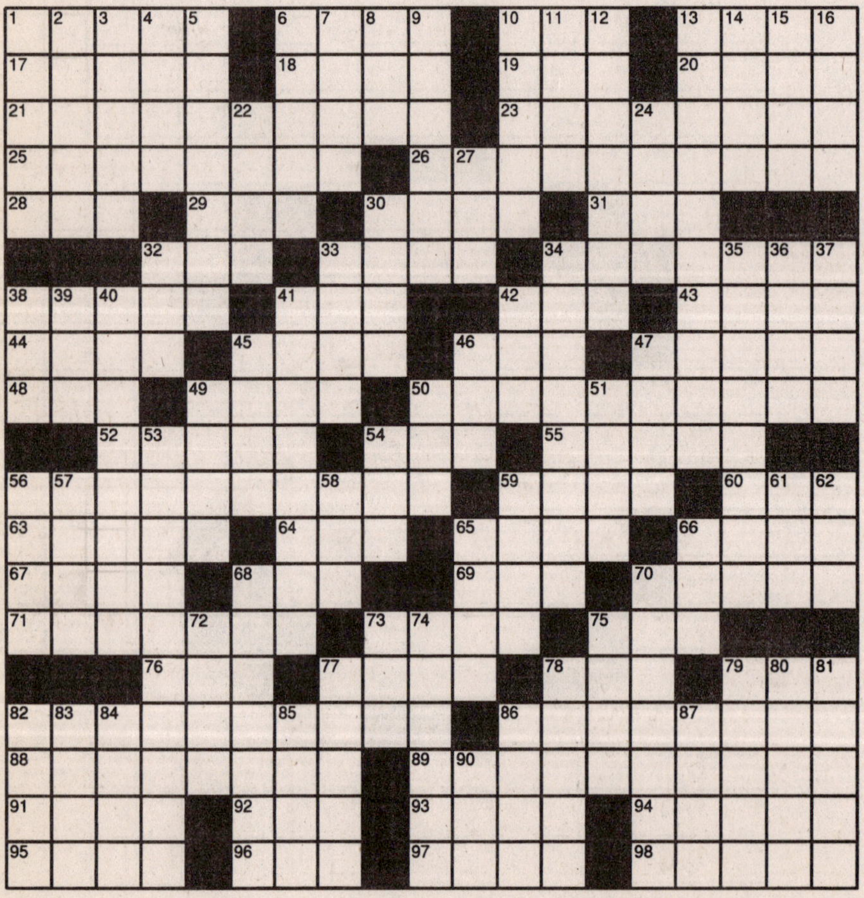

# PUZZLE 312

**• GET SMART •**

## ACROSS

1. ___ boy!
5. Shapeless
9. Martini additive
14. ___ patriae
18. Brood
19. Mother of Romulus and Remus
20. New Year's merrymaker
21. Stack
22. Narrow waterways
23. Classic cases
26. Gave permission
28. Ottomans
29. Distribute
30. Goat's coat
31. Jilt
32. See the light
35. Savoie season
36. Passes muster
39. Meadow, in France
42. Mix anew
44. Recurring midnight-movie film
46. Botanist Gray
47. Berlin, to friends
48. Above-the-ground locale
50. Osmose
51. One element of a cube
53. "The Pink Panther" star
55. MMMCLIII÷III
56. Antisocial one
57. Hervey and Cara
59. Lute's cousin
61. French vineyard
63. Take a bow!
71. Half a Latin dance
72. Not now
73. Having potential
74. Cradle's perch, in song
78. Belgian resort
81. Of an area
83. Sajak, e.g.
84. ___ time (never)
85. More minute
87. Kind of treatment
89. Byrnes or Roush
90. Necessities for baby
93. "I think my love ___ . . ." (Shakespeare)
95. Stolen
96. Like some suiting
100. Monk's title
103. ___ mer
104. Mrs. Mertz
105. Neptune, e.g.
107. Relative by marriage
110. Penned
111. Out of action
112. Reforms
117. Marcher on?
118. "Daily Planet" worker
119. Faucet
120. Wield a blue pencil
121. Baker
122. "___ at the Races"
123. Fifty minutes past
124. Has a virus
125. Square

## DOWN

1. Triangular support
2. Knitted fabric
3. Gable-Day movie
4. On the Atlantic
5. Intelligentsia
6. ___Yeu, France
7. Conglomeration
8. LaBelle and Page
9. Observed a warning
10. Lo mein cookers
11. Native: suffix
12. Topic for Dr. Ruth
13. ___-la-la
14. Bobbed-for item
15. Manufacturing site
16. Poor man's butter
17. Repose
20. Type of song
24. Cigar or pork
25. Productive one
27. Lowers, as a lamp
31. Moslem whirler
32. Thin as ___
33. "And he ___ yes . . ." ("Richard Cory")
34. Cooling quaff
37. Churn, in Spennymoor
38. 1/28 oz.
39. Worker in Oaxaca
40. Use a wrecking ball
41. Berleburg's river
43. ". . . could ___ fat"
45. Follower of boo
46. Prefix meaning gas
48. Gold, e.g.
49. Stunned
51. Malicious bit
52. Yosemite Park's ___ Hetchy Valley
54. What rivals do
56. Desi's daughter
58. Pipe down!
60. Spinning device
62. Preacher, for short
64. Section of London
65. Marsh
66. Hardship
67. Less convincing
68. "___ got a gal in Kalamazoo"
69. One-way vehicle
70. Notice
74. "Six English Suites" composer
75. Other, in Oviedo
76. Constituent
77. Navy man
79. Wedge
80. Naysayer
82. Struggle with sibilants
86. ___ Langerhans
88. Introduces
91. Be the source of
92. Goddess of Niflheim
94. Yemen's capital
97. This gives one a lift
98. Archaic pronoun
99. Waters off Saudi Arabia
101. German wineglass
102. Sum component
103. 1955 film
106. Knightly garb
107. Actress Chase
108. Necessity
109. A Turner
110. Lily
111. Cook three-minute eggs
113. Swift craft
114. Unlatch, to a poet
115. Writer Anais
116. "Star Wars," politically

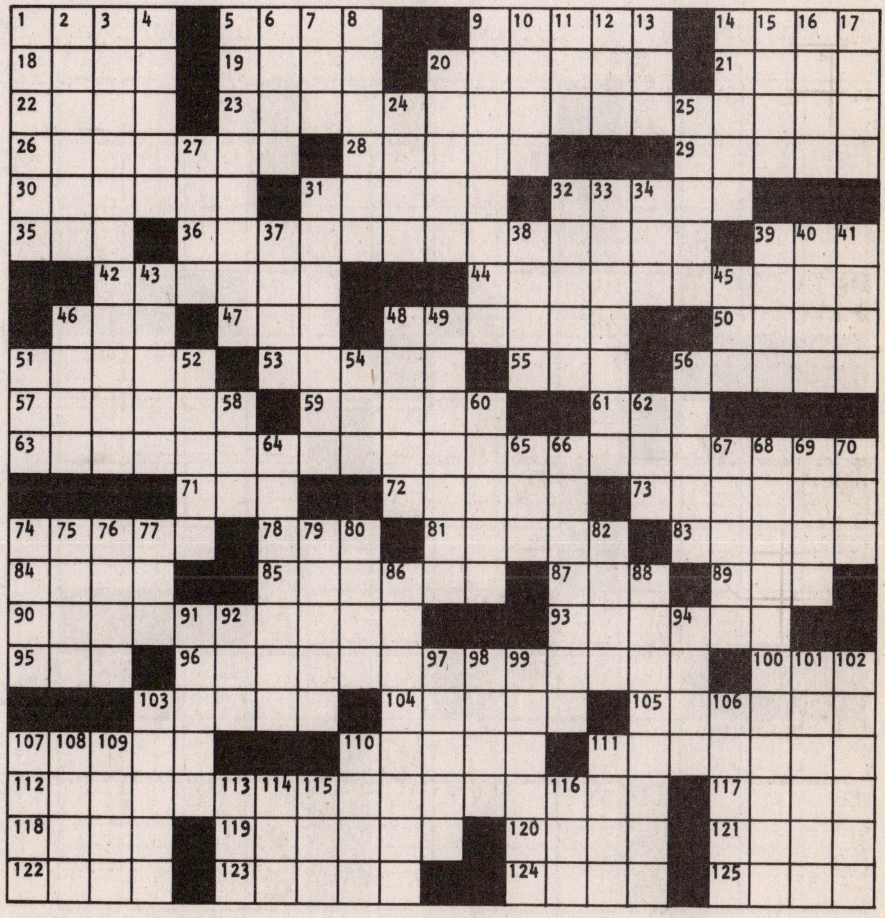

# PUZZLE 313

**ACROSS**

1. Apple's center
5. Morse or ZIP
9. Gallery display
12. Prayer ending
13. Highly impressed
14. Take to court
15. Curve
16. Elongate
18. Sleep
20. Herbal drink
21. "I ____ Forget You"
23. Cut violently
27. Baby bear
30. Lyric poems
32. Leer at
33. Dollar bills
35. Hatchet
36. Close by
37. What Santa checks twice
38. Speed contest
40. Change the color of
41. Garret
43. Confident
45. ____ Vegas, Nevada
47. Logic
51. Tiny bit
55. Clamping tool
56. Mine rock
57. Train track
58. Building wings
59. Marry
60. Follow orders
61. Coin opening

**DOWN**

1. Taxis
2. Sign of the future
3. Nevada gambling city
4. Establish a fund for
5. Date chart
6. Have debts
7. Fender-bender result
8. Borders
9. Fire remains
10. Regret
11. Twice five
17. Eagle's claw
19. Animal park
22. Dallas's state
24. Grew older
25. Do in
26. In this place
27. Soda flavor
28. Army group
29. Finest
31. Safely
34. Walking pole
39. Before, in poetry
42. Egypt's capital
44. Roof overhangs
46. Strikebreaker
48. Window ledge
49. Norway's capital
50. Bird's home
51. Sound of a punch
52. "We ____ the World"
53. Scarlet
54. Fib

# PUZZLE 314

**ACROSS**

1. Crow's call
4. Price
8. Wager
11. Public melee
13. ____ and above
14. ____ an egg
15. Fragrance
16. Actor Hackman
17. Pose a question
18. Foot lever
20. Proposed candidate
22. Mediter-ranean, e.g.
24. "____ of Ages"
25. Robin Hood's talent
29. Coral barriers
32. Auto
33. Taxi
35. Earl Grey, e.g.
36. Legislate
39. Used an iron
42. Apple center
44. Picnic pest
45. Ungainly
48. Unpaid bills
52. Cut off
53. Condemn
55. Female horse
56. Paid athlete
57. Boundary
58. Run-down neighborhood
59. Tennis unit
60. Take five
61. Hawaiian necklace

**DOWN**

1. Farm yield
2. General's assistant
3. Timber
4. Gear tooth
5. Baking appliance
6. Mister, in Spain
7. Quake
8. Quilts
9. Relieve
10. Small child
12. Garbage
19. Golfer Trevino
21. Frozen water
23. Joan of ____
25. Expert pilot
26. Sprinted
27. Eccentric person
28. Shrill bark
30. Service charge
31. Melancholy
34. Bikini top
37. Bull's mate
38. Swapper
40. Conclusion
41. Plant stalks
43. Deteriorate
45. Swiss peaks
46. Had on
47. Poodles, e.g.
49. Bowler's orb
50. Factual
51. Trucker's rig
54. Encountered

# PUZZLE 315

**ACROSS**

1. Used a loom
5. Polish
9. Savings plan: abbr.
12. Commotions
13. At a distance
14. Smidgen
15. Decays
16. Put up with
18. Give a sermon
20. Robert E. ____
21. Knitter's material
23. "Driving Miss ____"
27. Fish appendage
30. Frame of mind
32. Traveler Marco ____
33. "____ on a Grecian Urn"
34. Subsided
36. Paving goo
37. Show the way
39. Fitzgerald of jazz
40. Orangutan, e.g.
41. Saw socially
43. James ____ Jones
45. Notable period
47. Affluence
51. Personal magnetism
55. Peel
56. Rower's need
57. Untruthful one
58. Wicked
59. Brief farewell
60. Highway division
61. Lighting fixture

**DOWN**

1. Distort
2. Fragrance
3. Cast a ballot
4. College paper
5. Dressing gown
6. Flying saucer
7. Autumn
8. Gave liberty to
9. Actress Lupino
10. Mouse's kin
11. Actor Vigoda
17. Harvest
19. Arrived
22. High-minded
24. Tiny particle
25. Smack
26. Days of old
27. Crease
28. Thought
29. Tidy
31. Maryland's neighbor
35. Challenge
38. Stag or doe
42. Hole-making tool
44. Jacket flap
46. China's continent
48. Molten rock
49. Cut to size
50. Assist
51. Corn on the ____
52. Dried grass
53. "You ____ There"
54. Adult boy

# PUZZLE 316

**ACROSS**

1. "____ Heart of Mine"
5. Goes astray
9. Weed
12. Decorator's advice
13. Peek
14. Have
15. Territory
16. Enrolled
18. Oysters' treasures
20. Brace
21. Dines
23. Spring bulb
26. Morsel
28. Hard to come by
29. Edge
30. Fragrance
33. Waiter's reward
34. Matterhorn's mountains
36. 66 and 1
38. Cements
40. Agreeable
41. "____ Twist Again"
43. Ice Capades member
47. Jefferson City's state
50. Blacktop
51. Poem
52. Bride's accessory
53. Candid
54. Used to be
55. Swirl
56. Big top, for one

**DOWN**

1. Corner
2. Roll-call response
3. Brainstorm
4. Flew high
5. Springy
6. Dowel
7. Frolic
8. Mini or maxi
9. Small appliance
10. Have creditors
11. Finish
17. Sightsee
19. Places for experiments
22. Strict
24. Eye part
25. Vitality
26. Plow
27. Urges
29. Scrap of cloth
31. Loudly
32. Nip and ____
35. Catches sight of
37. Kitchen whistler
39. Kitchen cooker
42. Took to court
44. Cassette
45. Tied
46. Landlord's due
47. Tend the lawn
48. Actress Lupino
49. Free

# PUZZLE 317

**ACROSS**

1. Partly open, as a door
5. Expense
9. ____ down (recline)
12. Cook bread
13. Solemn vow
14. "____ to Joy"
15. Amend a manuscript
16. Of the East
18. Jeans material
20. ____ Grande
21. Actor's part
24. Lift up
28. Sidewalk surface
32. Wolf's cry
33. Drink cubes
34. Silky fabric
36. Used to be
37. Dispatch
39. Fragile
41. Daisylike flower
43. Nevada city
44. Corn unit
46. "Bald" bird
50. Unexpected event
55. Auto's path
56. Baseball stat
57. Genesis garden
58. Vocalized tune
59. Hill-building insect
60. Marsh plant
61. Swirling current

**DOWN**

1. In the sack
2. Green mineral
3. Related
4. Hit the hay
5. Pigeon's call
6. Rower's need
7. Mix
8. Belonging to them
9. Building parcel
10. Actress Lupino
11. Snaky fish
17. Ark builder
19. Dads' wives
22. Show the way
23. Go in
25. Des Moines's state
26. Smack, as a fly
27. What ____ is new?
28. Leaning Tower city
29. High cards
30. Air outlet
31. Mosaic piece
35. Cat-o'-____-tails
38. Profound
40. Rough-textured
42. More unusual
45. Go by horse
47. Virtuous
48. Come to earth
49. Nervous
50. Mediterranean, e.g.
51. Large vase
52. Ship deserter
53. Witness
54. Terminate

| | | | | | | | | | | | | |
|---|---|---|---|---|---|---|---|---|---|---|---|---|
| 1 A | 2 J | 3 A | 4 R | ■ | 5 C | 6 O | 7 S | 8 T | ■ | 9 L | 10 A | 11 E |
| 12 B | A | K | E | ■ | 13 O | A | T | H | ■ | 14 O | D | E |
| 15 E | D | I | T | ■ | 16 O | R | I | E | 17 N | T | A | L |
| 18 D | E | N | I | 19 M | ■ | ■ | 20 R | I | D | ■ | ■ | ■ |
| ■ | ■ | ■ | 21 R | O | 22 L | 23 E | ■ | 24 R | A | 25 I | 26 S | 27 E |
| 28 P | 29 A | 30 V | E | M | E | N | 31 T | ■ | 32 H | O | W | L |
| 33 I | C | E | ■ | 34 S | A | T | I | 35 N | ■ | 36 W | A | S |
| 37 S | E | N | 38 D | ■ | 39 D | E | L | I | 40 C | A | T | E |
| 41 A | S | T | E | 42 R | ■ | 43 R | E | N | O | ■ | ■ | ■ |
| ■ | ■ | ■ | 44 E | A | 45 R | ■ | ■ | 46 E | A | 47 G | 48 L | 49 E |
| 50 S | 51 E | 52 R | | R | O | 53 S | 54 E | ■ | 55 R | O | A | D |
| 56 E | R | A | ■ | 57 E | D | E | N | ■ | 58 S | O | N | G |
| 59 A | N | T | ■ | 60 R | E | E | D | ■ | 61 E | D | D | Y |

## TRIPLE PLAY

# PUZZLE 318

**Some of the clues in this crossword are Triple Play clues. They consist of three words separated by commas. The answer to a Triple Play clue is a word that can precede or follow each of the three words to form a common phrase, name, or compound word. For example, the answer to "Shelter, Income, Payer" is TAX (Tax shelter, Income tax, Taxpayer).**

**ACROSS**

1. Church recess
5. Melancholy
8. Plant stalk
12. Bellow
13. Railroad, Family, Clasp
14. Dream, Stove, Organ
15. Soft drink flavor
16. Chair, Pit, Rest
17. Portent
18. Pine substance
20. Concur
22. Table, Zone, Run
23. Tennis, Fish, Profit
24. Oak seeds
27. Gobi, Fever, Rat
31. Jig, Horse, Coping
32. Hold, Big, Dance
33. Already adjusted
37. Procession
40. In favor of
41. Stone, Old, Bronze
42. Begone!
44. Large parrot
47. Java's neighbor
48. Bottle, Baseball, Gun
50. Egg-shaped
52. Teheran's site
53. House, Wife, Ginger
54. Perform again
55. Crooner Crosby
56. Pine, Paper, Heel
57. Sketched

**DOWN**

1. Joan of ____
2. Richard, Boy, Box
3. Garage, Fire, Clearance
4. Pencil top
5. Tolerates
6. Rifle, Force, Brush
7. Insist upon
8. Spoil, Jacket, Cast
9. Bomb, Capsule, Warp
10. Dueling sword
11. Chess, Wise, Gentle
19. Small hotel
21. ____ whiz!
24. Deadly snake
25. Trolley, Hop, Wash
26. Have debts
28. Airport abbr.
29. Fishing, Curtain, Hot
30. Golf, Shirt, Off
34. Hand, Board, Training
35. Baseball stat
36. Male feline
37. Indulge
38. ____ Khan
39. Player, World, Public
42. Robe of India
43. Family group
45. Declare
46. Walk in water
47. Baby's napkin
49. Pie ____ mode
51. Brow, Key, Tide

# PUZZLE 319

**ACROSS**

1. Tavern order
4. Faucet problem
8. Peel
12. Neither here ____ there
13. Ethnic group
14. Zone
15. Mother Goose tales
18. Function
19. Supermarket lane
20. Coffee shops
23. Front of the leg
25. Colors
26. Caviar-producing fish
30. Wrath
31. Twosomes
32. Singer Eartha ____ Kitt
33. Flamenco dancer's instrument
35. Fielder's glove
36. Historic times
37. Tub soakings
38. Stringed instrument
41. Actor Vereen
42. Daring
48. Observed
49. At a distance
50. No vote
51. Sour
52. Dozes
53. Prior to, poetically

**DOWN**

1. Actress ____-Margret
2. Comedian Costello
3. Miscalculate
4. Gown
5. Uncommon
6. Frozen
7. Part of MPH
8. Remitting funds
9. "A Farewell to ____"
10. Film spool
11. Loosen
16. Prosecutes
17. Bristles
20. Fashionable
21. Atmosphere
22. Fixed charges
23. Pigs' homes
24. Injured
26. Mentally healthy
27. Give off
28. Vow
29. Brooklyn team
31. Heathen
34. Natural capability
35. Supplies with personnel
37. Pilsner and lager, e.g.
38. Huge
39. Brainstorm
40. Completed
41. Small nail
43. Light brown
44. Alien's ship
45. "A Chorus Line" number
46. Deface
47. Sight organ

# PUZZLE 320

**ACROSS**

1. Thing
5. Actor Baldwin
9. Strange
12. Steak order
13. Game on horseback
14. Actor Majors
15. Sprightly
17. News anchor Rather
18. Auto fuel
19. Bowed down
21. Cozy
24. Foreign goods
26. Fusses
27. Apple, e.g.
28. Stitch
29. Lift up
30. Change the color of
33. Solo
34. Neckwear items
35. Horses' pens
38. Air ducts
39. Little green man?
40. Goal
41. Short swim
42. Stevenson children's classic
48. First lady
49. Revise copy
50. Rip
51. "The ____ Commandments"
52. Labels
53. Nimble

**DOWN**

1. Wrath
2. Sun-bronzed
3. Before, in verse
4. Unites
5. Gorillas, e.g.
6. House site
7. Yale grad
8. Pilot's perch
9. More ancient
10. Distributed, as cards
11. Fender-bender results
16. Merry
20. Believe it or ____!
21. Possesses
22. "____ on a Grecian Urn"
23. Cut the lawn
24. Presses
25. Ponder
27. Hoodwink
29. Quilt
30. Loud commotion
31. Until now
32. Double curve
33. "We ____ the World"
34. Entices
35. West Point student
36. Martini garnish
37. Mature
38. By route of
40. Picnic pests
43. Actress Lupino
44. Excavate
45. Energy
46. Play it by ____
47. Thirsty

# PUZZLE 321

**ACROSS**

1. Owned
4. Yearn
8. Nip
12. Bullfighter's cheer
13. Slipper
14. Paradise
15. Wind toy
17. ____ a hand
18. Chop
19. Swimming holes
20. Embrace
23. Search
24. Follow orders
25. Crooning
28. Shake a ____
29. Cheerful
31. Dove's comment
32. Now
34. At the ____ time
35. Hearing organs
36. Evening wraps
38. Actress Davis
40. Lyricist Gershwin
41. Overdue
42. Hydrant
47. "____ the Rainbow"
48. Region
49. Before, in poetry
50. Gets hitched
51. Landlord's fee
52. ____ and all

**DOWN**

1. Jump
2. Famous boxer
3. Library
4. Ruins
5. Gnaws
6. Toolshed item
7. Moray, e.g.
8. Feel at home
9. Matching
10. Take care of
11. Finishes
16. Curd's companion
19. Undersized
20. Soft drink
21. Cain's brother
22. Was sorry for
23. Rose fruit
25. Mata Hari, e.g.
26. Alaskan seaport
27. Leaves
29. Rabbit
30. Newspaper items
33. Diners
34. Lather
36. Tornado warning
37. Handle
38. Gust
39. Roof overhang
42. ____ and wide
43. Wrath
44. Zodiac sign
45. Coffee server
46. Haw's opposite

# PUZZLE 322

**ACROSS**

1. "The Bell ____" (Plath work)
4. Ashen
8. No longer owing
12. Malt beverage
13. Spoken
14. Alan ____ of "M*A*S*H"
15. Nonconformist
17. Gambling machine
18. Student's workplace
19. Manner
20. Counsel
23. Pair
24. Outer garment
25. Got on, as a train
29. Chicago trains
30. Sigourney Weaver film
32. Sugar ____ Leonard
33. Tobogganed
35. ____-and-dime
36. Tattered cloth
37. Aided
39. Water vapor
42. Inlet
43. Public-land area
44. Sharp drop
48. Farmland measure
49. So be it!
50. Actor Aykroyd
51. Prepare salad
52. Finest
53. "Night ____ Day"

**DOWN**

1. Fruit spread
2. Chicken ____ king
3. Gun, as a motor
4. Tiny skin openings
5. Stand up
6. Need
7. Broad-antlered deer
8. Minister
9. Friendly nation
10. Rocker Billy ____
11. Escort
16. Prepare for publication
19. "____ Lake" (ballet)
20. Experts
21. Child's plaything
22. Urn
23. Foot part
25. Auction offer
26. Faucet problem
27. Overhanging roof edge
28. ____-in-the-wool
30. Eve's partner
31. Lower limb
34. Male ducks
35. Ran away
37. Tubes
38. Happening
39. Minor quarrel
40. Filled-tortilla dish
41. Blunders
42. Arrive
44. Catch
45. Neighbor of Mont.
46. Small bus
47. Finish

# PUZZLE 323

**ACROSS**

1. Coat sleeve
4. Specks
8. Jungle animals
12. Twosome
13. Do a laundry chore
14. Title
15. Lovable
17. Adhesive
18. Olympic trophy
19. Small valley
21. Saturated
23. Spun
27. Hubbub
30. Papa
32. Thicket
33. Took the bus
35. Halfway
37. Whirl
38. Flee to wed
40. Bubble or chewing
42. Cunning
43. Swat
45. Large snake
47. Individual
49. Enjoyed
53. Besides
56. Energy
58. Guide
59. Constantly
60. Foot part
61. Errand boy
62. Rough waters
63. Conclude

**DOWN**

1. First man
2. Fresh
3. Temperament
4. Tuned
5. Globe
6. Informed
7. Smile scornfully
8. Fishermen
9. Companion
10. Ostrich's kin
11. Notice
16. Uncooked
20. Lower limb
22. Highlander's cap
24. Chops off
25. Mischievous
26. Declare untrue
27. Son of Zeus
28. Fool
29. Smell
31. Use a spade
34. Event
36. Bestow
39. Piece out
41. Grinding teeth
44. Brownies
46. Be in pain
48. Half a decade
50. Wind toy
51. Short jacket
52. Colored
53. Swiss peak
54. Grazing land
55. Cave in
57. British beverage

# PUZZLE 324

**ACROSS**

1. Information
5. Eden dweller
9. Leather-working tool
12. Spoken
13. Break bread
14. Untruth
15. Challenge
16. Bosses
18. Metal fastener
20. Medicine measures
21. Recognition
24. Director Reiner
25. Desired
26. Knuckle under
27. ____ of luxury
30. Once at any time
31. Milk provider
32. Feeling
33. Cost
34. Careless
35. Color wood
36. Shoot the breeze
37. Fool
38. Male performer
41. Length times width
42. Homeowner's due
44. Baptize
48. Rage
49. Flock mamas
50. Makes a knot
51. Poor grade
52. Cincinnati baseball team
53. Skills

**DOWN**

1. Show sleepiness
2. Generation
3. Battle
4. Thin
5. Confess
6. Tune
7. Dancer Miller
8. Pasture
9. Tavern drinks
10. Metal thread
11. Minus
17. Lump
19. Provide help
21. Cook
22. Ramble
23. Dueling sword
24. Column
26. Crate
27. Hawaiian feast
28. Extremely dry
29. Sheet of glass
31. Baseball ____
32. Georgia's capital
34. Bigger
35. Witness
36. Spoil
37. Outfit
38. Among
39. Apple's center
40. Forest plant
41. Ancient
43. Fear
45. Ventilate
46. Encountered
47. Snaky curve

# PUZZLE 325

**ACROSS**

1. Grown boy
4. Gather in, as crops
8. Part of speech
12. "____ to Billy Joe"
13. Boundary
14. Actress Bancroft
15. Perplex
17. President's no
18. Speaks
19. Buffalo
20. Like a reptile's skin
23. Grand ____ Opry
24. Earring's place
25. Wooded
30. Ostrichlike bird
31. Allotted
32. Route
33. Swamps
35. Knitted
36. Finale
37. Soothed
38. Selected
41. Cab
43. Fishing poles
44. Proclaimed
48. Woodwind instrument
49. Actor Guinness
50. Type of whiskey
51. Shabby
52. Bed support
53. Certain evergreen

**DOWN**

1. Crowd
2. Fruit cooler
3. Modern
4. Type of race
5. Whirlpool
6. Eons
7. Part of RPM
8. Sea forces
9. Dollar bills
10. Do ____ others . . .
11. Colorful sign gas
16. Small land mass
19. Ran, as colors
20. Struck down
21. Approach
22. Adjoin
23. Mine rocks
25. Affectionate
26. Ancient
27. Pairs
28. Roof overhang
29. Colored, as hair
31. Copenhagen native
34. Reduce
35. Lament
37. Precise
38. Blackbird
39. Vagabond
40. Aroma
41. Inform
42. Territory
44. Owns
45. Like a desert
46. Look at
47. Morning moisture

# PUZZLE 326

**ACROSS**

1. Bridge
5. Butter serving
8. Get the word
12. Pitch
13. Regret
14. Eye suggestively
15. What ____ is new?
16. Amusing account
18. Kitten's cry
19. The same
20. Turf
21. Flightless birds
23. Once owned
25. Cavalcade
27. Banishes
31. Place for a roast
32. Father
33. Monotony
36. Admittance chit
38. Dined
39. Fireman's need
40. Actor Vigoda
43. Fiery crime
45. Soaked
48. Gaudier
50. Telegram
51. Atmosphere
52. Decade number
53. Largest continent
54. Depend
55. Firmament
56. Antlered animal

**DOWN**

1. Goblet feature
2. Skier's stick
3. Replied
4. Formerly named
5. Compliment
6. Uncle's wife
7. Grow the pearly whites
8. Coal scuttle
9. Selves
10. Choir singer
11. Bulrush
17. Cajole
19. Flop
22. Obsession
24. Records
25. Lobster trap
26. Blvd.
28. Similarly
29. Sooner than, in poems
30. Matched group
34. Beehive State
35. Deserves
36. Prickly
37. Charged atom
40. A long way off
41. Azure
42. Actor James ____ Jones
44. Search
46. Cleveland's lake
47. Salty eye drop
49. Utter
50. Roll of bills

# PUZZLE 327

**ACROSS**

1. Cobra
4. Daniel ___ Lewis
7. Duo
11. ___ beer
13. Ogle
14. Sailor's greeting
15. Sort
16. Big ___ (London landmark)
17. Baseball's Rose
18. Unit between game and match
20. "I Remember ___"
21. Tall, in Madrid
23. Baltic or Black
25. Cunning
26. Governess
28. Electrical unit
31. Poet's beyond
32. Clump
33. Pasture
34. Small
35. Poet's output
37. Wield
38. Citrus drink
39. Sudden wind
41. Tale
44. Obtained
45. Tender
46. Gawain's title
48. Pot builder?
52. Tug
53. Group of years
54. Put on the payroll
55. Epic city?
56. Path
57. Caustic

**DOWN**

1. Creative product
2. Kind of bean
3. Weasel's sound
4. Obligation
5. Pro vote
6. Monetary unit of Japan
7. Family member
8. Throat clearer
9. Speck
10. Deli bread
12. Evaluate
19. Eternity
20. "___ Fools"
21. To the sheltered side
22. Apollo's instrument
23. Web, e.g.
24. Concludes
25. Plant
27. Astonished
28. European range
29. Thaw
30. Stipend
35. Actor Dick ___ Dyke
36. Conceit
40. Provo's state
41. "___ Cheatin' Heart"
42. Singer Guthrie
43. Depend
44. Actress Erin ___
45. Vessel's destination: abbr.
46. Darn
47. Nest egg
49. Zilch
50. Attempt
51. Cobbler's width

# PUZZLE 328

**ACROSS**

1. Big fiddle
5. Sheep bleat
8. Raised
12. Way out
13. Have title to
14. Bathe
15. Worth a dime
17. ____ code
18. Overwhelm
19. "The ____ of Oz"
21. Follow
24. Pump
25. Racetrack boundary
26. Seattle ____
27. Pie ____ mode
30. Zilch
31. Crown
32. Male turkey
33. Big deer
34. Feed the kitty
35. Corn bread
36. Egg on
37. Jesse or Frank
38. Makes amends
41. Blemish
42. Actress Anderson
43. Boss
48. Help
49. Society-page word
50. Spanish pot
51. Dried up
52. "Annie ____ Your Gun"
53. Cleo's river

**DOWN**

1. Make a wager
2. Lumberjack's tool
3. Offend
4. City in Minnesota
5. Treat for Fido
6. Bristle
7. To whatever extent
8. In a ____ of glory
9. ____ avis
10. Always
11. ____ to the world
16. Meadow grazer
20. Hawkeye State
21. Sea eagle
22. Toolbox item
23. Tie fabric
24. Roofing tile
26. Monotonous verse
27. Smallest particle
28. Unaccompanied
29. Actor Leon ____
31. Weed of the Bible
35. Clergyman
36. Come together
37. Canning item
38. Woe is me!
39. "____ or not . . ."
40. Unique thing
41. Run into
44. 22nd letter
45. Inventor Whitney
46. House wing
47. Actress ____ Dawn Chong

# PUZZLE 329

**ACROSS**

1. B'way musical
5. Sore throat
10. Bridge term
14. Step ____!: 2 wds.
15. Bay window
16. Musician's concern
17. Vincent Lopez's theme
18. French common soldier
19. Air ____
20. Old sailing vessels
22. Tailor's tool
24. Zhivago's beloved
25. Theaters, to Demosthenes
26. Vocal townsmen
29. Always
33. Descends
34. Alligator ____ (avocado)
35. One-armed bandit opening
36. Promising phrase: 2 wds.
37. Earthy deposits
38. Kwa language
39. Lion's pride
41. "Trinity" author
42. Flatware item
44. Shade of hair
46. "Bless the ____ and ____ Children"
47. Ancient country on the Peloponnesus
48. Former coins of Riga
49. Rickenbacker, e.g.
52. Where to see 20 Across: 2 wds.
56. Asian mountains
57. Call forth
59. Vacant
60. Actor Auberjonois
61. Art stand
62. Streak in marble
63. Superlative endings
64. Orchestra members
65. Ms. Bagnold

**DOWN**

1. Viet ____
2. Wild ox
3. Treasury
4. Played for time
5. Deep sleeps
6. Mineral found in a lake basin
7. "The Making of an American" author
8. Grown-up elver
9. Ravages
10. Waterways
11. Freight
12. Source of indigo
13. Persian native
21. Flopsy features
23. Eternally, in verse
25. Ellipses
26. Ascend
27. Detection device
28. Turkish statesman
29. Creepy
30. Potpourris
31. "R.U.R." character
32. Some collars
34. Fractions
37. Fletcher Christian, e.g.
40. Foes
42. Clockman Thomas
43. Grammatical voice
45. High note
46. Bakery buys
48. Took to
49. Rhine feeder
50. ____ du Salut
51. Carry on
52. Nylons
53. Heavenly place
54. Hawaiian royalty
55. Export
58. ____ victis (woe to the vanquished)

# PUZZLE 330

**ACROSS**

1. Fertilizer
5. Kind of myrtle
10. Strikebreaker
14. Mr. Kazan
15. Norse gods
16. Expectation
17. Military man, of sorts
19. Dueling weapon
20. Ready and willing
21. From ___ Z
22. Records: abbr.
23. Iranian coin
26. Rocky ridge
28. Confined
32. Evening party
35. Elephant's flapper
36. Lecture reminders
38. Zubin ___
39. Tokyo, once
40. Zany
42. Continent: abbr.
43. Wash cycle
46. French fathers
48. Fruit drink
49. Melt
51. Delayed
53. Architectural order
55. Mound
56. Question
57. Building projection
59. Lab containers
63. Liturgy
64. Graphite marker
67. River to the Baltic
68. Hawaiian veranda
69. Austen title
70. Sorenson and Knight
71. Chimp's cousin
72. Profound

**DOWN**

1. Allot
2. Inter ___
3. Best man's item
4. Light beams
5. Presidential nickname
6. Mr. Buttons
7. Nepal's locale
8. Michelangelo masterpiece
9. Inaccuracies
10. Sheep dog
11. Pit viper
12. Primates
13. Busy one
18. Heavenly hunter
24. Soon
25. Ease
27. Store-sale letters
28. Jury panel
29. Auto accessory
30. Ruthless
31. Inhibit
33. Musical exercise
34. Like some seals
37. ___ throat
41. Abominable Snowman
44. Fire feeders
45. Night, to a poet
47. Balm for wounds
50. Enamellike alloy
52. Checked
54. Net
56. Adjutant
58. Miss Turner
60. Top
61. Rickey ingredient
62. Affront
63. Decay
65. Dapper one
66. Overeater

# PUZZLE 331

**ACROSS**

1. Obstruct
5. Fruit types
10. Meadow sounds
14. Pit
15. Fred's sister
16. Actor Ray
17. "____ the ears of all the congregation . . ." (Deut. 31:30): 4 wds.
20. To a ____
21. "____ World Turns": 2 wds.
22. Garments
23. CEO: abbr.
24. Ger. article
25. Lawn
27. Hockey name
28. Cushion
31. Smell ____: 2 wds.
32. Mars
33. Mature
34. "And ____ unto the king . . ." (1 Kings 1:15): 3 wds.
39. Falsehood
40. Wear out
41. Congers
42. Nav. rank
43. Lyric poem
44. Dial
46. Have being
47. French river
48. Swiftly
51. Squelched: 2 wds.
53. ____ la la
56. "So ____ came to the people . . ." (1 Sam. 26:7): 3 wds.
59. ____ Scott
60. Blues street
61. Bucket
62. Lip
63. Demeter
64. Wheat beards

**DOWN**

1. Gab
2. Solo
3. Ye ____ Shoppe
4. Jewel
5. Goes by
6. Clifford ____
7. Entangle
8. Otherwise
9. Ninth mo.
10. Cooker
11. Stouts
12. Mine access
13. Heirs
18. Paddles
19. Loath
23. Narrow lane
24. Sketched
25. Oat, e.g.
26. Grades
27. Mouths: Latin
28. Church dish
29. Spry
30. Bears' lairs
31. Competent
32. Honest ____
35. Stashed
36. Secrete
37. Bard's before
38. B'way sign
44. Digs deep
45. "____ soit qui mal . . ."
46. Etching fluids
47. "____ of Two Cities": 2 wds.
48. Totals
49. India rubber
50. Prayers
51. Blade
52. Jewish month
53. Melt
54. Drizzle
55. Is sick
57. Letter trio
58. Bath, e.g.

# PUZZLE 332

**ACROSS**

1. Greek peak
5. Square-dance locale
9. Musicians' gp.
14. Bogus
15. Inter ____
16. Elbowroom
17. Violent upheaval
19. Russian co-op
20. "____ Maria"
21. Needed
23. Toward the rising sun
24. Put in other words
26. "Love Story" author
28. Sky altar
29. Bullfighters
32. Mother-of-pearl
35. Put up your ____!
36. One-thousand smackers
37. Mr. Lendl
38. Piper of pickle prominence
39. Fair
40. Kettle
41. Buenos ____
42. Chompers
43. Bandaged
45. Spanish article
46. Christie Brinkley, e.g.
47. Irons
51. "____ Mullins"
53. Godlike
55. Inlet
56. Delight
58. Two-hulled boat
60. Obsession
61. Excursion
62. Strong tie
63. Enroll
64. "Auld Lang ____"
65. Pretentious

**DOWN**

1. Film award
2. Remove whiskers
3. Gluts
4. Candlenut
5. Golf-ball cover
6. ____ clover
7. Subject of insurance
8. Juniors
9. King of Judah
10. Coverlet
11. Library file
12. Experts
13. Animal skin
18. ____ Boothe Luce
22. Hinder
25. Mountain lake
27. Vapor
29. Softened
30. Remainder
31. Clockmaker Thomas
32. Pinches
33. Swear
34. Cougar
35. Vagrants
38. Heaped
39. Kid
41. Append
42. Tribal symbol
44. Unlucky, to Scots
45. New Jersey Indian
47. Mix well
48. Foul-up
49. Cheerful
50. Annie's dog
51. "Auntie ____"
52. Arabian gulf
54. Diversify
57. Jug handle
59. Desert wear

# PUZZLE 333

**ACROSS**

1. ___ right up!
5. Diplomacy
9. Hockey player
11. Bar
13. Orator's stand
14. Specter
16. Ashen
17. Bidding event
19. One ___ many
20. Says further
22. "Plaza ___"
23. Former Spanish coin
24. Flat-topped hills
26. ___ the world
27. Discharged
28. Imposing old woman
30. Like embroidery silk
31. Prejudice
32. Harness part
33. Leaped
36. "The ___ Bears"
39. Vote into office
40. Yale person
41. Lengths in office
43. ___ of lamb
44. General movement
46. Public disorder
47. Shame!
48. Entertainment, to "Variety"
50. Ring decision: abbr.
51. Smothered
53. Simple dance
55. Mate
56. Distorted
57. Arboretum sight
58. Certain horse

**DOWN**

1. Unspecified person
2. Spigot
3. Exile isle
4. Devout
5. Western lake
6. Comedy King
7. Swindle
8. Staggers
9. Persuaded
10. Alibis
11. Malice
12. Rope loops
13. Emulated Spitz
15. Brooding
18. Layer
21. Tenner
23. Settler
25. Canonized one
27. Spark maker
29. Joke
30. Nourished
32. ___ trout
33. Slaves
34. Braids
35. Sales chit
36. Huffed and puffed
37. In print
38. Enjoyed a cigar
40. Wear away
42. Quit
44. "___ Foolish Things"
45. Iraqi coin
48. Turn on an axis
49. Mr. Mostel
52. In favor of
54. Vichy, e.g.

# PUZZLE 334

**ACROSS**

1. Toward the stern
4. Ocean vessel
8. Thick slice
12. Pigeon sound
13. Mexican specialty
14. Hearty
15. Columbus or Magellan, e.g.
17. Prayer ending
18. Lo ____ behold
19. Pounded down
21. Glue
24. Female horse
25. Mature
26. Money owed
27. Pod vegetable
30. Smell
31. Everything
32. Pile
33. Was introduced to
34. Cuddly
35. Otherwise
36. Mists
37. Make changes in
38. One of the 4-H's
41. Building addition
42. Need liniment
43. Assume control
48. Leaf home
49. Pitcher
50. Anger
51. Totals
52. Relax
53. Very angry

**DOWN**

1. Top card
2. Actor Michael J. ____
3. Highest point
4. Rock
5. Difficult
6. Frost, as a cake
7. Easily carried
8. Disgrace
9. Light
10. To the sheltered side
11. Curve
16. Sooner or ____
20. Sculptures, e.g.
21. School dance
22. Military assistant
23. Stain
24. Thaws
26. Female child
27. Animal hide
28. Comfort
29. One who mimics
32. Friendly greeting
34. Folding bed
36. Runs away
37. Warn
38. Headgear
39. Light beige
40. Attention-getting word
41. Makes do
44. Admiration
45. Vigor
46. Important age
47. Stop-sign color

# PUZZLE 335

**ACROSS**

1. Punctuation mark
6. Literary monogram
9. Baking needs
13. Benefit
14. Fr. honorific
15. Leave out
16. Finicky
18. Skirt style
19. Wapiti
20. Patron saint of Norway
21. Michigan county
22. Critical
25. Elf
27. Society-page word
28. Egyptian capital
29. Reimbursed
32. Lamprey
35. Criticism of a particular person
39. Singleton
40. Poker bet
41. Host
42. Roman bronze
44. Roman gods
45. Like a tough customer
51. Avoid
52. Gold: pref.
53. Between, in Roma
56. Fine or goal
57. Precise
60. Out's mate
61. Norman city
62. Tolls
63. Mrs. Dick Tracy
64. Elected ones
65. Roly-poly

**DOWN**

1. Bistro's kin
2. Aqueduct is one
3. Ball item
4. With, in Wittenberg
5. ____ Baba
6. Crow
7. Deceptive ploy
8. French possessive
9. Fragrant ointment
10. Famous fiddle
11. 37th president
12. Smart
14. Pepper grinder
17. Gifted, to Gigi
21. Opposite of WSW
22. Road division
23. Chinese port
24. Racing's ____ 500
25. Pick up
26. Riviera city
28. Navy title: abbr.
29. Coup for Hulk Hogan
30. Vaudeville feature
31. Harry's successor
32. ____ homo
33. Augments
34. Soap ingredient
36. El ____
37. Snow and chick
38. Hungary's Nagy
42. Mathematical snakes?
43. Aout's season
44. Secular
45. Slave of Sparta
46. Vibrant
47. Ancient writings
48. Hymn
49. Minstrels' instruments
50. ____ go bragh
53. Ripped
54. Laments
55. South African fox
57. 1101, to Caesar
58. Mysterious spacecraft
59. Science room

# PUZZLE 336

**ACROSS**

1. Rose essence
6. Charley horse
11. Cherished
14. Unattached
15. Greek poet
16. ____ pro nobis
17. Yam
19. On ____ of the world
20. Macaw
21. Swap
23. Sixth sense: abbr.
26. Banqueted
27. More dulcet
29. Lazy posture
31. Rodeo rope
32. Book name
33. Ticker
35. Grimalkin
38. Holland export
39. Abounds
40. Buckeye State
41. Soak flax
42. Closes
43. Small broom
44. Aquatic animal
46. Specimen
47. Echo
49. Mountain pass
50. Japanese coin
51. Warning bell
52. Peruses
54. Sesame
55. Steak adjunct
61. Greek vowel
62. Climbing plant
63. Speed check
64. Headed
65. Gantry or Fudd
66. Facade

**DOWN**

1. Jolson and Hirt
2. Pull behind
3. Water tester
4. Bewildered
5. Go back over
6. Task
7. Church court
8. "I ____ Camera"
9. Ran into
10. Complaint
11. Dip accompaniments
12. Wear away
13. Come to a point
18. Lane
22. ____ judicata
23. Chemical compound
24. Chute
25. Picnic dish
27. Bridge coups
28. ____ of the Roses
30. German city
33. Was all ears
34. Conger
36. Bride's runway
37. Keepsake
39. "Harold ____"
40. Electrical unit
42. Take a spill
43. Salad type
45. Rocky crag
46. Detergent
47. Badgerlike animal
48. High society
49. Fragrant wood
52. Actor Auberjonois
53. Headliner
56. Feel poorly
57. Actor Fong
58. Fuss
59. Make leather
60. Plate scraping

# PUZZLE 337

**ACROSS**

1. Recreational area
5. Sail support
9. Howl
12. Destroy
13. Aroma
14. Mine find
15. Formerly
16. Brown syrup
18. Precipitous
20. Lassos
21. Tempts
23. Facial features
26. Conflict
29. Pop
30. Skirt feature
31. Power
33. Yeltsin's country
34. Bait
35. Forbid
36. Attempt
37. Dog-paddled
38. Likewise
40. Master
42. Perplex
46. Denver's state
49. Genuine
50. Tavern fare
51. Hymn ending
52. Caviar
53. Sunburn shade
54. Nude
55. Take it easy

**DOWN**

1. Paid athletes
2. Female relative
3. Pilaf ingredient
4. Bow down
5. "Mr. ____"
6. Worshiped
7. Arias
8. Snare
9. Most domineering
10. "We ____ the World"
11. Of course!
17. Vends
19. Chubby
22. Sunbeam
24. Au ____ (nanny)
25. Stick around
26. Marries
27. Again
28. Remembered
30. Kicks
32. Juliet's love
33. Tattle
35. Notebook
38. Play
39. Weasellike swimmer
41. Sheik
43. Persuade
44. Coffee cups
45. Annoyance
46. Sedan
47. Flamenco cheer
48. Washington bill

# PUZZLE 338

**ACROSS**

1. Belfry inhabitant
4. Golly
8. Marble slice
12. Hollywood's Gardner
13. Actress Moreno
14. Caesar's garb
15. Jumped the track
17. Ready for business
18. Was aware of
19. Lock of hair
20. Rip
23. Postpone
25. Let
27. Wipe gently
28. Select
31. Brief snooze
33. Widespread affliction
35. Lennon's wife
36. Vat
38. Deserves
39. "Full ____ Jacket"
41. Remainder
42. More senior
45. Actor Mostel
47. Tree's anchor
48. Rhythmic beats
52. Fit
53. Fury
54. Fearful reverence
55. Lascivious look
56. Baseball's Hershiser
57. Stroke

**DOWN**

1. Flawed
2. Madison or Park: abbr.
3. Roofing material
4. Wide smile
5. Lubricated
6. Simmered
7. Possessed
8. Anecdote
9. Easy gait
10. Ripens
11. Forbids
16. Ohio city
19. Dining surface
20. Mexican dish
21. Verve
22. Choir voice
24. Lick, like a dog
26. Irrigate
28. Mean monster
29. Plays on words
30. Try out
32. Place
34. Slugger Henry ____
37. Eastern market
39. Gauge
40. Sill
42. Type of exam
43. Ear part
44. Mete
46. Film spool
48. ____-Magnon
49. Beret, e.g.
50. Ram's mate
51. Matched group

# PUZZLE 339

**ACROSS**

1. Register
4. Folding beds
8. Sprinted
12. Shock
13. Table spread
14. Protagonist
15. Insisted
17. Bridle part
18. Caesar's date
19. Longs for
20. Din
23. Costa del ____, Spain
24. Sunbeams
25. Expression of regret
29. Tennis term
30. Foot lever
32. Constrictor
33. Meaning
35. Drench
36. Tango's need
37. Vinegar vessels
39. World carrier
42. Abel's brother
43. Trench ____
44. Haughty
48. Eternal city
49. Competition
50. Fawn's mom
51. Supplemented
52. Caresses
53. Have

**DOWN**

1. Youth
2. Be in the red
3. Sapphire, e.g.
4. Apartment
5. More mature
6. Casual shirts
7. Turf
8. Piercing
9. Hammer part
10. Pennsylvania port
11. Knotts and Rickles
16. Points
19. Billiards
20. Stuff
21. Frilly trim
22. Yes votes
23. Baden-Baden, e.g.
25. Summer refresher
26. Woodwind
27. Ruminant
28. Gabs
30. Furry feet
31. Conceit
34. Uttered
35. Warbled
37. Insertion mark
38. Public disorders
39. Farm unit
40. Stole
41. Ornate fabric
42. Northern Indian
44. Current measure, for short
45. Fuss
46. Immediately
47. Hamilton bill

# PUZZLE 340

**ACROSS**

1. Not cooked
4. Territory
8. Quick
12. Manipulate
13. Floral necklaces
14. Irritate
15. Cinemas
17. Notion
18. Strong wind
19. Poppy and sesame
20. Lid
23. Pleasure
24. Poems
25. Food fish
29. Buck's mate
30. Paces
32. Honey maker
33. Missions
35. Shoe part
36. Gloomy
37. Hex
38. Poet Robert ____
41. Sycamore, e.g.
43. Solitary
44. Large stones
48. "____ the Rainbow"
49. Jelly ____ Morton
50. Nautical response
51. Annoyance
52. Brewery products
53. Suit to a ____

**DOWN**

1. Furrow
2. ____ Wednesday
3. Diminutive
4. Church table
5. Film spool
6. Irish republic
7. Donkey
8. Pal
9. Military assistant
10. Toboggan
11. Oriental beverages
16. Matures
19. Lather
20. Morse ____
21. Aroma
22. Swerve
23. Plump
25. Towel word
26. Woodwind
27. Prison unit
28. Ship's centerboard
30. Tiny fly
31. Attach
34. Affirm
35. Raced
37. Retails
38. Fiasco
39. Drift
40. Smallest bills
41. Instrument
42. Reign
44. Bikini part
45. Have lunch
46. Deli bread
47. Understand

# PUZZLE 341

**ACROSS**

1. Butter portion
4. Canine comment
7. Transmit
11. Sherbet
12. Fish bait
14. Beseech
15. Tot's game
17. Weak, as an excuse
18. Before
19. Made fun of
21. Tacked on
24. Portable beds
25. Skinny
26. Grove
30. Nosh
31. Wet snow
33. Director Spike ____
34. Saltine, e.g.
36. Actor Alda
37. Suggestion
38. Land of the Pharaohs
39. Runways
42. Hatchet
43. Crude metals
44. Signed up
49. Go on horseback
50. Perches
51. Author Levin
52. Wrench or hammer
53. Kettle
54. Snoop

**DOWN**

1. Small seed
2. Expert
3. Football stand
4. Prize
5. Judge's garb
6. To and ____
7. Daryl Hannah film
8. Epochs
9. Title
10. Changed colors
13. Engines
16. Sharp
20. Engrave
21. Actor Guinness
22. Cherished
23. Information
24. Woo
27. Comrade
28. Harvest
29. Fender bender mark
31. Hop, ____, and a jump
32. Contact ____
35. Sculptor's device
36. Grows older
38. Have being
39. Type
40. Threesome
41. Update
42. Choir voice
45. Bite
46. Point
47. Go astray
48. Doris or Dennis

# PUZZLE 342

**ACROSS**
1. Notable time
4. Young cow
8. Surpasses
12. Replacement, for short
13. Opera solo
14. Wicked
15. Headstrong
17. California wine valley
18. Clamor
19. Capital of Oregon
20. Not fastened
22. Writing implement
23. Wander
24. Meteorologist's concern
28. Rifle or pistol
29. Leaks
31. Summer drink
32. Name
34. Very dry
35. Water barrier
36. Rides the air
38. Appraiser
41. Swap
42. Lamb's pseudonym
43. Gifts
46. Plummeted
47. Ceremony
48. Moray or conger
49. Notices
50. Actor Sharif
51. "One ____ at a Time"

**DOWN**
1. Dangerous curve
2. Boring routine
3. Plentiful
4. Log structure
5. Got up
6. Italian money, once
7. Ventilating device
8. Resident
9. Egg-shaped
10. Smoking device
11. Bang
16. Flourish
19. Oceans
20. Egg on
21. Part of speech
22. Energy
24. Tiny
25. Congealed
26. Singer Adams
27. Cincinnati nine
29. Celebrity
30. Nightmare street of film
33. High standards
34. Assistant
36. Actress Garbo
37. Surgical light beam
38. Umps
39. Toward shelter
40. Floor covering
41. Slim
43. In favor of
44. Oolong or pekoe
45. Crafty

# PUZZLE 343

**ACROSS**

1. Insect
4. Zone
8. Quote
12. Dollar
13. Christmas
14. Chess piece
15. Moral wrong
16. Hairstyling aids
17. Poker bet
18. "____ Magnolias"
20. Group
22. Morning moisture
24. Bread ingredient
28. Smooth wood
31. Oriental staple
34. Untruth
35. Follow orders
36. Have being
37. Carbonated beverage
38. Pub drink
39. Unlock
40. Abound
41. Piano part
43. Couple
45. Image of worship
48. Kitchen garment
52. Supporting limbs
55. Accustomed
57. Actor Vigoda
58. Elliptical
59. Fencing blade
60. Cut the grass
61. Used to be
62. Doe
63. Domestic animal

**DOWN**

1. Supervisor
2. Part of a whole
3. Actor Hackman
4. Viewpoint
5. Fish eggs
6. Wiggly swimmers
7. Too
8. Wooden container
9. Charged particle
10. Small child
11. Squeak by
19. Whirlpool
21. Type of whiskey
23. Shawl
25. Succulent plant
26. "West ____ Story"
27. Lakers, e.g.
28. Sudsy substance
29. Qualified
30. Deficiency
32. Anger
33. Penny
37. Traffic sign
39. Ancient
42. Theater lane
44. Seltzer, e.g.
46. Was indebted to
47. Gait
49. Incline
50. Woodwind instrument
51. Salamander
52. Not high
53. Night before a holiday
54. Elongated fish
56. Born as

# PUZZLE 344

**ACROSS**

1. Transparently thin
6. In front
11. Greeting
12. Films
14. Fragrance
15. Green gem
17. Officer
18. Monarch
20. Author Tolstoy
21. Understood
23. Title of respect
24. Sports competition
25. Neighborhood
27. Audacity
28. Rated
31. Flipped, as a coin
32. Resided
33. Moistens
34. Poetic works
35. Male heir
36. Three feet
40. Actor Vereen
41. Highlanders
43. Mr. Gehrig
44. Exploded
46. Sedates
48. Peaceful
49. Take on as one's own
50. Planted
51. Full of information

**DOWN**

1. Hut
2. Long-legged bird
3. Wed on the run
4. Shade tree
5. Bellow
6. Aviator Earhart
7. "Iliad" poet
8. Always
9. Melody
10. Merchants
13. Garment part
16. Was overly fond
19. Secondhand
22. Walks in water
24. Untidy
26. Ruby
27. Believe it or ____
28. Orb
29. Passengers
30. Streets
31. Camper's shelter
33. Covered with trees
35. Landscape
37. Let
38. Frolics
39. Powdery
41. Goulash
42. Read hastily
45. Expert
47. Fruit drink

# PUZZLE 345

**Diagramless crosswords are solved by using the clues and their numbers to fill in the answer words and the arrangement of black squares. Insert the number of each clue with the first letter of its answer, across and down. Fill in a black square at the end of each word. Every black square must have a corresponding black square on the opposite side of the diagram to form a diagonally symmetrical pattern.**

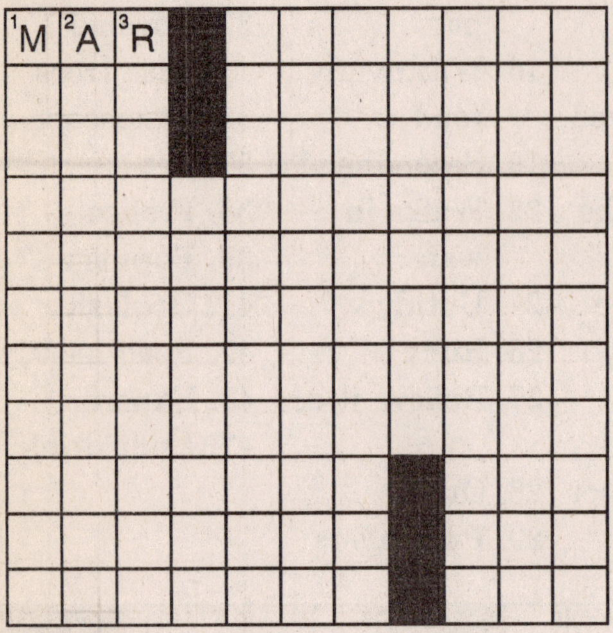


**ACROSS**
1. Deface
4. Do sums
7. Lyricist Gershwin
10. Reverence
11. Former Chinese leader
12. Negative
13. Tree fluid
14. Hockey great
15. Pair
16. Heavy curls
18. Doctrine
19. Son of Adam
20. Moves to music
22. Charged particle
24. Meadow
25. Rain sound
28. Store away
31. Inventor Whitney
32. Of touch
34. Also
35. Aunt: Sp.
36. Lyric poem
37. Actress Blythe
38. Superlative suffix
39. Composer Rorem
40. Bandleader Brown
41. ____ Moines
42. Fourth-year students: abbr.

**DOWN**
1. Spars
2. Cognizant
3. Dittos
4. Biblical prophet
5. Ventured
6. Of the back
7. Signs
8. Awaken
9. Tiny particles
17. Fired
21. Bird's home
23. Trapped
25. Flower part
26. Solo
27. Elevate
29. More ancient
30. Unwanted plants
33. Tabbies

# PUZZLE 346

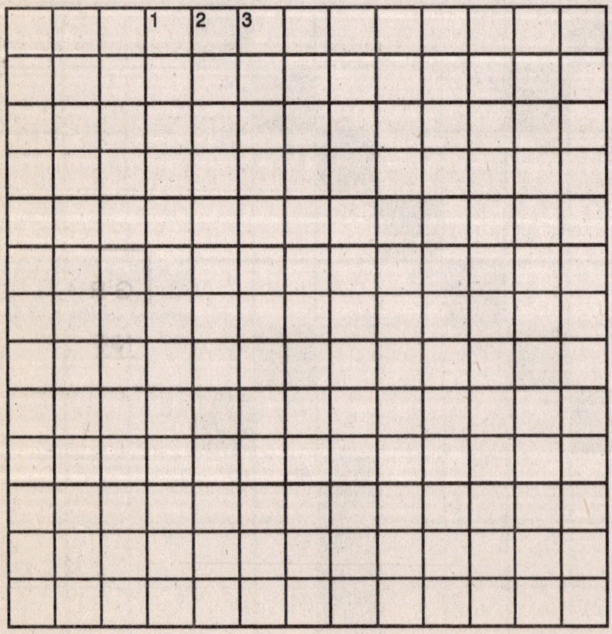


**ACROSS**
1. Cinder
4. Worked as a blacksmith
6. Wrapping material
8. Interoffice notes
10. Drain of strength
13. Not tipsy
15. Christmas carol
17. Empire State
21. Arrow poison
22. Donkey
23. Hear ____ drop
24. Continue on
26. Snow field
27. Smile smugly
29. Born
30. "A Bell for ____"
32. Musical study
34. English school
35. Work unit

**DOWN**
1. Small snake
2. Pretense
3. Fond wishes
5. Show how
7. Togas
9. Take stitches
10. Small cut
11. First-rate
12. Equal
14. Actor O'Neal
16. Minus
18. Unwrap
19. Split
20. Leg joint
22. Stage whisper
25. Miss Hogg
28. Coach Rockne
31. Fragrance
33. Chang's twin

# PUZZLE 347

**ACROSS**

1. Foreman
5. Buccaneer
7. Pizza herb
9. Desertlike
11. Qatar natives
13. Health resort
14. Feather scarf
15. Soupy meat dish
16. Young hooter
18. Persuade
19. Blinding light
21. Utilize
24. Upper limb
25. White with age
26. Danger color
27. Energy
28. Strong ties
29. Pindar poems
30. Gladden
32. Dutch cheese
33. Period
34. Judge Bean
35. Go in
38. Fly high
40. Army commander
42. President Reagan
43. Dispatched

**DOWN**

1. Feathered animal
2. Mineral source
3. Epic
4. Leading actor
5. Taro product
6. Make possible
8. Woodwind
9. Summit
10. Uncooked
12. Part of the weekend
13. Animal charge
15. Painful
16. Paddles
17. Twisted
18. Bottle top
19. Departed
20. Boy
22. Appear
23. Magazine execs
25. Torrid
28. Pancake mix
29. Smell
31. Lengthy
32. Historic period
36. Grandson of Adam
37. M. Coty
38. Season
39. Up in years
41. Sprinted

**Starting box on page 562**

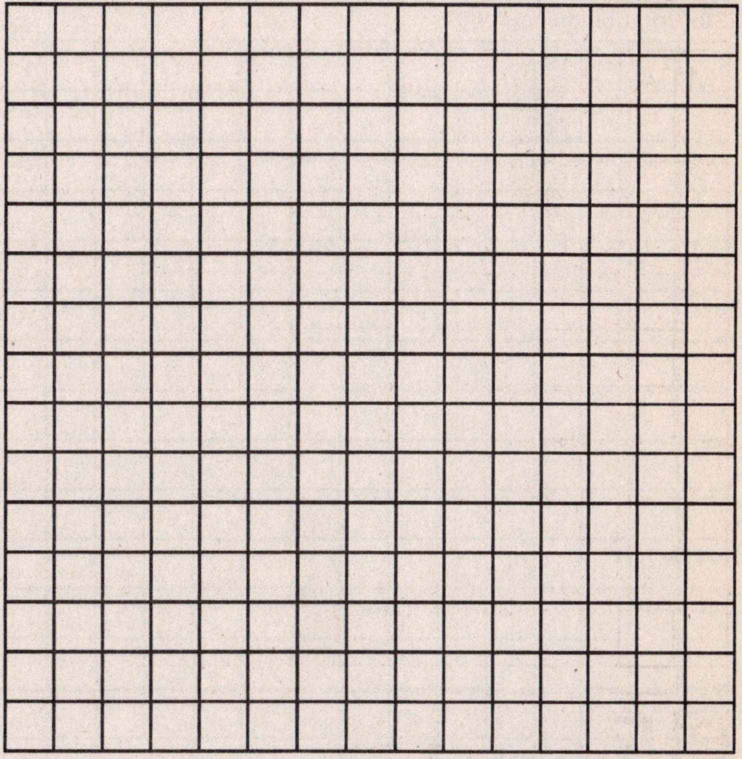

# Word Math

# PUZZLE 348

**In these long-division problems, letters are substituted for numbers. Determine the value of each letter. Then arrange the letters in order from 0 to 9, and they will spell a word or phrase.**

**1**

| 0 | 1 | 2 | 3 | 4 | 5 | 6 | 7 | 8 | 9 |
|---|---|---|---|---|---|---|---|---|---|
| | | | | | | | | | |

```
        PAL
EEL ) LAPEL
      ONA
      EIRE
      PNMP
       EEML
       EISM
        POA
```

**2**

| 0 | 1 | 2 | 3 | 4 | 5 | 6 | 7 | 8 | 9 |
|---|---|---|---|---|---|---|---|---|---|
| | | | | | | | | | |

```
         HAD
PET ) SEARCH
      SCRT
       ITAC
       ITAD
         CH
```

**3**

| 0 | 1 | 2 | 3 | 4 | 5 | 6 | 7 | 8 | 9 |
|---|---|---|---|---|---|---|---|---|---|
| | | | | | | | | | |

```
        FEE
AND ) GRAIN
      NFE
      AFYI
      ADRN
       AYRN
       ADRN
        ALL
```

# PUZZLE 349

**ACROSS**
1. Money holder
5. Garden path
6. Highway
10. Kiln
11. Fifty percent
15. Doing nothing
16. Breach
17. Western show
18. Plateau
19. Sinner
22. Rioting crowd
25. Be indebted
26. In the past
27. Angry
29. Indulgent
34. Hindu dress
35. Hint
36. Willowy
40. Necklace units
41. Spanish cheer
42. Mineral spring
44. Clear profit
45. Detail
51. African lily
52. Claw
53. Little devil
56. Bit of land
57. Fencing sword
58. Cure
59. Show the way
60. Hodgepodge
61. Small whirlpool

**DOWN**
1. Stop up
2. Molten rock
3. Awkward
4. Sty
6. Verges
7. Keats poems
8. In addition
9. Cherished
11. Sharpen
12. TV commercials
13. Lawful
14. Smithy
17. Uncooked
20. Caviar
21. Long, long time
22. Overlook
23. Spoken
24. Uncover
28. Can metal
30. Frozen water
31. Spirit
32. Unclothed
33. Exam
37. Oxford tutor
38. Cream of society
39. Summarize
40. Flying mammal
42. Wild plum
43. Dowel
45. Dog's wagger
46. Otherwise
47. Soda
48. Pay attention
49. Pub brew
50. Give way
54. Alice or Hazel, e.g.
55. Stratagem
58. Garden tool

Starting box on page 562

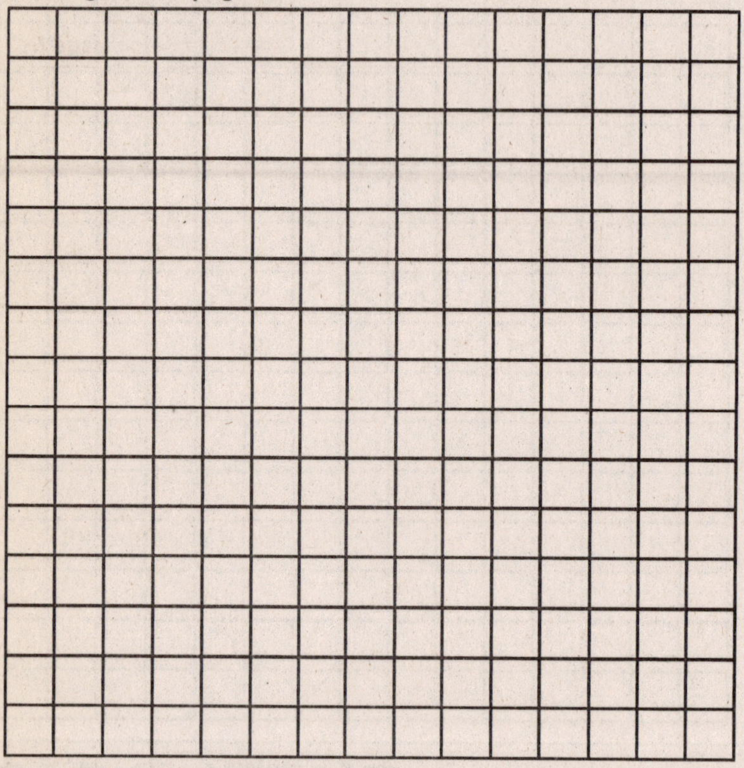

# PUZZLE 350

## Quotagram

**Fill in the answers to the clues. Then transfer the letters to the correspondingly numbered squares in the diagram. The completed diagram will contain a quotation.**

1. Past events ___ ___ ___ ___ ___ ___ ___ (9 16 39 23 36 20 28)
2. Musical drama ___ ___ ___ ___ ___ (29 18 42 35 25)
3. Forest ___ ___ ___ ___ ___ (8 4 43 13 17)
4. Stroking ___ ___ ___ ___ ___ ___ ___ (21 22 31 11 6 30 38)
5. Cries ___ ___ ___ ___ ___ (34 10 40 26 7)
6. Tirade ___ ___ ___ ___ ___ ___ ___ ___ (32 1 5 12 37 15 24 19)
7. Inundated ___ ___ ___ ___ ___ ___ ___ (44 27 14 3 41 33 2)

| | | | | | | | | | | | | | | | | | | |
|---|---|---|---|---|---|---|---|---|---|---|---|---|---|---|---|---|---|---|
| 1 | | 2 | 3 | 4 | 5 | | 6 | 7 | | 8 | 9 | 10 | 11 | | 12 | | 13 | 14 |
| 15 | | 16 | 17 | | 18 | 19 | 20 | 21 | 22 | 23 | 24 | 25 | 26 | 27 | 28 | | 29 | 30 |
| | 31 | 32 | 33 | | 34 | 35 | 36 | 37 | 38 | | 39 | 40 | 41 | 42 | | 43 | 44 | |

## PUZZLE 351

**ACROSS**
1. Secret language
5. Great Lake
6. Quit walking
7. Brusque
8. Figure out
11. DJ's platter
15. Gambling game
16. Settle a debt
19. Aware about
20. Wood menace
21. Banish
22. Press
23. Wiles
24. Against
25. Tithe
27. Friend: Fr.
28. Boxing matches
30. Epoch
31. Roman statesman
34. Make a mistake
35. Moved through water
36. Praise
37. Honking birds
40. Fibbers
41. Taj Mahal site
42. Direct affronts
43. International friend
44. Look like
45. Unaffected
47. Inquires
48. Hits
51. Copier powder
52. Gabs

**DOWN**
1. The arts
2. Food scrap
3. Female deer
4. Conclusion
5. Heavenly instrument
6. Wit
7. Apple centers
8. Gristle
9. Cowboy Ritter
10. Pursuer of pleasure
11. ____-yourself
12. As to
13. Block intentionally
14. Adverse
15. Fixed methods
17. Thanks ____!
18. Itches
20. Lamb sounds
26. Amateur actors
28. Entreats
29. Pitcher Hershiser
32. Entice
33. Actor West
35. "____ Marner"
38. Health club
39. Manors
40. Innocent frolics
46. Consumer
48. Pigpen
49. Extinct bird
50. Writing fluid

**Starting box on page 562**

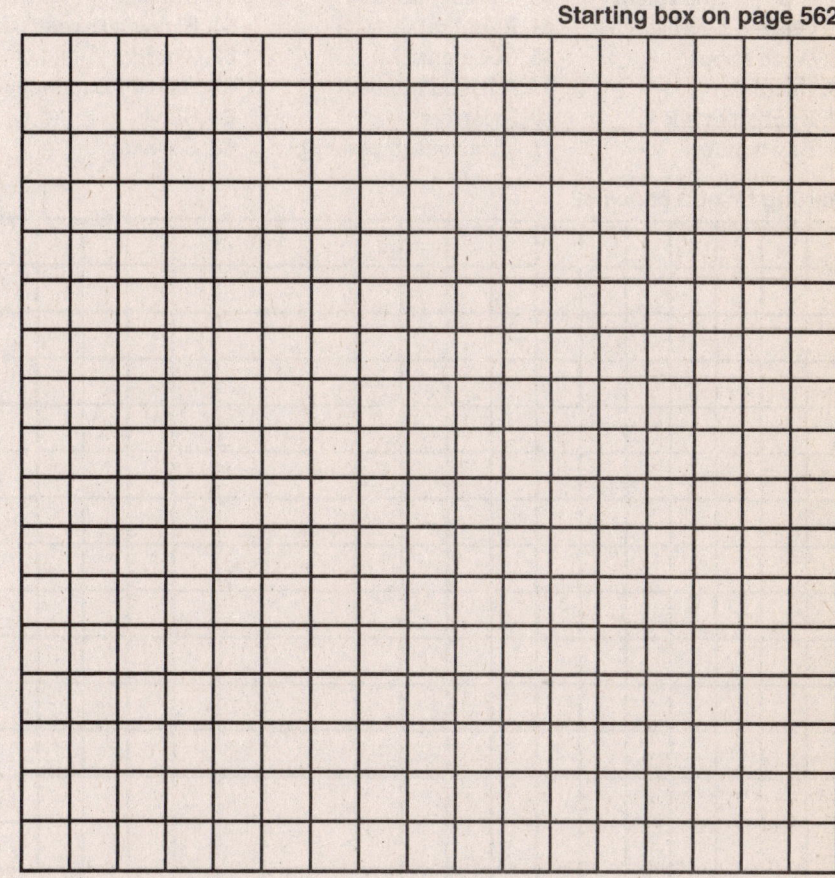

---

## Changaword — PUZZLE 352

**Can you change the top word into the bottom word in each column in the number of steps indicated in parentheses? Change only one letter at a time and do not change the order of the letters. Proper names, slang, and obsolete words are not allowed.**

| 1. WINE (3 steps) | 2. BILL (4 steps) | 3. TOUR (4 steps) | 4. LEFT (5 steps) |
|---|---|---|---|
| LIST | FARE | BOOK | BANK |

# PUZZLE 353

**ACROSS**
1. Thrash
5. Humorous picture
8. Celebration: Ger.
12. Falls in a heap
14. Curved monument
15. Church recess
16. Wood strips
18. Customer
19. English drink
20. Bay window
22. Hawaiian goose
23. ____ Speedwagon
24. Sailor
26. Robust
28. Stood up to
33. Weighty books
34. Rapid talk
36. Got along
37. A friend in need
40. Incorrect
41. Voracious grasshopper
42. Sheer fabric
43. Annoy
45. Actress Corcoran
46. Part of i.e.
48. Help
49. Anthracite
52. Slipper
55. Cup handle
58. Female singer
59. Strange
61. Sleeveless coat
62. Trudge
63. Asked for money
65. Slave
66. Earned
67. First garden

**DOWN**
1. Light wood
2. Author Gardner
3. "One Day ____ Time"
4. Spinning toys
5. Manage
6. Capital of Norway
7. Close by
8. "Afternoon of a ____"
9. Gaelic
10. Perfume
11. Filament
12. Feline pet
13. Mixed
17. Kernels
21. Actress Myrna ____
25. Rest
26. Israeli dance
27. Prayer ending
29. Lose color
30. "____ Magic"
31. And others: abbr.
32. Fiend
33. Tell on
35. Marathon
36. Clenched hand
37. Acquire
38. Spanish jar
39. Boring routine
40. Cheese dishes
42. Utterance
44. Flee
45. "____ Boot"
47. Turnpike payments
50. Like ____ of bricks
51. Ore vein
53. Out of
54. Office cabinet
55. Devoured
56. Copied
57. Crimson
60. Ireland
61. Quote
64. Spanish hero El ____

**Starting box on page 562**

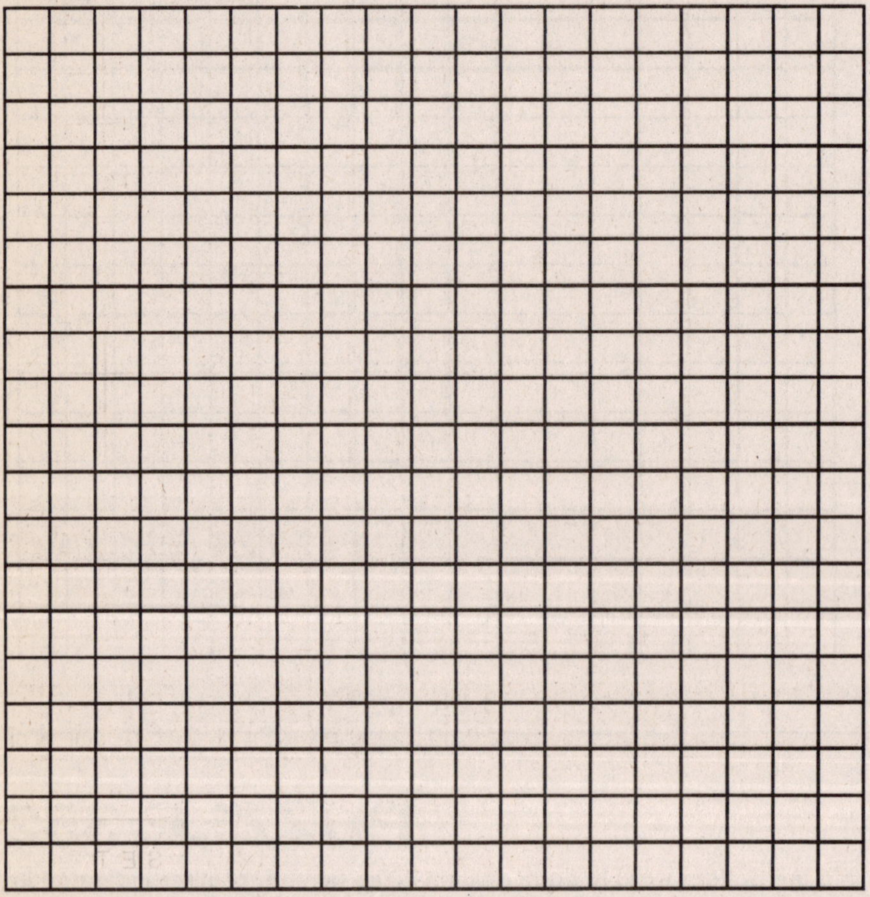

# PUZZLE 354

## Mix 'Em Maxim

**Rearrange the letters in this silly sentence to spell out a familiar saying.**

DIET SPELL LONG SIEGE

Saying: ___ ________ ____ ___

# PUZZLE 355

**ACROSS**
1. Distant
4. Price
8. Base
11. Keyboard instrument
13. Against
14. Hail
15. Biting
16. Orderly
17. Blemish
18. Abound
19. Bow
21. Secure
23. ____ Ike
25. Chop
26. Calm
27. Swift
31. Health resort
33. "You ____ Your Life"
34. Impolite
35. Orient
37. Fencing blade
38. Quote
39. Male descendant
42. Average
43. London buses
45. Kin
47. Church bench
49. Limber
50. Swipe
53. Posed
54. Weathercock
58. Haul
59. Defeat
61. Eatery
62. Roe
63. Other
64. Say
65. Remit
66. High-school student
67. Pigment

**DOWN**
1. Passenger
2. ____, vegetable, or mineral
3. Staff
4. Frank
5. Washington bill
6. Cache
7. Giggle
8. Ewe's young
9. Elliptical
10. Used to be
11. Caress
12. Frozen water
19. Kind
20. Newspaper notice
22. Cognizant
24. Research room
26. Trattoria offering
28. Canine offspring
29. Concept
30. Doe
31. Cult
32. Duo
36. Entice
39. Epic
40. Leave out
41. Nothing
44. Hidden
45. Latch
46. Frivolity
48. Entire
50. Cease
51. Star
52. Gone
55. Poker stake
56. Born
57. Make a faux pas
60. Employ
61. Flop

**Starting box on page 562**

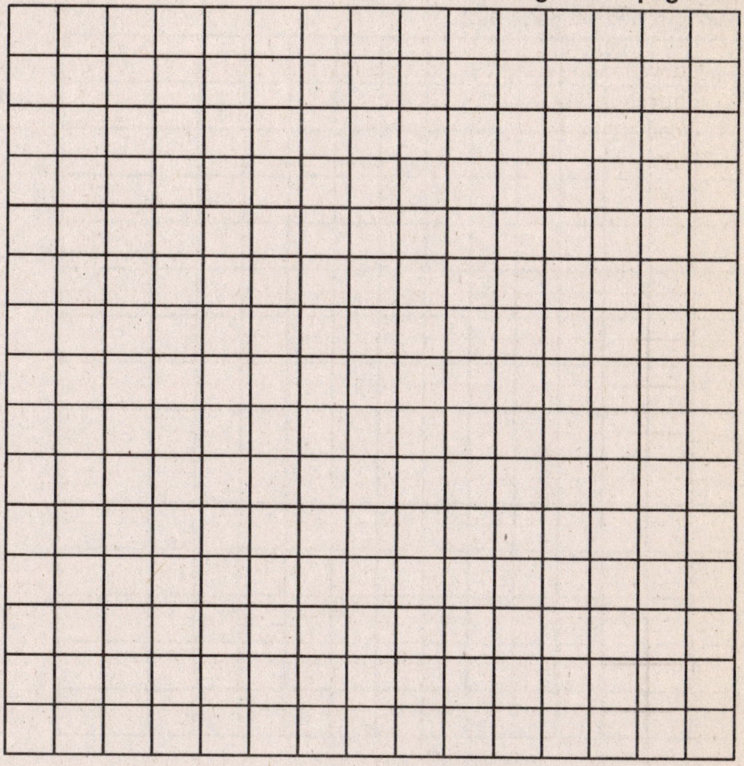

# Word Math

# PUZZLE 356

**In these long-division problems, letters are substituted for numbers. Determine the value of each letter. Then arrange the letters in order from 0 to 9, and they will spell a word or phrase.**

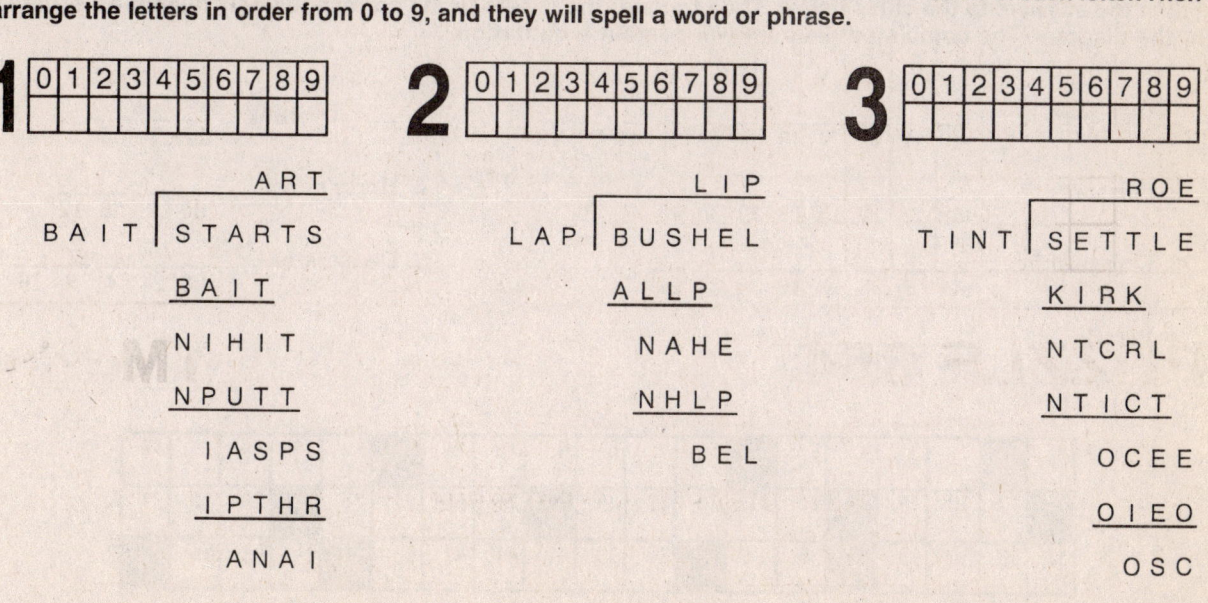

**1**

| 0 | 1 | 2 | 3 | 4 | 5 | 6 | 7 | 8 | 9 |
|---|---|---|---|---|---|---|---|---|---|
| | | | | | | | | | |

ART
BAIT | STARTS
BAIT
NIHIT
NPUTT
IASPS
IPTHR
ANAI

**2**

| 0 | 1 | 2 | 3 | 4 | 5 | 6 | 7 | 8 | 9 |
|---|---|---|---|---|---|---|---|---|---|
| | | | | | | | | | |

LIP
LAP | BUSHEL
ALLP
NAHE
NHLP
BEL

**3**

| 0 | 1 | 2 | 3 | 4 | 5 | 6 | 7 | 8 | 9 |
|---|---|---|---|---|---|---|---|---|---|
| | | | | | | | | | |

ROE
TINT | SETTLE
KIRK
NTCRL
NTICT
OCEE
OIEO
OSC

# PUZZLE 357

**ACROSS**

1. Once around a track
4. Exist
5. Chair
7. Gazed fixedly
9. Drama division
11. Actress Remick
12. Regret
13. Upon
17. Tree juice
20. Ground corn
22. Function
23. "____ Abner"
24. Trim grass
26. Espy
27. March date
29. Lass
32. Male child
33. Distribute cards
34. Payable
35. Classified items
38. Conclusion
39. Cold season
42. Well-behaved
43. Unrefined metal
44. Sty

**Starting box on page 562**

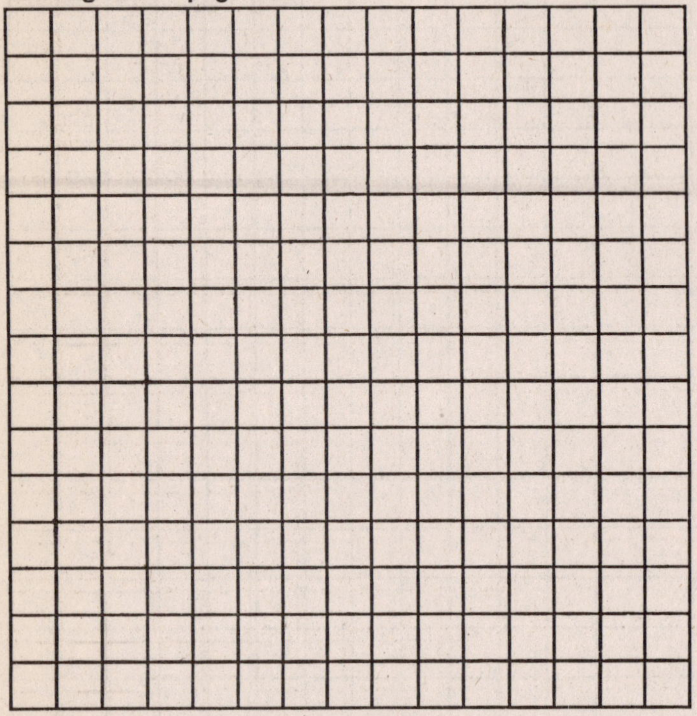

**DOWN**

1. Final
2. Region
3. Oyster gem
6. Golfing aid
7. Water vapor
8. Precious
9. Upper limb
10. Billiards stick
14. Flip
15. Margarine
16. Hammer head
17. Slipped
18. Assistant
19. Defense argument
21. Flight record
25. Broader
28. Cabbage salad
30. Sprint
31. Guided
36. Excavate
37. Pry
40. Shredded
41. Adam's garden

# PUZZLE 358 Quotagram

**Fill in the answers to the clues below. Then transfer the letters to the correspondingly numbered squares in the diagram. The completed diagram will contain a quotation.**

1. Rich person ___ ___ ___ ___ ___ ___ ___ ___ ___ ___ ___
   40 22 32 5 45 37 14 9 41 27 19
2. For sure ___ ___ ___ ___ ___ ___ ___ ___ ___ ___
   39 28 29 13 18 33 36 43 7 10
3. Flag position ___ ___ ___ ___ ___ ___ ___ ___
   44 6 23 2 46 38 34 21
4. Portals ___ ___ ___ ___ ___
   15 31 17 42 11
5. ____ Tse-tung ___ ___ ___
   25 1 30
6. Horse's foot ___ ___ ___ ___
   35 3 26 12
7. Decelerates ___ ___ ___ ___ ___
   20 24 4 8 16

| | | | | | | | | | | | | | | | | | | |
|---|---|---|---|---|---|---|---|---|---|---|---|---|---|---|---|---|---|---|
| 1 | ■ | 2 | 3 | 4 | 5 | ■ | 6 | 7 | 8 | 9 | 10 | 11 | ■ | 12 | 13 | 14 | 15 | 16 |
| ■ | 17 | 18 | 19 | ■ | 20 | 21 | 22 | 23 | 24 | ■ | 25 | 26 | 27 | 28 | ■ | 29 | 30 | 31 |
| 32 | 33 | 34 | 35 | ■ | 36 | 37 | ■ | 38 | 39 | 40 | 41 | 42 | 43 | ■ | 44 | 45 | 46 | ■ |

# PUZZLE 359

**ACROSS**
1. Float on a breeze
5. Zodiac ram
7. Gorilla
10. Commences
12. Reduce prices sharply
14. Shoulder bands
16. Verb forms
18. Aid in crime
19. Frenzied
20. Saloons
22. Garrison
23. Speak
24. Mutual give-and-take
28. Sauteed
29. Collision
30. Golf-club employee
33. Speed contest
34. Colonial insect
35. Deposited
36. United
37. Pamper
39. Paris's river
40. Drawing near
42. Herd of whales
45. Remain
46. Cairo's river
47. Published text
49. Russian city
51. Slander
52. Cowardly
55. Chalons's river
56. Kind of sofa
58. Modern: prefix
59. Inhibit
60. Went on horseback

**DOWN**
1. No longer is
2. ____ and crafts
3. Decree
4. ____ firma
6. Pierced
7. Watchful
8. Skillets
9. Double curves
11. Blade of grass
12. Unyielding
13. Wife of Zeus
15. Soda sipper
17. Pilot's milieu
19. Tome
21. Ready to fight
22. Novels and short stories
24. Persia
25. Pleasant
26. Ball holder
27. Male voice
28. To and ____
30. Ache
31. Resound
32. "____ on a Grecian Urn"
35. Hawaiian garland
37. Bridge
38. Congregation members
39. Removed peas from pods
40. Make amends
41. Hints
42. Jewel
43. First gardener
44. Site of La Scala
45. In hoc ____ vinces
48. Exhaust
50. Change
53. Director Preminger
54. Unwanted plant
57. Before, in poetry

**Starting box on page 562**

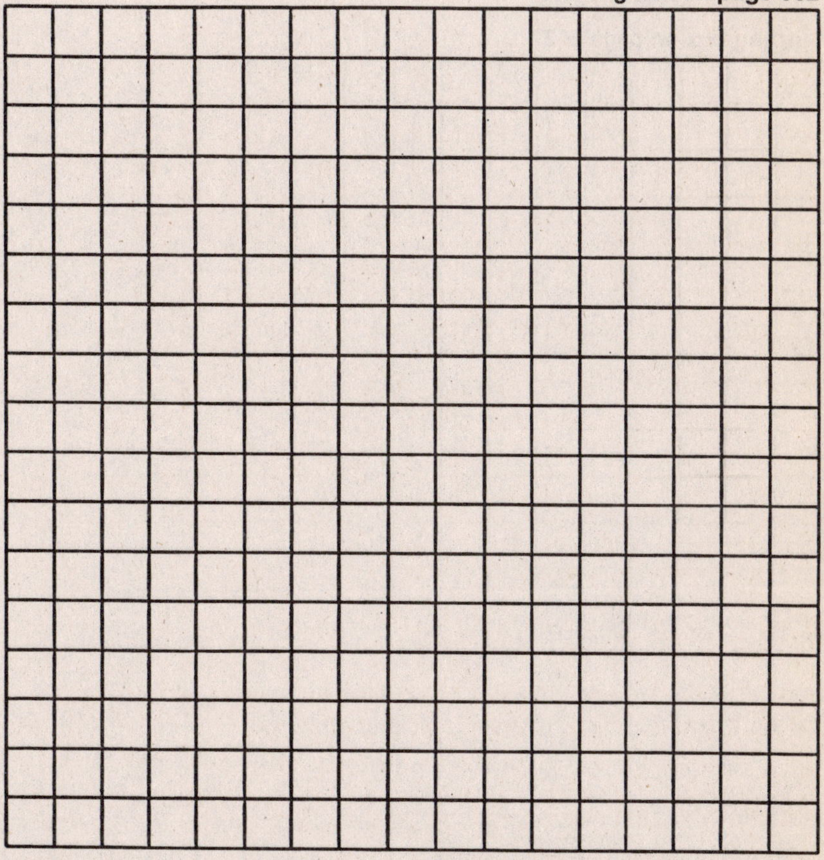

# Changaword

# PUZZLE 360

**Can you change the top word into the bottom word (in each column) in the number of steps indicated in parentheses? Do not change the order of the letters, and change only one letter at a time. Proper names, slang, and obsolete words are not allowed.**

| 1. **WORK** (3 steps) | 2. **CAKE** (3 steps) | 3. **SHED** (4 steps) | 4. **READ** (6 steps) |
|---|---|---|---|
| **LOAD** | **WALK** | **TEAR** | **PALM** |

# PUZZLE 361

**ACROSS**
1. Note
5. Nuisance
9. Madagascar mammal
10. Dull finish
11. Ridicule
12. Musical drama
13. Send back
14. Status ____
17. Products
18. Automaton
19. Bluefin
20. Born
21. Astronaut Shepard
22. Characteristic
23. "Sultan of ____" (Babe Ruth)
25. Tennis-court divider
26. Suit of cards
27. Holbrook or Linden
28. Most strange
31. Male child
32. Haul
33. Biddy
35. Father's sister
37. To the ____ degree
38. Barnyard strutter
40. Falsehood
41. Nursery decoration
43. Play part
46. Acorn, e.g.
47. Expunge
48. Yearning
49. Munch
50. Ethnic group
51. Glossy fabric
52. Wedding site
55. Large deer
56. Nobleman
57. Gravy
58. Modify
60. Roast host
61. Director Woody ____
62. Molds
63. Tropical tree

**DOWN**
1. Kind of Scout badge
2. Send out
3. Wet dirt
4. Mined matter
5. Hemingway's nickname
6. Everlasting
7. "Sesame ____"
8. Ridicule
9. Defective purchase
10. Cut the lawn
11. Argued
13. Actor's part
14. Gridiron leader
15. Apartment
16. Horse food
18. Operated
19. Garbage
22. Golf-ball stand
23. Yell
24. Singer Newton
26. "____ Noon"
29. Tennessee ____ Ford
30. Gave a "PG"
31. Diamond corner
34. Din
36. Farm vehicle
39. Spanish cheer
40. Salad greens
41. Nothing more than
42. Spoken
44. Facial feature
45. Hamilton bill
46. Spicy cold cut
48. Baseball's Hank ____
49. Relieved
51. Oregon capital
53. King-beaters
54. Female ruff
56. Invoice
58. Hit lightly
59. ____ carte

**Starting box on page 562**

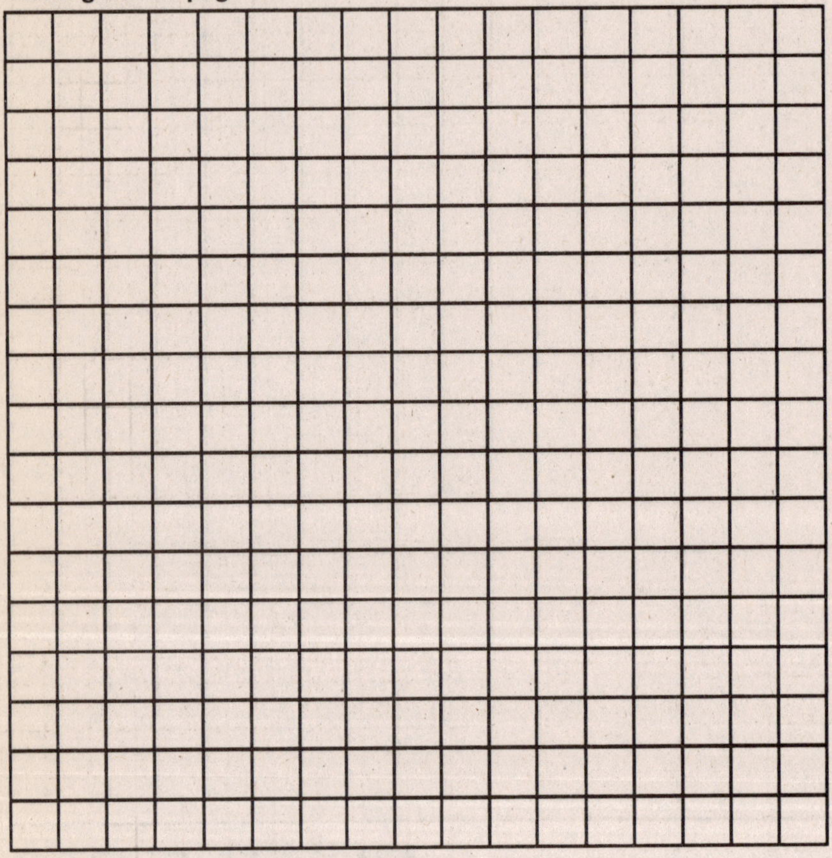

# PUZZLE 362

## Changaword

**Can you change the top word into the bottom word in each column in the number of steps indicated in parentheses? Change only one letter at a time and do not change the order of the letters. Proper names, slang, and obsolete words are not allowed.**

| 1. FARM (3 steps) | 2. YARD (4 steps) | 3. PICK (4 steps) | 4. FIRE (5 steps) |
|---|---|---|---|
| HAND | SALE | CORN | WOOD |

## PUZZLE 363

**ACROSS**

1. Shark's companion?
7. Sang
8. Sometimes it's receding
9. Repair, as a book
12. Diving bird
13. Eat
14. ____ Dhabi (Persian Gulf sheikdom)
17. Formosa Strait island
18. Door to ore
19. Wood strips
21. Cotton cloth
24. Drenches
26. Fine French porcelain
27. Certain Scandinavian
29. Marble, e.g.
30. Neither ____ (not a trace)
34. Sports palace
36. Predatory sea bird
37. Of heat
39. Oklahoma city
41. Enliven
42. Iroquoians
45. Corn bread
46. Italian lake
47. United
48. Here's ____ your eye!
49. "____ brillig, and the slithy toves"
53. Beaus
54. Refuges
56. Descendant of Shem
57. Simply

**DOWN**

1. Foray
2. Go astray
3. "____ Flanders"
4. Hodgepodge
5. Gambling town
6. Arabian gulf
7. Walking stick
8. Place for concealment
9. Actual
10. Author Bombeck
11. Footwear
14. Verona's river
15. Twining plant stem
16. Shoshoneans
18. Egyptian deity
20. Bridges
21. Actress/author Maxwell
22. South American monkey
23. God of love
25. Wheel part
28. Dried fruit
30. Queen of the gods
31. What's ____ for me?
32. Carp's cousin
33. Barbershop specialties
34. Dress style
35. City of the Seven Hills
37. Guitar device
38. Presently
40. Electron tube
43. Arabian prince
44. Offspring
48. Partner
49. Those people
50. Prank
51. Hebrew month
52. Dotted, in heraldry
53. Chore
55. Black gold

Starting box on page 562

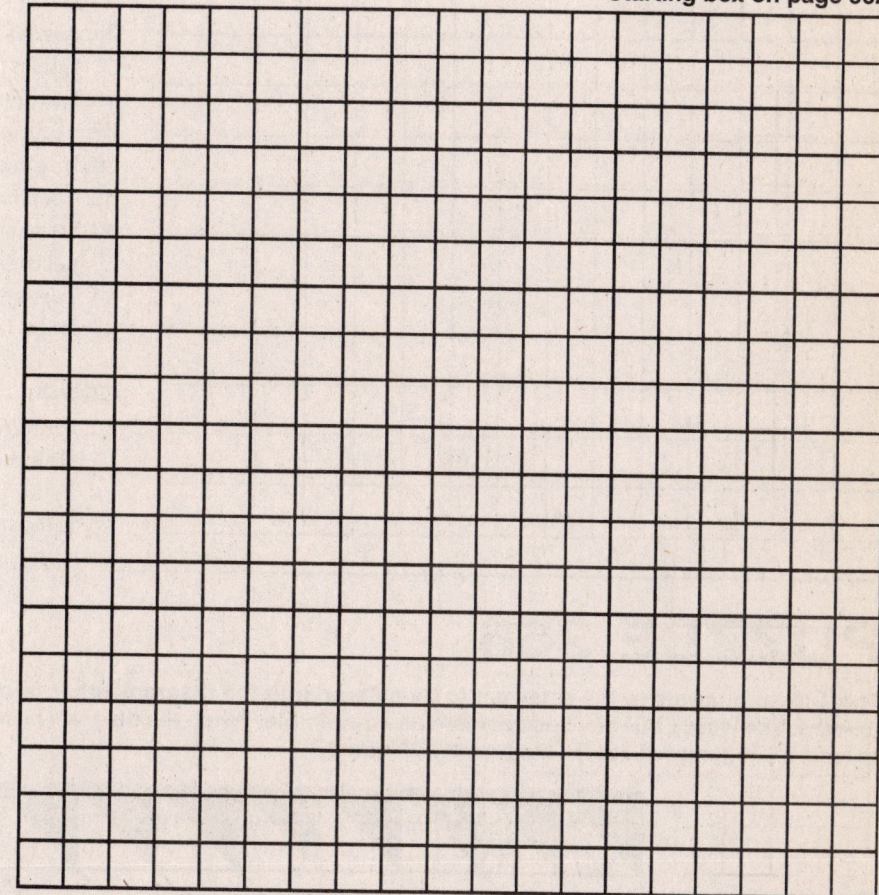

# Finish the Fours

## PUZZLE 364

**Place letters into the diagram to form a string of overlapping 4-letter words. A 4-letter word begins in each numbered square. If you choose the correct letters, they will reveal the name of a literary character, reading in order from left to right.**

| | | | | | | | | | | | | | | | | | | | | |
|---|---|---|---|---|---|---|---|---|---|---|---|---|---|---|---|---|---|---|---|---|
| 1 L | O | | 2 T | O | 3 | E | | 4 P | 5 L | A | 6 | E | C | 7 | I | T | 8 | V | E | 9 |
| O | 10 T | E | 11 | T | O | 12 P | A | 13 S | | E | 14 M | | L | 15 T | R | | 16 P | I | | K |

# PUZZLE 365

**ACROSS**
1. Cup edge
4. That woman
7. King beater
8. Artfully shy
9. Chicks' sounds
12. Curtain
14. Gratuities
16. Diving area
17. Halt
18. Otherwise
19. Celebrity
21. Fable, e.g.
22. Detroit athlete
24. Hideout
25. Lori or Tom
27. Stinging insects
29. Carpenters' tools
32. "____ the Clock"
33. Darn!
35. Aardvarks' tidbits
36. Doodled
37. Sections
39. Intelligent
42. Coop product
43. Neither's partner
44. Teensy
45. Hog's home

Starting box on page 562

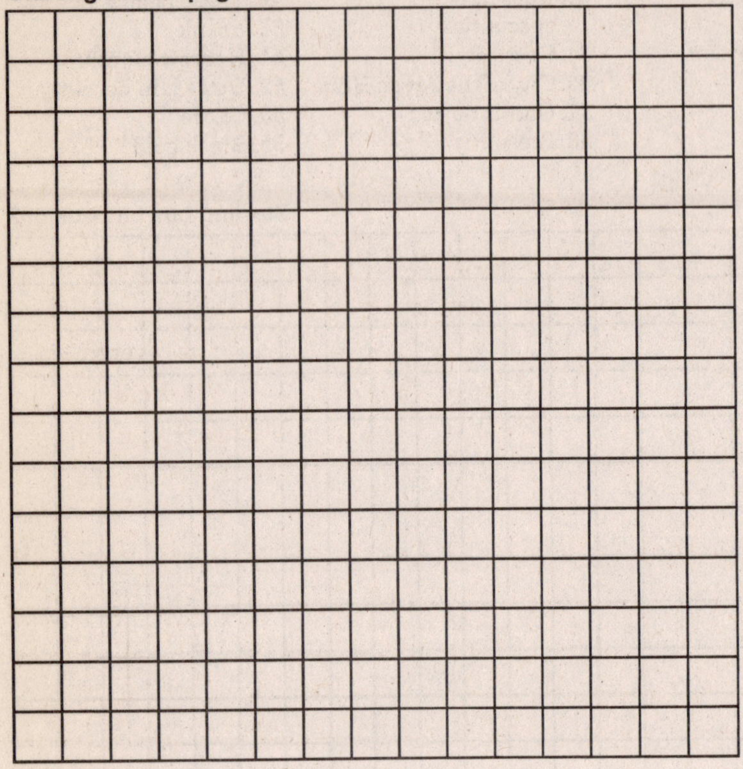

**DOWN**
1. Emulate Hammer
2. Polar sight
3. Encounters
4. Weighing device
5. Bunny's motion
6. View closely
10. Peach leftovers
11. Leopard's marking
12. Tot's toy
13. Gypsy ____ Lee
15. Tiff
16. Juicy fruit
20. Goes by bus
21. Hikers' shelters
23. Understand
25. Hamsters, e.g.
26. Football measure
27. Flexed
28. Diner offering
30. Armed conflicts
31. Wineglass feature
32. River vessel
34. Graceful birds
37. Chapel chair
38. Mature
40. Decay
41. Take to court

# PUZZLE 366 Crozzle

**The 4-letter answers to the clues are to be entered into the diagram either from top to bottom or diagonally upward. The word LIAR has been entered as an example. When the diagram is correctly filled, you will be able to read a 9-letter word across the top row of letters.**

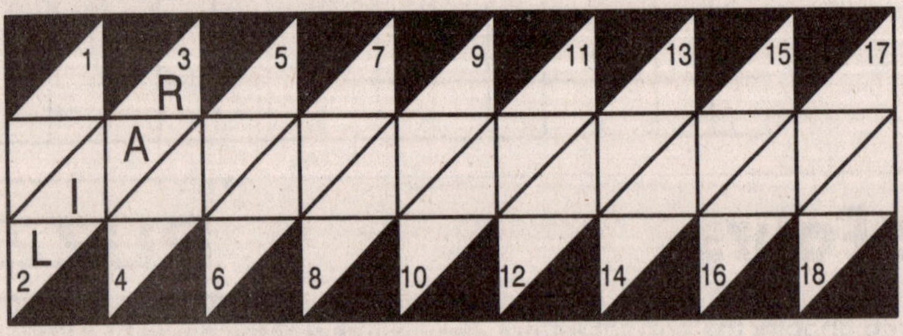


1-2. Bucket
2-3. Tall-tale teller
3-4. Surprise attack
4-5. Plunge
5-6. Fifty-fifty
6-7. Brooklyn team
7-8. Interrupt
8-9. Prod
9-10. ____ out (barely made)
10-11. College official
11-12. Metal fastener
12-13. Roster
13-14. Ivan the Terrible, e.g.
14-15. Great review
15-16. Always
16-17. Enjoy a book
17-18. Moist

# PUZZLE 367

**ACROSS**

1. French priest
5. Koweit's neighbor
6. Come up
7. War tactic
9. Grasslands
10. Vassal
11. For the life ____ . . .
15. Glorify
17. Guilty lover from the "Inferno"
19. Yokemates
21. Perfuming
24. Type of party
28. Being rejected in love
32. Book of Hebrew law
33. See-through wrap
34. Not trained
36. Certain comparisons: abbr.
38. More dreadful
40. Forest goddess
41. Sheer fabrics
43. Lacking self-confidence
45. Of the ear
46. On cloud nine
50. Hawaiian goose
51. Strutting
52. Kind of opera
55. Suppress
56. Middle Eastern dish
59. Painter Bonheur
60. Sitarist Shankar
61. Whirlybird, shortly
63. Stuffy
64. Notions
65. College official
66. "Das Lied von der ____" (Mahler song cycle)

**DOWN**

1. BB gun, e.g.
2. Actor Keith
3. Foundation
4. Supplemented
6. Well-known Biblical mount
7. Church area
8. Holm oak
11. Public
12. Snake's weapon
13. U.S. abolitionist/ women's rights advocate
14. Man who talked to Job
16. Labels
18. Upright
20. Honey drink
21. Gaping
22. Moving pictures
23. Metal cylinder used in dam building
24. Beginning for us
25. Like a ____ bricks
26. Thin as ____
27. Fast gait
29. Sea god
30. Incensed
31. Kidney enzyme
35. Minnow
37. Burns
39. U.S. journalist
42. Step
44. Dump
47. Division word
48. Sgts.
49. Miss Lollobrigida
53. Aviator's vehicle
54. License and dinner
57. Thoroughfares: abbr.
58. Some evergreens
61. Fall drink
62. Mountain nymph
63. Staff member

Starting box on page 562

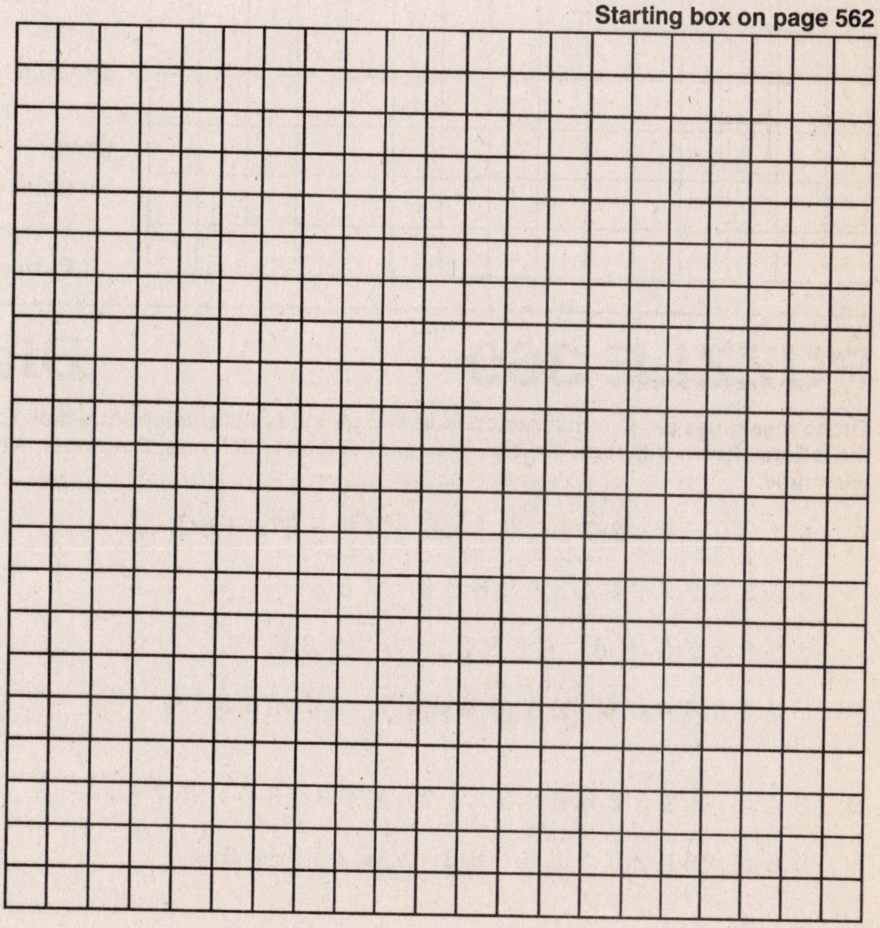

# PUZZLE 368

**ACROSS**
1. Bunny's movement
4. Bleat
7. Light breeze
8. Tractor-trailer
9. Flash
12. Window covering
14. Cut with scissors
16. Dog breed, for short
17. Exchange for money
18. "The ____ King"
19. Not strong
21. Submerged
22. Neat!
24. Sock part
25. Guide
27. Waiter's order carrier
29. Liquid measure
32. Small branch
33. Cage
35. Port, e.g.
36. Sharpen
37. Tendency
39. Draws closer
42. Affirmative vote
43. Billiard stick
44. Cot
45. Chop

**DOWN**
1. Crone
2. Furnace fuel
3. Push against
4. Muscular strength
5. Assist
6. Grow older
10. Turn over ____ leaf
11. ____ High City (Denver)
12. Leg part
13. Bait holder
15. Scheme
16. Brick material
20. Poker pot
21. Sharply inclined
23. Enemy
25. Wise
26. Wealthy
27. Double
28. Peel
30. Midday
31. Musical sound
32. Scottish cloth
34. Freestone fruit
37. Running bill
38. Type of bread
40. Regret
41. Stitch

**Starting box on page 562**

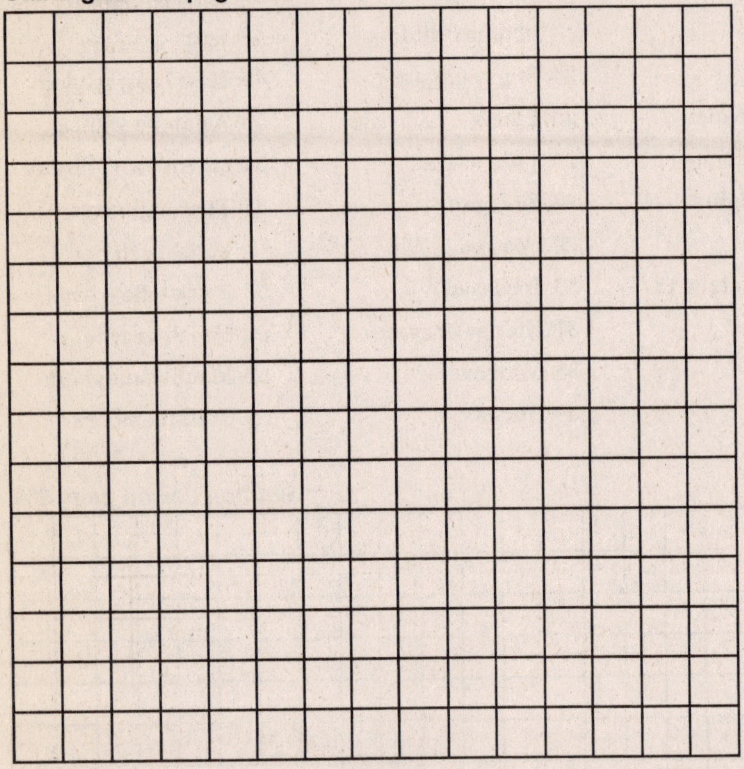

# PUZZLE 369

## Dial-A-Grams

**These messages are in a number code based on the familiar telephone dial. Each number represents one of the letters shown with it on the dial. You must decide which one. A number is not necessarily the same letter each time.**

**A.** 9436 93279 67 6837562333, 552627 543 3696 263 733873 86 6683, 63836 77488464 28 84347 3748377.

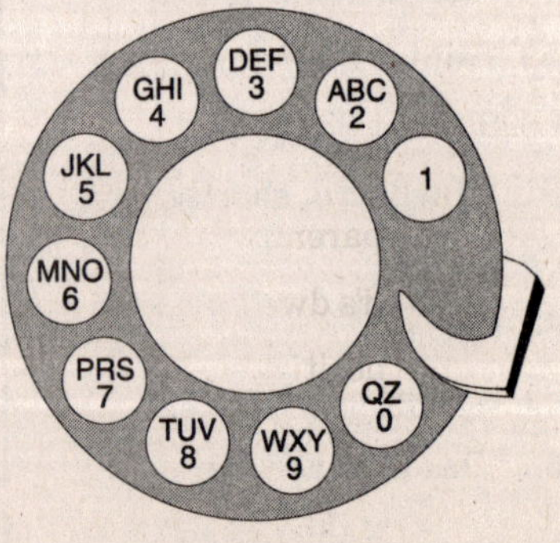


**B.** 843 62526883 47 843 653378 56696 27333 63 2527526 364.

# PUZZLE 370

**ACROSS**

1. Of the ear
5. ___ Alto
6. Subdivision of the American Devonian period
8. Certain fuel carriers
11. Son of Adam
12. Willing
16. Do a grammatical chore
17. ___ IX (king of Thailand)
18. Supervise
20. Chunky
22. Spoiled children
23. ". . . officers stood there, who had ___" (John 18:18)
29. Fine
30. Harangue
31. French novelist
35. Singer Loggins
36. Takes out
37. Makes defective
38. Aware of
39. Treated with mercy
41. Soap opera, e.g.
42. Carry ___ (do something unnecessary)
46. Run after
47. Despotic ruler
48. Flower parts
51. British gun
52. Transparent wrap
53. Nomad's dwelling
54. State positively
55. Certain fuel
59. "The Velvet Fog"
60. Corrosive
61. Actress Turner

**DOWN**

1. Oil gp.
2. Poi source
3. Pelvic bones
4. Train components
7. Approaches
9. Get up
10. Dagger
12. U.S. composer
13. Notes between so and do
14. Asian border river
15. Scandinavian
16. Favorite ones
18. Toward the mouth
19. Poetic lowland
20. Risque
21. Fools for love
22. Anacondas
23. Kind of shark
24. Hymn word
25. Depression
26. Orchestra conductor Rapee
27. ___ mignon
28. Beliefs
31. King Porsena
32. Forget
33. River duck
34. Man or Wight
36. Hill's companion
37. ___ of faith
39. Fly high
40. Go by
41. Meager
42. Chinese dynasty
43. Political cartoonist
44. Diminutive suffix
45. Famed English architect
46. Barbecue need
48. Relative of PDQ
49. Church part
50. Goodie
56. Killer whale
57. Ugandan dictator
58. Mother of Pollux

**Starting box on page 562**

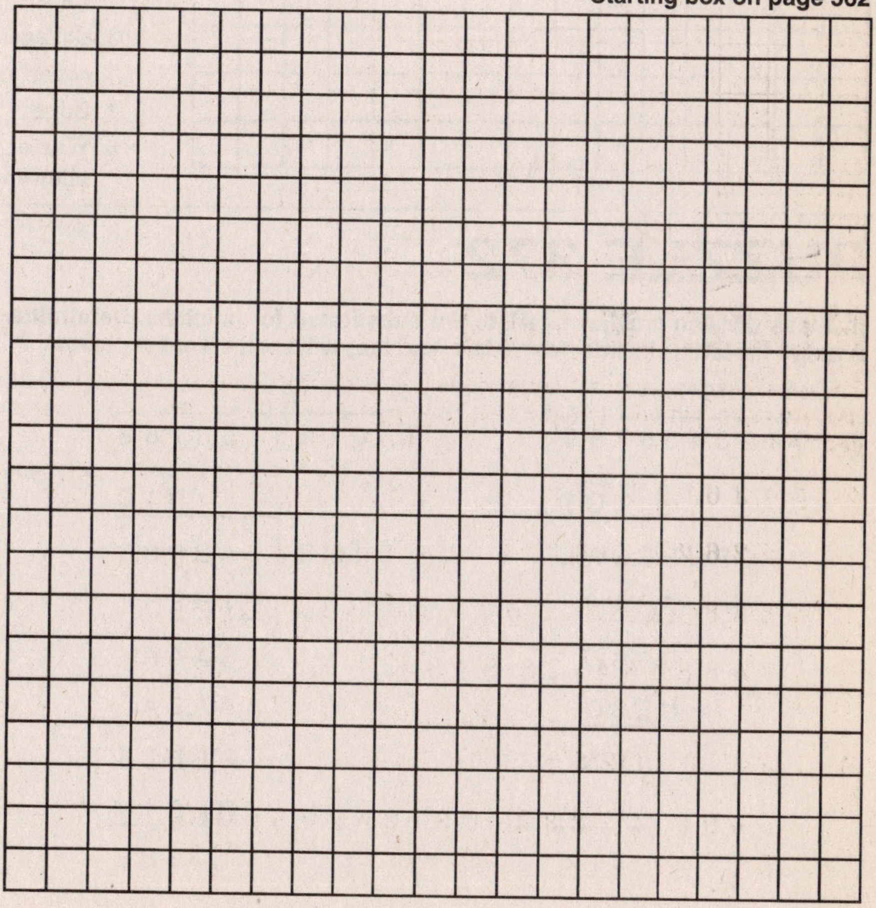

# PUZZLE 371

**ACROSS**

1. Speedy
6. Shake with cold
7. Author Bracken
10. Milk glass
11. Rowboat tool
12. Most unhappy
13. Egg-shaped
15. Attempts
16. Beirut native
18. Wrongdoers
20. Crimsons
21. Russian information service
25. Game fish
28. Left a jet
31. Taj ____
33. Window part
34. Greek galley
36. Relations
37. Misters, in Madrid
38. Pittsburgh clock setting: abbr.
39. Entertained
40. Stately flowers

Starting box on page 562

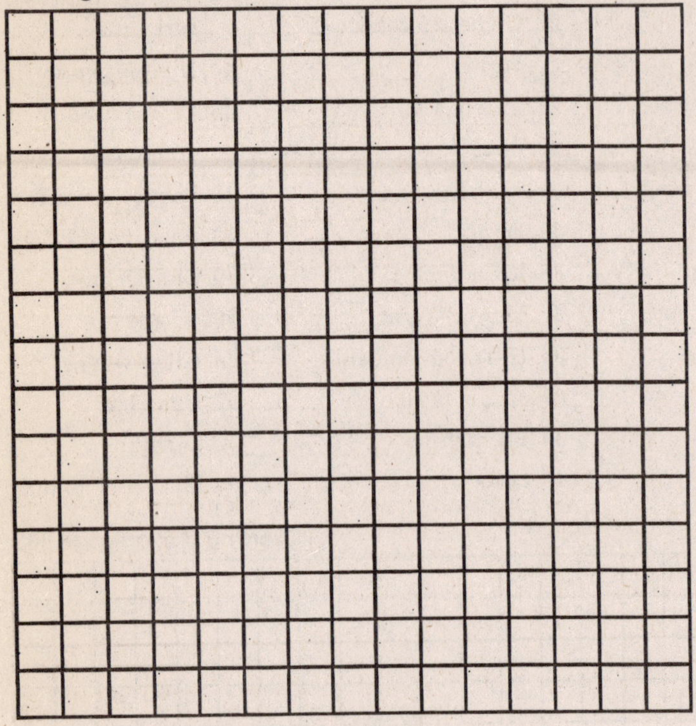

**DOWN**

1. More questionable
2. Playwright Oscar
3. College coverings
4. Bogs
5. Waste allowance
6. Most widely dispersed
7. Swimming hole
8. Roof edge
9. Snatches
10. Belgian city
14. Den
17. Wind dir.
19. Flowed
22. Russets, e.g.
23. Scale tone
24. Cookie
26. Sticks
27. Adder or asp
29. Geraint's beloved
30. Small impression
31. Less
32. Got up
34. Russian autocrat
35. San ____, Italy

# PUZZLE 372

## WORD MATH

**In these division problems, letters are substituted for numbers. Determine the value of each letter. Then arrange the letters in order from 0 to 9, and they will spell a word or phrase.**

**1.** 0 1 2 3 4 5 6 7 8 9

```
          TOT
    FOR | SCOWL
          EUW
          URSW
          UESC
           UCWL
            EUW
            FLR
```

**2.** 0 1 2 3 4 5 6 7 8 9

```
             RID
    DIME | LABORS
           DIME
           ASAAR
           AAALA
             REDLS
             REBIM
               DBE
```

**3.** 0 1 2 3 4 5 6 7 8 9

```
             PAL
    LAIC | RADIAL
           TPRD
           PLUIA
           PUOTD
            UPTAL
            UDRLC
             UOPO
```

# PUZZLE 373

**ACROSS**

1. Created
5. Cranshaw, for one
6. Milk producer
9. Make believe
11. Actor Lugosi
12. ____ to lunch
13. Actor Griffith
14. Brewed drink
15. Thwack
16. Sass
19. Ignited
20. Lassoed
22. Sharpened
23. Spear
24. Highland headgear
25. BPOE member
27. Use a shovel
28. ____ a girl!
31. Sit as judge on
33. Even score
34. Fairy-tale monster
35. Pupil
39. Sock part
40. Skin openings
41. Meara or Murray

**DOWN**

1. Faced
2. Brewed drink
3. Actor Johnson
4. Finale
5. "Full ____ Jacket"
6. Copper coin
7. Aged
8. Path
9. Flower holder
10. Regret
11. Earthworm, e.g.
15. Secreted
17. Press
18. ____ de Leon
19. Headed
21. Pare
22. Easter meat
23. Fall behind
24. Grow weary
26. March toys
27. Challenge
29. Soft metal
30. Matched group
31. Fiery
32. Self
35. Health resort
36. Heavy weight
37. Samovar
38. Actress Sandra

Starting box on page 562

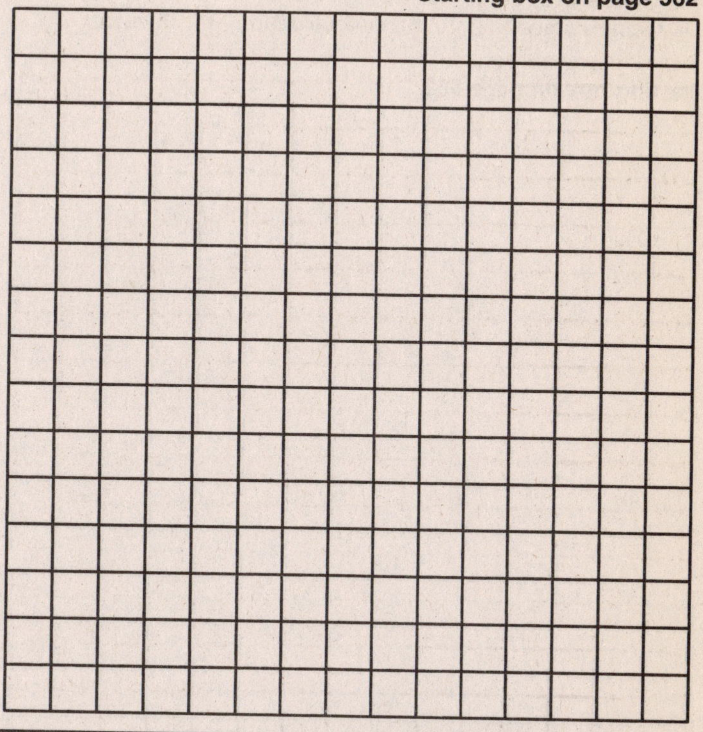

# QUOTAGRAM — PUZZLE 374

**Fill in the answers to the clues below. Then transfer the letters to the correspondingly numbered squares in the diagram. The completed diagram will contain a quotation.**

1. Circus laborer ___ ___ ___ ___ ___ ___ ___ ___ ___ ___
   68 15 28 63 1 13 71 45 73 21

2. Uppity: hyph. ___ ___ ___ ___ ___ ___ ___ ___ ___ ___
   2 59 64 37 26 8 56 75 32 23

3. Mexican dog ___ ___ ___ ___ ___ ___ ___ ___ ___
   66 33 5 22 16 70 9 46 20

4. Without choice ___ ___ ___ ___ ___ ___ ___ ___ ___ ___ ___
   10 65 35 27 50 60 31 17 34 47 44

5. Right on target: 3 wds. ___ ___ ___ ___ ___ ___ ___ ___ ___ ___ ___ ___ ___ ___
   14 67 43 57 3 41 11 52 55 36 39 58 49 54

6. Hope ___ ___ ___ ___ ___ ___ ___ ___ ___ ___ ___
   69 40 19 62 6 74 18 76 24 30 4

7. Smithies ___ ___ ___ ___ ___ ___
   51 72 42 12 7 48

8. Movable barriers ___ ___ ___ ___ ___
   29 38 53 61 25

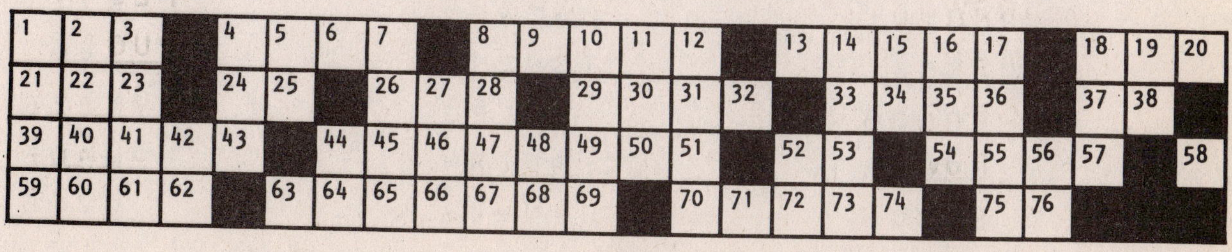

# PUZZLE 375

**ACROSS**

1. Command to Fido
4. Genie's place
8. Center
9. Song from "Faust"
10. Strenuous dance
11. Set of tables
12. Cartoonist Peter
13. 1978 Travolta film
15. ____ Vegas
16. Actress West
17. Pismire
18. Savoir-faire
20. Battle memento
22. Baby's toy
24. Author Bagnold
26. Tonic's partner
27. Warble
29. Muss
31. First gardener
33. Tupelos, e.g.
34. Before, in poems
35. Flower holder
36. Literary collection
37. Reception: hyph.
41. Hot spot
42. Cut of meat
43. Wit
45. After-dinner candy
46. Roman road
47. Choir voice
48. Corral

**DOWN**

1. Unaccompanied
2. Annoy
3. Gunpowder or jasmine
4. Narrow path
5. Zone
6. "____ Otis Regrets"
7. Top of the head
8. Unchanging
10. Cavort
12. Oh dear!
13. Method of moving
14. Takes ten
16. Low, sad sound
18. Snoops
19. Noted essayist
21. Public disorder
23. Try
25. Kind of wheat
26. Valley
28. Star of "The Rockford Files"
30. Parched
32. Intend
37. Singer Gluck
38. Labor
39. Clue
40. Atop
41. Portent
43. With it
44. Southwest Indian

**Starting box on page 562**

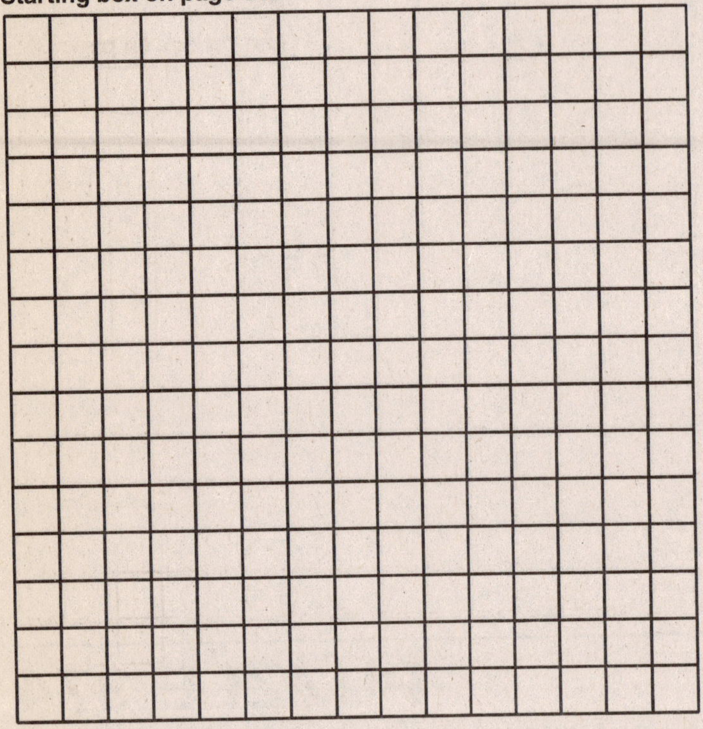

# PUZZLE 376

## WORD MATH

**In these long-division problems, letters are substituted for numbers. Determine the value of each letter. Then arrange the letters in order from 0 to 9, and they will spell a word or phrase.**

**1**

| 0 | 1 | 2 | 3 | 4 | 5 | 6 | 7 | 8 | 9 |
|---|---|---|---|---|---|---|---|---|---|
| | | | | | | | | | |

```
            AHA
SHAG ) CARPING
       CRRGA
        RGURN
        RANCS
         CRGRG
         CRRGA
           SCH
```

**2**

| 0 | 1 | 2 | 3 | 4 | 5 | 6 | 7 | 8 | 9 |
|---|---|---|---|---|---|---|---|---|---|
| | | | | | | | | | |

```
            DOE
SLOW ) DONATED
       NSOWL
        OWTWE
        TSNLH
         EALED
         WLSSN
          NLLA
```

**3**

| 0 | 1 | 2 | 3 | 4 | 5 | 6 | 7 | 8 | 9 |
|---|---|---|---|---|---|---|---|---|---|
| | | | | | | | | | |

```
            RIM
SUIT ) ASSISTS
       AAUMZ
        UMEZT
        UIIAM
         IAEZS
         IMAQE
          UZIE
```

## PUZZLE 377

**ACROSS**

1. Spring
4. Wane
7. Caress
10. Afresh
12. Meadow
13. Repent
14. Direct
16. Bernstein opus
18. Anger
19. Reflect
21. Zilch
22. Family vehicle
23. Spoil
25. Long legend
27. Conceit
28. Humor
29. Staff
32. Unhearing
34. Turn down
37. Solidarity
39. Sludge
41. Under
42. Interlock
43. Kind of star
45. Itch
46. Embrace
48. Auto
49. Smell
51. Outfit
52. Decade
54. Sorrow
56. Irritate
61. Bullring shout
62. Unfeeling
64. Rustic
65. Fuel
66. Bind
67. Deities
68. Pismire
69. Before, to a poet
70. Golfbag item

**DOWN**

1. Catch
2. Aware of
3. Hammer part
4. Lofty tree
5. Pinto or pea
6. Foundation
7. In confidence
8. Atmosphere
9. Adolescent
11. Marry
15. Cure
17. Cole ____
20. Wrath
24. Wander
26. Donate
29. Pirate's drink
30. Undivided
31. Deceitful
33. Jollity
35. Water tester
36. Possess
38. Dull bang
40. Pier
41. Trade
44. Futile
47. Ball dress
50. Course
52. Roman robe
53. Spirit
55. Mideast ruler
57. Harbor craft
58. Horse's gait
59. Put on cargo
60. Otherwise
63. Honeymaker

**Starting box on page 562**

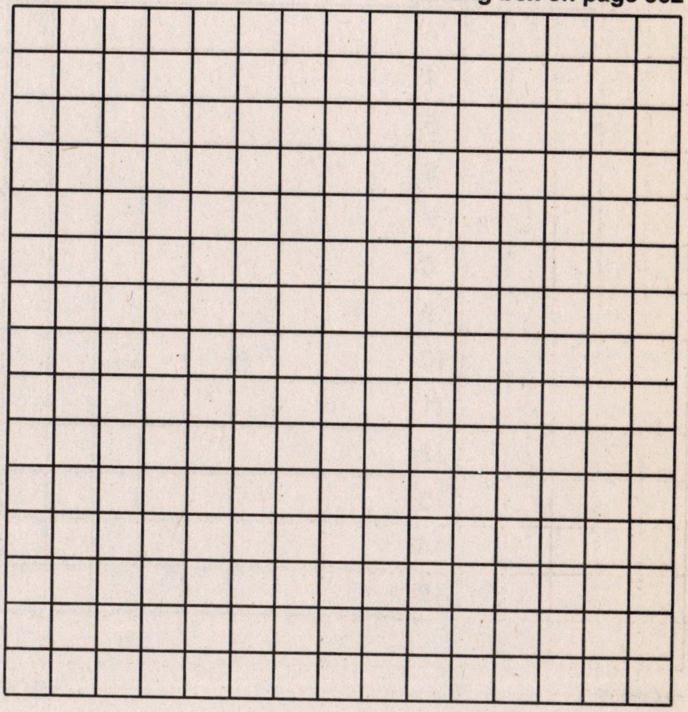

---

## MIX AND MATCH

## PUZZLE 378

**The letters of each word in the left-hand column can be rearranged and then placed in front of a word in the right-hand column to form a new word. For example, LAIR in the first column, matched with ROAD in the second, would lead to RAILROAD.**

| | |
|---|---|
| 1. LAIR | a. RUDE |
| 2. RATS | b. LICE |
| 3. TRADE | c. ROAD |
| 4. TINGE | d. BOARD |
| 5. REAPS | e. CANT |
| 6. SPUR | f. HEAD |
| 7. PURSE | g. MILL |
| 8. PORT | h. VISE |
| 9. MINED | i. RATE |

# PUZZLE 379

## WORDSWORTH

**Fill in each row and column of the Wordsworth diagram with at least two words. The number of words in a row or column is indicated by the number of clues. Words are not separated by extra squares, so all the squares are to be filled in when the diagram is completed.**

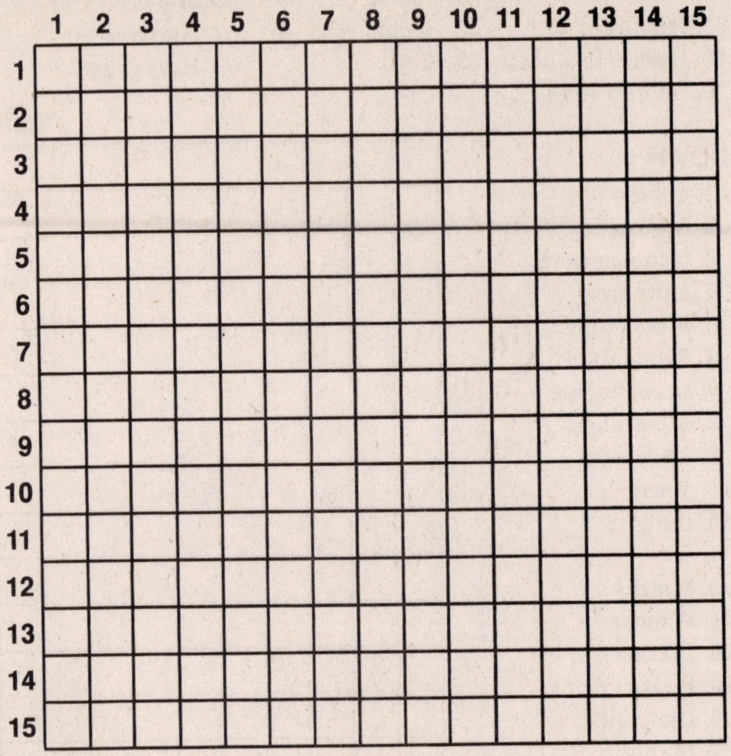


**ACROSS**

1. Unconscious state • Shade tree • U.S. playwright • Lumps
2. Stead • College official • Spray
3. Unselfish • Satire
4. NY city • Late-night TV offerings
5. Earth's satellite • Excited • Seep • Short rest
6. Compose • Leaf • Italian coin, once
7. Innocent • ____ live and breathe! • Half-size newspaper
8. Hurried • Old car • "Ben ____" • Formerly
9. Period of time • Prejudiced • Hound variety
10. Inactive • Symbol of peace • Consume • Competent
11. Caused intense fear • Luge • Operated
12. California wine valley • Small spar • Inventor's safeguard
13. ____ bien • Capital of Taiwan • Discovers
14. Piece out • Long time • Revolve • Subcontinent
15. Sigmoid figure • Storms • Seine • Diplomacy

**DOWN**

1. Assertion • Concerning • Charged particle • Golf mound
2. Lubricate • Heavy weight • Anteaters
3. Painstaking • Fencing swords
4. Emanation • Actor David • Pencil part
5. Schooled • Oklahoma city • Portico
6. Garland • Grow old • Pointed shaft • Sudden pain
7. Sail support • See • Ceremony
8. Incised carving • Legendary king of Thebes
9. Brad • Curse • Cowboy movie
10. Harmless lizard • Paint crudely • Of Swiss mountains
11. Goddess of discord • Horselike animal • Pekoe • Appropriate
12. And not • Greeting • Dejected • Shade
13. Servicemen's gp. • Pungent bulbs • Singer Lee
14. ____ voyage! • Feud • Of Reykjavik
15. Cunning • Shovel • Portable shelter • Perched

# PUZZLE 380

**ACROSS**

1. New York City vehicle
4. Make cookies
8. Envelop
12. Tint
13. Arab chieftain
14. Overhang
15. Generation
16. Chromosome
17. Sector
18. Alarm
20. Salesman
21. As well
22. Perched
23. Dress
26. Shy
30. Self
31. Fragment
33. Mineral
34. Conference
36. Darn
37. Egg layer
38. Dove call
40. Tooth
43. Trash
47. Spirit
48. Ground
49. Offer
50. Connect
51. Medicinal plant
52. Night before
53. Little piggies
54. Bar drink
55. Finger count

**DOWN**

1. ___ the fat
2. Atmosphere
3. Grizzly, for one
4. Start
5. Revise
6. Royal ruler
7. Previously, in poetry
8. Riches
9. Uncommon
10. Profess
11. Summit
19. Seize
20. Valise
22. Pouch
23. Jewel
24. Eternity
25. Caviar
26. Plead
27. Enemy
28. Footed vase
29. Conducted
31. Wharf
32. "Holiday ___"
35. Gratitude
36. Throng
38. Dugout
39. Command
40. Defrost
41. Medley
42. Alley
43. Wind gust
44. Help
45. Donate
46. Adam's garden
48. Research room

# PUZZLE 381

## MOVIES AND TELEVISION

### ACROSS

1. "That Certain ___" (1938 film)
4. "Happy Days" actress
9. Locale of "Golden Girls": abbr.
12. Actress Witherspoon
14. "___ in the Head" (1959 film): 2 wds.
15. "True ___" (1969 film)
16. Actress Markey (original Jane)
17. Michael or George
18. Reporter Lois ___
19. "The ___ Was Indiscreet" (1947 film)
21. "The ___ of Iwo Jima" (1949 film)
22. Actress Munson of "GWTW"
23. "The Night ___ Eyes" (1942 film)
24. "___ Street"
27. 1979 David Soul film: 2 wds.
33. Comedian Dean ___
35. Actress Thompson et al.
36. "___ Got a Secret"
37. Alan or Robert
38. More unusual
40. Actor Burl
41. TV's 66, e.g.: abbr.
42. Backwater
43. Arthur Godfrey's "___ Scouts"
45. 1953 film with Actor Cameron: 2 wds.
48. Singer Diana
49. Larry's friend
50. Actress Joanne of "Wagon Master"
52. "The Enemy ___" (1957 film)
55. 1927 Buster Keaton film, with "The"
60. "___ in my Heart" (1933 film)
61. Ruth or Susan
64. ___ Jill Miller of "Gimme a Break"
65. "What's My ___?"
66. On to
67. Comedian Kamen
68. Jolson and namesakes
69. Actress Sharon of "Cagney & Lacy"
70. "Meet John ___" (1941 film)

### DOWN

1. "Four ___," 1950s singing group
2. "___ Are the Days" (1963 film)
3. Actress Gray
4. "___ Fire" (1957 film): 2 wds.
5. Maureen and Catherine
6. ___ Serling's "The Twilight Zone"
7. Tavern brew
8. King Saul's grandfather
9. Ollie's pal
10. Peter ___ Hayes
11. Actor Roscoe
13. 1961 Hayward film
15. "The ___ Menagerie" (1950 film)
20. Singer Tennille
21. Waterston and Elliott
23. "Dear ___" (1964 film)
24. "The ___ Story" (1953 film)
25. Eve or Mary
26. Carol ___ White
28. Terri ___ (Priscilla Barnes TV role)
29. Grant or Majors
30. "Private ___" (1931 film)
31. Props for Julia Child
32. "___ Pilot" (1938 film)
33. "Presenting Lily ___" (1943 film)

# PUZZLE 381

34. Actor Nick of "48 Hours"
39. "The Dynamic ____" (Batman and Robin)
40. Labor initials
42. "The ____ Queen" (1959 film)
44. "____ for Your Money" (1949 film): 2 wds.
46. "That's ____" (Martin song from "The Caddy")
47. Buchanan and Barrier
51. Auberjonois and Clair
52. Lugosi or Bartok
53. "The ____ Mind" (1934 film)
54. Camera part
56. "A Nightmare on ____ Street" (1984 film)
57. "____ on Rommel" (1971 film)
58. Woody Guthrie's son
59. "The ____ George Apley" (1947 film)
61. Dusting cloth for "Hazel"
62. "The ____ and the Pussycat" (1970 film)
63. Actress West

# PUZZLE 382

**ACROSS**

1. Inner hand
5. Shock
10. Thrust
14. Balm
15. Unite
16. Bern's river
17. Bass tuba
19. Future sign
20. Lazy ____
21. Defeat
23. Vampire
24. Game fish
27. Region for Eisenhower: abbr.
29. Instruments for Benny Goodman et al.
33. Wine jug
36. Houston University
37. Inhabitant: suff.
38. Tibetan
39. Rise
41. Watches
42. Shortstops' equipment
43. Park it
45. Cleves lady
46. More dried out
47. Flamenco instruments
49. Medal initials
50. Gas consumers
51. Greek letter
53. Progeny
55. Bid
60. Ship call
62. Keyboard instrument
65. Not a soul
66. Rile
67. Old cars
68. Trial
69. Yorkshire city
70. Depression

**DOWN**

1. ____ judgment on
2. Baseball family
3. Costello and Rawls
4. High land
5. Stereo component
6. Exclamation of disgust
7. Will procedure
8. Actor James ____
9. Sodium hydroxides
10. ____ Paulo
11. Gypsy's instrument
12. Place
13. Committed
18. Opposed
22. Cal and Georgia, e.g.
25. Singles
26. Minnow catcher
28. Boring tool
29. Rugged rocks
30. Cloth type
31. Instruments for Judy Tenuta et al.
32. Actor Keanu ____
34. Worn out
35. Lets up
38. Fracas
40. Franco and Peter
43. Meat link
44. Suffix with novel or social
47. Dog
48. Until
51. Gasp
52. If the ____ fits . . .
54. October stone
56. Harrison or Henry
57. Liberate
58. Harrow's rival
59. Remainder
61. Thus far
63. Composer Rorem
64. Correlatives

# PUZZLE 383

**ACROSS**

1. Moon exploration vehicle
4. Squeal
7. Go out with
11. Met offering
13. Ms. Maxwell
15. Challenges
16. Spot's breed, perhaps?
18. Brilliance
19. Part of U.S.A.: abbr.
20. Healthcare facility
22. Spanish galleon's loot
23. Marvin and Trevino
24. Football scores, for short
27. ___ de France
29. Outlines sharply
32. Does more business
35. Dummy
36. Cheeky
37. Tree
39. Vincent Lopez's theme song
41. Orchestra members
44. Fixed a cushion
47. Music maker
49. Drench
50. Compass heading: abbr.
51. Teheran money
52. Singer Zadora
54. Accrued
58. Discover
60. More of the same
61. Racing breed
65. Wakes up
66. Gratify
67. Wipe out
68. Pass
69. Roll of money
70. Summer on the Seine

**DOWN**

1. Young man
2. Memorable time
3. Uris's "___ 18"
4. Fish again
5. Actress MacGraw
6. Russian ruler
7. Short-legged dog
8. Woody's boy
9. Sports group
10. Noted Italian family
12. Bullets
14. Anoint
15. Discover
17. Eagle's nest
21. Parts of a tennis match
24. Spinning toy
25. Singing twosomes
26. Prance
28. Fairy
30. Poem
31. Tennis champ Monica ___
33. Brandy carrier
34. Knight's title
38. Second notes of the scale
40. Summer drink
42. Gazelles
43. Scorch
45. Having bulging peepers
46. Silly
48. Designer Cassini and namesakes
53. Punctuation mark: abbr.
54. Stream
55. Dog in "The Thin Man"
56. Mar
57. Tie
59. Christmas season
62. Airport initials
63. Slave-leader Turner
64. Change color

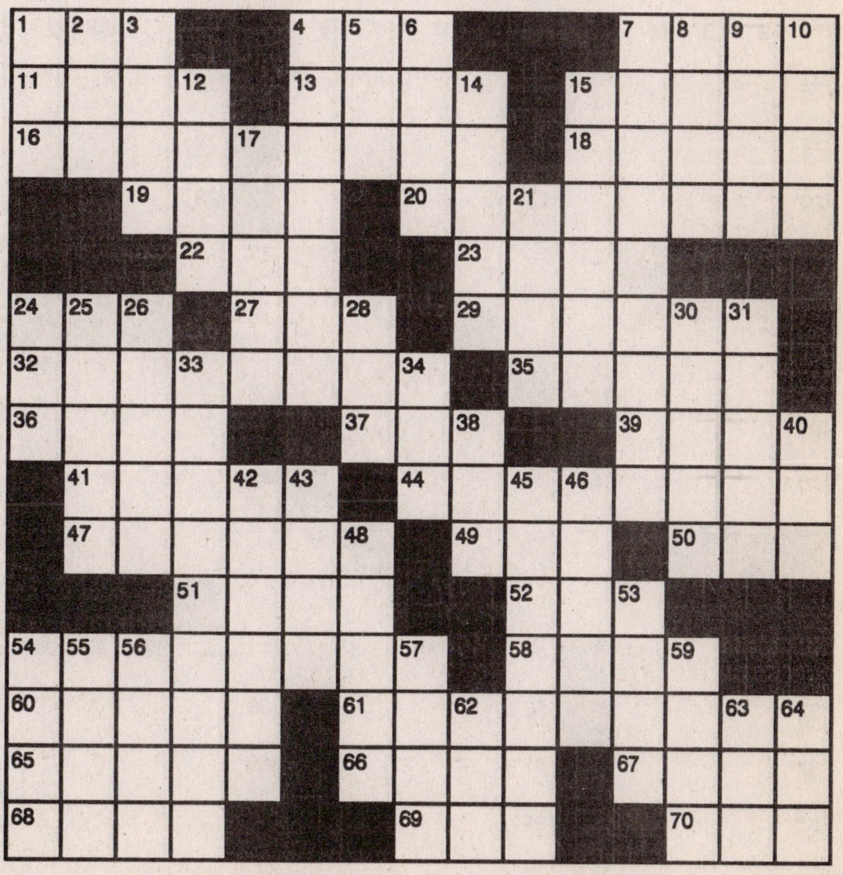

# PUZZLE 384

**ACROSS**

1. Eva or Zsa Zsa
6. ___ on the vine
10. Artist Chagall
14. Crockett's last stand
15. Sulk
16. African shrub
17. Deceives
18. Kimono features
19. Noisy
20. Breakfast drink
22. Roman garment
23. Van Gogh's loss
24. Short jacket
26. Uphold
30. Destined
32. Guinness and others
33. "Quoth the Raven, ___"
37. On this spot
38. Went with
39. Inventor Sikorsky
40. Jacksnipe
42. Dimness
43. Nat and Natalie
44. Cookie cookers
45. Sea creatures
48. "___ the ramparts . . ."
49. Medieval sharecropper
50. Soft drink
57. Treble or bass
58. Demonic
59. Major artery
60. Away from the weather
61. Hawaiian bird
62. Twinkle
63. Took a cab
64. Peter or Nicholas, e.g.
65. Millay and Ferber

**DOWN**

1. Fisherman's hook
2. Winglike
3. Azerbaijan capital
4. Buddhists' sacred mountain
5. Registers
6. Love affair
7. Mongolian desert
8. Spectacular
9. Abandoned
10. Soda-fountain treat
11. Distant
12. Red, in Paris
13. Aromatic wood
21. Wedge
25. Byron's eternity
26. Delightful sounds
27. Fido's bane
28. Houseplant
29. Java drink
30. Celebrations
31. Allege as fact
33. Neck part
34. Double curve
35. Laugh loudly
36. Goes astray
38. Thorough
41. Burst
42. Heavy fire
44. Social insect
45. Hollywood prize
46. Violin's kin
47. Cornered
48. Girl watcher
51. Currier and ___
52. Columbus's ship
53. Aggressive
54. Literary Ireland
55. Volcano in Sicily
56. Charlie Brown's exclamation

# PUZZLE 385

**ACROSS**

1. Word of regret
5. Foreman
9. Harness part
13. Stillness
14. A la ____
15. West of Afghanistan
16. Anderson fairy tale
19. Common verb
20. French kings
21. Bulrushes
22. Cut
23. Right and left, e.g.
24. Punishment method of yore
28. New York city
29. Electrical particles
30. Auto trip need
33. Carry on
34. Movie film units
36. Ditto
37. "High Hopes" insect
38. Breathing: abbr.
39. Southeast of Cleveland
40. Easy targets
43. Auspices
44. Author Bombeck
45. Playful act
46. Wild plum
47. Literary collection
50. Had ____ (was prepared)
53. Habit
54. Apply
55. Liturgy
56. Inside: pref.
57. Genesis home
58. Dressed

**DOWN**

1. Proceedings
2. Cowardly Lion
3. Aweather's antithesis
4. Dallas sch.
5. Howling
6. Commands: abbr.
7. Original Beatle Sutcliffe
8. Parts
9. Famous Jewish scholar
10. Northern constellation
11. Supplies the crew
12. A Siamese twin
14. Emmet Kelly, e.g.
17. Rye or wheat
18. Praise
22. Old card game
23. Converti-plane: abbr.
24. Dumb girl
25. ____ Bator
26. Wallet coin
27. Basso Cesare ____
30. Artist Chagall
31. Frenzied
32. Writes
34. Small purse
35. Assessments: abbr.
36. Seagull's relative
38. Unbending
39. Madison Avenue denizens
40. Begins
41. Actor Craig T. ____
42. Architectural joint
43. Concerning
45. Soon
46. Terrier type
47. Seed covering
48. Part of N.B.
49. Thunderstruck
50. Have bills
51. Heel
52. Circle part

# PUZZLE 386

**ACROSS**

1. Parking attendant
6. Poplar trees
12. Components
17. Likeness
18. Germinates
20. Bay window
21. Rocky Mountain tree
22. Pennsylvania: 2 wds.
24. Remnant
25. Quaker pronoun
27. Meager
28. ____ the mark
29. Crucifix
31. Totaled
34. Tease
35. Tirade
36. Type assortment
38. Festive nights
40. Timber wolf
42. Wild plum
43. Coarse files
45. Harvester
49. Stopwatches
52. Plugs
54. Mohawk, e.g.
55. Cooking utensil
56. "____ of Wine and Roses"
58. Iraqi's neighbor
60. Baseballer Slaughter
61. Killer whales
63. Purpose
65. Fender-bender mark
66. Pack away
67. "____ Rae"
68. Writer Ephron
70. "____ the season to . . ."
71. Fitzgerald and Logan
73. Twosomes
75. Sahara or Mohave
77. Contradicts
79. Lindens
81. Perennial plant
82. Actress Patricia
84. Complete defeat
85. Sugar plant
86. Automobiles
89. Brooks of "Blazing Saddles"
91. Approaches
93. Jacob's twin
96. Fuss
97. French painter
99. Scan
101. Sandboxer
102. West Virginia: 2 wds.
106. Divided
108. Unit of work
109. ____ glass
110. Ms. Midler
111. English city
112. Artemis's nymphs
113. Lance

**DOWN**

1. Fanged one
2. ____ acid
3. Illinois: 3 wds.
4. Conceit
5. Scout's shelter
6. Catechized
7. Radar trap's quarry
8. Use leverage
9. Greek's Aurora
10. From soup to ____
11. Business share
12. Station
13. Ovid's "____ of Love"
14. Lariat
15. Wyoming mountain
16. Winter precipitation
19. Sluggard
23. The witch of ____
26. Fedora or beret
30. Tragic fate
32. Gabor and LeGallienne
33. Goal
35. Bellowed
37. If ____ be
39. Athletic activity
41. "You ____ Your Life"
42. Shock
44. Basque country
46. Maine: 3 wds.
47. Vulcanite
48. Slumbers
50. April shower
51. Church council

# PUZZLE 386

53. Hairnet
55. Modeled
57. Swagger
59. Concerning: 2 wds.
62. Beaus
64. Arabian ruler
69. Movie dog
72. Bishop's jurisdiction
74. Swing around
76. Ocean eagle
78. Formerly Navigators Islands
80. Embarked on
83. Unaspirated consonant sound
85. Civil War govt.
86. Dromedary
87. Dote on
88. Cosmetic
90. Slow, in music
92. Oboes
94. Way to the heart
95. Speak
97. Rockies: abbr.
98. Russian ruler
100. Pats softly
103. Land of sleep
104. Cravat
105. Literary collection
107. Energy

# PUZZLE 387

**ACROSS**

1. Cicatrix
5. Hunters' settlement
9. ____ au rhum
13. Podium
17. Meat paste
18. Ellipsoidal
19. Cain's victim
20. In addition
21. Excited
22. Back of the neck
23. Bedouin shelter
24. Wheat grinder
25. Meal
27. Flavor
29. Contended
31. Smirk
33. Curling marks
35. Area or scatter
36. Degraded
40. Nancy of fiction
42. Obtuse
46. Welcome!
47. Spread widely
49. Time period
51. ____ to the world
52. Money-maker?
54. New Orleans Bowl
56. Stage item
58. Ice or Iron
59. Senior
61. Part of USNA
63. Dampen
65. Wail
67. Cut in two
69. Fellows
70. Desert hazard
74. Stately
76. Ballplayer Maris
80. "Mr. ____" (George Raft film)
81. Vault
83. Not now
85. Expansive
86. British streetcar
88. Place for money
90. Even
92. Perjure oneself
93. Horse or truth
95. Lounge
97. Chose
99. Russian fighter jet
101. Stumble
103. Truckee city
104. Falls down
108. Cogwheel
110. Expiated
114. Unwritten
115. Snout
117. Talks
119. Mound
120. Gawk
121. Emulates Bojangles
122. Genealogy diagram
123. Actress Martinelli
124. "____ Fall in Love"
125. Tiff
126. Darns
127. Spool

**DOWN**

1. Bandy words
2. Confine
3. At the acme
4. Entertain
5. Appeases
6. At all: Scot.
7. Charts
8. Skirt fold
9. Flashlight need
10. Humorist Burrows
11. South ____, Ind.
12. Change
13. Broken
14. Dismounted
15. Key
16. Vended
26. Caspian and Andaman
28. Showed the way
30. Potential flower
32. Second showing
34. Ooze
36. Female knight
37. Corrupt
38. Get better
39. French painter
41. Enthusiastic
43. Straight
44. Wise
45. Actress Barbara ____
48. Vacillate
50. Chamber
53. Final
55. Perplex
57. Dock
60. Bakery purchase
62. Lawful

# PUZZLE 387

64. TV static
66. Red vegetable
68. Ranks
70. Squeals
71. Farm unit
72. Kind of duct
73. Sora
75. Crowbar
77. Young female swine
78. Plimpton book
79. Clarinet, e.g.
82. Conspire
84. Press ____
87. Mutters
89. Most capacious
91. Fasting time
94. Wire measurement
96. Piffle!
98. Barrelmaker
100. Refined guys
102. Hair lines
104. Useful item
105. Coax
106. Beer ingredient
107. Detergent
109. Scarce
111. Cleo's river
112. Where's preceder
113. Business transaction
116. Belgian resort
118. Church seat

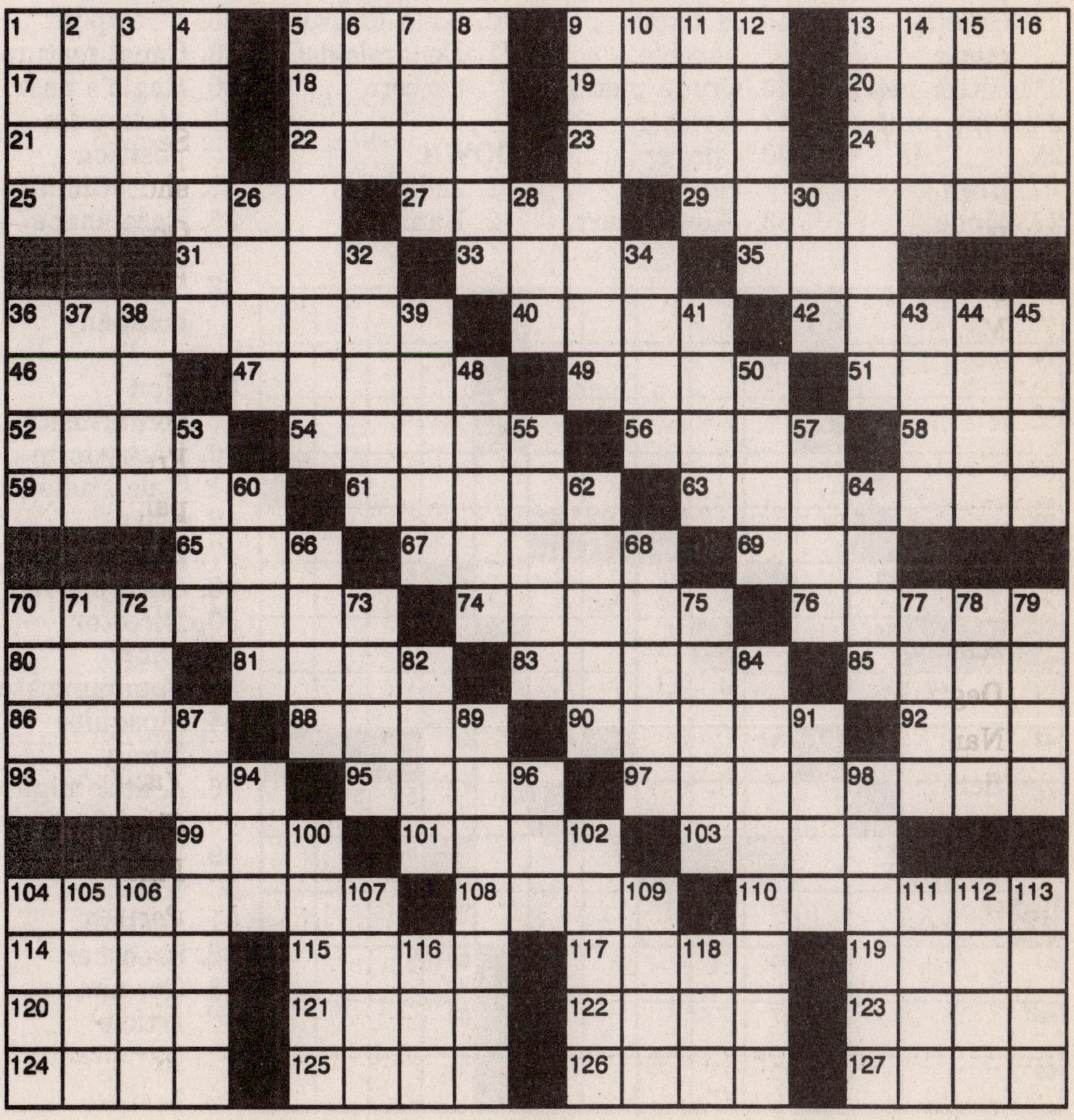

# PUZZLE 388

**ACROSS**

1. Bookies' quotes
5. Trances
10. Quarrel
14. Antitoxins
15. Weaken
16. European river
17. Footless
18. Actress Berger
19. Weird
20. Horace Greeley quote
23. Bitter vetch
24. Pipe joint
25. "___ Is Born"
27. Mode
29. Letterman
33. Actress Claire
34. Lennon's lady
36. German article
37. "The King ___"
38. Conestoga
43. Bandleader Lawrence ___
44. "The Greatest"
45. Hockey notable
46. Crude metal
47. Aviator
49. Conger catcher
53. Flower part
55. CIA predecessor
57. Actress Arden
58. Famous pioneer route
63. Pair
64. Muse of poetry
65. ___ St. Vincent Millay
66. Complexion woe
67. Tanker
68. Clan
69. Concordes
70. Kind of drum
71. Dendrologist's concern

**DOWN**

1. Indians
2. Banish
3. Sleepy
4. Marquis de ___
5. Rank
6. Carried out
7. Spanish hand
8. Aleutian island
9. Penn of films
10. Abounds
11. Thinking
12. Actor Lamas
13. Saute
21. Office worker
22. Flit about
26. Downpour
28. Canal feature
30. Eagle's nest
31. Jockey for position
32. ___-China
35. Face shape
37. Swiss river
38. "___ company . . ."
39. Non-conformists
40. Pachyderm
41. Yale student
42. Seize
47. Ziegfeld
48. Cheering fan
50. Director
51. Show
52. Communicate
54. Mosquito family
56. A little night music?
59. Vintage cars
60. Ireland
61. Festive
62. Breather
63. German article

# PUZZLE 389

**ACROSS**

1. Dough
5. Originate
9. Fictional elephant
14. Nora's dog
15. Comic Johnson
16. Informed
17. Legume
18. Japanese seasoning
19. Pianist Peter et al.
20. Wayne-Agar film
23. Type type: abbr.
24. Former king of Albania
25. More secure
28. Jane Austen novel
31. Stag
35. Alarm
37. Ventilates
39. Beetle
40. Southern constellation
41. Wayne-O'Hara film
43. Grow older
44. Edge
45. Yodeling feedback
46. Monument
48. ____ off (irritated)
50. Trumpeter Al ____
52. Suit material
53. Fish eggs
55. Willow
57. Wayne-Janssen film
64. Self-confidence
65. Seaweed
66. Seep
67. Telegraph inventor
68. Layer
69. Logan or Fitzgerald
70. Weaver's reeds
71. Impudence
72. Bambi, e.g.

**DOWN**

1. Taxis
2. On the briny
3. Comedian Laurel
4. More convenient
5. South Pacific islands
6. Treat lightly
7. Although: Lat.
8. The cat's ____
9. " . . . with a ____ on my knee"
10. "Anchors ____"
11. Brewer's yeast
12. Venezuela city
13. Legal matter
21. Photographic device
22. Missouri mountains
25. Begin
26. Lofty shelter
27. Casing
29. "____ Dad"
30. Actress Farrow
32. "____ With Judy"
33. Scoundrel
34. Cornered
36. Wealthier
38. Seat for two
42. Alphabet trio
47. Gave a medal to
49. Showy
51. Colors lightly
54. Moldings
56. Ski-lift components
57. Pickax, e.g.
58. Rent
59. Cafe sign
60. Lamb's pseudonym
61. First name in mystery
62. Mosaic piece
63. Boxers do it
64. Afternoons: abbr.

# PUZZLE 390

**ACROSS**

1. Dogpatch cartoonist
5. Official deeds
9. Skillful
13. Eastern nobleman
14. Unsharpened
16. "Dies ___"
17. Aquarelle
19. Actress Thompson
20. Pointed instruments
21. Seacoast
23. Street: abbr.
25. Mexican coins
26. ___ tell: 2 wds.
30. Spare
34. Bandleader Brown
35. Globes
38. Sierra ___
39. Oscar winner for Kazan: 3 wds.
43. Descendant
44. Talking Francis of films
45. East Indian hemp
46. Gave audience
47. "___, pick up sticks": 2 wds.
50. ___ pole
54. Fort ___
55. Strong drink
59. Day's march
63. Wrought ___
64. Having serious problems: 3 wds.
66. Untruths
67. Door part
68. Songstress Carter
69. Villa d'___
70. Rice wine
71. Pierre's head

**DOWN**

1. Certain bird calls
2. Amo, Amas, ___
3. Feel for
4. D.A.'s undergrad program
5. Three of twenty-six
6. Congeal
7. Spring flower
8. Battery part
9. Popular film genre
10. Part of QED
11. Diminish
12. Salty drop
15. Very French
18. ___ Ridge
22. Mrs. Dalloway's creator
24. " . . . were Paradise ___!"
26. Go through a puddle
27. Ergo
28. Ancient Roman port
29. Sixty grains
31. Circlets
32. Boredom
33. Demand further tribute
36. Energy abbr.
37. Ego
40. Maid in "Bleak House"
41. Provide with income
42. Actor Wallace
48. Panorama
49. Surviving
51. Shadow
52. Lab burners
53. Conductor Zubin
55. Drum's partner
56. Rainbow goddess
57. ___ E. Lee: abbr.
58. Before bottom or candy
60. Suit to ___: 2 wds.
61. Fur
62. Perry's creator
65. Article

# PUZZLE 391

**ACROSS**

1. Fashionable
5. Unwritten
9. Austere
14. Reckless
15. Soccer notable
16. Golfer Palmer
17. Vehicle
18. Idi ___
19. Consumer-advocate Ralph ___
20. Is inconsistent
23. Threw
24. Carbohydrate: suff.
25. Actress Arlene ___
27. Tallinn native: abbr.
30. Lost in
34. Fortune-teller's card
35. Pigeon sound
36. China's former ruler
37. Boast
42. Capone et al.
43. Monk's title
44. Uncanny
45. Bread grains
47. Use a stopwatch
49. God of war
50. Before, to poets
52. Get by
54. Venting one's anger
62. Animate
63. Amo, amas, ___
64. Unemployed
65. Hebrew measures
66. Speed contest
67. Quote
68. Keyed up
69. ___ Fox
70. RBI, e.g.

**DOWN**

1. Grouch
2. Lug
3. Ratio phrase
4. Dog breed
5. Colorful fish
6. Far off
7. Dismounted
8. "Stormy Weather" singer
9. Smoothes
10. Investigator
11. Within: pref.
12. Cambodian money
13. Dull person
21. Like some pretzels
22. Not in any way
25. Dawdle
26. Originated
28. Beat it!
29. Furthermore
31. Love, Italian style
32. Capital of France
33. Quality
34. Aspen conveyance
38. Frequently
39. Swiss lake
40. Approaches
41. Dissenters
46. Quilters
48. Expunge
51. Laundry cycle
53. Subsequent
54. Smudge
55. Key ___ pie
56. Baking chamber
57. Costume
58. Actor Sharif
59. Reword
60. Canadian prov.
61. Convene

# PUZZLE 392

**ACROSS**

1. Car protector
4. Support
8. It goes moo
11. Desert dweller
12. Feeling
13. Strong beer
14. Train track
15. Salty drop
16. ____ and board
17. Map feature
19. Arm or leg
21. Grape drink
22. Reporter's question
25. Foamy
28. ____ of the trade
30. Dreaded person
31. Went by horse
34. Lemon meringue ____
35. Broadway sign
36. Thought
37. Tinker to ____ to Chance
39. Compact
41. Australian bird
42. Place
45. Period of time
47. Model wood
49. Actor Wallach
51. Out of the ordinary
54. Go by schooner
55. Word of permission
56. Skunk's defense
57. English queen
58. Chow down
59. Singer McEntire
60. Tent stake

**DOWN**

1. Tattoo, western style
2. Elevate
3. Up to the task
4. TV host Sajak
5. Regret
6. Spoken
7. Capital of France
8. Corned beef and ____
9. Mexican cheer
10. Join
11. Diva's solo
18. Duet number
20. Planets' satellites
23. Faith
24. Martini garnish
26. Not a beginner
27. Longing
28. Razz
29. Appear
31. Do away with
32. "____ on a Grecian Urn"
33. Tooth doctor
38. Massage
40. Mistake
42. Hangar occupant
43. Handling
44. Fib
46. Constructed
48. Right away: abbr.
49. Organ of sight
50. Actress Thompson
52. Director Reiner
53. Dynasty

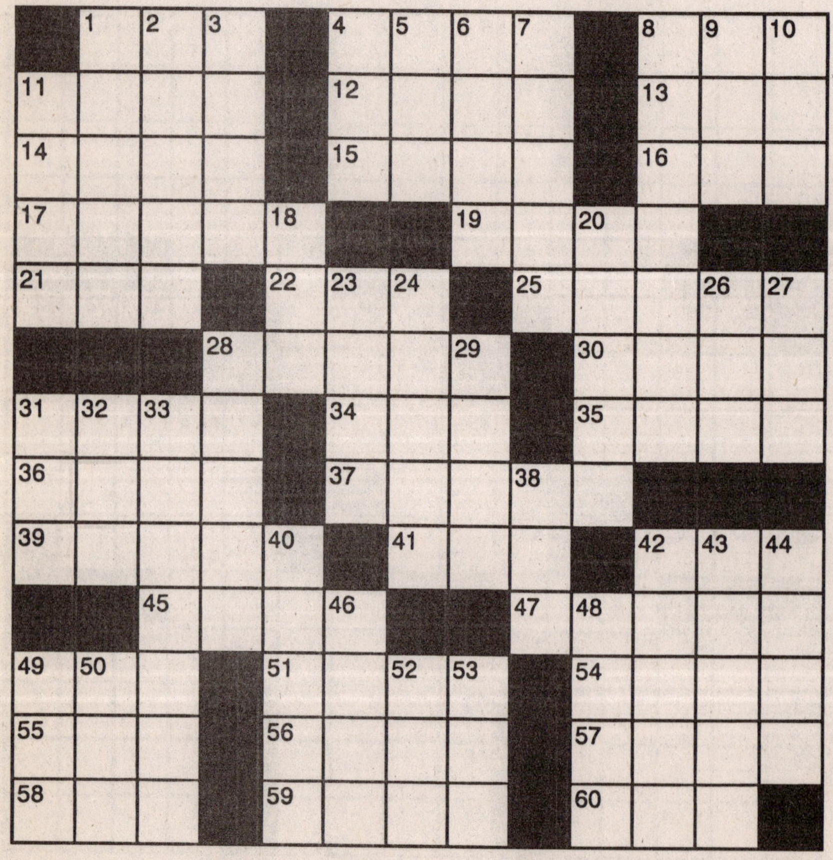

# PUZZLE 393

**ACROSS**

1. Large tart
4. Bucket
8. Worry
12. "We ___ the World"
13. Land measure
14. ___-de-camp
15. Naturally gifted
17. Manipulates
18. Absolutely!
19. Odor
20. Cigar residues
23. Adhesive substance
25. Noisy
26. Fertile
30. Beaver's construction
31. Oven-baked meat
32. Pitcher's stat
33. Come close
35. Embraces
36. Not working
37. Military student
38. Small lakes
41. Chum
42. Surrounded by
43. Catch up to
48. Prison room
49. Fibber
50. Unused
51. Leg joint
52. Simple
53. Coloring agent

**DOWN**

1. TV host Sajak
2. Nest egg fund
3. Elongated fish
4. Glass units
5. Performs
6. Anger
7. Went in front
8. Spigot
9. Go up
10. Garden of Paradise
11. Large quiz
16. Looked at
19. Set of clothing
20. Alan ___ of "M*A*S*H"
21. Cleansing bar
22. Camel's feature
23. Mealtime prayer
24. Abundant, as vegetation
26. Newborn horse
27. Quarrel
28. Encourage
29. Endure
31. Fishing poles
34. Puzzling question
35. Cease
37. Tote
38. Fill a suitcase
39. Sign of the future
40. Egyptian river
41. Soup vegetables
43. Grand ___ Opry
44. By way of
45. "Night ___ Day"
46. Lock opener
47. Ram's mate

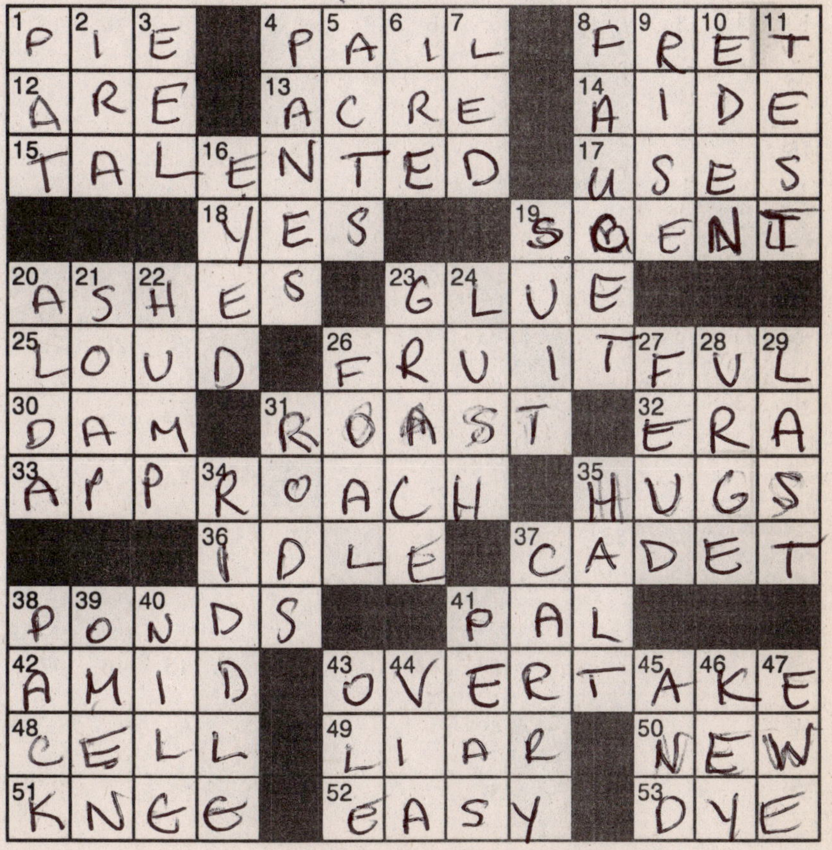

# PUZZLE 394

**ACROSS**

1. Topple
4. Aloud
8. Secret writing
12. Fruit drink
13. Flower holder
14. Territory
15. Saloon
16. Richard Mulligan TV series
18. Fish features
20. Caravan stop
21. Pals
23. Kiss-and-____
25. Reading light
26. Stopper
27. Method
30. Ginger ____
31. Flies high
32. Hooray, in Spain
33. Votes against
34. Youngsters
35. ____ pop
36. Healthy grains
37. Fragrant wood
38. Separate
41. Wharf rodents
42. Autumn wildflower
45. Not hers
48. Otherwise
49. ____-de-camp
50. Sooner than, in verse
51. Entrance
52. Wordsworth, for one
53. Morning wetness

**DOWN**

1. Label
2. Neighbor of Mont.
3. Scents
4. Kitchen appliances
5. Flock papas
6. Viper
7. Said yes
8. Panama or Suez
9. Mines' products
10. Bandleader Arnaz
11. Has a taco
17. Eggs' centers
19. Scamp
21. Extended family
22. Heavenly headwear
23. Pond creatures
24. Goes wrong
26. Paint layer
27. Farm building
28. Hawkeye portrayer
29. Twelve months
31. Roof covering
35. Collection
36. Law and ____
37. West Point student
38. Ripened
39. Marco ____
40. In addition
41. Galloped
43. Doze
44. ____ Grande
46. Fury
47. Make a blouse

# PUZZLE 395

**ACROSS**

1. Strike
5. Too
9. Mother's Day month
12. Journey
13. Fly high
14. Grand ____ Opry
15. "____ Karenina"
16. Provisions
18. Went to bed
20. Owns
21. Put
22. Spring holiday
25. Sidled
28. Light brown
29. Pitcher's stat
30. Tack
31. Successful song
32. Clip
33. School transport
34. "Great Expectations" hero
35. Baseball bags
36. Cured, as meat
38. Manner
39. Guided
40. Picky
44. Sign of a shower
47. Not any
48. Country hotel
49. Pool division
50. Expanded
51. Certain poem
52. Halts
53. Looks at

**DOWN**

1. Constellation member
2. Sole
3. Mother's sister
4. Applauded
5. Thing of value
6. Earsplitting
7. Tree's fluid
8. "Little ____ Annie"
9. Dampens
10. Beer's kin
11. Of course!
17. ____ Vegas
19. Color of rubies
22. Dine
23. New York canal
24. Talk sessions
25. Wanes
26. Percussion instrument
27. Car's fuel
28. Waiter's reward
31. Concealed
32. Proverbs
34. Sell
35. Outlaw
37. Barbie's beau
38. Rubs with a cloth
40. Loving
41. Central part
42. Leg hinge
43. Evergreen trees
44. ____ Grande (river)
45. Plus
46. Managed

# PUZZLE 396

**ACROSS**

1. "To ___ With Love"
4. Molten rock
8. Not on time
12. Gardening tool
13. Mineral-bearing rocks
14. Genesis garden
15. East Coast ocean
17. Sell
18. Perhaps
19. Musical tone
21. Santa's helper
23. Natural ability
27. Obtain
30. Sweet-potato lookalike
32. At no time
33. Wood-chopping tools
35. Knock
37. Showroom model
38. Keyboard instrument
40. Lawn moisture
42. Serling or Steiger
43. Kite cord
45. Seize
47. Enliven
49. Security officer
53. Ambush
56. Forefather
58. Had on
59. Close
60. "___ to a Nightingale"
61. Was indebted to
62. Bears' caves
63. Church seat

**DOWN**

1. Fake
2. Tiny bit
3. Depend
4. Friendless
5. Picasso's work
6. Blood vessel
7. Type of tie
8. Evened
9. Summer fruit cooler
10. Number of fingers
11. Stop
16. Honest ___ (Lincoln)
20. Sunbather's goal
22. Distant
24. Continuously
25. Captain ___ (Verne hero)
26. Trampled
27. Mountain passes
28. Way out
29. Rip
31. Furious
34. Clipped
36. Animal's cage
39. ___ in a million
41. Bets
44. Arizona's ___ Canyon
46. Public transit vehicle
48. Leg hinge
50. Upon
51. Was a passenger
52. Sketched
53. "Tea for ___"
54. Paddle
55. "___ You Sincere"
57. Is able to

# PUZZLE 397

**ACROSS**

1. Information
5. Hooded snake
10. Cancun's country
12. Bowling lanes
13. In dreamland
14. Moves a bit
15. ___ in the sky
16. Break ___
18. Have being
19. Earns
24. King Kong, e.g.
27. Sales ___
28. Idiot
29. Avoids
31. Skin design
33. Tops
34. Knows how
35. Picnic pest
36. Bangs
38. Actress Irving
39. Keep the faith
41. Baseball stat
44. Made a happy face
48. Holy
51. "Easter ___"
52. Gets in shape
53. Swift horses
54. Worry

**DOWN**

1. Mr. Arnaz
2. Wheel rod
3. Father's Day gift, perhaps
4. Top card
5. Adhered
6. Ancient
7. Whine
8. Whiskey
9. Donkey
10. Tourist's need
11. "Carmen" and "Aida"
12. Mr. Lincoln
17. Annoy
18. Had a snack
20. Toward the rear
21. Little bit
22. "High ___"
23. Suggestion-box opening
24. Clare and Maris
25. Swimmer's hole
26. Author Ferber
30. Precious stone
31. Gentlest
32. ". . . have you ___ wool?"
34. Head cover
37. Storage huts
40. Keats creation
41. New York canal
42. Apartment fee
43. Newspaper fillers
44. Healthy place
45. Dent
46. Savings plan: abbr.
47. Hunting dog, for short
49. Canine comment
50. Jalopy

# PUZZLE 398

**ACROSS**

1. Purse
4. Pesky insect
7. Chewing and bubble
11. Balloon filler
12. Smirk
14. Fiery gem
15. Orange or lemon drink
16. Aware of
17. Came to
18. Mania and trip
20. Censored
22. ____ down (softened)
24. Kramden's vehicle
25. In charge of
26. Sharp
28. Cup handle
31. With great compassion
34. Foxy
35. Picnic crashers
36. Beatles' meter maid
37. Nieces and uncles
38. Conductor's stick
39. Referee
42. Lucy's ex
43. Uprising
44. Costly
46. Uneven
49. Mirth
50. Time past
51. And not
52. Shade trees
53. Court divider
54. Hog's place

**DOWN**

1. Barnyard sound
2. Benefit
3. Foliage
4. Overwhelm
5. Camera eye
6. Still
7. Graduates' attire
8. "When You Wish ____ a Star"
9. Create
10. Toboggan
13. Thieves
19. Seed
21. Bee, to Opie
22. Pulls
23. Face shape
26. New York airport
27. Dine
28. Printings
29. Choir member
30. Actor O'Neal
32. Bristle
33. Epochs
37. High fliers
38. Artist's hat
39. Beg
40. Pepper grinder
41. Kilmer product
42. Challenge
45. Eternity
47. Speck
48. Lacking water

## REVELATION

# PUZZLE 399

**Solve this puzzle as you would a regular crossword. Then read the circled letters from left to right, and they will reveal a quotation.**

**ACROSS**

1. Television host Leno
4. "___ Miner's Daughter"
8. Plenty
12. Unrefined metal
13. "Mona ___" (Da Vinci painting)
14. Bone in the forearm
15. Relatives
17. Appear
18. Lets up
19. Prophet
21. Take care of
24. Daisylike fall flower
27. Church part
30. Kiln for drying hops
32. Novelist Levin
33. Trim
34. Aids
35. Small bite
36. Jackie's second husband
37. Jai ___
38. Grows older
39. Soda-sipper
41. One-twelfth of a foot
43. River of Florence, Italy
45. Interprets
49. Erase
51. Put together
54. Unlock
55. ___ accompli
56. "___ Abner" (comic strip)
57. Nothing: Sp.
58. Achy
59. One of the Gabor sisters

**DOWN**

1. Standup comic's material
2. Operatic solo
3. Hankerings
4. Near
5. Grease
6. Inquire
7. Young lady
8. Ponders
9. Warning
10. Compass pt.
11. Sweet-potato lookalike
16. Gala party
20. Has a meal
22. Christmas
23. ___ Lama
25. A Great Lake
26. Sharp knocks
27. Woe is me!
28. Harbor
29. Coiled
31. Twirl
34. Actress Goldie ___
38. Throat-clearer
40. Coliseum
42. Greek island
44. Blockheads
46. Qualified
47. Roman numeral 554
48. Actress Ward of "Sisters"
49. Comic actor Knotts
50. Gov. pollution-control dept.
52. ___ Paulo, Brazil
53. Knight's title

# PUZZLE 400

**ACROSS**

1. Drink like a cat
4. Entranced
8. Cloth scrap
11. Smell
13. Not working
14. Have unpaid bills
15. Clinton's VP
16. Pinto or navy
17. Every bit
18. Sewing joint
20. Steps
22. Building site
24. Conclusion
25. Room
29. Dining-room feature
33. "____ Miss Brooks"
34. Signal yes
36. Atmosphere
37. Flower part
40. Partition
43. Decay
45. Pop
46. Think highly of
49. Sports group
52. Expected
53. Matador's foe
55. Desert dweller
57. Unrefined metal
58. Wicked
59. Peru's capital
60. Sticky pitch
61. "The Donna ____ Show"
62. Newsman Rather

**DOWN**

1. Ship's diary
2. Fusses
3. Tiny skin opening
4. Chest bone
5. Fruit coolers
6. Dish
7. Renter
8. Lion's sound
9. Hole-punching tools
10. Hairstyling product
12. Kingdom
19. Unruly crowd
21. Actress Lupino
23. "The ____ Commandments"
25. Police officer
26. Color
27. Mr. Garfunkel
28. Fishing pole
30. Naughty
31. Deceive
32. Make a mistake
35. Performed
38. Upper limb
39. Hang around
41. Tub
42. Perfect
44. Treasure stash
46. Ambiance
47. Forest creature
48. A Great Lake
50. Very dry
51. Doll's cry
52. I-topper
54. Ancient
56. Prohibit

# PUZZLE 401

**ACROSS**

1. Dad's spouse
4. Gorillas, e.g.
8. Donkey's call
12. "____ on a Grecian Urn"
13. ____ up (support)
14. Oriental staple
15. Put off
17. The ____ of March
18. Train track
19. Winter slider
21. Church bench
23. Roman army unit
27. Strike
30. Use needle and thread
32. Windowsill
33. Be mistaken
34. Price label
36. Unrefined metal
37. Carpenter's spikes
40. Chewing ____
42. Guided
43. Investigates
45. At this time
47. Favorable votes
49. Hundred yard ____
52. Brought into life
55. Forefather, e.g.
58. ____ vera
59. Send by post
60. Night before
61. Marsh plant
62. Mineral springs
63. Marry

**DOWN**

1. Swab
2. Aroma
3. Butte
4. Winesap and Granny Smith
5. Paid athlete
6. Long time periods
7. Magic incantation
8. Spanning structure
9. Disen-cumber
10. Serve for a point
11. Certainly!
16. Lean
20. Snaky fish
22. Drenched
24. Graven image, e.g.
25. Fairy tale monster
26. Require
27. Mother chickens
28. Iraq's neighbor
29. Threesome
31. Shake, as a tail
35. Firearm
38. Gave temporarily
39. Secret agent
41. Poses, as for an artist
44. Cloth joints
46. Existed
48. Break sharply
50. Goulash, e.g.
51. Lifted with effort
52. Saloon
53. Spanish cheer
54. Caviar
56. U.S. security group: abbr.
57. Crimson

# PUZZLE 402

**ACROSS**

1. Basil or parsley, e.g.
5. Type of meat
9. Female deer
12. Scent
13. Presidential office shape
14. Vase
15. Mexican coin
16. Came back
18. Athletic shoe
20. Tractor-trailer
21. Accomplished
22. Chooses from the menu
25. Old-fashioned
28. Some
29. Lubricate
30. Iraq's neighbor
31. Compete
32. Formerly
33. Permit
34. Hearing organ
35. Pondered
36. Tardiest
38. Bowler or Stetson, e.g.
39. Large deer
40. Perils
44. Depot
47. Banister
48. Fury
49. Thaw
50. Norway's capital
51. Angry
52. Is obligated
53. Shed tears

**DOWN**

1. Short leaps
2. Biblical garden
3. ____-colored glasses
4. Expand
5. Drilled
6. Always
7. Nibble
8. Light snow shower
9. Castle jails
10. Metallic rock
11. Outcome
17. Make free of
19. Young goat
22. Half of a pair
23. Asian staple grain
24. Sleigh
25. Kind of pickle
26. Territory
27. Ragged
28. Broadcast
31. Tub
32. Get too big for
34. Native Alaskan
35. Adult male
37. Shade tree
38. Stops
40. Cowgirl Evans
41. Relax
42. Upset
43. Swill
44. Comic actor Conway
45. Age
46. Unused

# PUZZLE 403

**ACROSS**

1. Politician Quayle
4. Cultivating tool
8. Goulash, e.g.
12. Freezer cube
13. Impolite
14. Heap
15. Took an alternate route
17. Take five
18. Writing fluids
19. Aspects
20. Although
23. Heavy weight
24. Horse's dinner
25. Strive
30. Bravo!
31. Bow down
32. Canoeist's need
33. Ladylike
35. Sandwich fish
36. Small drink
37. Sees socially
38. Wide-awake
41. Wild pig
43. Pop flavor
44. Toothache causers
48. Not working
49. Verbal
50. Atlas entry
51. Agreement
52. Merely
53. Snoop

**DOWN**

1. Accomplished
2. High card
3. Fisherman's tool
4. Dried plum
5. Prowl
6. Poems
7. Marry
8. Season after winter
9. Bound
10. You are something ____!
11. Moistens
16. Lubricates
19. Eternal spirit
20. Dog's bark
21. Patriot Nathan ____
22. Thing
23. Hickory or elm, e.g.
25. Trim
26. Half a score
27. Inflammation of the small joints
28. Highway division
29. Epochs
31. Purl's counterpart
34. Tel Aviv's site
35. Sour
37. Every morning
38. Vinegar, e.g.
39. Ore deposit
40. Singer Fitzgerald
41. Hay-storage structure
42. Egg-shaped
44. Dove's comment
45. Rascal
46. Sense organ
47. Secret agent

# PUZZLE 404

**ACROSS**
1. Ocean liner
5. Saloon
8. Writing fluid
11. Overdue
12. Iniquitous
14. Lair
15. Always
16. Opera soloist
17. Lamb's mom
18. Take objection
20. Stray
22. Total
24. Light brown
25. Income
29. Snout
33. Native mineral
34. Arid
36. Gorilla, e.g.
37. Cab
39. Unaffected
42. Destiny
45. "The ___ I Love"
46. Mug
50. Guide
54. Bullring bravo
55. Hard work
57. Duration
58. Employ
59. Sharpen
60. Level
61. Staff
62. Caress
63. Hollow

**DOWN**
1. Winter toy
2. "___ a Heart"
3. Article
4. Read through
5. Berth
6. Eager
7. Metal fastener
8. Concept
9. Salamander
10. Patella's joint
13. Molten rock
19. Seek to be elected
21. Stopping place
23. Mire
25. Drivel
26. Paleozoic, e.g.
27. Annoy
28. Coastal flier
30. Paddle
31. Baden-Baden, e.g.
32. Moray
35. African tuber
38. Sort
40. Knock lightly
41. Joined
43. Solemn promise
44. Boy Scout group
46. Sightseeing journey
47. As well
48. Lack
49. Sup
51. Dwell
52. Portent
53. Camper's cover
56. Allow

# PUZZLE 405

**ACROSS**
1. Use the phone
5. Copycat
9. Children's game
12. "God's Little ___"
13. Extra
14. Malt beverage
15. People nearby
17. Operated
18. Stat for Clemens
19. "___ by Myself"
20. Discontinue
22. Pastry dessert
23. Mongrel
24. Beer
27. Originates
31. On the sheltered side
32. Author Talese
33. Bargain event
34. Elementary schoolbook
36. Earn
37. Elongated fish
38. TV host Serling
39. Swap
42. Club
43. Driver's compartment
46. Edge
47. Inn
50. Hole in one
51. Actress Lanchester
52. Without cost
53. Writing tool
54. Forest ruminant
55. Level

**DOWN**
1. Copenhagen native
2. Cake decorator
3. Soprano's solo
4. Part of a journey
5. Mosey
6. Billiards
7. Do wrong
8. Liberation
9. O'Hara home
10. Regretful word
11. Actor Hackman
16. Filament
21. Expunged
22. Removed the skin from
23. Loud call
24. ___ Vegas
25. Swiss peak
26. Turn to the right
27. Caboose, e.g.
28. Roofing liquid
29. Yale alumnus
30. Fixed
32. Solidify
35. Gave an evil look
36. Feathery insect
38. Airport device
39. Pitfall
40. Paddy product
41. Prayer ending
42. Underpinning
43. Tress
44. On the waves
45. Red vegetable
48. Corrida shout
49. Not up to par

## CODEWORD

# PUZZLE 406

**Codeword is a special crossword puzzle in which conventional clues are omitted. Instead, answer words in the diagram are represented by numbers. Each number represents a different letter of the alphabet, and all of the letters of the alphabet are used. When you are sure of a letter, put it in the code key chart and cross it off in the alphabet box. A group of letters has been inserted to start you off.**

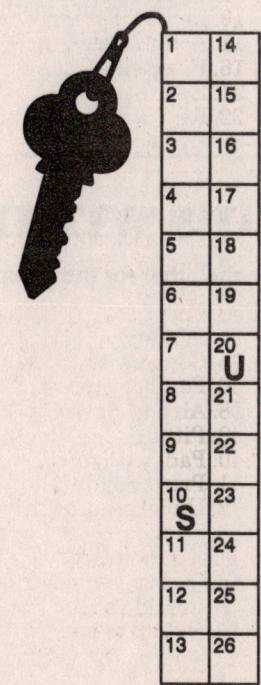

| | |
|---|---|
| 1 | 14 O |
| 2 | 15 |
| 3 | 16 |
| 4 | 17 |
| 5 | 18 |
| 6 | 19 |
| 7 | 20 |
| 8 | 21 |
| 9 | 22 |
| 10 | 23 |
| 11 N | 24 |
| 12 | 25 |
| 13 | 26 |

| | | | | | | | | | | | | |
|---|---|---|---|---|---|---|---|---|---|---|---|---|
| 16 | 21 | 1 | 14 | 13 | 6 | 19 | ■ | 14 | 10 | 20 | 11 | 26 |
| 21 | ■ | 19 | ■ | 6 | ■ | 13 | ■ | 10 | ■ | 11 | ■ | 19 |
| 2 | 21 | 16 | 5 | 19 | ■ | 6 | 11 | 5 | 6 | 17 | 8 | 22 |
| 17 | ■ | 20 | ■ | 4 | ■ | 20 | ■ | ■ | ■ | 6 | ■ | 4 |
| 25 | 19 | 1 | ■ | 2 | 20 | 11 | 22 | ■ | 12 | 1 | 19 | 19 |
| ■ | ■ | 2 | ■ | 20 | ■ | 19 | ■ | 17 | ■ | ■ | ■ | 1 |
| ■ | 4 | 25 | 14 | 14 O | 8 | ■ | 15 | 14 | 20 | 11 | 2 | ■ |
| 26 | ■ | ■ | ■ | 11 N | ■ | 19 | ■ | 11 | ■ | 6 | ■ | ■ |
| 1 | 19 | 21 | 3 | ■ | 19 | 9 | 20 | 2 | ■ | 18 | 20 | 24 |
| 20 | ■ | 3 | ■ | ■ | ■ | 24 | ■ | 1 | ■ | 18 | ■ | 21 |
| 19 | 9 | 24 | 5 | 14 | 7 | 19 | ■ | 20 | 11 | 5 | 21 | 10 |
| 23 | ■ | 5 | ■ | 12 | ■ | 11 | ■ | 23 | ■ | 19 | ■ | 19 |
| 19 | 15 | 19 | 17 | 2 | ■ | 7 | 1 | 19 | 21 | 7 | 19 | 7 |

| | |
|---|---|
| A | ~~N~~ |
| B | ~~O~~ |
| C | P |
| D | Q |
| E | R |
| F | S |
| G | T |
| H | U |
| I | V |
| J | W |
| K | X |
| L | Y |
| M | Z |

---

## CODEWORD

# PUZZLE 407

| | |
|---|---|
| 1 | 14 |
| 2 | 15 |
| 3 | 16 |
| 4 | 17 |
| 5 | 18 |
| 6 | 19 |
| 7 | 20 U |
| 8 | 21 |
| 9 | 22 |
| 10 S | 23 |
| 11 | 24 |
| 12 | 25 |
| 13 | 26 |

| | | | | | | | | | | | | |
|---|---|---|---|---|---|---|---|---|---|---|---|---|
| 25 | 2 | 17 | 21 | 1 | 25 | 11 | ■ | 26 | 13 | 17 | 20 | 11 |
| 17 | ■ | 11 | ■ | 17 | ■ | 25 | ■ | 3 | ■ | 8 | ■ | 3 |
| 18 | 19 | 17 | 24 | 1 | ■ | 16 | 3 | 2 | 8 | 19 | 15 | 25 |
| 25 | ■ | 7 | ■ | ■ | ■ | 13 | ■ | ■ | ■ | 16 | ■ | 10 |
| 13 | 20 | 1 | ■ | 16 | 17 | 19 | 8 | 19 | 14 | 19 | 21 | 15 |
| ■ | ■ | 25 | ■ | 17 | ■ | 10 | ■ | 8 | ■ | ■ | ■ | 19 |
| 25 | 20 | 13 | 25 | 15 | 17 | ■ | 22 | 19 | 13 | 21 | 3 | 24 |
| 24 | ■ | ■ | ■ | 25 | ■ | 10 | ■ | 17 | ■ | 17 | ■ | ■ |
| 9 | 20 | 17 | 11 | 13 | 20 | 7 | 25 | 11 | ■ | 5 | 17 | 1 |
| 20 | ■ | 24 | ■ | ■ | ■ | 17 | ■ | ■ | ■ | 25 | ■ | 20 U |
| 19 | 24 | 1 | 17 | 15 | 25 | 10 | ■ | 12 | 20 | 23 | 7 | 10 S |
| 13 | ■ | 19 | ■ | 19 | ■ | 23 | ■ | 17 | ■ | 17 | ■ | 15 |
| 4 | 17 | 21 | 6 | 1 | ■ | 10 | 17 | 13 | 3 | 24 | 18 | 10 |

| | |
|---|---|
| A | N |
| B | O |
| C | P |
| D | Q |
| E | R |
| F | ~~S~~ |
| G | T |
| H | ~~U~~ |
| I | V |
| J | W |
| K | X |
| L | Y |
| M | Z |

# PUZZLE 408

**ACROSS**

1. Type of teacher, for short
4. Sweetsop
8. Protrude
11. Having gall
14. Writer Silverstein
15. Passport endorsement
16. Pseudonym
17. Wife of Zeus
18. Allege
19. Figured out
21. Excursionists
23. Scent
25. Resort
26. Grouch
29. Theater box
31. Waned
35. Vagrant
36. Of an epoch
37. Actress Esther ___
38. Arabian gulf
39. Shut out
41. Call
42. Canasta plays
44. Memo
45. Small drink
46. Law-enforcement group
47. Unique person
48. Camera's eye
49. Excessive actor
51. Argentinian statesman Luis Maria ___
53. Bird
57. Works of fiction
61. Cry of revelry
62. Superman's girlfriend
64. Indian pepper plant
65. Sawbucks
66. Sea eagle
67. Muslim decree
68. "The King ___ I"
69. Wise man
70. Melancholy

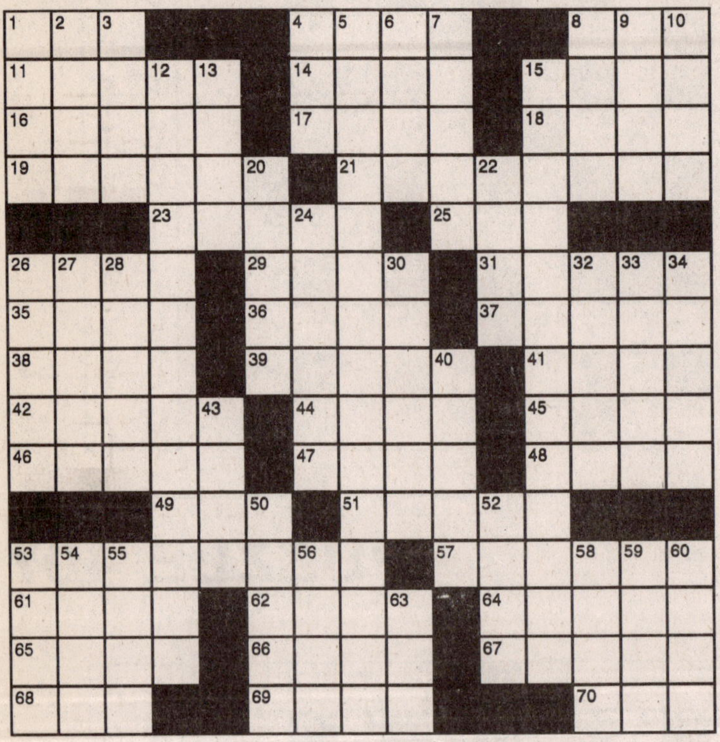

**DOWN**

1. Cinch
2. Congo river
3. Cell area, at sea
4. Tree
5. Rudolf Friml operetta
6. Architect Saarinen
7. Overwhelms with humor
8. Swing music
9. Consumer
10. Sailors
12. Footwear bound for "New York, New York"?
13. Belgian river
15. Vallee's "I'm just a ___"
20. Apportioned
22. Mimic
24. Actress Rita ___
26. Victor, for short
27. Cowboy contest
28. Actor Walter et al.
30. Beetle
32. Fanfare
33. Violinist Mischa ___
34. Surmises
40. Showed again
43. Glue
50. Actress Vera ___
52. Desert
53. Phi ___ Kappa
54. Baking chamber
55. Covenant
56. Mrs. Charles
58. Greek letters
59. Helen's mother
60. Luge
63. Witness

---

# PUZZLE 409

## WORDS WITHIN

**Each clue contains two parts, one for the 3-letter answer you place on the dashes, the other for the complete 5-letter word.**

1. Bossy in a sullen look — S ___ ___ ___ L
2. Armed conflict in a hive — S ___ ___ ___ M
3. A rowing blade in a plank — B ___ ___ ___ D
4. A knock in a diagram — G ___ ___ ___ H
5. Light brown color in a booth — S ___ ___ ___ D
6. Period of time in a showy flower — P ___ ___ ___ Y

# PUZZLE 410

**ACROSS**

1. Mayberry boy
5. Part of a mine
10. White House dog
14. Early day, in poetry
15. Viper's kin
16. Hodgepodge
17. Cry of dismay
18. Buttery spreads
19. Stink
20. Necessitate
22. Put on a show
24. Shad delicacy
25. Pillar
26. Egg carton quantity
29. Reticent
30. Off-white
34. Pre-holiday nights
35. Hawaiian staple
36. Fifth or Park
37. Saul's grandfather
38. Befuddle
40. Vermont founder Allen
41. Did a pressing job
43. Exclamation of commiseration
44. Battle memento
45. Signal booster
46. Suit to a ___
47. Shoe parts
48. Studied carefully
50. Fast plane
51. Enters a port
53. Ballroom dance
57. South American country
58. Parlor
60. Worship
61. Sues or Webb
62. French school
63. Level
64. Remove
65. Interprets
66. Transmitted

**DOWN**

1. General Bradley
2. Lech Walesa, e.g.
3. Baghdad's site
4. Guarantees
5. Play's music
6. Black ___
7. Humorist Burrows
8. "___ the Snowman"
9. Tidbit
10. Pardoned
11. To the sheltered side
12. Told a whopper
13. Thumbs-up
21. Atomic particle
23. Spirited
25. Moved
26. Jeans material
27. ___ barrel
28. Actor Mostel and namesakes
29. Heir
31. In reserve
32. Part of RFD
33. Birthday counters
35. Group of whales
36. Inquire
38. Mackerellike species
39. Apply
42. Eighth planet
44. Inhabits
46. Bridge term
47. Bewitch
49. Stair part
50. Davy ___
51. Soccer great
52. Asian river
53. Withdraw, in poker
54. Ramble
55. Hot spot
56. Wigwam
57. Apartment
59. Mauna ___

# Hop, Skip, and Jump

# PUZZLE 411

**What is the longest word you can find in this row of letters, starting with any letter and picking out letters, moving only from left to right? You may Hop, Skip, and Jump over any number of letters, but once you choose a letter you may not backtrack. A word of 4 to 6 letters is good; 7 to 9 letters is very good; a word with 10 letters is excellent.**

V P D I O R N C K T U B S V G H Y I X O W S O F N

# PUZZLE 412

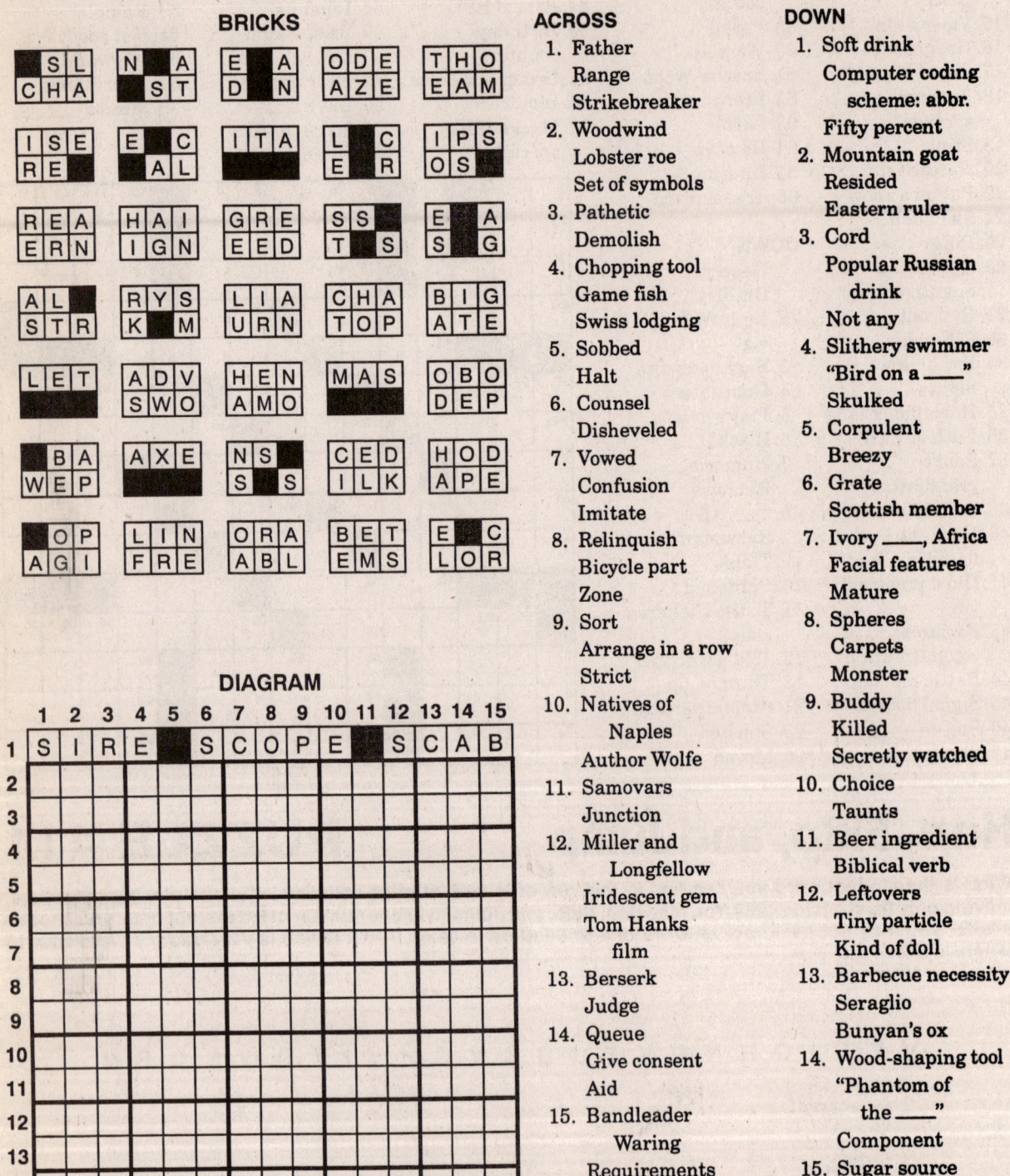

## BRICK BY BRICK

**Rearrange this stack of bricks to form a crossword puzzle. The clues will help you fit the bricks into their correct places. Row 1 has been filled in for you. Use the bricks to fill in the remaining spaces.**

### BRICKS

| | | | | |
|---|---|---|---|---|
| ■SL / CHA | N■A / ■ST | E■A / D■N | ODE / AZE | THO / EAM |
| ISE / RE■ | E■C / ■AL | ITA / ■■■ | L■C / E■R | IPS / OS■ |
| REA / ERN | HAI / IGN | GRE / EED | SS■ / T■S | E■A / S■G |
| AL■ / STR | RYS / K■M | LIA / URN | CHA / TOP | BIG / ATE |
| LET / ■■■ | ADV / SWO | HEN / AMO | MAS / ■■■ | OBO / DEP |
| ■BA / WEP | AXE / ■■■ | NS■ / S■S | CED / ILK | HOD / APE |
| ■OP / AGI | LIN / FRE | ORA / ABL | BET / EMS | E■C / LOR |

### DIAGRAM

| | 1 | 2 | 3 | 4 | 5 | 6 | 7 | 8 | 9 | 10 | 11 | 12 | 13 | 14 | 15 |
|---|---|---|---|---|---|---|---|---|---|---|---|---|---|---|---|
| 1 | S | I | R | E | ■ | S | C | O | P | E | ■ | S | C | A | B |
| 2 | | | | | | | | | | | | | | | |
| 3 | | | | | | | | | | | | | | | |
| 4 | | | | | | | | | | | | | | | |
| 5 | | | | | | | | | | | | | | | |
| 6 | | | | | | | | | | | | | | | |
| 7 | | | | | | | | | | | | | | | |
| 8 | | | | | | | | | | | | | | | |
| 9 | | | | | | | | | | | | | | | |
| 10 | | | | | | | | | | | | | | | |
| 11 | | | | | | | | | | | | | | | |
| 12 | | | | | | | | | | | | | | | |
| 13 | | | | | | | | | | | | | | | |
| 14 | | | | | | | | | | | | | | | |
| 15 | | | | | | | | | | | | | | | |

### ACROSS

1. Father
   Range
   Strikebreaker
2. Woodwind
   Lobster roe
   Set of symbols
3. Pathetic
   Demolish
4. Chopping tool
   Game fish
   Swiss lodging
5. Sobbed
   Halt
6. Counsel
   Disheveled
7. Vowed
   Confusion
   Imitate
8. Relinquish
   Bicycle part
   Zone
9. Sort
   Arrange in a row
   Strict
10. Natives of Naples
    Author Wolfe
11. Samovars
    Junction
12. Miller and Longfellow
    Iridescent gem
    Tom Hanks film
13. Berserk
    Judge
14. Queue
    Give consent
    Aid
15. Bandleader Waring
    Requirements
    Jewels

### DOWN

1. Soft drink
   Computer coding scheme: abbr.
   Fifty percent
2. Mountain goat
   Resided
   Eastern ruler
3. Cord
   Popular Russian drink
   Not any
4. Slithery swimmer
   "Bird on a ____"
   Skulked
5. Corpulent
   Breezy
6. Grate
   Scottish member
7. Ivory ____, Africa
   Facial features
   Mature
8. Spheres
   Carpets
   Monster
9. Buddy
   Killed
   Secretly watched
10. Choice
    Taunts
11. Beer ingredient
    Biblical verb
12. Leftovers
    Tiny particle
    Kind of doll
13. Barbecue necessity
    Seraglio
    Bunyan's ox
14. Wood-shaping tool
    "Phantom of the ____"
    Component
15. Sugar source
    School officials
    Acquires

# PUZZLE 413

**ACROSS**
1. "I came, I ____, I conquered"
4. Sick
7. Pasture
10. Paid athlete, for short
11. Sorrow
12. Hearing organ
13. O'Hare or LaGuardia, e.g.
15. Inquire
16. Fell to the bottom
17. Secure
19. Compassion
21. Female chicken
22. Melancholy
23. Photograph
27. Salad-dressing ingredient
28. Lid
29. Confederate soldier, for short
30. Get ready
33. Talk
34. Chilly
35. Raced
37. Desire
39. Wound remainder
41. Faint
42. Depot
45. Function
46. Crone
47. West of films
48. Cozy room
49. Seeing organ
50. Summer: Fr.

**DOWN**
1. Health resort
2. Business-man Onassis
3. Most terrible
4. Golf club
5. Wait out of sight
6. Allow
7. Tree greenery
8. Free from difficulty
9. Noah's vessel
14. Compensate
17. Dry, as wine
18. Colony insect
19. Couple
20. Not working
21. Haunch
22. Dunk, as a donut
23. Author Edgar Allan ____
24. Push
25. Enjoy a book
26. Kind of tide
28. Attempt
31. Brooch
32. Emulate Meryl Streep
35. Took a chair
36. First-rate
37. Like an owl
38. Church word
39. Remain
40. Bird enclosure
41. Flop
42. "Ain't ____ Sweet"
43. Bran type
44. Formerly named

# PUZZLE 414

**ACROSS**
1. Orient
5. Used a loom
9. Closemouthed person
13. Napped leather
14. Singer Burl
15. Praise highly
16. Rose essence
17. Schoolbook
18. Dill
19. Wool eater
20. Shabby
22. Water lily
24. Pigpen
25. One-spot
27. Choir member
29. Make possible
34. Young boy
35. Jungle cats
37. Goofed
38. Son of Seth
40. Sits for a portrait
42. Croon
43. Mountain ash
45. Bus station
47. Tool and ___
48. Sore
50. Story
51. Terminate
52. Mug
54. Fruit skins
56. Have a meal
61. Roman god of love
64. Forsaken
65. Sailing ship
66. Money wagered
67. Malt kiln
68. Being: Latin
69. Inheritors
70. Forest plant
71. Clarinet mouthpiece
72. Norse epic

**DOWN**
1. Car
2. Forgo wanderlust
3. Gem State
4. Atmospheric prefix
5. Resisted successfully
6. Finished
7. Riles
8. Landed property
9. Grouchy person
10. Ms. Turner
11. Affirm
12. Allot
13. Sleuth Spade
20. Dutch flower
21. Unit of force
23. Hindu cymbals
25. Wide-awake
26. Birchbark
28. Assault
30. ___ longa, vita brevis
31. Wedding attendant
32. Communist hero
33. Moved sideways
36. Divided
39. Unhappy
41. Not hollow
44. Narrow bottle part
46. Decade
49. Tire material
53. Ordinary writing
55. Went steady with
56. Ink smudge
57. Lion's cry
58. Gaelic
59. Poker stake
60. Comfort
62. Gumbo vegetable
63. In medias ___
66. That woman

# PUZZLE 415

## Complete-A-Word

**Fill in the 4-letter answers to the clues onto the blanks to complete 7-letter words.**

1. Pastime — _ _ R _ _ N T
2. Lawyer's assignment — _ _ P _ I Z _
3. Starring role — A _ R _ _ _ Y
4. Transport by cart — _ _ N D F _ _
5. Disorderly defeat — P _ _ D _ C _
6. Finest — _ R A V _ _ _
7. Fond wish — S _ _ P _ _ R
8. Profound — _ _ V _ L O _
9. Formerly — M _ _ O _ L _
10. Extensive — _ _ R _ I _ Y

# PUZZLE 416

**ACROSS**

1. "You ____ So Beautiful"
4. Cry of woe
8. Playwright Hart
12. ____ Quixote
13. Pretty
14. Gray's subject: abbr.
15. Peculiar
16. Maple, e.g.
17. Kitchen flooring
18. Lighten
20. Young cat
22. Blemish
24. Extensive
25. Small pie
26. Laziness
30. Intense anger
31. Sharp teeth
33. Jump
34. Scarlet tanager
36. Summon
37. Hearing organs
38. Actor Dillman
39. Roof of the mouth
42. Permit
44. Uproar
45. Wait for a moment
47. Make lace
50. Boundary
51. Exhaust
52. Self-esteem
53. Observed
54. Matched groups
55. Cozy place

**DOWN**

1. Turmoil
2. Fishing pole
3. Made beloved
4. Deeds
5. Entice
6. Wolfed down
7. Asking for
8. As a ____ of fact
9. Step ____!
10. Auction
11. British gun
19. Mr. Linkletter
21. Roman date
22. Mix
23. Feel concern
24. Coils
27. Hungered (for)
28. Greek vowel
29. Mimicked
31. Decree
32. Nabs
35. Defeated
36. Rival of NBC
39. Head honcho: abbr.
40. Assistant
41. Theater section
42. Become separated
43. Affirmative votes
46. ____ the knot
48. Get older
49. Heavy weight

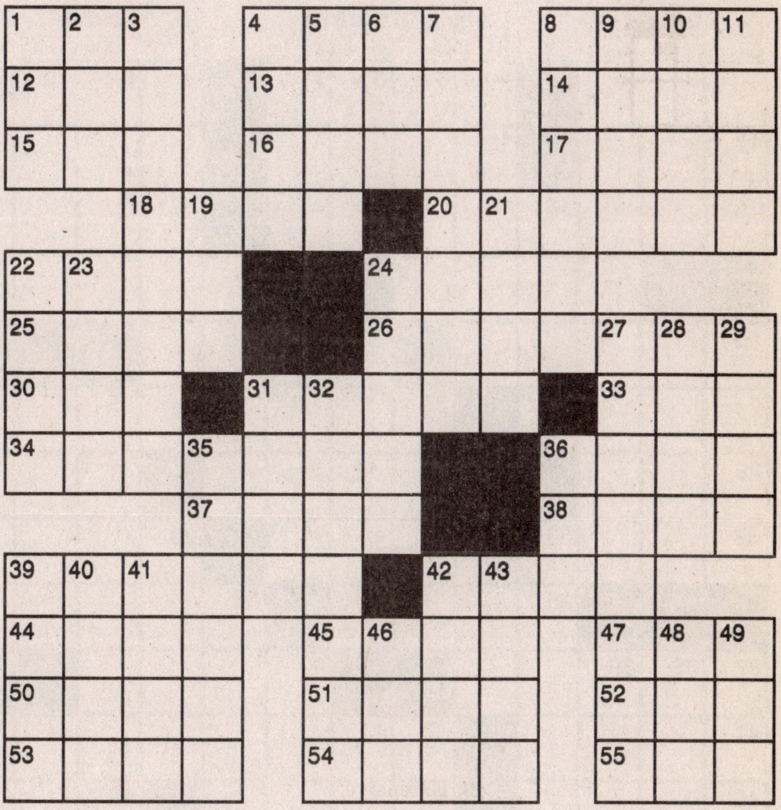

# PUZZLE 417

**ACROSS**

1. Sum up
4. An apple ____
8. Number one
12. Paris street
13. North or South
14. Face shape
15. News
17. "The Way We ____"
18. Rowers' needs
19. "The Turn of the ____"
20. ____ decision
22. Father
24. Frog's cousin
25. Left
29. Three strikes
30. Irrigate
31. Beam of light
32. Makes ready
34. Bottom
35. Always
36. Plate and run
37. Chop
40. Mound
41. District
42. Scares
46. Complain
47. Lend a ____
48. Nosh
49. "B.C." insects
50. Hen products
51. ____ as a bone

**DOWN**

1. Escort's offering
2. Give the Devil his ____
3. Deserted
4. Separately
5. Puppies
6. Pub drink
7. Okey-dokey
8. Wrecker
9. ____ the hill
10. Peel, as an orange
11. Seattle ____
16. Stated
19. Box
20. Street sign
21. Serve tea
22. Pickled-pepper picker Piper
23. Jungle inhabitants
25. Challenge
26. Crushed
27. Soothe
28. Colors, as shoes
30. Surfer's quest
33. Pie nuts
34. Ship
36. Elephant groups
37. "I Remember ____"
38. Golf club
39. Tidy
40. ____ by a thread
42. "____ Loves You"
43. Price ticket
44. Hearing organ
45. Pig place

# PUZZLE 418

**ACROSS**

1. Model
5. Informer
8. Servants
12. Shakespeare's river
13. Night before a holiday
14. Opera tune
15. Concerning
16. Counts (on)
19. Yes, to Pedro
20. Period
22. Short and sweet
23. Piece of corn
24. "____ Sir With Love"
26. Devoured
27. "____ American in Paris"
28. ____ slippers
31. Opposite of creditor
35. Repeatedly
36. Bangor's locale
37. City in Colorado
39. Made a short golf stroke
40. Spanish pronoun
41. Easily bruised item
43. Overhead train
44. Pie ____ mode
46. Fourth month
48. Leprechaun
51. ____ and behold
52. Appreciative
54. "Truth ____ Consequences"
55. Massive book
57. High card
58. Fairy-tale meanie
60. ____ -and-shut case
61. ____ Zeppelin
62. Set of regulations

**DOWN**

1. Trim
2. Above
3. Thus
4. Wrap up
5. Say twice
6. Head off
7. Stiffened
8. Enjoys
9. Hesitation sound
10. Actress Bonet
11. Matched twosome
17. Movie alien
18. Ponce ____ Leon
21. Georgia city
23. Name
25. Popeye's sweetie
27. Lessen
28. Improper
29. Driver's license information
30. Opposite of WSW
32. Australian bird
33. Single unit
34. "____ Badge of Courage"
38. Cancel
39. Balanced
42. Actress Kelly
44. Female voice
45. Chicago area
46. Cartoonist Capp
47. Cartoon's Pepe ____ Pew
49. "____ of the Flies"
50. At no cost
52. It's mightier than the sword
53. Musician Severinsen
56. "I've Got to Be ____"
59. Shove off

# PUZZLE 419

**ACROSS**

1. Actress Moreno
5. Club or dance
8. Scientist's workplace
11. Hat
14. Mr. Onassis et al.
15. Saloon offering
16. Melody
17. Iron source
18. May wish
24. Society-page word
25. Observed
26. "____ Maria"
27. Night before a holiday
28. Hiatus
29. Truck part
32. Fruit drink
33. Contend
34. Sub detector
36. "____ the land . . ."
37. Stringed instrument
39. Identical
42. Type of math: abbr.
44. Eureka!
46. Liza, to Judy
50. Mike, to Archie
52. Choice word
53. Psychic Geller
54. Shine
55. Each
56. Actress Remick
57. Raincoat, for short
58. "Cara, ____"
60. Uncle Sam's country: abbr.
62. Spout
65. Bare
67. Foot the bill
68. To the sheltered side
70. Expressing gratitude
73. Bidding
75. Comparative ending
76. Earth
77. Actress Carter
78. Ball wear
82. Wind pt.
83. Senior
87. Recite
88. Put on years
91. D.C. figure: abbr.
92. Plant
94. Large bird
95. Whopper
96. Ceremony
98. "You ____ My Sunshine"
99. Fragrant bloomer
105. Old salt
106. Gadget for Palmer
107. ____ to a customer
108. Be very fond of
109. Urban trains
110. Fast jet
111. ____ of 1812
112. Turkish officials

**DOWN**

1. Stadium word
2. Author Levin
3. Hint
4. Horned snakes
5. Renowned
6. Detached
7. Butterfly trap
8. ____ Vegas
9. Military helpers
10. Wonderful!
11. Wedding sentiments
12. Vicinity
13. Nest sound
19. Pro vote
20. Get hold of
21. Wicked
22. Stagger
23. Desire
29. Camp beds
30. Aviation prefix
31. April showers ____
35. Fire residue
37. Crow's sound
38. "____ to a Nightingale"
40. Henri's mother
41. Buffalo's lake
43. ____ monster
44. Neighbor of Miss.
45. Stage hog
47. Tyrolean peak
48. ____ one's noggin
49. Bonn native
51. Drink of the gods
59. Printing fluids
60. "Once ____ a time . . ."

# PUZZLE 419

61. Ump's call
63. ____ Baba
64. Write
65. That lady
66. Auto
69. Chick source
70. Third word of "America"
71. Baseball team
72. Little valley
74. Pipe bend
79. Scandinavian capital
80. Orphan
81. No, to Boris
84. Dolores ____ Rio
85. Radiates
86. ____ the roost
88. NBA site
89. Donation source
90. Greek vowel
92. Satisfy fully
93. Unwritten
97. Singer Fitzgerald
100. So far
101. In what manner
102. Naval diary
103. Argentine Peron
104. ____ sirree!

# PUZZLE 420

**ACROSS**

1. Swift
6. Seldom seen
10. Straightens
12. Frogmen
14. Piggy-bank coin
15. "The ____ Cometh"
16. Army rank: abbr.
17. Cook in hot liquid
19. ____ rule
20. Writer Bagnold
22. ____ one's noggin
23. Kind of school
24. Broth or whisky
26. Antlered animals
27. College cheer
28. Tavern brew
29. Just
31. Fleet of warships
34. Charity
35. Evergreen
36. Business section: abbr.
38. Poke
39. Multiplied by
41. Numbers man: abbr.
42. Entertains
44. Counter seats
46. Take offense at
47. Small tower
48. ____ some light on
49. Domineering

**DOWN**

1. "Home on the ____"
2. Strangers
3. Cookout
4. Squid's camouflage
5. Knee-____
6. Wealthy
7. St.
8. Say casually
9. Wipes clean
11. Lazy person
12. Game cubes
13. ____ out of it!
18. Fire residue
21. Singer Day
23. Implore
25. Paving material
26. Nightmare street
28. Take into custody
29. Blazes
30. Trap
31. Purpose
32. Room themes
33. Granny Smith and Winesap
34. Partly open
35. Boxer's weapon
37. Yummy
39. Care for
40. Receipt
43. Date
45. Spanish gold

# PUZZLE 421

**ACROSS**

1. Scored on a serve
5. Highland wear
9. Type of angle
10. Gladden
12. "Murder on the ___"
15. Actor Beatty
16. Tapestry
17. Greek letter
18. Military division
20. Possess, in Scotland
21. Actor Savage
22. "South ___"
24. Billiards shot
25. Basker's quest
26. Cocktail lounge
27. Church instrument
30. "Saturday in the Park" rock group
34. Singer Chaka ___
35. Actor Jack ___
36. Cupid
37. "___ Tin Tin"
38. Circus performer
40. Collapsible bed
41. "On the Atchison, Topeka, ___"
44. Weird
45. Wants
46. Preoccupied
47. ___ of Capri

**DOWN**

1. Corrosive
2. Actor's signal
3. Lab burner
4. Get off the Amtrak
5. One from Houston
6. Swiss mountains
7. Deface
8. Guides
9. Stadium
11. Mr. Kefauver
12. "Movin' ___"
13. ___ the Red
14. Marquis de ___
19. Giant
21. Spoof
23. Groupie
24. Spring month, in Paris
26. "___ Junction"
27. Gumbo ingredient
28. German river
29. Male goose
30. Dove sounds
31. Penny ___
32. Flubs
33. Bone: pref.
35. Winter weather word
38. ___ off the old block
39. Wind dirs.
42. Refrain word
43. ___ Aviv

# PUZZLE 422

**ACROSS**

1. Comedian Soupy ____
6. "____ Came in Through the Bathroom Window"
9. Biceps's location
12. ____ and kicking
13. It's mightier than the sword
14. Boston cream ____
15. Relying
17. Distress call
18. 2,000 pounds
19. Helps in crime
21. Strive
25. Ripen
26. Waste time
27. Make a knot in
28. Becker boomer
31. Use a phone
32. Stuff
33. Diesel, for one
34. Tricky
35. Top
36. Relates
37. "Little Miss Muffet ____ on . . ."
38. Puzzling thing
39. Steam
42. "Peter ____"
43. Timetable abbr.
44. Drifter
50. Maiden-named
51. Belonging to us
52. Blunder
53. Opinion
54. Gain as profit
55. Suspicious

**DOWN**

1. Down in the dumps
2. Pub order
3. Rim of a cup
4. Actress Arden
5. Guard
6. Twirl
7. Female fowl
8. Hire
9. Church section
10. Read someone the ____ act
11. Clutter
16. Female deer
20. "To ____ or not . . ."
21. Puts two and two together
22. Sloop's need
23. Participate in a game
24. Unwell
25. Intention
27. Kind of dance
28. "____ Lang Syne"
29. Jail room
30. Or ____!
32. Cat's quarry
33. Supplied with nourishment
35. Box
36. Christmas trimming
37. Therefore
38. Flowed
39. Moving trucks
40. Neighborhood
41. Victim
42. For the most ____
45. Regret
46. Anger
47. Before, poetically
48. And not
49. Make an effort

# PUZZLE 423

**ACROSS**

1. Not a ____ to stand on
4. Deep purple
8. ____ as molasses
12. Yes, matey
13. Simple
14. Use concrete
15. Term of endearment
17. Safe place
18. Skate on thin ____
19. Unoccupied
20. Bring
23. Bird of peace
24. "God's Little ____"
25. Three singers
26. Call for help
29. Shopper's tab
32. Blow one's ____
33. Do a fall chore
34. Isinglass
35. ____ in point
36. Supply food
37. Getaway
40. Cheering sound
41. Topic
42. Distant
46. Cipher
47. Vocalize
48. Be in debt
49. Foot part
50. Upon
51. Hockey goal

**DOWN**

1. Lick up
2. Ogle
3. ____ the show on the road
4. Georgia fruit
5. Gold fabric
6. ____ one's noggin'
7. "____ Bodyguard"
8. Gap
9. Volcanic flow
10. Furnace
11. Made an exit
16. More agreeable
17. Disorder
19. Verbalize
20. Statistic
21. Yodeling sound
22. Lock up
23. Male duck
25. Torment
26. Coat and pants
27. ____ in a while
28. Asterisk
30. Raisin's start
31. Nebraska city
35. Desert transportation
36. Ship's load
37. Engrave, as on glass
38. Moccasin
39. Yield
40. Rave
42. Flipper
43. Triumphed
44. Reverence
45. Thus far
47. Therefore

# PUZZLE 424

**ACROSS**

1. Elbow poke
4. Noise
7. Salary
8. Revise copy
10. Speechless actors
11. Prank
13. Pro's opposite
14. Big trucks, for short
16. At this time
18. Monkeys
20. Small boy
21. Soft drink
22. Birds' homes
24. Resigned at 65, e.g.
26. "___ Miss Brooks"
28. Period
29. Amazed
33. Send payment
37. Evergreen tree
38. Transgression
40. Show or walk starter
41. "Romeo ___ Juliet"
42. Assistants
44. Persona ___ grata
45. Informs
47. Bicycle part
49. ___ beer
50. Eternities
51. Positive response
52. Buttons or Skelton

**DOWN**

1. Fruit preserves
2. Matures
3. Invade
4. Chose
5. Lupino and others
6. Small amount
7. Chardonnay and Chablis
9. Choir voice
10. Sulk
12. Took a train
13. Container
15. Deface
17. Roll of money
19. "Romancing the ___"
21. Locations
23. "Here Comes the ___"
25. Craggy hill
27. Withstands
29. Health resort
30. Hue
31. Beneath
32. Accomplished
34. Ore shafts
35. Object of worship
36. Decade number
39. More recent
42. Medicinal plant
43. Footwear
46. Actress Myrna ___
48. Finish

# PUZZLE 425

**• OCTOBER 31 •**

**ACROSS**

1. Emulated Olivier
6. "What's ___ is prologue"
10. Low island
13. Tugboat's burden
14. Inter ___
15. ___ and the Ants
17. Witch's transport
19. Ms. Naldi
20. Evergreen shrub
21. Body of poetry
22. Regard highly
24. Creepy abode: 2 wds.
26. Buddy
29. You in Arles
30. Theater locales
31. Funny man
33. Poet Merriam
36. Off kilter
37. Wee Highlander
38. Guitar part
39. Each
40. Ancient Greek coins
41. Fishing net
42. Neighbor of Rabat
43. Intones
44. All Hallows E'en choice: 3 wds.
49. Rabbit's milieu
50. Moneyed street
51. "A Boy Named ___"
54. ___ fixe
55. Witches' companions
58. Baseball team
59. Bronte heroine
60. Fragrant rootstock
61. British lexicon: abbr.
62. Take out
63. Discernment

**DOWN**

1. "Dear ___"
2. Supervision
3. Believe
4. Self
5. Disparages
6. Writer Alan
7. Heeling
8. ___ transit gloria mundi
9. Wrestling score
10. Ezra Pound verses
11. Au revoir
12. Author Edmund Hodgson
16. Lucille Ball role
18. Tater
23. Avoid
24. 'Umble Uriah
25. Portuguese city
26. Sensation
27. Part
28. Stravinsky
31. Gambol
32. Wagon-___
33. ___ go bragh
34. Outlet
35. St. Tropez summers
37. Was in one's element
38. Stunt
40. Victoria, for one
41. Onion's kin
42. Diatribe
43. French pronoun
44. Romulus or Remus
45. Fibber McGee's medium
46. Actress Papas
47. Spin
48. Marie Louise de la ___
51. Kay and Gawain
52. One
53. To be in old Rome
56. Deli bread grain
57. Malay isthmus

---

# KEYWORD

# PUZZLE 426

**To find the KEYWORD fill in the blanks in words 1 through 10 with the correct missing letters. Transfer those letters to the correspondingly numbered squares in the diagram. Approach with care—this puzzle is not as simple as it first appears.**

1. _ R I M E
2. W _ I T E
3. G R _ P E
4. C L A S _
5. S H A _ E
6. P _ T T Y
7. S T A I _
8. W H _ L E
9. C R E _ E
10. _ I E L D

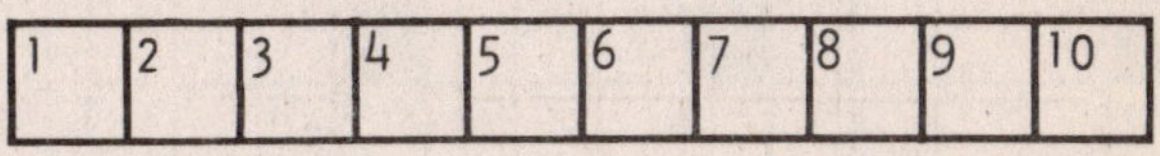

# PUZZLE 427

**ACROSS**

1. Space between
4. Kind of meat
8. Show concern
12. "Cakes and ____"
13. Relieve
14. Done
15. Ill-fated fleet: 2 wds.
18. Last month: abbr.
19. Hoover ____
20. Pieces
23. Agreements
27. War god
28. Western Indian
31. Slithery fish
32. Playful child
33. Done in
34. Thai language
35. "____ any drop to drink"
36. European river
37. ____ egg
38. Moves briskly
40. Ear parts
41. 7th Greek letter
43. Oolong, for one
44. North African region, of yore: 2 wds.
51. Butter portions
52. Pikes ____
53. Pinnacle
54. Nautical direction
55. Agile
56. "____ for the Road"

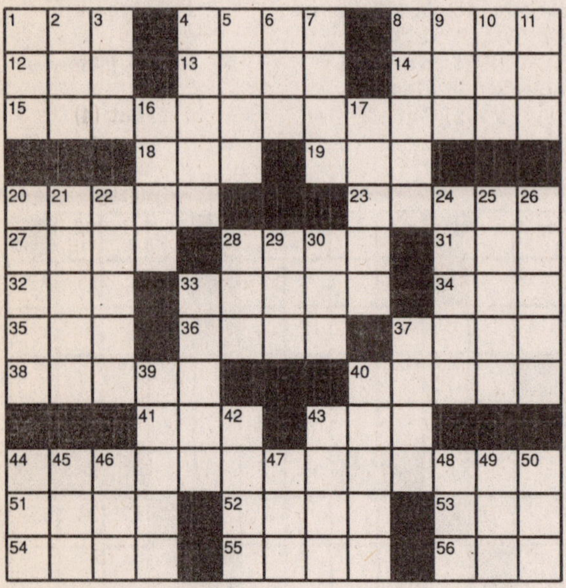

**DOWN**

1. Idle talk
2. Jungfrau, for one
3. Coal size
4. Shrouds
5. Orient
6. ____ Wednesday
7. Show the way
8. Punctuation mark
9. Gardner of films
10. Thomas Jefferson's hair color
11. Geological stage
16. Streisand film
17. ____ transit
20. "____ Your Wagon"
21. Chain mail
22. Copy, for short
24. Star, for short
25. Make fun of
26. Niches
28. Secreted
29. Mine's yield
30. For each
33. Italian composer
37. Actor Beery
39. Uptight
40. Like some faucets
42. Common vipers
43. Winter Palace resident
44. Health farm
45. O'Hara's Joey, e.g.
46. Blind impulse
47. With it
48. Lawyer: abbr.
49. File
50. GI's address

# PUZZLE 428

**ACROSS**

1. Deep voice
5. Slant
9. Health club
12. Spiced stew
13. Before: prefix
14. "El ____" (Heston film)
15. Coward's features: 2 wds.
18. 605, to Pliny
19. Clay, today
20. Ms. Miles
21. Superlative suffix
23. Adroitness
25. Playground
27. Sesame
28. High note: 2 wds.
31. Whole
34. Banged up
36. "Blame It on ____"
37. Work unit
39. Plains Indian
40. Pearly substance
42. Bother
43. Eye coquettishly
44. Badger
46. That guy
49. Speechless from exhaustion: 4 wds.
52. Comic Olsen
53. Despicable
54. ". . . maids all in ____": 2 wds.
55. Roll of bills
56. Type of school: abbr.
57. Summer acquisitions

**DOWN**

1. Actor William
2. Pianist Templeton
3. Eloquent: hyph.
4. Sun
5. Wail
6. Be firm
7. Siamese coin
8. Abject
9. Bonnie Butler's mother: 2 wds.
10. Rocky Mountain rodent
11. Commercials
16. Morsel for Dobbin
17. Slithery one
22. Emulate Franz Klammer
24. "The Yellow ____"
25. Each
26. Tropical cuckoo
29. Zodiac lion
30. Humorist George
32. Play end
33. Blunder
35. Fall asleep
38. Docile
41. Lager's kin
42. ____ of discretion
43. Jar: Sp.
45. Throaty sound
47. Church image
48. Feline cries
49. Kind of tie
50. Zip
51. Diet no-no

# DOUBLE TROUBLE

# PUZZLE 429

**Not really double trouble, but double fun! Solve this puzzle as you would a regular crossword, EXCEPT place one, two, or three letters in each box. The number of letters in each answer is shown in parentheses after its clue.**

## ACROSS

1. Perplexing situation (7)
4. Water pipes (5)
6. Moves slowly (6)
8. California city (7)
11. Press for payment (3)
12. Ready for harvesting (4)
13. Leave out (4)
14. Hebrides island (4)
15. Conflict (6)
16. Resident (8)
18. Stirring (7)
19. Supermarket (5)
21. Unexpected pleasure (5)
22. Characteristic (5)
23. Husband: Fr. (4)
25. Fraudulent cooperation (9)
27. Dramatist Henrik and family (6)
29. Likeness (5)
31. "More ___ You Know" (4)
32. Solidarity leader Walesa (4)
33. Moldy English cheese (7)
34. Antic (5)
35. Small crown (7)
37. Equivalence (6)
38. Consults together (7)
39. Bullfight (7)
40. Talking bird (6)
41. Sandy particles (4)
42. Beginning (5)
44. Upright (5)
45. Naval standard (6)
46. A few (7)
47. Modify (5)
48. Utter confusion (5)
49. Largest living bird (7)
51. Theme (5)
53. Ice (5)
55. With two chambers (9)
57. Cloaks (5)
60. Very heavy (6)
61. High, in music (3)
62. TV diner owner (3)
63. Rudolph Valentino's co-star in "Blood and Sand" (7)
64. Old Gallic chariot (5)
65. Balm (6)
66. Expired (4)
67. Speak imperfectly (4)

## DOWN

1. Performed, of old (5)
2. Madagascar mammal (5)
3. Sovereign declaration (9)
4. Writer Puzo (5)
5. Formal review (10)
6. Disharmony (15)
7. Uncertain (8)
8. Indic language (8)
9. Jubilant (6)
10. Viewing (6)
17. Heal (4)
20. Remember (9)
22. Across: prefix (5)
23. First First Lady (6)
24. Erroneous (9)
26. Luxuriant (4)
28. Mother ___ (U.S. saint) (5)
29. Aloof (10)
30. Ripening agent (4)
33. Begin (5)
34. Restaurant (4)
36. Lake near Syracuse (6)
37. Forecast (15)
38. Operatic voice (9)
39. Kitchen tool (5)
40. Indian Zoroastrian (5)
41. Mourn (6)
43. Irish or type (6)
45. Son of Seth (4)
46. Plotted (7)
48. Punished (9)
50. Margin (3)
52. Spiced relish (10)
53. Runs away (5)
54. Highways (5)
55. Vote (6)
56. Revived (7)
58. Rings (5)
59. Flow through (4)

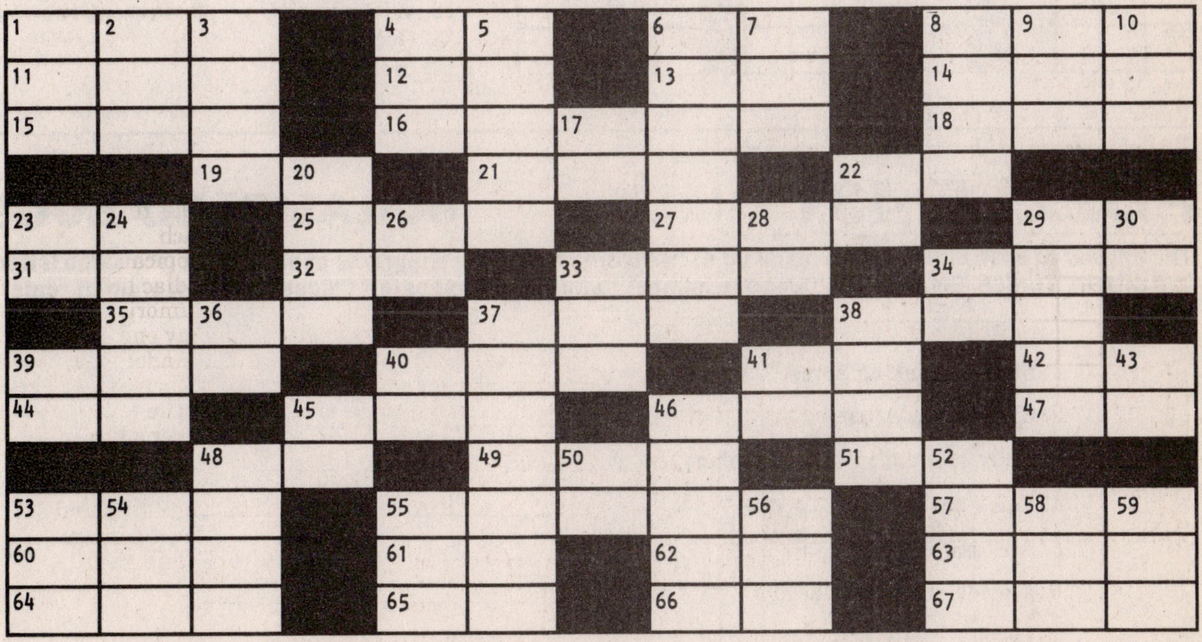

# PUZZLE 430

**• COWPOKE'S BEAT •**

**ACROSS**

1. On the ocean
5. Hang in folds
10. Talon
14. Drags
15. Artist's stand
16. Precept
17. "Deep in ____"
20. Neither's partner
21. Sink outlet
22. Motionless
23. Rep.
24. Hosiery shade
25. State song of Kansas
33. Challenged
34. Fragrance
35. Stevedores' union: abbr.
36. Mideast land
37. Rascal
38. Russian emperor
39. Superlative suffix
40. The Velvet Fog
41. Gardeners, sometimes
42. "Oh, Bury Me Not on ____"
45. Officeholders
46. Compass pt.
47. River to the Humber
50. "____ My Shadow"
53. Recede
56. "Let me ride thru the ____ . . ."
59. Champagne bucket
60. Friendship
61. Lulu
62. Coal units
63. Carbonated beverages
64. Hospital wing

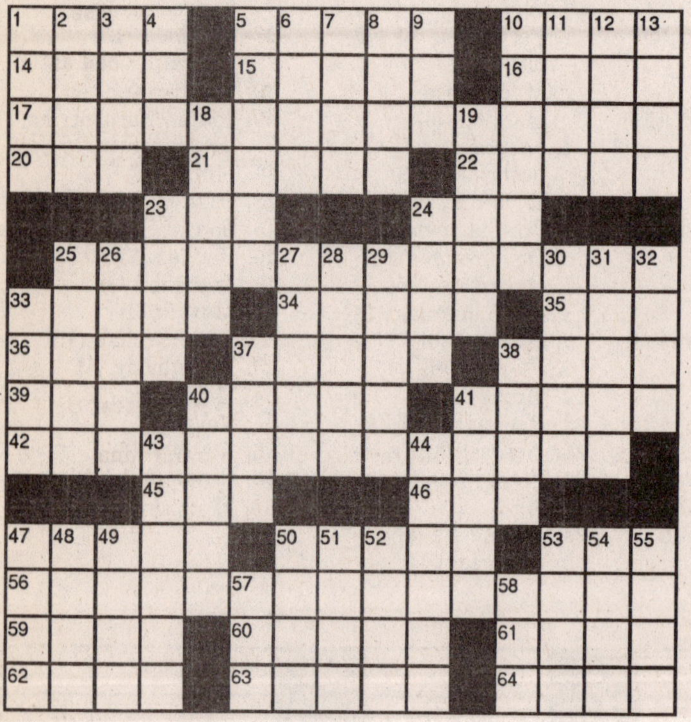

**DOWN**

1. Envelope abbr.
2. London restaurant area
3. Water pitcher
4. Cigar residue
5. "Plato is ____ me" (Aristotle)
6. ____ avis
7. Piedmont city
8. Unskilled worker
9. Pixy
10. Actor Richard
11. Elegance
12. Wing-shaped
13. Occident
18. Sidled
19. Coronet
23. Word of approval
24. Extra hand, for short
25. Severe
26. Speechify
27. Mother-of-pearl
28. Hobo
29. Greek poet
30. Japanese-American
31. Blinding light
32. What a husker husks
33. Food plan
37. "My Three ____"
38. Shredded
40. Scout's rider
41. Native of India
43. Passenger ships
44. Pesters
47. Taunt
48. Puerto ____
49. Paradise
50. Office note
51. Geraint's wife
52. Recorded proceedings
53. Alcohol burner
54. ____ Fox
55. Polar explorer
57. Dance step
58. Present time

---

# PUZZLE 431

## SCRAMBLED EGGS

**The answer to each clue below is made up of two words which are anagrams of each other (the same letters in a different order). For example, "Begone felines!" would be "Scat cats!" ("scat" is an anagram of "cats").**

1. Start a drinking spree ______ ______
2. Chef James's loaf ______ ______
3. Daily account in the milk plant ______ ______
4. Fears snakes _______ _______
5. Autographed pattern _______ _______
6. Alerted the prison head _______ _______
7. Peculiar red gems ________ ________

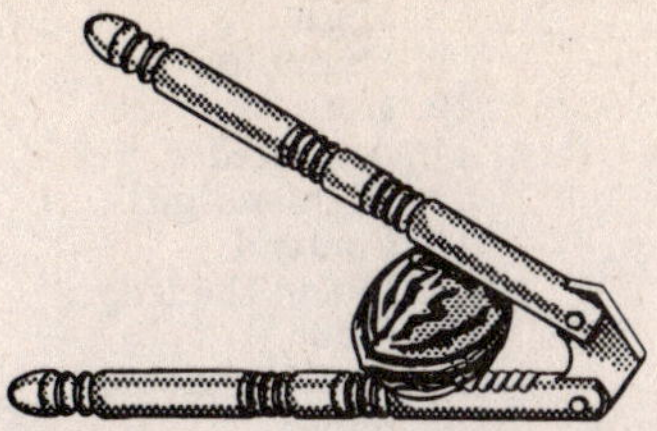

**NUTTY**

# PUZZLE 432

**Here is a puzzle with more than the expected crossword challenge—and rewards. Each clue involves a pun, an anagram or some form of wordplay. Look out for traps! With a little practice, you will soon catch on to these tricky clues and enjoy the extra challenge.**

## ACROSS

1. One who lives poor to die rich
6. Use it in a pinch to make lobster thermidor
10. Dale's boyfriend?
14. Entrance to a place of worship?
15. The same old grind for lunch
16. Ready to come down out of the tree
17. It can't be understood by everyone
18. You're little, sir, and yet you always talk back
19. Confused on your voyage
20. In the know, a generation ago
21. She grew up to be an American Beauty
23. Dannish
25. He's little, but he's refined
26. Spa-cialty
27. Raise a hand to an army officer
30. Ache to see the outside world?
31. Be tween?
34. Lengths and breadths at times
35. Endless parish in France
36. Miss O'Connor is just one of the girls in Rome
37. A Met? All Mets
38. A man's man
39. Chokes on jokes
40. Short response
41. Fought for more pay
42. They're right in the heart of things in apple country
43. Tan his rear
44. Poet on the other side of Mt. Palomar
45. He's in the doghouse with Pierre
46. World's first satellite
47. Where's your brain?
48. Michel was a cherubic Italian
51. Leaves in stitches
52. Just beginning to understand
55. Left-handed monkey wrench?
56. What goods in a hardware store are for
58. He's always high when he sings
60. Cleves to her
61. Live through a bad setback
62. Posh! I say! Posh, 400 times!
63. Know-it-all
64. Brings "Old Man River" to a halt
65. Did a rank thing

## DOWN

1. It's just chicken feed
2. Loaf that yields no bread
3. Add a little water to it and clean up
4. Earn only enough to keep a bird alive
5. Right thing to send when you can't attend
6. Good place to drawer a breath
7. It's made up out of hole cloth
8. Type of tray on which the bride might serve her first biscuits
9. What's his name's writing is a mystery to me
10. "A Raisin in the Sun"?
11. It's how you say it, baby
12. Piece of fencing
13. Close to an ear
22. First half of "Tea for Two"
24. Both sides appealed to him when Greek fought Greek
25. Grounds Under American Management
26. Started a package concern
27. The devil you say
28. It's where the action is, Caesar
29. Rented the smallest apartment?
30. Fainter, but not swooner
31. He's at the beach for life
32. Halo, there! Got any play money?
33. Passenger trains are beginning to be out of date
35. He believes otherwise
38. Got gone
39. It's not bad, not bad at all
41. Sheep's clothing
42. Seaside native?
45. Board of deacons, perhaps
46. The beat, beat, beat of the tom-tom
47. Women get high on them
48. Cry of the also-ran
49. Not one religious person?
50. Last word at an auction
51. Not a fat chance
52. One type of arian
53. Jot down a thought about music
54. Have no fear, Great Scott is here
57. Gardner in Havana
59. Guido got high drinking it up

# PUZZLE 433

**• STARTING NOW •**

## ACROSS

1. Canada's ___ Peninsula
6. Actor Baldwin
10. Figure out
15. Ump's ruling
19. Greek marketplace
20. Moselle tributary
21. Clemens
22. Pipe bends
23. Author Zona et al.
24. Israeli port
25. Beginning
26. Ms. Le Gallienne et al.
27. Friend of Porthos
29. Allows
31. Salad ingredient
33. ___ the finish
35. Nailed obliquely
36. Links figure
37. Nantes negative
38. Beginning
43. Beginning
45. Crocus-to-be
46. Idea
47. Stiff
48. Greek vowel
49. Glossy cloth
50. Hairless
51. Radon
55. Beginning
57. Pronoun
58. Spanish inn
60. S. Amer. balsam
61. Irish sea god
63. Passover feast
65. Breathed
67. Scurries about
71. VP under Coolidge
73. Make mad
74. Make rapt
76. Travel permits
78. River island
79. Greek portico
80. Beginning
82. Meadow
84. Requires
88. African antelopes
90. Boys
91. Enticement
93. Dyeing vessel
94. Refines metal
96. Bakery units
97. Corn Belt state
98. Frequently
101. Beginning
103. Cheer
104. Flip one's ___
105. Reaction
106. Famed Irish hill
107. Refrigerant deliverers
109. Beginning
112. Ginger ___
116. Willing
117. Correct
119. Singles
121. Number
122. Concept
123. "El ___ "(1983 film)
124. Hankering
125. Maternal relation
126. Cozy spot
127. Race official
128. Bender
129. City on the Meuse

## DOWN

1. Round the bend
2. Culture medium
3. Topee plant
4. Bonus
5. Letting up
6. King of Judah
7. Tatting product
8. Merit
9. Beginning
10. Hot
11. Admitted
12. Highland girl
13. Contend
14. Put in the ledger
15. Plant
16. Of the abdomen
17. Sapor
18. Hebrew ascetic
28. Health-club fixture
30. Kind of companion
32. Gens name
34. Pledge
36. Impelled
38. Chilled
39. Memo
40. Omani, e.g.
41. Monkshood
42. Layered
43. Extreme
44. Make a beginning
47. Existed
49. Inscribed monument
50. Puts to sleep
52. Rent
53. First name in fashion
54. "___ Descending a Staircase"
56. Radical
58. Flycatcher
59. On the briny
62. Truckee River city
64. Garroway and Brubeck
66. Some of it is fine
67. Defeat
68. Biblical preposition
69. Cease
70. Rowed
72. Oriental salutation
75. Fr. states
77. Wimbledon offering
81. '60s campus gp.
83. "___ We All?"
85. Bacchanalian cry
86. Eos's realm
87. RBI, e.g.
89. Grin
91. Makes a beginning
92. Famed statuette
95. Distinguished
96. Misplace
97. Lennon song
98. Beginning
99. Front
100. Topics
101. Combustion residue
102. Wears down
105. Fr. income
108. Pith
109. Antiseptic's target
110. Obi adjunct
111. Utah's lily
113. Mild oath
114. "Rio ___"
115. British carbine
118. Miss Piggy's pronoun
120. Coterie

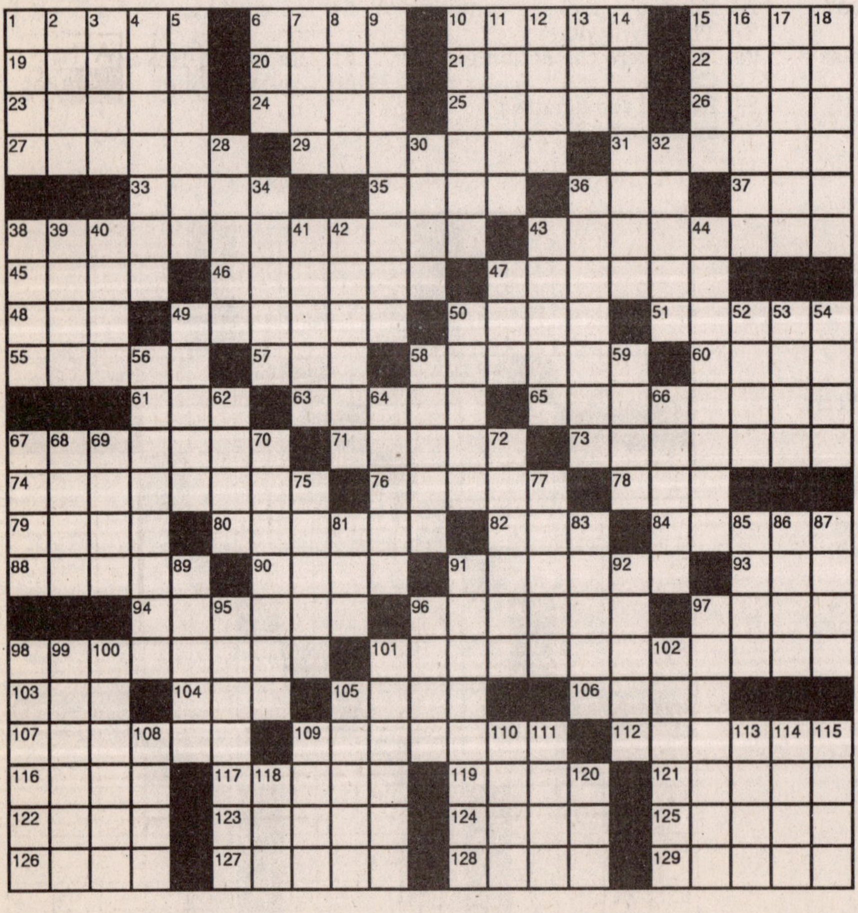

## BRICK BY BRICK

# PUZZLE 434

**Rearrange this stack of bricks to form a crossword puzzle. The clues will help you fit the bricks into their correct places. Row 1 has been filled in for you. Use the bricks to fill in the remaining spaces.**

**ACROSS**

1. TV's Jack
   Bamboo
   Divine Miss M
2. Theater award
   Always
   Maui good-by
3. Flops
   Romantic missives
4. Brewed
   Waterlogged
   Rancor
5. Additional
   Salami servings
6. Jabber
   Regularly
7. Lithe
   Slammer
   Deli pickle
8. Actress Lee
   Strong point
   Comedienne McClurg
9. Viewed
   Arden et al.
   Fencing blades
10. Belief
    Scrubs up
11. Morning fare
    Director Parker
12. Harem room
    Seine
    Dressing
13. Signatures
    Generations
14. Play part
    Harvest
    Aerie
15. Tryouts
    Crags
    Record

**DOWN**

1. Okra units
   Stripes
   Shoreline
2. Border on
   Flu's kin
   Evoke
3. Girl Friday
   Morsel
   Deserves
4. Similarity
   Toronto's prov.
5. Vaulting tool
   Grazing grounds
6. Esteem highly
   Ant's antenna
7. Dodge
   Jupiter
   Sensitivity
8. Conger
   Rowed
   Dab hand
9. Attracted
   Tantrums
   Detest
10. Cuddle
    Holds
11. Conflict
    Verve
12. Actor Wallach
    Nonpartisan
13. Bracer
    Inkling
    ____ code
14. Yonder
    Mortgage
    Huff and puff
15. Slows
    Inferior
    Villa d'____

**BRICKS**

| | | | | | | | | | | | | | | |
|---|---|---|---|---|---|---|---|---|---|---|---|---|---|---|
| P | ■ | N | E | D | ■ | O | R | T | ■ | ■ | ■ | D | I | E |
| S | ■ | T | ■ | ■ | A | V | E | S | I | L | L | E | E | S |
| N | E | ■ | A | ■ | F | O | D | A | A | N | D | R | U | T |
| T | S | ■ | N | ■ | E | A | U | T | S | ■ | E | S | E | E |
| O | H | A | E | T | ■ | I | R | E | T | E | N | V | E | R |
| N | E | S | S | L | I | C | E | S | L | ■ | D | A | L | E |
| ■ | ■ | ■ | C | R | O | C | R | E | ■ | N | E | E | P | E |
| C | E | R | T | O | R | E | A | L | O | G | R | M | O | R |
| A | G | E | D | ■ | W | S | T | E | ■ | A | L | C | L | E |
| R | A | S | E | ■ | ■ | ■ | ■ | ■ | N | T | I | L | A | N |
| S | C | E | B | L | E | T | ■ | B | ■ | O | F | B | A | B |
| T | E | S | L | E | ■ | A | P | H | J | A | I | A | G | I |
| E | ■ | E | E | S | T | O | B | I | E | ■ | E | A | N | S |
| ■ | E | P | A | P | E | D | U | D | S | ■ | V | ■ | ■ | ■ |

**DIAGRAM**

| | 1 | 2 | 3 | 4 | 5 | 6 | 7 | 8 | 9 | 10 | 11 | 12 | 13 | 14 | 15 |
|---|---|---|---|---|---|---|---|---|---|---|---|---|---|---|---|
| 1 | P | A | A | R | ■ | R | E | E | D | ■ | B | E | T | T | E |
| 2 | | | | | | | | | | | | | | | |
| 3 | | | | | | | | | | | | | | | |
| 4 | | | | | | | | | | | | | | | |
| 5 | | | | | | | | | | | | | | | |
| 6 | | | | | | | | | | | | | | | |
| 7 | | | | | | | | | | | | | | | |
| 8 | | | | | | | | | | | | | | | |
| 9 | | | | | | | | | | | | | | | |
| 10 | | | | | | | | | | | | | | | |
| 11 | | | | | | | | | | | | | | | |
| 12 | | | | | | | | | | | | | | | |
| 13 | | | | | | | | | | | | | | | |
| 14 | | | | | | | | | | | | | | | |
| 15 | | | | | | | | | | | | | | | |

# PUZZLE 435

**• X-TRA •**

## ACROSS

1. Siouan people
6. Of a time period
10. Enforce an embankment
15. Puzzle abbr.
19. Kind of orange
20. Gull genus
21. Banish
22. Metal fabric
23. Surprising
25. Civil War line
27. Wheys
28. Ceremonies
29. Astronaut Shepard
30. Put forth
31. Overcome
33. Table scraps
34. Certain photographs
35. Put in
38. Acorns, later
39. Trip
40. Vaquero equipment
41. Columnist Buchwald
42. ____ pas
43. Copy
46. Time's yield
50. Saved
53. Color for Stendahl
54. Tease
55. Dolphins' home
56. French department
57. Make ____ (get by)
59. Amerind craft
60. Church custodian
62. Print measures
63. Bodies of print
64. Ms. Farrow
65. Treatises
69. Information sources
70. Fanfares
75. Blood: prefix
76. Capital of Oregon
77. Verdi opus
78. Hold on
79. Not subject to question
82. What A suggests
84. Red or White
85. Alliance
86. Exist
87. Postulate
88. Pet
89. Reverberate
91. Works very hard
94. Widow
97. Ethereal
98. Hide
99. Kind of fig
100. Sailor's saint
101. Statesman Silas
102. Telephone
106. Color
108. Suitableness
110. October stone
111. Holy, in Mantmartre
112. Chevrons
113. Hag
114. Hawaiian goose
115. Daub
116. Aide: abbr.
117. Anglo-Saxon drudges

## DOWN

1. Burden
2. Leonine ruff
3. State
4. Certain poetic lines
5. Swiss peak
6. Stir up
7. Soaked flax
8. Arab noble
9. Boys
10. Comment
11. Praises
12. Country passes
13. N.C. college
14. Mark for Ms. Retton
15. Tonic
16. Made demands on
17. Love Italian style
18. Fast times
24. Once, once
26. Fancy
32. Sandarac tree
33. Stable staple grain
34. From ____ to nuts
35. Peace goddess
36. Johnson's successor
37. Tasty
38. Native mineral
39. Judd Hirsch vehicle
41. Perform
42. Woman, in law
43. Collier's ingress
44. Coin in Juarez
45. Paradise
47. Bits
48. She-sheep
49. Louse egg
50. Utah range
51. Ancient temple
52. Goddess of night
55. Saying
58. Encountered
59. Gave up
60. Of a facial cavity
61. Have a bite
63. Distant: prefix
64. Fashioned
65. So
66. City on the Truckee
67. Wall St. acronym
68. Loser to Harding
69. Netman Wilander
70. Fixation
71. 8 Popes
72. Arrested
73. Necktie
74. Shoots
76. Promontory
77. Hew
80. Invalidate
81. Leave
82. Work unit
83. Wash
86. "____ Wednesday"
88. Elementary
89. Shark sucker
90. Laundry worker
91. Scenic views
92. Author Hemingway
93. Actor Oliver
94. Scout's task, for short
95. Run away
96. Lac ____ (Lake Geneva)
97. Linda Lavin role
98. Genders
100. Test
101. Hindu divine
103. Party to
104. Skin problem
105. Caustic solutions
107. Kind of curve
109. Yegg's jewelry

## WORDBENDERS

# PUZZLE 436

**The answers for this crossword puzzle might be just around the bend! Solve the puzzle as you would a regular crossword. The clues for the words which bend in the diagram are listed under the heading BENDERS.**

**BENDERS**

1. Open to question
2. Dress
8. In the same book: abbr.
9. Needy persons
17. Neglectful
18. Doesn't eat
28. Melancholy
29. Make believe
30. Subdued
32. Limber
43. Japanese sacred mountain
49. Indonesian island

**ACROSS**

1. Stray calf
6. Caribbean republic
10. Began
13. Yarn-knotting craft
14. Scottish county
19. Greek letter
21. Golf mound
22. Cereal grain
23. Fall behind
24. Poplars
25. Anger
26. Pitch
33. Goal
34. Apartment dweller
36. Door
38. Food scrap
39. Time past
40. Adam's wife
41. Used to be
42. Ocean
44. Go before
50. Spray-can contents
51. Scottish landowner
52. Choice

**DOWN**

3. Doctrine
4. Greek letter
5. Make a mistake
6. Skirt edge
7. Summer drink
11. Boldly confronts
12. Food samplers
15. Affirmative response
16. Acts as agent for
19. Fellow students
20. Old witch
27. Italian wine city
29. Marcher
31. Inflicts
35. Time period
37. Hail!
44. Golfer's goal
45. Crimson
46. Folding bed
47. Female deer
48. Building extension

# PUZZLE 437

**ACROSS**

1. Gouda's kin
5. Rabbi ____ Hillel Silver
9. Schnitzel meat
13. Hack
17. Prima donna
18. Smear
19. Mystery maker Gardner
20. ____ avis
21. Finished by frosting
22. Aberdeen miss
23. Actress Bonet
24. Eons
25. Actress Wright
27. Coin flip question
30. Poetic contraction
32. Crackpot
33. Actor Pendleton
34. Content
38. Nip and ____
40. Most timid
44. Gemstone
45. Ploy
46. Startle
47. Jitney
49. Adventure
51. Pipes
52. Harem room
53. Fate
54. Arias
55. Seamstress Ross
57. Pull
58. Actress Ringwald
59. Big ____ (London site)
60. Baikal and Titicaca
63. Humble
64. Chic
68. Kimono sash
69. Duct and masking
70. Young adult
71. Actor Brynner
72. Quenched
73. Machu Picchu site
74. "Sommersby" lead
75. Added up
77. City on the Adda
78. Thin
79. Wing
80. Speck
81. Self-respect
83. Salon
89. Waning
94. One
95. Protagonist
96. Greater number
98. Brainstorm
99. Nonflying bird
100. Wise to
101. Woe is me!
102. Abandoned
103. Leda's seducer
104. Stalk
105. Grant
106. Further

**DOWN**

1. Revise
2. Gambling cubes
3. Swear to
4. Fabricated
5. Politician Stevenson
6. Bleat
7. Singer Kate ____
8. "____ of Malice"
9. African grassland
10. Goddess of discord
11. Too
12. Students, usually
13. Make
14. Mata ____
15. Mr. Roberts
16. Permit
26. Pigpen
28. Diving bird
29. Capture
31. Research
34. Cultivated
35. Basilica part
36. Snow boots
37. Missouri tributary
39. Purpose
40. The real ____
41. Devours
42. Glasgow native
43. Boys
45. Phoned
46. Tarnish
48. Howl
50. Pope's name
51. "Guys and ____"
54. Planted
55. Has-____
56. Hire
58. Pouted
59. ____ cheese
60. Actress Myrna ____
61. Adjoin
62. Metric pound
63. Overdue
64. Spooky
65. Author James ____
66. Clod
67. Low card
69. Fox hunting cries
70. Williams or Koppel
72. Seasoning
73. District of Columbia river
76. German of yore
77. "Diamond ____"
78. Actor Lowe
80. Housekeeper's tool
82. Silly ones
83. Develops
84. Poet's sufficiency
85. Verdi opera
86. Confined
87. Comedian Johnson
88. Part
90. Bodily humor
91. Baal
92. Promontory
93. Wicket
97. Wonderful

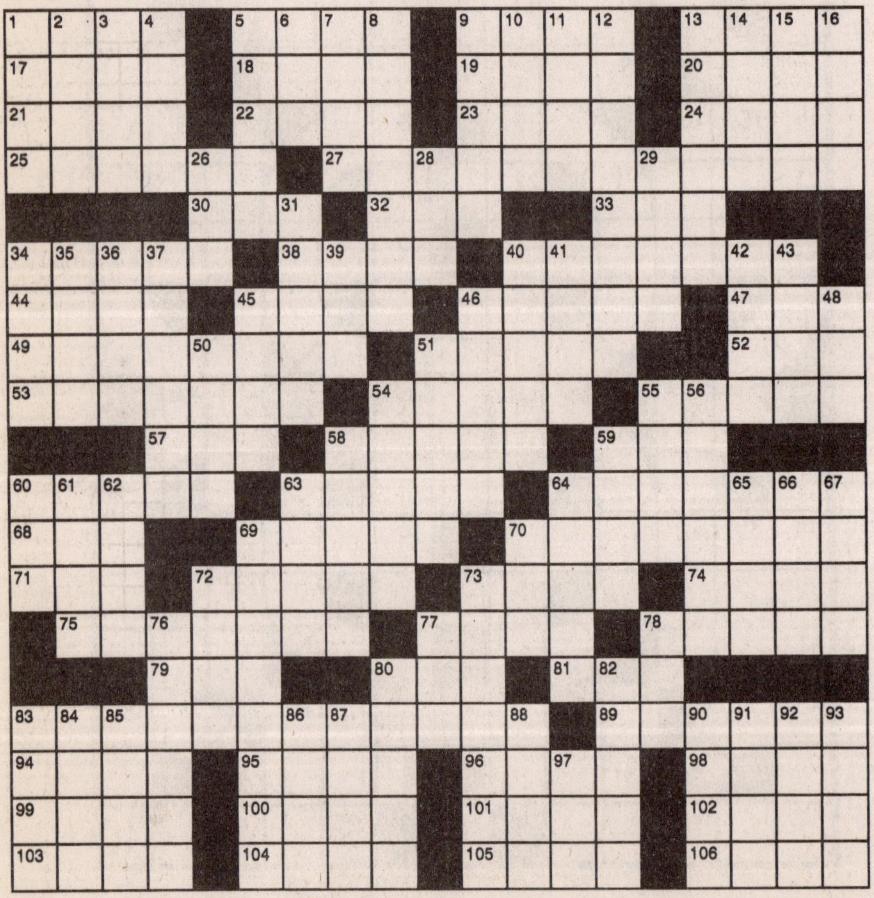

# PUZZLE 438

**• BRIDGE •**

**ACROSS**

1. Meadow sound
4. Rod
7. Small paving stone
11. French painter
16. Totality
17. Repented
19. Film robot, for short
20. In concert
21. Fen
22. Spindle
23. Delaware
26. Long
28. Shade of green
30. Come in second
31. Refrain syllable
32. Pericarp
34. Exercise vigorously
37. Sacred songs
38. Drunken cry
39. Greek letter
40. Boys of free birth, in old Rome
43. Balloon trips
46. Saphead
50. Dinnerware
52. "Bonanza" son
53. Ancient Balkan country
56. Actor Roger
57. Borodin prince
59. Abundance
60. ____ Dinh
61. Reliable
63. Genus of leaf-cutting ants
64. Blended whiskey
65. Was befriended
69. Doleful
72. Stubborn animal
73. Cold and rainy
74. Stage light transparencies
77. 1955 Wimbledon champ et al.
79. "M*A*S*H" star
80. Writer Zola
82. 1953 Ryan film
83. Hopalong Cassidy
85. Try to find blindly
88. Church court
89. Actor Tucker
92. Female praying figures
93. Molasses liquor
96. Stingy
97. Claim
99. Positions in enemy territory
103. Banqueting
106. Actor Piazza
107. "He had ____ like Castlereagh" (Shelley)
108. Celebrity
109. Claws
111. Memorize
115. Road distance
117. Hiatus
118. Derisive
119. Synthetic fiber
120. Calendar span
121. Historic age
122. Ventriloquist Bergen
123. Chinese dynasty
124. Bro's sib
125. Fiery

**DOWN**

1. ____ blue
2. "A Lesson from ____"
3. Water plants
4. Hit scoring four runs
5. ____ Cayes
6. "It's a Sin to ____"
7. ____ Lanka
8. Greek H
9. Muzzle plugs: var.
10. Workman's kit
11. Zany
12. Evaluate
13. Touch-me-____
14. Growing out
15. Tropical fish
18. Belief in God
19. Cool drink
24. Highlands negative
25. Consume
27. Grumbling
29. Tableland
33. Wolframites
34. Turntables
35. Prayers
36. Expand
40. Roman 205
41. OT king
42. South of France
44. Sand bars
45. Forge
47. Polish river
48. Nosegay
49. First word of the Massachusetts motto
51. Contributes a tenth
54. Official proceedings
55. Song from "Carefree"
58. ____ whiz
59. Motley crowd
61. "Ye are the ____ the earth"
62. Produces
66. Go bad
67. Actor Sparks
68. Mental impairment
69. Prison
70. Italian river
71. Loco
75. Hoist
76. Blackthorn
78. Whiskers
81. Vetch
83. Newport mansion, with "The"
84. Toward the mouth
86. Nuns' beads
87. Metallic finds
90. Single appearance
91. 27th President
94. Neighbor of Kenya
95. "____ of the Wedding"
98. Sordid
99. Oil measure: abbr.
100. Della ____
101. "Go ____ out the windows"
102. Dried grass
104. Neighbor of Chad
105. Blinding light
108. Broadcast outlet: abbr.
110. Plummet hook
112. Manipulate
113. Actress MacGraw
114. Baseballer Kittle
116. Love poem

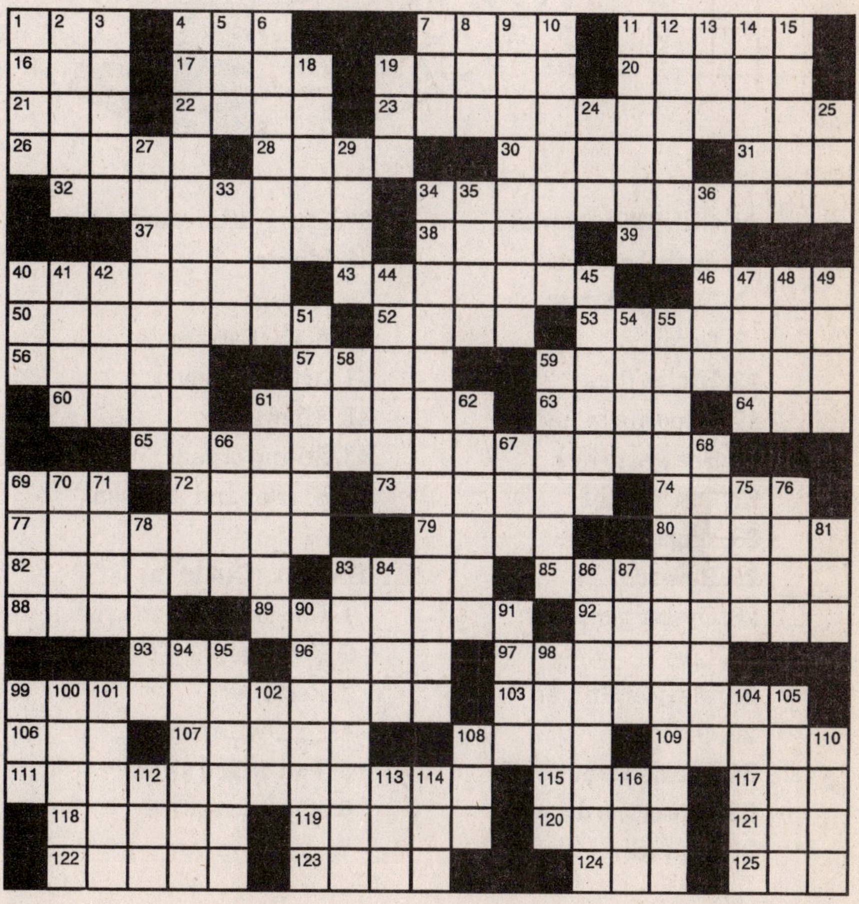

# PUZZLE 439

## CIRCULAR CROSSWORD

**To complete this Circular puzzle fill in the answers to the Around clues in a clockwise direction. For the Radial clues move from the outside to the inside.**

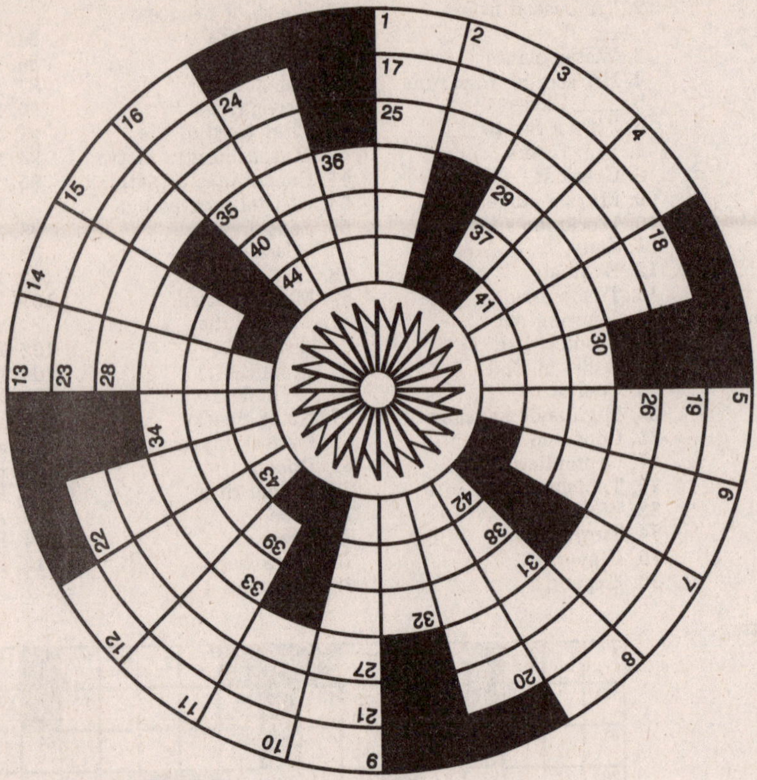

**AROUND (Clockwise)**

1. Strikebreaker
5. Large rodents
9. Deceit
13. Hit, as flies
17. Opposite in nature
19. See eye to eye
21. Office notes
23. Engages
25. Revere
26. Oyster gem
27. Live
28. Mexican Indian
29. Get
31. Hawkeye State
33. Chessboard space
35. Ripped
37. Furry little animal
38. Mimic
39. Abrupt
40. Actor Estrada
41. Active person
42. Allows
43. Seeing organs
44. Scarlet and crimson

**RADIAL (Out to in)**

1. Doesn't spare the rod
2. Food fish
3. Reserved
4. ____-wire fence
5. Two-edged sword
6. Representative
7. ____ la la
8. Soap opera, e.g.
9. Daubs
10. Bewitch
11. Wrong
12. Moslem temple
13. Portions
14. Dry up
15. Actor Carney
16. Wobble
18. Reverse: pref.
20. Marry on the lam
22. Hit the books
24. Make points
30. Have being
32. Damp
34. Summer drink
36. Clear

# PUZZLE 440

**ACROSS**

1. Cartoonist Peter ____
5. Sage or thyme
9. Dull
14. Fare
15. Zone
16. "Home ____"
17. Actor John ____
18. Hampers
19. Saturn moon
20. Monroe-Lemmon movie
23. Harpsichord
24. Wine: pref.
25. Put two and two together
28. Vessel
30. More slender
33. Jocks
38. Awkwardness
39. Sand bar
40. Two, in Toledo
42. Negotiations
43. Soaked
45. Fearfulness
47. Electrical measurements
49. Statute: abbr.
50. Recent: pref.
51. Printers' measures
53. Pince-nez
58. Vegas cry
62. Panache
64. Godiva's title
65. Reduce
66. Joyce Carol ____
67. Bald eagle's kin
68. Leak
69. Lyric poem
70. Bolt or end
71. Itchings

**DOWN**

1. Lay up
2. Swab again
3. Judd the singer
4. Comedian Ole ____
5. Milieu
6. Actor Rhodes
7. Tennis-player Richards
8. Inlets
9. "Lord ____ taken away ..."
10. Stew
11. Mexican entree
12. Actress Merkel
13. Guys
21. Smoother
22. Perfume resin
26. Work stations
27. Kind of code
29. Broadcaster Turner
31. Number
32. Signify
33. Nile dam
34. Motif
35. Risky situation
36. Off schedule
37. Greensward
41. English senor
44. Act
46. Passed on
48. Beamed
52. Intimidate
54. Indigent
55. Divvy up
56. Silk dye
57. Dancers' concerns
59. Scooted
60. Celtic language
61. Author Ferber
62. Contender
63. Once around the track

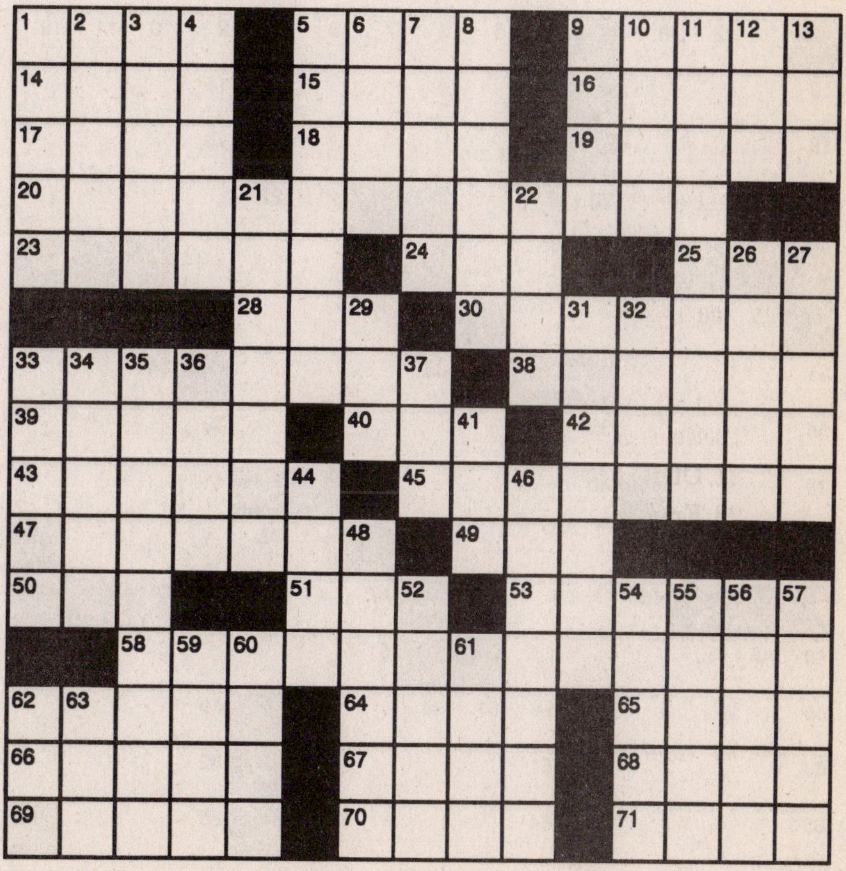

# PUZZLE 441

**ACROSS**

1. Actor Mineo
4. Hindu title
9. Rest against
13. Civil-rights pioneer Parks
14. Rink
15. Oom-pah instrument
16. "Iliad," e.g.
17. Nonets
18. Journey
19. Grant-Hepburn thriller
21. Refugee
23. Girasol
24. Fourth person
25. Swiss city
27. Lancelot comrade
31. Flubs a grounder
32. Bathroom item
34. Highest note, to Guido
35. Joe South tune
39. Gardner of Hollywood
40. Shade
41. Charged particles
42. Go down
44. Dollar makers
46. ____ to riches
47. Han ____ of "Star Wars"
48. Set up a bivouac
51. Night noisemaker
55. String
56. Frequently
59. Conceal
60. Certain exam
61. Not a soul
62. Advance
63. Vital statistic
64. Actress Garson
65. ____ Marie Saint

**DOWN**

1. Senior to a frosh
2. Tibet's locale
3. American Indian sport
4. Summer footwear
5. "The Tempest" sprite
6. Layer
7. Made of: suff.
8. Gooden's sport
9. Noted Hun
10. Hamlet
11. Over, in Bonn
12. Snatch
13. Family room
20. Tarzan's neighbor
22. Brawl
24. Wide open
25. Valiant
26. Former Red Sox Tony ____
28. Spartan slave
29. Arkin and Alda
30. Doris and Dennis
31. Mild expletive
32. Ships
33. Gear part
36. Engine or bath
37. Paddle sport
38. Card game
43. Baby's bed
44. Jack Horner's place
45. "Ace ____ and Rodger of the Skies" (Spielberg story)
47. Play part
48. Business subj.
49. Nick's wife
50. Crowd
52. Russian port
53. Author Ferber
54. Senator Kennedy
57. In favor of
58. Tip of Italy

## CAMOUFLAGE

# PUZZLE 442

**The answers to the clues can be found in the diagram, but they have been camouflaged. Their letters are in the correct order, but sometimes they are separated by extra letters which have been inserted throughout the diagram. You must black out all the extra camouflage letters. The remaining letters will be used in words reading across and down. Solve Across and Down together to determine the correct letters where there is a choice. The number of answer words in a row or column is indicated by the number of clues.**

| | 1 | 2 | 3 | 4 | 5 | 6 | 7 | 8 | 9 | 10 | 11 | 12 | 13 |
|---|---|---|---|---|---|---|---|---|---|---|---|---|---|
| 1 | K | E | E | R | N | E | L | A | B | A | R | K | D |
| 2 | E | N | T | E | N | R | A | L | I | T | O | R | E |
| 3 | P | L | A | T | E | E | R | A | B | O | V | I | E |
| 4 | Y | A | L | L | E | M | I | V | A | P | S | O | R |
| 5 | W | R | E | U | I | C | K | N | P | O | E | M | D |
| 6 | I | G | N | U | A | E | N | A | P | I | E | E | R |
| 7 | T | E | N | S | T | O | A | T | O | L | I | N | E |
| 8 | B | E | T | R | G | Y | S | A | L | O | L | N | E |
| 9 | T | O | A | N | A | L | B | L | E | R | R | O | D |
| 10 | A | P | H | I | T | D | B | E | P | D | A | T | E |
| 11 | G | W | O | E | N | E | E | D | D | E | N | A | N |
| 12 | S | A | N | C | A | W | T | S | A | R | T | E | D |
| 13 | S | L | E | E | T | W | A | M | D | E | E | N | D |

**ACROSS**

1. Seed • Poet
2. Join • Landed • Miner's find
3. More tardy • Overhead
4. Elihu ____ • Steam
5. Demolish • Verse
6. Large lizard • Wharf
7. Dress type • Grain • Fib
8. Attempt • Solo
9. Heavy weight • More fit • Reel's partner
10. Plant insect • Cot • Consumed
11. Left • Paradise
12. Behaves • Comic Johnson
13. Icy rain • Walked in water

**DOWN**

1. Lock opener • Humor • Stubs
2. Expand • Milky gem
3. Knack • Garden tool
4. Come back • Frozen water
5. Tidy • Pismire
6. Bard's before • Shy • Moisture
7. Spree • Catch • Greek letter
8. Hot rock • Stories
9. Baby apron • McIntosh, e.g. • Mom's man
10. On • Lubricant • Command
11. Wander • Angry
12. Italian city • Memo
13. Doe • Stem • Stop

# PUZZLE 443

**ACROSS**

1. Traffic problem
4. Forearm bone
8. Fencing weapon
13. Continent
15. Tag or football
16. Pseudonym
17. Malt beverage
18. Horsehair
19. Dagger handles
20. Don Quixote's sidekick
23. Golf-ball location
24. Parasite's home
25. Catherine of ____
27. Throw out
29. African antelope
31. Wading bird
32. Faux pas
33. Cain's nephew
36. Anglo-Saxon letter
37. Alike
40. Forty winks
41. Fairy's rod
43. Of the earth
44. Irish writer Thomas ____
46. Commanded
48. Anthony and Barbara
49. Slow, musically
51. Arab chieftain
52. Wrestler's surface
53. Secret Squirrel's sidekick
59. Short-lived David Soul TV series
61. Woodwind
62. Skating jump
63. Lime or brim
64. Soccer great
65. Football's Anderson
66. Male voice
67. "The ____ of Laura Mars"
68. New Deal org.

**DOWN**

1. Short punches
2. Cruising
3. Appearance
4. Extreme
5. Jumped
6. Darling dog
7. Sherman Hemsley TV series
8. Desert
9. Actress MacGraw
10. Joe Friday's sidekick
11. 7:1
12. German city
14. Actress Anne ____
21. Pawns
22. Mothers of Invention leader
26. Tankard contents
27. Kett, e.g.
28. Sherlock Holmes's sidekick
29. Homer epic
30. Factory
31. Baste
32. "Peter Pan" villain
34. Crew members
35. Mole
38. Snow house
39. Marconi's medium
42. Excavate
45. "Call Me Madam" star
47. Supple
48. Game-show hosts
49. "____ to Avoid" (Herman's Hermits)
50. "Divine Comedy" author
51. French school
54. Alfred Hitchcock film
55. Heed
56. Yoke animals
57. Limerick writer Edward
58. Fitzgerald of jazz
60. Numero ____

# PUZZLE 444

**ACROSS**

1. Nick and Nora's pet
5. Beaver creations
9. Mil. ranks
13. Highway
14. Inventor Howe
16. Seed coat
17. Part of BPOE
18. Biblical mount
19. Stuff
20. Summer drink
21. Midnight rider
22. Ski slope covering
23. Mall components
25. Skirt opening
27. Most secure
29. Church tower
32. Jogs
33. Has a different opinion
35. Always, in verse
36. Food scrap
37. Hosp. workers
38. Absorbs
42. Ike's wife
44. Former prisoner
45. Small houses
46. Prayer ending
47. Shows consideration for
49. Miracle site
51. Conceive
53. Gal of song
56. Italian city
57. Harangue
58. Water conduit
59. Mortgage
60. Scorer
61. Gypsy ____ Lee
62. Load cargo
63. Rocky crags
64. Extraordinary thing

**DOWN**

1. Locality
2. Realtor's sign
3. Assumes
4. Newspaper notices, for short
5. Wasteland
6. Active
7. Excavations
8. German territory
9. More impudent
10. Allow
11. Josip Broz
12. Large amount
15. Afternoon nap
21. Singer Diana ____
24. Asian holiday
26. Lower limb
27. Exorbitant
28. Amphitheater
29. Fast jets
30. Soviet premier
31. Dangerous curves
33. Doctor's amount
34. Dander
39. Kind of lettuce
40. Corrida cry
41. Certain college student
42. Colt's mom
43. Judge Fortas
45. Provides food
47. Defense gp.
48. Father: Lat.
49. Phone
50. China's continent
52. Darn!
54. Church recess
55. Sideways glance
58. Opposite of con

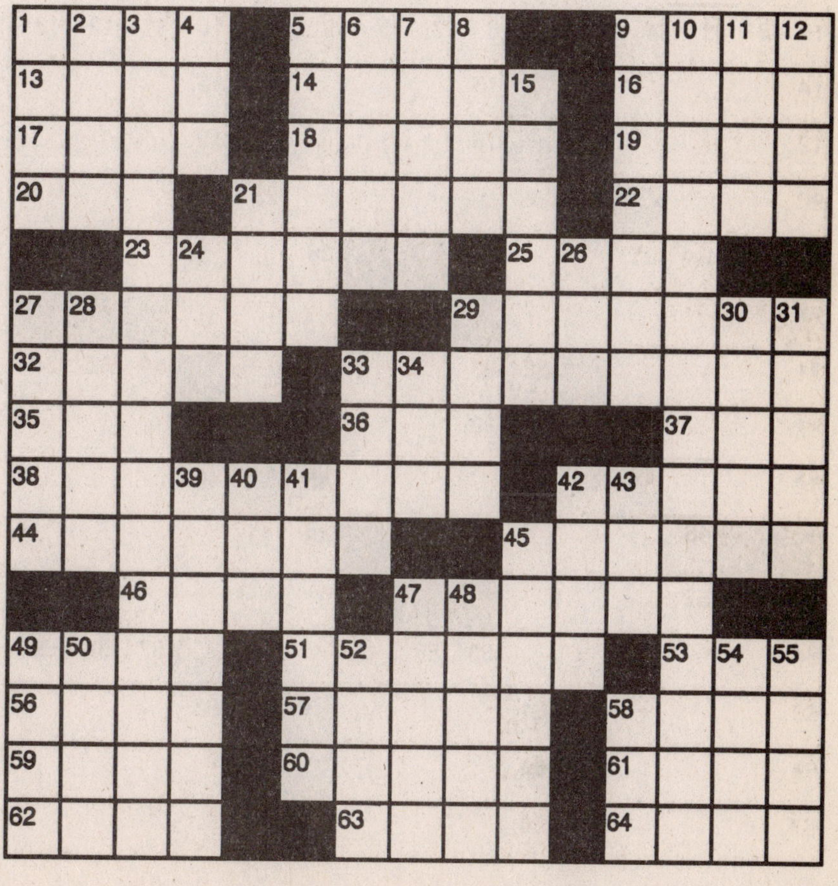

# PUZZLE 445

**ACROSS**

1. Called
6. Flop
10. Lhasa ____
14. Nod
15. Eros
16. Pro ____
17. Sing
18. Change the decor
19. Small insect
20. Summer color
21. "Albert's Son" artist
24. Strives
26. French rooms
27. Ivanhoe's love
29. Spectacle
31. English school
32. Warhol's forte
34. ____ Cuarto
37. Set upright
39. Witticism
40. Used
42. Mass of ivy
43. Kind of show
46. Mine: Fr.
47. Hum
48. Red dyes
50. Belfast's county
53. Roasting bird
54. "The Bath" artist
57. Opening
60. Eye part
61. Sullen
62. Yucca fiber
64. Go first
65. Pliny's road
66. Picked
67. Superlative suffixes
68. French statesman
69. Spanish title

**DOWN**

1. Treaty
2. Turkish general
3. "American Gothic" artist
4. Poetic contraction
5. Hold up
6. Poets
7. Hebrew measure
8. Way
9. Shopper, sometimes
10. Sock pattern
11. Triptych part
12. Washington
13. Vows
22. Kind of tide
23. Needs
25. Splitsville
27. Musical pause
28. ____ von Bismarck
29. Froth
30. Miracle site
33. Available
34. "Downing the Nigh Leader" artist
35. Party to
36. Elevator name
38. Classical order
41. El ____
44. Like the Bedouins
45. Undiluted
47. Woodland nymphs
49. Science of light
50. Stubborn as ____
51. Church areas
52. Pick up the tab
53. Convey
55. Hernando De ____
56. Tallow source
58. In addition
59. Nobleman
63. "Thar ____ blows!"

# PUZZLE 446

**ACROSS**

1. Market wagon
5. Quote
9. Reserved
12. Garden worker
13. Fighting ring
15. Greek porch
16. Singer Gibb
17. Tears at
18. Lanky
19. Fresh
20. Apartment payment
21. Party
23. ____ of cards
25. Rains heavily
26. ____ and dines
27. Section
28. Loudspeaker, for short
31. Detests
32. Lingers
33. Modernist: pref.
34. Affirm
35. Raggedy ____
36. Utopia
37. Meadow
38. Plebe
40. Dated
41. Aquatic bird
42. Singing brothers
43. Speed
44. Challenged
46. Kitchen gadget
47. Kind of check or stamp
49. Eternal City
50. Rhoda's mom
53. Mystery writer Gardner
54. Hanker for
56. Bridge piece
57. Chills and fever
58. Consumer
59. Nuisance
60. Billy ____ Williams
61. Towel word
62. Tennis great

**DOWN**

1. Chinese detective
2. Topnotch: 2 wds.
3. Old Glory: 4 wds.
4. Attempt
5. Pet
6. "Good Night" girl
7. Wigwam
8. Cease
9. Old Glory: 3 wds.
10. Golf goal
11. Ivy League school
14. Classify
15. Fidget
20. Grieves about
22. There are three per inning
24. Humdinger
25. Sketch
26. Teeter
27. Window squares
29. Edwin ____
30. Corn cake
31. Regretful American patriot
32. Walked through water
36. At ____!
38. Have feelings
39. Punish
40. Flay
43. Simpson patriarch et al.
45. Busy as ____: 2 wds.
46. Lid
47. Study
48. Egg on
49. Fee
51. Sprint
52. Pot-filler
55. Cheer
56. Fitness resort

# PUZZLE 447

**ACROSS**

1. Loser's place
5. Gossip
9. "____ Out of Control"
13. Requisite
17. Tennis great Arthur ____
18. ____ avis
19. Young horse
20. Writer Stanley Gardner
21. Have in mind
22. Unwritten
23. Korea's continent
24. Workbench item
25. Tatum O'Neal film, with "The"
28. More timid
30. Motel
31. Stir ____
32. Son of Venus
33. Violet
36. Astringent
38. Climb down
42. Southern constellation, the Altar
43. Heavenly messenger
45. Twosome
47. Comedienne Martha ____
48. More or ____
50. Columnist Buchwald
51. Florence's river
52. North Sea feeder
53. Gospel singer Jackson
55. Gather
56. Mas that baa
57. Actor Kilmer
58. Sports field
59. Andy Capp's wife
60. Ball of yarn
62. Sip
63. Greenbacks
67. Teasdale, e.g.
68. Oliver or Rex
69. Corp. chairman
70. Defect
71. Chinese nurse
72. Permit
73. Thin rock
75. "Three ____ Match"
76. Bouquet
78. Tennis tournament
79. Flight of fancy
81. Hardy's heroine
82. Lancelot's title
83. Coconut cream, e.g.
84. Illinois city
87. 1986 animated film
93. Enthusiastic
94. Atop
96. Mrs. James Joyce
97. Theater award
98. Nobel Peace Prize winner Cassin
99. Called up
100. ____ and bear it
101. Columnist Barrett
102. Prophet
103. Sommer of Hollywood
104. To a degree
105. Eye drop

**DOWN**

1. Mary's follower
2. At a loss
3. Food fish
4. Ken Rosewall's racket
5. Mahogany
6. Papa Hansen on "Mama"
7. Steed breed
8. Hurtful
9. Hair-raising
10. Little Joe's brother
11. Part of REO
12. Speech defect
13. Farley Mowat filmization
14. Actor Estrada
15. Or ____ (ultimatum)
16. White-tailed animal
26. Singer of "Orinoco Flow"
27. Prepare for battle
29. Goddess of the dawn
32. Tijuana ta ta
33. Grease one's ____
34. Precinct
35. Humorous poet
36. Indian city
37. Give the go-ahead
39. Alleviate
40. Bill and Louis
41. "____ Rosenkavalier"
44. Catch in the act
45. Practical joke
46. Vase handle
49. Jack Lemmon film
51. Modify
54. Statute
55. The Ram
56. Building wing
58. Hera's son

# PUZZLE 447

59. Stooge
60. Crooner Perry ____
61. Grazing grounds
62. Carts
63. Jagger or Jones
64. Burn reliever
65. Frog genus
66. Emulated Spitz
67. Find fault
69. Latin American revolutionist Guevara
72. Put out to ____
73. Mattress components
74. Actress Sedgwick
77. Teamster's command
78. Mineral or olive
80. Write-up
82. "Riders to the Sea" author
83. Woodworking tool
84. Startles
85. Double curve
86. Solitary
87. Friar
88. Pamplona bull
89. Svelte
90. Hautboy
91. 1492 ship
92. Vintage
95. Comrade

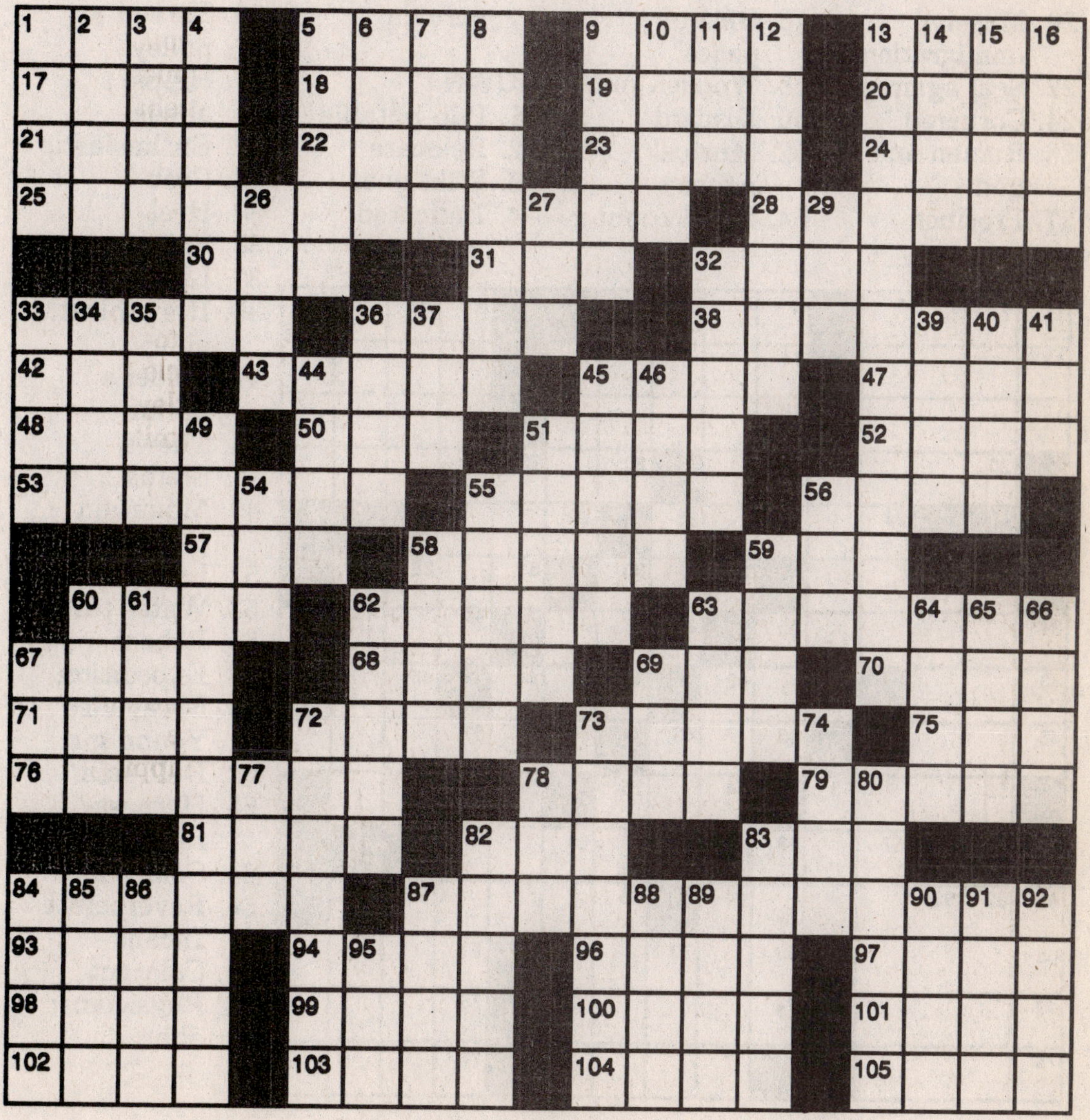

# PUZZLE 448

**ACROSS**

1. In the center of
5. Atoll
9. Campus spot
13. Place for an earring
14. Cereal fungus
16. Unfasten
17. Divisible by two
18. Unclear
19. Harrow's rival
20. Massive immigration
22. Seal again
24. Cornered
26. Roman sun god
27. Precinct
29. Scoop out
31. Profound
34. Financial approval
36. Doze
38. Sudden fast movement
40. Thirst quencher
41. At this time
43. Beaver's construction
45. ____ and tonic
46. Bird of peace
48. Wooden pin
50. Discard
52. Musical pause
54. Salad counter
56. Attract
57. Portable bed
59. Animal skins
61. Foams
65. Pale color
68. Farm measure
69. Church official
71. Frosted
73. Exhibit
74. Eskimo canoe
75. Burn to a cinder
76. Solidifies
77. Understands
78. Long time periods

**DOWN**

1. Pub potable
2. Relocate
3. Wild goat
4. Indicated
5. Theatrical satire
6. Expunged
7. Easter edible
8. Two pairs
9. Curbed
10. "Do ____ others . . ."
11. Commotions
12. Fully cooked
15. Summer wearables
21. Storm sewer
23. North Atlantic fish
25. Loud noises
27. Fervor
28. Thread a pulley
30. Hippie's abode
32. Enthusiastic
33. Cost
34. Heel
35. Spinning toy
37. Link's figure
39. It's a blast!: abbr.
42. Spider's parlor
44. Thaws
47. Shuns
49. Mountain pass
51. Lawfulness
53. Water tester
55. Rehash
58. Expedition
60. Escapades
61. Young girl
62. Dull pain
63. Harness-racing gait
64. Coal waste
66. Reverberate
67. Incline
70. Colorant
72. Physicians: abbr.

# PUZZLE 449

**ACROSS**

1. ____ and kin
5. Observes Lent
10. So long, and ciao
14. Zone
15. City on the Missouri River
16. Frolic
17. Cab
18. Alpine music
19. Diva's tune
20. Menu options
22. Bulb homes
24. Golf score
25. Moses' mountain
26. Send money
29. Those against
30. Midges
34. Draft animals
35. Deli delight
36. Extent
37. Grease
38. Spoke
40. Primate
41. Nodding
43. Sprinted
44. Snoozing
45. Young people
46. Tissue layer
47. Votes in favor
48. Postpone
50. Auricle
51. Salad garnish
54. Pungent cleanser
58. Back
59. Expensive fur
61. Ballad
62. Poker stake
63. Coal
64. ____ and for all
65. Overseer
66. Brazen
67. Clue

**DOWN**

1. Actress Capshaw
2. Modern Persia
3. Manual
4. Sharp curve
5. Lobby
6. Biblical prophet
7. Melancholy
8. Dissertation
9. Drawing room
10. Slowing down
11. Time past
12. Put out
13. Hot tubs
21. Snack
23. Cooped up
25. Gravely
26. Rule the ____
27. Napoleon's punishment
28. Skirmish
29. Edible seed
31. Certain steeds
32. Indian dwelling
33. Pods
35. Shoat's home
36. Family room
38. Topple
39. Author Bradbury
42. Holds out
44. Ecological no-no
46. Straw hat
47. Sweet potato
49. Forfeits
50. Manicurist's board
51. Grouch
52. Gambling town
53. Equine fodder
54. Malt drinks
55. "____ But the Brave"
56. Machu Picchu builder
57. Ripened
60. Air rifle ammo

# PUZZLE 450

**ACROSS**

1. Omelet ingredients
5. Social engagement
9. Clip
12. Bell the cat
13. Mexican mister
14. Pedestal base
15. Amo, amas, ____
16. Tumbling feats
18. Males
19. Did a cobbler's job
20. Wipe out
21. Station
23. Desolate, poetically
25. Valuable item
26. Letter opener
27. "____ Loves You"
30. Davis or Midler
31. Gaelic
32. Tic-____-toe
33. Periods
34. Mountain top
36. Meat dish
37. Envy or greed, e.g.
38. "The Bad ____"
39. Role for Silverheels
40. Spread hay
41. High mountains
42. Long-winded
43. Pot builder
44. Hawaiian veranda
45. Hoist
48. Put in a row
50. Seine
53. Get the picture
55. Distant
56. Actor Lugosi
57. "____ Dragon"
58. Misplace
59. Lamb's dam
60. Arabian gulf
61. Unleashed

**DOWN**

1. Party cheese
2. Mah jongg, e.g.
3. Stadium part
4. Collection
5. Handed out a hand
6. Ms. Baxter
7. Infants
8. Bitter vetch
9. Turner of films
10. Gambler's concern
11. Strike a ____
13. Sprout
14. Mend, as an argyle
17. ____ Haute
19. "Graf ____"
22. Superlative suffixes
24. Hops kiln
25. Eagle's nest
26. Titles
27. Take one's place
28. Rash
29. Resound
30. Greatest
34. Ancient Irishman
35. Said again
36. Dance of Israel
38. More sensible
39. Mood
42. Magic sticks
43. Confused
44. Hall closet
45. Yokel
46. Freshly
47. Inactive
49. Tardy
51. Lighten
52. Ginkgo, e.g.
54. Where to get a mudpack
55. TV alien

# PUZZLE 451

**ACROSS**

1. Border upon
5. Pierce
9. Italy's capital
13. Easy gait
14. More pristine
16. Cookie baker
17. Ump's call
18. Ease up
19. ____ of Avon
20. Spanish gold
21. Not yet certain
23. Schedule of fees
26. Pub order
27. ____ on (goaded)
28. Took leave
33. Small bird
34. Spelunker's delight
35. Sugar suffix
36. Glass drop
37. Famous
38. Ponder
39. Globe
40. Above
41. Shoe fastener
42. Agreed
45. Lanes
46. Kauai keepsake
47. Entree item in 9 Across
48. Not yet certain
52. Grab
55. Antiquated weapon
56. Large antelope
57. Poet St. Vincent Millay
58. Garlic feature
59. From that time
60. I's
61. Sportscaster Meredith et al.
62. Just managed
63. Without others

**DOWN**

1. In addition
2. Porky's wild kin
3. Available
4. Summer shirt
5. Turned the soil
6. Toothpaste containers
7. Steed breed
8. Alpha follower
9. Wrongful taker
10. Shaped like an egg
11. Scant
12. Conclude
15. Recorded anew
22. ____ carte
24. On in years
25. Toe count
27. Pitchers
28. Worn
29. "Be it ____ so humble . . ."
30. Iffy
31. Double curves
32. Fourth in series
34. Mariner's refuge
36. Constrictor
37. Ads
38. Actor Dillon
41. Palmas or Cruces
43. Church officials
44. Marriage-announcement word
45. Made larger
47. British coins
48. Take apart
49. Broadway sign
50. Netman Nastase
51. Damp
53. Presently
54. Home, for one
55. Turf
57. Serpentine swimmer

# PUZZLE 452

**ACROSS**

1. Author Ferber
5. Arrests
9. Pealed
13. Lemon candy
14. Hebrew month
15. River embankment
16. Store event
17. Actress Turner
18. Moslem ruler
19. Caldwell novel
22. One, in Bonn
23. Mork's planet
24. Share equally
27. Presidential nickname
29. Actress Moran
33. High home
34. Where belles dance
36. Exist
37. Supposedly better places
40. Geologic time period
41. Severe
42. Concerning
43. Word before dragon or shot
45. "Bali ____"
46. Catch
47. The Roaring Twenties, e.g.
49. Turkish hat
50. Cowboy song
58. Minced oaths
59. Mistreat
60. Spanish pot
62. Free-for-all
63. Pollster Roper
64. Singer Martin
65. Sampras of tennis
66. No, in Frankfurt
67. ____ packing (dismissed)

**DOWN**

1. Asner and Begley
2. Type of race
3. ____ contendere
4. Copied
5. Nervous ____
6. Actor Delon
7. Diamond ploy
8. Bed part
9. Update, as a film
10. With, to Renee
11. ____ -do-well
12. "Breathless" actor
15. Ogle
20. Lucky rolls
21. Lazes about
24. Wading bird
25. Concert locale
26. Tell a tall tale
27. Isle of ____
28. King of comedy
30. Less common
31. Papas or Castle
32. Hawk's home
33. Bronze and Stone, e.g.
34. La ____ Tar Pits
35. Hymn part
38. "____ Frome"
39. Actress Merkel
44. South Carolina river
46. Parson's speech
48. American Beauty, e.g.
49. Scientist Enrico ____
50. Rope fiber
51. Curved molding
52. Brewer's need
53. At that time
54. Patriot Nathan ____
55. Dozes
56. Type of club
57. Verve
61. Hill builder

## QUOTEWORD

# PUZZLE 453

**A quotation runs clockwise around the edge of this diagram. To find the quotation work the puzzle as a regular crossword, filling in the remaining blank squares with the given letters.**

**C D H H L O S T**

**ACROSS**
10. Church center
11. Part of RPM
12. Zone
13. Imitates
14. Lend an ____ (listen)
15. Mountain lake
16. Roofing
18. Station
19. Affirmative answer
22. Squander
25. Overact
27. Eat
31. Conceal
32. Straw's relative
33. Frolic
34. Door crosspiece
36. Trousers
37. Delicious or Winesap
39. Fireplace residue
40. Type of paint
44. Some
46. Ambiance
47. Fish's limb
49. Japanese ethnic group
52. Bullfight shouts
53. Chicken ____ king
54. Sheep's hair

**DOWN**
1. Atlas entry
2. Night before a holiday
3. Tree house?
4. "Tosca," for one
5. Meadow
6. Goof
7. Overindulge
8. Snare
9. Champion
17. Reverence
18. Study
20. Arabian prince
21. Fizzy drink
23. Rascal
24. Trifle
26. "The ____ Commandments"
28. Mineral spring
29. Forearm bone
30. Small rugs
32. Bunny's jump
35. Kenny G.'s tool, for short
36. Cage
38. Hawaiian porch
41. "____ Lang Syne"
42. Three, in cards
43. Soothe
45. Sign of sleepiness
47. Overweight
48. Ailing
50. Debtor's note
51. Indicate agreement

# PUZZLE 454

**ACROSS**
1. Yield
5. Chanted
9. Quoted
14. Kitchen hot spot
15. Locale
16. Stood up
17. Chicago's nickname
19. Washer cycle
20. Cunning
21. Blackboard cleaner
23. Plant stalk
24. Employs
25. Cowboy contests
27. Brought up
30. ____ Vegas
31. Signs of boredom
32. Talked wildly
35. Knock sharply
38. Misjudges
39. Lessens
40. Small brook
41. Undercover agent
42. Correct
43. TV and radio
44. Hairpiece
45. Eighty plus ten
46. Prize
49. Burden
50. Emblem
51. Boredom
53. "Mr. ____" (Keaton film)
56. Strays
58. Latitude's partner
60. Thing of value
61. Guilty, e.g.
62. Piece of gossip
63. Poor
64. Dispatched
65. Mexican coin

**DOWN**
1. Bovines
2. Wicked
3. Refuse
4. Stop
5. Holy
6. Singers' solos
7. Butterfly catchers
8. Merrier
9. Vehicle
10. Spring flowers
11. Lone Ranger's sidekick
12. Hairpin curves
13. Reckon
18. Affirmatives
22. Parts
24. Coffee servers
26. Pop
27. Cereal grains
28. O.K. Corral gunfighter
29. Amiss
32. Tatter
33. Fire's residue
34. Animal doc
35. Ferris wheel, e.g.
36. Landed
37. Drama
39. "____ Is Enough"
40. Tear apart
42. Actor Torn
43. "____ Vice"
44. Gulped
45. Chewy candy
46. Kid
47. Salary increase
48. Shrill cries
49. Flaxen fabric
50. Graceful waterfowl
52. Senator from Kansas
53. Silent
54. Poems
55. Reminder
57. Pigpen
59. Point

# PUZZLE 455

**ACROSS**

1. Bridge
5. Price
9. Walking rhythm
13. Openwork fabric
14. Zodiacal ram
16. Wedding missiles
17. Chooses
18. Heavenly food
19. Thought
20. Spendthrift
22. Aridity
24. Vietnam's neighbor
25. Bear's cave
26. Daisylike flowers
29. Hung around
34. "____ Dreams" (Heart song)
35. Swerve
36. Valley
37. Drink like a cat
38. Blacksmith's furnace
39. Brooch
40. District
42. Signs a deal
43. Port-au-Prince's locale
45. Spots
47. Bicycle built for two
48. Strike
49. Bovines
50. Lions and tigers, e.g.
54. Clumsy
58. ____ vera
59. Jewish cleric
61. Eastern prince
62. Czech, e.g.
63. Male admirer
64. Mechanical learning method
65. Domesticated
66. Crooned
67. Twist

**DOWN**

1. Sluggish
2. Hemingway's nickname
3. Deeds
4. Snuggles
5. Stars' bit parts
6. Some exams
7. Transgression
8. Watch over
9. Smiled
10. Staffer
11. Chills
12. Herbal drinks
15. Canned fish
21. Seldom-seen
23. Still
26. Mythical strongman
27. Pointy
28. Indian tent
29. Lies in wait
30. Assns.
31. Speedy
32. Upper crust
33. Jeans material
35. Sound quality
38. Strains
41. Accomplish
43. Peddle
44. Responds
46. Relatives
47. Hauling
49. Rustic dwelling
50. Go without food
51. Actress Raines
52. Rich soil
53. Woodcutting tools
55. Berserk
56. Ceremony
57. Actress Barrymore
60. Sheepish sound?

# PUZZLE 456

**ACROSS**

1. Look to be
5. Acknowledged applause
10. Quarrel between families
14. Molten rock
15. Proverb
16. Author Rice or Tyler
17. Above
18. Low bell chimes
19. Hairdo
20. Sweat
22. Pleasantly warm
24. Color
25. Encircle
26. On a ship
29. Feeler
33. Syrup tree
34. Fluster
36. Chimney dirt
37. Short farewell
38. Greased
39. Nipped
40. Billions of years
42. Drew a ____ on
43. Northeast Oklahoma city
45. More corroded
47. Surface layer
48. Actor Griffith
49. Delighted sigh
50. Two-piece suit
53. Vivacious
58. Biblical garden
59. Actress Barkin
61. Short letter
62. High spirits
63. Tibet's neighbor
64. Eat in style
65. Dispatch
66. Delicious
67. Smack

**DOWN**

1. Swill
2. Roof overhang
3. Always
4. Matt Dillon, e.g.
5. Coddled
6. Stink
7. Diminish
8. Hen's product
9. Meant to be
10. False fronts
11. Baseball's Slaughter
12. Army group
13. Resist openly
21. Undiluted
23. Table scrap
25. Stared
26. Yellowish brown
27. Louisiana marsh
28. Unwraps
30. High-minded
31. Din
32. Perfume oil
34. Blazing
35. Chicken ____ king
38. Compliant
41. Discolored
43. Sports group
44. Lets loose
46. Country hotel
47. Fruitlessly
50. Pleads
51. Not working
52. Eager
53. European peaks
54. Tidy
55. Slave away
56. Sicilian volcano
57. Profound
60. Pasture

# PUZZLE 457

**ACROSS**

1. Polluted air
5. Ran, as a color
9. Light tint
14. Zeus's wife
15. Ireland
16. Unique
17. Shipping instructions: abbr.
18. Come up short
19. Sprite
20. Big blows
23. Hesitant sounds
24. Seine dry spot
25. Scarab, i.e.
29. Helpful clue
31. Mine cart
35. Film Flynn
36. Divided Asian country
38. Anger
39. Dorothy and Toto didn't hear them
42. Clamor
43. Shopper's come-on
44. Bygone birds
45. Spanish artist
47. Young man
48. Like French bread
49. ____ standstill
51. Lager
52. Eye on the eye
60. Card: Fr.
61. Italian noble house
62. Stir up
63. Body part
64. Flower garlands
65. General Bradley
66. Deplete
67. Tatter's result
68. Meander

**DOWN**

1. Carpet style
2. Flat-topped rise
3. Evangelist Roberts
4. Stare
5. Earlier
6. Fact twisters
7. Clapton the singer
8. Printer's instructions
9. Escargot
10. Wasp kin
11. Excited
12. Poor grades
13. Building addition
21. Scorsese's are good
22. Windshield adjunct
25. Certain rays
26. Rust
27. Inaccuracy
28. Ship's weight unit
29. Pulled along
30. Savings plans: abbr.
32. Peelings
33. Street slang
34. Cluttered
36. African nut
37. President Jackson
40. ____ Lama
41. Debt letters
46. Plaid
48. "A Fish Called Wanda" actor
50. Popular tendency
51. Prank
52. Nag repeatedly
53. Yen
54. Leavenworth accommodation
55. Lost
56. Lined up
57. Capsule or limit
58. Family group
59. Elephant gathering
60. Lettuce

# PUZZLE 458

**ACROSS**

1. Star of "Moonstruck"
5. Healer
10. Staircase part
14. Sharpen
15. Over
16. Close
17. Prayer ender
18. Foot bottoms
19. Fairy-tale starter
20. Monument
22. Unrefined
24. Move with leverage
25. Picnic nuisance
26. Infant
27. Quiche ingredient
28. Ringlet
29. "Tea for ____"
32. Locales
35. Rumba or tango, e.g.
36. Chicken
37. Wagon
38. Flaming light
39. Cotillion
40. Cycle or angle
41. Tree limb
42. Useful
43. Behold
44. Additionally
45. Stick-in-the-____
46. Merriment
47. Auto
48. One of Santa's helpers
51. Phone user
54. Buttonless shirt
56. Toledo's state
57. Separated
59. Earned
60. Some parents
61. Kid
62. Advantage
63. Sight organs
64. Having hearing organs
65. Depend on

**DOWN**

1. Victor, for short
2. "Iliad" author
3. Foe
4. Gambling town
5. Door frame
6. German submarine
7. Dinner bread
8. Actress Plumb
9. Library work
10. Sleeper's sound
11. Circus big top
12. Apiece
13. Hunted animal
21. Tatters
23. Competent
26. Cluster
27. Ingest
28. Freight
29. In comparison with
30. Fuse
31. Lone
32. Play units
33. Steak order
34. Cleveland's lake
35. Drench
38. Put up with
39. Unfavorable
41. Cotton bundle
42. Throw
45. Type of milkshake
46. Sheen
47. Use profanity
48. Dodge
49. Shelf of rock
50. Let loose
51. Arrive
52. Nautical call
53. Daiquiri ingredient
54. Carson's predecessor
55. Forewarning
58. Garden vegetable

# PUZZLE 459

**ACROSS**

1. Frost
4. Arrayed
8. Source of fiber
12. Cowboy Rogers
13. Doer of brave deeds
14. Clinton's attorney general
15. Sufficient
17. Dines
18. Footed vase
19. Outlaw James
20. Ball of yarn
23. Storage buildings
25. Gasp for breath
26. Bucket
27. Employ
30. "This ____ House"
31. Hole-boring tool
32. Carrot-top's nickname
33. Golfer's peg
34. Small stream
35. Watch over
36. Tiny particles
38. Yummy
39. Leather thong
41. Repair
42. Idle of "Monty Python"
43. Phoenix player
48. Quick as a ____
49. Clarinet's kin
50. ____ Baba ("Arabian Nights")
51. Holiday egg drinks
52. Pleads
53. Bachelor's home

**DOWN**

1. Gershwin brother
2. Food fish
3. Sight organ
4. Butter-making tool
5. Low in fat
6. Gallery display
7. Buck's mate
8. Produce offspring
9. Comforts
10. Picnic crashers
11. Schnoz
16. Give up
19. Congeal
20. Common dog name
21. Cabbagelike plant
22. "Those ____ Young Charms"
23. Puts to sea
24. Knoll
26. Demure
28. Transmitted
29. Whirlpool
31. Sharp decline
35. Cab
37. Small nails
38. Ocean movements
39. Stitched
40. Threesome
41. Prince in disguise?
43. Corn on the ____
44. Honest ____ (Lincoln)
45. Siesta
46. Chicken ____ king
47. Cover

# PUZZLE 460

**ACROSS**
1. Protozoan
7. Motives
14. Bearcats
20. Dancer Ann
21. Navy chief
22. Develop
23. Chaperone
25. Lighter
26. Former UK coin
27. Hesitation sounds
28. Stiff
29. Service inst.
30. Indignation
31. TV knobs
33. Wiring experts: abbr.
34. Divine fluid
36. Morning song
39. U.S. novelist Wister
41. Luncheon or kitchen ending
42. Cupid
46. "As well be hanged for ____"
48. Farthest
51. Hail
53. Bontok wards
54. Unpolished
56. "Prince ____"
57. Geronimo, for one
58. Tiny bit
60. Religious statue
61. Infernal
62. Soften
63. Pampered
65. Before, before
66. Sequence
68. Gully
70. Wood sorrel
73. Canned fish
75. Figures of speech
79. Saudi ____
81. Postdated, to the bank
82. Furious
84. Author Rachel ____
85. Great many
86. Spanish painter
87. Ramie fiber
88. Listen
89. Senior citizen
91. Bricklayers
93. ____ Rusk
94. Cougar
96. Passion
98. Spanish gulf
99. Concise
101. Train unit
103. Ache
105. Grease
108. Struggle
109. Mead island
111. Kanga's child
112. Sock end
115. Flies on the wind
117. Heman-gioma
120. Rehabilitate
121. Smaller
122. Play a flute
123. Wields
124. Moderately slow, in music
125. Analyzes

**DOWN**
1. Elec. units
2. Venus de ____
3. Saint of Norway
4. Actor Ron
5. West Indian dance
6. Perfume
7. Ethiopian prince
8. German river
9. Moving freely
10. Bout
11. Gold braid
12. Ointment
13. Foxy
14. Complexion type
15. Dispatch boat
16. And not
17. Roman 552
18. Claim
19. Dried up
24. European capital
29. After Sept.
31. Truck fuel
32. Scandinavian
34. Say again
35. Have empathy
36. Queen's title
37. U.S. fur merchant
38. Oar fulcrum
40. English river
41. Hams
43. Collar trim
44. Something else
45. Oracle
47. Affectations
49. Journalist Jacob
50. Discharged
52. Baboon
55. Far-out
59. These: Fr.
60. Assumed
63. Pronuncia-tion symbol
64. Foyer

# PUZZLE 460

67. Tedious
69. Sweetie
70. Declaim
71. Magna ____
72. Away
74. Tidings
76. Human
77. Group culture
78. City in Tuscany
79. Institute: abbr.
80. Charged atom
82. Raid
83. "____ Timberlane"
86. Turn right!
90. Add, as a bonus
92. Dry gulches
95. Employ
97. Prov.
100. Chris of tennis
101. Minded
102. Iowa society
104. Main artery
105. Bogeyman
106. Holly
107. Biography
109. British gun
110. Encourage
112. So long
113. Paris airport
114. Makes do
116. June bug
117. Depot: abbr.
118. Before, in poems
119. May and June: abbr.

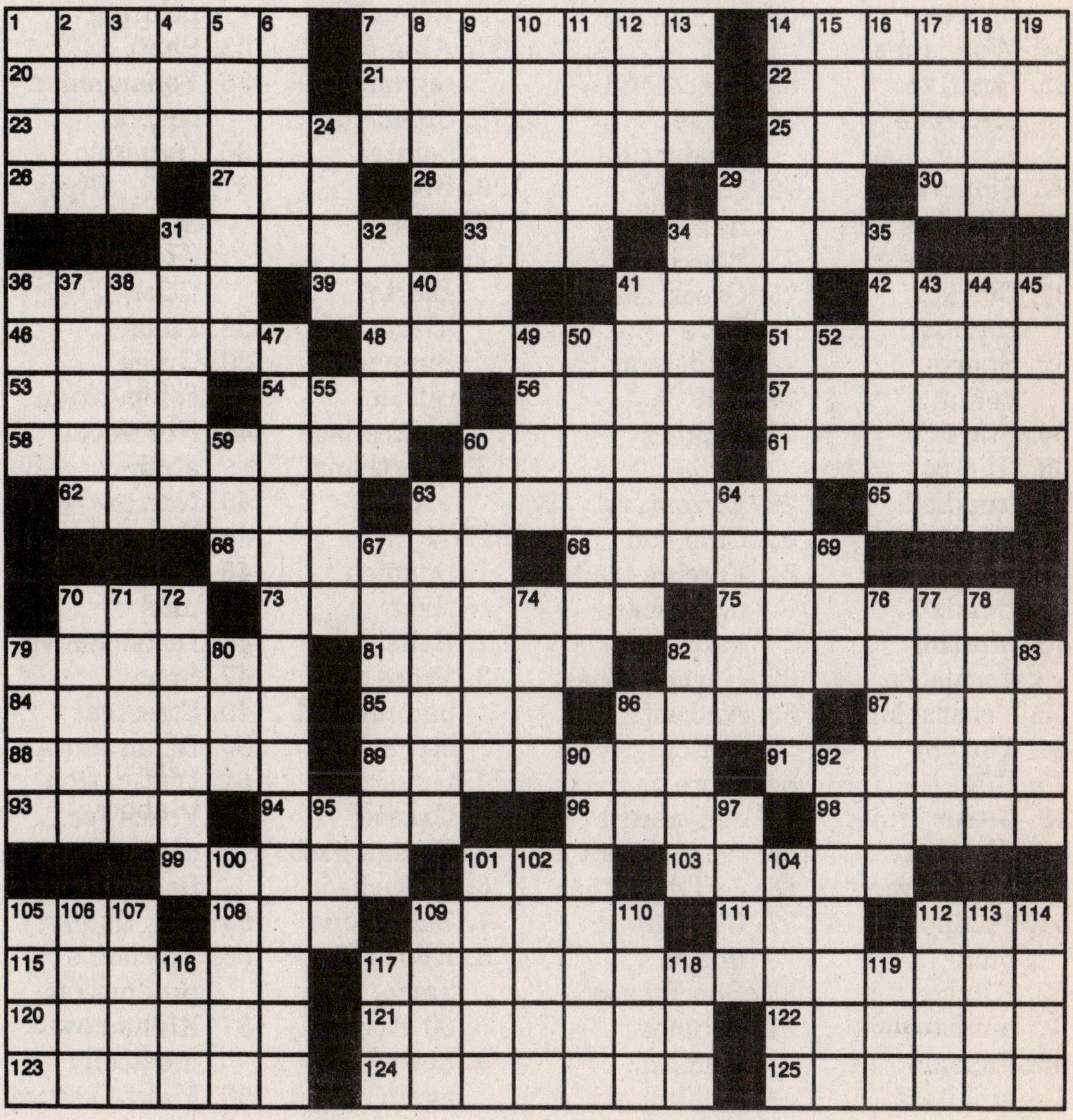

# PUZZLE 461

**ACROSS**

1. Glacial deposit
6. Jewish month
10. Bridge moves
15. Pealed
19. Beautiful girl
20. See 8 Down
21. Conviction
22. Chemical compound
23. Vigorous dances
24. Woe is me!
25. Positive electrode
26. I sing: Lat.
27. Singly
29. Watches and clocks, e.g.
31. Corrida sounds
32. Sports venue
34. Starts
35. ___ to (coddled)
39. Biblical prophet
40. Bonds
42. Martini garnishes
43. Venerable
44. The end
45. Bilge
48. Citrus fruits
49. Stepped
50. Force away
51. Philippines palm
52. Kitchen appliance
53. Famous architect
54. U.S. poet
55. Romeo
56. Napoleonic military leader
57. Official place
58. Litigation
59. Conspicuous
60. Wolfe novel
65. Of the eyes
67. Subject of many a painting
68. ___ move on!
69. Successful stage production
72. Zagreb native
73. Shabby
75. Greek cheese
76. TV's Anderson
77. SOS
78. Talking birds
79. Effrontery
80. Chili con ___
81. Foreign-trade document: abbr.
82. Harbor cities
83. Ancient Briton
84. More convenient
85. Amendment
86. Jeff's partner
87. Certain drinks
88. Blackbeard
91. Cabinet-member Hobby
93. Syria, Biblically
94. "Up ___" (Carmichael/Arodin song)
96. Certain drainage area
102. In ___ (as a whole)
103. Coeur d'___
104. Fateful March date
105. Author Jong
106. Remaining
107. Alpine region
108. Spanish painter
109. Boca ___
110. Cape
111. "___ shorts!" (Bart Simpson refrain)
112. Makes lace
113. Shorthand

**DOWN**

1. Spanish river
2. Beheld
3. Swiss painter and etcher
4. Governor Grasso
5. Brings back
6. Quenched
7. Sub shops
8. Eliot title name, with 20 Across
9. Sewed again
10. Elucidates
11. Communist hero
12. Quirks
13. Ancient Persian's kin
14. Hurry!
15. Take a break
16. Have ___ up one's sleeve
17. Singing group
18. Patina
28. Heady drinks
30. Readies for printing
33. Shaft
35. Panamanian seaport
36. Dynamic
37. "___ Gipsy Man" (Hodgson title)
38. Plane
39. Greek competition
41. Not vocal: abbr.
43. Narrow ridge
44. Foam
45. Hippopotamus
46. Inconclusive
47. Spicy
49. Streetcar
50. Be an author
51. Distinction
53. Fence for catching fish
54. ___-duddy
55. Volcano's production
57. Right now, medically
58. Makes secure

# PUZZLE 461

59. Round, flat bread
61. Oscillate
62. Magnani and Sten
63. Void
64. Soaks flax
65. Newspaper publisher Adolf Simon ___
66. Canadian Indian
70. Sanctum or sole
71. Rows
73. Acute
74. Shy one
75. Item of data
76. Land for Luang Prabang
78. Reasonable
79. Shankar, e.g.
80. Climbs with effort
82. Compassion
83. Set down
84. Sear
85. Shavers
86. No more than
87. Peaks
88. South African novelist Alan ___
89. "___ You to Death"
90. Grades
92. Malice
93. Turn aside
95. Pelvic bones
97. Impression
98. I smell ___
99. Locus
100. Emblem
101. 1,000,000,000: pref.

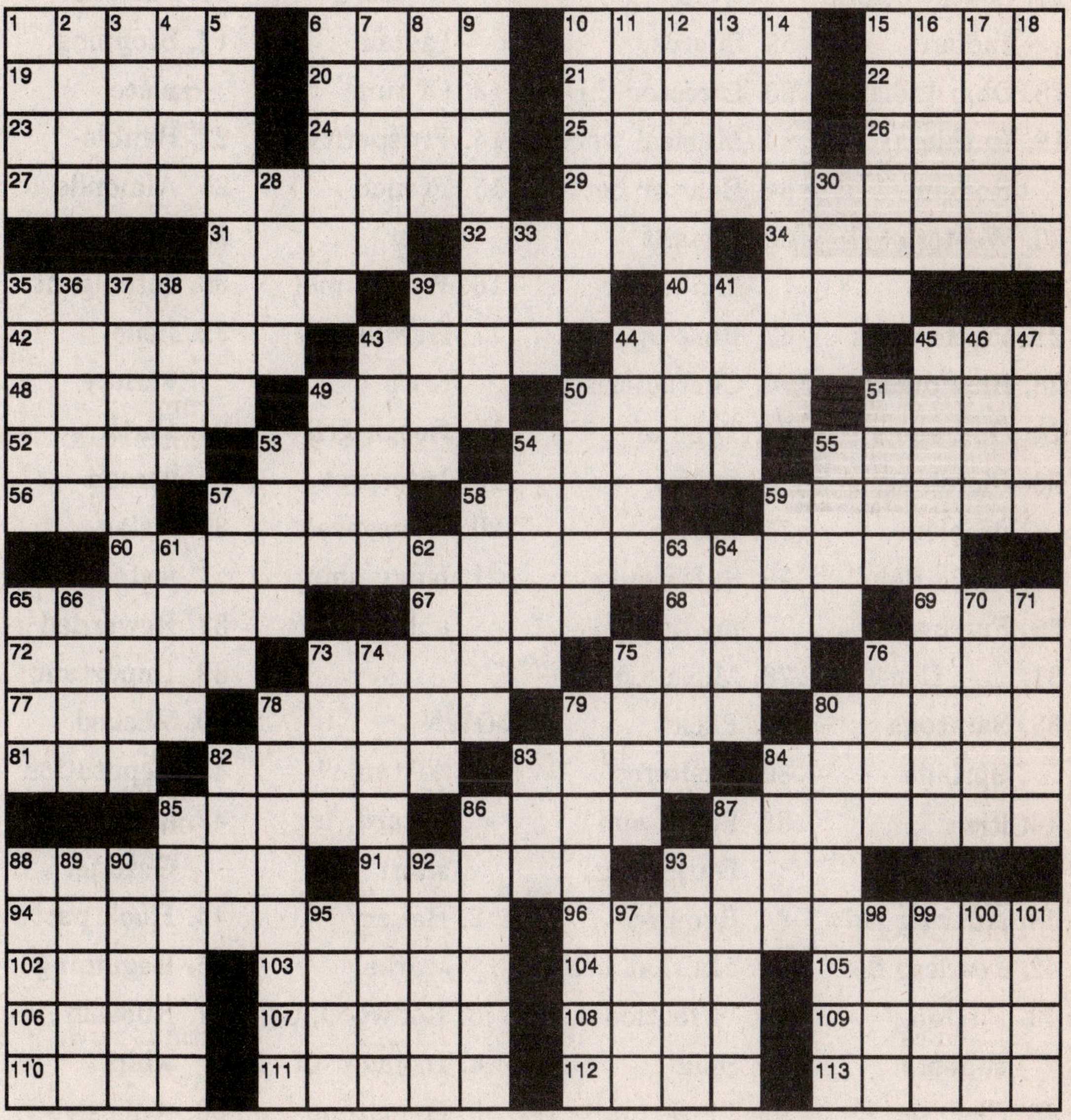

# PUZZLE 462

**ACROSS**

1. Chomped
4. Dandy
7. Chinese fabric
11. Kind of cheese
15. Ivory shade
17. Southwestern Indian
18. Ohio Indian
19. Ruthless Roman
20. Western Indians
21. Picnic drink
23. Blue duck
24. Golf spots
26. Plumbing problem
27. "____ Rain"
29. Furrows
31. ____ Canal
33. Saratoga Springs
34. Plan
36. Fall
38. Alluring lady
42. Fearless flier
43. Pitching rubbers
46. Cleanser
48. Russian river
49. Electrical unit
51. Drat!
53. Venus de ____
55. Faint
56. Reference work
58. Snares
60. Director C.B.
62. Musical work
64. Bear or betty
66. Weight allowance
67. Rose up
70. Characteristic
72. Type of rocket
75. Letter
76. Sufficient, poetically
78. Mosaic piece
79. Pack
80. Sheltered
82. Pekoe and Darjeeling
84. Requires
87. Ma that baas
88. Is footloose
90. Spill
92. Linear units
94. Munch
96. Yale students
98. Self-satisfied
99. Foe of Athens
102. Presently
104. Metal masses
108. Miss Fitzgerald
109. Western Indian
113. Of time
114. Prosperity
115. French river
116. Woe is me!
117. Gambling town
118. Beach grit
119. Interpret
120. Nonsense!
121. Navy ship: abbr.

**DOWN**

1. "Titanic" hazard, for short
2. Bakery worker
3. Redwood, e.g.
4. In favor of
5. Gemstone
6. Longs
7. Searchers
8. Author Levin
9. Cover
10. Retains
11. Board Amtrak
12. Immersed
13. Inland sea
14. Tunneler
16. Patrons
17. Stopping place
22. Bauble
25. Almonds
28. High points
30. Intelligent
32. Lens variety
34. Perth person
35. Asian waters
37. Rewarded
39. Important
40. Wicked
41. Reputation
42. Miss Gardner
44. Hook part
45. Beginning
47. Russian whip
50. Adhesive

# PUZZLE 462

52. Hockey or soccer
54. Actor Sharif
57. Positive
59. Lover
61. Angers
63. Dispatched
65. Cleo's river
67. Rip
68. European city
69. Lady rabbits
71. Abounds
73. Quarrels
74. Be indebted
77. Welt
81. Certain isle
83. Comforted
85. Resigns
86. Stupefy
89. Held session
91. In the ____
93. Goader
95. Small drum
97. Up to now
99. Fastens
100. Request
101. Comedian King
103. ____ contendere
105. Russian city
106. Beach colors
107. Opening
110. Be situated
111. ____ rule
112. Grain

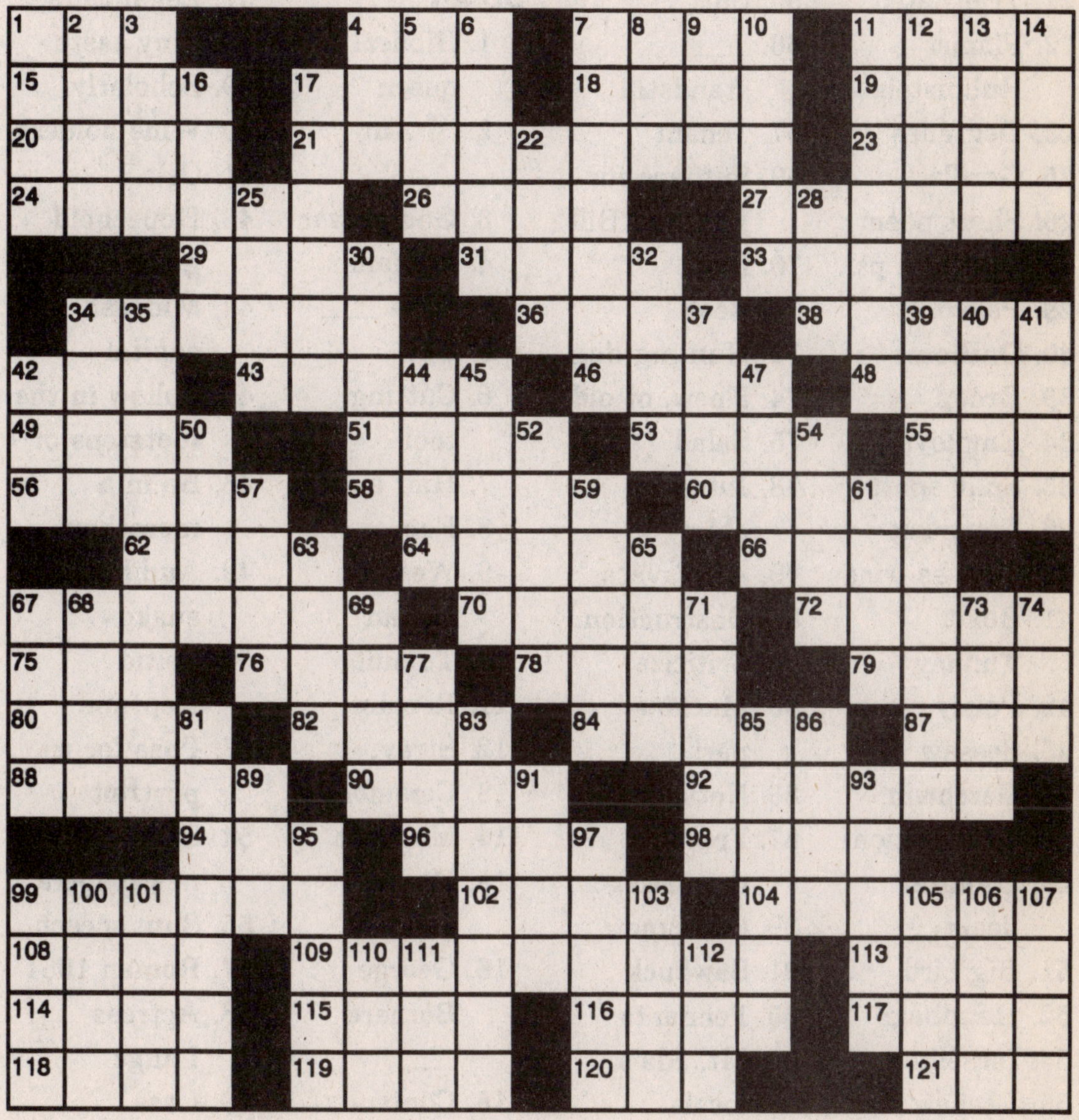

# PUZZLE 463

**ACROSS**

1. Mop
5. Pernicious
8. Entitle
11. Ice pinnacle
16. Seaside
17. Perform
19. Clan
20. Virile fellows
21. Translated
22. Pianist Rubinstein
23. Degrades
25. Gorilla
26. Short poem
28. Compass pt.
29. Pale
30. Outburst
33. Droop
34. Employs
35. Split apart
36. Comment
38. Dry, as wine
41. Boxer Tunney
42. Pokey
43. Seesaw
47. Gershwin
48. Conjunction
49. Used-car deals
51. Big bird
52. Handbags
54. Israelites
55. Eschew
56. ___ Eireann
57. Bullfighter
58. Scoundrel
59. Present
60. Sparkle
61. Ranch structure
63. Eroded
64. Gratings
65. Cut
66. ___ standstill
67. Tenant
69. Suffixes for Will and Bill
70. Dry
71. Beak
72. Hunting dog
74. Knew, of old
75. Salad
78. Integers: abbr.
79. Aggravate
81. Obstruction
84. Criticize
85. Machine part
86. Notice
87. French dramatist
89. Of sound
91. Sawbuck
95. Pennants
96. Mt. Ida's locale
97. New York city
98. Berlin's output
99. Facilitated
100. Sweater size: abbr.
101. "___ the ramparts . . ."
102. Emblem

**DOWN**

1. Biblical queen
2. "I Am ___"
3. God of war
4. William Rose ___
5. Cot
6. Cutting tool
7. Half a score
8. Fop
9. Western Indian
10. Tumult
11. Remain
12. Stray
13. Ceremonies
14. Maltreat
15. Harvest goddess
16. George Bernard ___
18. Contend
24. Dangerous damsels
27. Marbles
31. Fruit skin
32. Prayer beginning
33. Elected official
34. Godfrey's instrument, for short
36. Lives
37. Legal thing
38. Tiny taste
39. Scholarly
40. Wine holders
41. Celt
42. Household gods
44. Mideast capital
45. Follow in the footsteps of
46. Be in a marathon
49. Audible snake
50. Celtic Neptune
53. Pose for a portrait
54. Some newspapers
55. Sun. speech
57. Roman 1051
58. Actress Lange
59. Lass

60. ____ Green
61. Chopper
62. Sci. workroom
64. ____ whiz!
65. Itemize
68. Opposite of NNE
70. Midwest st.
73. Indian drum
74. "____ more, my lady"
75. "Star Trek" locale
76. Mrs. Rob Petrie
77. South American range
79. Spend it in Mexico
80. Floats
81. Ross or Rigg
82. Cherub
83. Untidy state
85. "Betty ____"
86. Prune
88. Fingerprint, e.g.
90. Adherent: suff.
92. Chemical suffix
93. Suffix denoting origin
94. Roofing liquid

# PUZZLE 463

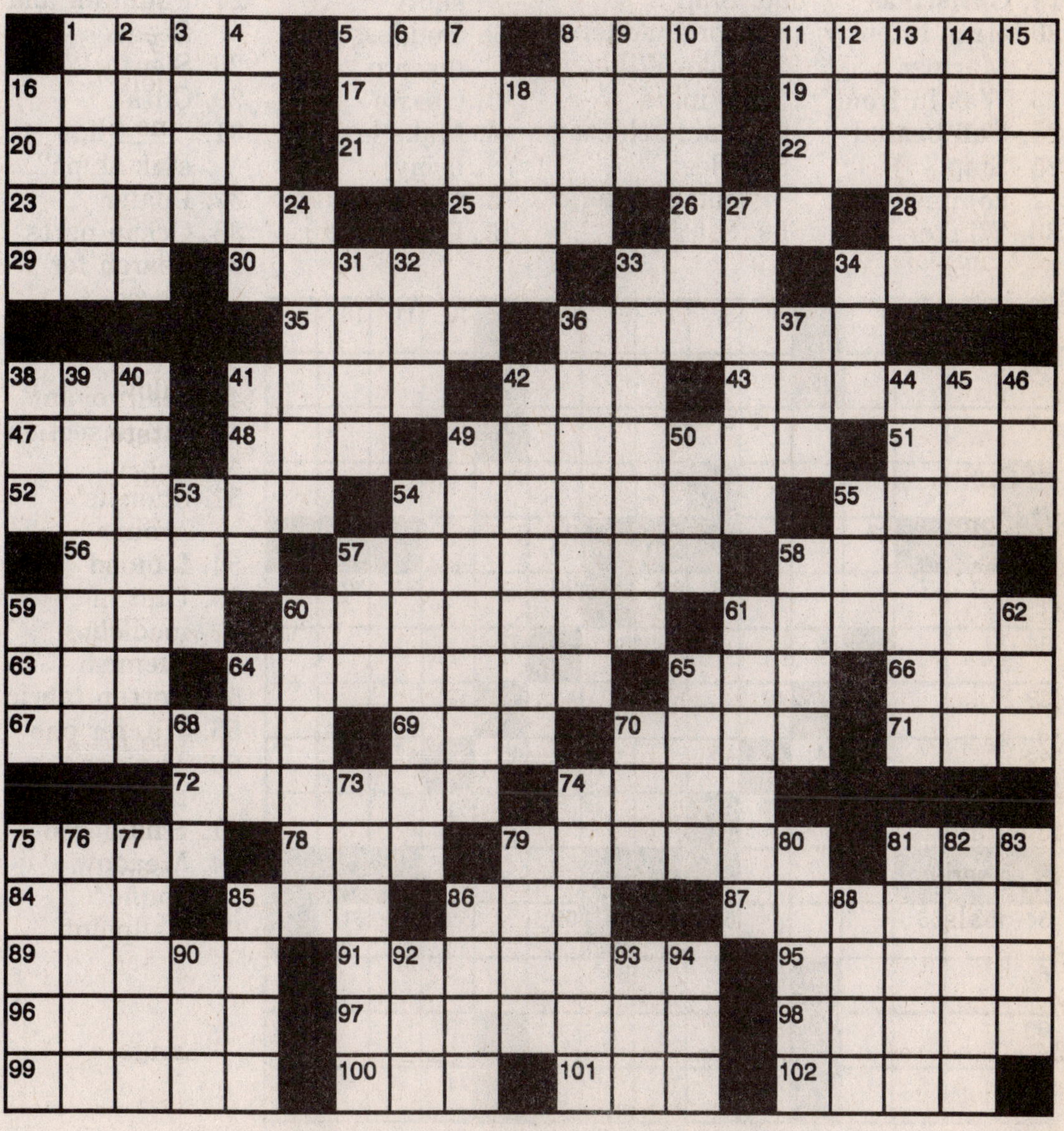

# PUZZLE 464

**ACROSS**

1. Foxx of TV
5. "M*A*S*H" man
10. Winery vessels
14. Clinton's canal
15. Author Zola
16. Forget
17. Deck officers: 2 wds.
19. Christmas
20. Gaze intently
21. Mariner
23. Was in front
24. Fall behind
25. Ship commanders
30. Winker
34. Exist
35. Adolescents
37. Wear away
38. Fixed routine
40. Dehydrated
42. Fillet of ____
43. Portents
45. "Faust," for one
47. Fall mo.
48. Lord and ____
50. Ship commanders
52. Like Willie Winkie
53. Paid athlete
54. Fleet commanders
59. Stations
62. Diving bird
63. Mariner's forte
66. Man or Capri
67. Stew vegetable
68. Roof edge
69. Golf pegs
70. Defendants' pleas, for short
71. Mr. Musial

**DOWN**

1. Soccer official, for short
2. Goddess of discord
3. Gossip
4. Make less briny
5. Cured
6. Doctors' gp.
7. Morse code units
8. Nautical term
9. Second vending
10. Travelers
11. Asian river
12. Fired clay
13. After gang or lob
18. Goodie
22. WWII pinup Alice ____
25. Billiards shot
26. Fragrance
27. Fountain and Seeger
28. Sleuth Wolfe
29. Cuts
31. "____ lips sink ships"
32. Loafer
33. Ocean parts
36. Search for
39. Laces
41. Stove parts: 2 wds.
44. Clairvoyant
46. Stage section
49. Sense
51. Sheriffs' groups
54. Landed
55. Unit of medicine
56. Blemish
57. Cotton fabric
58. Jib, for one
60. The one there
61. Hindu god
64. Meadow sound
65. Ballpoint

# PUZZLE 465

**ACROSS**

1. Fishhook connector
6. I smell ____: 2 wds.
10. Feline sound
14. Vampire
15. Earring spot
16. Ye ____ Shoppe
17. Japanese, e.g.
18. Diving bird
19. Orderly
20. Standard for fun: 3 wds.
23. Female hog
24. French cheese
25. Catchall file heading: abbr.
29. Kids
31. No, in Omsk
34. Beehive State
35. Compass pt.
36. Church sections
38. Actress Moore
39. Discharge
42. Director Preminger
43. Racecourse: suffix
45. ____ Guevara
46. Trillion: prefix
47. Weakens
48. Sandal
49. Brand
50. Helper: abbr.
52. Mel, the swatter
54. 1968 Heston movie: 4 wds.
62. Tease
63. "____ want for Christmas . . .": 2 wds.
64. Upstairs
65. Bitter drug
66. "Where Have You ____?"
67. Applejack
68. Turn, in chess
69. Hitch
70. "Steppenwolf" author

**DOWN**

1. Thick slice
2. Space agcy.
3. Moslem prince
4. Prevaricator
5. Penny and Lois
6. Permitting
7. Raise the ____
8. Nuclear explosives: hyph.
9. Chorus member
10. South American trees
11. Robt. ____: 2 wds.
12. Songstress Anita
13. Moistens
21. Actor Greene
22. Columbus's ship
25. Anchorman Roger
26. Roman roads
27. S. Pacific island
28. Simian
30. Chestnut's cousin
32. Ms. Lauder
33. Four: prefix
37. Fly high
40. Gallery or star
41. Canines
44. Being: Latin
48. Purloined
51. Thrusts
53. Impart knowledge
54. British buggy
55. French composer
56. Arm of the Black Sea
57. Circus performer
58. Rose's love
59. Seed vessels
60. 12/24 and 12/31, e.g.
61. Withered

# PUZZLE 466

**ACROSS**

1. Cinch
5. Charger, e.g.
10. Subsides
14. Corrida opponent
15. Tough guy
16. Cabbage dish
17. Wild goat
18. ____ -out
19. Biblical weed
20. Bog
21. David's weapon
22. Islamic religious center
23. Kind of light
25. Tongue-lash
26. Soft shoe
27. Strengthen
28. Otto's realm: abbr.
29. Grudge
31. Punch
33. Lout
34. Seedy dwelling
37. Shopping center
38. ____ d'Azur
39. Aweather's opposite
40. Adherent: suff.
41. Condensation
42. Park or Lexington, e.g.: abbr.
43. Fence crossings
45. Eggs ____
50. Madrid gentleman
51. Woodland plants
52. Capek drama
53. Curling ____
54. Persian
55. Italian seaport
56. Unaspirated
57. The Count
58. Suit to ____
59. River in Germany
60. Stakes
61. Actor Foxx

**DOWN**

1. Unbending
2. Dynamite inventor
3. Battleground
4. Curse
5. Elizabeth's husband
6. Russian dictator
7. Included with, in Edinburgh
8. Zest
9. Remnant
10. Chemical compound
11. Heavenly phenomenon
12. Gondolier's song
13. Pullover
21. Form
22. Frantic
24. Hushed
25. Two-wheeler
27. Suffer
29. Prated
30. Golf feat
31. Cover for Rainier
32. Baseballer Mel ____
33. Bundled
35. Frozen treats
36. Gives the high sign
37. Polaris, e.g.
41. German article
42. Oakley et al.
44. Hermit
45. Beauty's antithesis
46. Bert's pal
47. Fit to be tied
48. Preserved
49. Sampled
51. Friend of Kukla and Ollie
54. Philippine tree
55. Hurdle

# PUZZLE 467

**ACROSS**

1. Machine parts
5. Recorded
10. Reach across
14. Eliminate
15. Existing
16. Musical sound
17. Tableland
18. Baseball teams
19. Sea swooper
20. Doorway
22. Seafood sauce
24. Forest filler
25. Gardner of mystery
26. Climbed
29. Pops the question
33. Submissive
34. Serving receptacles
35. Fedora
36. Time periods
37. Attire
38. Put away
39. Naval rank: abbr.
40. Self-assurance
41. Workmen
42. Earns
44. Emphasize
46. Virginia family
47. Withered
48. Finally
51. The First State
55. Plunder
56. ____ Fool's Day
58. Duel memento
59. Dig for coal
60. One of the Horae
61. Footed vases
62. Coaster
63. Debase
64. Seeger or Fountain

**DOWN**

1. Draw near
2. Hymn ending
3. Slight fog
4. Frightens
5. Brown from the sun
6. Linda Lavin role
7. Desire
8. Genesis woman
9. Ruins
10. Sound system
11. Any ____ in a storm
12. Siam visitor
13. ____ do-well
21. "We ____ the World"
23. Swiss peaks
25. Clean the chalkboard
26. Spirited horse
27. Chili con ____
28. Pile up
29. Kind of agent
30. Stock unit
31. Roof edges
32. Mulligan and Irish
34. Attempts
37. Fit closely
38. Bungles
40. Bush, e.g.: abbr.
43. Very happy
44. Vendor
45. Song syllable
47. Net
48. Charity
49. Labor
50. The ____ Ranger
51. Sketched
52. Land measure
53. Bombast
54. Highlander talk
57. Player for pay

# PUZZLE 468

**• BEST FRIENDS •**

**ACROSS**

1. "____ Can I Turn To"
4. ____ Angeles
7. Angels and Padres
9. Assistance
10. Fireman's friend
14. Large dog breed
19. Chicago trains
20. Mountain group
21. Attempts
22. Fresh
23. Mimic
25. Sheepshank, e.g.
26. Borscht or chowder
27. Clamp
28. Walking stick
30. Longfellow, for example
31. Nick's wife
32. "The ____ and the Pussycat"
33. Body
34. Come up
38. Marsh
39. "The ____ from Laramie"
42. Solo
43. Schuss
44. Mahogany-colored dog
48. Heat meas.
51. Santa ____
52. Miner's goal
53. Guitarist Paul
54. Main subject
55. Singer Pat ____
57. Green vegetable
59. Atop
60. Fly high
61. Wall support
62. Lure
63. Snare
67. Distinctive region
70. "Pygmalion" playwright
73. Columnist Landers
74. Singer McEntire
75. Oratorio solos
77. Be in debt
78. Furry fetcher
81. Racing dog
83. Roof overhang
84. Cloudless
85. Seeded bread
86. Actor Beatty

**DOWN**

1. Cardiff canine
2. Overact
3. ____ Sharif
4. Tennis call
5. Former
6. Springer or cocker
7. Powder
8. Money at risk
9. Door clasp
10. Below-average grade
11. Tavern
12. In the past
13. Clear profit
14. Auto's need
15. ____ Grande
16. Flightless bird
17. Comfy home
18. Ram's mate
24. Rowboat propellers
27. Solemn promise
29. Model Campbell
30. "The Raven" author
31. Cranny
33. Cable network: abbr.
34. Porter or stout
35. Hogwash
36. Division word
37. Soothsayer
40. Foot part
41. African river
42. Pack animal
45. Newsman Donaldson
46. Shade

# PUZZLE 468

47. Argue against
48. Doggy detective
49. Nashville's state: abbr.
50. Utilize
54. ____ with the same brush
56. Comic penguin
57. Hunter's helper
58. Consume
60. Rational
61. Remains
62. Forbid
63. Oak or cherry
64. Gun a motor
65. Actor Vigoda
66. Average
67. Satchel
68. Make a mistake
69. Untruth
71. Bristly
72. Unite
76. Avoid
79. Author Bradbury
80. "____ Got a Secret"
82. Washington bill

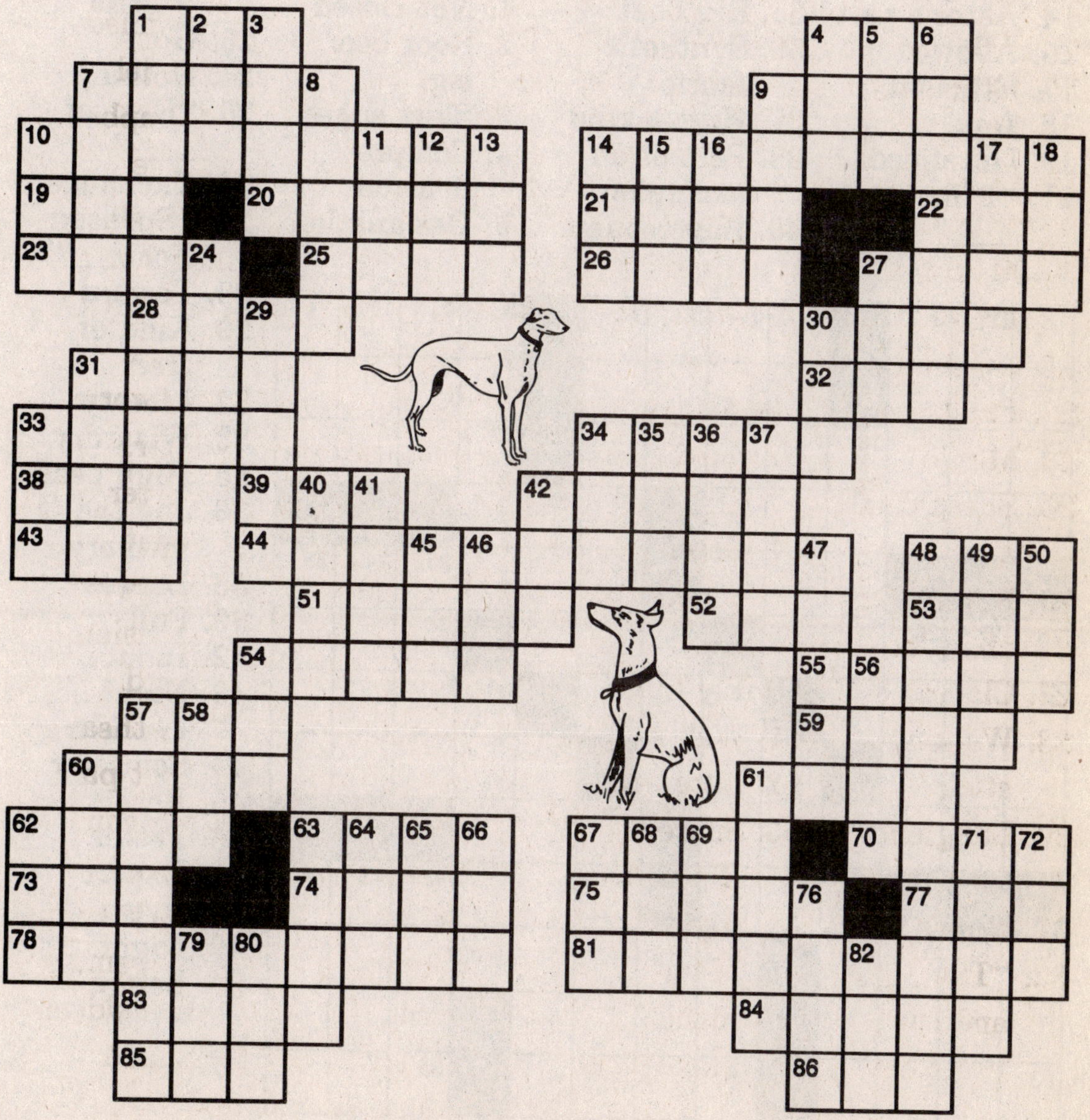

# PUZZLE 469

**ACROSS**

1. Cigarette leftover
4. Salt Lake City's state
8. Gloat
12. DiMaggio or Garagiola
13. Feel compassion for
14. Actor's part
15. Allowed in
17. Efficient
18. Imp
19. Unrefined
21. "I like ____"
22. Flaming
26. Glow
29. Individual
30. Get hitched
31. Bird appendage
32. Lard
33. Certain horse
34. Sculpture or pottery, e.g.
35. Big boat
36. Synthetic fabric
37. Humankind
39. Part of an excursion
40. Impersonate
41. Among
45. Obstacle
48. Devote
50. Cadence
51. Baking place
52. Road-surfacing material
53. Eons
54. Correct
55. Twist my ____

**DOWN**

1. Not closed
2. Root beer, e.g.
3. Skirt edges
4. Compre-hension
5. Designation
6. Consumed
7. Firefighter's spigot
8. Fight
9. Character on "The Dick van Dyke Show"
10. "____ the President's Men"
11. Golly
16. Frosting
20. Actor Vigoda
23. Gone
24. Nothing
25. "East of ____"
26. Exchange
27. "Spenser: For ____"
28. Toward
29. Kind of tree
32. Liberty
33. Wizardry
35. High peak
36. Jog the memory
38. Leaves
39. Full
42. Input
43. Night twinkler
44. Semester
45. Resort
46. Pester
47. Expert flyer
49. Night before

# PUZZLE 470

**ACROSS**

1. High card
4. Deface
7. Howl at the moon
10. Parcel of land
11. Comedian Carvey
12. Colt's mom
13. Honda riders
16. Shorthand, for short
17. Lets up
18. Atop
21. Society girl
22. Roofing stuff
25. Ages
27. Frenzy
30. Singer-actor Burl ____
32. Wire measure
33. Cabbage dish
34. Opposite of fem.
35. Freshly
37. Soap ingredient
38. ____ la la
40. Did the backstroke
42. Bea Arthur role
44. Rule the ____
48. Boat pusher
51. "Cheers" orders
52. Dead and Black
53. Water tester
54. Blushing color
55. "____ Little Indians"
56. Song from "A Chorus Line"

**DOWN**

1. Charity
2. Crotchety person
3. Suffix with luncheon or major
4. Singer Davis
5. Unspecified amount
6. Track event
7. Game for Strawberry
8. ____ and crafts
9. Okey-dokey
11. Herd
12. Stingy ones
14. Yoko ____
15. Lassie's pal
19. Author Bombeck
20. Sprinkles
22. Comedian Conway
23. A Gardner
24. Said again
26. Killed
28. "Enola ____"
29. Flock member
31. Cleanses
36. Heats up
39. Fuss
41. Cow call
42. Stubborn animal
43. "____ of Eden"
45. Director Preminger
46. In the near future
47. Playhouse locale
48. Dory stick
49. Ruff's mate
50. Quayle or Rather

# PUZZLE 471

**ACROSS**

1. Public vehicle
4. Pack down
8. Word before house or robe
12. Viper
13. Affirm
14. Dull pain
15. Media story part
17. Equipment
18. Ancient
19. ____ chango
21. Sarcasm
24. Drive a spike
25. Today's paper
26. Maidenhair
27. In the dumps
30. High note
31. ____ down (became quiet)
32. Sash
33. Say further
34. Cry of woe
35. Glen
36. Satisfied
37. French cap
38. Sigh
41. Golfer's peg
42. Small amount
43. Storage shack
48. Strong wind
49. Wicked
50. Paddle
51. Ogled
52. Author Carnegie
53. Snoop

**DOWN**

1. Exclamation of contempt
2. Put to work
3. Mineral spring
4. Add up
5. Zealous
6. Crew
7. Sets up
8. Roll with a hole
9. Fighter pilots
10. "____ Girl"
11. The good guy
16. Spanish noblemen
20. Cheese skin
21. Ancient Peruvian
22. Singer Lou ____
23. Was in debt
24. Site of the Himalayas
26. Deboned
27. Glide aloft
28. Proficient
29. Count calories
31. Painter Gauguin
35. Goose formations
36. Celebrated
37. ____ of the ball
38. Border
39. Medical photo
40. Patriot Nathan ____
41. Labor
44. Roe
45. Jump
46. Corn unit
47. Parched

# PUZZLE 472

**ACROSS**

1. Amusement
4. Sibling, for short
7. Edge of a cup
10. Climbing plant
11. Drag
12. Comfort
13. Flower
14. Sorrow
15. Suffers
16. Strength
18. Points of view
20. Singer Peggy ____
21. Caviar
22. Warnings
26. Pick up the check
30. Tint
31. Algonquian
33. Abel's mother
34. Bestow
37. Propelled
40. Assistance
42. ____ Alamos
43. Reliable
46. "The Scarlet ____"
50. Rabbit's kin
51. Colonist Yale
53. Ambience
54. "Green ____ and Ham"
55. Relieved
56. Skinny
57. Formerly called
58. Notice
59. Envelope abbr.

**DOWN**

1. Blaze
2. Compartment
3. Snuggle
4. "The ____ of San Francisco"
5. Debt letters
6. Curse
7. Wading bird
8. ____ of Man
9. Hodgepodge
10. Energy
12. Avid
17. Meadow
19. Forget-me-____
22. Article
23. Attila, e.g.
24. Crimson
25. Drain
27. Always, to a poet
28. Road: abbr.
29. Kennedy or Danson
32. Run together
35. Desert havens
36. Humor
38. Grief
39. Landed property
41. Colorists
43. "That Was ____, This is Now"
44. Indignation
45. Prod
47. Revolve
48. Journalist Sevareid
49. Ewe's mate
52. Fabricate

# PUZZLE 473

**ACROSS**

1. Alan or Robert
5. Golly!
8. Iowa city
12. Dirt
13. Raced
14. "Miami ___"
15. Trespassers
17. Tennis great Arthur ___
18. Ripen
19. Souvenir
21. Cover
22. Play on words
23. Richard ___ of "Pretty Woman"
25. Take for granted
28. In the vicinity
31. ___ d'etat (overthrow)
32. Bambi, e.g.
33. Subjects
36. Card suit
38. Napoleon's island
39. ___ capita
40. Damage
42. Grin
44. Ecology group: abbr.
47. Bullets
49. William Shatner series
51. Not nice
52. Baseball's Mel ___
53. All: pref.
54. "___ of Green Gables"
55. Negatives
56. Horace or Thomas

**DOWN**

1. Largest continent
2. Endless
3. Plunge
4. Chicken ___ king
5. Lorne of "Bonanza"
6. British nobleman
7. Certain navy officer
8. Gardner of films
9. TV's talking horse
10. Reverberate
11. Leak
16. Snare or kettle
20. Average grade
22. Student
24. Walter O'Reilly on "M*A*S*H"
25. Perform
26. Jack ___ of "Barney Miller"
27. Christopher Reeve role
29. Spelling contest
30. Calendar units: abbr.
34. Certain network: abbr.
35. Delilah's mate
36. Smacks
37. Equal
40. Mother
41. Prayer ending
43. Tell ___ the marines
44. Columnist Bombeck
45. William or Sean
46. Related
48. Dollar bill
50. Jerry's cartoon nemesis

# PUZZLE 474

**ACROSS**

1. Tidbit for Flicka
4. Expensive
9. NBC rival
12. Evergreen
13. Dance for two
14. Squeal
15. Pink birds
17. ___ was saying
18. Standard
19. Preference
21. Western Indians
23. ___-and-cream complexion
25. Adam's son
26. Canal vessel
27. Can top
28. Pickle juice
29. Cribbage counter
32. Across: pref.
33. Salve plant
34. Says again
37. Author Stephen ___
38. Indebted to
39. Tennis call
40. D.C. VIP
41. Alumni
47. Dander
48. Spooky
49. Zsa Zsa's sis
50. Kind of curve
51. Legal documents
52. Blushing color

**DOWN**

1. On one's way
2. Be under the weather
3. Caught in a snare
4. Blends
5. Summer hue
6. Part of G.B.: abbr.
7. ___ trip
8. Meter or stamp
9. Attend uninvited
10. Stitch loosely
11. Pigs' havens
16. Letter-carrier's burden
20. King's better
21. Actor Holbrook
22. Kimono sash
23. Aches
24. Sea eagles
26. Spoiled tot
28. Boasted
29. Dish
30. Vast time frame
31. ___ whiz!
32. Sawbuck
33. Neighborhood
34. ___ the Riveter
35. Water pitchers
36. Maine's trees
37. Indications
42. Ruff's mate
43. "___ You Lonesome Tonight?"
44. Performed
45. New Year's ___
46. Downcast

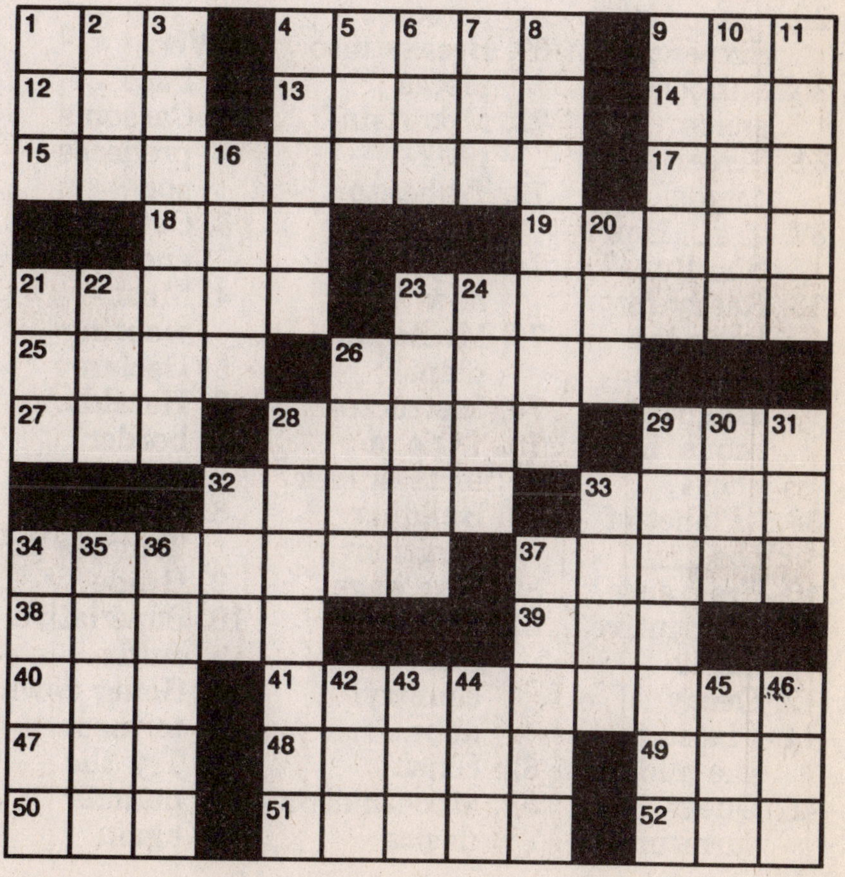

# PUZZLE 475

**ACROSS**
1. Bridge
5. Tippler
8. Angered
12. Outer edges
16. Cassette, e.g.
17. Cut back
19. Flower jar
20. Cleveland's lake
21. Soothe
22. To the sheltered side
23. Waiting servant
25. Decide in advance
28. Aim a finger
29. "____ Got Sixpence"
30. Suffocating snake
31. Screen star Lugosi
32. "____ How She Runs"
33. Ready for business
35. Played a king-rook move, in chess
38. "Planet of the ____"
40. Fragrance
41. Diminutive suffix
42. Decay
44. Placed in the middle
46. Queen ____ furniture
48. In the ____ (healthy)
49. Terminate
50. Roofing substance
51. African fly
53. Aware of
54. Wager
55. Fishing cords
56. Shoe tip
58. Johnson of "Laugh-In"
61. Worn away
63. ____ Na Na
64. Everyman John ____
67. Lunch time
68. Unique person
69. Breaks into pieces
71. Mountain peak
72. To be, to Caesar
74. Anytime now
75. Medicinal plant
76. Instructor
78. Type of football kick
79. Building addition
80. Fish eggs
81. Former Mideast country: abbr.
82. Exist
83. Moonshiner's device
85. One who trades places
91. Unending
93. Withered
94. "A ____ of Two Cities"
95. Peel
96. Perry's creator Gardner
97. Swarm
98. Songstress Fitzgerald
99. Hymn closing
100. Venison source
101. "____ Miser-ables"
102. Hold as an opinion

**DOWN**
1. Pace
2. Carson's predeces-sor
3. Cathedral end
4. Most wanting
5. Declare
6. Heraldic border
7. Row
8. Donald Trump's ex
9. Grade
10. Superlative suffix
11. Going down farthest
12. Try the number again
13. Persia, today
14. Money factory
15. Tennis match unit
18. Part of a group
24. Actor Nick ____
26. Adam's wife
27. Charged particle
31. Actress Kathy ____
32. Dispatch
33. Baltic feeder
34. Pea envelope
35. Pennies
36. Ireland, to poets
37. "____ Tread on Me"
38. Hole in one
39. Enclosure
40. Speak pompously
43. Boxing de-cision: abbr.
45. French summer
46. Actor Ed ____
47. Lack
48. Author of "The Raven"
51. Spring, neap, or flood
52. American patriot Allen
54. TV's Matlock

# PUZZLE 475

55. Lover of solitude
57. Cereal grain
58. Picnic pest
59. Tree's anchor
60. Ripped
62. Fragrant red flowers
63. Struck by a bullet
64. "The Farmer in the ____"
65. Spanish gold
66. Opposite of WNW
69. Boy baby
70. Naturally skillful
72. School, in Paris
73. Removed the husk from
74. Most certain
77. Gotten up
78. TV host Sajak
79. Historic age
81. Racecar driver Bobby ____
82. Attention getters
83. Joint
84. Weight allowance
85. ____ of Wight
86. Spool
87. Algonquin tribe
88. High wind
89. French fashion magazine
90. Measure of paper
91. Auditor: abbr.
92. Before

# PUZZLE 476

**ACROSS**

1. Sport fish
5. Rips
10. Bridge
14. Bouncing sound
15. Large black bird
16. Gap
17. Parched
18. Out of the way
19. Total defeat
20. Asked for insistently
22. Bells, whistles, etc.
24. Snaky fish
25. Dermal layer
26. Expand
30. Glossiest
34. Wide-awake
35. Pledged
36. Blemish
37. Rural road
38. Small stores
39. Skeletal material
40. Carpenter or army
41. Expositions
42. Palm fruits
43. Left alone
45. Apple beverages
46. Family quarrel
47. Female deer
48. Would rather have
51. Spaghetti's partner
56. Advertising emblem
57. Songs for two
59. Europe's neighbor
60. Aroma
61. Thing of value
62. Film critic Rex ____
63. Trial
64. Many ____ ago . . .
65. Alleviate

**DOWN**

1. Necklace component
2. Farm measure
3. Thin wedge
4. Bicarbonate of ____
5. Swapped
6. Painter's stand
7. Eager
8. Comedian Buttons
9. Athletic footwear
10. Reduced
11. Destitute
12. Grad
13. Receives after taxes
21. Orderly
23. Legal claim
25. Spills
26. Dish of fresh greens
27. Aircraft
28. Leases
29. Sooner than, poetically
30. Saber, e.g.
31. Show feeling
32. Mentally healthier
33. Long lock of hair
35. Flinched
38. Seventh day of the week
39. Not good
41. Without charge
42. Eat less
44. Exertion
45. Slides
47. Prevent
48. Story line
49. Went by horse
50. Selves
51. Plateau
52. Uncover
53. On the ocean
54. Falsehoods
55. Put a burden on
58. Utilize

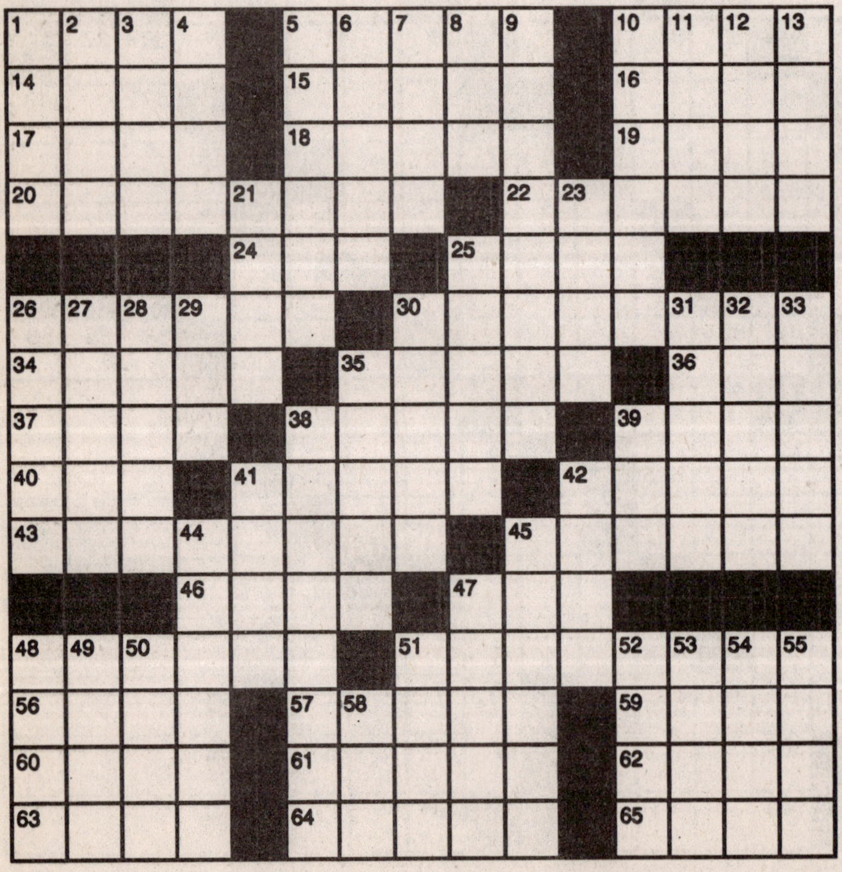

# PUZZLE 477

**ACROSS**

1. Frolic
5. Incline
10. Shut hard
14. State with confidence
15. Swiss call
16. Role model
17. Fence opening
18. Frown
19. Garage entrance
20. Lift
22. Wash
23. Frozen treat
24. Chowder ingredient
26. Buy back
29. Wrestled
33. Promises
34. Original source
35. Chopping tool
36. Small child
37. Weary from overwork
38. Health resort
39. ____ out a living
40. Fortune-telling card
41. Guide
43. Confine
45. Unsatisfactorily
46. Ace in the ____
47. Close to the ground
48. Noted
51. Adolescent
56. Butter substitute
57. "La Boheme," e.g.
59. Move quickly
60. Back
61. Dreads
62. Extreme
63. Refute
64. Inaccurate
65. Wall support

**DOWN**

1. Fury
2. Egg-shaped
3. Allot
4. Advance showing
5. Method
6. Crazy
7. Smell
8. Church seat
9. Building addition
10. Prawn
11. Slender
12. Weapons
13. Sulk
21. Experts
22. Fascinated
24. Glass bottle
25. Touch down
26. Estimator
27. Call forth
28. Loves to excess
29. "Waiting for ____"
30. Focused beam
31. Oust
32. Darling
34. Mockery
37. Hoosegow
40. Walked
41. Before long
42. In the direction of
44. Supposition
45. Gratify
48. Tennessee Ernie ____
49. To shelter
50. Intend
51. Greenish blue
52. Sins
53. Horse's stride
54. Light brown
55. Marsh grass
57. ____ and running
58. Green vegetable

# PUZZLE 478

**ACROSS**

1. Dominate
5. Alert
10. Scarlets
14. Spanish jar
15. Private teacher
16. Lamb's pen name
17. Garden pest
18. Boredom
19. Competes
20. Foster strife
23. Take it on the ____
24. Destroy
25. Ignobility
30. Invalidate
34. Sheep mother
35. Expanse of land
37. Evil spirit
38. Actor Alan
40. Golf norm
41. Papal court
42. Peculiarity
44. Sniff
47. ____ King Cole
48. Felt
50. Ern
52. But: Sp.
54. Battle
55. Commit youthful follies
63. Pub brews
64. In reserve
65. Eye tunic
66. Egyptian river
67. Mr. Standish
68. Male children
69. Precious metal
70. Appears
71. Terminates

**DOWN**

1. Curtsies
2. Bread spread
3. Killed
4. Seat on a horse
5. Soft-shell clam
6. Suspended
7. ____ time
8. Circular
9. Pokey
10. Retaliator
11. Writer Wiesel
12. Eating plan
13. Cummerbund
21. Carry on
22. Knotted
25. Waistbands
26. Cognizant
27. Family car
28. Weakens
29. Con games
31. Surrounded by
32. Sum up
33. Maternally related
36. Coatrack
39. Inclined
43. Adolescent
45. Unruly
46. Show the way
49. Reveries
51. Excite
53. Actor Davis
55. Crooned
56. Hodgepodge
57. Healthy
58. Stratagem
59. Same: Lat.
60. Bard's river
61. Baby-sit
62. Nerve

# PUZZLE 479

**ACROSS**

1. Equal
5. "The ___ Luck Club"
8. Astringent
12. Press
13. Sooner, poetically
14. Get up
15. Hire
16. Stockpiles
18. Looks for
20. Achievers
21. Misguided
23. Sunday bench
24. Applaud
25. Ashen
26. Typewriter key
29. Cattle group
30. Diaper fastener
31. Speed contest
32. McMahon and Sullivan
33. Like father, like ___
34. Hooded snake
35. Baseball stick
36. Wine glass
37. Guardian ___
40. Perhaps
41. Rewards
43. Kind of collar
46. Direct
47. Head cover
48. Actor's part
49. Shade providers
50. Chicago Loop trains
51. Gush out

**DOWN**

1. Baronet's title
2. Part of to be
3. Creatures
4. Signed up
5. Beef ___
6. Unrefined metals
7. Okay
8. Bow's missile
9. Not taped
10. Consumer
11. Confusion
17. Adam's garden
19. Hearing organ
21. In need of a massage
22. Cast off
23. Skillet
25. Triumph
26. Family's eating surface
27. Farmhold
28. Throb
30. Spaghetti cooker
31. Thieves
33. Seasoning
34. Modest
35. Zigzags
36. Puffs
37. Qualified
38. Yuletide
39. Pacific island
40. Repast
42. Winter driving hazard
44. "Grand ___ Opry"
45. Just bought

# PUZZLE 480

**ACROSS**

1. Remove moisture from
4. Drill
8. Water vehicle
12. Nautical response
13. Persia, today
14. Entice
15. Number of bowling frames
16. Split apart
17. Sector
18. Credit
20. Melancholy
22. Nautical greeting
25. Opposite of east
28. Fibber
31. Agreement
33. Enrage
35. Eternity
36. Rake over the ____ (reprimand)
37. Ess follower
38. Pismire
39. Blunders
40. Touch
41. Bird food
43. Exclusive
45. Guided
47. Conscious
51. Wearing boots
54. Merit
57. Pea container
58. Whet
59. Hint
60. Slump
61. Washstand vessel
62. Liquid containers
63. Prior to, poetically

**DOWN**

1. Computer fodder
2. Certain breads
3. Hankerings
4. Lineage
5. Unrefined mineral
6. Sought office
7. Football positions
8. Skate part
9. Belonging to you and me
10. Exist
11. London brew
19. Hearing organ
21. Shoemakers' tools
23. Smell
24. Century units
26. Locale
27. Corner
28. Meadow
29. Charged atoms
30. Contribute a share
32. Likewise
34. Sniggler's catch
36. Surrender
40. Not many
42. Church official
44. Bowling alleys
46. Card pack
48. Church recess
49. Lion's sound
50. Brink
51. That girl
52. ____ do you do?
53. Undivided
55. Beerlike beverage
56. Carpet

## PUZZLE 481

**ACROSS**

1. "The ___ Is High" (Blondie tune)
5. Brush's counterpart
9. Actor Pesci
12. Early man
13. Unwritten
14. Author Beattie
15. Cut
16. Went a roundabout way
18. Campers' shelters
20. 2000 pounds
21. Sorts
24. Catchers' gloves
28. Legendary Baba
30. Ticks off
32. Exhaust
33. Caviar
34. Tricks
36. ___ and tonic
37. West's opposite
39. Astonish
40. Very warm
41. Following
43. Explode
45. Corn serving
47. Yelps
50. A seasoning
55. Not any
56. Owed
57. Matinee figure
58. Blemish
59. Kind of trip
60. Morning moistures
61. Evergreens

**DOWN**

1. Diplomacy
2. At rest
3. Most delicate
4. Vacant
5. Cape ___, Massachusetts
6. Pay dirt
7. Actor Dillon
8. Flourish
9. Container
10. Song from "A Chorus Line"
11. Goal
17. Segment
19. Sputter
22. Makes a mistake
23. Glide
25. Acrobat's walkway
26. Threesome
27. Dispatched
28. Domain
29. Bread shape
31. Cowboy's prod
35. Rebuff
38. Kickoff props
42. Swift
44. Flower
46. Fair feature
48. Be cognizant of
49. Stage decorations
50. Fruit drink
51. Pull with effort
52. Sign before Virgo
53. Female bovine
54. Overhead trains

# PUZZLE 482

## ACROSS

1. "____ Glory"
4. Slashes
8. Turn upside down
12. Broadcast
13. Japan's continent
14. Leprechaun land
15. Cover charge
16. Landlord's due
17. Mass response
18. Pesters
20. Fondle
22. Extremely small
24. "____ Magic Moment" (Drifters song)
25. Pang
26. Prompted
27. Land parcel
30. Kind of shoe
31. Outlaw Starr
32. Summer refresher
33. Off the deep ____
34. Blue flag
35. Harbinger
36. Staircase part
37. Intertwine
38. Insignia
41. Bank holding
42. Bundle
43. Hautboy
45. Adder
48. Flowed out
49. Close by
50. Afternoon social
51. Mends
52. Craves
53. Sniggler's catch

## DOWN

1. Clumsy person
2. Falsehood
3. Saturated
4. Freight
5. Consumes
6. Can
7. Small bags
8. Dreads
9. Shade of green
10. Enrages
11. Writing instruments
19. "Car 54, Where ____ You?"
21. Adjutant
22. Aussie's buddy
23. Religious image
24. Spring flower
26. Solemn rite
27. Split into layers
28. Lyrical poems
29. Portable shelter
31. Mouthful
35. Part of IOU
36. Winter transports
37. Rows
38. Declines
39. Cob or buck
40. Tooted
41. Bank transaction
44. Buzzing insect
46. Lay eyes on
47. Friend

# PUZZLE 483

**ACROSS**
1. Tepid
5. Fades
9. In favor of
12. China's continent
13. Portent
14. Lend an ___
15. Small store
16. Current
18. Research center
20. Wipes out
21. Most skilled
24. Race in neutral
25. Sheep's cry
26. Beer barrel
28. Passenger
32. Shade trees
34. Pat
36. Cold-cut mart
37. Bus station
39. Cushion
41. Chicago Loop trains
42. Marry
44. Not fine
46. Seem
49. Boxer Norton
50. Stack of lumber
52. Slopes down
56. Beer's cousin
57. Completed
58. Famous canal
59. Nevertheless
60. ___ off (annoys)
61. Stuffing herb

**DOWN**
1. Used to be
2. Pulverized lava
3. ___ Grande
4. Syrup source
5. Questioned
6. Little devil
7. Gauge
8. Noisy sleeper
9. Pod vegetables
10. Assess
11. Crude metals
17. Comedian Letterman
19. Question
21. Retired for the night
22. Cotton unit
23. Illuminating device
27. Delaware Water ___
29. Stag or roe
30. Extensions
31. Get up
33. Planted
35. Supporters
38. Spouted vessel
40. Buck's mate
43. Ambition
45. Peruvian range
46. "Far and ___" (Cruise film)
47. North or South
48. Keats or Browning
51. Golfer Trevino
53. Author Levin
54. Swine
55. Notice

# PUZZLE 484

**ACROSS**

1. Pastry desserts
5. Social insect
8. Columnist Landers
11. First man
12. Bodies of water
14. Ghost's greeting
15. Be defeated
16. Water containers
18. Mrs. Roosevelt
20. Bowling center
21. Decompose
22. Everyone
23. Statement of belief
26. Be in debt
27. Skirt edge
30. Street
31. Spanish cheer
32. Sped
33. Thus far
34. Do sums
35. Special goody
36. Expert
37. Split ____ soup
38. Gush forth
41. Cattle farms
45. Shopper
47. Ocean movement
48. "Where the Boys ____"
49. Talk wildly
50. Baking chamber
51. Stop-sign color
52. Plaything
53. Tenant's fee

**DOWN**

1. Ashen
2. Role model
3. Relax
4. Blurred
5. Broad necktie
6. Approach
7. Sunbather's goal
8. Eve's son
9. Not any
10. Prying
13. Not fresh
17. Building addition
19. Bow the head
22. Reverence
23. Weep
24. Caviar
25. Snack
26. On in years
27. Gardening tool
28. Age
29. Encountered
31. Certain poem
32. Farm vehicle
34. Role player
35. Countdown starter
36. Gallery display
37. Celebration
38. Wound memento
39. Unaltered
40. Secondhand
41. Nevada town
42. Honey-maker's home
43. First garden
44. Mailed
46. Small rug

# PUZZLE 485

**ACROSS**

1. Pepper's partner
5. Hockey great
8. Mrs. Dithers
12. Smell
13. One of the Three Stooges
14. You can hear ____ drop
15. Meadow-dwelling songbird
17. Nimble
18. Favorite
19. Cara and Dunne
21. Wash up
24. Pesky fly
25. Follow orders
26. Puts in grass
27. Secret agent
30. Lager's kin
31. Musical range
32. Bend the truth
33. Newscaster Koppel
34. Funnyman Johnson
35. Festive
36. Cry of sorrow
37. At some future time
38. One behind the other
41. Wear away
42. Dry
43. Small quail
48. Legend
49. Ad-____
50. Buffalo's lake
51. Sleeping
52. Some railways, for short
53. Film spool

**DOWN**

1. Cry
2. Stir
3. Toss
4. Bowler's prize
5. Leave out
6. Howard of "Happy Days"
7. Excite again
8. West Pointer
9. Ready for business
10. Overflowing
11. Pismires
16. Confederate general
20. Demolish, in London
21. Water vehicle
22. Proficient
23. ____ off (angry)
24. Grazing animals
26. Mix together confusedly
27. Bed board
28. Heap
29. 365 days
31. Retail transaction
35. Collect
36. Summed
37. Regulation
38. Good-bye, in Yorkshire
39. Saudi, e.g.
40. African river
41. Recedes
44. It floats on water
45. Rage
46. Fasten
47. Moray

# PUZZLE 486

**ACROSS**

1. Caesar, e.g.
6. Fixed look
11. Spice
12. Weasel
14. Age
15. "____ of the Lost Ark"
17. Honest ____ Lincoln
18. Shy
20. ____ West (life jacket)
21. Tower town
23. Wayne's word
24. Knowledgeable
25. City on the Rhine
27. Belief
28. Stadiums
31. Prim
32. Iron-rich dish
33. Bolger and Milland
34. In excess of
35. Seed vessel
36. Checks
40. Egg layer
41. Rope
43. Friend
44. Grand Canyon site
46. Frightening
48. Noisy sleeper
49. Enormous
50. Pious
51. Aquatic mammal

**DOWN**

1. Fragment
2. Excuse
3. Easy runs
4. Wide st.
5. Depression
6. Speech
7. Characteristic
8. Surrounded by
9. Free
10. Adversaries
13. Rubs out
16. Run-down
19. Taverns
22. Mr. Kravitz on "Bewitched"
24. Bracelet's place
26. Rower's need
27. Yell
28. Island greeting
29. Talk show host Joan ____
30. Dusk
31. Cushions
33. Prayer's beads
35. Group of judges
37. Separate
38. Flatboat
39. Craftier
41. Nobleman
42. Capital of Norway
45. Animal park
47. Mouser

# PUZZLE 487

**ACROSS**

1. ____ Pan Alley
4. Speak wildly
8. Audacious
12. Serve for a point
13. Region
14. Away from the wind
15. Formal request
17. Skinny
18. College official
19. Lumps of dirt
20. Curved
23. Feather wrap
24. Busy insects
25. Small pools
29. Youth
30. Portrayal
32. Citrus cooler
33. Put up
35. Prayer ending
36. "____ It Be"
37. Use money
38. Coffee additive
41. Cotton bundle
43. Assists
44. Joker
48. Radar spot
49. Very dry
50. Pindaric poem
51. Adjusts, as a watch
52. Cincinnati team
53. "It's ____ or Never"

**DOWN**

1. Knock gently
2. Rink surface
3. Butterfly snare
4. Assessed
5. Diva's forte
6. Sign gas
7. Light brown
8. Romantic song
9. Mock butter
10. Heavy metal
11. Bears' lairs
16. March date
19. Zip ____
20. Up to the job
21. Posterior
22. Give up
23. Hidden microphone
25. Cushion
26. Gold fabric
27. First garden
28. Dispatch
30. List entry
31. Convened
34. Grips
35. Mimicked
37. Winter sliders
38. Taxis
39. Make angry
40. Revise copy
41. Use a drill
42. In the center of
44. Train component
45. Charged particle
46. Fuss
47. Modern

# PUZZLE 488

**ACROSS**

1. Social insect
4. Not working
8. Shout to a cat
12. "A Boy Named ___"
13. Close securely
14. Tramp
15. Backpack
17. Raw minerals
18. Entice
19. Parent's sisters
20. Binges
23. Every
24. Length times width
25. Annapolis, e.g.
29. Coral, e.g.
30. Tunnels
32. Green vegetable
33. Fireman's water source
35. Watch face
36. Beame of politics
37. Ring
39. Gap
42. Ms. Horne
43. Converse
44. Return to lower prices
48. Orderly
49. Capri or Man
50. Female rabbit
51. Bothersome child
52. Most favorable
53. Lassie, e.g.

**DOWN**

1. Interrogate
2. Religious sister
3. Earl Grey, e.g.
4. Emanate
5. Darlings
6. Curtain material
7. Wapiti
8. Ought to
9. Eared vegetable
10. Assist in a crime
11. Prepare, as salad
16. Defendant's response to charges
19. Word of sorrow
20. Belt
21. Target
22. Peruse
23. Flying pro
25. Music or literature
26. Heroic
27. Repast
28. New Haven university
30. Ruth of baseball
31. Buck
34. Tennis equipment
35. Dreary
37. Tissue units
38. Bay
39. Guess
40. Couple
41. "M*A*S*H" star
42. Be an also-ran
44. Chest bone
45. Total
46. Dove's murmur
47. Nail holder

# PUZZLE 489

**ACROSS**

1. Small amount
4. Provo's state
8. Swindle
12. Had a meal
13. Mama's mate
14. Ripped
15. Sugar syrup
17. Prayer ending
18. Liveliness
19. Rose part
20. Fruit drink
21. Breakfast food
24. Pay off
27. Actress Doris ____
28. ____-la-la
29. Disencumbers
30. Upper limb
31. Action
32. High card
33. Frosty
34. Present time
35. Renter
37. What person
38. Can metal
39. Archer's missiles
43. Corrosive liquid
45. Pastry store
47. Brief message
48. Concept
49. Anger
50. Child's treasures
51. James ____ (007)
52. Not even

**DOWN**

1. Scottish caps
2. On the peak
3. Sandwich shop
4. ____ down (inverted)
5. Flavor
6. Gorilla, e.g.
7. Possesses
8. One of a flight
9. Vied
10. Exist
11. Grown boys
16. Saudis, e.g.
19. ____, you!
21. Machine part
22. Region
23. Gentlewoman
24. Mischievous child
25. Paddy product
26. Card or crisis
27. Arid
30. Play unit
31. Entryways
33. Country hotel
34. Sewing cord
36. Assistants
37. Rouse
40. The Buckeye State
41. Sentence component
42. Hurried
43. Picnic pest
44. Dove's cry
45. Baby's apron
46. Fuss

# PUZZLE 490

**ACROSS**
1. Lowe or Reiner
4. Workbench jaws
8. Money-operated phonograph, for short
12. Summer drink
13. Vexes
14. Again
15. Garden plants
17. Soft wood
18. Cozy retreat
19. Electrical units
20. Chaos
23. Long-legged bird
25. Let in
27. Pair
28. Tree juice
31. Antenna
33. Changed into
35. Beige
36. ____ Cruces
38. Ladies' titles
39. Sacred table
41. Crooked
42. Board game
45. Disgusting
47. Greases
48. Zipper or pin
52. Still
53. Region
54. Raw mineral
55. Clean
56. Plate
57. Bankroll

**DOWN**
1. Hit sharply
2. "____ to Billy Joe"
3. Gamble
4. Grape plant
5. Whiskey or wolfhound
6. Glided
7. Road curve
8. Nippon
9. Division
10. Actor McCord
11. Wool producers
16. Up to the time that
19. Courted
20. Float
21. Notion
22. Harbinger
24. Chafe
26. Relates
28. Ditto
29. Prayer ending
30. Gnat, for one
32. Large rodent
34. Telegram
37. Hunting expedition
39. Credit
40. American Beauties
42. Dime or penny
43. Secrete
44. Jazz singer Fitzgerald
46. Idaho's neighbor
48. Craze
49. At this time
50. Epoch
51. Maroon

# PUZZLE 491

**ACROSS**

1. At a distance
5. Dined
8. Sailor's greeting
12. Curved roof
13. Earnings
14. Adore
15. Crude metals
16. Incense
17. Pub brews
18. Dagger
20. Failure
22. One of the Seven Dwarfs
23. Squid squirt
24. Globe
27. Church official
31. Antique auto
32. Astonish
33. Cherubs
37. Semitic language
40. Tatter
41. Past
42. Healer
44. Pleasing treat
47. Mama's mate
48. Hen product
50. Emblem
52. Strong metal
53. Lamprey
54. Fictional work
55. Baby-sit
56. Visit
57. Winter transport

**DOWN**

1. Confusion
2. Eating implement
3. It is so
4. Dwell
5. Each
6. Gooey substance
7. Facial feature
8. Baked ____
9. Jackson ____, Wyoming
10. Above
11. Word of assent
19. In behalf of
21. Small number
24. Sp. married woman
25. Enclosure
26. Swine
28. Convertible, e.g.
29. Be obligated to
30. York or Zealand
34. Chore
35. Recline
36. Flings
37. Barter
38. Freudian self
39. Intensifies
42. Feel concern
43. Once ____ a time
45. Agreement
46. Ivy League school
47. Cavity
49. Horse command
51. Took by the hand

# PUZZLE 492

**ACROSS**

1. Come ashore
5. Toga
9. Good-bye, Spanish style
11. Night-club charge
12. ____ Carlo
13. Works a cure
14. In favor
15. ____ rule: 2 wds.
17. Illuminated
18. Finish
20. Blot out
22. Articles
24. Severity
26. Chapeau
29. Young man
30. Poisonous snake
32. Border
34. Scents
36. Marketplace for Plato
38. Crocheted lace
39. Hearsay
40. Fling
41. Sail support

**DOWN**

1. Bulbed furnishing
2. Dote on
3. Curtain material
4. Speck
5. Small deer
6. Racetracks
7. Misrepresent
8. Before, formerly
10. Gull, horse, or urchin
11. Fascinate
16. Prophets
19. Gibe
21. ____ Wednesday
23. Warm thoroughly
24. Soap opera's first medium
25. Golden Calf and Baal
27. Fragrance
28. Weather satellite
29. Place for hay
31. Average
33. Store
35. Between dos and mis
37. Adhesive substance

# PUZZLE 493

**ACROSS**

1. Casualty
5. "____ will be done . . ."
8. Settee
12. Help in wrongdoing
13. Paris street
14. Homeric poem
15. Small horse
16. Bank-account accrual
18. Become firm
19. Cause for dieting
20. Peewees
21. Nobleman
23. Kind of wit
24. Church-social game
26. Is able to
27. Movie son of Tarzan
30. Formerly
31. Chicle
32. Function
33. "____ Day at a Time"
34. Dick Whittington's pet
35. Thick strings
36. Organized-crime group
37. Chess piece
38. Spring month
41. Spinning toy
42. Unlikely tale
45. Defames
47. ____ Stanley Gardner
48. Clark ____, aka Superman
49. Almond, e.g.
50. Find a buyer
51. Droops
52. ____ Plaines
53. Nuisance

**DOWN**

1. Licks
2. Woodwind
3. Punishment
4. Pigpen
5. Error's partner
6. Search
7. Nevertheless
8. Antitoxin
9. Not secret
10. 1978 Stallone film
11. Behaves
17. Ireland
19. To and ____
22. Years of one's life
23. Aswan sight
24. Jeer
25. Motel
26. Sever
27. Elsa's story: 2 wds.
28. Antique
29. Affirmative reply
31. Have a chin fest
32. Noisy quarrel
34. Frigid
35. Beanie
36. After-dinner sweets
37. Mails
38. Inquires
39. Earnest appeal
40. Pealed
41. Faithful
43. Sicknesses
44. Karate award
46. Conclude
47. Clairvoyant's skill, for short

**MOVIES AND TELEVISION**

# PUZZLE 494

**ACROSS**

1. "____ Bomber" (Erroll Flynn film)
5. "My Two ____"
9. Gregory Hines film
12. "The Man With the Golden ____"
15. Actress Gray
16. Final notice
17. Southern st.
18. "7 Faces of Dr. ____"
19. Rabbit ____ (antenna)
20. Gable/Tierney film
23. Actress Taylor of "I'll Fly Away"
25. "____ of the Needle"
26. "Johnny ____"
27. "____ Around" (Beach Boys hit)
28. "____ Yeller"
29. Jillian or Sheridan
30. Pat's partner on "Wheel of Fortune"
32. Sugary foods
34. Chancy
38. Actress Meyers
39. "____ Haw"
40. Judge
42. European ruminant
43. Patricia or Tom
45. Possesses
47. Stanwyck or Bain
49. Actor Martin ____
51. "My Gal ____"
53. "The ____ Mistress"
54. "____ to Beaver"
57. "The ____ of Living Dangerously"
59. Host Stephenson of "Real People"
62. "____ Prentiss"
63. Do as Lou Grant does
65. "____ Maria"
66. Sp. lady
67. "____ at the Top"
69. "Peer Gynt" enchantress
71. Dennehy or Donlevy
73. Trombonist Kid ____
75. Cask
76. Comedian Orson ____
77. Gawk
80. "____ and Away"
81. "Take the ____" (Duke Ellington theme song)
84. Bainter/Rains/Cooper film
88. Raison d'____
89. Bannen or Buchanan
90. "Cheers" bartender
91. Needlecase
92. Goddess of discord
93. "____ Jackson"
94. Prior to, to a bard
95. Director Clair
96. Back talk

**DOWN**

1. "The ____ Hunter"
2. "Dies ____"
3. Star of 53 Across
4. "____ Pulver"
5. Mr. Chips portrayer
6. Actor Vigoda
7. 504, to Pliny
8. "Remington ____"
9. "A ____ of Two Cities"
10. Falstaff's drink
11. Eucharistic plate
12. Shake ____ (hurry)
13. "A ____ to Live"
14. Othello, e.g.
21. Actress Winona ____
22. "The ____ Love" (Gershwin song)
24. Teachers' gp.
28. Co-host of 39 Across
29. Famous dancer
30. Dick ____ Dyke
31. "Butterflies ____ Free"
32. Use needle and thread
33. Actor Hunter
35. "Tony Rome" star
36. "____ Whom the Bell Tolls"
37. Pro vote
39. "Death Takes a ____"
41. Miscalculate
44. "P.S. I ____ U"
46. "____ Amen, Somebody"
48. Derek and Diddley
50. Kathie ____ Gifford
52. "Love and ____"
54. Actress Park-Lincoln
55. Comic Philips
56. "The ____ Drum"
58. Ms. Gardner
60. Lyricist Gershwin
61. "Peter ____"
64. "____—The Story of Michelangelo"
68. Comedian Sahl
70. Actress Lana ____
71. "You ____ Your Life"
72. Street shows
74. Singer Della ____
76. Musical Count
77. Loretta of "M*A*S*H"
78. "More ____ Friends"
79. "____ Misbehavin'"
80. Irene Cara film
82. "Stanley & ____"
83. Eliot ____ (Robert Stack role)
85. Scenery for "Love and War"
86. Hot time in Paris
87. River ____ ("Homefront" locale)

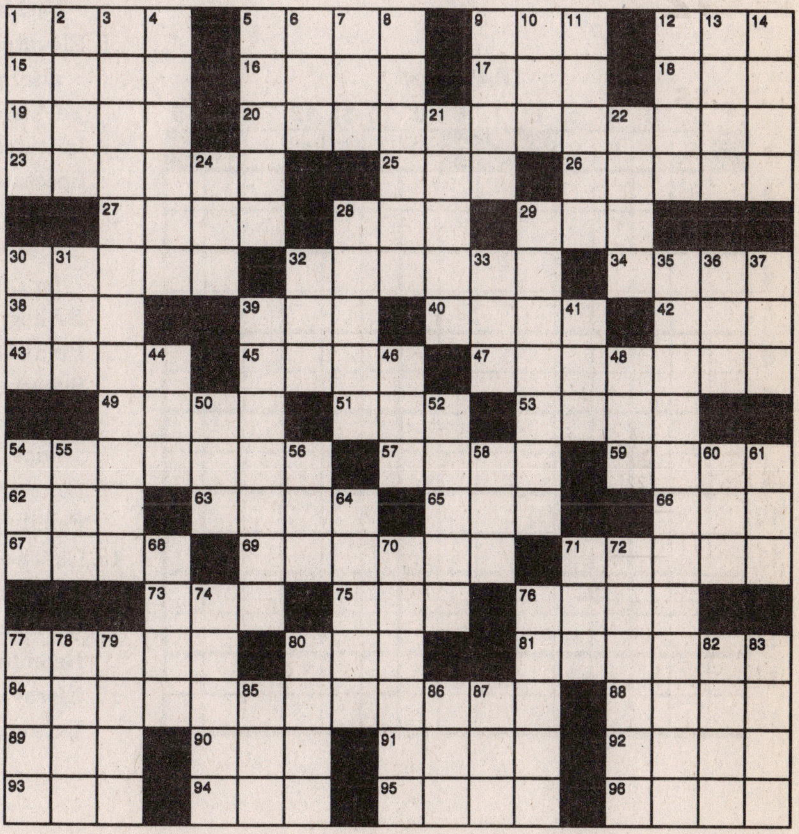

# PUZZLE 495

# BRICK BY BRICK

**Rearrange this stack of bricks to form a crossword puzzle. The clues will help you fit the bricks into their correct places. Row 1 has been filled in for you. Use the bricks to fill in the remaining spaces.**

## BRICKS

| | | | | |
|---|---|---|---|---|
| EPI<br>■ST | NKA<br>■AR | EUS<br>RE■ | E■A<br>S■R | ■AV<br>E■E |
| D■■<br>IBL | A■R<br>RAW | RRI<br>IML | STR<br>■SA | EN■<br>CIA |
| TES<br>HYT | ■ST<br>■■■ | EAT<br>SPE | DLE<br>■ED | ION<br>NGE |
| ■■R<br>L■A | ERS<br>■ET | COC<br>ACC | ANG<br>TEE | AIL<br>TTE |
| EUN<br>RRA | S■A<br>ED■ | RA■<br>ENA | TAL<br>ALI | LAC<br>ODE |
| VED<br>ICO | AIR<br>MOO | E■P<br>N■■ | E■A<br>D■P | BRI<br>LAD |
| T■E<br>HM■ | S■S<br>IM■ | HIS<br>EDE | EED<br>■■■ | ETE<br>DEN |

## DIAGRAM

| | 1 | 2 | 3 | 4 | 5 | 6 | 7 | 8 | 9 | 10 | 11 | 12 | 13 | 14 | 15 |
|---|---|---|---|---|---|---|---|---|---|---|---|---|---|---|---|
| 1 | ■ | S | A | S | S | ■ | ■ | ■ | C | A | E | S | A | R | ■ |
| 2 | | | | | | | | | | | | | | | |
| 3 | | | | | | | | | | | | | | | |
| 4 | | | | | | | | | | | | | | | |
| 5 | | | | | | | | | | | | | | | |
| 6 | | | | | | | | | | | | | | | |
| 7 | | | | | | | | | | | | | | | |
| 8 | | | | | | | | | | | | | | | |
| 9 | | | | | | | | | | | | | | | |
| 10 | | | | | | | | | | | | | | | |
| 11 | | | | | | | | | | | | | | | |
| 12 | | | | | | | | | | | | | | | |
| 13 | | | | | | | | | | | | | | | |
| 14 | | | | | | | | | | | | | | | |
| 15 | | | | | | | | | | | | | | | |

## ACROSS

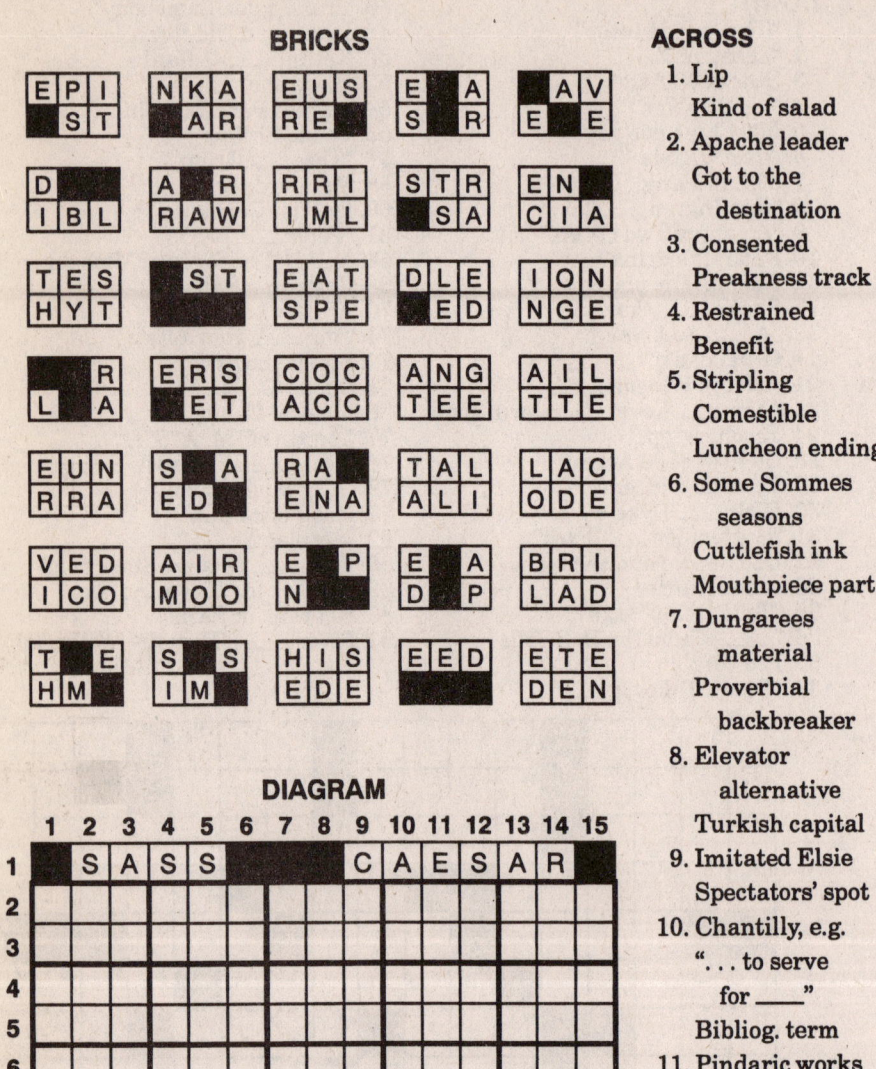

1. Lip
   Kind of salad
2. Apache leader
   Got to the destination
3. Consented
   Preakness track
4. Restrained
   Benefit
5. Stripling
   Comestible
   Luncheon ending
6. Some Sommes seasons
   Cuttlefish ink
   Mouthpiece part
7. Dungarees material
   Proverbial backbreaker
8. Elevator alternative
   Turkish capital
9. Imitated Elsie
   Spectators' spot
10. Chantilly, e.g.
    ". . . to serve for ____"
    Bibliog. term
11. Pindaric works
    Syncopation
    He had Clay feet, once
12. Consumed
    Family gathering
13. Chef's offering
    Put in order
14. Unusual
    He killed Medusa
15. Glossy fabric
    Raison d'____

## DOWN

1. Wired
   Fertile soil
2. Athenian philosopher
   Modifies
3. Collision, e.g.
   King of Siam's phrase, with et
4. Molted
   Certain feline
5. Move like a crab
   "O Sole ____"
   Supreme Court number
6. Sows
   Crowd sound
   Get on in years
7. Comedian Murphy
   Jessica Fletcher's friend
   Author Deighton
8. Modem speed abbr.
   "Love and War" actress
9. Gown's companion
   Actress Grey (Mrs. Charlie Chaplin)
   Watchband
10. "Exodus" hero
    Turn a penny
    "Over ____"
11. Humorist Bombeck
    Wanted poster abbr.
    Diving bird
12. Table utensils
    Political cartoonist
13. Take to the skies
    Dental device
14. Say from memory
    Corresponding item
15. Gave out
    Actress MacMahon and others

# DOUBLE TROUBLE PUZZLE 496

**Not really double trouble, but double fun! Solve this puzzle as you would a regular crossword, EXCEPT place one, two, or three letters in each box. The number of letters in each answer is shown in parentheses after its clue.**

**ACROSS**

1. Filled tortilla (4)
4. Performer (5)
7. Hidden (6)
10. Navy officer (6)
11. Group of four (7)
12. Bangkok citizen (4)
13. Carvey or Delaney (4)
14. Worldwide (13)
16. "Brian's Song" star (4)
18. Dynamic (6)
19. Lean-to (4)
20. Detergent (4)
22. Meat seller (7)
24. Hit (4)
26. Copper alloy (6)
28. Subsided (5)
30. Kind of cheese (7)
33. Boast (4)
35. Nook (6)
37. ___ King Cole (3)
38. Rotate (4)
40. Charlie Brown's oath (4)
42. More protracted (6)
44. Place of business (13)
47. Bedroom or key (6)
50. TV host Funt (5)
51. Attain (5)
52. Want (4)
53. Mr. Foxx (4)
54. Poor grades (4)
55. Whirlpool (4)

**DOWN**

1. Look after (4)
2. Chinese or Indian (5)
3. French brandy (6)
4. Personal knowledge (12)
5. Rich cake (5)
6. Take back (7)
7. Piece (7)
8. Go over again (6)
9. Shadowed (6)
15. Inhabitants (7)
17. Border on (4)
20. Weep (3)
21. Cook's garment (5)
23. Type of tea (6)
25. Observe (5)
27. Striped animal (5)
29. Sheets and blankets (10)
31. Author Ferber (4)
32. Move quickly (4)
34. Free (6)
36. Baking appliance (4)
38. Lance (5)
39. Set up (9)
41. Fragment (5)
43. Pertinent (7)
45. Mix (5)
46. Threat (6)
48. Spirited horse (5)
49. "Delta Dawn" singer (5)

# FAN WORDS PUZZLE 497

**Place the 5-letter answers to the clues into the fan to discover an 8-letter word reading across the outlined area. As an added help, pairs of answers are anagrams (1 is an anagram of 2, 3 is an anagram of 4, etc.).**

1. Shadow
2. Asian country
3. Pale
4. Alan Ladd film
5. Rye fungus
6. Thesaurus compiler
7. Damp
8. Leaves out

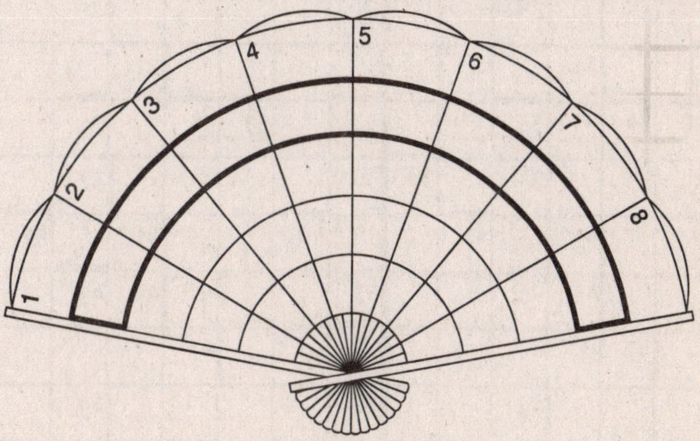

# PUZZLE 498 DILEMMA

**Except for 1 Across, there are 2 clues for each number and 2 identical sides of the diagram. Your dilemma is to discover which answer word goes on the right side and which answer word goes on the left. Note: The heavy lines indicate the ends of words as black squares do in regular crosswords.**

**ACROSS**

1. Future king
9. Uses a towel
   Evangelist's first name
10. Dolores ____ Rio
    Yodel site
11. Tremendous
    Disburse
12. Meadow
    Farrow
13. Over there
    Marie or Jeanne
15. Tammany boss
    Cut
17. Also
    Indian weight
18. Leading
    Weird
21. Relate
    Klutz
23. Bait
    Preposition
24. Elevating name
    Soaks
26. Story start
    Follow closely
28. Consent
    Failure
29. Mountain pass
    Oxford teacher
30. Gait
    Ship part
31. ____ boy!
    Noisy
32. Year's record
    Penetrators
36. Animal
    Edit
37. Function
    Tower gp.
39. Peruse
    Hotels
41. Prod
    Bruin
43. Midway buy
    Soft drink
44. Ms. Turner
    Type of admiral
46. Mineral rock
    Greek letter
47. Relatives
    Linen tape
48. ____ Haute
    Earns commissions
49. High trains
    Golf mound

**DOWN**

1. Nervous
   Russian news agency
2. Body part
   Hockey star
3. Eastern VIP
   Evil spirit
4. Five-year period
   Small carnivore
5. U.S.A. colors
   Soap opera
6. Looking for a job
   Limping
7. Hebrew judge
   Born
8. Dressed
   Box
14. 12:59
    Western Union specialty
16. Put on TV
    Consume
17. Bikini, e.g.
    Argument
19. Sonata part
    Pass laws
20. Buck
    Removes errors
22. Other: Sp.
    Speech problem
25. Observe
    Stitch
27. Bits
    Woo
32. Rabbit food
    Wading birds
33. Destroyer
    Ruler
34. Make beloved
    Attack
35. Payable
    Corn unit
38. Demeter's counterpart
    Rub out
40. Ireland
    Scale part
42. Wormwood
    Poker pot
45. Picnic pest
    Make do

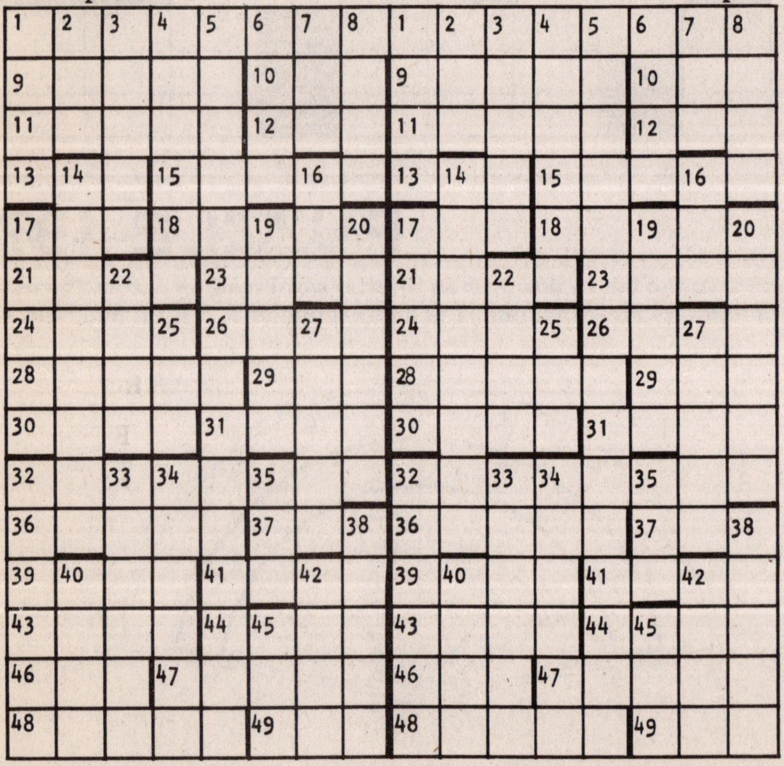

Note to Solvers: This Crossword does not have aids such as "2 wds." and "hyph."

# CODEWORD

# PUZZLE 499

**Codeword is a special crossword puzzle in which conventional clues are omitted. Instead, answer words in the diagram are represented by numbers. Each number represents a different letter of the alphabet, and all of the letters of the alphabet are used. When you are sure of a letter, put it in the code key chart and cross it off in the alphabet box. A group of letters has been inserted to start you off.**

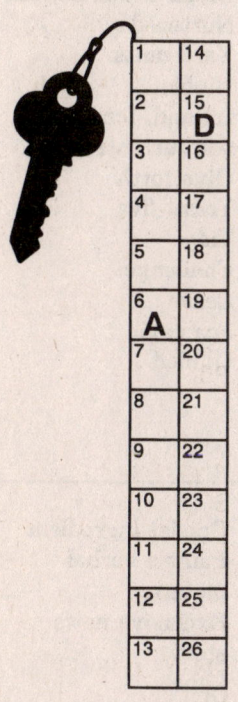

| | |
|---|---|
| 1 | 14 |
| 2 | 15 D |
| 3 | 16 |
| 4 | 17 |
| 5 | 18 |
| 6 A | 19 |
| 7 | 20 |
| 8 | 21 |
| 9 | 22 |
| 10 | 23 |
| 11 | 24 |
| 12 | 25 |
| 13 | 26 |

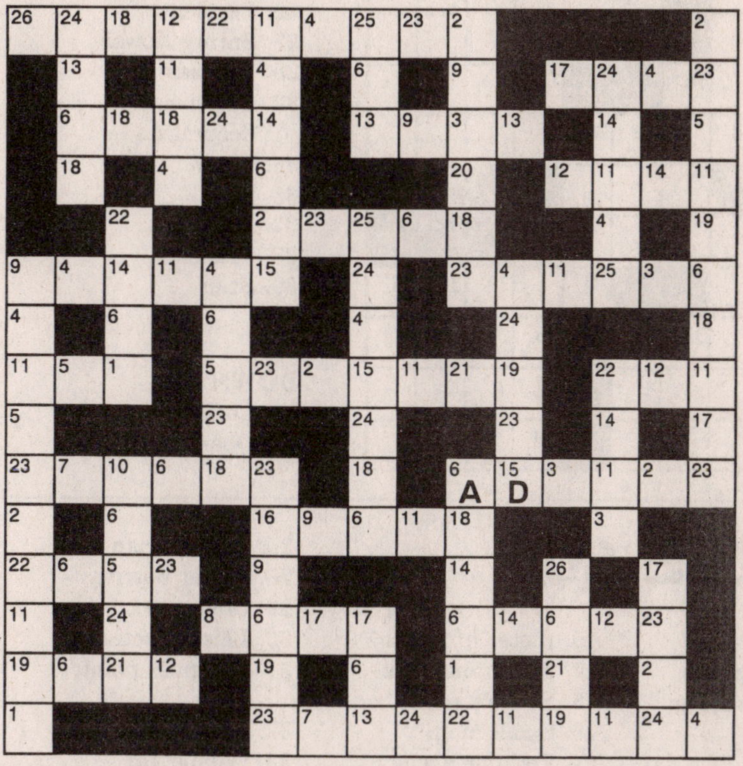


| | |
|---|---|
| ~~A~~ | N |
| B | O |
| C | P |
| ~~D~~ | Q |
| E | R |
| F | S |
| G | T |
| H | U |
| I | V |
| J | W |
| K | X |
| L | Y |
| M | Z |

# Ringmaster

# PUZZLE 500

**Place the letter groups in the diagram to form 24 five-letter words as indicated by arrows. The two-letter groups go in the circles in the outer ring, the three-letter groups in the inner ring. Two words have been given to start you off.**

**OUTER RING**

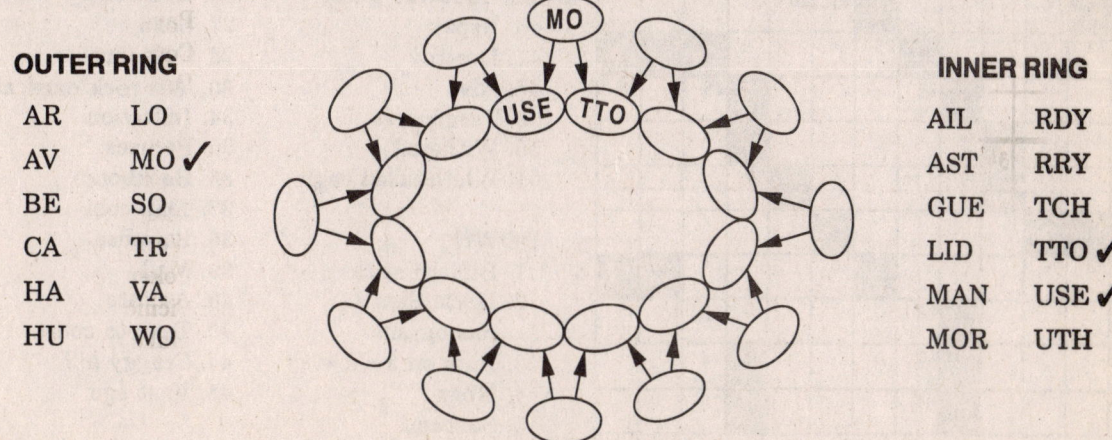

| | |
|---|---|
| AR | LO |
| AV | MO ✓ |
| BE | SO |
| CA | TR |
| HA | VA |
| HU | WO |

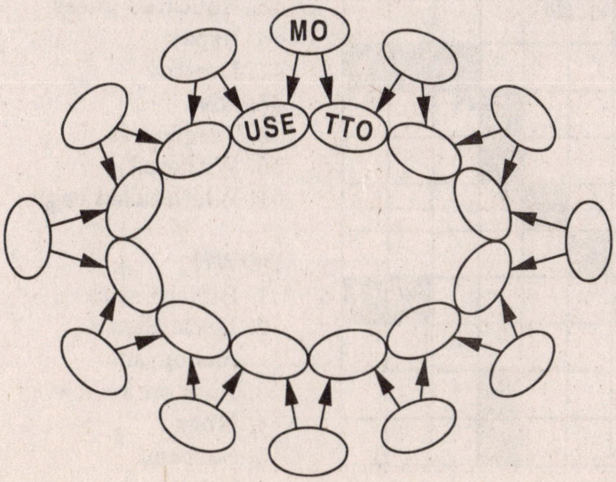


**INNER RING**

| | |
|---|---|
| AIL | RDY |
| AST | RRY |
| GUE | TCH |
| LID | TTO ✓ |
| MAN | USE ✓ |
| MOR | UTH |

# PUZZLE 501

**ACROSS**

1. Meadow youngster
5. Rapunzel's trademark

9. Vicinity
10. Spanning
13. Locate
14. Bronze figure
15. Artist's tripod
17. Ripped
18. Felt great pain
21. Actor Marvin
22. Perplex
27. Spring flower
28. Inclines
32. Christmas decoration
35. Chair
36. Last
37. Poi plant
38. Transmit
39. Stair

**DOWN**

1. Coffeehouse
2. Opera solo
3. Camera glass
4. Loses luster
5. Possesses
6. Behave
7. Angry
8. Helicopter blade
11. Certain
12. Plant-to-be
16. Break in the action
19. Nurtured
20. Yard units
22. Nibble
23. Ireland, fondly
24. Air currents
25. Give forth
26. Takes five
29. Tidy
30. Challenge
31. Cease
33. Sea eagle
34. Guided

# PUZZLE 502

**ACROSS**

1. Winner's trophy
4. Storage building
8. Stalk
12. Employ
13. Salary
14. Give a darn
15. Pieces of jewelry
17. Flirtatious look
18. Snake's tooth
19. Small room
21. Feel one's way
23. Snare
24. Dory propellers

25. ____ Marian
26. Water barrier
29. Chair part
30. Leisure activity
31. Compass point: abbr.
32. ____ Moines
33. Competent
34. Native of Edinburgh
35. Ascend
36. Glistened
37. Gobi, e.g.
40. Practice boxing
41. Brainstorm
42. Educated guess
46. Repair
47. Destroy
48. Also
49. Terminates
50. Withered
51. White-tailed eagle

**DOWN**

1. Billiard stick
2. Uncle Sam's monogram
3. Puts on a show
4. Hogs
5. Suspend
6. Omelet ingredient
7. Paint a verbal picture
8. Exclusive news story
9. Labels
10. ____ Stanley Gardner
11. Encounter
16. Tapping sounds
20. Gentlewoman
21. Prod
22. Unusual
23. Arthur's was round
25. Professional hoods
26. Embellish
27. Soon
28. Dole (out)
30. '60s rock musical
34. Imitation
35. Peruses
36. Backbone
37. Thin coin
38. Paradise
39. Mail
40. Agitate
43. Take to court
44. Craggy hill
45. Vast age

# PUZZLE 503

**• DON'T KIDD ME •**

**ACROSS**
1. Brace
5. Shade of blond
8. Lip
11. Nick's dog
12. Mauna ___
13. Tempo
14. Kidd's flag
17. Of an epoch
18. Casino employee
19. State
21. Small whale
22. Defeat at bridge
25. The Royal Navy, to Kidd
27. New York stadium, once
31. Holder for Kidd's loot
35. Asian salt lake
36. Pipe joint
37. Minuscule
38. Abet
41. Francis or Kendall
43. Causative agent
46. Antitoxins
49. Is put overboard by Kidd
52. Humorist George and family
53. ___ Amarna
54. Ponderosa or Scotch
55. Ruff's mate
56. Orange vegetable
57. Destroy

**DOWN**
1. Sajak or Nixon
2. Tennis great
3. Roman road
4. Indian princes
5. Whole
6. Vended
7. Rutherford or Helen
8. Storm
9. Cake finisher
10. Kidd's milieu, to Jacques
13. Shine
15. Norwegian kings
16. ___ Bareli, India
20. Second person pronoun
22. Depot: abbr.
23. Goof
24. Darjeeling or Bohea
26. Poet's before
28. Chop
29. Chemical suffix
30. Ingested
32. Exclamations of sorrow
33. Fraternal member
34. Necklace fastener
39. "___ De-Lovely"
40. Eccentric
42. Kennel sounds
43. Lose color
44. Helm position
45. Flightless bird
47. Track piece
48. Schoolmistress in "The King and I"
49. Armed conflict
50. Yale campus tree
51. Island

# PUZZLE 504

**ACROSS**
1. Sedan
4. Part of C.O.D.
8. Rotatable disk
12. Past
13. Nobel chemist
14. Repeat
15. Fairy queen
16. Raven's haven
18. Lion's family
20. Tolls
21. Capone's nemesis
23. Legitimate
27. Pang
29. Villainous
32. "___ Buttermilk Sky"
33. Cross
34. I.D. number
35. Fountain treat
36. Stir
37. Editor's word
38. Ivan or Peter
39. Scoop
41. Clarinet's relative
43. Singer Redding
46. Defeat unexpectedly
49. Wayward pedestrian
53. What one plus one make
54. Pulitzer prize-winning novelist
55. Prevaricator
56. Evening, to a bard
57. Deliver
58. Lively
59. Snoop

**DOWN**
1. Bivouac
2. Seaweed product
3. Famed archer
4. Dices
5. "Exodus" hero
6. Helot
7. London park
8. Extreme or intense
9. Driver's foe
10. Sounds of satisfaction
11. Destiny
17. Vendor's goal
19. Transfer legally
22. Virgo's mo.
24. Marching style
25. Robert or Alan
26. TV sitcom producer
27. Caspian Sea's neighbor
28. Musical ending
30. Contend
31. Involved with
35. Organ part
37. Bristle
40. Reduce
42. Covered with sticktights
44. Afflictions
45. Elide
47. Water jug
48. Marionette-maker Sarg
49. Poke
50. Iron or Bronze
51. Favorable vote
52. Lend an ___

# PUZZLE 505

**• FAMOUS SISTERS •**

**ACROSS**

1. Jazz dances
7. Outdated
12. Malaysian garments
19. Antenna
20. Of a branch
21. Fastening pin
22. The Brontes
25. Tennis player Richards
26. Group of Greek dialects
27. Therapeutic plant
28. Patriarchal nickname
29. Brain wave rec.
30. Dobbin's morsel
32. Young louse
33. Beams
35. The Gabors
41. Show Me State
45. Banking term: abbr.
46. Puma's sound
47. Star in Aquila
48. Tibet's capital
52. Scottish resort
56. Capp's Daisy ___
57. ___ acid
58. Genus of beetles
59. Vaudeville's Olsen
60. Drill attachment
61. Minnesota's capital: abbr.
62. Returner of goods
63. Sedimentary rock
66. The March sisters
69. Atomic attraction units
72. Captivate
73. Rend
76. GI's address
77. Set
78. ___ Gulf Resolution
79. Puts in position
81. Pod and dent starter
82. Belonging to Peer Gynt's mom
84. Racer Al ___
85. Uncompromising
86. Metallic element
88. Goat-legged god
90. Widespread
92. The Prozorovs
99. Predaceous insect
100. Career suffix
101. Prepare flax
102. Composer Franz Wilhelm ___
105. Expert one
108. Hired thug
109. "Hard" prefix
111. ___ alia
113. The Andrews Sisters
117. Expect again
118. Loire seaport
119. Abutting
120. Supergiant in Scorpius
121. Sabers' cousins
122. Literary works

**DOWN**

1. Consecrate
2. Giggling sound
3. Certain ape
4. Bog
5. Precambrian follower
6. ___-mo
7. Some metrical feet
8. Fielding heroine
9. Descendant of Shem
10. Levantine ketch
11. House extension
12. 1945 Yalta attendee
13. "Green Acres" pig
14. Clear by payment
15. "Three ___ Match"
16. Computer's ___ circuit
17. Actress Lollobrigida
18. Luge, for one
20. Map abbr.
23. Turkic language
24. Ancient Japanese
31. Assyrian deity
33. ___ Remo
34. Besieger's trench
36. Very large number
37. Roman streets
38. Okra
39. Deplete
40. Glacial ridge
41. ___-tai (Chinese liquor)
42. Afflictions
43. Editor's word
44. A Mariana
49. Ships' wheels
50. Indonesian island group, formerly
51. Medical specialist
53. Fondant-coated candy
54. Birch's kin
55. Cozy abode
58. Wheedle
62. Computer memory units
63. Copperhead, e.g.
64. Suitor
65. Prosper
67. "One million" prefix
68. Actresses Blyth and Sothern
69. Unleavened cracker
70. "___ Showers"
71. Attending
74. Piece of news
75. Persian fairy
78. Albacore
79. Calming agents
80. Dry, as wine
83. Giza sight
85. Trigonometry function
87. Neely of hockey
89. Certain lava flows
91. Golden oriole
93. Hungarian
94. Absence of social norms
95. Ermines
96. ___ Creed
97. Inform against
98. Goodnight girl et al.
102. Heart chambers
103. Flexible
104. Corners, in a way
105. ___ Harbor (Guam port)
106. French city
107. State, in Nice
109. Certain cookie
110. Blvds.
112. Promontory
114. Two, in Ayrshire
115. Cincinnati to New York dir.
116. Politician Beame

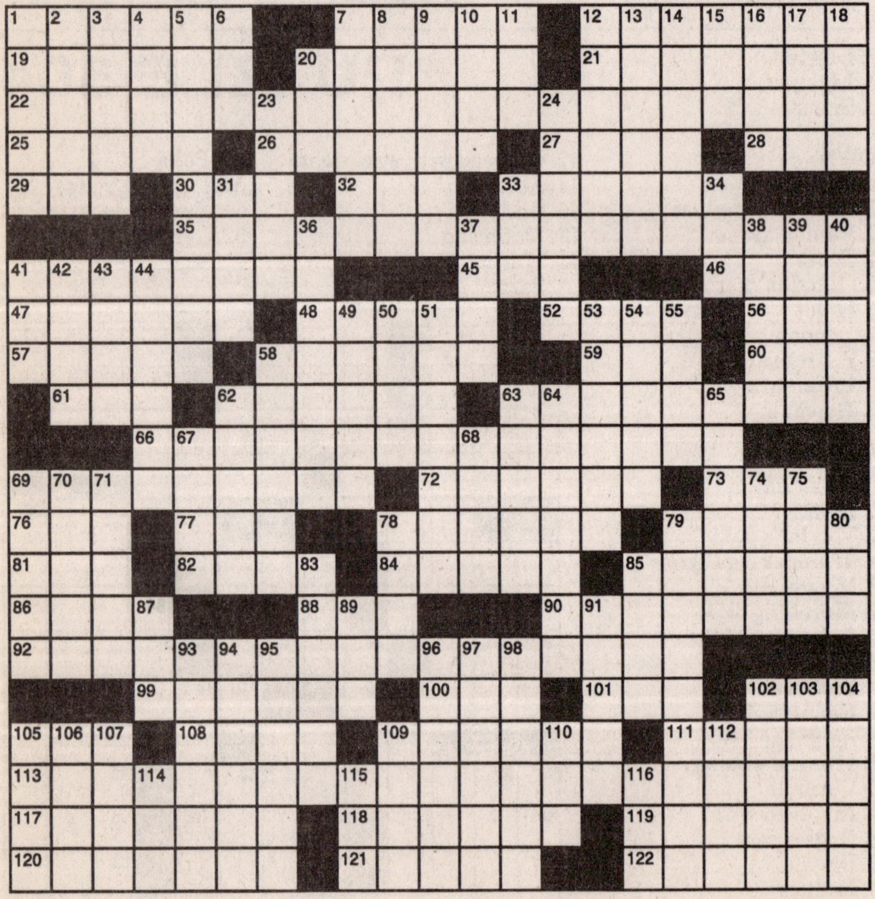

# PUZZLE 506

**• OF THE ESSENCE •**

**ACROSS**

1. Stare open-mouthed
5. Red-ink entry
10. Bullring cheer
13. Agenda tick-off
17. Parrot
18. Flooded
19. Points in time
20. Rustic crossover
21. Old song, with 69 Across
24. "___ Rookh"
25. Exclusive 100
26. Answer
27. Bee's pickup
28. Wee
29. Silvery fishes
30. Lapwing
31. Disorder
34. Vigoda and Fortas
35. Drained dry
38. Riata
39. Old song, with 50 Across
44. Guidonian note
45. Sound following a gaffe
46. ___-do-well
47. Items
48. Rip
49. NCO
50. See 39 Across
54. Kind of crayon
55. Hacienda lady
57. Like a galley
58. Got together
59. Cap
60. Onassis
61. Andrea del ___
62. Chateau rooms
64. Nimbi
66. Trial prints
68. Fish, in a way
69. See 21 Across
72. Scottish topper
74. Optimistic
75. Lounge around
77. Christie's "Death on the ___"
78. Opera star
79. Alliance letters
80. Old song
84. "___ a man who . . ."
85. Fuel for a torch
87. Imminent
88. Turn aside
89. Men
90. Bored
91. Go slack-jawed
93. Not so cool
95. Stiller's Anne
96. Very sensitive
100. Concorde, par exemple
101. Living it up
103. Send back
104. Ripened
105. Wife of Amphion
106. Israel's Abba ___
107. Exec.
108. Wire measure
109. Bancroft and Baxter
110. Impression

**DOWN**

1. Obtains
2. Hurt
3. Reporter's query
4. Vichyssoise base
5. Writer Runyon
6. Castle's place for linens
7. Nightsticks
8. Somewhat: suff.
9. Douglas novel
10. Exams
11. Gossamer
12. Native suff.
13. Like certain type
14. Old song
15. She: Fr.
16. Snide
19. City on the Rio Grande
20. Tapped the brakes
22. "How sweet ___!"
23. Biblical patriarch
27. Banana discards
29. Skier Phil ___
30. Deere product
31. Gator's cousin
32. Barrel features
33. "I'll Be with You in ___"
36. Happify
37. Found the nerve
39. Accustoms to hardship
40. Worm: pref.
41. Sun-god
42. My treat
43. Act
48. Role for Silverheels
50. French philosopher
51. Author Dahl
52. Gypsy's card
53. Dubliners
54. Yule song
56. Nice ___ (prude)
58. Keg
61. Overflow
62. Hone
63. Bellowing
64. Vagueness
65. Freshly
67. Collector
70. ___ nous
71. "___ me ae spark"
73. Dillon
75. Luxury boat
76. Singer Ed ___
78. Sidetracked
80. Star quality
81. Like some floors
82. Get word
83. Ristorante offering
86. Dialect
88. Mimicked
90. Chamfer
91. Sphere
92. Agalloch
93. Bard's prop
94. Through
95. Creche figures
96. Classical conflict
97. Poke fun at
98. "___ old cowhand"
99. Smallest of change
101. ___ it up
102. French department

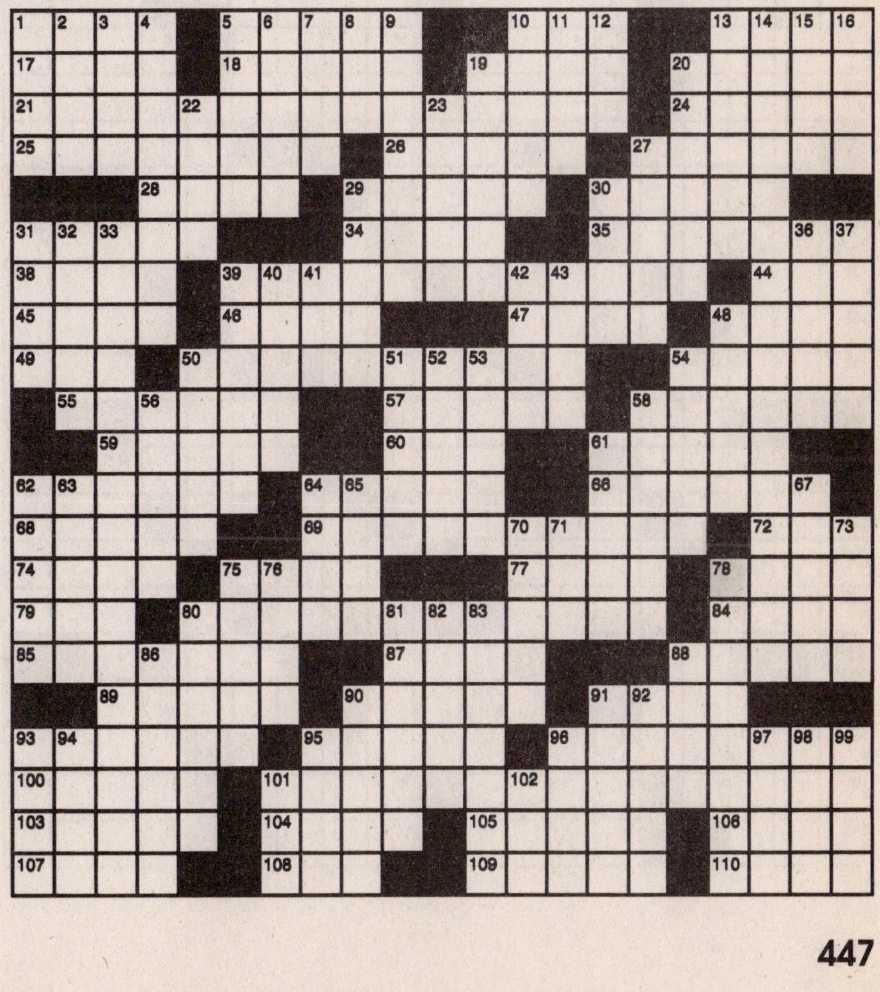

# PUZZLE 507

**• MUSICAL GREATS •**

**ACROSS**

1. Electrical unit
5. Multitude
9. Ring out
13. ____ Aviv
16. Roman road
17. Matty of baseball
18. Architect Saarinen
19. Drill
20. Type of skirt
21. Satchmo
24. Taker
26. Conservative
27. Stratagems
28. Does a gardening job
29. Window ledge
30. Uttered
32. Dwelling place
34. Sioux
35. Orchestra-leader Paul ____
39. Vehicles
40. At what time
41. Entryways
42. Vane letters
43. Cookie sheet
44. Joint
45. Golfer's helper
46. Bristle
47. Type of sofa
49. Alert to golfers
50. Hindu ascetic
51. Composer/orchestra leader
55. More ancient
58. "____ over Miami"
59. Recants
63. Needy
64. More foxy
66. "Strike up the ____"
67. Spanish queen
68. Building wing
69. Scoundrels
70. "____ Sit Under the Apple Tree"
71. Cut
72. Mr. Cab ____
74. Obey
75. Obnoxious plants
76. Sothern et al.
77. Billowy
78. Yip
79. Coeur d'____
82. Disconcert
83. Wish
85. Bop developer
89. Depose
91. Vegetable
92. Border lake
93. Snare
94. As far as
95. Ocean
96. New York team
97. Musical notes
98. German river

**DOWN**

1. Vigor
2. Of the ear
3. Female jazz great
4. Trivets
5. Rings of light
6. Swan genus
7. Old French coin
8. Fee for instruction
9. Oyster prize
10. Uncanny
11. Limb
12. ____ Angeles
13. Implement
14. Sea eagle
15. Table supports
19. Newlywed
22. Only
23. Nerds
25. Golf peg
29. Stalk
30. Fitted with shoes
31. Breezy
32. Performs
33. Surety
34. Chicago airport
35. Wednesday's god
36. Timid
37. Opposed to
38. Close by
40. Seven days
41. Singer Bobby ____
44. Incite
45. Hue
46. Of sound mind
48. German river
49. Floating ice masses
50. Affectionate
52. Pinky-extender Post
53. Magnificent
54. Canvas shelter
55. Oil-cartel letters
56. Kinks hit
57. Barbie, e.g.
60. Famed drummer
61. Camelot lady
62. Weakens
64. Stitched
65. Grasslands
66. Skinny
69. Nectar
70. Strips
71. Solemn
73. Opera-singer Mario ____
74. Labyrinth
75. Existed
77. Cardiff's country
78. Toots
79. Commotions
80. Similar
81. Poet Pound
82. Flutter
83. Clock face
84. This: Sp.
86. Jewel
87. Wrath
88. In favor of
90. Crag

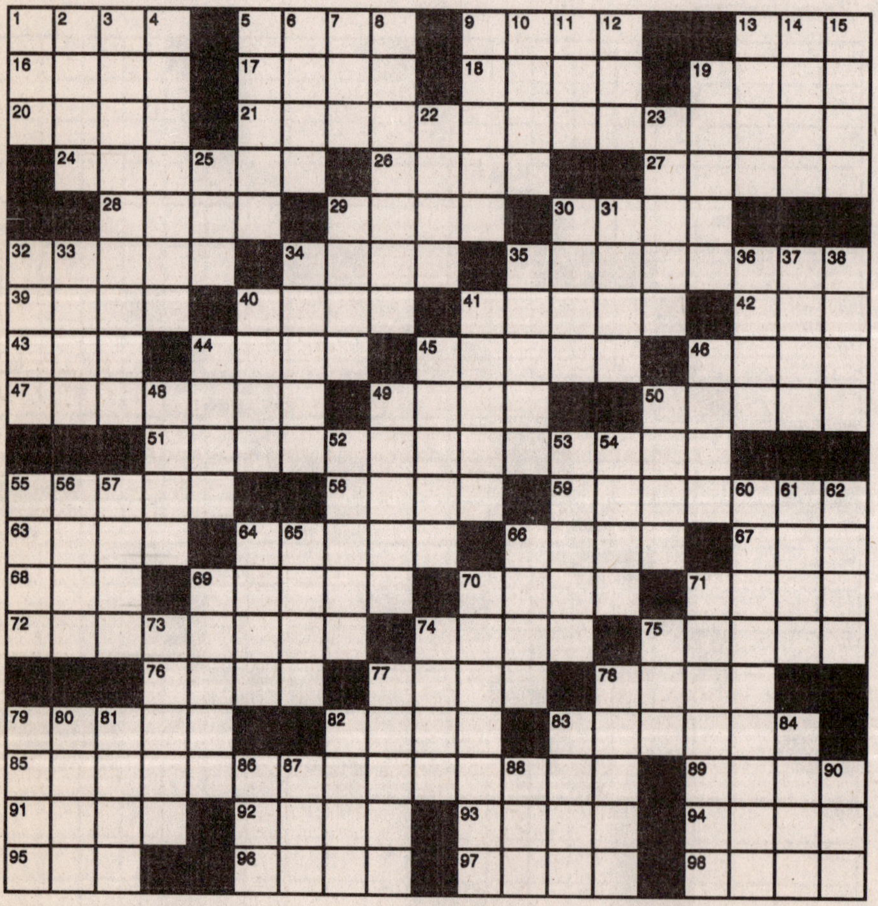

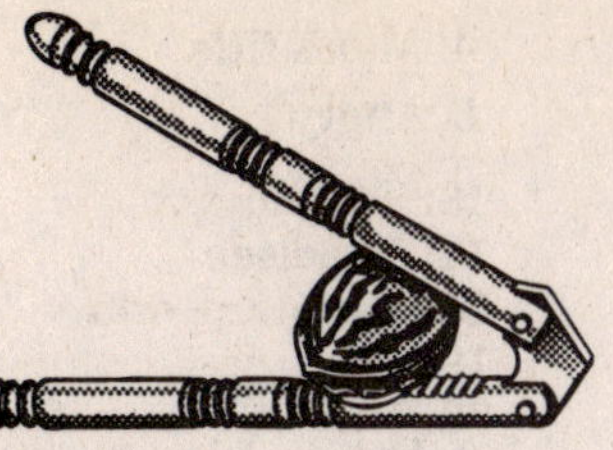

## NUTTY

# PUZZLE 508

**Here is a puzzle with more than the expected crossword challenge—and rewards. Each clue involves a pun or some form of nuttiness. Look out for traps! With a little practice you will soon catch on to these tricky clues and enjoy the extra challenge.**

**ACROSS**

1. They work undercover
6. Sunshade
10. Cut it out
14. Use a spear to take a sentence apart
15. Go around in circles
16. List heading
17. Rd. for Ms. Gardner
18. You hope to see his cousin after a while
20. Net the Hamilton
21. Work of a big author?
23. This is a warning!
24. Crazy type of stick and shtick
25. Cloak of authority
27. A twenty-sixth part
30. Mr. McCoy?
31. What do you say, kitten?
34. Ask any Frenchman what love is
35. This kind of paper goes in the circular file
36. Are you coming back in time?
37. Chicago, to Sinatra
38. They make a lot of hard cash
39. Be your own publicity agent
40. Hot time in Gay Paree
41. They turn a play into a musical
42. Give a lift
43. Buttons's color?
44. It puts zip in your mail
45. He gave a mad tea party
46. My, she was Fair on Broadway
47. Car-cleaning facility
48. He met a wolf in wolf's clothing
51. It's yesterday's roast
52. Scoop a pickpocket
55. Wrong type of sandwich for a poker player
58. Resident of the Society Islands?
60. See baby sit?
61. Not like doubting Thomas
62. Number of brides or brothers
63. Waves to a hairdresser
64. Went like the dickens
65. They can be made from onion peelings

**DOWN**

1. Taps on the row
2. Diamond setting
3. I came, I saw, I lost, ____
4. It's the end for the count's wife
5. He's got that pioneer spirit
6. Man from Hoboken?
7. It's just part of the acting game
8. This is the 12th epistle we've sent you about remodeling your house
9. Prophet or watch your Wallach
10. Don't get fresh with me
11. Walk around with a big chip on your shoulder
12. What nosy people might detect
13. Wine for a sailor's homecoming
19. Actor who was destined to reach the peak
22. It can help you get out of the doldrums
24. Nuts to you standing on your head
25. Ceases to blow his own horn for a while
26. Diet for the horsy set
27. What a Sooner can never be
28. Play too much of a part
29. Betrothed intention
30. Stove top to bottom
31. Timer, get your badge!
32. Rub the write 'way
33. "You Bet Your Life"
35. Stormy-eyed one, by Association
38. It's how you feel about it
39. Sitz just one of those things
41. Chow down dress accessory
42. Best bacon portion?
45. Laugh track tricks
46. Expects a return
47. Got your feed wet
48. Stop up
49. Aluminum foil, perhaps
50. Campy thing
51. This must be the place
52. Avid songstress
53. This way to the Colosseum
54. Cattle holdings
56. He's always in the last three-fifths of his class
57. Davis's mug
59. Eel turnaround

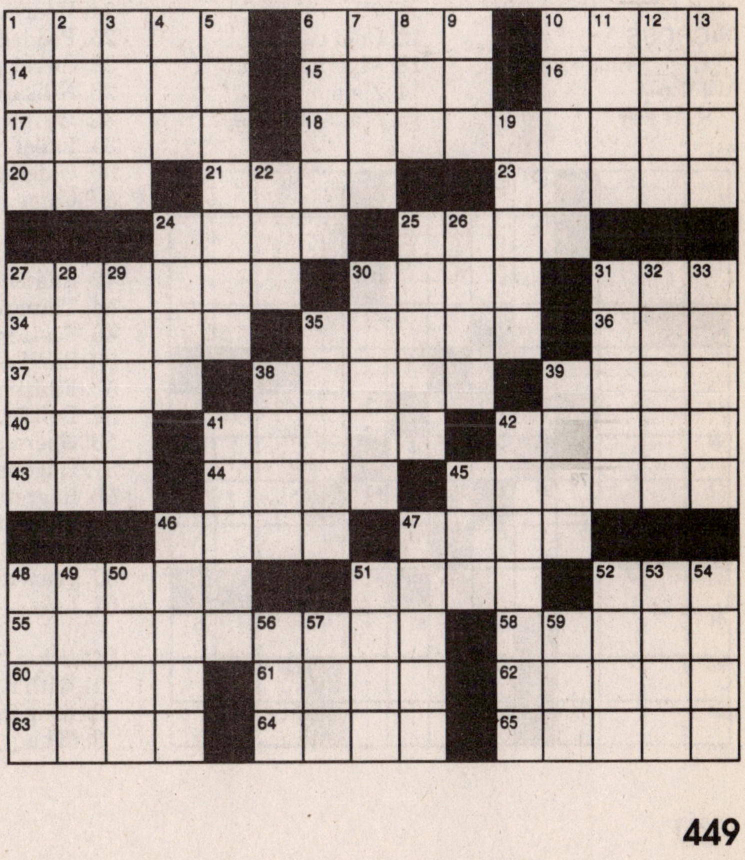

# PUZZLE 509

**ACROSS**

1. Settle a bill
4. Faction
8. Diet supplement
10. Weary
11. Rent
12. Speak publicly
13. Perform
14. Tank
16. Decade
17. Cry
19. Postpone
21. Scent
23. Goof
25. Slightly sour
29. Noise
30. Not many
32. Golly!
33. Wait for
35. Reflection
37. Bread ingredient
38. Giant
39. Care for
40. Diamond State: abbr.

**DOWN**

1. Bit
2. Subside
3. Sure!
4. Man's title
5. Angry
6. Hinder
7. Paradise
8. Defect
9. Accelerate
10. Indian pole
15. Worship
18. Woodland deity
20. Obese
22. Allude
23. Holy book
24. Shallot's kin
26. Playing marble
27. Stately
28. Adolescent
29. Foolish
31. Humor
34. Flop
36. Among

# PUZZLE 510

**ACROSS**

1. ____ and eggs
4. Step
8. Fewer
12. Cold cubes
13. Algerian port
14. Zone
15. Makes faultless
17. Bearing
18. Small bed
19. Hang
21. Stick
24. Hearing organ
25. Podded veggie
26. Sweet potato
28. Nuisances
32. Warbled
34. Label
36. Olden times
37. Come in
39. Buddy
41. Born
42. Snatch
44. Thumped
46. Scattered
50. San Francisco hill
51. Fibber
52. Deli buy
56. Opera song
57. Quiz answer
58. Regret
59. Alexander Graham ____
60. Transmit
61. Lair

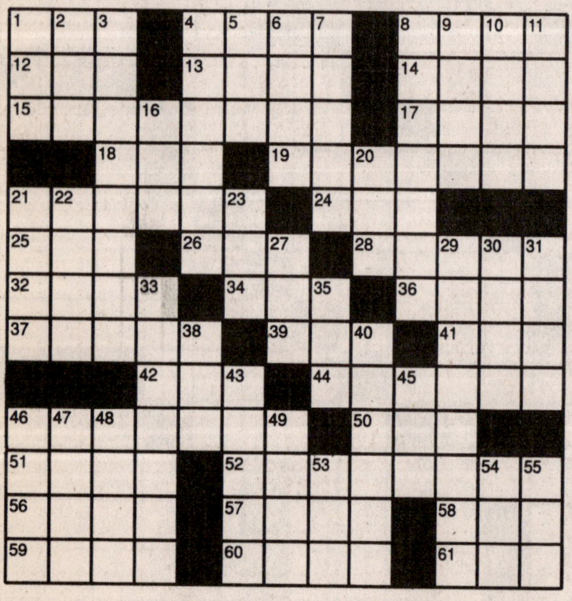

**DOWN**

1. With it
2. King topper
3. "The ____ of Venice"
4. Verse
5. Rainbow
6. Garfield and Morris
7. Follow
8. Eel
9. Great Lake
10. Observed
11. Beach material
16. Enemy
20. Pine juice
21. Church part
22. College head
23. Consume
27. Chart
29. Lark, e.g.
30. Maple, e.g.
31. Germ
33. Army officer
35. Chatter
38. Uncooked
40. Came down
43. Defeats
45. This minute
46. Thick slice
47. Car necessity
48. Train track
49. Challenge
53. Sister
54. Hint
55. Biddy

# PUZZLE 511

**• PEOPLE WITH CONNECTIONS •**

**ACROSS**

1. Humorous poet
5. "The first ___, the last prerogative"
10. Spiked clubs
15. Verve
19. Protective govt. org.
20. Janet or Vivien
21. In unison
22. Not any
23. Marc's exhibition site?
25. Frank's recordings?
27. Earth
28. Garbage receptacle
30. Agitation
31. Roundabout
33. Thousands of years
34. Rests
35. Apportionment: abbr.
36. Dynamite
37. More achy
38. Barbara Bel ___
41. Between the sheets
43. Free
44. Handle roughly
47. African lily
48. Piercing
49. Devour
50. Bristle
51. Portrays in words
53. Jesus: abbr.
54. Invitation inits.
56. Missive
58. ___ was saying
59. Latin being
61. Phrase of understanding
62. Late-day drizzle
63. Jack's title in '62, '67, '72, and '80?
67. Incapacitate
68. Declaim violently
69. Jug handles
70. Simian
73. Most attractive
74. Yodel
75. Hockey's Bobby ___
76. Theme
78. Dill
79. Bleat
80. Barber's service
82. Singer Adams
83. Gumshoes
84. ___ out (intimidate)
86. Ballet outfit
87. Credentials
89. Detests
90. Encountered
91. "___ good poem, see a fine picture"
93. Los ___
96. Gentleman
97. Check casher
101. High flyer
102. Went by
105. Classify
106. Harry's 1948 election outcome?
108. Actor Jack's film ads?
110. Storm
111. Lawn trimmer
112. Light measure
113. Russian city
114. Pindaric works
115. Donna and Rex
116. Banish
117. Beatty film

**DOWN**

1. Night: pref.
2. Pale
3. Fragment
4. Tormented
5. Malady
6. Choose
7. Falsehood
8. Taj Mahal site
9. Reasons
10. Army mule, e.g.
11. Type of flu
12. Neighbor of NY
13. Spanish queen
14. Bird dogs
15. Charm
16. Place
17. Tarsus
18. Cozy places
24. Eagle's abode
26. Pakistan money
29. Bandleader Skitch's vocalists?
32. Windpipe
34. Type of beer
36. Vietnamese festival time
37. Cleanser
38. Festive
39. Bulldogs
40. Music from Fats?
42. Motor coach
43. Embankment
44. With 104 Down, dance for choreographer Marius?
45. Solar disk
46. Conflict
48. Passageway
50. Check
52. Religious groups
55. Calendar abbr.
56. Annealing oven
57. Expunge
60. Variety-show segment
61. "No man ___ island"
62. Frighten
64. "___ Around" (Beach Boys)
65. Heep
66. Insect's wing vein
67. Search
71. Couple
72. Ogles
73. Bounder
74. Pouches
75. Grain
77. Dairy machine
79. Unplayed games
81. Shed
84. Flower part
85. More severe
87. Exploiting employer
88. Add splendor to
89. Greek herald
90. Tightwads
92. Glossy paint
93. Texas athlete
94. Mil. acronym
95. Standard measure
96. Full
98. Net
99. ___ on (urged)
100. Staggers
102. Capitol aide
103. She, in Arles
104. See 44 Down
107. After HST
109. Kubrick film, Roman style

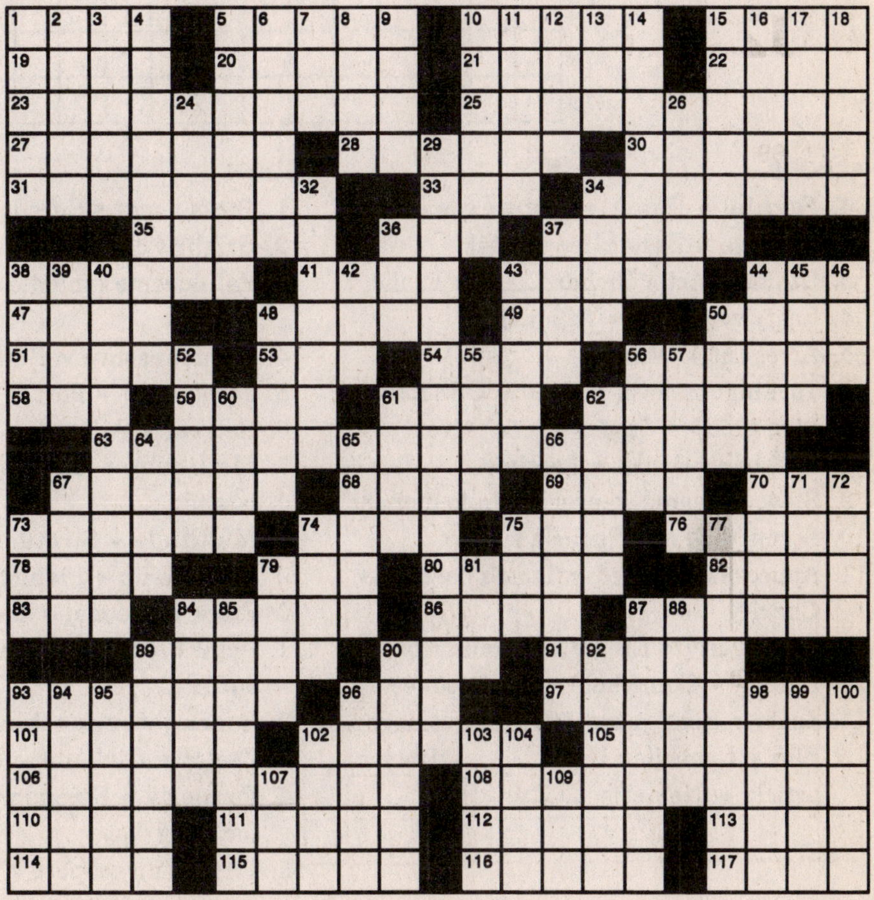

# PUZZLE 512

## WORDSWORTH

**Fill in each row and column of the Wordsworth diagram with at least two words. The number of words in a row or column is indicated by the number of clues. Words are not separated by extra squares, so all the squares will be filled in when the diagram is completed.**

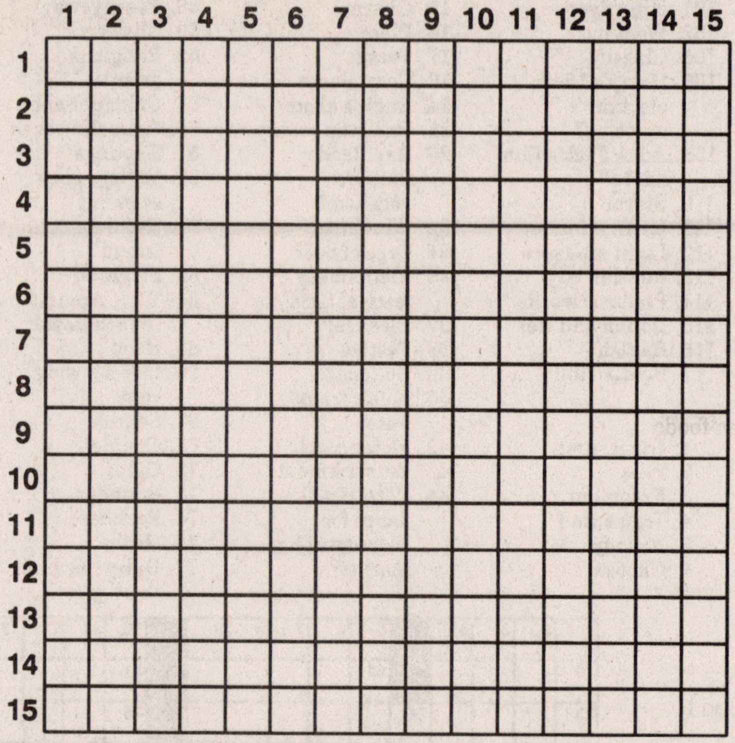


**ACROSS**

1. Faithful • Dowel • Pasture sound
2. Package • Zodiac lion • Task
3. Dillies • Actor Richard ____ • Frolic
4. Leafy vegetable • Affidavits
5. Arrogant • Weirs
6. Tarkington novel • Dine • OSS follower
7. Lion group • Stop • French river
8. Baseball's Banks • Pastime
9. Stew • Beanie wearer? • Auto pioneer
10. Scrub • Best • Fuchsia feature
11. Approves • Miffed • Time's partner • Charity
12. French city • Elf • Cooks outdoors
13. Python • Cubbyhole • Misfortunes
14. Zoom • Bear's cave • Orange variety
15. Flip • Comedian Louis ____ • French article • Nemesis

**DOWN**

1. Press agent • Speedy plane
2. Brightly colored bird • Store frame • Preposition
3. Palindrome's middle • Affectionate • Acting awards
4. Field measure • Boring • Augments
5. Foreordain • Part of EEC
6. Retreat • Auto part • Black
7. Math subj. • Cubic meter • Bend • Pierre's island
8. Multitude • Stratum • Faultfinding
9. Pick-me-up • Pianist Peter ____ • Draw • Scurry
10. Zip • Hoi polloi • Lawn tools
11. Actor Flynn • Ogden's state • Each • Chemical suffix
12. Super • Crock • Nourished • Athlete Lendl
13. Zealot • Civil unrest • Oily fruit
14. Formerly • Secondary • Bar none • Moon lander, for short
15. Ukrainian seaport • Perpetually

# CRYPTIC

# PUZZLE 513

**British-style or Cryptic Crosswords are a great challenge for crossword fans. Each clue contains either a definition or direct reference to the answer as well as a play on words. The numbers in parentheses indicate the number of letters in the answer word or words.**

**ACROSS**

1. Shrine also damaged by largest part (5,5)
6. Inside abstraction! (4)
10. Most favorable chrysanthemum — it points the other way (7)
11. Look in the direction of Toronto ward seven (7)
12. Appetizer against former goose egg (9)
13. It's said Hawaiian foods have tact (5)
14. Marx work is a piece of cake (4,4)
17. Good grade and $10 gold piece for Snoopy (6)
19. Profess to stir gel into ale (6)
20. Norse god captured by request for surplus (8)
23. Join traffic jam (3-2)
24. Express trains late? All but one (9)
27. Dignified by a state capital (7)
28. Save little Sir Edison and his company (7)
29. Looked at and listened to first person contraction (4)
30. Baking dishes broken — so careless (10)

**DOWN**

1. Broken toe dipped in fat acrobat's garment (7)
2. Eight trout, etc., originated upstream (5)
3. Wampum used to calculate returns (3,2)
4. Reportedly, Sherlock's play on words is common (8)
5. Portion lacks nothing in Ontario (6)
7. Bravery revealed by decoder ring document (7-2)
8. See the somber chateau stereo (7)
9. Crazy Pete swam to flea market (4,4)
15. Colonel has association with co-worker (9)
16. Assisi GNP ostensibly concealed by traveler's aid (8)
18. Sweeps away broken lens case (8)
19. Force taut cables to move over (7)
21. Eternal empress elegantly ascends (7)
22. Ivy League city covered with academia (6)
25. Sunlit scholar without small child (5)
26. Bring about end of travail (5)

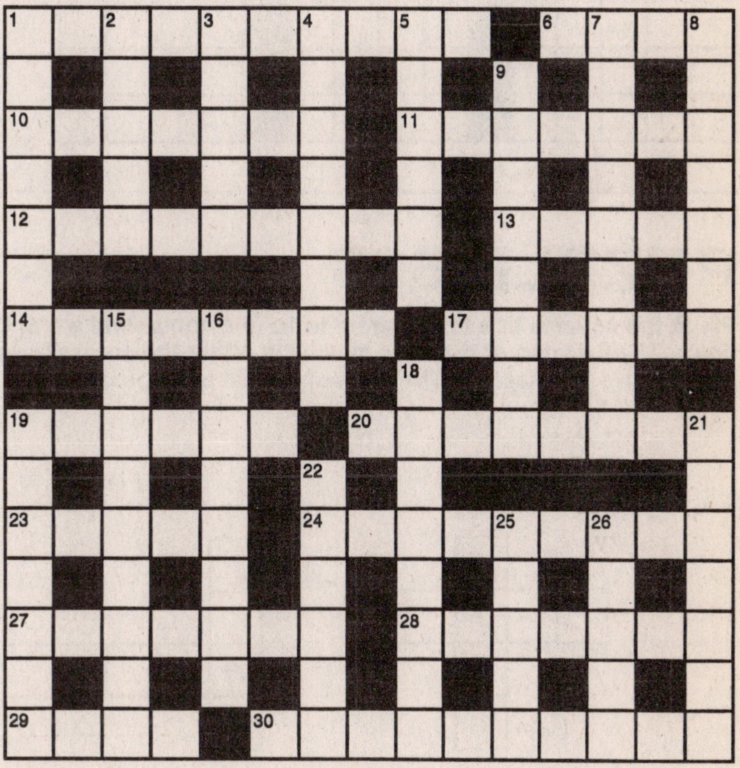

# PUZZLE 514

**ACROSS**

1. Phone
5. Ready a present
9. Fall flower
14. Largest continent
15. Israeli dance
16. Mothball
17. Raise
18. Culture medium
19. Dried plum
20. Large spiders
23. Actor Estrada
24. Function
25. Tumblers
27. Make tatters of
31. Certain horses
32. Throw
33. Do kitchen work
34. Links figure
37. Yen
38. Aspen incline
39. ____ and board
40. Pedal digit
41. Cut drastically
42. Insect stage
43. Dirt
44. Come in
45. Choir member
48. Health resort
50. Medicinal plant
51. Breakfast citrus
57. Two-wheelers, e.g.
59. Spoken
60. Cathedral part
61. Bakery chambers
62. Military group
63. Paddock youth
64. Of few words
65. Male offspring
66. Leg joint

**DOWN**

1. Two-wheeled wagon
2. Sailing
3. Prevaricator
4. Zhivago's love
5. "____ My Line"
6. Scoundrel
7. Asian sea
8. Essay segment
9. Common viper
10. Emphasize
11. Some are guided
12. Tennessee ____ Ford
13. Fumes
21. Unadorned
22. Schedule
26. Honest ____
27. Close
28. Star's role
29. Storm
30. Actress Arden
31. Came up
33. Like Marilyn Monroe
34. Tawny wine
35. Wander
36. Actor Sharif
38. David's weapon
39. Operated
41. Madrid Mrs.
42. Page
43. Golf areas
45. Wooden shoe
46. Martini garnish
47. Hearth tool
48. Iberian country
49. Skins
52. Florence's river
53. Pool-ball frame
54. Once ____ a time . . .
55. ____ of Man
56. Head: Fr.
58. Wind point: abbr.

---

# PUZZLE 515

## CROSSROADS

**Fill in the squares of each diagram to form a compound word. One part reads across and one part reads down. The first part of the word may be in either the across boxes or the down boxes. Use only the letters given above the diagram. The letter shown in each puzzle is shared by both parts of the compound word.**

**1.** E N O P T V W

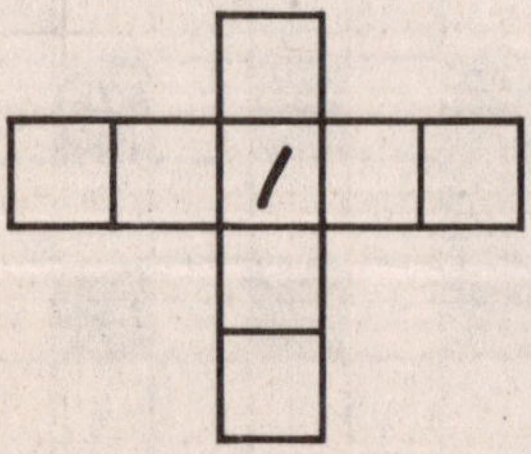

**2.** D E H O R R W

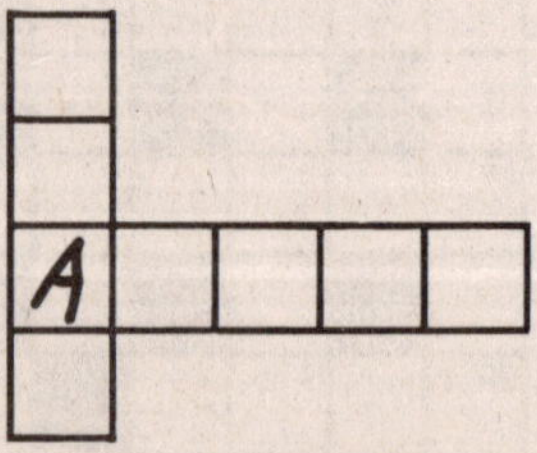

**3.** E I M M N R S T

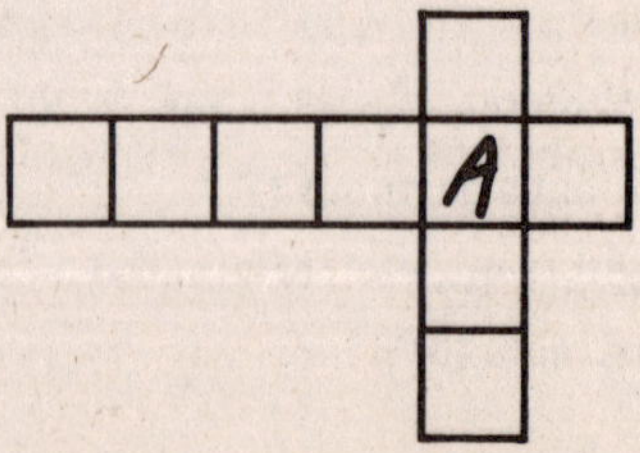

## BRICK BY BRICK

# PUZZLE 516

**Rearrange this stack of bricks to form a crossword puzzle. The clues will help you fit the bricks into their correct places. Row 1 has been filled in for you. Use the bricks to fill in the remaining spaces.**

### ACROSS

1. Enamel
   Brake part
   Patsy
2. Birch
   Listen!
   Irish river
3. "Dred" author
   Take turns
4. Sun
   Moon plain
   World holder
5. Up to
   Indites
6. Rook
   Vocalize
   Statute
7. Amalgam
   Stalk
   Sailor
8. Stray
   Blueprints
   Hue
9. Ms. Miller
   Well done!
   Slacks
10. Viet holiday
    Eternal City
    Carved gems
11. Ditto
    Hounds' prey
12. Let
    Ilk
    Ohio city
13. Hepatica
    Ingenious
14. Mr. Pound
    Goals
    Ills
15. Prophet
    Leg joint
    Wireless

### DOWN

1. Go by
   Gem weight
   Iowa city
2. Low voice
   Unaccompanied
   Take it easy
3. Baal
   Bias
   Small harp
4. Modern
   Molecule
   Yet
5. Quivering
   Melee
6. Porter
   School dance
   Sturdy tree
7. Portion
   Censure
   Victory
8. Robust
   Bondman
   Finely patterned
9. Table scrap
   Upright
   Steed
10. Make do
    Termini
    Limo
11. Gamut
    Co-owner
12. Blokes
    Gentle
    Eggs
13. Spoken
    Expiate
    Go-go
14. Tapir
    Poem section
    Food store
15. Golf pegs
    Curl
    Plus

### BRICKS

| | | | | |
|---|---|---|---|---|
| ONE<br>NTS | EZR<br>SEE | S■T<br>■PA | ACT<br>TAR | ALL<br>MAY |
| ■EV<br>■RA | ME■<br>E■H | CAM<br>ARE | ALD<br>STO | M■P<br>■BR |
| TET<br>■■■ | SOL<br>■■■ | RE■<br>E■P | ILS<br>DIO | ROA<br>ANN |
| ADA<br>VEL | RNE<br>ATE | ■AT<br>ENS | LAS<br>■■■ | EOS<br>■■■ |
| NG■<br>DE■ | RT■<br>■NO | ■SI<br>BLA | ■RO<br>SAM | HAR<br>ALT |
| IMS<br>NEE | OW■<br>FLO | A■A<br>R■K | CAS<br>ALL | ■MA<br>ABL |
| ER■<br>WE■ | K■E<br>ERN | LAN<br>AVO | ■SO<br>WER | TLE<br>OY■ |

### DIAGRAM

# PUZZLE 517

**• CLOTHESHORSE •**

**ACROSS**

1. Locks fixer
5. Quaker gray
10. Swollen
15. Do one's work
18. Seed covering
19. Numbers game
20. Harden
21. Quiz answer
22. Catamount
23. Texas plain
24. Effort
25. Kibbutz dance
26. Author Ambler
27. Spanish cookpot
28. Venues
29. Eatery
30. Save
32. Kind of baseball catch
34. Always
35. Ardor
36. ___ and file
37. Lashed
40. Go by
42. Model users
46. Colony dweller
47. Zest
48. Cost
50. Short cotton fiber
51. Aurora's counterpart
52. Lightning bolt
54. Poultry herb
55. Mediterranean island group
56. Requiem Mass hymn
58. Stir-fry
60. Lined with mother-of-pearl
61. Cultivators
62. Kind of drum
63. Famous tower town
64. Contract
67. Haitian rum
68. Put off
72. Tale tellers
73. Thrall
74. Baseball beginner
76. Lug
77. Landed
78. Look over
79. Range
80. White wine
82. Prop up
84. "She ___ to Conquer"
86. Proscenium drapery
87. Moon goddess
88. Down with: Fr.
89. Viragos
90. Miniature
93. Forte
97. Well-groomed
99. Peeler
100. Famous Texas family name
101. Church directory
102. City on the Dnieper
103. Coup ___
104. ___ cuisine
105. Phone
106. About
107. Actress Cara
108. Remove a brooch
109. Baby's perch
110. Actress Susan ___
111. City of Germany
112. Form of trapshooting
113. Kind

**DOWN**

1. Breton and May
2. City of Bolivia
3. Impersonate
4. Shiner
5. Licit
6. Eton, for one
7. Bari's country
8. Noted volcano
9. Kanga's child
10. Bird wings
11. Merge
12. Solders
13. Thwart
14. Of course!
15. Antler end
16. Entice
17. Twelvemonth
21. Studious frame of mind
28. Form
29. Force
31. Distastes
32. Eases up
33. Unusual
35. Noted essayist
37. Hightailed it
38. 5th-century pope
39. Church section
40. Fencer's blade
41. Muse of lyric poetry
43. Fly high
44. Flood, for one
45. Slithered
47. Mmes. of Madrid
49. Era
53. Hard journey
54. Make more acceptable
55. Spring hunt object
57. Straightforward
59. Cuckoo
60. Decree ___
62. Farm sights
63. Pig in a ___
64. Hefty chunk
65. Port of Hawaii
66. ___ at (scold loudly)
67. Hot or cold drink
68. Boston orchestra
69. "Miss ___ Regrets"
70. Zilch
71. Pitcher
73. Spunky fighters
75. Now I've done it!
78. Transmitted
79. Grave
81. Thick floor cushions
83. Rhino's implement
85. Relax
86. Touching
89. Hamper
90. Thrush
91. Joyce Carol ___
92. ___ one's neck
93. Jeweler's glass
94. Heavens: pref.
95. Machine gear
96. Realtor's sign
97. Lose control
98. Spiel
100. Aaron or Williams
103. Stamping machine
104. Czech reformer

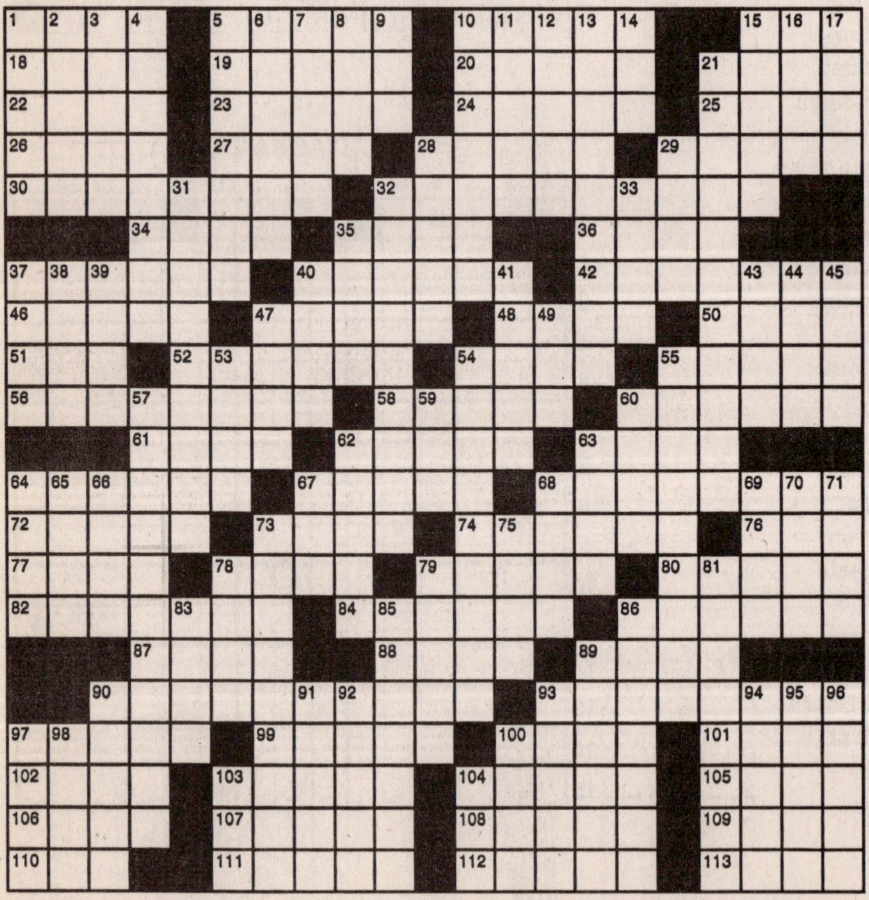

# PUZZLE 518

**ACROSS**

1. Chick's chirp
5. Surpasses
10. Competed
14. Regan's father
15. One of the Fords
16. Comedian Johnson
17. Too
18. "The ____ Mutiny"
19. Hatchet man
20. Court divider
21. Spring visitor: 2 wds.
23. Quiver
25. Disapproving exclamation
26. "A ____ with a View"
27. Cafe worker
32. ". . . ____ a tuffet": 2 wds.
34. Dissect a sentence
35. Likely
36. Exclude
37. Tithe
38. Wuhan's continent
39. Lend a hand
40. Questionable
41. Very small
42. Unequalled
44. Give up
45. Corn spike
46. Stripped sheep
49. Spring greeting: 2 wds.
54. Gabor
55. Gardner
56. Young chicken
57. Kitchen appliance
58. Spare
59. Edmonton player
60. Air hole
61. Gasp
62. Pep talk
63. Poker stake

**DOWN**

1. Aloe or agave
2. Lamprey hunter
3. Spring season
4. Money player
5. Strand at sea
6. Eradicate
7. Tizzy
8. Antler part
9. East Indian seas denizen
10. Less clear
11. Press
12. Thames school
13. Disclaim
21. Black
22. Quick lunch
24. Doubtful
27. Batons
28. Bohemian
29. Spring night: 2 wds.
30. ____ and polish
31. Remain
32. Detergent
33. Pierre's girl
34. Black-eyed veggies
37. In exchange
38. Verdi opera
40. Kill, as a dragon
41. Tavern staple
43. Rue
44. Bing or oxheart
46. Dark gray
47. Occurrence
48. "Inferno" author
49. Beatles movie
50. Neighborhood
51. Scheme
52. Song for Bumbry
53. Window section
57. Eggs

# PUZZLE 519

**ACROSS**

1. "Gorillas in the ____"
5. Soviet news agency
9. Mix
13. Run quickly
17. Redolence
18. Aleutian island
19. Type of hors d'oeuvre
20. Noted Italian family
21. Stewpan
22. Gather in
23. Singing brothers
24. Leading lady
25. Abound
26. Loathe
28. Communication
30. Snoop
32. Historical period
33. Society-page word
34. Fabric
37. By route of
39. Shock
43. Admiration
45. Noiseless
47. Stadium stratum
48. "Cakes and ____"
49. Encounters
51. More uncommon
54. Roofing material
55. Tales of olden times
57. Musical sound
58. Machine users
60. Person, place, or thing
62. Diminish
63. Fabulous
68. Molds
70. Slightly wet
74. Mellow
75. Songstress Della ____
76. Senior
78. Contend
79. Without dilution
81. Legislative body
83. Yearn for
85. Push, as a button
88. English river
89. At no time
90. Opposite of WNW
91. Halloween's month: abbr.
93. Weeding tool
94. Akin
98. Lure
100. Entangle
104. Door to ore
105. Statistical value
107. Rocker Billy ____
108. Hearty's partner
109. Food fish
110. Always
111. Lowland
112. Smooth
113. ____ off (angry)
114. Disavow
115. Zip
116. Legal document

**DOWN**

1. Theoretical
2. Not working
3. Shoe part
4. Stomp
5. Overdue
6. Fit to ____: 2 wds.
7. Condition
8. Act as boss
9. Fracas
10. Highlander cap
11. Unit
12. Begrudge
13. Dinner goodie
14. Spanish horn
15. All-male party
16. Roll-call reply
27. Cruise
29. Abundance
31. Atoll material
34. Shade of blue
35. Scandinavian city
36. Roman way
38. Of the atmosphere: pref.
39. Sprinkled
40. Yugoslav leader
41. Regan's father
42. Goes astray
44. Adult
45. Asian monetary unit
46. Take forty winks
50. Acknowledge
52. Obliterated
53. Sped afoot
56. Culmination
59. Weems or Williams
61. "... ____ the fields we go"
63. Magic stick
64. Arch
65. Wagon tongue
66. Utilize
67. ____-Lease Act
68. Private eye
69. ____ de la Cite
71. Tel ____
72. Entangle
73. Colleague
77. Nevada city
80. Handled
82. Years and years
84. Boiled
86. Id ____
87. Appeared
92. Type of pool
93. Lady from Troy
94. Engrossed
95. Mrs. Ernie Kovacs
96. Care for
97. Bird of peace
98. Strange
99. Soft drink
101. Rant's partner
102. Opposite of aweather
103. Await action
106. ____ of iniquity

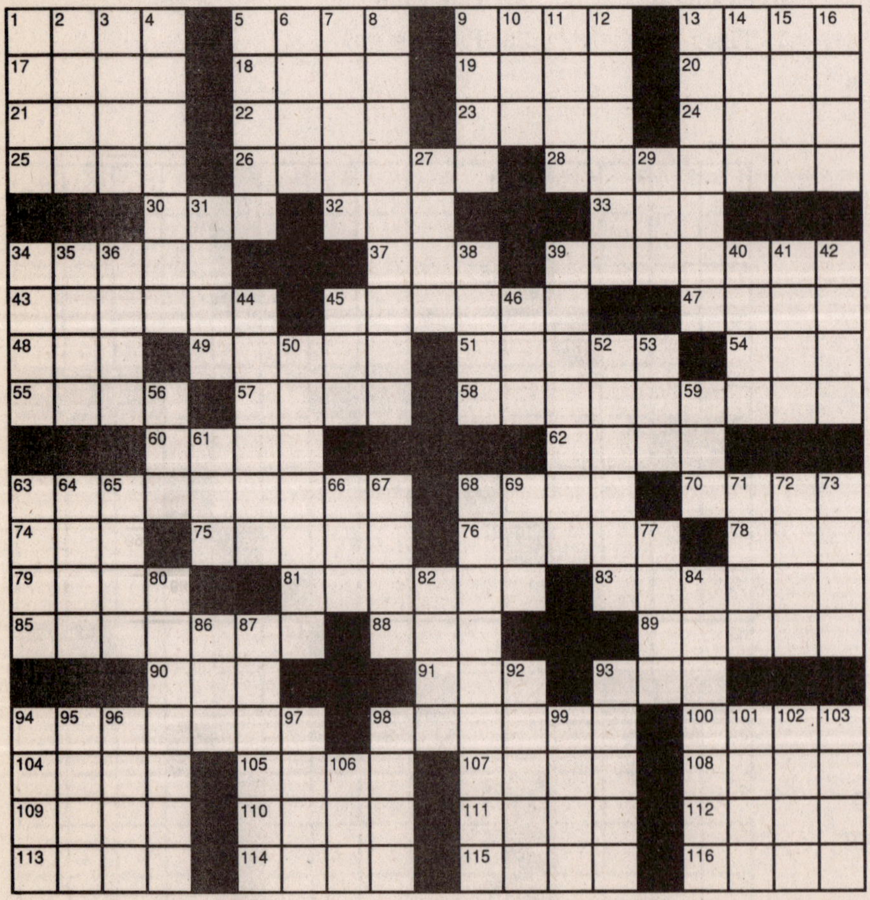

# PUZZLE 520

**• THE GOOD OLD DAYS •**

**ACROSS**

1. In good shape
4. Green veggie
7. Spring bloomer
9. Ring out
10. Old country-store feature
15. Gotcha!
17. Perfect
18. Cigarette leaving
21. Gets murky
23. Astronaut Grissom
24. Marcel Marceau, e.g.
25. Filch
27. Fragrant herb
29. Once again
30. Drink flavor
31. Actress Dunne
32. Pare
33. Word of disgust
35. Doggy doc
37. Ms. Lupino
39. Sci. room
42. The Greatest
43. Males
44. Historic period
46. Anger
47. Transgression
48. Pismire
49. Auto
50. Seine
51. Label
52. Lyric poem
53. Inquire
54. Auto fuel
55. Cleo's snake
56. Misdo
58. Spinoff of "Alice"
59. Sneaky
60. Tentmaker
63. Good golf score
67. Capital of Peru
70. Russian ruler
71. Wide
72. Play for time
74. To be: Fr.
75. Inventor Whitney
76. Mr. Preminger
77. Snaky letter
78. Trap
80. Sixth sense
81. Great-grandma's transport
88. Big defeat
89. Scottish hillside
90. Mr. Franklin
91. Comic Louis ___

**DOWN**

1. Evergreen
2. Lyricist Gershwin
3. Spasm
4. For each
5. Listener
6. Pub drink
8. Take to the slopes
9. Chum
10. Engraved gem
11. Mr. Poe
12. Utilize again
13. Bowl
14. Singer Frankie
15. Commercials
16. Parking spots for ponies
19. Old-time revivers
20. Chop down
22. "My Gal ___"
24. Ms. West
26. Old-time scent
27. Pony's mouthpiece
28. Garland for a wahine
32. Sunshades
33. Linguine, e.g.
34. A.K.A.
36. Go in
38. Windshield sticker
40. Of a zone
41. Ms. Ross
43. Chairman ___
45. Noah's boat
57. Johnny ___
58. Provided with lunch
61. Fen
62. Have being
64. Amphitheater
65. ___ Heights, Israel
66. Scottish landowner
68. Japanese statesman
69. Chummy
70. Golf gadget
73. Chop off
78. Tennis unit
79. Flow back
82. Sphere
83. Caviar
84. Old Sol
85. Vase
86. Joyous
87. Golly!

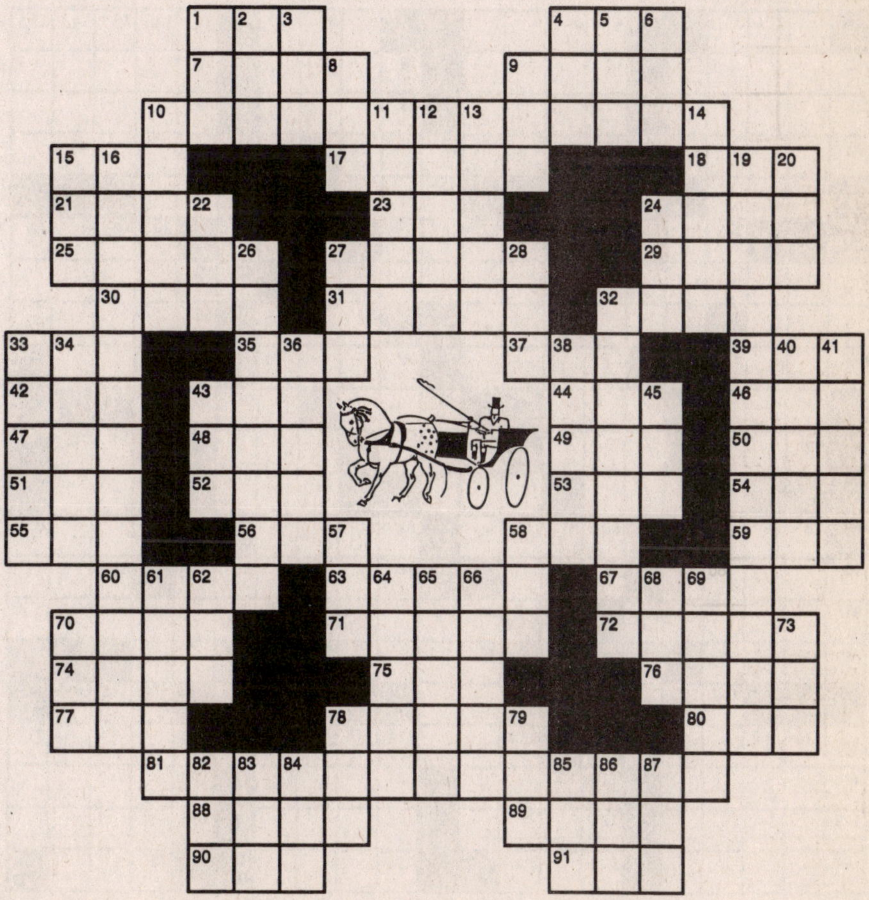

# PUZZLE 521

**• HOLLYWOOD •**

**ACROSS**
1. Punch
4. Questions
8. Soft food
11. Nerd
16. Street show
18. Brad
19. Stubbornness symbol
20. Audio device
21. Remove from a receptacle
22. Unoccupied
23. "The Sun ___ Rises"
24. Stews
25. "___ Mystery Theater"
28. Object
30. ___ Lanka
31. Fido's doc
32. Suburban ending
33. Gait
34. Haggard novel
36. Strange
38. Durocher
39. Schedule
43. Frederic March's 1936 role
49. Legendary
51. Constrictor
52. Hi-fi
53. Rearward
55. Pita
56. Shaw
58. Top-drawer
59. Essence
60. Smaller
61. Part of a yen
62. Auditing gp.
63. Zilch
64. Level
66. Work unit
67. Stout's kin
68. Zuider ___
69. Biol., e.g.
70. Torment
73. Rajah's lady
75. Bench
76. 20th in a series
77. Fuss
78. Facile
80. "High ___"
82. Ajar
84. Register
86. Commerce
87. Mail ctr.
88. Detective, at times
90. Nationality ending
91. Meander
93. 1949 Broderick Crawford flick
97. ___ fixe
98. Kin: abbr.
100. Popeye's greeting
101. Soak
102. Pour
104. Consumed
105. Baton Rouge campus: abbr.
107. Turkish general
110. Pulverized
113. "Cool Hand Luke" Oscar-winner
118. One at ___
119. Caesar's bad day
121. "Dies ___"
122. Positive terminal
123. Tooth
124. Air
125. Donated
126. TV, newspapers, etc.
127. In regard to
128. Superlative ending
129. Help
130. Old car

**DOWN**
1. Eyre et al.
2. Tree
3. Clumsy
4. Licoricelike flavoring
5. Former Egyptian leader
6. Oven
7. Luge
8. Beat
9. Jolson and Pacino
10. Humans
11. Cavalry unit
12. "Come and Get It" Oscar-winner
13. Ms. Adams
14. Grande et al.
15. Part of 87 Across
16. Covering
17. Breakfast fare
19. Principled sufferer
26. Occurrence
27. Ireland
29. "Fiddler on the ___"
35. Stockings
36. First address?
37. Bacchanalian cry
38. Departed
40. Spanish cheers
41. Brewed drinks
42. Sum up
43. Sleeveless gown
44. Scandinavian
45. Yam
46. Young animal
47. Stood
48. Cruise
50. Competent
54. Shelley's verse play
57. 1956 Best Actress
59. Large tart
62. Fleming
63. Unused
65. Rival
68. Kind of Buddhism
69. Turf, at dinner
71. Pertinent, to Cicero
72. Fowl
74. Genesis name
75. Combine
78. HS alum.
79. Disabled
81. Gemstone
82. Holy Roman emperor
83. Predator's quarry
84. Therefore
85. Cariou
86. Pod starter
89. Follow
92. New York canal
94. Most recent
95. Malcolm-Jamal Warner role
96. Wrench
99. Salad ingredient
103. Vigilant
104. Proxy
105. Holiday
106. Trapshooting
108. Hollow stone
109. Good-bye, in Milan
110. "I Remember ___"
111. Egyptian deity
112. Egyptian river
114. Baltic capital
115. Snatch
116. Thai river
117. Affirmative vote
120. ___ Plaines

**CLAPBOARD**

# PUZZLE 522

**In this crossword puzzle all words in the same line overlap by one or two letters.**

**ACROSS**

1. Accordion
9. "The ____ Incident"
14. Certain dollar bill
15. Mislead
16. Cowboy's show
18. Pound part
19. Proved human
21. Summer, in St. Tropez
22. Tips
23. 15th-century helmet
25. Italian peak
27. Skin growth
28. Greenish blue
30. Writer Anita ____
31. One-horse carriage
33. Man in orbit
36. Show position
37. Clogs, e.g.
38. Dispatches
41. Faun
44. In what way?
45. Roam
46. Rest
47. Wooden box
49. Lakers, e.g.
50. French impressionist
52. Pekoe
53. Embankment
54. Hammed it up
57. College residence
60. Exceeded
62. Unbeatable opponent
65. Rotate
66. Entitles
67. Comfort
68. Pianist Myra ____
69. Resorts
70. Step
71. Fink

**DOWN**

1. "The Taming of the ____"
2. Proportions
3. Riptide
4. Eve's home
5. Eat
6. Hera's husband
7. Author Ferber
8. Darken
9. Spotted wildcats
10. Sherry
11. Nativity
12. Kitchen appliance
13. Tied the knot
17. Beg
20. Reveries
23. Reasonable
24. Director Pakula
26. Not any
27. Small towel
29. Goddess of dawn
31. Designed
32. Strike
34. Coast
35. Wildflowers
38. Look of derision
39. Waxed cheese
40. Mild oath
41. Japanese coin
42. Dorothy's dog
43. Belgian river
45. Shows doubt
48. Stage offering
49. Sea birds
51. Verne hero
55. "That's My ____"
56. Trial
57. Food store
58. Glacial ridges
59. Costa ____
61. Ice Cube's forte
63. Flightless bird
64. Established

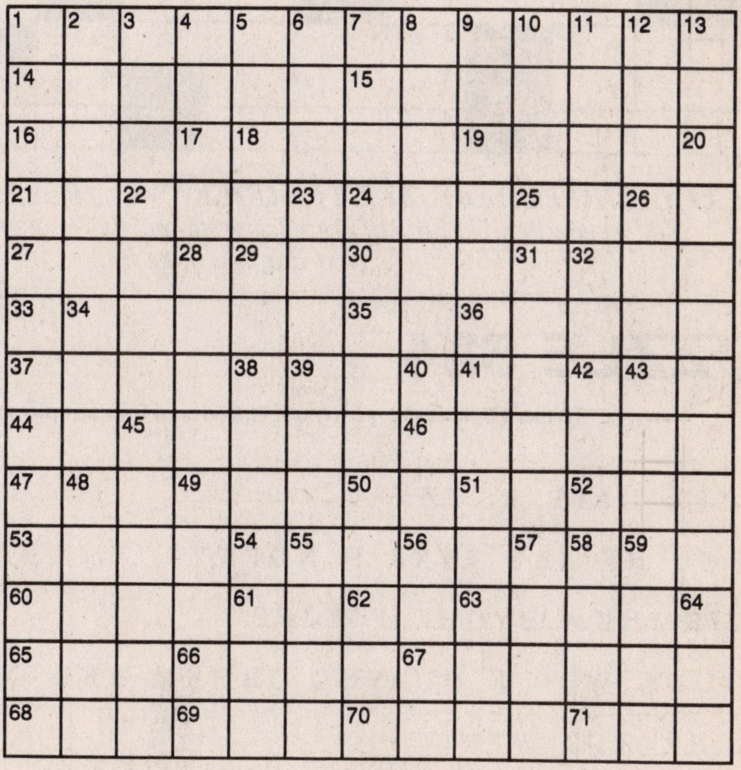

# PUZZLE 523

## DOUBLE TROUBLE

**Not really double trouble, but double fun! Solve this puzzle as you would a regular crossword, EXCEPT place one, two, or three letters in each box. The number of letters in each answer is shown in parentheses after its clue.**

**ACROSS**

1. Nursery rhyme shepherdess (6)
4. Error (5)
7. Condescends (6)
10. Scent (5)
11. Florida city (5)
12. Pinkish yellow (5)
13. Traveler's goal (11)
15. Be in first place (4)
16. Is able to (3)
18. Permit (3)
19. Sports building (5)
21. Manner (4)
23. Familiar with (4)
25. Hippo follower (5)
27. Marry on the sly (5)
28. Sorrow (5)
30. Slanted (5)
32. Legislative assembly (6)
34. Tender (4)
35. Dollars (4)
36. Copenhagen native (4)
38. Snake's weapon (4)
40. Paving material (3)
41. Excuse (5)
43. Irrelevant (11)
46. Banana ___ (5)
47. Customary practice (4)
48. Large families (6)
51. Simple (4)
52. Equipment (4)
53. Alternate route (6)

**DOWN**

1. Large snake (3)
2. Counterpart (4)
3. Hair goo (6)
4. Layering (10)
5. Porch (5)
6. College class (7)
7. Statement (11)
8. Leave out (6)
9. Dinner course (5)
14. Fence steps (5)
16. Dromedary (5)
17. Rope loop (5)
20. Finale (3)
22. Trustworthiness (13)
24. Conservatives (6)
26. Egg dish (6)
29. Hand digit (10)
31. Despot (4)
33. Egyptian sun god (4)
37. Develop (6)
39. Corners (6)
41. Sailing (4)
42. Brims (4)
44. Singer Baker (5)
45. Step (6)
49. Wager (3)
50. Vinegary (4)

★ ***LOOKING FOR DOUBLE TROUBLE?*** *You've found it! Treat yourself to* ★
*special collections of your favorite puzzles—over 50 in each!*
*To order, see page 63.*

# PUZZLE 524

## CRYPTO-VERSE

**To read this verse, you must first solve this simple substitution code.**

XJFPX UAYP XKUZ,

FKL HK JBY ZYXJ F NOFKYJ

XZHKMHKM SYOUZ F XJFP —

OUUE WUP F OUAYOQ JBHKM FKL QUC ZHOO WHKL HJ,

HJ HX KUJ WFP —

HJ KYAYP ZHOO SY WFP.

# PUZZLE 525

**ACROSS**
1. Tropical plant
5. Festive party
9. Read hastily
13. "Un Bel Di," e.g.
14. Fashion magazine
15. Cavities
17. Small parrot
19. More wintry
20. Have obligations
21. Scottish hillside
22. Turkish capital
23. Govt. sleuth gp.
24. Divided Asian land
26. Satirical mimicry
29. Comedienne Carol ____
33. Linen vestment
34. Grope
36. Three, in Ulm
37. Ooze
38. End
39. Restrain
40. Prefix for physical
41. Whetstone
42. Instruct privately
43. Asian ocean
45. Convicts
46. Les ____-Unis
48. Cuba: abbr.
49. Backslide
52. Agreement
54. Lanes: abbr.
57. Stop suddenly
58. Wildly gleeful
60. Ancient Greek area
61. Throw forcefully
62. Annapolis sch.
63. Hunt for
64. Suits to ____
65. Role for Kinski

**DOWN**
1. Mexican food
2. Queued up
3. Oriental staple
4. Furniture wood
5. Snitch on
6. Goddess of wisdom
7. Polished
8. Daughter of Loki
9. Small silvery fish
10. Kind of story
11. Inter ____
12. Not ever, poetically
16. Madrid Mrs.
18. Tolerate
22. As ____
23. Scottish soup
25. Overweight
26. Balearic capital
27. Arabian chieftain
28. Lasso
30. Muse of poetry
31. Wyoming range
32. Rows
34. Parade feature
35. Age
38. Con artist
42. Oat grain cover, e.g.
44. Lightning bolt
45. Inconstant
47. Nozzle
49. Baseball stat
50. Love god
51. Wind-direction indicator
53. Israeli seaport
54. Rambler of song
55. Puts on
56. Evian and Vichy
58. Half of a Latin dance
59. Shanty

# RINGMASTER

# PUZZLE 526

**Place the letter groups in the diagram to form 24 five-letter words as indicated by arrows. The two-letter groups go in the circles in the outer ring, the three-letter groups in the inner ring. Two words have been given to start you off.**

**OUTSIDE RING**

| | |
|---|---|
| AL | HE |
| AW | HO |
| BE | PR |
| CO | RE |
| DO | SH |
| GR✓ | ST |

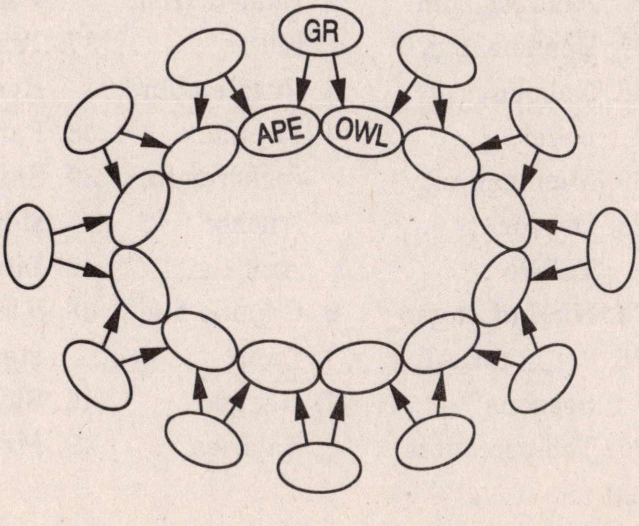


**INSIDE RING**

| | |
|---|---|
| ACH | LOW |
| APE✓ | NOR |
| ARD | OUD |
| ARE | OUT |
| AST | OWL✓ |
| DGE | VEL |

# PUZZLE 527

**ACROSS**

1. Summer in Saumur
4. Stick or happy
8. Smoke unit
12. Core
16. Charlie Brown oath
18. Pike fee
19. Con
20. Grimm heavy
21. Highfalutin
23. Guided inspection
25. Watering holes
26. Not windward
28. Greek mixing bowl
29. Equip
30. Summer coolers
31. Conspire
32. Actress Uta
35. Bucks
36. Shipping sites
40. "___ Town"
41. Plays to the crowd
44. Actor Carmichael
45. Greek letters
47. Tax shelter: abbr.
48. Onager sound
49. Sheep site
50. Shakespeare works
52. Cook, in a way
54. Primitive plants
55. Motivator Carnegie
56. Full and blue
57. Rigel, e.g.
58. Tuns
60. Author Bret
61. Cary Grant film
64. Tiger or Easter
65. Hereditary unit
66. Ursula Andress film
67. Bowline, e.g.
68. Nabokov novel
69. Michigan city
73. Day, in Toledo
74. Kind of sugar
76. "___ for All Seasons"
77. Ten-percenter
79. Air
80. Raceway gait
81. Neighbor of Ga.
82. Saw eye to eye
85. Spotted
86. Coast
90. Tsar's son
92. Car race
94. Carry on
95. Similar
96. Convinced
97. ___ Valley, California
98. "Lucky Jim" author
99. Gainsay
100. Curling marks
101. Hollywood locale

**DOWN**

1. Work units
2. Famed Irish hill
3. Puzzle abbr.
4. Popular rocker-actor
5. Author Anita ___
6. Capone and Capp
7. Begged
8. Salaries
9. As to
10. Terminal: abbr.
11. Cocktail
12. Spud
13. "___ the Sun in the Morning"
14. Faithful
15. Munster mister
17. Saw wood
22. Exploit
24. Decreases
27. Minus
30. "___ Christie"
31. Code or colony
32. Cultivates, in a way
33. Self: pref.
34. Bridge shutout
35. Trireme propellers
36. New Delhi wear
37. Texas-border river
38. Farewell
39. Snick's sidekick
42. Liturgy
43. Kind of steak
46. Sinuous
49. Mr. Kent

# PUZZLE 527

51. Raised railways
52. Feeling ennui
53. Poppycock
54. ___ glance
56. Heavenly fare
57. Storage structure
58. Attired
59. Assistant
60. Soul's mate
61. Shoot the breeze
62. Slay
63. French state
65. Family patriarch
66. Wee row
69. Avarice
70. Underdone
71. Included in
72. Waldorf ___
75. Track-meet units
78. Pants
80. Itsy
81. Wards off
82. Taj Mahal site
83. Small weight
84. Punjab princess
85. ___ and bones
86. Vendition
87. Rainbow
88. Thin coin
89. Egress
91. Hawaiian instrument, for short
93. Caviar

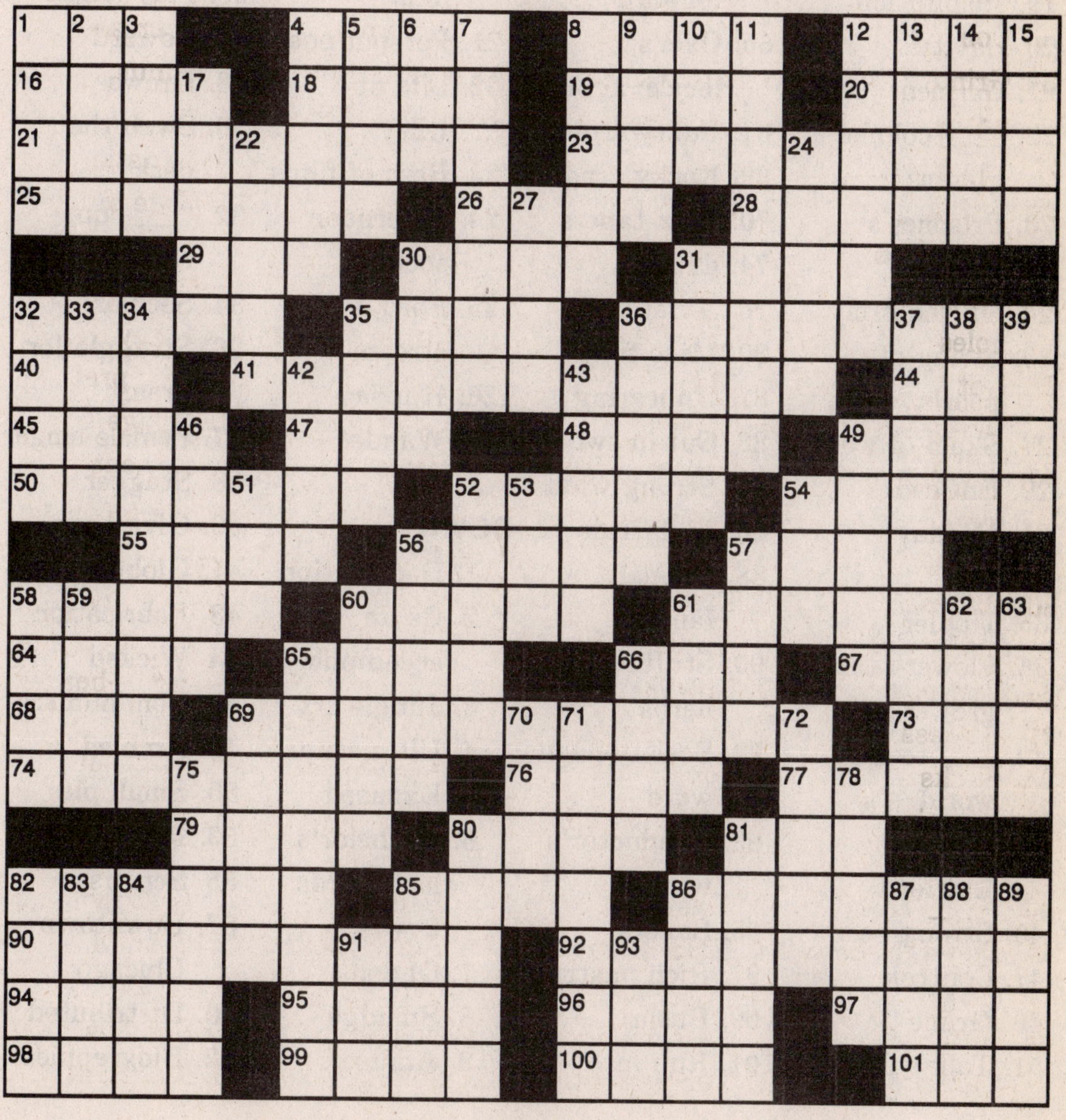

# PUZZLE 528

**ACROSS**

1. Shortening
5. Needles and ____
9. Bugle call
13. Scorch
17. Woodwind instrument
18. Actor West
19. Inspiration
20. Cavity
21. Garment joint
22. ____-colored glasses
23. Prisoner's room
24. On the briny
25. String of pearls
27. Skein of wool
29. Enticed
31. Midday
33. Bun
35. Tippler
36. Flower grower
40. ____ to the world
42. Actor Lawford
46. Strong beer
47. Control
49. Grime
51. Talk wildly
52. Goblet feature
54. Fiend
56. Anthracite
58. Pot cover
59. Warsaw residents
61. Competitor
63. Pushes forward
65. Oslo's locale: abbr.
67. Lukewarm
69. Rocky crag
70. Wax tapers
74. Cruel
76. Aviator
80. Mine find
81. Unhearing
83. Cut in two
85. Strong wind
86. Light rain
88. Dismal failure
90. Stuffing herbs
92. Society-page word
93. Conductor's wand
95. Sailors
97. Rich pastry
99. Basin
101. Run into
103. Ore vein
104. Gab
108. Legumes
110. Infant's toy
114. Employ
115. "Whatever ____ Wants"
117. Sulk
119. Amphibian
120. "____ in My Heart" (1933 Stanwyck film)
121. Persian poet
122. Life of Riley
123. Best of films
124. Afternoon socials
125. Ford a stream
126. Hurried
127. Wander

**DOWN**

1. Deprivation
2. Be an accomplice
3. Jungle cry
4. Ultimatum
5. Excused
6. Bachelor's last words: 2 wds.
7. Ogden ____
8. Smudge
9. Amused
10. Hoosier humorist
11. Untanned hide
12. Business transactions
13. Novel division
14. Party giver
15. Toward shelter
16. Peruse
26. Playwright Coward
28. Drowse
30. Swab the deck
32. "____ on Sunday"
34. Secular
36. Struggle for breath
37. Female singer
38. Stagger
39. Give back
41. Globule
43. Fabrication
44. Wicked
45. Communists
48. Ambled
50. Small pie
53. Repair
55. Scruffs
57. Downtown Chicago
60. Distributed
62. Biographies

# PUZZLE 528

64. Bluenose
66. Sandbar
68. Sofa
70. Rooster's crest
71. Opera song
72. Nidify
73. Sea mineral
75. Lawful
77. Highway division
78. Table spread
79. Bopper
82. Suds
84. Divulged
87. Walks uncertainly
89. Get ready
91. Fizz water
94. Pecan, e.g.
96. Diocese
98. Epistle
100. Beneath
102. Records
104. Mr. Huntley
105. Busy place
106. Length times width
107. "Arrivederci ___"
109. TV serial
111. Commotion: hyph.
112. Actress Turner
113. Dutch treat
116. Shaver
118. Function

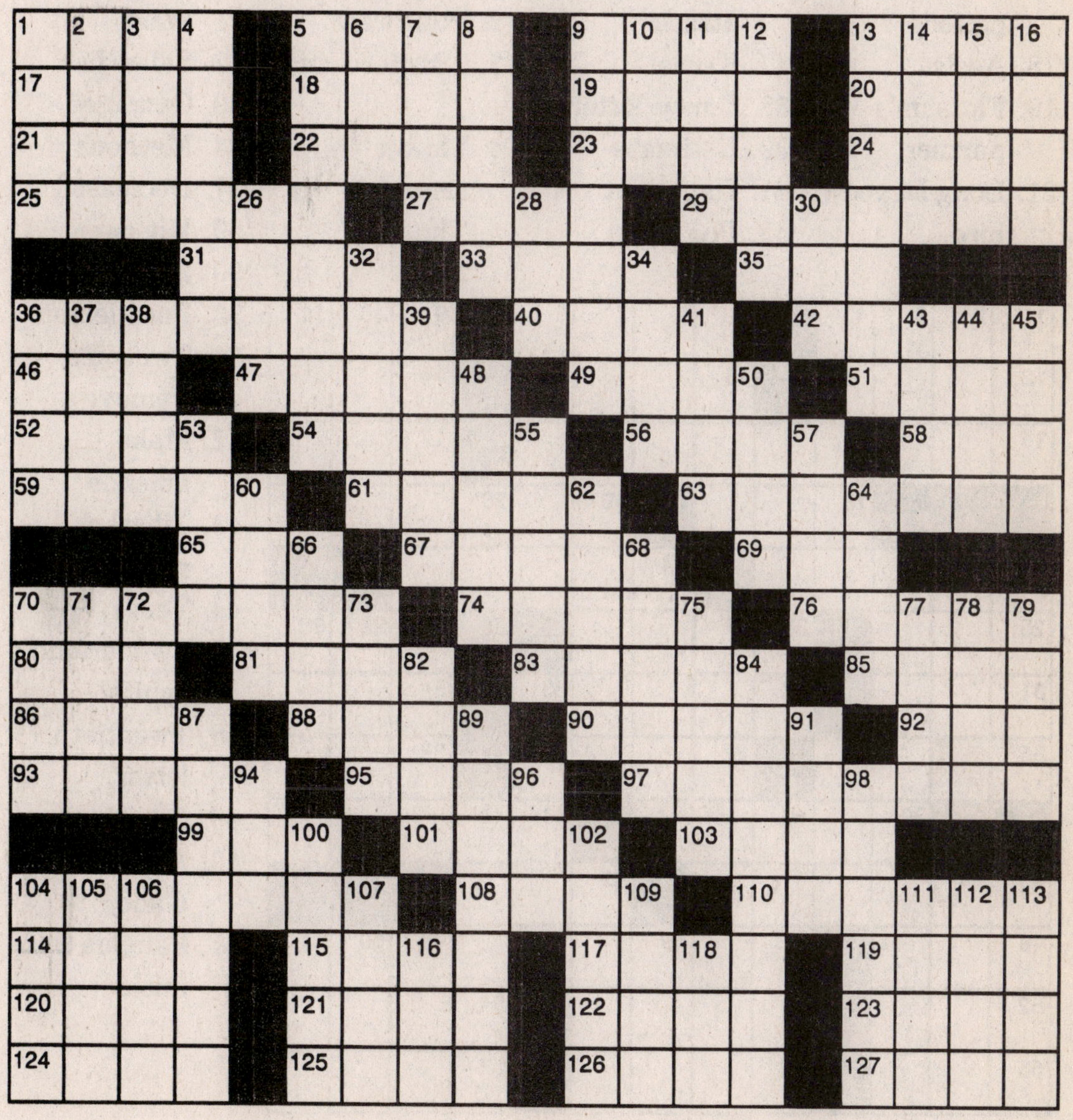

# PUZZLE 529

**ACROSS**

1. Short breath
5. Skirt edges
9. Golf score
12. Medicinal plant
13. Leave out
14. Lament
15. Rooftop dwelling
17. Historic period
18. Assist
19. Flotsam's partner
21. Long-legged bird
24. Work animals
25. Play on words
26. Dolt
28. Drop suddenly
31. Ampersand
32. Shrubbery
34. ___ de Janeiro
35. Sudden attack
37. Kernel
38. Curvy letter
39. Estimate
41. Impudent
43. Poe poem
45. Wager
46. ___ carte
47. Pronghorns
52. Fellow
53. Prophet
54. ___ Scotia
55. Hill dweller
56. Adam's residence
57. Dutch cheese

**DOWN**

1. Interval
2. Pub brew
3. "Sanford and ___"
4. Flower segment
5. Thug
6. Flightless bird
7. Estimate incorrectly
8. Modified iron
9. Strains
10. Subtle emanation
11. Paper measure
16. Catch
20. Kennedy or Knight
21. Mast
22. Salad fish
23. Outraged
24. Methods
27. Decreased
29. Hit or ___
30. Nosegay
33. Ford lemon
36. Twosome
40. Remove
42. Make amends
43. Tibetan monk
44. Verve
45. Switzerland's capital
48. Twentieth letter
49. Pea abode
50. Actress Gabor
51. Famous uncle

# PUZZLE 530

**ACROSS**

1. Miss Muffet's fare
5. Proper
9. Doctors' org.
12. Effortlessness
13. Wheels
14. Beverage for Jacques
15. Institution
18. Horse strap
19. Hawk's nest
20. Hags
23. Actress Gardner
24. Squealer
25. Interfering
30. Rara ____
32. ____ good deed
33. Dye source
34. Abuses
37. ____ de la Cite
38. Ethiopian prince
39. Hurry
41. Homeric epic
44. "Able was ____ . . ."
45. Metro stop
50. 52, in Old Rome
51. "Do-____"
52. Calif. school
53. Curved letter
54. List dimensions, etc., for short
55. Chick's sound

**DOWN**

1. Tiny
2. Possesses
3. Superlative suffix
4. Desire greatly
5. Cliffs along the Hudson
6. Destroy
7. Part of TGIF
8. Western Indian tribe
9. Assert
10. Skirt style
11. Poker pot
16. Root vegetable
17. Comedienne Anne ____
20. Stuff
21. Sitarist Shankar
22. Singer Redding
23. Showing little interest
26. Flightless bird
27. Monogram part: abbr.
28. River of Egypt
29. Singer Campbell
31. Sipper
35. Detection systems
36. Poetess Teasdale
40. Arrangement
41. ____ Royale
42. Baseball's Tiant
43. Wading bird
44. Woe ____!
46. Slangy agreement
47. Chill
48. Bullring cheer
49. Siesta

# PUZZLE 531

**• THE DUKE •**

**ACROSS**

1. Get going
7. Horse's kin
12. Flop
16. Wayne
20. Gaseous fuel
21. Florid
22. Bridget Fonda movie
23. Bread spread
24. Wayne film
26. Wayne film
28. Rebukes
29. Stubborn creatures
31. Contribute
32. Building extension
35. American composer
36. Baht
37. Cartoonist Groenig
38. New: pref.
39. Explorer Hedin
40. OT book
41. Rail
45. Shells
47. Rich Little, e.g.
48. Judah's son
49. Aspect
50. Wide-mouthed fish
51. Pressured
55. Spanish muralist
56. Left
57. Commerce
58. Roll call response
59. Stage setting
60. Front part
61. Pie cover
62. Lebanese leader Gemayel et al.
64. Baldachin
65. State
66. Wayne film
68. Wilde heroine
69. Estate
71. Obscured
72. Met offering
73. Exit
74. Seams
79. Pakistani waterway
82. Rains, in winter
83. Short hair: Scot.
84. Pulls
85. Pinnacle
86. Gleeful sounds
87. Project
88. First course
89. Yearns
90. Power source
91. Wayne film
94. African rulers
95. Moon vehicle
96. Saone
97. Murray and Marsh
98. Andy Capp's wife
99. Fisc
101. ___ Harbor, Guam
102. Hats
103. Unified
104. Blake work
105. Fashionable person
106. Alone
107. Stereo syst. outputs
108. Stalwart
111. Actress Picon
112. African republic
113. Furniture finish
115. Wayne film
122. Michigan town
123. Notion, in Nice
124. Herons
125. Dolores ___
126. Shuck
127. Wallet items
128. Takes it easy
129. Flattened at the poles

**DOWN**

1. Alternative
2. Icelandic letter
3. Haggard novel
4. Sigma follower
5. Stopover spot
6. Wayne film
7. Kilmer subjects
8. Literary collections
9. Contrived
10. List maker
11. Dieters
12. Confusion of voices
13. Hockey player and family
14. Actress Sara
15. Neck scarves
16. Dives
17. Vaclav Havel's wife
18. Vehemence
19. Canonical hour
21. Regularly
25. Mansard features
27. Absent
30. Grouse's courtship dance
32. Bivouacs
33. Tasso's love
34. Wayne film, with "The"
36. Indian dwelling
37. Parson's abode
39. Discard
41. Certain South Africans
42. Wayne film
43. Continent
44. Judge anew
46. Skein
47. Increase
51. Wild ox
52. U.S. humorist
53. "___ Happy Feeling"
54. Split
55. Granada mister
57. Curl
59. Valleys
61. Spassky's game
62. "...___ to dance"
63. French region
64. Wraps
66. Shipping allowances
67. Resistance units

# PUZZLE 531

68. " . . . lips are not ____"
70. Choice part
73. Beetle
74. French number
75. Turkish army corps
76. Frauds
77. Hacienda room
78. Polish lancer
80. Eskimo, e.g.
81. Tenants
82. Commandment word
83. Actor Noah ____
85. Box elder genus
87. ____ al-Sheikh
88. Pinch
89. Minor Prophet
91. Wayne film
92. Turbine rotor
93. At an ____
94. Wayne film
96. "____ to Remember"
98. Office worker
100. Footless
101. Punching tool
102. Divine word
105. Units of loudness
106. Filters
108. Exchange
109. Entice
110. Holy City
111. Bearing
112. Kiev refusal
114. Citrus beverage
116. Hosp. employees
117. Bill
118. Bad
119. Dear: Brit.
120. Club
121. Digit

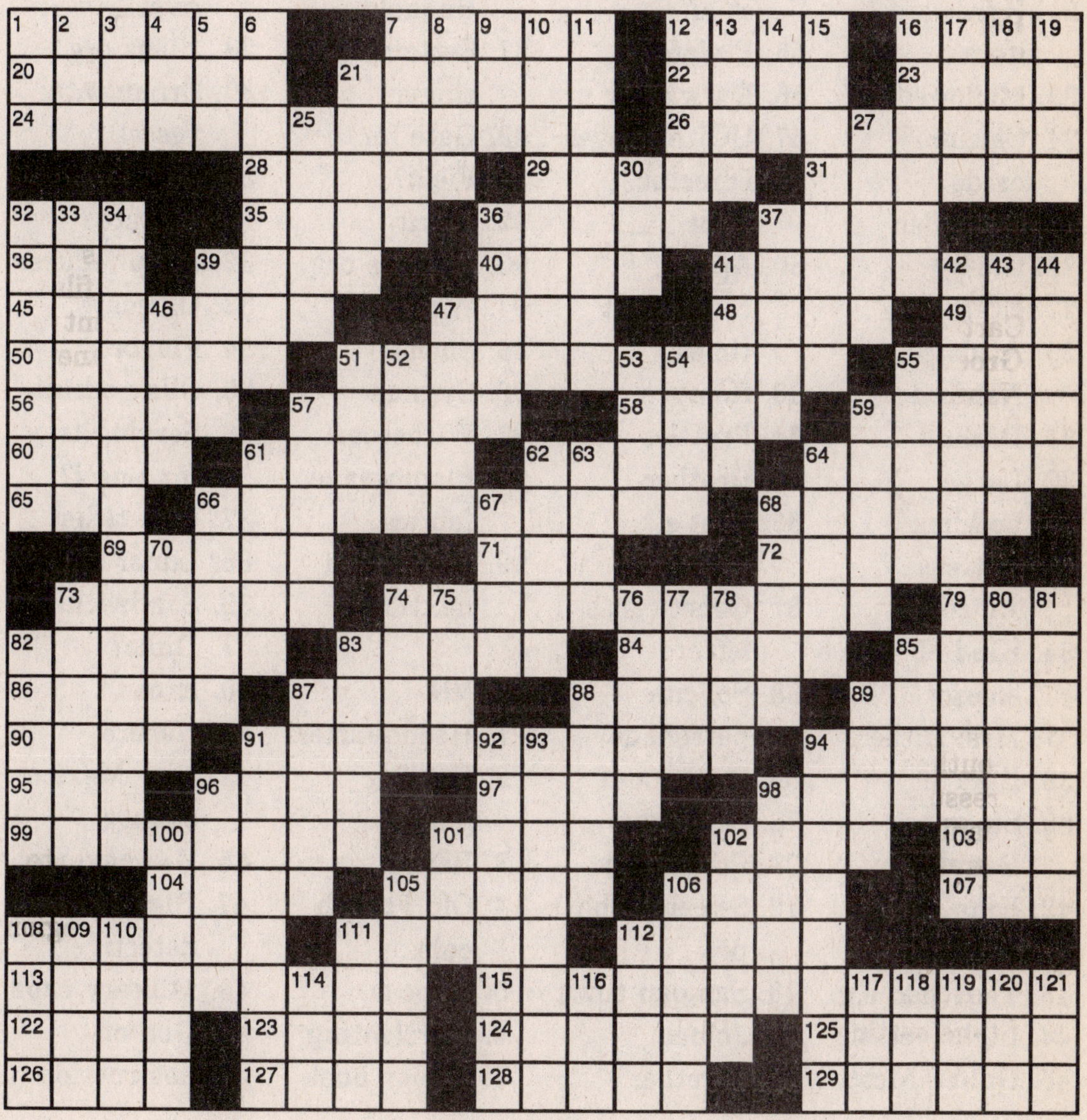

# PUZZLE 532

## ACROSS

1. Panamas
5. Vex
9. Greek promenade
13. Child of Hera
17. Cooking fat
18. Discordia
19. Threadbare
20. Georgia city
21. Hardware item
23. Mellowed
24. Calcium oxide
25. Long fish
26. Glory
27. Etats-____
29. Athlete Ashford
31. Darling
32. Large building
33. Actress Allison
34. Kind of energy
37. Mrs. Dithers
38. Escape
39. Singer Benatar
42. King of comedy
43. Thatcher, e.g.
44. Light vessel
45. Golfer Alcott
46. Columnist Smith
47. Extended
48. Sacred book
49. Prevent
50. North Pole establishment
52. Slant
53. Liturgical headdress
54. Hot Springs et al.
55. Prelates
56. Dark color
57. UCLA player
59. Director Rene ____
60. Apple coating, at times
63. Remove
64. Prattles
65. Brother
66. Poet's before
67. Geneticist's letters
68. Solicits patronage
69. Casa room
70. Arm bone
71. Propensity
72. Sweeten the pot
73. Samoan town
74. Joined together
75. Church feature
76. Iditarod vehicle
77. Elevator compartment
78. Sorrow
81. Responsive
82. William, to Diana
83. OSS successor
86. Author Bagnold
87. Certain singer
89. Gate for Field?
92. Spent
93. Defense org.
94. Way out
95. Shells
96. Cygnus
97. Withstood
98. Plain-weave fabrics
99. Plasterer's mixture

## DOWN

1. Headquarters
2. Healing plant
3. Reveal
4. Old French coin
5. Oppose
6. Unrelenting
7. Gypsy book
8. Water passage
9. Shepherd
10. Clothing
11. Swedish coin
12. Singer Marian ____
13. Composer Harold ____
14. Disturb
15. TV award
16. Recognized
22. European river
28. 1930s org.
30. Ornamental vessel
31. God of pastures
32. Sleep inducer
33. Ultimate
34. Flavor
35. Olla podrida
36. Serving tray for Lucci?
37. Free ticket
38. Lunar areas
39. Sandwich for Duke?
40. Eros
41. Nature
43. New Mexico county
44. Bar payment
47. Biggers's detective
48. Military caps
49. God of destruction

# PUZZLE 532

51. Point of land
52. Armada components
53. Characteristic
55. Full-page illustration
56. Darling dog
57. Text
58. Ancient character
59. Slide
60. Fizzy drink
61. Irish lake
62. Vanguard
64. Invariable
65. Manor employee
68. Finish line feature
69. English poet
70. Mideast fedn.
73. Rarebit ingredient
74. Large number
75. Actress Eve ___
76. Halloween visitor
77. Indianapolis team
78. Beatty film
79. Plenty, in verse
80. Lollobrigida
81. Holy Roman emperor
82. Small shoot
83. Lombardy commune
84. "My Friend ___"
85. Bit
88. Asian language
90. Cutting tool
91. Crony

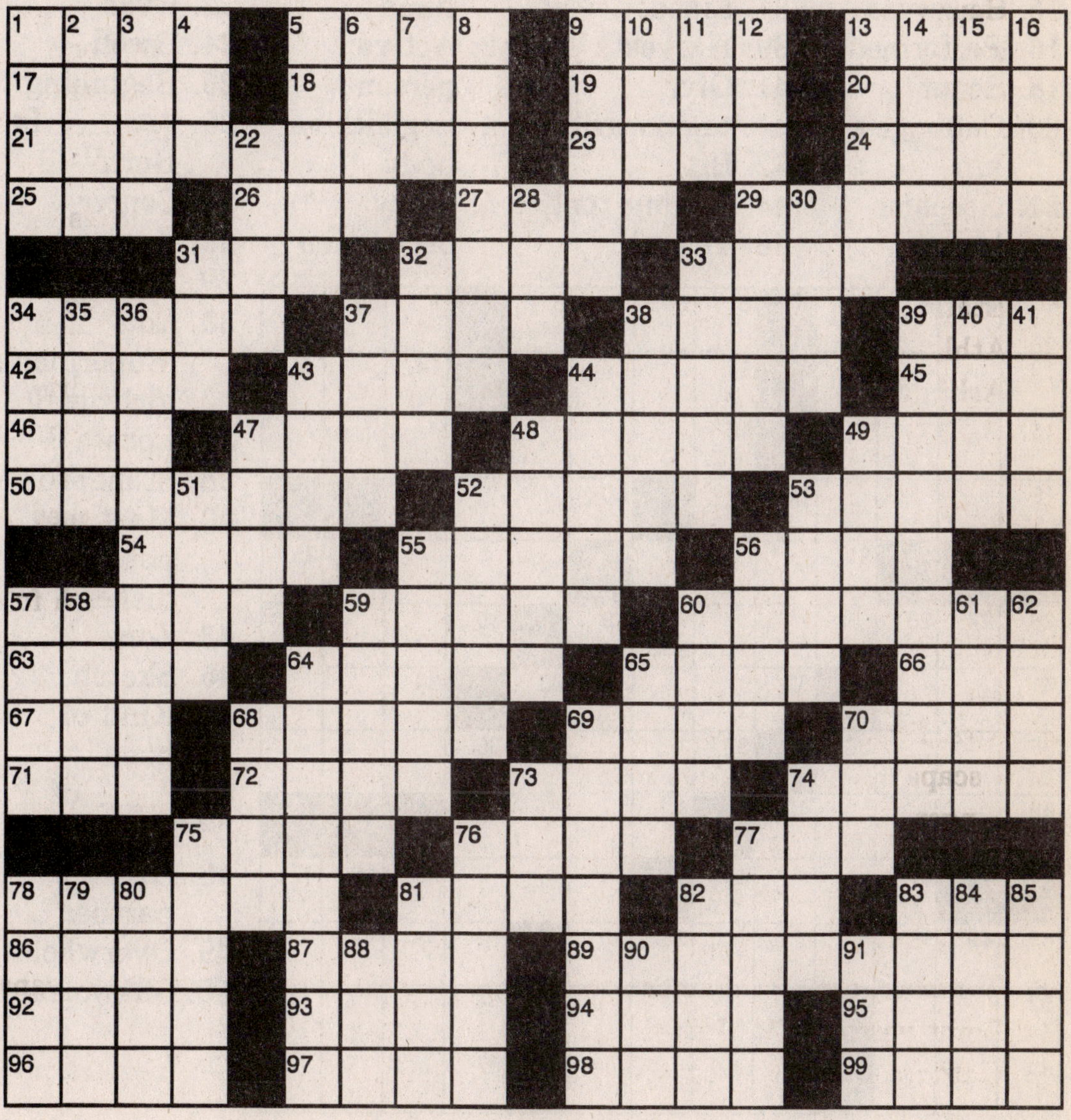

# PUZZLE 533

**ACROSS**

1. Writing tablets
5. Backtalk
9. "It's a ____
12. Succulent plant
13. Peter, Paul and Mary, for example
14. Paid athlete
15. Observed
16. Performed
18. Scour
20. Cabbage's kin
21. Greenish blue
23. Closes, as a package
26. Shouted
30. Singer Adams
31. Foot part
32. Frolic
34. Night before
35. Crafts' partner
37. Fixed
39. Harvests
41. Give temporarily
42. Bit
44. Sewing tool
48. Teased
51. Opera solo
52. Have debts
53. "The Way We ____"
54. Escapes
55. Marry
56. Stated
57. Hit hard

**DOWN**

1. Quarter-back's forte
2. Sir Guinness of films
3. Active person
4. Legislative body
5. Party decoration
6. "We ____ the World"
7. Kitchen feature
8. Beverages
9. Distributor
10. Anger
11. Sign of assent
17. Robert ____ (Confederate general)
19. Partridge's tree
22. Even
24. Dwell
25. Beginning
26. "A ____ Is Born"
27. Center
28. Kept
29. Trusted
33. Lois ____ (Superman's girlfriend)
36. Locate
38. Standards
40. Meat and potatoes dishes
43. Zone
45. Sketch
46. Kind of bean
47. "____ of Eden"
48. Arrow's partner
49. Overwhelm
50. Silkworm

# PUZZLE 534

**ACROSS**

1. Fragrance
5. Water barrier
8. Location
12. Shout wildly
13. Actor Wallach
14. Image
15. Rams' mates
16. ____ and ink drawing
17. Depressed area
18. Insulting
20. Diner patron
22. "The ____ Also Rises"
23. Deli bread
24. Subsided
27. Waits on tables
31. Cloth scrap
32. Unwell
33. Statements of principle
37. Only just
40. Propel a boat
41. Time period
42. Packing box
44. Makes a loan
47. Cry of sorrow
48. Everyone
50. Get one's ____
52. Ashen
53. Golf peg
54. Moslem prince
55. Watched
56. Affirmative response
57. Count on

**DOWN**

1. Mineral deposit
2. Black birds
3. Microwave ____
4. Oppose
5. Trust
6. Pub potable
7. Prospectors
8. "My ____ Sam"
9. Not working
10. Expedition
11. Graceful tree
19. Payable
21. Affirmative, at sea
24. Circle part
25. Drinking spot
26. Grow older
28. Contend
29. Building extension
30. Cunning
34. Rubbed out
35. Period
36. Soaked with perspiration
37. Southern beauties
38. "Car 54, Where ____ You?"
39. Park official
42. Flowerpot material
43. Breathing sound
45. Rounded roof
46. Spinnaker, for one
47. Monkey
49. Mr. Iacocca
51. ____ one's patience

# PUZZLE 535

**ACROSS**

1. Dice
5. Canter
9. Take to court
12. Cherish
13. Thought
14. Snoop
15. Help
16. House payment
18. Neither
19. Walking on ___
20. Soothes
21. Flip
23. Sphere
24. Brag
26. Cheerful
27. Driver's chart
30. Other
31. Pelt
32. Roman robe
33. Obtain
34. Storage box
35. Worn
36. Wagon
37. Corn bread
38. Knack
41. Crone
42. Jive talk
45. Site
47. Nimbus
48. Fire remainder
49. Coastal flier
50. Article
51. Tiny
52. Rod and ___
53. " . . . ___ in the heart of Texas"

**DOWN**

1. Family
2. Vagabond
3. Cloudy
4. Dog or cat
5. Boundary
6. Scent
7. Each
8. Diner
9. Health places
10. Prod
11. Potato buds
17. Chat
19. Creative work
22. Employ
23. Paddle
24. Plead
25. Corrida cry
26. Pistol
27. Mild
28. Generation
29. Mat
31. Fish flipper
32. Beige
34. Exchange
35. London mist
36. By way of
37. Discussion group
38. Defect
39. Misplace
40. Throb
41. Sharpen, as a razor
43. Toward shelter
44. Pageantry
46. Anger
47. Concealed

# PUZZLE 536

**ACROSS**

1. Spank
4. Wound remnant
8. Oaf
12. Polar cover
13. "GWTW" locale
14. Assistant
15. Bugged
17. Flesh
18. Unexciting
19. Purpose
21. Sediment
23. Carry
24. Clothes for poor Cinderella
25. Swayed
29. Good or rotten
30. Small orifices
31. Inventor Whitney
32. Horse operas
34. Asseverate
35. Heraldic insignia
36. Serious offense
37. Charlotte or Emily
40. By word of mouth
41. Thick outer covering
42. Anonymous
46. Away from the wind, to Popeye
47. ____ reminds me
48. Stadium shout
49. Beginning stage
50. Reasonable
51. Mata Hari

**DOWN**

1. Gratuity
2. High card
3. Reserve funds: 2 wds.
4. Checks
5. Concern
6. Exist
7. Shows happiness
8. Rook
9. Enjoy
10. Scand. war god
11. Car boo-boo
16. Touches
20. Fanatics
21. Barrymore of "E.T."
22. Fury
23. Trumpets e.g.
25. Afflicts
26. Those who malign
27. Sch. type
28. Dreadful
30. Flippant
33. One behind another
34. Asian sea
36. Minotaur's island
37. Boast
38. Irritate
39. Lollapalooza
40. Muscat and ____
43. Exclamation
44. Vital fluid
45. Bashful

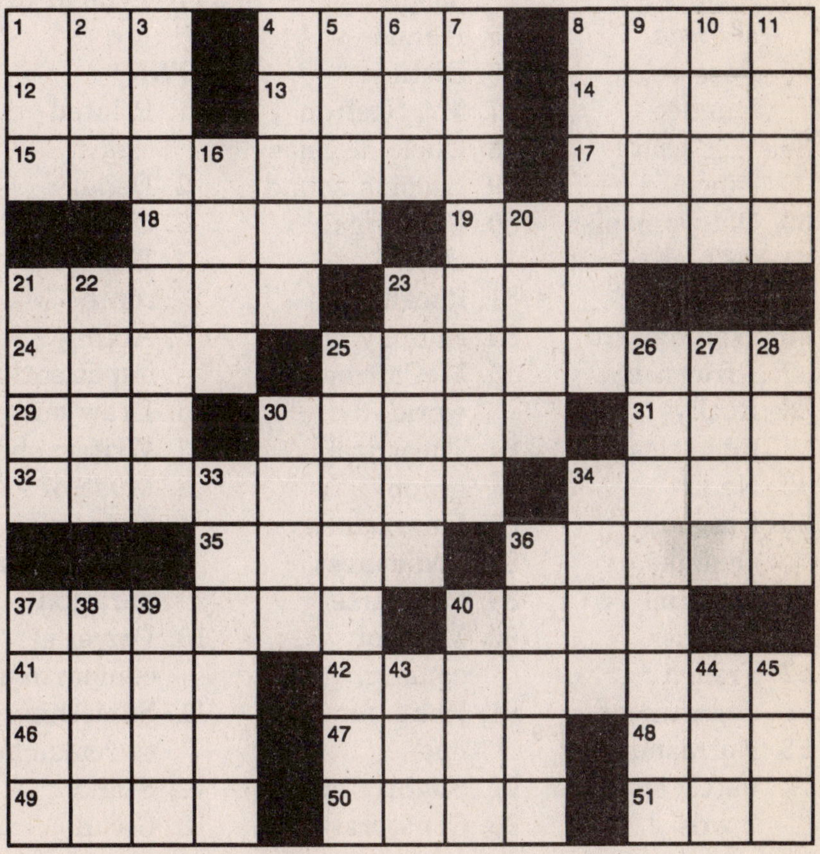

# PUZZLE 537

**ACROSS**

1. Brewer's 17 Down
5. Serenity
10. Whittle
15. Earth sci.
19. Stein filler
20. Of age
21. Man from Mars
22. Type of bean
23. Intention
24. ___ pie
25. Kernel
26. Time
27. Muse of dancing
30. Muse of tragedy
32. "Penny ___"
33. Claudius's stepson
35. Possess, in Dundee
36. ___ that (since)
39. Old-womanish
41. Of high quality
46. Wading bird
47. African fly
48. Rocky pinnacles
49. Nada
50. Emulate Godzilla
51. Like fall weather
52. French department
53. Normandy battle site: 2 wds.
54. Had a bite
55. Gee follower
56. Bowler
58. Biblical mountain
59. Muse of sacred songs
61. WWII fighters
62. Hirsute
63. Subclans of old
64. Gets word
65. Cadence
66. Military hats
69. Sledges
70. Muse of epic poetry
74. Wealthy people
75. Humid
76. Ditties
77. Mr. Skelton
78. Uncle of Enos
79. Leonine sound
80. Figurings: abbr.
81. Recall
82. Rummy cry
83. McCaffrey world
84. Theatrical group
86. Megacalorie
87. Ordinances
89. Main artery
90. Muse of comedy
91. Koko, for one
92. Slightly open
93. Consecrate
94. Abode of the Muses
99. Keats honoree
105. Rhodes or Satie
106. Oncle's femme
108. Senior member
109. Wicked
110. Human or rat
111. Record
112. Medieval headware
113. City in Italia
114. ___-friendly
115. "Light My Fire" group, with "The"
116. Enraptures
117. Type of dive

**DOWN**

1. Printed elegy
2. Deputy
3. Oracle
4. Hunter's route
5. Acting impatiently
6. Draw out
7. Writer: abbr.
8. Muse of history
9. True love's duration
10. Driver's compartment
11. Something to remember
12. Stand
13. Cloud
14. Place in an orb
15. Cloisonne
16. Actor Nicholas ___
17. Stove part
18. Muse's instrument
28. Compos mentis
29. "Princess Bride" sea beasts
31. Bireme propellers
34. Female ruff
36. Throw out
37. Muse of love poetry
38. Artist's support
39. Humane org.
40. Relative: abbr.
41. Playgoer's mementos
42. Royalist
43. Beginning, for short
44. City in Illinois
45. Orb
47. S. Amer. monkeys
51. Dressed to the ___
52. Cupid, to Greeks
53. Conductor Georg ___
55. Pulpits
56. Distributed
57. Flubs

# PUZZLE 537

58. Rome has seven
60. Bumpkin
61. Father of the Muses
62. Foundation spars
64. "Aquarius" musical
65. Spear
66. Plush rugs
67. Garb
68. Oat genus
69. Gripes
70. Mea ____
71. Bay window
72. Kind of dish
73. Swelling
75. Cry for seconds
76. Stretched
79. Tried again
80. Bullfights
81. Converters
83. Imago predecessor
84. Moslem cap
85. Horse hue
86. Narrow
88. Big boat
90. Sullies
92. Mitosis structure
93. Uhlan's mount
94. Land of the Incas
95. Kura feeder
96. "Vampire Lestat" author
97. I cure: Latin
98. "Thy word is a lamp ____ . . ."
100. Skirt feature
101. Church song
102. Confess
103. Capital of 94 Down
104. Zeal
107. European vetch

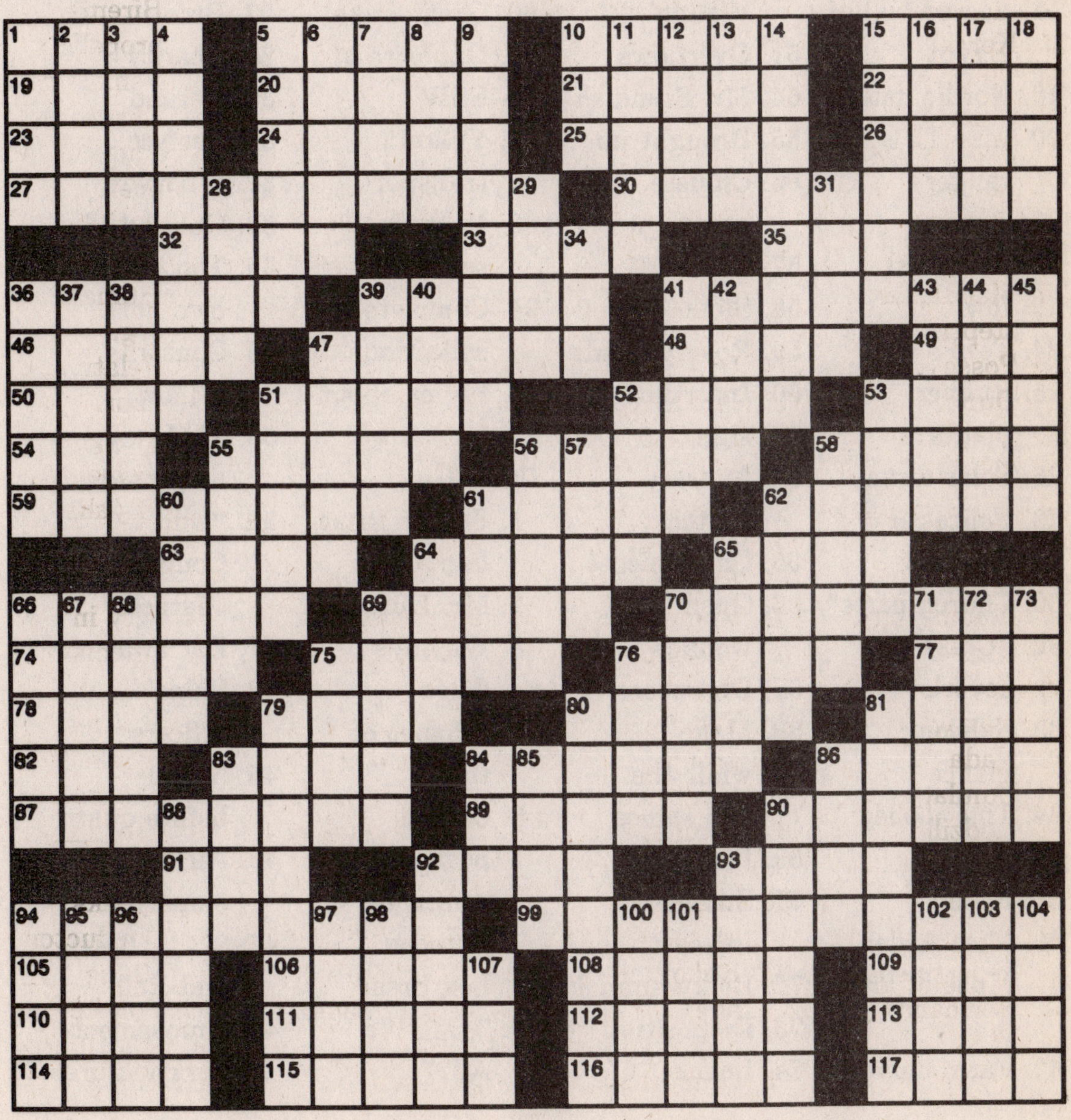

# PUZZLE 538

**ACROSS**

1. Top of Guido's scale
4. "I Remember ___"
8. Cleo's craft
13. Tickled pink
17. Precious stone
18. Sacred bull of Egypt
19. Nordic native
20. Like TV's ranger
21. Turkeys
23. Barnyard fowl
24. Teen's woe
25. Rubber plants
26. Solar disks
28. Police-car features
30. Church parts
32. "Crazy" coverlet
33. Sidelong glance
34. Thai money
35. Sects
36. Reds
40. Miss Arden
41. Muse of love poetry
42. Farm moms
43. Eat
44. Wrecks
46. Cancan locale
47. Parent
48. Tiers
49. Religious practices
50. "___ Boots Are Made for Walkin' "
51. Overflows
54. Mr. Standish
55. Brought up
56. Chinese perennial
57. Capers
58. Slink
59. Rosary beads
60. Insertion sign
61. Literary sketch
65. Chess pieces
66. Open wounds
67. Doorposts
68. Make ___ while the sun shines
69. Perfumes
71. Summer forecast
72. Balky animal
73. Disposition
74. Loans
75. Cripples
76. Renounce claim to
79. Sticky
80. ___ waist
81. Check before publication
82. Official decree
84. Scarf
88. Mention
89. Bushed
90. Great Lake
91. Opposite of SSW
92. Yukon transport
93. Nocturnal sound
94. Complete collections
95. Fly or about

**DOWN**

1. French-toast ingredient
2. Mr. Durocher
3. Waylays
4. Guys
5. "Planet of the ___"
6. Czarist peasant commune
7. Attacks
8. Lox bread
9. "___ We All?"
10. Bread and whiskey
11. Home utility
12. Driving forces
13. Wood clearings
14. Places
15. ___ Domini
16. Sandra and Ruby
22. Fruit decay
27. Broz
29. Charity
30. Retired
31. Surface
32. Wharves
33. Gold braid
35. Toots one's own horn
36. Concerns
37. Willow
38. TLC dispenser
39. "Odd Couple" character
41. Eat away
42. Ships' officers
45. Number before quatre
46. Airline employee
47. "___, Rattle and Roll"
49. Amusement-park features

# PUZZLE 538

50. Marine birds
51. Skeleton
52. Washes
53. Prophetic signs
54. Bogs down
55. British sport
57. Risked
58. Delineates
60. Sources of milk
61. Pointed beards
62. Whopping
63. Fabrication
64. Optics
66. Winter weather word
67. ____ bond
70. Overacted
71. Withdraw
72. Crush
74. Contemporary beam
75. Shoestrings
76. Animal retreats
77. Heathen god
78. Plot of ground
79. Arum's kin
80. Court order
83. Blood relatives
85. Bard's before
86. Last queen of Spain
87. Provided with dinner

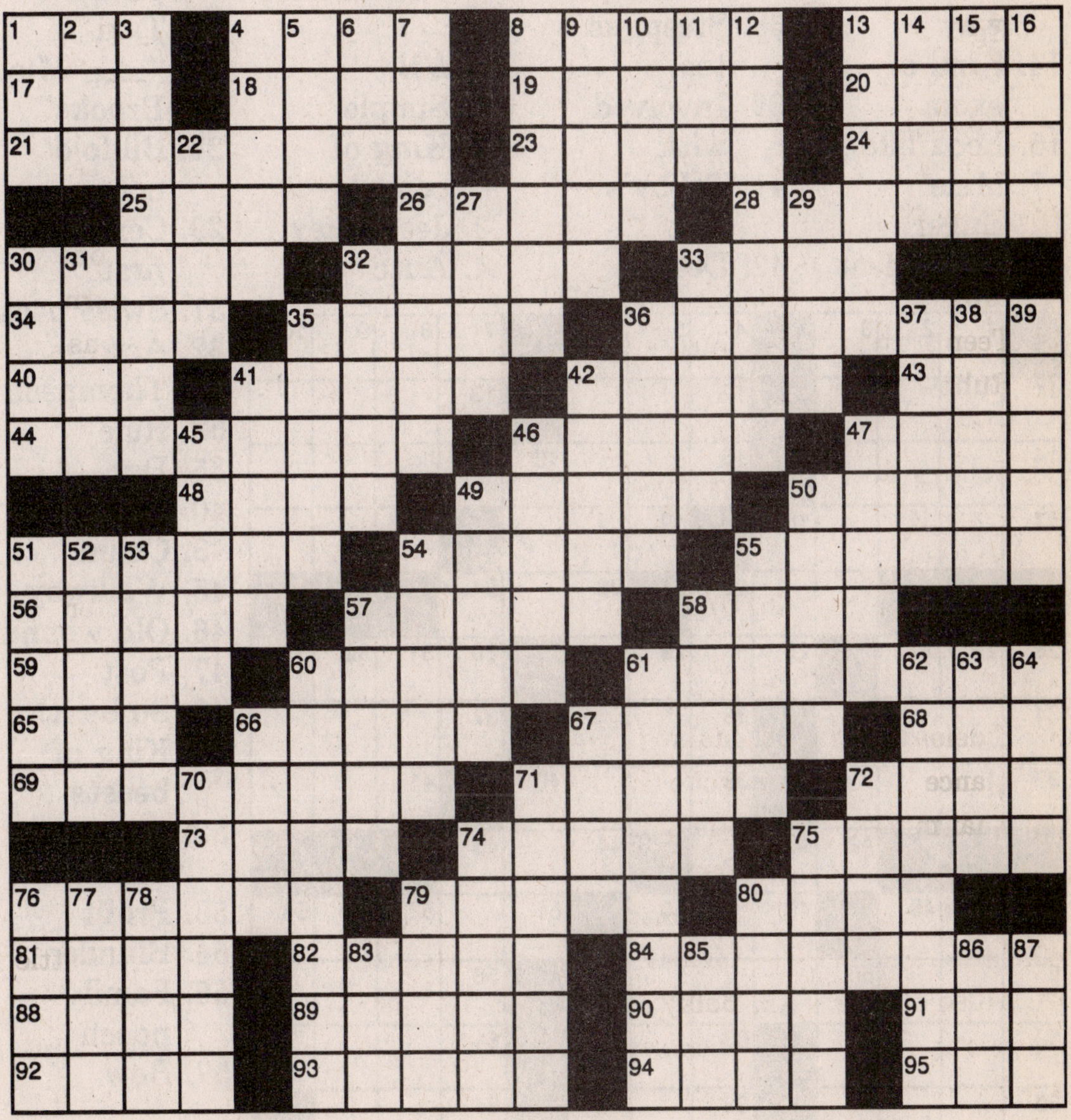

# PUZZLE 539

**ACROSS**

1. Tourist's need
4. Angler's catch
7. Have an ____ on
11. Grinder shop
12. Broad st.
13. ____ the way
14. Kind of exam
15. Look like
17. Male singer
19. Equipment
20. Hamilton bill
21. Heavy weight
23. Sticky stuff
25. Dove call
28. City
30. Autumn
34. Bee, to Opie
36. Through
37. Canine pest
38. Steep, as tea
39. Involved with
41. Tabby's foot
42. Decide
44. Time period
46. Health resort
49. Feel unwell
51. Spree
55. Gripe
58. Burn
59. Opposite of aweather
60. As well
61. Den
62. Lease
63. Finish
64. Coastal flier

**DOWN**

1. Simple
2. King of comedy
3. Jet jockey
4. Auto
5. Done
6. Specify
7. Shade provider
8. Liability
9. Wind gust
10. Adam's place
11. Polka ____
16. Conceit
18. Decompose
22. Beginner
24. Switch position
25. Taxi
26. "____ Miss Brooks"
27. Billfold note
29. Come in first
31. Swiss peak
32. Actress Thompson
33. Rule
35. Duo
40. Sphere
43. Chum
45. Walkway
46. Old wound
47. Post
48. So be it!
50. King of beasts
52. ____ at hand
53. Profit
54. Blunder
56. Family pooch
57. Bow

# PUZZLE 540

**ACROSS**

1. Kills flies
6. Blemish
9. Health club
12. Aviator
13. Frozen water
14. Paraffin
15. Texas attraction
16. Breathe
18. Caesar's X
19. Mine find
21. Egged on
22. Ripen
23. Foxy
24. Appliance
28. Suggestion
31. Booty
32. Street: abbr.
33. Top-notch
34. Clip
35. Therapy
37. Biblical boat
38. Answer
39. Sew
42. Change the color
43. Type of sandwich
46. Cost
48. Coil
50. Pub drink
51. Pool stick
52. Uncanny
53. Novel
54. Feminine pronoun
55. Naps

**DOWN**

1. Quarrel
2. Trickery
3. Poet Seeger
4. Author Clancy
5. Larry, Curly or Moe
6. Bog
7. High card
8. Outcome
9. Gulp
10. Use a kitchen gadget
11. Chopped
17. Snoop
20. Say
22. Model Carol ____
23. Conniving
24. Sickly
25. Cow's cry
26. Dad
27. Holiday lead-in
28. Pedal digit
29. Lodge
30. Favored one
33. Gospel singer Grant
35. Ditch
36. Reel
37. Took food
39. Pinto or lima
40. Wheel shaft
41. Jet
42. Antlered animal
43. Gentlemen
44. One
45. Wasps
47. Take to court
49. Tiny

# PUZZLE 541

**ACROSS**

1. Cap, in Scotland
4. Diva's song
8. Type
12. Famous boxer
13. "Star ___"
14. Entreaty
15. Makes into a different form
17. Enjoy a novel
18. Sailors
19. Expressions
21. Dish
23. Wide-eyed with curiosity
24. Lawn tool
25. Tennis court official
29. Single unit
30. Diamond bags
31. Actor Vigoda
32. Capable of being fixed
34. Say no to seconds
35. Woodwind
36. Furs
37. Bank employee
40. Location
41. Asian sea
42. Burden
46. Isinglass
47. Oliver or Donna
48. Set down
49. Equal
50. Dry
51. Bard's before

**DOWN**

1. Pitch
2. Tavern order
3. In error
4. Informed
5. Knocks
6. Rage
7. Trust recipient
8. Parsley units
9. Muffin topper
10. Paper measure
11. Little fellows
16. Despise
20. Female rabbits
21. School dance
22. Path
23. Corridor
25. Workmen
26. Approved by the post office
27. Aid
28. Gains
30. Baseballer Ruth
33. Buck
34. Consider
36. Overly modest person
37. Force down
38. Great Lake
39. Chantilly, e.g.
40. Maple genus
43. Formerly named
44. Corn unit
45. Bread choice

# PUZZLE 542

**ACROSS**

1. Actor Alan ____
5. Fedoras
9. That girl
12. Jai ____
13. Overlook
14. Skirt fold
15. Offers
16. Fork prong
17. Clockmaker Terry
18. Piled
20. Conform
22. OPEC concern
23. Actress MacGraw
24. Show an old show
27. Assignment
31. "____ the Rainbow"
32. Armed conflict
33. Frozen-yogurt holder
34. Argued
36. ____ up (studied hard)
37. Chat
38. Clergy mem.
39. Antic
42. Food supplier
46. Frost a cake
47. Moral
49. Took the bus
50. X
51. Mother Bloor
52. Level
53. Curvy letter
54. Shred
55. Hollow

**DOWN**

1. Test sites
2. Came down
3. Early 20th-century art form
4. Deter
5. Inn
6. Between
7. Badge metal
8. Thieves
9. Former Mets' stadium
10. Assist
11. Expel
19. Aunts and uncles
21. Found
23. Broadcast
24. Staff
25. Actress Brenner
26. Confederate soldier
27. Teed off
28. Charged particle
29. Dollar bill
30. Comedian Sparks
32. Spider's creation
35. Bull's-eye
36. Chance
38. Detecting device
39. Quote
40. High cards
41. Writing tools
42. Soft drink
43. Meander
44. Utopia
45. Lease
48. Bullring cry

# PUZZLE 543

**ACROSS**

1. Pistol ___ Maravich
5. Club's golf expert
8. Iraqi, e.g.
12. Section
13. "Swing ___, Sweet Chariot"
14. ___ Ranger
15. Laces, as shoes
16. Vigoda of "Fish"
17. Spouse
18. Guard
20. Baseball competitions
21. With no difficulty
24. Rigid
27. Cover
28. Kitten's foot
31. Advance
32. Falsehood
33. Zoo building
34. Neverthe-less
35. "The Streets of ___ Francisco"
36. Lubricated
37. Trimming
39. Kind of diving
43. Church official
47. Misplace
48. Witness
50. Bicycled
51. What's the big ___
52. Split ___ soup
53. Ceases
54. Student's table
55. "___ the king's horses . . ."
56. Tryout

**DOWN**

1. Touches lightly
2. Great Lake
3. High-school senior
4. Not western
5. Broadway offerings
6. Steal
7. Be indebted to
8. ___ mater
9. Meander
10. Poker stake
11. Buzzing insects
19. Fled
20. Swindle
22. Cake topping
23. Kind of dog, for short
24. Crafty
25. ___ the line
26. Have a snack
28. Chum
29. Time period
30. Marry
32. Craze
33. Smoke
35. "___ of Love" (Pacino film)
36. Small bill
38. Standard
39. Glided
40. Secret message
41. Takes ad-vantage of
42. Bird's nose
44. Pine or ice-cream
45. Betting probability
46. House of sticks
48. Health club
49. Long fish

# PUZZLE 544

**ACROSS**

1. Gigantic
5. Amino ____
9. Top pilot
12. Kind of exam
13. Army's kin
14. Promise
15. Gape
16. Elm, e.g.
17. Certain poem
18. Nectarines' relatives
20. Speed contests
22. Brown in the sun
23. Mountain resort
24. Crone
27. Fastener
30. Knife blade
33. Self
34. Skins, as fruit
36. Rowing need
37. Spider's creations
39. Browse
40. Columbus to Savannah direction: abbr.
41. Stake
43. Wail
45. Certain tooth
47. Unruly
51. Lincoln's nickname
52. Prayer ending
54. African succulent
55. Neither hide ____ hair
56. Castle's protection
57. Beer ingredient
58. Affirmative answer
59. "My Three ____"
60. Results

**DOWN**

1. Basketball player's target
2. Encourage
3. Celebration
4. Choose by vote
5. Aerials
6. Automobiles
7. "____ Got a Secret"
8. Tinters
9. Guacamole ingredients
10. Area or zip
11. Rams' mates
19. Yarn spindle
21. Gorilla
24. Cut
25. Period in history
26. Turkeys
28. Circle part
29. Laborers
31. Fuel
32. Poetic before
35. Winter precipitation
38. Baltic or Yellow, e.g.
42. Cable vehicles
44. Hold responsible for
45. Various
46. Reed instrument
47. Not fatty
48. Excitement
49. Convinced
50. Places
53. Cow sound

# PUZZLE 545

**ACROSS**

1. Police officer
4. Grand story
8. Accomplishment
12. Have being
13. Pianist Peter ____
14. Pay to play
15. Marine
17. Notion
18. Northern Indian
19. Directed
21. Vereen or Gazzara
22. Capture
26. Inn
29. Summer beverage
30. Date
31. Done
32. Frozen water
33. Tiers
34. Males
35. Social insect
36. Postpone
37. Goes in
39. Paddock
40. Slide downhill on snow
41. Unobstructed
45. Too bad!
48. Maryland's neighbor
50. Festive occasion
51. At any time
52. Container
53. Heed
54. Take it easy
55. Place

**DOWN**

1. Lawsuit
2. Metal sources
3. Pike's ____
4. Lacquer
5. Argentine leader
6. Wrath
7. Rot
8. Vague
9. Termination
10. Devoured
11. Oolong or Earl Grey
16. Thread
20. Lincoln, familiarly
23. Military infraction
24. Midwestern state
25. Inquisitive
26. Dwelling
27. Kiln
28. Canvas hut
29. Carry out
32. One in the know
33. Subscribe again
35. Noah's vessel
36. Leave
38. Composition
39. Posts
42. Grabs
43. One of the Great Lakes
44. Scar on a car?
45. Before
46. Research place
47. Lager's kin
49. First woman

# PUZZLE 546

**ACROSS**

1. Performs
5. Big boats
9. Warsaw's locale: abbr.
12. Sigh of relief
13. Runs with the pres.
14. One-spot
15. Small quantity
16. Light opera
18. Visually pleasing
20. Small spike
21. Married women in Madrid: abbr.
23. Faux pas
27. Cultivating tool
30. First garden
32. Effortless
33. Competent
35. Have bills
36. Mosaic piece
37. Whine
38. Place in office
40. Show agreement
41. Transports
43. Fall
45. Female wool producer
47. Requisite
51. Annoyance
55. Pressing
56. Limb
57. Rainbow
58. Blood-related
59. Break
60. Crackpots
61. Eyepiece

**DOWN**

1. Sacred bull of Egypt
2. Milk shake flavor: abbr.
3. Head, to Chantal
4. "The Wild ____ at Coole" (Yeats)
5. Pear-shaped fruits
6. Corded fabric
7. Protect
8. Celebration
9. Author Conroy
10. Tenth month: abbr.
11. Pasture
17. Long-plumed heron
19. Rage
22. Hemmed a skirt
24. Shower
25. Capital of Norway
26. Hollow stalk
27. Amateur actors
28. Woodwind
29. Enthusiasm
31. Closeness
34. Wrapped up
39. Shoe tip
42. Gentleman friend
44. Bicycle part
46. Off-white
48. Water barrier
49. Paddy's land
50. Hiding places
51. Crone
52. Period in history
53. Unit of current: abbr.
54. Punch

# PUZZLE 547

**ACROSS**

1. Observes
5. Canary, e.g.
8. War memento
12. ___ moss
13. Time period
14. Saga
15. Singing voice
16. Signed a check
18. Tennis score
20. Ceremonies
21. Tranquil
24. Knock
25. Wipe out
26. Set free
30. Goal
31. Mortar tray
32. Olive center
33. Answered
36. Belief
38. High card
39. Made of oak
40. Elf
43. Wedding band
44. Went back
46. Rim
50. Neighbor of Turkey
51. "___ to Billie Joe"
52. Genuine
53. Blockhead
54. Refusal abroad
55. Vend

**DOWN**

1. Health resort
2. Moray
3. Have a burger
4. Fur pieces
5. Make angry
6. Marine bird
7. Boy
8. Bar
9. Hurl
10. Sea call
11. Cubs' rival
17. Spoken
19. Unit
21. Dry up
22. Pennsylvania port
23. Incline
24. Senator Kennedy
26. Staff
27. Copied
28. Flank
29. Jacket type
31. "___ Haw"
34. Rue
35. Bakery employee
36. Prisoner
37. Cowboy Roy ___
39. Broaden
40. Metal grating
41. Roman emperor
42. Arena shape
43. Make over
45. Heir
47. Passing grade
48. "My ___ Sal"
49. House wing

# PUZZLE 548

**ACROSS**

1. Venerable
4. Draw a ____ on
8. Genre
12. Cow sound
13. At rest
14. Next in line
15. Tavern
16. Fine sand
17. Wide-mouthed jug
18. Hot water vessel
20. New Haven tree
22. Two thousand pounds
23. Technology
27. Parched
29. Appointment
30. Biblical craft
31. Bill and ____
32. Lucky number
33. Foot part
34. Managed
35. Emulated
36. Gratuities
37. Made certain
39. Disapproving sound
40. Brooch
41. Fair-haired
44. Lucid
47. Valley
49. Assist
50. Harbinger
51. Self-images
52. Relay part
53. Hurried
54. Obligation
55. Animal enclosure

**DOWN**

1. Pass over
2. Singular
3. Contributions
4. North American buffalo
5. Blue-pencil
6. "____ by Myself"
7. Discovered
8. Motif
9. Evergreen tree
10. Tart
11. Do wrong
19. Seedcase
21. Hold on property
23. Put aside
24. Citizens
25. Prune
26. Supplements
27. "God's Little ____"
28. Horse color
29. Relied
32. Eastern draped garment
36. Additionally
38. Affect drastically
39. Consecrated
41. Lump
42. Regimen
43. Tense
44. Call of alarm
45. Stereo component, for short
46. Born
48. Iron or Bronze

# PUZZLE 549

**ACROSS**

1. Baseball cap, for one
4. Play players
8. Pea holders
12. ____ Marie Saint
13. Before: pref.
14. Wicked
15. Newspaper employee
17. Tennis star Lacoste
18. Genuine
19. Lasted
21. Surf sound
23. "____ the World Turns"
24. Swiss mountain
27. ____ -fi
28. Wooden duck
32. Garment edge
34. Terminate
36. Challenge
37. Syngman Rhee's land
39. "I ____ Rhythm"
41. Little Indians number
42. Hirt or Capone
43. "The Way We ____"
45. Equip
49. "____ Three Lives"
52. Toledo's lake
53. Kiddie game
56. Souffle ingredient
57. Of flying
58. Actress Gardner
59. Exam
60. Begged
61. Tennis unit

**DOWN**

1. That girl
2. State as truth
3. Gift-wrapping need
4. Musician Santana
5. Social insect
6. Car horn's locale
7. Sea bird
8. Read
9. Atop
10. Eat
11. Toboggan
16. Dory stick
20. June honoree
22. ____ up one's sleeve
24. Inquire
25. Durocher of baseball
26. Golfer's delight
29. Mouser
30. Bauxite, for one
31. Desire
33. Most ornery
35. Female deer
38. Actress MacGraw
40. Camera stand
44. Sprite
45. Place for shoes
46. Goad
47. Trucks
48. Hit in the face
50. Ages
51. Noah's bird
54. "You ____ So Beautiful"
55. Gangster's weapon

# PUZZLE 550

**ACROSS**

1. Like a jalapeno
4. Besides
8. Cried
12. Commotion
13. Broadway light
14. Moroccan native
15. Property
16. Timetables
18. Just picked
20. Lay eyes on
21. Voting place
24. Slip-up
28. Tweety Pie and others
32. Miffed
33. Expert pilot
34. Circus performers
36. Foundation
37. Cause to ravel
39. Pure
41. Weird
43. Influence
44. Wing of a building
46. Posteriors
50. Most slender
55. Persian or calico
56. Lacking rain
57. Supper, for one
58. Arctic abundance
59. Health clubs
60. She, in Paris
61. Mountain ____

**DOWN**

1. Fifty percent
2. Skunk feature
3. Transport
4. "____ Aweigh"
5. Meadow
6. The sun
7. Dollar bills
8. Waterproof boots
9. Distinctive period
10. ____ for the course
11. Kitchen measurement: abbr.
17. Born
19. Mineral spring
22. Stretches out
23. By ____ and bounds
25. Evening wear
26. Metals
27. Ruby and carmine
28. Bistro
29. Land parcel
30. Close at hand
31. Sluggish
35. Sneak up on
38. Surrenders
40. Caustic liquid
42. Wapiti
45. Lollipop flavor
47. Sour
48. Speed contest
49. Meat and vegetable dish
50. Droop
51. Make an effort
52. Point
53. Elongated fish
54. Actor Mineo

# PUZZLE 551

**ACROSS**

1. Distant
5. Seasoning
9. Concerning
14. Mr. Porter
15. Scheme
16. Spanish priest
17. Rushes
18. "____ of Eden"
19. Computer instructions: abbr.
20. Dumbo, for one
22. Weasel's kin
23. Rabbit features
24. Departed
25. Pants
28. Elates
32. Social class, in India
33. Dirties
34. Roman 52
35. Without alteration: 2 wds.
36. Coasts
37. Toolboxes
38. Rock group ____ Zeppelin
39. Skirt style: hyph.
40. Takes the bus
41. Fearing
43. Napa Valley business
44. Hits
45. "Pretty in ____"
46. Monkeylike animals
49. Joey's mom
53. Keep occupied
54. Hunger for
55. Actor Hirsch
56. Greasy spoon
57. Ye ____ Shoppe
58. S-shaped molding
59. Uses a wooden spoon
60. Not distant
61. WWII ally

**DOWN**

1. Hankering
2. Kitchen wrap
3. Toward shelter
4. Admires
5. Pickle slices
6. Alda and Ladd
7. Hindmost
8. Explosive: abbr.
9. Adds
10. Prohibited
11. Redolence
12. Press
13. Check out
21. Food fish
22. Horses
24. Move effortlessly
25. Heat milk
26. ____ beam
27. Stage whisper
28. Auction word
29. Suppress in speech
30. Gunpowder ingredient
31. Scaredy-cat
33. Hurts the knee
36. Paper scraps
37. Coati's relative
39. Worshipers
40. Toll
42. Mishandler
43. "The Lion in ____"
45. Ling-Ling, e.g.
46. Young fellows
47. Give off
48. Actor Paul
49. Curly green veggie
50. Carpets
51. Epic poems
52. River to the Baltic
54. Gained victory

# PUZZLE 552

**ACROSS**

1. Tam
4. Health spot
7. Canopy ____
10. Adam's mate
11. Road repair goo
12. Long period of time
13. Cozy place
15. Park seat
17. Group of cows
18. In that place
20. Foreboding occurrence
22. Finished
23. Nasser's gp.
24. Utilized
25. Entertained
28. Great!
30. Heavy cord
31. Crimson
34. Cobra
35. Residences
36. Cup handle
37. Forest creature
38. Prayer ending
39. In a rush
41. Roof support
44. Metal containers
45. Emcee Sajak
46. Suspend
47. Blaze
48. Beneath
50. Mend
52. Perch
55. Pilaf
58. Mine find
59. Printing fluid
60. 24 hours
61. Get the drift
62. Guitarist Paul
63. Before, poetically

**DOWN**

1. Female chicken
2. Roadway: abbr.
3. Exam
4. Beef animal
5. Skillet
6. Part of a circle
7. Once was, with "has"
8. Goof
9. June honoree
14. "____ Were the Days"
15. Raised
16. Living places
17. Present
19. Always
21. Welcome item
24. The ____ hand
25. Baseball score
26. Not shut
27. Frock
28. Down in the mouth
29. GI's hangout: abbr.
30. Eternal City
32. Devour
33. Desertlike
35. Mad as a ____
39. Mitten filler
40. Fury
42. Neat as ____: 2 wds.
43. Long way off
44. Is unable to
46. Corn coverings
47. At no cost
49. Journey
50. John ____ Passos
51. Exist
53. Black gold
54. Single
56. Train unit
57. Pupil's place

# PUZZLE 553

**ACROSS**

1. Elapse
5. Congeals
9. Hunt ____ peck
12. Against
13. By mouth
14. "Runaround ____"
15. Pact
16. Classify
18. Song bird
20. Pay dirt
21. At no time
24. Actor Cruise et al.
28. Hide
31. TV's Kathie ____ Gifford
32. Orchestra instrument
33. Pull
35. "Enemy ____" (Gossett film)
36. Cherry center
37. Skeptical
39. Ragout
41. Choir voice
42. Become older
44. Dress
47. Purchaser
52. Rope
54. Fuss
55. Nimble
56. Den
57. Mountain ____
58. Went like mad
59. Tense

**DOWN**

1. Mattress cover
2. Recently
3. Hollywood notable
4. Stillness
5. Acquired
6. Generation
7. Toil
8. Smear
9. ____ rule
10. Tough ____ to crack
11. Fourth letter
17. Allow
19. Society-page name
22. Cauldron
23. Dodge
25. Medley
26. Bill of fare
27. Spots
28. Police officers
29. Death notice, for short
30. Memo
34. "Annie Get Your ____"
35. Stroke of luck
38. Marsh
40. Used to be
41. Pace
43. Blast of wind
45. Street
46. Ship's jail
47. Bounder
48. Poem
49. Presently
50. Goof
51. Bread grain
53. Thirsty

# PUZZLE 554

**ACROSS**

1. Fresh
5. Mineral spring
8. Actor Conway et al.
12. Sky ram
14. Work units
16. "I cannot tell ____": 2 wds.
17. Name
18. Try to reduce
19. Arrive
20. Visit
21. Singer Gibb
22. Kiln
23. Fast time
25. Is an also-ran
27. Whitest
31. "Be it ____ so . . ."
33. Cheese variety
34. Land measure
36. Hamlet's phrase: 2 wds.
40. Frog's beginning
42. Lab workers, perhaps
45. Western sight
46. Scottish miss
48. Levin et al.
49. Cannes festival entrant
51. Snuggle
53. Explosion
56. Jug
58. Actor Arkin
59. Sea eagle
61. Globes
65. ____ ho!
66. Constructed
67. Actress Day
69. Story starter
70. Short distance
71. Circumvent
72. Gets by
73. Newspaper workers: abbr.
74. Utopia

**DOWN**

1. A ____ on the back
2. Norse seaman
3. Beatles' meter maid
4. Narrate
5. Large car
6. Computer adjunct
7. Became old
8. Mexican treats
9. "____ Lucy": 2 wds.
10. Acts without words
11. Noticed
13. Convinces
15. Fashion
24. And others: abbr.
26. Crumbs
27. Docile animal
28. "____ Bede"
29. Put cargo on a ship
30. Rulers: abbr.
32. Animal doctors
35. Jail section
37. Elevator name
38. "Sesame Street" character
39. Of an epoch
41. Bumpkins
43. Old worker
44. Wind dir.
47. Altered
50. Articles
52. Wear away
53. Kind of cartridge
54. Spear
55. S. Amer. mountains
57. Sobs
58. Lilylike plant
60. Proportion
62. Wander
63. Type of nail
64. Team
68. Elected official: abbr.

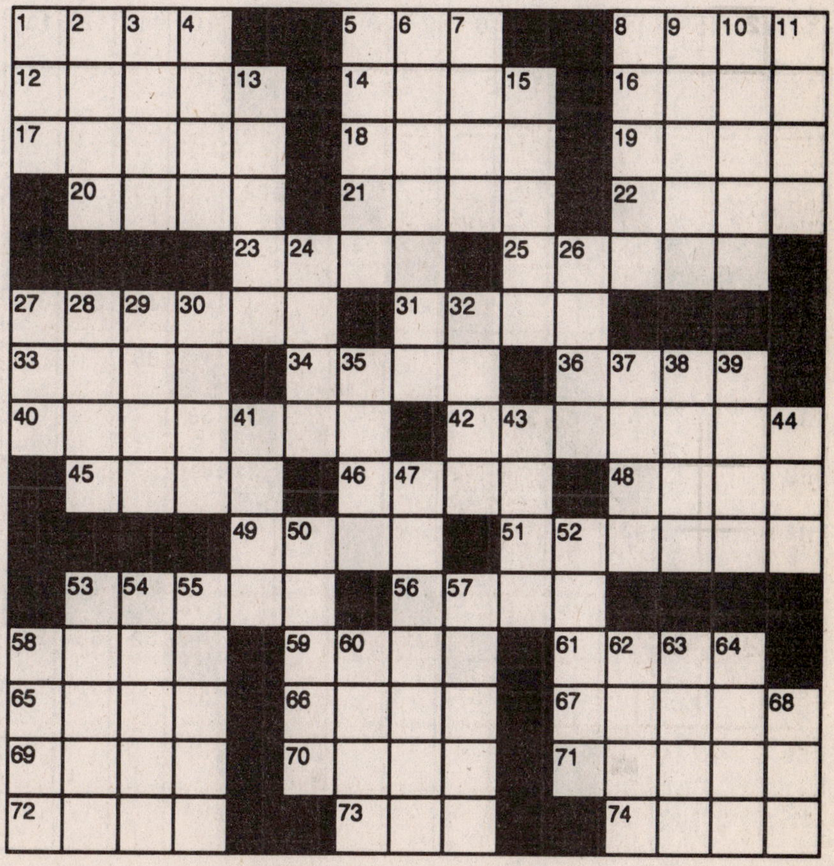

# PUZZLE 555

**ACROSS**

1. Ripped
5. Soda sipper
10. Gangster's gal
14. Woodwind
15. Ordinary writing
16. Samoan port
17. Gain control: 4 wds.
20. Nautical assent
21. Relaxation
22. Kirstie of "Cheers"
23. Red planet
24. Chablis, e.g.
26. Estates
29. Hoarders: 2 wds.
33. Fragrance
34. Radials
35. Plant seed
36. Tardy
37. Card game
38. Oxford
39. Lifetime
40. Ships' tracks
41. Fuse with metal
42. Kid's game: 2 wds.
44. Dance step
46. Prayer ending
47. Whip
48. Ladder rung
51. Certain
52. White lie
55. Make a habit of: 3 wds.
59. Inky black
60. Inclined, as a vessel
61. Before long
62. Knight's wife
63. Actress Davis
64. Lease out

**DOWN**

1. Roman garb
2. Mind orders
3. Repetition
4. Profit
5. Asparagus stalks
6. Bind firmly
7. Lasso
8. Viper
9. Very small
10. Austrian composer
11. Milky gem
12. Rule mark
13. English title
18. Listen to
19. Gradings
23. Additional
24. Merchandise
25. Bakery worker
26. Grinding tooth
27. Old saying
28. Illustrious
29. Cheap person
30. Fire remains
31. Implements
32. Scandinavian
34. Subway fare
37. Surface a road
38. Hit a fly
40. Madames
43. Gorge
44. Medicinal ointment
45. This one: Latin
47. Explode
48. Went fast
49. Brass instrument
50. Mighty particle
51. Roasting stick
52. Penalty
53. Religious image
54. Curved
56. Small flap
57. Corrida cheer
58. Veteran sailor

# PUZZLE 556

**ACROSS**

1. Stem
6. Lukewarm
11. Perform
14. "The —— Chase"
15. Silly
16. Three: prefix
17. Changes in fortune: 3 wds.
19. Impresario Hurok
20. Born
21. Morning moistures
22. Perfect
24. Health havens
26. Inflicts punishment
27. Ambush
30. Skin openings
32. Once more
33. Transfers
34. Actress Gabor
37. Lizard
38. Occupied
39. Hold fast
40. Cozy place
41. Provide food
42. Jet
43. Dwellings
44. Dancer Ruby
45. Adjust again
48. House plant
49. Leaves out
50. Russian ruler
52. Indian
55. Ballpoint
56. Suited to your abilities: 3 wds.
60. Work unit
61. Fable lesson
62. Wash lightly
63. Deli bread
64. Make an effort
65. Butcher's offerings

**DOWN**

1. Made thread
2. Horn or Cod
3. Church area
4. Pod vegetable
5. Sea bird
6. Ocean movements
7. Enough, old style
8. Animal feet
9. Hostel
10. Longs for
11. Confused: 2 wds.
12. Frog sound
13. Money drawers
18. June 6, 1944: hyph.
23. —— Moines
24. Long, narrow cut
25. Review harshly
26. English architect
27. Magic stick
28. Writer James
29. Fatigue sign
30. Jabs
31. Above
33. Spouse
34. Of an age
35. Climbing plant
36. Imitator
38. Domesticated
39. Small valley
41. Eat
42. —— diem
43. Shack
44. Actress Deborah
45. Lasso artist
46. Nail board
47. Hint of color
48. Defect
50. Phoenician city
51. Fly high
52. Forelimb bone
53. Exam
54. Flirts
57. Disease
58. Part of a sofa
59. Whopper

# PUZZLE 557

**ACROSS**

1. Arrived
5. Tree's fluid
8. Small brook
12. Baking chamber
13. ___ la la
14. Huron's neighbor
15. Outdo
16. ___ Tin Tin
17. Not any
18. Cook slowly
20. Steaks
22. Pool stick
23. Skid ___
24. Knack
27. New York baseballer
31. Self
32. Under the weather
33. Argue
37. Thickset
40. Reject
41. Egg producer
42. ___ cocktail
45. Gone up
49. Crew
50. Sea eagle
52. Floor piece
53. Song for a diva
54. Carpet
55. Gaelic
56. ___ weevil
57. Golf mound
58. Exploit

**DOWN**

1. Baseball great Ty ___
2. State
3. Flat-top hill
4. Lure
5. Easy or Main
6. Mr. Onassis
7. Food closet
8. Fame
9. Press, as clothes
10. "I Walk the ___"
11. Brenda and Pinky
19. "Empire of the ___"
21. ___ constrictor
24. Actor Danson
25. Birthday number
26. Tennis shot
28. Aunt and uncle
29. Large deer
30. TV's Ron ___
34. Creature
35. Actor Allen of "Home Improvement"
36. Specialist
37. ___ horses in midstream
38. That girl
39. ___ States
42. ___ in the back
43. Victor
44. Train track
46. Father
47. Choice word
48. Want
51. Regret

# PUZZLE 558

**ACROSS**

1. Shasta and Grand Coulee
5. Stories
10. Forbidding
14. Part of QED
15. Plant disease
16. Go by bus
17. Conflagration
18. Pitfalls
19. Epic poem
20. Flee: 4 wds.
23. Rajah's wife
24. Indian peasant
25. Witch town
28. Also
30. Seeger and Fountain
34. Wears away
36. Married woman's title
38. Blockhead
39. Excavate
40. Abhors
43. Whopper
44. Cruising
46. Medical test
47. Discolor
49. Cozy places
51. Fall behind
53. Nuisances
54. Family or shoe
56. Movie dog
58. Impose upon: 3 wds.
65. Desert robes
66. Scorch
67. Goad
68. Hat fabric
69. Organic compound
70. Robert ——: 2 wds.
71. Golf pegs
72. Rent
73. Bird food

**DOWN**

1. Dexterous
2. Scotto's specialty
3. Swimmer Spitz
4. Piloted
5. Wyoming range
6. Skillful
7. Spare
8. Supreme rulers
9. Impudent
10. Welcomed
11. Ready for picking
12. Object of worship
13. Hodgepodge
21. Bested a beast
22. Jump
25. Family car
26. Get up
27. Theater boxes
29. Greek letter
31. Highway charges
32. T.S. or George
33. Mulligan and Irish
35. Visualize
37. Eye problem
41. Broadcast on cable
42. Partitions
45. Certifies by oath
48. Alliances
50. Mrs.: Sp.
52. Indian river
55. Ford bomb
57. Cubic meter
58. 27th President
59. Busy as ——: 2 wds.
60. Cabbage
61. Theater org.
62. Perry's creator
63. S-shaped molding
64. Nourish

# PUZZLE 559

**ACROSS**

1. Houses in Seville
6. Marketed
10. Toga
14. Writer Jong
15. Cafeteria item
16. Tarzan's friends
17. Giddiness: hyph.
20. Rural road
21. Greasy
22. Concur
23. Devotee
24. Goodies
25. More certain
28. Lobby
30. Wall art
31. Disappearing seat
32. Which person
35. Ethereal: 4 wds.
40. Adherent: suffix
41. Tap
42. Garment
43. Menfolk
45. Limerick
46. Valentine words: 2 wds.
49. Purchase
50. Make amends
51. Alack!
53. Arrived
57. Explains: 3 wds.
60. Listen to
61. Excited
62. Beyond
63. Sea eagles
64. Numerous
65. Old Persians

**DOWN**

1. Prison pad
2. "Carmen" solo
3. Symbol
4. Pain
5. Perched
6. Mug
7. Kind of exam
8. Lord's wife
9. Tint
10. State trooper
11. Musical drama
12. Assail
13. Wiggly letters
18. Rime
19. Defy
23. Sensed
24. Sort
25. Spades, e.g.
26. Spur
27. Stadium yell
28. Irises
29. Simpleton
30. 1,051, to Caesar
32. Caprice
33. Present!
34. Table scrap
36. Efficient
37. Take to court
38. Wan
39. Quaker pronoun
43. Those under 21
44. Over again
45. Football tactic
46. Wash
47. Anesthetic
48. "Happy Days" actress
49. Ill-fitting
51. Pond vegetation
52. Pride patriarch
53. Geometric figure
54. Footless
55. Relocate
56. Hydrocarbon suffixes
58. Sleuth Spade
59. Highland hat

# PUZZLE 560

**ACROSS**

1. Gather
6. Large nail
10. Arab robe
13. Macaroni
14. Carry
15. Slip
16. Giant
17. Ancient Syria
18. Coil
19. Tolkien work, with "The": 4 wds.
22. Table piece
23. River to the Rhine
24. State
27. Curls
32. Chaps
33. Gelding
34. Egyptian king, for short
35. Mimic
36. Mighty tree
37. Fuss
38. Bakery item
39. Types
41. Fowl
43. Jewelry items
45. Very harsh
46. Overhead trains
47. Sensible
48. Sounds phony: 3 wds.
55. "—— Love Her": 2 wds.
56. Comfort
57. Less common
59. British gun
60. On the briny
61. Like a gymnast
62. Sweetie, for short
63. Exploit
64. Charter

**DOWN**

1. Fitting
2. Correspondence
3. Concerning: 2 wds.
4. Young actress
5. Actor George
6. Employees
7. Legal injury
8. Bryce Canyon's locale
9. Puts down
10. Similar
11. Cherry type
12. Does sums
15. Eddy
20. Granola grain
21. Craze
24. Open
25. Brown shade
26. Curl the lip
27. They all lead to Rome
28. Annoys
29. Storehouse
30. Royal name
31. Rock
33. —— Kong
39. Potter's oven
40. Preferably
41. In the middle
42. Unexceptional
44. Varnish ingredient
45. Droop
47. PGA champ
48. Elan
49. Atop
50. Utopia
51. Demolish, in England
52. Understanding phrase: 2 wds.
53. Murre genus
54. Slippery ones
58. Female ruff

# PUZZLE 561

**ACROSS**

1. Grate
5. "____ Dawn"
10. Openwork fabric
14. Piece together
19. Reed
20. River to the Rhone
21. Comic Johnson
22. Juan's January
23. After case or base
24. Step
25. TV knob
26. ____ in the bucket: 2 wds.
27. Hawaiian naval base: 2 wds.
30. Kind of sale
32. Band of color
33. Wind dir.
34. Weapons warehouse
36. Total
38. ____ terrier
40. Pastoral place
45. "____ Ballou"
48. Coed's digs
51. Senator Kefauver
54. Sea ducks
55. Mideast father
57. Clamor
59. Como ____?
61. Principle
62. Small vegetables: 2 wds.
65. Official policy: 2 wds.
67. Basin, e.g.
68. Encountered
69. ____ Grande
70. U.S. citizen
71. Nacre: hyph.
77. Stuff
81. Modern: prefix
82. King of France
83. Basket fiber
88. Wall decorator
91. "How-dee" sayer: 2 wds.
94. Marble
95. Island group off Ireland
97. Absorb knowledge
98. Small amount
99. Plaid of Scotland
101. Carved stone
103. Nixon and Boone
105. Rubber-stamps
106. Went on stage
108. Assists
110. Depot: abbr.
112. Pantries
115. Grade letter
118. Special persons
122. Cowboys
126. Dolly portrayer: 2 wds.
129. Screamer
130. Archaic verb
132. Spanish province
133. Domino
134. Chilean port
135. Kind of club
136. Varnish ingredient
137. To ____: 2 wds.
138. Like a gnat
139. Grade sch.
140. Printing unit
141. Allows

**DOWN**

1. Frolics
2. Red as ____: 2 wds.
3. Underwater detector
4. Lab containers
5. Plate
6. These, in Cadiz
7. Edward and Norman
8. Extended families
9. Gaseous prefix
10. Humor magazine
11. The Red et al.
12. No longer fresh
13. Mme. Rubenstein
14. Oahu locale: 2 wds.
15. "On a Wing ____ Prayer": 2 wds.
16. Seagull
17. Gator's kin
18. Hospital ship
28. Praise
29. Charles et al.
31. Swiss river
35. Network
37. Unvaried drone
39. Wailer
41. William the Conqueror's daughter
42. Jeans fabric
43. Goddess of peace
44. Starflower
45. Bottle tops
46. Support
47. Ski lift: hyph.
49. Director Howard
50. Roman 1,002
52. Clairvoyant's gift: abbr.
53. Gape
56. Exist
58. Any
60. Concert solo
63. Moon vehicle
64. "The Mortal ____"
66. Floods
72. Trillion: prefix
73. Farmers, at times
74. Stopped in time
75. Conifer
76. ____ of luxury
77. Packing box

# PUZZLE 561

78. King Lear's daughter
79. Separate
80. Photo finish
84. G-man
85. Game of chance
86. Foe of Khomeini
87. Charity
89. Neutral hue: 2 wds.
90. Ship-leaver
92. Snooze
93. A Gershwin
96. At hand
100. Actress Patricia
102. Speak incorrectly
104. Greek colonnade
107. Coat with flour
109. Mountain climber
111. ___ kingdom
113. Wryly humorous
114. Ms. Lauder
116. Expunge
117. Graceland's master
119. Cheer up
120. Adjust a watch
121. "Oliver Twist" villain
122. Do gift work
123. Out of the ordinary
124. Rara ___
125. Scarf locale
127. Lawman Wyatt
128. Forbids
131. Changing fashion line

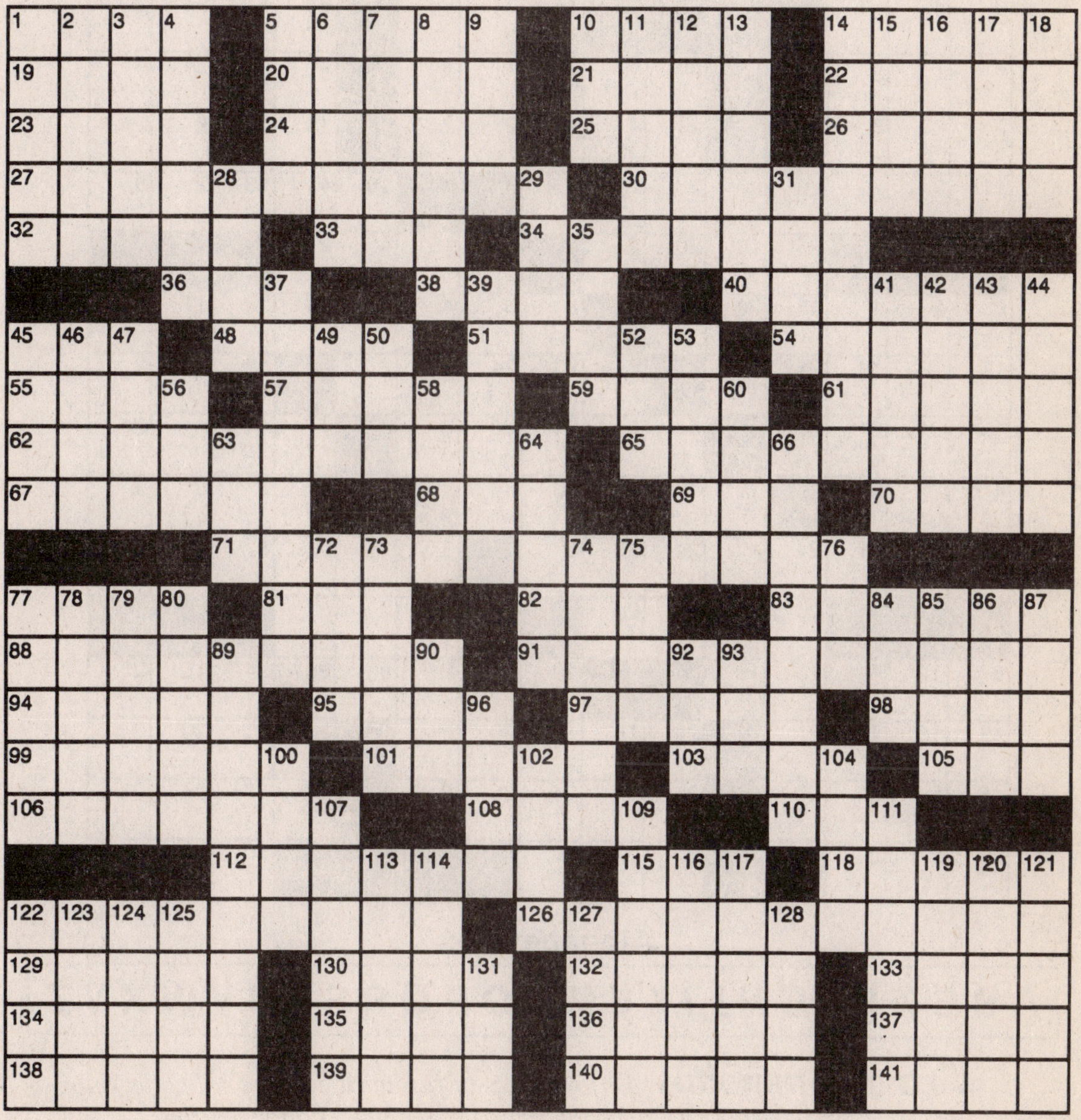

# PUZZLE 562

**CODEWORD**

**Codeword is a special crossword puzzle in which conventional clues are omitted. Instead, answer words in the diagram are represented by numbers. Each number represents a different letter of the alphabet, and all of the letters of the alphabet are used. When you are sure of a letter, put it in the code key chart and cross it off in the Alphabet Box. A group of letters has been inserted to start you off.**

| | | | | | | | | | | | | |
|---|---|---|---|---|---|---|---|---|---|---|---|---|
| 1 | 2 | 3 | 4 | 5 | 6 | 7 | 8 | 9 | 10 | 11 | 12 | 13 D |
| 14 | 15 | 16 | 17 | 18 | 19 | 20 | 21 | 22 | 23 L | 24 I | 25 | 26 |

| | | | | | | | | | | | | | | |
|---|---|---|---|---|---|---|---|---|---|---|---|---|---|---|
| 9 | 4 | 10 | ■ | ■ | ■ | ■ | 15 | 24 | 26 | ■ | 8 | 4 | 25 | 2 |
| 2 | 7 | 4 | 22 | ■ | 26 | 6 | 24 | 1 | 2 | ■ | 4 | 21 | 24 | 4 |
| 2 | 23 | 8 | 2 | ■ | 21 | 4 | 20 | 2 | 2 | ■ | 15 | 24 | 8 | 26 |
| 21 | 2 | 2 | 20 | 26 | 2 | 21 | 8 | ■ | ■ | 15 | 4 | 13 | 2 | 8 |
| ■ | ■ | ■ | 26 | 18 | 20 | 2 | ■ | 4 | 15 | 4 | 21 | ■ | ■ | ■ |
| 8 | 2 | 1 | 18 | 20 | 13 | ■ | 8 | 5 | 4 | 1 | 24 | 18 | 11 | 8 |
| 18 | 13 | 18 | 21 | 8 | ■ | 8 | 23 L | 24 I | 13 D | 2 | ■ | 18 | 20 | 2 |
| 15 | 24 | 21 | 8 | ■ | 8 | 5 | 24 | 20 | 8 | ■ | 1 | 14 | 4 | 21 |
| 4 | 1 | 2 | ■ | 18 | 6 | 24 | 20 | 3 | ■ | 1 | 21 | 2 | 5 | 2 |
| 8 | 26 | 21 | 24 | 17 | 24 | 20 | 3 | ■ | 3 | 11 | 2 | 8 | 26 | 8 |
| ■ | ■ | ■ | 20 | 4 | 22 | 2 | ■ | 12 | 11 | 2 | 8 | ■ | ■ | ■ |
| 8 | 12 | 4 | 13 | 16 | ■ | ■ | 19 | 11 | 2 | 8 | 26 | 24 | 18 | 20 |
| 12 | 18 | 22 | 2 | ■ | 20 | 18 | 11 | 20 | 8 | ■ | 2 | 21 | 20 | 2 |
| 18 | 5 | 2 | 20 | ■ | 2 | 13 | 24 | 26 | 8 | ■ | 13 | 18 | 26 | 2 |
| 26 | 2 | 20 | 26 | ■ | 6 | 2 | 26 | ■ | ■ | ■ | ■ | 20 | 18 | 13 |

**Alphabet Box**

**A B C ~~D~~ E F G H ~~I~~ J K ~~L~~ M N O P Q R S T U V W X Y Z**

★ ***LOVE CODEWORDS?*** *Enjoy hours of fun with our special collections of Selected Codewords! To order,* *see page 63 for details.* ★

# PUZZLE 563

**ACROSS**

1. Evergreen tree
4. Prevents
8. Foundation
12. King topper
13. Ireland
14. Egg-shaped
15. Explain
17. Hardy
18. Incline
19. Makes aware
21. Boulder
23. Lose traction
24. Sour
25. Monkeys
26. Favorite
29. Drink for Andy Capp
30. Prevent
31. Anger
32. Crimson
33. Lairs
34. Pine fruit
35. Scurry
36. Musical sounds
37. Enchants
40. Blaze
41. Fury
42. Upper canines
46. Mine finds
47. Lounge about
48. Fish eggs
49. Ties the knot
50. Christmas
51. Bart to Homer

**DOWN**

1. Fashion
2. Arctic abundance
3. Fixed
4. Swiss capital
5. Waterless
6. Make fun of
7. Court shoes
8. Arched
9. Affirm
10. Pepper's mate
11. Building wings
16. Penny
20. Roster
21. Celebrity
22. Story
23. Exhausted
25. Unwillingly
26. Early settlers
27. Sea eagle
28. Golf pegs
30. Rocker Ant
34. Center
35. Garb
36. Document
37. Black bird
38. Mad March creature
39. Grew older
40. Dropped
43. Second person
44. Also
45. Coop occupant

# PUZZLE 564

**ACROSS**

1. Bush-master
6. Swindle
10. —— -bellum
14. Gait
18. Worries
19. Goodbye: hyph.
20. David Copper-field's wife
21. Chicago terminal
22. Hoyle's forte
23. Particle
24. Portal
25. Unwanted sounds
26. Place for entertain-ment
27. Swedish seaport
29. Renowned frontiers-man: 2 wds.
31. Catkin plant: 2 wds.
33. Iranian sovereign
34. Navy man: abbr.
35. Chinese: prefix
36. Actress Carter
39. Old Testament book
41. Injure
45. Criminal team
47. Accommo-dation
49. Frome
52. Other name
54. Actor Car-michael
56. Peter, Paul, and Mary
58. Ankle
60. Climbing plants
62. Black Sea gulf
64. Gull
66. Catty
67. Central points
69. Less musical
70. Touches
72. Before, poetically
73. South African
74. Enthrone
78. Loose overcoat
80. French architec-ture style
85. Roman tourist attraction
87. "——, Brute?": 2 wds.
88. Kite
89. Watery swelling
90. Minestrone
92. Pouch
93. French girl
94. Loos
96. Revealing all
98. Mother of Helen
101. Catches
102. French composer
104. Places
106. Military VIP: abbr.
108. Current unit
111. Singer Horne
113. Awful event
119. 20th U.S. president and family
122. Puts out
123. Constella-tion
124. Foreigner
125. Perfume
127. Moderate
128. One given authority
129. Italian staple
130. Diva Gluck
131. Press
132. Spud
133. Columnist Bombeck
134. Tidy
135. Jargon
136. Trap

**DOWN**

1. Dogfight
2. Pacific republic
3. City on the Rhone
4. Laments
5. Specialty of Elia
6. Endurance
7. Certain Spaniards
8. Coral reef
9. Material wealth
10. Say further
11. Recess
12. Une, deux, ——
13. Miss Kitt
14. Thunder god
15. Rear
16. Bean or Welles
17. Youths
21. Spot for a Williams cat: 5 wds.
28. Indebted for
30. "Along —— a Spider"
32. False hair
37. Allow
38. Songbirds
40. Actor Dick
41. Semi
42. "I cannot tell ——": 2 wds.
43. Iranian coin
44. "The —— Love": 2 wds.
46. Mideast seaport
48. Roman 52
50. Asian range
51. Microwave, slangily
53. California island: 2 wds.
55. Work of fiction
57. Character in "A Fish Called Wanda"
59. Sunday talk: abbr.
61. Alliance acronym
63. Part of a poem
65. Layers
68. Lithuanian relatives
71. Prized things
73. American historian: 2 wds.
74. Frozen water
75. Nothing: Sp.
76. British gun
77. Dravidian language

# PUZZLE 564

78. Common
79. And others: Latin
81. First fratricide
82. Heraldic term
83. Stone ax
84. Mine finds
86. Bounce up and down
91. Paid athlete
95. Toward shelter
97. —— homo
99. Religious nonconformity
100. Colony insect
103. Borrowed: 2 wds.
105. Of certain metrical feet
107. Certain slavs
108. Wide open
109. Of the cheek
110. Light disperser
112. Confound
114. Crown
115. Pianolike instrument
116. Religious representation
117. Sharpener
118. —— nous
120. Goat cheese
121. Body of an organism
126. Cat's prey

# PUZZLE 565

**ACROSS**

1. —— party
7. Drawing room
12. Chicken part
18. Kind of goat
19. Writers
21. Simon ——
22. Mumble
23. "The —— Falcon"
24. Motor
25. Before: prefix
26. In one's dotage
28. Run aground
30. Mr. Spade
31. —— Cobb: 2 wds.
33. Ocean sunfish
34. African antelope
35. Festival
36. Letters
38. Modern
39. Roman three
40. Amerced
41. Excavation site
43. Harold or Richard
47. Reclined
49. Steeple
51. Auction word
52. Rent
55. Greek warrior
58. Was in session
59. Small boats
62. Reprocess leather
63. Innuendo
66. Resign voluntarily
67. Globe
68. Political faction
69. Raise
70. A king of Judah
71. Some tests
74. Traders in foreign goods
76. Serf
78. Small cigar
80. Mauna ——
81. Hair lightener
83. Kilt
84. Subject
86. Square columns
87. Paint layer
89. Bullfight area
90. Easter-egg dipper
91. Belt
94. Layer
96. Standard
98. Smooths
102. Cad
103. "—— Boatmen"
105. Gazetteer
107. Viewed
108. Power unit
109. Warship
110. Burned out the inside
112. Literary collection
113. "—— Tap" (film)
115. Arouse
117. Wise old man
119. Apartment dweller
120. Pittsburgh footballer
121. Take out
122. Mountain ridges
123. Surfeited
124. Germ cells

**DOWN**

1. Specimen
2. Habituates
3. Gives consent
4. Gypsy man
5. Shank
6. Seraglio
7. Rascal
8. City on the Rhone
9. Ignited
10. Fat
11. Baby bird
12. Mix
13. Tear
14. Incite to action
15. Out of bed
16. Washington group
17. Abounded
19. Show pleasure
20. Oriental inn
27. "And Then There Were ——"
29. Dye source
32. Daughter of Job
35. Conclusion
37. Temptress
40. Pasture
42. Actor Beatty
44. Pinkish red
45. Ananias
46. Amuse
48. Winglike part
49. Mountain ranges
50. Clayware locale
53. African country
54. Incident
55. Hang low
56. Iraq city
57. Comedienne Diamond
59. Steep slope
60. Drying framework
61. Condition
64. Dandy
65. Once named

# PUZZLE 565

72. Secular
73. Razor sharpener
75. Cowboy's line
76. Sharpens to a keen edge
77. Some film actors
79. Timetable letters
82. Light beam
84. Digressions
85. Caught
88. God of thunder
90. Fiddlesticks!
91. Daisy
92. State of mind
93. Complain
95. Presley
97. Change size
99. More tidy
100. Indicate
101. Certain drums
103. Electrical force units
104. "Victory ——": 2 wds.
105. Spry
106. Transmits
109. Sugar source
111. Profound
114. King Cole
116. Dino to the Flintstones
118. Road sign

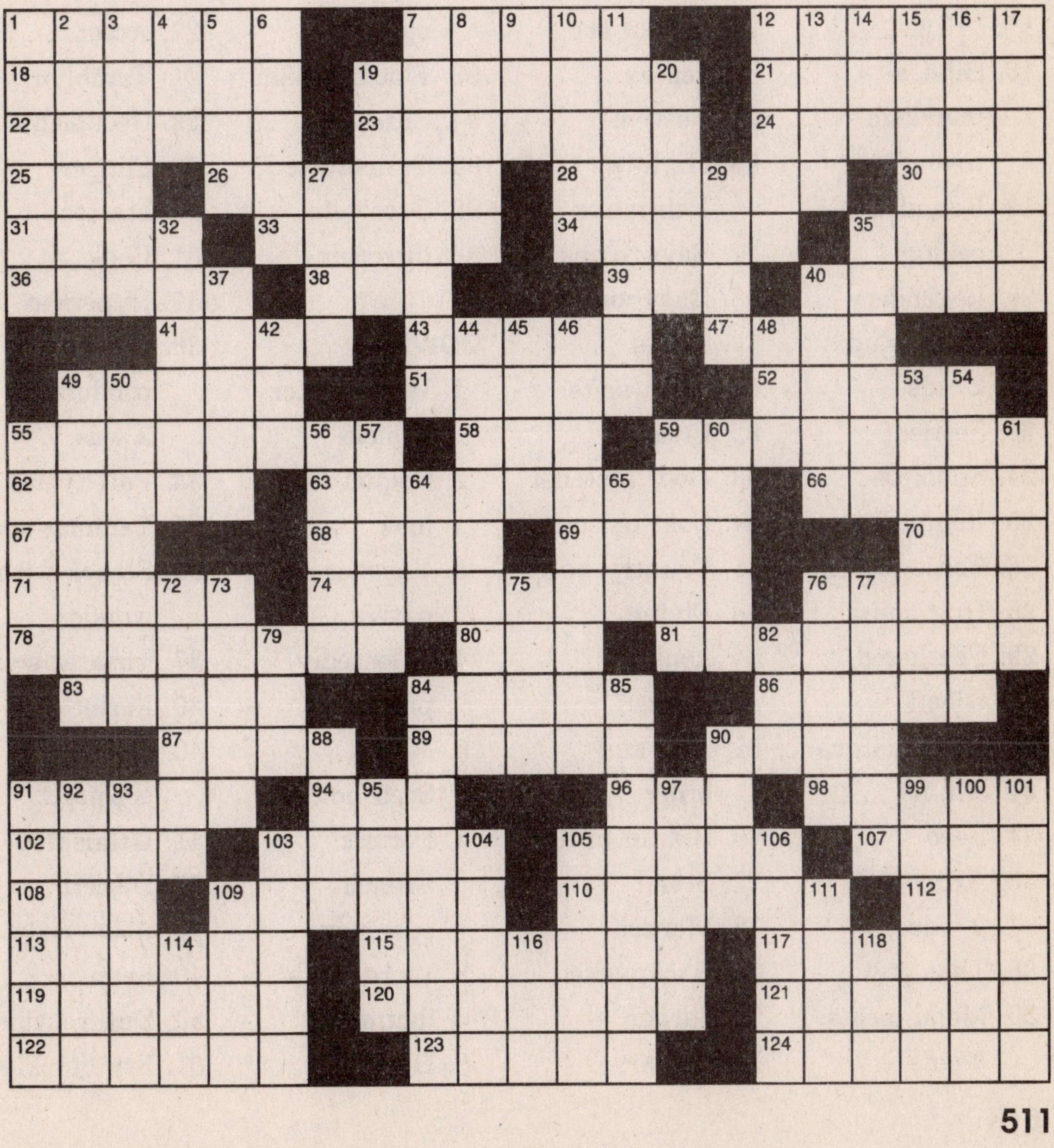

# PUZZLE 566

**ACROSS**

1. Noisy celebration
5. Church section
9. Furniture style
13. Infant food
16. Petri-dish medium
17. "High ____"
18. Biblical marriage town
19. Rounded ceiling
20. Legendary ghost ship: 2 wds.
23. Settled
24. Spoofers
25. Regrets
26. Celtic priests
28. Hog house
29. Feathered friend
30. Insect larvae
31. Ali, ne ____
34. Feed
35. Army VIP: 2 wds.
38. That guy
39. Menu meats: 2 wds.
42. Tea number
43. Abel bearer
44. Bohemian
45. Curtis's "The Great ____"
46. At that time
47. Spanking rods
49. Prop
51. Unkempt
52. ____ curtain
53. One of the senses
54. Festive
55. Highway to Fairbanks
57. Savage one
58. Busybody: 2 wds.
61. Anthracite
62. Create
63. Door fastener
64. Coat or soup
65. Country hotel
66. Flying honker: 2 wds.
69. ____ and order
70. Bid, in bridge
72. Stand
73. Market
74. Backpacker
75. Jargon
76. Drone
78. Vistas
80. Ceremonial staff
81. Says without proof
85. Nautical term
86. Rubdown: 2 wds.
89. Assemble
90. Relaxation
91. Incenses
92. Samoan capital
93. Flock mother
94. Curses!
95. Transmitted
96. Greeley's direction

**DOWN**

1. White-water vehicle
2. Coquettish look
3. Yucatan native
4. Affectedly proper
5. Mad
6. Seed holders
7. Former French currency
8. Words in a dictionary
9. Hurt
10. Beaver works
11. Anthology
12. Comic-strip magician
13. Score Brownie points: 3 wds.
14. Between
15. Favorites
19. Fingerpaints
21. Final
22. Corkscrew items
27. Actor Tamblyn
29. Occupied
30. Supper starter
31. Cook
32. In person
33. Dairy product: 2 wds.
34. Paroxysms
35. Tanning spot
36. Struck with wonder
37. Theater award
39. Parlor
40. English architect
41. Delineate
46. Discern
48. Asian river
49. Leap
50. Dull routine
51. Fry quickly

53. Musketeers, e.g.
54. Young dames
55. Caustic
56. Solitary
57. Howler
58. Impoverished
59. "___ People"
60. Sailing vessel
62. Patted
63. Rock the ___
66. Black Forest item
67. Adders' aid
68. "Land of Confusion" group
71. Salesmen's goods
73. Playground item
75. Military student
76. Crikey
77. City trains
78. Unchanged
79. Hammer part
80. Arizona town
81. Congregation's cry
82. Ogle
83. Protection
84. Ladderback
87. Card game
88. Charlemagne's realm: abbr.

# PUZZLE 566

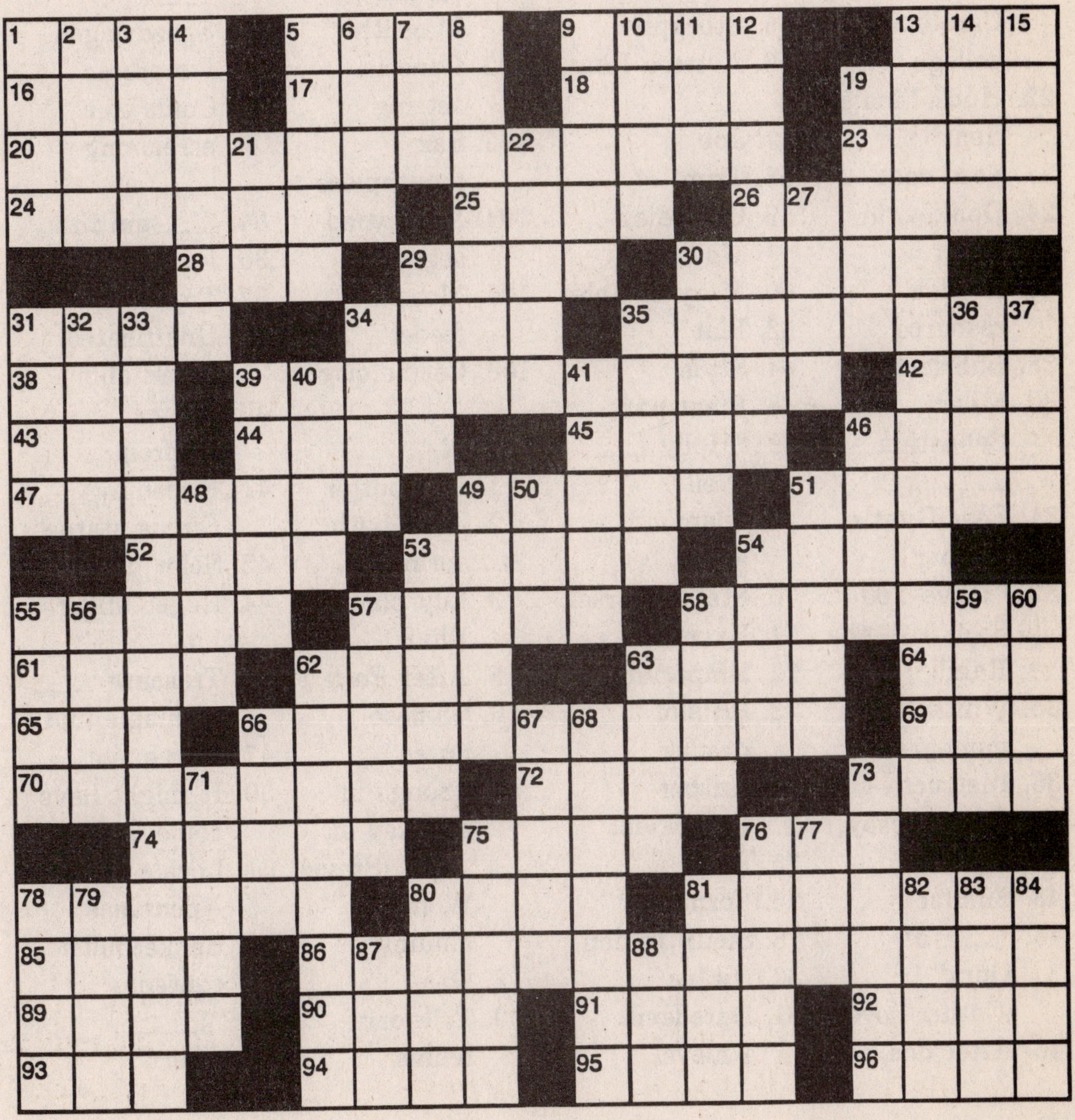

# PUZZLE 567

**ACROSS**

1. EMT's word
5. Still
9. Indian desert
13. Square
17. Nimbus
18. Pure Prairie League song
19. Verdi opera
20. Prod
21. North Carolina college
22. Huck Finn's float
23. Seed coat
24. Donkey, in Bonn
25. Hidden resource
28. Lubricate
30. Miler Sebastian ____
31. Peer Gynt's mother
32. "Have You Ever ____ the Rain"
33. White House monogram
36. Instructs
39. Bing Crosby, e.g.
43. Similar
45. "____ of Ours" (Cather novel)
46. After dos
48. Crenshaw's cry
49. Actress Anderson
50. Finale
51. Boxer Barkley
52. Easy gait
53. "I Was a ____ Werewolf"
55. Stockpile
56. Actress Ilka ____
57. Job
58. Trim
59. Comedian Howard
60. Mary or John
63. Flat
64. Style
68. Plant part
69. "Holly ____" (Neil Diamond song)
70. Stable morsel
71. Except
72. Emporium
73. Pribilof dweller
74. Author Lagerkvist
75. Bash
76. Formicary
78. Sioux Indian
80. Nibble
81. Daredevil Knievel
82. TV sitcom
83. Horned viper
85. Extent
88. Toy
94. Refrigerator item
95. Sulk
97. Rewrite
98. Part of ETA
99. Gumbo
100. Irish river
101. Belgian painter Magritte
102. Genesis setting
103. Sax mouthpiece
104. Hollywood segment
105. Moselle feeder
106. Casino city

**DOWN**

1. ____ butter
2. After-bath sprinkle
3. Lily plant
4. Elixir
5. After Ford
6. Chinese nurse
7. "Songs in the Key of ____" (Stevie Wonder album)
8. Gas
9. Talk or tennis
10. Give a job to
11. Drillers' gp.
12. NHL team
13. Bobby Darin hit
14. Major or Minor
15. Matures
16. Cross out
26. Take heed of
27. WWII intelligence agcy.
29. Rock group ____ Speedwagon
32. Panorama
33. Come to a screaming ____
34. ____ gin fizz
35. Fork prong
37. Top notch
38. Unaffiliated voter: abbr.
40. Writer Ephron
41. Piccadilly Circus statue
42. Solar plexus
44. Roger Miller hit
46. Treasure-____ (valuable find)
47. Infrequent
50. It might have come first
51. Locale of the Apennines
54. Basketball's contents
55. "I ____ return"

# PUZZLE 567

56. Romaine
58. Greek portico
59. Surface for Hulk Hogan
60. Michigan college
61. Playwright O'Casey
62. Sour
63. Beach-comber's find
64. Casino game
65. Concerning
66. Olive genus
67. Minsk refusal
70. Acorn, someday
73. Woody Allen film
74. Green Bay eleven
75. Obi
77. "____ Gotta Be Me"
78. "____ Hollywood"
79. Shred
82. Honey badger
84. Film director Weir
85. "Let's Make a Deal" choice
86. Actress Sommer
87. "Pretty Woman" star
88. Haver or Havoc
89. Thought
90. Designer Ricci
91. Remain
92. Portent
93. Alien: pref.
96. Siderite, e.g.

## PUZZLE 1

## PUZZLE 2

## PUZZLE 3

## PUZZLE 4

## PUZZLE 5

Acre, Agog, Away, Baby, Barb, Bare, Bawl, Brag, Bray, Brim, Brow, Care, Core, Cowl, Crab, Crag, Crop, Crow, Garb, Gaze, Gore, Heir, Herb, Here, Hero, Loco, Logo, Lore, Mica, Mice, Mire, Pica, Pier, Polo, Pore, Rare, Raze, Rice, Roar, Scab, Scar, Scow, Slop, Slow, Soar, Solo, Sore, Swab, Swag, Sway, Ware, Wore, Yawl, Zero.

## PUZZLE 6

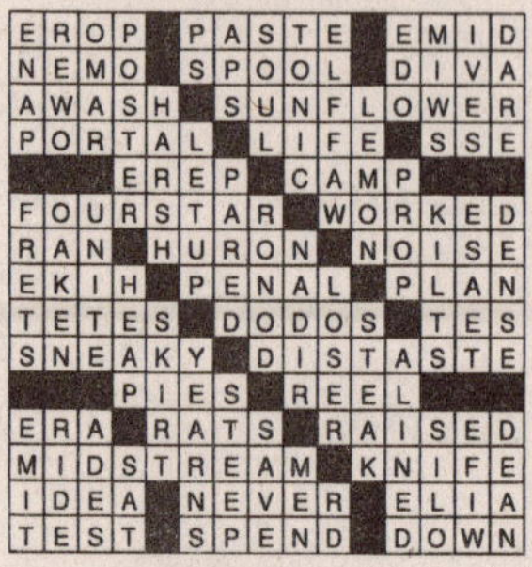

## PUZZLE 7

## PUZZLE 8

1. besEt, 2. purEe, 3. quiEt, 4. steEp, 5. harEm, 6. facEt, 7. carEt, 8. allEy, 9. basEs, 10. aidEs.

## PUZZLE 9

## PUZZLE 10

## PUZZLE 11

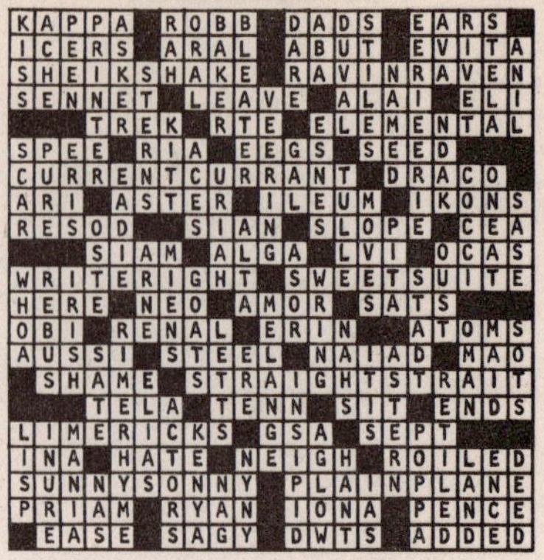

## PUZZLE 12

## PUZZLE 13

Reading is to the mind what exercise is to the body.

1. Exhibits, 2. Oddity, 3. Green, 4. Hoists, 5. Donate, 6. Cream, 7. White.

## PUZZLE 14

## PUZZLE 15

| | | | | | | | | | | | | |
|---|---|---|---|---|---|---|---|---|---|---|---|---|
| Y | O | R | E | | H | I | R | E | | P | U | T |
| A | M | E | N | | E | V | E | N | | A | N | Y |
| M | I | N | C | E | M | E | A | T | | T | I | P |
| S | T | O | O | P | | | P | E | T | I | T | E |
| | | | R | I | B | S | | R | O | E | | |
| E | A | V | E | | E | L | S | | E | N | I | D |
| S | P | A | | | G | E | T | | | C | O | O |
| S | E | L | F | | S | E | A | | S | E | N | T |
| | | U | R | N | | T | R | A | P | | | |
| B | R | A | Y | E | D | | | L | E | A | V | E |
| L | O | B | | C | O | N | T | I | N | U | E | D |
| E | L | L | | K | N | E | E | | D | R | A | G |
| W | E | E | | S | E | W | N | | S | A | L | E |

## PUZZLE 16

| | | | | | | | | | | | | |
|---|---|---|---|---|---|---|---|---|---|---|---|---|
| W | H | O | | A | C | H | E | | F | E | E | L |
| E | E | L | | M | O | O | N | | L | A | V | A |
| T | R | E | M | B | L | E | D | | U | S | E | S |
| | | | O | L | D | | | F | R | E | S | H |
| P | R | I | C | E | | H | E | I | R | | | |
| L | O | O | K | | B | O | B | B | Y | P | I | N |
| E | A | T | | S | L | A | B | S | | O | D | E |
| A | M | A | T | E | U | R | S | | M | O | L | E |
| | | | W | E | E | D | | B | O | R | E | D |
| F | A | C | E | S | | | J | U | T | | | |
| L | I | O | N | | O | V | E | R | H | A | U | L |
| E | D | I | T | | W | I | T | S | | D | R | Y |
| D | E | N | Y | | N | E | S | T | | O | N | E |

## PUZZLE 17

| | | | | | | | | | | | | |
|---|---|---|---|---|---|---|---|---|---|---|---|---|
| P | A | P | A | | J | E | T | | T | H | E | M |
| A | W | E | D | | A | G | O | | E | A | V | E |
| C | L | A | M | | C | O | M | P | A | R | E | S |
| E | S | K | I | M | O | S | | O | P | E | N | S |
| | | | T | A | B | | F | R | O | | | |
| V | E | R | S | E | | P | R | E | T | E | N | D |
| E | R | E | | | S | O | Y | | | S | E | A |
| T | A | D | P | O | L | E | | M | U | S | T | Y |
| | | | L | A | Y | | D | A | N | | | |
| S | T | O | U | T | | P | A | D | L | O | C | K |
| A | R | M | C | H | A | I | R | | I | R | O | N |
| S | E | E | K | | L | E | E | | K | A | T | E |
| H | E | N | S | | A | S | S | | E | L | S | E |

## PUZZLE 18

| | | | | | | | | | | | | | | | | | | |
|---|---|---|---|---|---|---|---|---|---|---|---|---|---|---|---|---|---|---|
| F | I | T | S | | N | A | I | L | | C | R | E | W | | P | R | I | M |
| A | B | U | T | | O | B | O | E | | H | E | R | E | | L | A | N | E |
| M | E | N | U | | B | L | U | E | B | E | A | R | D | | A | C | R | E |
| E | X | A | M | P | L | E | | C | L | A | D | | D | O | C | K | E | T |
| | | | B | E | E | | C | H | O | P | | H | I | K | E | | | |
| A | D | U | L | T | | P | O | E | T | | M | O | N | A | S | T | I | C |
| H | A | R | E | | B | O | S | S | | T | A | N | G | Y | | A | R | A |
| A | S | S | | T | O | O | T | | W | A | R | E | S | | W | R | E | N |
| S | H | A | D | O | O | F | | C | A | R | R | Y | | L | A | P | S | E |
| | | M | I | N | T | | F | A | I | R | Y | | G | A | L | A | | |
| M | A | I | N | E | | M | I | S | T | Y | | B | A | D | L | U | C | K |
| A | U | N | T | | H | O | L | E | S | | B | A | B | Y | | L | I | E |
| P | R | O | | T | A | L | E | S | | K | I | S | S | | M | I | T | E |
| S | A | R | D | I | N | E | S | | W | I | N | K | | P | A | N | E | L |
| | | | O | D | D | S | | F | I | N | E | | C | A | R | | | |
| A | L | L | O | Y | S | | B | I | N | G | | G | A | S | B | A | G | S |
| R | O | O | D | | O | L | I | V | E | D | R | A | B | | L | I | O | N |
| T | O | G | A | | F | O | R | E | | O | U | Z | O | | E | D | N | A |
| S | P | E | D | | F | A | D | S | | M | E | A | T | | S | E | E | P |

## PUZZLE 19

| | | | | | | | | | | | | |
|---|---|---|---|---|---|---|---|---|---|---|---|---|
| B | A | Y | | P | R | O | | | S | H | U | T |
| A | L | I | | L | O | R | E | | C | A | R | E |
| A | L | P | H | A | B | E | T | | R | I | G | S |
| | | | O | N | E | | E | Y | E | L | E | T |
| C | O | M | E | T | | F | R | E | E | | | |
| A | D | O | S | | B | O | N | A | N | Z | A | |
| P | O | P | | T | E | X | A | S | | O | L | D |
| | R | E | M | O | D | E | L | | N | O | T | E |
| | | | O | A | R | S | | D | E | M | O | N |
| O | V | E | R | D | O | | R | I | O | | | |
| P | A | R | T | | O | R | I | E | N | T | A | L |
| A | S | I | A | | M | A | S | T | | A | G | E |
| L | E | E | R | | | Y | E | S | | B | O | O |

## PUZZLE 20

| | | | | | | | | | | | | |
|---|---|---|---|---|---|---|---|---|---|---|---|---|
| A | C | T | S | | D | E | L | L | | S | P | A |
| C | O | N | E | | A | R | E | A | | L | I | P |
| E | N | T | E | R | T | A | I | N | M | E | N | T |
| | | | D | E | E | S | | C | E | D | E | S |
| | S | H | E | D | S | | Y | E | N | | | |
| H | E | E | D | S | | R | E | S | U | L | T | S |
| I | N | A | | | L | E | S | | | O | A | T |
| S | T | R | I | P | E | S | | B | E | N | D | S |
| | | | R | E | X | | L | O | V | E | S | |
| A | D | D | E | R | | S | A | N | E | | | |
| G | R | A | D | U | A | T | I | O | N | D | A | Y |
| T | A | N | | S | P | A | R | | T | I | D | E |
| S | T | E | | E | O | N | S | | S | P | O | T |

## PUZZLE 21

| | | | | | | | | | | | | |
|---|---|---|---|---|---|---|---|---|---|---|---|---|
| P | O | T | | I | D | E | A | | S | L | E | D |
| E | R | E | | N | E | A | R | | H | O | P | E |
| P | E | A | | T | A | S | K | | O | P | E | N |
| | | S | H | O | R | T | | K | N | E | E | S |
| T | A | P | E | | S | E | I | N | E | | | |
| A | B | O | R | T | | R | O | E | | D | O | G |
| C | L | O | S | E | T | | N | A | T | I | V | E |
| T | E | N | | A | I | R | | D | I | V | A | N |
| | | | A | S | P | E | N | | R | O | L | E |
| L | A | R | G | E | | C | A | P | E | R | | |
| A | L | O | E | | M | E | M | O | | C | A | P |
| D | E | A | N | | O | D | E | S | | E | R | A |
| S | E | N | T | | W | E | S | T | | D | E | W |

## PUZZLE 22

| | | | | | | | | | | | | |
|---|---|---|---|---|---|---|---|---|---|---|---|---|
| D | A | B | S | | P | A | L | | B | I | K | E |
| I | R | A | N | | A | C | E | | A | M | E | N |
| S | I | L | O | | T | H | O | U | S | A | N | D |
| C | A | L | O | R | I | E | | P | E | G | | |
| | | | Z | O | O | | P | O | S | I | N | G |
| G | L | U | E | D | | S | I | N | | N | O | R |
| O | I | L | S | | P | O | E | | D | E | S | I |
| O | A | T | | L | A | W | | C | A | D | E | T |
| F | R | I | D | A | Y | | S | O | N | | | |
| | | M | A | D | | L | I | N | C | O | L | N |
| A | N | A | L | Y | Z | E | D | | E | R | I | E |
| T | O | T | E | | E | E | L | | R | A | V | E |
| E | W | E | S | | E | R | E | | S | L | E | D |

## PUZZLE 23

| | | | | | | | | | | | | |
|---|---|---|---|---|---|---|---|---|---|---|---|---|
| F | U | S | E | | A | B | E | L | | A | C | E |
| O | R | E | S | | R | O | D | E | | U | R | N |
| A | G | E | S | | E | R | I | E | | R | I | D |
| L | E | D | | | N | E | T | | T | A | B | S |
| | | I | D | E | A | | E | M | U | | | |
| S | M | E | A | R | S | | D | A | N | C | E | D |
| P | A | S | T | A | | | | T | I | A | R | A |
| A | R | T | I | S | T | | R | E | N | T | E | D |
| | | | N | E | W | | E | D | G | E | | |
| P | L | U | G | | E | B | B | | | G | O | B |
| R | A | G | | F | L | E | E | | H | O | B | O |
| O | I | L | | O | V | A | L | | I | R | O | N |
| P | R | Y | | G | E | M | S | | D | Y | E | D |

## PUZZLE 24

| | | | | | | | | | | | | |
|---|---|---|---|---|---|---|---|---|---|---|---|---|
| L | I | E | S | | F | A | T | S | | F | R | O |
| A | C | R | E | | A | L | O | E | | L | O | W |
| P | E | N | E | T | R | A | T | E | | A | W | E |
| | R | E | D | O | | | O | M | I | T | | |
| | | | E | P | I | C | | S | A | T | E | S |
| S | H | A | D | | C | A | R | | N | E | R | O |
| H | O | B | | | O | R | E | | | R | I | N |
| E | R | A | S | | N | E | B | | D | Y | E | S |
| A | S | S | E | T | | D | A | T | E | | | |
| | | H | E | R | O | | | A | N | T | E | |
| A | L | I | | U | N | D | E | R | T | A | K | E |
| P | E | N | | S | C | A | R | | A | L | E | S |
| E | G | G | | T | E | N | S | | L | E | S | S |

## PUZZLE 25

| | | | | | | | | | | | | |
|---|---|---|---|---|---|---|---|---|---|---|---|---|
| C | A | R | E | | A | C | H | E | | B | A | T |
| A | R | E | A | | G | O | A | T | | I | C | E |
| M | I | N | T | | I | T | C | H | | R | E | D |
| P | A | T | E | N | T | | K | I | N | D | | |
| | | | R | E | A | L | | C | O | S | T | S |
| R | I | D | | A | T | O | M | | R | E | A | P |
| I | R | A | | R | E | G | A | L | | E | K | E |
| T | I | M | E | | S | I | T | E | | D | E | W |
| A | S | P | E | N | | C | E | N | T | | | |
| | | E | L | A | N | | R | O | A | S | T | S |
| S | I | N | | T | E | E | N | | L | O | R | E |
| A | R | E | | E | R | M | A | | O | M | E | N |
| W | E | D | | S | O | U | L | | N | E | E | D |

## PUZZLE 26

| | | | | | | | | | | | | |
|---|---|---|---|---|---|---|---|---|---|---|---|---|
| E | B | B | | H | E | A | D | | T | W | I | G |
| R | Y | E | | A | L | D | A | | W | I | D | E |
| R | E | F | O | R | M | E | R | | I | T | E | M |
| | | R | I | P | S | | K | A | N | S | A | S |
| P | A | I | L | S | | T | R | U | E | | | |
| O | R | E | S | | S | O | O | N | | S | H | E |
| D | E | N | | S | H | O | O | T | | T | O | Y |
| S | A | D | | C | A | L | M | | G | A | L | E |
| | | | H | A | M | S | | W | O | R | D | S |
| A | B | S | O | R | B | | G | O | O | F | | |
| N | E | A | R | | L | E | A | R | N | I | N | G |
| T | A | N | S | | E | V | I | L | | S | E | A |
| E | D | G | E | | S | E | N | D | | H | E | Y |

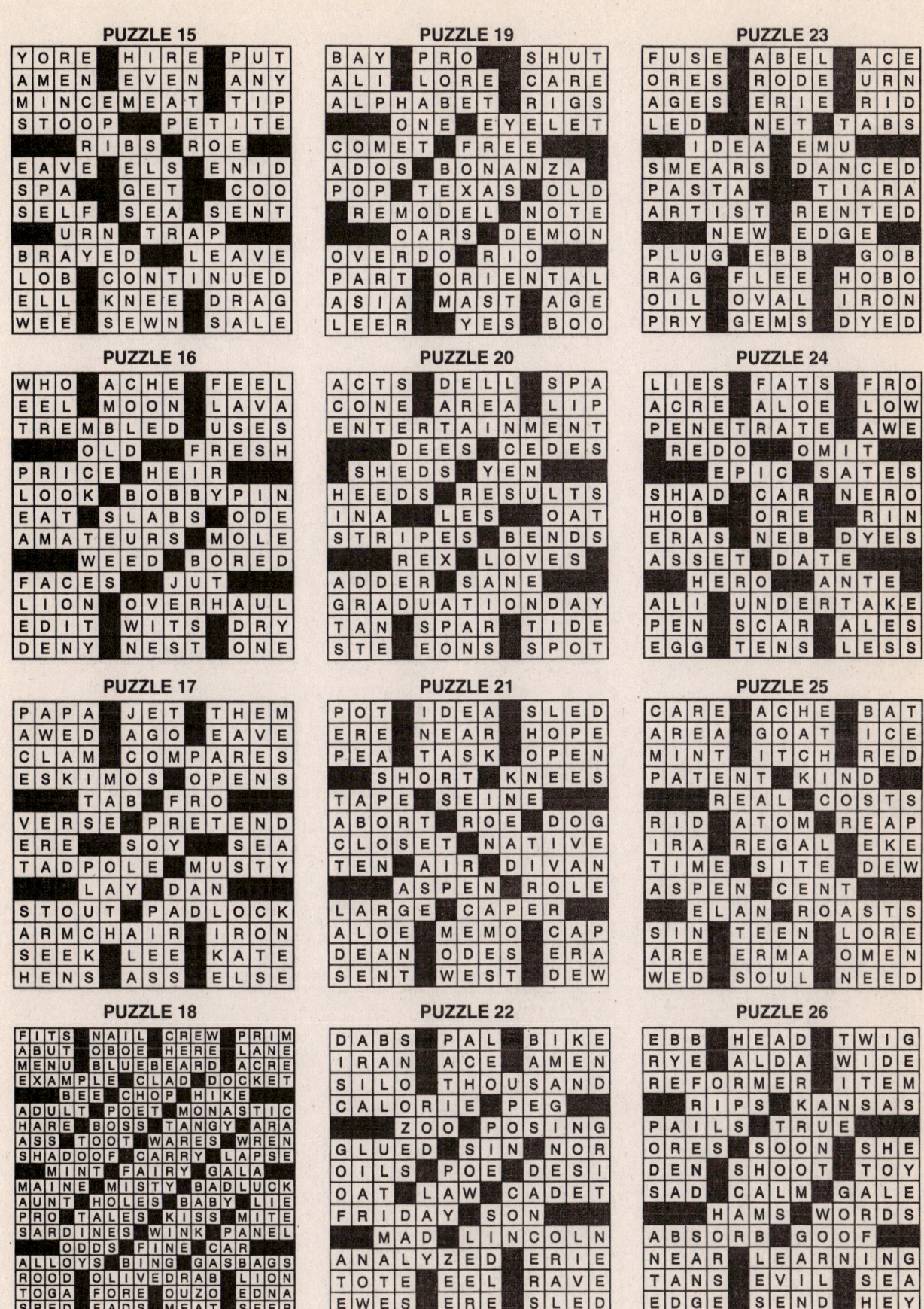

## PUZZLE 27

NEE EMITS ACES
OARS RANEE TARO
MRSMINIVER TSAR
ENTIRE MEDIATE
TASTE ORB
DEMENTED DUELS
ELY NOSES AHA
ELF AGT PIE NIL
SEA GESSO CPA
SISAL HOMEBASE
ROT ELUDE
GALLEON GARAGE
ALAI GOINGMYWAY
REDD EERIE LAVE
BEYS ELAND YES

## PUZZLE 28

MOB ACRE AMEN
AWE DUAL CAVE
DEW URGE ODES
IDLE PARENT
ALLOT CHIN
TIDE SLAM ADE
ONES TAN AMID
PER GRIT LANE
SEAM EATEN
HAPPEN BASE
ISLE GEAR UPS
LEAN EVIL RAP
LAND RELY SLY

## PUZZLE 29

NAPA AGENDA ABA
ALAN MARRON LIN
SINGLETRACKMIND
ANDEAN SLAKES
LEARN TIP EYETO
SAGEBRUSH
ADO IRENES EASE
HARDSET SHIMMER
ANTI TEASED INN
CHARTERED
SHAKO SAD AROSE
EIDERS PLANED
PREYSONONESMIND
TEL ELINOR ACTA
SSE SONANT SEAS

## PUZZLE 30

SNAP PRINT STOP
HOPI RESOW ARNO
OTIC OTTOI LEOS
TEATIME KNAVERY
UMP LIE
SERRATE TERRACE
ADEEM DEANS GEN
TIES TILLS HEAT
ILL ARTIE MANSE
NESTLES STINTER
ABA RAD
TOMCATS DISHPAN
ARAK ELGIN ELMO
RAIL RANEE LEON
ELLE STUNS DARE

## PUZZLE 31

ACID CHAT BRAES
MARE ROTE EERIE
AMEN EBON TSARS
SENT COP STILES
SLEIGHS SLOG
SUE FAIRNESS
SLATS LAND STOP
EAR HOARDED OAR
ASIS VIES HANKY
SHATTERS DOG
RUNS BEWAILS
ATTARS AIL IRON
CRANE ANTE NAPA
MERGE DIET STEP
ESSEN ELSE TESS

## PUZZLE 32

BEST OSRIC DEAN
AMOR STENO IDLE
TIDE CONAN ANON
STANDARD SEDATE
CORE SORE
LIGHT DETRIMENT
ARREST LUTE NEE
BEES HEINE STAR
ONE NEAT DETERS
REDRESSED WORSE
HOPE ALEC
BIKINI FRISKILY
ODIN ANITA AREA
RENO NINER DANK
NAGS SLEDS ENDS

## PUZZLE 33

HALF STROP LOTS
URAL AROMA ERIE
TINY WADER TAME
SAD BED NESTLED
SPADES SUE
FACED RED PRESS
ORANGE NOW SNIP
COP ENRAGED GEE
USED DOT DESIGN
SEDAN TOM PINED
GOT REMOTE
PROGRAM LIT ESS
LOVE PIVOT TRIO
AVER ELIDE HERO
YENS SLAYS EDEN

## PUZZLE 34

CAVE RIATA BLAB
APEX ENDER LENA
TEST ACERB AVON
OSTRICH MISSING
ANT TOT
RACCOON CELEBRE
ABUT RIGOR DRAM
BET COP ARE
ALEE SHOES LIEN
TERMITE DIVIDED
USE GAB
PRELATE ENTERED
AURA SCALA RAVE
CHIT ORIEL TRES
TREE NUDES YANK

## PUZZLE 35

FRO START DAM
OOPS OWNER SALE
ASEA SANTA ELEE
MERIT SAINTNICK
SALEM ECHO
ODES ERRAND
EVER LEAF EAGER
RAM ITEMIZE ERE
ASIAN MILE CROW
SETTLE LAME
TENT LANES
SPLATTERS STATS
ERIC EXITS EVIL
RISK RATES RENE
EMP SNAPS STD

## PUZZLE 36

SPAS ANA LAOS
PACT LOLA ANDES
ANNA IMAN STINT
NEER NANAS ENDS
THEN GEMS
STIRS ARIA ASP
CHINS FRANS PTA
HANG SLIME TROT
ORG RAYES TRIOS
WEE TIPS SHELL
BELA STEM
NATO SPITE BLAB
IRENE EVER LONE
PALES RAVE EONS
TESS NEO SPOT

## PUZZLE 37

FLAP FAST
ORATE LINES
TRIVIA ARENAS
PAD ALLOT EDGES
ALES TENT REGAL
PORES DEEP DELI
ANSWER SNOB DST
SLIP SEEP
CAR FORE TEASED
AWED TEAM SILLY
RAVEL TRUE LODE
PROSE ENTER WED
ELEVEN TRITER
TREND EIDER
TEES REED

## PUZZLE 38

HEMP SHRED SCAT
AMIR TEASE HALE
MILE EAGER IRON
STOPPERS RINSED
AIDS MINE
SPURNS BACKDOOR
TUNES LANKY LIE
ARID TIRES TILE
RET TONGS DIVED
KEEPSAKE CATERS
LASS PORT
DEPART BRAKEMAN
UPON ERROR ROBE
MERE ROADS ELLA
BEES SENSE DEER

## PUZZLE 39

| | | | | | | | | | | | | |
|---|---|---|---|---|---|---|---|---|---|---|---|---|
| S | O | U | R | | S | P | A | | F | O | R | M |
| A | N | T | E | | H | I | S | | O | B | O | E |
| P | E | A | S | | O | P | P | O | N | E | N | T |
| | S | H | I | F | T | | | A | D | D | | |
| | | | D | E | S | E | R | T | | I | C | E |
| S | P | E | E | D | | N | O | S | | E | A | R |
| H | E | N | S | | A | T | E | | A | N | N | A |
| E | E | L | | O | D | E | | R | I | T | E | S |
| A | L | I | | H | O | R | R | O | R | | | |
| | | S | K | I | | | A | B | L | E | R | |
| R | A | T | I | O | N | A | L | | I | D | E | A |
| A | G | E | D | | E | L | L | | N | E | E | D |
| P | O | D | S | | W | A | Y | | E | N | D | S |

## PUZZLE 40

| | | | | | | | | | | | | | | |
|---|---|---|---|---|---|---|---|---|---|---|---|---|---|---|
| B | O | W | L | | T | R | A | Y | | | D | A | R | E |
| A | L | O | E | | H | E | R | E | | S | I | L | A | S |
| N | E | O | N | | R | E | E | L | | T | A | I | N | T |
| G | O | L | D | M | E | D | A | L | | O | M | E | G | A |
| | | | E | Y | E | S | | | O | N | O | | | |
| | E | A | R | N | | | | S | C | E | N | T | E | D |
| A | N | N | | A | T | O | M | I | C | | D | I | R | E |
| I | N | N | | H | O | M | E | R | U | N | | D | O | E |
| R | U | E | S | | W | E | W | E | R | E | | A | D | D |
| S | I | X | T | E | E | N | | | | I | S | L | E | |
| | | | A | L | L | | | S | A | G | E | | | |
| C | H | I | D | E | | T | O | U | C | H | D | O | W | N |
| L | O | G | I | C | | A | B | E | T | | A | M | I | E |
| A | B | O | U | T | | N | O | D | E | | T | I | N | T |
| W | O | R | M | | | S | E | E | D | | E | T | E | S |

## PUZZLE 41

| | | | | | | | | | | | | |
|---|---|---|---|---|---|---|---|---|---|---|---|---|
| T | E | N | | C | A | F | E | | S | K | I | S |
| I | R | E | | A | B | E | L | | A | N | N | E |
| M | A | T | E | R | N | A | L | | R | I | C | E |
| | | | L | E | E | R | | O | A | T | H | S |
| F | L | U | E | | R | E | A | C | H | | | |
| O | U | N | C | E | | D | Y | E | | O | D | E |
| W | R | I | T | E | R | | E | A | R | N | E | D |
| L | E | T | | R | A | W | | N | O | T | E | D |
| | | | C | I | G | A | R | | B | O | D | Y |
| A | D | O | R | E | | R | I | P | E | | | |
| M | O | V | E | | S | P | L | A | S | H | E | S |
| I | D | E | A | | P | E | E | L | | I | R | A |
| D | O | R | M | | A | D | D | S | | M | E | N |

## PUZZLE 42

| | | | | | | | | | | | | |
|---|---|---|---|---|---|---|---|---|---|---|---|---|
| P | I | L | E | | S | P | A | | T | R | O | D |
| A | C | I | D | | L | A | G | | H | E | R | O |
| M | E | D | I | C | I | N | E | | R | E | A | L |
| | | | T | A | P | | N | E | E | D | L | E |
| A | G | L | O | W | | A | C | R | E | | | |
| B | O | O | R | | S | T | I | R | | P | E | T |
| L | A | B | | S | H | O | E | S | | A | D | E |
| E | L | S | | T | A | N | S | | G | L | E | N |
| | | | T | A | M | E | | T | R | E | N | D |
| D | E | S | I | R | E | | S | E | A | | | |
| O | P | E | N | | F | A | I | N | T | E | S | T |
| T | E | N | T | | U | R | N | | E | W | E | R |
| S | E | T | S | | L | E | G | | D | E | W | Y |

## PUZZLE 43

| | | | | | | | | | | | | | | |
|---|---|---|---|---|---|---|---|---|---|---|---|---|---|---|
| S | W | A | Y | | A | D | O | B | E | | B | E | G | S |
| L | A | K | E | | M | O | U | R | N | | R | A | R | E |
| A | R | I | S | T | O | C | R | A | T | | A | S | I | A |
| P | E | N | | A | U | K | S | | A | D | V | E | N | T |
| | | | F | I | R | S | | F | I | R | E | | | |
| R | A | V | E | L | S | | H | I | L | A | R | I | T | Y |
| A | L | I | A | S | | R | E | N | E | W | | S | E | A |
| G | I | L | T | | D | O | L | E | D | | C | L | A | N |
| E | E | L | | S | E | A | M | S | | F | L | E | C | K |
| S | N | A | P | P | E | R | S | | B | O | O | T | H | S |
| | | | L | A | P | S | | P | E | R | T | | | |
| S | E | N | A | T | E | | S | I | L | T | | A | P | E |
| I | R | O | N | | N | A | M | E | L | E | S | S | L | Y |
| R | I | T | E | | E | D | U | C | E | | E | P | E | E |
| S | E | E | D | | D | A | T | E | S | | T | S | A | R |

## PUZZLE 44

| | | | | | | | | | | | | |
|---|---|---|---|---|---|---|---|---|---|---|---|---|
| B | A | R | D | | S | T | O | W | | S | P | A |
| A | L | E | E | | K | I | W | I | | T | O | N |
| H | E | A | D | L | I | N | E | R | | A | P | T |
| | C | L | U | E | | | D | E | A | R | | |
| | | | C | E | D | E | | S | I | T | E | S |
| T | R | O | T | | A | R | M | | L | O | A | N |
| R | I | P | | | I | R | E | | | U | S | A |
| I | C | E | S | | S | E | T | | S | T | E | P |
| M | E | N | U | S | | D | E | M | O | | | |
| | | B | E | N | S | | | A | L | L | Y | |
| A | D | O | | I | N | T | E | R | V | I | E | W |
| D | U | O | | P | I | E | R | | E | L | L | A |
| E | E | K | | S | T | A | G | | S | I | P | S |

## PUZZLE 45

| | | | | | | | | | | | | | | |
|---|---|---|---|---|---|---|---|---|---|---|---|---|---|---|
| A | L | A | S | | R | E | C | A | P | | S | L | O | W |
| J | A | C | K | | O | X | I | D | E | | A | U | R | A |
| A | N | T | I | Q | U | A | T | E | D | | F | R | A | Y |
| R | E | S | | U | G | L | Y | | E | L | E | C | T | S |
| | | | M | E | E | T | | P | S | Y | C | H | E | |
| N | O | V | A | S | | | G | A | T | E | R | | | |
| E | X | I | S | T | | F | E | T | A | | A | R | O | W |
| C | E | N | T | | E | A | S | E | L | | C | A | G | E |
| K | N | E | E | | P | U | S | S | | S | K | I | R | T |
| | | | R | H | I | N | O | | | C | E | D | E | S |
| | L | A | P | E | L | S | | S | P | U | R | | | |
| C | A | S | I | N | O | | S | T | U | B | | T | O | O |
| A | N | T | E | | G | E | N | E | R | A | T | I | O | N |
| L | A | I | C | | U | T | I | L | E | | A | D | Z | E |
| F | I | R | E | | E | A | T | E | R | | B | E | E | R |

1-I, 2-J, 3-X, 4-O, 5-A, 6-E, 7-Z, 8-Y, 9-Q, 10-S, 11-D, 12-V, 13-P, 14-U, 15-C, 16-T, 17-W, 18-G, 19-R, 20-L, 21-B, 22-F, 23-K, 24-N, 25-M, 26-H.

## PUZZLE 46

| | | | | | | | | | | | | | | |
|---|---|---|---|---|---|---|---|---|---|---|---|---|---|---|
| S | T | A | G | | B | L | A | R | E | | C | O | L | A |
| K | A | L | E | | R | E | R | U | N | | A | R | A | B |
| I | L | E | S | | I | V | I | E | S | | R | A | T | E |
| D | E | S | T | I | N | E | D | | H | A | M | L | E | T |
| | | | U | R | G | E | | E | R | I | E | | | |
| M | A | D | R | A | S | | E | V | I | L | N | E | S | S |
| A | L | I | E | N | | C | L | A | N | S | | A | C | E |
| T | I | N | S | | B | L | A | D | E | | A | G | E | D |
| E | V | E | | B | R | U | T | E | | A | R | E | N | A |
| D | E | S | C | R | I | B | E | | B | A | R | R | E | N |
| | | | H | A | G | S | | A | U | R | A | | | |
| A | R | M | A | D | A | | A | B | S | E | N | C | E | S |
| W | O | O | F | | D | A | V | I | S | | G | A | V | E |
| A | L | O | E | | E | R | O | D | E | | E | P | E | E |
| Y | E | N | S | | S | E | W | E | D | | S | E | N | D |

## PUZZLE 47

GAG STOW CLAM
ERA TIDE LONE
MET AREA EATS
HATE TRADES
STEWED HER
CURED BED SEA
ONES WAR STAR
TED COG SWARM
MAN PEARLS
RECORD RANT
OVAL EVIL IRE
BERT RIDE NOW
ENDS SEED GEE

## PUZZLE 48

CALF AGA FILL
ALOE LIL ARIA
NEWZEALANDERS
ESS LITRE SAT
PAN MAR
NOLANS STEELE
ADOS LAID
TENTER SLATES
ERA HAY
TOM ATLAS AGE
ATASTEOFHONEY
RITA ROT NENE
ACED STS EWES

## PUZZLE 49

ROD WISH WIPE
OWE ARIA IVAN
ELL GARDENERS
IRON VEST
PECAN DEED
ADAM LEAN COT
SET BEAST HUR
ONE OGLE BASE
PAST PASTE
LEAS TART
HEARTLESS ICE
ANTI ALAS SAW
MASS WIRE ERE

## PUZZLE 50

AMI ETA ACRE
LIMA RED BOAR
EXPLORED ONCE
MAST MUTE
DEPOT EVITA
EROS ERIN IRA
LISTED LEANER
LET TETE WENT
PENNY WADES
SODA REEK
RING BARTERED
ALEE ANN NOME
PODS ATE BUN

## PUZZLE 51

CRAB ARM THE SHED
ROBE REO EAR HIDE
OVER RELEASE ARIA
PETER LENS SPEED
TAME DEBATE
FOR TIC TODO RIB
AREA STEP WAR ACE
DELL TEXAS MERGED
AIM DINES SOT
BOXTOP TILES MITE
ADE NET CLAW EMIT
RED DEAF SIN ENC
RANGES OMEN
DELAY LIEN WAFER
ASIS HAIRPIN MIRE
DAMP OWN ENE EVIL
SUES WEE EGO DENY

## PUZZLE 52

GAPE MAP CLAP
ALEX ERR ROVE
GULP ATE ASEA
MELON TOWER
OATMEAL
SCARF INK RAY
HUGE END SAVE
YEA AXE ETHAN
APPROVE
CIDER FEELS
AURA ELF PEAT
CROP SEE LAIR
TENT SIR EDDY

## PUZZLE 53

RIB SEWS CHOP
IRE PLEA HAIR
COLLIDED ONLY
ENTIRE AID
MAR ENRICH
LAPEL CAT CUE
ALES FAR DATA
ODD TIN VIPER
SAILOR SIN
GAP TEEPEE
BARN STANDARD
AGED EARN DIG
DOES AREA SEE

## PUZZLE 54

ARK PAPA SASH
BIN ARAM ALIE
COINCIDE FAZE
COED TEASED
LIKER CHAR
IDES PHYSIQUE
MER DAISY URN
BASSINET PEGO
LOAF POSES
EXPORT SENT
DRAW EXPEDITE
GATE LEER OWL
EYED ADDS NOM

## PUZZLE 55

NEWS COW SOFT
AREA LIE OVER
BILL OLD DALE
SELVES RALLY
AGENCY
CARGO IRE PUP
ALEE IVY WIFE
BED ACE WAGON
CENTER
SWEAT ABSENT
TAXI TIM HAIR
AVID WOE ISLE
BETS OUR PEEK

## PUZZLE 56

ALOT APOD WEBS DEAL
DESI RENO REAP ASSI
MALL GRAM ENNA NESS
SHOTPUT ITS CRICKET
IRE ENATE ELI
IRENE BROILER ENDED
BANG CONE ELOD GURU
INK SORES RESET DIN
SKITTLES REFEREES
AAL RAE
CRIBBAGE CHARADES
HID STILL CLAUS ERE
ALEC ELSA HIND BEIT
PLEAD DICKENS SODAS
NEB ERECT SOW
JAIALAI OAK PALLONE
ARCS RODS EVIL IDEA
DIET ONES RENA NEAT
EDDA NAME SEED GARS

## PUZZLE 57

DAMP SCAM AHA SATED
ERIE NOLA MEL IRATE
BONN ODIN ART OUTOF
SWEETWATER MONUMENT
TAI UNISEX
SHARING SLIT AFLAME
CORALGABLES RAININ
UNITS LOU ITS LIKED
DELE FLUES ITALIANS
GRANDRAPIDS
CONFRONT ISTLE BOLA
UVULA TYS OOT SAGAS
REDANS NEWPORTNEWS
BRENDA AITS NEATEST
FIESTA ARE
POTHOLES LITTLEROCK
OTHER LID SARI EVAN
STARK EGO ICES RUSE
TOTES RNS STEM SMEW

## PUZZLE 58

PIT ARK HABIT
ADE DEN ARENA
TEN APARTMENT
HAS MOVIE
LET RED SLIP
RAT EMPIRE
RAPID OUTER
ORATOR FOR
DELE USA NET
ITALY RAM
PARACHUTE ALE
AGAPE TEA SON
MEWED ERR END

## PUZZLE 59

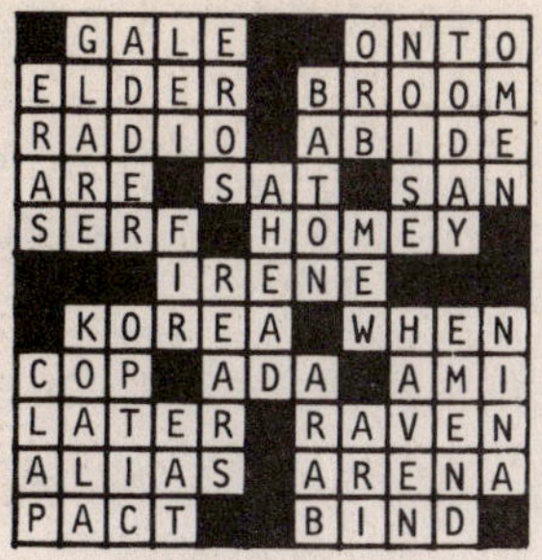

## PUZZLE 60

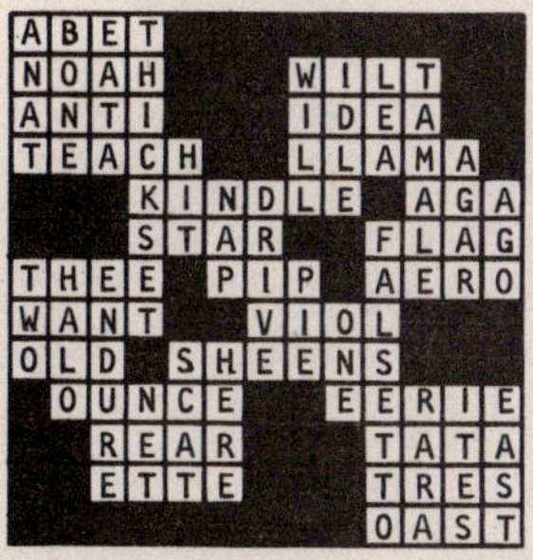

## PUZZLE 61

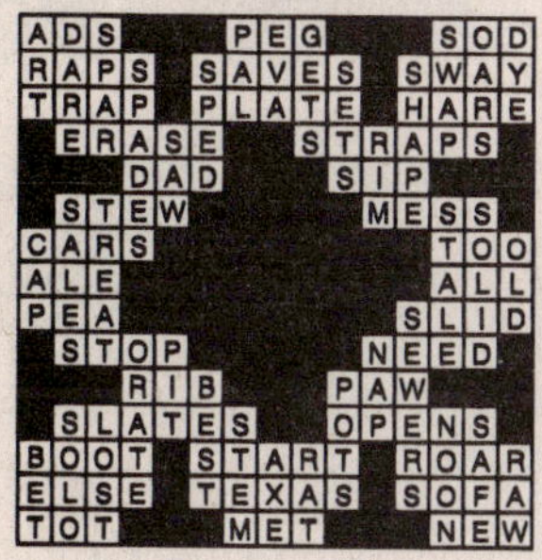

## PUZZLE 62

1. Ring, Rink, Rick, Rice, Rack, Race, Rage, Rags.
2. Pour, Pout, Port, Pore, Part, Pare, Pace, Pack.

## PUZZLE 63

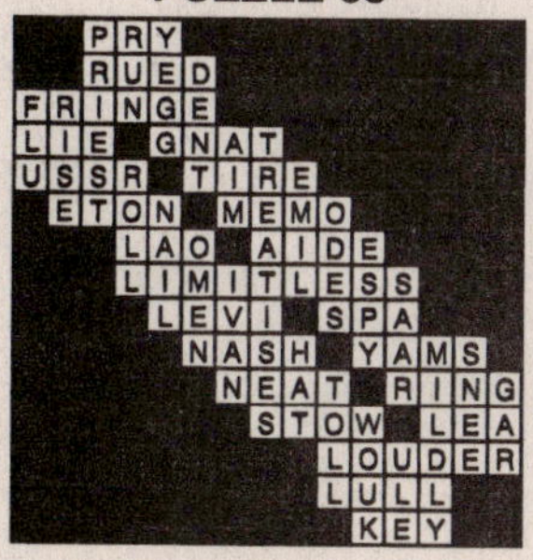

## PUZZLE 64

1. Inoculates, 2. Abductions, 3. Defaulting.

## PUZZLE 65

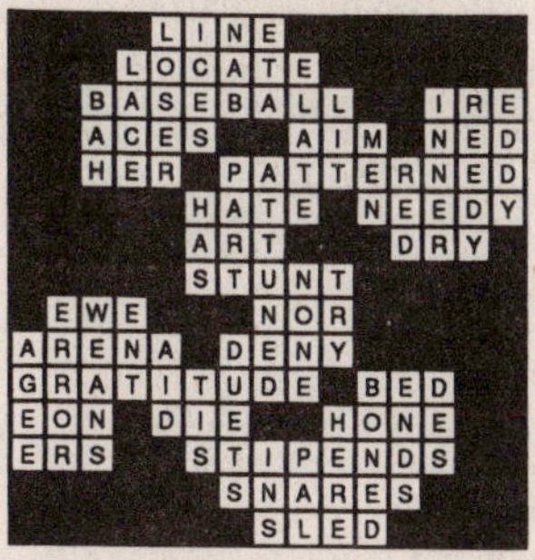

## PUZZLE 66

The greatest aid to adult education is children.

1. Toted, 2. Dish, 3. Suitor, 4. Ideal, 5. Educate, 6. Ethnical, 7. Grant.

## PUZZLE 67

## PUZZLE 68

Trying to make things work in government is like trying to sew a button on a custard pie. (Hyman G. Rickover)

1. Rip Van Winkle, 2. Twiggy, 3. Thanking, 4. Sensation, 5. Bounties, 6. Ousted, 7. Trick or treat, 8. Montgomery.

## PUZZLE 69

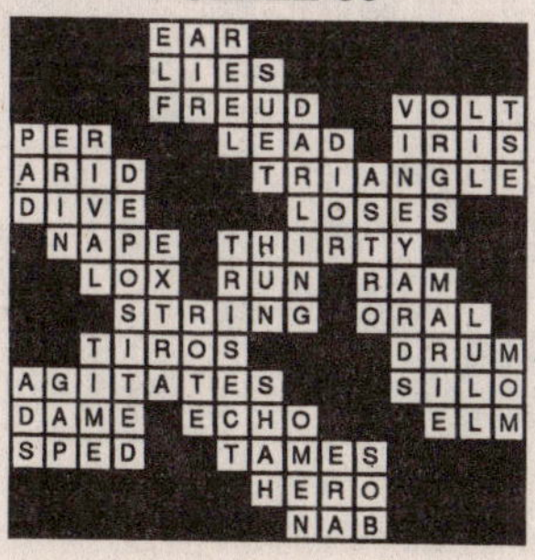

## PUZZLE 70

1. Moderating, 2. Mineralogy, 3. Manuscript.

## PUZZLE 71

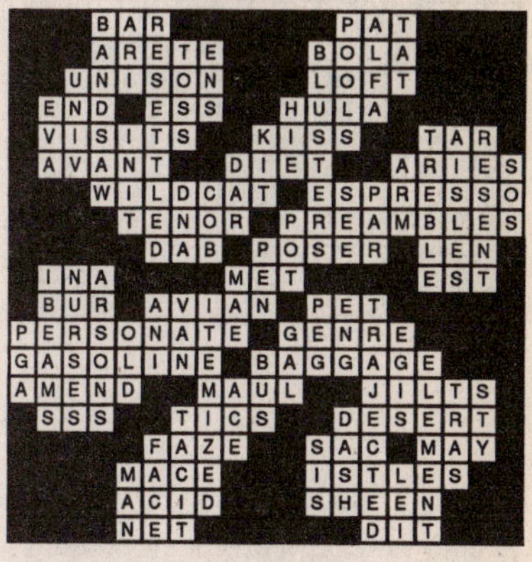

## PUZZLE 72

## PUZZLE 73

In wintertime I have such fun
When I play quoits with father.
I beat him almost every game.
He never seems to bother.
He looks at mother and just smiles.
All this seems strange to me,
For when he plays with grown-up folks,
He beats them easily.

## PUZZLE 74

## PUZZLE 75

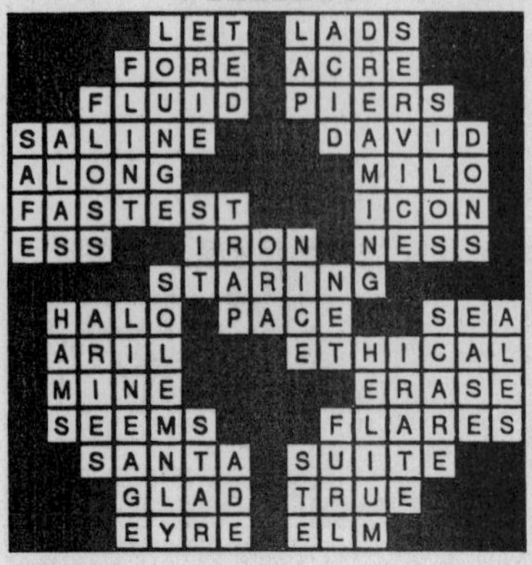

## PUZZLE 76

**A door is what a dog is perpetually on the wrong side of. (Ogden Nash)**

**1. People, 2. Odors, 3. Laos, 4. Wingding, 5. Hefty, 6. White, 7. Aurora, 8. Toads.**

## PUZZLE 77

## PUZZLE 78

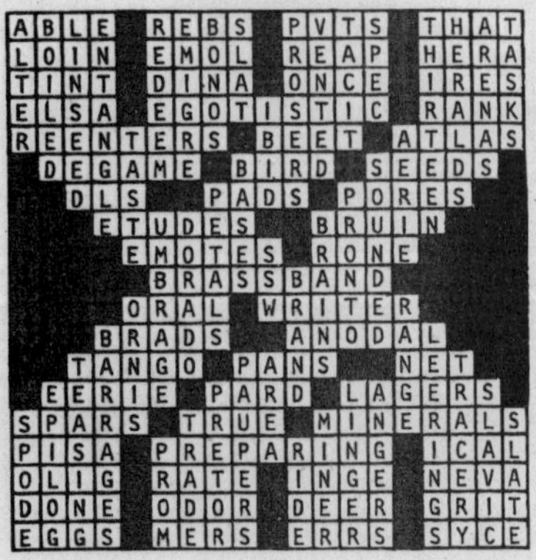

## PUZZLE 79

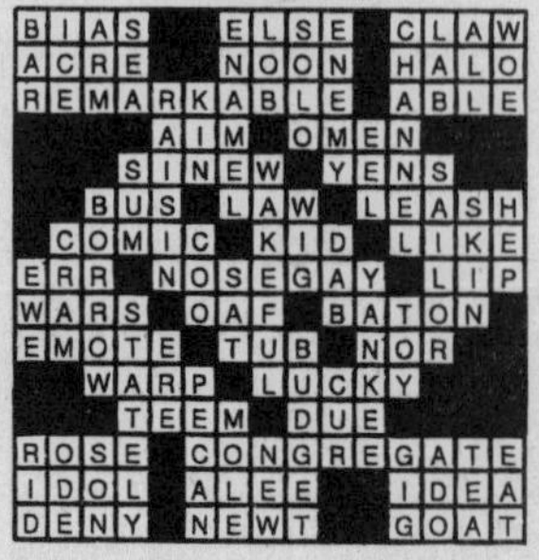

## PUZZLE 80

Few things have a shorter life than a clean garage.

1. Half, 2. Lavish, 3. Whine, 4. Teacher, 5. Arrogant, 6. Engage, 7. Feast.

## PUZZLE 81

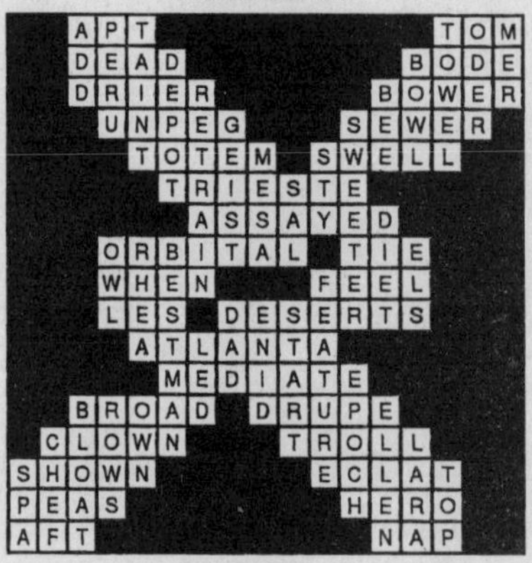

## PUZZLE 82

1. Less, Loss, Lose, Lore, More.
2. Good, Gold, Bold, Bolt, Belt, Best.
3. Slow, Slot, Soot, Loot, Lost, Last, Fast.
4. Dumb, Dump, Lump, Limp, Lisp, Wisp, Wise.

## PUZZLE 83

## PUZZLE 84

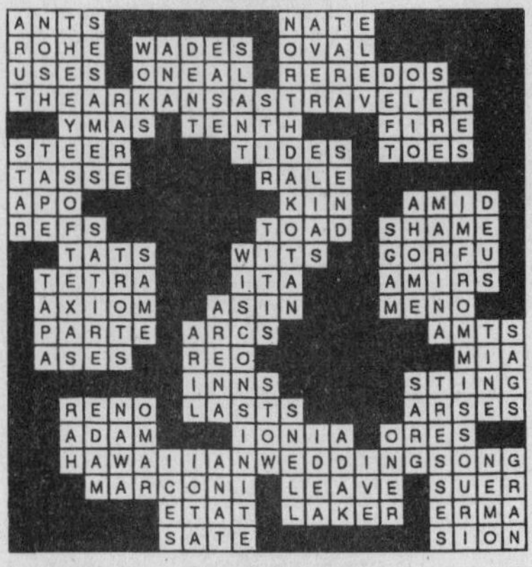

## PUZZLE 85

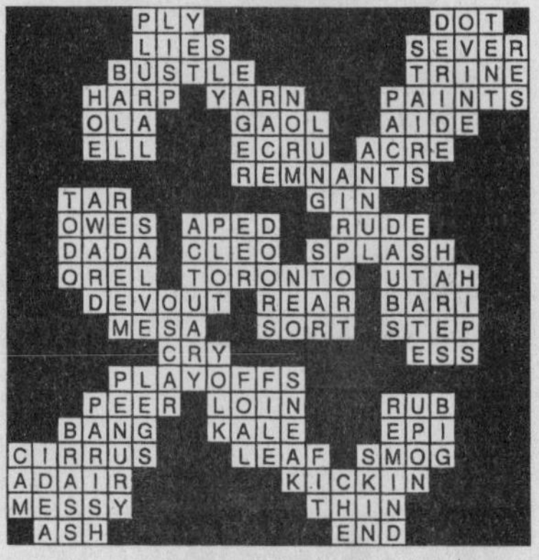

## PUZZLE 86

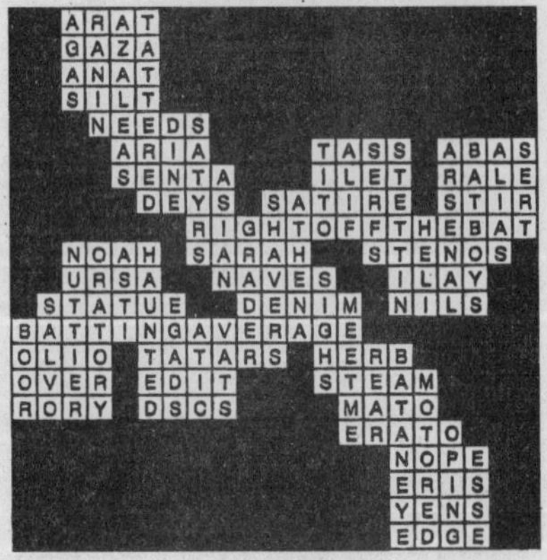

## PUZZLE 87

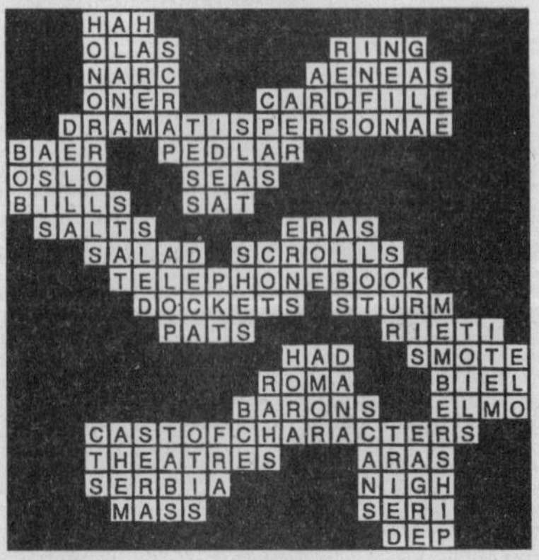

## PUZZLE 88

## PUZZLE 92

## PUZZLE 96

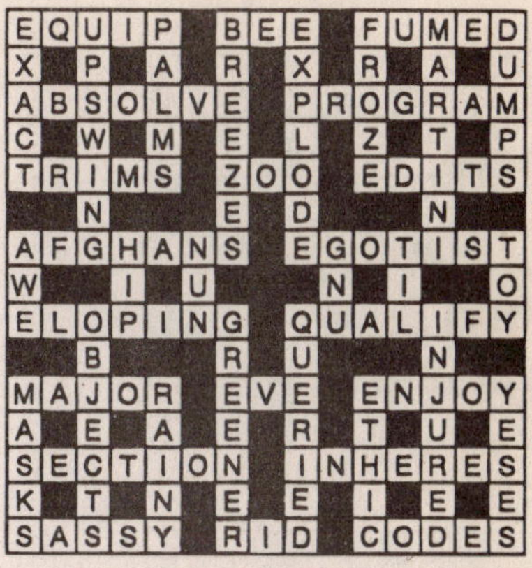

1-O, 2-I, 3-V, 4-Q, 5-S, 6-P, 7-H, 8-Y, 9-R, 10-M, 11-W, 12-N, 13-A, 14-X, 15-B, 16-K, 17-L, 18-C, 19-T, 20-G, 21-J, 22-U, 23-F, 24-Z, 25-D, 26-E.

## PUZZLE 89

## PUZZLE 93

## PUZZLE 97

1. Nimbus, 2. Easing, 3. Giggle, 4. Romper, 5. Indoor, 6. Gazebo.
GINGER ROGERS

## PUZZLE 90

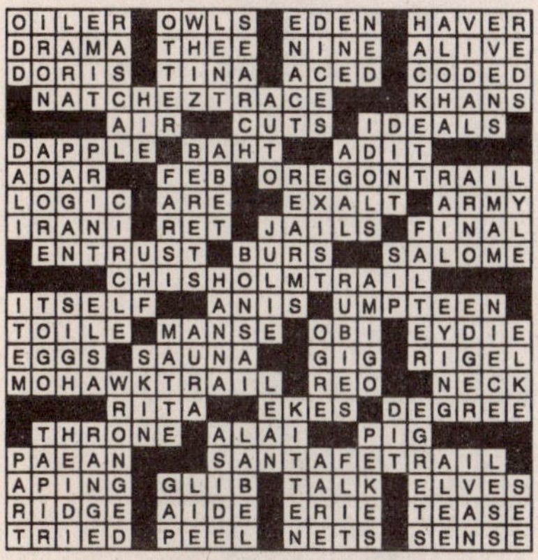

## PUZZLE 94

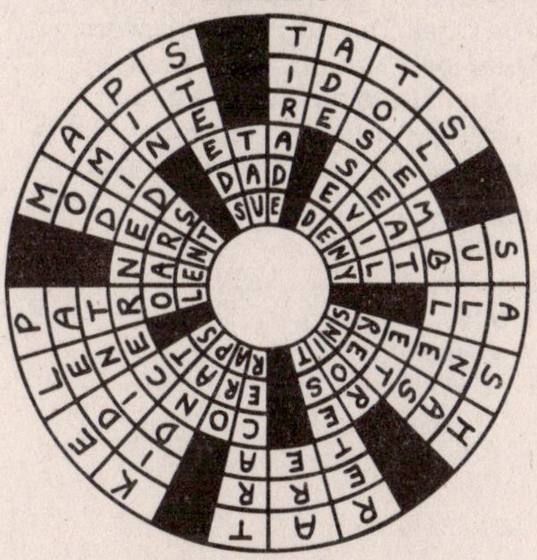

## PUZZLE 98

## PUZZLE 91

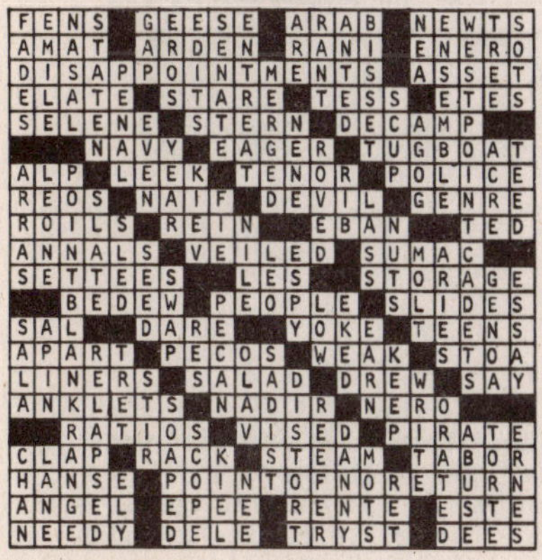

## PUZZLE 95

## PUZZLE 99

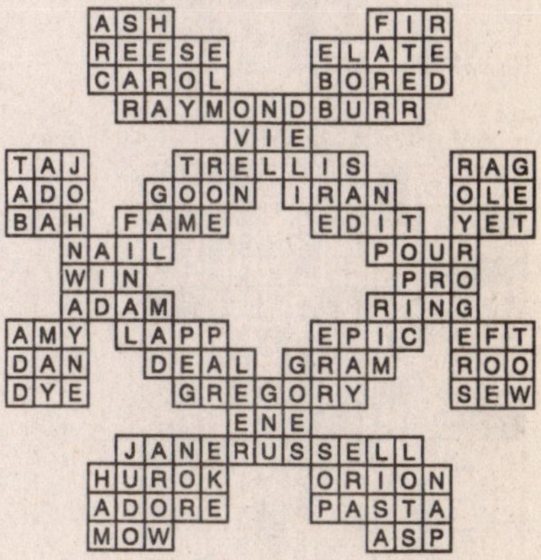

## PUZZLE 100

### A

ABEL POD RITA
GALA EVE EDAM
EDIT TIM COPE
EVADE ALES
TUNNEL RAN
UNITE LISTON
BIN RIOTS DAB
TENETS ELOPE
ODE STARED
CHAR ROAST
HARM APT TAFT
ELLA TEE ERIE
FOOL END REND

### B

FEED FAR URGE
ERLE ERE SOAP
WALL MID EDIE
ETUDE FETE
PASTOR EMU
OWLET SMILES
PEA TRUST VOW
STREAM THERE
ORB FEARED
TROD BARNS
HOPE IRE TARA
ALAN TIE EMIT
WELT SAD NAME

## PUZZLE 101

SPOT ACE STUB
RILE GAL EASE
INEXPERIENCED
TOTO DOORS
IDA SIR
ORAL PELT DAD
PINETREESTATE
TOT ROLE AMEN
WIN TOR
ALLIE AREA
FEEDSTHEKITTY
ANNE OUT ETTE
ROAR PEA DAYS

## PUZZLE 102

SMITE DEN GEM
TODAY ERE ROE
ADORE PRESENT
GEL SPA DOE
ELSE ORB STOW
BANTER EWE
FORBID CANDLE
EVE DEBATE
EASE RAM TAPS
TAD TEE PUP
PROTEST FLARE
EAR BEE TERSE
APE TAN SATED

## PUZZLE 103

MEAT NOTA FOE
ERLE ALAS LAP
GRILLEDCHEESE
LESE ELATE
SALSA ASI
AGO SEAL AGAS
VEGETABLESOUP
ERST SEAR ATA
HIT ACTOR
STAIN ASTI
CHICKENPOTPIE
OUR ERIE ERNE
TDS DALE SOAR

## PUZZLE 104

TIM DEAL TROT
AGO RAVE RENO
REDBARON ADEN
STEAK CALIF
CEDE ELATE
TORO UTES CIA
AMENDS CEMENT
BED ETCH ADES
UNCLE HOOD
RUMBA TRINE
RIOT INTHERED
ERSE AGEE ORE
PASS SEAR NOR

## PUZZLE 105

| | | | | | | | | | | |
|---|---|---|---|---|---|---|---|---|---|---|
| | RE | SEN | T | | | | W | AL | K | |
| RE | PU | D | IA | TE | | HE | AD | L | IN | ER |
| SI | GN | | RA | MP | | R | ING | | D | OS |
| DE | AN | S | | LE | TH | AL | | BO | R | E |
| | T | ACK | LES | | EN | DE | AV | OR | ED | |
| | | | SO | DA | | D | EN | | | |
| | TH | I | N | N | ER | | GE | LAT | IN | |
| T | I | LL | | CE | ASE | D | | IN | TER | N |
| RA | CK | | CA | R | | EA | SEL | | FE | ET |
| DE | SE | R | TER | S | | D | EC | LA | RE | S |
| | T | END | ED | | | | T | RA | NCE | |

## PUZZLE 106

The pearl (month of June) was not worn by June, Pearl, or Ruby; it was worn by Opal. The ruby was not worn by Ruby or Pearl; it was worn by June. Opal (June birthday) was born after Ruby; Ruby's birthday is January (garnet); Pearl wore the opal.

In summary:
June, ruby
Opal, pearl
Pearl, opal
Ruby, garnet

## PUZZLE 107

WAG TIC
SAGAS HASH
WATERWAYS WATERMAIN
EVE ALEE OMAR NRA
TERM PAST KIND SNOB
FIBS SEEN
ERLE AWL
ATOLL DERBY
DAN OBI SUGAR
ALT WATERINGCAN WOW
RELAX EGO AWE
REMIT MATES
WOO ALES
PALE ODOR
RETE LOOP RANG EWES
ARE ERNE OVAL HAT
FIREWATER WATERLESS
EARN SHEET
DRY OIL

## PUZZLE 108

GRAS GUSTS TARA
RIVE ANTES EVIL
IDEA GRUNT NINE
TERMAGANT LEDGE
SILT AIM
MAR LEAS CREASE
APED BLATANTLY
NAVE FLANS TRUE
TRUCULENT SEER
ATEASE THAN ESS
DEW ODES
STEER CALORIFIC
LIMN ARDOR GALL
OTIC DODGE HIKE
TOLE SWAYS SLAW

## PUZZLE 109

SENSE LISA NEAT
TROUT ANTS OPIE
ANTIC SCAN TIDE
TEETH AMERICAN
END PROM
LASER BELTS
STIR ROSES OAK
CALF VOILA GOBI
ATA EPSOM OPUS
BACON POSTS
NOEL EAT
SPRINGER OUTER
OLEO GATE ONETO
BEAN OVEN PIANO
SAPS NESS STRAD

## PUZZLE 110

1. Little League, 2. Ballet dancer, 3. Spring flower, 4. Purple martin, 5. Grease monkey, 6. Indian summer.

## PUZZLE 111

SPAR SMASH DART
ARTE TENSE ERIE
LOOP ALTER MILE
EMPLOYEE DWELLS
ALEE ASEA
SPACED REMANDED
PULE SORER RAE
IRIS SPAIN DIVA
NEE WHERE EVEN
SENTRIES CARESS
REND RATE
ASKING REPELLED
CHIP LEASE IOWA
TOLL ENTER CREW
SOLE SLATS TERN

## PUZZLE 112

1. Ira Gershwin, 2. Wyatt Earp, 3. Snow White, 4. Mickey Rooney, 5. Julia Child, 6. Milton Berle, 7. Mortimer Snerd, 8. Winston Churchill, 9. Danny Thomas, 10. Elizabeth Taylor.

## PUZZLE 113

```
POUR■GEM■BALL
INTO■IRA■ASIA
TEAS■RADISHES
■SHELL■■MET■■
■■■BISHOP■RAG
CLOUD■ELS■ALE
LOUD■BAD■HYMN
ANT■OAR■JESSE
WED■DASHER■■■
■■OLE■■ATOMS■
TROUSERS■IOTA
OURS■BAT■SLAB
MESH■BYE■MERE
```

## PUZZLE 114

```
PANT■RISK■ALL
IDEA■ERIE■DOE
PETS■BAREFOOT
■■■TEEN■PESTS
APPEAL■LEE■■■
MOIST■WORSHIP
ELL■■DIG■■ERA
SOLOMON■CORKS
■■■MEN■RAREST
AWAIT■WIDE■■■
CENTERED■GANG
END■ROPE■OBOE
STY■SETS■NEST
```

## PUZZLE 115

```
LADD■BATS■FEE
AIDE■AREA■LAY
PRESENTED■USE
■■■INDY■DOSES
HOARDS■SLIT■■
IDLES■REELED■
SOL■■AYE■■RIO
■RIDDLE■TREND
■■GAIT■LOADED
CLAMP■SONS■■■
HOT■POPPYCOCK
ADO■ERIE■ALOE
PER■REND■LEON
```

## PUZZLE 116

```
■GAS■SHE■HAG■
CARE■TON■OPAL
AMEN■ONT■PINE
READER■ICINGS
■■■ELM■RON■■■
SCARFS■ENGINE
EEL■■■■■■■ROY
TELLER■CHEESE
■■■ORE■RUN■■■
SLICES■ATTEND
OINK■CUT■EVIL
NOTE■USE■RENO
■NOT■END■SSE■
```

## PUZZLE 117

```
RASP■ROB■DOGS
ERIE■ARE■EPEE
STREAKED■PANT
■■■RYE■■MALES
SPREE■SEAR■■■
SLID■CHATTER■
TOP■SHORT■VAT
■WESTERN■MERE
■■■CORE■CURED
STRAP■■BUD■■■
HAIR■SHREDDED
ELSE■PEA■LIVE
DEED■YET■EDEN
```

## PUZZLE 118

```
ELF■SWAP■ACRE
WEE■TARO■WOOL
ENTRANCE■ANTI
STEER■■MARC■■
■■■SETH■PERIL
SEPT■ROME■EGO
MAE■DOLED■TON
ERN■ODES■BERG
ENDOW■SHOE■■■
■■ANNA■■TASTE
SENT■RESTRAIN
HATH■TAPE■NED
ERSE■STAR■ESS
```

## PUZZLE 119

```
POTS■■PAY■ARE
ARRAY■ALE■LAD
LEAVE■TINTING
■■PELLET■RAGE
APE■PEN■VASE■
DAZE■ATTIC■■■
DWELLS■REELED
■■■DITTO■SERE
■FEED■ITS■TAN
AIRS■RESULT■■
BLOTTER■ROUSE
LED■ODE■FACES
ERE■POD■■NEWS
```

## PUZZLE 120

```
AFT■■LAB■■PRO
PLOW■ERR■COOP
TYPE■AMI■ALVA
■■■BATON■NOEL
AGE■SHREWD■■■
NOR■HEY■ALTER
TAILOR■SLEEVE
STEER■ACT■AIL
■■■SEETHE■SLY
SPAS■STERN■■■
HOBO■TIM■URGE
OPEN■ERE■TANK
WET■■RED■■HUE
```

## PUZZLE 121

```
MOAT■FLAP■ELF
IDLE■RAIL■NEE
SOON■INDEBTED
TREATED■AIR■■
■■■NOD■ESTATE
CRATE■AGE■NEW
HATS■BIG■ACME
ACT■BUM■STEPS
PEARLS■SAT■■■
■■CUE■ALGEBRA
REHEARSE■NOUN
ORE■RAID■DALE
WED■SPAS■STEW
```

## PUZZLE 122

```
NET■GAPE■CUTE
ERA■OBOE■OPAL
AIR■LOLL■MOBS
RESTFUL■DENSE
■■■WET■TOT■■■
ACTOR■FRESHER
RUE■■COY■■EGO
TRAITOR■LUNGE
■■■CAN■NOS■■■
SWAIN■PAPERED
TIDE■FLIP■ELI
ENDS■ROVE■ALA
PEST■OWED■PAL
```

## PUZZLE 123

```
HAS■TONS■PAPA
ART■UNIT■ALEC
LEO■RELUCTANT
FACET■■MAR■■■
■■KALE■PROBES
WAITERS■SLURP
OWN■■EAR■■LIE
RAGES■DABBLED
MYSELF■MOOD■■
■■■RIO■■LOOKS
ESTIMATED■ZIP
NEIL■LIME■ELI
DENY■SPUR■RON
```

## PUZZLE 124

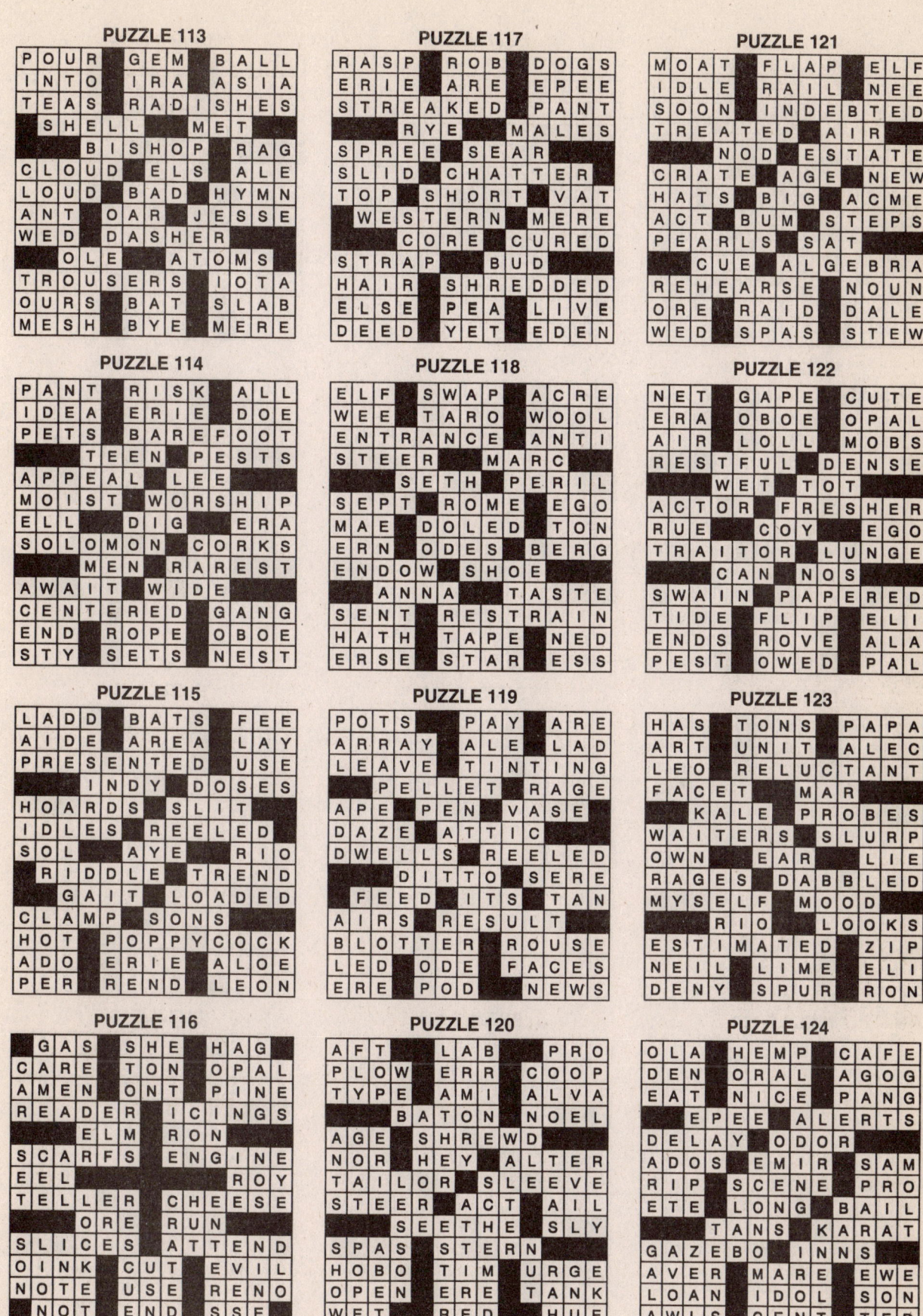

```
OLA■HEMP■CAFE
DEN■ORAL■AGOG
EAT■NICE■PANG
■■EPEE■ALERTS
DELAY■ODOR■■■
ADOS■EMIR■SAM
RIP■SCENE■PRO
ETE■LONG■BAIL
■■■TANS■KARAT
GAZEBO■INNS■■
AVER■MARE■EWE
LOAN■IDOL■SON
AWLS■CENT■TED
```

## PUZZLE 125

STARE AHEAD ACTED
LABOR EDIBLES MARCY
APATONTHEBACK ONION
NET SYNOD LEASABLE
TRET LAC STAIR SEES
EPOS STERNEST
LAPIN CHASE STAPLE
HELEN SHAFT ASIAN
OGLE SCARF ORAN NEV
TEE STATEOFMIND TRI
TNG LENS FOIST FATE
EDEMA SLATE FLIES
ASSIST TOILS TOOLS
SHOWOFFS LOBO
ADIT DANTE MAP DELL
SENATORS LOUIS ROE
SNAKE PICKANDCHOOSE
ESNES SLEEVES OLDER
TEENS SENAT PEERS

## PUZZLE 126

EGG OFF ERAS
ARAB WOO VILE
RETAILER EMIT
WELL TON
ELMS ASKED
SAGS ALIT IRE
ALA DEN TIN
PAL MEET BEET
SNARE POLE
OWE ELBA
SHAD RESTLESS
PANE RAH SAIL
ALTO STY RAY

## PUZZLE 127

DINA REP TAMP
ABEL AGE ERIE
REAL VOW AINT
EXPOSE TRADE
WINTER
ALLEN RAY SPA
FEED BIT REAR
TAG PET HEART
REELED
STORY ESCAPE
HIVE ERA ALAN
AMEN LOS POND
DENT LEE SEES

## PUZZLE 128

LIFE EBBS ODE
ODOR LALA BOA
TORO FRONTIER
SLEDS OWES
FELONS AFRO
ERR OWS ERROL
LOOSEN RESOLE
BUNTS HER NEO
ETTE RESIST
ELIA EIDER
AFFRONTS NOTE
CAR OGEE GOAT
TRY TORN ERLE

## PUZZLE 129

SCOT BARER
LEHAR ARMORED
UNITE FOOTAGE
ROC YARNS SAN
ERAS COT PELT
SAGEST EEL
SOLO REAP
MOP BRAVOS
GOYA UPI TALL
INA FRANK RIA
SILLIER EDICT
TOTALED RICES
NAMES NEED

## PUZZLE 130

MAC APSE ASIA
ORE SEAT RING
OER HAWTHORNE
NAVIES AIM
ANN TAHOE
RANK EPIC ERA
ART LEACH MAR
VIE ALLY BILL
EASED DIN
LEO SINGLE
STEINBECK WAD
PORT OTOE AVA
YORE EATS YAM

## PUZZLE 131

TACK APT CHEW
RULE SEASHORE
IRAN HASTIEST
PAWNS SKIN
EAR RASPS
POOLROOM ELI
LAW IDIOT MAN
EKE ELBOWING
ASSAY SPA
BOWL SIDLE
VALOROUS TEAL
ELEVENTH ELMS
TIDE TEE RIPE

## PUZZLE 132

ALE SPA BAG
DENT LANE USO
SIDEBURNS RIN
NAG TENSE
EMBERS GELS
POUT PARADES
ORR EEL ORE
SENATOR TWIT
IRON TWINES
BASIN ARE
ASH EDDBYRNES
RTE SOIL SIRE
TAD GEE LAW

## PUZZLE 133

GOLD ISLE TAM
LAIR MEAN OLE
ETNA MANDOLIN
ESKIMO DOME
NABS WARES
TRUSTIER RAGE
EAT ELDER TON
STEM EAGEREST
TENOR NILE
SOAR MYSELF
COINCIDE TSAR
OWL EDEN EASE
YES RENT DUST

## PUZZLE 134

COAT RIP ANTE
OUCH IDA LOOK
TREE FOLKLORE
BALL NINES
POLITE PIG
ADAGE GETAWAY
COMB BAG TILE
TREATED ROSIN
DOG CARETS
STEWS POMP
COLOSSAL EARL
ABEL ACT ARIA
REEF YES REDD

## PUZZLE 135

MESS SOW SHE
AMEN TIE STOW
TUNE ALE EASE
ESTEEM DANGER
ZAP SIS
ANGERED LEARN
DOE DIG BEE
SWEET PRECEDE
MOD AWL
BARBER NEATER
ALOE APT WAVE
NEAR FEE EPEE
GEM TAD DESK

## PUZZLE 136

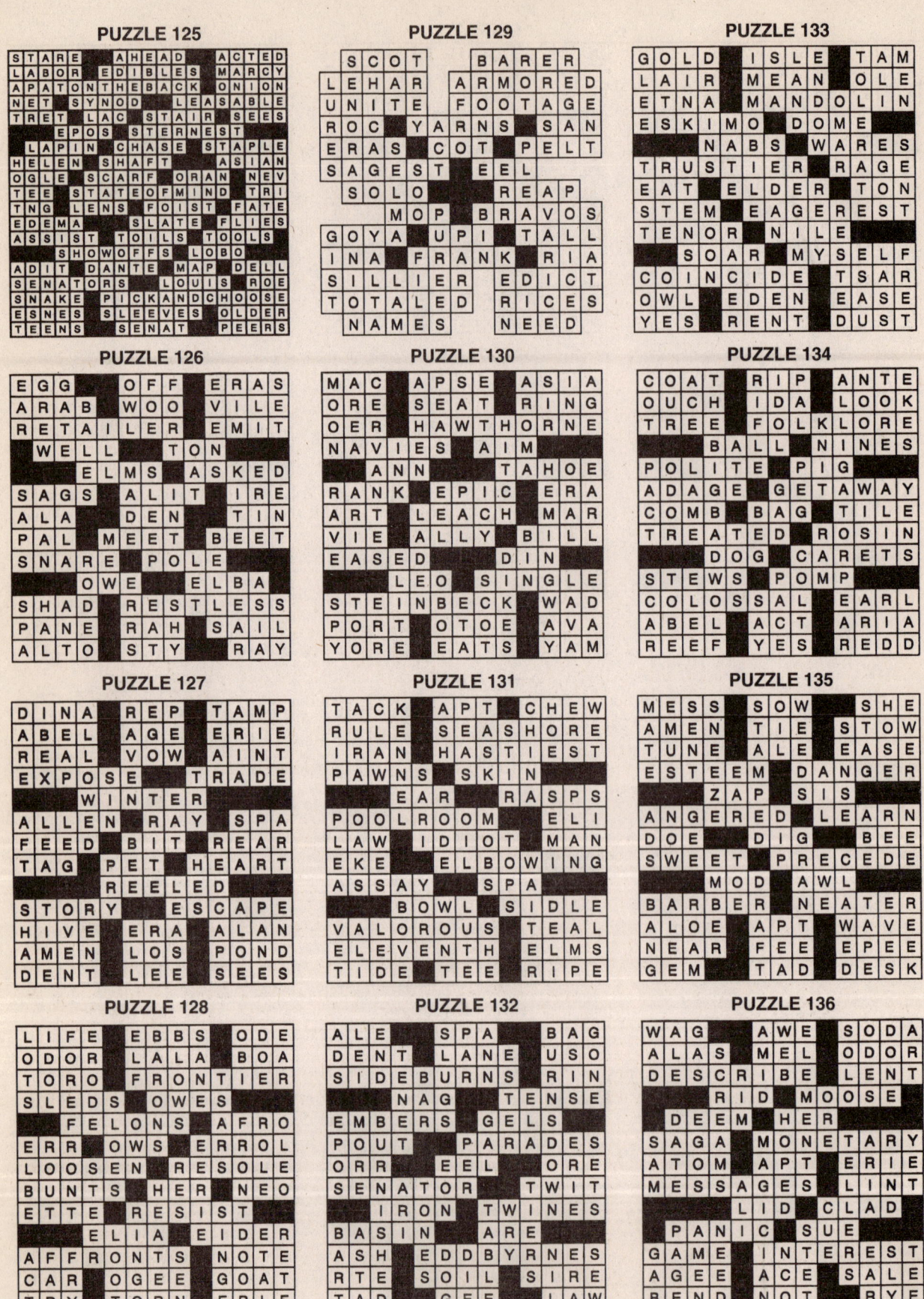

WAG AWE SODA
ALAS MEL ODOR
DESCRIBE LENT
RID MOOSE
DEEM HER
SAGA MONETARY
ATOM APT ERIE
MESSAGES LINT
LID CLAD
PANIC SUE
GAME INTEREST
AGEE ACE SALE
BEND NOT RYE

## PUZZLE 137

RAT EBIR DP AT
SOLI D NEW ARK
PLO DEL FOIL
HE NUSE D IRE
AL TO EE RIESON
CHAR TSTRE WEND
OWEN ICESMA SH
A GEN DAPLA Y
APR ON LAGE R
TENE TSA DT IM
CRIBLASTMEET
ED ITH O RN
HON EBLEATRA W
EV ENLOR E PIE
REGR ESSTAB LE

## PUZZLE 138

BRED PART CELT
AESOP ARIA AREA
SANTA STOREROOM
ERE PITS NESS
PETS SATE
STAIRS ANGERED
PATES FLIER ARE
AMOR CROPS STOW
TEN BOONE STEVE
REMORSE PLANES
AINT SEAN
HALL ROAN ALA
SEBASTIAN TOMES
TREY RANG SPEAK
SODA ANTS ENDS

## PUZZLE 139

ARAS TVA BABE
MOTH GRAD SAVER
ABIE RATE ANEAR
HOMERUNS START
TEPEES SPIN
MAL TEENAGER
VOTED RAVES AMO
ALAN CAPED SLID
SEN FAKIR STELE
TAKEOVER SER
ARES STEAMS
BASED SOURNOTE
TOTES STUN GORE
ABOLT EAST ERAL
MOPS ERE REDS

## PUZZLE 140

ARISTOCRAT

## PUZZLE 141

GOAT OLD PTA
ARLO MOOT HAG
STARLINGS ERE
TAT WARAND
LACES PORES
ORO TRIO BATS
BURN END SNAP
EMMA ITSA TRA
OPENS PESOS
GERALD AIR
ERA MERGANSER
TIN SEAT EASE
SET RNS SPED

## PUZZLE 142

ELSE CAR REVS
LEER ODE OVAL
FEARLESS DESI
AID OPENED
GLINT OLEO
RIND ISUP BET
ARK SNITS ARA
BAY ATEE TRIP
BIRR DANCE
TAMALE TON
OVER PLUCKILY
TORE ION EDIE
OWES DUE RAPT

## PUZZLE 143

CATHEDRALASKA
EQUIPROJECTOR
LUCKIEVAGRANT
LASEDGEREERIE
ORODESSANNUAL
PINERTOLDANCE
HUERMALARCTIC
ASSAILIPATENT
NOONSERAIMAGE
EGOISMANNERED
DONSUAVEININE
ABELEXEMPTSUE
MIRESILOSSEED

## PUZZLE 144

MOLAR RELAY HORDE
ILONA EMILE ORION
SOLON DOVES NAMED
CRATER TIE VOTERS
HEADED MARE
ANTE RID MUSS NET
CARRIED EAST LIRA
EPI BLONDIE VALET
BEY ODD FEW
RELAX GLISTEN EGO
AWED HOLE ENTERED
YET WINE OLD TAME
PALE GREECE
STRAIT ORA DORMER
HOIST AVANT SNIPE
ERASE LEDGE TALES
DOLED PREEN SLEET

## PUZZLE 145

SLICED SLOUCH
CANAPE WATERLOO
ANDRIA EMANATES
MDI STRAINS IVE
PLAN HIKED AMAS
SENOR DES DIAL
SAGEHEN FOR
SNARES POOLED
LIP PUERILE
SEEP MAN SNAPS
DAMS CASKS EMIT
ALE DENTATE ILE
CONDENSE AVATAR
INDENTED TERETE
ASSESS ERASES

## PUZZLE 146

ALARM BEG PAL
CAMEO ORE ABE
TYPED NATIVES
DEEDS NETS
NUTS KEEPS
ONE FED LEASE
DIALED HOTBED
STRUT BAY LEG
NEARS CEDE
SONG VIPER
KNEELED DIVAS
ICE ERE IMAGE
TED ITS TENET

## PUZZLE 147

PERK CRAM CAR
AMEN HOME ADO
SILO ANIMATED
STYLES DOT
LOTS SOLOS
GUM NILE LOOP
ARAB SAL LAZE
UGLY EVES FEW
DELLS ECHO
ALP TEASES
ANSWERER TOLL
TOE DEMO HOSE
ERE SPUN STEW

## PUZZLE 148

PROP SODAS ADAS
ROIL IRATE DISH
ABLE EERIE ETTA
MESA SGTPRESTON
SAT STORE
BANANA TERSE
ELAND AARE OSS
CAPTAINMIDNIGHT
KEA COPE ATREE
ARENA STEEDS
ADANO TOM
NICKCARTER IDOL
OVAL MOORE ZONE
DOGE ANNIE EVEN
ETES TAINT SERT

## PUZZLE 149

1. Hand, 2. Point, 3. Monkey.

## PUZZLE 150

SWIT ALBA OBIT
WINE NOELS PLEA
ATTA ISLET EERO
THOMASSTEARNS
HAN SEE MASSES
ELECT SOPPY YAH
AEC MOE DOSE
JOHNRONALDREUEL
UNES NUN EHS
SEC ATTIC OILER
TATAMI HED OLE
ALANALEXANDER
CARL USURP AGVA
OLEO EUBIE PEEK
BEST REEL ARNE

## PUZZLE 151

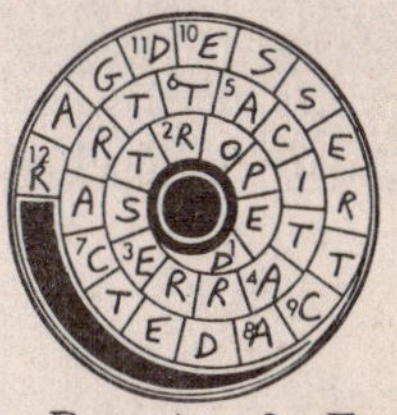

OUT: 1. Deports, 3. Erratic, 5 Attracted, 8. Actress, 10. Edgar.
IN: 12. Rag, 11. Dessert, 9. Cadet, 7. Cart, 6. Tacit, 4. Arrest, 2. Roped.

## PUZZLE 152

SALAD EDAM
OXIDES STAVES
TETONS CAMERA
ITCH RED
MODEM ROD
OPAL YOU ESS
LURKED LEGATE
EST GAT ASIA
GNU ALERT
ASH UTES
SCARAB AKIMBO
PALACE REREAD
METE DANTE

## PUZZLE 153

BAND TOM SALT
ABEE EEE ALOE
SEAT ARC LAST
STRESS COURSE
SEE ART
PASTA TENSE
ADO EEL
DETER PRANK
MAP WEE
DELETE ARMADA
OVER ENS OLIO
SING VET TORN
ELSE EWE ETTE

## PUZZLE 154

## PUZZLE 158

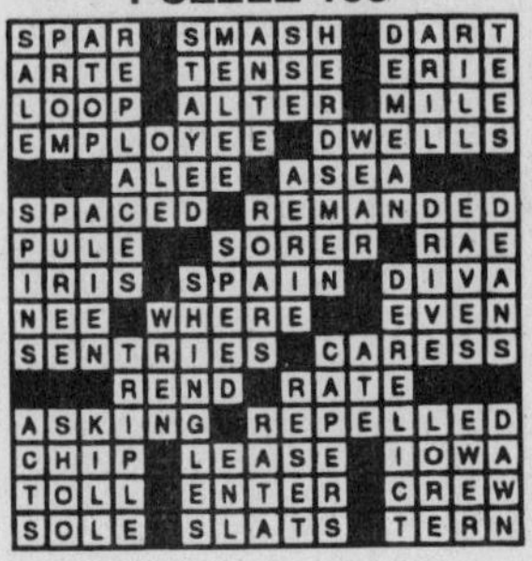

## PUZZLE 163

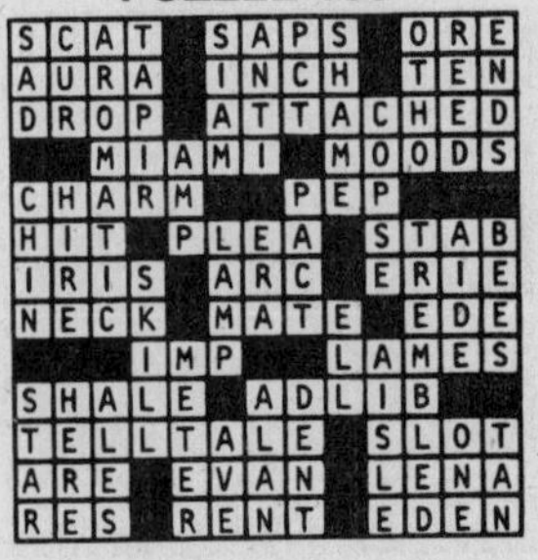

## PUZZLE 164

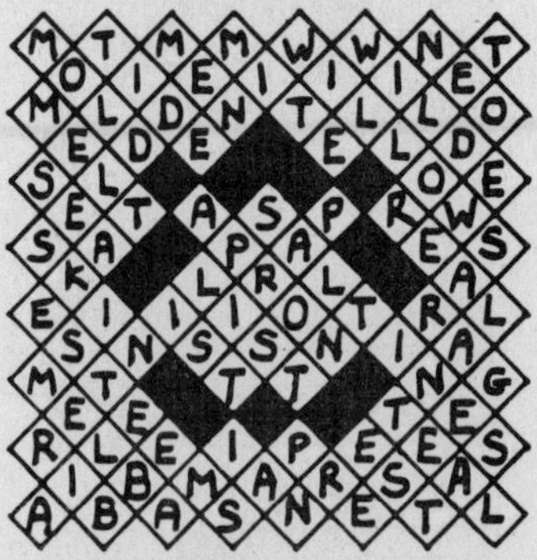

## PUZZLE 155

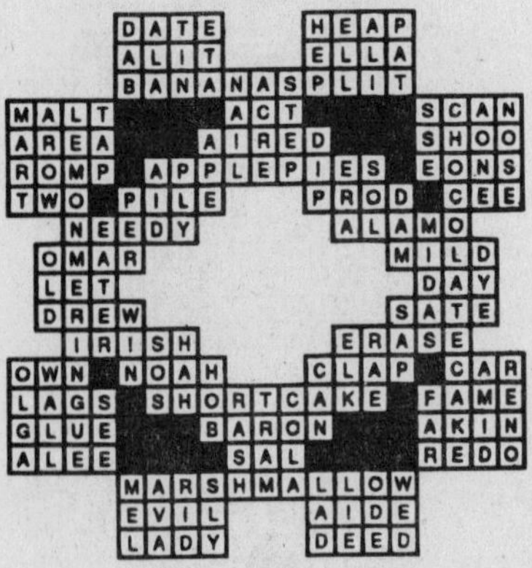

## PUZZLE 159

| | | | | |
|---|---|---|---|---|
| L | CALLER | CLEAR | RACE | L |
| O | PIANOS | SPAIN | NIPS | A |
| V | SHAVED | HEADS | ASHE | D |
| E | ELIDES | SLIDE | SLED | I |
| L | LEADER | EARED | DEAR | E |
| Y | SYSTEM | STEMS | METS | S |

## PUZZLE 160

## PUZZLE 165

1. 2. 3.

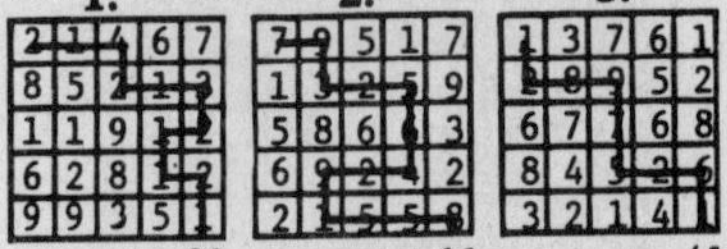

20 66 41

## PUZZLE 156

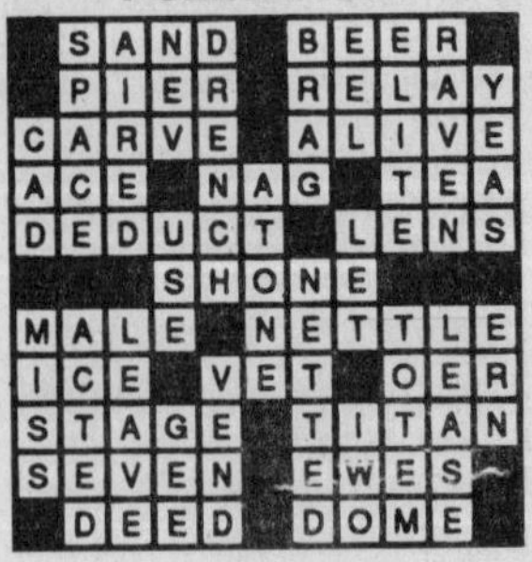

## PUZZLE 161

## PUZZLE 166

**5-Letter Words:** After, Alack, Cadet, Canal, Caper, Carat, Cared, Caret, Cater, Clack, Clash, Clasp, Deter, Etape, Fatal, Flack, Flare, Flash, Later, Nasal, Natal, Papal, Paper, Pared, Peach, Petal, Prate, Radar, Rated, Reach, Salad, Shack, Shade, Shaft, Shape, Share, Sharp, Spade, Spare, Speak, Spear, Taper, Teach.

**6-Letter Words:** Aerate, Caftan, Canape, Canter, Carpet, Claret, Facade, Flared, Harped, Karate, Palate, Parade, Pedant, Preach, Rafter, Reader, Reaper, Redeal, Repeal, Repeat, Spread.

## PUZZLE 157

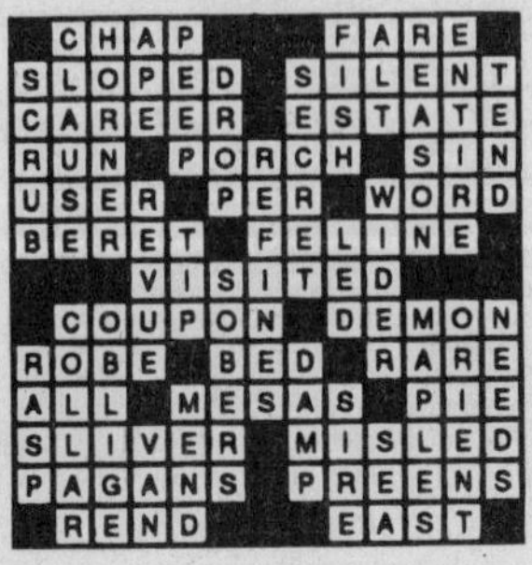

## PUZZLE 162

## PUZZLE 167

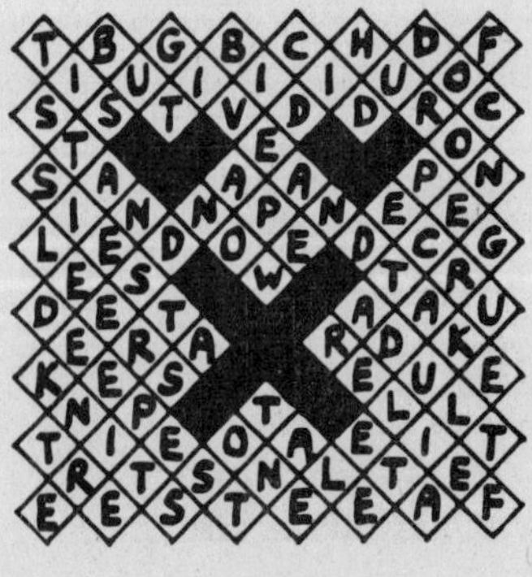

## PUZZLE 168

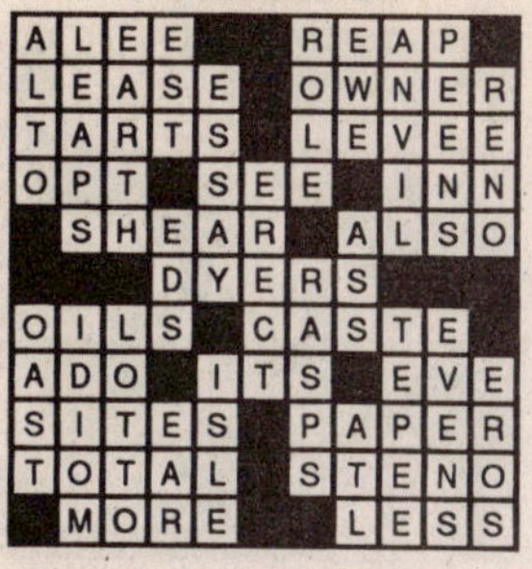


## PUZZLE 169

## PUZZLE 170

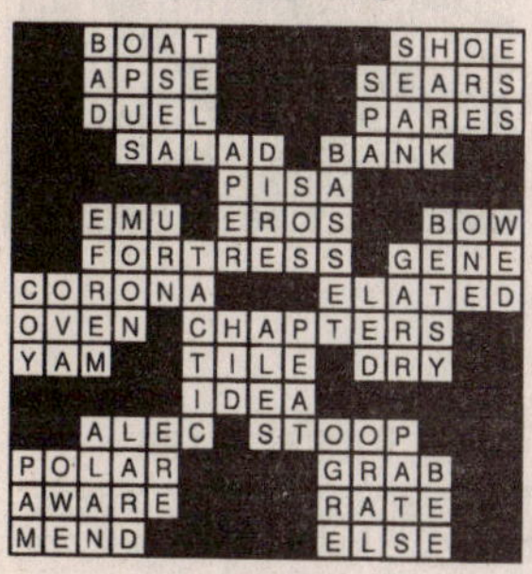


## PUZZLE 171

1. Bush clover, 2. Wet laundry, 3. Flight deck.

## PUZZLE 172

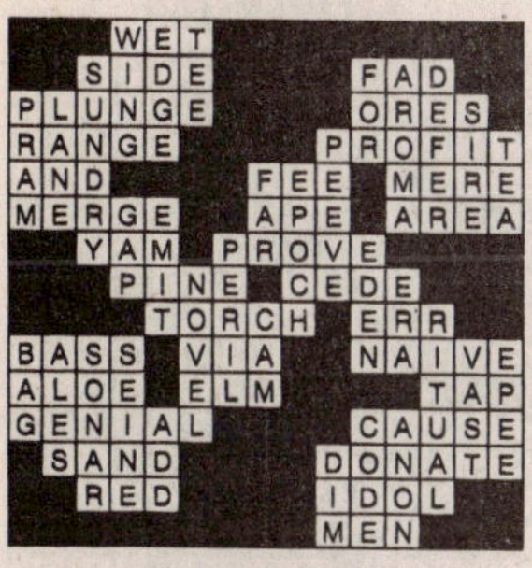


## PUZZLE 173

To whom nothing is given, of him can nothing be required.

1. Quiche, 2. High Noon, 3. Midnight, 4. Forgive, 5. Bonnet, 6. Woman, 7. Tires.

## PUZZLE 174

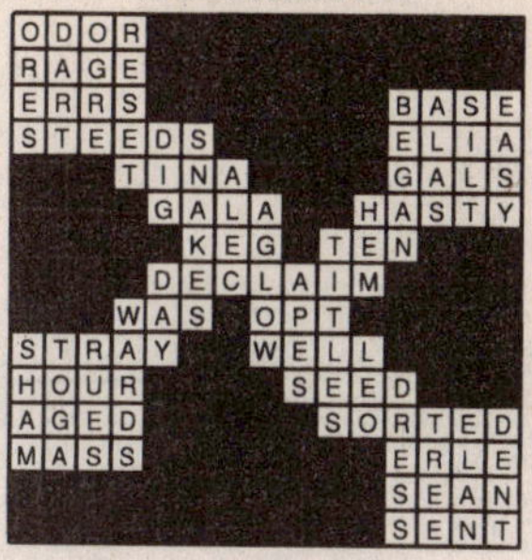


## PUZZLE 175

A. 25 (+1 +2 +3 +4...)
B. 36 (/3 x6 /3 x6...)
C. 49 (+1 /2 +3 /4 +5 /6 +7 /8)
D. 64 (x2 -4 x6 -8 x10 -12 x14 -16)
E. 81 (add two previous numbers)
F. 100 (x1 -100 x2 -100 x3 -100 x4 -100)
G. 121 (-11 x11 -11 x11...)
H. 144 (x8 /7 x6 /5 x4 /3 x2 /1)

BONUS: $5^2$, $6^2$, $7^2$, $8^2$, $9^2$, $10^2$, $11^2$, $12^2$.

## PUZZLE 176

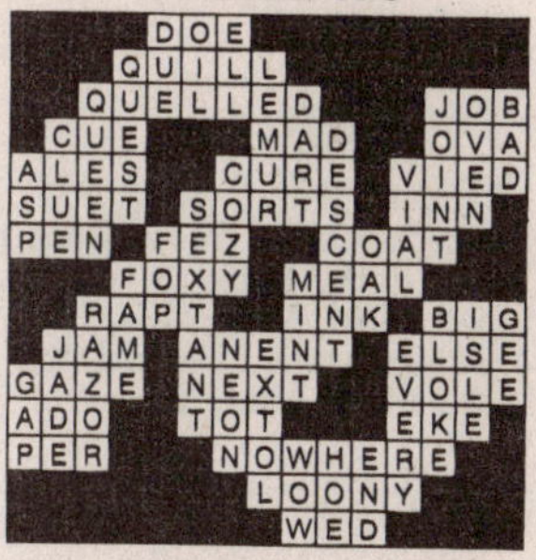


## PUZZLE 177

| | | | | |
|---|---|---|---|---|
| PASTOR | T | PROAS | O | SPAR |
| TENORS | O | STERN | N | REST |
| CRATER | R | CARET | T | RACE |
| SALOME | O | MEALS | A | ELMS |
| REMIND | N | MIRED | R | DIME |
| TINSEL | T | LINES | I | LENS |
| SOONER | O | SNORE | O | ERNS |

## PUZZLE 178

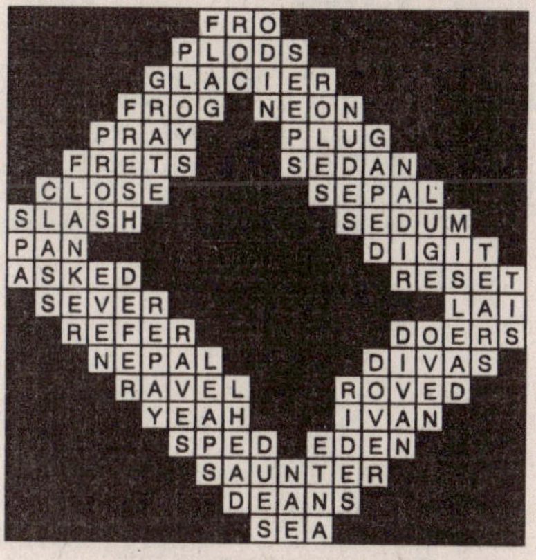


## PUZZLE 179

MODIFY

## PUZZLE 180

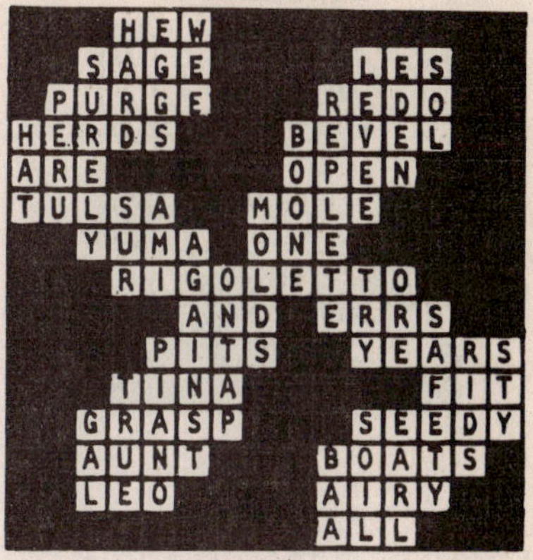


## PUZZLE 181

Be yourself is the worst advice you can give to some people. (Tom Masson)

1. Receiving, 2. Footloose, 3. Because, 4. Stopper, 5. Stymie, 6. Heavy, 7. Would.

## PUZZLE 182

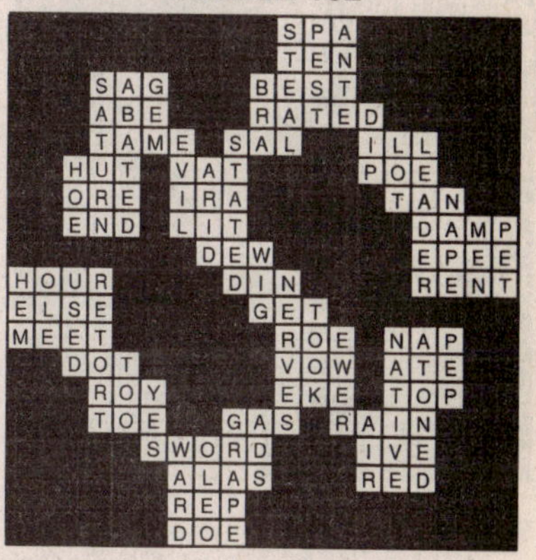


## PUZZLE 183

Jerk, Perk, Pert, Pest, Nest, Vest, West, Zest, Fest, Fist, Gist, List, Last, Cast, Cost, Most, Must, Dust, Bust, Bush, Busy.

## PUZZLE 184

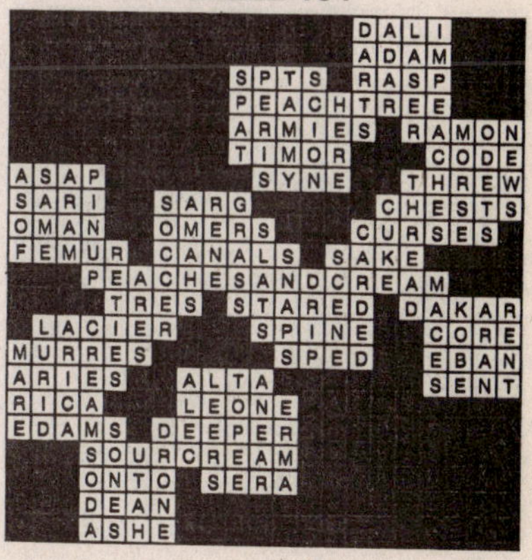

## PUZZLE 185

## PUZZLE 186

1. Heat, Head, Held, Hold, Cold.
2. Diet, Died, Hied, Hoed, Hood, Food.
3. Bird, Bind, Wind, Wing, Sing, Song.
4. Flour, Floor, Flood, Blood, Brood, Broad, Bread.

## PUZZLE 187

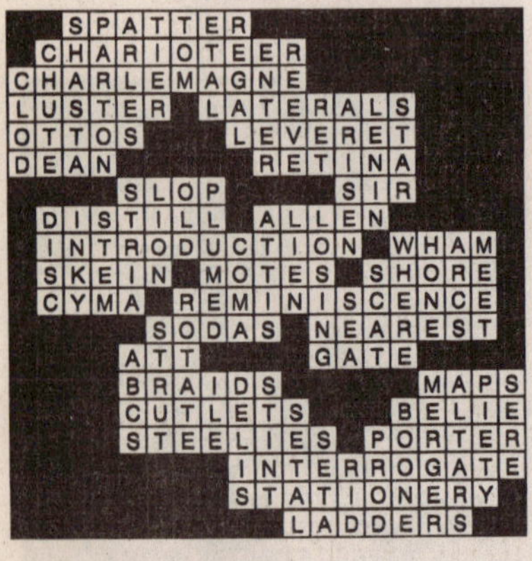


## PUZZLE 188

Quiz, Quit, Suit, Slit, Slim, Slip, Flip, Blip, Clip, Chip, Chin, Coin, Corn, Cork, Cord, Card, Care, Cage, Wage, Wave, Wavy, Waxy.

## PUZZLE 189

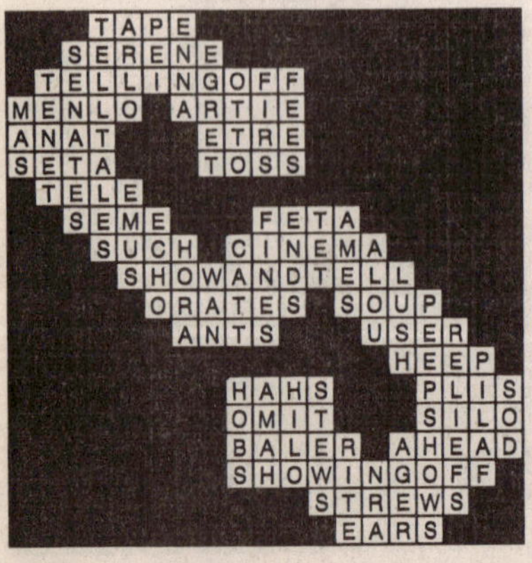


## PUZZLE 190

FINGERPRINT

## PUZZLE 191

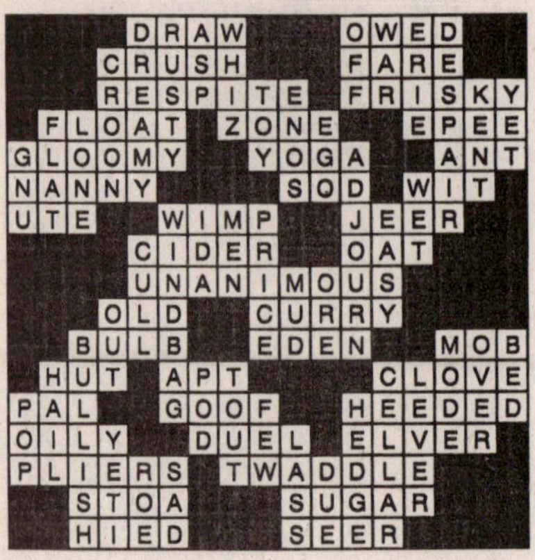


## PUZZLE 192

1. Snow, Slow, Slot, Slit, Suit; 2. Coat, Coot, Root, Rook, Rock, Rack; 3. Wood, Mood, Mold, Mild, Mile, Pile; 4. Down, Dawn, Darn, Dart, Mart, Mast, Vast, Vest.

## PUZZLE 193

## PUZZLE 194

1. Road, Roar, Soar, Sour, Tour.
2. Fast, Cast, Case, Cane, Lane.
3. Rest, Pest, Peat, Pear, Sear, Seer, Seep, Step, Stop.
4. Next, Neat, Seat, Slat, Slit, Alit, Adit, Edit, Exit.

## PUZZLE 195

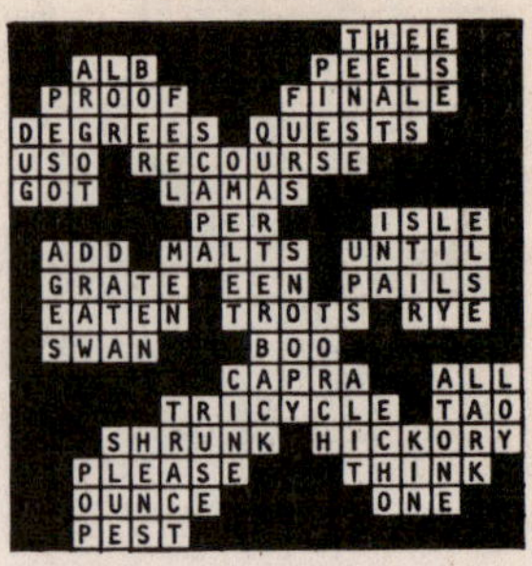


## PUZZLE 196

LIBERATION

## PUZZLE 197

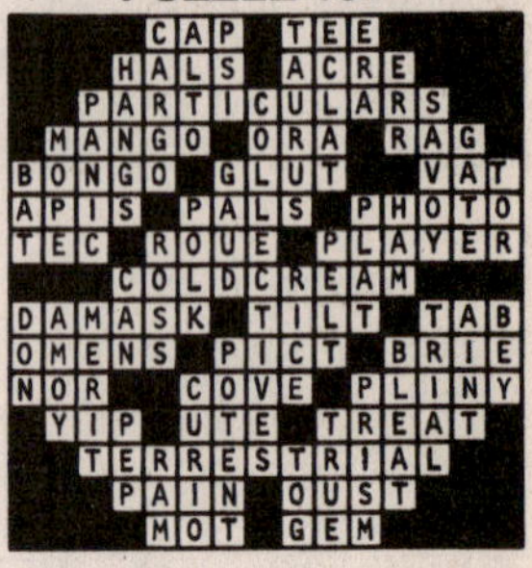


## PUZZLE 198

Impossible is a word only to be found in the dictionary of fools. (Napoleon)

1. Promotions, 2. Nobody, 3. Historical, 4. Definite, 5. Slowly, 6. Buffoon, 7. Sadie.

## PUZZLE 199

## PUZZLE 200

270

## PUZZLE 201

LATER ALEC DEAN
AGILE CATO ARNO
BULLDURHAM MITE
SET SER PENCIL
MOE TOBY
ABOARD RHUBARB
BANJO YARN NELL
ALSO DOTED KNEE
SEER AGEE BEENE
STLOUIS STEEDS
ERGS AUS
SHEATH FAR TWO
HANG THENATURAL
ALOU EIRE ATONE
DOSE RENT MATEO

## PUZZLE 205

OSSA PACTS AMEN
FLEW ALLOW HOLE
FATHERTIME STLO
WHITE PEAT HEN
LANG STARE
ABETTED SPARTA
HER SATED ETHER
EROS LUNAR SORT
RITES PIKES ONE
BEHELD MALTEDS
ERIES RAIL
ERR PICA TRAMP
TARA SOBSISTERS
CRAB TRURO ESAU
HATE SETON DAMP

## PUZZLE 209

SMOKE CAT SERGE
EAVES ONE ANEAR
TREES NIM LLAMA
SERPENT POMADES
ENERGETIC
SPAR BOOST EDDY
ALES SLOTS DIRE
PEG SEA
IBIS GEESE SCAR
DESK AARON TORN
ESOTERICA
PASTELS ODOROUS
ARACA OAR PRONE
TIGHT USA SEPIA
SLAYS TEL EDSEL

## PUZZLE 202

BARN GALE SALON
OMOO URAL LEONE
MOTO SINK ARNEL
BRANCHEDOUT GAL
LES PEBBLY
TABLED SEEDER
ARROW SOON LAIN
SNAG STAND ANNE
SONG TARS LYCEE
CITERS MESHED
SAHARA POA
AIR OLIVEBRANCH
BLOOP RAKI TORO
REAVE ARIL ONER
ADDIS SANE MOWN

## PUZZLE 206

LOBE ATTIC RAY
IDOL BRACE OLEO
ROOM OILER BETA
ARK TUBE ELIXIR
MAINE AMEN
AROUND PLOT BAG
BIBLE GIANT ORE
OVID DIZZY JOIN
DEL TIZZY BAKER
ETE ERMA BUCKLE
CLEO BROKE
ZODIAC FRAY ERA
AGOG TALON OPAL
PLEA OREAD PELL
ERR READY TREY

## PUZZLE 210

ATTN GLIB SLAP
BRAE DRONE TOGA
AIMS OASTS ANON
SEPTEMBERSONG
ERASE LAIR SOL
NED MEA PHI
ALAN PERU CREAM
MADASAMARCHHARE
INAPT OMAR OKAY
SAP ATL LYE
SIT NAIS LOTUS
AUGUSTBELMONT
EBBS THOLE BRIE
TALE LEMUR ETTA
EYED YSER REEL

## PUZZLE 203

STOP BASTE DIAL
HOLE AREEL ONTO
EWER TIERS UTES
SOUTHERNACCENT
EEL OER
CACHES OBEY VAN
ABOUT SHAM DENE
SOUTHSEAISLANDS
ANNS TART ALERT
SET ASTA ASIDES
IAM PSS
SONGOFTHESOUTH
ALGA ROUTE POET
CLOT ARRAS OGLE
KANE YELLS NAME

## PUZZLE 207

EMMA MATS PEASE
LIER UPON INCOG
ADDINGTWOANDTWO
PADDA ORO
SILENTP ZENANAS
ERE KISSES TOCK
LIEIN STUDY
SUMANDSUBSTANCE
AXING BLEAR
IOTA ROSARY GAI
DREISER HEPBURN
TIA URIAH
YOUCANCOUNTONME
EATER LENA KEIR
SKEET EDIE EASE

## PUZZLE 211

WELSH KISS SPUD
ABATE AREA TAME
KERRY VIED ALBA
ERGO SASS PRIOR
STEPON HABITS
SLOG WALLACE
TIL DRIP DEEDED
ADAM KLIEG SEND
DENIAL ABEL STY
SADDLER BRIG
GLARED ENLACE
KORAN FEED AGOD
EGAN TUFT AMATI
REND STOA MONET
NETS PEEL BRASH

## PUZZLE 204

LUSH FLIP BERN
ASIA RAISE OLIO
CAPTAINFRACASSE
TRACT ORIEL
SMELLY PURSE
HIRES BANK VAR
MIDAS BANDY ELA
ENDS TORSO SNIP
DEL TARRY TENET
ERE URGE HAVEN
MARNE EATERS
CLARK FLIER
OURMUTUALFRIEND
MICE OSTIA NANA
ASHE TESS GREW

## PUZZLE 208

PARADOX STAFF
HOMERULE PELLET
ONELINER ORIOLE
RABID AXIOM TIN
SPIC STEAK PICO
EEC CHESS ALLIN
BLAS INSULTS
GALOP ESSAY
DAMAGES SHAH
OMENS CHARY ACT
REND POILU ACRO
SPA GETAT UNCAS
ELBERT TIMEZONE
TALKAT UNALASKA
NEEDY SELECTS

## PUZZLE 212

LUCE AQUA BLUES
OPEN TURN LINDY
GOLD TASK ADDIN
ONTIME ALEC ETE
VISA ELKS
MAGENTA METTLE
OUR TERSE DORIA
ODES ROAST WETS
RIELS NOTED ARE
SONATA ENACTED
MARS RATA
EGO MILE CERISE
MAXIM ANTI AMIR
ILEDE TOOT FALA
TENOR ESPY EMOS

## PUZZLE 213

DEBTS KORAN POSH
SALAAM INEVITABLE
EMERGE MEDICATION
APE ADO DEMISE
TEMPERANCE TEN
ROAD MOULDY APSE
SUIT TAR ROW
CRYSTALS PET PONE
HONE POI SAY ALAR
EGAD SOL EMPERORS
CUR SET ERIN
KEYS DENOVO RAGS
PSI TRANSSHAPE
SPICES UTE TOY
COLLATERAL EMPIRE
ADULTERANT KAYOED
RAMS DENTS SPANS

## PUZZLE 217

FLIT UNTIL ADAM
AONE TORSO DELI
DAREDEVILS OVAL
EDEMA AMEER IRK
ETA STROLL
SADDENS WEST
AGE DOLED SABER
WAVY NAMES PIPE
SPIES TUNIC TEA
ELLA SPARSER
SPICED SRO
LAC DOMED LOTTO
OLLA DEVILSFOOD
STUD ERODE ERNE
SOBS SYNOD DYES

## PUZZLE 214

EFTS ABOUTFACED
N R F O N R L O
COATI ROBBERIES
O N N E O N N E
UPSIDEDOWNCAKE
N I E O E H A
THEOREM DEDUCED
E N S R A V
RETAKES TREMBLE
S E U R S L R
REVENGEISSWEET
D T P G E I C I
ACHIEVERS NEARS
M I R S T G R E
PACESETTER USED

## PUZZLE 218

**PO/STA/GE**

## PUZZLE 219

LEAD SNAPS URGE
ACME OILER SEER
THEMARXBROTHERS
EON AREA RELET
TROD PAIR
NARROW LONESTAR
ALIEN MASTS ITA
DOVE HADES IGOT
ENE SATES IRENE
RETRACTS SNARED
ELKE SHED
STATE ATOP NEA
THEAMESBROTHERS
LARK PILOT UNIT
OTOE ITEMS GENA

## PUZZLE 215

| | | | | | | | | | | | | |
|---|---|---|---|---|---|---|---|---|---|---|---|---|
| AR | TE | | DI | N | ED | | F | AM | OUS | | QU | E |
| M | E | S | S | EN | GER | | R | US | T | L | E | R |
| OR | N | A | T | E | | PR | ON | E | | I | ST | LE |
| | | LE | I | | V | ES | T | ME | N | T | | |
| SU | R | | N | AT | AN | T | | N | OT | E | BOO | K |
| S | E | AN | C | E | | ID | IO | T | | RA | S | E |
| PE | T | I | T | | SK | I | N | | STA | TU | T | E |
| N | OR | MAL | | D | I | GIT | | S | C | RE | E | N |
| SE | T | F | RE | E | | A | L | AC | K | | R | EST |
| | | A | DO | R | A | T | ION | | TH | OR | | |
| GE | A | R | | AN | CH | OR | | SH | E | A | RE | R |
| S | CRI | M | MA | G | E | | R | E | CA | N | T | ED |
| TE | D | | SH | E | D | | AW | A | RDS | | RO | AN |

## PUZZLE 220

1. Skunk, 2. Bison, 3. Hyena, 4. Tiger, 5. Horse, 6. Camel.
BONUS: Cougar.

## PUZZLE 216

MISS PAMS SKY
ALIE RAMONA TIE
DERN OLIVER ANN
DEANS ERRAND
TOES DELL
SENOR TOR SEAS
AVER TENANT UTA
GAL ELSIE RAT
ANS TALENT PETE
SOME ATE TALES
NONE SEAN
FENDER VIDOR
JED ELAINE OVEN
OLD REMAIN RENE
ELY DANS ARTE

## PUZZLE 221

LOAF BIRD PAW
ANNES ERIE BLUE
PETAL LAMB RANT
RESORT AWAITS
TOAST SHINS
GASPS OLEOS
GAB PINE REATA
EVEREST SOLDIER
MELON EAST DAM
STAMP HOSES
DATES EVENT
RIVERS ORIOLE
OVER EMIT ORATE
MARS RACE NESTS
ANT TEES STAT

## PUZZLE 222

## PUZZLE 227

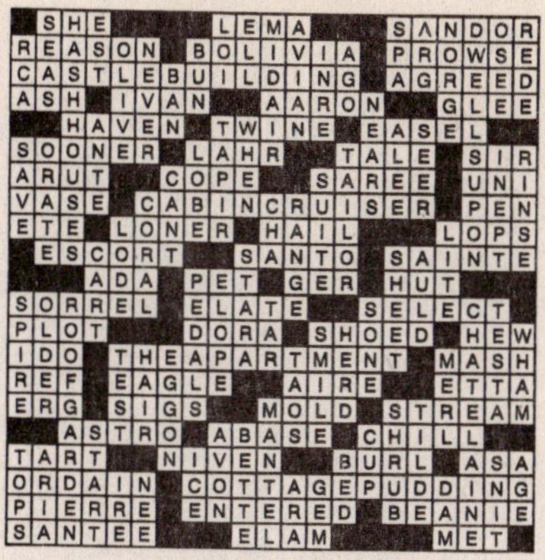

## PUZZLE 231

1-W, 2-M, 3-Y, 4-C, 5-S, 6-V, 7-N, 8-A, 9-U, 10-D, 11-E, 12-G, 13-J, 14-B, 15-Z, 16-I, 17-K, 18-T, 19-Q, 20-X, 21-H, 22-P, 23-F, 24-O, 25-R, 26-L.

## PUZZLE 223

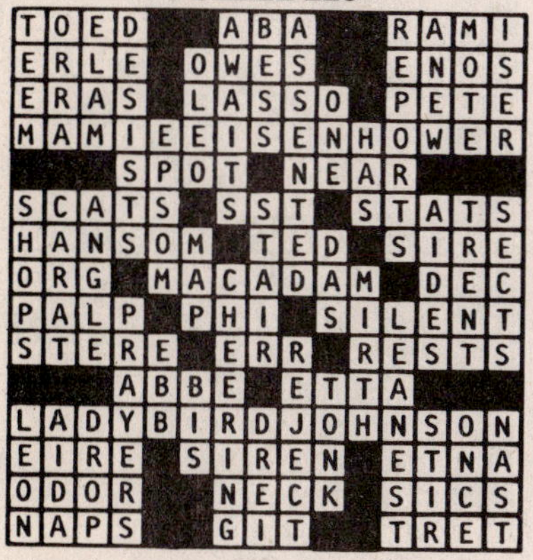

## PUZZLE 228

## PUZZLE 232

## PUZZLE 224

A. Idaho is the only state in the U.S. over which no foreign flag has ever flown.

B. One followed by forty-five zeros is a quattuordecillion.

## PUZZLE 229

## PUZZLE 233

## PUZZLE 225

## PUZZLE 230

## PUZZLE 234

## PUZZLE 226

A=3, B=6, C=1, D=9, E=7, F=2, G=8, H=4.

## PUZZLE 235

LOW TEE MUM
ASH URN ONE
SLY BLED SWIM
TOSSES TONTO
PLAYPEN
HABIT ERA BAT
EDIT RAY RENO
ROB AIR PENNY
SIGNALS
SOLID BUTLER
LIAR RIBS ELI
ELK ODE ASP
DYE DAY FEE

## PUZZLE 236

LAW BATH SPA
IRIS AREA TAP
PANE DIAL ADE
BEAD ALTARS
MOP SEW
BERSERK REPLY
AGE OIL AYE
RODEO TAMALES
ARE DIM
METALS LAMB
CAD TOES ZEAL
ODE OPAL EASE
PEN RELY TEE

## PUZZLE 237

PAD TAP SPA
USE AIRS BEAD
RIB BLOT ONCE
RATTLE ACUTE
RED BAT
DENY ALL LED
AGO TOTEM AWE
MOD ACE OPEN
ALE ASH
VILLA CEMENT
ZOOS NOTE MOO
ALTO SLED INN
PEA EDS TEE

## PUZZLE 238

MOTE BERT SHOE BIDE
EMIR ADOS PAPA UKES
SANG HIMALAYAS SEEP
ARSON SARI LENT
UPON SIP LILACS
CHAGRIN STOOD BELLE
REFUSE SCENTED SPED
ARTIE BEANS BAA HAG
WOES FOALS POUR ARE
REWROTE CORNCOB
ELS HATS PLEAT VEEP
RAH YUL SLOTH BETTE
AGAR DEFEATS TUNICS
SEVEN GIRTH BORSCHT
ERECTS NET BONG
RHEA ECRU SABER
OAHU UNDERLINE SORE
ALAI SKID INCA KILN
REST SAGS PEER SLED

## PUZZLE 239

CRAB ANET STAT STOP
LOCO NENE TORE ARGO
OUTOFDATE OMEN LARD
GESTE LEPERS DRONES
HAM REAM LEANS
BRASSERIES DIRT LOP
OAT TWIN THIEF TAPE
AVOW LATE ANNOTATES
TEPID TONITE ORIENT
MAMA DOT STOW
STAPLE JUNEAU TAMER
COLLECTOR RUGS NAPA
OGLE HIKES GAIN GEM
WOO VANE COURTESIES
RAINY MARS EWE
BONSAI PIRATE ELATH
AROW COAX LITTLEJOE
NANA ABLE ENNA CARE
GLEN LIED SEAT TROD

## PUZZLE 240

ERA LAMP GLAND GRAM
TAR OLEO LALIA RIME
CHESTERWNIMITZ ELBA
THUS DINES ZEALOT
COHOS VENTS ILLS
ROAD FARES PRESERVE
ALF MUSES SHIRE ION
BARTERED FLOSS ACTA
AUTOS PLATH ETHER
PINTER ALAMO CESARE
ASKED GLASS SURER
ISLE SLACK PLEIADES
LEI SCONE BLARE RAE
SINATRAS POETS POSE
BOAT TEXAS NODED
BEDLAM AIDES BORG
ERIE BARBARAWALTERS
ELMS LINEN NAST RAT
TEST EXERT TREE SPY

## PUZZLE 241

EVES COLA GRIP DRAY
SECT AMOR HADA RIPE
PERI BEND ONER OPEN
PULLINGUPSTAKES
TIN HOST LESSER
LAZED POUT STAR PRO
AMID BARS SHIN BARA
RIO SAWN STRAD ONOR
KENNEL HIRER SIRS
CONESTOGAWAGONS
ETAT TAMMY RASHER
LINE COMMA CHAR DAY
SOYS HOPE MOAB ROSE
AGO EELS GENT CENTS
SANITY KALI SAG
THESANTAFETRAIL
LAIC NONO NERO LOON
ARCH NAST GRIN ENNA
PREY ERAS ESNE DEEP

## PUZZLE 242

SHOO ALAD PLAY ALLS
TERM LOCO AONE LOUT
RANI LOOKERSON DUNE
ALATE TREATED RANGE
NET SEEN SERENE GEL
DRESSED HER SINLESS
OER PADRE BEE
PROWS FIT EAT GOOSE
LENS BATCH REPENTED
ANI BAN HID NED TIE
STONEAGE SETON PENN
MANIC SOD FOR DARES
PAR NEVER TEL
COWSLIP SER ARMORER
ERE MOROSE AGIO ENE
LILTS OVERAGE NESTS
LODE OVERSPEND DIRE
ALEE VERT ENDO ADEN
REDS ANTS STAR MEET

## PUZZLE 243

VANE AVID ABED TEST
ECOL WARE GIBE ASEA
ROTE ARES IDOL TAEL
BRAVERY PAL NEPTUNE
AGE VIXEN GAL
SOTTO CITE AMATEURS
TORE POLE STET SPOT
ONE LURE FLUTES ALI
PATTERN GLARE LOSER
AVE ORATE SOU
GROPE SPITE APPROVE
LED REMISS BLUE PAY
ATEN RUNT CAIN GALE
DESOLATE PORT MALES
MUS STERN NIL
MINIMUM WAS ROLLERS
ANON RITA ATOM AVOW
PELA ECON IOTA NOVA
SEAL SANG ROAD TEEM

## PUZZLE 244

CAT TEARS OFF
FACE ARROW LEAF
SANTA CITYOFDAVID
ADO CAKE BOA TONE
MONTHLY TESTS RAN
REL SHAH EMILY
MAJOR LOIN BRUT
ALOP WARN LOUDEST
UGH LAST ROOM SIR
LANCERS COST COLA
QUAY SOME LANKY
PIPES BITE FEN
ECU HERBS RAFTERS
NIBS DUE DART BAT
DELLASTREET IRONY
RIOT AISLE SINK
CEE LASER TOY

## PUZZLE 245

BAG SCAT RADIO DENS
EGO OHIO EBONY EXIT
TOLERATE FASTS PINA
FLAT HOUSE TOOLER
RAILS NORSE DEPRESS
EDNA BULGE BERET
DOG MIDDY LIVEN FES
BONES TAPIR ALLA
SPREADS VOWEL CLOUT
CLEANS BOUND CLOUDY
READS FAIRS GRAFTER
ABLY BIRDS TRUST
PES ZEROS CROSS DEE
HELEN FLOAT MEAN
RESEATS BRAWN WEARS
ORIELS PRONE RIND
TOED AGAIN LEADUPTO
EDGE WORST ERGO AIR
SEED SOAKS DREW NAT

## PUZZLE 246

TITO HAP POMS DRAG
ONER CEIL RAIN AIDE
OTEA HIRE OKRA IDOL
ORCHID ALF TRES
LILIESOFTHEFIELD
SERENE LENES STEREO
EMU TARE GRAB SIAM
AMIR NOVA RENE EKE
LANE SENNA GOLF
GOLDENDAFFODILS
SEER SERIN ETTA
LAD ANEW ODIC WARP
ASOP DATA DAIS LEE
THREAD CAROL TAILED
HEATHERONTHEHILL
USIA ASI AZALEA
DAWN GROG ORLE INNS
ALAI NEVE ATEN NINE
MAYA SEAR NEY IDEA

## PUZZLE 247

ASPIC LAC DUB DELLA
DIANA SOHO POKE IDEAL
ENACT ALEC OWED SWAPS
GRANDMAMOSES HIPPO
AIS NAME AGENTS
ENRAPT POUR TIES
REAL AUNTIEMAME CLAD
ANTAL PRY TILES HOBO
SNORE SIX SHRED FARES
INMATES UNIT MIDDLE
SISTINECHAPEL
SODDEN REES WETLAND
TBARS FRIAR PAL ELIOT
IOTA GROSS ORE RANGE
REAM MOTHERLODE INGE
PACE AAHS CANYON
SHRANK EAST EAR
FLAIR POPCORNBALLS
LORCA AKIN HOOD ROAMS
OPTED LICE ENOS ABOUT
GEESE IDS SAT TESTY

## PUZZLE 248

DORM BIBS ABA
ASEA BRAT BAN
FLAX LAMANCHA
TOPIC BRO
MYFAIRLADY
YOU DAD AREA
OPT STORY ILK
DEAD PIE ALS
ACHRISTMAS
ABE HELLO
WESTSIDE LEAD
ARE ENOS MAME
REX NESS APES

## PUZZLE 249

ARM JAMS FLAP
YOU OFIT LOSE
NAN NASA ONIT
RIVERCITYIA
ISM NOD
TRON OER ERA
ROBERTPRESTON
INS ORE LADY
WOO ASA
THEMUSICMAN
ORAL BADE BIG
HILL LIEN ELY
SOTS ELSE DEM

## PUZZLE 250

SPAT CUBE LITER BET
LULU ASEA AGAVE OWE
OMAN YENS TORAH ZEE
PAINTEDDESERT ACORN
ERN SLUR SASH
INKLING NAP SHABBY
FIE PEACH LOCH LORE
FLAP LOOT POI KNEW
YESES LABEL LEGENDS
NOD TONER RED
EPICURE SONAR TULSA
DALI ADA RICE POOR
NAIL WOLF NEARS LOT
ARABLE BAA PENALTY
OARS CAST CAB
PROXY CHARCOALGRILL
AUK MOOED RAVI ARIA
PIA ADORE EDEN DISC
ANY NAPES EYRE ESPY

## PUZZLE 251

KINGPIN FATHERS
E O U I R E R A
EATEN GREENLAND
N R G H I A S D
EVEREST GENTEEL
S D N H T E
TOASTIEST SEWED
M P E E
STEEP INDONESIA
E R C A T N
CABOOSE ARMREST
T A T N D E R H
ORCHESTRA TANGO
R O S E G A E N
SENATOR EAGERLY

## PUZZLE 252

SCAD WASH JOKER
HUGE AXLE ALIVE
ORAL YEAR GENIE
ASPIC MENU ELK
LEE HAS OAF
PAINT TRIFLE
HAZARDOUS DEED
IRIS ERROR GANG
LINT EPAULETTE
LAGOON SPLIT
RUE YEN ORB
GEM TWIN EQUAL
AMASS TOME UNDO
PIXIE EVER ICON
STINT MANE TEND

## PUZZLE 253

A fanatic is a man who can't change his mind and won't change the subject.

1. Jamaica, 2. Watches, 3. Hatchet, 4. Channing, 5. Bound, 6. Wafted, 7. Aching, 8. Tennis, 9. Mason.

## PUZZLE 254

EELS FLOP
TROT OAR LIMA
CANOE VIE ALARM
PAL STEVEMARTIN EBB
ALAS PEN LAW MAUL
RARE PER SAL EDGE
EMIT ASS PRY LOLA
DOC CUTE END WET
ERAL NELL
SAND STOA
TEAR WEAR
ABA LAB SCAR KOP
NERO KAY PAN OLLA
ELLA ENE ANN NEDS
ALIT IAN VII AMES
RAN MRSROBINSON ORE
GREET MAN THORN
ETTE EYE EIRE
DEER ROAM

## PUZZLE 255

PIT ARM
MADE BOAT
TALON CAMEO
FUN LOT RAMPS
ANON RAT PET
DARED RIBBONS
ROE PAR
BELONGS GAMES
EVE GAB TIDE
TEMPT GAL SIT
ROLES RIVET
NEAT NEAR
DRY SST

## PUZZLE 256

ALEC WAS LIED
CELL IDA IDLE
TOMORROW LOSE
SOY HAILED
THREE WORE
REED CARESSED
IRA TULSA MAY
POPSICLE LOVE
PLUS CAGED
ESTEEM BUT
BLUE BARBECUE
BAND EGO SOFA
STAY ROW TOOT

## PUZZLE 257

SPA COAT BEAT
NAP IDLE LACE
ONE DEAN AREA
WEDGE STIR
ART CEDAR
DORM RATE AXE
ALOE AGO ELLS
RED EPEE BEET
NOSEY DAB
LEFT ISLES
CARD OILS EVE
OBOE REEL NIX
BEER EDGE SLY

## PUZZLE 258

PEG SPAS BRAY
ERA HIRE LURE
AIL ANEW AGES
REALM ASPS
ASH OTHER
SETS ACID EWE
ADOS TOO FREE
WIN BENT LORD
STEER ATE
LADE ADULT
CARD OVER SOW
OBOE DEED EGO
WEER ONLY SOS

## PUZZLE 259

MANOR EAR AND
ADORE LYE FOR
PETER FESTIVE
GUN STORES
AMMONIA FUELS
SOON FLOUR
HOP STILL SEA
TOYED GULF
STRAP NEAREST
CHOIRS RIO
REPLACE SPRAY
USE NAY LEAVE
BED ONE EDGES

## PUZZLE 260

THIS TAN GONE
AIDE USE ARIA
PLEA ESS RANT
SLATES TABLES
SAD SPA
PEN RAG EGRET
AREA YET EIRE
RATIO MAR DEN
RIP BAR
SAMPLE LEADER
OLEO AWE COPE
REAR ROT EVEN
TENT LES REED

## PUZZLE 261

AGES PLUM BAR
DEBT RISE ACE
EMBROIDER SHE
ABE GREED
CLAWED LEO
LOUSY MYSTERY
URN WEE LIE
BETWEEN PASTA
ART TEPEES
BINGO OAR
ROE DESTROYER
OWE ERIE NERO
WAD SAND STEW

## PUZZLE 262

PA U SEK NO W
IG NO R E FAR
L OUD IRAT E
INS ISTRI D
FLE E T ALE
E RU P T F AN
E AR NINGS
R OAS T D IET
M U S HYSA RI
ASS E NT OAR
A L IA S
G ROWA C T
PE TT YYON

## PUZZLE 263

ALMS BEAU SHE
SEEP ADDS COD
KIWI WISHBONE
GILT EATEN
ACTORS ERR
ROUTE INSECTS
MOB ODD ARE
SPATULA REBEL
AND WEASEL
SAUCE WEDS
MUSTACHE EBBS
ORE SUED LEAK
GAS YEWS STAY

## PUZZLE 264

IFAT HEWS IDA
SANE AREA NOR
NINE PRIM SET
TRANSPARENT
SPEND EASE
HIP AND PINED
ADOPTS SALTED
ROLLS TAR SKY
ELLA DUCKS
UNDERHANDED
FAT ANTE AIDE
LYE TILT PAGE
YES AMES SLED

## PUZZLE 265

HAT BASH HERO
ARE ALEE OVAL
LEA NEAR REND
TAMPA DEN
INNS LENDS
TOENAIL STORE
ADD PIT TON
ROGUE CONCEPT
TREND EPEE
ASP SOFAS
LAMB LOFT IRA
IDOL ALOE SIN
DOME NEED HAD

## PUZZLE 266

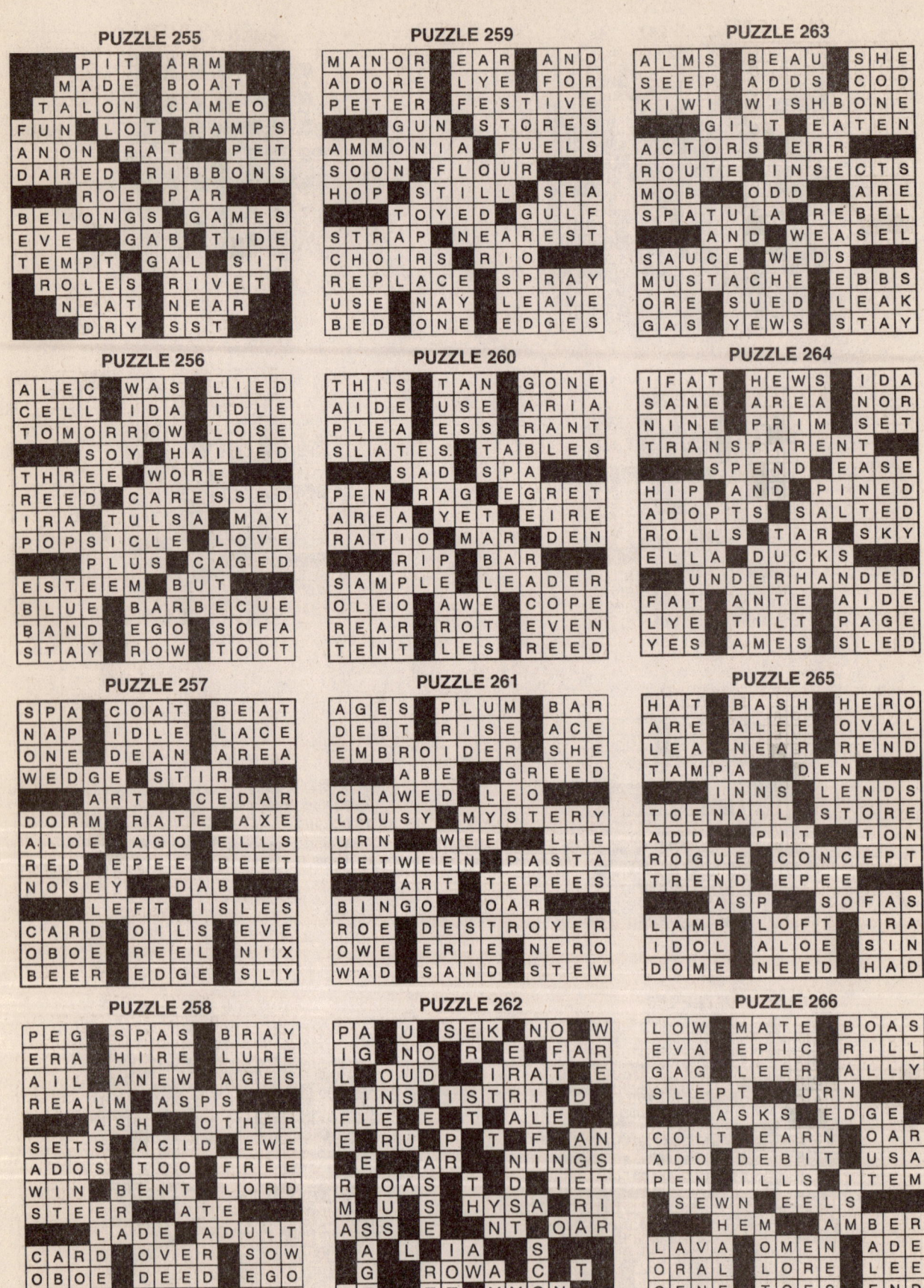

LOW MATE BOAS
EVA EPIC RILL
GAG LEER ALLY
SLEPT URN
ASKS EDGE
COLT EARN OAR
ADO DEBIT USA
PEN ILLS ITEM
SEWN EELS
HEM AMBER
LAVA OMEN ADE
ORAL LORE LEE
GENE TOES END

## PUZZLE 267

ACER ATHOS ETNA
RODE BRIDESMAID
AVID LANDLOCKED
BET VOID FLEECE
EROSION GREENER
STREAM MOULD
QUILL FOLLY NOM
URAL HORDE DESI
EEL HADES LOFTS
SOTOL DEPART
ADAPTER SEVERAL
MEDIAL TINY ICE
AFICIONADO DOIT
SOMERSAULT OUZO
SEED THREE ISEE

## PUZZLE 271

LAME IPSO SCAB
ENOL SUAVE ALLA
VEALCUTLET BUSS
EATER OKRA OBOE
ERS ELF SPOTS
BEEFSTEW TEA
RESOLE PASSKEYS
OCHO BAY NARK
CROSSBAR STAKES
SUR PORKCHOP
THANE AYN STE
CARA EBAN OATER
OBIT RACKOFLAMB
ROBE SCREW TIPI
MUSS KERN OREL

## PUZZLE 275

LAG WADES RAGE
ONE DEVINE EVEN
TEN ORANGE VEND
SWERVE UMPIRES
RUE PULSES
FROG PUFF RENDS
LOS COMO ASSURE
OBI ALA DUO TOE
POTATO BURN ROD
STYLE LANA PIPS
TRAINS OUT
ATTESTS EMPIRE
DEAR OTTAWA OAR
DALE NEARER URN
SLED ENTER SEE

## PUZZLE 268

DASH BASAL SCOW
UPTO ELENA RAKE
CARPETBAGS IRIS
TRIERS ESS PET
STARR SCROOGE
OLIO DONNA
MACAROON CARTON
IRAS ANITA GENA
CARSON CARTERET
ELMER ARTE
ESCUELA NOOSE
CAL ANT CORSET
AMIN CARVINGSET
ROTE AGAIN AIDE
EKED PENCE NESS

## PUZZLE 272

LOADS MALL IRS
ANGER AREA ANET
PERFORMASERVICE
STET EBBS HETER
EWE STAS DERIDE
DODGERS LEA AES
LEO PAC STD
PERFORMANCE
SON IVY DEA
SES ERA RESTERS
TATTLE PANT NUT
ABEAM ERIC ANSA
PERFORMONESDUTY
LENT SITE EDILE
ESS TROD EASED

## PUZZLE 276

NARC GAIT USES
OMAR ONER ATOLL
SOLITAIRE SOUSA
EYEBALL ENDPLAY
BRIE III
SPADE BACCARAT
STOGY SANK HIE
POKE SLITS NORA
EME MAZE CANER
CARDGAME CAPED
EER FARO
CANASTA IDOLIZE
ORALS SINGLETON
CAMEO CREE ONNA
OBER HERR NOES

## PUZZLE 269

SITE CRISP STEW
ADEN AORTA HIRE
GOLDENMEAN ULNA
ELL WOE MEDDLER
SEE GELID
CIDER DEN VENAL
AREA ROT MORALE
RAM AUTOMAT BOA
ATONCE VOW DONS
TENET MET TIBET
SOFAR SON
BEATNIK ACE ARA
ORNE NEATASAPIN
SING ADDER WENT
SNAG LOOSE EDGE

## PUZZLE 273

LAW SCAT PEA BOA
ALIT AMOLE SELMA JINX
MALA BILLYTHEKID ELEE
BILLFOLD WINO OPAL
ILOVE BIN RANI
SEABEE GMEN BRENNAN
ELMO AIR ROE TIRED
BUSY BOONE SHIER EDNA
ADO WILLIAMHOLDEN SEN
ENSILE IONS FIT
ARLO PLATE SOSO
LEO BEAM CRUMBS
ELS SWEETWILLIAMS ITS
RAHS STEIN YEARS CLAP
RIOTS AFT RON ALTO
CEREALS DENS BARBET
BEAR BUS CAIRO
IANA AARE WILLIAMS
BALK BUFFALOBILL ERAT
ALLY SMART OASIS DDAY
GAS PRO HAHA STE

## PUZZLE 277

APSE PHASE SOFT
LAOS ROLES OMAR
ONUS ONTAP MENU
HIT EPEE ORANGE
ACHATES DUAL
FOR FISSIONS
KORAN DINAH DIP
EVER PANEL ZOLA
PEN SOLAR BORER
TROPICAL BIN
SAKI HATEFUL
AFLAME SERE UKE
MAIL TAPIR AGAS
ATOM ELIDE MIST
TENS DEVIL STES

## PUZZLE 270

ABBA SAVES SCAM
NEAL AWARE ILLY
NATL MANNA MOAT
THEHORSESMOUTH
ROAD ANDES
SAGE ADALE
NOLI SENATE POE
THECATSWHISKERS
HOC BASALT ISNT
WAGER ONTO
ETHIC TREE
CHICKENHEARTED
LINK TIERS IMAS
ANTE CLASP CITE
TEST HERES STEW

## PUZZLE 274

TRAP STEP AJAR
AIDE TAHOE ROLE
LAMP ATONE RHEA
ELI SKIM PLANED
ROWENA ASP
GALAS SHAM HIM
ALLAN JUNE ICE
GAFF FLEET FLOE
ERA FIEF TAINT
DER LEAF CARPS
RUE ELATES
PHASES RANA OAF
LOGE PASTE FUSE
AMUR ALOHA ASHE
NETS TINE DAYS

## PUZZLE 278

MEIN TRIBES RIM
OTTO HODIAK OHO
CHARCOALBRIQUET
HEL ARNEL UTAH
ALOFT REPLIERS
OARS SUEZ
OMOO AAA DOZERS
CAPTAINMIDNIGHT
TIEPIN ALL COOK
EROS LEIA
TRIDENTS SLUMP
RAMA ATSEA NEO
INBLACKANDWHITE
PIE DIETED ETAS
END DORSEY RELY

## PUZZLE 279

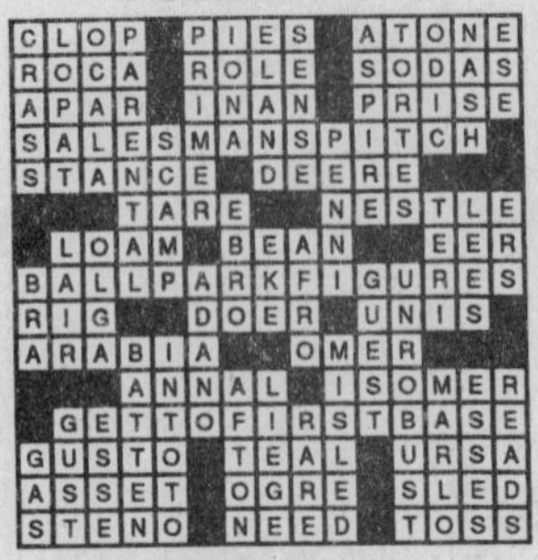

## PUZZLE 280

Belt, Boot, Cape, Clog, Hood, Hose, Kilt, Mule, Sari, Sash, Shoe, Slip, Suit, Vest.

## PUZZLE 281

## PUZZLE 282

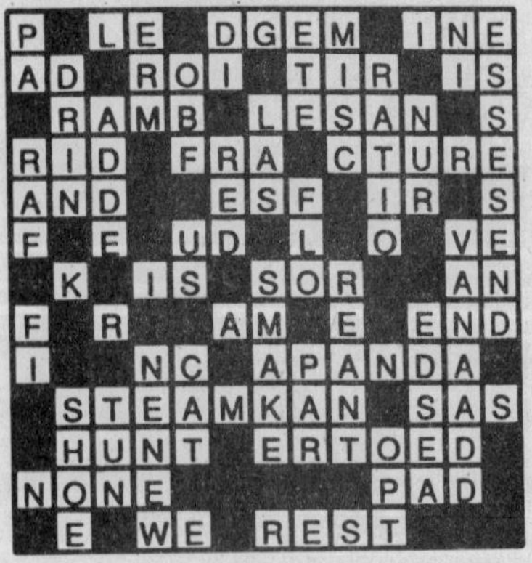

## PUZZLE 283

## PUZZLE 284

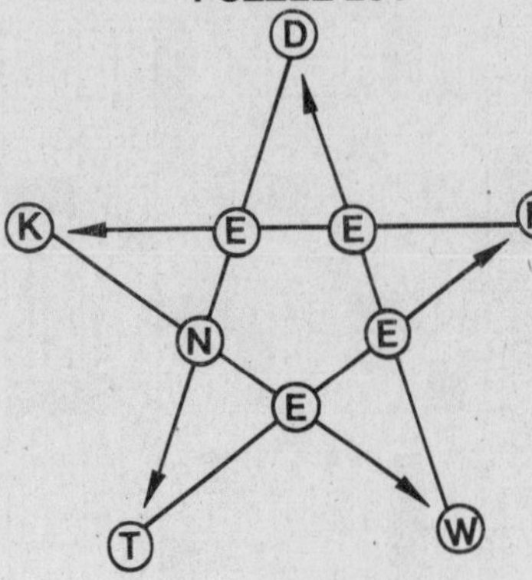


## PUZZLE 285

## PUZZLE 286

## PUZZLE 287

## PUZZLE 288

A hitter named Slugger McFate
Was rapidly putting on weight.
Said the coach, an old duffer,
"You're great, but you suffer
From too many trips to the plate."

## PUZZLE 289

1-L, 2-R, 3-P, 4-I, 5-G, 6-V, 7-U, 8-A, 9-W, 10-B, 11-F, 12-O, 13-J, 14-C, 15-Q, 16-Y, 17-H, 18-M, 19-E, 20-S, 21-T, 22-K, 23-Z, 24-D, 25-X, 26-N.

## PUZZLE 290

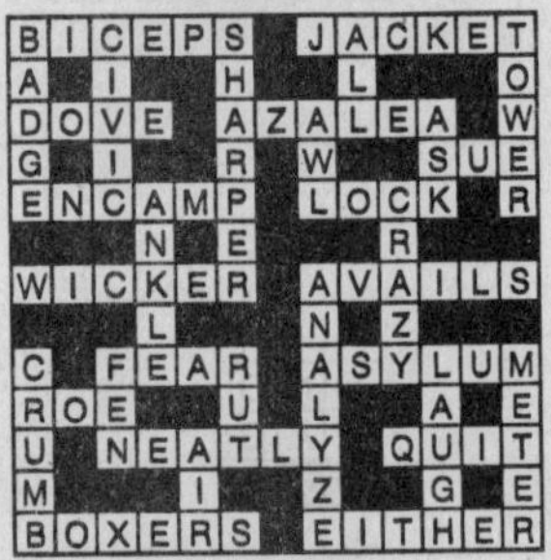

1-K, 2-I, 3-M, 4-X, 5-H, 6-R, 7-D, 8-Y, 9-T, 10-W, 11-F, 12-A, 13-E, 14-P, 15-J, 16-V, 17-Z, 18-S, 19-B, 20-N, 21-C, 22-L, 23-G, 24-Q, 25-O, 26-U.

## PUZZLE 291

## PUZZLE 292

1. The pen is mightier than the sword.
2. One swallow does not make a summer.

## PUZZLE 293

COPE OPTED MCII
ORES PAREE OATS
MIRE APOSTROPHE
MOI CLAM AANI
ALONE SPRIG TIN
EDILE EAN BANE
BLEEDS BALES
RIBBONS PRESSES
ANILS SISTER
FROE DEN STARE
TET FONDA LHASA
YOUR ENTE ITS
AMPERSANDS SNAP
LIES ANTRA PETE
POSE LASER ADEN

## PUZZLE 294

CHOSE CAMEL CROSS
RIVEN INURE RIATA
OVENS DETRIMENTAL
PEND LES ITCHY
SHARES OLEO
DIM OLES CPL NICE
UTE ULT MOES MOD
DESIRE SEAR LOANS
SCINTILLATING
SPIES ADES RETIRE
ORE AXLE SAD NUN
TERN BEE DICE EGG
OPUS BISTRO
APORT TOR MASS
PREDESTINED SELAH
SEALS EDUCE AGATE
TARES NESTS CARED

## PUZZLE 295

PATH STEEL ISON
ALIA TABLE CURE
LONGARMOFTHELAW
SEAGREEN TUMULT
LIED SEME
SOVIET VERANDAS
OPENS WOVEN ONA
BING CITED COIL
END ROVER GORSE
RESTORED LENSES
OURS BENT
SOIREE DECREASE
PLAINCLOTHESMAN
TIME TASTE TYRO
SOBS STEER SLAW

## PUZZLE 296

STERE SONS BET
HONOR TREE ATEE
ANDDAVIDWASTHEN
MESS ALES ITEMS
ONER TERSE
DING SPED
FUROR BLUE LED
APOMEGRANATEARE
DEN AIDS IVORY
IDLE LESS
PATRI BRAE
ASHES SLED PICA
WHENHEHADOPENED
NERI SORA OARED
REC STEN TRESS

## PUZZLE 297

HORNS ARAL GAS
ALOOP BOCA WENT
LEASE ENID ANNE
LONELYLADY SEER
LEE JANSEN
BERLES PIANO
ILIAD FUNNYLADY
LIND PENCE AMIE
LADYDIANA EDINA
LINTY GAYNOR
UNCORK DOG
MERV LADYBEGOOD
BRIE ABRA RHONE
EVES DIEN LENIN
RES YEWS YEATS

## PUZZLE 298

PASHA EYRA SPA
OTHER BOOTS HRE
SHOWSYOUTHEDOOR
SOW EVER LEEWAY
ESSENE STERNE
OVIS HOT EDIT
PANIC HOWE ORO
OREL PAWNS UNIT
LAS RIOS CREDO
ABCS ELF MESS
OPUSES ELAPSE
ARLENE HIRE LED
SHOWINGONESHAND
HER SCOWS TACNA
YES EAST AREAS

## PUZZLE 299

TESS VOW JAB SAWS
UNIT AMI ORE UTAH
NINA TEN UTE POLO
ADEPT NEAR TOPPLE
LOW SIN SUE
WAVERED MAP TRUTH
ICE DIP LEO FOE
TEXAS GAB PLATOON
NAP ROB DIE
SCUTTLE BED LARGE
OUR YAM TOP YES
BENNY TUB GOBLETS
EAU NAG PEA
STREWS DYED EDGED
ARID IDA RIP DIVA
PIPE NUN MAR EVER
SPED GEE SLY RENT

## PUZZLE 300

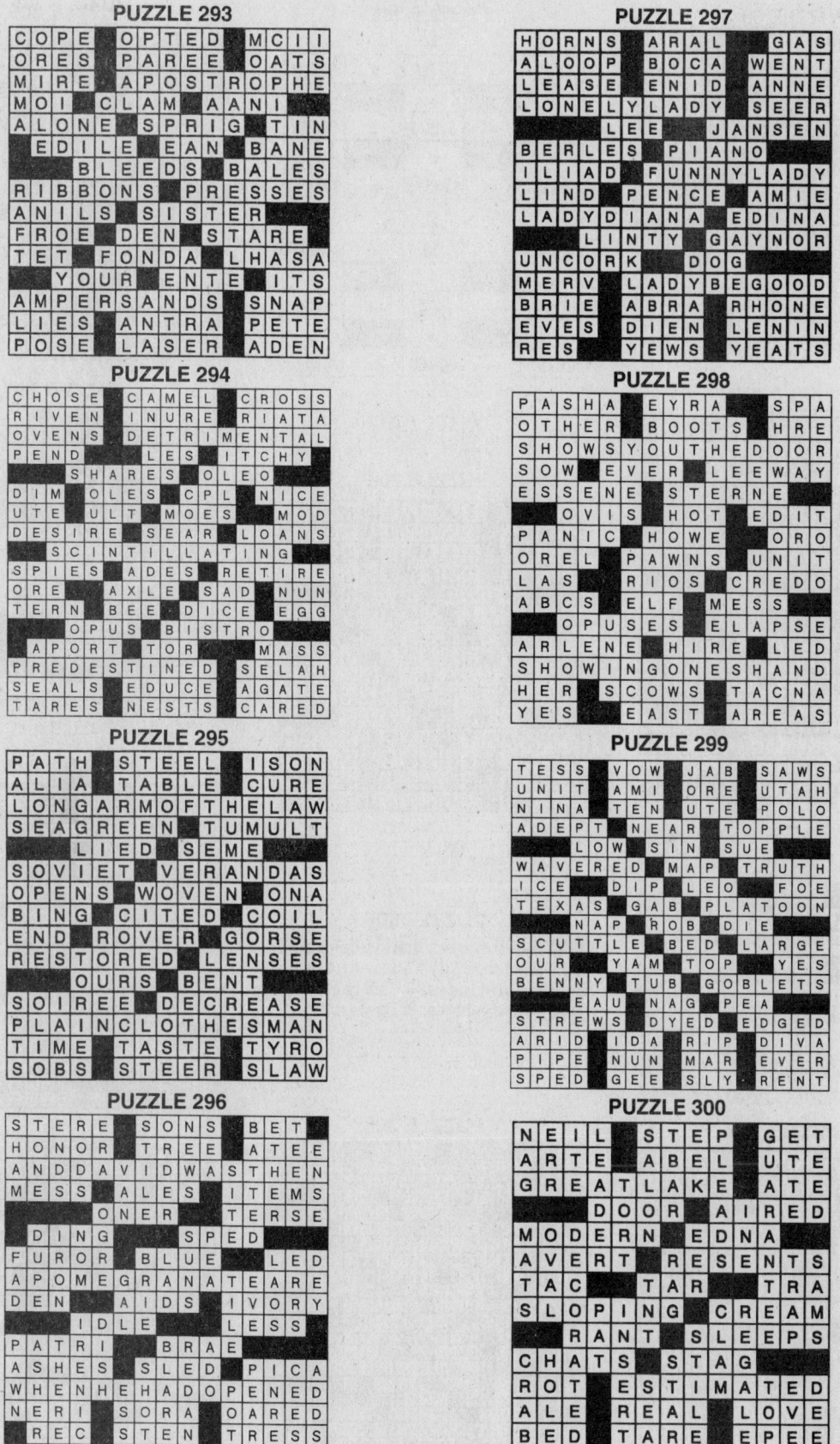

NEIL STEP GET
ARTE ABEL UTE
GREATLAKE ATE
DOOR AIRED
MODERN EDNA
AVERT RESENTS
TAC TAR TRA
SLOPING CREAM
RANT SLEEPS
CHATS STAG
ROT ESTIMATED
ALE REAL LOVE
BED TARE EPEE

## PUZZLE 301

DOSED TROLL FOE SAB
ANWAR AERIE INCLUDE
DEERE SWEETENTHEPOT
TENDSTO SURE ONERS
BITS HERR SOAP TREY
EMP SARDIS SNOW
DEODAR SOWS DEADSEA
TILES TENT SCOWLS
PEARTREE EARS SLEEK
AMT SWEETPEAS EVE
LOOSE SLOT SATIATED
ETERNE SNAG RENEW
RESIDUE SLED ENTIRE
ORRS KNEELS LAG
WISH ORAN TALE ALTO
ATTAR ANES RAREBIT
SHORTANDSWEET DIALS
PORTEND TASSE ADMEN
STY SIS STETS MESSY

## PUZZLE 302

ENDS REACT WHEN
LEAP ERROR HERE
SEMI TEMPO OMIT
EDEN ICY PULSES
SORT RISE
STATUE FACE ACT
TOWER SALAD MOO
ODOR CHILL SEAM
OAK SHINY SENSE
DYE LEFT FEASTS
DUCT DREW
REMARK WAY AFRO
AVID ELITE TIES
SEND REFER EVIL
PREY SEEDS RENO

## PUZZLE 303

1. Unfounded, 2. Manganese, 3. Heartbreak, 4. Industrious, 5. Maintain, 6. Condition, 7. Velvety, 8. Distinguish, 9. Dependence, 10. Hardware.

## PUZZLE 304

MASK DAMA CATS
ONCE EWER ARECA
STAG CART RATON
SIR HARVESTMOON
ELAND POINTS
ACCOST NEONS
WURST SOLO TSP
ABO AUTOMNE OOO
YEW SASS LAMPS
INURE SMITHY
LOANER OTARU
ONTHEPUNKIN ROW
BATED ROIL OKRA
SNARE ALEE BEAK
DRED LASS SYNE

## PUZZLE 305

**1.**

| | | | | |
|---|---|---|---|---|
| 5603 | + | 63115 | = | 68718 |
| + | | + | | + |
| 2860 | + | 57200 | = | 60060 |
| = | | = | | = |
| 8463 | + | 120315 | = | 128778 |

**2.**

| | | | | |
|---|---|---|---|---|
| 33040 | ÷ | 40 | = | 826 |
| — | | × | | + |
| 6279 | — | 504 | = | 5775 |
| = | | = | | = |
| 26761 | — | 20160 | = | 6601 |

## PUZZLE 306

COMB SALAD WHAT
AREA CHILI IOWA
MASS HEALS TOOL
ELSE OAR BUCKLE
MOOD HUSH
APPEAL CARE ALE
CRANK BLISS GIN
RUNT SLATE LENT
END MIAMI GONER
SEA ADDS PANTRY
FREE DALE
UNMASK MRS SASH
REAL IDIOT OHIO
ARTS COLOR MORE
LOSE KELLY EYES

## PUZZLE 307

1. Will-o'-the-wisp, 2. Aide-de-camp, 3. Out-of-doors, 4. Touch-and-go, 5. Jack-of-all-trades, 6. Off-the-cuff, 7. Down-at-the-heels, 8. Do-or-die.

## PUZZLE 308

DAW SWAB SAKI MASTS
RUR SPIRO PINTA EVOKE
ARI HARRYJAMESMADISON
MASTERY SAREE PLEA
ASTA PER GELATIN
REM SPA AIRY ERAS
JOHNMILTONBERLE EMU
APE IDIOM ETTA CRONES
VIM LIBRA LYE LOWERS
ANAT BECALM SEEN
ENE HERES OILOF EGG
AVER TANNER DRAB
DECREE HEN OATHS ATE
AMUSED LORE URIAH POE
MOP JOHNWAYNEROGERS
ATIP GOGO GET EWE
EDUCATE ADO ARIA
ROOT SNERD PEERING
SHARILEWISCARROLL ODE
TOKEN DATER EARLS TIN
YEARS RELY WETS SAT

## PUZZLE 309

JOT COAST FIEND ADO
AVE RUSTY RADIO SOL
BAR ETHER ENACT TEE
ROAM PODS METER
AVIATOR LACE REVOLT
DAFFODIL YOGA DINER
ALI REDYE SACK LOVE
PLED DERBY DEAF MEN
TIDES REBEL STRAYED
EON SEALS EAR
ALADDIN DRAMA YALTA
MUD ABAS SMART LARD
EAVE SILL ALLAN FAD
BUOYS LOAF LEMONADE
ASCENT EMIR SAMOYED
ASIAN PEAS RISE
JET FREER SUSAN TAB
ALE FORGE PEACE TRY
RID STOGY STOKE EKE

## PUZZLE 310

ARC BAA RAE
PARED END INERT
THESOUNDOFMUSIC
TEEN LANE
STE SHAPE ESS
SHAH EERIE DEMO
PORE SEXTETS TIDE
ADAM YON SET SLED
HURON POSTERS
SODA TARO
CABINET EDAMS
OPEC LAS ITS UTAH
TERM STRINGS SAGE
SLAM RERUN IRON
ENE AMATI ACE
ALAI TALL
MUSICTOONESEARS
INLET ARE HOMES
DAY TEE ODE

## PUZZLE 311

SLOOP SPAS AFT STAD
HINDI TAPE LAR HUGO
ACTINHASTE ORATORIO
CHANTEYS STOODUPFOR
KIP ARS TANK ELA
FIB NEWT PIERCES
TRAIL COE BIN OAST
WEIR JOSS GUN SUNNY
OAR BONY SIDEWINDER
CLUBS EOS TOADY
STAIRSTEPS PROM BUS
HADON ALI SLED EAST
AMEN INK HOE ARRAY
GETSHOT SPAT MUG
SAM FILM DIS PRE
LIGHTOPERA CASTIRON
OLEASTER COUNTEDOUT
REAR HER EURE REATA
AXLE SPY RIBS EASEL

## PUZZLE 312

ATTA LIMP TWIST AMOR
FRET ILIA TOOTER PILE
RIAS TEXTBOOKEXAMPLES
ACCEDED TURKS ALLOT
MOHAIR DITCH AWAKE
ETE MAKESTHEGRADE PRE
RESTIR ERASERHEAD
ASA IRV MIDAIR OOZE
DEPTH NIVEN MLI LONER
IRENES SITAR CRU
GOTOTHEHEADOFTHECLASS
CHA LATER VIABLE
BOUGH SPA ZONAL EMCEE
ATNO TINIER VIP EDD
CRIBSHEETS ASRARE
HOT PENCILSTRIPED FRA
MALDE ETHEL SEAGOD
INLAW STIED BENCHED
LEARNSONESLESSON TIME
KENT SPIGOT EDIT OVEN
ADAY TENOF AILS NERD

## PUZZLE 313

| | | | | | | | | | | | | |
|---|---|---|---|---|---|---|---|---|---|---|---|---|
| C | O | R | E | | C | O | D | E | | A | R | T |
| A | M | E | N | | A | W | E | D | | S | U | E |
| B | E | N | D | | L | E | N | G | T | H | E | N |
| S | N | O | O | Z | E | | T | E | A | | | |
| | | | W | O | N | T | | S | L | A | S | H |
| C | U | B | | O | D | E | S | | O | G | L | E |
| O | N | E | S | | A | X | E | | N | E | A | R |
| L | I | S | T | | R | A | C | E | | D | Y | E |
| A | T | T | I | C | | S | U | R | E | | | |
| | | | L | A | S | | R | E | A | S | O | N |
| P | A | R | T | I | C | L | E | | V | I | S | E |
| O | R | E | | R | A | I | L | | E | L | L | S |
| W | E | D | | O | B | E | Y | | S | L | O | T |

## PUZZLE 314

| | | | | | | | | | | | | |
|---|---|---|---|---|---|---|---|---|---|---|---|---|
| C | A | W | | | C | O | S | T | | B | E | T |
| R | I | O | T | | O | V | E | R | | L | A | Y |
| O | D | O | R | | G | E | N | E | | A | S | K |
| P | E | D | A | L | | N | O | M | I | N | E | E |
| | | | S | E | A | | R | O | C | K | | |
| A | R | C | H | E | R | Y | | R | E | E | F | S |
| C | A | R | | | C | A | B | | | T | E | A |
| E | N | A | C | T | | P | R | E | S | S | E | D |
| | | C | O | R | E | | A | N | T | | | |
| A | W | K | W | A | R | D | | D | E | B | T | S |
| L | O | P | | D | O | O | M | | M | A | R | E |
| P | R | O | | E | D | G | E | | S | L | U | M |
| S | E | T | | R | E | S | T | | | L | E | I |

## PUZZLE 315

| | | | | | | | | | | | | |
|---|---|---|---|---|---|---|---|---|---|---|---|---|
| W | O | V | E | | B | U | F | F | | I | R | A |
| A | D | O | S | | A | F | A | R | | D | A | B |
| R | O | T | S | | T | O | L | E | R | A | T | E |
| P | R | E | A | C | H | | L | E | E | | | |
| | | | Y | A | R | N | | D | A | I | S | Y |
| F | I | N | | M | O | O | D | | P | O | L | O |
| O | D | E | | E | B | B | E | D | | T | A | R |
| L | E | A | D | | E | L | L | A | | A | P | E |
| D | A | T | E | D | | E | A | R | L | | | |
| | | | E | R | A | | W | E | A | L | T | H |
| C | H | A | R | I | S | M | A | | P | A | R | E |
| O | A | R | | L | I | A | R | | E | V | I | L |
| B | Y | E | | L | A | N | E | | L | A | M | P |

## PUZZLE 316

| | | | | | | | | | | | | |
|---|---|---|---|---|---|---|---|---|---|---|---|---|
| T | H | I | S | | E | R | R | S | | H | O | E |
| R | E | D | O | | L | O | O | K | | O | W | N |
| A | R | E | A | | A | D | M | I | T | T | E | D |
| P | E | A | R | L | S | | P | R | O | P | | |
| | | | E | A | T | S | | T | U | L | I | P |
| | T | I | D | B | I | T | | | R | A | R | E |
| R | I | M | | S | C | E | N | T | | T | I | P |
| A | L | P | S | | | R | O | U | T | E | S | |
| G | L | U | E | S | | N | I | C | E | | | |
| | | L | E | T | S | | S | K | A | T | E | R |
| M | I | S | S | O | U | R | I | | P | A | V | E |
| O | D | E | | V | E | I | L | | O | P | E | N |
| W | A | S | | E | D | D | Y | | T | E | N | T |

## PUZZLE 317

| | | | | | | | | | | | | |
|---|---|---|---|---|---|---|---|---|---|---|---|---|
| A | J | A | R | | C | O | S | T | | L | I | E |
| B | A | K | E | | O | A | T | H | | O | D | E |
| E | D | I | T | | O | R | I | E | N | T | A | L |
| D | E | N | I | M | | | R | I | O | | | |
| | | | R | O | L | E | | R | A | I | S | E |
| P | A | V | E | M | E | N | T | | H | O | W | L |
| I | C | E | | S | A | T | I | N | | W | A | S |
| S | E | N | D | | D | E | L | I | C | A | T | E |
| A | S | T | E | R | | R | E | N | O | | | |
| | | | E | A | R | | | E | A | G | L | E |
| S | U | R | P | R | I | S | E | | R | O | A | D |
| E | R | A | | E | D | E | N | | S | O | N | G |
| A | N | T | | R | E | E | D | | E | D | D | Y |

## PUZZLE 318

| | | | | | | | | | | | | |
|---|---|---|---|---|---|---|---|---|---|---|---|---|
| A | P | S | E | | S | A | D | | S | T | E | M |
| R | O | A | R | | T | I | E | | P | I | P | E |
| C | O | L | A | | A | R | M | | O | M | E | N |
| | R | E | S | I | N | | A | G | R | E | E | |
| | | | E | N | D | | N | E | T | | | |
| A | C | O | R | N | S | | D | E | S | E | R | T |
| S | A | W | | | | | | | | T | O | E |
| P | R | E | S | E | T | | P | A | R | A | D | E |
| | | | P | R | O | | A | G | E | | | |
| | S | C | R | A | M | | M | A | C | A | W | |
| B | A | L | I | | C | A | P | | O | V | A | L |
| I | R | A | N | | A | L | E | | R | E | D | O |
| B | I | N | G | | T | A | R | | D | R | E | W |

## PUZZLE 319

| | | | | | | | | | | | | |
|---|---|---|---|---|---|---|---|---|---|---|---|---|
| A | L | E | | D | R | I | P | | P | A | R | E |
| N | O | R | | R | A | C | E | | A | R | E | A |
| N | U | R | S | E | R | Y | R | H | Y | M | E | S |
| | | | U | S | E | | | A | I | S | L | E |
| C | A | F | E | S | | S | H | I | N | | | |
| H | U | E | S | | S | T | U | R | G | E | O | N |
| I | R | E | | P | A | I | R | S | | M | A | E |
| C | A | S | T | A | N | E | T | | M | I | T | T |
| | | | A | G | E | S | | B | A | T | H | S |
| V | I | O | L | A | | | B | E | N | | | |
| A | D | V | E | N | T | U | R | E | S | O | M | E |
| S | E | E | N | | A | F | A | R | | N | A | Y |
| T | A | R | T | | N | O | D | S | | E | R | E |

## PUZZLE 320

| | | | | | | | | | | | | |
|---|---|---|---|---|---|---|---|---|---|---|---|---|
| I | T | E | M | | A | L | E | C | | O | D | D |
| R | A | R | E | | P | O | L | O | | L | E | E |
| E | N | E | R | G | E | T | I | C | | D | A | N |
| | | | G | A | S | | | K | N | E | L | T |
| H | O | M | E | Y | | I | M | P | O | R | T | S |
| A | D | O | S | | F | R | U | I | T | | | |
| S | E | W | | B | O | O | S | T | | D | Y | E |
| | | | A | L | O | N | E | | T | I | E | S |
| C | O | R | R | A | L | S | | V | E | N | T | S |
| A | L | I | E | N | | | A | I | M | | | |
| D | I | P | | K | I | D | N | A | P | P | E | D |
| E | V | E | | E | D | I | T | | T | E | A | R |
| T | E | N | | T | A | G | S | | S | P | R | Y |

## PUZZLE 321

| | | | | | | | | | | | | |
|---|---|---|---|---|---|---|---|---|---|---|---|---|
| H | A | D | | A | C | H | E | | B | I | T | E |
| O | L | E | | S | H | O | E | | E | D | E | N |
| P | I | N | W | H | E | E | L | | L | E | N | D |
| | | | H | E | W | | | P | O | N | D | S |
| C | A | R | E | S | S | | H | U | N | T | | |
| O | B | E | Y | | | S | I | N | G | I | N | G |
| L | E | G | | H | A | P | P | Y | | C | O | O |
| A | L | R | E | A | D | Y | | | S | A | M | E |
| | | E | A | R | S | | S | T | O | L | E | S |
| B | E | T | T | E | | | I | R | A | | | |
| L | A | T | E | | F | I | R | E | P | L | U | G |
| O | V | E | R | | A | R | E | A | | E | R | E |
| W | E | D | S | | R | E | N | T | | O | N | E |

## PUZZLE 322

| | | | | | | | | | | | | |
|---|---|---|---|---|---|---|---|---|---|---|---|---|
| J | A | R | | P | A | L | E | | P | A | I | D |
| A | L | E | | O | R | A | L | | A | L | D | A |
| M | A | V | E | R | I | C | K | | S | L | O | T |
| | | | D | E | S | K | | S | T | Y | L | E |
| A | D | V | I | S | E | | T | W | O | | | |
| C | O | A | T | | | B | O | A | R | D | E | D |
| E | L | S | | A | L | I | E | N | | R | A | Y |
| S | L | E | D | D | E | D | | | F | I | V | E |
| | | | R | A | G | | H | E | L | P | E | D |
| S | T | E | A | M | | C | O | V | E | | | |
| P | A | R | K | | N | O | S | E | D | I | V | E |
| A | C | R | E | | A | M | E | N | | D | A | N |
| T | O | S | S | | B | E | S | T | | A | N | D |

## PUZZLE 323

| | | | | | | | | | | | | |
|---|---|---|---|---|---|---|---|---|---|---|---|---|
| A | R | M | | D | O | T | S | | A | P | E | S |
| D | U | O | | I | R | O | N | | N | A | M | E |
| A | D | O | R | A | B | L | E | | G | L | U | E |
| M | E | D | A | L | | D | E | L | L | | | |
| | | | W | E | T | | R | E | E | L | E | D |
| A | D | O | | D | A | D | | G | R | O | V | E |
| R | O | D | E | | M | I | D | | S | P | I | N |
| E | L | O | P | E | | G | U | M | | S | L | Y |
| S | T | R | I | K | E | | B | O | A | | | |
| | | | S | E | L | F | | L | I | K | E | D |
| A | L | S | O | | V | I | T | A | L | I | T | Y |
| L | E | A | D | | E | V | E | R | | T | O | E |
| P | A | G | E | | S | E | A | S | | E | N | D |

## PUZZLE 324

| | | | | | | | | | | | | |
|---|---|---|---|---|---|---|---|---|---|---|---|---|
| N | E | W | S | | A | D | A | M | | A | W | L |
| O | R | A | L | | D | I | N | E | | L | I | E |
| D | A | R | E | | M | A | N | A | G | E | R | S |
| | | | N | A | I | L | | D | O | S | E | S |
| C | R | E | D | I | T | | R | O | B | | | |
| H | O | P | E | D | | B | O | W | | L | A | P |
| E | V | E | R | | C | O | W | | A | U | R | A |
| F | E | E | | L | A | X | | S | T | A | I | N |
| | | | R | A | P | | D | E | L | U | D | E |
| A | C | T | O | R | | A | R | E | A | | | |
| M | O | R | T | G | A | G | E | | N | A | M | E |
| I | R | E | | E | W | E | S | | T | I | E | S |
| D | E | E | | R | E | D | S | | A | R | T | S |

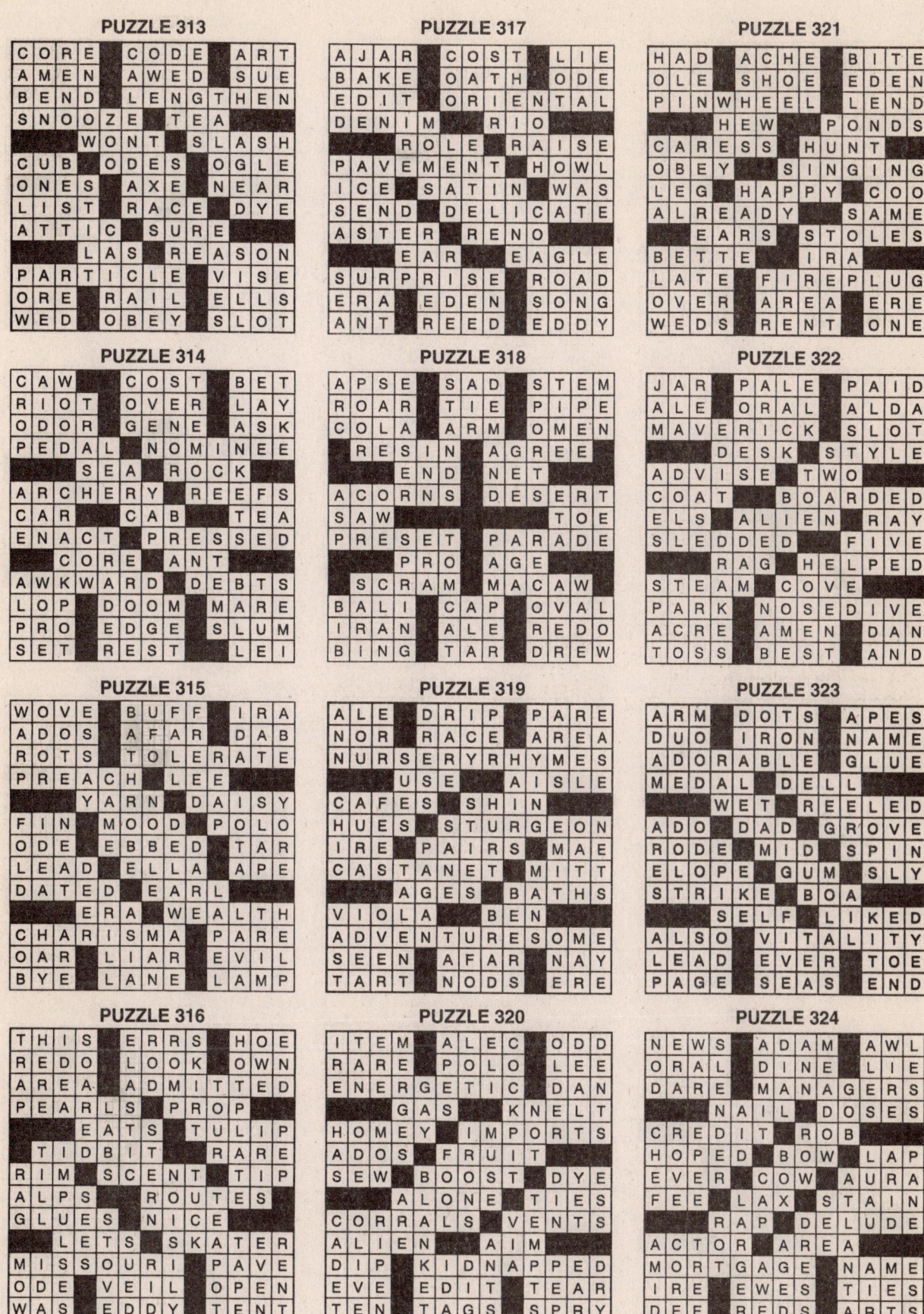

## PUZZLE 325

MAN REAP NOUN
ODE EDGE ANNE
BEWILDER VETO
SAYS BISON
SCALY OLE
LOBE FORESTED
EMU DOLED WAY
WETLANDS WOVE
END EASED
CHOSE TAXI
RODS HERALDED
OBOE ALEC RYE
WORN SLAT YEW

## PUZZLE 326

SPAN PAT HEAR
TONE RUE OGLE
ELSE ANECDOTE
MEW DITTO SOD
EMUS HAD
PARADE EXILES
OVEN SIRE
TEDIUM TICKET
ATE HOSE
ABE ARSON WET
FLASHIER WIRE
AURA TEN ASIA
RELY SKY DEER

## PUZZLE 327

ASP DAY PAIR
ROOT EYE AHOY
TYPE BEN PETE
SET MAMA
ALTO SEA
SLY NANNY AMP
OER WAD LEA
WEE VERSE PLY
ADE GUST
YARN GOT
SORE SIR ANTE
PULL ERA HIRE
TROY WAY LYE

## PUZZLE 328

BASS BAA BRED
EXIT OWN LAVE
TENPENNY AREA
AWE WIZARD
ENSUE SHOE
RAIL SLEW ALA
NIL TIARA TOM
ELK ANTE PONE
URGE JAMES
ATONES MAR
LONI OVERSEER
ABET NEE OLLA
SERE GET NILE

## PUZZLE 329

CATS STREP SLAM
ONIT ORIEL TONE
NOLA POILU RAID
GALLEONS NEEDLE
LARA ODEA
CRIERS EVERMORE
LANDS PEAR SLOT
IDO MARLS IBO
MANE URIS SPOON
BRUNETTE BEASTS
ELIS LATS
AIRMAN HIGHSEAS
ALAI EVOKE IDLE
RENE EASEL VEIN
ESTS REEDS ENID

## PUZZLE 330

MARL CRAPE SCAB
ELIA AESIR HOPE
TINSOLDIER EPEE
EAGER ATO LPS
RIAL ARETE
PRISONED SOIREE
EAR NOTES MEHTA
EDO NUTTY EUR
RINSE PERES ADE
SOFTEN RETARDED
IONIC PILE
ASK ELL VIALS
RITE LEADPENCIL
ODER LANAI EMMA
TEDS ORANG DEEP

## PUZZLE 331

CLOG POMES BAAS
HOLE ADELE ALDO
ANDMOSESSPAKEIN
TEE ASTHE VESTS
PRES DER
GRASS ORR PAD
ARAT ARES AGE
BATHSHEBAWENTIN
LIE TIRE EELS
ENS ODE PHONE
ARE ARON
APACE SATON TRA
DAVIDANDABISHAI
DRED BEALE PAIL
SASS CERES AWNS

## PUZZLE 332

OSSA BARN ASCAP
SHAM ALIA SPACE
CATACLYSM ARTEL
AVE LACKED EAST
RESTATE SEGAL
ARA MATADORS
NACRE DUKES GEE
IVAN PETER JUST
POT AIRES TEETH
SWADDLED LOS
MODEL FETTERS
MOON DIVINE RIA
AMUSE CATAMARAN
MANIA TRIP BOND
ENTER SYNE ARTY

## PUZZLE 333

STEP TACT
GOALIE SALOON
SOAPBOX PHANTOM
WAN AUCTION TOO
ADDS SUITE PESO
MESAS SEE FIRED
DOWAGER FLOSSY
BIAS REIN
SPRUNG BADNEWS
ELECT ELI TERMS
RACK TREND RIOT
FIE SHOWBIZ TKO
STIFLED ONESTEP
SPOUSE WARPED
TREE ROAN

## PUZZLE 334

AFT SHIP SLAB
COO TACO HALE
EXPLORER AMEN
AND TAMPED
PASTE MARE
RIPE DEBT PEA
ODOR ALL HEAP
MET CUTE ELSE
FOGS ALTER
HEALTH ELL
ACHE TAKEOVER
TREE EWER IRE
SUMS REST MAD

## PUZZLE 335

COMMA GBS PANS
AVAIL MLLE OMIT
FASTIDIOUS MAXI
ELK OLAF EATON
FAULTFINDING
GNOME NEE
CAIRO PAID EEL
PICKYPICKYPICKY
ONE ANTE EMCEE
AES LARES
HARDTOPLEASE
ELUDE AURI TRA
LINE METICULOUS
OVER CAEN FARES
TESS INS OBESE

## PUZZLE 336

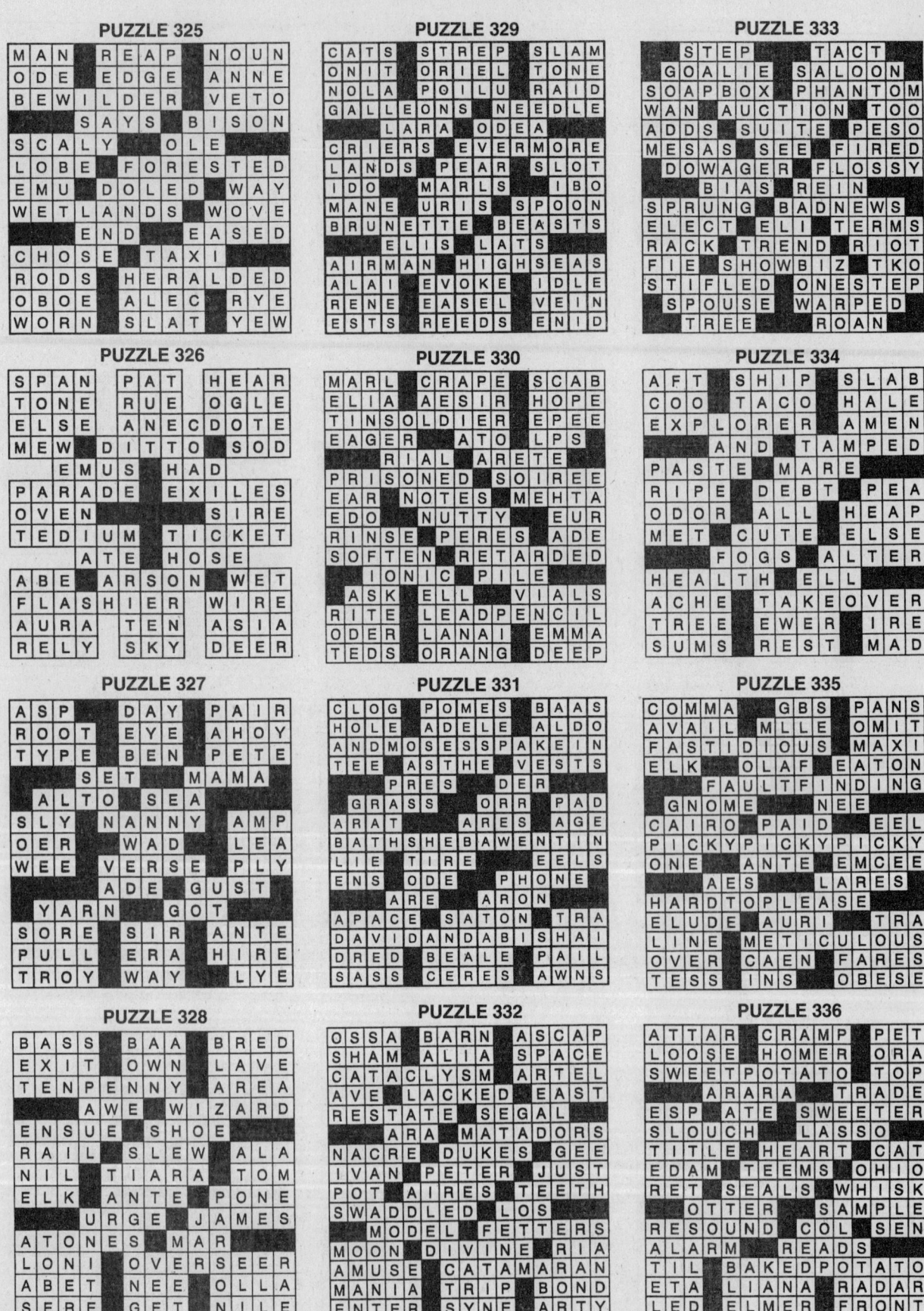

ATTAR CRAMP PET
LOOSE HOMER ORA
SWEETPOTATO TOP
ARARA TRADE
ESP ATE SWEETER
SLOUCH LASSO
TITLE HEART CAT
EDAM TEEMS OHIO
RET SEALS WHISK
OTTER SAMPLE
RESOUND COL SEN
ALARM READS
TIL BAKEDPOTATO
ETA LIANA RADAR
LED ELMER FRONT

## PUZZLE 337

| | | | | | | | | | | | | |
|---|---|---|---|---|---|---|---|---|---|---|---|---|
| P | A | R | K | ■ | M | A | S | T | ■ | B | A | Y |
| R | U | I | N | ■ | O | D | O | R | ■ | O | R | E |
| O | N | C | E | ■ | M | O | L | A | S | S | E | S |
| S | T | E | E | P | ■ | R | O | P | E | S | ■ | ■ |
| ■ | ■ | ■ | L | U | R | E | S | ■ | L | I | P | S |
| W | A | R | ■ | D | A | D | ■ | P | L | E | A | T |
| E | N | E | R | G | Y | ■ | R | U | S | S | I | A |
| D | E | C | O | Y | ■ | B | A | N | ■ | T | R | Y |
| S | W | A | M | ■ | D | I | T | T | O | ■ | ■ | ■ |
| ■ | ■ | L | E | A | R | N | ■ | S | T | U | M | P |
| C | O | L | O | R | A | D | O | ■ | T | R | U | E |
| A | L | E | ■ | A | M | E | N | ■ | E | G | G | S |
| R | E | D | ■ | B | A | R | E | ■ | R | E | S | T |

## PUZZLE 341

| | | | | | | | | | | | | |
|---|---|---|---|---|---|---|---|---|---|---|---|---|
| P | A | T | ■ | A | R | F | ■ | ■ | S | E | N | D |
| I | C | E | ■ | W | O | R | M | ■ | P | R | A | Y |
| P | E | E | K | A | B | O | O | ■ | L | A | M | E |
| ■ | ■ | ■ | E | R | E | ■ | T | E | A | S | E | D |
| A | D | D | E | D | ■ | C | O | T | S | ■ | ■ | ■ |
| L | E | A | N | ■ | ■ | O | R | C | H | A | R | D |
| E | A | T | ■ | S | L | U | S | H | ■ | L | E | E |
| C | R | A | C | K | E | R | ■ | ■ | A | L | A | N |
| ■ | ■ | ■ | H | I | N | T | ■ | E | G | Y | P | T |
| S | T | R | I | P | S | ■ | A | X | E | ■ | ■ | ■ |
| O | R | E | S | ■ | E | N | L | I | S | T | E | D |
| R | I | D | E | ■ | S | I | T | S | ■ | I | R | A |
| T | O | O | L | ■ | ■ | P | O | T | ■ | P | R | Y |

## PUZZLE 338

| | | | | | | | | | | | | |
|---|---|---|---|---|---|---|---|---|---|---|---|---|
| B | A | T | | G | O | S | H | | S | L | A | B |
| A | V | A | | R | I | T | A | | T | O | G | A |
| D | E | R | A | I | L | E | D | | O | P | E | N |
| | | | K | N | E | W | ■ | T | R | E | S | S |
| T | E | A | R | ■ | D | E | L | A | Y | | | |
| A | L | L | O | W | ■ | D | A | B | ■ | O | P | T |
| C | A | T | N | A | P | ■ | P | L | A | G | U | E |
| O | N | O | ■ | T | U | B | ■ | E | A | R | N | S |
| | | | M | E | T | A | L | ■ | R | E | S | T |
| O | L | D | E | R | ■ | Z | E | R | O | | | |
| R | O | O | T | | C | A | D | E | N | C | E | S |
| A | B | L | E | | R | A | G | E | | A | W | E |
| L | E | E | R | | O | R | E | L | | P | E | T |

## PUZZLE 342

| | | | | | | | | | | | | |
|---|---|---|---|---|---|---|---|---|---|---|---|---|
| E | R | A | ■ | C | A | L | F | ■ | T | O | P | S |
| S | U | B | ■ | A | R | I | A | ■ | E | V | I | L |
| S | T | U | B | B | O | R | N | ■ | N | A | P | A |
| ■ | ■ | N | O | I | S | E | ■ | S | A | L | E | M |
| U | N | D | O | N | E | ■ | P | E | N | ■ | ■ | ■ |
| R | O | A | M | ■ | ■ | W | E | A | T | H | E | R |
| G | U | N | ■ | S | E | E | P | S | ■ | A | D | E |
| E | N | T | I | T | L | E | ■ | ■ | A | R | I | D |
| ■ | ■ | ■ | D | A | M | ■ | G | L | I | D | E | S |
| R | A | T | E | R | ■ | T | R | A | D | E | ■ | ■ |
| E | L | I | A | ■ | P | R | E | S | E | N | T | S |
| F | E | L | L | ■ | R | I | T | E | ■ | E | E | L |
| S | E | E | S | ■ | O | M | A | R | ■ | D | A | Y |

## PUZZLE 339

| | | | | | | | | | | | | |
|---|---|---|---|---|---|---|---|---|---|---|---|---|
| L | O | G | ■ | C | O | T | S | ■ | S | P | E | D |
| A | W | E | ■ | O | L | E | O | ■ | H | E | R | O |
| D | E | M | A | N | D | E | D | ■ | R | E | I | N |
| ■ | ■ | ■ | I | D | E | S | ■ | P | I | N | E | S |
| C | L | A | M | O | R | ■ | S | O | L | ■ | ■ | ■ |
| R | A | Y | S | ■ | ■ | A | P | O | L | O | G | Y |
| A | C | E | ■ | P | E | D | A | L | ■ | B | O | A |
| M | E | S | S | A | G | E | ■ | ■ | S | O | A | K |
| ■ | ■ | ■ | T | W | O | ■ | C | R | U | E | T | S |
| A | T | L | A | S | ■ | C | A | I | N | ■ | ■ | ■ |
| C | O | A | T | ■ | A | R | R | O | G | A | N | T |
| R | O | M | E | ■ | M | E | E | T | ■ | D | O | E |
| E | K | E | D | ■ | P | E | T | S | ■ | O | W | N |

## PUZZLE 343

| | | | | | | | | | | | | |
|---|---|---|---|---|---|---|---|---|---|---|---|---|
| B | U | G | ■ | A | R | E | A | ■ | C | I | T | E |
| O | N | E | ■ | N | O | E | L | ■ | R | O | O | K |
| S | I | N | ■ | G | E | L | S | ■ | A | N | T | E |
| S | T | E | E | L | ■ | S | O | R | T | ■ | ■ | ■ |
| ■ | ■ | ■ | D | E | W | ■ | ■ | Y | E | A | S | T |
| S | A | N | D | ■ | R | I | C | E | ■ | L | I | E |
| O | B | E | Y | ■ | A | R | E | ■ | S | O | D | A |
| A | L | E | ■ | O | P | E | N | ■ | T | E | E | M |
| P | E | D | A | L | ■ | ■ | T | W | O | ■ | ■ | ■ |
| ■ | ■ | ■ | I | D | O | L | ■ | A | P | R | O | N |
| L | E | G | S | ■ | W | O | N | T | ■ | A | B | E |
| O | V | A | L | ■ | E | P | E | E | ■ | M | O | W |
| W | E | R | E | ■ | D | E | E | R | ■ | P | E | T |

## PUZZLE 340

| | | | | | | | | | | | | |
|---|---|---|---|---|---|---|---|---|---|---|---|---|
| R | A | W | ■ | A | R | E | A | ■ | F | A | S | T |
| U | S | E | ■ | L | E | I | S | ■ | R | I | L | E |
| T | H | E | A | T | E | R | S | ■ | I | D | E | A |
| ■ | ■ | ■ | G | A | L | E | ■ | S | E | E | D | S |
| C | O | V | E | R | ■ | ■ | F | U | N | ■ | ■ | ■ |
| O | D | E | S | ■ | ■ | H | A | D | D | O | C | K |
| D | O | E | ■ | G | A | I | T | S | ■ | B | E | E |
| E | R | R | A | N | D | S | ■ | ■ | S | O | L | E |
| ■ | ■ | ■ | S | A | D | ■ | ■ | S | P | E | L | L |
| F | R | O | S | T | ■ | T | R | E | E | ■ | ■ | ■ |
| L | O | N | E | ■ | B | O | U | L | D | E | R | S |
| O | V | E | R | ■ | R | O | L | L | ■ | A | Y | E |
| P | E | S | T | ■ | A | L | E | S | ■ | T | E | E |

## PUZZLE 344

| | | | | | | | | | | | | |
|---|---|---|---|---|---|---|---|---|---|---|---|---|
| S | H | E | E | R | ■ | A | H | E | A | D | ■ | ■ |
| H | E | L | L | O | ■ | M | O | V | I | E | S | ■ |
| A | R | O | M | A | ■ | E | M | E | R | A | L | D |
| C | O | P | ■ | R | U | L | E | R | ■ | L | E | O |
| K | N | E | W | ■ | S | I | R | ■ | M | E | E | T |
| ■ | ■ | ■ | A | R | E | A | ■ | N | E | R | V | E |
| G | R | A | D | E | D | ■ | T | O | S | S | E | D |
| L | I | V | E | D | ■ | W | E | T | S | ■ | ■ | ■ |
| O | D | E | S | ■ | S | O | N | ■ | Y | A | R | D |
| B | E | N | ■ | S | C | O | T | S | ■ | L | O | U |
| E | R | U | P | T | E | D | ■ | C | A | L | M | S |
| ■ | S | E | R | E | N | E | ■ | A | D | O | P | T |
| ■ | ■ | S | O | W | E | D | ■ | N | E | W | S | Y |

## PUZZLE 345

## PUZZLE 346

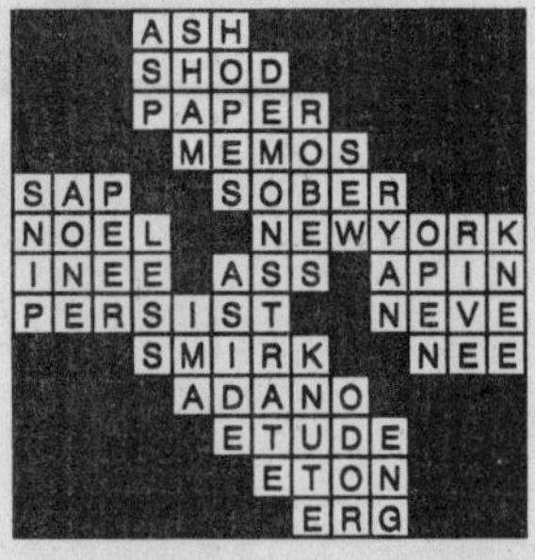

## PUZZLE 347

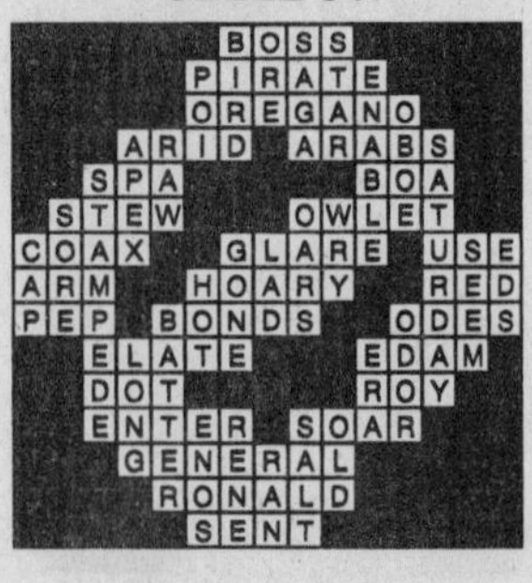

## PUZZLE 348

1. Impersonal, 2. Dispatcher, 3. Ladyfinger.

## PUZZLE 349

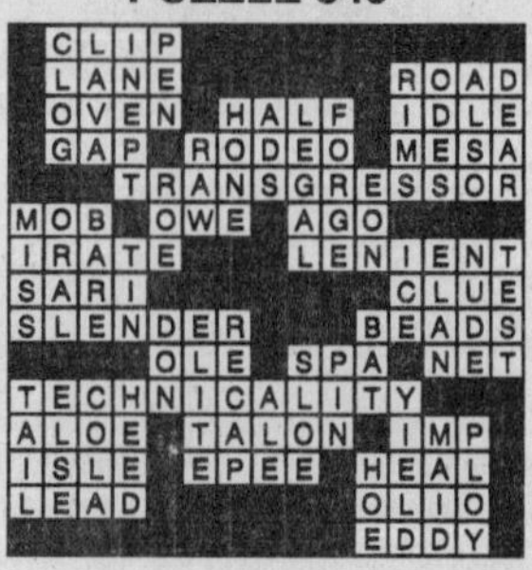

## PUZZLE 350

A door is what a dog is perpetually on the wrong side of.

1. History, 2. Opera, 3. Woods, 4. Petting, 5. Wails, 6. Harangue, 7. Flooded.

## PUZZLE 351

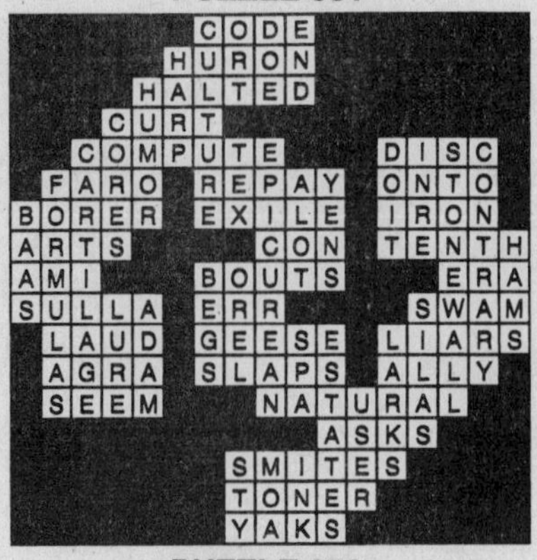

## PUZZLE 352

1. Wine, Line, Lint, List.
2. Bill, Ball, Bale, Bare, Fare.
3. Tour, Tout, Bout, Boot, Book.
4. Left, Lent, Bent, Bunt, Bunk, Bank.

## PUZZLE 353

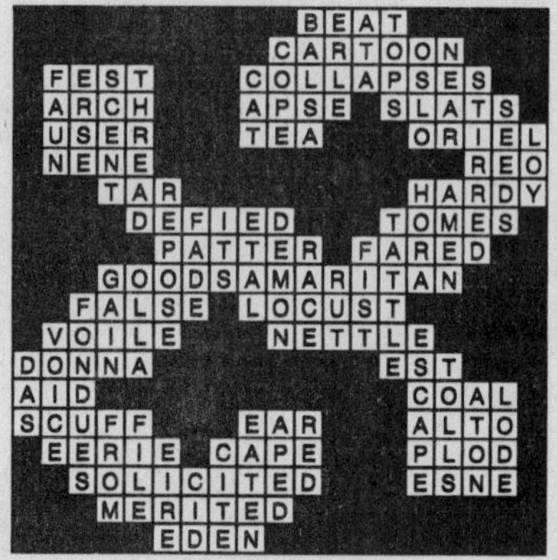

## PUZZLE 354

Let sleeping dogs lie.

## PUZZLE 355

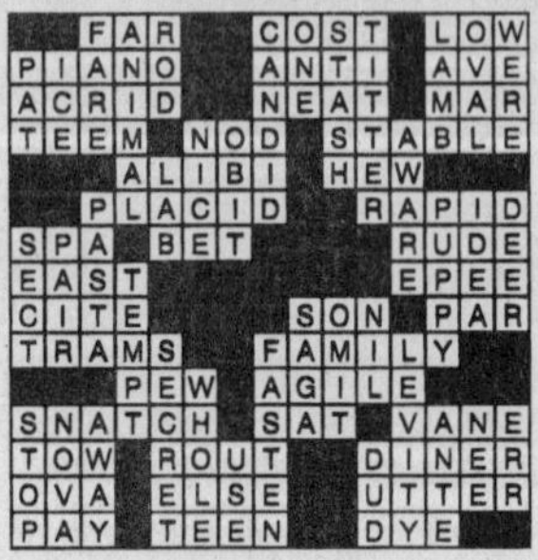

## PUZZLE 356

1. Paintbrush, 2. Punishable, 3. Interlocks.

## PUZZLE 357

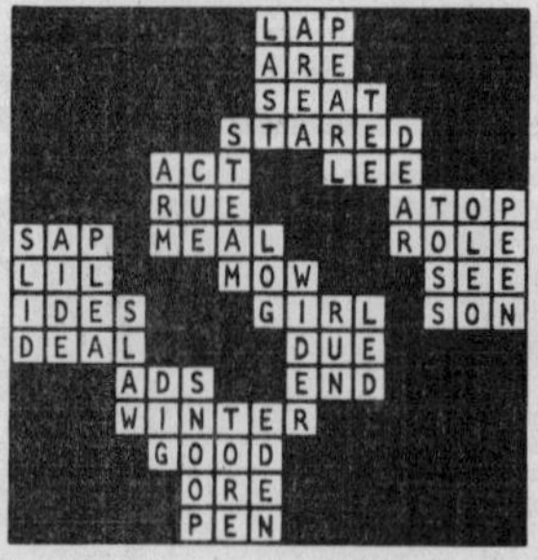

## PUZZLE 358

A fool always finds one still more foolish to admire him. (Boileau)

1. Millionaire, 2. Definitely, 3. Half-mast, 4. Doors, 5. Mao, 6. Hoof, 7. Slows.

## PUZZLE 359

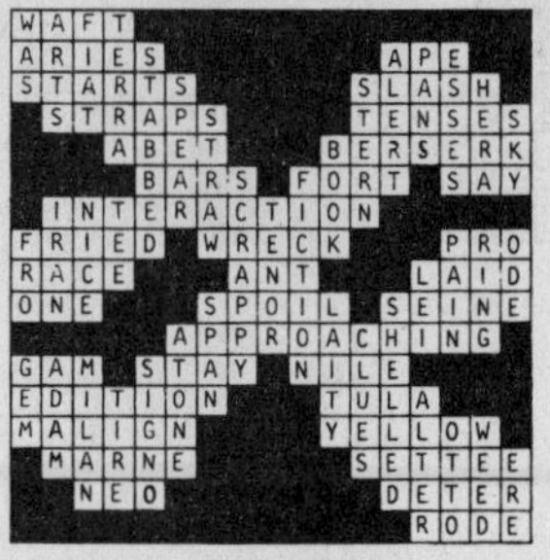

## PUZZLE 360

1. Work, Word, Lord, Load.
2. Cake, Wake, Wale, Walk.
3. Shed, Seed, Seer, Sear, Tear.
4. Read, Bead, Bend, Band, Bald, Balm, Palm.

## PUZZLE 361

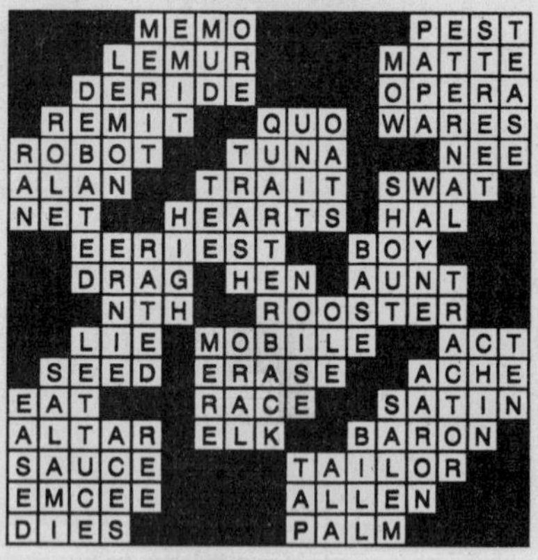

## PUZZLE 362

1. Farm, Harm, Hard, Hand.
2. Yard, Hard, Hare, Hale, Sale.
3. Pick, Pock, Pork, Cork, Corn.
4. Fire, Fine, Find, Fond, Food, Wood.

## PUZZLE 363

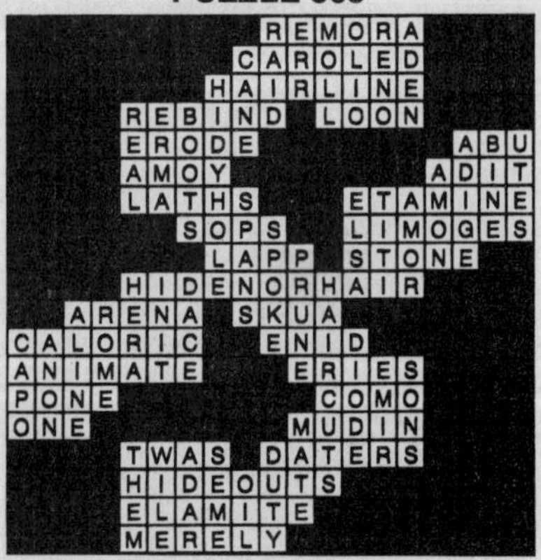

## PUZZLE 364

Literary character: Frankenstein

## PUZZLE 365

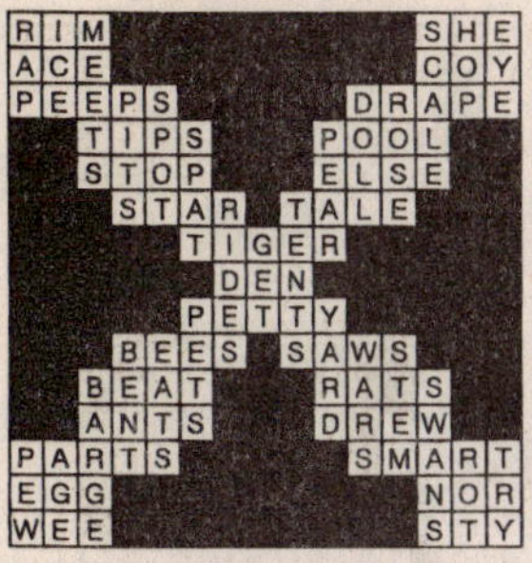

## PUZZLE 366

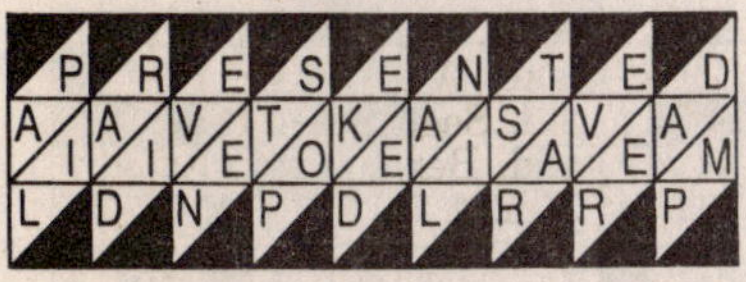

## PUZZLE 367

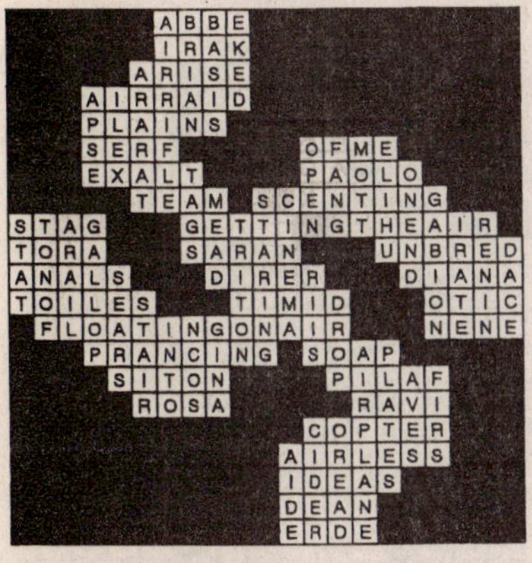

## PUZZLE 368

## PUZZLE 369

A. When weary or overloaded, llamas lie down and refuse to move, often spitting at their drivers.

B. The malamute is the oldest known breed of Alaskan dog.

## PUZZLE 370

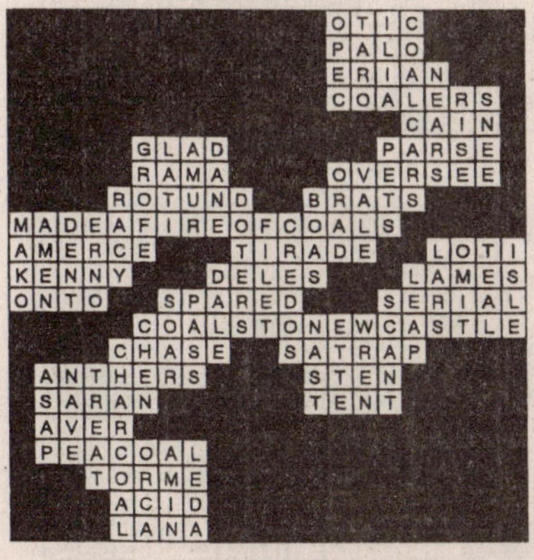

## PUZZLE 371

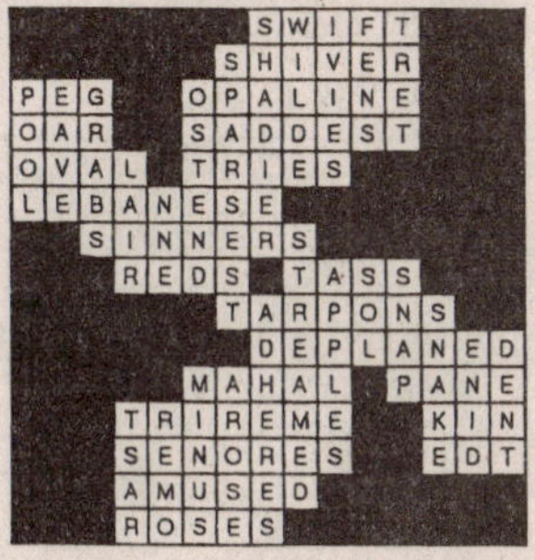

## PUZZLE 372

1. Cut flowers, 2. Broad smile, 3. Duplicator.

## PUZZLE 373

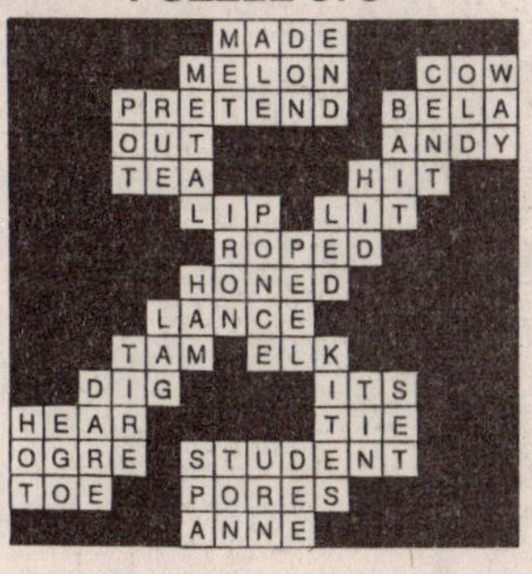

## PUZZLE 374

The nice thing about apathy is you don't have to exert yourself to show you're sincere about it.

1. Roustabout, 2. Hoity-toity, 3. Chihuahua, 4. Involuntary, 5. Between the eyes, 6. Expectation, 7. Forges, 8. Doors.

## PUZZLE 375

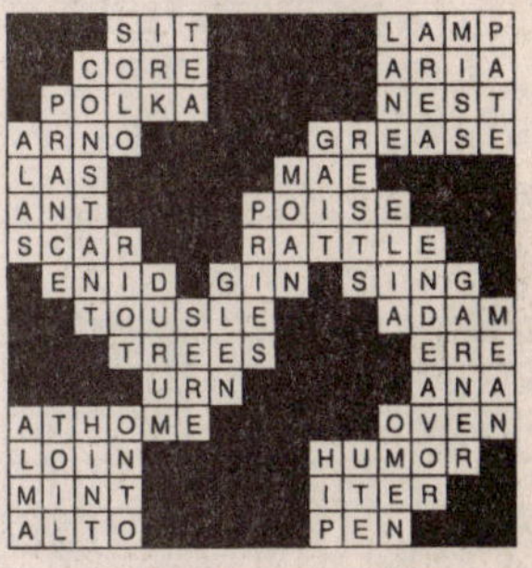

## PUZZLE 376

1. Purchasing, 2. Hand towels, 3. Quizmaster.

## PUZZLE 377

## PUZZLE 378

1c-Railroad, 2c-Starboard, 3g-Treadmill, 4i-Integrate, 5f-Spearhead, 6b-Surplice, 7h-Supervise, 8a-Protrude, 9e-Mendicant.

## PUZZLE 379

## PUZZLE 380

CAB BAKE WRAP
HUE EMIR EAVE
ERA GENE AREA
WARNING CLERK
AND SAT
GARB BASHFUL
EGO PIECE ORE
MEETING MEND
HEN COO
MOLAR GARBAGE
ELAN LAND BID
LINK ALOE EVE
TOES BEER TEN

## PUZZLE 384

GABOR AGED MARC
ALAMO MOPE ALOE
FAKES OBIS LOUD
FRUITJUICE TOGA
EAR REEFER
AFFIRM FATED
ALECS NEVERMORE
HERE DATED IGOR
SANDPIPER BLEAR
COLES BAKERS
OCTOPI OER
SERF GINGERBEER
CLEF EVIL AORTA
ALEE NENE GLINT
RODE TSAR EDNAS

## PUZZLE 388

ODDS COMAS TIFF
SERA ABATE EDER
APOD SENTA EERY
GOWESTYOUNGMAN
ERS TEE ASTAR
STYLE DAVID INA
ONO EIN ANDI
THECOVEREDWAGON
WELK ALI ORR
ORE FLIER EELER
SEPAL OSS EVE
THEOREGONTRAIL
DIAD ERATO EDNA
ACNE OILER SECT
SSTS SNARE TREE

## PUZZLE 381

AGE MORAN FLA
CORA AHOLE GRIT
ENID NADER LANE
SENATOR SANDS
ONA HAS
MAIN SALEMSLOT
MARTIN LEAS IVE
ALDA ODDER IVES
RTE SLUE TALENT
SANANTONE ROSS
MOE DRU
BELOW GENERAL
EVER ROMAN LARA
LINE AWARE MILT
ALS GLESS DOE

## PUZZLE 385

ALAS BOSS HAME
CALM CARTE IRAN
THEUGLYDUCKLING
ARE ROIS TULES
SAWN SIDES
DUCKINGSTOOL
OLEAN IONS MAP
RANT REELS SAME
ANT RESP AKRON
SITTINGDUCKS
AEGIS ERMA
ANTIC SLOE ANA
ONESDUCKSINAROW
WONT LAYON RITE
ENTO EDEN CLAD

## PUZZLE 389

CASH STEM BABAR
ASTA ARTE AWARE
BEAN MISO NEROS
SANDSOFIWOJIMA
ITAL ZOG
SAFER EMMA HART
TERROR AIRS DOR
ARA BIGJAKE AGE
RIM ECHO STATUE
TEED HIRT TWEED
ROE ITEA
THEGREENBERETS
POISE ALGA DRIP
MORSE TIER ELLA
SLEYS SASS DEER

## PUZZLE 382

PALM APPAL STAB
ALOE MARRY AARE
SOUSAPHONE OMEN
SUSAN BEST BAT
TUNAS ETO
CLARINETS CRUSE
RICE ITE SHERPA
ASCENT ESPIES
GLOVES SIT ANNE
SERER CASTANETS
DSO AUTOS
PSI SONS OFFER
AHOY PIANOFORTE
NONE ANGER REOS
TEST LEEDS DENT

## PUZZLE 386

VALET ASPENS PARTS
IMAGE SPROUTS ORIEL
PINON KEYSTONESTATE
END THEE SCANT TOE
ROOD ADDED KID RANT
FONT EVES LOBO
SLOE RASPS REAPER
TIMERS STOPS TRIBE
PAN DAYS IRANI ENOS
ORCS INTENTION DENT
STOW NORMA NORA TIS
ELLAS DUETS DESERT
DENIES TEILS TREE
NEAL ROUT CANE
CARS MEL NEARS ESAU
ADO MONET READ TOT
MOUNTAINSTATE APART
ERGON STAINED BETTE
LEEDS OREADS SPEAR

## PUZZLE 390

CAPP ACTA DEFT
AMIR BLUNT IRAE
WATERCOLOR SADA
STYLI TIDEWATER
AVE PESOS
SHOWAND OTHER
LES ORBS LEONE
ONTHEWATERFRONT
SCION MULE PUA
HEARD FIVESIX
TOTEM DIX
FIREWATER ETAPE
IRON INHOTWATER
FIBS LATCH NELL
ESTE SAKE TETE

## PUZZLE 383

LEM RAT DATE
ARIA ELSA DARES
DALMATIAN ECLAT
AMER RESTHOME
ORO LEES
TDS ILE ETCHES
OUTSELLS STUPE
PERT FIR NOLA
TUBAS REPADDED
STEREO SOP ESE
RIAL PIA
GARNERED ESPY
USUAL GREYHOUND
STIRS SATE SLAY
HAND WAD ETE

## PUZZLE 387

SCAR CAMP BABA DAIS
PATE OVAL ABEL ALSO
AGOG NAPE TENT MILL
REPAST SALT DEBATED
LEER TEES RUG
DEMEANED DREW DENSE
AVE STREW YEAR DEAD
MINT SUGAR PROP AGE
ELDER NAVAL MOISTEN
SOB SEVER MEN
RATTLER REGAL ROGER
ACE LEAP LATER WIDE
TRAM TILL LEVEL LIE
SERUM LOAF SELECTED
MIG TRIP RENO
TUMBLES GEAR ATONED
ORAL NOSE RAPS PILE
OGLE TAPS TREE ELSA
LETS SPAT SEWS REEL

## PUZZLE 391

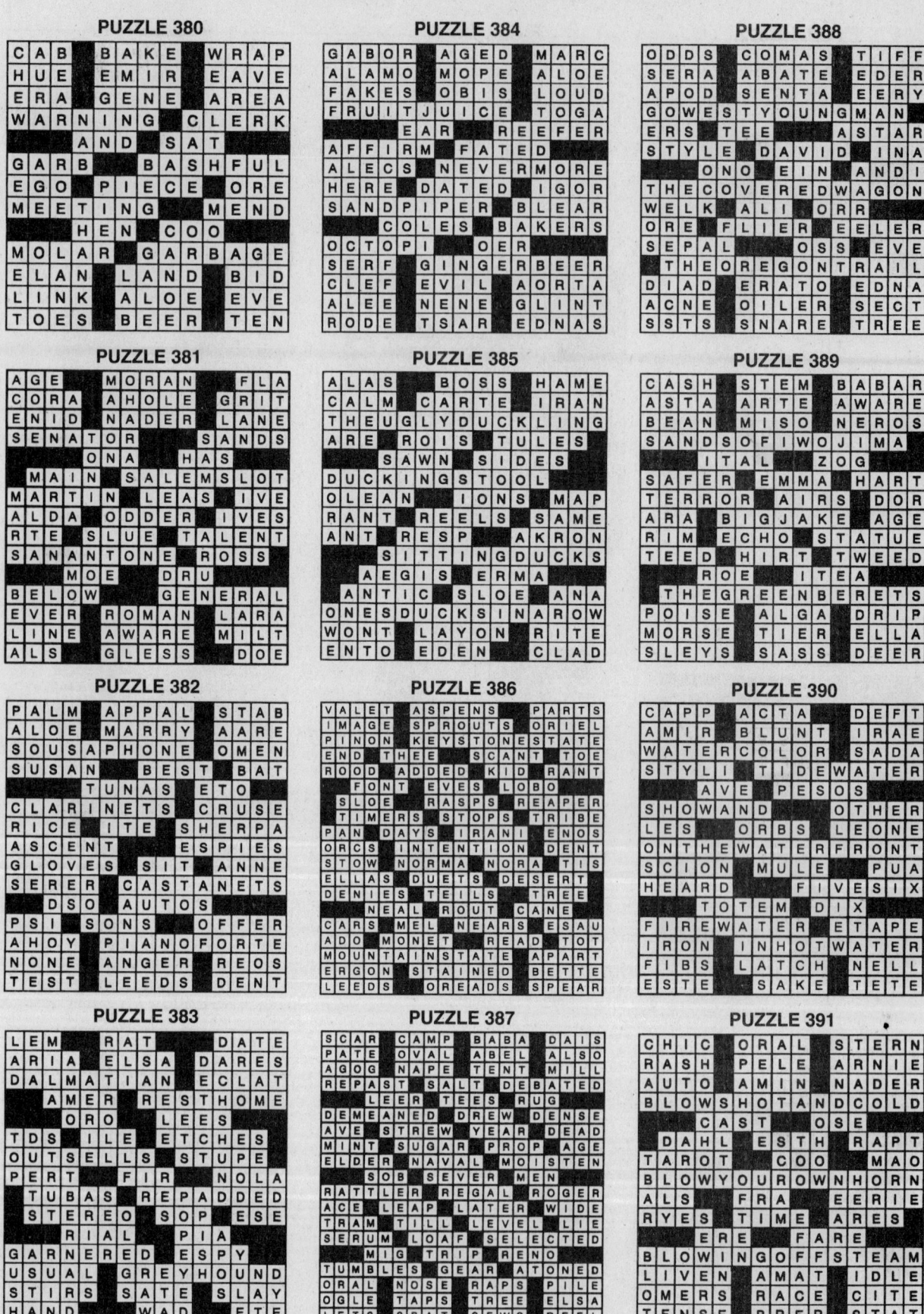

CHIC ORAL STERN
RASH PELE ARNIE
AUTO AMIN NADER
BLOWSHOTANDCOLD
CAST OSE
DAHL ESTH RAPT
TAROT COO MAO
BLOWYOUROWNHORN
ALS FRA EERIE
RYES TIME ARES
ERE FARE
BLOWINGOFFSTEAM
LIVEN AMAT IDLE
OMERS RACE CITE
TENSE BRER STAT

## PUZZLE 392

| | | | | | | | | | | | | |
|---|---|---|---|---|---|---|---|---|---|---|---|---|
| |B|R|A| |P|R|O|P| |C|O|W|
|A|R|A|B| |A|U|R|A| |A|L|E|
|R|A|I|L| |T|E|A|R| |B|E|D|
|I|N|S|E|T| | |L|I|M|B| | |
|A|D|E| |W|H|O| |S|O|A|P|Y|
| | | |T|O|O|L|S| |O|G|R|E|
|R|O|D|E| |P|I|E| |N|E|O|N|
|I|D|E|A| |E|V|E|R|S| | | |
|D|E|N|S|E| |E|M|U| |P|U|T|
| | |T|E|R|M| | |B|A|L|S|A|
|E|L|I| |R|A|R|E| |S|A|I|L|
|Y|E|S| |O|D|O|R| |A|N|N|E|
|E|A|T| |R|E|B|A| |P|E|G| |

## PUZZLE 393

| | | | | | | | | | | | | |
|---|---|---|---|---|---|---|---|---|---|---|---|---|
|P|I|E| |P|A|I|L| |F|R|E|T|
|A|R|E| |A|C|R|E| |A|I|D|E|
|T|A|L|E|N|T|E|D| |U|S|E|S|
| | | |Y|E|S| | |S|C|E|N|T|
|A|S|H|E|S| |G|L|U|E| | | |
|L|O|U|D| |F|R|U|I|T|F|U|L|
|D|A|M| |R|O|A|S|T| |E|R|A|
|A|P|P|R|O|A|C|H| |H|U|G|S|
| | | |I|D|L|E| |C|A|D|E|T|
|P|O|N|D|S| | |P|A|L| | | |
|A|M|I|D| |O|V|E|R|T|A|K|E|
|C|E|L|L| |L|I|A|R| |N|E|W|
|K|N|E|E| |E|A|S|Y| |D|Y|E|

## PUZZLE 394

| | | | | | | | | | | | | |
|---|---|---|---|---|---|---|---|---|---|---|---|---|
|T|I|P| |O|R|A|L| |C|O|D|E|
|A|D|E| |V|A|S|E| |A|R|E|A|
|B|A|R| |E|M|P|T|Y|N|E|S|T|
| | |F|I|N|S| | |O|A|S|I|S|
|C|H|U|M|S| |T|E|L|L| | | |
|L|A|M|P| |C|O|R|K| |W|A|Y|
|A|L|E| |S|O|A|R|S| |O|L|E|
|N|O|S| |L|A|D|S| |S|O|D|A|
| | | |O|A|T|S| |C|E|D|A|R|
|A|P|A|R|T| | |R|A|T|S| | |
|G|O|L|D|E|N|R|O|D| |H|I|S|
|E|L|S|E| |A|I|D|E| |E|R|E|
|D|O|O|R| |P|O|E|T| |D|E|W|

## PUZZLE 395

| | | | | | | | | | | | | |
|---|---|---|---|---|---|---|---|---|---|---|---|---|
|S|L|A|P| |A|L|S|O| |M|A|Y|
|T|O|U|R| |S|O|A|R| |O|L|E|
|A|N|N|A| |S|U|P|P|L|I|E|S|
|R|E|T|I|R|E|D| |H|A|S| | |
| | | |S|E|T| |E|A|S|T|E|R|
|E|D|G|E|D| |T|A|N| |E|R|A|
|B|R|A|D| |H|I|T| |S|N|I|P|
|B|U|S| |P|I|P| |B|A|S|E|S|
|S|M|O|K|E|D| |W|A|Y| | | |
| | |L|E|D| |F|I|N|I|C|K|Y|
|R|A|I|N|D|R|O|P| |N|O|N|E|
|I|N|N| |L|A|N|E| |G|R|E|W|
|O|D|E| |E|N|D|S| |S|E|E|S|

## PUZZLE 396

| | | | | | | | | | | | | |
|---|---|---|---|---|---|---|---|---|---|---|---|---|
|S|I|R| |L|A|V|A| |L|A|T|E|
|H|O|E| |O|R|E|S| |E|D|E|N|
|A|T|L|A|N|T|I|C| |V|E|N|D|
|M|A|Y|B|E| |N|O|T|E| | | |
| | | |E|L|F| |T|A|L|E|N|T|
|G|E|T| |Y|A|M| |N|E|V|E|R|
|A|X|E|S| |R|A|P| |D|E|M|O|
|P|I|A|N|O| |D|E|W| |R|O|D|
|S|T|R|I|N|G| |N|A|B| | | |
| | | |P|E|R|K| |G|U|A|R|D|
|T|R|A|P| |A|N|C|E|S|T|O|R|
|W|O|R|E| |N|E|A|R| |O|D|E|
|O|W|E|D| |D|E|N|S| |P|E|W|

## PUZZLE 397

| | | | | | | | | | | | | |
|---|---|---|---|---|---|---|---|---|---|---|---|---|
| |D|A|T|A| | | |C|O|B|R|A|
|M|E|X|I|C|O| |A|L|L|E|Y|S|
|A|S|L|E|E|P| |B|U|D|G|E|S|
|P|I|E| | |E|V|E|N| | | | |
| | | | |A|R|E| |G|A|I|N|S|
|A|P|E| |T|A|X| | |F|O|O|L|
|D|O|D|G|E|S| |T|A|T|T|O|O|
|A|O|N|E| | |C|A|N| |A|N|T|
|S|L|A|M|S| |A|M|Y| | | | |
| | | | |H|O|P|E| | |E|R|A|
|S|M|I|L|E|D| |S|A|C|R|E|D|
|P|A|R|A|D|E| |T|R|A|I|N|S|
|A|R|A|B|S| | | |F|R|E|T| |

## PUZZLE 398

| | | | | | | | | | | | | |
|---|---|---|---|---|---|---|---|---|---|---|---|---|
|B|A|G| |F|L|Y| | |G|U|M|S|
|A|I|R| |L|E|E|R| |O|P|A|L|
|A|D|E| |O|N|T|O| |W|O|K|E|
| | |E|G|O|S| |B|A|N|N|E|D|
|T|O|N|E|D| | |B|U|S| | | |
|O|V|E|R| |K|E|E|N| |E|A|R|
|W|A|R|M|H|E|A|R|T|E|D|L|Y|
|S|L|Y| |A|N|T|S| |R|I|T|A|
| | | |K|I|N| | |B|A|T|O|N|
|U|M|P|I|R|E| |D|E|S|I| | |
|R|I|O|T| |D|E|A|R| |O|D|D|
|G|L|E|E| |Y|O|R|E| |N|O|R|
|E|L|M|S| | |N|E|T| |S|T|Y|

## PUZZLE 399

| | | | | | | | | | | | | |
|---|---|---|---|---|---|---|---|---|---|---|---|---|
|J|A|Y| |C|O|A|L| |M|A|N|Y|
|O|R|E| |L|I|S|A| |U|L|N|A|
|K|I|N|F|O|L|K|S| |S|E|E|M|
|E|A|S|E|S| | |S|E|E|R| | |
| | | |T|E|N|D| |A|S|T|E|R|
|A|P|S|E| |O|A|S|T| |I|R|A|
|L|O|P| |H|E|L|P|S| |N|I|P|
|A|R|I| |A|L|A|I| |A|G|E|S|
|S|T|R|A|W| |I|N|C|H| | | |
| | |A|R|N|O| | |R|E|A|D|S|
|D|E|L|E| |A|S|S|E|M|B|L|E|
|O|P|E|N| |F|A|I|T| |L|I|L|
|N|A|D|A| |S|O|R|E| |E|V|A|

Joy runs deeper than despair.

## PUZZLE 400

| | | | | | | | | | | | | |
|---|---|---|---|---|---|---|---|---|---|---|---|---|
|L|A|P| | |R|A|P|T| |R|A|G|
|O|D|O|R| |I|D|L|E| |O|W|E|
|G|O|R|E| |B|E|A|N| |A|L|L|
| |S|E|A|M| |S|T|A|I|R|S| |
| | | |L|O|T| |E|N|D| | | |
|C|H|A|M|B|E|R| |T|A|B|L|E|
|O|U|R| | |N|O|D| | |A|I|R|
|P|E|T|A|L| |D|I|V|I|D|E|R|
| | | |R|O|T| |D|A|D| | | |
| |A|D|M|I|R|E| |T|E|A|M| |
|D|U|E| |T|O|R|O| |A|R|A|B|
|O|R|E| |E|V|I|L| |L|I|M|A|
|T|A|R| |R|E|E|D| | |D|A|N|

## PUZZLE 401

| | | | | | | | | | | | | |
|---|---|---|---|---|---|---|---|---|---|---|---|---|
|M|O|M| |A|P|E|S| |B|R|A|Y|
|O|D|E| |P|R|O|P| |R|I|C|E|
|P|O|S|T|P|O|N|E| |I|D|E|S|
| |R|A|I|L| |S|L|E|D| | | |
| | | |P|E|W| |L|E|G|I|O|N|
|H|I|T| |S|E|W| |L|E|D|G|E|
|E|R|R| | |T|A|G| | |O|R|E|
|N|A|I|L|S| |G|U|M| |L|E|D|
|S|N|O|O|P|S| |N|O|W| | | |
| | | |A|Y|E|S| |D|A|S|H| |
|B|O|R|N| |A|N|C|E|S|T|O|R|
|A|L|O|E| |M|A|I|L| |E|V|E|
|R|E|E|D| |S|P|A|S| |W|E|D|

## PUZZLE 402

| | | | | | | | | | | | | |
|---|---|---|---|---|---|---|---|---|---|---|---|---|
|H|E|R|B| |B|E|E|F| |D|O|E|
|O|D|O|R| |O|V|A|L| |U|R|N|
|P|E|S|O| |R|E|T|U|R|N|E|D|
|S|N|E|A|K|E|R| |R|I|G| | |
| | | |D|I|D| |O|R|D|E|R|S|
|D|A|T|E|D| |A|N|Y| |O|I|L|
|I|R|A|N| |V|I|E| |O|N|C|E|
|L|E|T| |E|A|R| |M|U|S|E|D|
|L|A|T|E|S|T| |H|A|T| | | |
| | |E|L|K| |D|A|N|G|E|R|S|
|T|E|R|M|I|N|A|L| |R|A|I|L|
|I|R|E| |M|E|L|T| |O|S|L|O|
|M|A|D| |O|W|E|S| |W|E|E|P|

## PUZZLE 403

| | | | | | | | | | | | | |
|---|---|---|---|---|---|---|---|---|---|---|---|---|
|D|A|N| |P|L|O|W| |S|T|E|W|
|I|C|E| |R|U|D|E| |P|I|L|E|
|D|E|T|O|U|R|E|D| |R|E|S|T|
| | | |I|N|K|S| |S|I|D|E|S|
|W|H|I|L|E| | |T|O|N| | | |
|O|A|T|S| |S|T|R|U|G|G|L|E|
|O|L|E| |K|N|E|E|L| |O|A|R|
|F|E|M|I|N|I|N|E| |T|U|N|A|
| | | |S|I|P| | |D|A|T|E|S|
|A|L|E|R|T| |B|O|A|R| | | |
|C|O|L|A| |C|A|V|I|T|I|E|S|
|I|D|L|E| |O|R|A|L| |M|A|P|
|D|E|A|L| |O|N|L|Y| |P|R|Y|

## PUZZLE 404

```
SHIP#BAR##INK
LATE#EVIL#DEN
EVER#DIVA#EWE
DEMUR#DEVIATE
###SUM#TAN###
REVENUE##NOSE
ORE##DRY##APE
TAXI##NATURAL
###LOT#MAN###
TANKARD#PILOT
OLE#TOIL#TIME
USE#HONE#EVEN
ROD##PET#DENT
```

## PUZZLE 405

```
DIAL#APER#TAG
ACRE#MORE#ALE
NEIGHBORS#RAN
ERA#ALL#CEASE
###PIE#CUR###
LAGER#CREATES
ALEE#GAY#SALE
SPELLER#MERIT
###EEL#ROD###
TRADE#BAT#CAB
RIM#ROADHOUSE
ACE#ELSA#FREE
PEN#DEER#FLAT
```

## PUZZLE 406

```
BAROQUE#OWING
A#E#U#Q#W#N#E
TABLE#UNLUCKY
C#I#S#I###U#S
HER#TINY#FREE
##T#I#E#C###R
#SHOOK#JOINT#
G###N#E#N#U##
REAM#EXIT#ZIP
I#M###P#R#Z#A
EXPLODE#INLAW
V#L#F#N#V#E#E
EJECT#DREADED
```

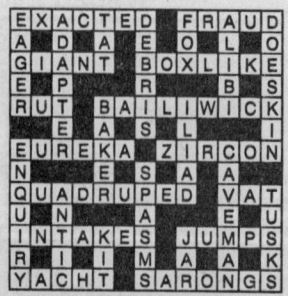

1-R, 2-T, 3-M, 4-S, 5-L, 6-U, 7-D, 8-K, 9-X, 10-W, 11-N, 12-F, 13-Q, 14-O, 15-J, 16-B, 17-C, 18-Z, 19-E, 20-I, 21-A, 22-Y, 23-V, 24-P, 25-H, 26-G.

## PUZZLE 407

```
EXACTED#FRAUD
A#D#A#E#O#L#O
GIANT#BOXLIKE
E#P###R###B#S
RUT#BAILIWICK
##E#A#S#L###I
EUREKA#ZIRCON
N###E#S#A#A##
QUADRUPED#VAT
U#N###A###E#U
INTAKES#JUMPS
R#I#I#M#A#A#K
YACHT#SARONGS
```

1-T, 2-X, 3-O, 4-Y, 5-V, 6-H, 7-P, 8-L, 9-Q, 10-S, 11-D, 12-J, 13-R, 14-W, 15-K, 16-B, 17-A, 18-G, 19-I, 20-U, 21-C, 22-Z, 23-M, 24-N, 25-E, 26-F.

## PUZZLE 408

```
SUB###ATES##JUT
NERVY#SHEL#VISA
ALIAS#HERA#AVER
PEGGED#VOYAGERS
###AROMA#SPA###
CRAB#LOGE#EBBED
HOBO#ERAL#ROLLE
ADEN#DEBAR#NAME
MELDS#NOTE#DRAM
POSSE#ONER#LENS
###HAM#DRAGO###
BOBOLINK#NOVELS
EVOE#LOIS#BETEL
TENS#ERNE#IRADE
AND##SAGE###SAD
```

## PUZZLE 409

1. Cow in Scowl, 2. War in Swarm, 3. Oar in Board, 4. Rap in Graph, 5. Tan in Stand, 6. Eon in Peony.

## PUZZLE 410

```
OPIE#SHAFT#FALA
MORN#COBRA#OLIO
ALAS#OLEOS#REEK
REQUIRE#STAGED#
###ROE#STELA###
DOZEN#SHY#IVORY
EVES#POI#AVENUE
NER#CONFUSE#IRA
IRONED#TSK#SCAR
MASER#TEE#HEELS
###PORED#JET###
#PUTSIN#FOXTROT
PERU#SALON#LOVE
ALAN#ECOLE#EVEN
DELE#READS#SENT
```

## PUZZLE 411

PINCUSHION

## PUZZLE 412

```
SIRE#SCOPE#SCAB
OBOE#CORAL#CODE
DEPLORABLE#RAZE
AXE#BASS#CHALET
###WEPT#STOP###
ADVISE#SLIPSHOD
SWORE#CHAOS#APE
CEDE#CHAIN#AREA
ILK#ALIGN#STERN
ITALIANS#THOMAS
###URNS#SEAM###
HENRYS#OPAL#BIG
AMOK#MAGISTRATE
LINE#AGREE#ABET
FRED#NEEDS#GEMS
```

## PUZZLE 413

SAW ILL LEA
PRO RUE EAR
AIRPORT ASK
SANK SAFE
PITY HEN
SAD PICTURE
OIL TOP REB
PREPARE GAB
ICY SPED
WANT SCAR
DIM STATION
USE HAG MAE
DEN EYE ETE

## PUZZLE 414

ASIA WOVE CLAM
SUEDE IVES RAVE
ATTAR TEXT ANET
MOTH THREADBARE
LOTUS STY
ACE ALTO ENABLE
LAD LIONS ERRED
ENOS POSES SING
ROWAN DEPOT DIE
TENDER TALE END
CUP RINDS
BREAKBREAD AMOR
LORN BOAT STAKE
OAST ESSE HEIRS
TREE REED EDDA

## PUZZLE 415

1. Game, 2. Case, 3. Lead, 4. Haul, 5. Rout, 6. Best, 7. Hope, 8. Deep, 9. Once, 10. Vast.

## PUZZLE 416

ARE ALAS MOSS
DON CUTE ANAT
ODD TREE TILE
EASE KITTEN
SCAR WIDE
TART INERTIA
IRE FANGS HOP
REDBIRD CITE
EARS BRAD
PALATE PASS
RIOT STAY TAT
EDGE TIRE EGO
SEEN SETS DEN

## PUZZLE 417

ADD ADAY TOPS
RUE POLE OVAL
MESSAGES WERE
OARS SCREW
SPLIT PAPA
TOAD DEPARTED
OUT WATER RAY
PREPARES BASE
EVER HOMES
MINCE HEAP
AREA STARTLES
MOAN HAND EAT
ANTS EGGS DRY

## PUZZLE 418

POSE RAT HELP
AVON EVE ARIA
RE DEPENDS SI
ERA TERSE EAR
TO ATE AN
BALLET DEBTOR
AGAIN MAINE
DENVER PUTTED
TE EGO EL
ALA APRIL ELF
LO PLEASED OR
TOME ACE OGRE
OPEN LED CODE

## PUZZLE 419

RITA FAN LAB CAP
ARIS ALE AIR ORE
HAPPYMOTHERSDAY NEE
SEEN AVE EVE GAP
CAB ADE VIE SONAR
OER CELLO SAME
TRIG AHA DAUGHTER
SONINLAW ELSE URI
GLEAM PER LEE
MAC MIA
USA TAP SCANT
PAY ALEE THANKING
OFFERING IER SOIL
NELL GOWNS NNE
OLDER SAY AGE SEN
SOW EMU LIE RITE
ARE LILYOFTHEVALLEY
TAR TEE ONE LOVE
ELS SST WAR AGAS

## PUZZLE 420

RAPID RARE
ALINES DIVERS
NICKEL ICEMAN
GEN POACH ASA
ENID USE PREP
SCOTCH ELKS
RAH ALE
FAIR ARMADA
ALMS FIR DEPT
JAB TIMES CPA
AMUSES STOOLS
RESENT TURRET
SHED BOSSY

## PUZZLE 421

ACED TAMS
ACUTE ELATE
ORIENTEXPRESS
NED ARRAS ETA
UNIT AIN FRED
PACIFIC MASSE
TAN BAR
ORGAN CHICAGO
KHAN SOO EROS
RIN CLOWN COT
ANDTHESANTAFE
EERIE NEEDS
RAPT ISLE

## PUZZLE 422

SALES SHE ARM
ALIVE PEN PIE
DEPENDING SOS
TON ABETS
ASPIRE AGE
DALLY TIE ACE
DIAL RAM FUEL
SLY CAP TELLS
SAT RIDDLE
VAPOR PAN
ARR TRANSIENT
NEE OUR ERROR
SAY NET LEERY

## PUZZLE 423

LEG PLUM SLOW
AYE EASY PAVE
PETNAME HAVEN
ICE VACANT
FETCH DOVE
ACRE TRIO SOS
CHARGEACCOUNT
TOP RAKE MICA
CASE CATER
ESCAPE RAH
THEME FARAWAY
CODE SING OWE
HEEL ONTO NET

## PUZZLE 424

JAB DIN
WAGE EDIT
MIMES CAPER
CON SEMIS NOW
APES TAD SODA
NESTS RETIRED
OUR DOT
STUNNED REMIT
PINE SIN SIDE
AND AIDES NON
TELLS WHEEL
ROOT EONS
YES RED

## PUZZLE 425

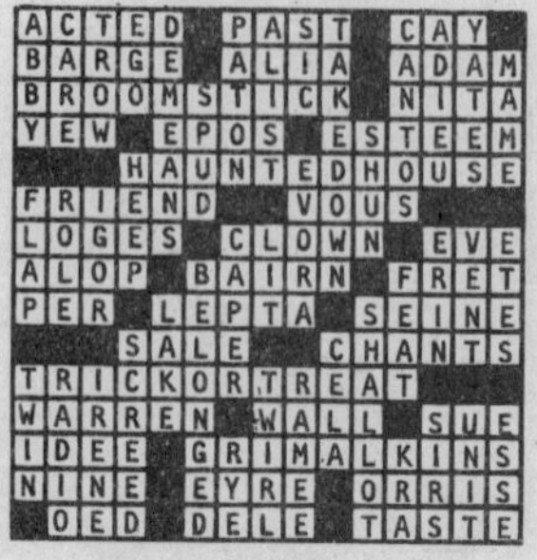

## PUZZLE 426

PROSPERITY

## PUZZLE 427

## PUZZLE 428

## PUZZLE 429

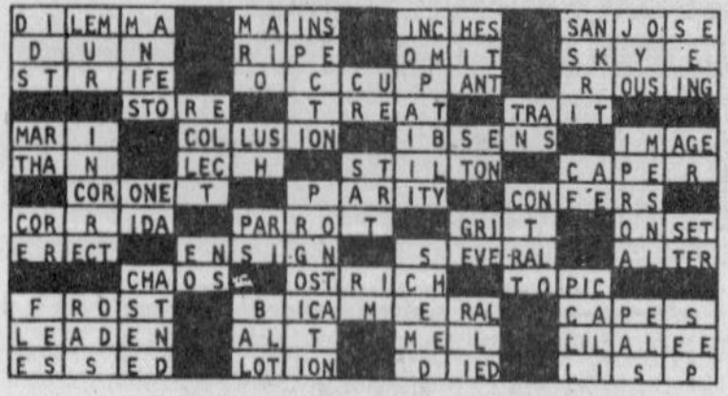

## PUZZLE 430

## PUZZLE 431

1. Begin binge, 2. Beard bread, 3. Dairy diary, 4. Dreads adders, 5. Signed design, 6. Warned warden, 7. Strange garnets.

## PUZZLE 432

## PUZZLE 433

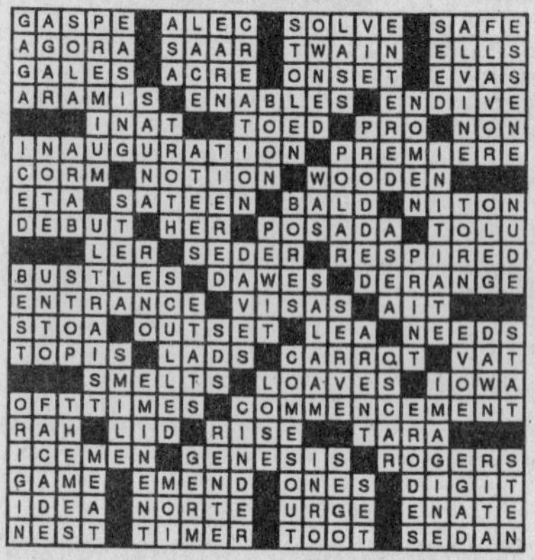

## PUZZLE 434

## PUZZLE 435

## PUZZLE 436

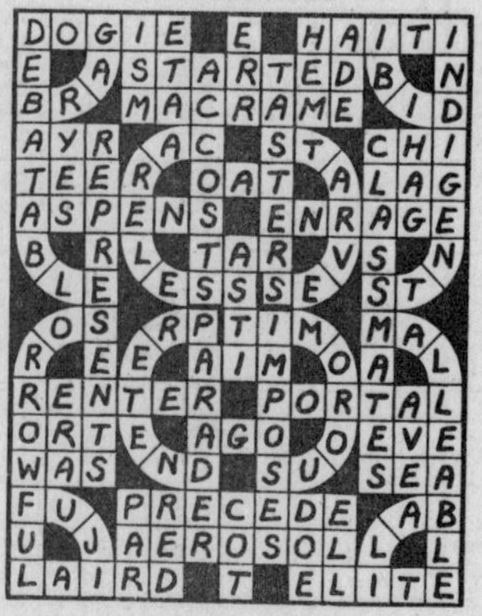

## PUZZLE 437

## PUZZLE 438

## PUZZLE 439

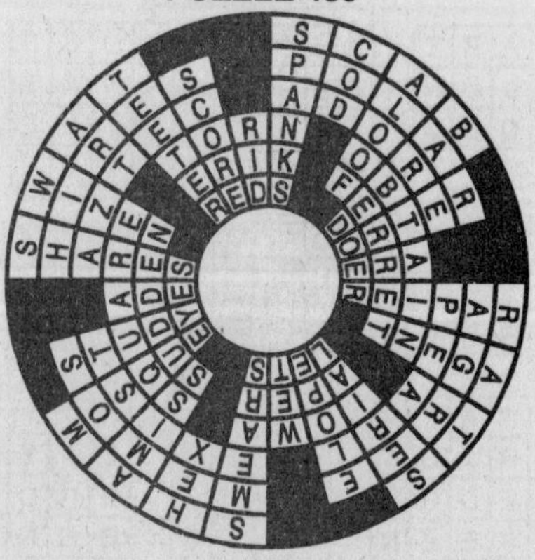

## PUZZLE 440

ARNO HERB HOHUM
MEAL AREA ALONE
AMOS BINS TITAN
SOMELIKEITHOT
SPINET ENO ADD
VAT SLIMMER
ATHLETES UNEASE
SHOAL DOS TALKS
WETTED DIRENESS
AMPERES REG
NEO EMS LENSES
THEDICEAREHOT
FLAIR LADY EASE
OATES ERNE DRIP
EPODE DEAD YENS

## PUZZLE 441

SAL SAHIB ABUT
ROSA ARENA TUBA
EPIC NINES TREK
CHARADE EMIGRE
OPAL ABEL
BASEL GALAHAD
ERRS SCALE ELA
GAMESPEOPLEPLAY
AVA TINGE IONS
DESCEND CENTS
RAGS SOLO
ENCAMP CRICKET
CORD OFTEN HIDE
ORAL NOONE LEND
NAME GREER EVA

## PUZZLE 442

KE RNEL BAR D
ENTE RALITORE
LAT ERABOV E
YAL E VAP OR
WRE CK POEM
IG UA NAPI ER
TEN TOAT LI E
TR Y ALO NE
TO NA BLERROD
APHI DBE DATE
G O NEE DE N
A C TSARTE
SLEETWA D E D

## PUZZLE 443

JAM ULNA SABRE
ASIA TEAM ALIAS
BEER MANE HILTS
SANCHOPANZA LIE
HOST ARAGON
EJECT IMPALA
STORK SLIP ENOS
ETH SIMILAR NAP
WAND GEAL AMORY
WILLED EDENS
ADAGIO EMIR
MAT MOROCCOMOLE
UNSUB OBOE AXEL
STONE PELE NEAL
TENOR EYES NRA

## PUZZLE 444

ASTA DAMS SGTS
ROAD ELIAS ARIL
ELKS SINAI SATE
ADE REVERE SNOW
STORES SLIT
SAFEST STEEPLE
TROTS DISAGREES
EER ORT RNS
ENGROSSES MAMIE
PAROLEE CABINS
AMEN SPARES
CANA IDEATE SAL
ASTI ORATE PIPE
LIEN RATER ROSE
LADE TORS ONER

## PUZZLE 445

PAGED BOMB APSO
AGREE AMOR RATA
CHANT REDO GNAT
TAN ANDREWWYETH
TRIES SALLES
ROWENA SCENE
ETON POPART RIO
STOOD PUN SPENT
TOD ONEMAN AMOI
DRONE EOSINS
ANTRIM CAPON
MARYCASSATT GAP
UVEA DOUR ISTLE
LEAD ITER CHOSE
ESTS COTY SENOR

## PUZZLE 446

CART CITE SHY
HOER ARENA STOA
ANDY RENDS TALL
NEW RENT SOIREE
HOUSE POURS
WINES PART AMP
HATES WAITS NEO
AVER ANN EDEN
LEA CADET PASSE
ERN AMES HASTE
DARED CORER
RUBBER ROME IDA
ERLE CRAVE SPAN
AGUE EATER PEST
DEE HERS ASHE

## PUZZLE 447

LAST BLAB SHES NEED
ASHE RARA COLT ERLE
MEAN ORAL ASIA VISE
BADNEWSBEARS MEEKER
INN FRY AMOR
PANSY ALUM DESCEND
ARA ANGEL PAIR RAYE
LESS ART ARNO YSER
MAHALIA AMASS EWES
VAL ARENA FLO
CLEW DRINK DOLLARS
POET REED CEO FLAW
AMAH PASS SHALE ONA
NOSEGAY OPEN DREAM
TESS SIR PIE
JOLIET MYLITTLEPONY
AGOG UPON NORA OBIE
RENE RANG GRIN RONA
SEER ELKE SOME TEAR

## PUZZLE 448

| | | | | | | | | | | | | | | |
|---|---|---|---|---|---|---|---|---|---|---|---|---|---|---|
|A|M|I|D| |R|E|E|F| | |Q|U|A|D|
|L|O|B|E| |E|R|G|O|T| |U|N|D|O|
|E|V|E|N| |V|A|G|U|E| |E|T|O|N|
| |E|X|O|D|U|S| |R|E|C|L|O|S|E|
| | | |T|R|E|E|D| |S|O|L| | | |
| |A|R|E|A| |D|I|P| |D|E|E|P| |
|C|R|E|D|I|T| |N|A|P| |D|A|R|T|
|A|D|E| |N|O|W| |D|A|M| |G|I|N|
|D|O|V|E| |P|E|G| |R|E|J|E|C|T|
| |R|E|S|T| |B|A|R| |L|U|R|E| |
| | | |C|O|T| |P|E|L|T|S| | | |
|L|A|T|H|E|R|S| |P|A|S|T|E|L| |
|A|C|R|E| |E|L|D|E|R| |I|C|E|D|
|S|H|O|W| |K|A|Y|A|K| |C|H|A|R|
|S|E|T|S| | |G|E|T|S| |E|O|N|S|

## PUZZLE 452

| | | | | | | | | | | | | | | |
|---|---|---|---|---|---|---|---|---|---|---|---|---|---|---|
|E|D|N|A| |N|A|B|S| | |R|A|N|G|
|D|R|O|P| |E|L|U|L| |L|E|V|E|E|
|S|A|L|E| |L|A|N|A| |E|M|E|E|R|
| |G|O|D|S|L|I|T|T|L|E|A|C|R|E|
| | | | |E|I|N| | |O|R|K| | | |
| |H|A|L|V|E| |C|A|L| |E|R|I|N|
|A|E|R|I|E| |B|A|L|L|S| |A|R|E|
|G|R|E|E|N|E|R|P|A|S|T|U|R|E|S|
|E|O|N| |S|T|E|R|N| |A|N|E|N|T|
|S|N|A|P| |H|A|I| |S|N|A|R|E| |
| | | |E|R|A| | |F|E|Z| | | | |
|H|O|M|E|O|N|T|H|E|R|A|N|G|E| |
|E|G|A|D|S| |H|A|R|M| |O|L|L|A|
|M|E|L|E|E| |E|L|M|O| |D|E|A|N|
|P|E|T|E| | |N|E|I|N| |S|E|N|T|

## PUZZLE 456

| | | | | | | | | | | | | | | |
|---|---|---|---|---|---|---|---|---|---|---|---|---|---|---|
|S|E|E|M| |B|O|W|E|D| |F|E|U|D|
|L|A|V|A| |A|D|A|G|E| |A|N|N|E|
|O|V|E|R| |B|O|N|G|S| |C|O|I|F|
|P|E|R|S|P|I|R|E| |T|O|A|S|T|Y|
| | | |H|U|E| | |G|I|R|D| | | |
|A|B|O|A|R|D| | |A|N|T|E|N|N|A|
|M|A|P|L|E| |F|A|Z|E| |S|O|O|T|
|B|Y|E| | |O|I|L|E|D| | |B|I|T|
|E|O|N|S| |B|E|A|D| |T|U|L|S|A|
|R|U|S|T|I|E|R| | |V|E|N|E|E|R|
| | | |A|N|D|Y| | |A|A|H| | | |
|B|I|K|I|N|I| |A|N|I|M|A|T|E|D|
|E|D|E|N| |E|L|L|E|N| |N|O|T|E|
|G|L|E|E| |N|E|P|A|L| |D|I|N|E|
|S|E|N|D| |T|A|S|T|Y| |S|L|A|P|

## PUZZLE 449

| | | | | | | | | | | | | | | |
|---|---|---|---|---|---|---|---|---|---|---|---|---|---|---|
|K|I|T|H| |F|A|S|T|S| |B|Y|E|S|
|A|R|E|A| |O|M|A|H|A| |R|O|M|P|
|T|A|X|I| |Y|O|D|E|L| |A|R|I|A|
|E|N|T|R|E|E|S| |S|O|C|K|E|T|S|
| | | |P|A|R| |S|I|N|A|I| | | |
|R|E|M|I|T| |N|O|S| |G|N|A|T|S|
|O|X|E|N| |S|U|B| |D|E|G|R|E|E|
|O|I|L| |U|T|T|E|R|E|D| |A|P|E|
|S|L|E|E|P|Y| |R|A|N| |A|B|E|D|
|T|E|E|N|S| |P|L|Y| |Y|E|S|E|S|
| | | |D|E|L|A|Y| |E|A|R| | | |
|C|R|O|U|T|O|N| |A|M|M|O|N|I|A|
|R|E|A|R| |S|A|B|L|E| |S|O|N|G|
|A|N|T|E| |E|M|B|E|R| |O|N|C|E|
|B|O|S|S| |S|A|S|S|Y| |L|E|A|D|

## PUZZLE 453

| | | | | | | | | | | | | |
|---|---|---|---|---|---|---|---|---|---|---|---|---|
| |M|E|N|D|O|L|E|S|S|T|H| |
|N|A|V|E| |P|E|R| |A|R|E|A|
|A|P|E|S| |E|A|R| |T|A|R|N|
|C| | |T|A|R| | |D|E|P|O|T|
|Y|E|S| |W|A|S|T|E| | | |H|
|E|M|O|T|E| |C|O|N|S|U|M|E|
|H|I|D|E| |H|A|Y| |P|L|A|Y|
|T|R|A|N|S|O|M| |P|A|N|T|S|
|L| | | |A|P|P|L|E| |A|S|H|
|L|A|T|E|X| | |A|N|Y| | |O|
|A|U|R|A| |F|I|N| |A|I|N|U|
|O|L|E|S| |A|L|A| |W|O|O|L|
| |D|Y|E|H|T|L|I|T|N|U|D| |

Men do less than they should until they do all they can.

## PUZZLE 457

| | | | | | | | | | | | | | | |
|---|---|---|---|---|---|---|---|---|---|---|---|---|---|---|
|S|M|O|G| |B|L|E|D| |S|H|A|D|E|
|H|E|R|A| |E|I|R|E| |N|O|V|E|L|
|A|S|A|P| |F|A|I|L| |A|R|I|E|L|
|G|A|L|E|F|O|R|C|E|W|I|N|D|S| |
| | | | |E|R|S| | |I|L|E| | | |
|B|E|E|T|L|E| |T|I|P| |T|R|A|M|
|E|R|R|O|L| |K|O|R|E|A| |I|R|E|
|T|O|R|N|A|D|O|W|A|R|N|I|N|G|S|
|A|D|O| |S|A|L|E|S| |D|O|D|O|S|
|S|E|R|T| |L|A|D| |C|R|U|S|T|Y|
| | | |A|T|A| | |A|L|E| | | | |
| |H|U|R|R|I|C|A|N|E|W|A|T|C|H|
|C|A|R|T|E| |E|S|T|E| |R|I|L|E|
|O|R|G|A|N| |L|E|I|S| |O|M|A|R|
|S|P|E|N|D| |L|A|C|E| |W|E|N|D|

## PUZZLE 450

| | | | | | | | | | | | | | | |
|---|---|---|---|---|---|---|---|---|---|---|---|---|---|---|
|E|G|G|S| | |D|A|T|E| | |L|O|P|
|D|A|R|E| |S|E|N|O|R| |D|A|D|O|
|A|M|A|T| |H|A|N|D|S|T|A|N|D|S|
|M|E|N| |S|O|L|E|D| |E|R|A|S|E|
| | |D|E|P|O|T| |L|O|R|N| | | |
| |A|S|S|E|T| |D|E|A|R| |S|H|E|
|B|E|T|T|E| | |E|R|S|E| |T|A|C|
|E|R|A|S| |C|R|E|S|T| |H|A|S|H|
|S|I|N| |S|E|E|D| | |T|O|N|T|O|
|T|E|D| |A|L|P|S| |W|O|R|D|Y| |
| | | |A|N|T|E| |L|A|N|A|I| | |
|R|A|I|S|E| |A|L|I|N|E| |N|E|T|
|U|N|D|E|R|S|T|A|N|D| |A|F|A|R|
|B|E|L|A| |P|E|T|E|S| |L|O|S|E|
|E|W|E| | |A|D|E|N| | |F|R|E|E|

## PUZZLE 454

| | | | | | | | | | | | | | | |
|---|---|---|---|---|---|---|---|---|---|---|---|---|---|---|
|C|E|D|E| |S|A|N|G| |C|I|T|E|D|
|O|V|E|N| |A|R|E|A| |A|R|O|S|E|
|W|I|N|D|Y|C|I|T|Y| |R|I|N|S|E|
|S|L|Y| |E|R|A|S|E|R| |S|T|E|M|
| | | |U|S|E|S| |R|O|D|E|O|S| |
|R|E|A|R|E|D| | | |L|A|S| | | |
|Y|A|W|N|S| |R|A|V|E|D| |R|A|P|
|E|R|R|S| |E|A|S|E|S| |R|I|L|L|
|S|P|Y| |R|I|G|H|T| |M|E|D|I|A|
| | | |W|I|G| | | |N|I|N|E|T|Y|
| |T|R|O|P|H|Y| |L|O|A|D| | | |
|S|E|A|L| |T|E|D|I|U|M| |M|O|M|
|W|A|I|F|S| |L|O|N|G|I|T|U|D|E|
|A|S|S|E|T| |P|L|E|A| |I|T|E|M|
|N|E|E|D|Y| |S|E|N|T| |P|E|S|O|

## PUZZLE 458

| | | | | | | | | | | | | | | |
|---|---|---|---|---|---|---|---|---|---|---|---|---|---|---|
|C|H|E|R| |C|U|R|E|R| |S|T|E|P|
|H|O|N|E| |A|B|O|V|E| |N|E|A|R|
|A|M|E|N| |S|O|L|E|S| |O|N|C|E|
|M|E|M|O|R|I|A|L| |E|A|R|T|H|Y|
|P|R|Y| |A|N|T| |B|A|B|E| | | |
| | | |E|G|G| |C|U|R|L| |T|W|O|
|A|R|E|A|S| |D|A|N|C|E| |H|E|N|
|C|A|R|T| |T|O|R|C|H| |B|A|L|L|
|T|R|I| |B|O|U|G|H| |H|A|N|D|Y|
|S|E|E| |A|L|S|O| |M|U|D| | | |
| | | |G|L|E|E| |C|A|R| |E|L|F|
|C|A|L|L|E|R| |P|U|L|L|O|V|E|R|
|O|H|I|O| |A|P|A|R|T| |M|A|D|E|
|M|O|M|S| |T|E|A|S|E| |E|D|G|E|
|E|Y|E|S| |E|A|R|E|D| |N|E|E|D|

## PUZZLE 451

| | | | | | | | | | | | | | | |
|---|---|---|---|---|---|---|---|---|---|---|---|---|---|---|
|A|B|U|T| |S|T|A|B| | |R|O|M|E|
|L|O|P|E| |P|U|R|E|R| |O|V|E|N|
|S|A|F|E| |A|B|A|T|E| |B|A|R|D|
|O|R|O| | |D|E|B|A|T|A|B|L|E| |
| | |R|A|T|E|S| | |A|L|E| | | |
| |E|G|G|E|D| |D|E|P|A|R|T|E|D|
| |W|R|E|N| |C|A|V|E| | |O|S|E|
|B|E|A|D| |N|O|T|E|D| |M|U|S|E|
|O|R|B| | |O|V|E|R| |L|A|C|E| |
|A|S|S|E|N|T|E|D| |P|A|T|H|S| |
| | | |L|E|I| | |P|A|S|T|A| | |
| |U|N|D|E|C|I|D|E|D| | |N|A|B|
|S|N|E|E| |E|L|A|N|D| |E|D|N|A|
|O|D|O|R| |S|I|N|C|E| |E|G|O|S|
|D|O|N|S| | |E|K|E|D| |L|O|N|E|

## PUZZLE 455

| | | | | | | | | | | | | | | |
|---|---|---|---|---|---|---|---|---|---|---|---|---|---|---|
|S|P|A|N| |C|O|S|T| | |G|A|I|T|
|L|A|C|E| |A|R|I|E|S| |R|I|C|E|
|O|P|T|S| |M|A|N|N|A| |I|D|E|A|
|W|A|S|T|R|E|L| |D|R|Y|N|E|S|S|
| | | |L|A|O|S| | |D|E|N| | | |
|A|S|T|E|R|S| |L|O|I|T|E|R|E|D|
|T|H|E|S|E| |T|U|R|N| |D|A|L|E|
|L|A|P| | |F|O|R|G|E| | |P|I|N|
|A|R|E|A| |I|N|K|S| |H|A|I|T|I|
|S|P|E|C|K|L|E|S| |T|A|N|D|E|M|
| | | |H|I|T| | |C|O|W|S| | | |
|F|E|L|I|N|E|S| |A|W|K|W|A|R|D|
|A|L|O|E| |R|A|B|B|I| |E|M|I|R|
|S|L|A|V| |S|W|A|I|N| |R|O|T|E|
|T|A|M|E| | |S|A|N|G| |S|K|E|W|

## PUZZLE 459

| | | | | | | | | | | | | |
|---|---|---|---|---|---|---|---|---|---|---|---|---|
|I|C|E| |C|L|A|D| |B|R|A|N|
|R|O|Y| |H|E|R|O| |R|E|N|O|
|A|D|E|Q|U|A|T|E| |E|A|T|S|
| | | |U|R|N| | |J|E|S|S|E|
|S|K|E|I|N| |S|H|E|D|S| | |
|P|A|N|T| |P|A|I|L| |U|S|E|
|O|L|D| |D|R|I|L|L| |R|E|D|
|T|E|E| |R|I|L|L| |T|E|N|D|
| | |A|T|O|M|S| |T|A|S|T|Y|
|S|T|R|A|P| | |F|I|X| | | |
|E|R|I|C| |C|A|R|D|I|N|A|L|
|W|I|N|K| |O|B|O|E| |A|L|I|
|N|O|G|S| |B|E|G|S| |P|A|D|

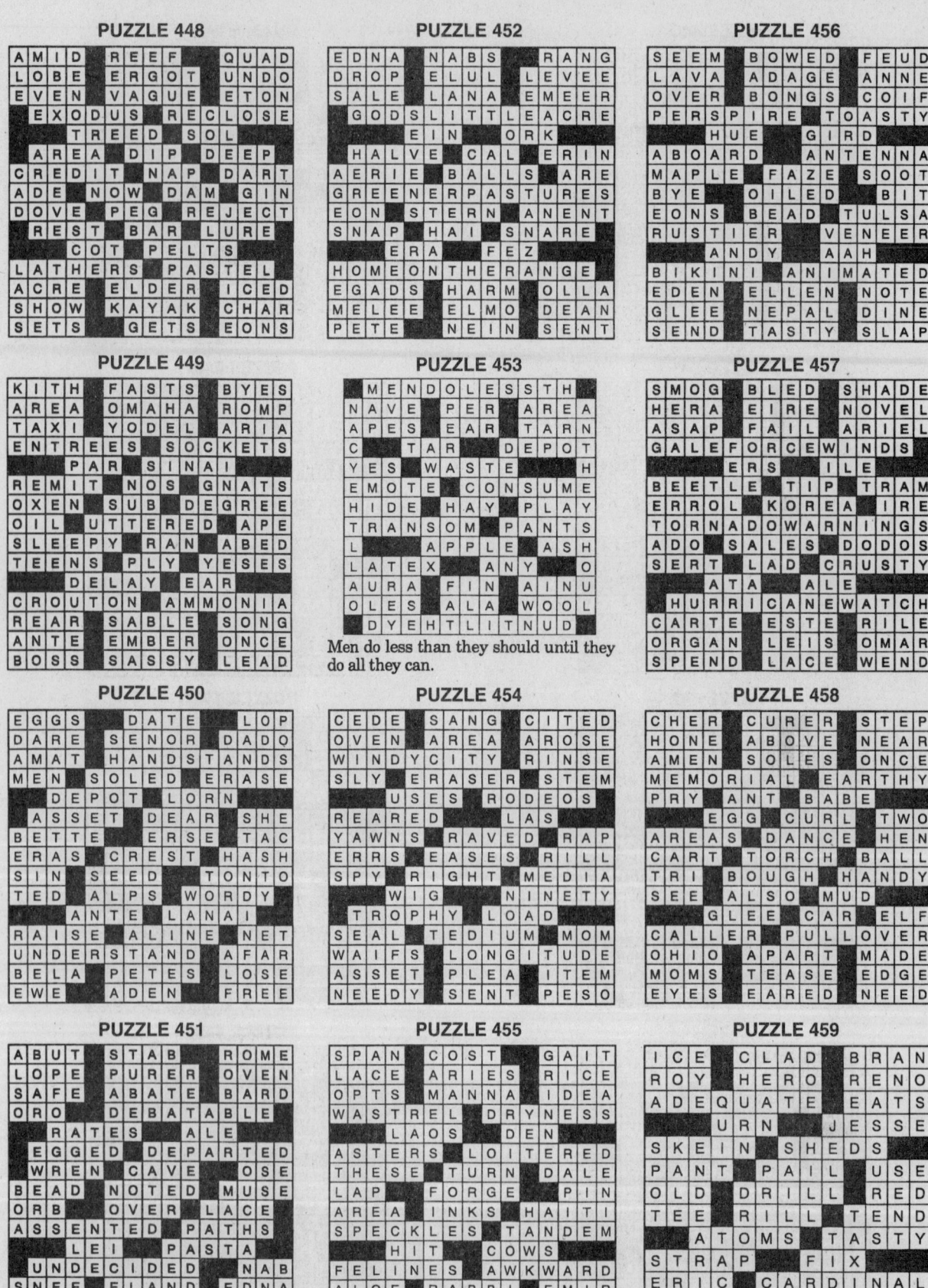

## PUZZLE 460

AMOEBA REASONS PANDAS
MILLER ADMIRAL EVOLVE
PLAYGOOSEBERRY AIRIER
SOV UMS RIGID OCS IRE
DIALS EES ICHOR
MATIN OWEN ETTE EROS
ASHEEP EXTREME SALUTE
ATOS RUDE IGOR APACHE
MOLECULE PIETA NETHER
RELENT COSSETED EER
SERIES TRENCH
OCA SARDINES TROPES
ARABIA KITED FRENETIC
CARSON SLEW GOYA RHEA
ATTEND OLDSTER MASONS
DEAN PUMA HEAT ROSAS
TERSE CAR YEARN
OIL VIE SAMOA ROO TOE
GLIDES STRAWBERRYMARK
REFORM TEENIER TOOTLE
EXERTS ANDANTE ASSAYS

## PUZZLE 461

ESKER ADAR SLAMS RANG
BELLE BEDE TENET ENOL
REELS ALAS ANODE CANO
ONEATATIME TIMEPIECES
OLES ARENA ONSETS
CATERED AMOS LINKS
OLIVES AGED FINIS ROT
LIMES TROD WREST NIPA
OVEN WREN FROST LOVER
NEY SEAT SUIT PATENT
OFTIMEANDTHERIVER
OCULAR NUDE GETA HIT
CROAT DINGY FETA LONI
HELP MINAS SASS CARNE
SED PORTS PICT CLOSER
RIDER MUTT CHASERS
PIRATE OVETA ARAM
ALAZYRIVER RIVERBASIN
TOTO ALENE IDES ERICA
OVER TIROL SERT RATON
NESS EATMY TATS STENO

## PUZZLE 462

BIT FOP SILK EDAM
ECRU HOPI ERIE NERO
REES ORANGEADE TEAL
GREENS LEAK PURPLE
RUTS SUEZ SPA
SYSTEM DROP SIREN
ACE SLABS SOAP NEVA
VOLT RATS MILO DIM
ATLAS TRAPS DEMILLE
OPUS BROWN TARE
TOWERED TRAIT RETRO
ESS ENOW TILE STOW
ALEE TEAS NEEDS EWE
ROAMS SLOP METERS
EAT ELIS SMUG
SPARTA ANON INGOTS
ELLA BLACKFOOT ERAL
WEAL OISE ALAS RENO
SAND READ ROT LST

## PUZZLE 463

SWAB BAD DUB SERAC
SHORE EXECUTE TRIBE
HEMEN DECODED ARTUR
ABASES APE LAY ESE
WAN TIRADE SAG USES
RIVE REMARK
SEC GENE PEN TEETER
IRA AND RESALES EMU
PURSES DANITES SHUN
DAIL MATADOR HEEL
GIFT GLITTER CORRAL
ATE GRILLES LOP ATA
LESSEE IES WIPE NEB
SETTER WIST
SLAW NOS PESTER DAM
PAN CAM SEE RACINE
AUDIO TENSPOT FLAGS
CRETE ONEONTA TUNES
EASED MED OER SEAL

## PUZZLE 464

REDD RADAR VATS
ERIE EMILE OMIT
FIRSTMATES YULE
STARE SEAFARER
LED LAG
CAPTAINS EYELID
ARE TEENS ERODE
ROTE DRIED SOLE
OMENS OPERA SEP
MASTER SKIPPERS
WEE PRO
ADMIRALS POSTS
LOON SEAMANSHIP
ISLE ONION EAVE
TEES NOLOS STAN

## PUZZLE 465

SNELL ARAT MEOW
LAMIA LOBE OLDE
ASIAN LOON NEAT
BARRELOFMONKEYS
SOW BRIE
MISC RIBS NYET
UTAH NNE APSES
DEMI EGEST OTTO
DROME CHE TERA
SAPS SHOE SEAR
ASST OTT
PLANETOFTHEAPES
RAZZ ALLI ABOVE
ALOE BEEN CIDER
MOVE SNAG HESSE

## PUZZLE 466

SNAP PLATE EBBS
TORO HEMAN SLAW
IBEX INAND TARE
FEN SLING MECCA
FLASHING BARKAT
TAP AID HRE
CHIP SOCK BOOR
HOLEINTHEWALL
MALL COTE ALEE
ITE DEW AVE
STILES BENEDICT
SENOR FERNS RUR
IRON IRANI BARI
LENE BASIE ATEE
EDER ANTES REDD

## PUZZLE 467

CAMS TAPED SPAN
OMIT ALIVE TONE
MESA NINES ERNE
ENTRANCE TARTAR
TREE ERLE
SCALED PROPOSES
TAME TRAYS HAT
ERAS DRESS SAVE
ENS POISE CREW
DESERVES STRESS
LEES SERE
ATLAST DELAWARE
LOOT APRIL SCAR
MINE IRENE URNS
SLED LOWER PETE

## PUZZLE 468

WHO LOS
TEAMS HELP
DALMATIAN GREATDANE
ELS RANGE AIMS NEW
ECHO KNOT SOUP VISE
CANE POET
NORA OWL
TORSO ARISE
BOG MAN ALONE
SKI IRISHSETTER BTU
CLAUS ORE LES
THEME BOONE
PEA UPON
SOAR STUD
BAIT TRAP BELT SHAW
ANN REBA ARIAS OWE
RETRIEVER GREYHOUND
EAVE SUNNY
RYE NED

## PUZZLE 469

ASH UTAH BRAG
JOE PITY ROLE
ADMITTED ABLE
RASCAL RAW
IKE ABLAZE
SHINE ONE WED
WING FAT MARE
ART ARK RAYON
PEOPLE LEG
APE AMIDST
SNAG DEDICATE
PACE OVEN TAR
AGES MEND ARM

## PUZZLE 470

ACE MAR BAY
LOT DANA MARE
MOTORCYCLISTS
STENO EASES
OVER DEB
TAR ERAS RAGE
IVES MIL SLAW
MASC ANEW LYE
TRA SWAM
MAUDE ROOST
OUTBOARDMOTOR
ALES SEAS TOE
RED TEN ONE

## PUZZLE 471

BUS TAMP BATH
ASP AVER ACHE
HEADLINE GEAR
OLD PRESTO
IRONY NAIL
NEWS FERN SAD
CEE PIPED OBI
ADD ALAS VALE
FULL BERET
EXHALE TEE
DRAM TOOLSHED
GALE EVIL OAR
EYED DALE PRY

## PUZZLE 472

FUN SIS RIM
VINE TOW EASE
IRIS RUE AILS
METTLE ANGLES
LEE ROE
THREATS TREAT
HUE SAC EVE
ENDOW POWERED
AID LOS
TRUSTY LETTER
HARE ELI AURA
EGGS RID TRIM
NEE SEE ENC

## PUZZLE 473

ALDA GEE AMES
SOIL RAN VICE
INVADERS ASHE
AGE RELIC TOP
PUN GERE
ASSUME NEARBY
COUP DEER
TOPICS SPADES
ELBA PER
MAR SMILE EPA
AMMO STARTREK
MEAN OTT OMNI
ANNE NOS MANN

## PUZZLE 474

OAT STEEP CBS
FIR TANGO RAT
FLAMINGOS ASI
PAR TASTE
HOPIS PEACHES
ABEL BARGE
LID BRINE PEG
TRANS ALOE
REPEATS CRANE
OWING LET
SEN GRADUATES
IRE EERIE EVA
ESS DEEDS RED

## PUZZLE 475

SPAN SOT IRED RIMS
TAPE TRIM VASE ERIE
EASE ALEE ATTENDANT
PREDETERMINE POINT
IVE BOA BELA
SEE OPEN CASTLED
APES ODOR ETTE ROT
CENTERED ANNE PINK
END TAR TSETSE ONTO
BET LINES TOE
ARTE ERODED SHA DOE
NOON ONER SHATTERS
TOR ESSE SOON ALOE
TEACHER PUNT ELL
ROES UAR ARE
STILL INTERCHANGER
CEASELESS SERE TALE
PARE ERLE TEEM ELLA
AMEN DEER LES DEEM

## PUZZLE 476

BASS TEARS SPAN
ECHO RAVEN HOLE
ARID ASIDE ROUT
DEMANDED ALARMS
EEL SKIN
SPREAD SLEEKEST
ALERT SWORN MAR
LANE SHOPS BONE
ANT FAIRS DATES
DESERTED CIDERS
FEUD DOE
PREFER MEATBALL
LOGO DUETS ASIA
ODOR ASSET REED
TEST YEARS EASE

## PUZZLE 477

ROMP SLOPE SLAM
AVER YODEL HERO
GATE SCOWL RAMP
ELEVATOR RINSE
ICE CLAM
REDEEM GRAPPLED
AVOWS FOUNT AXE
TOT JADED SPA
EKE TAROT STEER
RESTRICT POORLY
HOLE LOW
FAMED TEENAGER
OLEO OPERA RACE
REAR FEARS DIRE
DENY FALSE STUD

## PUZZLE 478

BOSS SHARP REDS
OLLA TUTOR ELIA
WEED ENNUI VIES
SOWDRAGONSTEETH
LAM DOIN
BASENESS NEGATE
EWE TRACT DEMON
LADD PAR ROTA
TRAIT SMELL NAT
SENSED SEAEAGLE
PERO WAR
SOWONESWILDOATS
ALES ASIDE UVEA
NILE MILES SONS
GOLD SEEMS ENDS

## PUZZLE 479

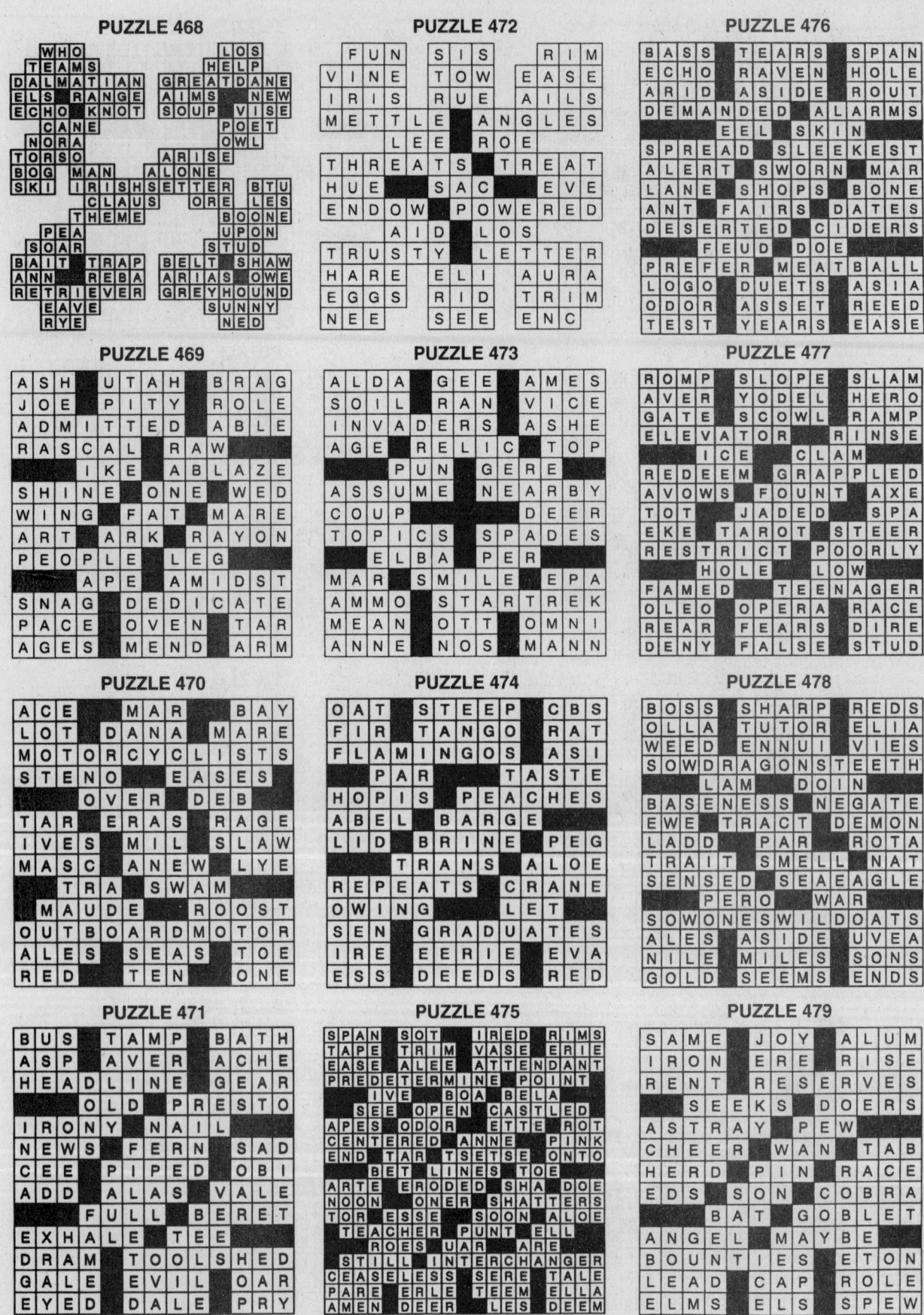

SAME JOY ALUM
IRON ERE RISE
RENT RESERVES
SEEKS DOERS
ASTRAY PEW
CHEER WAN TAB
HERD PIN RACE
EDS SON COBRA
BAT GOBLET
ANGEL MAYBE
BOUNTIES ETON
LEAD CAP ROLE
ELMS ELS SPEW

## PUZZLE 480

| | | | | | | | | | | | | |
|---|---|---|---|---|---|---|---|---|---|---|---|---|
| D | R | Y | ■ | B | O | R | E | ■ | B | O | A | T |
| A | Y | E | ■ | I | R | A | N | ■ | L | U | R | E |
| T | E | N | ■ | R | E | N | D | ■ | A | R | E | A |
| A | S | S | E | T | ■ | ■ | S | A | D | ■ | ■ | ■ |
| ■ | ■ | ■ | A | H | O | Y | ■ | W | E | S | T | ■ |
| L | I | A | R | ■ | D | E | A | L | ■ | I | R | E |
| E | O | N | ■ | C | O | A | L | S | ■ | T | E | E |
| A | N | T | ■ | E | R | R | S | ■ | F | E | E | L |
| ■ | S | E | E | D | ■ | S | O | L | E | ■ | ■ | ■ |
| ■ | ■ | ■ | L | E | D | ■ | ■ | A | W | A | R | E |
| S | H | O | D | ■ | E | A | R | N | ■ | P | O | D |
| H | O | N | E | ■ | C | L | U | E | ■ | S | A | G |
| E | W | E | R | ■ | K | E | G | S | ■ | E | R | E |

## PUZZLE 481

| | | | | | | | | | | | | |
|---|---|---|---|---|---|---|---|---|---|---|---|---|
| T | I | D | E | ■ | C | O | M | B | ■ | J | O | E |
| A | D | A | M | ■ | O | R | A | L | ■ | A | N | N |
| C | L | I | P | ■ | D | E | T | O | U | R | E | D |
| T | E | N | T | S | ■ | ■ | T | O | N | ■ | ■ | ■ |
| ■ | ■ | T | Y | P | E | S | ■ | M | I | T | T | S |
| A | L | I | ■ | I | R | K | S | ■ | T | I | R | E |
| R | O | E | ■ | T | R | A | P | S | ■ | G | I | N |
| E | A | S | T | ■ | S | T | U | N | ■ | H | O | T |
| A | F | T | E | R | ■ | E | R | U | P | T | ■ | ■ |
| ■ | ■ | ■ | E | A | R | ■ | ■ | B | A | R | K | S |
| A | L | L | S | P | I | C | E | ■ | N | O | N | E |
| D | U | E | ■ | I | D | O | L | ■ | S | P | O | T |
| E | G | O | ■ | D | E | W | S | ■ | Y | E | W | S |

## PUZZLE 482

| | | | | | | | | | | | | |
|---|---|---|---|---|---|---|---|---|---|---|---|---|
| O | L | D | ■ | C | U | T | S | ■ | F | L | I | P |
| A | I | R | ■ | A | S | I | A | ■ | E | I | R | E |
| F | E | E | ■ | R | E | N | T | ■ | A | M | E | N |
| ■ | ■ | N | A | G | S | ■ | C | A | R | E | S | S |
| M | I | C | R | O | ■ | T | H | I | S | ■ | ■ | ■ |
| A | C | H | E | ■ | C | U | E | D | ■ | L | O | T |
| T | O | E | ■ | B | E | L | L | E | ■ | A | D | E |
| E | N | D | ■ | I | R | I | S | ■ | O | M | E | N |
| ■ | ■ | ■ | S | T | E | P | ■ | T | W | I | S | T |
| E | M | B | L | E | M | ■ | L | I | E | N | ■ | ■ |
| B | A | L | E | ■ | O | B | O | E | ■ | A | S | P |
| B | L | E | D | ■ | N | E | A | R | ■ | T | E | A |
| S | E | W | S | ■ | Y | E | N | S | ■ | E | E | L |

## PUZZLE 483

| | | | | | | | | | | | | |
|---|---|---|---|---|---|---|---|---|---|---|---|---|
| W | A | R | M | ■ | D | I | M | S | ■ | P | R | O |
| A | S | I | A | ■ | O | M | E | N | ■ | E | A | R |
| S | H | O | P | ■ | U | P | T | O | D | A | T | E |
| ■ | ■ | ■ | L | A | B | ■ | E | R | A | S | E | S |
| A | B | L | E | S | T | ■ | R | E | V | ■ | ■ | ■ |
| B | A | A | ■ | K | E | G | ■ | R | I | D | E | R |
| E | L | M | S | ■ | D | A | B | ■ | D | E | L | I |
| D | E | P | O | T | ■ | P | A | D | ■ | E | L | S |
| ■ | ■ | ■ | W | E | D | ■ | C | O | A | R | S | E |
| A | P | P | E | A | R | ■ | K | E | N | ■ | ■ | ■ |
| W | O | O | D | P | I | L | E | ■ | D | I | P | S |
| A | L | E | ■ | O | V | E | R | ■ | E | R | I | E |
| Y | E | T | ■ | T | E | E | S | ■ | S | A | G | E |

## PUZZLE 484

| | | | | | | | | | | | | |
|---|---|---|---|---|---|---|---|---|---|---|---|---|
| P | I | E | S | ■ | A | N | T | ■ | ■ | A | N | N |
| A | D | A | M | ■ | S | E | A | S | ■ | B | O | O |
| L | O | S | E | ■ | C | A | N | T | E | E | N | S |
| E | L | E | A | N | O | R | ■ | A | L | L | E | Y |
| ■ | ■ | ■ | R | O | T | ■ | A | L | L | ■ | ■ | ■ |
| C | R | E | E | D | ■ | O | W | E | ■ | H | E | M |
| R | O | A | D | ■ | O | L | E | ■ | T | O | R | E |
| Y | E | T | ■ | A | D | D | ■ | T | R | E | A | T |
| ■ | ■ | ■ | A | C | E | ■ | P | E | A | ■ | ■ | ■ |
| S | P | U | R | T | ■ | R | A | N | C | H | E | S |
| C | U | S | T | O | M | E | R | ■ | T | I | D | E |
| A | R | E | ■ | R | A | N | T | ■ | O | V | E | N |
| R | E | D | ■ | ■ | T | O | Y | ■ | R | E | N | T |

## PUZZLE 485

| | | | | | | | | | | | | |
|---|---|---|---|---|---|---|---|---|---|---|---|---|
| S | A | L | T | ■ | O | R | R | ■ | C | O | R | A |
| O | D | O | R | ■ | M | O | E | ■ | A | P | I | N |
| B | O | B | O | L | I | N | K | ■ | D | E | F | T |
| ■ | ■ | ■ | P | E | T | ■ | I | R | E | N | E | S |
| B | A | T | H | E | ■ | G | N | A | T | ■ | ■ | ■ |
| O | B | E | Y | ■ | S | O | D | S | ■ | S | P | Y |
| A | L | E | ■ | S | C | A | L | E | ■ | L | I | E |
| T | E | D | ■ | A | R | T | E | ■ | G | A | L | A |
| ■ | ■ | ■ | A | L | A | S | ■ | L | A | T | E | R |
| T | A | N | D | E | M | ■ | E | A | T | ■ | ■ | ■ |
| A | R | I | D | ■ | B | O | B | W | H | I | T | E |
| T | A | L | E | ■ | L | I | B | ■ | E | R | I | E |
| A | B | E | D | ■ | E | L | S | ■ | R | E | E | L |

## PUZZLE 486

| | | | | | | | | | | | | |
|---|---|---|---|---|---|---|---|---|---|---|---|---|
| S | A | L | A | D | ■ | S | T | A | R | E | ■ | ■ |
| C | L | O | V | E | ■ | E | R | M | I | N | E | ■ |
| R | I | P | E | N | ■ | R | A | I | D | E | R | S |
| A | B | E | ■ | T | I | M | I | D | ■ | M | A | E |
| P | I | S | A | ■ | N | O | T | ■ | W | I | S | E |
| ■ | ■ | ■ | B | O | N | N | ■ | C | R | E | E | D |
| A | R | E | N | A | S | ■ | P | R | I | S | S | Y |
| L | I | V | E | R | ■ | R | A | Y | S | ■ | ■ | ■ |
| O | V | E | R | ■ | P | O | D | ■ | T | A | B | S |
| H | E | N | ■ | L | A | S | S | O | ■ | P | A | L |
| A | R | I | Z | O | N | A | ■ | S | C | A | R | Y |
| ■ | S | N | O | R | E | R | ■ | L | A | R | G | E |
| ■ | ■ | G | O | D | L | Y | ■ | O | T | T | E | R |

## PUZZLE 487

| | | | | | | | | | | | | |
|---|---|---|---|---|---|---|---|---|---|---|---|---|
| T | I | N | ■ | R | A | N | T | ■ | B | O | L | D |
| A | C | E | ■ | A | R | E | A | ■ | A | L | E | E |
| P | E | T | I | T | I | O | N | ■ | L | E | A | N |
| ■ | ■ | ■ | D | E | A | N | ■ | C | L | O | D | S |
| A | R | C | E | D | ■ | ■ | B | O | A | ■ | ■ | ■ |
| B | E | E | S | ■ | ■ | P | U | D | D | L | E | S |
| L | A | D | ■ | I | M | A | G | E | ■ | A | D | E |
| E | R | E | C | T | E | D | ■ | ■ | A | M | E | N |
| ■ | ■ | ■ | L | E | T | ■ | ■ | S | P | E | N | D |
| C | R | E | A | M | ■ | B | A | L | E | ■ | ■ | ■ |
| A | I | D | S | ■ | C | O | M | E | D | I | A | N |
| B | L | I | P | ■ | A | R | I | D | ■ | O | D | E |
| S | E | T | S | ■ | R | E | D | S | ■ | N | O | W |

## PUZZLE 488

| | | | | | | | | | | | | |
|---|---|---|---|---|---|---|---|---|---|---|---|---|
| A | N | T | ■ | I | D | L | E | ■ | S | C | A | T |
| S | U | E | ■ | S | E | A | L | ■ | H | O | B | O |
| K | N | A | P | S | A | C | K | ■ | O | R | E | S |
| ■ | ■ | ■ | L | U | R | E | ■ | A | U | N | T | S |
| S | P | R | E | E | S | ■ | A | L | L | ■ | ■ | ■ |
| A | R | E | A | ■ | ■ | A | C | A | D | E | M | Y |
| S | E | A | ■ | B | O | R | E | S | ■ | P | E | A |
| H | Y | D | R | A | N | T | ■ | ■ | D | I | A | L |
| ■ | ■ | ■ | A | B | E | ■ | C | I | R | C | L | E |
| S | P | A | C | E | ■ | L | E | N | A | ■ | ■ | ■ |
| T | A | L | K | ■ | R | O | L | L | B | A | C | K |
| A | I | D | E | ■ | I | S | L | E | ■ | D | O | E |
| B | R | A | T | ■ | B | E | S | T | ■ | D | O | G |

## PUZZLE 489

| | | | | | | | | | | | | |
|---|---|---|---|---|---|---|---|---|---|---|---|---|
| T | A | D | ■ | U | T | A | H | ■ | S | C | A | M |
| A | T | E | ■ | P | A | P | A | ■ | T | O | R | E |
| M | O | L | A | S | S | E | S | ■ | A | M | E | N |
| S | P | I | R | I | T | ■ | ■ | H | I | P | ■ | ■ |
| ■ | ■ | ■ | A | D | E | ■ | C | E | R | E | A | L |
| B | R | I | B | E | ■ | D | A | Y | ■ | T | R | A |
| R | I | D | S | ■ | A | R | M | ■ | D | E | E | D |
| A | C | E | ■ | I | C | Y | ■ | T | O | D | A | Y |
| T | E | N | A | N | T | ■ | W | H | O | ■ | ■ | ■ |
| ■ | ■ | T | I | N | ■ | ■ | A | R | R | O | W | S |
| A | C | I | D | ■ | B | A | K | E | S | H | O | P |
| N | O | T | E | ■ | I | D | E | A | ■ | I | R | E |
| T | O | Y | S | ■ | B | O | N | D | ■ | O | D | D |

## PUZZLE 490

| | | | | | | | | | | | | |
|---|---|---|---|---|---|---|---|---|---|---|---|---|
| R | O | B | ■ | V | I | S | E | ■ | J | U | K | E |
| A | D | E | ■ | I | R | K | S | ■ | A | N | E | W |
| P | E | T | U | N | I | A | S | ■ | P | I | N | E |
| ■ | ■ | ■ | N | E | S | T | ■ | W | A | T | T | S |
| R | I | O | T | ■ | H | E | R | O | N | ■ | ■ | ■ |
| A | D | M | I | T | ■ | D | U | O | ■ | S | A | P |
| F | E | E | L | E | R | ■ | B | E | C | A | M | E |
| T | A | N | ■ | L | A | S | ■ | D | A | M | E | S |
| ■ | ■ | ■ | A | L | T | A | R | ■ | B | E | N | T |
| C | H | E | S | S | ■ | F | O | U | L | ■ | ■ | ■ |
| O | I | L | S | ■ | F | A | S | T | E | N | E | R |
| I | D | L | E | ■ | A | R | E | A | ■ | O | R | E |
| N | E | A | T | ■ | D | I | S | H | ■ | W | A | D |

## PUZZLE 491

| | | | | | | | | | | | | |
|---|---|---|---|---|---|---|---|---|---|---|---|---|
| A | F | A | R | ■ | A | T | E | ■ | A | H | O | Y |
| D | O | M | E | ■ | P | A | Y | ■ | L | O | V | E |
| O | R | E | S | ■ | I | R | E | ■ | A | L | E | S |
| ■ | K | N | I | F | E | ■ | L | O | S | E | R | ■ |
| ■ | ■ | ■ | D | O | C | ■ | I | N | K | ■ | ■ | ■ |
| S | P | H | E | R | E | ■ | D | E | A | C | O | N |
| R | E | O | ■ | ■ | ■ | ■ | ■ | ■ | ■ | A | W | E |
| A | N | G | E | L | S | ■ | H | E | B | R | E | W |
| ■ | ■ | ■ | R | I | P | ■ | A | G | O | ■ | ■ | ■ |
| ■ | C | U | R | E | R | ■ | G | O | O | D | Y | ■ |
| P | A | P | A | ■ | E | G | G | ■ | S | E | A | L |
| I | R | O | N | ■ | E | E | L | ■ | T | A | L | E |
| T | E | N | D | ■ | S | E | E | ■ | S | L | E | D |

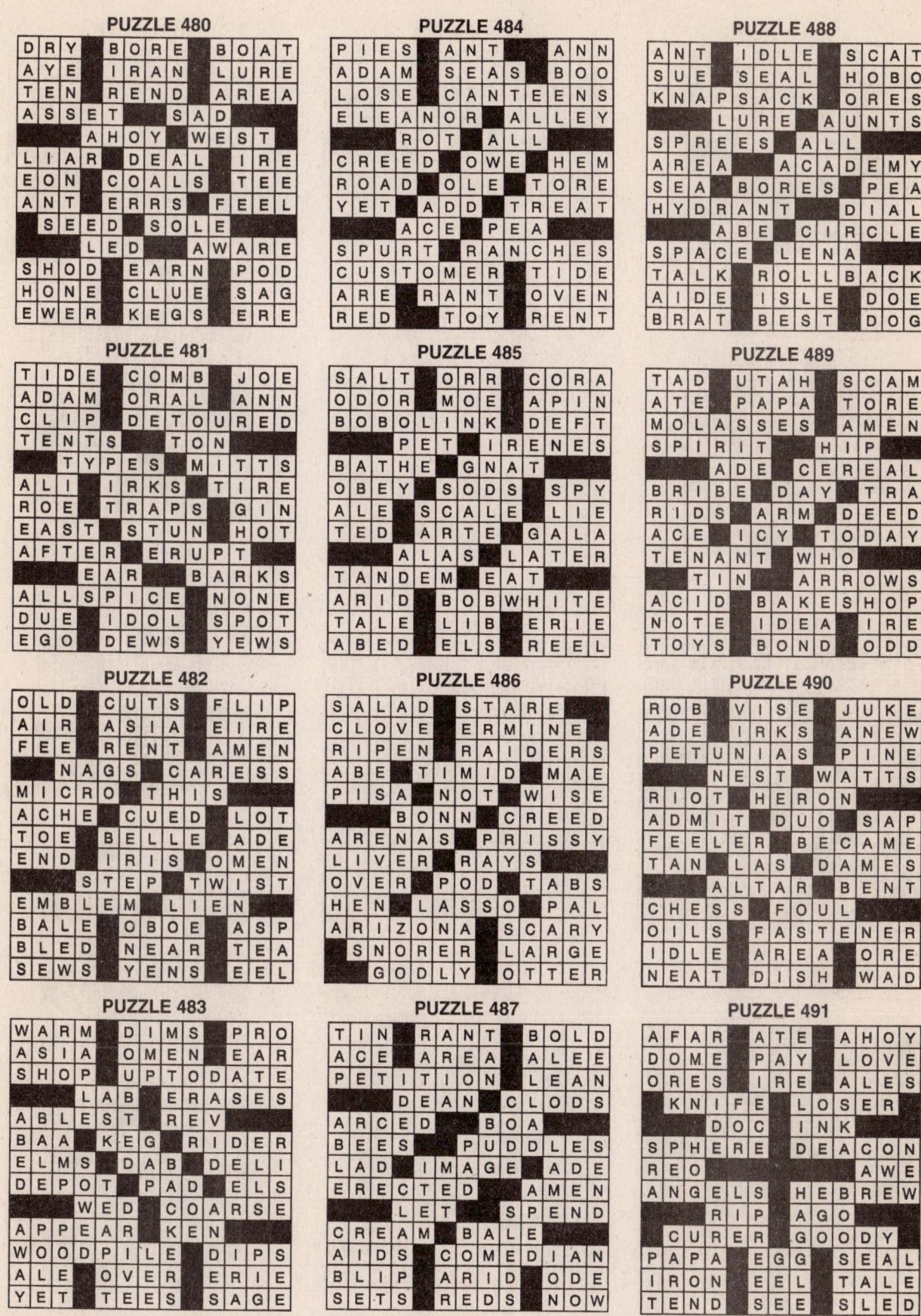

## PUZZLE 492

LAND ROBE
ADIOS COVER
MONTE HEALS
PRO ASA LIT
END ERASE
ITEMS
RIGOR HAT
LAD ASP RIM
ODORS AGORA
FILET RUMOR
TOSS MAST

## PUZZLE 493

LOSS THY SOFA
ABET RUE EPIC
PONY INTEREST
SET FAT RUNTS
EARL DIM
BINGO CAN BOY
ONCE GUM ROLE
ONE CAT CORDS
MOB PAWN
APRIL TOP FIB
SLANDERS ERLE
KENT NUT SELL
SAGS DES PEST

## PUZZLE 494

DIVE DADS TAP ARM
ERIN OBIT ALA LAO
EARS NEVERLETMEGO
REGINA EYE EAGER
IGET OLD ANN
VANNA SWEETS IFFY
ARI HEE RATE ROE
NEAL OWNS BARBARA
MULL SAL IRON
LEAVEIT YEAR SKIP
AMY EDIT AVE SRA
ROOM ANITRA BRIAN
ORY TUN BEAN
STARE FAR ATRAIN
WHITEBANNERS ETRE
IAN SAM ETUI ERIS
TNT ERE RENE SASS

## PUZZLE 495

SASS CAESAR
COCHISE ARRIVED
ACCEDED PIMLICO
BRIDLED AVAIL
LAD EDIBLE ETTE
ETES SEPIA REED
DENIM STRAW
STAIRS ANKARA
MOOED ARENA
LACE ATEST ETAL
ODES RHYTHM ALI
EATEN REUNION
SPECIAL ARRANGE
STRANGE PERSEUS
SATEEN ETRE

## PUZZLE 496

| | | | | | | | | | | |
|---|---|---|---|---|---|---|---|---|---|---|
| T | A | CO | | AC | TO | R | | SEC | RE | T |
| EN | SI | GN | | QUA | RT | ET | | T | H | AI |
| D | AN | A | | INT | E | R | NAT | ION | A | L |
| | | C | A | AN | | ACT | IVE | | SH | ED |
| SO | AP | | BUT | C | HER | | S | WAT | | |
| B | RON | ZE | | E | B | BED | | CH | ED | DAR |
| | | BRA | G | | AL | C | OVE | | NA | T |
| SP | IN | | RAT | S | | LO | N | GER | | |
| E | STA | BL | IS | H | MEN | T | | MA | STE | R |
| A | LL | EN | | RE | AC | H | | N | E | ED |
| R | ED | D | | D | E | ES | | E | D | DY |

## PUZZLE 497

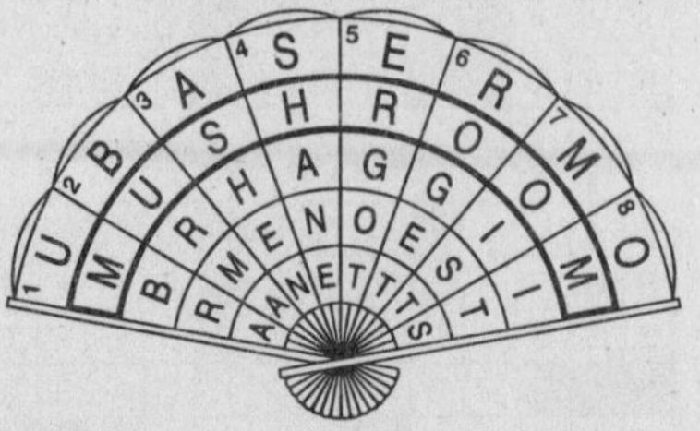

1. Umbra, 2. Burma, 3. Ashen, 4. Shane, 5. Ergot, 6. Roget, 7. Moist, 8. Omits.

8-LETTER WORD: Mushroom

## PUZZLE 498

T H E P R I N C E O F W A L E S
A I M E E D E L D R I E S A L P
S P E N D L E A G R E A T M I A
S T E T W E E D Y O N S H E A R
S E R A H E A D A N D E E R I E
C L O D I N T O T E L L W O R M
R E T S T A I L O T I S O N C E
A G R E E C O L L O S E R D O N
P R O W A T T A L O P E L O U D
C A L E N D A R I N V A D E R S
A M E N D U S E B E A S T A T C
R E A D B E A R I N N S U R G E
R I D E L A N A S O D A R E A R
O R E A U N T S E T A I N K L E
T E R R E T E E S E L L S E L S

## PUZZLE 499

| | | | | | | | | | | | | | | |
|---|---|---|---|---|---|---|---|---|---|---|---|---|---|---|
| F | O | L | K | S | I | N | G | E | R | | | | | R |
| | P | | I | | N | | A | | U | | Z | O | N | E |
| | A | L | L | O | W | | P | U | M | P | | W | | V |
| | L | | N | | A | | | | B | | K | I | W | I |
| | | S | | | R | E | G | A | L | | | N | | T |
| U | N | W | I | N | D | | O | | E | N | I | G | M | A |
| N | | A | | A | | | N | | | O | | | | L |
| I | V | Y | | V | E | R | D | I | C | T | | S | K | I |
| V | | | | E | | | O | | | E | | W | | Z |
| E | X | H | A | L | E | | L | | A | D | M | I | R | E |
| R | | A | | | Q | U | A | I | L | | | M | | |
| S | A | V | E | | U | | | | W | | F | | Z | |
| I | | O | | J | A | Z | Z | | A | W | A | K | E | |
| T | A | C | K | | T | | A | | Y | | C | | R | |
| Y | | | | | E | X | P | O | S | I | T | I | O | N |

1-Y, 2-R, 3-M, 4-N, 5-V, 6-A, 7-X, 8-J, 9-U, 10-H, 11-I, 12-K, 13-P, 14-W, 15-D, 16-Q, 17-Z, 18-L, 19-T, 20-B, 21-C, 22-S, 23-E, 24-O, 25-G, 26-F.

## PUZZLE 500

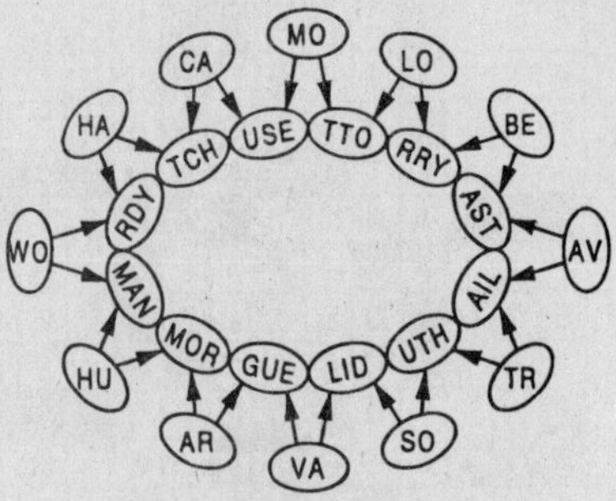


## PUZZLE 501

CALF HAIR
AREA ACROSS
FIND STATUE
EASEL TORE
SUFFERED
LEE
BEWILDER
IRIS TENDS
TINSEL SEAT
ENDURE TARO
SEND STEP

## PUZZLE 502

CUP SHED STEM
USE WAGE CARE
EARRINGS OGLE
FANG CLOSET
GROPE TRAP
OARS MAID DAM
ARM HOBBY ENE
DES ABLE SCOT
RISE SHONE
DESERT SPAR
IDEA ESTIMATE
MEND RUIN TOO
ENDS SERE ERN

## PUZZLE 503

PAIR ASH RIM
ASTA LOA PACE
THEJOLLYROGER
ERAL DEALER
SAY SEI
SET FOE SHEA
TREASURECHEST
ARAL ELL WEE
AID KAY
FACTOR SERA
WALKSTHEPLANK
ADES TEL PINE
REE YAM SLAY

## PUZZLE 504

CAR CASH DIAL
AGO UREY ECHO
MAB BIRDSNEST
PRIDE FEES
NESS LEGAL
ACHE EVIL OLE
ROOD PIN SODA
ADO STET TSAR
LADLE OBOE
OTIS UPSET
JAYWALKER TWO
AGEE LIAR EEN
BEAR SPRY PRY

## PUZZLE 505

STOMPS PASSE SARONGS
AERIAL RAMEAL TRENAIL
CHARLOTTEEMILYANDANNE
RENEE AEOLIC ALOE DAD
EEG OAT NIT SMILES
ZSAZSAEVAANDMAGDA
MISSOURI INT PURR
ALTAIR LHASA OBAN MAE
OLEIC CLERUS OLE BIT
STP BAILOR SANDSTONE
AMYJOMEGANDBETH
MAGNETONS ENAMOR RIP
APO GEL TONKIN SITES
TRI ASES UNSER SEVERE
ZINC PAN EPIDEMIC
OLGAMASHAANDIRINA
MANTIS IER RET ABT
ACE GOON SCLERO INTER
PATTYMAXENEANDLAVERNE
REAWAIT NANTES BESIDE
ANTARES EPEES ESSAYS

## PUZZLE 506

GAWP DEBIT OLE ITEM
ECHO AWASH ERAS STILE
THETIMETHEPLACE LALLA
SENATORS REPLY POLLEN
TINY MOLAS PEWIT
CHAOS ABES LEECHED
ROPE INTHEGOODOLD ELA
OOPS NEER NEWS TEAR
CPL SUMMERTIME CONTE
SENORA OARED BANDED
BERET ARI SARTO
SALLES HALOS PROOFS
TROLL ANDTHEGIRL TAM
ROSY LAZE NILE DIVA
OAS TIMEWILLTELL IMET
PROPANE NEAR AVERT
MALES BLASE GAPE
HOTTER MEARA ALLERGIC
AVION HAVINGAGOODTIME
REMIT AGED NIOBE EBAN
PRES MIL ANNES DENT

## PUZZLE 507

VOLT HOST PEAL TEL
ITER ALOU EERO BORE
MINI LOUISARMSTRONG
CAPTOR TORY WILES
HOES SILL SAID
ABODE OTOE WHITEMAN
CARS WHEN DOORS ENE
TIN SEAM CADDY SETA
SLEEPER FORE FAKIR
DUKEELLINGTON
OLDER MOON RENEGES
POOR SLIER BAND ENA
ELL HEELS DONT SNIP
CALLOWAY MIND WEEDS
ANNS WAVY BARK
ALENE FAZE DESIRE
DIZZYGILLESPIE OUST
OKRA ERIE TRAP UPTO
SEA METS SOLS SAAR

## PUZZLE 508

SPIES TREE STOP
PARSE ROLL TODO
AVAST ALLIGATOR
TEN TOME ALERT
SLAP ROBE
LETTER REAL MEW
AMOUR WASTE ERA
TOWN MINTS BRAG
ETE SONGS RAISE
RED CODE HATTER
LADY WASH
PETER HASH DIP
OPENFACED ELITE
TEND SURE SEVEN
SETS SPED TEARS

## PUZZLE 509

PAY SIDE
FIBER TIRED
LEASE ORATE
ACT VAT TEN
WEEP DEFER
AROMA
BONER TART
DIN FEW GEE
ABIDE IMAGE
FLOUR TITAN
TEND DEL

## PUZZLE 510

HAM PACE LESS
ICE ORAN AREA
PERFECTS MIEN
COT SUSPEND
ADHERE EAR
PEA YAM PESTS
SANG TAG YORE
ENTER PAL NEE
NAB BANGED
STREWED NOB
LIAR SANDWICH
ARIA TRUE RUE
BELL SEND DEN

## PUZZLE 511

NASH ISLAW MACES ELAN
OSHA LEIGH ASONE NONE
CHAGALLERY SINATRACKS
TERRENE ASHCAN TUMULT
INDIRECT EON REPOSES
DISTR TNT SORER
GEDDES ABED LOOSE PAW
ALOE ACUTE EAT SETA
LIMNS IHS RSVP LETTER
ASI ESSE ISEE SEREIN
NICKLAUSOPENCHAMP
HOGTIE RANT EARS APE
CUTEST SING ORR ESSAY
ANET BAA SHAVE EDIE
DTS PSYCH TUTU PAPERS
HATES MET READA
ANGELES SIR ENDORSER
SOARER PASSED ARRANGE
TRUMANDATE LEMMONTAGE
RAGE EDGER LUMEN OREL
ODES REEDS EXILE REDS

## PUZZLE 512

STEADFASTPEGMOO
PARCELLEOERRAND
ONERSEGANPRANCE
KALETESTIMONIES
EGOTISTICALDAMS
SEVENTEENSUPCIA
PRIDEARRESTORNE
ERNIERECREATION
RAGOUTFROSHFORD
SCOURELITEPETAL
OKSSORETIDEDOLE
NICEPIXIEGRILLS
SNAKENICHEEVILS
STREAKLAIRNAVEL
TOSSNYELESENEMY

## PUZZLE 513

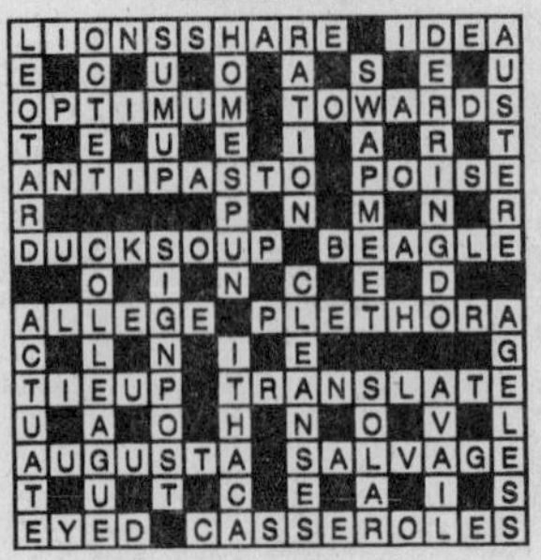


## PUZZLE 518

## PUZZLE 522

## PUZZLE 514

## PUZZLE 519

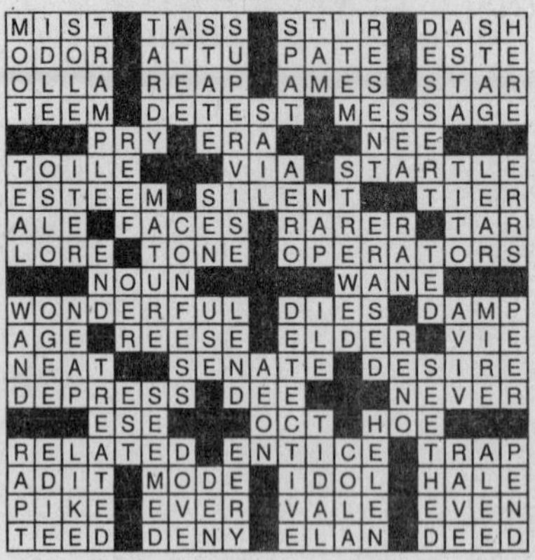


## PUZZLE 523

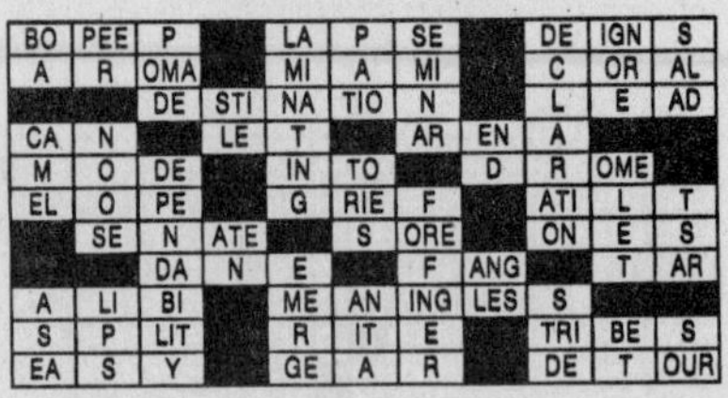


## PUZZLE 524

Stars over snow,
And in the west a planet
Swinging below a star—
Look for a lovely thing and you will find it,
It is not far—
It never will be far.

(Sara Teasdale)

## PUZZLE 515

1. Viewpoint, 2. Arrowhead,
3. Mainstream.

## PUZZLE 520

## PUZZLE 516

## PUZZLE 525

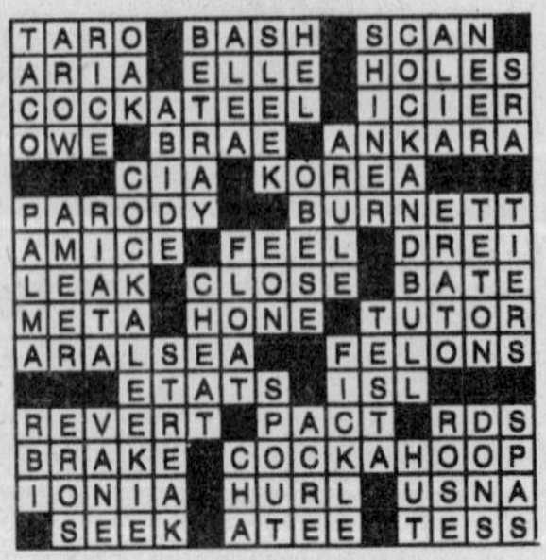


## PUZZLE 517

## PUZZLE 521

## PUZZLE 526

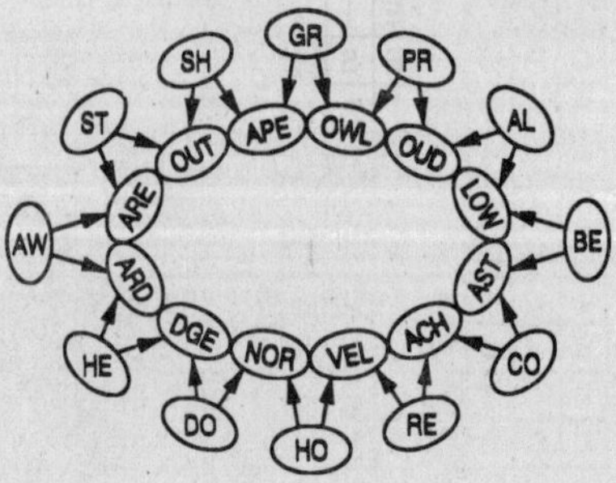

## PUZZLE 527

```
ETE SLAP WISP PITH
RATS TOLL ANTI OGRE
GRANDIOSE GRANDTOUR
SALOONS ALEE KRATER
RIG ADES PLOT
HAGEN ONES SEAPORTS
OUR GRANDSTANDS IAN
ETAS IRA BRAY COTE
SONNETS BROIL ALGAE
DALE MOONS STAR
CASKS HARTE CHARADE
LILY GENE SHE KNOT
ADA GRANDRAPIDS DIA
DEMERARA AMAN AGENT
VENT TROT FLA
AGREED SEEN SEASIDE
GRANDDUKE GRANDPRIX
RANT AKIN SOLD SIMI
AMIS DENY TEES SET
```

## PUZZLE 531

```
BESTIR TAPIR BOMB JOHN
ETHANE ORNATE ARIA OLEO
THEUNDEFEATED BRANNIGAN
RATES MULES DONATE
ELL IVES TICAL MATT
NEO SVEN EZEK BANISTER
CONCHES APER ONAN HUE
ANGLER UNDERSTRESS SERT
MOVED TRADE HERE DECOR
PROW CRUST AMINS CANOPY
SAY THESHOOTIST SALOME
ACRES HID OPERA
EGRESS COMMISSURES NAL
SLEETS BIRSE HALES ACME
HAHAS SEND SALAD ACHES
ATOM THEQUIETMAN EMEERS
LEM ARAR MAES FLORRIE
TREASURY APRA LIDS ONE
POEM SWELL SOLO SDS
STRONG MOLLY NIGER
WOODGRAIN LADYFORANIGHT
ALMA IDEE EGRETS DELRIO
PEEL TENS RESTS OBLATE
```

## PUZZLE 535

```
CHOP LOPE SUE
LOVE IDEA PRY
ABET MORTGAGE
NOR AIR EASES
CURT ORB
BOAST GAY MAP
ELSE FUR TOGA
GET BIN FADED
VAN PONE
FLAIR HAG RAP
LOCATION HALO
ASH ERNE ITEM
WEE REEL DEEP
```

## PUZZLE 528

```
LARD PINS TAPS CHAR
OBOE ADAM IDEA HOLE
SEAM ROSE CELL ASEA
STRAND HANK TEMPTED
NOON ROLL SOT
GARDENER DEAD PETER
ALE LEVER DIRT RAVE
STEM DEMON COAL LID
POLES RIVAL PROPELS
NOR TEPID TOR
CANDLES DEVIL PILOT
ORE DEAF SEVER GALE
MIST FLOP SAGES NEE
BATON TARS NAPOLEON
TUB MEET LODE
CHATTER PEAS RATTLE
HIRE LOLA POUT TOAD
EVER OMAR EASE EDNA
TEAS WADE SPED ROAM
```

## PUZZLE 532

```
HATS RILE STOA ARES
OLEO ERIS WORN ROME
MOLLYBOLT AGED LIME
EEL SUN UNIS EVELYN
PET BARN FRAN
SOLAR CORA MISS PAT
ALAN TORY CANOE AMY
LIZ CAME KORAN STOP
TOYSHOP BEVEL MITRE
SPAS POPES NAVY
BRUIN CLAIR CARAMEL
OUST CHATS MONK ERE
DNA TOUTS SALA ULNA
YEN ANTE APIA MATED
APSE SLED CAR
REGRET OPEN SON CIA
ENID ALTO SALLYPORT
DONE NATO EXIT AMMO
SWAN TOOK REPS LOAM
```

## PUZZLE 536

```
TAN SCAR CLOD
ICE TARA AIDE
PESTERED SKIN
TAME INTENT
DREGS HAUL
RAGS TOTTERED
EGG PORES ELI
WESTERNS AVER
ARMS CRIME
BRONTE ORAL
RIND NAMELESS
ALEE THAT RAH
GERM SANE SPY
```

## PUZZLE 529

```
GASP HEMS PAR
ALOE OMIT RUE
PENTHOUSE ERA
AID JETSAM
STILT MULES
PUN CLOD DUMP
AND HEDGE RIO
RAID SEED ESS
GUESS SASSY
LENORE BET
ALA ANTELOPES
MAN SEER NOVA
ANT EDEN EDAM
```

## PUZZLE 533

```
PADS SASS SIN
ALOE TRIO PRO
SEEN RENDERED
SCRAPE KALE
TEAL SEALS
SCREAMED EDIE
TOE REVEL EVE
ARTS REPAIRED
REAPS LEND
IOTA NEEDLE
BANTERED ARIA
OWE WERE LAMS
WED SAID SWAT
```

## PUZZLE 537

```
OAST PEACE CARVE ECOL
BIER ADULT ALIEN NAVY
IDEA CUTIE BASIS AGER
TERPSICHORE MELPOMENE
LANE NERO HAE
SEEING ANILE STERLING
CRANE TSETSE TORS NIL
RASE NIPPY EURE STLO
ATE AITCH DERBY HOREB
POLYMNIA ZEROS PILOSE
OBES HEARS LILT
SHAKOS MAULS CALLIOPE
HAVES MOIST TUNES RED
ABEL ROAR CALCS CITE
GIN PERN TROUPE THERM
STATUTES AORTA THALIA
APE AJAR SAIN
PARNASSUS NIGHTINGALE
ERIK TANTE DOYEN EVIL
RACE ENTER ARMET ROMA
USER DOORS SENDS SWAN
```

## PUZZLE 530

```
WHEY PRIM AMA
EASE AUTO VIN
ESTABLISHMENT
REIN AERIE
CRONES AVA
RAT TAMPERING
AVIS DOA ANIL
MISTREATS ILE
RAS HASTEN
ILIAD IERE
SUBWAYSTATION
LII REMI UCLA
ESS SPEC PEEP
```

## PUZZLE 534

```
ODOR DAM SITE
RAVE ELI IDOL
EWES PEN SLUM
SNIDE EATER
SUN RYE
ABATED SERVES
RAG ILL
CREEDS BARELY
ROW ERA
CRATE LENDS
ALAS ALL GOAT
PALE TEE EMIR
EYED YES RELY
```

## PUZZLE 538

```
ELA MAMA BARGE GLAD
GEM APIS ARYAN LONE
GOBBLERS GEESE ACNE
ULES ATENS RADIOS
APSES QUILT OGLE
BAHT CULTS CRIMSONS
EVE ERATO MARES SUP
DESTROYS PARIS SIRE
ROWS RITES THESE
FLOODS MILES REARED
RAMIE DIDOS LURK
AVES CARET VIGNETTE
MEN SORES JAMBS HAY
ESSENCES SUNNY MULE
MOOD LENDS LAMES
DISOWN TACKY WASP
EDIT UKASE KERCHIEF
NOTE TIRED ERIE NNE
SLED SNORE SETS GAD
```

## PUZZLE 539

| | | | | | | | | | | | | |
|---|---|---|---|---|---|---|---|---|---|---|---|---|
| | M | A | P | | C | O | D | | E | D | G | E |
| D | E | L | I | | A | V | E | | L | E | A | D |
| O | R | A | L | | R | E | S | E | M | B | L | E |
| T | E | N | O | R | | R | I | G | | T | E | N |
| | | | T | O | N | | G | O | O | | | |
| C | O | O | | T | O | W | N | | F | A | L | L |
| A | U | N | T | | V | I | A | | F | L | E | A |
| B | R | E | W | | I | N | T | O | | P | A | W |
| | | | O | P | T | | E | R | A | | | |
| S | P | A | | A | I | L | | B | I | N | G | E |
| C | O | M | P | L | A | I | N | | S | E | A | R |
| A | L | E | E | | T | O | O | | L | A | I | R |
| R | E | N | T | | E | N | D | | E | R | N | |

## PUZZLE 543

| | | | | | | | | | | | | |
|---|---|---|---|---|---|---|---|---|---|---|---|---|
| P | E | T | E | | P | R | O | | A | R | A | B |
| A | R | E | A | | L | O | W | | L | O | N | E |
| T | I | E | S | | A | B | E | | M | A | T | E |
| S | E | N | T | R | Y | | | G | A | M | E | S |
| | | | E | A | S | I | L | Y | | | | |
| S | T | E | R | N | | C | A | P | | P | A | W |
| L | O | A | N | | F | I | B | | C | A | G | E |
| Y | E | T | | S | A | N | | O | I | L | E | D |
| | | | | E | D | G | I | N | G | | | |
| S | C | U | B | A | | | D | E | A | C | O | N |
| L | O | S | E | | S | E | E | | R | O | D | E |
| I | D | E | A | | P | E | A | | E | N | D | S |
| D | E | S | K | | A | L | L | | T | E | S | T |

## PUZZLE 547

| | | | | | | | | | | | | |
|---|---|---|---|---|---|---|---|---|---|---|---|---|
| S | E | E | S | | P | E | T | | S | C | A | R |
| P | E | A | T | | E | R | A | | T | A | L | E |
| A | L | T | O | | E | N | D | O | R | S | E | D |
| | | | L | O | V | E | | R | I | T | E | S |
| S | E | R | E | N | E | | T | A | P | | | |
| E | R | A | S | E | | R | E | L | E | A | S | E |
| A | I | M | | | H | O | D | | | P | I | T |
| R | E | P | L | I | E | D | | C | R | E | D | O |
| | | | A | C | E | | W | O | O | D | E | N |
| G | N | O | M | E | | R | I | N | G | | | |
| R | E | V | E | R | S | E | D | | E | D | G | E |
| I | R | A | N | | O | D | E | | R | E | A | L |
| D | O | L | T | | N | O | N | | S | E | L | L |

## PUZZLE 540

| | | | | | | | | | | | | |
|---|---|---|---|---|---|---|---|---|---|---|---|---|
| S | W | A | T | S | | M | A | R | | S | P | A |
| P | I | L | O | T | | I | C | E | | W | A | X |
| A | L | A | M | O | | R | E | S | P | I | R | E |
| T | E | N | | O | R | E | | U | R | G | E | D |
| | | | A | G | E | | S | L | Y | | | |
| I | M | P | L | E | M | E | N | T | | T | I | P |
| L | O | O | T | | A | V | E | | A | O | N | E |
| L | O | P | | T | R | E | A | T | M | E | N | T |
| | | | A | R | K | | K | E | Y | | | |
| B | A | S | T | E | | D | Y | E | | S | U | B |
| E | X | P | E | N | S | E | | T | W | I | N | E |
| A | L | E | | C | U | E | | E | E | R | I | E |
| N | E | W | | H | E | R | | R | E | S | T | S |

## PUZZLE 544

| | | | | | | | | | | | | |
|---|---|---|---|---|---|---|---|---|---|---|---|---|
| H | U | G | E | | A | C | I | D | | A | C | E |
| O | R | A | L | | N | A | V | Y | | V | O | W |
| O | G | L | E | | T | R | E | E | | O | D | E |
| P | E | A | C | H | E | S | | R | A | C | E | S |
| | | | T | A | N | | | S | P | A | | |
| H | A | G | | S | N | A | P | | E | D | G | E |
| E | G | O | | P | A | R | E | S | | O | A | R |
| W | E | B | S | | S | C | A | N | | S | S | E |
| | | B | E | T | | | S | O | B | | | |
| M | O | L | A | R | | L | A | W | L | E | S | S |
| A | B | E | | A | M | E | N | | A | L | O | E |
| N | O | R | | M | O | A | T | | M | A | L | T |
| Y | E | S | | S | O | N | S | | E | N | D | S |

## PUZZLE 548

| | | | | | | | | | | | | |
|---|---|---|---|---|---|---|---|---|---|---|---|---|
| O | L | D | | B | E | A | D | | T | Y | P | E |
| M | O | O | | I | D | L | E | | H | E | I | R |
| I | N | N | | S | I | L | T | | E | W | E | R |
| T | E | A | P | O | T | | E | L | M | | | |
| | | T | O | N | | S | C | I | E | N | C | E |
| A | R | I | D | | D | A | T | E | | A | R | K |
| C | O | O | | S | E | V | E | N | | T | O | E |
| R | A | N | | A | P | E | D | | T | I | P | S |
| E | N | S | U | R | E | D | | B | O | O | | |
| | | | P | I | N | | B | L | O | N | D | E |
| S | A | N | E | | D | A | L | E | | A | I | D |
| O | M | E | N | | E | G | O | S | | L | E | G |
| S | P | E | D | | D | E | B | T | | S | T | Y |

## PUZZLE 541

| | | | | | | | | | | | | |
|---|---|---|---|---|---|---|---|---|---|---|---|---|
| T | A | M | | A | R | I | A | | S | O | R | T |
| A | L | I | | W | A | R | S | | P | L | E | A |
| R | E | S | H | A | P | E | S | | R | E | A | D |
| | | T | A | R | S | | I | D | I | O | M | S |
| P | L | A | T | E | | A | G | O | G | | | |
| R | A | K | E | | L | I | N | E | S | M | A | N |
| O | N | E | | B | A | S | E | S | | A | B | E |
| M | E | N | D | A | B | L | E | | D | I | E | T |
| | | | O | B | O | E | | P | E | L | T | S |
| T | E | L | L | E | R | | A | R | E | A | | |
| A | R | A | L | | E | N | C | U | M | B | E | R |
| M | I | C | A | | R | E | E | D | | L | A | Y |
| P | E | E | R | | S | E | R | E | | E | R | E |

## PUZZLE 545

| | | | | | | | | | | | | |
|---|---|---|---|---|---|---|---|---|---|---|---|---|
| C | O | P | | E | P | I | C | | F | E | A | T |
| A | R | E | | N | E | R | O | | A | N | T | E |
| S | E | A | F | A | R | E | R | | I | D | E | A |
| E | S | K | I | M | O | | R | A | N | | | |
| | | | B | E | N | | O | B | T | A | I | N |
| H | O | T | E | L | | A | D | E | | W | O | O |
| O | V | E | R | | I | C | E | | R | O | W | S |
| M | E | N | | A | N | T | | D | E | L | A | Y |
| E | N | T | E | R | S | | P | E | N | | | |
| | | | S | K | I | | O | P | E | N | E | D |
| A | L | A | S | | D | E | L | A | W | A | R | E |
| G | A | L | A | | E | V | E | R | | B | I | N |
| O | B | E | Y | | R | E | S | T | | S | E | T |

## PUZZLE 549

| | | | | | | | | | | | | |
|---|---|---|---|---|---|---|---|---|---|---|---|---|
| H | A | T | | C | A | S | T | | P | O | D | S |
| E | V | A | | A | N | T | E | | E | V | I | L |
| R | E | P | O | R | T | E | R | | R | E | N | E |
| | R | E | A | L | | E | N | D | U | R | E | D |
| | | | R | O | A | R | | A | S | | | |
| A | L | P | | S | C | I | | D | E | C | O | Y |
| S | E | A | M | | E | N | D | | D | A | R | E |
| K | O | R | E | A | | G | O | T | | T | E | N |
| | | | A | L | | W | E | R | E | | | |
| F | U | R | N | I | S | H | | I | L | E | D | |
| E | R | I | E | | L | E | A | P | F | R | O | G |
| E | G | G | S | | A | E | R | O | | A | V | A |
| T | E | S | T | | P | L | E | D | | S | E | T |

## PUZZLE 542

| | | | | | | | | | | | | |
|---|---|---|---|---|---|---|---|---|---|---|---|---|
| L | A | D | D | | H | A | T | S | | S | H | E |
| A | L | A | I | | O | M | I | T | | H | E | M |
| B | I | D | S | | T | I | N | E | | E | L | I |
| S | T | A | C | K | E | D | | A | D | A | P | T |
| | | | O | I | L | | A | L | I | | | |
| R | E | R | U | N | | M | I | S | S | I | O | N |
| O | V | E | R | | W | A | R | | C | O | N | E |
| D | E | B | A | T | E | D | | B | O | N | E | D |
| | | | G | A | B | | R | E | V | | | |
| C | A | P | E | R | | C | A | T | E | R | E | R |
| I | C | E | | G | O | O | D | | R | O | D | E |
| T | E | N | | E | L | L | A | | E | V | E | N |
| E | S | S | | T | E | A | R | | D | E | N | T |

## PUZZLE 546

| | | | | | | | | | | | | |
|---|---|---|---|---|---|---|---|---|---|---|---|---|
| A | C | T | S | | A | R | K | S | | P | O | L |
| P | H | E | W | | V | E | E | P | | A | C | E |
| I | O | T | A | | O | P | E | R | E | T | T | A |
| S | C | E | N | I | C | | P | E | G | | | |
| | | | S | R | A | S | | E | R | R | O | R |
| H | O | E | | E | D | E | N | | E | A | S | E |
| A | B | L | E | | O | W | E | | T | I | L | E |
| M | O | A | N | | S | E | A | T | | N | O | D |
| S | E | N | D | S | | D | R | O | P | | | |
| | | | E | W | E | | N | E | E | D | E | D |
| H | E | A | D | A | C | H | E | | D | I | R | E |
| A | R | M | | I | R | I | S | | A | K | I | N |
| G | A | P | | N | U | T | S | | L | E | N | S |

## PUZZLE 550

| | | | | | | | | | | | | |
|---|---|---|---|---|---|---|---|---|---|---|---|---|
| H | O | T | | A | L | S | O | | W | E | P | T |
| A | D | O | | N | E | O | N | | A | R | A | B |
| L | O | T | | C | A | L | E | N | D | A | R | S |
| F | R | E | S | H | | | S | E | E | | | |
| | | | P | O | L | L | | E | R | R | O | R |
| C | A | N | A | R | I | E | S | | S | O | R | E |
| A | C | E | | S | E | A | L | S | | B | E | D |
| F | R | A | Y | | S | P | O | T | L | E | S | S |
| E | E | R | I | E | | S | W | A | Y | | | |
| | | | E | L | L | | | R | E | A | R | S |
| S | T | A | L | K | I | E | S | T | | C | A | T |
| A | R | I | D | | M | E | A | L | | I | C | E |
| G | Y | M | S | | E | L | L | E | | D | E | W |

## PUZZLE 551

AFAR SALT ABOUT
COLE PLAN PADRE
HIES EAST PROGS
ELEPHANT FERRET
EARS GONE
SLACKS GLADDENS
CASTE SOILS LII
ASIS SKIDS KITS
LED ALINE RIDES
DREADING WINERY
BOPS PINK
LEMURS KANGAROO
AMUSE WANT JUDD
DINER OLDE OGEE
STIRS NEAR USSR

## PUZZLE 552

HAT SPA BED
EVE TAR ERA
NEST BENCH HERD
THERE OMEN
OVER UAR
USED HOSTED
SUPER ROPE RED
ASP HOMES EAR
DOE AMEN HASTY
RAFTER CANS
PAT HANG
FIRE UNDER
DARN ROOST RICE
ORE INK DAY
SEE LES ERE

## PUZZLE 553

PASS GELS AND
ANTI ORAL SUE
DEAL TABULATE
WREN ORE
NEVER TOMS
CONCEAL LEE
OBOE TUG MINE
PIT DUBIOUS
STEW TENOR
AGE GARB
CONSUMER CORD
ADO SPRY LAIR
DEW TORE EDGY

## PUZZLE 554

PERT SPA TIMS
ARIES ERGS ALIE
TITLE DIET COME
CALL ANDY OVEN
LENT LOSES
PALEST EVER
EDAM ACRE TOBE
TADPOLE TESTERS
MESA LASS IRAS
FILM NESTLE
BLAST EWER
ALAN ERNE ORBS
LAND MADE DORIS
ONCE STEP EVADE
EKES EDS EDEN

## PUZZLE 555

TORN STRAW MOLL
OBOE PROSE APIA
GETTHEUPPERHAND
AYE EASE ALLEY
MARS WINE
MANORS PACKRATS
ODOR TIRES SOW
LATE POKER SHOE
AGE WAKES WELD
REDROVER CHASSE
AMEN BEAT
STAVE SURE FIB
PUTINTOPRACTICE
EBON ALIST ANON
DAME BETTE RENT

## PUZZLE 556

SCAPE TEPID ACT
PAPER INANE TRI
UPSANDDOWNS SOL
NEE DEWS IDEAL
SPAS WREAKS
WAYLAY PORES
AGAIN MOVES EVA
NEWT TAKEN GRIP
DEN CATER PLANE
HOMES KEELER
RETUNE FERN
OMITS TSAR UTE
PEN UPYOURALLEY
ERG MORAL RINSE
RYE EXERT MEATS

## PUZZLE 557

CAME SAP RILL
OVEN TRA ERIE
BEST RIN NONE
BRAISE TBONES
CUE ROW
TALENT YANKEE
EGO ILL
DEBATE CHUNKY
NIX HEN
SHRIMP ARISEN
TEAM ERN TILE
ARIA RUG ERSE
BOLL TEE DEED

## PUZZLE 558

DAMS TALES GRIM
ERAT EDEMA RIDE
FIRE TRAPS EPOS
TAKETOONESHEELS
RANI RYOT
SALEM TOO PETES
ERODES MRS DOLT
DIG DETESTS LIE
ASEA EEG YELLOW
NESTS LAG PESTS
TREE ASTA
TAKEADVANTAGEOF
ABAS SINGE URGE
FELT ESTER ELEE
TEES LEASE SEED

## PUZZLE 559

CASAS SOLD ROBE
ERICA TRAY APES
LIGHTHEADEDNESS
LANE OILY AGREE
FAN TREATS
SURER FOYER
MURAL LAP WHO
LIGHTASAFEATHER
ITE BUG SHIRT
MALES RHYME
BEMINE BUY
ATONE ALAS CAME
THROWSLIGHTUPON
HEAR AGOG ABOVE
ERNS MANY MEDES

## PUZZLE 560

AMASS STUD ABA
PASTA TOTE SKID
TITAN ARAM WIND
LORDOFTHERINGS
LEAF AAR
ASSERT RINGLETS
GENTS HORSE TUT
APE OAK ADO
PIE KINDS CAPON
EARRINGS SEVERE
ELS SANE
DOESNTRINGTRUE
ANDI EASE RARER
STEN ASEA AGILE
HON DEED LEASE

## PUZZLE 561

RASP DELTA MESH PATCH
OBOE ISERE ARTE ENERO
MENT STAIR DIAL ADROP
PEARLHARBOR CLEARANCE
STRIA SSE ARSENAL
SUM SKYE ARCADIA
CAT DORM ESTES EIDERS
ABBA NOISE ESTA TENET
PEARLONIONS PARTYLINE
STREET MET RIO AMER
MOTHEROFPEARL
CRAM NEO ROI RAFFIA
REPAPERER MINNIEPEARL
AGATE ARAN LEARN DRAM
TARTAN STELE PATS OKS
ENTERED AIDS STA
LARDERS CEE ONERS
WRANGLERS PEARLBAILEY
RAVER DOTH ALAVA MASK
ARICA GLEE RESIN ATEE
PESKY ELEM PRESS LETS

## PUZZLE 562

JAB FIT SAVE
EXAM TWICE ARIA
ELSE RANEE FIST
REENTERS FADES
TONE AFAR
SECOND SPACIOUS
ODORS SLIDE ONE
FIRS SPINS CZAR
ACE OWING CREPE
STRIKING GUESTS
NAME HUES
SHADY QUESTION
HOME NOUNS ERNE
OPEN EDITS DOTE
TENT WET NOD

1-C, 2-E, 3-G, 4-A, 5-P, 6-W, 7-X, 8-S, 9-J, 10-B, 11-U, 12-H, 13-D, 14-Z, 15-F, 16-Y, 17-K, 18-O, 19-Q, 20-N, 21-R, 22-M, 23-L, 24-I, 25-V, 26-T.

## PUZZLE 563

FIR BARS BASE
ACE ERIN OVAL
DESCRIBE WELL
TEND ALERTS
STONE SKID
TART APES PET
ALE AVERT IRE
RED DENS CONE
DART TONES
CHARMS FIRE
RAGE EYETEETH
ORES LOLL ROE
WEDS YULE SON

## PUZZLE 564

SNAKE SCAM ANTE TROT
CARES TATA DORA OHARE
RULES ATOM DOOR NOISE
ARENA MALMO KITCARSON
PUSSYWILLOW SHAH ENS
SINO NELL AMOS
HARM GANG DEAL ETHAN
ALIAS IAN TRIO TALUS
LIANAS AZOV KITTIWAKE
FELINE NAVELS TINNIER
TAGS ERE BOER
INSTATE ULSTER ROCOCO
CATACOMBS ETTU SOARER
EDEMA SOUP SAC FILLE
ANITA BARE LEDA NETS
LALO LOCI CINC
AMP LENA CATASTROPHE
GARFIELDS EMITS ORION
ALIEN ODOR BATE AGENT
PASTA ALMA IRON TATER
ERMA NEAT CANT SNARE

## PUZZLE 565

SEARCH SALON BREAST
ANGORA SCRIBES LEGREE
MURMUR MALTESE ENGINE
PRE SENILE STRAND SAM
LEEJ MOLAS ELAND FETE
ESSES NEW III FINED
MINE ARLEN LAIN
SPIRE GOING LEASE
DIOMEDES SAT SHALLOPS
RETAN REFERENCE DEMIT
ORB BLOC REAR ASA
ORALS IMPORTERS HELOT
PANATELA LOA PEROXIDE
SKIRT TOPIC ANTAE
COAT ARENA DYER
STRAP HEN PAR SANDS
HEEL VOLGA ATLAS SEEN
AMP CORVET GUTTED ANA
SPINAL INSPIRE NESTOR
TENANT STEELER DELETE
ARETES SATED SPORES

## PUZZLE 566

ROMP APSE ADAM PAP
AGAR NOON CANA DOME
FLYINGDUTCHMAN ALIT
TEASERS RUES DRUIDS
STY BIRD GRUBS
CLAY FUEL BRASSHAT
HIM SWISSSTEAKS TWO
EVE ARTY RACE THEN
FERULES BRACE SEEDY
IRON TOUCH GALA
ALCAN BRUTE PAULPRY
COAL COIN BOLT PEA
INN CANADAGOOSE LAW
DECLARED BEAR SELL
HIKER CANT BEE
SCENES MACE ALLEGES
ALEE SWEDISHMASSAGE
MASS EASE IRES APIA
EWE DRAT SENT WEST

## PUZZLE 567

STAT CALM THAR QUAD
HALO AMIE AIDA URGE
ELON RAFT BRAN ESEL
ACEINTHEHOLE GREASE
COE ASE SEEN
HST TRAINS CROONER
ALIKE ONE TRES FORE
LONI END IRAN TROT
TEENAGE STORE CHASE
GIG SHAVE MOE
ASTOR STALE FASHION
LEAF HOLY OAT ONLY
MART SEAL PAR SPREE
ANTHILL DAKOTA EAT
EVEL ROC ASP
DEGREE JACKINTHEBOX
OLEO POUT EDIT TIME
OKRA ERNE RENE EDEN
REED REEL SAAR RENO

## DIAGRAMLESS STARTING BOXES

Puzzle 61 starts in box 1
Puzzle 63 starts in box 3
Puzzle 65 starts in box 5
Puzzle 67 starts in box 1
Puzzle 69 starts in box 5
Puzzle 71 starts in box 4
Puzzle 72 starts in box 5
Puzzle 74 starts in box 1
Puzzle 75 starts in box 5
Puzzle 77 starts in box 3
Puzzle 78 starts in box 1
Puzzle 79 starts in box 1
Puzzle 81 starts in box 3
Puzzle 83 starts in box 5
Puzzle 84 starts in box 1
Puzzle 85 starts in box 6
Puzzle 86 starts in box 3
Puzzle 87 starts in box 4
Puzzle 170 starts in box 3
Puzzle 172 starts in box 4
Puzzle 174 starts in box 1
Puzzle 176 starts in box 5
Puzzle 178 starts in box 8
Puzzle 180 starts in box 4
Puzzle 182 starts in box 11
Puzzle 184 starts in box 15
Puzzle 185 starts in box 12
Puzzle 187 starts in box 3
Puzzle 189 starts in box 4
Puzzle 191 starts in box 5
Puzzle 193 starts in box 4
Puzzle 195 starts in box 12
Puzzle 197 starts in box 5
Puzzle 347 starts in box 7
Puzzle 349 starts in box 2
Puzzle 351 starts in box 7
Puzzle 353 starts in box 11
Puzzle 355 starts in box 3
Puzzle 357 starts in box 8
Puzzle 359 starts in box 1
Puzzle 361 starts in box 5
Puzzle 363 starts in box 10
Puzzle 365 starts in box 1
Puzzle 367 starts in box 7
Puzzle 368 starts in box 1
Puzzle 370 starts in box 14
Puzzle 371 starts in box 8
Puzzle 373 starts in box 7
Puzzle 375 starts in box 4
Puzzle 377 starts in box 1

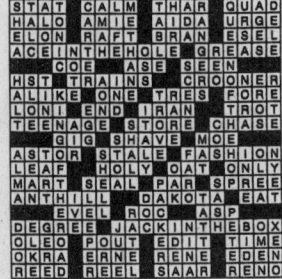